D1219193

The Professional Pastry Chef

The Professional
Pastry Chef

FOURTH EDITION

Fundamentals of Baking and Pastry

Bo Friberg

with Amy Kemp Friberg

JOHN WILEY & SONS, INC.

Library of Congress Cataloging-in-Publication Data

Friberg, Bo, 1940–

    The professional pastry chef : fundamentals of baking and pastry / Bo Friberg.-- 4th ed.

      p. cm.

    Includes bibliographical references and index.

    ISBN-13 978-0-471-35925-8 (cloth : alk. paper)

    ISBN 0-471-35925-4 (cloth : alk. paper)

    1. Pastry. 1. Title

TX773 .F75 2001

641.8'65--dc21

                     2001046952

Printed in the United States of America.

Book deisgn by Richard Oriolo

20 19 18 17 16 15 14 13 12 11

CONTENTS

In a sense, the fourth edition of *The Professional Pastry Chef* began as soon as the third edition was published. Right away I started to jot down ideas for new recipes, make notes regarding up-to-the-minute techniques, and consider ways in which I could improve the text. When it came time to begin the actual revision, it became clear rather quickly that there was more than enough material for two books rather than one. This book, *Fundamentals of Baking and Pastry*, is the first of a two-volume set. It covers all the techniques and recipes needed to complete a basic baking and pastry-making course.

Included here are all of my well-tested recipes for yeast breads, decorated cakes, tea cakes, cookies, plated desserts, ice creams, custards, sauces, fillings, and more— all of the classics from the first three editions that have stood the test of time. In addition, dozens of new recipes, illustrations, templates, and color photographs have been added to reflect the latest industry trends. For example, a new section is dedicated to today's popular Mediterranean-style flatbreads. Recipes for favorites such as ciabatta and lavash address consumers' growing demand for authentic artisan breads.

Notable is that each of the appendices—Ingredients, Equipment, and Weights, Measures, and Yields—has been greatly expanded. The ingredient and equipment sections combined are virtually "a book within a book" with over 1,000 and 500 entries, respectively.

Thanks to the teamwork of several people at John Wiley & Sons—publisher Rob Garber, who went out on a limb for me more than once to support this volume; my editor Susan Wyler, who treated the manuscript as if it were her own; Andrea Johnson, who never tired of my constant changes and additions; and the art and production departments, which offered great creative ideas and made the concept a reality—this edition has a brand new look and a contemporary, modular design. The recipes in each chapter are organized in a way that will make them easier to use whether you are a student, teacher, professional chef or amateur-cooking enthusiast. Among the many new design features are Chef's Tips and informational sidebars. These, along with the recipe introductions, point out potential challenges, give specific hints and advice, convey general information about the ingredients used, discuss the history of the dish, or offer an alternative presentation or usage. Subrecipes have been moved to follow a main recipe whenever possible to make them easier to access.

This new edition also contains innovative ideas for impressive plate presentations and incorporates techniques that utilize the tools that are needed to produce the latest novel creations. In the six years since the third edition was published, a multitude of new equipment has emerged in the baking and pastry field. Flexipan forms, made from special silicone-based compounds, are used more and more in place of tinned steel for baking everything from cake bases, to teacakes, madeleines and individual pastries. These pans are also used to mold custards, parfaits and other chilled or frozen creations. While the initial cost is higher than for metal forms, the expense is more than offset by the tremendous advantages they offer. The forms do not require greasing before use, they are easy to keep clean, the baked or frozen products are a cinch to unmold and, perhaps most importantly, these pans produce items that are perfectly consistent in appearance. Many other tools that were once made from metal are now made from composites that are heatproof, rustproof, and resistant to bacteria. Silpats (silicone baking mats), decorating stencils, plastic strips (acetate or polyurethane), transfer sheets for use with both chocolate and sponges, decorating combs used to create patterned sponge sheets, and, to some degree, dough sheeters, are no longer considered specialized equipment used only in large operations, but are now a must in any establishment that wants to keep up with the latest industry trends. These tools and others like them are discussed and utilized throughout both volumes.

Another big change in the pastry field over the past two decades is the ever increasing availability of reasonably priced imported produce, such as tropical fruits, and excellent quality "halfway" products like frozen fruit purees, gianduja, florentina mix, praline paste, chocolate truffle shells, and candy fillings. Other examples of new products that make our lives easier and allow today's pastry chefs much more creativity are food-grade coolant in an aerosol spray, specifically designed for rapid cooling and setting of melted chocolate and hot sugar when making decorations, and powdered gold leaf, also in aerosol form, to make precise application much easier.

A greater number of the recipes in this edition include alternative versions that produce a smaller yield, aptly titled "Small-Batch." This was done in an effort to make the book accessible to a wider range of readers and to both large and small professional operations. Recipes that do not include a small batch ingredient list are still easy to scale up or down as needed. Because none of the cake, tart, and pie recipes yield more than two, it is equally convenient for anyone to either multiply this amount as needed, depending on the occasion and/or demands, or for the home chef to divide the ingredients in half to make, for example, one birthday cake. As before, all of the recipes that produce individual servings, namely the plated desserts, custards, puddings, mousses, charlottes, and Bavarians, yield either eight, twelve, or sixteen servings, which again makes it easy to divide the ingredients to serve four, six, or eight.

The third edition of *The Professional Pastry Chef* was, I am pleased to say, a huge success for many reasons: the main one being that all the recipes work, period. This, of course, is the point of any cookbook, but unfortunately it is not always the case. Professional chefs especially, who work in an environment where not only are the cost and waste of ingredients significant, but time is of the essence, must have workable formulas they can rely on. Readers will be pleased to note that all of the recipes and procedures in my books have been tested by literally thousands of students in my classes and have been improved on over the course of many years. In the Chef's Tips and the recipe instructions, I point out typical pitfalls and explain why certain steps must be completed in a particular order or manner. I also offer suggestions for using more than one type of form or mold when applicable, knowing that not only does every operation not have the same equipment, but also that these items are not always readily available when needed. In several instances, instructions, complete with illustrations, are given for making your own forms and molds.

This book differs from many other cookbooks in several significant ways. My background allows me to approach the subject matter from numerous angles. This book is written by a working Certified Master Pastry Chef with forty-five years of professional experience in the industry. I have worked in both small shops and large retail and wholesale operations in the United States and in Europe. I worked for the Swedish-American cruise ship line, and I have demonstrated the art of pastry making in a number of instructional videos and television shows. I have spent half of my career teaching all levels of students at three different culinary schools: the California Culinary Academy in San Francisco, the Culinary Institute of America at Greystone, and the San Diego Culinary Institute, where I teach presently.

In writing this book, I have drawn from all of these experiences to create a comprehensive guide notably for those who aspire to make baking and pastry their career and for instructors who, like me, are guiding their students along this path. Additionally, this book is for working professionals who are looking for doable recipes for both the basics and more modern innovations. One is frequently called upon to prepare this or that as a special request or for a particular occasion, and a reference with numerous recipes and ideas is certainly a great help.

Some Thoughts On Teaching

Upon graduating from any culinary school, it is not enough that a student is simply able to perform; he or she must also be able to produce at a reasonable speed to make a living. These recipes are not designed just for practice or for all-day student projects where labor cost is not an issue. Instead, they are workable, practical recipes to be used in the real world of pastry and baking production. Students will certainly want to carry this text with them into the industry after graduation.

Depending on the institution and its curriculum, an instructor may want to use this book in different ways. Although the chapters follow a logical succession of procedures that is in keeping with students' skill development, this sequence does not necessarily need to be followed. However, it is imperative that students first learn to work with fundamental ingredients and practice preparing and handling formulas such as short dough, yeast doughs, laminated doughs, spongecakes and basic fillings before moving on to more complicated tasks. Even though the illustrations are of great help in showing students the particular steps for a given item, the instructor should still follow up a lecture on puff pastry, for example, by demonstrating how the turns are made, rolling and cutting the dough, making bouchées, and so on. Although these techniques are explained in this book in the way that I do them (and I do from time to time explain a variation), instructors are encouraged to give the students their own input.

As a teacher, as is true of anyone in a position of authority, it is important to realize that our students are observing and learning from us all the time—our demeanor, appearance, attitude, tone of voice, sense of humor, and our overall disposition all send a message. The knowledge we share and the lessons we teach are not limited to schoolwork assignments and our classroom or kitchen demonstrations.

To possess a skill and also have the ability to teach that skill to others is a gift that is not given to everyone. Most people working in a kitchen have at one time or another shown a subordinate, a fellow student, or a coworker how to perform a certain task or the accepted method used for a job in that particular workplace. I see and hear this everyday in my classes: the first student to successfully make pastry cream, for example, will then drop some little hint to whomever is in line to prepare the next batch. Working together, helping one another, and sharing information is a great thing provided that the information being shared is accurate.

As teachers, it is important that we not only possess the knowledge and the technical skills that relate to our subject matter, but also that we are able to convey information in a way that our students can comprehend and assimilate. Before you can teach, you must have the attention and the respect of your students. You must present the details and instructions in an interesting and entertaining way, and the students must feel motivated to learn. In other words, they must believe that what you are explaining or demonstrating will be of use to them.

I have found that a little humor goes a long way in keeping the attention focused and the class interested. Obviously, some subjects are much more appealing than others are. It is not hard to keep the class excited while they are watching a demonstration on pulled sugar or working with chocolate, but a lecture on the varying percentages of protein found in different types of flour is a bit more of a challenge. Again, students must know why they need this information and how it might be of use to them in the future. Another way to add interest to a lecture and to help the students retain the information more thoroughly is through visual effects. Students will retain more knowledge as more of their senses come into play. In the case of the aforementioned flour lecture, a chart or graph can be used to list the different ways that a particular type of dough or batter reacts when it is made with various types of flour. Or, better yet, combine the lecture and the graph or chart with samples of the food product. For example, make the same bread recipe using several different flours that vary in protein content so that the students can see, touch, and taste the bread. This way you have moved from engaging only one sense (hearing) to two (hearing and seeing) to all five (hearing, seeing, touching, smelling and tasting). Your boring flour lecture has not only become exciting, but the information has greater meaning and is far more likely to be remembered.

In a teaching kitchen, the instructor has a duty to point out a student's mistakes and to demonstrate the proper way that the procedure should have been performed. Even though it might be easier to "look the other way" or you may be afraid of hurting the student's feelings or might be concerned that they will become disappointed and give up, if you do not address the problem, you are not doing your job. In Scandinavia there is an expression that roughly translated says "The nail that sticks up will be hammered down." The meaning is that just because you did not trip over the nail doesn't mean someone else won't and if you simply walk around a problem; it is still going to be there later. One of the reasons that I like this expression is that building and woodworking are my hobby, but I also appreciate the underlying implication that a loose nail not only poses an immediate threat in that someone could trip or be cut, but it also has the potential to eventually bring down an entire structure. To me, the lesson here is to take care of small problems before they become larger.

As I said, a teacher must let his or her students know when they have made a mistake, but it is equally important that the message is conveyed in a diplomatic and professional manner. First of all, a teacher should never be condescending, rude, or cause embarrassment. Criticism can and must be constructive and should be done with a smile and a friendly reminder that "after all, you are here to learn." Explain what went wrong and show the student or the class the proper technique, even if you are doing so for the tenth time that day! If at all possible, try to find something positive to mention about the item in question at the same time. For example, let's say an apple tart is not acceptable for service because once it has been unmolded the crust falls apart. However, the filling was properly prepared and the tart was baked perfectly. By starting with comments about what was done right before moving into a discussion on what needs improvement, the student has something they can feel good about and be proud of. You can think of this as the "first the good news" technique.

I have always told my students that I will evaluate their technical skills based on how hard they try and how seriously they take their work. I emphasize that they must not be afraid of making a mistake and I tell them over and over "better to make a mistake here in school than when you are out working in the industry." Often a so-called mistake is the very best learning tool there is, provided that the student understands what went wrong and why. Another quote I particularly like is this one by F. P. Jones: "Experience is that wonderful thing that enables you to recognize a mistake when you make it again."

Two skills that are key to being successful in our industry are the ability to work as part of a team and to work efficiently in order to meet deadlines. In a lab setting, I divide the students into teams and assign each team at least as many projects as there are team members. I then leave it to the team as a group to "make a plan of attack" and to divide the assignments between them. Some of the projects are general mise en place, some are not needed until the next day but must be started right away, and others must be completed by the end of class. This exercise provides an excellent opportunity for the students to practice planning, delegating, and working with others, and to learn efficient production methods.

A sample of each project or recipe is set aside for review at the end of the day. I talk to the class about each item discussing what was done correctly and also how the item could be improved if applicable. As mentioned earlier, it is very important to find something good to say about each project and each student's efforts. Positive reinforcement is without question the best tool any teacher or manager can use. The desire to please and be recognized for one's efforts is a very basic part of human nature. Encouraging and recognizing a student's accomplishments in any situation—from a technical achievement, such as preparing a recipe correctly, to displaying a cooperative attitude toward classmates or coworkers, to simply trying one's best even if not entirely successful—will make any teacher or leader more productive.

In using this book I wish every reader—professional, nonprofessional, student, instructor, beginner, or experienced master—great success.

Please visit my web site **www.ChefBo.com** for inquiries, updates, and information.

Bo Friberg

INTRODUCTION

I started the first edition of this book twenty years ago when I returned from a trip to Europe, full of inspiration and new ideas. I began to catalog my new recipes along with the other recipes I was teaching. This fourth edition, like the first three, is a little different from other cookbooks in that it tells you not only what you should do, but also what not to do, based on common mistakes that I have observed in working with students.

Some of the selections are classic recipes made my way. Some date back to when I was an apprentice. A few I have adapted from restaurants and pastry shops in the United States and around Europe, where I would order something that looked interesting, pick it apart, literally and mentally, and then try to duplicate or even improve it. I developed many of the recipes by knowing what goes well together and what the American palate prefers. In addition to the classics, this fourth edition continues to expand on recipes and techniques that are in keeping with current trends in the industry. An old colleague once said to me, "Don't be concerned about someone stealing your ideas; show them all your cards, but always be working on something new."

Pastry is distinct from other types of cooking because you cannot just stick your spoon (or finger) in for a taste and then add a pinch of this and a pinch of that as you might when making a pot of soup. Most ingredients must be measured accurately because many formulas work on scientific principles. For this reason, the pastry chef must learn how different ingredients react with others and how and why ingredients respond to temperature, friction, and storage before he or she can create new recipes or troubleshoot existing recipes.

A competent chef's most important assets are common sense, self-confidence, and experience. These are the three things that cannot be taught. In the book *Siddhartha* by the German-born Swiss author Hermann Hesse, the wise sage tells his friend: "Wisdom is not communicable. Knowledge can be communicated, but not wisdom. One can find it, live it, be fortified by it, do wonders through it, but one cannot communicate and teach it."

To be a first-rate pastry chef, you must have some artistic talent, a good sense of coordination and taste, and a steady hand. You must also possess some people skills and earn the respect of those working with you. You must be able to solve problems and hire the right people. A good chef must be born with at least some of these talents, but keen interest and a lot of practice will improve these skills over the years. When you love what you are doing, believe in yourself, and believe that you can do the job, you will give everything your best effort. If the result is less than perfect, at least you will have learned something, and the next time you will try a little harder.

My first experiment with cooking took place in my mother's kitchen when I was eleven years old. When I came home from school and found the house empty, I attempted some kind of candy. I don't remember exactly what it was supposed to be, but I do remember my poor mother had great difficulty cleaning up the sticky pots and pans. We both learned something from this: my mom, to time her trips to the grocery store better; and I, to clean up my messes.

After graduating from school at fourteen, I started as an apprentice at one of the local *konditoris* (pastry shops). It was quite small—just two *commis*, the pastry chef, and myself. Without knowing it, I was lucky to have picked the best: my master and teacher for the next five years was a dedicated and skilled craftsman. When I began, I was a young boy who, of course, knew everything already. However, I soon found out about the real world, and especially how to take constructive criticism and learn from my mistakes. I remember his words: "One mistake is no mistake. But two mistakes are one too many."

I spent my first six months of training practicing the three Ls: listening, looking, and learning. While I was helping a little here and cleaning up a little there, I saw the breads and pastries being made. I had helped in making the dough for rye bread, but I had not done it on my own from start to finish. One morning when I arrived at work, my master said, "Bo! We are shorthanded today. Make up the rye bread!" I was startled and said, "I can't do that!" My master angrily replied, "Do not ever use that word here again! You can do anything you want to do if you want to do it badly enough. The least you can do is give it your very best try." I have always remembered and tried to live by those words. It is one of the philosophies that I try to instill in all of my students.

After I had become a regular on rye bread, the retired owner of the pastry shop used to come down to check me out. (At that time most bakeries in Sweden were in the cellar with small windows level with the street, so when the bakers looked out all they could see were shoes. Of course, to a young apprentice, some pairs of shoes were much more interesting than others.)

After a few lectures about the loaves that were not perfectly formed, I noticed that he would always walk in a straight line from the door to the shelves where the breads cooled and pick up a loaf in the center of one particular shelf to examine. After I started placing the almost-perfect loaves in this place, I could practice and improve in peace. But if I happened to pay too much attention to those shoes outside the windows, I used to hear from across the room, "Bo, throw some sheet pans on the floor. I don't see you doing anything, so at least let me hear you!" (And I have to admit the first time I did just that!) In the end my "yes-I-know-that" attitude must have improved too, for my master named his first and only son Bo, which I claimed as the ultimate victory. He assured me, however, that naming his son had nothing to do with a certain apprentice. I have a lot to thank John Håkanson for, and later on, Curt Anderson: two great Swedish Master Confectioners, who not only had the patience and craft to teach me what they knew of their profession, but also taught me a lot about life.

Unfortunately, very few restaurants and bakeries today can afford to train an apprentice thoroughly, because it costs too much in time and materials. Trade schools now provide the training that small businesses cannot, and this allows an employer to hire a graduate who has received instructions and experience in the basics.

Once the fundamentals are mastered, you can start to create, improve, and put your own style into the dishes you prepare. In our industry today, I am pleased to see more creativity and that "bit of self" going into dessert menus, and more recognition being given to the pastry chef and pastry kitchen. Ten years ago it was unheard of for a pastry chef to have his or her name on the menu; these days, many restaurants feature separate dessert menus, with written credit given to the pastry chef.

The first and last impressions of a meal are especially important. I do not expect anything of a meal if the kitchen cannot make a decent salad or serve the soup hot. However, even if the meal is mediocre, a dessert that looks and tastes terrific will leave the guest with a positive last impression. I have noted with pleasure the rebirth of interest in great desserts. And, of course, it is especially rewarding for me when I realize, glancing at a restaurant menu or tasting a dessert, that one of my former students is in the kitchen.

This book is about making desserts and baked goods that are both delicious and exciting. It is not meant to impress or to set any particular standards. The methods described and used in the recipes are not the only ones possible or necessarily the best methods. There are different ways to form a loaf of bread, frost a cake, or hold a pastry bag. One way is good for one person, another way better for someone else.

In this book I offer the best of my knowledge and experience, as I give it to my students. It is my hope that this knowledge will be useful to you as you seek to better yourself in our creative and honorable profession.

Before You Use This Book

Certain ingredient information is standard throughout the book. Please note the following conventions:

- Salt used in these recipes is common granulated salt. If you prefer using kosher salt see page 922.

- Butter is always specified as "unsalted butter." Salted butter can be substituted if the salt in the recipe is reduced by about ⅕ ounce (6 g) for every pound of butter. However, you cannot substitute salted butter if the recipe contains little salt or if the main ingredient is butter.

- The number of eggs specified in each recipe is based on 2-ounce (55-g) eggs (graded large). If you use eggs of a different size, adjust the number accordingly. For convenience in kitchens where a supply of separated egg yolks and whites is available, a volume measure is given when yolks or whites are used independently. The quantity of yolks, whites, and whole eggs per cup has been rounded to twelve, eight, and four, respectively, for these measures.

- Raw eggs: When egg yolks, whites, or whole eggs are included in a recipe in which they are not cooked, e.g. in a mousse or gelatin-fortified cake filling, they are first heated to at least 140°F (60°C) to pasteurize them (see page 883). This is done using different procedures depending on the recipe; often it involves whisking a hot syrup into the eggs or whipping the eggs over a bain-marie with another ingredient.

- Yeast is always specified as "fresh compressed yeast." To substitute dry yeast for fresh, reduce the amount called for by half. "Fast rising" yeast should be avoided. It is treated with conditioners that accelerate the yeast and give the chef less control. Furthermore, it impairs the flavor of baked goods in most cases.

- Gelatin is called for as unflavored powdered gelatin. To substitute sheet gelatin, see page 982, and also pages 889-890.

- The unsweetened cocoa powder called for in the recipes in this book refers to the alkalized (Dutch-process) type, preferred for its darker color and smoother flavor, and also because it dissolves more easily. Natural cocoa powder, which is somewhat acidic, may be substituted provided it is used in a recipe that contains a sweetener. However, it should not be used to sift on top of a pastry or to coat a truffle, because it can be bitter eaten alone.

- When recipes in this text call for both sweet dark chocolate and unsweetened chocolate, the combined weight of these two can be replaced with either semisweet or bittersweet chocolate, depending on the original ratio of sweet to unsweetened.

- Both metric and U.S. units are given throughout. However, to avoid unmeasurable fractions, metric amounts have been rounded to the nearest even number. The equivalent for 1 ounce, for instance, is given as 30 grams rather than 28.35 grams.

- When 1 ounce or less of an ingredient, dry or liquid, is needed, the quantity is always given in teaspoons or tablespoons and is based on an exact measurement. Hedges like "scant" or "heaping" are not used in this book.

- Avoid the temptation to convert ingredients into cups and tablespoons. Weight measurements are used in professional recipes for better accuracy, and a good scale can be purchased inexpensively. Make certain that your scale (old or new) is properly calibrated.

- Sheet pans are the standard American size. Full size is 16 x 24 inches (40 x 60 cm), and half size is 12 x 16 inches (30 x 40 cm). Both have a 1-inch (2.5-cm) slightly slanted border.

- In some recipes, instructions are given to spread a batter (most often a sponge batter) over a sheet of baking paper set on the work surface and then to drag the paper onto a sheet pan.

This is done to facilitate spreading the batter evenly without the sides of the sheet pan getting in the way, as the standard industry sheet pans in the United States have 1-inch (2.5-cm) sides. Readers throughout Europe and in other countries where regular sheet pans contain raised sides only on the short ends may eliminate this step.

- Some recipes in this text include instructions for making templates. Thin cardboard is one possibility because it is readily available and easy to work with; however, plain cardboard templates are intended for one-time use only. (A simple method to extend the life of a template is to spray or brush 2 or 3 layers of food-grade lacquer on both sides, so the template can be cleaned and reused.) A sturdier and more practical template can be made from $\frac{1}{16}$-inch (2-mm) plastic. These take a bit more effort to construct, but they can be used over and over. I prefer the laminated type of plastic (the type often used to cover office files or documents) since it will lie perfectly flat and will not tear, but polyurethane sheets also work well.

- Any recipe in this book can be scaled up or down in direct proportions as long as it is not multiplied or divided by any number greater than four. In calculating ingredients that do not divide straight across, e.g. to divide in half a recipe calling for 3 eggs or $1\frac{1}{3}$ cups of a liquid, round the number up (using 2 eggs or $5\frac{1}{2}$ ounces of liquid for the examples given).

- When a weight yield is given for baked goods (for example, four 1-pound, 4-ounce [570 g] loaves), it relates to the product before being baked. As a general rule, ten percent of the weight is lost in steam during the baking process of any item. When a large amount of liquid is part of the ingredients (such as for bread), up to 2 ounces (55 g) for every pound (455 g) of dough will expire.

- A properly calibrated thermometer is of great importance for both safe food handling and to obtain desired results whenever the exact temperature of the ingredients determines the outcome. Refer to page 967 for instructions on how to calibrate a thermometer.

- The ingredients and equipment used to produce these recipes are discussed in detail in the appendixes and the recipe introductions, sidebars, and chef's tips. These sections contain a tremendous amount of information, and I strongly urge readers to thoroughly familiarize themselves with the products used to make a particular item, not simply for the sake of curiosity, but to ensure the best possible result in the safest manner.

- When white flour is used in recipes in this book, cake flour, bread flour, or high-gluten flour is specified. All-purpose flour, pastry flour, and the dozens of other specialty white flours are not used. Many recipes combine cake flour and bread flour to create the desired protein content. If you do not have cake flour or bread flour, all-purpose flour may be substituted with a good result in most cases. When high-gluten flour is unavailable, bread flour may be used instead. The protein content of cake flour is generally around 7 percent. Bread flour has a protein content of approximately 12 percent, and high-gluten flour about 14 percent. When cake flour and bread flour are combined in equal amounts, they essentially create all-purpose flour, which has a protein content of approximately 9 to 10 percent. All of these protein percentages vary depending on the manufacturer.

The Professional Pastry Chef

Mise en Place

The literal translation of mise en place is "to put in place." In the professional kitchen, the term means getting ready the things we need to prepare ahead of time, or prep work. Preparation is an important factor for the professional pastry chef. In the pastry kitchen, many jobs should be done at the end of the day in anticipation of the next morning, such as making pastry cream and other fillings and removing butter from the freezer so it can thaw and soften.

Advance Planning and Stock Items

Before starting any project, the professional will make a plan of attack, first going through the recipe mentally and making sure all of the ingredients needed to complete it smoothly are at hand, then thinking through how to accomplish each step most efficiently. If toasted sliced almonds are called for to decorate the sides of poppy seed cake, they should be prepared first thing so they are cold by the time they are used. If melted chocolate is needed to finish a pastry, it can be placed over hot water and stirred from time to time while you complete the other steps. If you need to melt the butter and flour mixture so you can brush it on cake pans, there is no reason to put it on the top of the stove if the oven is closer; just put the pot in there for a few seconds.

Items that are used regularly should always be accessible. If you make croissants every morning, there is no reason to make fresh egg wash each day. Instead, make enough to last three or four days and store it, covered, in the refrigerator (in fact, egg wash actually works better if it is a day or more old). When going to the refrigerator for milk to make pastry cream, think about what you are making next, and if, for example, that happens to be apple filling, take out the apples at the same time instead of making two trips. If you can think one or two steps ahead, you will get a lot more done in less time. It is a bit like the old saying, "Don't walk across the river to fetch water," or, as my master used to tell me when I was an apprentice, "What you do not have in your head, you have to make up for with your feet."

Almond Paste yield: I pound 14 ounces (855 g)

Although it is simple to make almond paste if you have an almond mill (see page 937), the time involved does not justify the cost savings in today's industry, so it is rarely made in the pastry shop nowadays. The only disadvantage to purchasing a commercial brand is that consistency varies from one brand to another, and you will need to compensate for that in some recipes. Also, there can be tiny specks of brown skin from almonds that were not blanched properly in some batches. If you find that you cannot produce the specified powdery consistency in Step 1, very finely ground almonds will suffice. The quality of the finished product will not be as good, but the only recipe in which it will be noticeable is Marzipan.

10 ounces (285 g) dry blanched almonds	1¼ cups (300 ml) simple syrup
10 ounces (285 g) powdered sugar	

1. Place the almonds in a high-speed food processor and process to a powder (see Note).

2. Add the powdered sugar; then, with the machine running, gradually add the simple syrup until the mixture forms a paste. The amount of simple syrup needed will vary depending on how dry the almonds are. Freshly blanched almonds will need less syrup. Store the almond paste, tightly covered, for up to 1 week at room temperature. Refrigerate for longer storage.

NOTE: If the almonds are not completely dry, you will get a paste at this point rather than a powder. This is fine, provided that the paste is smooth.

Apricot Glaze <small>yield: 2 cups (480 ml)</small>

Melted sugar is extremely hot and can cause serious burns, so unless you have a chef's brass fingers, take great care in testing the glaze against your skin. Using two spoons is a safer bet.

1 pound (455 g) apricot jam	⅓ cup (80 ml) water
3 ounces (85 g) granulated sugar	

1. Place the jam, sugar, and water in a heavy-bottomed saucepan. Bring to a boil over medium heat, stirring constantly.

2. Lower the heat and continue cooking until the mixture can be pulled into a ¼-inch (6-mm) thread between your thumb and index finger or with the back of two spoons.

3. Quickly remove the pan from the heat, strain (discard the solids), and use immediately. Store the leftover glaze at room temperature. Reheat the glaze to use again; if it is too thick, add a small amount of water.

NOTE: If you overcook the glaze, it will become too thick to use properly. Unless it has started to caramelize, you can correct this by adding a small amount of water and cooking to the thread test again.

Beet Juice <small>yield: approximately 1¼ cups (300 ml)</small>

Beets are among the few red vegetables. They get their color from a group of pigments called anthocyanins. These are the same elements responsible for most of the color in red, purple, and blue fruits and flowers. Extracted beet juice can be used to color food products as an alternative to artificial red dyes. If added to foods that are too alkaline, the color will change from red to purple and begin to fade. Adding an acid will prevent this and will even reverse the effect after it has occurred, changing the purple color back to red.

1 pound (455 g) red beets

1. Wash and peel the beets, then process using a juice extractor (see Note).

2. Store the juice in a plastic squeeze bottle in the refrigerator. The juice will keep for several months.

NOTE: If you do not have a juice extractor, chop the beets and grind in a food processor or grate the beets fine and press the juice through a fine sieve. Using a food processor is not as desirable, as the yield of juice is much lower and both alternatives take more time. The freshness of the beets also affects the yield.

Blanched and Toasted Nuts

BLANCHED ALMONDS

To remove the brown skin from almonds, pour boiling water over the nuts, cover, and let them soak for 5 minutes. Drain the water and immediately pinch the almonds between your fingers to remove the skin. Another method is to place the almonds in a saucepan and add enough water to cover. Bring to a boil and simmer for 3 minutes. Strain off the water and remove the skin immediately. With both methods, do not forget and leave the almonds sitting in the water too long; the skin could stain the almond meat and turn it brownish.

TO REMOVE THE SKIN FROM HAZELNUTS

The skin on hazelnuts is easier to remove after they are toasted. Place the nuts in a 400°F (205°C) oven for about 10 minutes, or until they start to turn golden. Let cool, then rub the nuts between your hands or in a kitchen towel to remove the skin. This method will not remove all of the skin on all of the nuts. For recipes where that is necessary, one option is to toast more nuts than you will need, allowing you to pick out the better-looking ones and use the others where a little remaining skin does not matter.

To remove all of the skin from hazelnuts, or for recipes where the nuts are needed untoasted, pour boiling water with a little added baking soda (1 teaspoon/4 g to 1 quart/960 ml) over the nuts, let stand 5 minutes, drain, and remove the skins.

BLANCHED PISTACHIOS

Using a little salt in the blanching water for pistachios will accentuate their green color and allow you to remove the skin easily. Use approximately ½ teaspoon (2.5 g) salt per quart (960 ml) water. Pour the boiling salted water over the pistachios and let stand a few minutes. Drain, then rub the nuts in a towel.

CHESTNUTS: SHELLED OR ROASTED

To remove the shells from fresh chestnuts, cut a small X on the flat side of each shell and either roast in a 375°F (190°C) oven for 10 to 15 minutes or cook in boiling water for 5 to 15 minutes, depending on whether or not the chestnuts will be cooked further. Chestnuts are easier to peel while they are still warm.

GENERAL INSTRUCTIONS FOR TOASTING NUTS

Toasted shelled nuts—almonds in many forms, hazelnuts, walnuts, and pecans, for example—are frequently used in the pastry shop. All nuts should be toasted in a single layer (or a shallow layer, in the case of sliced hazelnuts and sliced or slivered almonds) at medium heat (350° to 375°F/175° to 190°C) for about 15 minutes for sliced hazelnuts or almonds, slightly longer for whole, broken, or slivered nuts. Nuts can become too dark very quickly, so it is important to keep an eye on them and move them about on the pan periodically while they are cooking.

Shake the pan to redistribute them and keep them in a single layer. The nuts nearest the edge of the pan will toast more rapidly and, in fact, due to their high oil content, it is quite possible to burn pine nuts that are close to the edge of the pan before those in the middle are even toasted. Sliced and slivered almonds also need extra attention and will continue to darken a bit after they are removed from the oven. If you are toasting nuts with the skin on, remove one or two before you think they are done, remove the skin, and check their progress.

Beurre Noisette

Also known simply as brown butter, this French term literally translates to "hazelnut butter." The word *noisette*, or hazelnut, refers to both the color and fragrance of the finished product. As the butter is cooked over low heat, the milk solids caramelize, turning the butter light brown and giving it a nutty flavor and aroma—hence the name.

To prepare beurre noisette, cook butter over low heat until it reaches a light brown color and is fragrant. Be careful not to burn the butter.

Butter and Flour Mixture

Using a butter and flour mixture is a quick and easy way to prepare cake pans, forms, and molds in any recipe that directs you to grease and flour the pan. Rather than applying the two separately, you brush on the flour at the same time you grease the pan. This method can save a great deal of time when the task is done over and over throughout the day. Many establishments use the commercially produced pan sprays instead, and these work fine as well. Although today more equipment is being made from nonstick material, there will always be a need for this old-fashioned method.

1. Stir together 4 parts melted butter or margarine with 1 part bread flour by volume until blended.

2. Apply the mixture with a brush.

NOTE: The combination can be left at room temperature for up to 1 week. If the mixture is refrigerated, warm it before using (but do not boil) and stir to combine.

Candied Chestnuts yield: I pound 4 ounces (570 g)

Candied chestnuts are expensive to purchase, so preparing your own can be economical, assuming you can justify the labor needed to remove the shells. If you want perfect whole candied chestnuts for garnish, start with more than you need, because some will break when you shell them; and don't let the chestnuts boil vigorously in the syrup, or all of them will break into small pieces. Broken pieces can, of course, be used in fillings and for chestnut puree. Pay close attention toward the end of the cooking process, as the thick syrup can burn easily.

1 pound (455 g) fresh chestnuts	8 ounces (225 g) granulated sugar
4 cups (960 ml) water	

1. Cut a small X in the flat side of the shell on each chestnut, using the tip of a paring knife.

2. Place the chestnuts on a sheet pan and roast at 375° (190°C) for approximately 15 minutes. (Or place in a saucepan with enough water to cover, simmer for the same length of time, and drain.)

3. While the nuts are still hot, remove the shells and the dark papery skin around the meat.

4. Place the chestnuts in a saucepan with the water and sugar. Bring to a boil, stirring gently, then simmer for approximately 45 minutes, or until the liquid has reduced to a thick syrup. Let cool.

5. Store the candied chestnuts in the syrup, covered, in the refrigerator. They will keep for several weeks.

Caramel Coloring yield: 3 cups (720 ml)

When I learned my trade in Europe, this was known as *blackjack*. It is basically just burned sugar, which, when cooked to 392°F (200°C), turns completely black. Once the mixture has cooled, a small amount is used to color baked goods, mainly breads. Caramel coloring will last indefinitely and does not need to be refrigerated.

I find many students do not cook the sugar long enough, especially when they make caramel coloring for the first time. There is probably some guilt involved in burning something intentionally, and no doubt they assume something must have gone wrong when they smell it, as sugar, when cooked to this extreme temperature, produces an aroma that should bring any executive chef worth his or her title into the kitchen in a hurry!

2 pounds (910 g) granulated sugar	4 drops of lemon juice
½ cup (120 ml) water	1½ cups (360 ml) water

1. Combine the sugar, the first measurement of water, and the lemon juice in a heavy saucepan. Cook over medium heat without stirring until the sugar begins to caramelize, brushing down the sides of the pan with water from time to time. Continue to cook, stirring frequently so that the sugar colors evenly, to 392°F (200°C)—blackjack stage. The sugar will be burned, and there will be smoke coming from the pan. Remove the pan from the heat, stand back, and very carefully pour in the second measurement of water. Stir until the mixture is smooth.

2. Let cool. Pour into a jar and store, covered, at room temperature.

Caramelized Sugar

Sugar starts to turn from golden to light brown in color and begins to caramelize when its temperature reaches 320°F (160°C). There are two ways of bringing sugar to this temperature: the dry method and the wet method. Caramelizing sugar dry takes about half the time, and you do not have to worry about recrystallization. It does, however, require more attention, as the sugar must be stirred constantly to prevent it from caramelizing too fast—that is, before all of the sugar granules have melted—or worse, from burning. If you use the dry method, do not use a skillet or pan that is any larger than necessary, or you will have a larger area to cover when stirring, and you may not be able to keep the sugar from getting too dark. With the wet method, a small amount of water added to the sugar means the caramel does not need to be stirred during the entire cooking process, but it takes longer to caramelize because you must wait for the water to evaporate.

Either way is much faster and easier if you use a sugar pan, an unlined copper pan made especially for cooking sugar. The acidity of the copper reacts with the sugar in such a way that some of the sugar breaks down into invert sugar, which is resistant to recrystallization. Invert sugar is a mixture of equal parts glucose and fructose. Be careful, though; because the copper is almost the same color as the caramelized sugar, the exact moment the pan should be pulled off the heat and placed in cold water to stop the cooking process is harder to identify. To be able to see the color of the sugar more clearly, use a folded piece of baking paper (do not use waxed paper) and dip the point of the folded paper in the sugar syrup. Remove and check the color.

Another option is to pour a few small test puddles on a silicone mat or a sheet of baking paper to determine the color more accurately. If the sugar is heated much above 320°F (160°C) and you are not using it immediately, you cannot stop it right there; the sugar will continue to darken, even as it sits in the water off the stove, from its own residual heat. This problem is intensified by using a copper pan. With caramelized sugar, you do not need to use a sugar thermometer, as the color of the sugar will tell you when it is done.

Caramelized Sugar, Dry Method yield: 2¼ cups (540 ml)

The addition of lemon juice or tartaric acid not only makes the sugar softer, it also delays the caramelization process, allowing more time to properly melt all of the sugar.

2 pounds (910 g) granulated sugar

1 teaspoon (5 ml) lemon juice *or* 12 drops tartaric acid solution (page 38)

1. Fill a bowl that is large enough to hold the pan used for cooking the sugar with enough cold water to reach halfway up the sides of the pan. Set the bowl aside.

2. Place the sugar and lemon juice in a copper or stainless-steel pan (see Note). Cook over low heat, stirring constantly, until the sugar is completely melted.

3. Continue to cook until the sugar has caramelized to just a shade lighter than the desired color.

4. Remove from the heat and immediately place the bottom of the pan in the bowl of cold water to stop the cooking process. Use the caramel as directed in individual recipes. If you need to reheat the caramel, stir the sugar constantly over low heat to prevent the sugar from getting any darker than necessary.

NOTE: You can help eliminate lumps of unmelted sugar by using the following procedure: Place the granulated sugar on a sheet pan lined with baking paper. Pour the lemon juice or tartaric acid solution on top of the sugar. Using your hands, rub the lemon juice or tartaric acid into the sugar as thoroughly as possible; take 2 or 3 minutes to incorporate it. Place this mixture in the saucepan and continue as directed in the second part of Step 2.

Caramelizing Sugar in Larger Quantities

If you are caramelizing more than 2 pounds (910 g) sugar at one time, it is easier if you do not add all of it at the beginning. Instead, start with about one-quarter of the total amount. Once it has melted but not changed color, add one-quarter more and repeat, adding the remaining sugar in the same way. This way, you do not have to stir the entire amount from the start.

If lumps of unmelted sugar remain when the rest of the sugar has caramelized, the temperature was too high and/or the sugar was not stirred properly, which is especially important once it begins to liquefy. These lumps cannot be melted without darkening the rest of the sugar, and it is not practical to strain them out unless the caramel is to be used for a sauce (in that case, strain after adding the water). Therefore, the best thing to do is pick them out of the syrup.

Caramelized Sugar with Water yield: 2¼ cups (540 ml)

While the sugar syrup here should not boil wildly at the start, you do want to reach the desired temperature as quickly as possible to reduce the chances of recrystallization (when this happens, we say in the industry that the sugar has died). Cooking as rapidly as possible is important in any situation where you are reducing a sugar syrup close to or all the way to the point of caramelization. Cooking quickly is not an issue when you are boiling a sugar syrup to a lower degree, such as for Italian meringue or simple syrup.

1 cup (240 ml) water
2 pounds (910 g) granulated sugar

¼ cup (60 ml) glucose *or* light corn syrup (see Note, page 12)

1. Fill a bowl that is large enough to hold the pan used for cooking the sugar with enough cold water to reach halfway up the sides of the pan. Set the bowl aside.

2. Place the water and sugar in a copper or stainless-steel pan. Stir to combine and dissolve the sugar in the water over low heat. Wash down the sides of the pan with water using a brush dedicated to sugar boiling.

3. Bring the mixture to a rolling boil, add the glucose or corn syrup, then lower the heat to ensure that the liquid will not boil too hard at the beginning. Do not stir once the sugar starts boiling. Instead, brush down the sides of the pan with water as needed until the sugar reaches 280°F (138°C)—the crack stage. Keep boiling until the sugar has caramelized to the desired color.

4. Quickly remove the pan from the heat and place the bottom of the pan in the reserved cold water to stop the cooking process. Use as directed in individual recipes.

Caramelized Sugar for Decorations yield: 2¼ cups (660 ml)

The old-fashioned dry method for caramelizing sugar is still the fastest and easiest way when only a small amount of caramel is needed, for a few ornaments or a batch of Crème Caramel, for example. If necessary, you can speed the process in the following recipe in a similar way by cutting both the water and glucose or corn syrup in half, provided you are very careful. By using the full amount of water and glucose or corn syrup called for, there will be plenty of liquid to help the sugar dissolve properly and prevent it from recrystallizing. If you are working during rainy weather or when there is a high level of humidity, you would be better off not taking the shortcut.

The most convenient way to caramelize sugar for decorations is to keep a stock of sugar syrup on hand (as described in Step 3 below). Simply pour off whatever amount is needed at the time and continue cooking it to the desired stage.

2 cups (480 ml) cold water (see Chef's Tip)
2 pounds (910 g) granulated sugar

7 ounces (200 g) glucose *or* light corn syrup (see Note)

1. Fill a bowl that is large enough to hold the cooking pan with enough cold water to reach halfway up the sides of the pan. Set the bowl aside.

2. Place the water and sugar in a copper or stainless steel pan. Dissolve the sugar in the water over low heat. Bring to a boil, stirring constantly, and skim off any scum that accumulates on the surface.

3. Add the glucose or corn syrup. Return the syrup to a boil. Wash down the sides of the pan with a clean brush dedicated to sugar boiling that is dipped in water. Remove any additional scum from the surface if necessary. If you are making sugar syrup for general mise en place, pour it into a clean container at this point (or just pour off the excess) and store until needed.

4. Continue cooking the sugar syrup, washing down the sides of the pan as long as sugar crystals are accumulating; do not stir from this point on. When the sugar begins to change from clear to light amber, watch it closely, as it will turn to golden brown very quickly because most of the water has evaporated at this point and the temperature is now around 315°F (157°C).

5. When the syrup just starts to show a hint of golden brown, remove the pan from the stove and set it in the bowl of cold water. Hold it there until all of the bubbles have subsided. Remove the pan from the water, wipe the bottom, and let the sugar cool at room temperature as necessary, depending on the intended use.

NOTE: Because glucose is not readily available in the United States, I use light corn syrup most of the time, and it works fine. Try to get the thicker 44° Baumé corn syrup if possible.

Chestnut Puree yield: 2¹/₂ cups (600 ml)

> 2 pounds 8 ounces (1 kg 135 g) fresh
> chestnuts in the shell

1. Cut a small X in the flat side of each nut using the point of a paring knife.

2. Place the chestnuts in a saucepan with enough water to cover. Bring to a boil, reduce the heat, and simmer for 15 to 30 minutes, or until soft inside. Be careful not to overcook the chestnuts. Peel one and check the inside; it should be dry and have a mealy texture, something like a baked potato.

3. Drain the chestnuts and let them cool until they can be handled comfortably. Do not cool completely, or they will be much more difficult to peel. Remove the shells and skin and puree the chestnuts in a food processor just until smooth. Do not overprocess, or the chestnuts will become gummy.

Cinnamon Sugar yield: 2½ cups (600 ml)

1½ ounces (40 g) ground cinnamon   1 pound (455 g) granulated sugar

1. Combine the ground cinnamon and sugar.

2. Store in a tightly covered container at room temperature.

NOTE: To make a smaller quantity, use 1 part ground cinnamon to 4 parts granulated sugar, measured by volume.

Citrus Segments from Oranges or Grapefruit

1. Cut the top and bottom off the fruit and set it, cut side down, on a cutting board.

2. Cut away the skin on the sides, slicing from top to bottom, removing all of the white pith and following the natural curved shape of the fruit (Figure 1-1).

3. Hold the fruit in your hand over a bowl to catch the juice. With a small, sharp paring knife, cut between the inside membranes to remove the segments (Figure 1-2), letting them fall into the dish.

FIGURE 1-1 **Cutting the peel and all of the white pith away from the orange flesh, making slightly rounded cuts to keep the natural shape of the orange**

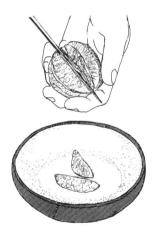

FIGURE 1-2 **Cutting between the membranes to release the orange segments, with the orange held over a bowl to catch the juice**

Clarified Butter

Clarified butter is butter with the milk solids removed. It has a higher burning point than whole butter, which makes it preferable for sauté work or any time you are cooking foods at a high temperature. Depending on the moisture content of the brand of butter you are using, the yield of clarified butter will be about 20 to 25 percent less than the amount of whole butter you start with. In other words, if you start with 16 ounces (455 g) butter, you will end up with 12 to 13 ounces (340 to 370 g) clarified butter.

1. Melt butter over low heat; let it bubble for a few minutes, but do not let it brown.

2. Remove the pan from the heat and let it stand for about 10 minutes.

3. Without moving or disturbing the pan, skim off all of the foamy solids that have risen to the top. This is easiest to do using a ladle.

4. Carefully spoon or pour the clear butterfat into a clean container, watching carefully so you do not add any of the milky portion that will have collected on the bottom.

5. Discard the milky residue in the bottom of the pan.

Coffee Reduction

This simple method of developing a good, strong coffee flavor can, of course, be modified to your own taste. Start with fresh coffee brewed from top-quality beans; do not use instant coffee.

1. Make coffee 10 times the normal strength.

2. Bring the coffee to a boil in a saucepan and reduce by half.

3. Let cool and use as needed. Coffee reduction can be stored at room temperature for a few days; it should be refrigerated if it is to be kept any longer.

Crepes yield: about 40 crepes, 6 inches (15 cm) in diameter

6 ounces (170 g) cake flour	6 egg yolks (½ cup/120 ml)
6 ounces (170 g) bread flour	6 ounces (170 g) unsalted butter, melted
3 ounces (85 g) granulated sugar	3 cups (720 ml) warm whole milk
2 teaspoons (10 g) salt	⅓ cup (80 ml) brandy
6 whole eggs	Clarified unsalted butter

1. Sift the cake flour and bread flour together. Combine with the sugar and salt in a mixing bowl.

2. Lightly beat the whole eggs with the egg yolks just to mix. Gradually stir the eggs into the dry ingredients. Add the melted butter, milk, and brandy. Stir until smooth. If the batter appears broken, the milk was probably too cool. To remedy this, warm the batter over simmering water, stirring constantly until smooth. Let the batter rest at room temperature for 1 hour.

3. Heat 2 crepe pans, each 6 inches (15 cm) in diameter. Brush with clarified butter (see Note); do not use a nylon brush. Using a small ladle, cover the bottom of the pans with a thin film of batter by quickly tilting and rotating them (Figure 1-3). Try to avoid making the batter run up the sides of the pans. Pour any excess batter back into the bowl. With practice, you should be able to add just the right amount of batter each time.

4. When the bottoms of the crepes have a nice golden brown color, flip them over using a spatula and the fingers of one hand, or flip them in the air, if you have the knack. The second side need cook for only a few seconds, until it is no longer sticky; overcooking the crepes will make them dry.

FIGURE 1-3 **Rotating the pan to distribute the crepe batter**

5. Slide the crepes out of the pans and stack them on a plate to prevent their drying out as you make the remaining crepes. Cover once you have a large stack. After you have made a few crepes, adjust the batter, if necessary. If large bubbles form as the crepes cook, the batter is probably too thin (or the pan may be too hot). Thicken the batter by whipping in additional flour. If the batter is too thick and does not pour in a thin film, add milk to thin it. Once you have the batter and the heat adjusted correctly, making a few dozen crepes is easy. If they will not be used within several hours, wrap and store in the refrigerator. Leftover refrigerated crepes are suitable for use in dishes where they will be served hot, but they should not be used in cold dishes because they tend to be a bit rubbery. Wipe the crepe pans clean with a towel; do not use water under any circumstances.

NOTE: If you are using properly seasoned crepe pans, you probably will have to grease them for the first few crepes only. In any case, avoid using too much butter, as this saturates the crepes and adds excess calories.

Crystallized Ginger yield: about 10 ounces (285 g)

Crystallizing ginger is rarely done in the professional bakeshop, although it is quite easy and not very time consuming. As with many homemade foodstuffs, which are free from artificial ingredients such as coloring, bleaching, and preservatives, the finished product will not look like the commercial product with which you are familiar. This crystallized ginger has a much darker color than the commercial golden or tan product you buy.

1 pound (455 g) fresh ginger (see Note)   ⅓ cup (80 ml) water
1 pound (455 g) granulated sugar, plus more
    for coating

1. Peel the ginger and slice ¼ inch (6 mm) thick.

2. Place the ginger slices in a saucepan and add enough water to cover. Simmer over low heat until the ginger is tender, approximately 40 minutes. Drain, discarding the liquid.

3. Place 1 pound (455 g) granulated sugar in the empty saucepan. Add ⅓ cup (80 ml) water and stir to moisten all the sugar. Bring to a boil, add the drained ginger slices, and boil gently, stirring frequently, until the ginger looks translucent, about 20 minutes.

4. Reduce the heat and simmer until the syrup is quite thick. The sugar syrup is likely to form lumps if you cook it too long. This is all right; however, you should remove any large lumps that stick to the ginger pieces.

5. Using two forks, remove the ginger slices from the syrup and toss them in granulated sugar to coat. Place the pieces in a single layer, spaced well apart, on a sheet pan. Let sit overnight in a warm place. Store the ginger in an airtight container for up to 6 months.

NOTE: Use ginger pieces that are as large as possible and cut smaller pieces on the bias to make the slices more uniform.

Egg Wash

Egg wash gives a shine to soft breads and rolls, croissants, and puff pastry items. It is also used as a glue to hold pieces of dough together or to make almonds or sugar adhere when sprinkled on a pastry or cookie before baking.

The best shine is obtained from egg wash containing only egg yolks and salt, thinned with a little water or milk. This is not really practical, however, unless you have egg yolks sitting around or have a use for the separated whites. It makes more sense to use the whole egg beaten with a little salt (but no water or milk) for everyday use (see Chef's Tip).

CHEF'S TIP EGG WASH

Although egg wash made from egg yolks alone (no egg whites) will produce a deeply colored shiny surface during baking, using egg yolks alone becomes too much of a good thing in most cases. Not only is egg yolk wash often too thick to be applied in a thin even layer, the resulting crust can be dark to the point of appearing over-baked. On the other hand, the addition of water and/or milk to egg wash made from whole eggs tones down the coloration, making the finished crust more pale. Adding salt to egg wash made from egg yolks, whole eggs, or a combination amplifies the shine on the final product and also works to thin the egg wash, which in turn makes it easier to apply correctly. The salt requires some time to break down and thin the egg substance, so this is only noticeable if the egg wash sits approximately 8 hours or overnight (in the refrigerator) before use.

Whole-Egg Egg Wash yield: I cup (240 ml)

4 eggs   ½ teaspoon (2.5 g) salt

1. Beat the eggs and salt together until the yolks and whites are combined.

2. Allow to stand 30 minutes before using or, preferably, cover and refrigerate overnight.

Yolks-Only Egg Wash yield: ³/₄ cup (180 ml)

8 egg yolks (²/₃ cup/160 ml)	2 to 3 tablespoons (30 to 45 ml) water *or* milk
½ teaspoon (2.5 g) salt	

1. Beat the egg yolks, salt, and water or milk together until well combined.

2. Cover and refrigerate overnight. If this is not possible, allow the egg wash to stand a minimum of 30 minutes before using.

NOTE: This egg wash might be too strong for items that are baked at temperatures above 400°F (205°C). The color will be too dark, giving the crust an overbaked appearance. If so, thin further or use whole-egg egg wash.

Egg Wash for Spraying yield: 2 cups (480 ml)

Applying egg wash with a spray bottle powered by compressed air, electricity, or elbow grease instead of a brush (the more typical and time-consuming method) has been common in European bakeries since the early 1960s. The spray technique makes a lot of sense. Not only is it faster, but it also produces a smooth, even application. Moreover, because you do not actually touch the product, you do not risk damaging the soft dough. The only disadvantage is that you will, of course, be applying egg wash to the sheet pan or baking paper around the items you are spraying, but this small amount of waste is offset by the advantages.

It is a good idea to designate an easy-to-clean area in the kitchen for spraying, or be sure to place a few sheets of baking paper around where you are working to aid in cleanup. For the best result, egg wash for use in a spray bottle should be prepared a day ahead to give the salt time to make the eggs less viscous.

6 whole eggs	½ teaspoon (2.5 g) salt
4 egg yolks (¹/₃ cup/80 ml)	

1. Combine whole eggs, egg yolks, and salt. Process for 10 to 15 seconds in a food processor. Strain through a fine mesh strainer (chinois) to remove the chalazae (the thick white cords attached to the yolk).

2. Cover the mixture and refrigerate for a minimum of 12 hours.

3. Pour the egg wash into a spray bottle set to fine mist.

4. Spray the item to be baked, holding the bottle about 10 inches (25 cm) above it and turning the sheet pan as necessary to ensure even coverage all over.

5. To achieve the maximum amount of shine, let the egg wash dry for a few minutes, then apply a second coat.

Fondant yield: 2 quarts (1 L 920 ml)

Fondant is sugar syrup that is recrystallized to a creamy white paste. It is widely used in the pastry shop for glazing and decorating. If properly applied, fondant dries to a silky-smooth icing that not only enhances the appearance of a pastry, but preserves it as well by sealing it from the air. Glucose and cream of tartar are used to invert part of the sugar to achieve the proper amount of recrystallization. Without these ingredients, the cooked sugar will harden and be impossible to work with. Conversely, if too much glucose or cream of tartar is used, there will not be enough recrystallization, and the fondant will be soft and runny.

Although fondant is inexpensive and relatively easy to make (once you get the hang of it), it is almost always purchased in a professional kitchen either ready to use or as a powder to which you add water. To make your own fondant, you will need a precise sugar thermometer (test in boiling water to determine accuracy), a sugar pan (see page 966) or heavy saucepan, a wide spatula or bench scraper, a marble slab (2 x 2 feet/60 x 60 cm for this recipe), 4 steel or aluminum bars, and, as in all sugar work, quick reaction time when the sugar has reached the proper temperature.

Vegetable oil for the equipment	⅔ cup (160 ml) glucose or light corn syrup, warmed
3 cups (720 ml) cold water	
4 pounds (1 kg 820 g) granulated sugar	½ teaspoon (1 g) cream of tartar

1. Clean, dry, and lightly oil the marble slab and metal bars with vegetable oil. Place the bars at the edge of the marble to make a frame to hold the hot syrup when it is poured on the slab. Oil a stainless-steel scraper and place 1 cup (240 ml) cold water close by.

2. Combine 2 cups (480 ml) water and the granulated sugar in a saucepan. Bring to a boil, stirring to dissolve the sugar. Reduce the heat to medium, stop stirring, and brush the sides of the pan with additional water. Be sure to brush down all of the crystals. It takes only a few particles of sugar left on the sides to make the mixture recrystallize (before you want it to) when the sugar becomes hotter.

3. When the temperature reaches 225°F (108°C), add the warm glucose or corn syrup and the cream of tartar dissolved in a little hot water. Continue boiling until the syrup reaches 238° to 240°F (114° to 115°C). Pay close attention; the syrup will reach this temperature quicker than you might think.

4. Immediately pour the syrup onto the prepared surface and sprinkle about 2 tablespoons (30 ml) of the cold water on top. It is critical that the temperature not exceed 240°F (115°C), so if your marble is not right next to the stove, place the saucepan in a bowl of cold water for a few seconds first to prevent overcooking. Insert the sugar thermometer into the thickest part of the puddle and let the sugar cool to 110°F (43°C).

5. Remove the metal bars and start to incorporate air into the sugar mixture: Using the oiled stainless-steel scraper, work the sugar by sliding the scraper under the edge of the puddle, lifting it, and folding in toward the center. After awhile, the sugar will start to turn white and become firmer. Continue to work the fondant slowly, either by hand or in a mixing bowl (see Note), until it has a smooth and creamy consistency.

6. Pack the fondant against the bottom of a plastic container and pour the remaining cold water on top to prevent a crust from forming. Store at room temperature. The fondant must rest about 24 hours before it is soft enough to use. Fondant will keep for weeks if covered properly. Pour off the water before using and keep the bowl covered with plastic wrap while you are working. Add a new layer of water, then cover to store until the next use.

NOTE: If you are making a large batch of fondant, you can work the sugar in a mixer instead of by hand. Carefully pour the cooled syrup into the mixing bowl. Do not get any on the sides of the bowl (hold the bowl next to the table and scrape the mixture in with the bench scraper). Use the paddle and mix on low speed until the fondant is smooth and creamy. You may need to scrape down the sides of the bowl to ensure that all of the fondant is mixed evenly. Scoop the fondant into a container and cover with the cold water, as above.

Graham Crackers and Crumbs

yield: 70 crackers, 2 × 2 inches (5 × 5 cm), or 1 pound 8 ounces (680 g) crumbs

I'm sure many of us have, on occasion, found that the pantry was fresh out of graham cracker crumbs when they were needed for cheesecake. While it is less convenient to make the crackers and crumbs the old-fashioned way, doing so sets you back only about 30 minutes (in an emergency, keep the dough fairly firm to speed the baking and drying process). Once you try these, I think you will find producing your own to be an advantage in both cost and quality. It is a good idea to keep the crumbs on hand as part of your regular mise en place so they are available when needed. Graham cracker crumbs can be stored at room temperature for several weeks.

6 ounces (170 g) bread flour

6 ounces (170 g) cake flour

2 ounces (55 g) whole wheat flour

2 ounces (55 g) dark brown sugar

1 teaspoon (4 g) baking soda

1 teaspoon (5 g) salt

3 ounces (85 g) unsalted butter, at room temperature

½ cup (120 ml) or 6 ounces (170 g) honey

1 teaspoon (5 ml) vanilla extract

⅓ cup (80 ml) water

GRAHAM CRACKERS

1. Thoroughly combine the bread flour, cake flour, whole wheat flour, brown sugar, baking soda, and salt in the bowl of an electric mixer.

2. Using the dough hook attachment, incorporate the butter, honey, vanilla extract, and water. Mix until a smooth and pliable dough has formed, adding additional water if necessary. Do not overmix.

3. Roll the dough out to a rectangle, 10 × 14 inches (25 × 35 cm), using flour to prevent it from sticking. Mark the dough with a docker or the tines of a fork.

4. Cut the rectangle into 2-inch (5-cm) squares. Transfer the squares to a sheet pan lined with baking paper.

5. Bake at 325°F (163°C) for approximately 15 minutes, or until dry.

6. Store in an airtight container.

History of the Graham Cracker

The original graham cracker was a thin whole wheat cracker developed in the 1830s. It was named for Dr. Sylvester Graham, the developer of the coarse grade of whole wheat flour (graham flour), also named after him. Dr. Graham, a Presbyterian minister, believed that eating meat and fat led to sinful behavior. The unrefined flour was part of his overall regime of healthy eating, which included a strict vegetarian diet and no alcohol. Dr. Graham further cautioned that consuming ketchup and mustard could to lead to insanity. In an effort to cash in on his popular teachings, the graham cracker was developed and marketed as a healthy snack.

One of Graham's followers was Dr. Caleb Jackson, who invented a breakfast cereal made from bran and dubbed it *granula*, a combination of the word *bran* with the name of his teacher, Graham. Some 50 years later, another doctor with a well-known food name, Dr. John Kellogg (yes, the same as Kellogg's Corn Flakes), who was also a great believer in the power of graham crackers and was said to eat seven every morning, invented his own breakfast cereal, which he named *granola*.

Today, graham crackers are widely produced commercially and are popular as a snack food for children. Their other primary use is for graham cracker crusts for pies and cheesecakes.

GRAHAM CRACKER CRUMBS

1. Prepare the dough as for Graham Crackers (above), but roll the dough out ⅛ inch (3 mm) thick.

2. Cut into small pieces; it is not necessary to measure them. Transfer to a sheet pan lined with baking paper.

3. Bake at 325°F (163°C) until dark golden brown.

4. When cold, grind the pieces in a food processor to make fine crumbs. Store in an airtight container.

Hazelnut Paste yield: I cup (240 ml)

In most professional operations, this product is typically purchased rather than made. The commercial product is more concentrated, so if you substitute purchased paste you may need to decrease the amount specified in the recipes.

8 ounces (225 g) hazelnuts   **⅓ cup (80 ml) simple syrup**

1. Toast the hazelnuts and remove the skins (see page 6).

2. Process the hazelnuts and simple syrup together in a food processor until the mixture becomes a thick paste.

3. Store in an airtight container at room temperature to use as needed.

Marzipan yield: approximately 4 pounds 6 ounces (1 kg 990 g)

Marzipan is used extensively in European pastry shops. It will keep almost indefinitely if you take proper care in mixing and handling it. It should be stored in airtight containers in a very cool place or in the refrigerator. It can also be stored in the freezer, should you need to keep it for a long time. If the oil separates from the marzipan after it thaws, add a small amount of water and some powdered sugar. Continue to knead until smooth and elastic.

2 pounds (910 g) almond paste

½ cup (120 ml) glucose *or* light corn syrup

2 pounds (910 g) sifted powdered sugar

1. In a stainless steel mixing bowl, use the hook attachment to mix the almond paste with the glucose or corn syrup at low speed until combined.

2. Start adding the sugar, scraping the sides of the bowl down as necessary. Add enough of the powdered sugar to make a fairly firm yet malleable dough.

3. Store the marzipan, wrapped in plastic, inside an airtight container in a cold place.

NOTE: The amount of powdered sugar needed depends on the consistency of the almond paste. Always mix at low speed and take care not to overmix. The friction will make the marzipan warm, thereby softening it, and you will end up adding too much powdered sugar.

All About Marzipan

Due to its high sugar content (60 to 70 percent), marzipan dries quickly when exposed to air and should be kept covered at all times. If it dries reconstitute by kneading in a little water. Use a stainless steel bowl to prevent discoloration. Keep your tools and workplace scrupulously clean, and always wash your hands. The almond oil brought to the surface will absorb even a small trace of dirt, which not only ruins the off-white color of the marzipan, but can lead to spoilage.

Marzipan is rolled out in the same manner as pastry dough, except powdered sugar is used instead of flour to prevent the paste from sticking. It can be left smooth or may be textured before being used to cover cakes, petits fours, and pastries. It is an ideal surface to decorate and pipe on. It is also used on petits fours and pastries that are to be coated with fondant or chocolate; the marzipan keeps the coating from soaking into the sponge and helps achieve an even surface. A thin layer of marzipan on a bûche de Noël or chocolate cake prevents the thin layer of chocolate coating from mixing with the buttercream. Not only does the marzipan make a smooth finish possible, but the combination of chocolate and marzipan also gives the pastry a distinctive flavor. With few exceptions, marzipan should not be rolled out thicker than ⅛ inch (3 mm), or it can look clumsy and unattractive and may be overwhelming in flavor.

Water-soluble food coloring can be used to tint marzipan, but add it with discretion to keep the colors soft. Green (such as for Princess Cake [page 530]) should usually be toned down with the addition of yellow. When adding color to a small amount of marzipan, or when you need only a hint of color, put a drop on a piece of baking paper and add some of it to the marzipan with the tip of a knife. Knead the marzipan until the color is completely worked in. Unsweetened cocoa powder can be used to produce brown in various shades, unless for some reason you do not want the chocolate flavor. Work the desired amount of cocoa powder into the marzipan, kneading it until you have a smooth, evenly colored marzipan. If you are adding a large amount of cocoa powder, you may have to compensate by working in some simple syrup or water to prevent the marzipan from getting too dry. To color marzipan bright white for decoration only, use 4 to 6 drops titanium dioxide for every 1 ounce (30 g) untinted marzipan. This should be done only for pieces that will not be eaten.

Mascarpone Cheese yield: 1 pound 8 ounces (680 g)

Mascarpone cheese is made from fresh cream derived from cow's milk. The cream is reduced to near triple-cream consistency to give the cheese its soft, smooth, rich texture. This cream cheese originated in the Lombardy region of Italy but is now made throughout the country. The flavor of mascarpone blends beautifully with other food, especially fruit. Fresh figs with mascarpone is a classic combination, although tiramisu is probably the dessert that most people think of first when it comes to mascarpone.

Uses for mascarpone are certainly not limited to sweets. A mixture of mascarpone, anchovies, mustard, and spices is a specialty of Trieste, in the northeast corner of Italy. Another popular appetizer preparation is a layered torte alternating mascarpone with pesto or smoked salmon. Because mascarpone is highly perishable and the imported product is expensive, the time involved in making it yourself is worthwhile.

2 quarts (1 L 920 ml) heavy cream	1 teaspoon (5 ml) tartaric acid solution (page 38)

1. Bring the cream to a boil in a heavy oversized saucepan. Boil over medium heat until reduced by one-third to about 5¼ cups (1 L 260 ml). As the cream is reducing, it should be bubbling but not boiling hard; if it reduces too quickly, the fat can separate as it cools (see Note).

2. Remove the pan from the heat, place in an ice bath, and stir the reduced cream until it is cold.

3. Stir in the tartaric acid solution, return the saucepan to the heat, and bring the mixture to 118°F (48°C). Remove from the heat.

4. Line a strainer with a triple layer of cheesecloth. Set the strainer over a bowl or pan to catch the liquid. Pour the cream mixture into the strainer. Refrigerate overnight.

5. Remove the thickened mascarpone from the cheesecloth and discard the liquid. If the cheese has not thickened properly, add another ½ teaspoon (2.5 ml) tartaric acid solution, reheat to 118°F (48°C), and repeat Steps 4 and 5. Store, covered, in the refrigerator.

NOTE: If the fat should separate (accumulate on top) while the mixture is draining, let the mascarpone sit at room temperature for 1 to 2 hours, then blend until smooth in a food processor.

Meringue

Meringue can be loosely defined as a mixture of beaten egg whites and granulated sugar. While the name is French, its origin is not documented, although history tells us that meringue may have been named for either the Swiss town of Meringen or the German city of Mehrinyghen. We do know that meringue has been around since the early sixteenth century.

COMPOSITION

Meringue is made of egg whites and sugar whipped together to incorporate air and form soft or stiff peaks. Egg whites whipped without sugar are not meringue; they are simply beaten egg whites.

In the recipes that follow, egg whites are measured by volume rather than by number. This measurement is not only more precise, but also easier to apply in professional kitchens, where a supply of egg whites is usually on hand. There are 7 to 8 egg whites in 1 cup (240 ml). Using the even number (8) makes it easier to divide when measuring fractions of a cup and is simple to remember, as are 4 whole eggs and 12 egg yolks per cup.

HOW EGG WHITES EXPAND

The white portion of the egg is referred to scientifically as albumen. The protein found in the egg white, or albumen, is albumin. Egg whites have excellent foaming ability. When egg yolks, which contain a fatty substance that destroys the albumen's ability to foam, are removed, egg whites alone can increase in volume by up to 8 times. This is possible through close teamwork by the two proteins albumin and ovalbumin. When the egg whites are beaten, the albumin protein forms a stable mass of tiny air bubbles, while some of the protein molecules bond and form a fragile network that holds the moisture in place (an egg white contains about 85 percent water). This alone would suffice if the beaten egg whites were not to be cooked, but because air expands when it is heated, the network of denatured proteins on the surface would be destroyed and immediately collapse if it were not for the ovalbumin protein. While the ovalbumin does not play an important role when the egg whites are simply beaten, it coagulates when heated, forming its own network in the meringue and making it resistant to collapse as the water evaporates. In other words, the ovalbumin protein makes it possible to change a liquid foam into a solid dry mass with heat.

THE EFFECTS OF SUGAR

Meringue would be bland without the addition of sugar, which also helps stabilize the foam, especially in the oven. Its addition, however, is something of a mixed blessing, as sugar also delays the foaming process and decreases the volume and lightness of the meringue. This is especially noticeable when meringue is whipped by hand, but even when using an electric mixer, the granulated sugar must be introduced gradually and, in most cases, never before the whipped egg whites have increased approximately 4 times in volume, so that the sugar will not prevent the albumin from working to stiffen the foam. As an example of what it means to add the sugar gradually, when making the recipe for French Meringue, it should take approximately 3 minutes to add the 2 pounds (910 g) of sugar to the egg whites—a little longer if the egg whites are cold.

The amount of sugar used in a meringue varies with the desired texture and intended use of the finished product. Soft meringues, which are typically used for toppings on tarts and pies, can be made with equal quantities of sugar and egg white by weight. Hard meringues, which are baked dry, usually have a 2 to 1 ratio of sugar to egg white.

SALT

Just like sugar, salt has a mixed effect on meringue. While it acts as a flavor enhancer, salt also increases the amount of time needed to whip the whites and decreases the foam's stability, although both of these occur to a very small degree only.

THE ADDITION OF ACID

Citric acid (lemon juice), tartaric acid solution, and cream of tartar (which is the solid salt of tartaric acid mixed with cornstarch) have no effect on the volume of the meringue, but they help stabilize the foam by decreasing the pH level in the albumen, making the foam less apt to collapse. Only a small amount of any of these acids should be used, as too much, in addition to adversely changing the taste of the meringue, will impede coagulation during baking.

It has been commonly accepted that a copper mixing bowl produces a superior and more rapidly whipped egg white foam. However, current research indicates that the degree to which a copper bowl is preferable to a stainless steel bowl is questionable. While you should certainly avoid plastic and wood, which are hard to clean of fat, aluminum, which is corrosive and tends to impart a grayish color, and glass, which is not suited for use in the kitchen, copper's alleged ability to impart an acidity to the whites as it comes in contact with the albumin is now disputed. Although there is certainly no proof of any disadvantage to using a copper bowl, the addition of acids generates the same result.

Chef's Tips for Perfect Meringue

1. Although this is not critical, if at all possible, use egg whites at room temperature.

2. Be sure the egg whites are not so old that they have started to deteriorate. Egg whites become thinner and clearer as the protein starts to diminish.

3. Because fat prevents the albumin in egg whites from expanding, make certain they are clean and free of any egg yolk particles. The mixing bowl and whip or whisk must also be perfectly clean.

4. Make sure there are no foreign particles (such as flour) in the sugar.

5. Using a copper bowl and a balloon whisk can be helpful when making meringue, but they are not absolutely necessary.

WHIPPING

Meringue whipped to a soft peak will not hold its shape; it will slowly settle or fall. Meringue properly whipped to a stiff peak will not change shape as you pipe it from a pastry bag or work with it; you should actually be able to turn the bowl of meringue upside down after it is finished whipping with no problem (or mess). Be observant: There is a fine line between stiff peaks and overwhipped, dry peaks. Meringue that is overwhipped and dry is hard to pipe into precise shapes and is impossible to fold into a batter without getting small lumps of meringue throughout. Meringue whipped to stiff peaks should still appear shiny, not dry or broken.

USES

Meringue is a key ingredient in the pastry kitchen. Baked layers of meringue are used in cakes and pastries, such as the famous marjolaine. Meringue is piped into ornate shapes for vacherin and dacquoise; it is made into cookies, added to buttercream, and used to top desserts such as baked Alaska and lemon meringue pie. In Europe today, many pastry shops do not make their own meringue, but to save time and money they buy it from companies that specialize in baked meringue products. This makes sense, as meringue formulas are basically generic, and it is what you create with them that makes the difference.

VARIETIES

The three basic types of meringue are French, Swiss, and Italian. The ingredients for each are essentially the same, but the methods of preparation and the results are different. A fourth type, Japonaise, is a French meringue with the addition of almond meal and a small amount of cornstarch.

FLAVORING AND COLORING

Nuts, cocoa powder, and other flavorings, as well as coloring, can be added to meringue just before the meringue is finished being whipped to the proper stiffness. Use regular water-soluble food coloring, adding just a small amount at a time.

BAKING

Meringue should be baked at a low temperature. For most types of meringue, this is between 210° and 220°F (99° and 104°C). In the case of a meringue containing ground nuts, such as Japonaise, the nuts will absorb some of the moisture in the egg whites and allow the meringue to dry more quickly.

Meringue is not baked so much as it is dried out. Baked meringue should not color, but rather remain white. However, a slight hint of color (off-white) is acceptable.

STORAGE

While meringue batter is never prepared in advance as a mise en place item, generally speaking, the more sugar that has been whipped into the whites, the longer the batter will maintain its volume and stiffness without deflating as it is shaped. French and Japonaise meringues should be piped or spread into the desired shape immediately after whipping, even if the batter cannot be baked right away, as it should be. The meringue will have less stability and will deflate to a greater degree as it is agitated (through spreading or being placed in a piping bag) after sitting for even as short a time as 10 minutes. Italian and, to a lesser degree, Swiss meringues will hold their shapes for much longer. The Italian variety has greater stability because it is partially cooked during preparation. If made properly, it will keep for several hours. However, if too much sugar ends up sticking to the side of the bowl or the whip, the keeping time will decrease.

All cooked (dried) meringue is susceptible to becoming soft from absorbing moisture in the air. It should always be stored airtight in a warm, dry place. Plain baked meringue will keep fresh this way for many weeks. Japonaise, or other meringues that contain nuts, can turn rancid if stored too long.

Figure 1-4 contrasts the formulas and characterizes some of the differences in the basic varieties of meringue.

Comparison of Meringue Formulas Relative to One Pint
(approximately 16) Egg Whites

	French	Italian	Swiss	Japonaise	Noisette
Egg White	1 pint (480 ml)	1 pint (480 ml)	1 pint (480 ml)	1 pint (480 ml)	1 pint (480 ml)
Granulated Sugar	2 pounds (910 g)	1 pound, 8 ounces (680 g)	1 pound, 8 ounces to 2 pounds (680 to 910 g)	1 pound, 6 ounces (625 g)	2 pounds (910 g)
Cornstarch	0	0	0	2 ounces (55 g)	2 ounces (55 g)
Corn Syrup	0	1 cup (240 ml)	0	0	0
Water	0	1 cup (240 ml)	0	0	0
Nuts	0	0	0	1 pound (455 g)	8 ounces (225 g)
Other	lemon juice	0	0	0	vanilla extract
Preparation Method	The lemon juice is added to egg whites at room temperature. The whites are whipped until they have quadrupled in volume. The sugar is added gradually as the mixture is whipped to stiff peaks.	The sugar, corn syrup, and water are boiled to 240°F (115°C). The hot syrup is added to partially whipped whites at medium speed. The mixture is whipped at high speed until it has cooled and formed stiff peaks.	The sugar and egg whites are placed in a bain-marie and heated to 140°F (60°C) while being whipped constantly. The mixture is then whipped off the heat until it has cooled and formed soft or stiff peaks, depending on the amount of sugar used and the application.	Finely ground blanched almonds and cornstarch are combined. The sugar is gradually added to partially whipped whites as they are whipped to stiff peaks. The nut mixture is then folded in by hand.	Ground hazelnuts and cornstarch are combined. The sugar is gradually added to partially whipped whites as they are whipped to stiff peaks. The vanilla is added, and the nut mixture is then folded in by hand.
Uses					
Cake Layers	Yes	No	Occasionally	Yes	Yes
Dessert Topping	No	Yes	Yes	No	No
Fillings	No	Yes	Yes	No	No
Meringue Glace	Yes	No	Occasionally	No	Yes
Cookies and Pastries	Yes	No	Occasionally	Yes	Yes
Buttercream	No	Yes	Yes	No	No
Sherbet	No	Yes	Yes	No	No

FIGURE 1-4 **A comparison of meringue formulas relative to 1 pint (480 ml) of egg whites**

French Meringue yield: approximately 5 quarts (4 L 800 ml)

French meringue is best for baking *au naturel*, for piping into various shapes for cookies and dessert shells, for mixing with nuts, and for use as a cake base. If it is made and baked correctly, French meringue is tender, light, and fragile. It should be piped or spread immediately after whipping, or the egg whites may start to separate from the sugar. It should also be baked immediately after forming. This type of meringue should not be added to fillings that will be eaten raw, unless the meringue is made with pasteurized egg whites to guard against salmonella.

2 cups (480 ml) egg whites, at room temperature

3 drops lemon juice or tartaric acid solution (page 38)

2 pounds (910 g) granulated sugar

1. In a copper or stainless steel bowl, whip the egg whites with the lemon juice or tartaric acid until the mixture has quadrupled in volume and has the consistency of a thick foam, 1 to 2 minutes.

2. Still whipping at high speed, gradually add the sugar; this should take about 3 minutes. Continue to whip the meringue at high speed until stiff peaks form. Do not overwhip.

3. Immediately pipe or spread the meringue into the desired shape.

4. Bake at 210° to 220°F (99° to 104°C) until dry, or follow the instructions given in individual recipes.

Italian Meringue yield: approximately 5 quarts (4 L 800 ml)

Italian meringue is a good choice if the meringue must stand for some time before baking. It is denser than French or Swiss meringue because the egg whites are partially cooked; therefore, it holds up longer before starting to deflate. Italian meringue is also preferable for use in desserts where the meringue is eaten raw, or with only partial further cooking—for example, when it is added to a filling or when only the outside is browned, as in baked Alaska. When Italian meringue is baked all the way through, it is harder than French meringue and not very pleasant to eat.

2 cups (480 ml) egg whites

12 ounces (340 g) or 1 cup (240 ml) light corn syrup

1 pound 8 ounces (680 g) granulated sugar

1 cup (240 ml) water

1. Place the egg whites in a mixing bowl so you will be ready to start whipping them when the sugar syrup is ready.

2. Boil the corn syrup, sugar, and water. When the syrup reaches 230°F (110°C), begin whipping the egg whites at high speed. Continue boiling the syrup until it reaches 240°F (115°C) —the soft-ball stage.

3. Remove the syrup from the heat and lower the mixer speed to medium. Pour the syrup into the egg whites in a thin, steady stream between the whip and the side of the bowl (if the syrup hits the whip, it will splatter and cause lumps). Return the mixer to high speed and continue to whip the meringue until it has cooled completely and has formed stiff peaks.

NOTE: If you do not have a sugar thermometer, boil the sugar to the soft-ball stage using the following directions for determining this level without a thermometer. When a drop of the sugar syrup can be formed into a soft, pliable ball after being dropped into ice water, it has reached the soft-ball stage. If the sugar dissolves and cannot be formed, it has not cooked long enough. If it becomes hard once it has cooled in the water, it is overcooked.

Japonaise Meringue Batter

yield: 4 shells, 10 inches (25 cm) in diameter, or 90 shells, 2¹/₂ inches (5.6 cm) in diameter

8 ounces (225 g) finely ground blanched
    almonds (see Note)

1 ounce (30 g) cornstarch

1 cup (240 ml) egg whites

11 ounces (310 g) granulated sugar

1. Prepare your sheet pans, pastry bag, and a template, if you are using one.

2. Combine the ground almonds and cornstarch; reserve.

3. Whip the egg whites to a foam; they should quadruple in volume. Gradually add the sugar and whip to stiff peaks.

4. Gently fold the almond mixture into the egg whites by hand. Pipe or spread into the desired shape immediately.

5. Bake as directed in individual recipes.

NOTE: If you do not have blanched almonds already ground (almond meal), combine 8 ounces (225 g) whole or sliced blanched almonds with one-third of the sugar and grind together in a food processor to a fine consistency. Process by pulsing on and off to prevent the mixture from heating up and sticking together.

Meringue Noisette

yield: 4 shells, 10 inches (25 cm) in diameter, or about 60 shells, 3 inches (7.5 cm) in diameter

4 ounces (115 g) hazelnuts, toasted	1 pound (455 g) granulated sugar
1 ounce (30 g) cornstarch	1 teaspoon (5 ml) vanilla extract
1 cup (240 ml) egg whites	

1. Draw 4 circles, 10 inches (25 cm) in diameter, on 2 sheets of baking paper. Place the papers upside down on sheet pans and set aside.

2. Remove as much skin from the toasted hazelnuts as comes off easily, then grind the nuts to a fine consistency. Combine with the cornstarch.

3. Whip the egg whites to a thick foam; they should quadruple in volume. Still whipping, gradually add the sugar, taking 3 to 4 minutes to add all of it. Continue to whip the meringue until it forms stiff peaks. Add the vanilla. Gently fold the nut and cornstarch mixture into the meringue by hand.

4. Place the batter in a pastry bag with a No. 4 (8-mm) plain tip (use a No. 3 [6-mm] tip if making the smaller size). Pipe the batter in a spiral within the 4 circles drawn on the papers, starting in the center and working to the outside (Figure 1-5).

5. Bake immediately at 250°F (122°C) for approximately 1 hour or until dry.

FIGURE 1-5 Piping meringue noisette batter into a spiral within the circle drawn on a sheet of baking paper

Swiss Meringue **yield: 2 to 3 quarts (1 L 920 ml to 2 L 880 ml)**

Swiss meringue could be described as a mixture of French and Italian meringues. It can be eaten raw, as the egg whites are pasteurized by being heated to 140°F (60°C) with the sugar. Swiss meringue is quicker and easier to produce than its Italian counterpart, but it is not as stable and should be used fairly soon once it has been prepared. It is typically used in buttercream and fillings, but it can also be piped into cookies or made into other shapes, then baked or dried in the same way as French meringue. However, for this use, Swiss meringue should be made with less sugar to ensure better volume and stiff peaks.

2 cups (480 ml) egg whites	1 pound 4 ounces to 1 pound 12 ounces (570 to 795 g) granulated sugar (see Note)

1. Combine the egg whites and sugar in a mixing bowl. Place the bowl over simmering water and heat to 140°F (60°C), whipping constantly to avoid cooking the egg whites.

2. Remove from the heat and whip the mixture at high speed until it has cooled completely.

NOTE: If the meringue is to be piped or spread on top of a dessert, or if it will be dried in the oven, less sugar should be used to ensure a stiffer and lighter meringue. If the meringue is to be added to a filling or used to make buttercream, use the full amount of sugar.

Orange Glaze yield: approximately 1 cup (240 ml)

1 cup (240 ml) orange preserves *or* marmalade

3 ounces (85 g) granulated sugar
⅓ cup (80 ml) water

1. Place the preserves or marmalade, sugar, and water in a heavy-bottomed saucepan. Bring to a boil over medium heat, stirring constantly.

2. Reduce the heat to low and continue to cook, stirring from time to time, until the mixture has reduced sufficiently to hold a thread ¼ inch (6 mm) long when pulled between your thumb and index finger or the backs of 2 spoons.

3. Quickly remove the pan from the heat and strain the glaze. Discard the solids in the strainer. Use the glaze immediately. Store leftover glaze at room temperature. To reuse, add a small amount of water and heat to boiling.

Pectin Glaze yield: approximately 3 cups (720 ml)

Pectin glaze is used in combination with tartaric acid solution, which acts as a catalyst to make the glaze gel and also gives it a slightly tart flavor that is especially complementary to fruit. The ability to gel quickly prevents the glaze from soaking into the fruit; instead, it leaves a thin, shiny coat on the top.

3 cups (720 ml) water
1 tablespoon (9 g) pure pectin powder (grade USP-NF)

1 pound 6 ounces (625 g) granulated sugar
Tartaric acid solution (page 38)

1. Heat the water to the scalding point in a saucepan.

2. In the meantime, mix the pectin powder with 3 ounces (85 g) of the sugar. Whisk into the scalded water, making sure it is thoroughly combined. Bring the mixture to a boil, then stir in the remaining sugar. Return to a boil, but this time check to see exactly when the mixture begins to boil, then reduce the heat and boil for 8 to 12 minutes (see Note). Remove from the heat and let cool.

3. Skim off any foam or scum that appears on the surface. Pectin glaze will keep for months at this stage if stored, covered, in the refrigerator.

4. To set (gel) the glaze, use approximately 4 drops tartaric acid solution for every 1 ounce (30 ml) pectin glaze; stir in the tartaric acid quickly and use the glaze immediately. The amount required will vary with the consistency of the glaze. The flavor should definitely be tart, but not to the point where it is unpleasant; also, adding too much liquid can prevent the glaze from setting. Add tartaric acid only to the amount of glaze you are ready to use at the moment, because it will not work as well if it has to be softened again once it has set. You can keep the glaze from setting up while you are working by stirring it every few seconds.

NOTE: For a quick test, remove 1 to 2 tablespoons (15 to 30 ml) glaze and chill it. Add the appropriate amount of tartaric acid as described in Step 4. If the glaze does not set properly, return the solution to a boil and cook for 1 to 2 minutes. If the glaze sets up too fast or too thick, add a small amount of water. Always make a small test portion of glaze first before applying it to the food.

Plain Cake Syrup yield: 5 cups (1 L 200 ml)

Plain cake syrup is basically plain poaching syrup without any citric acid. If you have leftover poaching syrup after cooking fruit, keep it on hand to use as cake syrup instead; the subtle flavor from the fruit is a bonus. If the liquid has been reduced significantly during the poaching process, add water accordingly before using. Leftover poaching liquid must be stored in the refrigerator. If you have simple syrup made up, you may use that as a substitute for cake syrup as well. Add ¼ cup (60 ml) water to 1 cup (240 ml) simple syrup. Dilute only the amount required for each use.

1 quart (960 ml) water	1 pound (455 g) granulated sugar

1. Place the water and sugar in a saucepan and bring to a boil. Remove from the heat and let cool.

2. Store, covered, to use as needed. This syrup does not need to be refrigerated; it can be kept at room temperature for several weeks.

Plain Mirror Glaze yield: 1 cup (240 ml)

1 tablespoon (9 g) unflavored gelatin powder	½ cup (120 ml) simple syrup
½ cup (120 ml) cold water	

1. Sprinkle the gelatin over the cold water and set aside until softened. Heat the mixture over a bain-marie until dissolved; do not overheat.

2. Stir the simple syrup into the gelatin mixture. Use the glaze as soon as it begins to thicken. If the glaze becomes too thick before you can apply it, warm it to liquefy and let it thicken again.

Plain Poaching Syrup yield: 5 cups (1 L, 200 ml)

The basic ratio in poaching liquid is 2 parts water to 1 part sugar by weight. This can be modified depending on the desired sweetness of the finished product. After the first use, the syrup can be used again to poach fruit (you may need to replace the evaporated water), or as cake syrup. After poaching, any fruit that is susceptible to browning should be kept in the syrup until needed to prevent oxidation. Apricots are especially delicate and turn brown quickly. To keep the fruit submerged, place a towel or a sheet of baking paper on top and place a plate on top of that.

1 quart (960 ml) water	½ lemon, cut into wedges
1 pound (455 g) granulated sugar	1 teaspoon (5 ml) vanilla extract

1. Combine all of the ingredients in a saucepan and bring to a boil.

2. Proceed as directed in individual recipes or see directions on page 32.

SPICED POACHING SYRUP

Follow the preceding recipe but in Step 1, add 6 whole cloves and 1 cinnamon stick.

Instructions for Poaching Fruit

TO POACH PEARS OR APPLES

1. Peel and core apples or pears. Cut in half, if desired, and add to the poaching syrup in the saucepan. Place a lid or plate that fits down inside the saucepan on top of the fruit to keep it submerged; otherwise, the fruit will bob on top of the syrup and the exposed part will oxidize, turn brown, and not cook.

2. Boil gently for about 5 minutes. Even if the fruit is fairly ripe, the poaching syrup should be brought to a boil so the center of the fruit will cook through and will not become brown.

3. Lower the heat and simmer very slowly until the fruit is tender and cooked all the way through. Do not poach the fruit too rapidly, or it will become overcooked on the outside and remain raw inside.

4. To check if pears or apples are done, pinch them gently with your fingers. They should feel soft but not mushy, having about the same amount of resistance as the fleshy part of your hand.

TO POACH PLUMS, PEACHES, APRICOTS, CHERRIES, AND OTHER FRAGILE FRUITS

1. Bring the syrup to a boil, add the fruit, and lower the heat immediately to simmer very gently; do not boil.

2. Cook the fruit until it is tender.

NOTE: Remove peaches after they have cooked for a few minutes, peel off the skin using a small pointed knife, then return them to the syrup and continue cooking until soft.

TO POACH OR RECONSTITUTE DRIED FRUIT

Allow the fruit to soak in cold water overnight, then add the appropriate amounts of sugar and lemon to make a poaching liquid. Poach as directed for fresh fruit.

Praline yield: I pound (455 g)

Praline is hard to work with in a humid climate or in wet weather because the sugar starts to break down and the praline becomes sticky. However, sticky praline is suitable to use in making Praline Paste (recipe follows).

4 ounces (115 g) hazelnuts

4 ounces (115 g) blanched almonds

Corn oil *or* other bland oil

8 ounces (225 g) granulated sugar

1 teaspoon (5 ml) lemon juice

1. Toast the hazelnuts and remove the skin (see page 6). Toast the almonds lightly. Reserve the nuts.

2. Lightly oil a marble slab or sheet pan.

3. Caramelize the sugar with the lemon juice to a light golden color (see page 10).

4. Immediately add the toasted nuts, stir to combine, and pour onto the oiled marble.

5. Let the praline cool completely, then crush with a dowel or rolling pin to the desired consistency.

PRALINE PASTE yield: I cup (240 ml)

Praline paste is used mainly for making candy and for flavoring cake and pastry fillings. As with hazelnut paste, making your own is time consuming, and you will be hard pressed to achieve the same result as the ready-made commercial product. Commercial praline paste is passed through a grinding machine equipped with stone rollers (known as an almond mill), which produces a superior result. Either this recipe or a purchased paste can be used in recipes in this book that call for praline paste.

1 recipe Praline (above)

¼ cup (60 ml) simple syrup

1. Crush the praline as fine as possible.

2. Place in a high-speed food processor and process, using the metal blade, gradually adding the simple syrup until the mixture becomes a fine paste. To prepare a small amount, you can use a coffee grinder.

Red Currant Glaze yield: 2 cups (480 ml)

1 pound (455 g) red currant jelly

4 ounces (115 g) granulated sugar

1. Place the jelly and sugar in a saucepan. Stirring constantly, bring to a boil over low heat. Keep stirring until all lumps have dissolved.

2. Lower the heat and simmer for a few minutes or until the mixture has a glossy shine. Strain, then use immediately. Store leftover glaze in a covered container. Reheat to a liquid consistency to use again.

Ricotta Cheese yield: 2 pounds (910 g)

Ricotta translates to "recooked" or "cooked again." The name for this wonderful cooking cheese came about because it was originally (and still is, in many parts of Italy) made from the whey drained from cow's, goat's, or ewe's milk after making other cheeses, such as mozzarella. Today, ricotta is most often made starting with whole or low-fat milk. In addition to numerous applications in the pastry kitchen, ricotta is used in savory dishes such as lasagna and ravioli. Ricotta is easy to make; however, most consumers today prefer to purchase it ready-made. The main drawback in making your own ricotta is the time involved, but the finished cheese will keep for up to 2 weeks stored, covered, in the refrigerator.

6 quarts (5 L 760 ml) low-fat milk	1 tablespoon (15 g) salt
6 drops lemon juice	½ cup (120 ml) heavy cream
1 pound (455 g) unflavored yogurt	

I. Pour the milk into a plastic container and stir in the lemon juice. Cover, then place the mixture in the refrigerator for approximately 24 hours.

2. Using a wooden spoon, stir in the yogurt and the salt. Transfer to a heavy-bottomed saucepan. Stirring constantly, bring the mixture to a boil and boil for 2 minutes; a thick layer of curds should form on the top.

3. Remove from the heat. Strain into a bowl, pouring it through a fine mesh strainer (chinois) lined with cheesecloth. Reserve ½ cup (120 ml) of the whey (liquid) and discard the remainder.

4. Spread the hot curds to cool on a sheet pan lined with baking paper. Separate the curds as much as possible by rubbing them between your hands.

5. Once the cheese has cooled, place it in a bowl and stir in the reserved whey and the heavy cream.

Royal Icing yield: 6 cups (I L 440 ml) or 3 pounds 7 ounces (I kg 565 g)

This type of icing is also called *decorating icing*, because that is its principal use. Royal icing is one of the best materials with which to practice piping. It is inexpensive and easy to make, and it can be piped and formed into almost any shape. Royal icing is used a great deal around Christmastime to decorate gingerbread and Christmas cookies, and is essential for making gingerbread houses. Because it becomes hard and brittle when dry, royal icing is used more for decorating than for eating. However, it is traditional in some countries to use it on special-occasion cakes, such as wedding cakes. Personally, I limit its use to showpieces, or for piping a small amount on a cake or pastries. Be careful to keep royal icing covered at all times, and clean off any icing on the side of your cup or bowl. The icing dries quickly, and the small lumps will interfere with your piping. A wet towel on top functions well while you are working, but you should pour a layer of water on the icing and wrap the container in plastic for longer storage.

1 cup (240 ml) egg whites (see Note)	½ teaspoon (1 g) cream of tartar
2 pounds 8 ounces (1 kg 135 g) sifted powdered sugar	

1. Pour the egg whites into a mixer bowl. Using the paddle attachment with the machine set at low speed, gradually add all but a few handfuls of the powdered sugar and the cream of tartar. Mix until it forms a smooth paste, adding the remaining powdered sugar if necessary.

2. Beat at high speed for just a few seconds if you are using the royal icing for piping. If you will be spreading the icing—on the top of a gingerbread house, for example—beat the icing a bit longer to make it light and fluffy.

3. Immediately transfer to a clean container and cover to prevent a skin from forming. If you are going to use it within a few minutes, place a damp towel on top instead. Stored, covered, in the refrigerator, royal icing will keep for up to 1 week.

NOTE: As mentioned above, royal icing is used mostly for decorating showpieces and, as such, is rarely intended for consumption. If it is used as a major component of an item that will be eaten (more than just a decorative touch on a pastry, for example), pasteurized egg whites should be used for safety (see pages 881 to 882).

CHEF'S TIP
This recipe makes a large amount of royal icing. If you need only a small amount (to pipe the eyes on Porcupine Pastries, for example), simply add powdered sugar to 1 egg white until the icing reaches the proper consistency; stir rapidly until the mixture is light and fluffy. Add a small pinch of cream of tartar to prevent the icing from yellowing. This will make approximately ¾ cup (180 ml) of icing.

Simple Icing yield: 3 cups (720 ml)

This icing is also known as *flat icing* and *water icing*. If you use simple icing as part of your daily routine, here is an easy way to make it. Fill a storage container with powdered sugar and add as much hot water as the sugar will absorb; do not stir, but let it settle for a few minutes. Pour enough additional water on top to cover the surface in a 1-inch (2.5-cm) layer. Let the icing sit overnight. The next day, not only will you have perfectly fine simple icing, but the water on the top of the icing can be poured off and used instead of simple syrup on Danish pastries or puff pastry items.

2 pounds (910 g) powdered sugar	¾ cup (180 ml) hot water
3 tablespoons (45 ml) corn syrup (see Note)	

1. Place the powdered sugar in a mixing bowl. Pour the corn syrup into the hot water and stir until melted. Add the liquid to the powdered sugar and mix until smooth.

2. Adjust the thickness with additional water as needed. The icing should be the consistency of sour cream.

3. Cover the surface with a thin layer of water to prevent a crust from forming (pour off before using). Store, covered, at room temperature.

NOTE: The corn syrup prevents the icing from crystallizing when it is stored for several weeks. If the icing will be used within a few days, the corn syrup may be omitted.

Simple Syrup (28° Baumé) yield: 3 quarts (2 L 880 ml)

Simple syrup is a useful ingredient to have on hand. If proper hygiene is observed during preparation and storage, it keeps almost indefinitely. Besides everyday uses, such as sweetening sorbets and parfaits, this syrup is used to thin fondant to the proper consistency before it is applied and to thicken chocolate for piping. I also use it as a quick cake syrup by adding ¼ cup (60 ml) water for every 1 cup (240 ml) simple syrup, plus an appropriate liqueur or other flavoring.

2 quarts (1 L 920 ml) water

2 pounds 8 ounces (1 kg 135 g) granulated sugar

2 cups (480 ml) or 1 pound 8 ounces (680 g) glucose *or* light corn syrup (see Chef's Tip)

CHEF'S TIP
To avoid mess when measuring glucose or corn syrup, first weigh the sugar and leave it on the scale, then make a well in the sugar (adjust the scale) and pour the corn syrup into the well until you have the right amount. Glucose is too thick to pour but can easily be scooped with a wet hand. (The glucose or corn syrup is added to prevent the syrup from recrystallizing when stored.) If you are using a small amount of corn syrup in a recipe that does not have any sugar, it may be easier to measure the syrup by volume; both measurements are given throughout this text. Converting dry to liquid ounces is simple for corn syrup: Fluid ounces are two-thirds of dry ounces (e.g., 6 ounces by weight = 4 fluid ounces.)

1. Place the water, sugar, and glucose or corn syrup in a saucepan; stir to combine.

2. Heat to boiling and let boil for a few seconds (see Note).

3. Set aside to cool. If any scum has developed on the surface, skim it off before pouring the syrup into bottles. Simple syrup should be refrigerated if kept for more than 2 to 3 weeks.

NOTE: Because it is impossible to know exactly when the syrup will come to a boil—and, I trust, you do not have the time to stand there watching it—do not be concerned about boiling the syrup just a little longer than specified in the recipe; its viscosity will not be adversely affected. However, boiling the syrup for as much as 5 minutes longer than the specified time will increase the Baumé to 30°; 10 minutes of boiling will bring it to 34°. Should this happen, let the syrup cool to approximately 60°F (16°C), check the sugar content using a Baumé thermometer, and replace the evaporated water as needed to bring it to 28° Baumé. The water that you add should first be boiled and then cooled to 60°F (16°C) to get an accurate reading and also to sterilize it so the syrup can be stored. Although it is simple enough to test the Baumé level, going through this procedure is really practical only for a large batch of syrup.

Streusel Topping yield: 2 pounds 10 ounces (1 kg 195 g)

This topping, as the name suggests, was originally intended for sprinkling on top of the German delicacy Streusel Kuchen; *streusel* means "to sprinkle" or "to strew" in German. You will find that I have borrowed it for use in a number of recipes throughout the book—Danish pastries, tarts, muffins, and apple mazarins, to name a few. The crunch of the baked topping adds a nice contrast in each case.

6 ounces (170 g) light brown sugar
6 ounces (170 g) granulated sugar
11 ounces (310 g) unsalted butter
1 tablespoon (5 g) ground cinnamon

2 teaspoons (10 g) salt
1 teaspoon (5 ml) vanilla extract
1 pound 2 ounces (510 g) bread flour

1. Mix the brown sugar, granulated sugar, butter, cinnamon, salt, and vanilla.

2. Stir in the flour. The mixture should be crumbly and should not come together like a dough; you may need to add extra flour.

3. Store, covered, in the refrigerator to prevent the topping from drying out.

VARIATION
HAZELNUT STREUSEL

Add 10 ounces (285 g) chopped or coarsely crushed untoasted hazelnuts when you add the flour.

Sweetened Condensed Milk yield: 1¼ cups (300 ml)

As with so many other stock ingredients or mise en place products used in the industry (and sometimes at home also), condensed milk is easy to make—it simply takes time. Because of the long cooking process and the fact that the canned product is inexpensive, widely available, and does not require refrigeration, in most cases, it makes sense to go ahead and buy it in cans. However, for those times when Plan B has to be put into action (you run out, or you forgot to order or buy it), here are the instructions. Another reason to consider making your own sweetened condensed milk is that you can make it less sweet than the commercial product, which may be too sweet for your taste or for a particular application. You can also use nonfat milk to make a fat-free version. If using nonfat milk, reduce the sugar to 2 ounces (55 g).

3½ cups (840 ml) whole milk

8 ounces (225 g) granulated sugar

1. Pour the milk into an oversized heavy-bottomed saucepan. Add the sugar and stir to incorporate.

2. Bring the mixture to a boil, then reduce the heat so the liquid is just simmering. Cook for 40 to 50 minutes, stirring occasionally, until the liquid is reduced to 1½ cups (360 ml).

3. Strain through a fine mesh strainer (you should have 1¼ cups/300 ml after straining) and let cool completely before using. Store, covered and refrigerated, for up to 5 days.

Tartaric Acid Solution yield: approximately ³⁄₄ cup (180 ml)

½ cup (120 ml) hot water   4 ounces (115 g) tartaric acid

1. Mix hot water and tartaric acid until all of the granules are dissolved.

2. Pour the liquid into an eyedropper bottle (available in pharmacies and through professional pastry supply stores).

Unflavored Yogurt yield: 4 cups (960 ml)

Making your own yogurt will take only about five minutes away from your other work while you monitor the temperature of the milk in Step 1. The incubation takes care of itself, thanks to the bacteria cultures *lactobacillus bulgaricus* and *streptococcus thermophilous*. Basically, they consume lactose as a source of energy, thereby producing lactic acid during the incubation period, which, after the pH has reached 4 to 4.5, sets the liquid.

Fermented milk is nothing new. Yogurt was almost certainly consumed in some form as early as 6000 B.C., invented most likely by accident and then used as a convenient way to preserve milk. Yogurt made its way to Europe as early as the fifteenth century, but it was not until well into the 1900s that it became fashionable as a health food. Later, plain yogurt was mixed with fruits and flavorings to balance the sourness, and it became a popular commercial product. Frozen yogurt, which is similar in texture to soft ice cream but generally lower in fat, has been a big seller over the last decade or so. Just how healthy yogurt really is has been the source of debate for a long time. It is, no doubt, a good source of vitamin B, calcium, and protein, but it is, of course, only low in fat if made from low-fat milk to begin with.

5 cups (1 L 200 ml) milk, whole or nonfat   ¼ cup (60 ml) unflavored yogurt

1. In a heavy-bottomed saucepan, heat the milk to a simmer, about 185°F (85°C), while stirring frequently. Remove from the heat and let cool to 110°F (43°C) (see Note).

2. Place the yogurt in a mixing bowl that measures about 9 inches (22.5 cm) in diameter. Gradually stir in the cooled milk, continuing to stir until the mixture is smooth before adding the next portion. Cover the bowl with a plate, wrap two or three towels around the bowl and the lid, and set aside in a warm location to set the yogurt. This usually takes about 5 hours, depending on the temperature in your kitchen. If this is not 80°F (26°C) or above, and I sincerely hope it is not, place the bowl in a 90° to 100°F (32° to 38°C) oven. You can usually achieve this temperature by turning the oven off and on a few times during the first hour. Be careful not to let the oven get too hot or you will kill the bacteria.

3. Remove the towels and the plate and cover the bowl with plastic wrap. Store the yogurt in the refrigerator. Use part of this batch to make the next batch, and so on.

NOTE: If you do not have a dairy thermometer that can be placed in the saucepan, you can make a convenient holder by laying a large spoon across the center of the pan. Place an inverted dinner fork at a 90-degree angle to the spoon with the tines of the fork balanced on the spoon handle. You can now insert your instant-read pocket thermometer through the tines of the fork and let it hang in the milk.

YOGURT CHEESE yield: 1³/₄ cups (420 ml)

While not a true cheese, yogurt (homemade or store-bought) thickened to the consistency of mascarpone can be substituted in some recipes for sour cream, crème fraîche, and cream cheese to reduce fat and calories. The substitution can be made in an equal quantity in recipes where the ingredient is not cooked—for example, Sour Cream Mixture for Piping, Romanoff Sauce, or when crème fraîche is used to accompany a dessert. You will get a better result if you drain some of the liquid out of the yogurt before you use it, as this thickens it and improves the texture.

2 cups (480 ml) yogurt

1. Place yogurt in a strainer lined with cheesecloth and set the strainer over a bowl to catch the liquid. Cover and refrigerate for 24 hours.

2. Discard the liquid and store the yogurt cheese as you would yogurt.

Vanilla Extract yield: 1 quart (960 ml)

Making your own vanilla extract is as easy as 1, 2, 3—it merely requires advance planning. The two whole beans added at the end are purely for decoration, but the extract does make a great place to store them.

8 long, soft vanilla beans   **1 quart (960 ml) good-quality vodka**

1. Split 6 of the beans lengthwise, then cut them into small pieces.

2. Put the vanilla pieces and the vodka in a jar with a lid and seal tightly.

3. Let stand in a dark, cool place for about 1 month, shaking the bottle from time to time.

4. Strain the liquid through a fine-mesh strainer lined with a double thickness of cheesecloth.

5. Clean the bottle and return the vanilla extract to the bottle.

6. Add the 2 remaining whole vanilla beans. Store tightly sealed.

Vanilla Sugar

There are a number of recipes for making vanilla sugar. A simple way that also protects the beans from drying out when stored is to place split or whole vanilla beans in a jar of granulated sugar. The jar should be tall enough to hold the beans standing up and allow room for plenty of sugar around them. Make sure the jar is tightly sealed. Shake it once a day to circulate the sugar and increase the fragrance. After 1 week, the vanilla sugar is ready. As you use the vanilla sugar and the beans, keep adding to the jar. Naturally, the more beans you store in the jar in relation to the amount of sugar, the stronger the flavor and fragrance.

Zested Citrus Peel, Citrus Zest Strips, and Grated Citrus Zest

I find beginning students are often unclear about the differences between zested citrus peel, grated citrus zest, and strips of citrus zest. The word *zest* refers to the colored part of the skin on the citrus fruit. The pith (the white part of the peel underneath the zest) can be bitter and is usually avoided. While the zest is removed in distinct ways that have differing uses, the technique used for each procedure is the same for lemons, limes, oranges, and grapefruit.

If you will be extracting the juice from the citrus fruit, you should do so after removing the zest using any of the methods described below, because it is difficult to remove the zest properly once the fruit is cut in half.

ZESTED CITRUS PEEL

To make zested citrus peel, you need to use a citrus zester, which should not be confused with a citrus stripper. Figure 1-6 shows the tool used to make citrus zest on top and the tool used to make citrus strips on the bottom. If you are producing zested peel for decoration, you may want to make the thin threads as long as possible, but if the zest is to be mixed into a batter, for example, shorter strokes that produce shorter pieces are more appropriate. If you do not have a citrus zester and must make do, shave off the colored part of the rind as thinly as possible with a citrus stripper or vegetable peeler, then chop the zest as finely as possible.

1. Place the sharp edge of the zester against the fruit at one end and, pressing hard against the fruit, drag it down to the opposite end, letting the threads of zest fall into a bowl or onto a sheet of baking paper. Move the zester to an intact section of the peel and repeat (Figure 1-7).

2. To remove some of the bitter flavor from the zest, place it in a saucepan with enough cold water to cover. Bring to a boil, strain, and repeat with fresh cold water. Chill in ice water, blot dry, and store, covered, in a jar in the refrigerator. The zest will keep well for several days.

FIGURE 1-6 A citrus zester and a citrus stripper

FIGURE 1-7 Using a citrus zester to remove thin threads of lemon zest

CITRUS ZEST STRIPS

Strips of citrus zest are cut using a citrus stripper—although, accurately speaking, the tool removes the rind and not just the zest. These strips are much thicker than the strips removed with the zester and are used for garnish. They can also be used as string to tie a package closed. The strips are chopped finely if they are to be added to a batter or other mixture.

1. Place the citrus stripper against the fruit with the notched edge of the blade touching the fruit. Pressing firmly, move the tool in long strokes, allowing the strips of zest to fall off into a bowl or onto a sheet of baking paper (Figure 1-8).

2. The citrus zest strips can be blanched as described above, if desired.

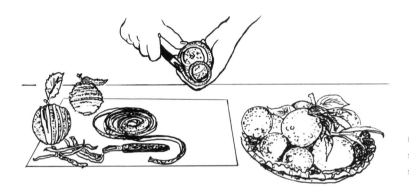

FIGURE 1-8 **Using a citrus stripper to remove long, thin strips of orange zest**

GRATED CITRUS ZEST

Grated citrus zest is produced by lightly grating the fruit over the very tiny holes on a box grater or hand grater, taking care not to remove any more of the white pith than is necessary. Turning the fruit as you work so that you grate the peel in a new spot with each stroke facilitates that result (Figure 1-9).

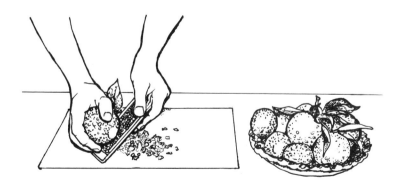

FIGURE 1-9 **Grating orange zest using a hand grater**

The following recipes don't really fit into any of the other chapters in this book. They are included here because, in my experience, the pastry department is usually called upon to help with the preparation and baking of such items as quiches, cheese puffs, and puff pastries like ham or cheese croissants and cheese straws. This, of course, makes sense, as these items are all variations on basic pastry doughs and products, and we usually have much better ovens in which to bake them. Also, in the old classical menus (which typically consisted of as many as 14 courses, each accompanied by the appropriate wine), a savory dish was always served between the sweet, which could be just about anything sweet that did not interfere with the dessert, and the actual dessert. Typical favorites for the sweet course were blancmange, Bavarian creams, and ices. Then a savory such as cheese straws was served, followed by the final dessert course.

Many of the puff pastry hors d'oeuvres in this chapter, such as Anchovy Sticks, Cheese Straws, Cumin Bow Ties, Ham or Cheese Croissants, and Sausage Cuts, can be made up in advance and frozen to bake as needed.

Anchovy Sticks yield: 56 pieces, 2 inches (5 cm) long

Anchovy sticks, together with cheese straws, ham or cheese croissants, and cumin bow ties, are always included in European assortments of puff pastry hors d'oeuvres. Anchovies should be used with restraint, as their salty flavor is an acquired taste; it almost seems as if you have to be raised in Europe to fully appreciate the salted fillets of these small silvery fish.

There are many species of anchovy; all are members of the herring family and bear a strong resemblance to the English sprat fish. In fact, the Norwegian anchovy is actually a young sprat. The true anchovy is found along the southern European coastline, most abundantly in the Mediterranean. Anchovies are a must in Caesar salad and are most popular in the cuisine of southern Europe, in such classics as salade Niçoise, pissaladière, and, of course, pizza—at least on the pizza of yours truly. Anchovies have also found their way to many other countries; an extremely popular dish in Sweden, for example, is *Janson's Frestelse* (Janson's Temptation), which is a gratin of anchovies and potatoes.

1 pound 10 ounces (740 g) Puff Pastry (page 74)	**14 ounces (400 g) canned anchovy fillets** **Egg wash**

I. Roll the puff pastry out to a rectangle measuring 21 × 16 inches (52.5 × 40 cm). If the dough shrinks back excessively as you roll it, do this in two stages, letting the dough relax for 30 minutes in the refrigerator in between.

2. Cut the sheet in half lengthwise to make 2 pieces measuring 16 × 10½ inches (40 × 26.2 cm) each. Measure and mark (without cutting through the dough) both short ends of one piece every 1½ inches (3.7 cm). Use the back of a chef's knife to draw lines lengthwise between the marks.

3. Cut the anchovy fillets in half lengthwise. Brush egg wash over the entire marked sheet of puff pastry. Place a row of anchovies lengthwise down the center of each of the 7 marked rows.

4. Place the second puff pastry sheet on top of the anchovy-covered sheet. Using a thin dowel (½ to ¾ inch/1.2 to 2 cm), press down between the rows of anchovies and on the long edges to seal the puff pastry sheets together.

5. Cut the strips apart with a chef's knife or pastry wheel. Brush egg wash over the strips. Transfer the strips to a sheet pan and place in the refrigerator or freezer until the egg wash is dried.

6. Score the tops of the strips crosswise every ½ inch (1.2 cm) by pressing a serrated knife lightly into the dough. Cut each strip into 8 pieces measuring 2 inches (5 cm) long. Place the pieces on sheet pans lined with baking paper.

7. Bake at 425°F (219°C) for 8 minutes. Lower the heat to 375°F (190°C) and continue baking 10 minutes longer or until baked through and golden brown.

Blini yield: 40 to 45 blini, 3 inches (7.5 cm) in diameter

The name *blini* is a western modification of the Russian word *blin,* which means "pancake." Although they are enjoyed in Russia all year round, blini are traditionally associated with Maslenitsa, the week-long pre-Lenten Butter Festival. This is a lively and joyous celebration signifying the end of the long, cold winter and the beginning of spring. As a famous Russian once said, "Blini are round and hot and beautiful like a glorious sun." During the festival, it is traditional to serve hot, freshly made blini at every meal, topped with melted butter, sour cream, and caviar, salmon, or herring—usually in that order—with the toppings becoming a bit more humble as the week goes by.

These little pancakes can be found in many sizes and variations. An authentic blini pan is slightly over 5 inches (12.5 cm) in diameter. I find this size too large in many instances, considering the richness of the toppings and the fact that blini are generally served as an appetizer. I like to make them using the small Swedish pancake iron called plättiron, which has indentations a little less than 3 inches (7.5 cm) across. It is excellent for this purpose and produces blini that are small enough to serve stacked Napoleon-style, giving height to the presentation.

While blini and Beluga caviar are almost inseparable—being a traditional must-order appetizer by tourists in Russia and a classic part of the captain's farewell dinner on many cruise ships—I have had blini served with many other types of fish eggs in Scandinavia—salmon, whitefish, trout, herring. They are usually accompanied by diced onions or chives and sour cream. Regardless of where and with what blini are served, they should always be served warm and shining with melted butter on top.

½ ounce (15 g) or 1 tablespoon (15 ml) fresh compressed yeast *or* 2 ½ teaspoons (6 g) active dry yeast	¼ teaspoon (2 g) granulated sugar
½ cup (120 ml) warm water	1 cup (240 g) warm whole milk
3 ounces (85 g) bread flour	3 eggs, separated
3 ounces (85 g) cake flour	3 ounces (85 g) unsalted butter, melted
½ teaspoon (2.5 g) salt	Clarified butter for greasing the pan

1. Dissolve the yeast in the warm water. If using dry yeast, allow it to proof for 10 to 15 minutes before continuing.

2. Place the bread flour, cake flour, salt, and sugar in an oversized bowl to allow room for the batter to proof. Using a whisk, stir the dry ingredients together.

3. Add the milk, yeast mixture, and egg yolks. Whisk until the batter is completely smooth, 3 to 4 minutes.

4. Cover the bowl and set aside in a warm place to proof for at least 1 hour or up to 3 hours for more sourdough flavor.

5. Whip the egg whites to stiff peaks and fold into the batter.

6. Heat a griddle, skillet, or small Swedish pancake pan until very hot but not smoking. Brush the surface with clarified butter and add 1-ounce (2-tablespoons/30-ml) portions of batter to the pan by pouring it or by using an appropriate-sized ladle; this will be the correct amount of batter to fill the indentations if using the Swedish pancake pan. Flip the blini when they are brown and set on the bottom; the edges on the top side will begin to look dry, but the center should still look moist (a small offset spatula works well to turn the blini). Brush clarified butter over the cooked tops and cook 30 to 60 seconds on the second side. Remove to a warm platter or warm serving plates. If well covered, the blini may be kept warm in a very low oven for up to 15 minutes but, preferably, they should be served as soon as they have finished cooking.

Buckwheat Blini yield: approximately 20 blini, 4¹⁄₂ inches (11.2 cm) in diameter

½ ounce (15 g) or 1 tablespoon (15 ml) fresh compressed yeast

1½ cups (360 ml) whole milk, at room temperature

5 ounces (140 g) buckwheat flour

2 ounces (55 g) bread flour

½ cup (120 ml) buttermilk

½ cup (120 ml) beer

3 eggs, separated

1 teaspoon (5 g) salt

1 tablespoon (15 g) granulated sugar

Clarified butter for greasing the pan

1. Dissolve the yeast in the milk. Incorporate the buckwheat flour and mix to form a smooth paste. Cover and set aside in a warm place for 1 hour to rise.

2. Add the bread flour, buttermilk, beer, and egg yolks, stirring until smooth. Cover and set aside in a warm place for 1 hour to rise again. After the second rising, the blini batter may be reserved in the refrigerator for several hours.

3. When you are ready to cook the blini, whip the egg whites with the salt and the sugar until stiff but not to the point where dry peaks form. Fold into the batter.

4. Generously butter a heavy 10- to 12-inch (25- to 30-cm) skillet or a griddle. Heat until the surface is hot but not smoking. Pour 3 or 4 small pools of batter onto the skillet, using slightly less than ¼ cup (60 ml) batter for each pancake (see Note). Cook for about 4 minutes, then turn and cook approximately 1 minute longer on the second side. You can usually judge when the blini are ready to turn by watching the bubbles as they form on the surface. Brush additional butter on the skillet as you turn the blini, if necessary, to avoid a dry appearance. Transfer to an ovenproof pan or platter, cover, and keep warm while you cook the remaining blini.

NOTE: The blini should be about ³⁄₈ inch (9 mm) thick. If the batter does not spread properly, thin it with milk. If you are making a fair amount of blini and do not have the benefit of a griddle, try this technique using 2 skillets: When the first batch of 3 or 4 blini is ready to turn, flip them all at once into a second hot skillet instead of turning them individually. Pour another 3 or 4 pools of batter into the first skillet while the group in the second skillet finishes cooking, then repeat.

Cheese Soufflé yield: 8 servings

Soufflé is a French word meaning "to blow," "to breathe," or "puffed up." This latter is, of course, how we like to see our finished soufflés. Whether sweet or savory, soufflés should always be made in round forms with straight sides to help them rise. Although a savory soufflé will never rise as high as a properly prepared dessert soufflé, it must still be served hot, straight from the oven.

Melted unsalted butter	7 eggs, separated
5 ounces (140 g) freshly grated Parmesan cheese	2 ounces (55 g) grated Gruyère cheese
3 ounces (85 g) bread flour	$\frac{1}{4}$ teaspoon (1 g) cayenne pepper
3 ounces (85 g) unsalted butter, at room temperature	$\frac{1}{4}$ teaspoon (1 g) ground nutmeg
2 cups (480 ml) whole milk	2 teaspoons (10 g) salt

1. Brush melted butter over the insides of 8 soufflé molds 3¼ inches (8.1cm) in diameter that hold 5 ounces (150 ml) each. Dust with enough Parmesan cheese to coat; reserve the remaining cheese for the batter. Set the forms aside.

2. Blend the flour and butter to a smooth paste.

3. Heat the milk in a saucepan to the scalding point.

4. Whisk in the flour mixture and cook to a thick paste, stirring constantly.

5. Remove from the heat. Mix in the egg yolks a few at a time, continuing to stir constantly so they do not cook. Add the remaining Parmesan cheese, Gruyère cheese, cayenne, nutmeg, and salt.

6. Whip the egg whites to stiff peaks (be careful not to whip them dry). Gently fold the egg whites into the batter one-third at a time.

7. Fill the prepared forms three-quarters full.

8. Bake immediately at 400°F (205°C) for approximately 15 minutes or until puffed, with a nice golden color on the side. Serve at once.

Cheese Straws yield: 64 cheese straws, 3¹/₂ inches (8.7 cm) long

In addition to making a nice before-meal snack with your favorite aperitif, cheese straws are often served as an accompaniment to soups or salads. As with many puff pastry products, these can be made up in advance and conveniently stored in the freezer, well wrapped, for up to 1 month. Bake as needed directly from the freezer.

3½ ounces (100 g) grated Parmesan cheese	1 pound (455 g) Puff Pastry (page 74)
1 teaspoon (2 g) paprika	Egg wash

1. Toss the Parmesan cheese and paprika until evenly mixed; set aside.

2. Roll out the puff pastry to ⅛ inch (3 mm) thick in a rectangle 14 x 10 inches (35 x 25 cm).

3. Brush the entire surface of the dough heavily with egg wash.

4. Sprinkle the paprika-cheese mixture over half of the dough, starting from one of the long sides.

5. Fold the plain half of the dough over the cheese. Roll the dough to 6 inches (15 cm) in width, sealing and pressing the cheese into the dough at the same time.

6. Place the dough in the refrigerator for 30 minutes to relax and firm up.

7. Cut the dough lengthwise into 16 strips, each ⅜ inch (9 mm) wide. Twist each strip into a spiral as for Pretzel Pastries (see Figure 12-15, page 581), stretching the strips to 16 inches (40 cm) at the same time.

8. Place on sheet pans lined with baking paper, securing both ends of each twisted strip to the paper by pressing hard with your thumbs. This will help keep them straight; they still tend to curl and twist somewhat but can easily be straightened before they are completely baked through. Let rest for at least 30 minutes before baking.

9. Bake at 400°F (205°C) for approximately 15 minutes or until golden brown and done.

10. Immediately cut each strip into quarters, each 3½ inches (8.7 cm) long. Cheese straws are best served the same day they are baked.

Cumin Bow Ties yield: 48 bow ties, 1¹/₂ x 3 inches (3.7 x 7.5 cm) each

These little bow ties are part of a long list of puff pastry hors d'oeuvres. You might say they come dressed for the occasion, requiring only egg wash and a sprinkling of cumin after they are cut, unlike anchovy sticks and ham and cheese croissants, which are a bit more involved.

Adjust the amount of cumin used to suit your preference. The distinctive warm flavor of the seeds blends well with both Mexican and Middle Eastern dishes. These bow ties should not be restricted to simply a before-dinner tidbit but could be served as an accompaniment or garnish to a curry or lamb dish.

1 pound 10 ounces (740 g) Puff Pastry (page 74)

Egg wash

2 tablespoons (14 g) whole cumin seed

1. Roll out the puff pastry, using flour to prevent the dough from sticking, to make a rectangle that is slightly larger than 12 x 18 inches (30 x 45 cm). Place the dough in the refrigerator to chill and become firm.

2. Trim the sides of the dough to make them even and make the rectangle exactly 12 x 18 inches (30 x 45 cm). Cut 4 strips lengthwise, then cut across into 1½-inch (3.7-cm) pieces to make 48 rectangles measuring 1½ x 3 inches (3.7 x 7.5 cm).

3. Leaving the pieces in place, brush egg wash over the dough. Immediately sprinkle the cumin seeds evenly over the cut pieces. Lightly sprinkle salt on top.

4. Twist each piece twice in the center to form a bow-tie shape. The side of the dough with the cumin seeds will be facing up on both ends. Place the pieces on sheet pans lined with baking paper.

5. Bake at 400°F (205°C) for approximately 15 minutes or until golden brown and baked through. Let cool completely, then store in a dry place. The bow ties taste best the day they are baked. If needed, you can refresh them by placing them in a hot oven for a few minutes.

Gougères yield: approximately 50 pieces, 1 inch (2.5 cm) in diameter

These savory French cheese puffs from Burgundy make a quick and easy hors d'oeuvre, excellent with, of course, red wine. Traditionally, the dough is piped into a large ring shape, but individual gougères are more common and, perhaps, more practical. The addition of cheese greatly affects the ability of the paste to puff, so do not expect that these will increase in volume to the extent of profiteroles piped the same size. If you must substitute another cheese for either of the two listed in the recipe, Parmesan adds a nice flavor, but you probably should not suggest it to a French chef.

5 ounces (140 g) Gruyère or Emmenthaler cheese, finely diced or grated

¼ recipe Pâte à Choux (page 83)

1. Draw 2 circles, 10 inches (25 cm) in diameter, on a sheet of baking paper. Invert the paper on a sheet pan and set aside.

2. Reserve ¼ cup (60 ml) cheese. Mix the remaining cheese into the pâte à choux. Place in a pastry bag with a No. 6 (12-mm) plain tip.

3. Pipe approximately 25 mounds around each circle to form a ring. If you have pâte à choux left over, pipe it into individual mounds inside the ring; do not pipe on top of the ring. Sprinkle the reserved cheese over the mounds.

4. Bake immediately at 400°F (205°C) for approximately 25 minutes or until fully baked and golden brown. Gougères should be eaten the same day they are baked.

Ham or Cheese Croissants yield: approximately 50

These hors d'oeuvres can, and often seem to be, made into a full meal. Be forewarned—you would be wise to bake a few extra, as these savory croissants have a tendency to disappear. If they are made ahead and frozen, bake the croissants directly from the freezer; they will require a slightly longer baking time.

6 ounces (170 g) ham and/or Swiss cheese

Whole milk

1 pound (455 g) Puff Pastry (page 74)

Egg wash

1. Process the ham in a food processor to make a puree (this makes it easier to roll the croissants). If using cheese and ham, finely dice or grate the cheese and mix it with the ham. If using cheese alone, grate it and mix in enough milk to make a paste, or the cheese will fall off when you roll the croissants.

2. Roll the puff pastry out to a rectangle measuring 16 × 18 inches (40 × 45 cm), which should be slightly thinner than ⅛ inch (3 mm). Let rest, then cut into 4 strips, each 4 inches (10 cm) wide. Cut 3-inch (7.5-cm) triangles from the strips.

3. Place a small amount of filling on top of the puff pastry at the wide end of each triangle. Roll up tightly, stretching and pinching the ends underneath to prevent them from unrolling, and place on sheet pans lined with baking paper. Shape each croissant into a crescent as you set it down.

4. Brush with egg wash. Bake at 400°F (205°C) for about 20 minutes or until golden brown and baked through. Serve the croissants the same day they are baked.

Quiche Lorraine yield: 2 quiches, 11 inches (27.5 cm) in diameter

Quiche, which originated in Lorraine, took its name from the German word *Kuchen*, which means "little cake." Quiches can be loosely defined as unsweetened custards with various fillings. In some areas of Lorraine, any dish containing custard (eggs and cream), onion, and/or cheese is called a quiche.

1 recipe Flaky Pie Dough (page 62)

3 cups (720 ml) heavy cream

½ teaspoon (2.5 g) salt (see Note)

Pinch white pepper

Pinch ground nutmeg

12 egg yolks (1 cup/240 ml)

14 ounces (400 g) bacon, cut in small pieces, cooked, and drained

14 ounces (400 g) diced Gruyère cheese

1. Roll out pie dough ⅛ inch (3 mm) thick and line 2 false-bottomed tart pans, 11 inches (27.5 cm) in diameter (see Figure 7-1, page 325). Prick the bottom of the shells lightly and let rest for at least 30 minutes.

2. Combine the cream, salt, pepper, nutmeg, and egg yolks; blend thoroughly. Distribute the bacon and cheese evenly over the bottom of the shells. Pour the custard on top, dividing it between the two pans.

3. If you are using a conventional oven, place the pans on the lowest rack. If using a deck oven, place them directly on the hearth. Do not use a sheet pan. Bake at 375°F (190°C) for approximately 30 minutes or until the custard is set. Serve warm.

NOTE: You can substitute diced ham for the bacon. Adjust the amount of salt according to the saltiness of the ham or bacon.

Sausage Cuts in Puff Pastry   yield: 54 pieces, approximately 1¼ inches (3.1 cm) long

These great-tasting tidbits are a welcome addition to an assortment of passed hors d'oeuvres at any gathering. Sausage cuts are often referred to as pigs in a blanket, although the term is probably more commonly used for cocktail sausages wrapped in pastry or for small breakfast sausages wrapped in pancakes. If you make the sausage cuts ahead of time, or if you freeze part of the recipe, wait to apply the egg wash until you are ready to bake the pastries.

1 pound 8 ounces (680 g) Puff Pastry (page 74)	**¼ teaspoon (.5 g) cayenne pepper**
½ teaspoon (1 g) dried oregano	**1 pound 8 ounces (680 g) ground pork (not too lean)**
½ teaspoon (1 g) dried thyme	**3 medium cloves of garlic, finely chopped**
½ teaspoon (1 g) fennel seeds, chopped	**2 eggs**
¼ teaspoon (.5 g) ground cloves	**Egg wash**

1. Roll out the puff pastry to a rectangle measuring 13½ x 24 inches (33.7 x 60 cm), using flour to prevent the dough from sticking. The dough should be about ⅛ inch (3 mm) thick. Refrigerate the sheet to relax and firm the dough.

2. Combine the spices, then thoroughly mix them into the ground pork together with the garlic and the eggs.

3. Cut the puff pastry sheet lengthwise into 3 strips, each 4½ inches (11.2 cm) wide. Brush egg wash over the strips.

4. Place the pork mixture in a pastry bag with a No. 7 (14-mm) plain tip. Pipe a rope of filling next to one long edge on each strip, dividing the filling evenly among the strips. Roll the dough around the filling, enclosing it in a spiral of dough.

5. Place the finished ropes seam-side down on a sheet pan lined with baking paper. Press lightly with the palm of your hand to flatten the ropes slightly. Brush egg wash over the tops.

6. Bake at 375°F (190°C) for approximately 35 minutes or until light brown and baked through. Cool slightly, then cut each strip into 18 equal pieces using a serrated knife. Serve warm.

Special Reward Dog Biscuits yield: 30 dog biscuits, 3 × 1½ inches (7.5 × 3.7 cm)

You may be a bit surprised to find this recipe in a pastry book, but it is important to me. I am sure that anyone who has been fortunate enough to share their life with a dog (they truly are man's or woman's best friend) will understand why I am including it.

Any close reading of this text will reveal that I was lucky enough to grow up on a farm; it was rather small, but it still had a nice assortment of animals. The only drawback was that I was never allowed to have a dog because there were always several cats close at hand to keep the mice in check. I did a lot of traveling as a young adult, and it was not until I was 30 years old that I was ready to settle down and buy a house, but it did not take very long after that for me to get my first Akita puppy.

While I was writing the third edition of this book, the two Akitas that were part of the family—Kuma (also known as Mama Dog) and her son Shiro (also known as The Baby even though he weighs 140 pounds!)—received a dog-bone cookie cutter as a gift from one of my classes. Anyone who takes my classes is bound to hear my dog stories sooner or later. Once this recipe was developed, Kuma and Shiro would have nothing more to do with store-bought biscuits, given the choice! I am sure the same thing will happen at your house, should you decide to reward your best friend with these treats.

As you will see, these biscuits are fairly large (perhaps because I have large dogs). If you have a small dog, you should make the biscuits quite a bit smaller and roll the dough out thinner as well. If you do not have a bone-shaped cutter or you are short on time, use the quick biscuit method that follows. Although we dog lovers can tell the difference, our doggie friends understand that we can be pressed for time.

12 ounces (340 g) whole wheat flour	3 eggs
12 ounces (340 g) bread flour	1 cup (240 ml) vegetable oil
2 ounces (55 g) wheat germ	3 ounces (85 g) powdered dry milk
1 teaspoon (5 g) salt	1 cup (240 ml) water
2 tablespoons (30 g) brown sugar	

1. Combine the whole wheat flour, bread flour, wheat germ, salt, and brown sugar in a large mixing bowl. Stir in the eggs and the vegetable oil.

2. Dissolve the milk powder in the water, then incorporate the mixture.

3. Mix to form a very firm dough that is smooth and workable. Adjust by adding a little extra flour or water as required.

4. Cover the dough and set it aside to relax for 15 to 20 minutes.

5. Roll the dough out to ½ inch (1.2 cm) thick. Cut out biscuits, using a bone-shaped cutter measuring 3 × 1½ inches (7.5 × 3.7 cm). Place the biscuits on sheet pans lined with baking paper.

"Shiro"

"Kuma"
8-15-87 to 7-24-99

6. Bake at 375°F (190°C) for approximately 40 minutes or until the bones are brown and, more importantly, rock-hard. Let the bones cool, then store them in a covered container 5 to 6 feet off the floor. Use as needed to reward your four-legged friends.

QUICK METHOD FOR DOG BISCUITS

1. Prepare biscuits following Steps 1 through 3.

2. In Step 4, knead and shape the dough into a uniform square. Cover and place in the refrigerator to relax.

3. In Step 5, divide the dough into 2 equal pieces. Roll out 1 piece to make a rectangle measuring 15 x 6 inches (37.5 x 15 cm). Set this piece aside to relax and roll the second piece to the same size. Cut the first piece in half lengthwise, then cut each half across into 12 equal pieces. Repeat with the second piece of dough.

4. Pan, bake, and store as directed for main recipe.

MISCELLANEOUS TECHNIQUES

TO STRAIN A SAUCE OR OTHER LIQUID

The best method for straining a thick liquid, a fruit puree, or anything with a large amount of fiber or seeds is to force the contents through a strainer or chinois with the aid of a ladle. Not only does using a ladle make the job go considerably faster, but the yield of strained product is much higher.

1. Place the item to be strained in a strainer or chinois set or held over a bowl or other container (see Note).

2. Choose an appropriate-sized ladle; if using a chinois, you need a ladle small enough to reach close to the bottom of the cone. Press the outside of the ladle against the mesh of the strainer and move it either in a circular motion, if using a round strainer, or an up-and-down motion with a quick twist as you come down, if using a chinois (Figure 1-10), to force the contents through the strainer. From time to time, use a rubber spatula to scrape the product from the outside of the strainer into the bowl and, if needed, use a scraper or a small soupspoon to scrape the inside of the strainer if it becomes clogged.

3. Once nothing but solids remains in the strainer, discard them and add more of the liquid to be strained. It is more efficient to strain several small batches consecutively than to work with a large portion of liquid or to puree all at once.

NOTE: If using a chinois, placing it in a tall, round steam table insert helps hold it steady as you work.

FIGURE 1-10 **Using the bowl of a ladle to force the contents through a strainer by pressing the ladle against the strainer while moving it in a circular motion**

FILLING AND PIPING WITH A PASTRY BAG

Use a pastry bag that is large enough to allow you to fill the bag only half to two-thirds full. This will prevent the contents from being forced out through both ends.

1. Cut the opening of a new bag so that the point of your largest piping tip just barely shows through; this ensures that the opening will not be too large for the smaller tips.

2. Fold open the top half or third of the empty bag.

3. Place the tip in the bag. Turn the bag upside down and force a small part of it, closest to the tip, inside the tip to lock the bag and prevent the filling from running out (Figure 1-11). This is a good habit all of the time but essential when you are piping a thin or runny filling.

4. Use one hand to hold the bag under the folded section and place the filling in the bag with the other (Figure 1-12).

5. Straighten out the fold and slide the top of the bag between your thumb and forefinger from the top to where the filling is, on both sides of the bag, to move the filling away from the top and remove any air pockets. Twist the bag closed at the top. Turn the bag upside down and pull the tip up to release the inverted (locked) bag. Twist to temporarily relock it before pointing the bag down to pipe (Figure 1-13).

6. Hold the bag by resting the top between your thumb and fingers and apply pressure to the top of the bag with the palm of your hand only. Use your other hand to guide the tip or to hold onto the item being filled or decorated; do not apply pressure with this hand.

7. Squeeze some of the filling back into the bowl to make sure there are no air pockets near the tip before piping on the item you are decorating. When you are ready to pipe, untwist to open the flow, then twist again as you move between items so that the filling does not continue to run out (Figure 1-14). This is not necessary with a thick filling, such as cookie dough, that will stay in the bag without running.

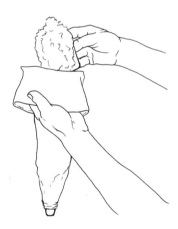

FIGURE 1-11 Pushing the top of the pastry bag inside the tip to prevent the filling from leaking out as it is added

FIGURE 1-12 Adding the filling to the pastry bag

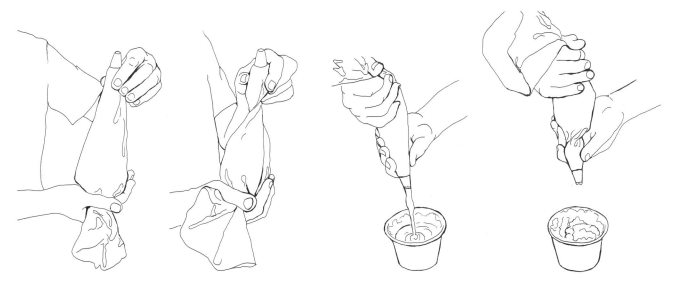

FIGURE 1-13 **Releasing the portion of the bag that was pushed inside after adding the filling; twisting the bag below the tip to temporarily relock the opening**

FIGURE 1-14 **Untwisting the top while piping; twisting again to close and stop the flow while moving between items**

PASTRY BAG SANITATION

Because pastry bags are used for so many dairy items—buttercream, pastry cream, and whipped cream—that are susceptible to food-borne illness, they must be washed after each use in warm, soapy water. The piping tip should be removed and washed separately, and the bag should be turned inside out to clean the inside thoroughly. Never wash the bag with the piping tip inside; there is almost always some amount of foodstuff trapped between the tip and the bag. Rinse the bag and wipe dry before turning right-side out and drying the outside of the bag. Hang the bag on a pastry bag rack or invert over a bottle so that air can circulate around the bag until it is completely dry. To sanitize pastry bags after washing them, submerge them in water that is at least 180°F (82°C) or in water containing a chemical sanitizing solution. While it is not practical to go through this procedure after each use in a busy shop, it is important to do at the end of each workday. Not only are these rules important from a health and safety standpoint, but your bags will last longer if cared for properly.

TO MAKE A PAPER PASTRY BAG

What constitutes a pastry bag versus a piping bag, by definition, is that a pastry bag, being larger, must be held in your hands when piping, while a piping bag is held with the fingers only. Therefore, technically speaking, the size determines the name. However, in general, people referring to a pastry bag are speaking of a reusable bag made of canvas or other material; a piping bag is usually a handmade paper cone meant for a single use. These directions, combining the two, are for making a disposable pastry bag from baking paper. This is fast and easy to do and is a practical solution in many instances. I simply tear a sheet of baking paper in half when I need a bag, but you could certainly cut sheets ahead of time so you always have 12- x 16-inch (30- x 40-cm) pieces handy. In several European countries, including my own, Sweden, professionals are required by law to use disposable pastry bags when working with dairy products.

1. Tear a full sheet (16 x 24 inches/40 x 60 cm) of baking paper in half crosswise against the edge of a table. The cut edge will be a bit ragged, but this doesn't matter. Set one piece of paper aside to use another time.

2. Hold the paper so that the rough edge is at the top (the opening of the bag) and fold the paper into a cone as you do to make a piping bag (Figures 1-15 and 1-16). See Figures 1-22 to 1-25 (page 55) for a more detailed example.

3. To keep the bag from coming apart, fold up about 2 inches (2.5 cm) of the tip.

N O T E : Moist fillings, such as whipped cream, pastry cream, and some jams, must be piped out within 5 to 10 minutes after filling the bag or the paper may burst.

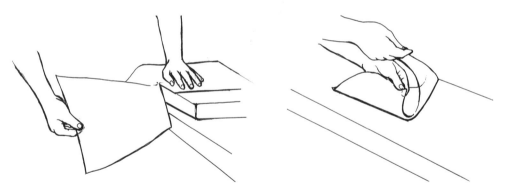

FIGURE 1-15 **Tearing the paper in half; starting to form a disposable pastry bag**

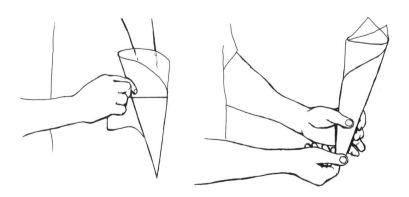

FIGURE 1-16 **Completing the pastry bag; folding the tip to prevent the bag from coming apart**

TO MAKE A PIPING BAG

1. Cut a standard full-size sheet (24 × 16 inches/60 × 40 cm) of baking paper into 6 pieces, each 8 inches (20 cm) square. Fold each square diagonally and cut into 2 triangles.

2. Start by holding a triangle horizontally so that the longest side is in front of you. Fold into a cone shape so that the long side becomes the tip and the point of the original triangle (the opposite side) becomes the opening of the cone (Figures 1-17 through 1-20). Fold the top into the cone to secure the shape (Figure 1-21). Fill the cone only halfway. Close the top securely and cut the tip into the desired size opening.

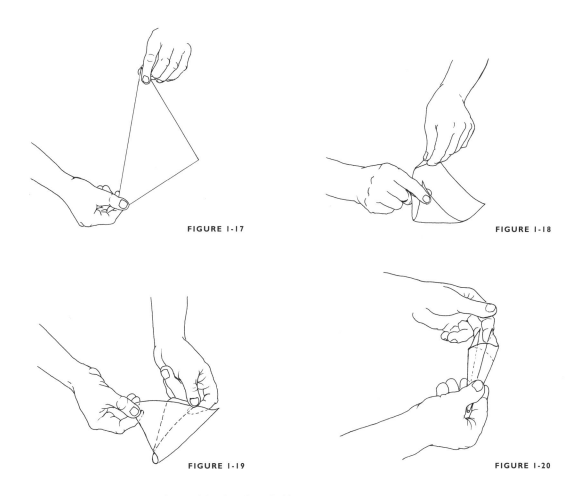

FIGURE 1-17

FIGURE 1-18

FIGURE 1-19

FIGURE 1-20

FIGURES 1-22, through 1-25 Making a piping bag from baking paper

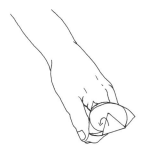

FIGURE 1-21 Securing the top of the cone inside the piping bag to prevent the bag from unfolding

TO LINE DEEP SQUARE OR RECTANGULAR PANS WITH BAKING PAPER

1. Place the pan in the center of a square or rectangle of baking paper large enough so that the paper that extends beyond the pan will cover the sides.

2. Place a ruler against one side of the pan and draw a line along the edge next to the pan, continuing to the end of the paper. Repeat on all 4 sides of the pan to create intersecting lines with a box the same size as the bottom of the pan in the center. Take into consideration that you are drawing on the outside of the pan, so make the square or rectangle slightly smaller.

3. Cut away the corner squares (Figure 1-22), leaving a cross-shaped piece of paper (Figure 1-23).

4. Place the paper in the pan.

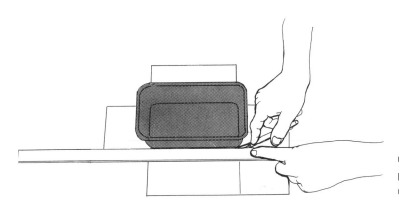

FIGURE 1-22 **Cutting baking paper to line the inside of a rectangular pan**

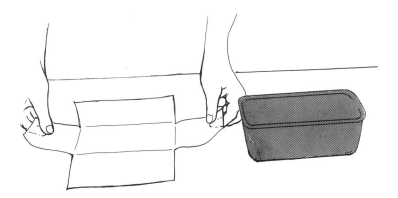

FIGURE 1-23 **The paper ready to line the pan**

TO LINE THE BOTTOM OF ROUND PANS WITH BAKING PAPER

It is fast and easy to cut a circle of paper to fit in the bottom of a round pan. Describing it actually takes more time than doing it.

1. Start with a rectangle of baking paper; if you are lining a 10-inch (25-cm) round cake pan, half of a standard sheet of baking paper will suffice. Fold the paper in half by bringing the short sides together and in half again the same way. Fold the 2 short folded edges in toward the long folded edge (Figure 1-24). Fold again in the same direction (Figure 1-25). The point of the triangle should be in the center of the original rectangle. You may need to fold 1 or 2 more times in the same direction, depending on the size of the circle you are creating. The more times you fold the paper, the more rounded the finished edge will be because each straight cut you make later will be shorter.

2. Hold the folded cone over the pan with the pointed end in the center. Cut the opposite end of the paper even with the edge of the pan.

3. Unfold the paper; you should have a circle the same size as the bottom of the pan (Figure 1-26). If the paper circle is too large, refold and cut again.

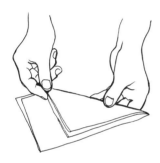

FIGURE 1-24 **Folding a rectangle of baking paper to create a circle for lining a cake pan**

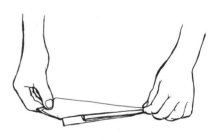

FIGURE 1-25 **Folding again in the same direction**

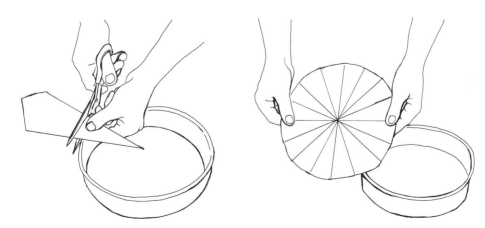

FIGURE 1-26 **Cutting the folded paper to make it as long as half the diameter of the pan; the circle after unfolding, ready to place in the pan**

Basic Doughs

Basic Doughs

A mastery of dough making is critical to the success of a professional pastry kitchen. Different techniques are required to create short dough, puff pastry, pâte à choux, pâte brisée, and flaky pie dough. However, in making any basic dough, it is important to use a good, workable recipe and to follow the proper procedures for preparation.

SHORT DOUGH

Short dough, along with its many variations, such as Linzer dough and cornmeal crust, is, without question, the dough used most frequently in the majority of pastry shops. A proficient pastry chef will always keep a supply of short dough in the refrigerator, ready to use as a base for cakes and pastries or to line tart pans. Short dough is also irreplaceable for preparing what I call nothing-left-in-the-showcase cookies. With one basic dough, you can make a variety of cookies and pastries quickly and efficiently.

Comparison of Doughs

Figure 2-1 (pages 60 and 61) compares the formulas of several of the doughs in this chapter, as well as other basic dough recipes throughout the text, relative to 1 pound (455 g) flour.

Ingredient Ratios in Basic Doughs Relative to One Pound of Flour

(Percentages of the other ingredients are expressed in relation to the flour weight which is calculated as 100 percent, not as a percentage of the total recipe weight)

	Puff Pastry		Quick Puff Pastry		Pie Dough		Danish Dough		Croissant Dough	
Flour	1 pound (455 g)	100%	1 pound (455 g)	100%	1 pound (455 g)	100%	1 pound (455 g)	100%	1 pound (455 g)	100%
Butter (margarine in Danish)	1 pound (455 g)	100%	1 pound (455 g)	100%	10 ounces (285 g)	63%	17 ounces (485 g)	106%	11½ ounces (325 g)	72%
Fresh Yeast	0	0	0	0	0	0	1½ ounces (40 g)	9%	1¼ ounces (37 g)	8%
Sugar	0	0	0	0	0	0	1½ ounces (40 g)	9%	7 teaspoons (35 g)	7.5%
Eggs	0	0	0	0	0	0	two (100 g)	22%	0	0
Water	6½ ounces (195 ml)	41%	3 ounces (90 ml)	19%	3 ounces (90 ml)	19%	0	0	0	0
Milk	0	0	0	0	0	0	6½ ounces (195 ml)	41%	9 ounces (270 ml)	56%
Salt	2½ teasp. (12.5 g)	3%	2½ teasp. (12.5 g)	3%	2½ teasp. (12.5 g)	3%	⅔ teasp. (3 g)	0.7%	2½ teasp. (12.5 g)	3%
Other	1½ teasp. (7.5 ml) lemon juice	2%	0	0	3 ounces (85 g) lard	19%	⅔ teasp. cardamom	0.3%	Few drops lemon juice	n/a
Mixing/ Production Method	The majority of the butter is mixed with the lemon juice and one-third of the flour, and the mixture is formed into a block. The remainder of the flour is mixed with the water, salt, and the balance of the butter to form a dough. The butter block is layered with the dough. The dough is given four double turns.		The flour and salt are combined. The butter is cut into large chunks, which are added to the flour mixture but are not fully incorporated. The water is mixed in just until the dough holds together. The dough is given three single turns followed by one double turn.		The flour and salt are combined. The butter and lard are added and mixed until the fat pieces are the size of marbles. Water is added, and the dough is mixed only until it holds together.		The margarine is shaped into a block. The yeast is dissolved in the cold milk and eggs. Salt, sugar, and cardamom are added, and the flour is incorporated to form a dough. The margarine block is layered with the dough. The dough is given four single turns.		The lemon juice, butter and a portion of the flour are formed into a block. The yeast is dissolved in the milk. The sugar, salt, and the balance of the flour are kneaded in with the dough hook. The butter block is layered with the dough. The dough is given three single turns.	

FIGURE 2-1 A comparison of basic dough formulas relative to 1 pound (455 g) flour

Ingredient Ratios in Basic Doughs Relative to One Pound of Flour

(Percentages of the other ingredients are expressed in relation to the flour weight which is calculated as 100 percent, not as a percentage of the total recipe weight)

	Brioche Dough		One-Step White Bread Dough		Pre-Ferment Style Bread Dough		Short Dough		Pâte à Choux	
Flour	1 pound (455 g)	100%	1 pound (455 g)	100%	1 pound (455 g)	100%	1 pound (455 g)	100%	1 pound (455 g)	100%
Butter (margarine in Danish)	5 ounces (140 g)	31%	2 ounces (55 g)	12%	½ ounce (15 g)	3.5%	14 ounces (400 g)	88%	6½ ounces (185 g)	41%
Fresh Yeast	1 ounce (30 g)	6%	1 ounce (30 g)	6%	½ ounce (l5 g)	3.5%	0	0	0	0
Sugar	2½ ounces (70 g)	16%	1 ounce (30 g)	6%	2½ teasp. (12.5 g)	3%	6 ounces (170 g)	38%	0	0
Eggs	four (200 g)	44%	0	0	0	0	one (50 g)	11%	14 (700 g)	154%
Water	0	0	0	0	1¼ cups (300 ml)	63%	0	0	3⅓ cups (800 ml)	163%
Milk	1½ ounces (45 ml)	9%	1 cup (240 ml)	50%	0	0	0	0	0	0
Salt	2 teasp. (l0 g)	2%	2¼ teasp. (11.25 g)	2.5%	1¾ teasp. (8 g)	1.8%	0	0	1¼ teasp. (6.25 g)	1.4%
Other	0	0	0	0	0	0	1 teasp. (5 ml) vanilla extract	1%	0	0
Mixing/ Production Method	The yeast is dissolved in the milk. The sugar, salt, and eggs are added. The flour, and then the butter, are incorporated. The dough is kneaded with the dough hook and then proofed in the refrigerator. The dough is formed and then proofed a second time prior to baking.		The yeast is dissolved in the milk. Salt, flour, and sugar are incorporated using the dough hook. Butter is mixed in, and the dough is kneaded for 10 minutes. The dough is proofed, formed, and proofed a second time before baking.		A pre-dough is made with one-third of the water, 20 percent of the yeast, a touch of sugar and one-third of the flour. It is kneaded for 10 minutes then left to proof 12 to 24 hours. The remaining yeast, water, salt, sugar, and butter are added, followed by the remaining flour, and the dough is kneaded for 10-15 minutes. The dough is proofed, punched down and proofed again before forming. Once formed, the dough is proofed again and then baked.		Sugar, soft butter, egg, and vanilla are mixed for a few minutes at low speed. The flour is added, and the dough is mixed only until the flour is fully incorporated.		The water, butter and salt are brought to a boil. The flour is stirred in over the heat. The roux is cooked for a few minutes and then cooled slightly. The eggs are incorporated gradually off the heat. The paste is immediately piped into the desired shape and baked.	

PUFF PASTRY

Another basic dough used continually in the pastry kitchen is puff pastry. It is one of the most exciting and also one of the most challenging doughs to work with. The use of puff pastry dates back many centuries; cookbooks and food reference books are filled with theories about its origin. It is impossible to say which story is accurate, but the one that I particularly like (having once been a 15-year-old apprentice myself) tells of a pastry apprentice in France. The young man was given the responsibility of making up all of the pastry doughs for use the following day. When he was finished, he realized that he had forgotten to add the butter in one of the recipes. Knowing that the master would certainly find out, but not wanting to start over, he quickly mixed in the missing butter, flattening and turning the dough over several times in an effort to hide his mistake. The next day, the master let it be known that he intended to have a few words with the apprentice. The apprentice, fearing he was to be scolded for ruining the dough, ran away. When he was found at last and brought trembling before the master, he was astonished to find out that rather than intending to punish him, the master wanted to praise him and learn the secret of the wonderful new flaky dough he had invented!

PÂTE À CHOUX

Pâte à choux, also known as *éclair paste,* is a basic and versatile paste used to make many items in the pastry kitchen, including cream puffs or profiteroles, swans, croquembouche, and, of course, éclairs. Like short dough, pâte à choux is also used in combination with puff pastry to make delicious sweets such as Gâteau Saint-Honoré and Choux Surprise. The translation of pâte à choux is "cabbage paste," referring to the baked cream puff's resemblance to a small cabbage head.

SIMPLE AND DECORATIVE DOUGHS

Pie dough, pizza dough, and pasta dough are much quicker and less complicated to master than puff pastry and pâte à choux. This chapter also contains four recipes for decorative doughs. Of these, only the Whole Wheat Weaver's Dough is intended for consumption. The salt doughs and the weaver's dough are used for purely decorative purposes.

Flaky Pie Dough yield: approximately 3 pounds 4 ounces (1 kg 480 g), or 4 shells, 10 inches (25 cm) in diameter

Making pie dough is quick and easy as long as the ingredients are kept cold and they are mixed only until just combined. In a good pie dough, most of the fat should still be visible in small, separate lumps. Overmixing or using soft fat will cause too much fat to be blended into the flour instead of remaining in separate pieces. The result is a dough that is hard to work with—and worse, a baked crust that is tough instead of flaky. The flakiness of pie crust also depends a great deal on the flour-to-fat ratio. As with short dough, the more flour in the dough, the harder the finished shell. Therefore, you should use the smallest amount of flour possible when rolling out a pie dough.

Scraps from pie dough should be treated with the same care as puff pastry. They should be layered on top of each other to roll out a second time; never knead the scraps together. These precautions will help to keep the dough from becoming rubbery and hard to work with.

While some chefs insist on the exclusive use of lard in their pie crust, I feel that even though it does produce a beautiful, flaky crust, its flavor of the lard can be overwhelming, especially when the pie has a sweet fruit filling. In my opinion, a compromise using both lard and butter gives the best overall result. If you prefer not to use lard, it is preferable to substitute margarine or vegetable shortening rather than to make the dough with all butter. Because of butter's high water content and low melting point, a pie dough made using 100 percent butter is very hard to work with, and the texture of the baked crust can be mealy.

1 pound 9 ounces (710 g) bread flour	5 ounces (140 g) cold lard
2 teaspoons (10 g) salt	⅔ cup (160 ml) ice water
1 pound (455 g) cold unsalted butter	

1. Combine the flour and salt in a bowl. Add the firm butter and lard to the flour and pinch the fat to the size of hazelnuts with your fingertips.

2. Add the ice water and mix with your hands just until the dough comes together; the butter should still be lumpy. Gather the dough into a ball. Flatten into a disc to help it chill faster.

3. Cover the pie dough and allow it to rest in the refrigerator for at least 1 to 2 hours before using. This step is important to allow the dough to hydrate; the flour absorbs some of the moisture in the dough.

NOTE: Unless you are making a large amount, always mix pie dough by hand, because it is easy to overmix the dough by machine. The pie dough should rest for an additional 30 minutes after it has been rolled out to prevent shrinkage as it is baked.

To Make a Decorative Fluted Edge

If it is important that your decorative edge hold a precise shape after baking, use Cream Cheese Pie Dough or Pâte Brisée rather than Flaky Pie Dough. The chunks of butter in the Flaky Pie Dough can cause small holes in the decorative edge.

Roll the dough out ⅛ inch (3 mm) thick, large enough so that it will extend about 1 inch (2.5 cm) beyond the edge of the pie pan. Roll the dough up on a dowel and unroll over the pan (see Figure 7-1, page 325). Fold the edge under and form it into a ½-inch (1.2-cm) lip standing up around the edge of the pan.

Method I: Use the knuckle of your right index finger and the tips of your left thumb and index finger to bend the lip of dough into an evenly spaced fluted design (Figure 2-2).

Method II: Pinch the lip of dough between your thumb and the side of your bent index finger and twist to make the fluted pattern (Figure 2-3).

FIGURE 2-2 **Method I: Creating a fluted edge using the knuckle and fingertips**

FIGURE 2-3 **Method II: Creating a fluted edge by pinching and twisting the dough**

Pâte Brisée yield: approximately 3 pounds 8 ounces (1 kg 540 g), or 4 shells, 10 inches (25 cm) in diameter

The French term *pâte brisée* refers to a type of pie dough or tart dough that is made without any sugar; in English, this is sometimes called *mealy pie dough*. Pâte sucrée, on the other hand, is a sugar dough, or short dough, that is used for the same applications. Both are known as *1, 2, 3 doughs*, although the formulas differ. Pâte sucrée is made with 1 part sugar, 2 parts fat, and 3 parts flour by weight. Pâte brisée is made with 1 part liquid (typically water), 2 parts fat, and 3 parts flour by weight. Both doughs generally contain 1 egg for every 1 pound of flour and may include additional flavoring ingredients, such as salt, lemon juice, or vanilla extract.

Pâte brisée is often confused with traditional flaky pie dough, as both are used to create tart and pie shells. The difference between the two is in the way that the ingredients are mixed—specifically, the distribution of the fat. Pie dough is made to be flaky. The desired texture is achieved by cutting the cold fat into the flour, being certain that it remains in small lumps, then binding the dough with ice-cold water. A true pâte brisée has the same consistency as short dough. It is produced by mixing the soft fat with the flour on low speed using the paddle attachment. The liquid is then incorporated and the ingredients are mixed just until a dough has formed. Just as with pie dough, it is important not to overmix and to let the dough rest, covered, in the refrigerator for at least 2 hours. Pâte brisée, or mealy pie dough, is preferable to flaky pie dough for use with a moist filling, such as a custard. Because the fat particles are evenly dispersed throughout the dough (the opposite of a flaky pie dough), they create a barrier that helps prevent the crust from becoming soggy. Pâte brisée is also a good choice when making a decorative fluted edge.

1 pound 4 ounces (570 g) bread flour	4 ounces (115 g) lard, at room temperature
12 ounces (340 g) cake flour	2 eggs
1 tablespoon (15 g) salt	⅓ cup (80 ml) ice water
12 ounces (340 g) unsalted butter, at room temperature	1 tablespoon (15 ml) lemon juice

1. Using the paddle attachment on the mixer, blend together the bread flour, cake flour, salt, butter, and lard at low speed, scraping down the bowl as necessary.

2. Combine the eggs, water, and lemon juice. Incorporate the liquid and blend only until the mixture forms a dough; do not overmix.

3. Cover the dough and refrigerate for a minimum of 2 hours.

Cream Cheese Pie Dough

yield: 2 pounds 4 ounces (1 kg 25 g), or 3 shells, 11 inches (27.5 cm) in diameter

This fast, uncomplicated pie dough was one I used frequently in the mid-1980s and was included in my first book. Why I dropped it from the second and third editions I do not remember. I had all but forgotten about this technique until a chef from one of the country's top restaurants happened to be at Greystone to do a plated dessert demonstration that included his version of this dough. Here, then, is my version, born again.

13 ounces (370 g) unsalted butter, at room
temperature

11 ounces (310 g) cream cheese, at room
temperature

1½ teaspoons (7.5 g) salt

1 teaspoon (5 ml) lemon juice

13 ounces (370 g) bread flour

I. Slowly combine the butter, cream cheese, salt, and lemon juice, using the hook attachment.

2. Incorporate the flour, scraping down the sides of the bowl once or twice and mixing just until the dough comes together.

3. Refrigerate, covered, and use as you would traditional pie dough.

Linzer Dough yield: I pound I4 ounces (855 g)

At first glance, this dough appears fairly simple, and although that is true, for the most part, Linzer dough is a bit deceiving in that it can become unusable if you are not careful. It is critical that the hazelnuts are ground to a fine consistency. (If this is done in a food processor, add half of the sugar to the nuts while grinding to absorb the oil and keep the nuts from turning into a paste.) When the ground nuts are too coarse, it becomes virtually impossible to move a rolled sheet of dough without it falling apart. Overmixing the dough will cause the same problem—in this case, a result of incorporating too much air.

In addition to this recipe, see the one for piped linzer dough on page 335. The piped method works especially well if you are making a large quantity of tarts.

6 ounces (170 g) granulated sugar

8 ounces (225 g) unsalted butter, at room
temperature

3 egg yolks (¼ cup/60 ml)

8 ounces (225 g) bread flour

2 teaspoons (3 g) ground cinnamon

½ teaspoon (1 g) ground cloves

6 ounces (170 g) finely ground hazelnuts

2 teaspoons (12 g) grated lemon zest

I. Combine the sugar, butter, and egg yolks in a mixer bowl, using the dough hook on low speed.

2. Sift the flour with the cinnamon and cloves.

3. Add the flour mixture, hazelnuts, and lemon zest to the butter mixture; mix just until all ingredients are incorporated and smooth. Overmixing will make this dough very hard to work with.

4. Cover the dough and refrigerate on a paper-lined sheet pan.

Short Dough

The name short dough makes more sense if you realize that short refers to its crumbly quality, which is produced by the shortening (butter or margarine).

BUTTER VERSUS MARGARINE

Short dough can be prepared with butter, margarine, or a combination of the two. Although butter produces the best flavor, it makes the dough hard to manage. Because the temperature range when butter is just the right consistency is so narrow, the butter in the dough will be rock-hard if the dough is stored in the refrigerator and too soft if the dough is left at room temperature. Another disadvantage to using butter is that if too much flour is worked into the dough while it is being rolled out, the dough will not only crumble and be harder to work with, but also will become rubbery and shrink when it is baked. In cold climates, all or part butter can be used more successfully.

A short dough made with high-quality margarine may not be as tasty, but it is less complicated to handle. By comparison, if you work too much flour into a dough made with margarine, the dough will crumble and be hard to work with, but it will not shrink during baking. Margarine is often a better choice if you are in a hurry, because it may be used straight from the refrigerator, whereas butter must first be brought to room temperature to soften. A compromise is to use half butter and half margarine to benefit from the advantages of each. When using both butter and margarine in a short dough, it is essential that they have the same consistency before mixing the dough. If the butter is harder than the margarine, you will end up with small lumps of butter in the finished dough.

MIXING THE DOUGH

If short dough is overmixed, mixed using the wrong tool, mixed at the wrong speed, or if any combination of these occurs, too much air will be incorporated into the dough. This will result in a soft product that could well, in the worst scenario, be piped out using a pastry bag. When this happens, you can imagine the problems and frustrations the baker has attempting to roll the "dough" into a thin sheet to line tart pans, for example. However, trying to compensate for the softness by adding too much flour to the short dough, either when making the dough or while rolling it out, will make the baked crust unpleasantly tough and hard instead of crumbly. (The best way to salvage a dough that has been improperly mixed is to combine it with a larger portion of properly prepared dough.)

Being cautious about working in excess flour is especially important when working with a short dough made with butter. The toughness that can occur is the result of hydration and the development of insoluble proteins in a gluten-rich flour. The water contained in the butter, together with that in the eggs, forms a gluten structure when combined with flour. The strength of the gluten structure is proportionate to the amount of flour used and the amount of time the dough is worked. A short dough in which the gluten structure has been allowed to develop will also shrink when baked. When used properly, the butter (or other fat) insulates the insoluble proteins and keeps them from coming into contact with the water. If the dough is overmixed or handled in a rough manner, the water is forced through the fat instead.

WORKING WITH SHORT DOUGH

To work at a reasonable production speed, the dough should be somewhat elastic so that it does not break as it is molded and fit into pans, but, as previously discussed, it should not be too soft. When making the dough, use the dough hook of the mixer at low speed and mix just until combined. Remember, overmixing will incorporate too much air. Before you start working with chilled short dough, knead it with your hands until it is smooth. This will minimize cracking around the edges when you roll it out and help prevent it from breaking as it is shaped. Use bread flour to roll out the dough, but only the minimum amount needed to prevent the dough from sticking to the table. Add new dough, cold and firm from the refrigerator, as needed to the scraps from the batch you are working with.

STORAGE

Short dough can be stored in the refrigerator for several weeks and can be frozen for up to 2 months if well wrapped.

BAKING

A short dough that has been made correctly does not need to rest before it is baked, and it should neither shrink nor puff during baking. It is not essential to prick short dough before baking, but doing so will deflate any air pockets that may have formed. Short dough can be baked at any temperature between 325° and 425°F (163° and 219°C), but 375°F (190°C) is ideal. Short dough made according to this recipe is one of the few doughs where simply looking at the color of the baked product will tell you if it is done (provided the dough was rolled out to the proper thickness). This is not necessarily true of other short dough recipes, some of which contain a different proportion of sugar. But if you use this recipe and follow the directions as given, you can be certain baking is complete when the dough turns golden brown.

Short Dough

yield: 4 pounds 14 ounces (2 kg 220 g), or enough to line about 90 tartlet pans, 2¹/₂ inches (6.2 cm) in diameter, or 6 tart pans, 11 inches (27.5 cm) in diameter

12 ounces (340 g) granulated sugar

1 pound 12 ounces (795 g) unsalted butter, at room temperature, *or* margarine

2 eggs

2 teaspoons (10 ml) vanilla extract

2 pounds 2 ounces (970 g) bread flour

> ### *Small-Batch Short Dough*
>
> **yield: 2 pounds 6 ounces (1 kg 80 g)**
>
> 6 ounces (170 g) granulated sugar
>
> 14 ounces (400 g) unsalted butter, at room temperature, *or* margarine
>
> 1 egg
>
> 1 teaspoon (5 ml) vanilla extract
>
> 1 pound (455 g) bread flour

1. Place the sugar, butter or margarine, eggs, and vanilla in a mixing bowl; mix at low speed with the dough hook just until combined.

2. Add the flour and mix only until the dough is smooth.

3. Place the dough on a paper-lined sheet pan; press out as flat as possible so that the dough takes up less space and cools quickly.

4. Cover and refrigerate until firm enough to work with, about 30 minutes.

Note: If overmixed, the dough will be much harder to roll out. This is especially true if you use all butter or a large percentage of butter.

Cocoa Short Dough yield: 4 pounds 12 ounces (2 kg 160 g)

8 ounces (225 g) granulated sugar

1 pound 12 ounces (795 g) unsalted butter, at room temperature, *or* margarine

2 eggs

2 teaspoons (10 ml) vanilla extract

2 pounds 4 ounces (1 kg 25 g) bread flour

1 ounce (30 g) unsweetened cocoa powder

Small-Batch Cocoa Short Dough

yield: 2 pounds 6 ounces (1 kg 80 g)

4 ounces (115 g) granulated sugar

14 ounces (400 g) unsalted butter, at room temperature, *or* margarine

1 egg

1 teaspoon (5 ml) vanilla extract

1 pound 2 ounces (510 g) bread flour

2 tablespoons (16 g) unsweetened cocoa powder

---

1. Place the sugar, butter or margarine, eggs, and vanilla in a mixing bowl. Mix on low speed using the dough hook, just until the ingredients are combined.

2. Sift the flour with the cocoa powder; add to the dough and mix only until smooth.

3. Place the dough on a paper-lined sheet pan; press the dough as flat as possible.

4. Cover and refrigerate.

Hazelnut Short Dough yield: 3 pounds (1 kg 365 g)

8 ounces (225 g) granulated sugar

1 pound (455 g) unsalted butter, at room temperature, *or* margarine

1 egg

½ teaspoon (2.5 ml) vanilla extract

1 pound 2 ounces (510 g) bread flour

4 ounces (115 g) hazelnuts, finely ground

1. Place the sugar, butter or margarine, egg, and vanilla in a mixing bowl; mix on low speed using the dough hook, just long enough to incorporate the ingredients.

2. Add the flour and hazelnuts and mix just until the dough is smooth.

3. Place the dough on a paper-lined sheet pan; press out as flat as possible so that the dough takes up less space and cools quickly.

4. Cover and refrigerate.

Short Dough Cake Bottoms yield: I cake bottom, 10 inches (25 cm) in diameter

9 ounces (255 g) Short Dough (page 67)

1. Work the short dough smooth with your hands, shaping it to a thick circle in the process.

2. Start to roll out the dough to ⅛ inch (3 mm) thick and slightly larger than the size you need. Sprinkle just enough bread flour on the board to keep it from sticking. Keep moving and turning the dough over as you roll it, first with your hands and then, as the dough gets thinner, by rolling it up on a dowel. Look closely at the dough as you roll it out. If only the edge of the dough is moving and not the middle, the middle is sticking to the table. Try to roll the dough into the general shape of what you plan to make. Trim the ragged edge that always develops when the dough starts to get thin; this edge often tears away from the dough when you are picking it up or rolling it.

3. When the short dough is ⅛ inch (3 mm) thick, roll it up on a dowel (avoid using a rolling pin) and place on a sheet pan lined with baking paper or a Silpat.

4. Place a 10-inch (25-cm) cake ring or template on top of the short dough and cut around the outside edge; remove the leftover dough. If you cut the dough circle first and then transfer it to the sheet pan, you will probably stretch the dough as you move it, resulting in an oval rather than a circle.

5. Prick the dough lightly so that any trapped air can escape.

6. Bake at 375°F (190°C) for about 10 minutes.

Lining Small Individual Forms

1. Prepare the dough and roll out as instructed for Short Dough Cake Bottoms, rolling the dough into a rectangle ⅛ inch (3 mm) thick. If you are lining forms that are very small, roll the dough slightly thinner so as to leave room in the forms for the filling.

2. Stagger the forms, 1 to 2 inches (2.5 to 5 cm) apart, in the approximate shape of the dough. The taller the forms, the more space you need to leave between them, so the dough will line the sides.

3. Roll the dough up on a dowel and unroll over the forms (Figure 2-4).

4. Push the forms together with your hands to create enough slack for the dough to fall into the forms without overstretching and breaking (Figure 2-5).

FIGURE 2-4 **The first step in lining small forms with short dough: rolling the dough up on a dowel and unrolling it over the forms**

FIGURE 2-5 **Pushing the forms together to make the dough fall into the forms**

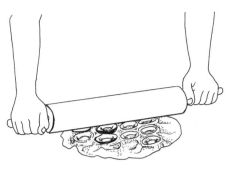

FIGURE 2-6 **Using the ball of dough to press the dough into place**

FIGURE 2-7 **Rolling over the top of the lined forms with a rolling pin to trim away the excess dough**

5. Dust the dough lightly with bread flour and using a ball of dough about the same size as the inside of the forms, gently pound the dough in place (Figure 2-6).

6. When all the air pockets are eliminated, roll the rolling pin over the forms to trim away the excess dough (Figure 2-7). You can also press down on the forms with the palm of your hand to achieve the same result. Place the finished forms on a sheet pan. Bake as directed in the individual recipes.

NOTE: For instructions on lining large tart shells, see page 325.

Short Dough Cookies

1. Prepare and roll the dough as for Short Dough Cake Bottoms, rolling it into a rectangle ¹⁄₈ inch (3 mm) thick. Make sure the dough does not stick to the table.

2. Cut the cookies with a plain or fluted cutter, holding your other hand next to where you are cutting.

3. As you cut each cookie, flip the dough in one smooth motion into your waiting palm (Figure 2-8). Smaller cookies are the easiest to flip but, with a little practice, this method works well with sizes up to 3½ inches (8.7 cm). If you are doing this for a living, you simply must learn this technique to save time.

4. When you have about 6 cookies in your hand, place them on a sheet pan lined with baking paper or a Silpat. Continue to cut the remaining cookies in the same manner. Stagger the cutting and the placing of the cookies for the least amount of wasted dough and space.

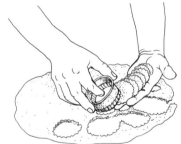

FIGURE 2-8 **Flipping Short Dough Cookies into the palm of the hand as they are cut**

5. Bake the cookies at 375°F (190°C) until golden brown, 10 to 12 minutes, depending on their size.

Semolina Dough **yield: approximately 3 pounds 12 ounces (1 kg 705 g)**

In making semolina dough, as in producing flaky pie dough, it is of the utmost importance that you start with cold butter and that the butter remain cold and in small chunks as the dough is mixed. If you are making the dough when the weather is warm, or if you are working in a warm kitchen, do not ignore the suggestion in Step 1. If this dough is mixed improperly, it can become tough and hard. Semolina dough is particularly useful for pies and tarts with a moist filling.

12 ounces (340 g) cake flour	1 tablespoon (15 g) salt
12 ounces (340 g) bread flour	1 pound 6 ounces (625 g) cold unsalted butter
6 ounces (170 g) semolina flour	1½ cups (360 ml) cold water

1. Combine the cake flour, bread flour, semolina flour, and salt in a bowl. Add the butter in ½-inch (1.2-cm) chunks; stir to mix well. (If the butter feels soft, spread the mixture on a paper lined sheet pan and refrigerate until firm before proceeding.)

2. Using the paddle attachment of a mixer or your hands, slowly incorporate the cold water, adding only enough to form a dough. Do not overmix; pieces of butter should be visible in the dough when you are finished. Cover and refrigerate until needed.

Cornmeal Crust

yield: 4 pounds 10 ounces (2 kg 105 g), or enough to line 6 tart pans, 11 inches (27.5 cm) in diameter

Yellow cornmeal gives this type of short dough a great robust texture and a rich buttery color. It also makes the dough easy to work with. I use a medium-textured grind in this recipe, but fine or coarsely ground cornmeal can be used as well. Very coarsely ground cornmeal (the type used to make authentic polenta) makes the crust exceptionally crisp, but some people do not care for it, finding it unpleasant to eat the hard grains. I previously called this recipe Polenta Short Dough until I was informed by an Italian colleague that polenta is the name of the cooked cornmeal mush, not the grain. His exact words were, "It isn't polenta until your Italian grandmother stirs it on top of the stove."

1 pound 6 ounces (625 g) unsalted butter, at room temperature

1 pound (455 g) granulated sugar

8 ounces (225 g) pine nuts, finely ground (optional)

1 teaspoon (5 g) salt

2 teaspoons (10 ml) vanilla extract

½ cup (120 ml) or 5 ounces (140 g) honey

6 egg yolks (½ cup/120 ml)

Grated zest of 2 lemons

1 pound (455 g) bread flour

1 pound (455 g) yellow cornmeal

Small-Batch Cornmeal Crust

yield: 2 pounds 5 ounces (1 kg 50 g)

12 ounces (340 g) unsalted butter, at room temperature

8 ounces (225 g) granulated sugar

4 ounces (115 g) pine nuts, finely ground (optional)

½ teaspoon (2.5 g) salt

1 teaspoon (5 ml) vanilla extract

¼ cup (60 ml) or 2½ ounces (70 g) honey

3 egg yolks (¼ cup/60 ml)

Grated zest of 1 lemon

8 ounces (225 g) bread flour

8 ounces (225 g) yellow cornmeal

1. Using the dough hook in a mixer set on low speed, thoroughly combine the butter, sugar, pine nuts (if using), salt, vanilla extract, honey, egg yolks, and lemon zest.

2. Blend in the flour and cornmeal, mixing only until the ingredients are combined.

3. Chill the dough before using.

Puff Pastry

The preparation of puff pastry demands great care. To produce a light, flaky product, everything must be done properly start to finish, or the results will be disappointing.

BASIC DOUGH

Making the basic dough correctly (the flour and water mixture also commonly referred to as *détrempe*) is extremely important. If you add too much flour or work the dough too long, it does not matter how carefully you roll in the butter; the paste will be glutenous and rubbery, hard to work with, and will shrink when baked. When the dough shrinks to this extent, not only are the texture and appearance affected, but the baked dough can taste salty as well because the same amount of salt is now concentrated within a smaller portion of product.

CREATING THE LAYER STRUCTURE

Great care must also be taken when rolling in the butter and turning the dough to get the optimum rise, or puff. If rolled in properly, each layer of dough is separated by a layer of butter. In a hot oven, the moisture in the dough layers produces steam that, if properly sealed in by the butter, will push up as it evaporates. This is how puff pastry rises without the addition of a leavening agent.

Creating an even layer structure can be accomplished only if the butter and the dough have the same consistency, which is why a small amount of flour must first be worked into the butter. As in a bread dough, gluten is formed when flour and water (here, the water in the butter) are combined and agitated. Although not necessary, adding a small amount of citric acid (lemon juice, for example) to both the butter and the dough is beneficial for two reasons: (1) it gives the butter an extra measure of pliability to ensure that it will stretch with the dough as the two are rolled out together; and (2) it tightens the gluten that has formed, as explained above—which in turn helps prevent the finished dough from shrinking.

BUTTER

Many fats specially designed for puff pastry are on the market, but none stands up to butter when it comes to taste. Also, because butter has a much lower melting point, it will not leave an unappetizing film in one's mouth the way some shortening products do.

NUMBER OF LAYERS

There are actually 513 layers of butter and dough in puff pastry made with 4 double turns, as directed in the following recipe. When the dough is given 6 single turns, which is the classic

Working with Puff Pastry

Even after you have made perfect puff pastry, there are many things to watch for as you work with it:

- Be careful not to damage the layer structure when rolling the dough. Never let your rolling pin roll over the edge of the dough, which mashes down the sides, and always apply even pressure as you are rolling so that the butter is evenly distributed.

- As a general rule, puff pastry dough should rest 5 to 10 minutes between rolling out and cutting. It should then rest an additional 15 minutes after it has been made up (for example, into turnovers) before baking to eliminate shrinkage. (If the dough seems particularly rubbery and shrinks back a lot as you roll it, it will need to rest a bit longer.)

- As you cut the dough, hold the knife at a sharp 90-degree angle, so the edges of the dough are perfectly straight. This way, the dough will rise straight up in the oven.

- When using egg wash on a product made with puff pastry dough, take care not to let any drip on the side. This can seal the dough to the pan and prevent it from rising.

- Start baking puff pastry in a hot oven. If the oven is not hot enough, you will lose the effect of the steam, and the butter will run out of the dough.

- Ideally, puff pastry made according to the recipe in this book should be ready to use the day after it is started, with all four turns having been made before it is placed in the refrigerator overnight. If the situation demands, the dough can be given two turns only, then finished the following day to be ready for use on day three. Puff pastry should not be started if there is time to make only one turn before leaving it overnight. The butter layer will be too thick and will break when the dough is rolled out the following day.

French technique, the finished dough has almost 1,500 layers of dough and butter combined. The French word for puff pastry is *feuilletage*, from *feuilles*, meaning "leaves"; the pastry we call a napoleon is known as *mille-feuille*, or "a thousand leaves."

FREEZING PUFF PASTRY

Puff pastry freezes well both as a dough and made up, ready to be baked. However, it should not be stored in the refrigerator for more than 5 days after it is finished. If held longer than that, the flour and water in the dough will start to ferment, eventually causing the dough to turn gray. It will gradually become darker, and both taste and appearance will suffer. The ideal way to use puff pastry, provided you have the freezer space, is to make up as many apple turnovers or fleurons (or whatever items you are making) as you will need for the week and freeze them to take out and bake fresh every day. If this is not practical, freeze the dough, divided into suitably sized pieces, to use as required. Puff pastry dough must be kept well covered at all times, especially in the freezer, to prevent the top from drying and forming a skin (freezer burn).

USING SCRAP DOUGH

Scraps from puff pastry dough (as with any other flaky dough, such as Danish, pie, and croissant) will not be as good rolled out the second time, but they can be used successfully in some recipes. Puff pastry scraps are actually preferable to fresh dough for pastries that should not puff up much. Scrap pieces can be frozen until needed or combined with fresh dough. Never knead the scraps together to form a larger piece; lay them on top of each other and roll to retain the layered structure. Scraps from puff pastry can also be used for Butter-Wheat Bread (page 114).

NOTE: In the recipes for Fleurons, Vol-au-Vents, and Bouchées, the amount of dough required and the thickness specified for rolling out assume you are using properly layered puff pastry dough freshly made according to the recipe in this book. If you are using another recipe or a dough that you know (or suspect) is getting old—more than 5 days in the refrigerator—you may need to adjust the thickness of the dough when rolling it out. Bake a few samples before making a large batch. A good puff pastry dough should rise to 4 times its original height.

Puff Pastry yield: approximately 11 pounds (5 kg)

BUTTER BLOCK

4 pounds 6 ounces (1 kg 990 g) cold unsalted butter

1 teaspoon (5 g) salt

3 tablespoons (45 ml) lemon juice

1 pound 2 ounces (510 g) bread flour

DOUGH

3 tablespoons (45 g) salt

1 quart (960 ml) water

7 ounces (200 g) unsalted butter, melted

1 tablespoon (15 ml) lemon juice

14 ounces (400 g) cake flour

2 pounds 4 ounces (1 kg 25 g) bread flour

Small-Batch Puff Pastry

yield: approximately 2 pounds 12 ounces (1 kg 250 g)

BUTTER BLOCK

1 pound 2 ounces (510 g) cold unsalted butter

Pinch of salt

2 teaspoons (10 ml) lemon juice

4½ ounces (130 g) bread flour

DOUGH

2 teaspoons (10 g) salt

1 cup (240 ml) water

2 ounces (55 g) unsalted butter, melted

1 teaspoon (15 ml) lemon juice

3½ ounces (100 g) cake flour

11 ounces (310 g) bread flour

TO MAKE THE BUTTER BLOCK

1. Work the cold butter into the proper consistency (see Note) with the warmth of your hand. Dissolve the salt in the lemon juice. Mix into the butter together with the bread flour.

2. Shape into a 12-inch (30-cm) square (6-inch/15-cm for the small-batch recipe) and refrigerate until firm.

NOTE: The butter block should not be so soft that it is hard to handle; you should be able to transfer the finished block easily from one hand to the other. It should not be so firm that it cracks or breaks if you press on it. Ideally, the dough and the butter block should have the same consistency. A dough that is softer than the butter will be forced to the sides by the firmer butter; a dough that is too firm will force the butter out on the sides. Either will result in poor-quality puff pastry. Take into consideration that the dough needs to rest for 30 minutes and try to time your work so that both the dough and the butter block are ready at the same time.

TO MAKE THE DOUGH USING A MIXER (PRODUCTION METHOD)

1. Using the dough hook in a mixer on low or medium speed, dissolve the salt in the water. Add the melted butter, lemon juice, cake flour, and enough of the bread flour to make a soft, smooth dough. Do not overmix. If you add too much flour, the dough will be too glutenous and rubbery.

2. Shape the dough into a tight ball. With a sharp knife, cut a cross halfway into the ball. Let rest for 30 minutes, covered, in the refrigerator.

TO MAKE THE DOUGH BY HAND (CLASSIC EUROPEAN METHOD)

In this preparation method, the order of the ingredients is reversed. You start by using the full measurement of both flours and, instead of adjusting the consistency of the dough with bread flour, adjust the amount of water added at the end. The butter should be firm rather than soft. The dough is worked much less and, when finished, should be not soft, smooth, and elastic but quite the opposite.

1. Sift both flours together onto your work surface—preferably a marble slab or table. Cut the firm butter into chunks, place on top of the flour, and, using your fingertips, cut it into the flour, pinching it down until the mixture resembles coarse crumbs.

2. Shape into a mound, make a well in the center, and add the salt and most of the cold water to the well. Stir to dissolve the salt. Gradually mix the flour and butter into the water, using the fingers of both hands. If necessary, gradually add more water to form a dough that holds together but is fairly sticky and rough looking.

3. Form the dough into a ball, kneading it as little as possible. Flatten the dough a little and cut a cross halfway into the ball. Cover and let rest for 30 minutes in the refrigerator.

TO ASSEMBLE

1. Pull the corners of the cuts out to make the dough square-shaped (Figure 2-9).

2. Roll the opened dough out to a square slightly thicker in the center than on the sides and slightly larger than the butter block.

3. Place the butter block diagonally within the square so there are 4 triangles around the sides (Figure 2-10). Fold the dough triangles in so they meet in the center. Pinch the edges together to seal in the butter block (Figure 2-11).

4. Roll the dough into a rectangle ½ inch (1.2 cm) thick. Do not roll the dough wider than a sheet pan is long.

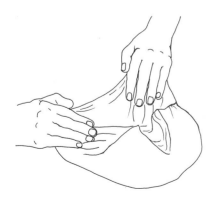

FIGURE 2-9 **Opening the cut ball of dough to make it square**

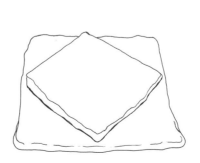

FIGURE 2-10 **Positioning the butter block diagonally on the dough square**

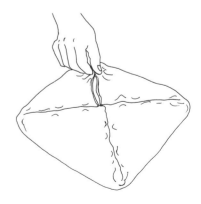

FIGURE 2-11 **Sealing the butter block inside the dough**

5. Give the dough 4 double turns (instructions follow), refrigerating it for approximately 30 minutes between each turn. Be sure the dough is well covered at all times.

6. After the last turn, roll the puff pastry out to approximately ¾ inch (2 cm) thick. If this is difficult to do, refrigerate the dough for a few minutes to relax the gluten. Place the dough on a sheet pan lined with baking paper, cover, and refrigerate or freeze. Remember that you should not keep puff pastry dough in the refrigerator more than 5 days.

CHEF'S TIP

When rolling the dough for the small-batch recipe to make a double turn, it is difficult to avoid it becoming so thin that the layer structure is compressed and the dough's ability to rise is significantly decreased. A better option is to give the dough 5 single turns, as it does not have to be rolled out as large for a single turn as it does for a double turn. The single turns take slightly less time to complete and you can be assured of a high-puffing dough at the end. See page 212 for instructions on making a single turn.

Start by rolling the dough to 16 x 12 inches (40 x 30 cm), then make 5 single turns, resting the dough between each turn (the dough does not have to rest as long as for a double turn, however). When the dough is finished, it will have 487 layers of butter and dough—slightly less than with 4 double turns, but more than adequate.

TO MAKE A DOUBLE TURN

1. As carefully and evenly as possible, roll out the dough to a rectangle 30 x 20 inches (75 x 50 cm), or 15 x 10 inches (37.5 x 25 cm) for the small-batch recipe (see Chef's Tip). Arrange the dough rectangle with a long side closest to you.

2. Make a vertical mark in the center of the rectangle. Fold both ends of the dough in to this mark (Figure 2-12).

3. Brush excess flour from the top of the dough and fold once more, as if you were closing a book (Figure 2-13). The dough now has one double turn.

4. Carefully place the dough on a sheet pan, cover, and refrigerate for 30 minutes.

5. When you begin the second double turn, place the dough in front of you so that the short ends of the rectangle are on your left and right, opposite to the way the dough lay when you "closed the book" with the first turn. Roll out and turn as above; repeat as you make the remaining turns.

FIGURE 2-12 **The first step of a double turn: folding both short edges in to meet in the center**

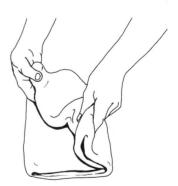

FIGURE 2-13 **Completing a double turn: folding the dough in half as if closing a book**

Quick Puff Pastry yield: 11 pounds 2 ounces (5 kg 60 g)

If you do not have time to make traditional puff pastry, quick puff pastry (also known as blitz puff pastry) is an efficient compromise. You will not get the height of the authentic version, but this recipe can easily be made—from scaling through baking—in 2 hours. It is perfect for lining tart pans or making fleurons and napoleons, when the dough must not puff up too much. In Europe, this type of dough is known as *American puff pastry*. The name has nothing to do with the lesser quality of dough you get from mixing all of the ingredients together in a rapid fashion but simply came about because this method resembles the technique used to make pie dough, and in Europe pies are synonymous with America.

5 pounds (2 kg 275 g) bread flour

5 pounds (2 kg 275 g) cold unsalted butter

2 tablespoons (30 g) salt

3 cups (720 ml) cold water

Small-Batch Quick Puff Pastry
yield: 2 pounds 12 ounces (1 kg 250 g)

1 pound 4 ounces (570 g) bread flour

1 pound 4 ounces (570 g) cold unsalted butter

1½ teaspoons (7.5 g) salt

¾ cup (180 ml) cold water

---

1. Place the flour in a mixer bowl.

2. Cut the butter, which should be firm but not hard, into 2-inch (5-cm) pieces (or about half this size for the small-batch recipe). Add to the flour while mixing on low speed with the dough hook; be careful not to knead.

3. Dissolve the salt in the water. Add to the flour and butter mixture and mix only until the dough can be handled. Mix carefully and for only a short time so that lumps of butter remain whole; the dough should look like well-made pie dough.

4. Shape the dough into a square and allow it to rest for 10 minutes. If it is warm in your kitchen, place the dough on a sheet pan lined with baking paper and let it rest in the refrigerator until it becomes firm enough to work with.

5. Roll the dough out ½ inch (1.2 cm) thick and in the shape of a rectangle. Give the dough 3 single turns, followed by 1 double turn (see single-turn instructions on page 212 and double-turn instructions on page 76). If the dough feels rubbery after you have completed the 3 single turns, let it rest for a few minutes and finish with a fourth single turn rather than making a double turn at the end. Cover and refrigerate.

NOTE: This dough does not need to rest between turns and is ready to use immediately after the last turn. However, after the dough has been rolled, it must rest 20 to 30 minutes before baking to prevent it from shrinking.

Fleurons yield: 28 pieces

Fleurons are small crescent-shaped puff pastry garnishes. They are used in classic French cooking, usually as a garnish with seafood and as an accompaniment to soup.

1 pound (455 g) Puff Pastry (page 74)   **Vegetable oil**
Egg wash

1. Roll out the puff pastry to a 12-inch (27.5-cm) square about ⅛ inch (3 mm) thick (see Note). Prick the dough lightly.

2. Place the dough on a sheet of cardboard or an inverted sheet pan. Brush with egg wash.

3. Using the back of a chef's knife, mark a diamond pattern in the egg wash.

4. Refrigerate or freeze the dough until firm. The egg wash will dry slightly. It is much easier to brush on the egg wash and mark the dough before you cut it than to try to do each fleuron individually.

5. Starting from the bottom edge of the square on the left side, cut away a little less than a half-circle of dough using a 3-inch (7.5-cm) fluted cookie cutter dipped occasionally in oil. Cut straight down and do not twist the cutter. Make a second cut parallel to the first and 1½ inches (3.7 cm) higher to form a crescent (Figure 2-14). The cut that makes the top of one crescent becomes the bottom of the next. Continue cutting until you have made the first row of 7 fleurons. Cut 3 more rows of 7 fleurons each in the same way. The only scraps of dough will be at the beginning and at the end of each row. Place the individual pieces on a sheet pan lined with baking paper.

6. Bake at 400°F (205°C) for about 10 minutes or until golden brown and baked through. You may need to lower the heat and leave the fleurons in a few minutes longer to finish drying (Figure 2-15). Fleurons can be frozen before baking; bake directly from the freezer for about 12 minutes following the same procedure.

NOTE: If you are making a great many fleurons and you are not sure about the quality of the dough, make a few samples so you can adjust the thickness as necessary.

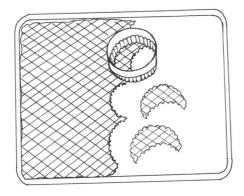

FIGURE 2-14 **Cutting crescents to create fleurons**

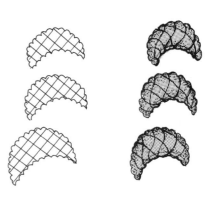

FIGURE 2-15 **The fleurons before and after baking**

Vol-au-Vents

yield: 1 shell, 10 inches (25 cm) in diameter, for 10 to 12 servings

Y ou could say that a vol-au-vent is a big bouchée or, conversely, that a bouchée is a small vol-au-vent; in principle, they are the same thing. *Vol-au-vents* (the term literally means "flying in the wind," a reference to the delicate nature of the baked puff pastry) were invented by the famous French chef Antoine Carême, who according to history is said to have proclaimed, "*s'envola au vent,*" referring to the lightness of his creation as he removed it from the oven. These pastry shells can be made around 8 to 10 inches (20 to 25 cm) in diameter for multiple servings, 4 to 5 inches (10 to 12.5 cm) for individual servings. Ten inches is the largest shell it is practical to make. If this is not large enough for the number of servings needed, it is best to make two smaller shells.

1 pound 8 ounces (680 g) Puff Pastry (page 74)	Egg wash

1. Roll out the puff pastry to a square slightly larger than 10 inches (25 cm) and approximately ½ inch (1.2 cm) thick (see Note, page 74).

2. Refrigerate the dough first if it has become soft; then, using a 10-inch (25-cm) template as a guide (a cake pan is a good choice), cut out a circle of dough. Be sure to cut at a 90-degree angle to prevent the vol-au-vent from falling to one side as it puffs up in the oven.

3. Place an 8½-inch (21.2-cm) template in the center of the circle and cut again. Carefully transfer the ring-shaped piece of dough to a sheet pan, cover, and place in the refrigerator.

4. Roll out the remaining circle of dough to ⅛ inch (3 mm) thick and to a shape that will allow you to cut one circle, 10 inches (25 cm) in diameter, which will be the bottom, and a smaller circle, 8½ inches (21.2 cm) in diameter, to use for the lid of the vol-au-vent (if desired). Cut out the circles, prick the dough thoroughly, and refrigerate for approximately 30 minutes. (If you have enough scrap dough on hand, you can roll and cut these circles first, then allow them to rest in the refrigerator while you make the ring.)

5. Place the 10-inch (25-cm) circle on an even sheet pan. Brush the outer 1 inch (2.5 cm) with egg wash; place the chilled ring on top so it sticks to the egg wash. Adjust to make the vol-au-vent perfectly round.

6. With the back side of a knife held vertically, mark the vol-au-vent every 1½ inches (3.7 cm) around the outside, pressing from the bottom to the top and pushing in just a little to create a scallop pattern (Figure 2-16). Prick the top of the ring and brush lightly with egg wash; do not let any drip down the sides.

CHEF'S TIP

One of the best ways to keep the sides of a vol-au-vent from falling in as it puffs up is to arrange a cake cooling rack above the vol-au-vent on baking forms or coffee cups set at the edges of the baking pan. Place them at a height slightly below the point to which you expect, or want, the dough to puff. This acts as a mold, preventing the vol-au-vent from puffing too high and helping keep the edges straight.

To make a smaller vol-au-vent, follow the same directions using whatever size is required for the outside template; just use a ring 1 inch (2.5 cm) smaller to create the frame.

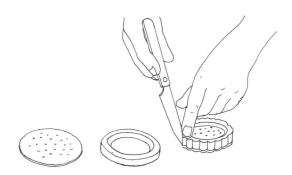

FIGURE 2-16 Pressing the back of a knife into the dough to create vertical marks and a scalloped edge on a vol-au-vent

7. Remove the 8½-inch (21.2-cm) circle from the refrigerator and place it on the pan next to the vol-au-vent. Brush the lid with egg wash and mark it with a diamond pattern using the back of a chef's knife.

8. Bake at 400°F (205°C), double-panned to prevent the bottom from getting too dark, for about 15 minutes or until puffed. Reduce the temperature to 375°F (190°C) and continue baking until dry and golden, 30 to 35 minutes. If the top gets too dark before it is dried through, cover it with a piece of baking paper or aluminum foil. The lid will, of course, be finished baking long before the case of the vol-au-vent; remove it carefully.

Individual Vol-au-Vents yield: 15 shells, 3¼ inches (8.1 cm) in diameter

There are two basic ways of making individual vol-au-vents: the production method and the classic method. If you use the production method, they won't get quite as high, but they can be made very quickly, and you can be sure that the sides will not fall in as they bake. The classic method produces higher and more elegant vol-au-vents, but they take a little longer to finish.

2 pounds (910 g) Puff Pastry (page 74)   **Egg wash**
Vegetable oil

CLASSIC METHOD

1. Roll out the puff pastry to a rectangle measuring 7 x 10 inches (17.5 x 25 cm) and slightly less than ½ inch (1.2 cm) thick (see Note, page 74). Place the dough in the refrigerator for a few minutes to relax and firm.

2. Using a 3¼-inch (8.1-cm) plain or fluted cookie cutter, cut out 15 circles of dough. Dip the edge of the cutter in oil periodically and push the cutter straight down without twisting.

3. Using a 2-inch (5-cm) cutter, cut a circle out of each round to form rings. Carefully place the rings on a sheet pan and refrigerate.

4. Layer the scrap dough, including the circles cut out of the centers, and roll out to ⅛ inch (3 mm) thick. Prick the dough and place in the refrigerator to firm and relax.

5. Cut out 15 circles (not rings), 3¼ inches (8.1 cm) in diameter, from the sheet of rolled scrap dough, plus 15 circles, 2 inches (5 cm) in diameter, to use as lids if desired.

6. Brush egg wash on the larger circles and place the reserved rings on top. If you wish, brush the top of the rings with egg wash, but be careful not to let any run down the sides.

7. Bake the vol-au-vents and the lids at 400°F (205°C) until puffed, about 10 minutes. Reduce the heat to 375°F (190°C) and bake until they are dry enough to hold their shape, about 30 minutes. (You might have to use a second pan underneath to prevent the bottoms from becoming too dark, and you may need to remove the vol-au-vents on the edges of the pan if they are done before those in the middle. The lids will finish baking sooner.)

PRODUCTION METHOD

1. Roll out the puff pastry to a rectangle measuring 7 x 10 inches (17.5 x 25 cm) and slightly less than ½ inch (1.2 cm) thick (see Note, page 74). Place the dough in the refrigerator for a few minutes to relax and firm.

2. Using a 3¼-inch (8.1-cm) plain or fluted cookie cutter, cut out 15 circles of dough. Dip the edge of the cutter in oil periodically and push the cutter straight down without twisting.

3. Place the circles on a sheet pan about ¾ inch (2 cm) apart. Rather than cutting all the way through the dough and removing the 2-inch (5-cm) center, as in the classic method, cut only two-thirds of the way through the dough (Figure 2-17). Do not forget to continue dipping the cutter in oil as you work to produce a clean cut.

4. Thoroughly prick the 2-inch (5-cm) center of the circles.

5. Bake the vol-au-vents and the lids at 400°F (205°C) until puffed, 10 minutes or more. Reduce the heat to 375°F (190°C) and bake until they are dry enough to hold their shape, 30 minutes or more. (You might have to use a second pan underneath to prevent the bottoms from becoming too dark, and you may need to remove the vol-au-vents on the edges of the pan if they are done before those in the middle. The lids will finish baking sooner.)

6. When the vol-au-vents have cooled slightly, lift off the lids and use a fork to scrape out the unbaked dough inside. If necessary, put the shells back in the oven to dry further.

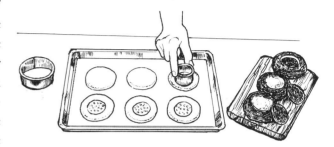

FIGURE 2-17 **Using a small plain cookie cutter to cut halfway into the puff pastry circles for the production method of making vol-au-vents. In the bottom row on the sheet pan, these smaller circles have already been cut and the dough has been pricked within the small circles. Three baked vol-au-vents are shown on the side; the lids have been removed from the two in the front.**

Bouchées yield: 24 shells, 1½ inches (3.7 cm) in diameter

Bouchée is a French word that means "mouth-size" or "mouthful." These petite pastry shells are usually made with savory fillings and served as hors d'oeuvres. It is best to use the production method described in the recipe for individual vol-au-vents to make these bouchées.

2 pounds (910 g) Puff Pastry (page 74)   **Vegetable oil**

1. Follow the instructions given in the production method for individual vol-au-vents, using a 1½-inch (3.7-cm) cutter to cut out 24 circles of dough. Then use a 1-inch (2.5-cm) cutter to cut two-thirds of the way through the center. Continue as directed; these will require a shorter baking time.

Pâte à Choux

Pâte à choux, or choux paste, is not really a dough in the strictest sense, but rather a thick paste that could be described as a roux with the addition of eggs. There are many different recipes and philosophies to choose from when it comes to making this classic pastry. However, the one factor that holds true in each case is that the more eggs you are able to add to the base mixture (without causing it to lose its shape when piped), the higher and lighter your finished product will be, ideally becoming just a hollow shell.

COMPOSITION AND PREPARATION OF THE BATTER

Pâte à choux begins as a cooked mixture of water or milk, fat (usually butter), and flour, with a small amount of salt added if sweet butter is used. Sifted flour is added to the boiling water and fat and stirred in quickly. The resulting roux is then cooked for a few minutes while being stirred constantly to allow as much liquid as possible to evaporate so that the maximum number of eggs can be incorporated. Although some chefs use a slightly different formula that incorporates a stronger flour (especially for larger items, such as Paris-Brest, as opposed to profiteroles), I find it satisfactory to compromise and use a combination of bread and cake flours (in a sense, creating an all-purpose flour).

You should add as many eggs as the paste can absorb and still stay in a precise shape once it is piped out; the paste will have a slightly shiny appearance if the correct amount of eggs has been added. On the other hand, if not enough eggs are used, the baked pastries will be low and heavy with a gluey mass inside that must be removed before the pastries can be filled. Add the eggs a few at a time; you can then mix them in more easily and also avoid accidentally adding too many. Add a small amount of ammonium carbonate with the eggs to give an extra lift. The ammonium gas released during baking helps increase the volume; the strong-smelling gas quickly dissipates as the pastry cools. If you do not have ammonium carbonate, you need not substitute another leavener; simply leave it out.

ADVANCE PREPARATION OF INDIVIDUAL PIECES

Pâte à choux is never prepared ahead of time and refrigerated or frozen in batter or dough form before being shaped, as is, for example, puff pastry dough. It must be piped out first, then either baked or frozen immediately, before the paste develops a skin.

BAKING

The formed paste is put into a hot (425°F/219°C) oven (directly from the freezer without thawing, if frozen) to produce the maximum amount of steam, which rapidly expands the paste and leaves a large, empty space in the center. The heat coagulates the gluten and proteins that set the structure and make a firm shell. After approximately 10 minutes, the heat is reduced (375°F/190°C) to finish baking and allow the shells to become firm and dry without getting too dark. Simply turning the thermostat control will not lower the heat quickly enough. Open the oven door partway as well to reduce the temperature, but do not open it fully; a sudden drop in temperature at this stage can cause the shells to collapse.

Using Egg Wash

It isn't necessary to brush pâte à choux pastries with egg wash before baking. The egg wash usually dries before the pastries have finished expanding, which gives them an unattractive cracked appearance. In most applications, the pastries are to be finished with a glaze or powdered sugar on top and, provided that the roux was cooked properly and an adequate number of eggs was added, plain pâte à choux (without egg wash) will have a shiny surface.

As long as you do not let it become too brown, you cannot overbake pâte à choux, so make sure that the shells have been baked long enough to hold their shape and not fall. The baked shells—for éclairs and profiteroles, for example—can be stored covered for a day or so before being filled, but once filled, they should be served the same day.

Pâte à Choux

yield: 5 pounds 8 ounces (2 kg 500 g), or enough for approximately 70 to 100 profiteroles, 1½ to 2 inches (3.7 to 5 cm) in diameter, or about 60 éclairs, 4 to 5 inches (10 to 12.5 cm) long

8 ounces (225 g) cake flour

11 ounces (310 g) bread flour

1 quart (960 ml) water

12 ounces (340 g) unsalted butter

1½ teaspoons (7.5 g) salt

1 quart (960 ml) eggs

1 teaspoon (3.5 g) ammonium carbonate

Small-Batch Pâte à Choux
yield: 2 pounds 12 ounces (1 kg 250 g), or enough for approximately 35 to 50 profiteroles, 1½ to 2 inches (3.7 to 5 cm) in diameter, or about 30 éclairs, 4 to 5 inches (10 to 12.5 cm) long

4 ounces (115 g) cake flour

5½ ounces (155 g) bread flour

1 pint (480 ml) water

6 ounces (170 g) unsalted butter

½ teaspoon (2.5 g) salt

1 pint (480 ml) eggs

¼ teaspoon (1 g) ammonium carbonate

---

1. Sift the flours together on a sheet of baking paper and reserve.

2. Heat the water, butter, and salt to a full rolling boil, so that the fat is not just floating on the top but is dispersed throughout the liquid.

3. Form the ends of the baking paper into a pouring spout. Then, using a heavy wooden spoon, stir the flour into the liquid, adding it as fast as it can be absorbed. Avoid adding all of the flour at once, as this can make the paste lumpy.

4. Cook, stirring constantly and breaking up the inevitable lumps by pressing them against the side of the pan with the back of the spoon, until the mixture forms a mass and pulls away from the sides of the pan, about 2 to 3 minutes.

5. Transfer the paste to a mixer bowl. (If you are making the small recipe, adding the eggs by hand is quite easy; use the spoon and leave the paste in the saucepan.) Let the paste cool slightly so the eggs will not cook when they are added.

6. Mix in the eggs, 2 at a time, using the paddle attachment on low or medium speed. After the first few eggs are incorporated, add the ammonium carbonate. Add as many eggs as the paste can absorb and still hold its shape when piped.

7. Pipe the paste into the desired shape according to the individual recipe.

8. Bake at 425°F (219°C) until fully puffed and starting to show some color, about 10 minutes. Reduce the heat to 375°F (190°C) and bake about 10 to 12 minutes longer, depending on size.

9. Let the pastries cool at room temperature. Speeding the process by placing them in the refrigerator or freezer can cause them to collapse.

Pasta Dough yield: approximately 1 pound (455 g)

I have included a basic pasta recipe not so much because I love pasta, but because the bakeshop is often asked to make the dough when a large amount is required. I use semolina flour, which, in my opinion, produces a far superior pasta dough to one made with bread flour. It gives the dough a much better color, makes it easier to work with, and gives the cooked pasta a slightly chewy bite. You can, however, replace all or part of the semolina flour with bread flour or even all-purpose flour if desired. Try to use the least amount of water possible at the start; then, if the dough can not be formed into a ball, add more drop by drop. Eggs are considered optional; they give the pasta a more appealing color and a richer texture, but they can be replaced with an additional ¼ cup (60 ml) of water. This recipe gives you a fundamental, plain pasta dough. Many ingredients, such as vegetables or vegetable juices and fresh or dried herbs, can be added to change the flavor of the pasta.

12 ounces (340 g) semolina flour	1 teaspoon (5 ml) olive oil
½ teaspoon (2.5 g) salt	2 tablespoons (30 ml) water
2 eggs	

TO MIX USING A FOOD PROCESSOR

1. Combine all of the ingredients in the food processor bowl with the steel blade. Process until the dough forms a crumbly mass, 2 or 3 minutes. The dough should hold together when you gather it into a ball with your hands but should not feel sticky. Add more flour or water (only a few drops at a time) if required. It is best to keep the dough as dry as possible while still having it hold together. The texture of a pasta dough made with semolina flour is coarse and sandy compared to pasta dough made with bread or all-purpose flour.

2. Cover the dough and let it rest for 1 hour before rolling it out.

TO MIX USING AN ELECTRIC MIXER

1. Place all of the ingredients in the mixer bowl. Mix at medium speed, using the dough hook, for about 3 minutes. Add more flour or water as required. The dough should form a smooth ball that pulls away cleanly from the sides of the bowl.

2. Cover the dough and let it rest for 1 hour before rolling it out.

TO MIX BY HAND

1. Place the dry ingredients on your work surface in a mound and make a well in the center. Pour the remaining ingredients into the well. Working quickly, incorporate the eggs, water, and oil into the flour until the mixture forms a crumbly mass. Knead the dough against the table until it becomes smooth and pliable, about 6 to 10 minutes.

2. Cover the dough and let it rest for 1 hour before rolling it out.

Salt Dough yield: approximately 4 pounds 6 ounces (1 kg 990 g)

This is an inexpensive and easy-to-make dough used for bread ornaments or to practice braiding. Try to keep the dough as firm as possible, as there is no gluten structure and the dough will therefore stretch and fall apart easily if the consistency is too soft. Because of the nonexistent gluten structure, salt dough is excellent for patterns that are assembled after they are baked. The pieces will not shrink or change shape.

2 pounds (910 g) bread flour	1 pint (480 ml) water
1 pound (455 g) salt	Egg wash

1. Combine the flour and salt.

2. Mix in just enough water to make a fairly stiff dough.

3. Roll out to the desired thickness—¼ inch (6 mm) for most uses. Should the dough seem to drag as you cut around your templates, refrigerate it until firm. Dipping the tip of the knife in oil from time to time will also help prevent a ragged finish.

4. Brush the pieces with egg wash.

5. Bake at 375°F (190°C) until the pieces have a pleasant light-brown color.

NOTE: When making large pieces, check to be sure they are dry enough not to break before removing them from the oven. Keep the dough covered at all times while working. Store, covered, in the refrigerator no longer than 3 days. For a sturdier dough, use up to a 1-to-1 ratio of flour and salt. To color the dough, see Chef's Tip.

Unbaked Salt Dough yield: 4 pounds 5 ounces (1 kg 960 g)

This dough is ideal for small, intricate showpieces, as it is pliable and easy to work with. Figures made with this dough are not baked; they are left to air-dry instead. Typically, pieces take up to 3 days to dry completely, so you must allow more time than usual to complete your project. If the figure you are making is more than ¼ inch (6 mm) thick, it should be made in layers, letting each layer dry before adding the next, or the dough will shrivel from the moisture trapped inside. The drying process may be accelerated by placing the finished pieces in a gas oven, using the heat from the pilot light only, or by placing the pieces outside to dry in the sun.

The ingredients in this recipe can alternatively be measured by volume, using 1 part each cornstarch and water and 2 parts salt.

9 ounces (255 g) cornstarch

2 cups (480 ml) water

2 pounds 12 ounces (1 kg 250 g) popcorn salt (see Note)

1. Mix the cornstarch and water in a saucepan. Heat the mixture over medium heat, stirring constantly with a heavy spoon, until it starts to gelatinize, approximately 10 minutes. As the mixture thickens, it will be rather difficult to stir, and you may need help during the last few minutes.

2. Remove the mixture from the heat and transfer the paste to a mixer bowl. Using the dough hook on low speed, incorporate the salt plus 1 to 2 tablespoons (15 to 30 ml) additional water as needed to make a stiff but pliable dough. Mix until the dough is completely smooth, about 5 minutes. Store the dough, covered, in the refrigerator.

NOTE: Popcorn salt is a very finely ground salt. If it is not available, use an almond mill to grind table salt to a very fine consistency. A coffee grinder can also be used, but it makes the job rather time-consuming.

Weaver's Dough yield: 8 pounds 2 ounces (3 kg 695 g) dough

Like salt dough, weaver's dough is used to make ornaments and decorations, but because this dough has some elasticity, it is better suited to long pieces—making a bread basket, for example. Because the dough does not contain yeast, baked ornaments look exactly as you shaped them. For the same reason, the ornaments are quite hard and not very appetizing. They are intended for purely decorative purposes.

¼ cup (60 ml) vegetable oil

2 eggs

¼ cup (60 g) salt

2 ounces (55 g) granulated sugar

4½ cups (1 L 80 ml) water

5 pounds 12 ounces (2 kg 615 g) bread flour

Egg wash

1. Add the oil, eggs, salt, and sugar to the water. Incorporate all but a handful of the flour. Using the dough hook, knead for approximately 10 minutes to make a smooth and elastic dough. Adjust with additional flour as needed.

2. Cover the dough and let it rest for about 1 hour before using. Weaver's dough can be stored, covered, in the refrigerator for up to 4 days without deteriorating and can be kept frozen for months.

3. Shape as desired. Before baking the ornaments, brush with egg wash (if you let the first layer dry, then brush a second time, you will get the maximum amount of shine on the finished pieces).

4. Bake at 350°F (175°C) until the ornaments have a nice deep golden color.

Whole Wheat Weaver's Dough yield: 6 pounds 2 ounces (2 kg 785 g)

This is another dough intended for ornaments and decorating pieces, but because it contains a small amount of yeast, the baked goods are soft enough to be pleasant to eat. Whole wheat weaver's dough is especially suitable for rolled, cut-out flat pieces. To make nice clean edges, place the rolled dough in the freezer for a few minutes to harden so it won't drag as you cut it.

½ ounce (15 g) fresh compressed yeast

1 quart (960 ml) cold water

½ ounce (15 g) granulated malt extract *or* 2 tablespoons (30 ml) honey

2 ounces (55 g) granulated sugar

2 tablespoons (30 g) salt

3 pounds 8 ounces (1 kg 590 g) finely ground whole wheat flour

6 ounces (170 g) unsalted butter, at room temperature

Egg wash

1. In a mixer bowl, dissolve the yeast in the water. Add the malt extract or honey, granulated sugar, and salt. Incorporate about half of the flour using the dough hook. Add the soft butter, then the remaining flour.

2. Knead until the dough is smooth and elastic, approximately 8 to 10 minutes. Adjust with additional flour as necessary. Do not overknead or the dough will become too soft to work with.

3. Cover the dough and let rest for 1 hour in the refrigerator. Punch the dough down and form as desired. If the pieces are to be eaten, allow them to proof in a warm, draft-free location until slightly less than doubled in volume.

4. Brush the pieces with egg wash and bake at 375°F (190°C) until they are golden brown.

Yeast Breads

Fundamental Procedures in Bread Baking

The preparation and baking of yeast breads can be summarized in 12 basic steps, as follows. Each of these steps is discussed in greater detail following this list.

CHAPTER

THREE

- **Step 1—Selecting the raw ingredients.** Because bread doughs are composed of relatively few ingredients, each is significant. Use the best possible flours, grains, and salt (kosher salt is ideal), be certain your yeast is viable, and pay close attention to the temperature of liquids.

- **Step 2—Weighing the ingredients.** Accuracy of measurement is essential to producing a balanced and workable formula, to creating consistency in quality, and to controlling cost. Digital scales are particularly accurate.

- **Step 3—Mixing and kneading.** The order in which the ingredients are combined and the way they are mixed together influence both the flavor and texture of the baked bread. If these jobs are done improperly, the yeast may be damaged to the point where the bread will not rise. The different objectives for choosing among the sponge, straight-dough, old-dough, and sourdough starter methods are discussed below.

  Once all of the ingredients are combined, the gluten in the dough must be developed through kneading. The kneading process also distributes the yeast cells evenly throughout the dough so they are able to receive proper nutrition and expand the dough uniformly.

- **Step 4—Fermentation.** Yeast fermentation is an ongoing process that begins as soon as the yeast is added to the dough and ends during baking when the bread reaches approximately 145°F (63°C) and the yeast is killed. Either underproofing or overproofing will have a negative effect on the finished product.

■ **Step 5—Punching down the dough.** When using the straight-dough method, the dough is punched down after it has reached its maximum volume during the proofing/fermentation stage. By flattening the expanded dough and kneading it gently for a few seconds, the yeast cells are redistributed, which allows them to find a new food supply, and the trapped gas is expelled, which equalizes the temperature and prevents the dough from developing a sour flavor.

■ **Step 6—Portioning.** The bread dough must be accurately divided into equal portions for bread loaves or rolls so that the finished pieces will bake uniformly and have a professional appearance. This step must also be completed quickly to prevent the yeast from overreacting and/or the dough from forming a skin. This step should be completed in no more than 20 minutes.

■ **Step 7—Bench proofing.** This resting period allows the gluten in the dough to relax before the dough is formed into a particular shape; 10 to 15 minutes is generally sufficient. The dough should be covered to prevent a skin from forming, and it should be protected from drafts.

■ **Step 8—Shaping.** In this step, the relaxed, pliable dough is formed into the desired shape for loaves or rolls.

■ **Step 9—Panning.** The dough is placed on or in its baking pan, which may be lined with baking paper, greased with butter or oil, or dusted with cornmeal. If bannetons (special woven baskets) are to be used to form a pattern on the loaves as they rise, the dough is placed in them at this stage.

■ **Step 10—Final proofing.** The dough is left to rise in a warm, humid proof box (or other location) so that it can expand without forming a hard crust on the surface.

■ **Step 11—Baking.** The application of heat at the proper rate transforms the well-risen dough into a pleasant and digestible product.

■ **Step 12—Cooling.** It is essential that the bread be allowed to cool completely before it is sliced or stored.

History

The baking of bread dates back to the Stone Age, when people first learned to grind seeds —probably barley and millet—in mills made from stone. It was not a huge leap from the first porridge to bread. Early bread, heavy and unleavened, was cooked on heated stones (this period was not called the Stone Age for nothing). Over the centuries, the process of milling grain was improved. With the aid of wind-powered fans and sieves, people developed a way to remove parts of the chaff and bran. The Romans and Greeks further advanced cultivation and milling methods and produced different kinds of flour in various stages of refinement.

Baking bread has always had an important place in the European home. Local regions of various countries produce breads that differ not only in flavor, but also in shape. Although today most bread is baked commercially, home baking is still a favorite hobby of many.

Basically, there are four types of bread products:

1. *loaf breads* made with yeast

2. *breakfast items,* such as croissants and Danish pastries, made with laminated doughs

3. *quick breads,* which are leavened with baking powder or baking soda

4. *flatbreads,* which may or may not be leavened

This chapter pertains to those in the first category.

Effects of Ingredients

Baking with yeast demands that ingredients be in proper proportion. Yeast needs sugar to grow, but too much sugar can slow the process to the point where it stops altogether. As it melts and caramelizes, sugar adds color and flavor to the bread. Salt is used in yeast dough to add color and flavor and to retard the action of the yeast just a little. When I see a loaf of baked bread that is pale instead of a healthy brown color, I know that the loaf was either baked at too low a temperature or that the salt was left out.

Yeast

Yeast fermentation is damaged in temperatures above 115°F (46°C), and yeast is killed at 145°F (63°C). At the other end of the scale, yeast fermentation is slowed but not damaged at temperatures below 65°F (19°C) and becomes nonexistent at 40°F (4°C) or lower. Although fermentation ceases, this does not mean that the yeast is killed. Once the dough is thawed and warmed, the yeast becomes active again. In certain types of yeast dough, such as for Danish pastry, braided white bread, and croissants, it is essential that the yeast be kept cold to prevent fermentation while the dough is being shaped.

The easiest bread to make is plain white bread, which contains all white glutenous flour and only the amount of sugar that is healthy for the yeast. White bread can, therefore, be made with cold milk, which slows the fermentation long enough to allow time to braid the dough into various shapes. In breads with a high proportion of sugar or a sweet flour, such as rye, that has little or no useable gluten structure, it is important to keep the dough from getting too cold.

RISING TEMPERATURE

The ideal temperature for yeast to develop is between 78° and 82°F (25° and 27°C), with 85 percent humidity. The dough should be kept as close to this temperature as possible by starting with a warm liquid, 105° to 115°F (40° to 46°C). However, if the liquid is too hot, the yeast will be damaged or killed. Use a thermometer until you know your judgment is accurate. Take care to keep the dough covered and away from drafts at all times.

YEAST FERMENTATION

There are two basic methods of fermenting the yeast in bread dough: the one-step or straight-dough method, and the pre-ferment method, in which the dough is produced in stages. The pre-ferment category includes the sponge-method, the pre-dough method, the use of sours and starters, and the use of old dough.

Straight-Dough or One-Step Method

In the straight-dough method, all of the ingredients, including the yeast, are mixed together at the beginning and, in most cases, are kneaded to form a gluten structure. The dough is then given one or two periods to rise before being punched down for the last time and formed into loaves or rolls.

Pre-Ferment Sponge Method

In the sponge method, a very soft dough or paste is made using a small amount of flour, water, sugar (although sugar is not necessary if milk is used because milk contains lactose, which is natural milk sugar), and, most of the time, all of the yeast. This sponge rises in a warm place, covered, until it has doubled in volume. The sponge is then mixed with all of the remaining ingredients to make the dough. This method allows the yeast to ferment in peace and develop strength without interference from other ingredients. The flavor from the alcohol (produced by the fermented yeast) also becomes stronger during the longer time this method requires. In breads with a high sugar content, such as Swedish Orange Rye, the sponge method is essential for a satisfactory result.

Pre-Ferment Pre-Dough Method

A pre-dough is used for primarily the same reasons as the sponge method, but the pre-dough is intentionally made firmer to allow the dough a longer time in which to develop a fremented flavor and to soften the gluten, giving the final product increased volume. To make the pre-dough, a small percentage of the yeast is mixed with the liquid (usually water) and flour to form a stiff, smooth dough. The firmness of the dough depends on the planned length of time for the rising period and the conditions under which it is left to rise. The stiffer the dough, the longer it will take for the yeast to leaven it. The mixture is then covered and left to rise for 12 to 24 hours.

Pre-Ferment Sours and Starters

Sours and starters are used for the same reasons as sponges and pre-doughs, but here the mixture is soft and somewhat fluid, and it is left to develop for an extended period to produce a much stronger fermented or sour flavor.

Terminology

- Autolysis—A process that occurs when the initial ingredients in a bread dough (typically a mixture of flour and water only) are allowed to rest. During this time, the flour is able to absorb the maximum amount of water before any preferments (sponge, pre-dough, old dough) are incorporated. Autolysis allows the gluten to develop and shortens the final mixing period, reducing the chances of oxidation that may occur if too much air is incorporated into the dough.

- Barm—The English name for a sourdough starter made from wild yeast using the sponge method, except that the starter is left to ferment for several days. Most often made using whole wheat flour.

- Biga—The biga is a firm pre-ferment, like the pre-dough described above. The term is Italian.

- Leavened breads—Breads made using a natural or wild yeast starter for leavening.

- Levain—A starter made from wild yeast; also a type of sourdough bread. *Levain* means "leaven" in French, and the bread *pain au levain* is made by using the starter to leaven the loaf. Levain is milder in flavor than either the barm-style starter or the traditional sourdough starter used, for example, to make San Francisco–style sourdough bread. Country-style levain is made with the addition of whole grains.

- Old dough—The method of incorporating a piece of fermented dough from a previous batch of bread into a new bread dough to add both flavor and leavening. The old dough, or pâte fermentée, is mixed in after the dough is formed, giving this method the ease of the straight-dough method (with no waiting time, although some variations retard the dough further) combined with the added flavor that comes from the pre-ferment techniques.

- Pâte fermentée—The French name for old dough.

- Poolish—A French word for a type of pre-ferment made using the sponge method. It may be left to ferment for several hours or even a full day to develop a sour flavor. The poolish is named in honor of Polish bakers who are said (confusingly enough) to have first developed the technique to make French-style breads in Vienna. A poolish is very soft—in some cases, almost a batter.

- Pre-ferment—Any procedure where the bread dough is produced in stages by starting with a fermented yeast mixture that is made separately, ahead of time, from the bread dough itself.

- Rustic breads—Also known as *stretch breads*, these are made from a very wet dough with only a small amount of yeast. Well-known examples are Ciabatta (page 165) and Pugliese. The moist, pastelike dough cannot be formed into a conventional loaf, hence the rustic appearance of the finished bread. The large amount of hydration in combination with a long fermentation period (sometimes lasting several days) produces loaves with large, irregular holes.

- Scalding method—In principle, this is the same as autolysis. The difference is that in the scalding method the water is heated before it is mixed with the flour or, in recipes where the scalding method is used with whole or cracked grains, before it is poured over the grains and left to sit without mixing. The purpose is to allow the flour or grain to absorb a greater amount of water than it would if the water was not heated or the mixture was not allowed to stand.

- Sourdough starter—This term is often shortened to simply *sour* or *starter*. A sourdough starter technically is made using wild yeast only. It is a mixture of flour, preferably organic, and water that is used to trap air-borne yeast and left to ferment for many days to produce a strong sour flavor (see "About Sourdough Breads," page 106).

- Yeasted breads—Breads made using commercial yeast instead of, or in addition to, a pre-ferment of any kind.

Forming Freestanding Loaves of Bread

To make round or oval loaves of bread, put the required weight of dough on the table in front of you and cup your hand around it. Using primarily the section of your palm at the base of the thumb, knead and move the dough around counterclockwise as you lift one section at a time from the outside and press it down in the center, forming a tight skin around the dough (Figure 3-1). When you have worked all the way around the circle a few times and the dough is tight, gradually turn it upside-down, using the same movements, so that the seam is now on the bottom. Hold the side of your hand against the table and form the loaf into a round or oval as desired (Figure 3-2).

You can form two loaves of bread simultaneously by working a second piece of dough with your other hand in the same way, moving this one clockwise so that the two loaves press up against each other in the center. This technique also is used to form and tighten the skin around individual rolls, but here the kneading motion is reversed. With rolls, the kneading motion moves clockwise with your right hand and counterclockwise with your left—both hands moving to the outside. With loaves, it is the opposite: your hands move in circles toward the center and each other.

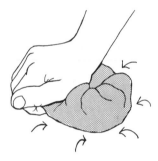

FIGURE 3-1 **Forming a tight skin around the bread dough by lifting the outer edges and pressing them into the center with the palm of the hand**

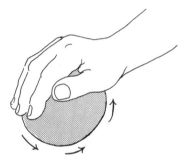

FIGURE 3-2 **Forming the loaf into a round or oval shape using the palm of the hand, after the dough has been turned seam-side down**

FORMING BAGUETTES

Baguettes are formed using the same method as for bread strings used for braided loaves. The oblong piece of dough is repeatedly folded and pounded with the heel of the hand to remove air bubbles and form a tight skin. The loaves are then rolled against the table to the desired length (see Figures 3-16 to 3-18, page 148).

Shaping Loaves for Bread Pans

Forming loaves that are to be baked in bread pans is a little different—and much easier—than forming freestanding loaves, because the pan helps develop the shape during proofing and baking. Start by punching down each piece of dough with the heels of both hands to flatten. Tuck in stray end pieces and roll the dough against the table to form a tight, wrinkle-free cylinder. At the same time, stretch the loaf, if necessary, to make it the same length as the pan. Place seam-side down in the prepared pan.

Proofing

Most bread doughs should rise to double in volume, but this includes the rising that will occur in the oven before the bread reaches 145°F (63°C), when the yeast is killed. Therefore, prior to baking, the bread should rise to just before it doubles in volume (approximately 1½ times the original size) to allow for the final rise in the oven. Test by pressing the dough lightly with your fingertip; a slight indentation should remain. A loaf that has risen too much is crumbly, dries out faster because of the extra air, and has less flavor. On the other hand, if the bread is not allowed to rise long enough, the gluten will not have formed all the elasticity it needs to expand and, as a result, the loaf will crack (usually on the side) and will be compact and heavy. Not enough rising time for Danish pastry and croissants will cause some of the butter in the dough to run out onto the pan simply because there is not enough dough volume to absorb the fat as it melts. This results in a drier and heavier pastry. Last, but certainly not least, it is important that the proof box (the box where the yeast ferments in a dough in industrial baking) or other rising area is not too hot. Ideally, the temperature should be about 80°F (26°C), with 85 percent humidity.

Slashing

Slashes are cut on the top of breads and rolls before baking not simply for appearance, but as an aid to relieving pressure. The product increases in volume at a greatly accelerated speed during the first 5 minutes of baking. This can cause the surface to break or crack at any weak point. By slashing the skin into decorative patterns, these points become predetermined, and the expansion is uniform and controlled. In most cases, the cuts are made just under the skin of the loaf and not deep toward the center. The slashes can be made with a small serrated knife designed especially for this purpose or with a razor blade. Thin, narrow strips of metal may be purchased that are specifically designed to provide a handle for a standard razor blade and at the same time, force the blade into a slight curve, which is desirable. These handles are often referred to by the French name, *lamis*. The metal strip is woven in and out through the openings in the center of the blade; a thin piece of wood (like a miniature popsicle stick) can be used for the same purpose. Several slashing tools are pictured in Figure 3-7, page 120. Figure 3-3 shows var-

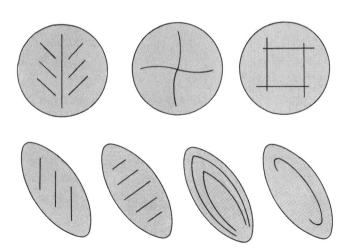

FIGURE 3-3 **Designs for slashing round and oval bread loaves**

ious ways to slash the tops of round and oval loaves. Other slashing designs are shown in Figures 3-5, 3-7, 3-9, 3-10, and 3-14 (all included in this chapter). Bread will occasionally develop cracks around the base despite being slashed. As stated previously, this is generally related to the bread not having proofed long enough.

The Baking Process

The baking of bread (and of most other yeast-leavened products) is a three-stage process that ultimately transforms the raw dough into a digestible product that is pleasant to eat. The first part of this process is the rapid rise that takes place when the partially proofed loaf (referred to in this text as slightly less than doubled in volume) is placed in a hot oven, typically 375° to 425°F (190° to 219°C). This expansion occurs during the first 5 minutes or so of baking and stops when the interior of the loaf has reached about 145°F (63°C) and all of the yeast cells are dead.

This first stage is commonly referred to as the oven-spring. Because this phenomenon cannot be altered or eliminated, it must be anticipated and is the reason that the loaf is allowed to expand only partially during the proofing stage. The oven-spring is caused by a temporary increase in the production of carbon dioxide as well as the rapid expansion of the carbon dioxide that was created during the proofing process.

Baking temperature is an important consideration. It must be selected to balance the effects of three processes that take place within the dough at almost the same time: the expansion of gas cells, as previously discussed; the gelatinization of the starch, and the coagulation of the gluten. If the oven temperature is too low, the gas cells—and therefore the loaf—will expand before the gluten and starch are set. Without the necessary structure, this loaf will fall. Too high a temperature will cause the outer crust to form prematurely and prevent maximum expansion. As a general rule, doughs with a high sugar content must be baked at a lower temperature, or the surface may become too brown before the interior has gelatinized.

In the second stage, the interior of the loaf reaches its maximum temperature of 212°F (100°C). Due to the evaporation of moisture and alcohol, this internal temperature is not exceeded, and the starches and gluten complete their coagulation. The coagulating process begins at 140°F (60°C) in the case of the starches and at 160°F (71°C) for proteins and continues until the bread is fully baked. The interior temperature of a baked loaf is 180° to 200°F (82° to 94°C) in the case of a loaf made using the straight-dough or any of the pre-ferment methods, or 210°F (99°C) for a loaf made with a sourdough starter.

In the final stage, the crust formed from starch and sugar on the surface of the dough becomes brown due to a chemical reaction known scientifically as the "Malliard browning reaction," named for the scientist who first described it. This browning process involves the effect of sugars reacting with proteins. To obtain a surface crust that has a glossy shine in addition to a pleasant color, egg wash is applied before baking or, in the case of loaves baked with steam, not at all since moisture is added during the initial phase of the baking process. The starch on the surface in conjunction with the applied moisture (steam) gelatinizes into a glossy thin coat.

When baked loaves of bread are removed from the oven, the composition throughout is far from homogenous. The outside is dry, brown, and close to the temperature of the oven, while the interior is moist and even sticky. The internal temperature, as described above, is about half that of the outside. As moisture from the interior of the loaf escapes and the room temperature cools the outside, the difference in temperature begins to stabilize, and simultaneously the starches begin to solidify. This is why it is not possible to cut into a loaf of bread to check for doneness; instead, one must rely on feel and the customary method of tapping the bread sharply on the bottom to check for a hollow sound. To be absolutely certain, a thermometer can be inserted to check the temperature using the guidelines on the previous page.

Pan breads should be unmolded at once after they are removed from the oven and placed on a cooling rack to allow air to circulate around all sides. The loaves are still exhausting their moisture as they finish the baking process. If left in the pans, the moisture will have nowhere to go, which will result in a wet surface on the loaf where it touches the pan.

Baking with Steam

Some of the recipes in this chapter give baking instructions for ovens with steam injectors. Steam creates a moist environment that prevents the dough from forming a crust too soon. After a specified length of time, a damper is opened to let the steam out, and the bread finishes baking. The resulting crust is much thinner and crisper, fragile enough to crack and break. The steam also produces a glossy surface. As explained above, sugar is present in any bread dough. The moisture from the steam mixes with the sugar on the surface of the dough, which then caramelizes and turns golden brown as it bakes. For this reason, breads and rolls that are baked with steam need not—and should not—be brushed with egg wash. It takes some experimenting with a steam oven to determine the proper length of time for the steam period. If too much steam is used, almost no crust will form. If the steam is not left in the oven long enough, you will not achieve the desired effect either. The trick is to use exactly enough steam for the correct length of time in combination with the proper temperature, so that the crust is thick enough to stay crisp and dry after the bread is removed from the oven but is not so thick that it will not crack from the sudden change in temperature.

CREATING STEAM WITHOUT STEAM INJECTORS

If your oven is not equipped with steam injectors, you can keep bread moist for the prescribed length of time by quickly opening the oven door every 1 or 2 minutes during this period and spritzing water into the oven or onto the bread using a spray bottle. In this case, start baking the loaves at a higher temperature to compensate for the heat loss from the open door. An alternative method is to place a pan containing 4 or 5 ice cubes in the oven and to add more ice cubes, a few at a time, to create steam during the initial baking period. After the length of time specified in the individual recipe, remove the pan and continue baking as directed.

INDIVIDUAL BREAD PANS FOR STEAM BAKING

Several bread pans available on the market today were created so that the home baker can produce a lean bread, such as a baguette, with the same thin, crisp, glossy, and crackling crust that a professional baker creates in a steam injection oven. These pans are a much easier alternative to the old tricks of spraying water or placing a pan of ice cubes in the oven during the initial baking stage. The science and the intention, however, are the same: to keep the surface of the bread moist and prevent it from developing a crust during the early stages of baking. These pans are designed to bake only one loaf per pan, so their use in a commercial operation is unlikely, but they do produce a very good result.

The bread pan comprises three sections: a shallow base with reservoirs to hold a precisely measured amount of water, a perforated pan that fits on top and holds the formed bread dough in a long, shallow indentation to help shape the loaf, and a tight-fitting lid. The bread loaf proofs and bakes in the covered pan. The water in the bottom evaporates and passes through the perforations to create moisture and steam in the sealed upper chamber. At a certain time during the baking process (calculated scientifically by the manufacturer of the pan based on the amount of water used and the thickness of the pan), all of the water will have evaporated, and the bread finishes baking with dry heat in the same way that it does when the damper of a steam injection oven is opened after a specified time.

Staling and Storage

Our common sense might lead us to believe that bread will start to become stale as soon as it has cooled. This is not so; unfortunately, the process is already at work even before the starch has solidified to the point that the bread can be sliced! Exactly how and why bread and other baked goods become stale has been studied by researchers for ages. One study showed that even if bread is hermetically sealed, it still loses moisture—that is, becomes stale. The crust becomes stale at a different rate than the interior. As moisture from the body of the loaf moves outward, it transforms the dry crust into a chewy, leathery, and tough skin, far from the crisp covering it was when freshly baked. The interior, or body, of the bread becomes dry at a slower rate because it is protected by the crust. If the staling process has not progressed too far, it can be remedied temporarily by reheating the loaf, which will make the body soft and pleasant to eat; the crust, however, will remain tough.

Baked bread is best preserved by freezing. The bread should be properly wrapped and placed in the freezer as soon as possible once it has cooled. Bread that is not to be frozen should be stored, wrapped, at room temperature. Baked loaves should not be stored in the refrigerator. Wrapped or not, refrigerating the bread will actually accelerate the staling process up to 6 times.

REDUCING STALING

Specially formulated emulsifying agents that act as preservatives have been added to bread made by commercial bakers for years. Granulated malt extract or malt syrup, milk powder, and soybean oil have all been found to retard the staling process. Increasing the fat content is also beneficial but is not possible with certain types of bread. Durum and other high-gluten flours aid in absorbing a larger percentage of moisture during the kneading process, which produces a loaf that stays moist longer. Bread that is made by the scalding method or with the inclusion of the autolysis step during mixing will also have a higher moisture content. Lastly, correct proofing is essential. Bread that is overproofed or left to dry and form a skin will get old much faster than properly fermented and cared-for bread.

If you keep to all of these rules and guidelines, I can assure you that you will be satisfied with the results of the following recipes.

Baguettes yield: 6 loaves, 12 ounces (340 g) each, or 4 loaves, 1 pound (455 g) each

The word *baguette* literally translates as "small rod"; however, most people today would immediately identify it as a French type of chewy white bread with a crisp crust. Baguettes are far and away the most popular bread in France—or in any other French-speaking country for that matter. Currently, about 25 million baguettes are sold in France each day. Baguette loaves are long, thin, and crusty, usually weighing between 10 ounces and 1 pound. When I travel to France by car, a baguette is always one of the first things I buy after crossing the border and I never have to look too far. It seems that even the smallest village in France has a church, a city hall, a pâtisserie, and a boulangerie. If I am able to buy a baguette freshly baked first thing in the morning, I need nothing else for breakfast but a good cup of coffee.

6 cups (1 L 440 ml) cold water

3 pounds (1 kg 365 g) bread flour

1 pound 6 ounces (625 g) cake flour

3 tablespoons (45 g) salt

1 recipe or 1 pound (455 g) Baguette Pâte Fermenté (recipe follows)

1 ounce (30 g) fresh compressed yeast

Vegetable oil or pan spray

Cornmeal

Small-Batch Baguettes
yield: 3 loaves, 12 ounces (340 g) each, or 2 loaves, 1 pound (455 g) each

3 cups (720 ml) cold water

1 pound 8 ounces (680 g) bread flour

11 ounces (315 g) cake flour

1½ tablespoons (22 g) salt

½ ounce (15 g) fresh compressed yeast

½ recipe or 8 ounces (225 g) Baguette Pâte Fermenté (recipe follows)

Vegetable oil or pan spray

Cornmeal

When you make the small-batch recipe, follow the instructions as given but scale the dough into 11-ounce (310-g) pieces and roll each piece to 20 inches (50 cm) in length.

1. Place 5 cups (1 L 200 ml) water (2½ cups /600 ml for the small recipe), all but a handful of the bread flour, the cake flour, and the salt in a mixer bowl. Combine the mixture, using the dough hook attachment at low speed, and continue mixing until smooth. Allow the dough to rest for 15 minutes (the process that occurs during this step is called *autolysis*; see Chef's Tip).

2. Add the pâte fermenté to the contents of the mixer bowl. Dissolve the yeast in the remaining water, then add it along with the remaining handful of flour. Knead for 4 to 6 minutes; the ingredients should be well incorporated, and the dough should have a smooth texture.

3. Lightly oil the top of the dough or use pan spray. Cover and set aside to rise for 1½ hours; this is known as *bulk rising*.

4. Divide the dough into pieces weighing 12 ounces (340 g)

CHEF'S TIP
Autolysis occurs during one of the first steps in making a bread dough before mixing and kneading. It involves allowing a well-combined mixture of flour and water to rest for 15 to 30 minutes so that the flour has time to fully absorb the water. It has the same effect as the scalding method, the only difference being that with autolysis, the water is not heated. See page 92 for further information. If you are pressed for time, this step can be left out.

The Baguette of France

The French government has regulated the size and price of baguette loaves produced and sold in France since the end of World War II. Unfortunately, once the size and price were fixed, the quality of the bread itself suffered in many of the high-production bakeries. In an effort to circumvent the regulations, some bakers began adding flavorings, such as nuts, herbs, dried fruits, olives, and onions, and selling their breads labeled as something other than baguettes. These breads were not new; they were simply not as well known in the cities and were at that time more of a homemade or provincial specialty. Ironically, when these flavored breads were brought to the markets in Paris and other big cities, they became immensely popular and are the moving force behind much of the current interest in flavored breads found in the United States and elsewhere today.

As a perfect example of how seriously the French take their baguettes, a decree was issued in 1993 that called for specific labeling of all baguette loaves sold. A 1912 law already stated that baguettes must contain nothing other than flour, water, salt, and yeast. The new decree took the matter a step further and specified that if the bread is kneaded and baked on the seller's premises, it shall be labeled *pain maison* (homemade bread). If it is labeled *de tradition française* (traditional French), this means that no additives were used and the dough was never frozen; however, it may be baked in one location and sold in another.

or 1 pound (455 g). Pound, fold, and roll each piece against the table to form short torpedo-shaped loaves, 6 to 8 inches (15 to 20 cm) long. Line the loaves up on the workbench as you set them down. Very lightly spray vegetable oil (or pan spray) over the loaves. Cover the loaves and let them rest for 30 minutes to 1 hour on the worktable; this is known as *bench resting* or *bench proofing*.

5. Using the same method as for forming bread strings (see Figures 3-16 to 3-18, page 148), pound and roll each piece into a 23-inch (57.5-cm) baguette. Place the baguettes on floured breadboards or sheet pans lined with baking paper (see Note). Spray the tops of the baguettes lightly with water and let them rise until slightly less than doubled in size.

6. Dust a baker's peel with cornmeal and carefully transfer the baguettes, 2 or 3 at a time, onto the peel. Using a baker's blade, a dough cutter, or a serrated knife, cut well-defined slits, 4

Sizes and Shapes of Baguettes and Other French-Style Loaves

- The classic *baguette* loaf weighs 8 ounces (225 g) and is 30 inches (75 cm) long by comparison, a typical baguette in the United States is likely to weigh about 12 ounces (340 g) and be 24 inches (60 cm) long.

- The *bâtard* loaf is also 8 ounces (225 g) like the classic, but only 24 inches (60 cm) long. The word literally means "bastard," referring to the loaf not being the standard size.

- The *ficelle* is a 4-ounce (115-g) loaf that is 30 inches (75 cm) long, the same as the classic baguette. This makes it quite thin, almost like a bread stick, and it is eaten in much the same way.

- The *parisienne* is 16 ounces (455 g) by weight and, like the classic baguette and the ficelle, 30 inches (75 cm) long.

- The largest of all is the *marchand du vin* (literally, "merchant of wine"), a 16-ounce (455-g) loaf that is 42 inches (1 m 5 cm) long. These breads are served in wine bars cut in half lengthwise, filled, then cut across into small sandwiches for guests to consume with wine.

to 5 inches (10 to 12.5 cm) long and approximately 3 inches (7.5 cm) apart, at a sharp angle on top of each baguette. Transfer the baguettes to the hearth of a deck oven preheated to 450°F (230°C). Repeat slashing and transferring the remaining baguettes in the same manner.

7. Bake the baguettes, using steam for the first 6 to 10 minutes; depending on your oven, you may need to have the injector open the whole time or just for 15 to 20 seconds to fill the oven with steam. Open the damper to let the steam out and continue baking approximately 10 minutes longer or until the loaves are golden brown and have a hard crust.

8. Transfer the loaves to racks to cool. Do not slice the bread until it has cooled to room temperature. Wrap and freeze any loaves that will not be served the same day.

NOTE: If you do not have a hearth oven, there is no reason to place the baguettes on breadboards in Step 5 nor do you need to use a peel to transfer them to the oven. Although the difference will be noticeable, a good result can still be obtained by baking the baguettes on paper-lined sheet pans.

BAGUETTE PÂTE FERMENTÉ yield: 1 pound (455 g)

½ teaspoon (2.5 ml) fresh compressed yeast (see Note)

¾ cup (180 ml) water, at room temperature

10 ounces (285 g) bread flour

1 teaspoon (5 g) salt

Vegetable oil or pan spray

1. In a mixer bowl, dissolve the yeast in the water. Add the flour and the salt. Knead at medium speed, using the dough hook attachment, until the dough is soft and pliable; scraping down the dough a few times, and, if it seems necessary, dust a little flour around the bowl. It will be somewhat tacky without being sticky and will take aproximately 10 minutes.

2. Pinch off a small amount of dough and stretch it between your hands until very thin. If the dough has been kneaded long enough, it will form a thin, translucent sheet that does not tear; this is known as the *windowpane test*.

3. Lightly oil the dough or use pan spray, cover, and set aside to proof at room temperature until doubled in size, approximately 1 hour.

4. Punch the dough down, you will see it has "matured" (the dough feels firmer now) knead it into a tight, firm ball, and place it back in the bowl. Oil lightly or use pan spray, cover, and refrigerate overnight. The refrigeration step is known as *retarding* the pre-dough (see Note). Ideally, you should remove the pre-dough from the refrigerator 1 hour before using it in the baguette dough.

NOTE: If you have no other dough and do not have time to wait for this to fully develop, retard the pâte fermanté as long as possible, or as a last resort, skip this step and instead double the yeast and use water at 105° to 115°F (40° to 46°C). Follow the directions as given but, after fermenting the dough at room temperature for 1 hour (you have to punch down the dough once or twice), add it to the baguette recipe rather than retarding overnight as directed. Please note that even though both shortcuts will produce a good result the baguettes will lack the ovenspring of the slow retardation.

Epi Baguettes yield: 4 loaves, about 1 pound (455 g) each

If you have the opportunity to drive through farm country in the fall, you may be lucky enough to see the beautiful golden ripe wheat sheaves bending into shallow waves in the wind. This picture-perfect display of nature's bounty inspires the shape of these loaves.

Epi is the French word for an ear of wheat—the top part of the wheat sheaf. Forming the baguettes in this shape is not only fitting, but also attractive. Epi baguettes add visual appeal to a bread display on a buffet table or in a shop window. The shape is also practical for use in bread baskets, as it allows the guests to break off individual rolls as they please. The épi design can be made using any gluten-rich bread dough in this book with excellent results.

I first came across these shapely baguettes in a small restaurant in Provence, which served an individual épi loaf to each diner, placing it directly on the tablecloth next to the plate. To make the individual size, divide the dough into 4-ounce (115-g) pieces. Shape them as described for the larger size, but make them 5 inches (12.5 cm) long. The individual loaves will require less time in the oven.

Although it is not necessary to start this dough with ice-cold water (this is usually done when making a large batch so that the dough will not get too warm from friction during the kneading process), using cold water generates a slower and longer proofing period, which allows the dough to absorb more flavor from the alcohol produced by the yeast. This, and the use of old bread dough, give these baguettes their special taste and character (see page 92 for more information on the use of pre-doughs).

1½ ounces (40 g) fresh compressed yeast	1 tablespoon plus 2 teaspoons (25 g) salt
2½ cups (600 ml) ice-cold water	1 teaspoon (4 g) ascorbic acid (see Note 2)
1 pound (455 g) bread dough scraps (see Note 1)	Olive oil
2 pounds 6 ounces (1 kg 80 g) bread flour	

1. Dissolve the yeast in the cold water. Add the bread dough scraps and all but a handful of the bread flour. Knead with the dough hook on low speed for 8 minutes, adjusting the consistency if necessary by adding the remaining bread flour. The dough should be soft but not sticky.

2. Incorporate the salt and the ascorbic acid. Knead 4 minutes longer on low speed.

3. Cover the dough and let it rest in a warm place for 30 minutes.

4. Reserve 1 pound (455 g) dough to use in the next batch (see Note 3). Divide the remaining dough into 4 equal pieces, about 1 pound (455 g) each.

5. Form the pieces into baguette loaves 16 inches (40 cm) in length (see Figures 3-16 to 3-18, page 148). Place on sheet pans that have been lightly greased with olive oil; do not place more than 3 per full sheet pan.

6. Hold scissors at a 45-degree angle and cut an épi or wheat sheaf design into the loaves, alternating left and right (Figure 3-4). Let the loaves rise until doubled in volume.

7. Bake the loaves at 425°F (219°C), using steam for the first 10 minutes. Open the damper (or the oven

FIGURE 3-4 **Cutting the épi design in the loaves before baking**

door) to let the moisture out, then continue baking approximately 10 minutes longer or until the baguettes are baked through (see Note 4).

NOTE 1: You can use either dough left over from a previous batch of this recipe or any white bread dough. If you do not have any suitable bread dough scraps, use the following recipe for Epi Baguette Pre-Dough.

NOTE 2: Ascorbic acid is pure vitamin C. Although it is destroyed on exposure to high heat in the oven, it is beneficial as the yeast is growing. The microorganisms seem to thrive on it and grow stronger. If you do not have this ingredient on hand, simply leave it out of the recipe; in that case, increase the salt by 1 teaspoon (5 g).

NOTE 3: If properly covered, the leftover dough can be stored in the refrigerator for up to 3 days. If you do not plan to make another batch of épi baguettes within this time, either make a fifth loaf or freeze the dough until needed.

NOTE 4: If your oven is not equipped with steam injectors, see "Creating Steam Without Steam Injectors," page 97.

EPI BAGUETTE PRE-DOUGH yield: I pound (455 g)

¼ ounce (7.5 g) or 1 slightly rounded teaspoon (5 ml) fresh compressed yeast *or* ½ teaspoon (2.5 ml) active dry yeast

¾ cup (180 ml) warm water (105° to 115°F/40° to 46°C)

10 ounces (285 g) bread flour

1 teaspoon (2 g) ground cumin (optional)

1. Dissolve the yeast in the water. Add the flour and ground cumin, if desired, and mix until smooth.

2. Cover and refrigerate overnight.

NOTE: The cumin is added to enhance the fermentation. If you do not care for the flavor, it may be omitted.

Sicilian White Bread yield: 4 loaves, I pound 6 ounces (625 g) each

This gluten-rich bread from Italy brings back memories of my first visit to the spectacular island of Sicily. I was in my early twenties and working in the pastry department on board the Swedish American Lines proud ship *MS Kungsholm*. Having never been to that part of the world before, my palate was unaccustomed to tasting bread without any salt (what I referred to, with the arrogance of youth, as "tasteless bread"). I later learned that the bakers of Sicily have a very good reason for not adding salt to some of their breads: the milder taste complements the richly flavored, often spicy cuisine.

Yes, there is salt in this bread, and I have added garlic for more flavor, though it can be omitted if you want. This dough makes up well into traditional baguette-shaped loaves, scaled to half the normal size. The gluten generates a pronounced oven-spring, which is attractive on the slashed baguettes and also on rolls formed as for Rustica rolls (page 203). Try proofing the rolls in fine or medium semolina flour instead of bread flour. The appearance and flavor are wonderful.

2 ounces (55 g) fresh compressed yeast

1 quart (960 ml) warm water (105° to 115°F/40° to 46°C)

2 tablespoons (18 g) granulated malt extract or ¼ cup (60 ml) or 3 ounces (85 g) honey

1 pound (455 g) bread flour

¼ cup (60 ml) olive oil

3 tablespoons (45 g) salt

4 teaspoons (12 g) garlic powder or 2 tablespoons (30 ml) pureed fresh garlic

2 pounds 8 ounces (1 kg 135 g) finely milled semolina flour (durum wheat)

Small-Batch Sicilian White Bread
yield: 2 loaves, 1 pound 6 ounces (625 g) each

1 ounce (30 g) fresh compressed yeast

2 cups (480 ml) warm water (105° to 115°F/40° to 46°C)

1 tablespoon (9 g) granulated malt extract or 2 tablespoons (40 g) honey

8 ounces (225 g) bread flour

2 tablespoons (30 ml) olive oil

4 teaspoons (20 g) salt

2 teaspoons (6 g) garlic powder or 1 tablespoon (15 ml) pureed fresh garlic

1 pound 6 ounces (625 g) finely milled semolina flour (durum wheat)

---

1. Dissolve the yeast in the warm water. Using the dough hook, mix in the malt extract or honey, bread flour, olive oil, salt, garlic powder or pureed garlic, and all but a handful of the semolina flour. Once the ingredients have formed a dough, continue kneading for about 10 minutes, adding the remaining semolina flour as necessary to form a smooth, soft dough.

2. Place the dough in an oiled bowl and turn to coat with oil. Cover and let it rise in a warm place until doubled in volume.

3. Punch the dough down. Let rise again until it has doubled in volume a second time.

4. Divide the dough into 4 equal pieces (2 for the smaller recipe), approximately 1 pound 6 ounces (625 g) each. Shape the pieces into round loaves (see Figures 3-1 and 3-2, page 94).

5. Let the loaves rise until they are 1½ times the original size.

6. Bake at 410°F (210°C), using steam for the first 10 minutes, until the loaves are golden brown and baked through, about 40 minutes total.

NOTE: If your oven is not equipped with steam injectors, see "Creating Steam Without Steam Injectors," page 97.

Mediterranean Olive Bread yield: 4 loaves, 1 pound 4 ounces (570 g) each

This bread is marbled throughout with flavorful brine-cured Greek kalamata olives. It goes well with antipasto or carpaccio, or try it toasted, topped with creamy goat cheese and fresh basil, and served with a glass of chardonnay. I have not had good results when substituting other olives for the kalamatas. The Greek-style California olives lose all of their flavor after being baked in the bread. If the kalamata olives you are using are very salty, reduce the amount of salt in the recipe by 1 to 2 teaspoons.

When making the dough, be sure not to add too much flour. If the dough is too firm, you will find it hard, if not impossible, to incorporate all of the olives—and kalamata olives are too good, and too expensive, to end up burned on the sheet pan next to the loaves. If you find it difficult to incorporate the olives into the dough, bake the loaves in greased, paper-lined bread pans, to avoid losing the olives. Due to the moisture in the olives, this bread will keep fresh longer than the average loaf.

PRE-DOUGH

1½ ounces (40 g) fresh compressed yeast

1 cup (240 ml) warm water (105° to 115°F/40° to 46°C)

1 tablespoon (15 g) granulated sugar

10 ounces (285 g) high-gluten flour

DOUGH

2¼ cups (540 ml) warm water (105° to 115°F/40° to 46°C)

⅓ cup (80 ml) olive oil

2 ounces (55 g) granulated sugar

2 tablespoons (30 g) salt

1 pound (455 g) high-gluten flour

1 pound (455 g) bread flour

1 pound 8 ounces (680 g) kalamata olives, pitted and coarsely chopped, *or* 1 pound 3 ounces (540 g) pitted kalamata olives (2¾ cups/660 ml)

Olive oil (optional; see Note)

1. Start the pre-dough by dissolving the yeast in the warm water. Add the sugar and high-gluten flour. Knead for about 5 minutes using the dough hook. Let the pre-dough rise in a warm place just until it starts to fall.

2. Add the remaining warm water, olive oil, sugar, salt, high-gluten flour, and all but a handful of the bread flour to the pre-dough. Knead until the dough is smooth and elastic, adding the last handful of flour if necessary. Cover the dough and let rise in a warm place until it has doubled in volume.

3. Add the olives to the dough and knead by hand just until they are incorporated. Do not mix so long at this step that the olives break up completely and turn the dough an unpleasant gray color. However, the dough should have a slightly marbled look from the olives. This not only enhances the appearance, but also adds to the flavor of the finished bread. Cover the dough and let it rise a second time until it has doubled in bulk.

4. Punch the dough down and divide it into 4 equal pieces, approximately 1 pound 4 ounces (570 g) each. Shape the pieces into oval loaves (see Figure 3-13, page 143). Let the loaves rise until they are 1½ times their original size.

5. Bake at 375°F (190°C), using steam and leaving the damper closed for the first 10 minutes. Open the damper, lower the heat slightly, and continue to bake approximately 35 minutes longer or until baked through.

NOTE: Should you prefer not to use steam, or do not have a steam oven, baking this bread in a regular dry-heat oven will produce a very good soft-crust loaf. The baking time will be a little shorter, about 35 minutes. If you use this method, brush the loaves with olive oil immediately after removing them from the oven. To add steam, see "Creating Steam Without Steam Injectors," page 97.

About Olives

Olives are found all over the Mediterranean, where more than 90 percent of the world's cultivated olives are grown. The ragged-looking trees are among the heartiest of species and can live to be hundreds of years old. Their main harvest, of course, is olive oil, but what would we do without the popular small pitted fruit? It is hard to imagine a *salade Niçoise* without the dark olives of Provence, or a martini without a pimento-stuffed Spanish green olive, or my favorite martini olive—stuffed with anchovies. The dozens of varieties, sizes, and colors have one thing in common: they are all green before they are ripe and turn black when left on the tree to ripen. Either way, when first picked, olives are very bitter, and if they are not pressed for oil, they are always cured in brine or oil before they are eaten.

About Sourdough Breads

Although making sourdough bread using your own starter is a lengthy and sometimes frustrating procedure, that just makes it all the more rewarding to sample the finished product when you succeed. Sourdough starters provide a unique flavor as they leaven the bread. The starter, a fermented mixture of flour—ideally organic—and water, is used to trap the natural wild yeast present in the air. Natural airborne yeast is abundant in a kitchen or bakery where bread has been baked for many years. To assure a predictable result, especially in a kitchen where these organisms are less plentiful, a small amount of fresh yeast is used to help the starter develop. Even then, the performance of the starter will be affected by temperature and climate, and it requires careful tending to achieve the desired result. As you will see, making bread with a sourdough starter is not completed in a few hours like most other types of bread. Instead, it requires several days while the starter, affectionately referred to as the mother, ferments. You may replace the water called for in the starter recipe with water left after boiling potatoes; the starch and sugar from the potatoes can enhance the starter's development.

If you are a purist who refuses to use anything other than natural wild yeast in your sourdough, you can try making a natural starter (directions follow), but unfortunately, that is the one recipe in this book I cannot guarantee will always work. However, if you have the time and the patience and you are up for a real challenge, give it a try. As a third option, commercial starters are available to make life a little easier; just follow the directions on the package.

Using sourdough starter alone to leaven the bread will produce a reasonably good but fairly dense product. The bread will take much longer to proof than other breads, making this technique impractical, especially in a commercial operation. Therefore, we again help the starter along by including fresh or dry yeast in the recipe to guarantee a light and flavorful bread.

Sourdough Starter yield: approximately 3 pounds (1 kg 365 g)

If you do not use starter very often, replenishing may present a small problem, as the volume grows with each feeding. A way around this is to remove the starter from its container, discard half (or give it to a friend—one who will appreciate it and not think it is some kind of bad joke), wash and rinse the container, place the remaining starter back inside, and feed as directed.

1½ ounces (40 g) fresh compressed yeast	1 ounce (30 g) granulated sugar
3 cups (720 ml) warm water (105° to 115°F/40° to 46°C)	1 pound 8 ounces (680 g) unbleached bread flour

1. In a plastic or crockery container with a large opening and plenty of room for expansion, dissolve the yeast in the water, then add the sugar. Stir in the flour using a wooden spoon; keep stirring until you have a smooth paste.

2. Cover loosely to allow gases to escape and let stand at approximately 80°F (26°C) for at least 2 to 3 days, preferably a little longer. The mixture should bubble and have a strong sour smell. Stir down the starter once a day during the time it is fermenting, also stirring in any crust that forms on top. After that, the starter should be stored in the refrigerator (see Note). The starter, or part of it, may also be frozen; before using, allow it to slowly thaw and start to bubble again at room temperature.

NOTE: The starter should always be replenished after each use. Even if not used, it must be fed every 10 days or so. If left alone too long, it will perish in its own residue. To feed the starter, add half as much flour and water as in the original recipe relative to the amount of starter you are feeding. For example, if the full amount of the recipe above was left unused and had to be fed, you would add 12 ounces (340 g) unbleached bread flour and 1½ cups (360 ml) water stirring until completely smooth again. If you are replenishing the starter after using about half of it for the sourdough bread recipe, you would add ¾ cup (180 ml) water and 6 ounces (170 g) flour. Let the starter proof, loosely covered, in a warm place for 24 hours before refrigerating again.

Natural Sourdough Starter yield: approximately 3 pounds (1 kg 365 g)

Remember, this will not work unless natural yeast is present in the air of your kitchen from recent bread baking.

> 3 cups (720 ml) milk, at body temperature   1 pound 8 ounces (680 g) bread flour
> 2 ounces (55 g) granulated sugar

1. Follow the preceding directions for Sourdough Starter.

2. When ready to replenish, add 1 cup (240 ml) warm milk, 8 ounces (225 g) bread flour, and 1 ounce (30 g) granulated sugar.

San Francisco Sourdough Bread yield: 4 loaves, 1 pound 2 ounces (510 g) each

Producing a bread with a sour flavor was long looked upon as a serious fault—a bread fit only for peasants, whose rye bread commonly had a sour taste, not necessarily by choice. While sourdough bread, made from either rye or wheat, is still regarded as a country-style bread, its characteristic flavor is now popular in Scandinavia and other parts of Europe. In France, they call their sourdough wheat bread *pain de campagne.*

First the pioneers and later on, the gold miners of California and the Yukon (whose sharing of sourdough starter was considered the ultimate act of friendship) made sourdough bread popular in the United States. As there was little access to fresh supplies, and certainly not to yeast, they utilized the method of including a piece of leftover dough to start a new fermentation. The leftover starter became known as the mother dough.

Much has been written about the renowned San Francisco sourdough bread; many say it simply cannot be made to taste the same (read *as good*) anywhere else. Some give the famous San Francisco fog all the credit. The basic explanation is this: Because the yeast present in the starter is dependent on the type or characteristics of the microflora of the area, and as this, of course, is not the same in, for instance, New York as in San Francisco, then even if the starter is transferred to another part of the country, the bread baked with it naturally will not taste the same. This is the reason the bakers in San Francisco get away with saying that their bread cannot be duplicated. I say they also have a few tricks up their sleeve that they are not telling. To be fair, while I haven't really tried that hard, I must admit I can't copy that wonderful aroma—and I lived and worked in the San Francisco Bay Area for over 30 years!

1 ounce (30 g) fresh compressed yeast

2 cups (480 ml) warm water (105° to 115°F/41° to 46°C)

2 tablespoons (30 g) salt

2 tablespoons (18 g) granulated malt extract *or* ¼ cup (60 ml) or 3 ounces (85 g) honey

1 pound 4 ounces (570 g) Sourdough Starter (page 106)

2 pounds 6 ounces (1 kg 80 g) bread flour

Cornmeal

Small-Batch San Francisco Sourdough Bread

yield: 2 loaves, 1 pound 2 ounces (510 g) each

¾ ounce (22 g) fresh compressed yeast

1 cup (240 ml) warm water (105° to 115°F/41° to 46°C)

2 teaspoons (10 g) salt

1 tablespoon (9 g) granulated malt extract *or* 2 tablespoons (30 ml) or 1½ ounces (40 g) honey

10 ounces (285 g) Sourdough Starter (page 106)

1 pound 3 ounces (540 g) bread flour

Cornmeal

---

1. In a mixer bowl, dissolve the yeast in the warm water. Add the salt, malt extract or honey, and the starter. Kneading with the dough hook at low speed, incorporate enough of the bread flour to make a dough that is quite firm but not sticky. Continue kneading at medium speed for about 8 minutes, until the dough is elastic and pliable.

2. Place in a lightly oiled bowl and turn to coat with oil. Cover and let rise in a warm place for 2 hours.

3. Punch the dough down and scale into 4 equal pieces (2 for the smaller recipe), approximately 1 pound 2 ounces (510 g) each.

4. Pound and roll each piece into a 16-inch (40-cm) loaf (see Figures 3-16 to 3-18, page 148, but do not taper the ends; also, see Note).

5. Let rise until slightly less than doubled in volume. Be patient here; the loaves will take quite a bit longer to rise than regular bread. While proofing, spray the loaves with water to prevent a crust from forming on the top. Before baking, spray the loaves again, then dust with cornmeal. Slash the tops of the loaves using a sharp serrated knife or razor blade, cutting lengthwise at a slight angle as for baguettes.

6. Bake at 425°F (219°C) with steam, leaving the damper closed for the first 10 minutes. Open the damper and bake approximately 30 minutes longer or until done. Allow the bread to cool on a rack.

NOTE: In addition to long oval loaves, sourdough bread is also typically made in a large, flat, round shape in San Francisco. Scale the dough into 2 equal pieces, approximately 2 pounds 4 ounces (1 kg 25 g) each, then form the pieces into tight round loaves (see Figures 3-1 and 3-2, page 94). Let relax for a few minutes, then flatten them to approximately 9 inches (22.5 cm) in diameter. Proof and spray as for the long loaves. Dust heavily with bread flour so that it shows after baking. Slash the tops of the loaves first in a series of parallel lines, then with additional parallel lines at a 45-degree angle to the first set to form a diamond pattern (see Figure 3-10, page 132). Bake as directed in Step 6 for approximately 35 minutes.

Sourdough Multigrain Bread yield: 6 loaves, 1 pound 6 ounces (625 g) each

As you will see when you read through the instructions, this recipe must be started 2 to 3 days before you can enjoy the finished product. To use an old, tired phrase, though, it really is well worth waiting for. Admittedly, a fair amount of prep work is involved. Besides soaking the grains (which should not scare anyone off, as this is simple and takes just a few minutes), you have to make both the starter and a baguette dough. However, once you (or the bakeshop you are working in) make the necessary mise en place for producing pre-fermented bread part of your regular routine, you will already have these items on hand. Once this happens, adding these ingredients to the dough becomes as effortless as adding flour or water. The starter—all or part of it—can be frozen, and the same goes for the pre-fermented dough; thaw the dough slowly in the refrigerator.

Because this recipe is rather involved and requires quite a few steps if you are starting from scratch, it intentionally produces a fairly large yield. If you do not need the full amount, the recipe can, of course, be scaled down to make a half-recipe or even one-third. A better choice would be to produce the full amount of bread dough following the recipe through Step 4, omitting the proofing step, then freeze part of it to thaw, form, and bake another time. If you do this, scale the dough so you are freezing a quantity that will produce a loaf or loaves of the proper size. Press the dough flat before you freeze it so it will freeze quickly and thaw evenly.

1 pound 2 ounces (510 g) Sour Wheat Starter (recipe follows)

2 pounds (910 g) Fermented Dough (recipe follows)

6 ounces (170 g) rye flour

6 ounces (170 g) cracked wheat

6 ounces (170 g) rolled oats

4 ounces (115 g) sunflower seeds

1 ounce (30 g) salt

3 cups (720 ml) hot water

DOUGH

1 cup (240 ml) water, at room temperature

1 ounce (30 g) fresh yeast

2 pounds 6 ounces (1 kg 80 g) bread flour

¼ cup (60 ml) molasses

Mixed grains and seeds, such as cracked wheat, rolled oats, and sunflower seeds

1. Make the Sour Wheat Starter and the Fermented Dough.

2. Combine the rye flour, cracked wheat, rolled oats, and sunflower seeds. Stir the salt into the hot water, then pour over the dry ingredients and stir to combine. Let the grains stand, covered, at room temperature for 24 hours.

3. To make the dough, in a mixer bowl with a dough hook, add the water and the yeast. Mix to dissolve, combine the sour wheat starter, and the soaked grain mixture, mixing at low speed for 1 minute. Hold back a handful of the bread flour and add the remainder to the mixer, together with the molasses. Mix until all the ingredients are fully combined.

4. Add the fermented dough. Knead the dough on medium speed, adding the reserved and additional bread flour as necessary until you have a fully developed, soft, and elastic dough. Cover the dough and proof in a warm location for 1 hour.

5. Divide the dough into 6 equal pieces, approximately 1 pound 8 ounces (680 g) each. Cover the pieces and bench proof for 20 minutes.

6. Shape the dough pieces into rounds or oblongs as desired. Place them seam-side up in bannetons dusted with mixed grains and seeds. Proof until the loaves are 1½ times their original size, approximately 1 hour.

7. Carefully invert the loaves onto sheet pans lined with baking paper and remove the baskets. Make 4 to 5 slashes on top of the loaves.

8. Bake at 425°F (219°C) using steam for the first 15 minutes (see Note). Open the damper and continue baking approximately 45 minutes longer or until baked through.

NOTE: If your oven does not have steam injectors, see "Creating Steam Without Steam Injectors," page 97.

SOUR WHEAT STARTER yield: 1 pound 2 ounces (510 g)

½ ounce (15 g) fresh yeast

1 cup (240 ml) warm water (105° to 115°F/40° to 46°C)

1 ounce (30 g) granulated sugar

8 ounces (225 g) whole wheat flour

1. In a plastic or crockery container with a large opening and plenty of room for expansion, dissolve the yeast in the water, then add the sugar. Stir in the flour using a wooden spoon; keep stirring until you have a smooth paste.

2. Cover loosely to allow gases to escape and let stand at approximately 80°F (26°C) for at least 2 to 3 days, preferably a little longer. The mixture should bubble and have a strong sour smell. Stir down the starter once a day during the time it is fermenting, also stirring in any crust that forms on top. After that, the starter should be stored in the refrigerator. The starter, or part of it, can be frozen; before using, allow it to thaw and start to bubble again at room temperature.

NOTE: See note on feeding (page 107). For more information on starters see page 106.

FERMENTED DOUGH yield: 2 pounds (910 g)

1 teaspoon (5 ml) fresh compressed yeast

1½ cups (360 ml) water, at room temperature

1 pound (455 g) bread flour

2 teaspoons (10 g) salt

Vegetable oil or pan spray

1. In a mixer bowl, dissolve the yeast in the water. Add the flour and salt. Knead at low speed, using the dough hook attachment, until the dough is soft and pliable; it will be somewhat tacky without being sticky.

2. Pinch off a small amount of dough and stretch it between your hands until very thin. If the dough has been kneaded long enough, it will form a thin, translucent sheet that does not tear; this is known as the windowpane test.

3. Lightly oil the dough or use pan spray, cover, and set aside to proof at room temperature until doubled in size, approximately 1 hour.

4. Punch the dough down, knead it into a tight, firm ball. Place it back in the bowl and refrigerate overnight.

Basil Baguettes Stuffed with Spinach and Cheese

yield: 2 loaves, approximately 2 pounds 5 ounces (1 kg 50 g) each

This delicious bread can be served as a snack or as an hors d'oeuvre. The cut slices are attractive due to the spiral design of the filling, and the taste is similar to a cheesy vegetarian pizza. Be sure to heed the instructions when it comes to removing as much moisture as possible from the spinach. If the filling is too wet, the interior of the loaf will not bake properly and the bread swirls around the filling will be soggy. The same thing can happen if the bread is not allowed to cool sufficiently (see Step 10).

PRE-DOUGH	DOUGH
3 ounces (85 g) semolina flour	2½ teaspoons (12 g) salt
1½ cups (360 ml) warm water (105° to 115°F/40° to 46°C)	15 ounces (430 g) bread flour
¾ ounce (22 g) fresh compressed yeast	¼ cup (60 ml) finely chopped fresh basil, loosely packed
½ teaspoon (2 g) granulated sugar	Spinach and Cheese Filling (recipe follows)
½ teaspoon (1 g) dried thyme	

1. Place all of the pre-dough ingredients in the bowl of a mixer. Stir to combine thoroughly and dissolve the yeast. Some grains of the coarse semolina will still be visible in the liquid. Cover the bowl and set aside in a warm place for a minimum of 45 minutes and no longer than 2 hours while you make the filling.

2. Add the salt to the pre-dough. Place on the mixer and mix with the dough hook attachment for 2 or 3 minutes, stopping the machine and scraping down the sides of the bowl 3 or 4 times to thoroughly dissolve the salt. Incorporate the bread flour; the dough should form a ball. Knead the dough for approximately 8 minutes, until soft and elastic.

3. Place the dough on a work surface (you should not need to use any flour) and knead in the chopped basil by hand. It will take 3 or 4 minutes to incorporate it evenly. Do not knead the basil in using the mixer or the dough will become green and sticky.

4. Return the dough to the bowl, cover, and let sit at warm room temperature for about 45 minutes or until the dough has doubled in volume.

5. Punch down and scale the dough into 2 equal pieces. Using a rolling pin and shaping the dough with your hands, form 1 piece of dough into a rectangle measuring 16 x 8 inches (40 x 20 cm).

6. Spread half of the chilled filling over the dough in an even layer, spreading it to within ½ inch (1.2 cm) of the edge on all sides. Fold the uncovered portion on the short ends of the dough rectangle in on top of the filling. Press these edges down so that the rectangle has an even thickness. Starting from the top of the rectangle (the long edge farthest away from you), roll the dough into a tight spiral, keeping the short edges lined up evenly. When you get to the bottom, pinch the seam closed as tightly as possible to prevent the filling from leaking out during baking; it is very important to get a good seal here.

7. Lightly flour the work surface and roll the loaf between your palms and the table to make it even and about 16 inches (40 cm) in length. Form and fill the second loaf in the same way.

8. Place the loaves, seam-side down, on a sheet pan lined with baking paper. Stretch the loaves a little bit as needed to keep them 16 inches (40 cm) long. Let the loaves rise to 1½ times their original size. Cut 3 slashes on top of each loaf.

9. Bake the loaves for 30 to 35 minutes at 375°F (190°C), using steam for the first 15 minutes (if your oven is not equipped with steam injectors, see page 97). The loaves should be dark golden brown. Be careful not to underbake, or the moist filling will cause the loaves to sag as they cool.

10. Let the loaves cool at room temperature. Because the filling is moist, the crust will soften as the bread cools and the steam from the filling is trapped inside. Once the bread is completely cool and the filling has solidified (this takes 45 minutes to 1 hour), it will slice easily, but if you attempt to slice it while it is still warm, you will compress the loaves, making the interior doughy and ruining the attractive spiral appearance of the filling.

SPINACH AND CHEESE FILLING
yield: 2 pounds 10 ounces (1 kg 195 g), enough for 2 loaves, 16 inches (40 cm) long

Frozen chopped spinach works fine in this recipe. If you use fresh, you will need 2 or 3 bunches, depending on their size. Cook the fresh spinach or thaw frozen spinach, weigh out the amount needed, then squeeze all of the water out and blot it dry with paper towels before adding it to the filling.

2 ounces (55 g) unsalted butter

1 medium yellow onion, finely chopped (5 ounces/140 g or about 1 cup /240 ml after chopping)

1 pound (455 g) cooked chopped spinach, thawed if frozen, blotted dry

¼ teaspoon (1 g) garlic powder

1½ teaspoons (7 g) salt

½ teaspoon (2.5 ml) freshly ground black pepper

¼ teaspoon (1 g) ground nutmeg

¼ teaspoon (1 g) dried marjoram

3 ounces (85 g) pine nuts, lightly toasted

¾ cup (180 ml) chopped fresh basil, loosely packed

6 ounces (170 g) cream cheese, at room temperature

10 ounces (285 g) mozzarella cheese, grated

1. Melt the butter in a large skillet over medium heat. Add the onions and cook, stirring from time to time, for about 5 minutes or until they are soft and translucent; do not let them brown.

2. Add the spinach to the skillet and stir to combine. Cook for 2 to 3 minutes, stirring to prevent the spinach from sticking to the skillet.

3. Place the spinach and onion mixture in a bowl and let cool to room temperature. Do not skip this cooling step, or the cheese will melt when you add it and the texture of the filling will not be as pleasant.

4. Add the remaining ingredients to the spinach and onions and mix thoroughly. Refrigerate the filling until needed.

Black Forest Bread with Cocoa and Dried Cherries

yield: 4 loaves, 1 pound 14 ounces (855 g) each

This wholesome multigrain bread takes a little longer to knead than most breads. You may find it difficult to judge when the loaves are baked through, because the bread dough is so dark to begin with. To be absolutely certain the loaves are baked, you can check the internal temperature using a thin probe-style thermometer. The temperature should read 180° to 200°F (82° to 94°C). If you do not use a thermometer and, after removing the loaves from the pans, you find that the bread is still soft on the sides or bottom, place the loaves directly on a sheet pan and return them to the oven for 5 to 10 minutes. If necessary, cover the tops of the loaves with a sheet of baking paper or foil to keep them from overbaking. Black Forest bread can also be made into freestanding loaves (baked without using bread pans). In that case, make a firmer dough, to support the shape of the loaves until the crust has formed.

I like to use European Montmorency dried cherries in this bread because of their distinctive tart flavor. Unfortunately, I sometimes have trouble getting them from the suppliers. The sweeter variety is more readily available commercially. These taste and even look like miniature prunes, and because they are about 3 times more expensive than prunes, you might as well just go ahead and use prunes, cut into smaller pieces; or try substituting dried cranberries, which taste good and are easy to come by.

10 ounces (285 g) dried cherries, preferably tart

1 cup (240 ml) apple cider

2 ounces (55 g) fresh compressed yeast

3½ cups (840 ml) warm coffee (105° to 115°F/40° to 46°C) (see Note 1)

2 tablespoons plus 2 teaspoons (40 g) salt

½ cup (120 ml) or 6 ounces (170 g) molasses

4 eggs

4 ounces (115 g) unsweetened cocoa powder

1 pound 12 ounces (795 g) high-gluten flour

5 ounces (140 g) whole wheat flour

5 ounces (140 g) pumpernickel flour

5 ounces (140 g) multigrain flour (see Note 2)

3 ounces (85 g) cornmeal

¾ cup (180 ml) vegetable oil

1 pound (455 g) high-gluten flour

> ### Small-Batch Black Forest Bread with Cocoa and Dried Cherries
>
> **yield: 2 loaves, 1 pound 8 ounces (680 g) each**
>
> 4 ounces (115 g) dried cherries, preferably tart
>
> ½ cup (120 ml) apple cider
>
> 1½ ounces (40 g) fresh compressed yeast
>
> 1½ cups (360 ml) warm coffee (105° to 115°F/40° to 46°C; see Note 1)
>
> 1 tablespoon (15 g) salt
>
> ¼ cup (60 ml) or 3 ounces (85 g) molasses
>
> 1 egg
>
> 1½ ounces (40 g) unsweetened cocoa powder
>
> 10 ounces (285 g) high-gluten flour
>
> 2 ounces (55 g) whole wheat flour
>
> 2 ounces (55 g) pumpernickel flour
>
> 2 ounces (55 g) multigrain flour (see Note 2)
>
> 1 ounce (30 g) cornmeal
>
> ¼ cup (60 ml) vegetable oil
>
> 6 ounces (170 g) high-gluten flour

1. Combine the dried cherries and apple cider and set aside for 30 minutes to soften and plump the cherries. Strain, reserving the cider and cherries separately.

2. Dissolve the yeast in the warm coffee. Add the salt, molasses, reserved apple cider, and eggs.

3. Thoroughly combine the unsweetened cocoa powder and the first measurement of high-gluten flour. Add to the coffee mixture.

4. Using the dough hook at medium speed, mix in the whole wheat flour, pumpernickel flour, multigrain flour, and the cornmeal. Add the vegetable oil and mix until incorporated.

5. Reserve a few handfuls of the remaining high-gluten flour, then add the rest to the dough. Once it is incorporated, turn the mixer to medium speed and knead for about 12 minutes. The dough should be smooth, quite soft, and elastic. Adjust by adding the reserved flour as necessary while kneading.

6. Place the dough in an oiled bowl and turn to coat it completely with oil. Cover and let rise in a warm place until doubled in volume.

7. Knead the reserved cherries into the dough by hand. Let rise again until it is doubled in volume.

8. Scale the dough into 4 pieces, 1-pound 14 ounces (855 g) each (2 pieces, 1 pound 8 ounces/680 g each for the small recipe). Form the pieces into rectangular loaves as described in "Shaping Loaves for Bread Pans," page 94; if you prefer to make freestanding loaves, see Figures 3-1 and 3-2, also on page 94.

9. Place the loaves in oiled bread pans measuring approximately 10 x 4½ x 3 inches (25 x 11.2 x 7.5 cm). Let rise until slightly less than doubled in volume.

10. Make 3 slashes lengthwise in the center of each loaf.

11. Bake at 350°F (175°C) with steam, leaving the damper closed for the first 10 minutes (If your oven is not equipped with steam injectors, see page 97.) Open the damper and continue to bake approximately 30 minutes longer or until baked through. Take the bread out of the pans as soon as possible to prevent the sides and bottom from becoming soggy from trapped moisture. Finish cooling on racks.

NOTE 1: It is not necessary to use freshly brewed coffee here. This is a good way to utilize left-over coffee (regular or decaffeinated), which would otherwise be wasted.

NOTE 2: This is a special flour containing a mixture of whole grains. It is often found in health-food stores. If it is not available, substitute an additional 2½ ounces (70 g) each of pumpernickel flour and whole wheat flour (1 ounce/30 g each for the small recipe).

Butter-Wheat Bread with Dutch Crunch Topping

yield: 6 loaves, 1 pound 4 ounces (570 g) each

This is a great way to use up puff pastry, croissant, or Danish dough scraps that might otherwise go to waste; you might call it the baker's version of rum balls. I put pieces of scrap dough in the freezer until I have enough scraps to make a batch. The scraps freeze well for several weeks. To use this dough for braiding, start with cold water, keep the dough rather firm, and, instead of letting it rise until doubled in volume, just let it relax for 10 minutes before you begin to form it.

3 ounces (85 g) fresh compressed yeast

1 quart (960 ml) warm water (105° to 115°F/40° to 46°C)

1 pound (455 g) whole wheat flour

2 pounds 8 ounces (1 kg 135 g) bread flour

3 tablespoons (45 g) salt

2 pounds (910 g) puff pastry, croissant, *or* Danish dough scraps (see Note)

Egg wash

Whole wheat flour *or* Dutch Crunch Bread Topping (optional; recipe follows)

Small-Batch Butter-Wheat Bread with Dutch Crunch Topping
yield: 2 loaves, 1 pound 4 ounces (570 g) each

1¼ ounces (35 g) fresh compressed yeast

1⅓ cups (320 ml) warm water (105° to 115°F/40° to 46°C)

5 ounces (140 g) whole wheat flour

13 ounces (370 g) bread flour

1 tablespoon (15 g) salt

11 ounces (310 g) puff pastry, croissant, *or* Danish dough scraps (see Note)

Egg wash

Whole wheat flour *or* Dutch Crunch Bread Topping (optional; recipe follows)

---

1. In a mixer bowl, dissolve the yeast in the warm water. Add the whole wheat and bread flours and mix 3 minutes on medium speed using the dough hook.

2. Add the salt and dough scraps. Knead until the dough is smooth and elastic, about 5 minutes. Add more bread flour if needed to make a medium-firm dough.

3. Place the dough on a sheet pan and let rise in a warm place, covered, until the doubled in volume, about 45 minutes.

4. Divide the dough into pieces weighing 1 pound 4 ounces (570 g), keeping them covered as you weigh them to prevent a skin from forming.

5. Knead each piece between your palm and the table until the loaf is tight and round and the dough has enough tension to spring back when pressed (see Figures 3-1 and 3-2, page 94). If kneaded too much, the skin will break, giving the loaf a ragged look.

6. After kneading each loaf, flatten it slightly with your hand, brush with egg wash, and invert it in whole wheat flour. Shake off the excess. If using Dutch Crunch topping, skip the egg wash and flour coating.

7. Place the loaves, flour-side up, on sheet pans, 4 to a pan.

8. Using a sharp paring knife, cut a fan pattern ⅛ inch (3 mm) deep by first making 1 vertical slash in the center, then 3 fanned slashes on either side, all joining at the bottom (Figure 3-5). Do not slash if using the Dutch Crunch topping.

9. Let the loaves rise until slightly less than doubled in volume. Spread the Dutch crunch topping, if using, over the proofed loaves, following the directions with the topping recipe.

10. Bake at 400°F (205°C) until the loaves have a healthy brown color and test done (they should feel light when you pick them up and sound hollow when tapped), about 50 minutes. Place on racks to cool.

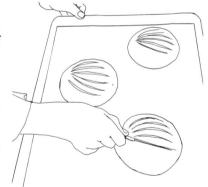

FIGURE 3-5 **Slashing the tops of the butter-wheat loaves before baking**

NOTE: If you are using all croissant and/or Danish dough scraps (no puff pastry scraps), reduce the amount of yeast in the dough by 10 percent. Conversely, if you do not have any dough scraps to use, add 1 pound (455 g) unsalted butter and an additional 10 ounces (285 g) bread flour.

DUTCH CRUNCH BREAD TOPPING yield: 2½ cups (600 ml)

If you have traveled much in Europe, you most likely have enjoyed breads or rolls with this baked-on crackled, crunchy topping. Breads baked with Dutch crunch topping are also known as *mottled bread*. These breads originated in Holland and have been popular there and in the northern part of Germany for many years. Other countries such as France and Italy have also adopted this style of bread topping.

After baking, Dutch crunch topping is similar in appearance to the short dough crust found on the Swedish pâte à choux pastries known as Maria Puffs (or Swedish Profiteroles), as well as the topping on the Swiss Triestine Bread. Another example along the same lines is the topping found on the Mexican breakfast buns known as Conchas. In each case, the topping cracks and pulls apart during the baking process due to the expansion of the product underneath, giving the finished item both an interesting and attractive appearance and an appealing contrasting crunchy texture. The topping is made in a dough form in the recipes for the profiteroles and the conchas, in which case it is rolled out or flattened, then pressed on top of the pâte à choux or the bun dough. The Triestine bread topping, like the following recipe, has the consistency of a paste, and both of these are applied with a brush. In trying to describe to my students the final appearance of the topping, I tell them it should resemble a dried-up riverbed in the middle of the summer.

2 ounces (55 g) fresh compressed yeast	8 ounces (225 g) rice flour
1 cup (240 ml) warm water	1 teaspoon (5 g) salt
1½ ounces (40 g) granulated sugar	¼ cup (60 ml) vegetable oil

1. Dissolve the yeast in the water. Stir in the sugar, rice flour, salt, and oil.

2. Cover and let rise until doubled in volume. Stir to deflate the mixture.

3. Brush or spread over proofed rolls or breads before baking (Figure 3-6). The baked loaves will have a crackled topping, as shown in the drawing.

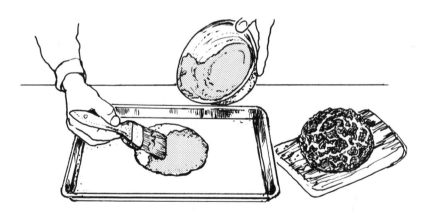

FIGURE 3-6 **Brushing the Dutch Crunch Bread Topping over a raw loaf of bread; the baked loaf with the crackled topping**

Challah yield: 5 loaves, 1 pound 8 ounces (680 g) each

This traditional Jewish egg bread is usually made in a 3-string braid when served at the Sabbath but is formed into other braids for specific holidays. The large quantity of eggs in the dough provides richness, high volume, and a long shelf life. It also gives the bread a pleasant golden color. Challah dough can be shaped following the instructions given for any of the braids described in the recipe for Braided White Bread (page 147), but keep in mind that it will rise much faster and therefore tends to dry out faster as well. After applying the egg wash, try dusting the center of the loaf with bread flour, using a small sifter so that the flour goes only in the center and the rest of the loaf keeps the shine from the egg wash. The flour will keep the strings separate during the oven-spring and give the challah an appetizing rustic look.

1½ ounces (40 g) fresh compressed yeast

1 quart (960 ml) cold milk (see Note)

1 tablespoon (15 ml) vanilla extract

3 ounces (85 g) vanilla sugar (see Note)

2 tablespoons (30 g) salt

6 whole eggs

6 egg yolks (½ cup/120 ml)

4 pounds 8 ounces (2 kg 45 g) bread flour

1 cup (240 ml) mild olive oil

Egg wash

Poppy and/or sesame seeds (optional)

Small-Batch Challah

yield: 2 loaves, 1 pound 8 ounces (680 g) each

1 ounce (30 g) fresh compressed yeast

1½ cups (360 ml) cold milk (see Note)

1 teaspoon (5 ml) vanilla extract

1 ounce (30 g) vanilla sugar (see Note)

1 tablespoon (15 g) salt

2 whole eggs

2 egg yolks

1 pound 8 ounces (680 g) bread flour

⅓ cup (80 ml) mild olive oil

Egg wash

Poppy and/or sesame seeds (optional)

---

1. Dissolve the yeast in the cold milk. Add the vanilla extract, vanilla sugar, salt, whole eggs, and egg yolks. Using the dough hook, mix in all but a few handfuls of the flour.

2. Add the olive oil and knead the dough on low speed for 15 minutes, adding the reserved flour, if necessary, to correct the consistency.

3. Cover the dough and let it rise in a warm place until it has doubled in volume.

4. Punch the dough down. Cover and let rise again until the dough doubles in volume a second time.

5. Punch the dough down and weigh it into 8-ounce (225-g) pieces.

6. Using 3 pieces for each braid, pound and roll the pieces into strings (see Figures 3-16 to 3-18, page 148), then braid them following the directions for a 3-string braid on page 150.

7. Transfer the braids to sheet pans and let them rise until they are 1½ times their original size. Brush with egg wash, then sprinkle with poppy and/or sesame seeds, if desired.

8. Bake at 350°F (175°C) for approximately 35 minutes. The loaves should be a deep golden brown and sound hollow when tapped on the bottom.

NOTE: If you do not have vanilla sugar, substitute granulated sugar and increase the vanilla extract by 1 tablespoon (15 ml) for the large recipe, 1 teaspoon (5 ml) for the small recipe.

Traditionally, challah does not contain vanilla or milk, but I find they give the bread a more well-rounded flavor and added depth. To produce a more authentic bread, use granulated sugar, omit the vanilla extract, and use water rather than milk.

Chocolate Apricot Bread yield: 3 loaves, 1 pound 6 ounces (625 g) each

Although this may not be the best choice of bread to serve on the dinner table, it is a great addition to a cheese and fruit platter and an ideal selection for a ham and cheese sandwich. Chocolate apricot bread is also the ultimate option for Chocolate Bread and Butter Pudding Kungsholm (page 769). Many other dried fruits, such as pears and cherries, can be used in combination with the dried apricots or as a substitution.

This bread is a bit difficult when it comes to judging if it is done, because the color does not give you any clue. You can check the internal temperature using a thin probe-style thermometer. The temperature will read 180° to 200°F (82° to 94°C) when the loaves are done. If you are more experienced, pick up the loaves to feel for lightness and tap them sharply on the bottom to check for a hollow sound.

2½ cups (600 ml) boiling water	1 tablespoon (15 g) salt
8 ounces (225 g) dried apricots	8 ounces (225 g) sweet dark chocolate, melted
2 ounces (55 g) fresh compressed yeast	
⅓ cup (80 ml) or 4 ounces (115 g) honey	Bread flour
1 pound 12 ounces (795 g) bread flour	

1. Pour the boiling water over the apricots and set aside for 30 minutes to soften.

2. Drain the apricots, reserving the water in a bowl. Cut the apricots into large chunks, reserve.

3. Make a sponge by dissolving the yeast in the water drained from the apricots (first warm it to 105° to 115°F/40° to 46°C if it has cooled beyond that point), then mixing in the honey and half of the bread flour until the mixture is smooth. Cover and allow to rise until more than doubled in volume.

4. Place the sponge in a mixer bowl. Add the salt, melted chocolate, and all but a handful of the remaining bread flour. Scrape down the sides of the bowl and knead with the dough hook for 8 to 10 minutes, adjusting the consistency by adding the reserved flour, if necessary. The dough should be soft and glutenous. Add the reserved apricots, mixing just long enough to incorporate them.

5. Cover the dough and let it rise in a warm place until it has doubled in volume.

6. Divide the dough into 3 equal pieces, about 1 pound 6 ounces (625 g) each. Form the pieces into oval loaves (see Figure 3-13, page 143). Place the loaves on sheet pans lined with baking paper. Brush water lightly over the top of the loaves, then dust with bread flour. Let rise until 1½ times the original size.

7. Make 3 slashes lengthwise on the top of each loaf (see Figure 3-14, page 143). Bake at 375°F (190°C) for approximately 40 minutes or until baked through.

Dill Bread with Quark Cheese yield: 3 loaves, 1 pound 8 ounces (680 g) each

I was somewhat surprised at the enthusiastic reception this bread received when I first made it with my class. The student who baked the first batch was quite proud when the three loaves he produced disappeared rather quickly.

Dill plays a big role in Scandinavian cooking and, to some degree, in the cuisine of many German-speaking countries as well. It is most often associated with seafood presentations; however, dill is also used in the Swedish kitchen to flavor lamb and veal dishes. The popularity of dill in Scandinavia can be compared to that of rosemary in Southern Europe. Its decorative, feathery green fronds dot the famous Swedish Smörgåsbord, and it is a must when cooking crawfish (crawdads). For crawfish, the crown containing the seeds must also be included to obtain the proper flavor.

As you might guess, this bread is a wonderful accompaniment to seafood and is especially good with smoked fish.

8 ounces (225 g) fresh yellow onions	1 ounce (30 g) granulated sugar
¾ cup (180 ml) olive oil	3 eggs
3 tablespoons (10 g) dried dill weed	6 ounces (170 g) quark or cottage cheese
4 teaspoons (20 g) salt	2 pounds 10 ounces (1 kg 195 g) bread flour
1½ ounces (40 g) fresh compressed yeast	
1½ cups (360 ml) warm water (105° to 115°F/40° to 46°C)	

1. Peel the onions and chop into small pieces. Sauté the onions in a small portion of the olive oil until they are soft. Remove from the heat and add the remaining oil, the dried dill, and the salt; reserve.

2. In a mixer bowl, dissolve the yeast in the warm water, then add the granulated sugar, eggs, and quark or cottage cheese. Using the dough hook, incorporate enough of the bread flour to form a soft dough.

3. Add the reserved onion mixture and adjust the consistency by adding enough of the remaining flour to make a fairly firm dough. Knead at medium speed for 8 to 10 minutes; the dough should be elastic but not sticky. Cover and set aside in a warm place until it is doubled in volume.

4. Punch the dough down, cover, and allow to proof a second time until doubled in volume.

5. Divide the dough into 3 pieces, approximately 1 pound 8 ounces (680 g) each. Shape the pieces into smooth, round loaves (see Figures 3-1 and 3-2, page 94). Allow the loaves to rise until slightly less than doubled in volume.

6. Bake at 400°F (205°C), using steam for the first 10 minutes. Open the damper to remove the steam and continue baking approximately 20 minutes longer. The loaves should feel light and sound hollow when tapped sharply on the bottom. Let cool completely before slicing.

NOTE: If your oven is not equipped with steam injectors, see "Creating Steam Without Steam Injectors," page 97.

Farmer's Rye Rings yield: 4 loaves, 1 pound 3 ounces (540 g) each

As late as just a century ago, rye bread was a significant part of the peasant diet in Northern Europe. Not only is rye easier to grow in poor soil than other grains, it retains moisture better, which made it possible to store the breads longer. A hearty slice of rye bread blended well with the simple peasant fare. Preparing the loaves in a ring shape had a practical purpose in the old days. The rings could be hung up high on dowels, where they stayed dry and were protected from pests. Today, the design is more an aesthetic touch than anything else.

The protein in rye flour forms a weak gluten structure. Therefore, unless you want a dense, flat bread, the amount of rye flour in any rye bread dough should not exceed 30 to 35 percent of the total flour weight. The following recipe contains 32 percent rye flour. This lack of gluten-producing help from the rye flour gives extra responsibility to the wheat flour, so it is especially important to pay close attention to the dough's temperature and consistency.

2 ounces (55 g) fresh compressed yeast	1 pound (455 g) medium rye flour
1 quart (960 ml) warm milk (105° to 115°F/40° to 46°C)	8 ounces (225 g) whole wheat flour
2 tablespoons (30 ml) white vinegar	1 pound 10 ounces (740 g) bread flour
3 tablespoons (45 ml) or 2 ounces (55 g) honey	Water
2 tablespoons (30 g) salt	Medium rye flour

1. Dissolve the yeast in the warm milk in a mixer bowl. Add the vinegar, honey, and salt. Mix in the rye and whole wheat flours using the dough hook.

2. Reserve one handful of the bread flour. Mix in the remainder and knead for 4 to 5 minutes until you have a smooth, elastic dough. Adjust the consistency, if required, by adding the reserved flour.

3. Place the dough in an oiled bowl, turn to coat both sides with oil, cover, and let rise in a warm place until it has doubled in volume.

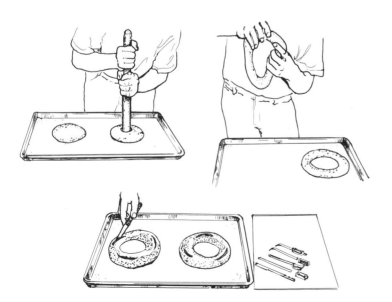

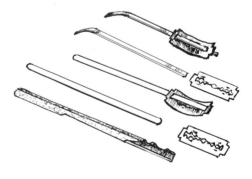

FIGURE 3-7 **Making the hole in the center of a loaf for Farmer's Rye Rings; stretching the ring to enlarge the hole; slashing the top of the loaves; the various tools used to slash bread loaves**

4. Punch down the dough. Divide into 4 equal pieces, approximately 1 pound 3 ounces (540 g) each. Form the pieces into tight, round loaves (see Figures 3-1 and 3-2, page 94). Flatten the loaves to about 1½ inches (3.7 cm).

5. Using a thick dowel, make a hole in the center of each loaf, cutting all the way through the dough. (The original technique for making the holes was to use your bare elbow; feel free to try this approach if it seems appropriate in your workplace.) Let the rings relax for a few minutes, then widen the holes by placing your fingers in the center and stretching the dough around the holes until the opening is approximately 6 inches (15 cm) in diameter.

6. Place the rings on sheet pans lined with baking paper. Spray or brush with water. Dust the top of the rings with enough rye flour to cover. Let rise until doubled in volume.

7. Using a sharp knife, make 3 evenly spaced slashes on top of each ring (Figure 3-7).

8. Bake at 425°F (219°C) with steam, leaving the damper closed for the first 10 minutes. Open the damper and bake approximately 20 minutes longer or until baked through.

N O T E : If your oven is not equipped with steam injectors, see "Creating Steam Without Steam Injectors," page 97.

Garlic-Herb Bread yield: 6 loaves, 1 pound 2 ounces (510 g) each

This is one of the most popular breads that I make with my students. Everyone loves the wonderful aroma and flavor of garlic. California produces 80 percent of the garlic grown in the United States. The annual garlic festival held in Gilroy, California (just south of San Francisco), draws tens of thousands of garlic worshipers eager to sample not only savory dishes but such oddities as garlic ice cream and garlic-flavored chocolate mousse.

2 ounces (55 g) minced fresh garlic (about 10 medium cloves)

3 tablespoons (45 ml) olive oil

2 ounces (55 g) fresh compressed yeast

1 quart (960 ml) warm water (105° to 115°F/40° to 46°C)

2 egg whites (¼ cup/60 ml)

2 ounces (55 g) unsalted butter, at room temperature

2 ounces (55 g) granulated sugar

4 tablespoons (60g) salt

2½ tablespoons (15 g) ground dried oregano

2½ tablespoons (15 g) ground dried basil

4 pounds 4 ounces (1 kg 935 g) bread flour

Water

Whole wheat flour

Small-Batch Garlic-Herb Bread
yield: 3 loaves, 1 pound 2 ounces (510 g) each

1 ounce (30 g) minced fresh garlic (about 5 medium cloves)

1½ tablespoons (22 ml) olive oil

1¼ ounces (35 g) fresh compressed yeast

1 pint (480 ml) warm water (105° to 115°F/40° to 46°C)

1 egg white

1 ounce (30 g) unsalted butter, at room temperature

1 ounce (30 g) granulated sugar

2 tablespoons (30 g) salt

4 teaspoons (8 g) ground dried oregano

4 teaspoons (8 g) ground dried basil

2 pounds 2 ounces (970 g) bread flour

Water

Whole wheat flour

About Garlic

The history of the bulb dates back to ancient times, when it was treasured as a medicine and an antidote to poison. In folklore, garlic is used to repel vampires. The Egyptians fed garlic to the slaves who built the pyramids with the idea that it would increase their strength. Research continues to this day regarding garlic's healing capacity. Some people believe garlic has antibacterial properties and, because it thins the blood and slows clotting, it may be useful for some heart conditions. Garlic is rich in minerals and vitamins C and B₁. Garlic was introduced to Europe from the Middle East during the Crusades in the eleventh century. Today it is popular all over the world, with the major exceptions of Japan, Scandinavia, and, to some degree, England.

1. Sauté the garlic in olive oil over low heat to soften the flavor; do not allow the garlic to brown. If the garlic is very strong, reduce the amount. Set the cooked garlic in the oil aside to cool.

2. Dissolve the yeast in the warm water. Stir in the egg whites, butter, sugar, salt, oregano, basil, cooked garlic, and all but a few ounces of the bread flour. Using the dough hook on medium speed, knead the dough, adding the reserved bread flour as required, until the dough is fairly stiff and smooth.

3. Place the dough in an oiled bowl, turn to coat both sides with oil, cover, and let rise for 1 hour.

4. Punch down the dough and divide into 6 equal pieces (3 for the smaller recipe), approximately 1 pound 2 ounces (510 g) each. Shape each piece into a round loaf (see Figures 3-1 and 3-2, page 94). Starting with the loaf formed first, shape each into a tight oval loaf. The loaves should spring back when pressed lightly.

5. Place the loaves seam-side down on sheet pans lined with baking paper. Brush with water and sprinkle lightly with whole wheat flour. Make diagonal slashes across each loaf, about ¼ inch (6 mm) deep. Let rise until doubled in volume.

6. Bake at 375°F (190°C) for about 30 minutes. Cool on racks.

Honey-Wheat Bread   yield: 4 loaves, 1 pound 4 ounces (570g) each

The combination of whole wheat and honey produces a wonderful, richly flavored bread that I frequently enjoyed as a child with nothing more than a spread of comb honey on top. As a variation, try substituting molasses for the honey in this recipe. It produces a heartier, more robust loaf. You can also add ⅓ cup (80 ml) chopped fresh parsley and 1 tablespoon (15 ml) chopped fresh rosemary (with either the honey or the molasses variation) for an herb bread that is delicious, especially with lamb dishes. Use a medium grade of whole wheat flour or, if not available, a coarse flour will do. Finely milled whole wheat flour will not produce the proper texture.

About Honey

Honey has been used as a sweetener in cooking far longer than sugar. Before the nineteenth century, sugar was considered a luxury for the masses, and honey was one of the most commonly used substitutes. As is true with molasses and other sweetening agents, the darker the color of the honey, the stronger the flavor. There are hundreds of types of honey; most are named for the flower from which the honey derives its fragrance. Two of the most common varieties in the United States are clover and orange blossom. Most types of honey are interchangeable, with the exception of the most strongly scented.

1¾ cups (420 ml) milk

4 teaspoons (20 g) salt

1 cup (240 ml) or 12 ounces (340 g) honey

7 ounces (200 g) unsalted butter, at room temperature

1 ounce (30 g) fresh compressed yeast

1 cup (240 ml) warm water (105° to 115°F/40° to 46°C)

1 pound 4 ounces (570 g) whole wheat flour

1 pound 4 ounces (570 g) bread flour

Egg wash

Wheat bran

1. In a small saucepan, combine the milk, salt, honey, and butter. Heat to 115°F (46°C), then set aside.

2. In a mixer bowl, dissolve the yeast in the warm water. Add the milk mixture, the whole wheat flour, and all but a handful of the bread flour. Knead, using the dough hook at low speed, until the dough has developed a smooth, elastic, glutinous consistency. Add the reserved bread flour while kneading if necessary.

3. Cover the dough and let rise in a warm place until it has doubled in volume.

4. Punch the dough down, cover again , and proof a second time until doubled in volume.

5. Punch the dough down and scale into 4 equal pieces, approximately 1 pound 4 ounces (570 g) each.

6. Form each piece into an oval loaf (see Figure 3-13, page 143). Brush egg wash on the loaves, then invert them in wheat bran. Place them, bran-side up, on sheet pans.

7. Let the loaves rise until they have slightly less than doubled in volume.

8. Using a sharp knife or a razor blade, slash 3 deep lines lengthwise on each loaf (see Figure 3-14, page 143).

9. Bake at 400°F (205°C), using steam and leaving the damper closed for 10 minutes. Open the damper and continue baking approximately 30 minutes longer or until dark golden brown and baked through.

NOTE: If your oven is not equipped with steam injectors, see "Creating Steam Without Steam Injectors," page 97.

Italian Easter Bread   yield: 4 loaves, 1 pound 2 ounces (510 g) each

This sweet Italian bread, also called *Columba Pasquale* or *Easter Doves*, is made from a dough very much like panettone. The shape, however, differs a great deal. Veiled with crystallized sugar and studded with whole almonds, these loaves are formed to resemble a dove in flight.

As is often the case when one travels far back in history, several stories can be found regarding the origin of this bread. One places it in Milan around 1176 and says the bread was created to celebrate a victory over a Roman general. Another story says the Columba was first made in the city of Pavia during the conquest over Albion. A woman who had been captured made a sweet bread in the shape of a dove to symbolize peace. When the bread was brought to the villain who had abducted her, he was so touched he granted her freedom.

Today, Columba Pasquale is offered in bakeries at Easter. Special baking pans are available to shape the dough into a rounded cross design. It is important that this bread is allowed to proof long enough to be light and airy; compared to a standard bread, it would actually be considered overproofed.

10 ounces (285 g) whole blanched almonds	½ teaspoon (2.5 ml) *fiori di sicilia or* orange flower water
2 ounces (55 g) fresh compressed yeast	3 ounces (85 g) granulated sugar
1¼ cups (300 ml) warm milk (105° to 115°F/40° to 46°C)	Grated zest of 1 lemon
1½ tablespoons (22 g) salt	6 ounces (170 g) candied orange peel, finely diced
1 pound 8 ounces (680 g) bread flour	Simple syrup
7 ounces (200 g) unsalted butter, at room temperature	Granulated sugar
10 egg yolks (⅞ cup/210 ml)	Powdered sugar

1. Reserve 32 almonds to use for decoration. Lightly toast the remaining almonds, chop finely, and reserve separately.

2. Dissolve the yeast in the warm milk. Add the salt and approximately two-thirds of the flour, or enough for a soft, spongelike consistency. Mix until smooth. Cover the sponge and let rise in a warm place until it has doubled in volume.

3. Mix the butter and the remaining flour into the sponge. Knead with the dough hook at medium speed until the dough is smooth and elastic, approximately 10 minutes.

4. Combine the egg yolks, fiori di sicilia or orange flower water, and sugar. Incorporate this mixture into the dough in 4 additions, letting the dough completely absorb each portion before adding the next. Add additional flour if required to make a fairly soft but workable dough.

5. Combine the lemon zest, candied orange peel, and reserved chopped almonds. Mix into the dough. Place the dough in an oiled bowl, turn to coat with oil, cover, and let rise in a warm place for 1 hour, punching the dough down twice during that period.

6. Divide the dough into 8 equal pieces, approximately 9 ounces (255 g) each. Working with 2 pieces at a time, pound and roll them into 8-inch (20-cm) ropes (see Figures 3-16 to 3-18, page 148), not tapered on the ends but shaped instead like sausages.

7. Place 1 piece on a sheet pan lined with baking paper. Using the side of your hand, make an indentation across and slightly off center. Lay the second piece in the indentation and bend

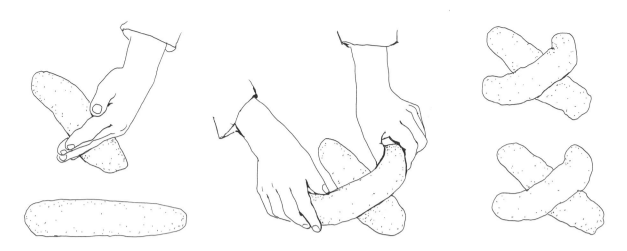

FIGURE 3-8 Using the edge of the hand to make an indentation across a dough rope; placing the second rope in the indentation and bending the ends back slightly; the formed Easter Doves before baking

both ends back slightly to form the wings of the dove (Figure 3-8). Repeat with the remaining pieces to form 3 more loaves. Let the loaves rise until doubled in volume.

8. Brush the top and sides of the loaves with simple syrup. Sprinkle with granulated sugar, then dust heavily with powdered sugar. Place 8 almonds, evenly spaced, on the top of each loaf, pressing them in so they adhere tightly.

9. Bake at 375°F (190°C) for about 20 minutes or until baked through. Remove the loaves from the pans and cool on racks.

Multigrain Bread with Walnuts yield: 3 loaves, 1 pound 10 ounces (740 g) each

Toasted walnuts set this bread apart from the run-of-the-mill health-food breads that are found everywhere these days—many of which, unfortunately, sound more interesting than they taste. The instructions call for making fairly large loaves, so you can still form two normal-sized loaves from half of the recipe. Because of its high sugar content, this bread proofs very slowly. Do not worry; just be patient (see Chef's Tip). The higher proportion of sugar makes this multigrain bread a great match for smoked meats and fish.

10 ounces (285 g) walnuts	4 teaspoons (20 g) salt
2 ounces (55 g) fresh compressed yeast	4 ounces (115 g) rolled oats
1¾ cups (420 ml) warm water (105° to 115°F/40° to 46°C)	4 ounces (115 g) coarse rye flour (pumpernickel flour)
4 ounces (115 g) light brown sugar	4 ounces (115 g) wheat bran
⅓ cup (80 ml) or 4 ounces (115 g) honey	1 pound 12 ounces (795 g) high-gluten flour
¾ cup (180 ml) buttermilk	Olive oil

If you have reason to believe that something other than the high sugar content and/or the cold liquid is keeping the dough from rising (for example, you may have let the dough get too hot), you can do a quick test to see if the yeast is still viable. Take a small piece of dough and shape it into a ring. Place the dough ring in a bowl of warm water, no hotter than 115°F (46°C). The dough ring will sink to the bottom of the bowl. If it remains on the bottom of the bowl after 10 minutes, the yeast is dead. If the yeast is growing, the dough ring will float near the top of the water after 10 minutes time. If the dough does not pass the test, you will know to start over and not waste anymore time waiting for the dough to progress.

1. Chop the walnuts coarsely without crushing. Toast lightly and reserve.

2. In a mixer bowl, dissolve the yeast in the warm water. Mix in the brown sugar, honey, buttermilk, and salt. Incorporate the rolled oats, rye flour, wheat bran, and most of the high-gluten flour; reserve a handful or so to add if necessary as you knead the dough. Knead at low speed using the dough hook for 5 minutes. Add the chopped walnuts and the reserved flour, if necessary, and continue kneading until the dough is smooth and elastic, 5 to 7 minutes longer.

3. Cover the dough and let rise in a warm place until it has doubled in volume.

4. Scale the dough into 3 equal pieces, approximately 1 pound 10 ounces (740 g) each. Form the pieces into round loaves (see Figures 3-1 and 3-2, page 94). Place the loaves on sheet pans and let rise until they have slightly less than doubled in volume.

5. Bake at 375°F (190°C) for approximately 40 minutes or until golden brown and baked through. Brush olive oil over the loaves as soon as they are removed from the oven.

Potato Bread yield: 4 loaves, 1 pound 2 ounces (510 g) each

This is another peasant-style bread, distinctive in its use of potatoes, which keep the dough nice and moist and contribute a pleasingly chewy texture. Because of the moisture, the baked loaves stay fresh longer than other breads. If you are not in a hurry, try Rosemary-Potato Bread (page 137). It requires slow rising—overnight in the refrigerator—but is well worth the wait.

SPONGE

1 cup warm water (105° to 115°F/40° to 46°C)

2 tablespoons (30 ml) or 1½ ounces (40 g) light corn syrup

½ ounce (15 g) fresh compressed yeast

8 ounces (225 g) bread flour

DOUGH

10 ounces (285 g) russet potatoes

2 ounces (55 g) fresh compressed yeast

1 pint (480 ml) warm milk (105° to 115°F/40° to 46°C)

1½ tablespoons (22 g) salt

1 ounce (30 g) granulated malt extract *or* 3 tablespoons (45 ml) or 2 ounces (55 g) honey

6 ounces (170 g) whole wheat flour

1 pound 14 ounces (855 g) bread flour

Egg wash

1. Combine the water and corn syrup and dissolve the yeast in the liquid.

2. Add the bread flour and mix until you have a very soft, smooth sponge.

3. Cover and let rise in a warm place until the sponge starts to fall.

TO MAKE THE DOUGH

1. Peel, cook, and mash the potatoes. Set aside to cool.

2. Dissolve the yeast in the warm milk. Add the salt, malt extract or honey, and the whole wheat flour. Mix the mashed potatoes and the sponge into the dough.

3. Reserve a handful of the bread flour, then mix in the remainder. Knead with the dough hook for about 8 minutes at medium speed, then adjust with the reserved flour if necessary. The dough will be smooth and elastic but not sticky. Cover the dough and let rest for 1 hour in a warm place, punching it down after 30 minutes.

4. Divide the dough into 4 equal pieces, approximately 1 pound 2 ounces (510 g) each. Pound each piece into a tapered oval loaf about 10 inches (25 cm) long (see Figure 3-13, page 143). The loaves should be thicker in the center and thinner on the ends.

5. Brush the loaves with egg wash, invert in whole wheat flour, and place right-side up on sheet pans lined with baking paper. Let the loaves rise until slightly less than doubled in volume.

6. With a sharp knife, make 3 slashes at a 45-degree angle across each loaf. Cut deep enough to go through the skin only.

7. Bake at 400°F (205°C), using steam and leaving the damper closed for the first 10 minutes. Open the damper and continue baking approximately 20 minutes longer.

NOTE: If your oven is not equipped with steam injectors, see "Creating Steam Without Steam Injectors," page 97.

Pullman Loaves

yield: 2 loaves, 4 × 4 × 16 inches (10 × 10 × 40 cm) each, or 3 loaves, 4 × 4 × 12 inches (10 × 10 × 30 cm) each

In lending his name to the Pullman railroad car, George Pullman inspired the name for this bread, so dubbed because of the loaf's resemblance to the long box shape of the car. The basic difference between a regular loaf of bread and a pullman loaf is that pullman loaves are baked in pans that are enclosed on all sides so the top of the loaf is flat rather than rounded. The top of the pan slides into place after the dough is put inside. Pullman bread pans have a larger capacity than the average bread pan. Pullman loaves are used primarily for sandwiches or toast in commercial food establishments.

If you do not have pans of the precise size specified here, adjust the amount of dough used accordingly. Because the dough cannot escape from the enclosed pan, you will be able to determine quite easily if you use too much by the dead dough trapped under the lid. This can also happen to a properly scaled loaf during the oven-spring if the bread has been overproofed.

SPONGE	DOUGH
2 ounces (55 g) fresh compressed yeast	2 ounces (55 g) dry milk powder
2½ cups (600 ml) warm water (105° to 115°F/40° to 46°C)	1½ cups (360 ml) warm water (105° to 115°F/40° to 46°C)
1 ounce (30 g) granulated malt extract *or* 3 tablespoons (45 ml) or 2 ounces (55 g) honey	2 ounces (55 g) granulated sugar
2 pounds (910 g) bread flour	2 tablespoons (30 g) salt
Melted unsalted butter	1 pound 8 ounces (680 g) bread flour
	3 ounces (85 g) unsalted butter, at room temperature

I. To make the sponge, dissolve the yeast in the first measurement of warm water. Add the malt extract or honey and the first measurement of bread flour. Mix for a few minutes until you have a smooth dough. Cover and let rise in a warm place until the sponge starts to fall.

2. Butter the inside and the underside of the lids of 2 pullman loaf pans measuring 4 x 4 x 16 inches (10 x 10 x 40 cm), 3 pans measuring 4 x 4 x 12 inches (10 x 10 x 30 cm), or other suitable bread pans (see Note).

3. To make the dough, dissolve the milk powder in the remaining warm water. Add the granulated sugar, salt, the prepared sponge, and all but a handful of the remaining bread flour. Incorporate the soft butter. Knead the dough with the dough hook for approximately 8 minutes, adjusting the consistency by adding the reserved flour, if necessary, to develop a soft but not sticky dough. Cover and let the dough rise until it has doubled in volume.

4. Divide the dough into 2 equal pieces, approximately 3 pounds (1 kg 365 g) each, for the larger loaves, or 3 equal pieces, approximately 2 pounds (910 g) each, for the smaller loaves. Form each piece into a tight round loaf (see Figures 3-1 and 3-2, page 94). Allow the loaves to relax on the table for a few minutes.

5. Form the loaves into thick ropes the length of the pans, using the same technique as for shaping baguettes (see Figures 3-16 to 3-18, page 148), but do not taper the ends. Place the ropes in the pans. Slide the tops of the pans in place, leaving them partially open so you will be able to check the loaves as they proof. Let proof until doubled in volume; the pans should be approximately three-quarters full.

6. Close the tops of the pans. Bake the loaves at 400°F (205°C) for 30 minutes. Slide the tops of the pans open partially to allow steam to escape. If the top sticks, bake a few minutes longer, then remove the tops completely. Remember that for every 1 pound (455 g) of bread dough, 2 ounces (55 g) are lost in steam during baking. Continue baking 15 minutes longer or until the loaves are baked through. Turn the loaves out onto a rack and let cool completely before slicing.

NOTE: Instead of pullman pans, you can use regular bread pans and cover the tops with a flat sheet pan as a lid. Weigh the pan down with a minimum of 16 pounds (7 kg 280 g) of weight on top to prevent the dough from seeping out during the oven-spring. Two 8-pound (3-kg 640-g) weights from a balance scale are a good choice.

Pumpernickel Bread yield: 4 loaves, I pound 8 ounces (680 g) each

This is my version of the well-known German dark bread. The name *pumpernickel* comes from two German words. The first, *pumper*, means "to break wind," and the second, *nickel*, which means "demon," are probably both references to the old-fashioned pumpernickel bread, which was unleavened, dense, and slightly sour. The small amount of yeast added to this recipe gives the bread a lighter texture, but it will still take much longer to proof than other breads. Pumpernickel bread is wonderful with cheese, especially a sharp cheese like Stilton or a sharp white cheddar.

1 ounce (30 g) fresh compressed yeast	1 pound (455 g) Sourdough Starter (page 106)
3 cups (720 ml) warm water (105° to 115°F/40° to 46°C)	3 tablespoons (24 g) caraway seeds
2 tablespoons (30 g) salt	1 pound 12 ounces (795 g) coarse rye flour (pumpernickel flour)
⅓ cup (80 ml) Caramel Coloring (page 8)	2 pounds (910 g) bread flour

I. In a mixer bowl, dissolve the yeast in the warm water. Add the salt and caramel coloring and mix to combine.

2. Incorporate the sourdough starter, caraway seeds, and rye flour. Reserve a few handfuls of the bread flour and knead in the remaining flour using the dough hook. Continue kneading the dough, adding the reserved flour as required, for approximately 8 minutes. The dough should be smooth yet somewhat sticky.

3. Place the dough, covered, in a warm place and let rise until it has doubled in volume.

4. Punch the dough down, cover, and let rise again until it has doubled in volume.

5. Scale the dough into 4 equal pieces, approximately 1 pound 8 ounces (680 g) each. Line the insides of 4 loaf pans (approximately 10 x 4 x 3 inches/25 x 10 x 7.5 cm) with baking paper (see Figures 1-22 and 1-23, page 56), or brush the pans with Butter and Flour Mixture (page 7). Fold the dough pieces into tight rectangles that will fit inside the pans. Place the dough in the pans, seam-side down, and let rise until the loaves have doubled in volume.

6. Bake at 350°F (175°C) for approximately 45 minutes or until baked through. The baked loaves should feel light when you pick them up and sound hollow when tapped sharply on the bottom. Turn out onto a cooling rack immediately.

NOTE: To make this recipe without a sourdough starter, see page 130.

PUMPERNICKEL BREAD WITHOUT A SOURDOUGH STARTER

Substitute the following for the 1 pound (455 g) sourdough starter called for in the recipe. The bread will not have the same flavor but will suffice.

1 ounce (30 g) fresh compressed yeast

1 cup (240 ml) warm water (110° to 115°F/40° to 46°C)

1 teaspoon (5 ml) Caramel Coloring (page 8)

1 teaspoon (5 ml) distilled white vinegar

8 ounces (225 g) bread flour

1. Dissolve the yeast in the warm water (see Note). Add the caramel coloring and vinegar. Using the dough hook, knead in the bread flour. Continue kneading until the sponge is smooth, approximately 10 minutes. The sponge will be quite soft, which helps the yeast react more rapidly.

2. Place the sponge, covered, in a warm place and let rise until it bubbles and starts to fall.

NOTE: For a much better flavor, start with cold water and let the sponge rise, covered, overnight in the refrigerator.

Russian Rolled-Wheat Bread yield: 4 loaves, 1 pound 4 ounces (570 g) each

This robust Russian peasant bread is one of my personal favorites, probably because it is one of the breads I ate while I was growing up. We called it *Ryskt Matbröd*, and it was very popular in Sweden at that time. Try serving Russian rolled-wheat bread spread with sweet butter and topped with Swedish *herrgårdsost* cheese (roughly translated, "estate or mansion cheese") or fontina cheese.

This bread is made using the scalding method: Boiling water is poured over the grain and the mixture left to sit overnight. This allows the grain to absorb the maximum amount of moisture and ensures the bread will stay moist longer.

A special cutter is available to mark the decorative pattern on the top of the loaves. It can be purchased from bakery suppliers.

2 cups (480 ml) water

½ cup (120 ml) or 6 ounces (170 g) light corn syrup

9 ounces (255 g) rolled wheat

2 cups (480 ml) warm water (105° to 115°F/40° to 46°C)

2½ ounces (70 g) fresh compressed yeast

1 tablespoon plus 2 teaspoons (25 g) salt

2 ounces (55 g) unsalted butter, at room temperature

8 ounces (225 g) whole wheat flour

2 pounds (910 g) bread flour

Egg wash

Rolled wheat

> *Small-Batch Russian Rolled-Wheat Bread*
>
> **yield: 2 loaves, 1 pound 4 ounces (570 g) each**
>
> 1 cup (240 ml) water
>
> ¼ cup (60 ml) or 3 ounces (85 g) light corn syrup
>
> 4½ ounces (130 g) rolled wheat
>
> 1 cup (240 ml) warm water (105° to 115°F/40° to 46°C)
>
> 1½ ounces (40 g) fresh compressed yeast
>
> 2 teaspoons (10 g) salt
>
> 1 ounce (30 g) unsalted butter, at room temperature
>
> 4 ounces (115 g) whole wheat flour
>
> 1 pound (455 g) bread flour
>
> Egg wash
>
> Rolled wheat

1. Heat the first measurement of water and the corn syrup to boiling; pour over the rolled wheat. Do not stir. Let stand overnight.

2. Pour the second measurement of warm water into a mixer bowl, add the yeast, and mix to dissolve. Add the rolled-wheat mixture, salt, butter, whole wheat flour, and all but a handful of the bread flour. Knead the mixture with the dough hook at medium speed for 6 to 8 minutes, adding the reserved handful of bread flour if needed to make a smooth, elastic dough. Let the dough rest, covered, in a warm place for 30 minutes.

3. Divide the dough into 4 equal pieces (2 for the smaller recipe), approximately 1 pound 4 ounces (570 g) each. Shape each piece into a smooth, round loaf (see Figures 3-1 and 3-2, page 94). Flatten lightly with your hand. Place the loaves on sheet pans lined with baking paper.

4. Brush egg wash over the loaves and sprinkle rolled wheat on top. Using a 3-inch (7.5-cm) plain cookie cutter, cut a circle ⅛ inch (3 mm) deep in the center of each loaf. Cut about 10 slashes to the same depth radiating from the circle (Figure 3-9). Let the loaves rise until they are slightly less than doubled in volume.

5. Bake at 400°F (205°C) for approximately 35 minutes. Place on racks to cool.

FIGURE 3-9 **Slashing lines on the top of Russian Rolled Wheat loaves before proofing**

CHEF'S TIP
This bread can be made with good results even if the resting time in Step 1 is reduced to 3 or 4 hours. The loaves will just not be as moist as they would be if the rolled wheat were given the full length of time to absorb the maximum amount of liquid.

Swedish Joggar Bread yield: 4 loaves, 1 pound 7 ounces (655 g) each

The name of this bread is a good example of how the English language is infiltrating Sweden. *Joggar* is the adopted Swedish word for "jogger." I have to admit it sounds more appealing than the proper Swedish word *lunka*, meaning "to run slowly at a steady pace." On a trip to China several years ago, I was doing my best to keep up with my exercise program by running when I had a chance. During one of these sessions, I happened to be wearing a Swedish t-shirt that had been given to me by a company that produces bread mixes. It said "Joggar Bröd" in big letters across the front. I was in a rural part of China where very few people spoke English, so I got a big kick out of it when an older Chinese gentleman looked at me running along, read my t-shirt, and said very carefully with a smile, "Jogger: running slowly!"

This bread is appropriately named, as it tastes great and is rich in fiber and carbohydrates, our bodies' preferred energy source.

1 cup (240 ml) warm water (105° to 115°F/40° to 46°C)

2 cups (480 ml) warm milk (105° to 115°F/40° to 46°C)

2 ounces (55 g) fresh compressed yeast

2 eggs

¼ cup (60 ml) or 3 ounces (85 g) honey

¼ cup (60 ml) or 3 ounces (85 g) molasses

2 tablespoons (30 g) salt

3 ounces (85 g) unprocessed wheat bran

6 ounces (170 g) cornmeal

4 ounces (115 g) rolled wheat

1 pound (455 g) whole wheat flour

3 ounces (85 g) unsalted butter, at room temperature

1 pound 8 ounces (680 g) bread flour

Water

Whole wheat flour

1. Combine the water and milk in a mixer bowl. Add the yeast and mix to dissolve.

2. Combine the eggs, honey, and molasses. Add to the liquid in the bowl, together with the salt, bran, cornmeal, rolled wheat, and whole wheat flour.

3. Using the dough hook, knead in the butter and the bread flour at medium speed, adjusting the amount of bread flour as necessary for a fairly stiff dough. Continue kneading until the dough is smooth and elastic, approximately 8 minutes.

4. Place the dough in an oiled bowl, turn to coat both sides with oil, cover, and let rise until doubled in volume.

5. Punch the dough down, then cover and let rise a second time until doubled in volume.

6. Punch the dough down and divide into 4 equal pieces, approximately 1 pound 7 ounces (655 g) each. Form the pieces into round loaves (see Figures 3-1 and 3-2, page 94). Flatten the loaves lightly. Spray or brush with water, then sprinkle enough whole wheat flour over the loaves to cover the tops.

7. Place on sheet pans lined with baking paper. Slash the tops of the loaves, cutting just deep enough to penetrate the skin, making a series of parallel lines approximately ¾ inch (2 cm) apart, first in one direction, then at a 45-degree angle, to create a diamond pattern (Figure 3-10). Let rise until slightly less than doubled in volume.

8. Bake at 400°F (205°C), using steam and leaving the damper closed for the first 10 minutes. Open the damper and bake approximately 30 minutes longer or until the loaves are baked through.

NOTE: If your oven is not equipped with steam injectors, see "Creating Steam Without Steam Injectors," page 97.

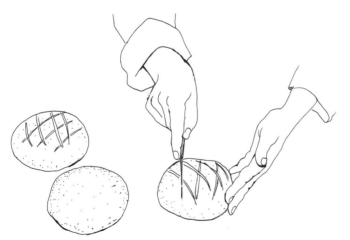

FIGURE 3-10 **Slashing the top of Joggar Bread loaves with 2 sets of parallel lines to form a diamond pattern**

Onion-Walnut Bread yield: 6 loaves, 1 pound 5 ounces (595 g) each

The Spanish introduced both yellow onions and walnuts to California in the 1700s. Today, California produces about 90 percent of the world's supply of the most common commercial walnut, the English variety.

Through the interaction of the tannin in their skins with the other ingredients and the metal in the mixing bowl, walnuts create a lavender-colored dough. If this is not desired, add the walnuts at the end, after most of the kneading is done. A stainless-steel bowl will also minimize the coloring. These loaves are proofed in round bannetons to mark a ring pattern. In the absence of these, follow the alternate directions in the Note.

8 ounces (225 g) yellow onions, minced

3 tablespoons (45 ml) butter *or* olive oil

2 ounces (55 g) fresh compressed yeast

5 cups (1 L 200 ml) warm milk (105° to 115°F/40° to 46°C)

2 ounces (55 g) granulated sugar

4 tablespoons (60 g) salt

1 cup (240 ml) olive oil

4 pounds 6 ounces (1 kg 990 g) bread flour

8 ounces (225 g) finely chopped walnuts

Whole wheat flour

> **Small-Batch Onion-Walnut Bread**
> yield: 2 loaves, 1 pound (455 g) each
>
> 2 ounces (55 g) yellow onions, minced
>
> 1 tablespoon (15 ml) butter *or* olive oil
>
> ³⁄₄ ounce (22 g) fresh compressed yeast
>
> 1¼ cups (300 ml) warm milk (105° to 115°F/40° to 46°C
>
> 1 tablespoon (15 g) granulated sugar
>
> 1 tablespoon (15 g) salt
>
> ¼ cup (60 ml) olive oil
>
> 1 pound (455 g) bread flour
>
> 2 ounces (55 g) finely chopped walnuts
>
> Whole wheat flour

1. Sauté the onions in the butter or olive oil in a skillet over medium heat until soft and golden, about 5 minutes. Set aside to cool to lukewarm.

2. Use a stainless steel bowl (or one made of another noncorrosive material) to mix the dough. Dissolve the yeast in the warm milk in the mixer bowl. Stir in the sugar, the salt, and the olive oil.

3. Mix in half of the bread flour using the dough hook. Mix in the walnuts and onions. Incorporate enough of the remaining bread flour to make quite a firm dough. Knead until smooth, at low or medium speed, approximately 8 to 10 minutes. Place the dough in an oiled bowl, turn to coat with oil, cover, and let rise until doubled in volume.

4. Dust the inside of bannetons heavily with whole wheat flour, but not so heavily that you obscure the ring pattern; reserve (see Note).

5. Divide the dough into 6 equal pieces, approximately 1 pound 5 ounces (595 g) each (2 equal pieces, about 1 pound/455 g each, for the smaller recipe). Knead the pieces into firm round loaves (see Figures 3-1 and 3-2, page 94).

FIGURE 3-11 Unmolding a loaf of Onion-Walnut Bread from a banneton after proofing the loaf in the basket; a baked loaf; an empty banneton

About Onions

Onions are now grown in every part of the world; the United States is one of the top producers. Onions are sometimes referred to as the king of vegetables, in part because of their widespread use, versatility, and year-round availability but also because of their distinctive, pungent, and sometimes overpowering flavor. Because the taste can be so strong (and lingering), it is important to avoid chopping the onions on a board or table where you will be working with other products later. Ideally, designate a cutting board for onions only. This is not as crucial in kitchens where the next item to be chopped might be carrots for a stock, but in the pastry kitchen or bakeshop, where the next task might be chopping chocolate for chocolate chip cookies, the lingering scent of onions could be a real disaster!

Invert the loaves in the prepared bannetons so that the smooth sides of the loaves are against the baskets. Cover and let the loaves rise in the baskets until they have doubled in volume.

6. Invert the loaves onto paper-lined sheet pans, dislodging them carefully from the baskets. Remove the baskets (Figure 3-11, page 133).

7. Bake at 400°F (205°C) for about 35 minutes. Cool on racks.

NOTE: If you do not have these baskets, you can create the same rustic-looking beehive pattern in the following way. Form the loaves as directed at the start of Step 5. Instead of placing the loaves in bannetons, brush with egg wash, then invert in whole wheat flour, completely covering the tops of the loaves with flour. Turn right-side up and immediately mark the top with 4 plain cookie cutters, using the back of the cutters so you can press firmly and leave a distinct mark without cutting the skin of the loaf (Figure 3-12). Start with a 5-inch (12.5-cm) cutter for the outside ring, then mark 3 additional rings in descending size using cutters approximately 3¾, 2½, and 1½ inches (9.3, 6.2, and 3.7 cm) in diameter, depending on the spacing of the particular set of cutters you are using. Let the loaves rise until they have doubled in volume. Bake as directed in Step 7.

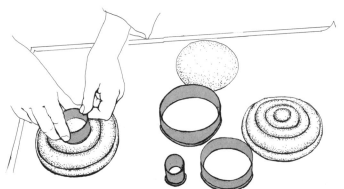

FIGURE 3-12 **Using cookie cutters to mark the top of Onion-Walnut loaves if bannetons are not available**

ONION-WALNUT ROLLS

Although, in principle, all bread doughs can be made into rolls, this dough makes a particularly pretty and unusual roll when shaped as described below.

I. Divide each 1-pound 5-ounce (595-g) piece of dough into 10 equal pieces.

2. Shape into rolls (see Figure 4-2, page 186) and finish as instructed in the Note, using 3 cutters approximately 2½, 1½, and ¾ inches (6.2, 3.7, and 2 cm) in diameter to mark the pattern.

3. Bake at 400°F (205°C) for about 20 minutes.

Raisin Bread yield: 4 loaves, I pound (455 g) each

The addition of raisins to baked goods will retard staling, since raisins, which are high in sugar, retain moisture. I do not soften the raisins before adding them to the dough because I have found that very soft raisins tend to crush or mash, leaving unpleasant dark streaks in the bread. However, if the raisins you are using are dry and hard, soak them in warm water for about 30 minutes, then drain well before adding them. Try thick slices of raisin bread toasted at breakfast, or use raisin bread to make French toast.

Melted unsalted butter

1½ ounces (40 g) fresh compressed yeast

2 cups (480 ml) warm milk (105° to 115°F/40° to 46°C)

1 tablespoon (15 g) salt

½ cup (120 ml) or 6 ounces (170 g) honey

1 pound 8 ounces (680 g) bread flour

2 ounces (55 g) unsalted butter, at room temperature

12 ounces (340 g) dark raisins

Egg wash

Cinnamon sugar

Small-Batch Raisin Bread
yield: 2 loaves, I pound (455 g) each

Melted unsalted butter

¾ ounce (22 g) fresh compressed yeast

1 cup (240 ml) warm milk (105° to 115°F/40° to 46°C)

1½ teaspoons (8 g) salt

¼ cup (60 ml) or 3 ounces (85 g) honey

12 ounces (340 g) bread flour

1 ounce (30 g) unsalted butter, at room temperature

6 ounces (170 g) dark raisins

Egg wash

Cinnamon sugar

---

1. Brush the inside of bread pans measuring 8 x 4 x 2½ inches (20 x 10 x 6.2 cm) with melted butter to coat.

2. Dissolve the yeast in the warm milk. Stir in the salt and the honey. Reserve a few ounces of the bread flour, then add the remainder. Mix in the soft butter.

3. Knead, using the dough hook, for 8 to 10 minutes to make a smooth, soft dough. Adjust the consistency by adding the reserved bread flour if necessary. Do not overknead or tighten the dough, or it will be difficult to work in the raisins later. Place the dough, covered, in a warm place and let rise until it has doubled in volume, about 1 hour.

4. Turn the dough out onto the workbench but do not punch it down. Incorporate the raisins by hand. Let the dough rest, covered, for 10 minutes.

5. Divide the dough into 8 equal pieces (4 for the smaller recipe), approximately 8 ounces (225 g) each. Keep the pieces covered. Starting with the first one weighed, pound and roll each piece into a 10-inch (25-cm) string (see Figures 3-16 to 3-18, page 148); do not taper the ends.

6. Twist 2 strings together loosely and place in one of the prepared pans. Repeat with the remaining strings.

7. Brush the loaves with egg wash and sprinkle heavily with cinnamon sugar. Let the loaves rise until just under doubled in volume.

8. Bake at 375°F (190°C) for about 40 minutes. Unmold and cool on racks.

NOTE: Due to the large amount of sugar in this bread, you must protect the dough from cooling below 75°F (24°C), or the capability of the yeast will be severely reduced.

Rosemary Bread yield: 6 loaves, 1 pound (455 g) each

The flavor of rosemary, a bushy herb native to the Mediterranean, where it grows wild, is a mixture of lemon and pine. While rosemary is used in many types of cooking, I think you will find its flavor especially pleasing in this classic Italian bread. Try reserving some rosemary bread dough to use for a pizza crust. If it is well wrapped, the bread dough can be stored in the freezer for several weeks.

2 ounces (55 g) fresh compressed yeast

1 quart (960 ml) warm water (105° to 115°F/40° to 46°C)

2 ounces (55 g) granulated sugar

1 cup (240 ml) olive oil

6 tablespoons (30 g) fresh rosemary, finely chopped

3 tablespoons (45 g) salt

3 pounds 12 ounces (1 kg 705 g) bread flour

Egg wash

Small-Batch Rosemary Bread
yield: 2 loaves, 1 pound (455 g) each

¾ ounce (22 g) fresh compressed yeast

1½ cups (360 ml) warm water (105° to 115°F/40° to 46°C)

1 ½ tablespoons (22 g) granulated sugar

⅓ cup (80 ml) olive oil

2 tablespoons (10 g) fresh rosemary, finely chopped

1 tablespoon (15 g) salt

1 pound 4 ounces (570 g) bread flour

Egg wash

---

1. Dissolve the yeast in the warm water. Stir in the sugar, oil, rosemary, salt, and enough of the flour to make a smooth, nonsticky dough.

2. Knead, using the dough hook, at medium speed for 6 to 8 minutes to develop the gluten structure. The dough will get a little looser as it becomes smoother.

3. Place the dough in an oiled bowl and turn to coat with oil. Cover and let rise for 30 minutes. Punch down the dough, then let it rise 30 minutes longer.

4. Punch the dough down again and divide into 6 equal pieces (2 pieces for the small-batch recipe), approximately 1 pound (455 g) each. Shape the pieces into tight oval loaves (see Figures 3-1 and 3-2, page 94) that spring back when lightly pressed but are not so taut that the skin on the dough breaks. Place the loaves on sheet pans lined with baking paper.

5. Brush egg wash over the loaves. Let rise until slightly less than doubled in volume.

6. Using a serrated knife and starting in the center, cut halfway into each loaf at a 45-degree angle.

7. Bake at 400°F (205°C) until the loaves sound hollow when tapped, about 35 minutes. Place the loaves on racks to cool.

Rosemary-Potato Bread yield: 5 loaves, 1 pound 10 ounces (740 g) each

Potatoes are not high on the list of culinary ingredients associated with Italy; however, they are plentiful all over the southern region (Puglia and Basilica in particular), and while it is certainly more common to find a baker in Northern or Eastern Europe adding this popular vegetable to bread, you will find it in Italy as well. This tuber, which is a member of the same family as tomatoes and eggplants, is added to the bread not for flavoring, but to retain moisture. The starch released by the potato helps trap liquid, producing, in turn, a soft, moist, long-lasting bread. One caution, however: Because of its high starch content, the bread will brown quickly, so it requires close attention during baking. For a traditional potato bread, omit the rosemary or try the Potato Bread recipe on page 126.

When the uncovered loaves are allowed a long, slow rising in the refrigerator overnight, the outside forms a crust. Once the loaves have proofed to their maximum potential, the interior creates irregular air pockets that give this bread its characteristic rustic appearance. The air pockets will be lost if the dough is too firm when it is shaped into loaves. If you cannot wait until the following day to bake—and taste—this absolutely delicious bread, you can let it rise as you would any other bread dough in a proof box, but the bread will not have the desired unusual-looking cross section when sliced.

SPONGE

1 ounce (30 g) granulated malt extract *or* 3 tablespoons (45 ml) or 2 ounces (55 g) honey

1 cup (240 ml) warm water (105° to 115°F/40° to 46°C)

2 ounces (55 g) fresh compressed yeast

12 ounces (340 g) high-gluten flour

DOUGH

2 pounds (910 g) red potatoes

1 quart (960 ml) cold water

3 pounds (1 kg 365 g) bread flour

12 ounces (340 g) high-gluten flour

1 teaspoon (4 g) ascorbic acid (see Note 2 on page 103 in the recipe for Epi Baguettes)

1½ ounces (40 g) salt

1½ ounces (40 g) fresh rosemary, finely chopped

1 cup (240 ml) olive oil

Small-Batch Rosemary-Potato Bread
yield: 2 loaves, 1 pound 12 ounces (795 g) each

SPONGE

2 tablespoons (18 g) granulated malt extract *or* 1 tablespoon plus 2 teaspoons (25 ml) honey

½ cup (120 ml) warm water (105° to 115°F/40° to 46°C)

1 ounce (30 g) fresh compressed yeast

4 ounces (115 g) high-gluten flour

DOUGH

12 ounces (360 g) red potatoes

1½ cups (360 ml) cold water

1 pound (455 g) bread flour

10 ounces (285 g) high-gluten flour

½ teaspoon (2 g) ascorbic acid (see Note 2 on page 103 in the recipe for Epi Baguettes)

1 tablespoon (15 g) salt

½ ounce (15 g) fresh rosemary, finely chopped

⅓ cup (80 ml) olive oil

---

1. To start the sponge, add the malt extract or honey to the warm water. Dissolve the yeast in this mixture. Add the high-gluten flour and mix with the dough hook until the sponge is smooth, about 5 minutes. Cover and let rise in a warm place until doubled in bulk.

2. Wash the potatoes, cut any large ones in half, and arrange in a single layer on a sheet pan or hotel pan. Cover with foil and bake at 400°F (205°C) for approximately 30 minutes or until somewhat softened; do not overbake. Once they have cooled, cut the potatoes into olive-sized chunks. Do not cut the pieces too small, as they will become smaller as they are worked into the dough; reserve.

3. Add the cold water, bread flour, high-gluten flour, and ascorbic acid to the sponge. Knead for 6 minutes using the dough hook at low speed. Add the salt, rosemary, and olive oil. Knead 6 minutes longer, then incorporate the potatoes. Knead just long enough to mix in the potato chunks. Do not mash them into the dough; whole pieces of potato should be visible in the finished bread. This Italian country-style bread dough will be soft and may seem too sticky at first. After the resting and punching-down periods, it will firm up considerably as the gluten matures.

4. Cover the dough and let it rest in a warm place for 30 minutes.

5. Punch the dough down, then let it rise again for 30 minutes.

6. Punch the dough down and weigh it into 5 equal pieces, approximately 1 pound 10 ounces (740 g) each (2 pieces, approximately 1 pound 12 ounces [795 g] each, for the smaller recipe). Form the pieces into tight round loaves (see Figures 3-1 and 3-2, page 94). Place on sheet pans and leave in the refrigerator overnight to rise and form a natural crust.

7. Remove the loaves from the refrigerator. They should be 1½ times their original size. Let rise further at room temperature if necessary.

8. Bake at 475°F (246°C) directly on the floor of a deck oven or on the bottom rack of a rack oven, using steam for the first 10 minutes. Open the damper to remove the steam and lower the temperature to 375°F (190°C). Continue baking 20 to 25 minutes longer or until the bread is baked through and has a dark golden crust.

NOTE: If your oven is not equipped with steam injectors, see "Creating Steam Without Steam Injectors," page 97.

Southwestern Corn and Cheese Bread yield: 6 loaves, 1½ pounds (680 g) each

To prepare the fresh corn kernels for this recipe, remove the corn husks, then cut the kernels away from the cob using a serrated knife. Blanch the kernels in boiling water (to cook the starch) for approximately 1 minute, refresh under cold water, and dry on paper towels. When corn is not in season, substitute thawed frozen corn kernels. You may want to consider sprinkling the peppers over half of the dough only so that you will have some cheese bread for those who would prefer it less spicy, or you can use roasted mild green chilies instead.

As with cinnamon rolls, the finished appearance of these loaves depends on how tightly you roll the logs. If they are rolled tightly, as instructed, the oven-spring will force the center of the coil up and into an attractive peak. If rolled too loosely, they will flatten as they bake, with the energy directed outward instead.

1 cup (240 ml) warm water (105° to 115°F/40° to 46°C)

2 cups (480 ml) warm buttermilk (105° to 115°F/40° to 46°C)

2 ounces (55 g) fresh compressed yeast

2 eggs

6 ounces (170 g) granulated sugar

10 ounces (285 g) yellow cornmeal

12 ounces (340 g) bread flour

2 tablespoons (10 g) garlic powder

2 teaspoons (4 g) ground paprika

2 teaspoons (4 g) cumin seed

2 teaspoons (4 g) ground cumin

4 teaspoons (20 g) salt

½ cup (120 ml) olive oil

2 pounds (910 g) bread flour

1 pound 2 ounces (510 g) fresh corn kernels (from about 5 ears), blanched and well drained

Egg wash

4 ounces (115 g) fresh jalapeño peppers, seeded and minced

1 pound 6 ounces (625 g) cheddar cheese, cut into ½-inch (1.2-cm) cubes

Small-Batch Southwestern Corn and Cheese Bread

yield: 3 loaves, 1 pound 8 ounces (680 g) each

½ cup (120 ml) warm water (105° to 115°F/40° to 46°C)

1 cup (240 ml) warm buttermilk (105° to 115°F/40° to 46°C)

1¼ ounces (37 g) fresh compressed yeast

1 egg

3 ounces (85 g) granulated sugar

5 ounces (140 g) yellow cornmeal

6 ounces (170 g) bread flour

1 tablespoon (5 g) garlic powder

1 teaspoon (2 g) ground paprika

1 teaspoon (2 g) cumin seed

1 teaspoon (2 g) ground cumin

2 teaspoons (10 g) salt

¼ cup (60 ml) olive oil

1 pound (455 g) bread flour

10 ounces (285 g) fresh corn kernels (from 2 to 3 ears), blanched and well drained

Egg wash

2 ounces (55 g) fresh jalapeño peppers, seeded and minced

12 ounces (340 g) cheddar cheese, cut in ½-inch (1.2-cm) cubes

1. Combine the warm water and buttermilk in a mixer bowl. Dissolve the yeast in this mixture. Add the eggs, sugar, cornmeal, first measurement of bread flour, garlic powder, paprika, cumin seed, ground cumin, salt, and olive oil. Mix until well blended, about 2 minutes.

2. Reserve a few handfuls of the second measurement of bread flour (1 handful, if making the smaller recipe). Add the remainder and knead with the dough hook for 6 to 8 minutes. While kneading, add as much of the remaining bread flour as required to make a smooth, elastic dough. Add the corn kernels and mix just until incorporated.

3. Form the dough into a ball. It will be a little sticky at this point; use flour as necessary. Cut an X halfway through the ball of dough using a sharp knife. Pull the cuts out a little to make a rough square (see Figure 2-9, page 75); this will make it easier to roll the dough into a rectangle later. Cover the dough and let rest for 30 minutes.

4. Roll out the dough into a rectangle measuring 15 x 20 inches (37.5 x 50 cm) (15 x 10 inches/37.5 x 25 cm for the smaller recipe). Brush egg wash over the dough. Sprinkle the minced jalapeño peppers and cubed cheddar cheese evenly over the top. Roll the dough into a tight log starting from the top.

5. Cut the dough into 6 equal slices (3 for the smaller recipe). Place the pieces on 2 paper-lined sheet pans cut-side down (all 3 will fit on a single pan if you are making the smaller recipe).

Using your fingers, spread the spirals apart, pushing down and out, to open up the loaves. Let proof until 1½ times the original size.

6. Brush the loaves with egg wash.

7. Bake at 375°F (190°C) for approximately 30 minutes.

Sun-Dried Tomato and Onion Bread *yield: 4 loaves, 1 pound 6 ounces (625 g) each*

This wonderfully distinctive bread gets its incomparable tang and meatiness from pieces of sun-dried tomatoes. Unfortunately, their terrific flavor does not come cheap. I have reduced the expense a bit by using plain sun-dried tomatoes rather than the oil-packed variety. If cost is not an issue, or if you already have oil-packed sun-dried tomatoes on hand, skip the ingredients and procedure in Step 1 and use 12 ounces (340 g) oil-packed tomatoes (including some of the oil) instead. If you have the time and space and use a lot of these, drying your own tomatoes in the oven makes a lot of sense. Directions follow the recipe.

If you prefer not to use steam when baking (or if you do not have a steam oven), brush the warm loaves just out of the oven with reserved olive oil from Step 1.

8 ounces (225 g) moist or reconstituted sun-dried tomatoes (see "About Sun-Dried Tomatoes")	5 ounces (140 g) yellow onion, finely chopped
½ cup (120 ml) olive oil	1 tablespoon (15 ml) minced fresh garlic (about 5 medium cloves)
2 ounces (55 g) fresh compressed yeast	2 tablespoons (30 g) salt
2½ cups (600 ml) warm water (105° to 115°F/40° to 46°C)	3 pounds (1 kg 365 g) bread flour

1. Cut the sun-dried tomatoes into ½-inch (1.2-cm) pieces. Combine with the olive oil in a small saucepan. Bring to a boil, remove from the heat, and set aside. When cool, strain and reserve the oil and tomatoes separately.

2. Dissolve the yeast in the warm water. Add the onion, garlic, salt, reserved oil from the tomatoes, and all but a handful of the bread flour. Mix on low speed using the dough hook for about 1 minute.

3. When the flour has been incorporated, turn the mixer to medium speed and knead for approximately 6 minutes or until the dough is smooth and elastic. Adjust the consistency during the kneading process, if necessary, by adding additional flour, turning the mixer back to low speed before each addition. Incorporate the reserved tomatoes on low speed.

4. Place the dough in an oiled bowl and turn to coat completely. Cover and let rise in a warm place until doubled in volume.

5. Without punching it down, turn the dough onto a lightly floured workbench. Divide into 4 equal pieces, about 1 pound 6 ounces (625 g) each.

6. Shape the pieces into round loaves (see Figures 3-1 and 3-2, page 94). Place on a sheet pan lined with baking paper.

7. Let proof in a warm place until just doubled in volume. Use a serrated paring knife or a razor blade to cut decorative slashes on top of the loaves.

Preparing Sun-Dried Tomatoes in Oil

Soak dried tomatoes (either the moist or the completely dry variety) in a mixture of equal parts distilled white vinegar and water long enough for the tomatoes to become perfectly soft, about 1 hour. Drain the liquid and discard. Pat the tomatoes dry on paper towels. Place in a jar; add a few bay leaves and add enough olive oil to cover. The tomatoes will keep for many weeks stored, covered, in the refrigerator.

About Sun-Dried Tomatoes

In addition to oil-packed sun-dried tomatoes, two types of plain dried tomatoes are sold. The moist type is similar in texture to dried fruit and is generally sold in a sealed package. The other type is completely dried out and crisp; it is often available in bulk at a lower cost. The latter must be reconstituted before using. You will need only 6 ounces (170 g) for this recipe. Soak the tomatoes in about 3 cups (720 ml) hot water (but no vinegar, as is used to make the oil-packed tomatoes). When they are soft, drain the tomatoes and save the water to use as part or all of the warm water called for in the recipe when you make the bread.

Drying Tomatoes Outdoors

You may have seen pictures from around the Mediterranean showing clusters of tomatoes hanging outside to dry slowly in the sun. But even if you live in Florida or the Southwest, drying tomatoes this way will take much longer due to the cooler and sometimes damp nights. If you want to try it, arrange the tomatoes just as you would for drying inside, but you must cover them with netting to prevent insects from landing on them. I dry my homegrown Italian prune plums this way in wooden frames covered with plastic screening (the same material used for screen doors) made to fit the size of a full sheet pan.

8. Bake at 400°F (205°C), using steam for the first 10 minutes. Open the damper to remove the steam and continue baking approximately 20 minutes longer. Let the loaves cool completely before slicing.

NOTE: If your oven does not have steam injectors, see "Creating Steam Without Steam Injectors," page 97.

OVEN-DRIED TOMATOES

yield: approximately 4 ounces (115 g) if dried through; 8 ounces (225 g) if left moist

There is no excuse for not drying your own tomatoes because, after you have spent a few minutes slicing and sprinkling them with salt, they need little attention other than turning the pans from time to time and making sure the oven temperature does not creep over 200°F (94°C). If you have a food dehydrator, you don't even have to worry about that. In a professional kitchen, the sliced tomatoes can be dried under the heat lamp when the space is not occupied by plates to be delivered to the dining room. This is probably the next best thing to utilizing the hot sun because, just as out in the open, this shelf allows plenty of air circulation.

6 pounds (2 kg 730 g) plum tomatoes, such as Roma

2 tablespoons (30 g) salt (optional)

1. Wash the tomatoes. Dry them thoroughly. Remove the cores and stems, if necessary.

2. Slice the tomatoes in half lengthwise. Arrange them cut-sides up on wire racks set on 3 half-size sheet pans or 1 full-size pan, if you crowd them a bit. Lightly sprinkle salt over the tomatoes, if desired. The salt helps to draw out moisture.

3. Place the tomatoes in a 170° to 200°F (77° to 94°C) oven; a convection oven is preferable. If you are using a conventional oven, convection or not, without the air vent found in commercial ovens, prop the door ajar slightly with a wooden spoon to increase air circulation.

4. The amount of time necessary to dry the tomatoes will vary considerably depending on the oven, the relative humidity, and how dry you want them. This quantity of tomatoes should take 12 to 20 hours to dry. If you plan to store the tomatoes for any length of time, they must be completely dry, actually brittle, or they can mold. If you will be using the tomatoes fairly soon, dry them just until leathery, then pack in olive oil to store. The tomatoes will become much darker in color after drying.

Swedish Limpa Rye *yield: 4 loaves, 1 pound 4 ounces (570 g) each*

The Swedish word *limpa* refers to a loaf of bread that is formed into an oblong shape, slightly tapered at the ends, and baked free-form without a bread pan. (The dough can be baked in a conventional rectangular bread pan, if you prefer.) Limpa breads usually contain spices and rye flour. This particular limpa is flavored with the popular Scandinavian spices fennel, anise, and caraway as well as orange peel. For a lighter taste and color, light corn syrup or golden syrup can be used in place of the molasses, or you can replace both the molasses and brown sugar with 1 cup (240 ml) or 12 ounces (40 g) of either light corn syrup or golden syrup. The golden syrup produces an authentic Swedish limpa.

1½ ounces (40 g) fresh compressed yeast	½ cup (120 ml) or 6 ounces (170 g) molasses
1½ cups (360 ml) warm water (105° to 115°F/40° to 46°C)	¾ cup (180 ml) vegetable oil
8 ounces (225 g) medium rye flour	4 ounces (115 g) light brown sugar
1 tablespoon (6 g) fennel seed	1 tablespoon (15 g) salt
1 tablespoon (6 g) caraway seed	Grated zest of 2 oranges
4 teaspoons (8 g) anise seed	2 pounds (910 g) bread flour
1½ cups (360 ml) warm milk (105° to 115°F/40° to 46°C)	Water
	Rye flour

1. Dissolve the yeast in the warm water. Add the rye flour and mix to make a smooth, sticky paste. Cover and let stand in a warm place until the sponge has doubled in bulk.

2. Crush the fennel, caraway, and anise seeds with a mortar and pestle. If one is not available, wrap the spices in a kitchen towel and crush them with a rolling pin.

3. Place the sponge in a mixer bowl and using the dough hook attachment at low speed, blend in the milk, molasses, vegetable oil, brown sugar, salt, and orange zest.

4. Add the crushed spices and enough of the bread flour to form a dough. Knead for 8 to 10 minutes, adding the remaining flour as necessary, to make a smooth and elastic yet fairly stiff dough.

5. Place the dough in a lightly oiled bowl and turn to coat it with oil. Let rise in a warm place until doubled in bulk.

6. Without punching the dough, turn it out onto a worktable. Divide into 4 equal pieces, approximately 1 pound 4 ounces (570 g) each. Pound and form each piece into an oval limpa loaf, slightly tapered on both ends (Figure 3-13). Place the loaves on a sheet pan lined with baking paper. Let the loaves rise until they have slightly less than doubled in volume.

7. Spray or brush the loaves with water. Dust heavily with rye flour. Use a razor blade or a small serrated knife to score the loaves lengthwise down the center (Figure 3-14).

8. Bake at 375°F (190°C) for approximately 35 minutes or until baked through. The loaves should sound hollow when tapped on the bottom. Let cool, then store the loaves covered.

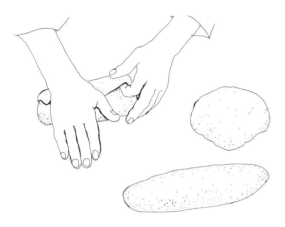

FIGURE 3-13 **Shaping slightly tapered oval loaves for Swedish Limpa Rye by folding and pounding the dough; the final shape after rolling the dough against the table**

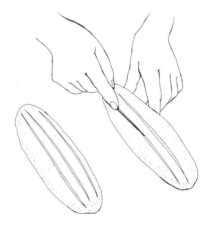

FIGURE 3-14 **Slashing the tops of Swedish Limpa Rye loaves before baking, making 3 cuts lengthwise**

Swedish Orange Rye Bread yield: 6 loaves, 1 pound 2 ounces (510 g) each

Because of the high amount of sugar in this recipe, the yeast needs a warm dough in order to work properly. It is very important that the temperature of the dough does not fall below 75°F (24°C). This bread differs from most in that the dough is not kneaded to develop the gluten. Do not be tempted to add extra flour. Just keep your hands and the table well floured and the dough will be manageable. Because the dough is so soft, I bake the loaves in bread pans. They can be baked free-form as limpa-style loaves, but they will be a little flat. The reduced flour and gluten structure make for a tender, moist bread with a distinctive flavor that combines molasses, orange, and rye.

SPONGE

1½ cups (360 ml) or 1 pound 2 ounces (510 g) molasses

3¾ cups (900 ml) warm water (105° to 115°F/40° to 46°C)

2½ ounces (70 g) fresh compressed yeast

1 pound 8 ounces (680 g) bread flour

3 ounces (85 g) medium rye flour

DOUGH

7½ ounces (215 g) candied orange peel

12 ounces (340 g) medium rye flour

2 tablespoons (30 g) salt

¼ cup (60 ml) vegetable oil

1 pound (455 g) bread flour

Unsalted butter, at room temperature

Vegetable oil

Small-Batch Swedish Orange Rye Bread

yield: 2 loaves, 1 pound 2 ounces (510 g) each

SPONGE

½ cup (120 ml) or 6 ounces (170 g) molasses

1¼ cups (300 ml) warm water (105° to 115°F/40° to 46°C)

1 ounce (30 g) fresh compressed yeast

1 ounce (30 g) medium rye flour

8 ounces (225 g) bread flour

DOUGH

2½ ounces (70 g) candied orange peel

4 ounces (115 g) medium rye flour

2 teaspoons (10 g) salt

2 tablespoons (30 ml) vegetable oil

5 ounces (140 g) bread flour

Unsalted butter, at room temperature

Vegetable oil

---

1. For the sponge, combine the molasses and warm water in a mixer, pouring some of the water into the measuring cup used for the molasses to rinse all of the molasses out. Add the yeast, bread flour, and rye flour. Mix with the dough hook to form a smooth sponge (for the small recipe, you can simply mix the sponge with a wooden spoon). Cover and let rise in a warm place until the sponge just starts to fall, about 1 hour.

2. Chop the orange peel to the size of currants and set aside.

3. To make the dough, add the candied orange peel to the sponge along with the rye flour, salt, vegetable oil, and all but a handful of the bread flour. Mix using the dough hook just until the ingredients are incorporated and the dough is smooth, adding the reserved flour if needed; do not overmix. The dough should be sticky and cling to the side of the bowl. Cover and let rest for 10 minutes.

4. Butter the inside of rectangular bread pans measuring 8 x 4 x 4 inches (20 x 10 x 10 cm).

5. Divide the dough into 6 equal pieces (2 for the smaller recipe), approximately 1 pound 2 ounces (510 g) each. Roll each piece into a tight circle and form into an oval loaf (see Figure 3-13, page 143). The dough should spring back when pressed lightly. Place the loaves in the prepared pans. Let rise until doubled in volume.

6. Bake at 375°F (190°C) for about 45 minutes. You may need to protect the loaves from overbrowning by placing a second pan underneath or by covering the tops with baking paper. Brush the loaves with vegetable oil as soon as they come out of the oven. Unmold and cool on racks.

Swedish Peasant Bread yield: 6 loaves, 1 pound 8 ounces (680 g) each

Breads made by the scalding method have been eaten for centuries by peasant farmers all over Europe. The shape, texture, and taste of the bread differ within as well as between countries, making each representative of a particular region. The common characteristics are that the breads are robust multigrain loaves made to last for several weeks. Years ago, this was necessary, as freezing food as we know it today was not an option. Peasant bread was traditionally stored in the bread chest that was central to every farmer's kitchen. Swedish peasant bread rings were threaded onto sticks and stored hung from the rafters.

SCALDING MIXTURE

3 cups (720 ml) boiling water

2 tablespoons (30 g) salt

9 ounces (255 g) whole wheat flour

9 ounces (255 g) medium rye flour

DOUGH

2½ cups (600 ml) warm water (105° to 115°F/40° to 46°C)

2 tablespoons (30 ml) distilled white vinegar

1 cup (240 ml) or 12 ounces (340 g) light corn syrup

2½ ounces (70 g) fresh compressed yeast

1 ounce (30 g) granulated malt extract *or* 3 tablespoons (45 ml) or 2 ounces (55 g) honey

6 ounces (170 g) unsalted butter, at room temperature

2 tablespoons (12 g) ground cumin

2 tablespoons (12 g) ground fennel

4 pounds (1 kg 820 g) bread flour

Egg wash

Whole wheat flour

Small-Batch Swedish Peasant Bread
yield: 2 loaves, 1 pound 8 ounces (680 g) each

SCALDING MIXTURE

1 cup (240 ml) boiling water

2 teaspoons (10 g) salt

3 ounces (85 g) whole wheat flour

3 ounces (85 g) medium rye flour

DOUGH

¾ cup (180 ml) warm water (105° to 115°F/40° to 46°C)

2 teaspoons (10 ml) distilled white vinegar

⅓ cup (80 ml) or 4 ounces (115 g) light corn syrup

1 ounce (30 g) fresh compressed yeast

1 tablespoon (9 g) granulated malt extract *or* 2 tablespoons (40 g) honey

2 ounces (55 g) unsalted butter, at room temperature

2 teaspoons (4 g) ground cumin

2 teaspoons (4 g) ground fennel

1 pound 4 ounces (570 g) bread flour

Egg wash

Whole wheat flour

---

1. For the scalding mixture, combine the boiling water with the salt, whole wheat flour, and rye flour. Mix until smooth and let stand, covered, for 1 hour.

2. For the dough, combine the warm water, vinegar, and corn syrup in a mixer bowl. Add the yeast and mix to dissolve. Stir in the scalding mixture, malt extract or honey, butter, cumin, and fennel.

3. Reserve a few ounces of the bread flour; add the remainder and knead for about 2 minutes using the dough hook at medium speed. Adjust with the reserved bread flour as required to make a dough that is not sticky. Knead until smooth, 2 to 4 minutes longer. Turn the dough onto a floured table and let rest, covered, for 10 minutes.

4. Divide the dough into 6 equal pieces (2 for the smaller recipe), approximately 1 pound 8

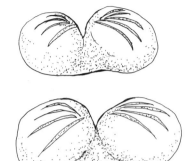

FIGURE 3-15 **Using the side of the hand to form Swedish Peasant Bread loaves in a double rounded shape; the loaves after slashing the tops**

ounces (680 g) each. Roll each piece into a firm round loaf (see Figures 3-1 and 3-2, page 94). The formed loaves should spring back immediately when you press lightly.

5. Using the side of your hand, press down on the center of each loaf and roll the loaf back and forth until you have almost severed the 2 halves (Figure 3-15).

6. Brush the loaves with egg wash, invert in whole wheat flour, and place flour-side up on sheet pans lined with baking paper. Slash a few lines across the top of each loaf with a sharp knife. Let rise until doubled in volume.

7. Bake at 375°F (190°C) for about 35 minutes. Cool on racks.

Braided White Bread yield: 6 loaves, 1 pound 2 ounces (510 g) each

Braided breads are found all over continental Europe, especially in Germany and Switzerland. There, you can find some version in virtually every bakery and in many pastry shops as well, even those that do not specialize in bread. These shops usually make a small quantity just to look—and smell—good on display. The braids you find most often are the two-string, four-string, and five-string, because they are quick and easy to make but appear just the opposite.

Basically, any firm bread dough that can be made with a cold liquid can be used for braiding. The following recipe is a firmer version of the dough for Milk Rolls (page 198) and is also used to make Knots (page 196). Egg bread and challah are the types of dough most commonly used, but try braiding Butter-Wheat Bread (page 114) and Honey-Wheat Bread (page 122) as well. For an unusual effect, combine strings of white and wheat breads in the same loaf.

4 ounces (115 g) fresh compressed yeast

1 quart (960 ml) cold milk

2 pounds (910 g) bread flour

2 pounds (910 g) cake flour

4 ounces (115 g) granulated sugar

2½ tablespoons (38 g) salt

8 ounces (225 g) unsalted butter, at room temperature

Egg wash

Poppy or sesame seeds (optional)

Small-Batch Braided White Bread
yield: 2 loaves, 1 pound 4 ounces (570 g) each

1½ ounces (40 g) fresh compressed yeast

1½ cups (360 ml) cold milk

12 ounces (340 g) bread flour

12 ounces (340 g) cake flour

1½ ounces (40 g) granulated sugar

1 tablespoon (15 g) salt

3 ounces (85 g) unsalted butter, at room temperature

Egg wash

Poppy or sesame seeds (optional)

---

1. Dissolve the yeast in the milk. Add the bread flour, cake flour, sugar, and salt. Mix, using the dough hook, until the dough forms a ball. Incorporate the butter.

2. Knead at medium speed until a fine gluten structure develops, 8 to 10 minutes. Test by pulling off a small piece of dough and stretching it lightly; if it forms an almost translucent membrane, the dough has been kneaded enough. Do not overknead. If the dough is overkneaded, the gluten structure will be permanently damaged, resulting in a loose and hard-to-work dough that will not rise properly, if at all, because the damaged gluten cannot trap enough air.

3. Place the dough in an oiled bowl, turn to coat both sides with oil, cover, and let rise until doubled in volume (see Note).

4. Punch the dough down. Place it on a sheet pan lined with baking paper and flatten it. Cover and chill for 30 minutes to 1 hour. If you will not be forming the braids until the following day, freeze the dough at this point.

NOTE: If your kitchen is unusually warm, or if you are inexperienced in braiding, skip Step 3 and chill the dough right after mixing it.

Instructions for Braided Loaves

1. Punch down the dough and divide it into pieces for braiding. The total weight of each braided loaf should be about 18 ounces (510 g). The weight and length of the pieces depend on how many strings are used. For example, if you want 3 strings per braid, make each piece 6 ounces (170 g); if you want 6 strings, make each piece 3 ounces (85 g). The length of the strings must be increased with the number of strings used to compensate for the greater number of turns and complexity. Weights and lengths of the strings for each braid are specified in the instructions that follow. Keep the pieces covered to prevent a skin from forming.

2. Form the pieces into strings by repeatedly folding the dough and pounding with the heel of your hand to remove any air bubbles or pockets (Figures 3-16 and 3-17). Then gently roll the string between your hands and the table until it has reached the desired length (Figure 3-18).

3. Pound and roll enough pieces for 1 loaf into tapered strings, thicker at the centers and thinner on the ends. (In most cases, it is possible to use strings of a uniform thickness instead of tapered strings, except when the instructions specify tapered strings). It is better not to roll all the dough into strings at once but to braid each loaf after rolling out 1 set of strings.

4. Lay the strings in front of you and join them at the top; for the braids that allow you to do so, it is preferable to start braiding in the center, then turn the loaf 180 degrees to braid the other side. Braid according to the instructions that follow. Take care not to braid too tightly and try not to stretch the strings any more than is necessary. This is usually a problem only if the dough has been overkneaded.

5. In following the numbers in the instructions for the different braids, count from left to right: when you move string number 1 in a 5-string braid over numbers 2 and 3, number 1 becomes number 3 and number 2 becomes number 1 (Figure 3-19).

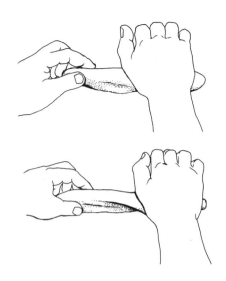

FIGURES 3-16 AND 3-17 Forming the dough strings by folding and pounding with the palm of the hand

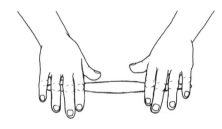

FIGURE 3-18 Rolling the dough string against the table to create the desired length

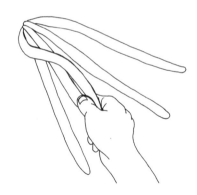

FIGURE 3-19 Moving string number 1 over string number 2 and string number 3

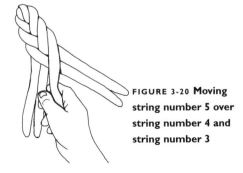

FIGURE 3-20 Moving string number 5 over string number 4 and string number 3

In Figure 3-20, number 5 is being moved over numbers 4 and 3; number 5 becomes number 3, and number 4 becomes number 5. Doing it is not as complicated as reading about it—give it a try!

6. As you come to the end of the braid, pinch the strings together and tuck underneath. When making a braided loaf with a large number of strings, it is often necessary to stop braiding before reaching the end because some of the strings may become too short to be usable. If this is the case, trim all of the remaining strings evenly and tuck the pieces underneath.

7. Place the braided loaves on sheet pans lined with baking paper, placing a maximum of 4 to a pan. If the loaves have shrunk during the braiding, which will happen in a 6- or 8-string braid, gently stretch them to about 14 inches (35 cm) as you put them on the pan. This will give you more attractive, uniform loaves.

8. Brush the loaves with egg wash and let rise until slightly less than doubled in volume (see Chef's Tip). For extra shine, brush the braids with egg wash again prior to baking. Sprinkle with poppy or sesame seeds if desired. Figure 3-21 shows some braided breads before baking.

9. Bake at 400°F (205°C) for about 25 minutes. Cool on racks.

CHEF'S TIP
Try this for a pretty and appetizing effect: Brush the braids with egg wash and proof them a little less than specified. Egg wash the braids a second time, then place the sheet pan in the freezer long enough for the loaves to become firm on the outside, 15 to 20 minutes. Bake directly from the freezer. The temperature change from the freezer to the hot oven, combined with the underproofing, makes the bread develop more oven-spring. This shows up between the strings as a lighter-colored area (without egg wash) and gives the pattern more definition.

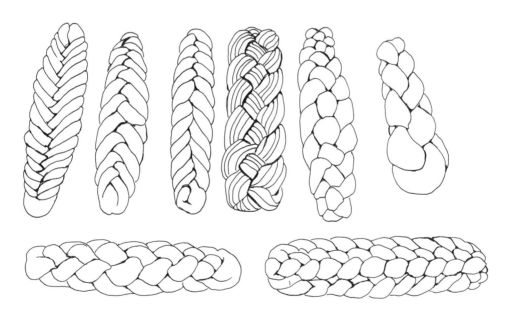

FIGURE 3-21 **The braided breads before baking. Top row, from left to right: Seven-String Braid, Five-String Braid, Three-String Braid, Eight-String Four-Braid Loaf, Four-String Braid II, and Two-String Braid. Bottom row: Six-String Braid, Eight-String Braid**

ONE-STRING BRAID

Refer to the technique shown for Double Knots, Figure 4-6, page 197. Because the string used for this braid is much larger, the loop will be much bigger than shown in the roll illustration, and the twisting motion is repeated several times to make the loaf. These instructions will produce a 12-inch (30-cm) loaf. However, this method can be used with a string as short as a few inches (as is done to make the Double Knot roll) or up to many feet to produce a wreath, for example.

1. Weigh out a 1-pound 2-ounce (510-g) piece of dough.

2. Pound and roll the dough out to make a 28-inch (70-cm) string that is tapered at both ends.

3. Place the string in front of you vertically.

4. Pick up the end closer to you and, forming a loop to the right, cross it over the top of the string just below the tip, so that one-third of the length is now in a straight line pointing to the left. The loop and the straight piece should be the same length.

5. In one continuous motion, twist the bottom of the loop one-half turn to the right and tuck the opposite end underneath and up through the opening.

6. Twist the bottom of the loop one-half turn to the left and tuck the opposite end underneath and up through the opening.

7. Repeat Steps 5 and 6 until the braid is finished.

TWO-STRING BRAID

1. Weigh the dough into 2 pieces, 9 ounces (255 g) each.

2. Pound and roll the pieces out to make 20-inch (50-cm) strings that are tapered at both ends.

3. Place the strings in a wide *X* shape in front of you.

4. Pick up the ends of the bottom string and move them straight across the other string so they change sides but do not cross over each other.

5. Repeat the procedure with the other string and repeat until the braid is finished.

THREE-STRING BRAID

1. Weigh the dough into 3 pieces, 6 ounces (170 g) each.

2. Pound and roll out to make 12-inch (30-cm) strings.

3. Braid 1 over 2. Braid 3 over 2.

4. Repeat braiding sequence.

NOTE: I find it much easier to start this braid in the center. I braid the bottom half first, then flip the loaf over to braid the other half. With any of the braids that use an odd number of strings, it is possible to either flip the loaf over in this manner or simply turn the loaf around 180 degrees, keeping it right-side up. There is no difference in the outcome.

FOUR-STRING BRAID I

1. Weigh the dough into 4 pieces, 4½ ounces (130 g) each.

2. Pound and roll out to make 12-inch (30-cm) strings.

3. Braid 2 over 3.

4. Braid 4 over 3 and 2.

5. Braid 1 over 2 and 3.

6. Repeat braiding sequence.

FOUR-STRING BRAID II

1. Weigh the dough into 4 pieces, 4½ ounces (130 g) each.

2. Pound and roll out to make 12-inch (30-cm) strings.

3. Line the strings up next to one another and start braiding in the center, working toward you.

4. Braid 4 over 3.

5. Braid 2 over 3.

6. Braid 1 under 2.

7. Repeat braiding sequence.

8. Squeeze the end pieces together and tuck underneath. Turn the braid around on its own axis (keeping it right-side up) and repeat the braiding sequence to braid the other half.

FOUR-STRING BRAID III

This variation folds two strings over each other to create four strands. It gives you the same pattern as the Four-String Braid I but uses the technique of the Two-String Braid.

1. Weigh the dough into 2 pieces, 9 ounces (255 g) each.

2. Pound and roll out to make 24-inch (60-cm) strings that are tapered on both ends.

3. Place the strings perpendicular to each other in front of you to form a + shape, with the vertical string underneath the horizontal string. Fold the top vertical string down and place it to the right of the bottom vertical string.

4. Braid 4 (the right horizontal string) over 3 and under 2 (Figure 3-22).

5. Braid 1 under 2.

6. Repeat from Step 4.

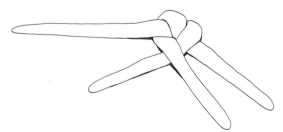

FIGURE 3-22 **The fourth step in forming the Four-String Braid III**

FIVE-STRING BRAID I

1. Weigh the dough into 5 pieces, 3½ ounces (100 g) each.

2. Pound and roll out to make 12-inch (30-cm) strings.

3. Braid 2 over 3.

4. Braid 5 over 4, 3, and 2.

5. Braid 1 over 2 and 3.

6. Repeat braiding sequence.

7. When the braid is finished, roll the whole loaf one-quarter turn to the left (on its side) before proofing and baking.

FIVE-STRING BRAID II

1. Weigh the dough into 5 pieces, 3½ ounces (100 g) each.

2. Pound and roll out to make 12-inch (30-cm) strings.

3. Braid 5 over 4.

4. Braid 2 over 3 and 4.

5. Braid 2 over 1.

6. Braid 5 over 4 and under 3.

7. Braid 2 over 1.

8. Repeat braiding sequence.

FIVE-STRING BRAID III

1. Weigh the dough into 5 pieces, 3½ ounces (100 g) each.

2. Pound and roll out to make 12-inch (30-cm) strings.

3. Braid 1 over 2.

4. Braid 3 over 2.

5. Braid 5 over 4.

6. Braid 3 over 4.

7. Braid 2 under 3.

8. Braid 4 under 3.

9. Repeat braiding sequence.

SIX-STRING BRAID

1. Weigh the dough into 6 pieces, 3 ounces (85 g) each.

2. Pound and roll out to make 14-inch (35-cm) strings.

3. Braid 1 over 2, 3, 4, 5, and 6.

4. Braid 5 over 4, 3, 2, and 1.

5. Braid 2 over 3, 4, 5, and 6.

6. Braid 5 over 4 and 3.

7. Braid 5 over 4, 3, 2, and 1.

8. Braid 2 over 3 and 4.

9. Repeat from Step 5.

SEVEN-STRING BRAID

1. Weigh the dough into 7 pieces, 2½ ounces (70 g) each.

2. Pound and roll out to make 14-inch (35-cm) strings.

3. Braid 7 over 6, 5, and 4.

4. Braid 1 over 2, 3, and 4.

5. Repeat braiding sequence. This is the same general procedure as is used for the Three-String Braid and can be used for any odd number of strings. Always place the odd string in the center (over half of the remainder), alternating between left and right.

NOTE: As with the Three-String Braid and Four-String Braid II, the Seven-String Braid not only looks better, but is easier to produce if you start braiding from the center. After you braid the first half and flip the loaf over, it is necessary to gently unfold the remaining strings before braiding the second half.

EIGHT-STRING BRAID

1. Weigh the dough into 8 pieces, 2 ounces (55 g) each.

2. Pound and roll out to make 14-inch (35-cm) strings.

3. Braid 2 under 3 and over 8.

4. Braid 1 over 2, 3, and 4.

5. Braid 7 under 6 and over 1.

6. Braid 8 over 7, 6, and 5.

7. Repeat braiding sequence.

Star or Sunburst Braid yield: 1 braid, 2 pounds 8 ounces (1 kg 135 g) in weight

This bread makes a striking centerpiece for any table. The recipe makes a star 15 inches (37.5 cm) in diameter. If you want a smaller star, reduce the weight and length of the pieces. Although you need only know how to make a four-string braid to make this loaf, you should not attempt it before you are fairly successful in rolling out and forming the strings. If you take too long, the first string will have risen while you are still shaping the last one. If you are not yet up to speed, or when the weather is warm, keep the dough in the refrigerator as you are forming the strings. It is also a good idea to place the completed outside of the loaf in the refrigerator while you are braiding the center.

Small-Batch Braided White Bread dough or 2
   pounds 8 ounces (1 kg 135 g) (page 147)

Egg wash

Poppy and sunflower seeds (optional)

1. Make the bread dough and weigh out 16 pieces, just over 2½ ounces (70 g) each. (Twelve pieces will be used for the points and 4 pieces for the center of the star.) Keep the pieces you are not working with covered to prevent a skin from forming.

2. Pound and roll 12 pieces into 12-inch (30-cm) strings that are tapered at both ends (see Figures 3-16 to 3-18, page 148).

3. Bend each string in a upside down U-shape and place them, overlapping, on a paper-lined inverted sheet pan in a wreath shape with the ends pointing out. Space each string one-third of the distance between the two halves of the previous string. When you add the last string, tuck one side under the first string (Figure 3-23). Place the strings so that you leave a 5-inch (12.5-cm) opening in the center. An easy way to do this is to arrange them around a cookie cutter or other round object of the proper size.

4. Divide the strings into 6 sections of 4 strings each (Figure 3-24), and form each section in a Four-String Braid II (Figure 3-25): Braid 4 over 3, braid 2 over 3, braid 1 under 2; repeat from the beginning. For more information on braiding, see pages 148 and 149.

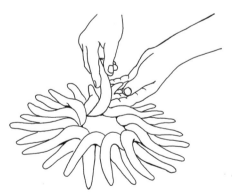

FIGURE 3-23 **Positioning the strings for out-side of the Star Braid**

FIGURE 3-24 **Dividing the strings into 6 sections of 4 strings each**

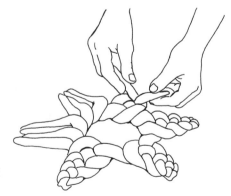

FIGURE 3-25 **Braiding each of the 6 sections, using the Four-String Braid II method**

FIGURE 3-26 **The outside of the Star Braid before adding the center**

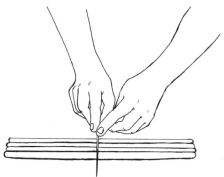

FIGURE 3-27 **Cutting the group of 4 strings in half to use for braiding the center of the star**

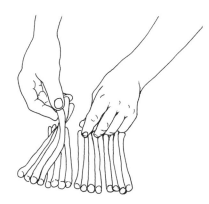

FIGURE 3-28 **Braiding the 4 groups of 4 strings each, using the Four-String Braid II method**

5. As you come to the end of each braid, pinch the ends together and tuck underneath (Figure 3-26). If the opening in the center becomes too large, move the sections closer together after you have finished braiding.

6. Pound and roll the remaining 4 pieces into 30-inch (75-cm) strings. Do this in sequence to give the gluten a chance to relax. Roll each string partway (keeping them in order), then go back and extend each one a little farther, and so on.

7. Place the strings next to each other and cut in half (Figure 3-27). Cut both resulting pieces in half again. The strings will shrink as you do this and will probably end up different lengths, but this will not show in the finished shape. You should now have 4 pieces, each consisting of 4 strings approximately 7 inches (17.5 cm) long.

8. Place the pieces next to each other and braid, following the directions for the Four-String Braid II in Step 4, braiding from the center out to one end (Figure 3-28). Turn the pieces around so the opposite side is facing you and braid from the center again, making sure that the pieces in each group remain together. Leave both ends of the braid open.

9. Pick up the braid with both hands and push the two ends under so that you form a round loaf (Figure 3-29). Place the loaf in the center opening of the star (Figure 3-30). Brush with egg wash. Let rise until slightly less than doubled in volume.

10. For a good shine, brush a second time with egg wash; sprinkle with poppy and/or sunflower seeds if you wish.

11. Bake at 375°F (190°C) until golden brown, about 40 minutes.

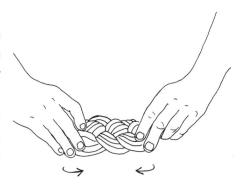

FIGURE 3-29 **Pushing both ends of the braid underneath to form a round loaf for the center of the star**

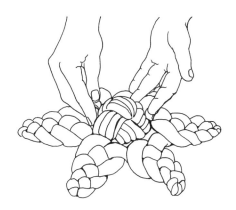

FIGURE 3-30 **Placing the center of the star within the outside frame; the completed Star Braid before baking**

Eight-String Four-Braid Loaf yield: I loaf, I pound (455 g) in weight

This loaf is impressive looking and is easier to produce than it sounds. It uses four thin bread strings to form each of the two main strings; these are then braided using the Four-String III method, where the two long pieces are arranged at the start in a + shape. The bread can be made into a rectangular loaf, as shown in Figure 3-21, page 149, or a round loaf, as shown in the center of the Sunburst Braid (see Figure 3-30, page 155). These variations take a bit more time, but they are well worth it. In the case of the round loaf, very few people will be able to figure out how it was done.

1 pound (455 g) Braided White Bread dough
(page 147)

1. Weigh the dough into 8 pieces, 2 ounces (55 g) each.

2. Pound and roll the pieces out to make 20-inch (50-cm) strings. Work on the strings in sequence, rolling each out partway, then allowing the gluten to relax before going back and rolling it a bit further. Keep the pieces in the same order as you roll them out. If your kitchen is warm, it may be necessary to refrigerate some of the strings as you work on the others.

3. Place the strings touching, side by side, in two groups of four; each of these groups will now be treated as a single string. Place the two strings in front of you in a + shape, with the vertical string underneath the horizontal string.

4. Keeping it right-side up, bring the top portion of the vertical string down and place it to the right of the bottom portion of the same string. Do not simply flip it forward; turn it clockwise to keep it right side up. Continue to use this technique of keeping the pieces facing up as you continue braiding.

5. Braid 4 (the right side of the horizontal string) over 3 and under 2 (see Figure 3-22, page 151).

6. Braid 1 under 2.

7. Repeat from Step 5.

8. To make a rectangular loaf, pinch the ends together and tuck underneath, as specified in the general directions for braiding. To make a round loaf, it is not necessary to pinch the ends together. Simply turn the braid so that it is in front of you horizontally, pick up each end in one hand and push the two ends together underneath, as shown in Figure 3-29, page 155). Shape and pinch the ends underneath as required to make the loaf round.

Simple Bread Basket

yield: 1 basket, approximately 12 inches (30 cm) in diameter and 15 inches (37.5 cm) tall

This basket may appear to be more difficult than the name implies as you first look through the instructions. However, when you consider that it does not require the use of a form such as the type used to make a sugar basket, you will agree that it is a comparatively quick and easy project.

Because this basket is made with a yeast dough, the strings will proof as you form and work with them, so you must work quickly. You should be fairly proficient in rolling dough into even ropes in order to produce a neat and professional-looking finished basket. The yeast does, however, actually make the braided white bread dough easier to work with in terms of stretching the strings.

The instructions suggest drying the pieces for 1 day before assembly. If you place the bowl and the other pieces in a low-temperature oven for approximately 1 hour after baking, however, the basket can be finished in a single day. In this case, glue the handle pieces together after drying them in the oven.

1 recipe Braided White Bread Dough (page 147) (see Step 1)	Royal Icing (page 34)
Unsalted butter, at room temperature	¼ recipe Caramelized Sugar for Decorations (page 11)
Egg wash	

1. Make the braided bread dough using only half the amount of yeast specified in the recipe. Weigh out 12 pieces, 3 ounces (85 g) each. Divide the remaining dough into 2-ounce (55-g) pieces; you will get about 35. Cover and refrigerate the 2 groups of pieces separately.

2. Butter the outside of an inverted mixing bowl approximately 12 inches in diameter and 5 inches high (30 × 12.5 cm).

3. Draw a 16-inch (40-cm) circle on a sheet of baking paper; invert on a sheet pan. Draw 3 additional circles 1 inch (2.5 cm) larger in diameter than the mixing bowl you set aside (i.e., if the bowl is 12 inches/30 cm in diameter, the circles will be 13 inches/32.5 cm in diameter), on 3 sheets of baking paper. Invert these papers on separate sheet pans.

4. Pound and roll the 2-ounce (55-g) dough pieces into 20-inch (50-cm) strings (see Figures 3-16 to 3-18, page 148). Do these in sequence by rolling out a few partway, working on the next group, then returning to the first strings; this allows the gluten to relax and avoids breaking the strings. When about half of the strings have been rolled out to the final length, place them in the refrigerator while you complete the remainder.

5. When you have finished forming the strings, place 20 strings in straight horizontal rows, about ½ inch (1.2 mm) apart, centered over the 16-inch (40-cm) drawn circle. Fold every other horizontal string back halfway. Place a vertical string in the center and cross the folded horizontal strings over the vertical string to start weaving (see Figure 7-7, page 368). Add vertical strings ½ inch (1.2 mm) apart in the same manner, placing the vertical strings so that they alternate over and under the center horizontal string, until the circle is covered with woven strings (see Figure 7-8, page 368). As you come to the edges of the circle, you can cut the strings shorter, but they should still extend about 2 inches (5 cm) beyond the drawn circle on all sides. Push the ends of the strings together where they extend beyond the circle to keep the pattern from unraveling. Place in the refrigerator for 30 minutes to firm the woven dough.

6. Place the buttered bowl right side up in the center of the woven circle. Place a sheet of baking paper and a sheet pan on top. Firmly hold both sheet pans and invert to transfer the dough to the outside of the bowl. The bowl should now be inverted on a sheet pan lined with baking paper. Adjust the dough as needed to center it over the bowl, then trim the excess dough around the rim. Brush the dough lightly with egg wash. If you apply too much, it will accumulate in the dimples between the woven strings and detract from the finished appearance.

7. It is not necessary to let the dough rise before baking, because it will have proofed the small amount that is required during the weaving process. Bake at 375°F (190°C) for approximately 40 minutes or until the crust is a rich, dark brown. Wait until the basket and the bowl are cool enough to pick up with your bare hands, then carefully turn the basket right side up, place it in a larger bowl to support the outside, and remove the bowl from the interior (see Note). Place the basket back in the oven for 15 minutes to dry and brown the interior. Set the basket aside to cool.

8. Roll out the reserved 12 pieces of dough, 4 at a time, to strings measuring 44 inches (1 m 10 cm) long. Braid 4 of the strings following the instructions for Four-String Braid I on page 51. Because this braid must be started at an end rather than in the center, it takes a little more effort. You must untangle the opposite end as you work. Place the finished braid in a ring on top of one of the reserved circles drawn on baking paper. Join the ends together and pinch to secure.

9. To make the first half of the two-part handle, braid the next set of 4 strings following the instructions for Four-String Braid II on page 151. Place this braid on another of the reserved circles, arranging it so that the ends of the braid are at the widest point of the edges of the circle and the braid forms a handle that is 14 inches (35 cm) tall. Bring both ends to the outside of the circle to widen the base slightly. Place in the refrigerator. Repeat to make an identical handle with the remaining 4 strings and place on the last drawn circle.

10. Remove the first section of the handle from the refrigerator; it should be firm. Leaving it on the baking paper, lift it off the sheet pan and place the first section on top of the second section, adjusting the two pieces to make them the same shape and size. Return the first section on its paper to its original sheet pan.

11. Brush egg wash over the 3 braided pieces. Refrigerate for 5 minutes, then brush with egg wash a second time.

12. Bake at 400°F (205°C) for approximately 20 minutes or until dark golden brown. Set aside to cool.

13. Place the royal icing in a pastry bag with a No. 2 (4-mm) plain tip. Turn one of the cooled handle pieces over and pipe a string of icing down the center, along the full length of the handle. Place the second half of the handle on top and press down firmly so that the pieces are glued together. Reserve the remaining royal icing. Set all of the pieces of the basket aside to dry overnight.

14. To assemble the basket: Trim the top of the basket, if necessary, so that it is even. Cut 2 notches on opposite sides of the basket the same width as the width of the assembled handle. Adjust the handle to fit by trimming the ends as needed so they are flush with the inside of the bowl. Using a palette knife, spread some caramelized sugar inside, just below the notches, where the ends of the handle will touch the inside of the basket. Quickly put the handle in place, holding it straight and firmly pressing the ends against the inside of the basket. It is helpful to have some assistance at this point. Hold the handle in place until the sugar hardens and the handle can support itself.

15. Place the remaining royal icing in a pastry bag with a No. 2 (4-mm) plain tip. Pipe icing around the ends of the handle inside the basket for additional support.

16. Cut the ring braid in half. Trim the ends of each half so that the pieces will fit snugly against the handles when placed on top of the bowl. Attach the pieces to the bowl with royal icing.

NOTE: It is not absolutely necessary, but a good idea, to have a second larger bowl 15 to 16 inches (37.5 to 40 cm) in diameter available when you invert the partially baked basket, just in case it is not ready to stand on its own.

Crown Bread Wreath yield: 1 wreath, 2 pounds 8 ounces (1 kg 135 g) in weight

To make this intriguing "now-how-did-they-do-that?" bread wreath, you will need a ring-mold style of banneton approximately 11 inches in diameter and 3½ inches deep (27.5 x 8.7 cm). It looks something like an oversized savarin mold, but the center is covered (not open like a tube pan), and this portion extends only halfway up the depth of the mold. The wreath is known as *Les Couronne Lyonnaise* in France, which means "Crown of Lyon." You can prepare the wreath using a rich dough, as is done here, or with a leaner dough, such as baguette dough. In fact, any of the dough formulas in this book that are shaped by kneading the dough into a loaf will work. You may also experiment by using more than one type of bread dough in the same wreath. A combination that works well is the braided bread dough used here with Butter-Wheat Bread dough (page 114). Alternating three loaves of each in the basket produces an attractive wreath. When selecting two or more types of dough, choose bread recipes with approximately the same rising and baking times.

1 Small-Batch Braided White Bread dough or 2 pounds 8 ounces (1 kg 135 g) (page 147)	Egg wash
	Poppy seeds and/or sesame seeds (optional)
Vegetable oil	

1. Make the bread dough and weigh out one 7-ounce (200-g) piece. Weigh the remaining dough into 6 equal pieces; they will weigh approximately 5½ ounces (155 g) each.

2. Refer to Figure 3-31 in forming the wreath. Roll the 6-ounce (170 g) piece of dough into a round 8 inches (20 cm) in diameter. Place this piece over the center mound in a banneton ring, 11 inches (27.5 cm) in diameter and dusted lightly with flour; the dough will extend over the mound and cover part of the bottom of the basket as well. Brush vegetable oil lightly over the

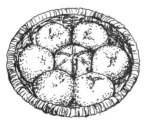

FIGURE 3-31 The sequence of steps in making the Crown Bread Wreath: A piece of dough placed over the center mound in a ring-shaped banneton; 6 round loaves spaced on top of the center dough piece, which is then cut into 6 wedges; the wedges folded back on top of the round loaves; the wreath after being inverted onto a sheet pan

outer 4 inches (10 cm) of the dough round, but do not brush oil in the center (the part covering the top of the mound).

3. Knead and roll the remaining pieces of dough into tight round loaves and arrange them in the basket, evenly spaced, on top of the oiled dough, placing the smooth side of each loaf touching the dough (facing down).

4. Cut the exposed center dough piece into 6 wedges (like a pie), extending the cuts only as far as the dough loaves. Brush egg wash over the wedges. Fold 1 wedge on top of each loaf and press to secure. Let the wreath rise until just under doubled in volume.

5. Carefully invert the wreath onto a sheet pan lined with baking paper. Remove the basket. Brush egg wash over the top and sides of the wreath and sprinkle poppy and/or sesame seeds on top if desired.

6. Bake at 375°F (190°C) until golden brown and baked through, about 50 minutes.

Winter Dough Figure yield: 4 dough figures, 12 inches (30 cm) long (Photo 60)

Forming these charming little bread figures is fairly straightforward and easy. However, because there are so many steps, if you are working in a hot climate or steamy kitchen, it is a good idea to decrease the yeast by one-fourth to allow more working time before the dough proofs. The same is true if you are producing a large number of figures in one batch.

If you prefer, the figures can be made to hold a fresh twig from an olive or redwood branch, for example, instead of the bare sticks, which will get a bit dark in the oven. The fresh twigs are inserted after the figures have baked rather than baked with the figures like the bare branches. Grease a narrow piping tip and insert it into the raw dough where the sticks will be placed to create a small hole. After the figures have baked and cooled, you can insert your choice of greenery.

By rolling the dough as long as directed (which will seem too long at first), you will end up with figures that are 12 inches (30 cm) tall once the legs and arms have been cut and stretched out. Consequently, all four will fit in a neat row on a full-size sheet pan if they are evenly spaced. Try to place each figure in his or her baking spot from the outset, as moving the figures once they have started to proof can easily damage and wrinkle the dough.

½ **full recipe Braided White Bread dough (page 147) (see Step 1)**	**Small sticks from bare branches**
32 golden and/or dark raisins	**Egg wash**
	Sesame and/or poppy seeds

1. Follow the recipe for the braided bread dough, but in Step 3, do not allow the dough to double in volume. Instead, refrigerate the dough or place it on the worktable and begin to weigh it out for the figures. Weigh out 6 ounces (170 g) of dough and divide this into 4 equal pieces. Cover and reserve them for use later. Divide the remaining dough into 4 equal pieces; they will weigh slightly over 12 ounces (340 g) each. Place all of the dough pieces on a paper-lined sheet pan, cover with plastic, and refrigerate for a minimum of 30 minutes.

2. Refer to Figure 3-32 in making the dough figures. Remove the dough pieces from the refrigerator (if the conditions are unusually warm where you are working, remove and work with only one set of dough pieces at a time—one large and one small for each figure). Pound, fold, and roll one of the large dough pieces into a 14-inch (35-cm) log, slightly tapered at both ends.

Holding your hand vertically with your fingers together at a 90-degree angle to the dough, use a back-and-forth motion to almost sever the log 3½ inches (8.7 cm) inches from the top, creating both the head and the neck of the dough person (see Figure 5-1, page 209, as an example). Tilt the head at a slight angle to the right and, using your fingers, pinch to narrow the top portion of the head, which will become a hat.

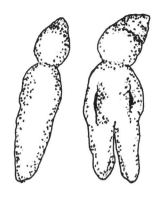

3. Place the log on a paper-lined sheet pan. Use the palm of your hand to flatten the head and the body portions to about ½ inch (1.2 cm) thickness; the body should be 4 inches (10 cm) wide in the center. Make a cut from the bottom halfway toward the neck, in the center of the dough, to create the legs.

4. Make a slit ¼ inch (6 mm) wide on either side of the chest, starting right below the neck and ending on opposite sides of the slit you made to create the legs. Spread the arms well apart, as if the elbows are sticking out or as if the hands were on the hips or in pants pockets; there are no actual hands.

5. Spread the legs apart. Cut short slits ½ inch (1.2 cm) up from the bottom on the inside of both legs. Turn the feet out to the left and right to create the look of boots, as shown in Figure 3-32.

6. Roll one of the reserved small dough pieces into a string ¼ inch (6 mm) thick and approximately 20 inches (50 cm) in length. Cut off about one-third of the rope and roll it against the table to make it about one-third thinner. Shape the top of the head according to the kind of dough figure you plan to create: Stretch the top to a point with a small ball at the end if you want the figure to resemble a Santa or a skier, or you can shape the top into a chef's toque. Use pieces from the thinner dough string to form a band for the hat (or the vertical stripes of a chef's hat) and to make the tops of the boots.

7. Brush egg wash over the entire top of the dough figure. Cut the ¼-inch (6-mm) rope in half. Secure one end of each resulting length behind the neck on either side. Twist the 2 pieces together down the chest to the waist, then tuck them under to the back, just below the end of the arms. Brush with egg wash again. Apply poppy and/or sesame seeds if desired.

8. Push some small, short sticks of wood into the body below the right armpit. (They should be no more than 6 inches/15 cm long.) Firmly (or they will pop up during baking) push 2 raisins into the head for the eyes and 3 raisins on either side of the jacket front (see note).

9. Repeat with the other dough pieces to make the rest of the figures. If the dough figures have not already started to proof slightly, proof just a little before baking (see introduction).

FIGURE 3-32 **The sequence of steps in making the Winter Dough Figure**

10. Bake the figures at 375°F (190°C) until they have a healthy golden brown color and are baked through, about 30 minutes.

NOTE: You may leave out the raisins for the eyes and instead make two deep indentations with your finger. After the figures are baked and cooled, follow the instructions for piping the eyes in the recipe for porcupines, page 580 step 5.

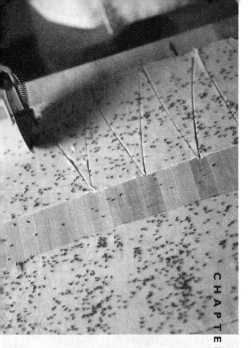

Flatbreads, Crackers, and Rolls

FLATBREADS

Flatbreads are the most popular type of bread worldwide.
They are also the oldest, having been made for more than
6,000 years. The original flatbreads were unleavened—nothing
more than a paste made of ground grain and water cooked on
a heated stone. Today, the term *flatbread* encompasses everything from simple pancake-style wrappers and tortillas made
with nothing more than flour, water, and salt to crisp, paper-
thin crackers and more complex creations that are leavened
with yeast and filled or topped with grilled vegetables, olives,
or herbs.

Many flatbreads contain only the four essential ingredients
of water, salt, leavening (unless they are the unleavened type),
and grain. Wheat, corn, sorghum, millet, barley, and rice are
among the grains most commonly used. Flatbreads can also

be made from starchy root vegetables, such as potatoes, or from legumes, such as lentils and chickpeas. In most cases, the type of grain used is indigenous to a particular region or country. For example, naan, a typical flatbread from India and Afghanistan, uses wheat flour. Because the wheat grown in that area is low in protein and uneven in quality, it would be difficult to create a large European loaf-style bread of good quality with it. Naan, however, being small and flat, makes use of the local wheat with a better outcome.

In addition to efficiently using products that are available locally, native flatbreads are simple, nourishing, and easier to prepare than most baked bread loaves. Also, many flatbreads can be made on the stovetop or over a fire and do not require a traditional oven—a convenience that most of us take for granted in the United States, but one that is not as widely available in other parts of the world. Even today, in many regions of the Third World, flatbreads are cooked on a sheet of metal heated over an open fire. Of course, the most popular cooking vessel used for flatbreads across Asia and in neighboring regions is the tandoor oven. Very different than the oven we are used to, tandoor ovens do not have racks. They are deep, ceramic ovens that are heated extremely hot. Thin pieces of bread dough are simply slapped onto the inside walls of the oven using a special protective mitten. The fact that these types of bread cook quickly and therefore require a minimum of heat also contributes to their popularity in countries where obtaining fuel for heating and cooking can be difficult.

Flatbreads are not limited to Asia, Africa, and Latin America; they have been popular in Europe and in the United States for a long time as well. Familiar flatbreads include the Italian ciabatta, focaccia, and pizza; Britain's English muffins and crumpets; Scandinavian unleavened crisp breads in many shapes and flavors; Norwegian lefse; and Mexican corn and flour tortillas. The pocket bread we know as pita, which is the most widely consumed bread in the Middle East, has become so popular in the United States that it is now available in most grocery stores and is even on the menu at many fast-food restaurants. And let's not forget the varieties of pancakes, crepes, waffles, blini, and blintzes—also technically categorized as flatbreads—that are made from a batter rather than a dough.

With the ever-increasing popularity of the so-called Mediterranean diet creating a small culinary revolution—or perhaps we should say evolution—we are continuously exposed to new types and flavors of flatbread. Naan and lavash, both of which are made in a multitude of variations, are cracker-style flatbreads commonly served as part of the bread-basket assortment in a growing number of restaurants today. In some cases, they are made on the premises and, in others, purchased from purveyors. The Culinary Institute of America at Greystone in the Napa Valley is a Mediterranean-influenced cooking school, and the five years I spent teaching there opened up a whole new world to me with respect to the many products that regional and ethnic groups around the world call their daily bread.

Ciabatta yield: 4 loaves, I pound (455 g) each (Photo 27)

The Italian word *ciabatta* literally translates to "slippers," and one look at the stubby, flattened shape of these bread loaves will tell you why they carry that name. Breads that are made from a very sticky dough, such as this one, are often categorized as rustic due to their rugged appearance. Because the consistency of what you are working with is closer to a paste than a dough (similar to that of a firm pâte à choux), the shape is a result of the baker's decreased control over forming these loaves compared to traditional bread dough. The first time you make this type of dough, you may feel a natural tendency to continue to add more flour, because it is so sticky. But if you do so, you will take away from the fabulous moist texture and unusual taste of this one-of-a-kind bread from the Lake Como region of Italy.

To give you an idea of the relatively high level of moisture in this dough, a typical bread—such as olive, whole wheat, or plain white bread—is made with 50 to 65 percent hydration, while ciabatta can have up to 80 percent. (This is using the bakers' percentage system for comparison, in which the flour always equals 100 percent and the other ingredients are calculated as a percentage of the weight of the flour.) To illustrate further, in a typical baguette dough, 10 pounds (4 kg 550g) of flour can be hydrated with 6 pounds (2 kg 730 g) of water for 60 percent hydration.

The ciabatta's wonderful flavor comes not only from the moist dough, but also from the long retardation in combination with a very small amount of yeast. With a little bit of practice and patience, you will find that handling this sticky dough is not as difficult as it seems in the beginning. Ciabatta dough can also be used to make great focaccias and pizzas by adding a few ingredients to the top and, of course, shaping the dough a little differently.

POOLISH

½ teaspoon (2.5 ml) fresh compressed yeast

1½ cups (360 ml) water, at room temperature

12 ounces (340 g) bread flour

DOUGH

1 teaspoon (5 ml) fresh compressed yeast

1 pint (480 ml) water, at room temperature

1 tablespoon plus 2 teaspoons (25 g) salt

8 ounces (225 g) cake flour

1 pound (455 g) bread flour

Coarsely ground cornmeal

I. To make the poolish, in a bowl large enough to hold both the poolish and the bread dough mixture once it expands, dissolve the yeast in the water. Stir in the flour by hand (see Note 1). Cover with plastic wrap and let stand at room temperature for 15 to 24 hours.

2. To make the dough, dissolve the yeast in the water. Add the dissolved yeast to the poolish in the bowl. Mix by hand until combined. Mix in the salt. Gradually add the cake flour and bread flour and continue mixing by hand until the flour is well incorporated. The dough will be very wet and sticky. Do not work the dough, just mix until blended.

3. Let the dough proof in the bowl at room temperature for approximately 1 hour; it should double in size.

4. With the dough still in the bowl, flour your hands and picking up the dough from the bottom, fold the 2 opposite sides in toward the center. Repeat, this time folding from the other 2 sides toward the center. Cover and proof for 30 minutes.

5. Turn out the dough onto a heavily floured work surface. Fold all 4 sides in toward the center the same way as you did when the dough was in the bowl. Clean and oil the inside of the bowl and place the folded dough back inside. Cover and proof for 30 minutes.

6. Prepare 2 bread boards or sheet pans by covering them with canvas and dusting the canvas with flour. If you do not have canvas, cut a full sheet of baking paper crosswise to make 4 pieces 16 x 6 inches (40 x 15 cm) each. Place the papers 2 to a sheet pan and dust the papers heavily with flour.

7. Turn the dough back out onto the floured surface. Be sure to use enough flour to keep the dough from sticking. Using your hands, carefully stretch the dough into a rectangle approximately 8 x 16 inches (20 x 40 cm). The dough will be very sticky and full of air bubbles; be careful not to release the air as you shape the dough.

8. Dip a pastry wheel or a knife into water and cut the dough rectangle crosswise into 4 equal pieces. Gently pull the pieces apart and flour all of the sides, including the cut ends. Flour your hands and lift the pieces, one at a time, stretching them lengthwise (and, if it seems necessary, crosswise as well); place them on a well-floured surface. They may shrink somewhat as you move them, but be certain they are oblong in shape. Using well-floured hands, move the pieces, one at a time, to the prepared bread boards or sheet pans (or to the cut pieces of baking paper, if used), at the same time stretching the dough pieces to the desired length and thickness.

9. Place the ciabatta in the proof box or cover them with towels or canvas and let proof in a warm location until doubled in size, approximately 30 minutes. Make sure your oven has been preheated to 425°F (219°C); see Note 3.

10. Sprinkle cornmeal lightly over a wooden peel and invert 2 ciabatta on top (remove the pieces of baking paper, if used). Transfer the loaves directly to the hearth of the oven by either sliding them off the peel (cornmeal-side down) or inverting them once again to place them cornmeal-side up. Repeat with the remaining loaves, transferring them 2 at a time.

11. Turn on the steam injectors and leave them on to steam the bread for 15 seconds with the damper closed. Bake with the steam in the oven for 15 minutes, then open the damper to let the steam out. Continue to bake approximately 20 minutes longer or until the ciabatta are golden brown and baked through.

NOTE 1: This works fine for both the poolish and dough for this size recipe. For a larger batch, use a mixer with the dough hook attachment, but take care not to overwork the dough.

NOTE 2: As ciabatta tastes best if eaten within the first 3 or 4 hours after baking (and absolutely should be enjoyed the same day it is baked), freeze any loaves that will not be eaten within 24 hours. The texture will still be acceptable, though not as good.

NOTE 3: If you do not have an oven with a hearth and/or steam injectors, place a baking or pizza stone in the oven and heat the oven at 425°F (219°C) for at least 1 hour before you bake the bread (see Note 4). One at a time, invert each loaf onto a cornmeal-dusted peel, remove the paper, and transfer the bread to the hot baking stone, cornmeal-side down. Quickly spray the sides of the oven using a plastic spray bottle filled with ice-cold water. Spray again every 5 minutes for the first 15 minutes. Bake until deep golden brown, about 30 minutes in total or until baked through. Cool on a rack.

NOTE 4: If you do not have a baking stone and need to bake the ciabatta on sheet pans, preheat the pans in the oven as directed for the stone before placing the loaves on the pans. Work as quickly as possible to return the pans to the oven after transferring the loaves, as immediate direct heat is necessary for the best result.

Crisp Rosemary Flatbread

yield: 12 pieces, 10 inches (25 cm) in diameter and 7 ounces (200 g) in weight, plus cutouts

This is a cracker-style flatbread with an interesting ring shape and the popular flavor of rosemary. The rings and cutouts make an attractive display when served with rectangular or wedge-shaped crackers, such as Sesame Crackers (page 176). Crisp rosemary flatbread is delicious topped or served with a soft goat's-milk cheese, sun-dried tomatoes and olives, or, for that matter, any of the toppings usually associated with pizza. Fresh mozzarella marinated in olive oil with garlic, basil, and more rosemary is another great combination.

2 ounces (55 g) fresh compressed yeast	6 tablespoons (30 g) finely chopped fresh rosemary
3½ cups (840 ml) warm water (105° to 115°F/40° to 46°C)	3 pounds 8 ounces (1 kg 590 g) bread flour
2 ounces (55 g) granulated sugar	Olive oil
1 cup (240 ml) olive oil	Kosher salt
3 tablespoons (45 g) salt	

1. Dissolve the yeast in the warm water. Stir in the sugar, oil, salt, rosemary, and all but a handfull of the flour to make a smooth, nonsticky dough.

2. Knead, using the dough hook, at medium speed for 6 to 8 minutes to develop the gluten structure. The dough will get a little looser as it becomes smoother, add remaining flour as needed.

3. Place the dough in an oiled bowl and turn to coat with oil. Cover and let rise for 30 minutes in a warm place.

4. Punch down the dough, then let it rise 30 minutes longer.

5. Punch the dough down again and weigh into eight pieces, approximately 8-ounce (225-g) each. Form into loose round loaves. Let stand a few minutes to relax the dough.

6. Starting with the loaf you formed first, roll each out to a 10-inch (25-cm) circle. If the dough is still rubbery, let it rest some more by rolling all the circles halfway, then coming back to finish.

7. Cut a 3-inch (7.5-cm) hole in the center of each circle.

8. Place the rings and the cutouts on sheet pans, brush with olive oil, and sprinkle lightly with kosher salt. Let rise until one-quarter larger in height, prick the rings well.

9. Bake at 375°F (190°C) for about 30 minutes or until golden brown and baked through.

Focaccia yield: I sheet, 16 x 24 inches (40 x 60 cm)

This Italian flatbread is a close cousin of the better-known pizza and has long been found all over the Italian Riviera; it is said to have originated in Genoa. Focaccia has become a popular bakery offering in both Europe and the United States, though sometimes in rather disguised variations. The original version started as a simple, unpretentious bread, traditionally flavored using the herbs and olive oil indigenous to the region where it was made. It was often topped with olives, sweet onions, potatoes, and/or anchovies. Use your imagination to suit your taste and requirements in choosing flavors and toppings, but keep in mind that without the herbed garlic oil to begin with, you are not making an authentic focaccia.

Focaccia is good as a snack or as an accompaniment to soups or salads. If you prefer to make the focaccia round, this recipe will yield 2 disks, 14 inches (35 cm) in diameter, or 15 individual rounds, 5 inches (12.5 cm) in diameter. The individual servings will bake in much less time.

SPONGE
1½ ounces (40 g) fresh compressed yeast

¾ cup (180 ml) warm water (105° to 115°F/40° to 46°C)

1 tablespoon (15 g) granulated sugar

8 ounces (225 g) high-gluten flour

DOUGH
2 cups (480 ml) warm water (105° to 115°F/40° to 46°C)

¾ cup (180 ml) olive oil

3 ounces (85 g) granulated sugar

2 tablespoons (30 g) salt

1 pound (455 g) high-gluten flour

14 ounces (400 g) bread flour

¼ cup (60 ml) olive oil

TOPPING
Herbed Garlic Oil (recipe follows)

1 teaspoon (5 g) kosher salt

I. To make the sponge, dissolve the yeast in the warm water. Add the sugar and high-gluten flour, and knead, using the dough hook, until the dough is smooth and elastic, about 5 minutes.

2. Cover and let rise in a warm place until the sponge starts to fall.

3. To make the dough, add the warm water to the sponge together with the olive oil, sugar, salt, and high-gluten flour. Start kneading with the dough hook and then add enough of the bread flour to develop a very soft, smooth, yet still elastic dough.

4. Form the dough into a ball, place on a floured surface, and cut an *X* halfway through it. Pull the cuts out slightly to form a rough square (see Figure 2-9, page 75); this will make it easier to shape the dough into a rectangle later. Cover and let rest for 30 minutes.

5. Using ¼ cup (60 ml) olive oil, coat the bottom and sides of a full sheet pan (do not use baking paper). Place the dough in the center of the pan. Oil your hands, then stretch out the dough as far as you can. Let rise in a warm place until the dough has doubled in bulk.

6. Use your hands to stretch the dough until it covers the entire sheet pan. Let the dough relax a few minutes if needed. Press your fingertips into the top to mark it with dimples.

7. Let the dough rise until it is 1½ times the original size.

8. Using your hand, very gently spread three-quarters of the herbed garlic oil evenly over the surface of the dough. Sprinkle the kosher salt evenly over the top.

9. Place the bread in an oven preheated to 475°F (246°C). Immediately reduce the heat to 375°F (190°C) and bake for 25 to 30 minutes or until baked through. Remove from the pan by placing a second sheet pan on top and inverting. This will keep the bottom of the focaccia from becoming soggy. Place another inverted pan on top and invert again to place the focaccia on the underside of the sheet pan (so that the sides do not hold in any steam). Immediately brush the remainder of the herbed olive oil on top. Allow to cool, then cut into pieces of the desired size.

HERBED GARLIC OIL yield: approximately 1¼ cups (300 ml)

1 ounce (30 g) fresh rosemary

1 ounce (30 g) fresh sage

1 ounce (30 g) fresh basil

1 cup (240 ml) olive oil, heated

2 heads of garlic, roasted and pureed (see Note)

1. Finely chop the herbs. Add to the heated olive oil along with the garlic.

2. Let stand for at least 1 hour or overnight.

NOTE: If there is no roasted garlic in the kitchen, cut off the tops of the garlic heads to reveal the individual cloves, which will look a little like a honeycomb. Rub the cut sides with oil and wrap the garlic heads in aluminum foil. Roast in a 350°F (175°C) oven for 30 to 45 minutes, until the garlic is soft and ivory colored but not browned. To use, simply squeeze the soft garlic out of the skin.

Potato-Topped Focaccia yield: 1 sheet, 16 x 24 inches (40 x 60 cm)

1 pound (455 g) small red potatoes

1 recipe Herbed Garlic Oil (above)

1 recipe Focaccia (page 168) (see Step 2 below)

1. Bake the potatoes until they are cooked through but still firm. Slice them thinly and toss them with the herbed garlic oil.

2. Follow the recipe for focaccia (at left) through Step 7.

3. Drain the herbed oil from the potatoes and brush it over the surface of the dough. Distribute the sliced potatoes and herbs evenly on top. Sprinkle the kosher salt over the potatoes.

4. Bake and unmold as directed in Step 9 of the focaccia recipe.

Lavash yield: 4 full sheet pans; approximately 150 wedge-shaped crackers

Lavash is a very thin variety of flatbread, most strongly associated with Armenia but made in other countries as well. Both the thin, single-layer lavash and its cousin, the softer two-layer pocket, or pita bread, have made their way into the mainstream of the American culinary world and are now offered in many restaurants and grocery stores. Lavash, in numerous sizes and shapes, is a staple bread in most parts of the Middle and Far East. Because it is so thin, it dries out very quickly and is pliable only when freshly made. In some cases, huge baked sheets of lavash—as large as 4 to 6 feet—are hung to dry on lines, just like clothing. This preserves the bread for many months, just as drying fruit or a meat product like beef jerky is a traditional way of conserving food for the winter. In some recipes, such as this one, the lavash is initially baked until crisp and dried like a cracker in the first place, so the further drying process is not necessary. To stay crisp, the crackers simply need to be stored in airtight containers.

Baking lavash on regular sheet pans in what we think of as a regular oven is unheard of in the regions of the world where this bread originated. In Armenia, it is typically made in a tandoor oven, which looks like a large, round ceramic planter. The thin pieces are placed on a special cushion and pressed against the extremely hot inside wall of the tandoor, which cooks the thin sheets in a matter of seconds. In other areas, a *sajj*, which is a large, slightly concave iron plate that is heated over an open fire, is used.

Lavash is traditionally baked without a topping or with just a small sprinkling of sesame seeds and/or salt, but it in the United States, it has become popular to brush the dough with olive oil and sprinkle a topping over it made from a mixture of nuts and seeds. Lavash, in one variation or another, is added to the bread basket in many restaurants today. The sheets may be broken into suitably sized pieces after baking, or the thinly rolled dough can be cut into rectangles or wedges, as in this recipe, before baking. Wedges and large irregular broken pieces are great for adding height to a bread basket or bread display.

¾ ounce (22 g) fresh compressed yeast	4 ounces (115 g) whole wheat flour
1 cup (240 ml) warm water (105° to 115°F/40° to 46°C)	2 tablespoons (30 g) salt
1 cup (240 ml) whole milk, at room temperature	¼ cup (60 ml) molasses
4 ounces (115 g) durum flour	10 ounces (285 g) bread flour
4 ounces (115 g) cake flour	Olive oil
	Lavash Topping (recipe follows)

1. Dissolve the yeast in the warm water. Mix in the milk. Add the durum flour, cake flour, and whole wheat flour. Mix until combined. Incorporate the salt and molasses.

2. Reserve a handful of the bread flour and add the remainder to the dough. Knead until the dough is elastic and fairly firm, adding the reserved bread flour as necessary place the dough in a lightly oiled bowl. Turn to coat with oil. Cover and let it proof at room temperature for 1½ hours.

3. Punch down the dough and allow it to rest for at least 15 minutes.

4. Divide the dough into 10-ounce (285-g) pieces. Flatten them and reserve the pieces you are not working on in the refrigerator to make them more manageable. Roll out each piece to make it close to the size of a full sheet pan, 16 x 24 inches (40 x 60 cm). This must be completed in several steps because the dough will be very glutinous. (If you have a dough sheeter, or even a manual pasta machine for small pieces, use it instead of rolling the pieces by hand.)

5. Place each sheet of dough on a sheet pan lined with baking paper. Brush olive oil over the

About Lavash

Freshly made lavash is traditionally served with thick soups and stews, where the bread itself is used as a spoon to scoop up the contents of the meal and absorb the sauces and juices. Crisp or dried lavash is served like a cracker with dips or spreads, or it can be softened by sprinkling water over the sheets and wrapping them in damp towels for several hours or overnight. The softened sheets are consumed as described for the fresh bread. They also may be topped with any number of vegetable or bean purees or pastes (a Westernized variation made with cream cheese is very popular in this country), along with thinly sliced meats, grilled vegetables, sliced tomatoes, lettuce, and fresh herbs, rolled up jelly roll style, and sliced crosswise into sandwiches. Softened lavash is also served with any of the aforementioned toppings offered separately for the guests to pile on the bread, roll up, and eat out of hand.

sheets and then sprinkle the lavash topping over them. Gently press the topping into the dough using a rolling pin. Let the sheets relax at room temperature for 30 minutes.

6. Prick the dough lightly over the top of each sheet. Use a rolling cutter to cut each sheet lengthwise into 5 strips (about 4½ inches/11.2 cm each), then cut the strips into wedges.

7. Bake at 425°F (219°C) for approximately 10 minutes or until the crackers are golden brown. Store in airtight containers.

LAVASH TOPPING yield: enough for 4 full-sized sheet pans

1 ounce (30 g) pistachio nuts, finely chopped

1 ounce (30 g) poppy seeds

1 ounce (30 g) black sesame seeds

1 ounce (30 g) white sesame seeds

1 ounce (30 g) sumac seeds

Combine all ingredients. Use as directed in the recipe.

Naan yield: 12 flatbreads, approximately 6 ounces (170 g) each

This soft, puffy flatbread, native to East India and popular in many neighboring countries, especially Afghanistan, is also known as *nan* and *nane* in the Hindu language. In these countries, it is as customary to serve naan (and/or any of the similar flatbread varieties) during a meal as it is for us to expect a basket of bread to be placed on the table when we are seated in a restaurant. In fact, because this type of bread is such a large part of the staple diet, it is often enriched with vitamin- and protein-rich grains, such as whole wheat, wheat germ and/or bran, soy flour, and coarse cornmeal. In addition to adding nutritional value, these variations also change the texture and flavor of the finished product; you may want to experiment with the formula given here. Baked naan have a soft, pliable texture and are usually eaten rolled around a filling of some type, see "About Lavash."

Traditionally, naan are baked in a tandoor oven, where the shaped pieces of dough are quickly slapped against the inside walls. In just moments, the high heat cooks the dough and the slightly puffed bread is speared with a skewer, peeled off the side of the oven, and served warm.

SPONGE	DOUGH
1 ounce (30 g) fresh compressed yeast	1 ounce (30 g) granulated sugar
2 cups (480 ml) warm water (105° to 115°F/40° to 46°C)	4 teaspoons (20 g) salt
2 tablespoons (18 g) granulated malt extract *or* 2 tablespoons or 1½ ounces (60 ml/40 g) honey	1 cup (240 ml) water
	1 ounce (30 g) soy flour (optional)
	1 ounce (30 g) wheat germ (optional)
1 pound 12 ounces (795 g) bread flour	1 pound 2 ounces (510 g) bread flour
	1 ounce (30 g) shortening, at room temperature

1. To make the sponge, dissolve the yeast in the warm water. Stir in the malt extract or honey.

2. Incorporate the bread flour and mix to form a smooth dough. Cover and set aside in a warm place until the dough has proofed and starts to fall.

3. To make the dough, place the sponge in a mixer bowl with the dough hook attachment. Add the sugar, salt, and water as well as the soy flour and wheat germ, if you are using them. Mix for a few minutes, incorporating all but a handful of the bread flour, until a dough has formed.

4. Add the shortening and the reserved flour, plus additional if necessary. Knead until you have developed a smooth, soft, elastic dough. Cover and let the dough rest for a few minutes.

5. Divide the dough into 12 equal pieces approximately 6 ounces (170 g) each. Roll each piece into a round, using flour to prevent the dough from sticking. Flatten each piece and roll it out to form a rectangle 8 × 6 inches (20 × 5 cm) and about ¼ inch (6 mm) thick.

6. Place on paper-lined sheet pans, cover, and allow to proof until 1½ times the original size.

7. Dock the dough pieces and let them proof slightly a second time.

8. Slide a baker's peel under each piece and transfer directly onto the hearth of the oven or onto preheated sheet pans (see Note). Bake at 450°F (230°C) for approximately 6 minutes or until the naan are golden brown and baked through. Transfer to a bread rack and repeat with the remaining pieces until you have finished baking all of them.

NOTE: If you do not have a hearth oven, place a pizza stone in a conventional oven and preheat at 450°F (230°C) for at least 30 minutes before baking. If you have to use sheet pans, preheat them at the same temperature before placing the naan on the pans, then quickly return the pans to the ovens. Immediate high heat is necessary to simulate the heat of a tandoor oven to achieve the desired effect.

Norwegian Potato Lefse yield: 30 lefse, 8 inches (20 cm) in diameter

Lefse are generally eaten for breakfast or for an afternoon snack. They are spread with butter, sprinkled with sugar, and folded into quarters, or served flat on a plate with butter, honey, or jam as accompaniments. Lefse are also served rolled around a filling of smoked meat and/or cheese.

For best results, the lefse dough should be prepared the day before cooking the breads, unless you have a specially made lefse skillet or a flattop griddle on your stove. If not, a well-seasoned cast-iron skillet is the next best thing, but any heavy skillet with even heat will do.

About Lefse

Every village in Norway—or for that matter, just about every family—seems to have its own version of this tortilla-style flatbread. The name is spelled *lefser* in Norwegian. The bread is made in numerous varieties. Some lefse are served only in the summertime; others are for special occasions, holidays, or weddings. Lefse vary in size from that of a small saucer to 12 to 14 inches (30 to 35 cm) in diameter, and from ¹⁄₁₆ inch to ¹⁄₂ inch (2 mm to 1.2 cm) in thickness. Depending on the recipe, the ingredient list might contain a dozen different items or just two: cooked potatoes and flour. Some lefse are served with toppings and some made with fillings. If you are traveling in Norway, you will no doubt find some variation year round. Potatoes are a staple food throughout Scandinavia, and I remember the Swedish version of this treat as being one of my favorites. The breads were usually made when my mom had leftover mashed potatoes. She served them for lunch or dinner with thin slices of smoked pork and lingonberries.

2 pounds 8 ounces (1 kg 135 g) russet potatoes

2 teaspoons (10 g) salt

4 ounces (115 g) unsalted butter, at room temperature

¹⁄₂ cup (120 ml) heavy cream

1 pound (455 g) sifted bread flour

Granulated sugar

Lingonberry or other jam

1. Peel the potatoes and cut into chunks. Place the pieces in a saucepan and add just enough water to cover. Bring to a boil, cover the pan, reduce the heat, and cook until the potatoes are soft and cooked through, about 20 minutes.

2. Drain the potatoes and return to the pan. Place the pan back on the stove and shake the potatoes in the pan over the heat for 1 or 2 minutes to evaporate excess moisture. Add the salt and mash until smooth. Stir in the butter and cream. Remove from the heat.

3. Gradually incorporate the flour into the potatoes, mixing until the dough forms a ball. Add more flour if necessary; the dough should be soft but not sticky.

4. Place the dough in a bowl and cover tightly. Refrigerate for a minimum of 12 hours or overnight.

5. Divide the dough into 2 equal pieces. Using flour to prevent the dough from sticking to your worktable, roll each piece into a rope and cut each rope into 15 equal pieces. Roll the pieces into balls.

6. To form each piece, begin by flattening a ball with the palm of your hand, flipping it over, back and forth, between your palms a few times, using flour to keep it from sticking. Place the flattened pieces on a sheet pan lined with baking paper and refrigerate for 10 to 15 minutes to firm the dough before proceeding to roll out the breads.

7. Using light pressure, use a rolling pin to roll each lefse into an 8-inch (20-cm) circle, continuing to pick it up and turn it as you are rolling to be certain it is not sticking.

8. Place the round on a sheet pan lined with baking paper and lightly dusted with flour. Continue to form the remaining balls of dough. If the lefse are very soft at this point, refrigerate them until firm before cooking.

9. To cook the lefse, heat a skillet over medium heat and cook the breads, 1 at a time, for about 1 minute on each side or until lightly browned. If they stick to the skillet, you can use a little clarified butter in the pan; however, the butter in the dough is usually sufficient.

10. Place the cooked lefse on a sheet pan lined with baking paper, or transfer them directly to a serving plate or platter. Once you get a feel for working with the dough, you will be able to roll them out and cook them at the same time. Serve warm, sprinkled with sugar, and topped with a dollop of jam.

11. To store cooked lefse, wrap tightly and refrigerate. Reheat in a skillet over medium heat.

Pita Bread yield: 16 breads, 7 inches (17.5 cm) in diameter

The most widely consumed bread in the Middle East is this classic pita, or flatbread, referred to in Arabic simply as *khubz*, meaning "bread." It is a bread with very little leavening that puffs up spectacularly, like an odd-looking balloon, after a few minutes in a hot oven. Throughout the Middle East, pita is served with meals whole, or cut or broken into wedges for dipping into local dishes, such as baba ghanoush or hummus. Sometimes the pocket breads are stuffed with meats, falafel topped with tahini sauce, or other ingredients to create a sandwich.

If your baked pita breads feel tough and cardboardlike, as so many store-bought pitas do, replace the bread flour with all-purpose flour or use ⅓ cake flour with ⅔ bread flour to reduce the gluten and make the bread more tender. As a variation, replace up to half of the bread flour with whole wheat flour. In any case, it is preferable to use unbleached bread flour.

SPONGE	DOUGH
½ ounce (15 g) or 2 tablespoons (30 ml) fresh compressed yeast	1½ cups (360 ml) warm water (105° to 115°F/40° to 46°C)
1 tablespoon (15 g) granulated sugar	4 teaspoons (20 g) salt
1½ cups (360 ml) warm water (105° to 115°F/40° to 46°C)	⅓ cup (80 ml) olive oil
14 ounces (400 g) bread flour	1 pound 4 ounces (570 g) bread flour

1. To make the sponge, dissolve the yeast and sugar in the warm water, then add the bread flour. Mix until well blended and smooth, then cover and let stand in a warm place until the sponge has doubled in bulk, approximately 30 minutes.

2. To make the dough, add the warm water to the sponge together with the salt, olive oil, and all but a handful of the bread flour. Knead, using the dough hook on low speed, until the dough forms a smooth and elastic ball, about 8 minutes.

3. Place the dough on a worktable and knead in as much of the reserved flour by hand as needed to prevent the dough from being sticky. Work the dough into a firm ball and place in a lightly oiled bowl. Turn to coat with oil, then cover and let proof in a warm place for 1½ hours.

4. Punch down the dough and divide into 16 equal pieces about 4 ounces (115 g) each. Shape the pieces into tight round balls (see Figure 4-2, page 186). Cover and set aside on a floured surface for 30 minutes to let the dough proof and the gluten relax.

5. Before starting to form the breads, preheat the oven to 475°F (246°C). Flatten and roll out each ball of dough to a 7-inch (17.5-cm) disk, using flour to prevent it from sticking. There

Chef Bo's First Encounter with Pita Bread

My first exposure to pita bread (although I did not know what it was at the time) was in Cairo, Egypt, where the local pita is known as *baladi*, in the days when I worked on cruise ships. As usual, I was ready with my camera hung around my neck looking for unusual local photos. On this occasion, I saw a man running down the street with a large board balanced on top of his head. It was covered with something that looked like flat loaves of bread, so I naturally pointed my camera and shot, then followed him to see what this was about. After I had run behind him for a few blocks, trying not to lose him in the crowded streets (although the big board on his head made him easy to spot), he stopped at what was literally a hole in the wall on the outside of a building on a street corner. This turned out to be an extremely hot brick oven and apparently a thriving business someone had set up solely for baking pitas and other types of flatbreads for the locals. I later learned that most households did not have ovens of their own. The process was quick and simple. A customer would deliver his tray of baladi or other bread dough rounds, which had, shall we say, already gotten a running start as far as proofing. The breads were slid into the oven for just the few minutes required, and the freshly baked pitas were carried back home.

should not be any wrinkles or cuts in the dough that can prevent the pitas from forming pockets as they bake. Lay the dough rounds on floured towels or baking pans after rolling them. Let stand at room temperature until they have puffed slightly.

6. Starting with the breads rolled out first, use a floured peel to slide 4 pitas at a time directly onto the hearth of the oven (see Note). Bake for approximately 4 minutes or until light golden brown on the bottom. The breads should puff up halfway through baking. If the breads become too dark on the bottom before they are firm on the top, lower the heat slightly. Place on wire racks to cool. Cover with a dry towel if you would like to keep the crust soft. Bake the remaining pita breads in the same way.

7. Once the breads have cooled, if they are not to be served right away, wrap them in plastic to keep them flexible. Freeze for longer storage.

NOTE: If you are using a noncommercial oven that does not have a hearth, use a homemade one (see page 949) or use a baking stone. Place the stone in the oven well ahead of time so it will be very hot when you are ready to bake the pitas. A nonstick or well-seasoned sheet pan can be used as well in a pinch. When you use sheet pans, the breads will require longer to bake, and the pitas will not be as crunchy on the bottom.

Pizza Dough yield: approximately 1 pound (455 g), or 2 pizza crusts, 10 to 12 inches (25 to 30 cm) in diameter

The Italian word *pizza* translates, of course, as "pie." It is unclear exactly where pizza originated, but the similarity of the name and the product to the French *pissaladière* (a provincial specialty typically topped with olives, onions, and anchovies) suggests that the Italians may have borrowed the idea they later made famous—especially in Naples, which is recognized for popularizing traditional Italian pizza. Another theory says that Italian pizza evolved from Middle Eastern flatbread. Who is to say, really, which came first hundreds, if not thousands, of years ago? One can certainly imagine that the idea of taking some raw dough from the daily bread, flattening it, and topping it with whatever was on hand before placing it in the oven would come naturally. Today, pizza has become a popular American fast food with so many changes and variations that the Neapolitans might not link it to their original creation.

½ ounce (15 g) fresh yeast

¾ cup (180 ml) water, at room temperature

1 teaspoon (5 g) granulated sugar

2 tablespoons (30 ml) olive oil

1 teaspoon (5 g) salt

1 tablespoon (15 ml) honey

10 ounces (285 g) bread flour

I. In a mixer bowl, dissolve the yeast in the water (help it along by squeezing it with your fingers).

2. Mix in the sugar, olive oil, salt, and honey.

3. Add the flour and knead with the dough hook until the dough has a smooth, elastic consistency, about 10 minutes.

4. Place the dough in an oiled bowl, turn to coat both sides with oil, cover, and let rise until slightly less than doubled in volume.

5. Place the dough, covered, in the refrigerator for at least 2 hours. Return to room temperature before proceeding.

6. Divide the dough in half. On a floured board, roll and stretch the dough with your hands to make each piece into a circle, 10 to 12 inches (25 to 30 cm) in diameter.

7. Top as desired and bake at 450°F (230°C) on a heated pizza stone or a thin sheet pan placed in the bottom of the oven to allow the crust to brown on the bottom.

Sesame Crackers yield: variable, depending on size

This recipe was given to me by a baker at the Ahwahnee Hotel in Yosemite National Park. At the hotel, they place one huge cracker wedge standing tall in the center of the bread assortment served to each table. When I first saw these crackers at dinner, I was impressed by how precise and evenly they were rolled out. During the many times I had worked in the Ahwahnee kitchen as a guest chef during their "Chef's Holidays" program, I had never seen a sheeter, and frankly, these were just too perfect to have been done by hand. Sure enough, when I checked the next day, there was, indeed, a sheeter hiding in the corner.

If you do not have access to a sheeter, try using a pasta machine to roll the crackers. You will need to start them by hand, rolling the dough to about ¼ inch (6 mm) thick with a rolling pin. Then pass the dough through the pasta rollers in succession to make it as thin as possible without tearing. If you have to, use a rolling pin to do the job; it will take a bit longer and the crackers will not look quite as professional, but the flavor will still be great as long as you make them very thin.

1½ ounces (40 g) fresh compressed yeast

3½ cups (840 ml) warm water (105° to 115°F/40° to 46°C)

1 tablespoon (15 ml) diastatic malt *or* 1 tablespoon (15 ml) honey

1 ounce (30 g) salt

⅓ cup (80 ml) Asian sesame oil

12 ounces (340 g) whole wheat flour

2 pounds 8 ounces (1 kg 135 g) bread flour

1 pound (455 g) sesame seeds, a mixture of black and white

1. In the bowl of an electric mixer, dissolve the yeast in the warm water. Mix in the malt or honey, salt, and sesame oil. Using the dough hook attachment, incorporate the whole wheat flour and all but a handful of the bread flour. Knead until a smooth, elastic dough develops, scraping down the sides of the bowl and adding the reserved flour if necessary. Incorporate the sesame seeds.

2. Cover and allow to proof in a warm location for 1 hour.

3. Divide the dough into 6 equal pieces. Roll the pieces into tight round balls (see Figure 4-2, page 186). Cover the balls of dough and allow them to relax for 15 minutes.

4. Roll each ball out to ¹⁄₁₆ inch (2 mm) thick, preferably by using a dough sheeter.

5. Cut the dough sheets into crackers of the desired size and shape. Large triangles or wedges work particularly well.

6. Place on sheet pans lined with baking paper and bake immediately (do not let them rise, or the crackers will be thick instead of thin and crisp) at 375°F (190°C) until deep golden brown. Store in airtight containers.

Swedish Peasant Rings

yield: 3 ring-shaped loaves, 9 inches (22.5 cm) in diameter and 1 pound (455 g) in weight, plus cutouts

This recipe contains a comparatively small amount of rye flour, so if you are looking for a heartier flavor, try the Farmer's Rye Rings in Chapter 3. They, too, are made in the same ring shape, which was long ago done for purposes of storage. The rings could be hung from a dowel, allowing air to circulate and prevent spoilage, and also to keep the breads safe from rodents.

1 cup (240 ml) water	1 tablespoon (9 g) granulated malt extract *or* 2 tablespoons (40 g) honey
1½ teaspoons (8 g) salt	
3 ounces (85 g) whole wheat flour	2 ounces (55 g) unsalted butter, at room temperature
3 ounces (85 g) medium rye flour	
⅓ cup (80 ml) or 4 ounces (115 g) light corn syrup	2 teaspoons (4 g) ground cumin
	2 teaspoons (4 g) crushed fennel seeds
¾ cup (180 ml) warm water (105° to 115°F/40° to 46°C)	1 pound 4 ounces (570 g) bread flour
2 teaspoons (10 ml) distilled white vinegar	Egg wash
1 ounce (30 g) fresh compressed yeast	Whole wheat flour

1. Heat the first measurement of water to boiling. Add the salt, whole wheat flour, and rye flour. Mix until smooth. Let stand, covered, for 1 hour.

2. Combine the corn syrup, warm water, and vinegar in a mixer bowl. Add the yeast and stir to dissolve. Blend in the flour-water mixture, malt extract or honey, butter, cumin, and fennel.

3. Reserve a few ounces of the bread flour; add the remainder to the mixer bowl and knead for about 2 minutes, using the dough hook at medium speed. Adjust with the reserved bread flour as required to make a dough that is not sticky. Knead until smooth, 2 to 4 minutes longer. Turn the dough onto a floured table and let rest, covered, for 10 minutes.

4. Scale the dough into 3 equal pieces, approximately 1 pound (455 g) each. Form into round loaves (see Figures 3-1 and 3-2, page 94), cover, and let the dough relax for a few minutes.

About Rye

Rye has an interesting history. It was once known as "the wheat of the peasant" because it could be grown in inferior soil, which was, of course, about all the impoverished farmers of Eastern Europe had to work with. Rye was considered nothing more than a weed to be removed and destroyed each time it sprang up in the fields. But as all of us who garden know, sometimes the weeds do better than whatever it is we are attempting to grow in the first place. In this instance, the crop was wheat, and after a time the farmers simply gave up trying to remove all the rye "weeds" from their wheat fields. They began to harvest this persistent and rather unusual-looking plant along with their wheat crop. The milled combination was called rye flour. Today, rye is cultivated on its own to produce 100 percent rye flour in various grades.

5. Flatten the loaves by rolling them to 9-inch (22.5-cm) circles. Do this in sequence, rolling each one just part of the way each time, so the gluten in pieces you are not working on has time to relax while you work on the others. Cut a 3-inch (7.5-cm) hole in the center of each circle.

6. Brush the rings and the cutouts with egg wash, invert in whole wheat flour, and place flour-side up on sheet pans lined with baking paper. Prick all over with a docker. Let rise until doubled in volume.

7. Bake the rings and the cutouts at 400°F (205°C) for approximately 25 minutes. The cutouts will be done a little sooner than the rings.

Vegetable-Topped Cracker Sheets

yield: 10 cracker sheets, approximately 6 × 15 inches (15 × 37.5 cm) each

These cracker sheets are not only delicious, they are very attractive and make a wonderful choice for a buffet presentation. They can be presented whole standing up in baskets or in a single layer lined up on a napkin-lined platter as a centerpiece. The flavors are especially nice to accompany an antipasto or cheese assortment. The herb and vegetable toppings can be varied to suit what you have on hand, but the suggested combination works particularly well. If you are looking for individual-size crackers, one of the other recipes in this chapter would make a better choice, as the special charm of these comes from presenting them whole as little pieces of artwork and allowing guests to break off their own servings.

2½ teaspoons (12.5 ml) fresh compressed yeast	¼ cup (60 ml) plus 2 tablespoons olive oil
1¼ cups (300 ml) warm water (105° to 115°F/40° to 46°C)	1 or 2 small red onions
½ teaspoon (2.5 g) granulated sugar	4 fresh tomatillos, husked
8 ounces (225 g) bread flour	30 red and/or yellow cherry tomatoes
7 ounces (200 g) cake flour	1 small fresh zucchini, crookneck, or patty pan squash
2 ounces (55 g) yellow cornmeal	1 or 2 bunches fresh sage (see Chef's Tip)
2 tablespoons (30 ml) minced fresh rosemary	Small sprigs fresh rosemary
1½ teaspoons (7.5 g) salt	Kosher salt
½ teaspoon (2.5 ml) freshly ground black pepper	

I. Dissolve the yeast in the water. Add the sugar and set aside for 10 minutes.

2. Place the bread flour, cake flour, cornmeal, rosemary, salt, and pepper in the bowl of an electric mixer. Stir to thoroughly combine the dry ingredients. Using the dough hook with the mixer on low speed, add the yeast mixture and the ¼ cup (60 ml) of the olive oil. Knead at low speed, scraping down the sides of the bowl and adding a small amount of either additional water or bread flour as needed, to form a dough that pulls sway from the sides of the bowl. Knead at medium speed for 5 to 6 minutes, until the dough is smooth and elastic.

CHEF'S TIP

If the sage leaves are not extremely fresh and moist, they will not stick to the crackers and instead will curl up and fall off. To remedy this, soak the leaves in water for a few minutes to rehydrate them, then blot dry before arranging them firmly on the dough sheets.

3. Place the dough in an oiled bowl, turn the dough to coat, cover, and set aside in a warm location until doubled in volume.

4. Transfer the dough to a worktable and scale into 10 equal pieces just over 3 ounces (85 g) ounces each. Roll each of the pieces into a ball and cover the balls with plastic wrap to keep them from forming a skin.

5. Roll out each ball of dough to make a very thin oval, approximately 6 x 15 inches (15 x 37.5 cm). Because the dough is rolled very thin, it is important that the thickness is even throughout, or the sheets will not bake evenly. If you have a dough sheeter, you may want to use it, but rolling the crackers by hand is fairly simple if you work on several pieces at the same time, rolling each one partway, then letting it relax for a few moments while you work on another.

6. Place the ovals on sheet pans; it is not necessary to grease them and you should not use baking paper, as it makes the thin dough buckle. Brush the surface of the dough sheets thoroughly with the remaining olive oil.

7. Slice the red onions lengthwise in half, cutting from the top to the root end. Slice the onions lengthwise as thinly as possible, leaving the pieces connected at the root end. Slice the tomatillos crosswise into very thin slices. Slice the cherry tomatoes in half and squeeze out some of the excess juice. Slice the zucchini or crookneck squash into rounds as thin as possible. If using patty pan squash, first cut in half crosswise, then place it cut-side down and slice very thinly to show the scalloped edge on the half slices.

8. Arrange the onion, fanning the slices, tomato halves (cut-side down), tomatillo slices, squash, sage leaves, and rosemary sprigs in a decorative pattern on each dough sheet (Figure 4-1). The cracker sheets are designed to be presented whole, so each one should be created as an individual display of artwork. Lightly dab additional olive oil over the herbs and vegetables. Sprinkle kosher salt and additional freshly ground pepper over the crackers.

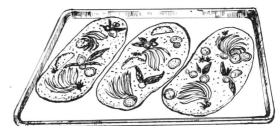

FIGURE 4-1 **Vegetable-Topped Cracker Sheets ready to be baked**

9. Bake at 400°F (205°C) for 12 to 15 minutes or until golden brown and baked through. Lightly brush olive oil over the crackers, being careful not to loosen the toppings after they come out of the oven.

Bread Sticks yield: 24 bread sticks, each 16 inches (40 cm) long

Bread sticks are a popular addition to a bread basket and also make a great snack. They are known as *grissini* in Italy, where the long, thin crackers seem to be included on the table at almost every meal. Instead of sesame seeds, the dough can be coated with chopped fresh rosemary, fennel seeds, poppy seeds, cracked black pepper, or a combination. For a more nutritious bread stick, use the dough from Swedish Whole-Grain Crisp Rolls (page 183), formed and baked as directed here.

1 ounce (30 g) fresh compressed yeast	1 tablespoon (15 g) salt
2½ cups (600 ml) warm water (105° to 115°F/40° to 46°C)	2 pounds 4 ounces (1 kg 25 g) bread flour
	¼ cup (60 ml) olive oil
1 ounce (30 g) granulated malt extract *or* 3 tablespoons (45 ml) or 2 ounces (55 g) honey	Sesame seeds *or* semolina flour

1. In a mixer bowl, dissolve the yeast in the warm water. Add the malt extract or honey and the salt. Incorporate about three-quarters of the flour. Add the olive oil and knead, using the dough hook, for 6 to 8 minutes, adding as much of the reserved flour as required to make a smooth, elastic dough.

2. Place the dough in a bowl oiled with olive oil and turn the dough to coat with the oil. Cover and let rise in a warm place until doubled in volume.

3. Punch down the dough and form into a rectangle measuring 10 x 6 inches (25 x 15 cm). Cover the dough and let it relax for 30 minutes.

4. Cut the dough lengthwise in half. Cut each half lengthwise into 12 equal strips.

5. Pound and roll the pieces into strings (see Figures 3-16 to 3-18, page 148) without using any flour. Roll and stretch the strings to make them 16 inches (40 cm) long.

6. Line up the pieces and spray lightly with water. Sprinkle sesame seeds or semolina flour on top, then roll each piece a half turn and sprinkle again to cover them all over. (If you want the bread sticks heavily coated with sesame seeds, place the seeds on a sheet pan and roll the bread strings on top.)

7. Place the bread sticks on sheet pans lined with baking paper, spacing them a few inches apart.

8. Bake immediately (without allowing the bread sticks to rise first) at 425°F (219°C) for approximately 10 minutes or until golden brown. They will still be soft inside. To dry them completely, reduce the oven temperature to 300°F (149°C) and bake about 20 minutes longer. If they are dried all the way through and stored in airtight containers, the bread sticks will stay crisp for several weeks.

Lemon Thyme–Sesame Butter Crackers yield: variable, depending on size

These crackers acquire an excellent and refreshing flavor from the combination of lemon thyme and lemon zest, but you could certainly vary the recipe by using another herb, such as fresh basil or sage. The dough is basically mixed like a pie dough, which makes the finished texture of the crackers short and flaky. For a faster production method, cut into squares or rectangles, instead of rounds, with a multiple-wheel pastry cutter.

4 ounces (115 g) bread flour	⅛ teaspoon (.25 g) cayenne pepper
3 ounces (85 g) cake flour	½ cup (120 ml) or 3 ounces (85 g) white sesame seeds
2 ounces (55 g) semolina flour	
Finely chopped zest of 1 lemon	2½ ounces (70 g) unsalted butter, cut into small chunks and frozen
1 tablespoon (15 ml) minced fresh lemon thyme leaves, firmly packed	½ cup (120 ml) ice-cold water
1 teaspoon (5 g) salt	Olive oil
1 teaspoon (2 g) freshly ground black pepper	Kosher salt *or* freshly grated Parmesan cheese

1. Place the bread flour, cake flour, semolina, lemon zest, thyme, salt, pepper, cayenne, and sesame seeds in the bowl of a food processor. Mix to thoroughly combine. Add the frozen butter and pulse a few times until the butter is reduced to tiny but still visible pieces, about the size of rice grains. With the machine running, add the cold water and mix only until the dough comes together; do not overmix.

2. Transfer to a worktable and, working with a portion of the dough a time, roll it out to about ¼ inch (6 mm) thick, then pass it through a dough sheeter or the rollers of a pasta machine to make it as thin as possible without tearing. If neither of these options is available to you, finish rolling the dough by hand, making it as thin and even as possible. Prick the dough all over with a docker.

3. Line sheet pans with baking paper and brush the paper generously with olive oil.

4. Using a round plain or fluted cutter, cut out rounds from the cracker dough and place the crackers on the pans. Reroll the scraps, adding some of the fresh dough, and continue rolling, docking, and cutting the crackers until you have used all of the dough.

5. Brush olive oil lightly over the crackers; then lightly sprinkle kosher salt or Parmesan cheese on top (as Parmesan is fairly high in salt, it is not necessary to use both).

6. Bake at 375°F (190°C) until deep golden brown and baked though. Store the crackers in airtight containers.

Swedish Thin Bread yield: 112 crackers, 2 x 3 inches (5 x 7.5 cm)

This type of cracker, called *Knäckebröd* in Swedish—hard, crisp, and healthy—is included in the daily diet of the majority of Scandinavians. The crackers are delicious eaten plain as a quick snack, or they can be cut into a larger size before baking and served topped with cheese or pâté as an appetizer.

4 ounces (115 g) vegetable shortening

2 ounces (55 g) unsalted butter, at room temperature

2 ounces (55 g) granulated sugar

6 ounces (170 g) rolled oats

1 pound 5 ounces (595 g) bread flour

1 teaspoon (5 g) salt

1 teaspoon (4 g) baking soda

1½ cups (360 ml) buttermilk

1. Cream the shortening, butter, and sugar, using the paddle until the mixture is light and fluffy.

2. Combine the rolled oats, flour, salt, and baking soda.

3. On low speed, incorporate the dry ingredients into the butter mixture in 2 additions, alternating with the buttermilk. Do not overmix; the dough will be fairly sticky. Adjust with a little additional flour if necessary to be able to roll the dough out very thin. Keep in mind, however, that the softer the dough, the crisper the finished product.

4. Divide the dough into 4 pieces, 12 ounces (340 g) each. Cover and place 3 pieces in the refrigerator (see Note).

5. Roll the remaining piece into a rectangle measuring 14 x 12 inches (35 x 30 cm), using flour to prevent sticking. The dough will be very thin.

6. Mark the top of the rolled sheet with a waffle roller or, if not available, prick well.

7. Roll up the dough on a dowel and transfer to a sheet pan lined with baking paper. Score the top, cutting approximately halfway through, marking 28 rectangles measuring 2 x 3 inches (5 x 7.5 cm)—7 rectangles on the long side by 4 on the short side. Repeat Steps 5, 6, and 7 with the 3 remaining pieces of dough.

8. Bake at 325°F (163°C) for approximately 30 minutes or until completely dry. Let the crackers cool on the pan. Break apart on the scored lines. Stored in airtight containers, the crackers will stay fresh and crisp for several weeks.

NOTE: If you do not need the full amount of crackers all at once, place the extra dough pieces in the freezer after Step 4. They will keep for several weeks.

Swedish Whole-Grain Crisp Rolls yield: 96 crackers, approximately 3¹/₂ × 1¹/₂ inches (8.7 × 3.7 cm)

Crisp rolls, or *skorpor*, as they are called in Scandinavia, are a delicious and hearty snack eaten plain, dipped in coffee or tea, or topped with butter, cheese, or marmalade. They are a type of cracker and should not be mistaken for dried leftover rolls. The characteristic fragile and crunchy texture, which is the trademark of a real crisp roll, is obtained only by making sure the dough as been prepared and proofed properly.

1 cup (240 ml) boiling water	1 tablespoon (15 g) salt
8 ounces (225 g) cracked wheat	4 ounces (115 g) bread flour
1¹/₂ ounces (40 g) fresh compressed yeast	1 pound (455 g) whole wheat flour
1 pint (480 ml) warm whole milk (105° to 115°F/40° to 46°C)	3 ounces (85 g) soft lard
2 tablespoons (30 ml) or 1¹/₂ ounces (40 g) honey	

1. Pour the boiling water over the cracked wheat and stir to combine. Cover and set aside until soft, 2 to 3 hours, or, preferably, overnight.

2. Dissolve the yeast in the warm milk. Mix in the honey and salt, then incorporate the bread flour, half of the whole wheat flour, and the reserved cracked wheat. Add the lard and knead, using the dough hook, for 6 to 8 minutes at low to medium speed, adding enough of the remaining whole wheat flour to make a fairly firm and elastic dough.

3. Place the dough in an oiled bowl, turn to coat with oil, cover, and let rise in a warm place until doubled in volume.

4. Punch down the dough and repeat Step 3 twice.

5. After the third rising, punch down the dough and divide it into 2 equal pieces approximately 1 pound 12 ounces (795 g) each. Roll each into a 24-inch (60-cm) string and cut the strings into 24 equal pieces each. Form the pieces into 2¹/₂-inch (6.2-cm) ovals, slightly tapered at the ends (see Figure 4-2, page 186).

6. Place the rolls on sheet pans lined with baking paper and let rise until doubled in volume.

7. Bake at 400°F (205°C) until light brown and baked through, approximately 15 minutes. Let cool.

8. Break the rolls in half horizontally in the traditional way, using a large fork (see Note). Return the pieces to the sheet pans, cut-side up.

9. Toast the roll halves at 400°F (205°C) until they have browned lightly. Reduce the oven temperature to 300°F (149°C) and leave the rolls in the oven until they are completely dried through. If stored in airtight containers, these crackers will keep fresh for many weeks.

NOTE: Avoid cutting the rolls with a serrated knife. This not only ruins their rustic look, but, more important, it will also make them less crispy.

WHEAT CRISP ROLLS yield: 80 crackers, approximately 2¹/₂ inches (6.2 cm) in diameter

1¹/₂ ounces (40 g) fresh compressed yeast

1 pint (480 ml) warm whole milk (105° to 115°F/40° to 46°C)

4 ounces (115 g) granulated sugar

1 tablespoon (15 g) salt

1 tablespoon (6 g) ground cardamom

1 pound 10 ounces (740 g) bread flour

2 ounces (55 g) lard, at room temperature

1. Dissolve the yeast in the warm milk. Add the sugar, salt, and cardamom.

2. Incorporate about two-thirds of the flour.

3. Add the lard and knead, using the dough hook, for approximately 6 minutes, adding enough of the remaining flour to make a smooth, elastic dough.

4. Place the dough in a lightly oiled bowl, turn over to coat with oil, cover, and let rise in a warm place until doubled in volume.

5. Punch down the dough and repeat Step 4 twice.

6. After the third rising, punch down the dough and divide it into 2 equal pieces approximately 1 pound 8 ounces (680 g) each. Roll each one into 20-inch (50-cm) strings and cut each string into 20 pieces. Shape the pieces into tight rounds.

7. Proceed with the directions for Swedish Whole-Grain Crisp Rolls, Steps 6 through 9.

Zwieback yield: about 70 toasts, 5 x 2¹/₂ x ³/₄ inches (12.5 x 6.2 x 2 cm)

Literally translated from German, *zwieback* means "twice baked." It is basically a breakfast bread dough that is baked, cut in half or sliced, and toasted until dry and pleasingly crunchy, like biscotti. When I was growing up, zwieback were made not only in factories and larger bakeries but even in the smallest pastry shop. Today, with few exceptions, zwieback are mass-produced exclusively in factories.

There are many ways to vary this basic recipe. By increasing or decreasing the amounts of sugar and/or eggs, you can produce differing flavors and textures. Zwieback are also made with a special highly nutritious flour for those on special diets and for infants and toddlers; these are especially popular for youngsters who are teething. My mother was a great believer in the theory that hard or stale bread was good for children (although all through my early childhood, I felt it was just an excuse to use up old bread). Zwieback make great croutons for soups, salads, and canapés.

To achieve the desired texture in the finished cracker, it is crucial to keep the dough a little firmer than you might expect and to take the time to allow the dough to mature fully, punching it down and letting it proof 3 times. Use a low oven for the final toasting to dry the crackers all the way through.

SPONGE

2 ounces (55 g) fresh compressed yeast

2 cups (480 ml) warm whole milk (105° to 115°F/40° to 46°C)

14 ounces (400 g) bread flour

DOUGH

1 cup (240 ml) warm whole milk (105° to 115°F/40° to 46°C)

3 ounces (85 g) granulated sugar

1 tablespoon (15 g) salt

3 eggs

2 pounds 6 ounces (1 kg 80 g) bread flour

5 ounces (140 g) unsalted butter

Potato Starch Solution (recipe follows)

1. To make the sponge, dissolve the yeast in the warm milk, then stir in the flour, mixing until you have a smooth paste. Cover and let stand in a warm place until the sponge has risen to its maximum volume. When the sponge is fully mature, it first begins to bubble on the surface and then gradually starts to fall; this takes approximately 30 minutes.

2. To make the dough, mix the milk, sugar, salt, and eggs into the sponge. Hold back a handful of the remaining flour and incorporate the rest. Knead in the butter and enough of the reserved flour to make quite a firm dough. Continue to knead at low speed until the dough is smooth and elastic, about 6 minutes.

3. Place the dough in a lightly oiled bowl, turn over to coat with oil, cover, and let rise in a warm place until doubled in volume.

4. Punch down the dough, then cover and let rise again until doubled in volume.

5. Punch down the dough and let rise once more, for a total of 3 risings.

6. Divide the dough into 3 equal pieces, approximately 1 pound 12 ounces (795 g) each. Pound and roll each piece into a 16-inch (40-cm) rope (see Figures 3-16 to 3-18, page 148); do not taper the ends as shown.

7. Cut each rope into 12 equal pieces. Form the small pieces into mini-loaves. Place the pieces side by side on sheet pans lined with baking paper, as shown for Tessiner Rolls (see Figure 4-15, page 205; do not cut these as shown in the drawing). Let rise to just under 1½ times the original size. Do not overproof. Brush the potato starch solution over the loaves.

8. Bake at 400°F (205°C) for approximately 25 minutes or until completely baked through. Remove from the oven and brush again with the potato starch solution. Set the zwieback loaves aside at room temperature until the following day.

9. Cut the loaves lengthwise into slices ¾ inch (2cm) thick. Place the slices cut-side down on sheet pans lined with baking paper.

10. Toast the slices at 325°F (163°C) until they are light golden brown on top, about 20 minutes. Turn the slices over and continue baking for about 20 minutes longer or until golden brown on the second side as well. Adjust the oven temperature if necessary. If the oven is too hot, the zwieback will not have a chance to dry properly in the center by the time they are brown on the outside, which will cause them to become chewy after just a few days of storage. Properly baked and stored in airtight containers, they will stay crisp for many weeks.

POTATO STARCH SOLUTION

1 cup (240 ml) cold water   1 ounce (30 g) potato starch

1. Stir the water into the potato starch.

2. Heat, stirring constantly, to just under boiling.

3. Use hot or cold.

MELBA TOAST

This is the lesser known of the culinary creations named for the opera singer Nellie Melba, the most famous being the dessert peach Melba, which is accompanied by Melba sauce. All were composed in her honor by the great chef Auguste Escoffier. History has it that having returned from a tour exhausted and in poor health, Nellie Melba was put on a strict diet which included thin slices of toasted bread. Chef Escoffier's plain dried bread then became known as Melba toast.

Although any rich bread can be used, zwieback is ideal due to its fine, crumbly texture. To make Melba toast, slice the baked zwieback loaves ¼ inch (6 mm) thick. Cut the slices into rounds, triangles, or squares as desired. Toast the slices as instructed in the main recipe; however, the thinner Melba toasts will require only about 10 minutes on each side.

ROLLS

With a few exceptions, virtually any bread dough can be made into rolls or knots and, conversely, the opposite is also true. Rolls can be defined simply as bread dough that is portioned into individual servings, usually around 2 ounces (55 g) each, before it is baked. Rolls, especially knots, take longer to form than loaves, but the results are worthwhile. Rolls look much more elegant served in a bread basket on the lunch or dinner table than do slices of bread, and rolls do not become stale as quickly as sliced bread. In many European countries, a kaiser roll or other type of crusty roll is considered an absolute must at breakfast.

TO FORM ROLLS

Forming a perfectly round, smooth, tight roll with the palm of your hand is easy if you use the right technique. As when forming bread loaves, your objective is to create a tight skin around the mass of dough. Place two balls of dough on the table with your hands cupped on top, fingers clenched like claws. Press down fairly hard on the dough as you move both hands simultaneously in tight circles. Move your left hand counterclockwise and your right hand clockwise, so both are moving toward the outside (Figure 4-2). As you press down, forming the dough into a tight round ball, let the dough stick to the table just a little, or it will not form a skin. For this

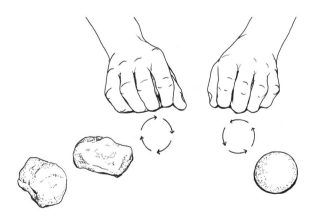

FIGURE 4-2 Forming rolls by moving the hands in circular directions, at the same time pressing the balls of dough against the table; a round roll and a roll made into an oval shape

reason, as little flour as possible should be used, and if the dough just slides and doesn't stick at all, try rubbing the table with a wet towel. If you are making oval rolls, such as Milk Rolls, first roll the dough round. Then, without lifting your hands, which remain cupped around the dough, move them away and back toward you a few times in a straight line.

An easier instructional method is to practice with just one hand. If you are right-handed, use the palm of your left hand as the tabletop, holding it flat, and work the dough into a round ball by cupping your right hand on top and moving it in a circle.

Bagels yield: 36 bagels, approximately 4 inches (10 cm) in diameter

The Yiddish word *bagel* comes from the German word *boug*, meaning "ring." These doughnut-shaped bread rolls are poached in a sweetened water solution before they are placed on sheet pans and baked in the oven. This reduces the starch, which, in combination with the gluten-rich flour and the absence of fat, gives bagels their characteristic chewy texture. Poaching also contributes to the bagel's glossy finish. Bagels are a traditional Jewish breakfast food served topped with cream cheese and smoked salmon (lox). Smaller cocktail-sized bagels are popular for hors d'oeuvres and snacks. As a variation, replace one-third of the flour with whole wheat or rye flour.

1½ ounces (40 g) fresh compressed yeast	4 pounds 4 ounces (1 kg 935 g) high-gluten flour
1 quart (960 ml) warm water (105° to 115°F/40° to 46°C)	Poaching Liquid for Bagels (recipe follows)
3 tablespoons (45 ml) or 2 ounces (55 g) honey	Egg wash (optional)
2 ounces (55 g) granulated sugar	Poppy, sesame, *or* caraway seeds, kosher salt, or chopped onion (optional; see Note)
2 tablespoons (30 g) salt	

1. Dissolve the yeast in the warm water. Mixing with the dough hook, add the honey, sugar, salt, and enough of the flour to make a stiff, smooth dough.

2. Cover tightly to prevent a skin from forming, then let the dough rest in a warm place for about 1 hour.

3. Punch down and divide the dough into 3 equal pieces, approximately 2 pounds 4 ounces (1 kg 25 g) each. Roll each piece into a 16-inch (40-cm) rope. Do not use any flour while forming the ropes. The dough should be stiff and elastic enough to form without flour.

4. Cut 12 equal pieces from each rope. Form and roll each of the smaller pieces into ropes about 9 inches (22.5 cm) long. Overlap the ends of the ropes about ½ inch (1.2 cm) and press them together firmly against the table, rocking the dough back and forth with your palm to seal the edges together. Try to make the rings a uniform thickness throughout.

5. Place the bagels on a sheet pan lined with cloth; canvas is ideal. Let the bagels rise until they have slightly less than doubled in volume.

6. Bring the poaching liquid to a boil, reduce the heat to a simmer, then carefully drop the bagels into the liquid and poach for about 2 minutes. They will sink in the liquid and then slowly rise to the surface. Once the bagels float to the top, remove them with a slotted spoon or skimmer. Place them 1½ inches (3.7 cm) apart on sheet pans lined with baking paper. If desired, brush with egg wash and top with poppy, sesame, or caraway seeds; kosher salt; or chopped onion.

7. Bake at 450°F (230°C) until the bagels are light brown, approximately 12 minutes. Flip the bagels over and continue baking about 10 minutes longer, until baked through and browned on the second side.

NOTE: Chop the onion fine, blanch in boiling water, then pat dry with paper towels.

POACHING LIQUID FOR BAGELS

This may seem like a lot of water and honey to use for poaching the bagels only 2 minutes. The large quantity is necessary to be able to poach a greater number at the same time. If this were not done, the bagels waiting their turn would overproof. If kept in the refrigerator, the poaching liquid can be reused many times.

1 gallon (3 L 840 ml) water	**1½ cups (360 ml) or 1 pound 2 ounces (510 g) honey**

1. Combine the water and honey in a large pan and bring to a boil.

2. Reduce the heat to a simmer to use for poaching.

VARIATION

EGG BAGELS yield: 24 bagels, approximately 4 inches (10 cm) in diameter

Egg bagels are less chewy than regular bagels and are not poached prior to baking. They have a lighter texture that is similar to challah. After they are fully proofed, egg bagels are often topped with poppy, sesame, or caraway seeds, or kosher salt before being placed in the oven. If you would like to top the bagels with onion, follow the directions in the note with the bagel recipe above.

1 ounce (30 g) fresh compressed yeast	1 pound 12 ounces (795 g) high-gluten flour
1½ cups (360 ml) warm water (105° to 115°F/40° to 46°C)	1 whole egg
2 ounces (55 g) granulated sugar	1 egg yolk
1 tablespoon (15 g) salt	Egg wash
¼ cup (60 ml) olive oil	Caraway, sesame, or poppy seeds, or kosher salt

1. Dissolve the yeast in the warm water. Add the sugar, salt, and olive oil. Mix in enough of the flour to form a pasty dough. Mix in the egg and egg yolk separately, blending after each addition. Incorporate all but a few handfuls of the remaining flour.

2. Knead for about 8 minutes, using the dough hook at medium speed and adding the reserved handfuls of flour if necessary, to make a stiff, smooth dough.

3. Place the dough in an oiled bowl and invert it to coat with oil. Cover and leave in a warm place until doubled in volume, about 40 minutes.

4. Divide the dough into 2 equal pieces approximately 1 pound 8 ounces (680 g) each.

5. Proceed as directed for traditional bagels, omitting the poaching step and placing the bagels directly on paper-lined sheet pans as you form them. Let the bagels rise until 1½ times the original size.

6. Brush the bagels with egg wash. Sprinkle with caraway seeds, poppy seeds, or kosher salt.

7. Bake as directed in the recipe for Bagels on pages 187 to 188.

Conchas yield: 40 buns, approximately 3¹/₂ inches (8.7 cm) in diameter

You will notice quite a few south-of-border influences in this new edition of my book—from cookies, desserts, and garnishes to these ever-popular conchas. During the five years that I worked for The Culinary Institute of America, I was dispatched to Mexico City on numerous occasions to teach classes at an adjunct facility. I also taught classes privately and conducted seminars at what is, in my opinion, the top cooking school in Mexico City, Gastronomía Maricu, run by the wonderful Señora Maricu Ortiz and her devoted crew.

Conchas, which translates to "shells," made their way to Mexico from Spain. These round sugar-topped buns are found everywhere from the fanciest *pastelería* (pastry shop) to the supermarket and just about any place in between. Conchas are often served for *merienda*, an afternoon snack.

The dough resembles a cross between a challah dough and a brioche dough. After proofing, the buns are topped with a sugar paste, which is etched into a spiral design using a special cutter. As the rolls bake and expand, the topping forms the spiral shell pattern for which the rolls are named. You will also see conchas made with a crisscross design on top, though I was told that, in this case, they should be called *chicharrones* (which is also the name for a fried pork skin snack). If you do not have a concha cutter to mark the topping, you can use three or four plain cookie cutters in descending sizes to imprint the paste, or you can use a knife to score a crosshatch pattern, in which case you will be making *chicharrones*.

STARTER

1 ounce (30 g) fresh compressed yeast

¾ cup (180 ml) water, at room temperature

2 eggs, beaten slightly

10 ounces (285 g) cake flour

DOUGH

6 eggs

½ cup (120 ml) warm water (115°F/46°C)

4 ounces (115 g) unsalted butter, at room temperature

1 teaspoon (5 g) salt

12 ounces (340 g) granulated sugar

1 pound (455 g) bread flour

1 pound (455 g) cake flour

TOPPING

6 ounces (170 g) unsalted butter, at room temperature

1 teaspoon (5 ml) vanilla extract

5 ounces (140 g) cake flour

6 ounces (170 g) powdered sugar

1 ounce (30 g) ground cinnamon *or* sifted unsweetened cocoa powder

Egg wash

1. To make the starter, dissolve the yeast in the water. Add the eggs and mix for a few moments. Gradually incorporate most of the cake flour, continuing to mix until you have a dough that is fairly sticky, yet is elastic enough to pull away from the sides of the bowl; add more flour if needed. Cover and let the starter rest in a warm location until doubled in volume.

2. To make the dough, place the starter in a mixer bowl with the dough hook attachment. Add the eggs, water, butter, salt, and half of the sugar. Hold back a handful of the bread flour; add the remainder together with the cake flour.

3. Knead the dough at medium speed for 6 to 8 minutes. Add the remaining sugar and continue to knead for another 5 minutes, adding some or all of the reserved flour as needed to create a soft, shiny, elastic dough. Place the dough in an oiled bowl; turn to coat. Cover with plastic and set in a warm location to proof for 1 hour.

4. To make the topping, work the butter smooth in a mixer bowl and, at the same time, incorporate the vanilla extract. Sift together the cake flour and powdered sugar and gradually add this mixture to the butter. Continue mixing until you have a smooth, pliable paste you can work with in your hands. Flavor the mixture with the cinnamon or cocoa powder. If desired, both the cocoa powder and cinnamon may be omitted, which will highlight the flavor of the vanilla.

5. Divide the dough into 4 equal pieces approximately 1 pound 3 ounces (540 g) each. Pound and roll each piece into a rope 16 inches (40 cm) long, using flour to prevent the dough from sticking to the table. Divide each rope into 10 equal pieces. Roll each piece into a smooth, round ball (see Figure 4-2, page 186), keeping the pieces you are not working with covered so they do not dry out or form a skin.

6. Place the balls of dough on sheet pans lined with baking paper or Silpats, spacing them about 3 inches (7.5 cm) apart. Use the palm of your hand to flatten the balls, making them approximately 3 inches (7.5 cm) in diameter.

7. Divide the topping into 4 equal pieces. Roll out each one to a 12-inch (30-cm) rope. Cut each rope into 10 equal pieces, then roll each small piece into a ball. Flatten the balls by pressing each one into the palm of your hand to make a 3-inch (7.5-cm) disk. Brush egg wash over the dough rounds, then press the topping disks on top, making sure they are well attached. Cut a curved pattern in the sugar topping with a small knife or razor blade, or use a concha cutter dipped in flour (Figure 4-3). Let the conchas proof until 1½ times their original size.

8. Bake at 375°F (190°C) until golden brown and baked through, about 20 minutes.

FIGURE 4-3 **Making Conchas. Left to right: A flattened disk of the topping mixture; balls of dough before being flattened; flattened balls of dough with the topping disks in place; the rolls after marking the topping with a Concha cutter; a close up of the tool**

Crumpets yield: approximately 30 crumpets, 3 inches (7.5 cm) in diameter

One can hardly mention crumpets without thinking of English tea. In fact, the phrase "tea and crumpets" is about as commonplace in the food world as "coffee and doughnuts" or "soup and a sandwich."

Crumpets can be enjoyed for breakfast as well as afternoon tea. Afternoon tea can be a very simple affair or, at the other end of the scale, it can be a significant social ritual governed by strict rules of etiquette and protocol. In addition to small sweets, an ornate afternoon tea menu features savory items that could include tiny crustless sandwiches filled with shrimp paste, thinly sliced cucumber and cream cheese, or finely minced chicken salad, and a selection of cheeses with crackers and fresh fruit. Rounding out the assortment might be scones served with jam and clotted cream and these freshly made crumpets offered with whipped sweet butter and lemon curd or orange marmalade.

2 ounces (55 g) fresh compressed yeast

2½ cups (600 ml) warm whole milk (105° to 115°F/40° to 46°C)

1 ounce (30 g) granulated sugar

1 teaspoon (5 g) salt

2 ounces (55 g) melted unsalted butter

4 eggs, at room temperature

8 ounces (225 g) cake flour

8 ounces (225 g) bread flour

Clarified butter

Accompaniments such as maple or golden syrup; marmalade, jam or jelly; Lemon Curd (page 844); clotted cream and/or whipped butter

1. In the bowl of an electric mixer, dissolve the yeast in the warm milk. Stir in the sugar and salt. Place the bowl on the mixer and, using the paddle attachment, incorporate the butter, eggs, and cake flour. Reserve a handful of the bread flour and mix in the remainder, beating until a smooth soft batter has formed; add the reserved flour if necessary. The batter should be fluid and approximately the same consistency as a buttermilk pancake batter. Cover the bowl and allow the batter to proof in a warm place until it has doubled in volume.

2. When you are ready to cook the crumpets, brush the inside of 6 to 8 crumpet rings, 3 inches (7.5 cm) in diameter, with clarified butter and heat a large skillet with a flat, even surface (or a griddle) until very hot but not smoking.

3. Stir down the batter. Brush clarified butter over the skillet or griddle and place the rings on top. Ladle 2 tablespoons (1 ounce/30 ml) batter into each ring. The batter will flow out and fill the rings and should start to bubble in less than 1 minute. When the bottoms of the crumpets begin to turn golden brown, lift off the rings and turn the crumpets over with a wide spatula. Continue cooking until the second side is also light brown, then transfer to warm platter or sheet pan. Keep the cooked crumpets covered and warm as you cook the remainder in the same way, adding more clarified butter to the rings and the cooking surface as needed.

4. Serve the crumpets warm with any of the accompaniments suggested in the ingredient list.

English Muffins yield: 25 muffins, 3½ inches (8.7 cm) in diameter

English muffins are a breed apart from the sweet, cupcake-like American muffin traditionally baked in a paper cup. English muffins are flat, barely sweetened yeast-leavened buns, closely resembling crumpets. Both English muffins and crumpets are baked on a griddle on top of the stove within small ring forms, usually about 3 inches (7.5 cm) in diameter. Crumpets are made with a softer dough—almost a batter—that cannot be rolled out and is instead poured into the rings. The softer crumpet dough produces larger air pockets (holes) than the English muffin dough does when baked.

1 ounce (30 g) fresh compressed yeast	1 egg
1½ cups (360 ml) warm water (105° to 115°F/40° to 46°C)	1 pound 8 ounces (680 g) bread flour
2 ounces (55 g) granulated sugar	3 ounces (85 g) unsalted butter, at room temperature
2 teaspoons (10 g) salt	Cornmeal

1. In a mixer bowl, dissolve the yeast in the warm water. Add the sugar, salt, and egg. Incorporate about two-thirds of the flour and mix with a wooden spoon to form a smooth paste.

2. Cover and let the sponge rise in a warm place until it has reached its maximum size and has started to fall.

3. Mix in the butter and the remaining flour, using the dough hook or paddle on your electric mixer. Adjust with additional flour if necessary; the dough should be soft and smooth but, because it is not kneaded, it will remain slightly sticky. Cover the dough and let rise in a warm place until doubled in volume.

4. Punch the dough down and let it rest for 10 minutes.

5. Roll out the dough ¼ inch (6 mm) thick, using flour to prevent sticking. Cut out 3½-inch (8.7-cm) circles, using a plain cookie cutter. If the dough shrinks as you cut the first few, let it relax for a few minutes before continuing, or you will end up with ovals instead of circles.

6. Line a sheet pan with baking paper. Sprinkle cornmeal lightly over the paper. Grease the inside of 3½-inch (8.7-cm) crumpet rings (or other metal rings) and set the rings on the cornmeal. Place the dough rounds inside the rings. (If you do not have crumpet rings or other suitable rings, you can make the muffins free-form. They will not be quite as high nor will they be perfectly round, but the taste will be the same.)

7. Stack the dough scraps, then roll out and cut more rounds until all of the dough is used. Let the muffins rise until doubled in volume.

8. Use a metal spatula to transfer the muffins (including the rings) to a hot, greased griddle (see Note). Remove the rings and cook the muffins for 2 minutes. Turn them over and cook for 2 minutes on the other side. Lower the heat and continue cooking for approximately 12 minutes or until baked through, turning the muffins again halfway through cooking. Carefully transfer the muffins to a cake rack to cool.

9. To split the muffins, pierce them horizontally all around the sides with a large fork, then break the halves apart. You should never cut an English muffin in half with a knife. Not only will they no longer look the way they are supposed to, they will not be as crisp after they are toasted.

10. Store leftover muffins in the freezer. The muffins will start to taste like the store-bought variety after a few days in the refrigerator.

NOTE: Although English muffins should be baked on a griddle, they can also, if necessary, be baked in the oven. Leave the muffins on the sheet pan after proofing. Bake at 450°F (230°C) for 2 minutes on each side. Remove the rings and lower the oven temperature to 400°F (205°C). Bake approximately 14 minutes longer or until done.

VARIATION
ENGLISH MUFFIN LOAVES

Try making half of the English muffin dough into loaf bread. It is great sliced and toasted, although this challenges the rule that says an English muffin must be pierced with a fork and pulled apart. The full recipe will yield 2 large loaves, about 1 pound 6 ounces (625 g) each before baking. Grease the inside of bread pans measuring 10 x 4 x 2½ inches (25 x 10 x 6.2 cm), form the dough to fit, let proof until doubled in volume, then bake at 375°F (190°C) until golden and baked through. Let cool slightly before unmolding.

Hamburger Buns yield: 24 buns

Hamburger, the small grilled or fried beef patty we are so familiar with today, comes from the city of Hamburg, Germany. The burger, as it is often called, became firmly established and synonymous with American cooking at the St. Louis World's Fair in 1904, and America never looked back—the fast-food chains made sure of that. Enclosing the cooked meat between toasted bun halves was popularized around 1940 with the birth of what is currently the oldest and largest of these establishments. From my point of view, at least, you could say, "It's the bun that makes the burger."

This recipe for hamburger or hot dog buns is not for the most common type, but I personally like them better. If you yearn for tradition, make the buns from the Milk Roll dough (page 198) instead, following the instructions below to form them.

SPONGE

1½ ounces (40 g) fresh compressed yeast

1 quart (960 ml) warm low-fat milk (105° to 115°F/40° to 46°C)

1 ounce (30 g) granulated sugar

3 tablespoons (27 g) granulated malt extract *or* 3 tablespoons (45 ml) or 2 ounces (55 g) honey

2 pounds 2 ounces (970 g) bread flour

DOUGH

1 pound 4 ounces (570 g) bread flour

2 tablespoons (30 g) salt

⅓ cup (80 ml) vegetable oil

Poppy or sesame seeds

1. To make the sponge, dissolve the yeast in the warm milk. Using the dough hook, mix in the granulated sugar, malt extract or honey, and the flour. Continue mixing until the sponge has a smooth, pastelike consistency, about 2 to 3 minutes. Cover and let rise in a warm place for 1 to 2 hours.

2. To make the dough, reserve 2 handfuls of the flour and mix the salt with the remainder. Add this to the sponge and knead for 1 minute or so to combine well. Add the oil and continue kneading for 8 to 10 minutes, adjusting the consistency by adding the reserved flour as required to make a medium-stiff dough that is smooth and elastic.

3. Place the dough in a lightly oiled bowl. Turn the dough to coat with oil, place a damp towel on top, and set aside to rise in a warm location until the dough has doubled in volume.

4. Punch down the dough, cover, and let rise a second time until doubled in volume.

5. Divide the dough into 3 equal pieces, approximately 1 pound 14 ounces (855 g) each (do not punch down the dough or otherwise tighten the gluten). Form the pieces into even strings.

6. Cut each string into 8 equal pieces. Form the pieces into round rolls (see Figure 4-2, page 186). Set the rolls on sheet pans lined with baking paper, leaving about 3 inches (7.5 cm) between them. Set aside in a warm place until the dough has relaxed and the rolls have just started to rise, about 10 minutes.

7. Using a flat, round object about 4 to 6 inches (10 to 15 cm) in diameter, flatten the rolls to make them 4 inches (10 cm) in diameter. Spray or brush with water, then sprinkle poppy or sesame seeds over the tops. Let rise until slightly less than doubled in volume.

8. Bake at 400°F (205°C) for approximately 15 minutes or until baked through and golden brown.

VARIATION
HOT DOG BUNS yield: 36 buns

When I was an apprentice in Sweden, the sausage, or hot dog, was king of what was the equivalent of today's takeout or fast-food outlets. (The burger had not yet arrived.) Every village in Scandinavia and the German-speaking countries of the continent—especially Germany itself, which is unsurpassed when it comes to making delicious wurst or frankfurters—had a hot dog stand, a mini-street kitchen serving various sausages and other quickly made specialties. The hot dog stand in the small village where I did my apprenticeship usually received its buns from the local bakery but would, in an emergency, order 100 or so from the pastry shop where I was one of several young trainees. Reporting to work and being told that part of your job was to make hot dog buns was considered just about as low as you could sink. You would, of course, respectfully reply "Yes, chef!" but at the same time try to figure out what you had done wrong to be handed this degrading task.

1. Prepare dough as for Hamburger Buns (above) through Step 5.

2. In Step 6, cut each of the 3 strings into 12 equal pieces instead of 8.

3. Pound and form each of the small pieces into 6-inch (15-cm) ropes, using the same technique as for baguettes (see Figures 3-16 to 3-18, page 148; do not taper the ends as shown).

4. Spray or brush with water. Let rise until slightly less than doubled in volume.

5. Bake at 400°F (205°C) for 12 to 15 minutes or until baked through and golden brown.

Kaiser Rolls yield: 60 rolls, approximately 2 ounces (55 g) each

Kaiser Franz Joseph I, emperor of Austria from 1848 to 1916 (and king of Hungary from 1867 to 1916), lent his name to many culinary creations, including the desserts Kaiser Schmarren and Franz Joseph Torte, as well as kaiser rolls, which are also known as *Vienna rolls*. Although the rolls can be formed by hand, most commercial operations mark the pattern on top using a special cutter with a fan-shaped blade, or they use a kaiser roll machine. You cannot have missed seeing these great-looking crusty rolls if you have walked into a deli almost anywhere in the world. In Germany and Austria, they are always on the breakfast table with cheese, cold cuts, and marmalade—what a way to start the day! I like them best the way the way I grew up with them in Europe—with plenty of poppy seeds on top.

2 ounces (55 g) fresh compressed yeast

1 quart (960 ml) warm water (105° to 115°F/40° to 46°C)

3 tablespoons (45 g) salt

2 ounces (55 g) granulated malt extract *or* ⅓ cup (80 ml) or 4 ounces (115 g) honey

3 ounces (85 g) unsalted butter, at room temperature

Kaiser Roll Pre-Dough (recipe follows; see Note 1)

3 pounds 5 ounces (1 kg 505 g) bread flour

Poppy seeds (optional)

Small-Batch Kaiser Rolls

yield: 20 rolls, approximately 2 ounces (55 g) each

1½ cups (360 ml) warm water (105° to 115°F/40° to 46°C)

¾ ounce (22 g) fresh compressed yeast

1 tablespoon (15 g) salt

1 ounce (30 g) granulated malt extract *or* 2 tablespoons (30 ml) honey

1 ounce (30 g) unsalted butter, at room temperature

Small-Batch Kaiser Roll Pre-Dough (recipe follows; see Note 1)

1 pound 3 ounces (540 g) bread flour

Poppy seeds (optional)

---

1. Dissolve the yeast in the warm water. Mix in the salt and the malt extract or honey. Add the butter and pre-dough. Using the dough hook at low to medium speed, mix in enough of the bread flour to form a dough. Knead until smooth and elastic, 10 to 15 minutes.

2. Place the dough in an oiled bowl. Turn to coat with oil, cover, and let rise for 30 minutes.

3. Punch the dough down to remove all air. Cover and let rise an additional 30 minutes.

4. Divide the dough into 3 equal pieces, approximately 3 pounds (1 kg 365 g) each. Form each piece into an even rope about 20 inches (50 cm) long, then cut each rope into 20 equal pieces. (For the smaller recipe, divide the dough in half evenly, roll each piece to a rope 16 inches (40 cm) long, and cut each rope into 10 equal pieces.) Form the small pieces into round rolls (see Figure 4-2, page 186). Place the rolls on sheet pans lined with baking paper. Sprinkle with poppy seeds, if desired.

FIGURE 4-4 Using a kaiser-roll cutter to flatten and mark the tops of kaiser rolls. The bottom row shows 3 rolls topped with the optional poppy seeds; the rolls on the far left have not yet been marked and flattened with the cutter.

5. Mark the rolls with a kaiser cutter (Figure 4-4, page 195), or cut an *X* on the tops using a razor blade. Let the rolls rise until slightly less than doubled in volume.

6. Bake the rolls at 400°F (205°C), with steam, leaving the damper closed for the first 10 minutes. Open the damper and continue baking approximately 10 minutes longer or until done.

NOTE 1: To make kaiser rolls without pre-dough, increase the yeast to 2½ ounces (70 g) and decrease the salt to 2 tablespoons (30 g). This will yield 45 rolls. For the small-batch recipe, increase the yeast to 1 ounce (30 g) and decrease the salt to 2 teaspoons (10 g). The small-batch recipe will then yield 12 rolls.

NOTE 2: If your oven is not equipped with steam injectors, see "Creating Steam Without Steam Injectors," page 97.

KAISER ROLL PRE-DOUGH yield: 2 pounds 12 ounces (1 kg 250 g)

½ ounce (15 g) fresh compressed yeast
1 teaspoon (5 g) granulated sugar
1 pint (480 ml) cold water
1 pound 12 ounces (795 g) bread flour

Small-Batch Kaiser Roll Pre-Dough
yield: 14 ounces (400 g)

1 tablespoon (9 g) fresh compressed yeast
½ teaspoon (2.5 g) granulated sugar
¾ cup (180 ml) cold water
8 ounces (225 g) bread flour

1. Dissolve the yeast and the sugar in the water (see Note).

2. Add all of the bread flour at once, mixing with the dough hook at low speed. Knead until the dough has developed a smooth consistency, about 10 minutes. The dough will be quite firm, which makes the yeast react more slowly and allows the dough to develop properly.

3. Cover the dough and leave at room temperature overnight.

NOTE: For a quick pre-dough, use warm water (105° to 115°F/40° to 46°C) and increase the yeast to 1 ounce (30 g) (1½ teaspoons/5 g for the small-batch recipe); let rise in a warm place until the dough begins to bubble and fall.

Knots yield: 27 rolls, 2 ounces (55 g) each

Knots, also called twisted rolls, always start out in the form of a string, which is then crossed or twisted in a wide variety of ways. (Simply joining the two ends of the string would not be considered a knot; it is simply a loop, or circle.) The single knot shown here is the fastest, easiest knot one can make. It is basically a circle that winds through itself, making 3 crossings along the way. I call these production knots because they can be formed quickly in midair on their way down to the sheet pan. Single knots are the most advantageous choice when you have to produce several hundred.

There are many more elaborate choices available if you are making a fairly small quantity. These fancier shapes are not necessarily more complicated; they are just more time-consuming because they must be formed on the tabletop after the string has been rolled out. Whichever shape you choose, a knot will always take more time than a plain round or oval roll because you can produce only one at a time, in contrast to the rolls that are made two at a time using both hands (see page 186).

A nice assortment of knots in a bread basket, shining from egg wash, always makes an impressive addition to a buffet table or display case. If you think any of these knots look complicated, consider this: Knot theorists have determined that almost 13,000 different knots contain 12 or fewer crossings!

1 recipe Braided White Bread dough (page 147)   **Egg wash**

SINGLE KNOTS

1. Punch down the dough and divide it into 2-ounce (55-g) pieces. Keep the pieces you are not using covered to prevent a skin from forming.

2. Roll one piece at a time into a 9-inch (22.5-cm) rope and tie it into a loose knot so that the ends protrude just slightly beyond the body of the roll (Figure 4-5).

3. Place the knots on a sheet pan lined with baking paper.

4. Let the knots rise until slightly less than doubled in volume.

5. Brush with egg wash and bake at 400°F (205°C) for approximately 15 minutes.

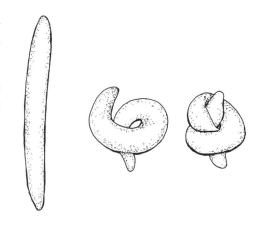

FIGURE 4-5 Forming a single knot

DOUBLE KNOTS

1. Punch down the dough and divide it into 2-ounce (55-g) pieces. Keep the pieces you are not using covered to prevent a skin from forming.

2. Roll one piece at a time into an 11-inch (27.5-cm) rope and place it in front of you vertically.

3. Pick up the end closest to you and, forming a loop on the right, cross it over the top of the rope just below the tip, so that one-third of the length is now in a straight line pointing to the left.

4. In one continuous motion, twist the bottom of the loop one-half turn to the right and tuck the top end underneath and up through the opening (Figure 4-6).

5. Place the knots on a sheet pan lined with baking paper.

6. Let the knots rise until slightly less than doubled in volume.

7. Brush with egg wash and bake at 400°F (205°C) for about 15 minutes.

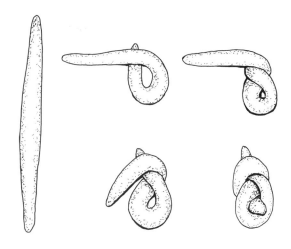

FIGURE 4-6 Forming a double knot

1. Punch down the dough and divide it into 2-ounce (55-g) pieces. Keep the pieces you are not using covered to prevent a skin from forming.

2. Roll one piece at a time into a 16-inch (40-cm) rope and place it in front of you in a U shape, with the inner edges touching.

3. Fold up the bottom to about ¾ inch (2 cm) from the top.

4. Using both hands, twist the sides in opposite directions as if you were opening a book. Repeat this motion (Figure 4-7).

5. Place the knots on a sheet pan lined with baking paper.

6. Let the knots rise until slightly less than doubled in volume.

7. Brush with egg wash and bake at 400°F (205°C) for approximately 15 minutes.

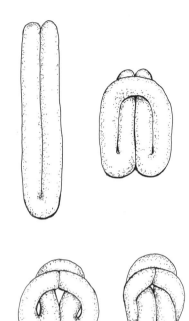

FIGURE 4-7 Forming a twisted knot

Milk Rolls yield: 48 rolls, approximately 2 ounces (55 g) each

Given the current favor shown toward so-called health breads made with whole grains and multiple grains, plain white bread and rolls seem to have dropped in rank to secondary status lately. Whole grain purists refuse to eat white bread, rationalizing that the nutritious part of the wheat kernel has been milled out, and there is some truth to that argument. There are times, however, when only buttery white bread or rolls will do. It may go against today's trend for the rustic and hearty types, but I feel that plain white bread rolls—with a hard crust like kaiser rolls, or these softer milk rolls—will never go out of style. They make such a good accompaniment to a meal because their flavor doesn't compete with other dishes, and what could be better for mopping up that last bit of gravy?

This basic recipe can be formed into several classic American dinner roll shapes, such as cloverleaf, butterflake, and Parker House, enabling you to offer an assortment in the bread basket. Soft-crust rolls are always a better choice if you plan to make the rolls ahead of time to freeze. If properly thawed and warmed before service, it is almost impossible to tell them from freshly baked. Rolls with a hard crust, on the other hand, tend to become a bit chewy after freezing because there is little or no fat in the dough.

4 ounces (115 g) fresh compressed yeast	3 tablespoons (45 g) salt
1 quart (960 ml) cold whole milk	8 ounces (225 g) unsalted butter, at room temperature
2 pounds (910 g) bread flour	
1 pound 10 ounces (740 g) cake flour	Egg wash
4 ounces (115 g) granulated sugar	Poppy seeds (optional)

1. Dissolve the yeast in the milk. Add the bread flour, cake flour, sugar, and salt. Mix, using the dough hook, until the dough forms a ball. Incorporate the butter. Knead the dough for 6 to 8 minutes, until it is smooth and elastic.

2. Place the dough, covered, in a warm place and let it rise until it has doubled in volume.

3. Punch down the dough and let rise until it has doubled a second time.

4. Divide the dough into 4 equal pieces approximately 1 pound 10 ounces (740 g) each. Pound and roll each piece into an 18-inch (45-cm) rope. Cut each rope into 12 equal pieces. Form the pieces into oval rolls (see Figure 4-2, page 186).

5. Place the rolls on sheet pans lined with baking paper. Let the rolls rise until slightly less than doubled in volume.

6. Brush with egg wash and sprinkle with poppy seeds if desired. Cut 4 shark's teeth on the top of each roll with a pair of scissors (Figure 4-8).

7. Bake the rolls at 425°F (219°C) for approximately 12 minutes or until golden brown.

NOTE: Refer to Figure 4-9 in making the three variations that follow.

FIGURE 4-8 **Cutting the shark's-tooth design on the top of Milk Rolls before baking**

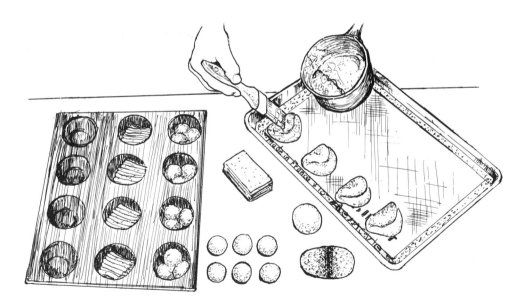

FIGURE 4-9 **Milk Roll variations: Butterflake and Cloverleaf Rolls in a baking pan; brushing melted butter on top of Parker House Rolls. The center of the drawing shows the stacked layers of dough that are sliced for Parker House Rolls; the small balls of dough to be grouped in threes to make Cloverleaf Rolls; and dough balls for the Parker House Rolls, one rolled round and one flattened and creased in the center.**

CLOVERLEAF ROLLS

1. Brush melted butter over the inside of 48 cups in standard-sized muffin tins.

2. Follow the recipe for Milk Rolls (page 198) through Step 3.

3. After dividing the dough into 48 pieces in Step 4, divide each piece again into 3 equal pieces. Roll the small pieces into smooth round balls.

4. Cluster 3 balls in each cup of the muffin tins.

5. Proof, brush with egg wash, and bake as directed in Step 7.

BUTTERFLAKE ROLLS

1. Brush melted butter over the inside of 48 cups in standard-sized muffin tins.

2. Follow the recipe for Milk Rolls (page 198) through Step 3. Divide the dough into 4 pieces as directed in Step 4, but do not form the pieces into ropes.

3. Roll each of the 4 pieces of dough into a 14 x 18-inch (35 x 45-cm) rectangle approximately ⅛ inch (3 mm) thick, using flour to prevent the dough from sticking. Transfer each rectangle to a sheet pan and place in the refrigerator while you are working on the next one.

4. Cut the sheet of dough that was rolled out first in half lengthwise. Brush melted butter over one half. Place the other half on top. Cut the stacked sheet lengthwise into 3 equal strips. Brush butter on top of 2 strips and stack again, placing the unbuttered piece on the top. The dough stack should now have 6 layers and measure 18 inches long and a little over 2 inches wide (45 x 5 cm).

5. Cut the strip across into 12 equal pieces. Place the pieces in the prepared muffin pans with the cut edges facing up.

6. Repeat Steps 4 and 5 with the remaining 3 dough rectangles.

7. Proof and bake as directed for Milk Rolls, but do not use egg wash. Instead, brush the tops of the rolls with butter as soon as they come out of the oven.

PARKER HOUSE ROLLS

1. Brush melted butter over the inside of 48 cups in standard-sized muffin tins.

2. Follow the recipe for Milk Rolls (page 198) through Step 3. After dividing the dough into 48 pieces in Step 4, roll each piece into a ball and set the pieces aside to relax for a few minutes on a lightly floured area of your worktable.

3. Using a dowel, press down on the center of each round and roll it into a 4-inch (10-cm) oval, keeping the ends thick and shaping the middle section flat.

4. Brush melted butter over the tops of the ovals. Fold one thick edge on top of the other, placing the top edge slightly behind the bottom edge. Press lightly with your palm to make the edges adhere.

5. Proof and bake as directed for Milk Rolls, brushing the rolls with melted butter rather than egg wash prior to baking.

Pretzels

yield: 30 traditional pretzels, 3 ounces (85 g) each, or 60 twisted pretzel sticks, 8 inches (20 cm) long

Pretzels are made in two variations, both from the same dough. The thicker soft pretzels are boiled before baking in the same way as bagels, which kills the yeast immediately and eliminates any oven-spring. This, in combination with the dough not proofing very much, produces a fairly dense and chewy pretzel of the type typically sold garnished with mustard by street vendors, especially in cities on the East Coast.

The other pretzel, the hard type, is proofed and baked in the oven just like any ordinary bread. These are generally made much smaller than the chewy pretzels and are a popular snack to accompany drinks. Both varieties are formed in either the traditional pretzel shape or in sticks. Due to the absence of fat in the pretzel dough, the finished pretzels will keep fresh for many weeks.

If you prefer not to make this number of pretzels or sticks at one time, the dough can be divided and frozen for several weeks if properly wrapped. Thaw the dough as needed and shape as desired.

1 ounce (30 g) fresh compressed yeast

1 quart (960 ml) warm water (105° to 115°F/40° to 46°C)

4 teaspoons (20 g) salt

2 tablespoons (30 g) granulated sugar

4 tablespoons (30 g) caraway seeds (optional)

3 pounds 12 ounces (1 kg 705 g) bread flour

Melted butter

Baking Soda Solution (recipe follows)

Coarse salt

Caraway seeds (optional)

1. Dissolve the yeast in the warm water. Add the salt, sugar, and caraway seeds if desired. Gradually mix in enough of the bread flour to make a stiff dough. Knead at medium speed with the dough hook, adding the remaining flour if necessary, until the dough is smooth and elastic, about 8 minutes.

2. Place the dough in a well-buttered bowl. Turn the dough to coat all over. Cover and set aside in a warm place until doubled in volume, approximately 45 minutes.

3. Brush melted butter over 3 full-size sheet pans or line the pans with Silpats, which do not need to be buttered.

4. Punch down the dough and divide it into 3 equal pieces approximately 2 pounds (910 g) each. Roll each piece into a rope 20 inches (50 cm) long. Cut each rope into 10 equal pieces.

5. Pound and roll each of the smaller pieces into a 20-inch (50-cm) tapered string, as instructed for Braided Bread (see Figures 3-16 to 3-18, page 148). A helpful guide in judging the length is to compare the strings to the sheet pans: a full-size pan is 16 inches (40 cm) wide and a half-size pan is 16 inches (40 cm) long. Form the strings into twisted pretzel shapes (Figures 4-10 and 4-11) and place them on a lightly floured board or sheet pan. Let the gluten in the pretzels relax for 1 or 2 minutes, then stretch each one to make it approximately 7 × 4 inches (17.5 × 10 cm) (Figure 4-12).

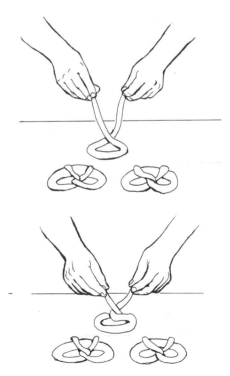

FIGURE 4-10 Starting the pretzel shape by crossing and twisting the string

History of the Pretzel Knot

You would be hard pressed to find a shape that can symbolize the baker's art better than the pretzel. The name comes from a Germanic word meaning "bracelet." Some sources say this twisted knot dates back to the sixth century; others suggest that the pretzel goes back to the Romans. I particularly like the story that tells of the heroic bakers of Vienna. While the city was held under siege by the Turks during the Ottoman reign, this group, upon seeing the enemy's flag raised above the cathedral, battled their way to the top and put their own flag in its place. With the Turkish flag torn down, the Viennese defenders gained new strength, rallied, and saved the city. The emperor rewarded these brave bakers with the royal coat of arms. The pretzel—which was the symbol of the bakers' guild—had been incorporated into the design.

FIGURE 4-11 Pressing the ends of the string firmly into the dough

FIGURE 4-12 Stretching the pretzel after the gluten has relaxed

6. Bring the baking soda solution to a boil. Drop 2 or 3 pretzels at a time into the liquid. Boil for 1 minute after they float to the surface. Remove them carefully with a slotted spoon and transfer to the buttered sheet pans. Use a razor blade to cut 4 or 5 small slits randomly on each pretzel.

7. As each sheet pan is filled, sprinkle coarse salt and caraway seeds, if desired, over the pretzels.

8. Bake at 475°F (246°C) until dark brown, approximately 20 minutes. Remove from the baking sheets and let cool on racks. Stored in an airtight container, the pretzels will keep for several weeks.

NOTE 1: Because this no-butter, no-egg dough can be very rubbery and hard to work with, a good method is to partially roll out 10 of the strings, then go back and finish stretching them to their full length, working on the strings in the same order. This will allow the gluten time to relax and make the job easier. Repeat this procedure twice with the remaining dough. It should not be necessary to use any flour in shaping the strings and pretzels. If you find you must use flour, this indicates the dough is too soft.

NOTE 2: Pretzels are traditionally dipped in a 5 percent solution of sodium hydroxide (caustic soda) and water, which creates a beautiful deep brown color on the baked pretzels. To use this method, follow the instructions with the following changes:

1. In Step 3, brush butter on 3 paper-lined pans instead of directly on the sheet pans (or use Silpats).

2. In Step 6, omit the baking soda solution and boiling.

3. Instead, dissolve 1½ ounces (40 g) sodium hydroxide U.S.P.-N.F. in 1 quart (960 ml) hot water. Keep the solution as hot as your hands can take and dip the pretzels into this solution, wearing latex food handling gloves to protect your hands and goggles to protect your eyes.

4. Transfer the dipped pretzels to the prepared pans and continue as directed.

WARNING: Sodium hydroxide is harmful when not properly diluted and baked. Store it in a safe place.

TWISTED PRETZEL STICKS

I. Follow the instructions in the main recipe through Step 4. However, cut each of the 3 ropes into 20 pieces rather than 10.

2. Pound and roll each of the small pieces into a 16-inch (40-cm) tapered string (see Figures 3-16 to 3-18, page 148). Work in batches to allow the gluten to relax (see Note 1, page 202).

3. Fold the strings in half. Hold the thicker folded end steady with one hand, then use the other hand to roll and twist the bottom of the stick (Figures 4-13 and 4-14).

4. Place on sheet pans lined with baking paper, pinching the ends together firmly as you place them to prevent the pretzels from unwinding.

5. Poach and bake as directed in the main recipe.

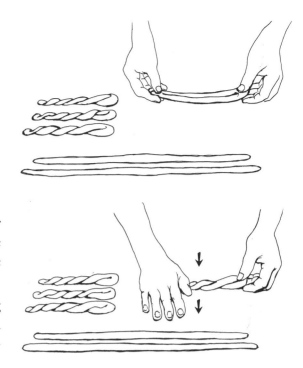

FIGURES 4-13 AND 4-14 Forming Twisted Pretzel Sticks by holding the folded end of the string steady while twisting the opposite end with the other hand

BAKING SODA SOLUTION

2 quarts (1 L 920 ml) water
3 tablespoons (36 g) baking soda

1 tablespoon (15 g) salt

I. Bring the ingredients to a boil in a large saucepan or sauté pan.

2. Use as directed in the Pretzels recipe on pages 201 and 202.

Rustica yield: 36 rolls, approximately 2 ounces (55 g) each

Chances are good that you will be served these homey-looking rolls in any small village in Switzerland; there they are known as *Schlumbergerli*. Rustica are simple to make and do not require any special cutter or form. The finished rolls have a very appetizing appearance. Because they are rolled in olive oil, the dough does not seal completely; consequently, the oven-spring causes the rolls to open up slightly as they bake. The contrast between the newly revealed crust and the flour-coated top looks great. As for most baking techniques, it may take some practice before you are able to form the rolls so they open up just right. Generally, if too much oil is used in shaping the rolls, they will open up too far. If not enough oil is used or if you overwork the dough as you form them, they will stay closed.

½ ounce (15 g) fresh compressed yeast

2 cups (480 ml) warm water (105° to 115°F/40° to 46°C)

2 tablespoons (30 g) salt

1½ ounces (40 g) granulated malt extract *or* ¼ cup (60 ml) or 3 ounces (85 g) honey

½ recipe or 1 pound 6 ounces (625 g) Kaiser Roll Pre-Dough (page 196)

1 pound 14 ounces (855 g) bread flour

3 tablespoons (45 ml) olive oil

Olive oil

Water

Bread flour

1. Dissolve the yeast in the warm water. Mix in the salt, malt extract or honey, and pre-dough. Incorporate approximately three-quarters of the flour. Mix in the olive oil together with most of the remaining flour. Knead, using the dough hook at low speed, for 8 to 10 minutes, adding the reserved flour if necessary for a smooth, elastic dough.

2. Place the dough in an oiled bowl, turn the coat with oil, and allow to rise in a warm location until the dough has doubled in volume.

3. Punch down the dough and divide into 2 equal pieces approximately 2 pounds 4 ounces (1 kg 25 g) each.

4. Roll each piece into a rope approximately 24 inches (60 cm) in length, then cut each rope into 18 equal pieces.

5. Lightly oil the area of the worktable where you are forming the rolls. Roll the dough pieces into round rolls (see Figure 4-2, page 186). Keep the table oiled as needed so that the rolls do not stick to the table and therefore do not close completely on the bottom.

6. Place the rolls bottom- (wrinkled) side up on the table next to you and spray them lightly with water.

7. Fill 2 sheet pans almost to the top with bread flour. Invert the rolls into the flour, leaving enough room around them for expansion. Let the rolls rise in the flour until slightly less than doubled in volume.

8. Gently transfer the rolls, inverting each one flour-side up, to a sheet pan.

9. Bake at 400°F (205°C) using steam and leaving the damper closed for 10 minutes. Open the damper and continue baking approximately 10 minutes longer or until baked through.

NOTE: If your oven is not equipped with steam injectors, see "Creating Steam Without Steam Injectors," page 97.

Tessiner Rolls yield: 60 rolls, approximately 2 ounces (55 g) each

These unusual Swiss pull-apart rolls borrowed their name from the Italian-influenced region (or canton, as it is called there) of Tessin (*Ticino* in Italian), which is located in the southern part of Switzerland at the Italian border. The restaurants in Tessin serve a whole "loaf" of these rolls in their bread baskets, which not only looks interesting, but keeps the rolls from drying out.

Malt, which is extracted from barley, is used as a powerful food for the yeast in a bread dough. It adds flavor to the finished product and color to the crust. Replacing part of the liquid in this recipe with beer in combination with the use of malt extract amplifies this effect. If you prefer not to use beer, 3 cups (720 ml) water can be used instead for a total of 6 cups (1 L 440 ml).

3 cups (720 ml) warm water (105° to 115°F/40° to 46°C)

3 cups (720 ml) warm beer (105° to 115°F/40° to 46°C)

1 ounce (30 g) fresh compressed yeast

3 ounces (85 g) granulated malt extract *or* ½ cup (120 ml) or 6 ounces (170 g) honey

2 tablespoons (30 g) salt

1 recipe or 2 pounds 12 ounces (1 kg 250 g) Kaiser Roll Pre-Dough (page 196)

3 pounds 12 ounces (1 kg 705 g) bread flour

⅓ cup (80 ml) olive oil

1. Combine the water and beer. Dissolve the yeast in the warm liquid. Mix in the malt extract or honey, salt, and pre-dough. Incorporate approximately three-quarters of the flour. Mix in the olive oil together with most of the remaining flour. Knead with the dough hook at low to medium speed for 8 to 10 minutes, adding the remaining flour as needed for a smooth, elastic dough.

2. Place the dough in an oiled bowl, turn to coat with oil, cover, and let rise in a warm place for 30 minutes.

3. Punch down the dough to remove all air, then let rise again for 30 minutes.

4. Punch down the dough and divide it into 3 equal pieces approximately 3 pounds (1 kg 365 g) each. Roll these out to 24-inch (60-cm) strings and cut each string into 20 equal pieces.

5. Form the pieces into round balls, then roll into tapered ovals 3 inches (7.5 cm) long (see Figure 4-2, page 186).

6. Place in rows of 6, with the long sides touching, on sheet pans lined with baking paper. Let rise until slightly less than doubled in volume.

7. Using a sharp, thin knife or a razor blade, make a cut down the full length of each loaf (6 rolls). Start the cut at one-third of the width of the rolls, and cut ½ inch (1.2 cm) deep at a 45-degree angle toward the center of each loaf (Figure 4-15).

8. Bake at 400°F (205°C) with steam, leaving the damper closed for 10 minutes. Open the damper and continue baking approximately 10 minutes longer or until done.

NOTE: If your oven is not equipped with steam injectors, see "Creating Steam Without Steam Injectors," page 97.

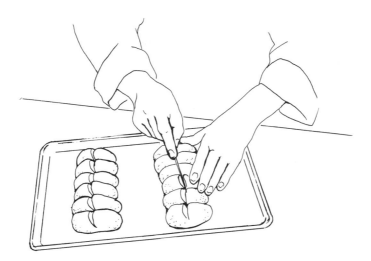

FIGURE 4-15 **Cutting a deep slash in the top of Tessiner Rolls before baking**

Breakfast Breads and Pastries

Unfortunately, breakfast, for a lot of us, simply means a cup of coffee gulped down on the run. This habit really is a shame because a good hearty breakfast is the most important meal of the day. Because our bodies have been without food for 10 hours or so, our brains need sugar. Breakfast can be a welcome opportunity to enjoy sweets, whether in the form of fruit or oat bran muffins, for the health-conscious, or the delicious indulgence of a pastry.

I grew up eating a big breakfast. There were always two or three types of home-baked bread on the table: rye bread, a whole grain bread, and white bread to toast (try toasting the Raisin Bread on page 135). We spread the bread with fresh sweet butter and piled on an abundance of wonderful things like ham, cheeses, and smoked fish.

Although an old-fashioned big breakfast is still available in many countries, travelers unfortunately often end up with the so-called continental breakfast, which does not provide much opportunity to try the local specialties. The typical restaurant breakfast in Scandinavia is served on a large buffet and contains everything from scrambled eggs to herring, caviar, and pâtés. It also includes, of course, the famous Wienerbröd, known in the United States as Danish pastries. Wienerbröd translates to "bread from Vienna." The story goes that long ago the bakers in Denmark, specifically in Copenhagen, went on strike, and the Danish shopowners hired replacement bakers from Germany and Austria. These chefs produced wonderful crisp, light, buttery pastries with a delicious variety of fillings and toppings. The pastries proved so popular that even when the Danish bakers returned to work, the pastries were still referred to as Wienerbröd, *Wien* being the German-Austrian name for Vienna, the capital of Austria and a city long associated with fine baked goods.

In Germany, you can have a breakfast sweet very familiar to American doughnuts. Called *Berliners*, German doughnuts have a different round shape and no hole, but basically they are the same pastry. And in France, you will naturally want to try the croissants. Fresh out of the oven, their taste and crispness are found nowhere else, and, plain or topped with sweet butter and marmalade, they are a wonderful breakfast treat.

Brioche

yield: 36 individual brioche, approximately 2 ounces (55 g) each, or 4 loaves, 1 pound 3 ounces (540 g) each

This light French specialty, so rich in butter and eggs, is said to have gotten its name from the French word *brier*, which means "to pound." I assume this relates to the dough's lengthy kneading process, which long ago, before electric mixers, simply meant pounding the dough until it reached the desired consistency.

The most typical shape for brioche is a round fluted base with slightly sloping sides and a round knot on top. This shape can be used for individual servings or for larger sizes equivalent to a standard loaf. For the classic shape, the dough is baked in fluted round brioche molds, which can be made of metal or ceramic, the latter being mostly for the larger sizes. Brioche can also be made into rectangular loaves. Brioche dough is versatile and is used frequently for encasing other foods. It can be wrapped around a wheel of cheese and is used for boeuf en croûte and in the Russian classic *kulebiaka* (often known by the French spelling *coulibiac*), where the dough is filled with layers of salmon, rice, eggs, and herbs. Individual baked brioche are sometimes hollowed out and filled with savory stews or with fruit and cream for dessert.

SPONGE

2 ounces (55 g) fresh compressed yeast

1 cup (240 ml) warm whole milk (105° to 115°F/40° to 46°C; see Note)

¼ cup (60 ml) or 3 ounces (85 g) honey

10 ounces (285 g) bread flour

DOUGH

4 ounces (115 g) granulated sugar

4 teaspoons (20 g) salt

8 eggs

1 pound (455 g) cake flour

1 pound (455 g) bread flour

8 ounces (225 g) unsalted butter, at room temperature

Egg wash

I. To make the sponge, dissolve the yeast in the warm milk in a mixer bowl, then add the honey and bread flour on low speed. Mix until soft and smooth. Cover the sponge and let it rise until it has doubled in volume.

2. To make the dough, add the granulated sugar, salt, and eggs to the sponge. Mix in the cake flour and all but a handful of the bread flour. Gradually mix in the butter, adding it in small pieces.

3. Knead with the dough hook until the dough forms a ball. Adjust the consistency by adding the reserved bread flour if necessary. The dough should not stick to the sides of the bowl and should have a slightly shiny appearance.

4. Cover the dough and set aside until doubled in volume. If you are not going to shape the dough until the following day, refrigerate it at this point (before it has proofed) so that the large amount of yeast does not make the dough sour.

5. Punch down the dough.

TO MAKE BRIOCHE

I. Divide the dough into 3 equal pieces, approximately 1 pound 10 ounces (740 g) each. Roll each piece into a 16-inch (40-cm) rope, then cut each rope into 12 equal pieces. Roll each piece into a firm ball (see Figure 4-2, page 186); set the balls to the side in order so you can form them in the same order they were rolled.

2. Place the ball of dough you rolled first in front of you and hold your hand above it. With your fingers held tightly together and your hand completely vertical, press down on the ball at one-third of the width, and move your hand back and forth in a sawing motion until you almost sever the ball into 2 portions (Figure 5-1).

3. You should now have 2 round balls of dough, one twice the size of the other, connected by a very thin string of dough. Gently pinch the connecting string between the thumbs and index fingers of both hands and, still holding it, force your thumbs and fingers straight down into the top of the larger ball, all the way to the bottom. Open your fingers slightly to create a hole, and let the smaller ball drop into it (Figure 5-2). Be sure the smaller ball of dough sits well inside the larger, or it can fall off as the dough expands in the proof box and, later, in the oven. Form the remaining brioche in the same way.

  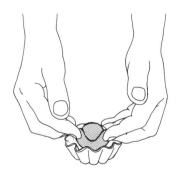

FIGURE 5-1 **Using the side of the hand with a sawing motion to form 2 connected balls of dough for brioche**

FIGURE 5-2 **Pushing the smaller ball of dough inside the larger one**

FIGURE 5-3 **Placing the brioche into the baking form**

4. Place the shaped brioche into buttered forms (Figure 5-3) and let them rise until slightly less than doubled in volume.

5. Brush the brioche with egg wash, being careful not to let any drip between the dough and the form, as this will make it difficult to remove the brioche after baking.

6. Bake at 400°F (205°C) for about 18 minutes. Unmold before completely cool and finish cooling on racks. A faster cooling method, and one that is more typically used in the industry, is to quickly turn each brioche on its side (leaving them in the forms) to allow air to circulate underneath.

NOTE: Do not overheat the milk. If the temperature is hotter than specified the yeast will be killed. This mistake happens frequently for two reasons: it is easy to overheat such a small quantity of milk, and the high fat content of the dough also makes the yeast more vulnerable.

TO MAKE LOAVES

1. Divide the dough into 4 equal pieces approximately 1 pound 3 ounces (540 g) each. Pound the pieces into tight loaves (see Figure 3-13, page 143) and place in buttered or paper-lined loaf pans measuring 8 x 4 x 4 inches (20 x 10 x 10 cm). Let rise until doubled in volume.

2. Bake the loaves at 375°F (190°C) until they have a healthy brown color and are baked through, about 40 minutes. Unmold and let cool on racks.

Croissants yield: 44 croissants, approximately 3 ounces (85 g) each

Today, croissants are one of the most popular yeast-leavened breakfast pastries anywhere in the world south of Scandinavia (there, the Wienerbröd or Danish pastry still reigns). In addition to the classic plain croissant, the French also bake them filled with chocolate, soft almond paste, or pastry cream. Instead of curving these pastries into the crescent shape, they are often left straight to signify that they are filled. In Austria, Germany, and Switzerland, bakers make a pastry called *Plunder*, which is sort of a cross between a croissant and a Danish pastry. The main distinction between Plunder, filled croissants, and Danish pastries is the amount of fat rolled into the dough. Genuine Danish pastry dough contains about twice as much fat as croissant dough and about twice as much fat as what I call the American-style Danish pastry. Most American-made Danish pastries are actually closer to Plunder than to the Scandinavian version of Danish. Another difference between these three is that a true croissant dough does not contain eggs, as a Danish pastry or Plunder dough does.

FORMING CROISSANTS: PRODUCTION SCHEDULE

Croissant dough is easier to work with if it is allowed to rest several hours between giving the dough 3 single turns and forming the croissants. Because you generally want to bake croissants early in the morning, here are two possible game plans, neither of which requires starting in the middle of the night. Make the dough in the morning a day ahead, leave it to rest until early afternoon, form the croissants, leave them overnight in the refrigerator, then proof and bake the next morning. An even better method is to prepare the dough the afternoon before, let the dough rest overnight in the refrigerator, then form, proof, and bake the croissants in the morning.

If your refrigerator does not keep a consistent temperature below 40°F (4°C)—in other words, a lot of traffic goes in and out—store the dough in the freezer instead. This is important to keep the yeast dormant; otherwise, the dough will start to proof in the refrigerator, lowering the quality of the finished product and possibly making it taste sour.

The instructions that follow assume that you will be making up all of the dough at once. If this is not the case and you want to freeze part of the dough to use later, roll the amount you are working with into a strip 10 inches (25 cm) wide, ⅛ inch (3 mm) thick, and as long as needed. After the dough has relaxed, cut triangles every 4½ inches (11.2 cm).

2 teaspoons (10 ml) lemon juice

3 pounds 4 ounces (1 kg 480 g) bread flour

2 pounds 8 ounces (1 kg 135 g) chilled unsalted butter

3 ounces (85 g) fresh compressed yeast

1 quart (960 ml) cold whole milk

3 ounces (85 g) granulated sugar

1 ounce (30 g) granulated malt extract *or* 2 ounces (55 g) or 3 tablespoons (45 ml) honey

3 tablespoons (45 g) salt

Egg wash *or* whole milk

Small-Batch Croissants
yield: about 15 croissants, 2 ounces (55 g) each

Few drops of lemon juice

12 ounces (340 g) bread flour

10 ounces (285 g) chilled unsalted butter

1 ounce (30 g) fresh compressed yeast

1 cup (240 ml) cold whole milk

4 teaspoons (20 g) granulated sugar

2¼ teaspoons (7 g) granulated malt extract *or* 1 tablespoon (15 ml) honey

2 teaspoons (10 g) salt

Egg wash *or* whole milk

---

1. Work the lemon juice and 4 ounces (115 g) flour (1 ounce/30 g for the smaller recipe) into the chilled butter by kneading it against the table or in a bowl with your hand. Do not use a mixer.

2. Shape the butter into a 10-inch (25-cm) square (5-inch/12.5-cm for the smaller recipe). Place the butter on a piece of baking paper and set aside. If the room is warm, place it in the refrigerator, but do not let it get too firm. If this happens, rework and reshape the butter back to the original consistency.

3. Dissolve the yeast in the cold milk. Add the granulated sugar, malt extract or honey, and the salt. Mix for a few seconds, using the dough hook, then start adding the remaining flour. Mix in enough flour to make a dough that is slightly firm but not rubbery. Take care not to mix any longer than necessary.

4. Place the dough on a table dusted lightly with flour; roll it out to a 14-inch (35-cm) square (7-inch/17.5-cm for the smaller recipe).

5. Check the butter to be sure that it is smooth and at the same consistency as the dough; adjust if necessary. Place the butter square on the dough diagonally so that there are 4 triangles on the sides, fold in the sides, and seal in the butter (see Figures 2-10 and 2-11, page 75).

6. Give the dough 3 single turns (directions follow). Refrigerate, covered, for at least 2 hours.

7. Roll the dough into a rectangle measuring 49½ x 30 inches (123.7 x 75 cm), slightly thinner than ¼ inch (6 mm) and as even as possible. (If you are making the smaller recipe, roll out the dough following the instructions given below.) Let the dough rest 5 minutes so that it will not shrink when you cut it, then cut it lengthwise into 3 strips, 10 inches (25 cm) wide.

8. On the bottom edge of the strip closest to you, start at the left corner, measure 4½ inches (11.2 cm), and make a mark in the dough. Continue making marks every 4½ inches (11.2 cm) from that point. Do the same on the top edge of the top strip.

9. Place a ruler from the lower left corner up to the first mark on the top strip (4½ inches/11.2 cm from the left edge) and cut the dough, using a knife or pastry wheel, following the ruler through the top strip. Then cut from the first mark on the bottom strip (4½ inches/11.2 cm from the left edge) to the second mark (9 inches/22.5 cm from the left edge) on the top strip. Repeat, cutting every 4½ inches (11.2 cm) for the length of the dough.

10. Beginning at the opposite end, follow the same pattern and cut from right to left (Figure 5-4). Form 2 or 3 croissants from the scrap dough or save for the next batch of Butter-Wheat Bread (page 114).

11. Make a ½-inch (1.2-cm) cut in the center of the short side on each croissant (Figure 5-5). Pull the cuts apart a little, then form the croissants by rolling the triangles toward you. Roll them up tightly, but do not stretch the dough too much.

12. Form each croissant into a crescent shape as you place it on a sheet pan lined with baking paper or a Silpat. The tip of the croissant should be inside the center curve and tucked underneath so that it does not unroll. Do not put more than 16 to 18 on a full-sized pan, to ensure that they bake evenly. If too crowded, they will get overdone on the ends before they are fully baked in the middle.

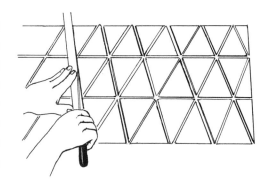

FIGURE 5-4 Cutting the dough into triangles for croissants

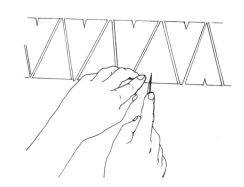

FIGURE 5-5 Cutting a small slit in the base of each dough triangle. Because the dough is elastic, the slit opens up into a wedge shape

13. Let the croissants rise until slightly less than doubled in volume in a proof box at 78° to 82°F (25° to 27°C) with 80 percent humidity. If the proof box gets too hot, the butter will start to leak out. (This can also happen while the croissants are baking if they have not proofed enough.)

14. Brush the croissants with egg wash (or milk, which is typical in France).

15. Bake at 425°F (219°C) until golden and baked through, about 25 minutes.

TO FORM CROISSANTS FOR THE SMALL-BATCH RECIPE

1. Roll out the dough to 18 x 31½ inches (45 x 78.7 cm) and ⅛ inch (3 mm) thick. Let the dough relax for a few minutes, then cut in half lengthwise to make 2 strips, 9 inches (22.5 cm) wide.

2. Continue as directed in the main recipe.

INSTRUCTIONS FOR MAKING A SINGLE TURN

1. Roll the dough into a rectangle ½ inch (1.2 cm) thick, as carefully and evenly as possible.

2. Divide the rectangle crosswise into thirds by sight alone or mark the dough lightly with the edge of your hand.

FIGURE 5-6 The first step in making a single turn: folding one-third of the dough toward the center

FIGURE 5-7 Completing the single turn: folding the remaining one-third over the folded section

3. Fold one-third of the dough over the middle section (Figure 5-6), then fold the remaining one-third over both of them (Figure 5-7), brushing away the excess flour from the inside as you fold. The dough now has one single turn.

4. Refrigerate, covered, for 30 minutes.

5. Position the dough so that the long sides run horizontally, roll the dough to the same size rectangle as before, and make the second single turn.

6. Chill the dough, covered, for 30 minutes; then make the last single turn.

German Butter Crescents yield: 48 pastries, about 3½ ounces (100 g) each

This variation on croissants is made in Germany and Switzerland, where the pastries are known as *Butter Gipfels*. Because they have a more pronounced crescent shape, almost circular, they require a different, slightly slower rolling technique. Although their fat content is almost the same as croissants, German butter crescents are lighter in texture due to much thinner layers as well as a greater number of layers, both of which are produced by stretching the dough while rolling up the triangles. Another contributing factor, and one that is quite unusual when working with a laminated dough, is that the crescents are baked using steam at the beginning. This gives a more rapid oven-spring, trapping additional air, so the pastries rise higher. They may also be baked without steam (as is typical for croissants) with excellent results.

8 ounces (225 g) cold unsalted butter plus 2 pounds 4 ounces (1 kg 25 g) unsalted butter, at room temperature

5 ounces (140 g) lard

4 ounces (115 g) bread flour

4 teaspoons (20 ml) lemon juice

3 ounces (85 g) fresh compressed yeast

3 cups (720 ml) cold water

2 ounces (55 g) granulated malt extract *or* ⅓ cup (80 ml) or 4 ounces (115 g) honey

¼ cup (60 g) salt

6 ounces (170 g) granulated sugar

4 eggs

3 pounds 6 ounces (1 kg 535 g) bread flour

Egg wash

1. Melt the 8 ounces (225 g) cold butter and brown lightly (see beurre noisette, page 7). Remove from the heat and set aside to cool to room temperature.

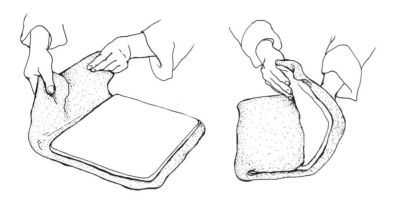
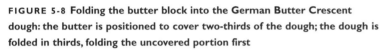

FIGURE 5-8 Folding the butter block into the German Butter Crescent dough: the butter is positioned to cover two-thirds of the dough; the dough is folded in thirds, folding the uncovered portion first

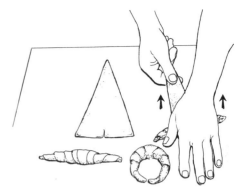

FIGURE 5-9 Forming German Butter Crescents by holding the tip of the triangle steady and stretching the dough while rolling the wide end toward you with the other hand

2. Combine the remaining soft butter, lard, 4 ounces (115 g) bread flour, and the lemon juice. Shape the mixture into a rectangle, 14 x 12 inches (35 x 30 cm), on a sheet of baking paper and reserve; place in the refrigerator if necessary.

3. Dissolve the yeast in the cold water in a mixer bowl. Add the malt extract or honey, salt, granulated sugar, eggs, and browned butter. Reserve a handful of the remaining bread flour and add the rest. Mix for approximately 1 minute until a smooth soft dough forms. Adjust by adding the reserved flour as needed. Cover the dough and place in the refrigerator for 30 minutes.

4. Roll out the dough to a rectangle measuring 14 x 18 inches (35 x 45 cm). Place the butter block on top of the dough, covering two-thirds of the rectangle. The butter block should have the same consistency as the dough.

5. Fold the uncovered third of the dough over half of the butter block. Fold the remaining butter-covered piece on top of the dough (Figure 5-8).

6. Roll out the dough to a rectangle ½ inch (1.2 cm) thick. Give the dough a single turn (see Figures 5-6 and 5-7, page 213). Cover and refrigerate for 30 minutes.

7. Make 2 additional single turns, refrigerating the dough for 30 minutes between them.

8. After completing the third turn, roll out the dough to the size of a full sheet pan, 16 x 24 inches (40 x 60 cm); refrigerate to relax the dough first if necessary. Cover the dough and place in the refrigerator or freezer for at least 2 to 3 hours or, preferably, overnight.

9. Cut the dough in half crosswise. Roll out one piece at a time to a rectangle measuring 16 x 42 inches (40 cm x 1 m 5 cm) and about ¹⁄₁₆ inch (2 mm) thick.

10. Let the dough relax for a few minutes (roll the second piece in the meantime), then cut lengthwise into 2 strips, 8 inches (20 cm) wide.

11. Cut each strip into 12 triangles measuring 7 inches (17.5 cm) across the base. You will need to miter the 2 end pieces together to make a total of 12 crescents. Cut a slit in the center of the base of each triangle, as for croissants (see Figure 5-5, page 212).

12. Roll the triangles tightly by holding the pointed end still with one hand while using the palm of the other hand to curl up the dough, lightly stretching it as you roll (Figure 5-9).

13. Roll each piece between your palms and the table to make it about 9 inches (22.5 cm) long and very tapered at the ends.

14. Place on sheet pans lined with baking paper or Silpats and curl each crescent into a full circle so that the ends meet. Pinch the ends together. Let the crescents rise until slightly less than doubled in volume.

15. Brush with egg wash and bake at 400°F (205°C) with steam, leaving the damper closed for 5 minutes. Open the damper and continue baking approximately 10 minutes longer or until baked through.

NOTE: If your oven is not equipped with steam injectors, see "Creating Steam Without Steam Injectors," page 97.

Danish Pastry Dough
yield: 12 pounds 8 ounces (5 kg 680 g), or about 90 pastries, 3 ounces (85 g) each

In making Danish dough, it is crucial that all of the ingredients be cold. On very hot days, you may want to decrease the amount of yeast slightly so that the dough does not rise too fast. Due to the limited amount of sugar, absence of fat, and soft consistency of the dough, these precautions keep the yeast from taking over before you have a chance to roll in the margarine. Margarine is used for this dough because it produces a lighter and flakier texture than butter. Also, because the fat and the dough need to be at the same consistency to give the best layered structure and margarine has a higher melting point than butter, margarine is preferable with such a soft dough. You may need to adjust the amount of salt called for in the recipe, depending on the salt content of the margarine you are using.

1 quart (960 ml) cold whole milk

8 eggs

5 pounds (2 kg 275 g) cold margarine

5 ounces (140 g) fresh compressed yeast

6 ounces (170 g) granulated sugar

1 tablespoon (15 g) salt

1 tablespoon (6 g) ground cardamom

4 pounds (1 kg 820 g) bread flour

Small-Batch Danish Pastry Dough
yield: 4 pounds 3 ounces (1 kg 905 g), or about 30 pastries, 3 ounces (85 g) each

1⅓ cups (320 ml) cold whole milk

3 eggs

1 pound 6 ounces (625 g) cold margarine

2 ounces (55 g) fresh compressed yeast

2 ounces (55 g) granulated sugar

1 teaspoon (5 g) salt

1 teaspoon (2 g) ground cardamom

1 pound 6 ounces (625 g) bread flour

1. Mix the milk and the eggs, then refrigerate the mixture, and the flour, for at least 1 hour before making the dough (see Note 1).

2. Shape the cold margarine into a 10-inch (25-cm) square (5-inch/12.5-cm for the small-batch recipe) and place in refrigerator so it will be firm when the dough is ready.

3. Dissolve the yeast in the milk and egg mixture (use your hand to speed this up, as yeast dissolves slowly in cold liquid). Stir in the sugar, salt, and cardamom. Reserve a handful of the flour and mix in the remainder. Add enough of the reserved flour to make a soft, sticky dough.

4. Place the dough on a floured table and shape it into a 14-inch (35-cm) square (7-inch/17.5-cm for the small-batch recipe). Place the chilled margarine square diagonally on the dough so that 4 dough triangles are showing. Fold in the triangles toward the center and seal in the margarine (see Figures 2-10 and 2-11, page 75).

5. Roll the dough as carefully and evenly as possible into a rectangle measuring 30 x 20 inches (75 x 50 cm) (12 x 8 inches/30 x 20 cm for the small-batch recipe). Use plenty of flour to prevent the dough from sticking to the table and the rolling pin.

6. Give the dough a single turn (see Figures 5-6 and 5-7, page 213) (see Note 2). Cover and refrigerate 30 minutes.

7. Roll the dough to the same size as before and make 3 additional single turns, resting the dough in the refrigerator for 30 minutes in between.

8. Roll out the dough to about ½ inch (1.2 cm) thick, cover with plastic wrap, and place it in the refrigerator or freezer, depending on how hot the room is where you are working and when you are going to make up the Danish. In either case, the dough should chill at least 30 minutes.

9. Make up the Danish according to the individual recipes and let the pieces rise until slightly less than doubled in volume. Watch carefully to check on their rising. If they rise too long, they will lose their flakiness and get spongy; if they do not rise enough, the fat will run out when they are baked.

NOTE 1: If you are working in an air-conditioned kitchen, the refrigeration time in Step 1 can be shortened or possibly even eliminated.

NOTE 2: If the dough does not seem to be rubbery after making the first turn, it does not have to rest between the first turn and the second turn. This is such a soft dough that it has less gluten structure than other laminated doughs, such as croissant and puff pastry, and is therefore more pliable.

Danish Filling I yield: 5 pounds (2 kg 275 g)

This filling will keep fresh at room temperature for several days. If stored longer, it should be refrigerated.

1 pound 4 ounces (570 g) cake or cookie scraps (see Note)

¾ cup (180 ml) water

2 pounds (910 g) almond paste

8 ounces (225 g) granulated sugar

1 pound (455 g) unsalted butter, at room temperature

I. Place the scraps in a mixer bowl and start mixing using the paddle. Mix in just enough water to make a firm paste and continue mixing until smooth.

2. Add the almond paste and sugar.

3. Incorporate the butter gradually and beat until smooth.

NOTE: Use any non-chocolate sponge cake, coffee cake, or cookie scraps that do not contain perishable filling or decoration.

Danish Filling II yield: 3 pounds (1 kg 365 g)

10 ounces (285 g) unsalted butter, at room temperature

2 pounds (910 g) almond paste

4 ounces (115 g) finely ground hazelnuts

6 ounces (170 g) Pastry Cream (page 845)

I. Mix the butter into the almond paste, adding it gradually to avoid lumps. Mix in the hazelnuts.

2. Stir in enough pastry cream to reach the desired consistency. If the filling is to be piped on the dough, it needs to be a little firmer than if it is to be spread; for spreading, you want it loose enough that you can apply it easily.

3. Store in the refrigerator.

Cream Cheese Filling for Danish yield: 2 pounds 9 ounces (1 kg 165 g)

1 pound 6 ounces (625 g) cream cheese, at room temperature

3½ ounces (100 g) sugar

3½ ounces (100 g) unsalted butter, at room temperature

3 eggs

1½ ounces (40 g) bread flour

½ teaspoon (2.5 ml) vanilla extract

4 ounces (115 g) dark raisins

¼ cup (60 ml) whole milk

I. Place the cream cheese and sugar in a mixer bowl. Blend, using the paddle at medium speed. Add the butter gradually and mix until smooth.

2. Mix in the eggs and flour, then add the vanilla, raisins, and enough milk so that the mixture can be piped.

3. Store, covered, in the refrigerator.

Bear Claws yield: 30 pastries

These are by far the most well known and probably the most popular of all the Danish pastry varieties. In Scandinavia, these pastries are called *kamm*, which translates to "comb" and refers to a cock's comb (the fleshy red decoration on the head of a rooster), not the type you use on your hair. The method for making the pastries is different in Scandinavia as well. There, the slits are cut with a special knife instead of the rolling cutter used in the United States.

4 pounds 3 ounces (1 kg 905 g) or 1 recipe
    Small-Batch Danish Pastry Dough
    (page 215)

1 pound (455 g) Danish Filling I (page 217)

Egg wash

12 ounces (340 g) sliced almonds

Simple syrup

Simple Icing (page 35)

1. Roll the dough into a rectangle measuring 55 x 12 inches (1 m 37.5 cm x 30 cm) and approximately ⅛ inch (3 mm) thick. Allow the dough to relax for a minute or so, then cut lengthwise into 3 strips, 4 inches (10 cm) long. Leave the strips in place.

2. Place the Danish filling in a pastry bag with a No. 6 (12-mm) plain tip. Beginning ¼ inch (6 mm) down from the top edge, pipe a ribbon of filling along the complete length of each strip.

3. Brush egg wash on the entire lower part of each strip below the filling. Fold the top edge down, over, and past the filling, and press the ¼-inch (6-mm) borders into the egg wash, just below the filling, to seal.

4. Fold up the lower part of the strip past the sealed point to just below the filling so the seam is in approximately the center of the strip; press again to secure (Figure 5-10). Lightly flatten and shape the strips with your palm.

5. Roll a bear-claw cutter along the unfilled edge to create the claw pattern (Figure 5-11). Be careful not to cut into the filling or it will leak out. Turn the strips over so the seams are underneath. Push the strips together next to each other with a ruler or a dowel.

6. Brush the strips with egg wash and sprinkle generously with sliced almonds (see Note 2). If you are making only one strip, it is more convenient to do this before cutting the claws, as shown in the illustration.

7. Cut each strip into 10 pieces, 5½ inches (13.7 cm) long. The pieces will weigh approximately 3 ounces (85 g) each.

8. One at a time, pick up the bear claws, shake off any almonds that are not stuck to the egg wash, stretch the pastries slightly, and place them on paper-lined sheet pans, bending each strip into a half-circle so that the cuts open up. Let rise until slightly less than doubled in volume.

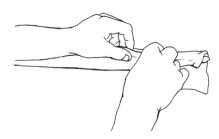

FIGURE 5-10 Folding the lower edge of the dough strip up to seal in the filling

FIGURE 5-11 Rolling the bear claw cutter along the unfilled edge of the strip

9. Bake at 410°F (210°C) for about 15 minutes. Brush the pastries with simple syrup as soon as you remove them from the oven. Let cool completely, then ice lightly with simple icing.

NOTE 1: If you do not have a bear-claw cutter, which looks like a miniature waterwheel with a handle, use a multiple pastry wheel with the wheels pushed together. If you do not have either of these tools, a chef's knife will do; it just takes a little longer. Make cuts ¾ inch (2 cm) long and ¼ inch (6 mm) apart along the length of each strip.

NOTE 2: The quantity of sliced almonds is specified because it is a fairly large amount. However, a faster and more practical method in a professional kitchen is to work with a greater amount of almonds, sprinkle them on top, and simply return the leftovers to the almond supply.

Butterhorns yield: about 30 pastries

This pastry is the one that my students seem to have the most success with when making Danish pastries for the first time. (Maybe this is the reason it is the teacher's favorite.) As butterhorns do not have any filling in the conventional sense, be sure you apply plenty of egg wash—enough so the dough is quite wet—and use all of the cinnamon sugar. When the sugar melts and mixes with the egg wash as the pastries bake, it creates a moist interior. The streusel topping contributes not only to the taste but also gives the Danish a nice finished appearance.

4 pounds 3 ounces (1 kg 905 g) or 1 recipe Small-Batch Danish Pastry Dough (page 215)

Egg wash

6 ounces (170 g) cinnamon sugar

1 pound 5 ounces (595 g) or ½ recipe Streusel Topping (page 37)

Simple Icing (page 35)

1. Roll the dough into a rectangle measuring 24 x 14 inches (60 x 35 cm) and approximately ¼ inch (6 mm) thick. If necessary, trim the edges of the strip to make them even.

2. Brush the entire surface of the dough heavily with egg wash. Sprinkle the cinnamon sugar over the dough.

3. Fold the long sides in to meet in the center. Brush again with egg wash, then fold in half in the same direction (double turn). Even the top by gently rolling with a rolling pin.

4. Cut the folded strip into pieces ¾ inch (2 cm) wide and, at the same time, use the knife to turn them over a quarter-turn so that the cut sides face up (Figure 5-12).

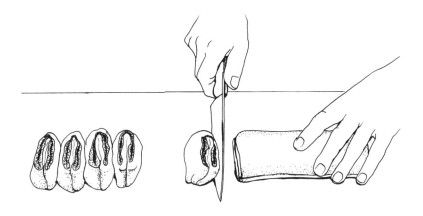

FIGURE 5-12 Slicing the Butterhorns and turning each piece cut-side up at the same time

5. Brush the top (cut sides) of the pieces with egg wash and sprinkle the streusel topping over them; be sure to use all of the topping. Press the streusel with the palm of your hand to help keep it in place.

6. Carefully place the pieces on sheet pans lined with baking paper or Silpats and let rise until slightly less than doubled in volume.

7. Bake at 425°F (219°C) until golden brown, about 15 minutes. Let the pastries cool completely, then spread a small amount of simple icing on top.

Danish Cinnamon Wreath yield: 1 wreath, 10 inches (25 cm) in diameter

Making breads and pastries in a wreath shape is very popular in Scandinavia. It makes sense for the customer who wants more than half a dozen Danish or rolls at the same time, and because forming wreaths is faster for the baker than making individual pieces, it is less expensive. A wreath also looks good displayed alone or on a tray with other rolls or pastries. The épi (wheat sheaves) design is definitely the most common. This shape can be made very quickly and looks appealing.

1 pound (455 g) Danish Pastry Dough (page 215)

6 ounces (170 g) Danish Filling I (page 217) *or* II (page 217)

4 tablespoons (48 g) cinnamon sugar

Egg wash

Sliced almonds

Simple syrup

Simple Icing (page 35)

1. Roll the dough into a strip 22 inches (55 cm) long, 7 inches (17.5 cm) wide, and approximately ⅛ inch (3 mm) thick.

2. Spread the Danish filling over the dough. (It is a common misconception that spreading on a little extra filling will make the wreath especially tasty, but this is not so! The filling will overpower the dough in the flavor of the baked wreath, and part of the filling will run out and burn on the sheet pan while the wreath is baking.)

3. Sprinkle cinnamon sugar over the filling and roll the strip into a tight string, starting from the top.

4. Roll the coiled string between your palms and the table to make it even and about 24 inches (60 cm) long.

5. Place the string on a sheet pan lined with baking paper or a Silpat and shape it into a ring 10 inches (25 cm) in diameter, making sure the seam is on the bottom. Seal the ends by pushing one inside the other.

6. Holding scissors at a 45-degree angle from the wreath, make cuts ½ inch (1.2 mm) wide, cutting almost to the bottom of the wreath. As you cut, use your free hand to turn these cuts to the side (Figure 5-13), alternating between left and right.

FIGURE 5-13 Cutting the filled coil of dough and turning each cut piece to the side to form the Danish Cinnamon Wreath

7. Brush with egg wash and sprinkle lightly with sliced almonds. Let the wreath rise until slightly less than doubled in volume.

8. Bake at 400°F (205°C) for about 30 minutes. Brush with simple syrup immediately after removing the wreath from the oven. Let the wreath cool completely, then spread simple icing lightly over the top.

Danish Twists yield: about 24 pastries

This is a very simple and quickly made Danish pastry. It does, however, require a carefully rolled and well-chilled dough in order to achieve the characteristic crispness on the top. The crispness is also lost if the dough is rolled too thin, if the strips are cut too wide, or if the Danish are left to rise too long before baking. Choose a good piece of dough (avoid end pieces). If you accidentally roll the dough too thin, make Custard Pockets (page 223) or turnovers from that piece and start over with a fresh piece of dough.

4 pounds 3 ounces (1 kg 905 g) or 1 recipe Small-Batch Danish Pastry Dough (page 215)

1 pound (455 g) Pastry Cream (page 845) *or* 1 pound (455 g) apricot jam or 1 pound (455 g) Cherry Filling (page 838)

Simple syrup

Simple Icing (page 35)

1. Roll the dough into a rectangle measuring 14 x 10 inches (35 x 25 cm) and approximately ³⁄₈ inch (9 mm) thick.

2. Chill the dough if needed; it should still be firm before going to the next step.

3. Cut the dough lengthwise into ³⁄₈-inch (9-mm) strips, using a sharp knife or pastry wheel and a ruler as a guide.

4. Twist the strips tight, stretching them slightly at the same time (see Figure 5-27, page 238).

5. Shape into Cherry Twists, Singles, or Figure Eights (Figures 5-14 and 5-15; instructions follow). Check to make sure the pieces weigh about 2½ ounces (70 g), which will make the finished pastries about 3 ounces (85 g) each. If any are too heavy, cut a piece off the end before you shape it; if too light, conceal a scrap piece under the pastry after forming it.

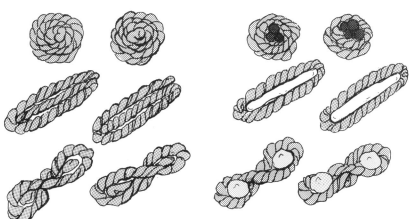

FIGURES 5-14 AND 5-15
Top to bottom: Cherry Twists, Singles, and Figure Eights, before and after the toppings are added

6. Place the pastries on sheet pans lined with baking paper or Silpats and let rise until slightly less than doubled in volume.

7. Bake at 425°F (219°C) until golden brown, about 15 minutes. Brush the pastries with simple syrup as soon as they are out of the oven. Let them cool completely, then ice with a small amount of simple icing.

CHERRY TWISTS

Twist the strips and shape into loose spirals. Secure the end piece underneath as you place each one on paper-lined sheet pans. Top with a small amount of cherry filling (1 generous tablespoon/15 ml) in the center of each twist.

SINGLES

Twist the strips and fold them in thirds, as in a single turn. Place them on paper-lined sheet pans and, at the same time, tuck the end piece underneath. Pipe a ribbon of pastry cream lengthwise down the center of each pastry.

FIGURE EIGHTS

Twist the strips and form into figure eights. Overlap both end pieces enough to protrude into the center and cover the openings in the eight. Invert onto paper-lined sheet pans. Pipe a dot of apricot jam into both indentations on the eight.

Double Curls yield: 30 pastries

These pastries are known as *Glasögon* in Swedish, which translates to "glasses" in English. Interestingly, they are fashioned after the distinctive marking—a double spiral design—found on the head of a cobra. This pattern resembles a pair of eyeglasses. For a different twist (literally) on this shape, omit brushing the egg wash between the two cylinders after rolling them. After slicing the pieces, turn one curl on each piece over to make an *S* shape as you place them on the pan.

4 pounds 3 ounces (1 kg 905 g) or 1 recipe Small-Batch Danish Pastry Dough (page 215)	12 ounces (340 g) Pastry Cream (page 845)
1 pound 4 ounces (570 g) Danish Filling I (page 217), softened	Sliced almonds
	Simple syrup
Egg wash	Simple Icing (page 35)

1. Roll out the Danish pastry dough, using flour to prevent the dough from sticking, to make a rectangle measuring 36 × 18 inches (90 × 45 cm); the dough should be about ⅛ inch (3 mm) thick.

2. Check the consistency of the filling to be certain it is soft enough to spread easily, then spread the filling evenly over the surface of the dough.

3. Starting with the long side farthest away from you (the top), roll the dough toward you, forming a tight spiral; stop when you reach the center of the dough. Repeat the procedure with the bottom half of the dough, rolling it away from you toward the center until it meets the other coil. Stretch the ropes as needed so that they are the same length and thickness. Brush egg wash on the dough where the 2 coils meet and push them together firmly.

4. Place the double rope at the edge of the table, keeping it right-side up. Using a sharp knife, cut 30 equal pieces, each about 1¼ inches (3.1 cm) wide. The individual pieces should weigh 3 ounces (85 g). Place the pastries cut-side up on sheet pans lined with baking paper or Silpats.

5. Pipe 2 dots of pastry cream on each pastry, placing them in the center of each spiral. Sprinkle sliced almonds lightly over the pastries. Let rise until the pastries are slightly less than doubled in volume.

6. Bake the double curls at 425°F (219°C) for about 15 minutes or until golden brown. Brush simple syrup over the pastries immediately after removing them from the oven. After the Danish have cooled, spread a small amount of simple icing over the tops.

Custard Pockets yield: 30 pastries

These envelope-shaped pastries are known as *Kuverts* in Sweden and *Spandaurs* in Denmark. Making an envelope—folding all 4 sides of a square in to meet in the center—is an excellent and convenient way to enclose a filling. These pastries are fast to produce and because you start by cutting squares, you don't have any scrap dough left over. Try these two variations on the same theme: Fold two opposite corners in to the center and leave two flat. Or fold as directed in the recipe, but invert the pastries as you place them on the sheet pans and pipe the jam or pastry cream on top of the bottom, so to speak.

4 pounds 3 ounces (1 kg 905 g) or 1 recipe Small-Batch Danish Pastry Dough (page 215)	**8 ounces (225 g) Pastry Cream (page 845)** *or* **apricot jam**
Egg wash	**Sliced almonds**
8 ounces (225 g) Danish Filling I (page 217) or II (page 217) or Cream Cheese Filling (page 217)	**Simple syrup**
	Simple Icing (page 35)

1. Roll the dough into a rectangle measuring 20 x 16 inches (50 x 40 cm) and approximately ¼ inch (6 mm) thick.

2. Let the dough rest for a few minutes before you cut the squares so that they will not shrink and become rectangles. Mark and cut the dough into 4-inch (10-cm) squares, using a ruler as a guide, or use a multiple pastry wheel adjusted to 4 inches (10 cm). The pieces will weigh approximately 2½ ounces (70 g) each.

3. Lightly brush egg wash along the cuts to cover all 4 edges of each square.

4. Place Danish or cream cheese filling in a pastry bag. Pipe a dot of filling the size of a cherry in the center of each square.

5. Fold all 4 corners of each square in to meet in the center (see Figure 5-31, page 243). Press the center down firmly with your thumb, pushing all the way down to the pan to prevent the dough from unfolding.

6. Place the pastries on sheet pans lined with baking paper or Silpats. Pipe a dot of either pastry cream or jam the size of a cherry on top of the pastries in the indentation created by your thumb. Or, if you used cream cheese filling inside, you can use it on top as well, to indicate what is inside.

7. Lightly sprinkle sliced almonds on the pastries; they will stick to the topping. Let rise until slightly less than doubled in volume.

8. Bake at 425°F (219°C) until golden brown, about 15 minutes. Brush the pastries with simple syrup immediately after removing them from the oven. Once the pastries have cooled, spread a small amount of simple icing on top.

Honey-Raisin Snails *yield: 30 pastries*

Brushing honey butter over the dough gives these snails a distinctive taste. Do not skimp on the raisins—no one likes a raisin snail when they can count the raisins using the fingers on one hand! Although you can use regular dry raisins in the snails, soaked raisins provide additional moisture for the pastries, which lack filling. The raisins should soak until they are nice and plump—several hours or, preferably, overnight. You can speed up the process by starting with hot water.

4 pounds 3 ounces (1 kg 905 g) or 1 recipe
    Small-Batch Danish Pastry Dough
    (page 215)

Honey Butter (recipe follows)

1 pound 8 ounces (680 g) dark raisins, soaked
    in water, then well drained

6 ounces (170 g) cinnamon sugar

Simple syrup

Simple Icing (page 35)

1. Roll the dough into a rectangle measuring 48 x 14 inches (1 m 20 cm x 35 cm) and approximately ⅛ inch (3 mm) thick.

2. Brush the surface of the dough with the honey butter, leaving a 1-inch (2.5-cm) strip uncovered along the bottom edge. Evenly distribute the soft raisins over the honey butter; do not discriminate against the ends. Sprinkle the cinnamon sugar on top. Roll over the top with a rolling pin to make the raisins stick to the dough.

3. Starting at the top, roll up the dough evenly, stretching it if necessary to make a tight rope. Place the rope at the edge of the table with the seam underneath.

4. Using a sharp knife, cut the rope into 30 pieces weighing approximately 3 ounces (85 g) each.

5. Place the snails on sheet pans lined with baking paper or Silpats, cut sides up, tucking the ends underneath so they will not unroll while baking. Let rise until slightly less than doubled in volume.

6. Bake at 425°F (219°C) until golden brown, about 15 minutes. Brush the pastries with simple syrup immediately after removing them from the oven. When the snails have cooled, spread a small amount of simple icing on the top of each one.

HONEY BUTTER yield: approximately 1 pound (455 g)

6 ounces (170 g) unsalted butter

2 ounces (55 g) light brown sugar

⅓ cup (80 ml) or 4 ounces (115 g) honey

½ cup (120 ml) half-and-half

1. Combine all of the ingredients in a heavy-bottomed saucepan. Stir over medium heat until the mixture comes to a boil. Remove from the heat.

2. Cool before using.

Mayor's Wreath yield: 1 wreath, 10 inches (25 cm) in diameter

The name suggests that this wreath is something special, and I think you will agree after your first bite. But there is a price to pay: The filling is made with a high percentage of almond paste, and the braiding is quite labor intensive. However, its elegant appearance and great taste have always made this pastry very popular, especially with anyone who doesn't care for cinnamon, as this is one of the few Danish pastries without it.

1 pound (455 g) Danish Pastry Dough (page 215)

6 ounces (170 g) Danish Filling II (page 217)

Egg wash

Sliced almonds

Simple syrup

Simple Icing (page 35)

1. Roll out the dough to a strip 8 inches (20 cm) wide, 18 inches (45 cm) long, and ⅛ inch (3 mm) thick. Cut the strip lengthwise into 3 equal pieces.

2. Check the Danish filling to be sure it is not too soft, as the strips will be braided later; adjust if needed. Place the filling in a pastry bag with a No. 3 (6-mm) plain tip. Pipe a ribbon of filling along the length of each strip approximately ½ inch (1.2 cm) from the top.

3. Brush egg wash along the bottom of the strips, then roll each one into a spiral, rolling from the top to the bottom.

4. Roll out each coiled strip to 20 inches (50 cm) in length by rolling it between your palms and the table.

5. Place the 3 strings, seam-side down, next to each other on the table. Braid them into a Three-String Braid (see page 150), starting from the middle and working to each end to avoid stretching the dough any more than necessary.

6. Carefully place the braided loaf on a sheet pan lined with baking paper or a Silpat. If necessary, stretch the braid slightly to make it 24 inches (60 cm) long.

7. Shape into a ring that is 10 inches (25 cm) in diameter. Fold the ends together so that the seam shows as little as possible.

8. Brush with egg wash and sprinkle lightly with sliced almonds. Let rise until slightly less than doubled in volume.

9. Bake at 375°F (190°C) about 30 minutes. Brush with simple syrup immediately after removing the wreath from the oven. Let cool completely, then lightly spread simple icing over the top.

Sister's Pull-Apart Coffee Cake yield: 1 cake, 10 inches (25 cm) in diameter

If you are wondering about this title, there is an explanation. In Sweden, whenever you pay a visit, you are always served coffee with some kind of coffee cake or Danish and also cookies. During one of my frequent visits to my sister's house, I jokingly remarked, "Isn't this the same type of coffee cake you served last time and the time before that? I hope it's not the same one!" She said that because this cake turned out great every time she made it, she figured why take a chance when her critical and always hungry brother was invited. This cake is traditionally known simply as Buttercake.

1 pound 4 ounces (570 g) Danish Pastry Dough (page 215)	Sliced almonds
6 ounces (170 g) Danish Filling I (page 217) *or* II (page 217)	Simple syrup
6 ounces (170 g) Pastry Cream (page 845)	Simple Icing (page 35)

1. Roll the dough into a strip 22 inches (55 cm) long, 7 inches (17.5 cm) wide, and ⅛ inch (3 mm) thick. Cut a 7-inch (17.5-cm) square from one end and set this piece aside.

2. Spread the Danish filling over the larger piece of dough.

3. Starting from the top, roll up the strip into a tight string. Roll the string between your palms and the table to make it even. Cut the strip into 12 equal pieces.

4. Roll and shape the reserved square of dough into a 10-inch (25-cm) circle. Place it on a sheet pan lined with baking paper or a Silpat.

5. Put about one-third of the pastry cream in a pastry bag with a No. 3 (6-mm) plain tip. Set aside. Using a metal spatula, spread the remainder of the pastry cream over the dough, covering the entire surface. Place a 10-inch (25-cm) adjustable cake ring around the dough (or use the ring from a springform pan).

6. Arrange the 12 pieces, cut-side up, on the cream. Press them in lightly with your knuckles. Pipe a dot of pastry cream about the size of a hazelnut on top and partially inside each piece. Sprinkle with sliced almonds. Let the cake rise until slightly less than doubled in volume.

7. Bake at 375°F (190°C) for about 35 minutes. Brush the cake with simple syrup as soon as you remove it from the oven. When the cake has cooled, remove the ring and ice lightly with simple icing.

Sugar Buns yield: 30 pastries

This is my number one favorite Danish pastry. One good reason I never get tired of sugar buns is that I so seldom get to enjoy one, as this is not a pastry that you are likely to find at most bakeries. They are a little delicate and time consuming to produce, but you are guaranteed plenty of favorable comments when you make them. The pastry cream inside bubbles up as the pastries bake, coating the inside of the shell and leaving the center hollow. The initial sensation of biting into thin air is fabulous.

4 pounds 3 ounces (1 kg 905 g) or 1 recipe Small-Batch Danish Pastry Dough (page 215)

Egg wash

1 pound 6 ounces (625 g) Pastry Cream (page 845)

Melted unsalted butter

Granulated sugar

1. Roll the dough into a rectangle measuring 24 x 20 inches (60 x 50 cm) and approximately ⅛ inch (3 mm) thick.

2. Mark and cut the dough into 4-inch (10-cm) squares, using a ruler as a guide, or use a multiple pastry wheel adjusted to 4 inches (10 cm). The pieces will weigh just under 2½ ounces (70 g) each.

3. Lightly brush egg wash along the cuts to cover all 4 edges of each square.

4. Place the pastry cream in a pastry bag. Pipe a mound about the size of an unshelled walnut in the middle of each square. You should use all the pastry cream. Be sure to divide it evenly. If you use too much, it will be difficult to seal the pastries; if you use too little, it will be absorbed into the dough and leave the inside dry.

5. Pick up the corners, stretch them if necessary to cover the filling, and fold in to meet in the center. Pinch the seams closed so the pastry cream will not leak out.

6. Place the buns, seam-side down, on sheet pans lined with baking paper or Silpats. Let rise in a warm place until slightly less than doubled in volume.

7. Bake at 400°F (205°C) until golden brown, about 20 minutes. Because of the pastry cream inside, the buns will puff up as high as a large profiterole, so they must bake long enough to hold their shape once removed from the oven. Let the buns cool completely.

8. Brush the tops and sides of the buns with melted butter. Fill a bowl with enough sugar to make a well in it deep enough to fit a bun without flattening it. Dip each bun into the sugar well; the sugar should stick to the melted butter.

Apple Pastries with Almond Cream yield: 24 pastries (Photo 19)

You can purchase special cutters to cut out the dough for the following apple-shaped pastries or use the template at right, as suggested. These pastries can also be made using Danish pastry dough instead of puff pastry. Either way, they make a great addition to a selection of breakfast items. However, made with puff pastry, they can really be enjoyed any time of the day and can even be turned into a plated dessert by adding a sauce and garnish. See Small Pear Tartlets with Caramel Sauce (page 679) for presentation ideas. Conversely, the pear-shaped tarts on that page can be served as a simple pastry, just like these.

12 small to medium apples	Cinnamon sugar
2 recipes Plain Poaching Syrup (page 31)	Simple syrup
5 pounds 8 ounces (2 kg 500 g) or ½ recipe Puff Pastry (page 74)	Pectin Glaze (page 30) *or* Apricot Glaze (page 5) (optional)
10 ounces (285 g) Pastry Cream (page 845)	
8 ounces (225 g) almond paste	

1. Peel the apples, using a swivel-bladed vegetable peeler to keep them as smooth and round as possible. Place the peeled apples into acidulated water as you work to prevent them from becoming brown. If the apples will be too tall to fit within the frame of the template (shown as a broken line in the drawing) after they are cut in half lengthwise, peel them down to size, keeping a natural rounded shape. This will produce a more attractive finished pastry than will trimming a flat piece from one end later. Core the apples and cut them in half.

2. Poach the apple halves in the poaching syrup until they begin to soften but are still shapely and intact. Avoid overcooking at this stage and keep in mind that the apples will cook further as they bake on the pastries. Let the apples cool in the syrup.

3. Trace the drawing shown in Figure 5-16, following the outside solid line, then cut the template out of cardboard that is ¹⁄₁₆ inch (2 mm) thick.

4. Divide the puff pastry in half. Roll out one piece at a time into a rectangle measuring 16 x 22 inches (55 x 40 cm). Place the dough rectangles on flat, even sheet pans lined with baking paper. Cover and refrigerate for approximately 30 minutes to relax and firm the dough.

5. Using the tip of a sharp paring knife and the template as your guide, cut 12 apple-shaped pieces of dough from each sheet of chilled puff pastry, spacing the pieces a few inches apart on sheet pans lined with baking paper as you cut them. Return the cut pieces to the refrigerator until the dough is chilled and firm. Gather the scrap pieces of dough, cover, and reserve for another use.

6. Again using the tip of a paring knife, cut halfway through the dough on each "apple" ¼ inch (6 mm) from the edge around the perimeter with the exception of the stem (shown as a broken line in the template). In order to create a neat frame, it is important that the dough be very cold and firm as you do this. Keep the pieces you are not working on in the refrigerator so they do not become soft. After cutting the borders, prick the dough inside the frame very well.

7. Mix the pastry cream into the almond paste, adding just a small amount at first to soften the paste so you do not create lumps. Place the mixture in a pastry bag with a No. 4 (8-mm) plain tip. Pipe a thin layer of filling over the puff pastry pieces, covering the pricked dough within the border only.

8. Remove the apple halves from the poaching syrup and pat them dry. Starting just below the stem end on each apple (leaving the stem end intact), slice the apple halves lengthwise, making the slices approximately ⅛ inch (3 mm) thick. Press down to fan out the slices. Transfer each apple half to a puff pastry piece, placing the stem end of the apple at the stem end of the dough and being careful to keep the slices and the filling within the cut frame. Sprinkle cinnamon sugar lightly over the apple slices.

9. Bake the pastries at 375°F (190°C) for about 35 minutes or until the apples are tender and the puff pastry is golden brown and baked all the way through. Brush simple syrup over the top of the pastries—both the dough and the apples—as soon as the pastries are removed from the oven. Once they have cooled, decorate with apricot glaze or pectin glaze, if desired.

FIGURE 5-16 The template used as a guide to cut the puff pastry for Apple Pastries with Almond Cream

Apple Turnovers yield: 20 pastries

Few pastries can compete with a well-made apple turnover to go with morning coffee. Ideally, turnovers should have a slightly tart, moist filling surrounded by very flaky puff pastry. The key is to have the baked puff pastry as dry and crumbly as possible. If the dough is rolled too thick or if the oven temperature is too high, you may very well produce a tall, golden brown pastry that looks great on the outside, but the inside will contain a thick layer of heavy, unbaked dough. Some soft dough is impossible to avoid due to the moisture in the apples, but the proper dough thickness and oven temperature will minimize the problem.

A more labor-intensive solution is to fold the puff pastry squares into triangles and prebake them (bake them blind without the filling) until they are almost done. Remove them from the oven, carefully lift up or cut off the top of each shell, and add the filling. Continue baking until done.

Served with Vanilla Ice Cream (page 734) or Créme Anglaise (page 817), turnovers can also make a lovely simple dessert. For variation, try Sour Apple and Cheese Turnovers (page 686).

2 pounds 8 ounces (1 kg 135 g) Puff Pastry (page 74)	Cinnamon sugar
	Crystal sugar
Egg wash	Sliced almonds, lightly crushed
1 pound (455 g) Chunky Apple Filling (page 840)	Simple syrup

I. Roll out the puff pastry to ⅛ inch (3 mm) thick, 22½ inches (56.2 cm) long, and 18 inches (45 cm) wide. Let it rest 5 to 10 minutes to relax.

2. Cut the dough into 5 rows of 4 squares each, making 20 squares, 4½ inches (11.2 cm) each.

3. Brush 2 adjoining sides of each square with egg wash.

4. Pipe a mound of apple filling in the center of each square, dividing it evenly, and sprinkle cinnamon sugar on the apple filling.

5. Fold the upper part of the squares onto the part brushed with egg wash to make triangles, making sure that apple filling does not get on the egg wash. Press the edges together with your fingers.

6. Mix equal amounts of crystal sugar and almonds. Brush the tops of the triangles with egg wash, invert into the sugar-nut mixture, then place the turnovers sugar-side up on sheet pans lined with baking paper or Silpats. Do not put more than 16 turnovers on a full-sized sheet pan.

7. Cut a small slit in the center of each turnover.

8. Bake at 375°F (190°C) until golden and completely baked through, about 25 minutes. You may need to use a second pan underneath and/or baking paper on the top to prevent the turnovers from overbrowning.

9. Brush the pastries lightly with simple syrup as soon as they come out of the oven to produce a light glaze.

NOTE: Apple turnovers are excellent to make up ahead and freeze. When needed, bake them directly from the freezer.

CHERRY TURNOVERS

Make the turnovers as directed above, substituting Cherry Filling (page 838) for the Chunky Apple Filling.

Flaky Cherry Coffee Cake Strips yield: 2 strips, 24 inches (60 cm) long, or 16 pastries

Back in the mid-1960s, when I worked on cruise ships, we used to make these with apple filling and call them apple strudel. The braided strips were faster to assemble than the real thing, and we got away with it because they resemble German apple strudel. Try making this recipe with Chunky Apple Filling (page xx) and sprinkle some cinnamon sugar on the filling before braiding the top. The assembled coffee cake strips freeze very well; bake as needed directly from the freezer.

2 pounds (910 g) Puff Pastry (page 74)   Egg wash
2 pounds (910 g) Cherry Filling (page 838)   Simple syrup
Crystal sugar   Simple Icing (page 35)
Sliced almonds, lightly crushed

1. Roll the puff pastry dough out to ⅛ inch (3 mm) thick, 23 inches (57.5 cm) long, and 16 inches (40 cm) wide. Cut the dough in half to make 2 strips, 23 inches x 8 inches (57.5 x 20 cm).

2. Fold each strip lengthwise over a 1-inch (2.5-cm) dowel so that the long cut edges meet and are closest to you. (The dough should be firm for easy handling; reserve the second strip in the refrigerator while you are working on the first if necessary).

3. Using the back of a chef's knife, lightly mark, but do not cut, a line about 2 inches (5 cm) away from and parallel to the long cut edges.

4. With the sharp edge of the knife, cut ¼-inch (6-mm) strips, up to the mark, along the entire length of the dough, leaving the folded edge uncut (Figure 5-17).

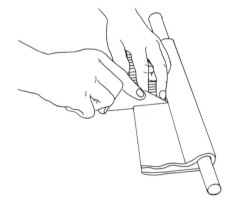

FIGURE 5-17 Cutting the short edges of the dough into strips, ¼ inch (6 mm) wide

5. Use the dowel to lift the strip and place it to one side on an inverted sheet pan lined with baking paper or a Silpat (2 strips will fit per pan). Remove the dowel carefully and separate the fringed edges so that the dough lies flat and open. Repeat with the second strip of dough.

6. Divide the cherry filling between the 2 strips, placing it down the uncut center of the strips. Spread the filling even with a small metal spatula, but do not let it get on or close to the cut strips.

7. Fold the left and right strips alternately over the filling, using both of your hands in an even rhythm (Figure 5-18). Make

FIGURE 5-18 Alternating the left and right strips over the filling

sure each left strip is folded on top of the right and each right is folded on top of the left so that they lock each other in place.

8. Place the dowel in the middle of each finished strip and press down hard enough to be sure the strips will not unfold in the oven (Figure 5-19). You will leave a small indentation, but you do not want to press the filling out.

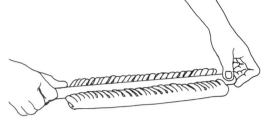

FIGURE 5-19 Pressing a dowel lengthwise in the center of the assembled Flaky Cherry Coffee Cake Strip to prevent the woven strips from unfolding

9. Mix equal amounts of crystal sugar and almonds. Brush the pastries lightly with egg wash, then sprinkle the sugar-nut mixture on top.

10. Bake, double-panned, at 375°F (190°C) for about 35 minutes. You may need to protect the top with baking paper to give the dough time to bake through completely.

11. Brush the strips with simple syrup as soon as they come out of the oven. When cool, ice with simple icing. Slice each strip into 8 pieces at an angle.

Choux Surprise yield: 24 pastries

These delicious pastries rank very high on my list of favorites, not only because of the wonderful combination of the main ingredients—puff pastry, pâte à choux, and pastry cream—but also for their practicality. Choux Surprise can be fully assembled and frozen, then plunged directly into a preheated oven (not only is it not necessary to thaw them, it is preferable not to do so). So in less than half the time it takes to proof and bake some of the more common breakfast pastries, such as Danish pastries and croissants, Choux Surprise are ready to eat.

In Sweden, we call these breakfast treats *Franska Wienerbröd*, which, translated into English, means "French Danish". Of course, the French elements are the puff pastry and the pâte à choux. As with most baked goods that comprise a combination of doughs, Choux Surprise can be a little tricky to bake correctly. In general, it is better to let them get a bit dark. If underbaked, the pastries become doughy and heavy.

2 pounds 4 ounces (1 kg 25 g) Puff Pastry (page 74)	**Sliced almonds, lightly crushed**
10 ounces (285 g) Pâte à Choux (page 83)	**6 ounces (170 g) Pastry Cream (page 845)**
Egg wash	**Simple syrup**
Crystal sugar	**Simple Icing (page 35)**

1. Roll the puff pastry dough to a rectangle measuring 22½ x 15 inches (56.2 x 37.5 cm) and ⅛ inch (3 mm) thick. Cut into 24 squares, 3¾ inches (9.5 cm) each (4 strips cut into 6 pieces each).

2. Divide the pâte à choux evenly among the puff pastry squares by piping a small mound about the size of a prune in the center of each. Brush the sides of each square with egg wash. Fold in the points to meet in the center like an envelope. With your thumb, press firmly, all the way down to the pan, in the spot where the points come together (see Note).

3. Mix equal amounts of crystal sugar and almonds. Brush the squares with egg wash, invert onto the sugar-nut mixture, then place right-side up on a sheet pan lined with baking paper or a Silpat.

4. Divide the pastry cream evenly between the pastries by piping a small amount of pastry cream in each indentation left by your thumb.

5. Bake, double-panned, at 375°F (190°C) for about 40 minutes. Be certain that the pastries are done. If the pâte à choux inside is not thoroughly baked, the pastries will collapse, becoming heavy and dense.

6. Brush the pastries with a small amount of simple syrup as soon as they come out of the oven. When cool, spread simple icing on top.

NOTE: It is important that you press firmly when you make the indentation for the pastry cream. You want to push all the pâte à choux underneath out of the way. Otherwise, as it bakes, the pâte à choux will puff up and force the pastry cream off the pastry and onto the pan.

Parisiennes yield: 24 pastries

Parisiennes cannot be produced as quickly as some of the more commonplace breakfast pastries, such as bear claws and cheese Danish, but the fact that they are a bit more original is a smart reason to include them in your selection of offerings. These pastries are also an excellent way to use up good puff pastry scraps. However, this makes sense only if you have the scrap dough stored in the refrigerator or freezer, previously rolled out and ready to use, as freshly rolled or sheeted scrap dough must be left to relax at least several hours or, better still, until the following day to avoid having the dough shrink.

Parisiennes can also be made by substituting croissant dough for the Danish dough to add more variety.

12 ounces (340 g) Quick Puff Pastry (page 77)
   or Puff Pastry (page 74)

1 pound 2 ounces (510 g) Pastry Cream
   (page 845)

2 pounds 8 ounces (1 kg 135 g) Danish Pastry
   Dough (page 215)

8 ounces (225 g) Danish Filling II (page 217)

1½ ounces (40 g) sliced almonds

Simple syrup

Simple Icing (page 35)

1. Roll the puff pastry out to a rectangle measuring 12 × 16 inches (30 × 40 cm) and about ⅛ inch (3 mm) thick. Place in the bottom of a half-sheet pan lined with baking paper or a Silpat. Prick the dough well and allow it to rest for at least 30 minutes in the refrigerator.

2. Bake the puff pastry sheet at 400°F (205°C) until light brown and baked through, approximately 20 minutes. Let cool.

3. Spread 12 ounces (340 g) pastry cream on top of the puff pastry sheet (leaving the sheet in the pan).

4. Roll the Danish dough out to a rectangle measuring 12 × 18 inches (30 × 45 cm). Spread the Danish filling over the dough. Starting from the long edge away from you, roll the dough

CHEF'S TIP
If you have a hearth oven and can therefore place the sheet pan with the assembled pastries directly on the bottom of the oven during baking, you don't have to prebake the puff pastry and can skip Step 2. In this case, also disregard the instructions for double panning in Step 8. Note, though, that the baking time will be slightly longer.

toward you to make a tight rope. Cut the rope into 24 equal slices.

5. Arrange the slices, evenly spaced and cut-side up, in straight rows over the pastry cream, placing 4 across and 6 lengthwise (see Note). As you place each slice, tuck the end piece of the dough underneath. Using your thumbs and index fingers on both hands, spread the top of each pastry apart a little (Figure 5-20).

6. Let the pastries rise until they have slightly less than doubled in volume.

7. Place the remaining 6 ounces (170 g) pastry cream in a pastry bag with a No. 3 (6-mm) plain tip. Pipe about 1 tablespoon (15 ml) pastry cream in the center of, and partially inside, each pastry using all of the cream. Sprinkle the sliced almonds over the pastries.

FIGURE 5-20 **Using the thumb and index finger on both hands to open up the spirals by pushing the dough gently to the outside**

8. Bake, double-panned, at 400°F (205°C) for about 35 minutes or until rich golden brown and baked through. Immediately brush simple syrup over the pastries. Let cool. Run a knife around the inside perimeter of the pan to loosen the sheet. Unmold, turn right-side up, and ice with simple icing. Cut the sheet into 24 pastries.

NOTE: When you cut the sheet after it is baked, you will appreciate the fact that you lined up the pastries evenly. The round snails will rise and bake together into squares. When you cut them apart, you should be able to cut straight lines that fall between the pastries without cutting into the snails. If they are not spaced evenly to begin with, the cut pieces will be different sizes, and you will have to cut into some snails to cut straight lines. If you have trouble, try this: Mark the pastry cream into 24 equal squares before you add the snails, then center a snail in each square.

Puff Pastry Diamonds yield: 20 pastries

This is a great versatile pastry shell for a breakfast treat, dessert, or to use with a savory filling. I have used this shape many times instead of individual vol-au-vents for large banquets (or when a customer's taste exceeded his or her budget). The diamonds are less costly to produce, because you can just about eliminate any scrap dough and being much faster to assemble, your labor cost is lower. Because they look good on top of all that—why not?

Instead of decorating with fresh fruit after baking, the pastries can be baked topped with apples or pears (see Sugar-Glazed Puff Pastry Waffles, page 592, to prepare the fruit; top with cinnamon sugar before baking). Or bake the pastries with fresh apricots or plums. Cut the fruit in half, remove the pits, slice, and fan the fruit over the pastry cream. Bake and glaze as directed in the recipe.

2 pounds (910 g) Puff Pastry (page 74)

Egg wash

14 ounces (400 g) Pastry Cream (page 845)

Fresh fruit

1 recipe Apricot Glaze (page 5)

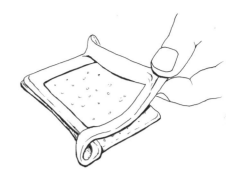

FIGURE 5-21 The folded square of puff pastry dough after making 2 cuts, starting from the folded edge

FIGURE 5-22 The square after unfolding

FIGURE 5-23 After moving the right cut edge to the left side, crossing the left cut edge over the top to form a frame

1. Roll out the puff pastry to ⅛ inch (3 mm) thick and into a rectangle measuring 16 × 20 inches (40 × 50 cm). Refrigerate, covered, for a few minutes to firm and relax the dough.

2. Cut lengthwise into 4 strips, 4 inches (10 cm) wide, then cut across the strips every 4 inches (10 cm) to make 20 squares, 4 inches (10 cm) each. Refrigerate the dough again if necessary. Do not attempt to cut and fold the squares when soft.

3. Fold the firm squares into triangles with the folded side toward you. Cut through ¼ inch (6 mm) from the edge on both the left and right sides, ending the cuts ¼ inch (6 mm) from the top (Figure 5-21). Do not cut all the way to the top so you cut the sides off; the dough should still be in one piece.

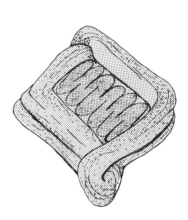

FIGURE 5-24 A Puff Pastry Diamond after baking

4. Unfold the triangles; the square will now have an *L* shape on each side (Figure 5-22). Brush egg wash over the squares. Prick the center of each square.

5. Cross the right *L* to the left side and the left *L* to the right side to form a frame (Figure 5-23). Brush egg wash lightly over the top of the frame, being careful not to get any on the sides.

6. Using a No. 4 (8-mm) plain tip, pipe an even layer of pastry cream on the inside of the frame.

7. Bake at 400°F (205°C) for about 20 minutes or until baked through and golden brown (Figure 5-24). Let the diamonds cool completely.

8. Decorate the pastry cream, staying inside the frame, with fresh fruit (see "Decorating with Fruit," page 564). Brush the entire pastry with apricot glaze.

NOTE: Puff pastry diamonds can be prepared up to the point of baking, then frozen to bake and decorate as needed; bake directly from the freezer.

Puff Pastry Pinwheels yield: 16 pastries

The pinwheel shape is a classic and can be produced from either croissant dough or Danish dough following the same directions given here for this puff pastry version; you must allow either of those to proof to about doubled in volume before applying the second coat of egg wash and any of the toppings/fillings. Made with any of the three doughs, pinwheels baked with pastry cream or cream cheese filling on top can be decorated after they have cooled with sliced fresh fruit or berries arranged on top of the filling.

If the pinwheels are baked blind (without any filling), you can pipe pastry cream or whipped cream in the center on top of the cooled pastries and again decorate with fresh fruit, or you can add either of the fruit fillings to the baked shells as well. Because the cream cheese filling contains raw eggs, it must be baked with the dough.

1 pound 12 ounces (795 g) Puff Pastry (page 74)

Egg wash

12 ounces (340 g) Pastry Cream (page 845); Cherry Filling (page 838); Chunky Apple Filling (page 840); *or* Cream Cheese Filling for Danish (page 217)

Fresh fruit and/or berries, if using pastry cream or cream cheese filling

Granulated sugar (optional, see Note)

Apricot Glaze (page 5) (optional, see Note)

I. Roll out the puff pastry to ⅛ inch (3 mm) thick and into a square just slightly larger than 16 x 16 inches (40 x 40 cm). Place the dough on a sheet pan lined with baking paper, cover, and refrigerate for a few minutes to firm and relax the dough (if you only have a half-sheet pan, fold the dough in half very gently to fit the pan).

2. Place the dough on your work surface and trim the sides of the square to make it exactly 16 x 16 inches (40 x 40 cm). Cut the square into 4 strips, 4 inches (10 cm) wide in one direction, then cut across the strips every 4 inches (10 cm) to make 16 squares, 4 inches (10 cm) each. Refrigerate the dough again if necessary before continuing; do not attempt to cut and fold the squares when the dough is soft.

3. Cut 4 slits in each square starting from each corner and extending 1½ inches (3.7 cm) toward the center. Place the squares on sheet pans lined with baking paper or Silpats, keeping the shape perfectly even.

4. Brush egg wash lightly over the squares of dough. Fold in every other corner to meet in the center to form a pinwheel. Press the points down firmly to make sure they adhere (Figure 5-25). Brush egg wash over the dough a second time. Invert the pinwheels into granulated sugar if desired (see Note), then return them right-side up to the baking pan.

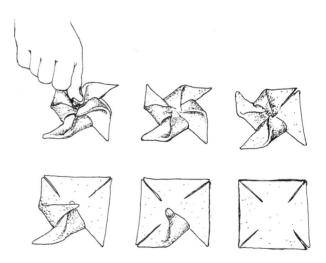

FIGURE 5-25 Forming Puff Pastry Pinwheels and firmly pressing the 4 ends down in the center to prevent the dough from unfolding as it bakes

5. Pipe pastry cream, cherry filling, apple filling, or cream cheese filling in the center of each pinwheel. Alternatively, you can blind bake the pinwheels and fill/decorate them after they have cooled, as discussed above.

6. Bake at 400°F (205°C) for approximately 12 minutes or until golden brown and baked through. Let cool. Brush the pastries with apricot glaze if desired (see Note).

NOTE: If the pinwheels are baked at the specified temperature, the coating of granulated sugar will caramelize and leave a nice shine on the dough, and it will add some sweetness and crunch as well. However, if you prefer to use apricot glaze after the pastries have cooled, omit the sugar.

Raspberry Choux Strips yield: 2 strips, 24 × 4 inches (60 × 10 cm) each (Photo 47)

Like Choux Surprise (page 232), these are nice, light pastries to try as a change of pace from the usual Danish or cinnamon rolls. Raspberry Choux Strips provide an excellent use for leftover scrap puff pastry dough. If you are using virgin puff pastry, be sure to prick the dough well or it will puff too high.

1 pound (455 g) Puff Pastry (page 74)	Crystal sugar
10 ounces (285 g) Pastry Cream (page 845)	Sliced almonds
1 pound (455 g) Pâte à Choux (page 83)	Simple syrup
4 ounces (115 g) raspberry jam	Simple Icing (page 35)

1. Roll out the puff pastry dough to a strip measuring 24 × 8 inches (60 × 20 cm). Let the puff pastry rest for a few minutes to avoid shrinkage. Cut into 2 strips, 4 inches (10 cm) wide.

2. Place the strips on a sheet pan lined with baking paper or a Silpat. Spread the pastry cream out evenly on top of the strips, spreading it almost all the way to the edges.

3. Place the pâte à choux in a pastry bag with a No. 3 (6-mm) plain tip. Pipe the pâte à choux in a figure-eight pattern, with the loops of the eights touching the long sides of the puff pastry rectangles, to cover each strip (Figure 5-26).

4. Place the raspberry jam in a pastry bag with a No. 3 (6-mm) plain tip. Pipe the jam in a line lengthwise down the center of each strip. Combine equal amounts of crystal sugar and almonds (measured by volume), and sprinkle on top.

5. Bake, double-panned, at 375°F (190°C) for about 45 minutes. Be sure the pâte à choux is baked through or it will fall after the pastries have been removed from the oven. Immediately brush simple syrup over the top of the strips. Let cool.

6. Ice with simple icing, then cut into the desired number of pieces.

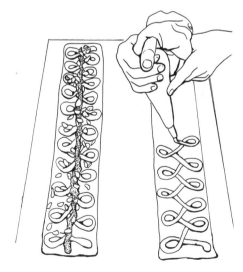

FIGURE 5-26 Piping the pâte à choux over the puff pastry dough in a figure-eight pattern. The strip on the left shows the jam and sliced almonds added.

Cinnamon Knots yield: 30 pastries, 3¹/₂ ounces (100 g) each

As you will see if you make or look through the recipe for Cinnamon Swirls (page 241), Cinnamon Knots contain exactly the same ingredients, but the way that the pastries are formed is much more unusual. Making the knots does require additional time, but they look very appetizing and taste great as well. Plus it is always a good idea to be able to offer something that isn't going to be found in every other shop in town.

Make sure that the filling is not too soft; it should be just spreadable, so refrigerate it if needed. If the filling is too soft, you will not be able to slice the narrow strips as easily or as neatly. It is better to refrigerate the filling alone, however, than to chill the dough after it has been filled.

1 recipe Rich Cardamom Yeast Dough (page 242)	Egg wash
	Crystal sugar
1 pound 8 ounces (680 g) or ¹/₂ recipe Danish Filling II (page 217)	Sliced almonds, lightly crushed
Cinnamon sugar	

1. Roll the dough into a rectangle measuring 14 x 36 inches (35 x 90 cm). Arrange the dough so that the long edges of the rectangle are on the top and bottom.

2. Spread the Danish filling over the left half of the dough only. Sprinkle cinnamon sugar over the filling.

3. Brush egg wash over the uncovered side of the dough and fold it over the filling. The dough should now measure 14 x 18 inches (35 x 45 cm).

4. Roll out to a rectangle measuring 16 x 24 inches (40 x 60 cm), dusting with flour underneath to prevent sticking. Cut into 30 strips, 16 inches (40 cm) long.

5. One at a time, place each strip in front of you horizontally. With one hand on top of each end of the strip, quickly move one hand up and the other hand down simultaneously to twist the strip (Figure 5-27). Wind the twists into a knot shape in the same way you would roll up a ball of yarn; each turn should cross over the previous one and hold it in place (Figure 5-28). As

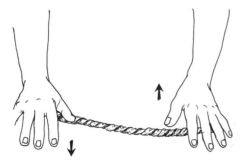

FIGURE 5-27 **Twisting the strip of filled dough by quickly moving the hands in opposite directions**

FIGURE 5-28 **Winding the twisted strip into a ball**

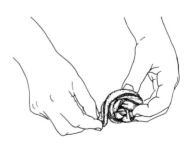

FIGURE 5-29 **Tucking the end underneath the assembled Cinnamon Knot**

you finish each knot, tuck the end underneath (Figure 5-29) and place it on a sheet pan lined with baking paper or a Silpat. Let the knots rise until slightly less than doubled in volume.

6. Combine equal parts crystal sugar and sliced almonds by volume. Brush egg wash over the pastries, then sprinkle the sugar-nut mixture on top.

7. Bake at 375°F (190°C) for approximately 25 minutes or until light brown and baked through. You may need to use a second pan underneath to keep the pastries from getting too brown on the bottom before they are baked through.

Cinnamon Loaves and Wreaths

yield: 6 loaves, 10 inches (25 cm) long, or 4 wreaths, 10 inches (25 cm) in diameter

These braided loaf and wreath shapes have always been very popular with both consumers and bakers in my part of Scandinavia. The simple reasons are that they are quick and easy for us to produce, and customers are attracted to the unusual, appetizing look of the exposed baked filling drizzled with sugar and almonds. They not only look and taste good, but the braids will stay fresh much longer than their close relatives, the individual Cinnamon Knots and Cinnamon Swirls. When I was in the retail business, I would make up either or both the loaves and wreaths to the point of rolling the dough and filling into (short or long) ropes. Because they could be placed close together on a sheet pan, storing the ropes in the refrigerator or freezer took up very little of my precious space and it was then no trouble at all to thaw, slice, form, proof, and bake fresh loaves or wreaths every day.

When making either the loaves or the wreaths, the same suggestions and warnings apply as mentioned at the end of the introduction to Cinnamon Knots (page 238). The consistency of the filling is key to a satisfactory result.

1 recipe Rich Cardamom Yeast Dough (page 242)

3 pounds (1 kg 365 g) or 1 recipe Danish Filling II (page 217)

Cinnamon sugar

Egg wash

Crystal sugar

Sliced almonds, lightly crushed

NOTE: If making the small-batch recipe, make the dough following the instructions for Rich Cardamom Yeast Dough on page 242.

> **Small-Batch Cinnamon Loaves and Wreaths**
> **Yield: 3 loaves, 10 inches (25 cm), or 2 wreaths, 10 inches (25 cm) in diameter**
>
> 1 ounce (30 g) fresh compressed yeast
>
> 1 cup (240 ml) warm whole milk (105° to 115°F/40° to 46°C) (see Note, page 210)
>
> 2½ ounces (70 g) granulated sugar
>
> 1½ teaspoons (7.5 g) salt
>
> 1 tablespoon (6 g) ground cardamom
>
> 2 eggs
>
> 1 pound 5 ounces (595 g) bread flour
>
> 3½ ounces (100 g) melted unsalted butter
>
> 1 pound 8 ounces (680 g) or ½ recipe Danish Filling II (page 217)
>
> Cinnamon sugar
>
> Egg wash
>
> Crystal sugar
>
> Sliced almonds, lightly crushed

TO MAKE LOAVES

1. Divide the dough into 6 equal pieces (3 for the small-batch recipe) weighing approximately 13 ounces (370 g) each. Roll out each piece to make a 12-inch (30-cm) square, working in stages so that each partially rolled piece of dough has time to relax while you work on the others.

2. Divide the Danish filling evenly between the dough squares and spread it out over the dough, leaving ½ inch (1.2 cm) of dough uncovered along the bottom edges (closest to you). Sprinkle cinnamon sugar over the filling. Brush egg wash over the uncovered edges of dough. Use a palette knife to gently press the cinnamon sugar into the filling in a spreading motion.

3. Starting at the top of one square, roll the dough toward the uncovered edge, pressing it together as you move down, to make a tight coil. Repeat with the remaining pieces.

4. Place the ropes in front of you vertically, seam-side down. Cut them in half lengthwise, using a sharp knife or a large pastry wheel. Refrigerate the pieces for a few minutes at this stage if they feel very soft.

5. Place 2 halves on your work surface side by side with the cut edges facing up. Join the pieces together by alternating one on top of the other, keeping the cut sides facing up the entire time (Figure 5-30). Pinch the ends together and tuck underneath. Repeat with the remaining pieces.

6. Transfer the loaves to sheet pans lined with baking paper or Silpats, at the same time stretching the loaves if necessary to make them about 10 inches (25 cm) in length. Let the loaves rise until slightly less than doubled in volume.

FIGURE 5-30 **After slicing the filled dough coil lengthwise, braiding the two halves to make a Cinnamon Loaf; on the left side of the pan are a braided loaf and a braided wreath ready to proof.**

7. Combine equal parts crystal sugar and almonds by volume. Brush egg wash over the loaves and sprinkle the sugar-nut mixture over the top.

8. Bake at 375°F (190°C) for approximately 25 minutes or until brown and baked through. You may need to use a second pan underneath to protect the loaves from becoming too dark before they are baked through.

TO MAKE WREATHS

1. Divide the dough into 4 equal pieces (2 for the small-batch recipe) weighing approximately 1 pound 4 ounces (570 g) each. Roll out each piece of dough to a rectangle measuring 8 x 22 inches (20 x 55 cm), working in stages so that each partially rolled piece of dough has time to relax as you work on the others.

2. Divide the Danish filling evenly between the dough squares and spread it out over the dough, leaving ½ inch (1.2 cm) of dough uncovered along the bottom edges (closest to you). Sprinkle cinnamon sugar over the filling. Brush egg wash over the uncovered edges of dough. Use a palette knife to gently press the cinnamon sugar into the filling in a spreading motion.

3. Starting at the top of one square, roll the dough toward the uncovered edge, pressing it together as you move down, to make a tight coil. Repeat with the remaining pieces.

4. Place the ropes in front of you vertically, seam-side down. Cut them in half lengthwise, using a sharp knife or a large pastry wheel. Refrigerate the pieces for a few minutes at this stage if they feel very soft.

5. Place 2 halves on your work surface side by side with the cut edges facing up. Join the 2 pieces together by starting in the center and alternating one piece on top of the other, keeping the cut sides facing up the entire time. Rotate the rope and repeat to braid the other side.

6. Transfer to a sheet pan lined with baking paper or a Silpat and join the ends together to form a 10-inch (25-cm) circle, stretching and forming the dough as needed, and disguising the seam as best as possible. Repeat to form the remaining wreaths. Let the wreaths rise until they have just under doubled in volume.

7. Combine equal parts crystal sugar and almonds by volume. Brush egg wash over the wreaths and sprinkle the sugar-nut mixture over the top.

8. Bake at 375°F (190°C) for approximately 25 minutes or until brown and baked through. You may need to use a second pan underneath to protect the wreaths from becoming too dark before they are baked through.

Cinnamon Swirls yield: 30 pastries, 3¹/₂ ounces (100 g) each

These spiraled pastries are made with a not-too-sweet, butter-enriched egg bread dough that complements the filling nicely. To avoid ending up with dry pastries, make sure the dough is not too firm, add all of the filling, use a heavy hand with the cinnamon sugar (no one buys a Cinnamon Swirl if they don't like cinnamon), and, finally, make certain that the oven is hot enough.

Rich Cardamom Yeast Dough (recipe follows)	**Egg wash**
1 pound 8 ounces (680 g) or ½ recipe Danish Filling II (page 217)	**Crystal sugar**
	Sliced almonds, lightly crushed
Cinnamon sugar	

1. Roll the dough into a rectangle measuring 14 x 36 inches (35 x 90 cm). Spread the filling over the dough, leaving a 1-inch (2.5-cm) strip uncovered along the bottom (long) edge. Sprinkle cinnamon sugar heavily over the filling. Roll up the rectangle from the top toward you, making a tight rope.

2. Cut the rope evenly into 30 slices. Place on paper-lined sheet pans, cut-side up, tucking the ends underneath to prevent the pastries from unrolling as they expand. Let rise until slightly less than doubled in volume.

3. Brush the pastries with egg wash. Sprinkle with a mixture of equal parts crystal sugar and sliced almonds (measured by volume).

4. Bake at 410°F (210°C) for approximately 15 minutes or until golden brown and baked through. Use a second pan underneath to prevent them from becoming too brown on the bottom.

RICH CARDAMOM YEAST DOUGH yield: 5 pounds (2 kg 275 g)

2 ounces (55 g) fresh compressed yeast

1 pint (480 ml) warm whole milk (105° to 115°F/40° to 46°C) (see Note, page 210)

6 ounces (170 g) granulated sugar

1 tablespoon (15 g) salt

2 tablespoons (12 g) ground cardamom

4 eggs

2 pounds 10 ounces (1 kg 195 g) bread flour

7 ounces (200 g) melted unsalted butter

I. In a mixer bowl, dissolve the yeast in the warm milk. Add the sugar, salt, cardamom, and eggs. Reserve a few ounces of the flour and mix in the remainder. Mix in the butter (it is important that the butter does not come in contact with the yeast before the yeast has had a chance to start expanding).

2. Using the dough hook, knead the dough for a few minutes, then adjust by adding the reserved flour, if required, to make the dough firm enough to roll out. Continue to knead until the dough is smooth and elastic, approximately 6 minutes. Cover and let rest 10 minutes before using.

Cream-Filled Coffee Cake Squares yield: 3 cakes, approximately 9 inches (22.5 cm) square (Photo 28)

These coffee cakes feature the delicious combination of rich cardamom dough and moist custard filling, but perhaps just as important, their shape is unusual, so they are not going to be found in every other pastry shop in town. The opposite is true in Denmark and Sweden, where this folded style is quite popular and is also made using Danish dough and an almond-based filling. If you substitute Danish dough, reduce the filling by about one-third, as it is so rich. Note: The small-batch version of this recipe is shaped into a rectangle rather than a square.

½ recipe Rich Cardamom Yeast Dough (above)

3 pounds (1 kg 165 g) or ½ recipe Pastry Cream (page 845)

Egg wash

1 ounce (30 g) sliced almonds (optional)

I. Divide the dough into 3 equal portions approximately 12 ounces (340 g) each. Roll each piece of dough into a 12-inch (30-cm) square. Trim the edges if necessary. Place the dough squares on sheet pans lined with baking paper or Silpats.

2. Place about 1 cup (240 ml) pastry cream in a pastry bag with a medium-size plain tip (or use a paper pastry bag and cut a ½-inch (1.2-cm) opening. Set aside.

3. Divide the remaining pastry cream evenly between the dough squares; you will use about 12 ounces (340 g) per square. Spread the cream out evenly over the squares, leaving a ½-inch (1.2-cm) uncovered edge on all 4 sides of each piece.

4. Fold all 4 corners of each square in to meet in the center and press down firmly in the center to attach the corners to the dough beneath (Figure 5-31). The folded pieces will measure 8½ inches (21.2 cm) square.

FIGURE 5-31 Making the first fold to form the Cream-Filled Coffee Cake Squares after spreading pastry cream over the dough; piping additional pastry cream along the seams after completing the folds

5. Brush egg wash over the tops of the cakes. Pipe the reserved pastry cream into the 4 open seams of each cake, piping from corner to corner. Sprinkle the sliced almonds over the cakes if desired. Let proof until 1½ times the original size.

6. Bake the cakes at 375°F (190°C) for approximately 35 minutes or until deep golden brown and baked through.

Small-Batch Cream-Filled Coffee Cake Squares
yield: I cake, approximately 6 × 12 inches (15 × 30 cm)

1 pound 2 ounces (510 g) or ¼ recipe Rich Cardamom Yeast Dough (page 242)

1 pound 8 ounces (680 g) or Small-Batch Pastry Cream (page 845)

Egg wash

½ ounce (15 g) sliced almonds (optional)

I. Roll out the dough to a rectangle measuring 12 × 14 inches (30 × 35 cm), using as little flour as possible to keep the dough from sticking. Trim the edges if necessary to make them even (press the trimmings into the center of the rectangle where they will not show). Place the dough on a sheet pan lined with baking paper or a Silpat.

2. Make a small paper pastry bag (see page 54) and place approximately ¼ cup (60 ml) pastry cream in the bag; reserve. Spread the remaining pastry cream over the dough, leaving ½ inch (1.2 cm) of dough uncovered on all 4 edges.

3. Brush egg wash lightly over the uncovered edges of dough. Fold the short edges in ¼ inch (6 mm) so they are next to but not on top of the pastry cream, doubling the thickness of the dough on the short sides. Press the folded edges with your fingers to help the folds adhere. Brush egg wash over the folded short edges.

4. One at a time, fold the long edges in toward the center leaving a ½-inch (1.2-cm) gap between them running the length of the envelope. Press lightly on top of the short ends to seal the sides well.

5. Brush egg wash lightly over the top of the cake. Cut a small opening in the pastry bag and pipe the pastry cream in a line all along the uncovered center. Sprinkle the sliced almonds over the cake if desired.

6. Proof and bake as directed in the main recipe.

Gugelhupf yield: 4 loaves, 15 ounces (430 g) each

A number of rather interesting stories credit people from Austria to France with the invention of this yeasted coffee cake. One theory says it was first made in Vienna in the seventeenth century and was modeled after the turban headdress of a sultan to celebrate Austria's defeat of the Turkish invaders. The cake is also closely associated with the French Alsace region. There it is called *Kugelhopf*, from two German words: *kugel*, meaning "ball" and *hopf*, which translates to "hump." Both are references to the rounded, fluted bundt-style pan that the cakes are baked in. In addition to being good as a snack or with a coffee break, Gugelhupf slices are excellent toasted. See also Chocolate Gugelhupf (page 388).

6 ounces (170 g) dark raisins	1 tablespoon (15 g) salt
¼ cup (60 ml) dark rum	4 ounces (115 g) granulated sugar
¾ ounce (22 g) fresh compressed yeast	4 ounces (115 g) unsalted butter, at room temperature
1 cup (240 ml) warm water (105° to 115°F/40° to 46°C)	2 eggs
½ ounce (15 g) granulated malt extract *or* 2 tablespoons (30 ml) honey	Finely diced zest of 1 lemon
8 ounces (225 g) bread flour	1 pound (455 g) bread flour
40 whole blanched almonds	Powdered sugar
¾ cup (180 ml) warm whole milk (105° to 115°F/40° to 46°C; see Note, page 210)	

1. Macerate (soak) the raisins in the rum.

2. Dissolve the yeast in the warm water in a mixer bowl. Add the malt extract or honey and the first measurement of flour. Mix with a wooden spoon to make a smooth sponge. Cover and let rise in a warm place until doubled in volume.

3. Grease 4 Gugelhupf forms, 1 quart (960 ml) in capacity, or other similar molds. Place 10 whole almonds in the bottom of each form, spacing them evenly around the ring.

4. Incorporate the milk, salt, and sugar into the sponge, using the paddle attachment. Mix in the butter, eggs, and lemon zest.

5. Hold back a handful of the second measurement of flour, mix the remainder into the dough, then adjust the consistency as needed with the reserved flour to make a smooth, soft dough. Cover and let rise in a warm place for 1 hour, punching down the dough once during that time.

6. Knead in the raisin-rum mixture by hand.

7. Divide the dough into 4 equal pieces approximately 15 ounces (430 g) each. Form the pieces into round loaves (see Figures 3-1 and 3-2, page 94).

8. Let the loaves relax for a few minutes, then use a thick dowel to punch a hole in the center of each (see Figure 3-7, page 120).

9. Place the loaves in the reserved pans, pressing the dough firmly into the forms. Let rise until slightly less than doubled in volume.

10. Bake at 375°F (190°C) for approximately 20 minutes or until baked through. Invert immediately onto a cake rack and remove the forms. When cool, dust very lightly with powdered sugar.

Honey-Pecan Sticky Buns

yield: 16 individual buns, or 2 pull-apart cakes, 9 inches (22.5 cm) in diameter

More than one American pastry chef has built a thriving business on some variation of these sticky, gooey, and irresistible buns. It is said that they originated in Philadelphia during the nineteenth century. I make my version (which I do not claim to be anything like the authentic Philadelphia bun) with Rich Cardamom Yeast Dough, but croissant or Danish dough works fine as well. The crucial parts here are the filling and, of course, the topping. If you can't invert the baked buns immediately, put the pan back in the oven to reheat the glaze before doing so, or the sticky part of their name will have a whole new meaning.

Honey Glaze (recipe follows)

3 ounces (85 g) coarsely chopped pecans

½ recipe Rich Cardamom Yeast Dough (page 242)

8 ounces (225 g) or ⅓ recipe Toffee-Coated Hazelnut Spirals filling (page 250)

1. Brush the glaze on the inside of 16 large muffin tins or 2 cake pans, 9 inches (22.5 cm) in diameter (see Note). Be sure the glaze is not too cold and thick, or you risk losing bristles from your pastry brush. Most of the glaze will settle at the bottom—this is okay. Sprinkle the pecans evenly over the glaze.

2. Roll the dough into a rectangle measuring 18 x 15 inches (45 x 37.5 cm), using the minimum amount of flour needed to prevent it from sticking. Spread the filling evenly over the dough. Starting from the top, roll lengthwise into a tight rope. Roll the rope against the table, stretching it at the same time, to make it 24 inches (60 cm) long.

3. With the seam underneath, cut the rope into 16 equal pieces. Place the pieces cut-side up in the prepared muffin tins or cake pans. Let rise until slightly less than doubled in volume.

4. Bake at 375°F (190°C) for approximately 35 minutes for the individual buns or 45 minutes for the cake pans. The top and bottom should have a pleasant brown color. Because the top will brown faster than the bottom, which is moist with glaze, use a fork to lift one of the buns out of the pan to check the color.

5. Remove from the oven, place a sheet pan large enough to cover over the top, and immediately invert. Be very careful of the hot glaze; it should run down the sides of the buns, but it could also end up on your hands. Use a palette knife to scoop up any excess glaze or nuts that fall onto the sheet pan and place back on the buns. Let the sticky buns cool for about 10 minutes. The glaze will set up quite fast on the outside, but any that has seeped inside can easily burn a too-eager taster.

NOTE: You should use up all of the glaze when you coat the pans. If you do, however, have any left over, spread (or brush) it over the dough before topping with the filling.

HONEY GLAZE yield: 2 cups (480 ml)

4 ounces (115 g) unsalted butter

10 ounces (285 g) light brown sugar

3 tablespoons (45 ml) or 2 ounces (55 g) honey

¼ cup (60 ml) or 3 ounces (85 g) light corn syrup

2 tablespoons (30 ml) water

1. Combine all of the ingredients in a heavy-bottomed saucepan. Stir over medium heat until the mixture just comes to a boil.

2. Cool to thicken slightly before using.

Hot Cross Buns yield: 36 buns, approximately 2 ounces (55 g) each

These lightly spiced buns filled with currants and, sometimes, dried fruit are slashed on top in the outline of a cross. The English institutionalized the custom of serving Hot Cross Buns, with their symbolic design, at Easter, specifically on Good Friday, at the beginning of the 1700s. Like Fat Tuesday Buns (also called Lenten Buns), Hot Cross Buns originated as part of the Lenten festivities celebrated by the Roman Catholic Church and some western Christian churches. Shrove Tuesday, or Fat Tuesday, marks the last day to enjoy the rich foods that will be given up during Lent. Don't forget—Hot Cross Buns should be served hot.

2 ounces (55 g) fresh compressed yeast

2 cups (480 ml) warm whole milk (105° to 115°F/40° to 46°C; see Note, page 210)

1 tablespoon (15 g) salt

½ cup (120 ml) or 6 ounces (170 g) honey

1 pound 12 ounces (795 g) bread flour

2 teaspoons (3 g) ground cinnamon

1½ teaspoons (3 g) ground nutmeg

½ teaspoon (1 g) ground cloves

6 ounces (170 g) unsalted butter, at room temperature

12 ounces (360 g) dried currants

Finely chopped zest of 2 lemons

Egg wash

12 ounces (360 g) or ½ recipe Small-Batch Pastry Cream (page 845)

Simple Icing (page 35)

Vanilla extract

1. In a mixer bowl, dissolve the yeast in the warm milk. Stir in the salt and the honey.

2. Combine the flour with the cinnamon, nutmeg, and cloves. Mix into the yeast and milk mixture, using the dough hook at low speed. Incorporate the soft butter.

3. Knead at medium speed for 8 to 10 minutes, adding bread flour if necessary. The dough should be smooth and soft. Do not overknead the dough, or it will be difficult to incorporate the fruit later. Place the dough, covered, in a warm place and let it rise until it has doubled in volume, about 1 hour.

4. Knead in the currants and lemon zest by hand, kneading until the dough is smooth and glutenous. Let the dough rest, covered, for 10 minutes.

5. Divide the dough into 2 pieces approximately 2 pounds (910 g) each. Roll the pieces into 18-inch (45-cm) ropes, then cut each rope into 18 equal pieces. Roll the small pieces against the table into tight round buns (see Figure 4-2, page 186). Place approximately 1½ inches (3.7 cm) apart on sheet pans lined with baking paper or Silpats.

6. Using a sharp knife or razor blade, cut a cross on top of each bun just deep enough to penetrate the skin. Let the buns rise until slightly less than doubled in volume.

7. Brush the buns with egg wash.

8. Place the pastry cream in a pastry bag with a No. 3 (6-mm) plain tip. Pipe a cross of pastry cream in the opened cut on top of each bun.

9. Bake at 400°F (205°C) for approximately 20 minutes or until done. Let cool slightly.

10. Flavor the simple icing with vanilla extract. Use a spatula to drizzle the icing on the buns.

CHEF'S TIP
Try spacing the buns just ½ inch (1.2 cm) apart on the baking pan. They will push up next to one another once they are fully proofed and baked, creating a square, slightly moister bun with soft edges. This method is helpful when making a large quantity because not only do more buns fit on each pan but also the process of cutting the crosses and piping on the pastry cream is speeded up, as both jobs can be done making straight lines across the pan instead of working on each bun individually.

Orange-Almond Twists   yield: 4 loaves, 1 pound 14 ounces (855 g) each

This recipe was given to me by a Hungarian colleague from Budapest. I haven't seen this particular shape of brioche-like dough stuffed with orange-almond filling anywhere else, though the idea of braiding plain and chocolate doughs, batter, or sponges for contrast is nothing new. These two-toned twists will keep fresh for several days.

2 ounces (55 g) fresh compressed yeast

1 pint (480 ml) cold whole milk

1 ounce (30 g) granulated malt extract *or* 3 tablespoons (45 ml) or 2 ounces (55 g) honey

3 ounces (85 g) granulated sugar

2 pounds 4 ounces (1 kg 25 g) bread flour

2 tablespoons (30 g) salt

Grated zest of 1 lemon

1 teaspoon (5 ml) vanilla extract

2 eggs

5 ounces (140 g) unsalted butter, at room temperature

1 ounce (30 g) unsweetened cocoa powder

⅓ cup (80 ml) water

Orange-Almond Filling (recipe follows)

Egg wash

Sliced almonds

1. In a mixer bowl, dissolve the yeast in the cold milk. Add the malt extract or honey and the granulated sugar. Reserve a few ounces of the flour and mix the remainder into the yeast and milk mixture.

2. Combine the salt, lemon zest, vanilla, and eggs. Add to the dough. Mix in the butter.

3. Knead the dough 8 to 10 minutes, using the dough hook. Halfway through the kneading, add more flour, if necessary, to make a fairly soft and elastic dough.

4. Divide the dough into 2 unequal parts, one 4 ounces (115 g) lighter than the other.

5. Combine the cocoa powder and the water and add to the lighter piece of dough, mixing well so it is uniform in color. Cover both pieces of dough and let them rest for approximately 10 minutes.

6. Divide the chocolate dough and the plain dough into 4 equal pieces, approximately 9 ounces (255 g) each. Form each piece into a rectangle without kneading or overworking it; cover the pieces.

7. Starting with the piece you formed first, roll out each piece to approximately 15 × 4 inches (37.5 × 10 cm).

8. Spread the filling out evenly over the 8 rectangles, leaving a ½-inch (1.2-cm) border on the bottom long sides.

9. Brush the borders with egg wash and roll the dough toward you (starting from the top long side) in a very tight spiral. Press the egg-washed border on the outside to seal the rolls.

10. Roll each rope between your hands and the table to make it 20 inches (50 cm) long.

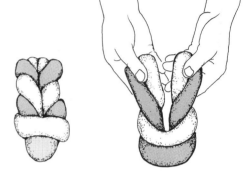

FIGURE 5-32 **Twisting the filled ropes of light and chocolate dough together to form Orange-Almond Twists**

11. Place a plain and a chocolate rope next to each other in an upside-down *U* shape, with the plain piece on the inside. Braid by twisting each side of the *U* 4 times toward the outside (Figure 5-32) (hold the pair of ropes on each side of the *U* in your hands and turn your hands as if you are opening a book). Make sure the chocolate and the plain dough line up evenly in the finished twist.

12. Place the twists on sheet pans, brush with egg wash, and sprinkle lightly with sliced almonds. Let rise until slightly less than doubled in volume.

13. Bake, double-panned, at 375°F (190°C) for about 40 minutes.

ORANGE-ALMOND FILLING yield: 3 pounds (1 kg 365 g)

8 egg whites (1 cup/240 ml)

5 ounces (140 g) almond paste

1 pound 6 ounces (625 g) blanched almonds
    or hazelnuts, finely ground

8 ounces (225 g) granulated sugar

5 ounces (140 g) candied orange peel,
    finely chopped

1. Incorporate the egg whites into the almond paste, adding them gradually so you do not create lumps.

2. Add the nuts, sugar, and orange peel.

3. If the filling feels too firm to spread (this will usually be the case if it is left overnight, as nuts absorb moisture), add enough additional egg whites to thin it to a spreadable consistency.

Fastlags Bullar

Fastlags Bullar is what these cream-filled buns are called in Swedish. They were originally created for Fat Tuesday, the day before Ash Wednesday, when fasting for Lent begins. Fat Tuesday (*Fet Tisdag*) is the day people traditionally eat large quantities of the goodies that will be off limits until Easter. In the old days, Fastlags Bullar ("fasting buns") were always made in the Swedish pastry shops beginning a few weeks before Lent. Then they became available a little earlier year by year, and of course, once one shop started making them, the others had to follow suit, until today, when you can enjoy these delicacies when the Christmas decorations have barely left the store windows.

Although they are filled with whipped cream, these buns are traditionally eaten with your hands as you would a Danish pastry or a cinnamon roll. The way I remember eating them with my friends as a child is first using the lid to scoop out some of the cream before biting into the rest of the bun. Even so, we would usually end up with a mustache from the remaining cream. A conventional presentation on Fat Tuesday is to serve a bun in a deep bowl with cinnamon sugar and warm milk.

Swedish Lenten Buns yield: 32 buns

If you didn't grow up with these treats, your first reaction may be the same as that of my students, who wondered, "What's so special about these?" But that was only before they tasted them—the buns might seem simple, but they are simply delicious! To be at their best, Swedish Lenten Buns should be served the same day they are baked, but they can be stored, covered, in a cool place (but not refrigerated) until the next day before they are filled. If they are then served with warm milk, none of their appeal will be lost.

1 recipe Rich Cardamom Yeast Dough (page 242)	4 teaspoons (20 g) granulated sugar
12 ounces (340 g) almond paste	Powdered sugar
2 ounces (55 g) Pastry Cream (page 845; see Note)	Warm whole milk (optional)
3 cups (720 ml) heavy cream	Cinnamon sugar (optional)

1. After it has rested, divide the dough into 2 pieces, about 2 pounds 4 ounces (1 kg 25 g) each. Form each piece into a rope about 20 inches (50 cm) long. Cut each rope into 16 pieces. Form the pieces into round rolls (see instructions and Figure 4-2 on page 186).

2. Place the rolls, staggered, on sheet pans lined with baking paper or Silpats. Let rise until doubled in volume.

3. Bake at 400°F (205°C) until brown and baked through, about 15 minutes. Set aside to cool.

4. Soften the almond paste by gradually mixing in the pastry cream; the mixture should be spreadable.

5. Whip the heavy cream and the granulated sugar until stiff peaks form. Place in a pastry bag with a No. 7 (14-mm) star tip.

6. Using a serrated knife, slice the top ½ inch (1.2 cm) off the buns, leaving a flat, even surface. You can also use scissors held at a 45-degree angle to remove the top of the buns in a triangular cut. Point the scissors toward the center of the bun and cut about ¾ inch (2 cm) deep. Spread the almond paste mixture over the cut surface. Pipe a ring of the whipped cream around the edge on top of the almond paste. Replace the tops of the rolls, setting them on the whipped cream ring. Sift powdered sugar lightly over the buns. Serve with warm milk and cinnamon sugar if desired. If the buns are not served at once, refrigerate until needed.

NOTE: The amount of pastry cream required depends on the starting consistency of the almond paste. If you do not have pastry cream on hand, you can soften the almond paste to a spreadable consistency with water. Conversely, if you do not care for almond paste, using all pastry cream tastes good combined with the roll and the whipped cream.

Toffee-Coated Hazelnut Spirals yield: 36 pastries, approximately 2 ounces (55 g) each

I acquired this recipe from an old Danish pastry chef (or so he seemed at the time) when I was a young apprentice. The pastries are made with a soft brioche-type dough and a cinnamon-hazelnut filling, and they are covered with a toffee mixture before baking. Toffee-Coated Hazelnut Spirals are baked in muffin cups or Flexipans so that none of the goodies are lost on this very special breakfast pastry.

DOUGH

1½ ounces (40 g) fresh compressed yeast

1 cup (240 ml) cold whole milk

3 eggs

3 ounces (85 g) granulated sugar

2 teaspoons (10 g) salt

1 pound 8 ounces (680 g) bread flour

10 ounces (285 g) unsalted butter, at room temperature

FILLING

10 ounces (285 g) unsalted butter, at room temperature

6 ounces (170 g) light brown sugar

6 ounces (170 g) granulated sugar

4 ounces (115 g) toasted hazelnuts, finely ground

1½ tablespoons (7 g) ground cinnamon

TOPPING

5 ounces (140 g) unsalted butter

2 tablespoons (30 ml) heavy cream

4 ounces (115 g) granulated sugar

2 tablespoons (30 ml) or 1½ ounces (40 g) light corn syrup

2 ounces (55 g) coarsely chopped or crushed hazelnuts

TO MAKE THE DOUGH

1. Dissolve the yeast in the milk; stir in the eggs, sugar, and salt.

2. Mix in enough of the flour, using the dough hook or the paddle, to make a sponge with the consistency of soft butter, then mix in the remaining flour and the butter. This method ensures that you will not get lumps of butter from adding it to a cold dough. Mix the dough until smooth; it will be very soft and will not come away from the sides of the bowl.

3. Place the dough on a sheet pan, press it flat and even, and refrigerate (or freeze, if you are in a hurry) until the dough is firm enough to roll out.

1. Cream the butter with the brown sugar and granulated sugar.

2. Add the hazelnuts and cinnamon. Blend well.

NOTE: If the filling is left overnight, the nuts will absorb much of the moisture and it may be necessary to soften the thickened filling to a spreadable consistency by adding some pastry cream or an egg.

TO MAKE THE TOPPING

1. Place the butter and cream in a saucepan over low heat. When the butter starts to melt, add the sugar and corn syrup.

2. Boil to 215°F (102°C), then add the hazelnuts.

3. Boil 5 minutes longer over medium heat. The hotter the sugar mixture gets (as it is being reduced), the smaller and slower the bubbles will become; with some experience, you will be able to judge the temperature by the appearance.

4. Remove the topping from the heat and let cool until it is firm enough to be spread with a spatula. If the topping becomes too hard, or if it is made ahead, you will need to reheat it. When you reheat it, the butter will separate; stir in 1 tablespoon (15 ml) heavy cream to bring it back together.

ASSEMBLY

1. Roll the dough to 14 inches (35 cm) wide, 3 feet (90 cm) long, and ⅛ inch (3 mm) thick.

2. Spread the filling evenly over the dough. If you are not making the spirals in paper cups or Flexipans, leave a ½-inch (1.2-cm) strip at the bottom without filling and brush it with egg wash; this will prevent the spirals from unrolling as they rise.

3. Starting from the top edge, roll the strip up tightly.

4. Cut the roll into 36 equal pieces. An easy way to ensure that the pieces will be uniform is to cut the roll into quarters and then cut each quarter into 9 pieces.

5. Place the spirals level in muffin-size paper cups; you can place the paper cups in muffin pans to keep the spirals from spreading too flat if desired.

6. Let the spirals rise until slightly less than doubled in volume; be careful not to let them rise too long or, when they expand in the oven, a lot of the topping will fall off onto the sheet pan and be lost.

7. Spread the topping on the spirals using a small spatula.

8. Bake at 375°F (190°C) until golden brown, about 40 minutes.

NOTE: The spirals can be made in Flexipan No. 3051. Place the pastries into the indentations of the pan as in Step 5, but omit the paper muffin cups. Allow the baked pastries to cool before unmolding them.

Berliners yield: 40 buns

A Berliner is simply a filled doughnut. But unlike traditional American-style doughnuts, which are always cooked first if they are to be filled, Berliners can be filled before or after cooking. The latter is more practical for commercial operations. The trademark of a perfectly prepared Berliner is a light-colored ring around the center where the dough was not in the oil as long. In addition to adding to the overall appearance, it shows that the oil was hot enough to make the pastry rise up high before the yeast was killed (the same as oven-spring for baked yeast products).

SPONGE

2 ounces (55 g) fresh compressed yeast

1½ cups (360 ml) warm whole milk (105° to 115°F/40° to 46°C; see Note, page 210)

12 ounces (340 g) bread flour

DOUGH

1½ ounces (40 g) fresh compressed yeast

½ cup (120 ml) warm whole milk (105° to 115°F/40° to 46°C)

4 ounces (115 g) granulated sugar

1 teaspoon (5 g) salt

Grated zest of ½ lemon

6 egg yolks (½ cup/120 ml)

6 ounces (170 g) unsalted butter, at room temperature

1 pound 2 ounces (510 g) bread flour

Vegetable oil *or* deep-frying oil

Cinnamon sugar

Chunky Apple Filling (page 840) *or* Cherry Filling (page 838), pureed

1. To make the sponge, dissolve the yeast in the warm milk, then add the flour and mix to a smooth consistency. Let the sponge rise, covered, in a warm place until it starts to fall.

2. Start making the dough by dissolving the yeast in the warm milk in a mixer bowl. Add the sponge and start kneading with the dough hook.

3. Add the sugar, salt, lemon zest, egg yolks, and butter as you continue to knead the dough. Knead in enough of the flour to make a medium-soft dough, kneading for a total of 5 to 10 minutes. The dough should not be too firm, so do not add all the flour at once.

4. Refrigerate the dough, covered, for 1 hour to relax it.

5. Divide the dough into 4 equal pieces, approximately 1 pound (455 g) each. Roll each piece into a rope, then cut each rope into 10 equal pieces.

6. Roll the small pieces into smooth, round buns (see Figure 4-2, page 186). Place them on a sheet pan covered with a cloth or towel. Try not to use any flour at all when working with Berliners, as it will burn when they are fried, making the outside too dark.

7. Let the buns rise in a warm place, around 80°F (26°C), until slightly less than doubled in volume (this will happen fairly quickly due to the softness of the dough).

8. Preheat the frying oil to 360°F (183°C). Use a frying thermometer to test the temperature, and try to time it so the oil is ready when the Berliners have risen. You should have at least 4 inches (10 cm) of oil. Use a good-quality vegetable oil or, better yet, an oil specifically made for deep frying. It is very important that the oil is at the correct temperature. If it is not hot enough, the buns will absorb too much oil and be heavy and unappetizing. If the oil is hotter than it should be, the Berliners will brown before they are cooked through, the flavor will not be as good, and the oil will darken so that you will not be able to use it a second time. See "About Deep Frying," page 257.

9. Pick up the Berliners one at a time and quickly add them to the oil, seam-side up. Do not fill up the pan completely, because the Berliners will increase in volume as they cook.

10. When they are golden brown, in about 5 minutes, turn them over and cook about 4 minutes longer on the other side. Try to turn them all over at about the same time so they are uniform in color.

11. As you remove the Berliners from the frying pan, place them on a rack or paper towels to drain.

12. While the buns are still hot, roll them in cinnamon sugar.

13. After the Berliners have cooled down a bit, inject them with chunky apple or cherry filling, using a special plain pastry bag tip made for that purpose, and pushing the sharp end of the tip halfway into the side of the Berliner. If you do not have a tip made for filling, use a No. 3 (6-mm) plain tip and be careful not to make the opening in the bun any larger than necessary. Berliners should be served the same day they are made.

KLENÄTER yield: 36 pastries, 1¼ x 4 inches (3.1 x 10 cm) each

Known as *Schüferli* in Germany and Switzerland, these pastries are very popular there and are considered a must at Christmastime in Sweden. They are traditionally leavened with baking powder rather than yeast but are even better made with Berliner dough, as they are here. Klenäter are served as part of a cookie or pastry assortment.

1. Make ½ recipe Berliners (page 252), preparing the dough through Step 4 with the following changes:

- Replace ¼ cup (60 ml) of the milk in the dough (not the sponge) with an equal amount of brandy.
- Add ½ teaspoon (1 g) ground cardamom with the flour.
- Omit Chunky Apple or Cherry Filling.

2. Roll the dough to a rectangle measuring 12 x 16 inches (30 x 40 cm), using as little flour as possible. (Let the dough relax for a few minutes as needed to keep it from shrinking.) Brush off any excess flour from the top and the bottom.

3. Preheat the frying oil to 360°F (183°C).

4. Cut the dough into 3 strips, 4 inches (10 cm) long, using a fluted pastry wheel. Leave the strips in place. Using the same tool and cutting crosswise, cut 12 pieces, approximately 1¼ inches (3.1 cm) wide, in each strip. Cut a 2-inch (5-cm) slit lengthwise in the center of each piece.

5. Pick up one piece and pull one end of the strip through the slit. Then, holding the rectangle by two diagonal corners, stretch lightly so it takes on a slight diamond-shape (Figure 5-33).

6. Repeat with the remaining pieces and place them on a sheet pan covered with a cloth or towel. They are ready to cook immediately and do not require additional proofing.

7. Carefully drop the pieces one at time into the hot frying oil. Cook approximately 2 minutes or until nicely browned; then turn and cook about 1 minute longer on the other side.

8. Remove from the oil with a slotted spoon or skimmer and place on paper towels or napkins for a few seconds to drain. While still warm, turn in cinnamon sugar to coat thoroughly.

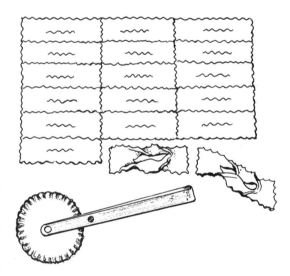

FIGURE 5-33 The dough for Klenäter after cutting the strips with a fluted pastry wheel; one piece turned inside out; a piece after stretching the diagonal corners

Viennese Apple Fritters yield: approximately 24 pastries

This type of fritter is called *Krapfen* in Austria, a name that translates from the German language to "doughnut." The fritters make a delicious breakfast pastry or, in my opinion, an enjoyable treat anytime of the day. As you will see, Krapfen are quite simple to make, and they contain only a few ingredients. The only trick is to be certain that your frying oil is at the correct temperature to be sure that the pastries will be cooked all the way through. If the oil is too hot, the fritters will become browned and cooked on the outside (and will appear done) even though the center may still contain raw pâte à choux, which is not too pleasant to eat, even in a small quantity. As is true for any type of fried pastry, the fritters should be served and enjoyed while still warm or, at the outside, within a few hours of frying. You can use all raisins or all apples rather than a combination of the two, should you desire.

1 small Granny Smith *or* other similar cooking apple (approximately 5 ounces/140 g)

¼ lemon

½ recipe Pâte à Choux (page 83)

4 ounces (115 g) dark raisins

Vegetable oil *or* deep-frying oil

Cinnamon sugar and/or powdered sugar

1. Peel and core the apple; cut into ¼-inch (6-mm) cubes. Place the cubes in a bowl, squeeze the lemon juice over the top, and toss the cubes to ensure they are all coated with lemon juice to prevent browning. Cover and set aside while you prepare the pâte à choux.

2. Stir the reserved apples and the raisins into the pâte à choux.

3. Heat the frying oil to 360°F (183°C). Using a 2-ounce (60-ml) ice cream scoop (No. 24), add scoops of the dough to the hot oil in batches. Do not crowd the frying pan to avoid lowering the temperature of the oil below 350°F (175°C). Cook the fritters for about 10 minutes, turning them as necessary to brown evenly (because of their round shape they tend to turn on their own) or until they are deep golden brown and cooked all the way through.

4. Use a slotted spoon to transfer the cooked fritters to sheet pans lined with paper towels to drain. While they are still warm, roll the balls in cinnamon sugar and/or sift powdered sugar over the tops. The fritters are best eaten warm but are almost as good at room temperature.

Yeast-Leavened Doughnuts yield: 30 doughnuts

True to my word in the recipe for Berliners, which I describe as "simply a doughnut without the hole," I am using an only slightly modified version of that dough here. To form the traditional doughnut shape, you will need either a doughnut cutter or two plain cookie cutters, one approximately 3 inches (7.5 cm) in diameter and the other about 1 inch (2.5 cm) for cutting out the holes. Because fried doughnut holes are a favorite of many (especially kids), you may want to fry the cutout holes for a special treat. If you do decide to fry the holes instead of rerolling them to cut out more doughnuts, this recipe will yield only about 24 doughnuts instead of 30. I enjoy my doughnuts just like my Berliners—rolled in cinnamon sugar after frying.

SPONGE

2 ounces (55 g) fresh compressed yeast

1½ cups (360 ml) warm whole milk (105° to 115°F/40° to 46°C; see Note, page 210)

12 ounces (340 g) bread flour

DOUGH

1½ ounces (40 g) fresh compressed yeast

½ cup (120 ml) warm whole milk (105° to 115°F/40° to 46°C; see Note, page 210)

4 ounces (115 g) granulated sugar

1 teaspoon (5 g) salt

Grated zest of 1 lemon

6 egg yolks (½ cup/120 ml)

4 ounces (115 g) unsalted butter, at room temperature

1 pound (455 g) bread flour

Vegetable oil *or* deep-frying oil

Cinnamon sugar *or* powdered sugar

1. To make the sponge, dissolve the yeast in the warm milk, then add the flour and mix to a smooth consistency. Let the sponge rise, covered, in a warm place until it starts to fall, approximately 30 minutes.

2. To make the dough, dissolve the yeast in the warm milk in the bowl of a mixer. Add the sponge. Using the dough hook, start mixing and incorporate the sugar, salt, lemon zest, egg yolks, and butter. Gradually add the flour and knead for 5 to 10 minutes, scraping down the bowl occasionally and incorporating additional flour if needed. The dough should be soft, but you must be able to roll it out.

3. Using enough flour on your hands and on your work surface to keep the dough from sticking, form the dough into a square or rectangle. Line a sheet pan with baking paper and dust flour over the paper. Place the dough on top, cover, and refrigerate for 1 hour to relax and firm.

4. Roll the dough out to ½ inch (1.2 cm) thick, using as little flour as possible (an excess of flour on the surface of the doughnuts will burn during the frying process, detracting from both the flavor and the appearance of the finished product). Cut out doughnuts using a doughnut cutter or 2 plain cookie cutters. If using cookie cutters, use a 3-inch (7.5-cm) cutter to cut the outside rings and a 1-inch (2.5-cm) cutter to cut out the holes. Place the doughnuts on sheet pans covered with a cloth or towel. Combine and reroll the scraps (with or without the holes) and continue cutting out doughnuts until you have used all the dough. You may need to let it rest and relax a bit while you are rerolling.

5. Set the doughnuts aside to proof in a warm location (ideally 80°F/26°C) until they have just about doubled in volume. This will happen fairly quickly due to the comparatively large

About Deep Frying

As is true when preparing any deep-fried item, you should use a fat made especially for this purpose. It will have a high smoking point and will give you the best result. Never use solid shortening for deep frying. Be certain to keep the oil clean during the frying process by skimming off any small bits of dough that would otherwise burn and affect the flavor of the fat.

When you are finished frying, allow the fat to cool in a safe place, strain it, and store it covered. While the fat can be reused several times, it will not last forever; once it shows signs of darkening or breaking down, discard it. Old fat can become rancid and even if it is not, it tends to cause the items being cooked to brown excessively once it has been heated several times. Lastly, be sure the fat or oil you are using for deep-frying pastries is not being used for any other purpose, especially for cooking any savory items.

amount of yeast and the softness of the dough, so be sure to have the frying oil preheated to the correct temperature when the doughnuts have finished proofing.

6. Heat the frying oil to 360°F (183°C), using a deep-frying thermometer to accurately test the temperature. You should have a minimum of 4 inches (10 cm) of oil in the pan. Use a good-quality vegetable oil or, better yet, an oil specifically made for deep-frying. It is very important that the oil is at the correct temperature. If it is not hot enough, the doughnuts will absorb too much oil and be heavy and unappetizing. If the oil is hotter than it should be, the doughnuts will brown before they are cooked through, the flavor will not be as good, and the oil will darken so that you will not be able to use it a second time.

7. Quickly add the doughnuts to the oil one at a time. Do not fill up the pan completely because the doughnuts will increase in volume as they cook and adding too many will lower the temperature of the oil.

8. When the doughnuts are cooked halfway, about 2 minutes, turn them over and finish cooking.

9. Remove the doughnuts with a slotted spoon or skimmer and place them on paper towels to absorb excess oil. While they are still warm, roll in cinnamon sugar or in powdered sugar, if you prefer.

Cookies

It is a tradition in Sweden to serve cookies and coffee at 3 o'clock each afternoon—our equivalent of English afternoon tea. Seven kinds of cookies are neatly lined up on trays. If it is not possible to have seven types, the custom is to serve another odd number of varieties such as five. When someone dropped by to visit during the day, we always served coffee and cookies. Cookies are also great for after-dinner treats. It has become popular in some restaurants to serve a platter of assorted small cookies when the check is presented, perhaps to cushion the shock a little.

Cookie comes from the Dutch word *koekje*, which translates to "small cake," as do both the Swedish name for cookies, *småkakor*, and the German *klein gebäck*. In England, cookies are known, of course, as biscuits. There are more varieties of these small, irresistible sweets than any other baked good—largely because so many variations in shape, flavor, texture, and size fall under this one heading. There are drop cookies, refrigerator cookies, meringue-type cookies, petit four sec, bar cookies, piped cookies, cookie-cutter cookies, cakelike cookies, twice-baked varieties (such as biscotti), and so on. Add to each of these seasonal and international modifications, and the list goes on indefinitely.

Texture

Some cookies are crisp; others are intentionally soft and/or chewy. Some cookies spread out flat during the baking process; others hold their shape. In order to produce the desired texture, to correct mistakes, or to modify cookie recipes, it is of the utmost importance that you have an understanding of the role played by each ingredient.

CHEWY TEXTURE

A chewy cookie needs a high moisture content, which is provided by eggs and other liquids. Eggs must be in higher proportion to the other ingredients, while the fat content must be lower. You should use a high-gluten flour and be certain that there is some gluten development when mixing the dough.

CRISP TEXTURE

For a cookie to be crisp, the dough must be relatively low in moisture. The cookies should be small and thin to allow them to dry properly as they bake. Most important, these cookies must be high in both fat and sugar. Crisp cookies can become soft if stored improperly, especially if they contain hygroscopic ingredients, such as ground nuts, that absorb moisture from the air. Crisp cookies must be stored in an airtight container.

SOFT (CAKELIKE) TEXTURE

Naturally, soft cookies are found at the opposite end of the scale from crisp cookies. They require a dough with a high proportion of liquid and a low sugar and fat content. Soft cookies are generally thick and comparatively large, which allows retention of the additional moisture during baking. They usually contain either corn syrup, honey, or molasses, which are hygroscopic (moisture-absorbing) sweeteners. Soft cookies should be slightly underbaked and must be stored in a covered container, or they will dry out. Storing moist or chewy cookies in the same container with a few slices of apple or quince will greatly prolong their shelf life.

Altering the Shape in the Baking Process

With any of the previous texture traits, you may want the cookies to spread out flat during baking, or it may be highly undesirable for the cookie to change shape at all. When the latter is preferable, the cookie dough generally will not contain any baking powder or baking soda, and the dough should be mixed only until the ingredients are well incorporated. Beating or creaming will incorporate air and cause the cookies to puff and fall as they bake. Using a chlorinated flour will also reduce spreading. Granulated sugar acts as an aid to incorporating air into fat, so a high sugar content can contribute to spreading when combined with overmixing. If the sugar and fat are mixed to a paste without incorporating air, however, this effect will not occur. In general, the higher the sugar content, the more the cookies will spread. Using powdered sugar or even a very fine granulated sugar, such as castor sugar, will reduce this tendency. Additional sugar will also make baked cookies harder. An overgreased baking pan and/or a soft dough will further cause cookies to spread.

If the cookies are intended to spread out, the dough should contain baking soda, baking powder, ammonium carbonate, potash, or a combination of these leaveners. Increased spread is also obtained by creaming the ingredients during mixing and by adding tenderizers such as fat, honey, molasses, and corn syrup. These can have an adverse effect if used in a quantity that disrupts the balance of the strengtheners (also called the binding ingredients) in the recipe: the eggs and flour.

Appearance

Cookies should look as good as they taste. You want to create petite, bite-sized morsels that your guests just can't resist, even if they are not hungry. With few exceptions, cookies should be small. They should always be uniform in size and thickness. Not only will they bake more evenly, your cookies will create an elegant presentation when displayed on a tray or mirror. Pay special attention when the following recipes call for chilling the dough at various stages in the preparation; skipping this important step will result in misshapen, unprofessional-looking cookies.

DECORATING

Cookies can be decorated and made more delicious by piping jam on top, dipping them in chocolate (completely or in part), sandwiching them together with preserves or buttercream, dipping them in fondant, or topping them with sifted, powdered sugar or an icing.

FORMING

Cookie dough is shaped in several ways. Some cookies, such as Coconut Macaroons and Spritz Rings, are piped out using a pastry bag with a specific tip. In other recipes, the dough is divided into equal portions; which are rolled into ropes of uniform thickness and cut into cookies. These are known as *icebox cookies*, and this technique is used with Macadamia Nut, Hazelnut Butter, and all variations of Vanilla Butter Cookies. This method not only gives you cookies of uniform size, but also makes storage easier. If well wrapped, the logs can be refrigerated for days or frozen for weeks. The cookies can be baked and finished as needed, allowing you to produce fresh cookies with a minimum of effort. A third way of forming cookies is to spread the dough in sheets on a pan or roll it into ropes and press these on the pan. The cookies are cut to size as soon as the baked dough comes out of the oven.

Baking

Most cookies have a high sugar content, which makes them susceptible to overbrowning. It is usually a good idea to bake them double-panned to prevent them from becoming too dark on the bottom before they have a chance to reach an appetizing golden brown color on the top. Generally, cookies should be baked around 375°F (190°C), except macaroons, which need high heat, 425°F (219°C), to ensure softness.

Cookie Recipes Categorized by Texture, Production Method, and Storage Capability

Soft Cookies	Chewy Cookies	Crisp Cookies	Pastry-like Cookies	Piped Cookies	Icebox Cookies	Good for Storage
Almond Macaroons	Almond Macaroons	Almond Shortbread	Almond Horseshoes	Almond Macaroons	Almond Shortbread	Biscotti
Brownies	Brutti ma Buoni	Biscotti	Apple-Coconut Points	Coconut Haystack Cookies	Austrian Hazelnut-Almond Cookies	Butter Crescents
Chewy Trail Mix Cookies	Chewy Trail Mix Cookies	Chinese Sesame Seed/Almond Cookies	Butter Crescents	Coconut Macaroons	Chewy Trail Mix Cookies	Chinese Sesame Seed/Almond Cookies
Chocolate Chip Cookies	Chunky White-Chocolate Chip	Cornmeal-Lime Cookies	Coconut Haystack Cookies	Oat Flakes	Chocolate Chip Cookies	Cocoa Cuts
Chunky White-Chocolate Chip Cookies	Coconut Haystack Cookies	Cocoa Cuts	Florentinas	Spritz Rings	Chunky White-Chocolate Chip Cookies	Florentinas
Coconut Haystack Cookies	Coconut Macaroons	Florentinas	Layered Florentina Squares	Strassburger Cookies	Cornmeal-Lime Cookies	Hazelnut Squares
Coconut Macaroons	Date Bars	Hazelnut-Almond Squares	Madeleines		Hazelnut Butter Cookies	Heide Sand Cookies
Gingersnaps	Gingersnaps	Heide Sand Cookies	Meyer Lemon Bars		Macadamia Nut Cookies	Honey Oatmeal Cookies
Macadamia Nut Cookies	Oat and Date Chews	Honey-Oatmeal Cookies	Palm Leaves		Marzipan Almond Cookies	Marzipan Almond Cookies
Madeleines	Orange Macaroons	Marzipan Almond Cookies	Pirouettes		Oat and Date Chews	Mexican Wedding Cookies
Oat and Date Chews	Triple Chocolate Indulgence	Moravian Spice Cookies	Spritz Rings		Peanut Butter Cookies	Moravian Spice Cookies
Orange Macaroons		Oat Flakes	Strassburger Cookies		Vanilla Butter Cookies and variations	Scottish Shortbread
		Palm Leaves		**Bar Cookies**		
				Brownies		Spritz Rings
		Peanut Butter Cookies		Cocoa Cuts		
				Date Bars		Vanilla Butter Cookies and variations
		Pirouettes		Hazelnut Squares		
		Spritz Rings				
		Scottish Shortbread		Meyer Lemon Bars		
		Vanilla Butter Cookies and variations		Scottish Shortbread		

FIGURE 6-1 Cookie recipes throughout the text categorized by texture, production method, and storage capability

Storage

In most instances, there is no reason to use anything but butter in cookie doughs. The buttery flavor is irreplaceable, and cookies baked with butter will taste fresh for at least 3 to 4 days if they are stored properly. Cookies baked with jam stay at their best for the shortest amount of time, as the jam tends to become rubbery. To keep cookies crisp, store them in a jar with a little air for circulation; or keep the cover on loosely. If cookies become soft anyway, due to high humidity or rain, dry them in a 200°F (94°C) oven, providing they are not iced, dipped, or filled. Other cookies, such as macaroons, need to be kept soft; store these in an airtight container. If they get a little dry, take them out of the container and place them on a sheet pan in the refrigerator overnight. The old-fashioned method mentioned previously of putting a few apple or quince slices in the jar is helpful with macaroons as well.

Almond Horseshoes yield: 48 cookies, 2¹/₂ inches (6.2 cm) in diameters

Horseshoe, or crescent, shapes are used for a number of cookie recipes, and they add variety to the more common round selections. They are easy to pipe out, as is done with Strassburger Cookies, or to form by hand, as here and in the recipe for Butter Crescents. All of these look especially nice when the open ends are dipped into chocolate. In this recipe, a semisweet or even bittersweet chocolate tastes best in contrast with the sweet almond flavor. To use one of these you will, of course, have to use tempered chocolate, as coating chocolate is not available in these variations.

2 pounds (910 g) almond paste

8 ounces (225 g) granulated sugar

4 to 6 egg whites (½ to ¾ cup/120 to 180 ml; see Note)

Bread flour

8 ounces (225 g) thinly sliced almonds (natural or blanched), slightly crushed

Simple syrup

Dark coating chocolate *or* tempered semisweet chocolate

I. Combine the almond paste and sugar in a mixing bowl using the paddle attachment. Gradually, to avoid lumps, incorporate the egg whites. Continue to mix at medium speed, scraping down the sides of the bowl as needed, until you have a smooth, soft paste.

2. Lightly flour the baking table and your hands. Divide the paste into 3 equal pieces. Roll each piece into a 20-inch (50-cm) log, using just enough flour to keep the paste from sticking to the table. Cut each log into 16 equal pieces.

3. Place the almonds on a sheet of baking paper or on a half-sheet pan. Roll each of the small dough pieces in the almonds, at the same time shaping them into small logs. Be sure that the almonds adhere all around; you might have to roll the pieces in your hands first to eliminate excess flour, which will prevent the almonds from sticking. Transfer the logs to the table and continue rolling the pieces between your palms and the table to make each one 5 inches (12.5 cm) long, with slightly tapered ends.

4. Bend the pieces into horseshoe shapes 2½ inches (6.2 cm) wide as you place them on a sheet pan lined with baking paper or a Silpat. Allow the cookies to dry at room temperature for a few hours.

5. Bake, double-panned, at 375°F (190°C) for approximately 15 minutes or until golden brown and baked through. Brush simple syrup over the cookies immediately after removing them from the oven. After they have cooled completely, dip the ends into dark chocolate.

NOTE: The exact quantity of egg whites required will depend on the consistency of the almond paste.

Austrian Hazelnut-Almond Cookies

yield: approximately 50 cookies, 2 inches (5 cm) in diameter

Bad Ischler was once a famous Austrian resort, located in a region where hazelnuts, almonds, and walnuts grew in abundance. It has given its name to a number of special miniature nut-flavored tidbits, including these cookies, also known as *Ischler Toertchen*, and the *Nuss Busserln,* or Nut Kisses, which you'll find on page 303.

When making the following recipe, take care to press the decorative whole almonds firmly into the tops of the cookies—all the way down to the sheet pan—or they will push up during baking and fall off as you handle the baked cookies. In the worst-case scenario, they will fall into the chocolate as you dip them. You can, of course, skip the dipping step, but it adds a nice touch, appropriate to the luxurious location where the cookies originated.

7 ounces (200 g) unsalted butter, at room temperature	5 ounces (140 g) bread flour
3½ ounces (100 g) powdered sugar	5 ounces (140 g) finely ground hazelnuts
5 ounces (140 g) cake flour	50 whole blanched almonds
	Melted dark coating chocolate

I. Using the paddle attachment, cream the soft butter for approximately 1 minute.

2. Sift together the powdered sugar, cake flour, and bread flour. Mix this into the butter, followed by the hazelnuts. Mix to form a smooth dough.

3. Place the dough on a sheet pan lined with baking paper, flatten it to help it cool down more rapidly, and refrigerate until firm.

4. Knead the dough against the worktable, using just enough flour to keep it from sticking, until it is smooth and pliable. Roll out the dough to ¼ inch (6 mm) thick, turning the dough and dusting flour underneath as needed to prevent sticking.

5. Using a 2-inch (5-cm) plain round cutter, cut out cookies and place them on sheet pans lined with baking paper or Silpats. Combine the dough scraps, reroll, and continue cutting the cookies until you have used all of the dough.

6. Press 1 blanched almond, flat side down, firmly in the center of each cookie. You must press the nuts in firmly, or they will fall off after the cookies are baked.

7. Bake at 375°F (190°C) until the cookies become golden brown, 15 to 18 minutes. Let cool completely.

8. Dip each cookie into the melted chocolate, coating it halfway, so that the chocolate edge ends right next to the almond.

Butter Crescents yield: 72 cookies, 2¼ inches (5.6 cm) in diameter

These pretty little cookies start with the same ingredients as Mexican Wedding Cookies (page 310), the differences being that here the nuts are ground instead of chopped and the cookies are shaped differently. Butter Crescents are also very similar to Viennese Crescents, which are formed the same way but use almonds rather than pecans. Any and all of these rich butter and nut confections can be positively addictive. While forming the individual crescent shape does take more time than producing a slice-and-bake cookie, the finished appearance adds an elegant touch to your cookie or pastry assortment. To melt the decorative powdered sugar into a glaze on top of the cookies, place the pan back in the oven for just a minute or so after applying the sugar.

4 ounces (115 g) powdered sugar	12 ounces (340 g) unsalted butter, at room temperature
6 ounces (170 g) pecans	
8 ounces (225 g) bread flour	1 tablespoon (15 ml) vanilla extract
8 ounces (225 g) cake flour	Powdered sugar
1 teaspoon (5 g) salt	

1. Place half of the measured powdered sugar and all of the pecans in the bowl of a food processor and grind together to a very fine consistency. Combine this mixture with the bread flour, cake flour, and salt; reserve.

2. Using the paddle attachment, cream the butter with the remaining 2 ounces (55 g) powdered sugar and the vanilla. Incorporate the nut and flour mixture at low speed, scraping down the sides of the mixing bowl as needed and mixing just until the ingredients are combined. Refrigerate the dough until it is firm enough to work with.

3. Divide the dough into 3 equal pieces; they will weigh about 12 ounces (340 g) each. Roll out each piece to make a rope 16 inches (40 cm) long. Cut each rope into 24 equal pieces. Roll each small piece into a 3-inch (7.5-cm) log that is slightly tapered on each end. Bend each cookie into a crescent shape as you place it on a sheet pan lined with baking paper or a Silpat. The cookies do not change shape much during baking, so you can place them fairly close together.

4. Bake at 375°F (190°C) for approximately 12 minutes or until golden brown and baked through. As soon as the cookies come out of the oven, sift powdered sugar over the tops, continuing to sift the sugar until it no longer melts into the cookies but instead leaves a white coating. Store the cookies in airtight containers; they will stay fresh for up to 1 week.

Hazelnut Butter Cookies yield: approximately 110 cookies, 2 inches (5 cm) in diameter (Photo 17)

This cookie is one of my personal favorites, and it is the one most frequently requested by my colleagues. Depending on your taste, walnuts, cashews, or pecans can be used in place of the hazelnuts, or you can combine different types of nuts for a more complex flavor.

One word of warning: Be sure to press the hazelnuts all the way to the bottom of the pan, or they will bake loose in the oven and fall off. I got into a little trouble with these cookies myself as an apprentice. My boss told me that half of the cookies in the showcase had just an empty hole in the center where the hazelnut used to be. He instructed me to "push the nuts down firmly," so I did. A few days later, it was the same story all over again, except this time, naturally, my boss was a bit angry. Because I knew for certain that I had pressed those nuts down all the way to the metal (yes, I'm afraid there was no baking paper way back then), I got a little suspicious and decided to conduct an investigation. The next time I made the cookies, I walked up to the shop a few moments after the counterperson had picked up the sheet pan and peeked around the corner. Sure enough, while transferring the cookies to the showcase tray, she was picking the nuts off and eating them as fast as she could chew.

1 pound 5 ounces (595 g) unsalted butter, at room temperature

11 ounces (310 g) granulated sugar

12 ounces (340 g) hazelnuts, lightly toasted and finely ground

1 pound 5 ounces (595 g) bread flour

½ teaspoon (2 g) baking soda

5 ounces (140 g) whole hazelnuts

1. Using the dough hook at low to medium speed, mix the butter and sugar together. Add the ground nuts.

2. Sift the flour with the baking soda. Blend into the butter mixture on low speed, mixing only until just combined. Refrigerate the dough if necessary.

3. Divide the dough into 3 pieces; this can be done by eye, as it need not be exact. Roll each piece into a rope 1½ inches (3.7 cm) in diameter. Refrigerate the ropes until firm.

CHEF'S TIP
For a slightly more elegant look, lightly toast enough hazelnuts to use for both the dough and for decoration (1 pound 1 ounce/ 485 g) total. Rub off the skin, select the nicest-looking hazelnuts to use on top of the cookies, then grind the remainder for the dough.

4. Slice the ropes into ⅜-inch (9-mm) cookies. Place the cookies, staggered, on sheet pans lined with baking paper or Silpats. Leave the cookies at room temperature until they are fairly soft.

5. Push a hazelnut, point up, into the center of each cookie. Push the nuts all the way down to the sheet pan so they will not fall off after the cookies are baked. If you try to do this while the dough is still firm, it will crack.

6. Bake at 375°F (190°C) for about 12 minutes or until the cookies are golden brown. Store the cookies in an airtight container to prevent softening.

Hazelnut-Almond Squares yield: 96 cookies, 2 inches (5 cm) each (Photo 18)

Here is another of my favorites, partly because I don't get to have them very often. I think you too will find it impossible to eat just one cookie, but try not to feel guilty, because at least the cookies are small and thin. Although not the best production cookie, because you have to stand by and cut them as soon as the sheet comes out of the oven, these are a good choice when you want an unusual addition to your assortment.

6 ounces (170 g) hazelnuts

15 ounces (430 g) granulated sugar

10 ounces (285 g) unsalted butter, at room temperature

3 eggs

1 teaspoon (5 ml) vanilla extract

8 ounces (225 g) bread flour

2 tablespoons (16 g) unsweetened cocoa powder

1 tablespoon (12 g) baking powder

1½ ounces (40 g) sliced almonds

1. Toast the hazelnuts and remove the skin (see page 6). Crush coarsely, using a rolling pin, and reserve.

2. Beat the sugar and butter together until light and creamy, using the paddle at medium speed. Add the eggs and vanilla.

3. Sift the flour, cocoa powder, and baking powder together. Mix into the batter together with the reserved hazelnuts.

4. Spread the batter evenly over a sheet of baking paper measuring 24 x 16 inches (60 x 40 cm). You will have to spread back and forth a few extra times to fill in the lines made by the crushed nuts as you drag them across. Sprinkle the sliced almonds over the batter.

5. Drag the baking paper onto a sheet pan (see Figure 9-4, page 443).

6. Bake at 375°F (190°C) for about 20 minutes. When the sliced almonds on top start to brown, it is a pretty good indication that the cookies are done.

7. Cut the sheet into 2-inch (5-cm) squares as soon as it comes out of the oven. Store the cookies in airtight containers so that they remain crisp.

Heide Sand Cookies yield: 75 cookies, approximately 2¹⁄₂ inches (62 cm) long (Photo 18)

Lünburger Heide is an area in northern Germany near the town of Bremen. It is flat, sandy, and desolate, with little vegetation other than shrubs and brushes. The closest English translation of the word *heide* is probably "prairie." While Heide Sand Cookies take their name from this region, they are made throughout Germany and also by the Scandinavian neighbors to the north.

After forming the ropes, you can store the dough in the freezer, or for up to 1 week in the refrigerator; then slice and bake as needed. Leave the ropes at room temperature for about 5 minutes before rolling them in decorating sugar.

1 pound 10 ounces (740 g) bread flour	¹⁄₂ teaspoon (2.5 ml) vanilla extract
7 ounces (200 g) powdered sugar	Pale pink decorating sugar (see "Making Your Own Decorating Sugar")
1 pound 5 ounces (595 g) unsalted butter, at room temperature	8 ounces (225 g) smooth apricot jam
Few drops of lemon juice	

1. Sift the flour with the powdered sugar. Place in a mixing bowl with the butter, lemon juice, and vanilla. Mix, using the dough hook at low speed, until smooth. Refrigerate the dough if necessary to make it easier to handle.

2. Divide the dough into 3 pieces, about 1 pound 2 ounces (510 g) each. Roll the pieces into 10-inch (25-cm) ropes, pressing the dough together to compact it. Do not use any flour as you roll, as it will prevent the colored sugar from sticking.

3. Place the ropes in the colored sugar and roll to make them 12 inches (30 cm) long. Remove the ropes from the sugar.

4. Using the palm of your hand, flatten the side nearest you to form a smooth teardrop shape (Figure 6-2). Refrigerate the ropes until firm.

FIGURE 6-2 Using the palm of the hand to flatten 1 side of the cookie dough rope to form Heide Sand Cookies into a teardrop shape

5. Cut each rope into 25 slices. Arrange the pieces on sheet pans lined with baking paper or Silpats. Let the cookie slices sit at room temperature until softened.

6. Make an indentation in the wider part of the cookies and fill it with apricot jam.

7. Bake at 375°F (190°C) for about 15 minutes or until the cookies are golden brown. Store the baked cookies in airtight containers to keep them crisp.

Marzipan Almond Cookies yield: 105 cookies, 2¾ inches (7 cm) each

If you are not able to purchase finely ground blanched almonds (also known as *almond meal*), place 7 ounces (200 g) of the blanched almonds from the recipe in a food processor along with a handful of sugar (removed from the recipe as well) and process to a very fine consistency. The sugar is added to absorb some of the oil from the nuts and prevent the mixture from caking.

If you find that you enjoy the flavor, crunchy texture, and ease of making these cookies, as I do, you may want to consider doubling the recipe, even if you do not need all of the cookies at once. Half of the shaped dough can be wrapped and placed in the refrigerator or freezer to slice and bake as needed.

To mold a double recipe, press the dough into a half-sheet pan (12 x 16 inches/30 x 40 cm) in Step 3. To form the cookies in Step 4, cut 4 equal strips lengthwise, then cut across each strip to obtain 48 cookies per strip, making the slices approximately ⅜ inch (9 mm) thick. A double recipe molded and cut in this fashion will yield 192 cookies.

14 ounces (400 g) unsalted butter, at room temperature	1½ teaspoons (6 g) baking powder
14 ounces (400 g) granulated sugar	7 ounces (200 g) finely ground blanched almonds (almond meal)
2 eggs	1 teaspoon (5 ml) vanilla extract
8 ounces (225 g) bread flour	9 ounces (255 g) whole natural almonds (skin on)
6 ounces (170 g) cake flour	

1. Place the butter, sugar, and eggs in a mixing bowl. Using the dough-hook attachment, thoroughly mix the ingredients at low speed.

2. Combine the bread flour, cake flour, baking powder, and ground almonds. Add to the butter mixture together with the vanilla and whole almonds, mixing until well combined.

3. Remove the dough from the bowl and shape into a rectangle measuring 7½ x 10 inches (18.7 x 25 cm) on a sheet pan lined with baking paper. Cover and refrigerate until firm, at least 2 hours or, preferably, overnight. The dough must be very firm to be able to slice cleanly through the whole almonds.

4. Using a serrated knife, cut the rectangle of dough lengthwise into 3 strips. Cut each strip into 35 cookies slightly thinner than ¼ inch (6 mm). Place the cookies on sheet pans lined with baking paper or Silpats.

5. Bake at 375°F (190°C) for approximately 10 minutes or until light golden brown. Store the cookies in airtight containers to keep them crisp.

Spritz Rings yield: about 100 rings, 2¼ inches (5.6 cm) in diameter, or 100 S shapes, 2¾ inches (7 cm) long (Photo 17)

In Scandinavia, these are considered an absolute must on an assorted cookie tray. *Spritz* in both Swedish and German refers to the fact that the cookies are piped out; the more literal translation is closer to "spray." While basically a plain sugar and butter cookie, it is the ring shape that makes these so pretty and decorative. If you are making lots of Spritz Rings all the time, a fast and easy production method is to pipe out several long strips of dough parallel to one another on top of the table. Cut through the strips every 6 or 7 inches (15 to 17.5 cm), then pick up the short pieces one at a time and quickly twist them into a circle around two fingers as you move them to the sheet pan.

1 pound 5 ounces (595 g) unsalted butter, at room temperature

10 ounces (285 g) powdered sugar

3 egg yolks (¼ cup/60 ml)

1 teaspoon (5 ml) vanilla extract

1 pound 11 ounces (765 g) bread flour

Raspberry jam (optional)

1. The butter must be quite soft, or you will have trouble piping out the dough. Beat the butter and sugar for a few minutes with the paddle at medium speed. Mix in the egg yolks and vanilla. Add the flour and mix until you have a smooth, pliable dough.

2. Place the dough in a pastry bag with a No. 4 (8-mm) star tip. Do not put too much dough in the bag at one time, or it will be much more difficult to pipe out. Pipe out 2-inch (5-cm) rings or 2½-inch (6.2-cm) S shapes on sheet pans lined with baking paper or Silpats. If you make the S shape, the ends should curl in and close.

3. Make an indentation in each curled part of the S. Place the jam in a disposable pastry bag and pipe a small amount into the indentations (Figure 6-3).

4. Bake at 375°F (190°C) until golden brown, about 15 minutes. Store Spritz Rings in airtight containers to keep them crisp.

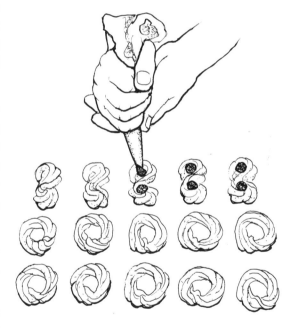

FIGURE 6-3 Spritz Rings dough piped into rings and S shapes; piping 2 dots of jam onto the S-shaped cookies

Strassburger Cookies yield: about 80 cookies, 2¹/₂ to 3¹/₂ inches (6.2 to 8.7 cm) each

This is one of the most common cookies found in Europe and also one of the most versatile. Strassburger Cookies can be piped out in an array of shapes, and two cookies may be sandwiched together with jam or another filling before they are dipped in chocolate.

1 pound 8 ounces (680 g) unsalted butter, at room temperature

1 pound (455 g) powdered sugar

6 whole eggs

3 egg yolks (¼ cup/60 ml)

2 teaspoons (10 ml) vanilla extract

2 pounds 8 ounces (1 kg 135 g) cake flour

2 teaspoons (4 g) ground cardamom

Dark coating chocolate, melted

1. Beat the butter and sugar together using the paddle attachment at medium speed until light and creamy, approximately 5 minutes. Mix in the eggs and egg yolks a few at a time. Add the vanilla. Add the flour and cardamom and stir on low speed until well combined.

2. Place the cookie dough (a portion at a time) in a pastry bag with a No. 6 (12-mm) star tip. Pipe the dough into one of the following shapes on sheet pans lined with baking paper (Figure 6-4). Attach the paper to the pan with a pea-sized piece of dough in each corner to keep the paper from moving as you pipe and draw parallel lines on the paper (invert the paper before attaching it to the pan) to serve as a guide in making the cookies the correct size.

3. Bake the cookies at 375°F (190°C) for approximately 12 minutes. Store in airtight containers.

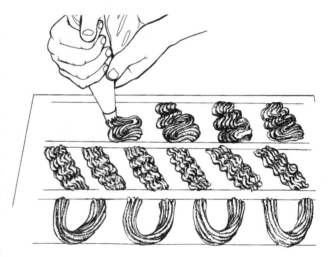

FIGURE 6-4 Piping Strassburger Cookies into, top to bottom: Cones, Pleated Ribbons, and Horseshoes

CONES

Pipe out cone-shaped cookies, 2½ inches (6.2 cm) long and wider at the top narrowing to a point at the bottom. Bake and cool, then dip the tips of the cookies into melted coating chocolate.

PLEATED RIBBONS

Pipe the cookies in 3½-inch (8.7-cm) flattened ribbons, holding the pastry bag close to the sheet pan so that the width of the dough is piped out flatter than the width of the tip. As you pipe, wiggle the tip back and forth a little so the dough forms pleats or gathers. Bake and cool the cookies, then dip half of each cookie into melted coating chocolate.

HORSESHOES

Pipe 3-inch (7.5-cm) lengths bent in a half circle. Bake and cool, then dip both ends in melted coating chocolate.

1. Frozen Mint Mousse with a Frosty Chocolate Shell

2. Variation of Caramel Toffee Almond Tart (as described in the recipe introduction)

3. White Chocolate Bavarian with Macadamia and Pistachio Nuts

4. Assorted Truffles

5. Dark Chocolate Bark, Milk Chocolate Bark, Ginger-Almond Bark, Macadamia Nut Toffee, Chocolate Cobblestones, and Rochers

6. Courting Swans

7. Apple Strudel, German Style

8. Lemon Fig Wedges

9. Assorted Breakfast Pastries

10. (clockwise from top) **Strawberry-Rhubarb Meringue Tart, Swedish Hazelnut Tart, Clafoutis with Cherries, and Walnut Caramel Tart**

11. **Chocolate Mint Torte with a Golden Touch**

12. **Chocolate Hearts with Orange Cream and Cape Gooseberries**

13. **Coconut Haystack Cookies and Financiers with a Soft Chocolate Filling**

14. (above left)
Peach and Berry Crisp

15. (above right)
Sour Apple and Cheese Turnovers

16. Assorted Breads and Rolls

17. (top)
**Assorted Cookies (left to right):
Hazelnut Butter Cookies, Cocoa Cuts,
Marble Butter Cookies, Walnut Bites,
Triple Chocolate Indulgence, Spritz
Rings, Chewy Trail Mix Cookies**

18. (middle)
**Assorted Cookies (left to right): Heide
Sand Cookies, Hazelnut-Almond Squares,
Florentinas, Checkerboard Cookies, Chewy
Trail Mix Cookies, Chocolate-Orange
Pillows**

19. (left) **Apple Pastries with Almond Cream**

20. (top)
Assorted Pastries (left to right):
Citrons, Fruit Tartlets, Orange Truffle
Cuts, Conversations, Rainbow
Pastries, and Small Saint-Honoré

21. (middle)
Assorted Pastries (left to right):
Small Saint-Honoré, Porcupines,
Senator Cuts, Florentina Cones with
Chantilly Cream, Citrons, and Fruit
Tartlets

22. (left) **Apple Puff Pastry Pyramids**
with Almond Ice Cream and
Caramel Sauce

COCOA STRASSBURGER COOKIES yield: about 80 cookies, 2¹/₂ to 3¹/₂ inches (6.2 to 8.7 cm) each

Replace 2 ounces (55 g) cake flour with an equal amount of sifted unsweetened cocoa powder.

Vanilla Butter Cookies yield: about 100 cookies, approximately 2 inches (5 cm) in diameter

These are also known as *Brysselkex* in the Scandinavian countries, *sablès* in some parts of Europe, and *Dutch biscuits* in others. It reminds me of the Swedish saying "kärt barn har många namn," which means "a loved child has many names." Many varieties of cookies can be made from this one basic dough; the most common are vanilla, marble, and checkerboard. Like most cookies that are divided into pieces from ropes, these can be refrigerated or frozen, well wrapped, then sliced and baked as needed.

1 pound 11 ounces (765 g) unsalted butter, at room temperature	2 pounds 3 ounces (1 kg) bread flour
1 teaspoon (5 ml) vanilla extract	Pale Pink Decorating Sugar (see "Making Your Own Decorating Sugar," page 268)
10 ounces (285 g) powdered sugar	

1. Using the dough hook at low to medium speed, mix the butter, vanilla, sugar, and flour to make a smooth dough.

2. Divide the dough into 3 equal pieces, 1 pound 8 ounces (680 g) each. Chill if needed.

3. Roll each piece into a rope 2 inches (5 cm) in diameter, using as little flour as possible.

4. If needed, brush excess flour from the ropes, then roll them in the tinted sugar to coat.

5. Transfer the ropes to a sheet pan. Roll them so they are even and just slightly thinner. Refrigerate until firm.

6. Cut the ropes into ¹/₄-inch (6-mm) slices. Place the cookies on sheet pans lined with baking paper or Silpats.

7. Bake at 375°F (190°C) until golden brown, about 15 minutes.

Checkerboard Cookies yield: about 150 cookies, approximately 1³/₄ inches (4.5 cm) square (Photo 18)

1 recipe Vanilla Butter Cookies (above), prepared through Step 1	2 pounds 10 ounces (1 kg 195 g) Short Dough (page 67) *or* Cocoa Short Dough (page 68)
1 ounce (30 g) unsweetened cocoa powder	Egg wash

1. Divide the dough in half. Mix the cocoa powder into one half. Chill the dough until it is firm enough to work with.

2. Roll out the plain and chocolate doughs into rectangles of equal size, ⁵/₈ inch (1.5 cm) thick.

3. Brush egg wash on the chocolate dough and place the plain dough on top. Refrigerate until firm.

4. Cut the rectangle into ⅝-inch (1.5-cm) strips (Figure 6-5). Lay half of the strips on their sides; brush with egg wash.

5. Arrange the remaining strips on top of the egg-washed strips, stacking them so that the chocolate dough is on top of the plain dough and vice versa, to create a checkerboard effect.

6. Roll out the short dough ⅛ inch (3 mm) thick and the same length as the strips. Brush the short dough with egg wash.

7. Place one of the stacked cookie strips on top and roll to enclose all 4 sides in short dough. Cut away the excess dough. Repeat with the remaining strips. You can omit wrapping the logs in short dough, or stack 3 or 4 strips together to create different patterns and sizes (Figures 6-6 and 6-7). Refrigerate the logs until firm.

8. Slice and bake as directed for Vanilla Butter Cookies (page 271).

FIGURE 6-5 Slicing the stacked rectangle of plain and chocolate doughs into strips, and laying half of the strips on their sides

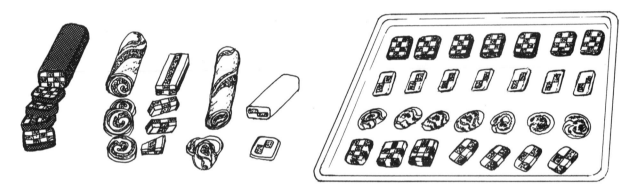

FIGURES 6-6 and 6-7 Examples of marble and checkerboard Vanilla Butter Cookies

Marble Butter Cookies yield: about 100 cookies, approximately 2 inches (5 cm) in diameter (Photo 17)

1 recipe Vanilla Butter Cookies (page 271), prepared through Step 1

1 ounce (30 g) unsweetened cocoa powder

1. Divide the cookie dough in half. Mix the cocoa powder into one half. Chill the dough until it is firm enough to work with.

2. Divide the plain and chocolate doughs into 3 portions each; this can be done by eye, as the pieces need not be exactly equal.

3. Roll all 6 pieces separately into ropes about 10 inches (25 cm) long.

FIGURE 6-8 **A plain rope and a chocolate rope in 1 group**

FIGURE 6-9 **One pair of ropes cut into thirds**

FIGURE 6-10 **Alternating 3 pieces of plain dough with 3 pieces of chocolate dough from 1 group, to form a stack**

4. Arrange the ropes in 3 groups, with 1 plain and 1 chocolate rope in each (Figure 6-8). Cut each pair into thirds, to yield 3 small chocolate and 3 small plain in each group (Figure 6-9).

5. Working with one group at a time, gently press the 6 pieces on top of one another, alternating plain and chocolate (Figure 6-10); keep each group separate.

6. Roll each group of stacked dough into a log 2 inches (5 cm) in diameter (Figure 6-11), twisting the logs as you form them to create a marbled effect (Figure 6-12).

7. Carefully transfer the logs to a sheet pan and refrigerate until firm. Slice and bake as directed for Vanilla Butter Cookies (page 271).

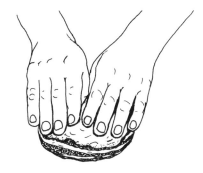

FIGURE 6-11 **Starting to roll the stacked pieces of dough into a log**

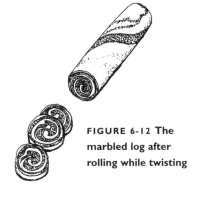

FIGURE 6-12 **The marbled log after rolling while twisting**

Vanilla Dreams yield: 75 cookies, approximately 2¼ inches (5.6 cm) in diameter

I suspect that these simple but unusual cookies got their name because they have a mysterious hollow center, not because cookie lovers can't get them out of their thoughts, although this would certainly be easy to understand. I loved to eat these cookies when I was a kid. We would dip them in milk or even water, so that the hollow space would fill up with liquid. Because of its high sugar content, the surrounding cookie would remain crisp, allowing us to suck the milk or water out of the center before we ate the cookie (it did not take very much to entertain kids in those days).

Ammonium carbonate, while not readily available in your local supermarket, can be obtained from the pharmacist. Alternatively, these cookies can be made using 1 teaspoon (4 g) baking powder, but only a tiny hollow center will form.

1 pound 10 ounces (740 g) granulated sugar

1 pound (455 g) unsalted butter, at room temperature

2 teaspoons (10 ml) vanilla extract

1 pound (455 g) bread flour

1 teaspoon (3.5 g) ammonium carbonate

1. Combine the sugar, butter, and vanilla, mixing until well blended.

2. Sift the flour with the ammonium carbonate and incorporate into the butter mixture.

3. Divide the dough into 3 pieces, 19 ounces (540 g) each. Roll each piece into a 20-inch (50-cm) rope. Cut each rope into 25 equal slices and roll the slices into round balls.

4. Place the balls of dough on sheet pans lined with baking paper or Silpats. Flatten each piece slightly, using the palm of your hand.

5. Bake at 300°F (149°C) until the cookies are a light golden brown, about 30 minutes.

NOTE: The ammonium carbonate causes the cookies to puff up, which creates a hollow space in the center, but they will fall easily if they are removed from the oven before they are done or if the oven door is opened early while they are baking.

Walnut Bites yield: 90 cookies, 2³⁄₄ × 1¹⁄₄ inches (7 × 3.1 cm) each (Photo 17)

It doesn't get much easier than this! The few ingredients, which by coincidence are all measured using the numerals 1 and 2, are a cinch to remember; and just one step is required to combine them. How you shape the dough and the size to which you slice the cookies are both fairly flexible. The size given here produces a relatively small butter cookie, which is probably just as well, as it is hard to stop eating these crumbly little morsels.

Walnut Bites are among the few cookies that can be baked at any temperature between 325° and 425°F (163° to 219°C). The only difference is that they will take a little longer at a lower temperature. You can gauge when they are done simply by looking at the color. Keep the dough wrapped in the refrigerator to slice and bake as needed. The dough must be firm when it is sliced so that you can cut cleanly through the walnuts without dragging them through the dough.

1 pound 12 ounces (795 g) unsalted butter, at room temperature

1 pound (455 g) granulated sugar

1 tablespoon (15 ml) vanilla extract

1 teaspoon (5 g) salt

2 pounds (910 g) bread flour

12 ounces (340 g) walnut halves or pieces

1. Cream the butter, sugar, vanilla, and salt together, using the paddle. Mix in the flour, then the walnuts.

2. Press the dough into a one-quarter sheet pan (12 × 8 inches/30 × 20 cm) lined with baking paper. It should be approximately 1 inch (2.5 cm) thick. Chill until firm.

3. Unmold and cut the dough lengthwise into 3 strips. Slice each strip across into 30 pieces. Place the cookies cut-side down on sheet pans lined with baking paper or Silpats. They will spread out slightly as they bake.

4. Bake at 375°F (190°C) for approximately 15 minutes or until golden brown.

Chewy Trail Mix Cookies yield: 64 cookies, approximately 3 inches (7.5 cm) in diameter (Photo 18)

These cookies are a favorite of many—colorful, crunchy, and chewy at the same time. They make a great snack with a glass of cold milk, even if you are not out hiking in the woods but just moving along in the kitchen or around the house. As with most refrigerator-type cookies, these are very practical, so I suggest that you don't bother to cut down the recipe even if you do not need the entire batch immediately. The dough will keep well in the refrigerator for a week and in the freezer for much longer.

6 ounces (170 g) cashews

6 ounces (170 g) walnuts

14 ounces (400 g) unsalted butter, at room temperature

12 ounces (340 g) light brown sugar

12 ounces (340 g) granulated sugar

½ cup (120 ml) or 6 ounces (170 g) honey

2 teaspoons (7 g) ammonium carbonate dissolved in a small amount of water (see Note 1)

4 eggs

1 tablespoon (15 ml) vanilla extract

1 pound 8 ounces (680 g) bread flour

2 teaspoons (8 g) baking soda

1 teaspoon (1.5 g) ground cinnamon

2 teaspoons (10 g) salt

12 ounces (340 g) pumpkin seeds

6 ounces (170 g) sunflower seeds

8 ounces (225 g) rolled oats

1 pound 8 ounces (680 g) raisins, preferably moluka (see Note 2)

1. Chop the cashews and walnuts into raisin-sized pieces and reserve.

2. In a mixing bowl and using the paddle attachment, mix the butter, brown sugar, granulated sugar, and honey just until combined; do not overmix or cream. Add the dissolved ammonium carbonate to the eggs, then incorporate the eggs in the butter mixture, 2 at a time. Add the vanilla extract.

3. Sift together the flour, baking soda, cinnamon, and salt. Mix into the batter together with half the pumpkin seeds, the sunflower seeds, and the reserved cashews and walnuts. Incorporate the rolled oats and the raisins, mixing until just combined. Place the dough on a sheet pan lined with baking paper and refrigerate until firm.

4. Divide the dough into 4 equal pieces, about 2 pounds (910 g) each. Roll each piece into a 16-inch (40-cm) rope, using flour to prevent the dough from sticking. Cut each rope into 16 slices and roll the pieces into round balls.

5. Place the balls of dough on top of the remaining pumpkin seeds. Flatten the cookies lightly with the palm of your hand. Place the cookies, seed-side up, staggered, on sheet pans lined with baking paper or Silpats. Flatten the cookies slightly with the palm of your hand to secure the seeds on top.

> **CHEF'S TIP** If you want to vary the flavor, use any nuts or seeds that you like instead of the varieties specified. Or try omitting the salt in the recipe and substitute lightly salted pumpkin seeds or cashews. If the unthinkable should happen and the cookies become overbaked and dry, place them in a covered container with an apple (or better yet, if you have one, a quince) cut into wedges; the cookies will become soft and chewy again overnight.

6. Bake at 300°F (149°C) for approximately 20 minutes or until the cookies are light brown and done.

NOTE 1: If you do not have ammonium carbonate, double the amount of baking soda to 4 teaspoons (16 g) total.

NOTE 2: If you are not able to locate the large juicy moluka raisins, use any other dark seedless raisin, such as Thompson.

Chocolate Chip Cookies yield: 48 cookies, approximately 2³/₄ inches (7 cm) in diameter

These all-American favorites were invented by a woman in Massachusetts, who had the brilliant idea of mixing small chunks of chocolate into her cookie dough. They are irresistible when eaten warm, fresh out of the oven, the way you get them at those little hole-in-the-wall cookie shops in the shopping centers—the ones that lure you in with their enticing aroma to make you an easy target. Chocolate chip cookies should be slightly underbaked so they stay soft and chewy. While ordinarily that would be a sign of a stale or improperly stored butter cookie, these are the exception to the rule.

9 ounces (255 g) unsalted butter, at room temperature

6 ounces (170 g) light brown sugar

6 ounces (170 g) granulated sugar

2 eggs

1 teaspoon (5 ml) vanilla extract

13 ounces (370 g) bread flour

1 teaspoon (4 g) baking soda

1 teaspoon (5 g) salt

12 ounces (340 g) dark chocolate chips

6 ounces (170 g) chopped walnuts

1. Beat the butter, brown sugar, and granulated sugar together, using the dough hook at medium speed. Add the eggs and vanilla.

2. Sift the flour, baking soda, and salt together; mix into the batter. Stir in the chocolate chips and walnuts.

3. Divide the dough into 3 equal pieces, approximately 1 pound 2 ounces (510 g) each. Roll each piece into a rope 16 inches (40 cm) long and cut each rope into 16 equal pieces.

4. Place the pieces, cut-side up (it is not necessary to roll the pieces round), on sheet pans lined with baking paper or Silpats; stagger the cookies so they do not bake together.

5. Bake the cookies at 375°F (190°C) until just done, about 10 minutes. The cookies should still be a bit sticky in the middle and just slightly brown at the edges.

Giant Chocolate Chip Cookies
To make the currently popular oversized chocolate chip cookies, use a 2-ounce (60 ml) ice cream scoop to portion the dough, evenly spacing 12 cookies on a full-size sheet pan. Bake at 350°F (175°C) for approximately 15 minutes. This recipe will make 24 cookies, 4 inches (10 cm) in diameter.

Chunky White-Chocolate Chip Cookies

yield: 60 cookies, approximately 2³/₄ inches (7 cm) in diameter

This variation tastes distinctively different from regular chocolate chip cookies, and the chunks of melted white chocolate on top give the cookies lots of visual appeal. Every once in a while, one of my students will produce a batch of white chocolate chip cookies in which the chunks of white chocolate have vanished. These always appear normal going into the oven, but they come out extremely flat with no visible chunks of chocolate left. What invariably causes this mysterious disappearance is that the student has accidentally chopped up chunks of cocoa butter instead of white chocolate (in all fairness, they do look very much alike, as "white" chocolate is actually an ivory color) and, of course, the cocoa butter just melts away in the oven. This reinforces the doctrine we teachers preach over and over: Always taste to be sure.

14 ounces (400 g) white chocolate	1 teaspoon (5 g) salt
12 ounces (340 g) walnuts	3 eggs
8 ounces (225 g) unsalted butter, at room temperature	¼ cup (60 ml) or 3 ounces (85 g) honey
8 ounces (225 g) light brown sugar	2 teaspoons (10 ml) vanilla extract
6 ounces (170 g) granulated sugar	1 pound 2 ounces (510 g) bread flour
	1½ teaspoons (6 g) baking soda

1. Chop the white chocolate and the walnuts into raisin-sized pieces and set aside.

2. Using the dough hook at low to medium speed, mix together the butter, brown sugar, granulated sugar, and salt until well combined. Add the eggs, honey, and vanilla.

3. Sift together the flour and baking soda. Add to the butter mixture. Stir in the chopped walnuts and white chocolate. Chill the dough if it is too soft to form.

4. Divide the dough into 3 equal pieces, approximately 1 pound 9 ounces (710 g) each. Roll each piece into a 20-inch (50-cm) rope; use flour as needed to prevent the dough from sticking.

5. Cut each rope into 20 pieces and place them, staggered, on sheet pans lined with baking paper or Silpats.

6. Bake the cookies at 350°F (175°C) just until they start to color, about 15 minutes. They taste best if still somewhat soft in the center.

Triple Chocolate Indulgence **yield: 80 cookies, approximately 2 inches (5 cm) in diameter** (Photo 17)

Here is the ultimate chocolate cookie—something like a fudgy brownie in the shape of a cookie. As with brownies, it can be tricky to know when to remove them from the oven the first time you try the recipe. Because looking at the color of a chocolate cookie doesn't tell you anything (unless they are burned!), you must rely on the oven temperature and the approximate baking time given, then touch the cookies to judge if they are baked. The edges should just feel firm, and the center should stay soft and gooey. Be careful not to overbake, or you will lose the fudgy quality.

1 pound (455 g) sweet dark chocolate

6 ounces (170 g) unsweetened chocolate

3 ounces (85 g) unsalted butter

5 eggs

14 ounces (400 g) granulated sugar

½ teaspoon (3 g) mocha paste *or* 2 tablespoons (30 ml) Coffee Reduction (page 14)

1 teaspoon (5 ml) vanilla extract

3 ounces (85 g) cake flour

2 teaspoons (8 g) baking powder

1 teaspoon (5 g) salt

8 ounces (225 g) dark chocolate chips

8 ounces (225 g) white chocolate, coarsely chopped

6 ounces (170 g) chopped walnuts

Powdered sugar

1. Chop the dark and unsweetened chocolates into small pieces. Place in a bowl with the butter and melt together over simmering water.

2. Whip the eggs and granulated sugar at high speed until light and fluffy. Blend in the mocha paste or coffee reduction and the vanilla. Fold the egg mixture into the melted chocolate.

3. Combine the flour, baking powder, salt, chocolate chips, chopped white chocolate, and walnuts. Add to the chocolate and egg mixture and stir just until combined. Refrigerate the dough until it is firm enough to handle.

4. Divide the dough into 4 equal pieces, approximately 1 pound 2 ounces (510 g) each. Roll each piece into a rope 16 inches (40 cm) long, using powdered sugar on your work surface to prevent the dough from sticking. Refrigerate the ropes until they are firm.

5. Using a sharp serrated knife, cut each rope into 20 equal pieces. Place the cookies, cut-side down, on sheet pans lined with baking paper or Silpats.

6. Bake the cookies, double-panned, at 375°F (190°C) for about 10 to 12 minutes.

Cocoa Cuts yield: about 60 cookies, approximately 3 x 1¼ inches (7.5 x 3.1 cm) each (Photo 17)

These are a typical Swedish cookie. I like to include them on cookie trays because their unusual shape contrasts with all of the other round cookies. Another plus is that because they are not shaped individually, they can be produced very quickly. If you do not have ammonium carbonate, use twice as much baking soda instead.

12 ounces (340 g) unsalted butter, at room temperature

7 ounces (200 g) granulated sugar

½ teaspoon (2 g) ammonium carbonate, dissolved in a small amount of water

3 tablespoons (45 ml) honey

14 ounces (400 g) bread flour

2 tablespoons (16 g) unsweetened cocoa powder

Egg wash

Crystal sugar

Sliced almonds

1. Using the dough hook at medium speed, beat the butter and sugar together until well combined. Mix in the dissolved ammonium carbonate and the honey.

2. Sift the flour and cocoa powder together and blend into the butter mixture. Mix until smooth.

3. Divide the dough into 4 equal pieces, about 8 ounces (225 g) each. Refrigerate the dough, if necessary, to make it easier to handle.

4. Roll each piece of dough into a 20-inch (50-cm) rope. Transfer the ropes to full-size sheet pans lined with baking paper; the cookies will bake out slightly, so do not put more than 3 ropes on a pan if you are increasing the recipe.

5. Roll the ropes on the pans to make them the full length of the pan, 24 inches (60 cm). Flatten the ropes slightly, using the palm of your hand.

6. Brush egg wash over the dough.

7. Combine equal parts of crystal sugar and sliced almonds. Sprinkle the mixture over the cookie dough.

8. Bake at 375°F (190°C) for about 12 minutes or until baked through. Because its color makes it hard to judge when chocolate dough is baked, look at the almonds; when they start to turn light brown, the cookies should be almost done.

9. As soon as the strips come out of the oven, cut them on a slight angle into 1¼-inch (3.1-cm) cookies using a metal dough scraper (Figure 6-13). If you are making several pans of these cookies, stagger the baking so you will have time to cut each pan before the cookies become crisp.

FIGURE 6-13 Using a metal dough scraper to cut Cocoa Cuts while they are soft right after baking

Cornmeal-Currant Cookies **yield: 100 cookies, 3 × 1½ inches (7.5 × 3.7 cm) each**

These delightful cookies dotted with currants are popular all over northern Italy, especially in Venice where they are known as *zaletti* (or *zalettini*, when they are made in a miniature version). The addition of cornmeal to the cookie dough produces a great crunchy texture that contrasts beautifully with the soft, sweet currants.

About Currants

Currants are miniature raisins, produced by drying a very small grape known as the Zante variety. Zante grapes originated in the eastern part of the Mediterranean in Corinth, Greece. In fact, the word *currant* comes from the name *Corinth*. The tiny purple grapes are available fresh in the late summer and fall, and small clusters on the stem make a very attractive decoration on fruit tarts and whole cakes. The fresh grapes are also called *champagne grapes*. Dried into currants, these sugar-rich raisins have been used in the kitchen for many, many years, mostly in sweet baked goods but, to a lesser extent, in savory dishes as well. Currants, like other dried fruits, are often macerated in a spirit or liqueur, or plumped in boiling water, before they are combined with the other ingredients in a recipe, to impart a particular flavor and/or to soften them.

7 ounces (200 g) dried currants

½ cup (120 ml) dark rum

14 ounces (400 g) granulated sugar

14 ounces (400 g) unsalted butter, at room temperature

2 egg yolks, at room temperature

14 ounces (400 g) bread flour

2 teaspoons (8 g) baking powder

½ teaspoon (2.5 g) salt

1 pound 2 ounces (510 g) yellow cornmeal

1. Macerate the currants in the rum for 30 minutes.

2. Combine the sugar and butter and beat until light and creamy. Incorporate the egg yolks.

3. Sift together the flour, baking powder, and salt. Stir into the butter mixture together with the cornmeal. Add the currant and rum mixture.

4. Divide the dough into 4 pieces, 1 pound 2 ounces (510 g) each. Roll each piece into a 12-inch (30-cm) log. Flatten the logs so that the sliced cookies will be rectangular with rounded corners. Refrigerate until firm; wrap in baking paper if storing to bake at a later date.

5. Slice each log into 25 equal pieces. Place the cookies on sheet pans lined with baking paper or Silpats.

6. Bake at 350°F (175°C) for approximately 12 minutes.

VARIATION

CORNMEAL-CURRANT COOKIES WITH PISTACHIOS
yield: 120 cookies, 2½ x 1½ inches (6.2 x 3.7 cm) each

Mix 6 ounces (170 g) blanched and coarsely chopped pistachio nuts into the dough at the end of Step 3. Shape the dough into a 10-inch (25-cm) square and refrigerate. Cut the firm chilled dough into 4 equal strips. Slice each strip crosswise into 30 equal pieces. The sliced green nuts and dark currants look especially attractive together in the finished cookies.

Cornmeal-Lime Cookies yield: 48 cookies, approximately 2½ inches (6.2 cm) in diameter

These crisp, buttery cookies feature the nonstandard additions of crunchy cornmeal, a generous amount of citrus zest, chopped pistachios, and a refreshing tart-sweet lime glaze. They provide a nice contrast served alongside the more typical chocolate and vanilla butter cookies. To achieve the best result, it is important to use fresh lime juice and zest in both the cookies and the glaze.

8 ounces (225 g) unsalted butter, at room temperature

7 ounces (200 g) granulated sugar

1 egg

1 tablespoon (15 ml) freshly grated lime zest

2 tablespoons (30 ml) fresh lime juice

1 tablespoon (15 ml) freshly grated orange zest

1 teaspoon (5 ml) vanilla extract

4 ounces (115 g) bread flour

3 ounces (85 g) cake flour

5 ounces (140 g) finely ground yellow corn meal

2 ounces (55 g) granulated sugar

2 ounces (55 g) finely chopped pistachios

Margarita Glaze (recipe follows)

1. Using the paddle attachment, cream the butter and the first measurement of sugar together for about 5 minutes, until light in color and texture. Add the egg, lime zest, lime juice, orange zest, and vanilla extract; mix until fully incorporated.

2. Add the bread flour, cake flour, and cornmeal. Mix at low speed until well blended. Remove the dough and transfer to a sheet pan lined with baking paper. Press it flat to help it chill faster, cover, and refrigerate for at least 2 hours, or longer if desired.

3. Divide the cookie dough into 3 equal pieces, 10 ounces (285 g) each. Roll the pieces into logs; cut 16 equal pieces from each log. Roll the pieces into round balls.

4. Combine the remaining 2 ounces (55 g) sugar and the pistachios. Place the mixture on a large plate or on a piece of baking paper. Pick up the balls of cookie dough, press them into the sugar-nut mixture and then invert them onto a sheet pan lined with baking paper or a Silpat, sugar-side up. Press each cookie into a round approximately 2½ inches (6.2 cm) in diameter, using your fingertips or a flat tool.

5. Bake at 375°F (190°C) for approximately 12 minutes or until the cookies are golden brown around the edges. Transfer the cookies to a rack to cool.

6. Leave the cookies on the cooling racks and place the racks on sheets of baking paper. Spoon or pipe the glaze on top of each cookie, letting the excess drip off the sides onto the paper. The cookies will stay crisp longer without the glaze, so you should glaze only as many as will be served or eaten the same day. Store the cookies, glazed or unglazed, in airtight containers.

MARGARITA GLAZE yield: approximately ½ cup (120 ml)

6 ounces (170 g) sifted powdered sugar

¼ cup (60 ml) fresh lime juice

2 teaspoons (10 ml) finely grated lime zest

1. Combine all the ingredients and mix until fully incorporated.

2. Apply as directed in the main recipe.

Gingersnaps yield: 120 cookies, approximately 2½ inches (6.2 cm) in diameter

As the name implies, these cookies should be dry and crisp. Nonetheless, I actually prefer them soft and chewy, which is how they get when they are left uncovered overnight. Be careful to mix the butter and sugar together just to combine. If you cream or beat them together, you will incorporate too much air, which causes the cookies to spread out too far as they bake, making them thin and unpleasant-looking. These are great refrigerator cookies. Form the dough into ropes, then slice and bake as needed.

8 ounces (225 g) unsalted butter, at room temperature

1 pound 6 ounces (625 g) granulated sugar

3 eggs

1 cup (240 ml) or 12 ounces (340 g) molasses

2 tablespoons (30 ml) distilled white vinegar

1 pound 12 ounces (795 g) bread flour

2 tablespoons (24 g) baking soda

4 teaspoons (8 g) ground ginger

1 teaspoon (1.5 g) ground cinnamon

1 teaspoon (2 g) ground cloves

1 teaspoon (2 g) ground cardamom

Crystal sugar

1. Using the dough hook at low speed, mix the butter and sugar together until well combined. Incorporate the eggs, molasses, and vinegar.

2. Sift together the flour, baking soda, ginger, cinnamon, cloves, and cardamom. Add to the butter mixture and mix on low speed just until combined. Cover and refrigerate until firm.

3. Divide the dough into 4 equal pieces, approximately 1 pound 2 ounces (510 g) each. Roll each piece into a rope 18 inches (45 cm) long and cut each rope into 30 pieces.

4. Form the pieces into round balls and press the balls in crystal sugar to cover the tops. Place the cookies sugar-side up on sheet pans lined with baking paper or Silpats.

5. Bake at 375°F (190°C) until light brown on top but still soft in the center, approximately 10 minutes.

Honey-Oatmeal Cookies   yield: 80 cookies, approximately 2 inches (5 cm) in diameter

While American kids grow up with peanut butter and chocolate chip cookies, their counterparts in Sweden enjoy oatmeal cookies with the same degree of enthusiasm. These cookies continue to be irresistible to me. The baked cookies don't really spread out much; they hold their shape and are crisp like shortbread. For a soft oatmeal cookie, try the recipe for Chewy Trail Mix Cookies (page 275) or Oat and Date Chews (page 283).

1 pound 3 ounces (540 g) unsalted butter, at room temperature	1 teaspoon (5 ml) vanilla extract
8 ounces (225 g) granulated sugar	¾ cup (180 ml) or 9 ounces (255 g) honey
9 ounces (255 g) dark raisins	1 teaspoon (4 g) baking soda
8 ounces (225 g) rolled oats	1 pound 5 ounces (595 g) bread flour

1. Beat the butter and sugar together lightly. Add the raisins, rolled oats, vanilla, and honey; mix until combined.

2. Sift the baking soda with the flour; mix into the batter. Refrigerate the dough if necessary.

3. Divide the dough into 4 equal pieces, about 1 pound 2 ounces (510 g) each. Roll each piece into a rope 16 inches (40 cm) long. Refrigerate the ropes until firm.

4. Cut each rope into 20 pieces. To save time, try placing 2 ropes together and cutting them simultaneously.

5. Place the slices, staggered, cut-side down, on sheet pans lined with baking paper or Silpats. If necessary, let the dough soften at room temperature so it will not crack when it is flattened. Flatten the cookies with a fork to about 2 inches (5 cm) in diameter while marking the tops at the same time.

6. Bake at 375°F (190°C) until golden brown, about 15 minutes. Keep the baked cookies in airtight containers to prevent them from getting soft.

Macadamia Nut Cookies yield: 80 cookies, approximately 2¹/₂ inches (6.2 cm) in diameter

Unfortunately, the scarcity of macadamia nuts keeps the price high, sometimes as much as 3 times that of walnuts, almonds, and hazelnuts. You can substitute any of those—chopped or coarsely crushed—for the macadamias, but I prefer pine nuts as an alternative. Leave them whole and toast them before mixing into the dough.

14 ounces (400 g) granulated sugar

3 ounces (85 g) light brown sugar

12 ounces (340 g) unsalted butter, at room temperature

3 eggs

1 teaspoon (5 ml) vanilla extract

1 pound 3 ounces (540 g) bread flour

¹/₂ teaspoon (2 g) baking soda

9 ounces (255 g) chopped macadamia nuts

9 ounces (255 g) shredded coconut

1. Using the dough hook at low to medium speed, cream the granulated sugar, brown sugar, and butter together until light and fluffy. Mix in the eggs and vanilla.

2. Sift the flour with the baking soda and incorporate into the batter at low speed, together with the nuts and the coconut.

3. Divide the dough into 4 equal pieces, about 1 pound 2 ounces (510 g) each. Roll each piece into a rope 10 inches (25 cm) long. Place the ropes in the refrigerator until firm.

4. Cut each rope into 20 equal pieces. Stagger the pieces cut-side down on sheet pans lined with baking paper or Silpats.

5. Bake at 375°F (190°C) until the cookies are just starting to color at the edges, about 12 minutes. Like chocolate chip cookies, these cookies taste best if they are a little chewy.

Oat and Date Chews yield: 64 cookies, approximately 3 inches (7.5 cm) in diameter

These easy-to-make, wholesome cookies don't require any fussy techniques. In fact, you don't even have to soften and cream the butter; it is actually preferable if a few small lumps of butter remain in the dough. Try using soft Medjool dates, which are available in most grocery and health food stores. You will have to pit them, but their flavor is well worth the extra effort. Lacking Medjool, use any packaged dates that are convenient or, for a change, replace the dates with dried cherries or dried cranberries. Cranberries not only provide color, they give the cookies a lively tangy flavor.

12 ounces (340 g) pitted dates

12 ounces (340 g) light brown sugar

12 ounces (340 g) granulated sugar

1 pound (455 g) firm unsalted butter, cut into chunks

¹/₂ cup (120 ml) or 6 ounces (170 g) honey

5 eggs

2 tablespoons (30 ml) vanilla extract

2 teaspoons (7 g) ammonium carbonate, dissolved in a small amount of water (see Note)

1 pound 8 ounces (680 g) bread flour

2 teaspoons (8 g) baking soda

1 pound (455 g) rolled oats

12 ounces (340 g) dark raisins

1 pound 8 ounces (680 g) chopped walnuts

1. Chop the dates into raisin-sized pieces.

2. Combine the brown and granulated sugars in a mixing bowl. Add the butter and the honey. Mix with the paddle attachment until combined. Do not cream the mixture together; small lumps of butter should remain.

3. Beat the eggs with the vanilla extract in a separate bowl. Stir in the ammonium carbonate. Add to the sugar mixture and mix to combine.

4. Sift together the flour and baking soda. Incorporate into the dough without overmixing. Mix in the oats, then the raisins, dates, and half of the walnuts. Refrigerate the dough until it is firm enough to work with.

5. Divide the dough into 4 equal pieces, approximately 2 pounds (910 g) each. Roll each piece into a 16-inch (40-cm) log, and cut each log into 16 equal slices. Roll the pieces into balls, then press the balls into the reserved chopped walnuts. Place the cookies walnut-side up on sheet pans lined with baking paper or Silpats.

6. Bake at 350°F (175°C) for approximately 25 minutes.

NOTE: If you do not have ammonium carbonate, you can get a good result by using twice as much baking soda (4 teaspoons/16 g) instead.

Peanut Butter Cookies yield: 60 cookies, approximately 2¼ inches (5.6 cm) in diameter

These cookies are always a big hit with kids. Instead of currants or raisins, try adding dates chopped to the same size. For something really special, dip the baked and cooled cookies halfway into melted dark coating chocolate.

8 ounces (225 g) unsalted butter, at room temperature	4 teaspoons (16 g) baking powder
8 ounces (225 g) granulated sugar	½ teaspoon (3 g) salt
6 ounces (170 g) light brown sugar	2 ounces (55 g) sweet dark chocolate, finely chopped
9 ounces (255 g) chunky peanut butter	4 ounces (115 g) toasted peanuts, coarsely chopped
2 eggs	6 ounces (170 g) currants *or* raisins
2 teaspoons (10 ml) vanilla extract	
13 ounces (370 g) bread flour	

1. Using the paddle attachment, cream the butter, granulated sugar, brown sugar, and peanut butter until fluffy. Add the eggs and vanilla.

2. Sift together the bread flour, baking powder, and salt. Add to the butter mixture along with the chocolate, peanuts, and currants or raisins, mixing at low speed only until the ingredients are combined. Chill the dough until firm.

3. Divide the dough into 3 equal pieces, 1 pound 3 ounces (540 g) each. Roll each piece into a rope 12 inches (30 cm) long and cut the ropes into 20 pieces each.

4. Place the small pieces on sheet pans lined with baking paper or Silpats. Flatten each cookie with a fork.

5. Bake at 375°F (190°C) for about 10 minutes.

Brownies yield: 1 half-sheet pan, 16 × 12 inches (40 × 30 cm)

I certainly cannot call myself an expert on brownies, which are very much an American sweet. They seem to come in all varieties, from fudgy and chewy to cakelike, and from tiny cookie-sized pieces to big squares. It is up to you how to portion the baked sheet. These brownies hold together well if you cut them small.

I happen to like raisins, so in the second edition of this book I added 6 ounces (170 g) raisins mixed in with the nuts. I have not gotten into so much trouble since I used someone's sewing scissors to cut paper! The word I get from my students and the customers at the school is that adding raisins to brownies is un-American. So, the raisins are now just an option.

14 ounces (400 g) walnuts	8 eggs
1 pound 8 ounces (680 g) sweet dark chocolate	1 teaspoon (5 ml) vanilla extract
1 pound (455 g) unsalted butter	1 pound (455 g) bread flour
1 pound 12 ounces (795 g) granulated sugar	$\frac{1}{2}$ teaspoon (2 g) baking powder
	6 ounces (170 g) dark raisins (optional)

1. Chop the walnuts into raisin-sized pieces and set aside.

2. Cut the chocolate into chunks, place in a bowl with the butter, and melt together over simmering water. Set aside to cool.

3. Line the bottom of a half-sheet pan (16 x 12 inches /40 x 30 cm) with baking paper or a Silpat.

4. Whip the sugar, eggs, and vanilla at high speed until light and fluffy. Fold into the cooled chocolate mixture.

5. Sift the flour with baking powder and stir into the chocolate. Add 12 ounces (340 g) walnuts and the raisins, if you are using them.

6. Spread the batter evenly in the prepared pan. Sprinkle the remaining 2 ounces (55 g) walnuts over the top.

7. Bake at 400°F (205°C) for about 30 minutes or until the cake is completely set but still slightly soft. Let cool, then slice into pieces of the desired size.

White Chocolate–Pecan Brownies yield: 1 half-sheet pan, 16 × 12 inches (40 × 30 cm)

These may not technically qualify as brownies because they are not brown, but I think they are much more appealing than the other brownie hybrid, the butterscotch-flavored blondie, which always seems to be too sweet. This white chocolate version has a slight caramel flavor, which pairs well with the pecans without being cloying. To dress up the bars a bit, you can finish them by streaking melted white chocolate over the cooled sheet before you cut it, or you can streak white or dark chocolate over the individual pieces after portioning.

1 pound 4 ounces (570 g) white chocolate

7 ounces (200 g) unsalted butter, at room temperature

Melted butter or pan spray

6 ounces (170 g) granulated sugar

6 ounces (170 g) brown sugar

4 eggs

1 tablespoon (15 ml) vanilla extract

7 ounces (200 g) bread flour

7 ounces (200 g) cake flour

2 teaspoons (8 g) baking powder

6 ounces (170 g) pecans, chopped to the size of raisins

1. Cut the white chocolate into chunks. Reserve one-third of the chocolate and place the remainder in a bowl with the butter. Melt the chocolate and the butter together over a bain-marie, stirring frequently. Chop the reserved white chocolate into small pieces about the size of raisins.

2. Line the bottom of a half-sheet pan with baking paper and brush melted butter over the paper and the sides of the pan (or use pan spray). Set aside.

CHEF'S TIP
Be sure to chop the white chocolate pieces that are added to the batter to the small size specified in the directions. If the chocolate chunks are too large, they will sink to the bottom of the pan and create a layer of chocolate on the base of the baked sheet instead of being dispersed throughout like chocolate chips, as they should be.

3. Beat the granulated sugar, brown sugar, eggs, and vanilla at high speed until light and fluffy.

4. Sift together the bread flour, cake flour, and baking powder. Add the flour to the sugar mixture and incorporate at low speed, scraping down the sides of bowl as necessary. Stir in the melted chocolate and butter mixture, followed by the reserved chopped white chocolate and two thirds (4 ounces/115 g) of the chopped pecans.

5. Spread out the batter evenly in the prepared pan. Sprinkle the remaining pecan pieces over the top.

6. Bake at 375°F (190°C) for 30 minutes or until the cake is set but still soft. Let cool completely, then cut into pieces of the desired size.

Date Bars yield: 1 half-sheet pan, 16 × 12 inches (40 × 30 cm)

Bars, as the name suggests, are pastries or cookies cut into shapes—usually squares, rectangles, or diamonds—after baking. They can be crumbly or moist and chewy like brownies, lebkuchen, and these date bars.

Try replacing the dates with other dried fruits, such as pears, prunes, or apricots, which are particularly refreshing. Reconstitute first in water as needed. Served warm and topped with a scoop of ice cream, date bars make a homey dessert. They are great to take along on picnics or outings.

1 pound 10 ounces (740 g) dates, pitted, *or* 1 pound 8 ounces (680 g) pitted dates

1½ cups (360 ml) water

10 ounces (285 g) granulated sugar

¾ cup (180 ml) lemon juice

1 pound 4 ounces (570 g) light brown sugar

14 ounces (400 g) bread flour

12 ounces (340 g) rolled oats

1 teaspoon (4 g) baking soda

1 teaspoon (5 g) salt

1 pound 4 ounces (570 g) melted unsalted butter

Ice Cream Sandwiches

These chewy date bars can be made into ice cream sandwiches as follows: Cut the baked sheet in half crosswise to make 2 rectangles, 8 × 12 inches (20 × 30 cm) each. Spread slightly softened ice cream over one half in a layer about ½ inch (1.2 cm) thick. Place the remaining date bar sheet on top and press down firmly. Freeze until hard. Use a serrated knife to cut the sheet into sandwiches of the desired size.

1. Combine the pitted dates and water in a saucepan. Cook over medium heat, stirring frequently, for approximately 5 minutes, until the mixture forms a thick paste. Remove from the heat and stir in the granulated sugar and lemon juice. Set the date filling aside.

2. Thoroughly combine the brown sugar, bread flour, rolled oats, baking soda, and salt. Stir in the melted butter.

3. Press half of the oat mixture in an even layer over the bottom of a half-sheet pan, 16 × 12 inches (40 × 30 cm). Spread the date filling evenly on top. Crumble the remaining oat mixture evenly over the date filling, then press it flat with your hands.

4. Bake at 350°F (175°C) for about 40 minutes. Let cool slightly, then cut into pieces of the desired size.

Meyer Lemon Bars yield: 24 bars, approximately 3 × 2³⁄₄ inches (7.5 × 7 cm) each

Lemon bars have a strong hold over some people, particularly those from the South. These cookies are sweet enough to satisfy any dessert lover. If you prefer your lemon bars a bit more tangy, either reduce the amount of sugar in the recipe by a few ounces or use an acid type of lemon and possibly increase the sugar a little.

10 ounces (285 g) unsalted butter, at room temperature

8 ounces (225 g) light brown sugar

1 egg

13 ounces (370 g) bread flour

Meyer Lemon Filling (recipe follows)

About Lemons

There are two types of lemons: sweet and acid. The latter are the more popular of commercially grown lemons, the bulk of which are either Eureka (recognizable by a short neck at the stem end) or Lisbon (on which the blossom end appears as a pointed nipple). Lisbons are just about seedless as well, which is also true of the sweet, roundish, thin-skinned Meyer lemon. Biologically not a true lemon, this hybrid was discovered near Beijing, China, by Frank Meyer. It was introduced to the United States in the beginning of the twentieth century and, since then, the compact size and shape of the tree has made this citrus variety the most popular among homegrown lemons.

1. Place the butter, brown sugar, and egg in a mixing bowl. Mix at low speed using the dough hook attachment until the ingredients are just combined. Add the flour and continue to mix until the dough is smooth, scraping down the sides of the mixing bowl once or twice; do not mix any longer than necessary. Refrigerate the dough until it is firm enough to work with.

2. Line the bottom of a half-sheet pan (12 x 16 inches/30 x 40 cm) with baking paper. Roll out the chilled dough to a rectangle slightly larger than the pan and line the bottom and sides of the pan with the dough; you should use up all of the dough. Prick the dough well over the bottom of the pan. Cut a sheet of baking paper to cover the bottom and long sides of the dough in the pan. Place the paper on top of the dough and fill with dried beans or pie weights.

3. Bake at 375°F (190°C) until the crust is golden brown around the top edges, approximately 15 minutes. Remove the beans or pie weights (be certain to get any that stick to the dough on the short ends) and the baking paper, then return the shell to the oven to finish baking, about 5 minutes longer.

4. While the crust is baking, make the filling. Pour the filling over the hot crust as soon as it is removed from the oven. Return to the oven and lower the oven temperature to 350°F (175°C). Bake for about 25 minutes longer or until the filling has thickened and a very light brown skin has formed on top.

5. Let cool completely. Cut lengthwise into 4 strips and crosswise into 6 pieces each to yield 24 bars.

MEYER LEMON FILLING yield: about 6 cups (1 L 440 ml)

4 tablespoons (32 g) cornstarch	4 egg yolks (⅓ cup/80 ml)
1 pound 8 ounces (680 g) granulated sugar	Finely grated zest of 4 Meyer lemons
12 whole eggs	2½ cups (600 ml) Meyer lemon juice

1. Stir the cornstarch into the sugar. Mix in the eggs, egg yolks, lemon zest, and lemon juice, stirring until the ingredients are well combined; do not whip or beat the mixture.

2. Place the lemon custard over a bain-marie and heat, stirring constantly, until the filling has thickened; do not overcook.

Biscotti yield: about 120 cookies, approximately 4 inches x 1 inch (10 x 2.5 cm) each

This Italian specialty is part of an international group of cookies and crackers that are baked twice: the French *biscotte*, the German *zwieback*, and the Swedish *skorpor*, which are known in America as rusks. Some of these are unsweetened or, in the case of biscotti, sweetened and flavored with nuts. If you like the flavor of anise, substitute 1 ounce (30 g) lightly crushed anise seed for the orange flower water; you can also add some anisette liqueur.

These cookies are another example of where it would really be worthwhile to go through the process of tempering real chocolate instead of using coating chocolate, which is sweeter. Just as with Florentinas and Butter Crescents, the bittersweet flavor pairs exceptionally well.

1 pound 4 ounces (570 g) bread flour

4 teaspoons (16 g) baking powder

12 ounces (340 g) granulated sugar

6 ounces (170 g) white bread crumbs

8 ounces (225 g) whole almonds, skin on

8 ounces (225 g) whole hazelnuts, skin on

¼ cup (60 ml) orange juice

1 teaspoon (5 ml) orange flower water

1 teaspoon (5 ml) vanilla extract

5 eggs

Egg wash

Crystal sugar

Melted dark coating chocolate *or* tempered bittersweet chocolate

1. Sift the flour with the baking powder. Add the sugar and bread crumbs; combine, using the dough hook at low to medium speed. Mix in the almonds and hazelnuts.

2. Combine the orange juice, orange flower water, vanilla, and eggs. Gradually add the liquid to the dry ingredients and mix for approximately 1 minute, until you achieve a firm dough.

3. Divide the dough into 4 equal pieces, about 1 pound (455 g) each. Roll each piece into a uniform rope 16 inches (40 cm) long. Place the ropes on sheet pans lined with baking paper. Brush egg wash on top of the ropes, then sprinkle with the crystal sugar.

4. Bake at 350°F (175°C) for about 25 minutes or until golden brown. Let cool for at least 1 hour or, preferably, overnight.

5. Slice the ropes diagonally into cookies ⅜ inch (9 mm) thick. Place the slices cut-side down on sheet pans lined with baking paper or Silpats.

6. Bake at 375°F (190°C) until the cookies start to turn golden brown around the edges, approximately 15 minutes.

7. When the cookies have cooled completely, dip them halfway into melted chocolate. Store in airtight containers.

NOTE: If making more cookies than you will use within 1 week, it is better to store some of the uncut baked ropes in the refrigerator (covered) to slice and dry as needed.

Chocolate-Walnut Biscotti yield: 90 cookies, approximately 4 × 1½ inches (10 × 3.7 cm)

This delicious version of biscotti, studded with raisins and toasted walnuts, differs a bit from tradition in that it is made with chocolate-flavored dough. Depending on the brut, or strength, of the cocoa powder you are using, you may want to adjust the quantity to suit your taste. The same holds true for the hauntingly fragrant anise seed. Many people love it, but for chocolate purists, you can certainly leave it out.

An old-fashioned method used for the second baking, or drying, of biscotti cookies is to stand them on end so the cookies develop an attractive uniform color on both sides. While some home cooks may still use this method, it is obviously not practical in a professional kitchen. Another option is to turn the cookies over once or twice during the second baking period to achieve the same result; this is by no means essential. What is definitely important is to ensure the cookies are completely dried through. Because properly made biscotti are dry and crisp, they are most often enjoyed dunked into a favorite fortified wine, a steaming cappuccino, or a cup of tea. Biscotti, as they say in Italy, are "cookies made for dipping."

10 ounces (285 g) bread flour	4 eggs
8 ounces (225 g) cake flour	1 tablespoon (15 ml) vanilla extract
1 tablespoon (12 g) baking powder	10 ounces (285 g) granulated sugar
1 teaspoon (4 g) baking soda	6 ounces (170 g) walnuts, coarsely chopped
2 ounces (55 g) unsweetened cocoa powder	5 ounces (140 g) dark raisins
1 teaspoon (5 g) salt	Egg wash
2 tablespoons (20 g) crushed anise seeds	

1. Sift together the bread flour, cake flour, baking powder, baking soda, cocoa powder, and salt. Mix in the anise seeds. Reserve.

2. In a mixer bowl and using the paddle attachment, beat the eggs, vanilla, and sugar until the mixture is thick and lighter in color, approximately 2 minutes.

3. Mix in the dry ingredients at low speed, followed by the walnuts and raisins.

4. Turn the dough out of the bowl onto a well-floured work surface; the dough will be quite sticky. Knead the dough gently until smooth, approximately 2 minutes. Divide the dough into 2 equal portions, 1 pound 8 ounces (680 g) each.

5. Roll each piece against the table to make a uniform rope 16 inches (40 cm) long, using flour as needed to keep the dough from sticking. Place the ropes, evenly spaced, on a full-size sheet pan lined with baking paper or a Silpat. Use the palm of your hand to flatten the ropes slightly. Brush egg wash on top of each rope.

6. Bake at 350°F (175°C) for approximately 30 minutes. The ropes should be firm to the touch; if you press lightly, your fingertips should not leave an indentation. Allow the cookie ropes to cool completely.

7. Using a serrated knife, cut each rope diagonally into slices ⅜ inch (9 mm) thick. Place the cookies, cut-side down (see introduction), on sheet pans lined with baking paper or Silpats.

8. Bake the sliced cookies at 350°F (175°C) for approximately 12 minutes or until dried through. Allow the cookies to cool before storing or serving. Packaged in airtight containers, biscotti can be kept for several weeks.

Almond Shortbread yield: 32 cookies, approximately 2¼ inches (5.6 cm) in diameter

Just about everyone loves shortbread cookies—the buttery taste and crumbly texture are all but irresistible. In this recipe, a portion of the butter has been replaced with almond paste. This makes it possible to roll the dough into logs and slice into cookies before baking, unlike the traditional bar-type of shortbread cookie, in which the fragile dough is rolled out flat, scored, baked, then cut into individual pieces after baking. Keep the logs of dough in the refrigerator and finish the cookies as needed. The baked cookies will stay fresh for several days, but, unfortunately, as the moisture dissipates, the jam becomes chewy and dry. If you do not have ammonium carbonate, this recipe works fine without it; the cookies will just be a little less crumbly.

2 eggs

7 ounces (200 g) almond paste

14 ounces (400 g) unsalted butter, at room temperature

7 ounces (200 g) granulated sugar

½ teaspoon (2 g) ammonium carbonate, dissolved in a small amount of water

1 tablespoon (15 ml) vanilla extract

1 pound 2 ounces (510 g) bread flour

4 ounces (115 g) smooth strawberry jam

1. Mix the eggs into the almond paste one at a time to avoid lumps. Incorporate the butter, sugar, ammonium carbonate, and vanilla. Add the flour and mix only until combined. Refrigerate the dough until it is workable.

2. Divide the dough into 2 equal pieces, about 1 pound 8 ounces (680 g) each. Roll each piece into a 12-inch (30-cm) rope and cut 16 equal slices from each. Refrigerate the ropes first, if necessary, to keep the slices round and even.

3. Place the slices on sheet pans lined with baking paper or Silpats. Make an indentation in the center of each cookie, using your thumb or an appropriate tool. If the dough cracks when you do this, let it soften at room temperature for a short time, then continue.

4. Place the strawberry jam in a disposable pastry bag made from a half-sheet of baking paper (see Figures 1-15 and 1-16, page 53). Pipe the jam into the indentation on each cookie.

5. Bake at 375°F (190°C) for approximately 30 minutes or until golden brown.

Scottish Shortbread yield: 20 pieces, 3¹/₄ × 3 inches (8.1 × 7.5 cm)

This delicious, delicate cookie is made from a mixture of sugar and flour that has been shortened (made soft and crumbly) by the addition of fat. In this case, butter is used, but lard, margarine, or oil would have the same effect—although they would not produce the same wonderful flavor. These cookies are the epitome of "buttery."

Scotland is probably the country best known for shortbread. There, the cookies are traditionally made around the Christmas and New Year's holidays. The dough is typically baked in a round, shallow ovenproof form, 8 to 10 inches (20 to 25 cm) in diameter. After baking, the circle is inverted, and the round is cut into wedges. The problem with this method is that the fragile nature of the cookie makes for a lot of broken pieces. A more practical alternative is to cut the cookies into squares, which are more durable.

The addition of rice flour gives this cookie a special crispness. If you do not have rice flour, cake flour can be substituted with a good result. You would be hard put to improve on these cookies but, if you like, try adding nuts or candied ginger to the dough. Scottish shortbread makes a perfect accompaniment to ice cream, especially vanilla.

1 pound 2 ounces (510 g) unsalted butter, at room temperature

1 tablespoon (15 ml) vanilla extract

6 ounces (170 g) powdered sugar

12 ounces (340 g) bread flour

6 ounces (170 g) rice flour

½ teaspoon (2.5 g) salt

1. Place the butter, vanilla, and powdered sugar in a mixing bowl. Beat with the paddle attachment until creamy. Incorporate the bread flour, rice flour, and salt at low speed. Place the dough in the refrigerator until firm.

2. Briefly work the dough with your hands to make it pliable, then roll it out to a rectangle measuring 16 x 12 inches (40 x 30 cm), using flour to prevent it from sticking. Roll up the dough on a dowel and transfer it to a half-sheet pan lined with baking paper. Adjust the size of the rectangle as needed if it becomes stretched in moving.

3. Mark the top of the dough with a pattern of wavy lines, using a fork. If the dough sticks to the fork, dip the fork into vegetable oil as you work.

4. Bake at 400°F (205°C) for approximately 30 minutes or until the top is golden brown. While the sheet is still warm, cut lengthwise into 4 strips, then crosswise into 5 pieces each. Allow the shortbread to cool completely before removing the pieces from the pan. Store in airtight containers. Do not stack too high, as the cookies are quite fragile.

MACAROONS AND MADELEINES

Almond Macaroons yield: about 60 cookies, 2 inches (5 cm) in diameter

These small cookies, crunchy on the outside and soft inside, can be positively addictive. They originated in Venice during the Renaissance and are still popular all over Europe. Numerous varieties are made(flavored with chocolate or liqueur, or sandwiched together with ganache, buttercream, or jam. One variety is sold still attached to its baking paper, an edible rice paper known as *oblaten*. A version of tiny macaroons was my favorite candy as a kid. They were a little less than 1 inch (2.5 cm) in diameter and sold in cellophane bags to prevent them from drying out.

2 pounds (910 g) almond paste	6 to 8 egg whites (¾ to 1 cup/180 to 240 ml)
1 pound (455 g) granulated sugar	

1. Place the almond paste and sugar in a mixing bowl. Using the paddle at low speed, blend in 1 egg white at a time, being careful not to get any lumps in the batter. Add as many egg whites as the batter will absorb without getting runny; this will vary depending on the firmness of the almond paste and, to some degree, the size of the egg whites.

2. Beat for a few minutes at high speed to a creamy consistency.

3. Place the batter in a pastry bag with a No. 6 (12-mm) plain tip. Pipe the batter in 1½-inch (3.7-cm) mounds onto sheet pans lined with baking paper. They will spread slightly, so do not pipe them too close together.

4. Bake the cookies, double-panned, at 410°F (210°C) for about 10 minutes or until light brown.

5. Let the macaroons cool attached to the baking paper. To remove them from the paper, turn

FIGURE 6-14 Peeling the baking paper away from the baked Almond Macaroons with the cookies turned upside down

them upside down and peel the paper away from the cookies rather than the cookies from the paper (Figure 6-14). If they are difficult to remove, brush water on the back of the papers, turn right-side up, wait a few minutes, then try again. For long-term storage, place the cookies in the freezer still attached to the baking paper. Macaroons can be served as is or dipped in melted coating chocolate.

VARIATION

MACAROON DECORATING PASTE

Make the recipe above, keeping the paste a bit firmer by using fewer egg whites. The paste should be soft enough that you can pipe it out without monumental effort, but it should not change shape at all when it is baked. It should always be baked in a hot oven; follow directions in the individual recipes in which the paste is used.

Apple-Coconut Points yield: 40 pastries, 2¹/₄ inches (5.6 cm) in diameter and 2 inches (2.5 cm) high

Apple Coconut Points are a combination of Coconut Haystack Cookies and Coconut Macaroons, with the addition of apple. My experience using different brands of desiccated coconut from various countries and suppliers is that the amount of moisture the coconut will absorb can vary greatly depending on how finely it was ground and how dry it is. In a recipe such as this, these factors affect the consistency of the paste. The degree to which you reduce the apple puree will also influence the moisture level in the paste. If the batter is too soft to shape, add additional coconut.

1 pound (455 g) Short Dough (page 67)	Apple Puree (recipe follows)
8 egg whites (1 cup/240 ml)	Granulated sugar
8 ounces (225 g) granulated sugar	Simple syrup
1 pound (455 g) unsweetened desiccated coconut (see "About Desiccated Coconut," page 296)	Melted dark coating chocolate *or* tempered semisweet chocolate (optional)

1. Roll out the dough to ¹/₈ inch (3 mm) thick, using flour to prevent sticking. Cut out cookies, using a 2¹/₄-inch (5.6-cm) fluted round cutter. Reroll the scrap pieces as needed to be able to cut out 40 rounds. Place the dough rounds on sheet pans lined with baking paper or Silpats.

2. Combine the egg whites, sugar, and coconut. Stir in the apple puree. The paste will be fairly soft but thick enough to work with.

3. Use a small ice cream scoop to distribute the paste over the dough rounds.

4. Wet your fingers lightly so that the paste will not stick, then pinch and shape the paste into points with 4 distinct vertical ridges. Sprinkle granulated sugar over the pastries.

5. Bake at 375°F (190°C) for approximately 15 minutes or until the cookies are golden brown. Lightly brush simple syrup over the tops as soon as the pastries are removed from the oven. Allow to cool completely.

6. If desired, dip the base of the cookie (the short dough) into chocolate.

APPLE PUREE yield: approximately 2 pounds (910 g)

If you do not have time to make the apple puree starting with fresh apples, you can substitute 4 cups (960 ml) prepared unsweetened apple puree for both the apples and the poaching syrup and begin with Step 2.

2 pounds 8 ounces (1 kg 135 g) Granny Smith apples (about 5 medium)

1 recipe Plain Poaching Syrup (page 31)

2 tablespoons (30 ml) lemon juice

4 ounces (115 g) unsalted butter

8 ounces (225 g) granulated sugar

1 vanilla bean

1. Peel and core the apples; cut them in half. Poach in the syrup until they become soft and just start to fall apart. Strain the apples, reserving the syrup for another use if desired. Puree the apples in a food processor until smooth.

2. Place the apple puree in a skillet together with the lemon juice, butter, and sugar. Split the vanilla bean lengthwise and scrape the seeds into the apple mixture. Add the vanilla bean pod as well.

3. Cook over medium heat, stirring constantly, until the puree has thickened and turned a light golden, almost caramel color. Remove and discard the vanilla bean pods.

Coconut Haystack Cookies

yield: 36 cookies, 1¼ inches (3.1 cm) in diameter, or approximately 100 cookies, ⅞ inch (2.3 cm) in diameter, using Flexipan No. 1562 (Photo 13)

Only one thing could possibly prevent you from gulping down these old-fashioned and absolutely delicious chewy cookies: not liking coconut at all!

In the mid-1950s, when I was starting out as an apprentice, coconut was just becoming readily available again (at least in my part of the world) after a long drought that followed World War II. Consequently, when we began making these cookies as well as the macaroon version that follows, they seldom made it as far as the showcase—they were usually sold right from the sheet pan in the bakery to customers who had been without these treats for a long time.

12 ounces (340 g) unsalted butter

1 pound (455 g) granulated sugar

6 eggs

1 pound 2 ounces (510 g) desiccated coconut (see "About Desiccated Coconut," page 296)

Simple syrup

Dark coating chocolate, melted (optional)

1. Place the butter and sugar in a saucepan and heat to 150°F (65°C) while stirring constantly. Remove from the heat and beat in the eggs a few at a time. Stir in the coconut.

2. Return to the stove and cook, stirring constantly, until the mixture pulls away from the sides of the pan. Let the batter cool to room temperature.

3. Place the cookie batter in a pastry bag with a No. 9 (18-mm) plain tip. Pipe out 36 tall mounds of dough shaped like large chocolate kisses on a sheet pan lined with baking paper or a Silpat.

4. Bake, double-panned, at 425°F (219°C) for approximately 15 minutes. Brush simple syrup over the cookies as soon as they come out of the oven. If you would like to dress them up a bit, dip the bottom of the cookies into chocolate, coating the base and just slightly up the sides (see Figures 12-25 to 12-29, page 599), or streak melted chocolate over the top of the cookies. Allow the cookies to cool completely before applying the chocolate.

DIRECTIONS FOR USING A FLEXIPAN

1. Make the batter as directed in Steps 1 and 2.

2. In Step 3, pipe the batter into a No. 1562 (small pyramid shape) Flexipan, filling the forms to the top. Using a palette knife, press the top of the filling flat so that when the cookies are inverted, the bottom will be even. At the same time, this will help force the batter into the precise shape of the molds.

3. Bake at 425°F (219°C) for about 15 minutes, or just until the coconut starts to become light brown on the sides; unmold one to check. Be careful not to let the cookies get too dark on either the top or the bottom before they are baked through. Depending on your oven, you may need to use a double pan or cover the top with foil if they are getting too dark.

4. Let cool before unmolding. The pastries do not need to be brushed with simple syrup because they will develop a glossy surface from being baked in the Flexipan, provided they are chilled in the pan before unmolding. Place in the refrigerator or, better yet, the freezer, and wait until they are thoroughly chilled. The pastries will then pop right out of the form, and the exterior will be as shiny as if you had brushed them with simple syrup. Decorate with chocolate if desired, as described above.

Coconut Macaroons yield: 40 cookies, 2 inches (5 cm) in diameter

These cookies, which fall somewhere between a fancy cookie and a simple pastry, may be too labor-intensive for some operations. But semantics aside, you can make a simplified version by omitting the short dough bottom and piping the batter directly onto paper-lined sheet pans, either in a star shape, as specified, or in small rosettes using a No. 6 (12-mm) star tip. In that case, also omit dipping the baked cookies in chocolate. Coconut macaroons taste best when they are freshly baked and still soft inside, so rather than baking more cookies than you can use right away, store the batter, covered, in the refrigerator for up to 1 week, and bake fresh macaroons as needed. Bring the batter to room temperature before piping it out.

6 ounces (170 g) almond paste	3 whole eggs
2 egg whites (¼ cup/60 ml)	1 pound (455 g) Short Dough (page 67)
5 ounces (140 g) unsalted butter	6 ounces (170 g) raspberry jam
7 ounces (200 g) granulated sugar	Simple syrup
12 ounces (340 g) unsweetened desiccated coconut (see "About Desiccated Coconut," page 296)	Melted dark coating chocolate

1. Soften the almond paste by mixing in the egg whites; reserve.

2. Melt the butter in a saucepan. Add the sugar and bring to a boil.

3. Transfer to a mixing bowl and combine with the coconut. Gradually blend in the whole eggs and the almond paste mixture; stir until smooth. Let the batter rest for a few minutes.

4. Roll out the short dough to ⅛ inch (3 mm) thick. Cut out 40 cookies, using a 2-inch (5-cm) fluted cookie cutter. Place the cookies on a sheet pan lined with baking paper or a Silpat.

5. Place the reserved coconut mixture in a pastry bag with a No. 8 (16-mm) star tip. Pipe the coconut batter onto the short dough, holding the bag straight up above the cookies to make a star design. If the batter seems difficult to pipe or is too runny, adjust with an additional egg or extra ground coconut.

6. Make a small indentation in the top of the coconut batter on each cookie. Put the raspberry jam into a piping bag and pipe it into the indentations.

7. Bake the cookies at 400°F (205°C) until the top of the coconut batter starts to brown and the short dough is golden, about 15 minutes.

8. Brush simple syrup over the pastries as soon as they come out of the oven, taking care not to soak them. Let cool completely.

9. Hold on to the baked coconut topping and dip the short dough, including the top of the cookie, into melted dark coating chocolate. Allow the excess to drip back into the bowl, scrape the bottom against the side of the bowl, and place the cookies on baking paper.

10. Move the cookies on the paper once or twice before the chocolate sets up completely to remove excess chocolate. If you have trouble with this dipping method, set the cookie on top of a dipping fork as you immerse it in the chocolate to prevent it from breaking and falling in the chocolate.

11. Store, covered, in a cool, dry place.

About Desiccated Coconut

Desiccated coconut is simply the term for ground, dried coconut. (Desiccate means "to dry up" or "to become dried up"; a desiccant is a drying agent.) Sometimes called *macaroon coconut*, it is available from baking suppliers. Dried coconut is made from the white portion of the coconut kernel after the brown skin has been removed. The coconut is dried, processed, and sorted into various grades of coarseness. Macaroon coconut, with a texture similar to that of coarse polenta, is the finest.

As a substitute for desiccated, if necessary, you can use flaked or shredded coconut, but it must first be dried. To dry prepared coconut, spread it out in a thin layer on a sheet pan and leave it at room temperature for a few days. Alternatively, the coconut can be dried in a very low oven, but you must be careful not to let it brown. Chop the dried coconut very fine or grind in a food processor. If you substitute sweetened coconut, be sure to decrease the sugar in the recipe.

Orange Macaroons **yield: 96 cookies, approximately 2 inches (5 cm) in diameter**

This variety of macaroon cookie is convenient if you do not have almond paste on hand. It is a good idea to bake a few test cookies to make sure they spread out properly before rolling all of the dough; they should spread out fairly flat, like chocolate chip cookies. If the cookies do not spread enough, add more egg white; if they spread too thin, add a small amount of flour.

1 pound 8 ounces (680 g) blanched almonds	½ teaspoon (2.5 ml) orange flower water
1 pound 6 ounces (625 g) granulated sugar	8 egg whites (1 cup/240 ml)
11 ounces (310 g) candied orange peel	Powdered sugar
1 pound 6 ounces (625 g) powdered sugar	96 whole natural almonds (skin on), about 4 ounces (115 g)
4 ounces (115 g) bread flour	

1. Grind the blanched almonds and granulated sugar to a coarse consistency. Add the candied orange peel and continue grinding to a very fine consistency. Transfer to a mixing bowl.

2. Add the powdered sugar, flour, orange flower water, and egg whites. Blend until all of the ingredients are incorporated.

3. Divide the dough into 6 equal pieces, approximately 1 pound (455 g) each. Roll each piece into a rope 16 inches (40 cm) long, using powdered sugar on your work surface to prevent the dough from sticking.

4. Cut each rope into 16 pieces. Roll the small pieces into balls, then roll the balls in powdered sugar to coat them completely. Place on sheet pans lined with baking paper or Silpats.

5. Flatten the cookies just enough so that they do not roll. Press a whole almond on top of each cookie in the center.

6. Bake at 325°F (163°C) for approximately 12 minutes or until very lightly browned. When cool, store covered to prevent the macaroons from drying out.

Madeleines yield: 40 cookies, about 3 × 2 inches (7.5 × 5 cm)

These small scallop-shaped sponge cakes were made immortal by the French writer Marcel Proust around 1912 in his celebrated novel *Remembrance of Things Past*, in which the protagonist recalls the taste of a madeleine dunked in lime blossom tea, given to him by his aunt. I particularly like what food writer A. J. Liebling had to say about the connection: "In the light of what Proust wrote with so mild a stimulus, it is the world's loss he did not have a heartier appetite; with a full meal he might have written a masterpiece."

Legend has it that these little cakes were named for their inventor, a French pastry chef from Commercy, a small town in Lorraine. Madeleines are served much as any fancy cookie or petit four sec, with the exception that dipping them in coffee or tea is more socially acceptable.

Butter and Flour Mixture (page 7)

9 ounces (255 g) granulated sugar

4 ounces (115 g) bread flour

4 ounces (115 g) cake flour

4 ounces (115 g) finely ground blanched almonds

6 eggs

1 teaspoon (5 g) salt

9 ounces (255 g) Beurre Noisette (page 7), at room temperature

2 teaspoons (10 ml) orange flower water

2 teaspoons (10 ml) vanilla extract

Powdered sugar

1. Brush the butter and flour mixture on the inside of 40 madeleine forms (see Note 1).

2. Sift the sugar, bread flour, and cake flour together. Mix in the ground almonds.

3. Whip the eggs and salt at high speed until foamy, about 2 minutes. Add the flour mixture in 2 parts, alternating with the beurre noisette. Mix in the orange flower water and vanilla.

4. Cover the batter and let it rest in the refrigerator for 1 hour.

5. Place the batter in a pastry bag with a No. 5 (10-mm) plain tip. Pipe the batter into the prepared forms, filling them to just below the rim.

6. Bake at 450°F (230°C) for approximately 8 minutes or until the tops are until golden brown and spring back when pressed lightly in the center. Unmold and sift powdered sugar lightly over the tops.

NOTE 1: If you are using Flexipan No. 1511 (shaped for madeleines), omit the butter and flour mixture and increase the baking time to approximately 15 minutes. Place the sheet pan directly on the hearth of a deck oven or on the bottom rack of a rack oven. You may also need to cover the top of the cookies with foil toward the end of baking if they become too brown.

NOTE 2: For a crisper crust, try brushing the pans with melted butter, then coating them with granulated sugar. Do not use this method if you are using Flexipans.

VARIATION
LEMON MADELEINES

Prepare madeleines as above, but use the grated zest of 2 lemons in place of the orange flower water.

Gianduja Madeleines yield: approximately 50 cookies, 3 × 2 inches (7.5 × 5 cm)

The addition of rich, creamy hazelnut-flavored gianduja chocolate not only imparts a wonderful flavor to these madeleines, it also contributes to their moist texture. It is crucial that the hazelnuts are ground very finely. If you do not have finely ground nuts on hand, grind them in a food processor together with about one-third of the granulated sugar from the recipe to prevent the nuts from caking and forming a paste. The remaining sugar will still be sufficient to whip the meringue.

Butter and Flour Mixture (page 7)	**8 egg whites (1 cup/240 ml)**
14 ounces (400 g) Beurre Noisette (page 7), at room temperature	**3 drops of lemon juice or 3 drops Tartaric Acid Solution (page 38)**
1 pound (455 g) gianduja chocolate, chopped	**8 ounces (225 g) granulated sugar**
5 ounces (140 g) bread flour	**2 teaspoons (10 ml) vanilla extract**
5 ounces (140 g) finely ground hazelnuts (see introduction)	**Tempered semisweet chocolate (optional)**

1. Brush the butter and flour mixture over the inside of 50 madeleine forms, or coat them with pan spray. If you are using Flexipans, disregard this step and simply place the Flexipan on a flat and even full-size sheet pan (see Note). Reserve the prepared molds or pans.

2. Place the gianduja in a bain-marie and melt, using low heat and stirring from time to time. Set aside but keep the chocolate warm.

3. Thoroughly combine the bread flour and the ground hazelnuts. Reserve.

4. In a mixer bowl, using the whip attachment at high speed, beat the egg whites with the lemon juice or tartaric acid solution for 30 seconds. Gradually add the sugar and whip until the egg whites just begin to form soft peaks, about 1 minute longer. Be careful not to overwhip, as incorporating too much air will cause the cookies to overexpand during baking and lose the classic madeleine outline that comes from baking the cakes in the forms.

5. Remove the mixer bowl from the machine. Using a spoon or rubber spatula, fold in the hazelnut-flour mixture, followed by the beurre noisette. Stir in the melted gianduja and the vanilla extract. If the batter is too soft to pipe out, refrigerate it for 5 to 10 minutes to firm the consistency.

6. Place a portion of the batter at a time in a pastry bag with a No. 6 (12-mm) plain tip. Pipe the batter into the prepared forms, filling them almost to the top.

7. Bake at 375°F (190°C) for approximately 15 minutes or until the cakes spring back when pressed gently in the center. Allow the cookies to cool to room temperature before unmolding. Serve the cookies inverted (rounded side up). If desired, dip the narrower half of the cookies in chocolate after they have cooled completely. Stored in an airtight container, the madeleines will stay fresh for up to 1 week.

NOTE: If you are using a Flexipan, place the sheet pan directly on the hearth of a deck oven or on the bottom rack of a rack oven.

Lemon Verbena Madeleines yield: approximately 40 cookies, 3 x 2 inches (7.5 x 5 cm)

One day, a student presented me with a tray of lovely looking, golden brown, freshly unmolded madeleines made from this recipe. When I told her they looked great, she surprised me by responding, "I don't really care for them that much, Chef." Although I personally have always found these cookies to be delicious, especially so when they are warm right out of the oven, I told her, "Well, of course, everyone has their own individual taste." I went on to explain that this is a good thing; our business would be boring if everyone had the same preferences, and so on. Then I tasted one of the cookies myself, and I had to admit the flavor was lacking. "Are you sure you added all of the ingredients?" I asked. "Yes, Chef," she replied, "except for the lemon verbena, because I could not find any." After I showed the student where the citrusy herb could be found, I said, "So, you complain about the flavor of the cookies even though you omitted the flavoring called for in the recipe? Have you ever heard the expression 'Don't complain about the government if you don't vote?'"

If you don't care for the flavor of lemon verbena, use lime zest instead or substitute 1 teaspoon (5 ml) vanilla extract and the seeds from 1 vanilla bean pod.

Melted unsalted butter

Finely ground blanched almonds (almond meal) or granulated sugar

5 ounces (140 g) granulated sugar

3 eggs, at room temperature

4 ounces (115 g) bread flour

1 ounce (30 g) cornstarch

1½ teaspoons (6 g) baking powder

5 ounces (140 g) unsalted butter, melted

2 tablespoons (30 ml) dark rum

½ ounce finely chopped fresh lemon verbena leaves (approximately 2 stalks, 12 inches long, or about 60 leaves) or finely grated zest of 2 limes

Powdered sugar

1. Brush melted butter over the inside of 40 small madeleine forms. Coat with almond meal and shake off the excess. For a crisper crust, coat the forms with granulated sugar instead of almond meal.

2. Whip the sugar and the eggs until the mixture is light, frothy, and doubled in size.

3. Sift together the flour, cornstarch, and baking powder. Stir into the egg mixture. Incorporate the butter, rum, and lemon verbena or lime zest.

4. Pipe the batter into the prepared forms.

5. Bake at 450°F (230°C) for 2 minutes; the edges should begin to rise. Reduce the oven temperature to 400°F (205°C) and continue baking until done. Invert the molds to remove the madeleines as soon as possible. Sift powdered sugar lightly over the top of the inverted cakes before serving.

NOTE: If you use Flexipan madeleine forms rather than metal forms, skip Step 1 and simply place the Flexipan on a flat, even sheet pan. Place the sheet pan directly on the hearth of a deck oven or on the bottom rack of a rack oven. The cookies will take a bit longer to bake, and you may need to cover the top of the cookies with foil toward the end of baking if they become too brown.

White Chocolate–Almond Madeleines yield: about 50 cookies, 3 × 2 inches (7.5 × 5 cm)

These delicious cookies came about as a variation of the Gianduja Madeleines. Here, white chocolate and almonds, which always make a good match, replace the gianduja and ground hazelnuts. I cannot stress enough to be cautious of overwhipping the egg whites. I have seen it happen too many times with my students, and it can ruin both the appearance and the texture of the cookies. The oven temperature is also critical; if you are not certain your oven is accurate, it is better to set the temperature a bit lower than instructed. High heat will cause the cookies to expand too rapidly and crack.

Melted unsalted butter

Finely ground almonds (almond meal)

1 pound (455 g) white chocolate, chopped

5 ounces (140 g) bread flour

5 ounces (140 g) finely ground almonds
(almond meal)

8 egg whites (1 cup/240 ml)

8 ounces (225 g) granulated sugar

14 ounces (400 g) Beurre Noisette (page 7),
at room temperature

2 teaspoons (10 ml) vanilla extract

1. Brush the inside of 50 madeleine forms with melted butter, then coat with finely ground almonds. Shake off the excess almond meal that does not stick to the butter. Set the prepared pan aside (see Note).

2. Place the chopped white chocolate in a bowl and set over a bain-marie. Melt the chocolate over low heat, stirring frequently. Remove from the heat but keep warm.

3. Combine the flour and the 5-ounce (140-g) measurement of ground almonds. Reserve.

4. Whip the egg whites at high speed for 30 seconds, using the whip attachment. Gradually add the sugar and beat approximately 1 minute longer, just until the egg whites begin to form soft peaks. Do not overwhip; if you incorporate too much air, the cookies will puff up too much during baking and lose their special shape.

5. Remove the mixer bowl from the machine. Using a spoon or rubber spatula, fold in the almond and flour mixture, followed by the beurre noisette. Fold in the reserved white chocolate and the vanilla extract. If the batter is too thin to pipe out, refrigerate for 5 to 10 minutes to thicken.

6. Place the batter in a large pastry bag with a No. 6 (12-mm) plain tip. Pipe the batter into the prepared forms, filling them to just below the rim.

7. Bake at 375°F (190°C) for approximately 15 minutes or until the cakes spring back when pressed lightly in the center. Let the cookies cool for a few minutes before unmolding. Serve the madeleines inverted (rounded-side up). Store the madeleines in an airtight container for up to 1 week.

NOTE: If using a Flexipan, omit the unmeasured melted butter and almond meal as well as Step 1. Instead, place the Flexipan on a flat, even sheet pan (a perforated sheet pan is preferable) and set aside while you make the batter. In Step 7, place the sheet pan directly on the hearth of a deck oven or on the bottom rack of a rack oven.

Brutti ma Buoni à la Venetia yield: about 50 cookies, 1¹/₂ inches (3.7 cm) in diameter

The appearance of these cookies may not be particularly tempting, but the old saying "Don't judge a book by its cover" certainly applies here. These delicious nut and meringue confections have been given a very appropriate name—*brutti ma buoni* translates to "ugly but good." And though not particularly fancy, good they are.

Brutti ma Buoni originated in the northern part of Italy, where the climate is cool and particularly well suited to growing hazelnuts and almonds, but they are especially popular in Florence and numerous versions of this rather homely little cookie can be found all over Italy; one variation follows the main recipe below.

Admittedly, the name Brutti ma Buoni is kind of fun to say and easy to remember, but please don't misuse it if you are traveling in Italy!

1 pound 4 ounces (570 g) hazelnuts

12 egg whites (1¹/₂ cups/360 ml)

¹/₂ teaspoon (2.5 g) salt

1 pound 8 ounces (680 g) granulated sugar

1 tablespoon (15 ml) vanilla extract

6 ounces (170 g) sweet dark chocolate, chopped into raisin-sized pieces

2 ounces (55 g) unsweetened chocolate, chopped into raisin-sized pieces

1. Toast the hazelnuts and remove the skins (see page 6). Grind the nuts and reserve.

2. Beat the egg whites until foamy; add the salt. Gradually incorporate the sugar and whip to stiff peaks. Fold in the chopped nuts and vanilla extract by hand.

3. Transfer the nut meringue to a heavy saucepan. Cook over medium heat, stirring constantly, until the mixture turns light golden brown and begins to thicken, about 15 minutes. Do not overcook; if you are not sure if the batter is cooked, it is better to undercook it. Place in a mixing bowl and let cool to room temperature. Stir in the chopped chocolates.

4. Using a small ice cream scoop (about 1¹/₂ tablespoons/25 ml in volume), scoop the batter onto sheet pans lined with baking paper or Silpats, spacing the rounds 1¹/₂ inches (3.7 cm) apart. Dipping the ice cream scoop into hot water from time to time will make this procedure much easier.

5. Bake at 325°F (163°C) for approximately 25 to 30 minutes. The cookies should feel firm to the touch but still be soft and chewy inside.

VARIATION

BRUTTI MA BUONI A LA MILANESE yield: about 40 cookies, 1¹/₂ inches (3.7 cm) in diameter

14 ounces (400 g) hazelnuts or equal parts hazelnuts and blanched almonds

16 egg whites (2 cups/480 ml)

1 pound (455 g) granulated sugar

2 teaspoons (10 ml) vanilla extract

1. Toast the hazelnuts and remove the skins (see page 6). Crush the nuts finely; the pieces should be approximately the size of grains of rice.

2. Beat the egg whites until foamy. Gradually incorporate the sugar and continue to whip until stiff peaks form; take care not to overwhip. Immediately stir in the vanilla and the reserved nuts.

3. Transfer to a heavy-bottomed saucepan and cook over medium heat, stirring constantly, until the mixture turns light golden brown and begins to thicken and pull away from the sides of the pan. (When you first start cooking, the mixture will become looser before evaporation occurs and it starts to thicken.) Transfer to a bowl and let cool to room temperature. If the mixture seems dry and crumbly, incorporate a few more egg whites, 1 at a time, to make it soft.

4. Follow Steps 4 and 5 in the main recipe to shape and bake the cookies.

Nut Kisses yield: approximately 50 large cookies

These delightful little cookies, called *Nuss Busserln* in German, are, like Austrian Hazelnut-Almond Cookies (page 264), originally from the Bad Ischler Alpine resort. Made from walnut meringue that is very fast to put together, Nut Kisses have a distinctive crackled exterior that comes from a surprise step: After the cookies are formed, they are placed in a proof box before baking to add moisture.

8 ounces (225 g) walnuts, toasted	1 pound (455 g) granulated sugar
2 ounces (55 g) cake flour	1 teaspoon (5 ml) vanilla extract
8 egg whites (1 cup/240 ml)	

1. Chop the walnuts to a coarse consistency. Combine with the cake flour.

2. Place the egg whites and half of the sugar in a mixer bowl over a bain marie. Whipping constantly, heat to 140°F (60°C). Place the bowl on a mixer and whip the egg whites to a thick foam. Still whipping, gradually add the sugar, taking 3 to 4 minutes to add all of it. Continue to whip the meringue until it forms stiff peaks. Add the vanilla extract. Carefully fold the nut mixture into the meringue by hand.

3. Using 2 tablespoons dipped in water, drop oval portions of the meringue mixture approximately 2½ inches long and 1½ inches wide (6.2 x 3.7cm), on a sheet pan lined with baking paper or a Silpat. Space them fairly well apart, since they will expand as they bake.

4. Place the cookies in a proof box for 1 hour. If no proof box is available, place them in a warm location and mist them lightly with water.

5. Bake at 200 to 225°F (94 to106°C) for 30 to 60 minutes, depending on size, until dried through but not browned. Store in airtight containers.

Chinese Sesame Seed Cookies yield: 50 cookies, approximately 2½ inches (6.2 cm) in diameter

This simple recipe was given to me by an old Chinese baker in the small village of Qufu, which is located northeast of Shanghai, off the main road on the way to Beijing. The village is famous as the birthplace of Confucius. It was certainly the highlight of my trip during a three-week culinary exchange I was invited to participate in, together with Jacques Pepin and Cindy Pawlcyn. We showed the Chinese chefs examples of Western cooking, and they taught us their specialties.

We were generally served litchi fruit, oranges, or cookies such as these almond or sesame cookies. When I questioned the use of lard in this recipe, I was told very firmly (through an interpreter) that under no circumstances should any fat other than lard be used. Lard is what gives the cookies their special character. Through my students, I have found that the average American does not care for this refined pork fat; however, when given a cookie to try, they rarely wrinkle their noses.

10 ounces (285 g) granulated sugar	1 pound (455 g) bread flour
1 pound (455 g) soft lard (do not substitute another fat)	1 teaspoon (3.5 g) ammonium carbonate, dissolved in a small amount of water
3 eggs, at room temperature	Sesame seeds

1. Place the granulated sugar and the lard in a mixing bowl and beat until creamy. Mix in the eggs 1 at a time.

2. Sift the bread flour. Add to the lard mixture together with the ammonium carbonate and blend until incorporated.

3. Place the dough on a sheet pan lined with baking paper. Refrigerate until well chilled.

4. Divide the dough into 2 pieces, 1 pound 7 ounces (655 g) each. Roll the pieces out to 16-inch (40-cm) ropes, using flour to prevent the dough from sticking.

5. Cut each rope into 25 equal pieces. Roll the small pieces between your hands to form balls.

6. Roll the balls in sesame seeds to coat all over. Place the cookies 1 inch (2.5 cm) apart on sheet pans lined with baking paper or Silpats. Press down on the top of each cookie just enough so that it will not roll.

7. Bake at 350°F (175°C) for about 20 minutes or until golden brown.

NOTE: Make sure your oven is not too hot, or the cookies will flatten and become too dark around the edges.

VARIATION
CHINESE ALMOND COOKIES

Prepare Chinese Sesame Cookies, but substitute whole natural almonds (skin on) for the sesame seeds. Place the balls of dough about 2 inches (5 cm) apart on sheet pans lined with baking paper or Silpats and press a whole almond firmly into the top of each cookie. Brush egg wash over the top of the cookies, covering the almond as well. Bake as directed.

NOTE: It is not really necessary to use the egg wash on the almond cookies. The almonds will stay in place without it, but the look of the glaze from the egg wash is traditional.

Large-Scale Production Florentinas

The method used here for making the Florentinas perfectly round is practical only if you are making a small quantity and you have a use for the scrap pieces—although, unless you hide them, they will be nibbled away in record time. To produce these cookies in a large quantity and/or on a regular basis, you should purchase special Florentina baking sheets. These are coated with silicone and feature very shallow, round indentations in which the batter spreads out into perfect circles. Special sheets are also available for forming the chocolate coating. These pans have round indentations with the same diameter as the cookie pans, but the indentations are even thinner and have the classic wavy pattern on the bottom. Chocolate is spread in the indentations and left to harden in the refrigerator; then the chocolate discs and the cookies are sandwiched together with a little additional melted chocolate. The latest timesaving tool is the Flexipan made in just the right size to shape and bake the batter (see page 307). If the chef is using one of these methods, he or she is probably using one of the convenient—and foolproof—Florentina mixes that are also available.

Florentinas yield: 36 cookies, 3¼ inches (8.1 cm) in diameter (Photo 18)

You will find these classic cookies in just about every pastry shop in continental Europe and Scandinavia, often with the addition of chopped candied fruit. The cookies can be left flat or molded into a curved shape by draping the soft cookies over a rolling pin and leaving them to set up, as in a Tuile. Most often, they are just over 3 inches (7.5 cm) in diameter, round and flat, with chocolate on one side combed into a wavy pattern. The chocolate is added not only because it looks and tastes good, but also because it helps prevent the cookies from becoming soft. Florentinas are also made into cookie shells shaped in the manner of pirouettes or in cones, and are used in many types of elegant desserts and filled pastries.

Florentina Batter (recipe follows)   Bittersweet chocolate, tempered (see Chef's Tip)

1. Draw 36 circles, 3¼ inches (8.1 cm) in diameter, on 2 full sheets of baking paper (18 circles per sheet), using a plain cookie cutter as a guide. Make 2 rows of 5 and 2 rows of 4 in a staggered pattern on each sheet of paper so the circles are evenly spaced. Invert the papers, place them on sheet pans, and set aside while you prepare the batter. If you are making a large number of cookies or making them regularly, you may want to make one template and reuse it by placing another sheet of paper on top, as described in Steps 3 and 4 of Florentina Cups (page 307).

2. Using 2 spoons, divide the batter between the circles, flattening and spreading it to within ¼ inch (6 mm) of the drawn lines. Wet the spoons to keep the batter from sticking. If the batter was made ahead and is therefore cold and firm, you can portion it instead by dividing it in half, rolling each half out to a rope, and cutting 18 equal pieces from each rope. In this case, simply place the small portions, 1 per circle, on the papers and flatten the dough with your fingers.

3. Bake at 375°F (190°C) for about 8 minutes or until light brown. Stagger the baking so you will have time to trim the edges of the cookies immediately as you take each pan from the oven, as follows.

FIGURE 6-15 Cutting Florentinas while they are still soft to even the edges; breaking off the uneven edges after they have hardened; a finished cookie with a clean edge

4. If the cookies are just a little uneven, place a plain round cookie cutter that is slightly larger than the baked cookie around the cookie, not on top. Using a circular motion, push the soft cookie into a nice even round shape. If the cookies are very uneven or have spread too far beyond the lines, transfer the baking paper with the baked cookies on it to a piece of cardboard or an even tabletop. Use a 3¼-inch (8.1-cm) cookie cutter to cut out the center of the cookie to the correct size. Pull the baking paper back on the pan, let the cookies cool, then break off the excess from the outside (Figure 6-15).

5. When the cookies are cold, brush a thick layer of bittersweet chocolate on the flat bottom side. For the classic Florentina look, use a cake-decorating comb to spread the chocolate into a wavy pattern before it hardens. Do not refrigerate Florentinas.

NOTE: To make a simplified Florentina cookie, just drop small portions of batter directly onto the baking paper and flatten the batter slightly before baking. Don't bother with drawing the circles, cutting the baked cookies, or coating them with chocolate. Do not bake more than you can use in a day, however, because without the chocolate coating, the cookies will become soft after 1 day.

FLORENTINA BATTER

7 ounces (200 g) unsalted butter	¼ cup (60 ml) heavy cream
7 ounces (200 g) granulated sugar	7 ounces (200 g) sliced almonds, lightly crushed
3 tablespoons (45 ml) or 2 ounces (55 g) glucose *or* light corn syrup	

1. Combine the butter, sugar, glucose or corn syrup, and heavy cream in a saucepan; bring to a boil.

2. Add the almonds and cook over medium heat for 2 to 3 minutes. Remove the batter from the heat.

3. Try baking a small piece of batter as a test. If the batter spreads out too thin, cook the batter in the saucepan a little longer. Conversely, if the batter does not spread enough, add a little more cream and test again; you will need to warm the batter to mix in the cream.

NOTE: Although the batter can be portioned and baked immediately, it is easier to work with if it is allowed to rest and become firmer in consistency; to speed this up, it can be refrigerated. If the batter has set up and you are using it in a recipe where it must be spread out very thin (for example, over the top of a cake or a sheet of pastries), you will need to reheat it. Reheating may cause the butter to separate, but mixing in a small amount of cream will remedy this.

FLORENTINAS MADE IN FLEXIPANS

yield: 40 cookies, 3¹/₂ inches (8.7 cm) in diameter using Flexipan No. 1299

The Flexipan(s) must be placed on perfectly flat, even sheet pans or, as with anything liquid, the batter will not bake evenly in the forms. If you have 3 Flexipans, you can bake all the cookies in one batch; simply divide the batter evenly among 40 indentations. If you are making one pan at a time, use approximately 1 rounded teaspoon of batter per cookie. Press the batter into the indentations in the pan to flatten it just a little. The glossy, smooth surface of the Flexipan will do the rest of the job of forming the cookies as they bake. The yield is slightly higher using the Flexipans, because you do not have any scrap pieces. You also save the time it takes to cut the cookies round using the traditional method.

VARIATION

FLORENTINAS WITH CANDIED FRUIT

Prepare Florentinas as directed on page 305, adding up to 6 ounces (170 g) diced candied and/or dried fruit to the batter at the end of Step 2 after removing the batter from the heat. A colorful combination is candied orange peel, candied angelica, and dried or candied cherries.

Florentina Cups yield: 20 to 24 cups

1 recipe Florentina Batter (page 306), chilled

1. Make the batter, pour it into a bowl, and refrigerate.

2. Have ready 1 or, preferably, 2 ladles, 6 to 8 ounces each, 1 or 2 oranges or small grapefruit that will fit loosely inside the ladles (chilling the fruit will make the shells harden more quickly), and a container that is close the same height as the length of the ladle handles (a round bain-marie insert usually works great). Hook the ladles to the top of the container so that the bowls of the ladles are resting on the table as level as possible (Figure 6-16). Set aside.

3. Make a template by drawing 10 circles, 5¹/₂ inches (13.7 cm) in diameter, on a sheet of baking paper with a black marking pen (see Note 1). Space the circles evenly and arrange them in a staggered pattern, making 3 rows and placing 3 rounds in both the top and bottom rows and 4 rounds in the center row. This template can be reused many times.

4. Place a second sheet of baking paper on top of your template (tape the edges to the table if necessary to keep the papers from sliding).

FIGURE 6-16 Using an orange to press a soft Florentina cookie into the bowl of a ladle to form a Florentina Cup. Left to right: 2 finished Florentina Cups; a bain-marie supporting 2 ladles in an upright position; a baked cookie waiting to be formed

5. Divide the chilled (and thickened) batter into 2 equal pieces. Using a small amount of flour, if necessary, to keep the dough from sticking to your hands and the table, roll out each piece into a rope, then cut each rope into 10 equal pieces.

6. Place 10 of the small slices inside the circles on the baking paper set over the template. Press each piece with your fingers to flatten it and bring it to ½ inch (1.2 cm) from the edge of the drawn circle. Remove the paper from the template and place it on a perfectly flat sheet pan.

7. Place a new sheet of baking paper over your template and repeat Step 5 with the remaining 10 slices of dough.

8. Bake 1 sheet pan of Florentinas at a time at 350°F (175°C) for approximately 10 minutes or until they are golden brown. Remove the pan from the oven and let the cookies cool for just a few minutes, until firm enough to be lifted off the pan with a spatula. Working quickly, transfer a cookie to the bowl of one of the ladles (right-side up) and press the cookie into the ladle with one of the oranges to form the cup shape (Figure 6-16). If you are using 2 ladles, as suggested, leave the first cup in place, form a second cup in the other ladle, then go back and remove the first one. Repeat until you have formed all 10 cups (see Note 2). If the cookies on the pan become too firm to shape, return the pan to the oven for 1 or 2 minutes to soften them again. Repeat Step 8 to form the remaining 10 cups.

NOTE 1: Alternatively, you can bake the Florentinas using Flexipan No. 2455. Follow the directions on page 307, then proceed to Step 8. This will yield 24 cups.

NOTE 2: If you want the top edge of the cups to be perfectly even, follow the procedure for trimming the baked cookies as described in Step 4 on page 306 in the recipe for Florentina Cookies, using a 5½-inch (13.7-cm) cookie cutter to trim the cookies.

CHEF'S TIP

If you do not have the proper size ladles or prefer not to use that method to shape the cups, they can also be formed in one of the following two ways:

- As soon as the warm cookies are firm enough to work with, immediately bend ½ inch (1.2 cm) of the edge of each cookie up 45 degrees to form a shallow hexagon-shaped basket (with the top of the cookie facing out).
- Press the cookie between 2 large brioche molds, or fold the warm, soft cookies over the back of a small bowl or jar and press into shape with your hands (Figure 6-17).

Shaping the cookies with the brioche molds or over the back of a small bowl will result in fairly uniform baskets. The ladle method produces more of a freeform shape.

FIGURE 6-17 Forming Florentina Cups by pressing the soft cookies between 2 identical molds; folding the soft cookie over the back of a small inverted mold and shaping it by hand

COCOA NIB FLORENTINA CUPS

Add 4 ounces (115 g) cocoa nibs to the Florentina Batter in Step 1 before chilling the batter.

Layered Florentina Squares yield: 70 cookies, 1¹/₂ inches (3.7 cm) square

This is another version of chocolate-coated Florentinas. Layered Florentina Squares provide the same well-liked combination of nuts, caramel, and candied fruit covered with chocolate, but, by sandwiching a layer of short dough between them here, you introduce a whole new textural dimension. Take great care not to overbake the sheet in Step 2 or 3, or it will become too brittle, and the cookies will be difficult to cut attractively.

Another method, which makes it easier to cut the pieces nicely but takes more time, is to cut the cookies out as directed in Step 6 after baking the sheet and before spreading out the chocolate. Keep the pieces in each row together. Spread out the chocolate and quickly place the cut Florentina squares, short dough-side down on the chocolate, row by row in straight lines, keeping the pieces as close together as possible and recreating the same shape that the sheet was in before it was cut. If you are working in a cool location, you should do this in two steps, spreading the chocolate into a rectangle measuring 6 x 8 inches (15 x 20 cm) and placing 7 rows of 5 cookies on top, or the chocolate will set up before you have time to place all of the cookies (see Note). Allow the chocolate to set, then cut through the chocolate between each row, first in one direction and then in the other. Refrigerate briefly to make it easier to remove the cookies from the paper.

1 pound 5 ounces (595 g) Short Dough (page 67)

¹/₂ recipe Florentina Batter (page 306)

2 ounces (55 g) candied orange peel

2 ounces (55 g) candied *or* dried cherries

12 ounces (340 g) Sweet dark chocolate, tempered

1. Line the bottom of a half-sheet pan (12 x 16 inches/30 x 40 cm) with baking paper. Roll the dough out to ¹/₈ inch (3 mm) thick and cover the bottom of the pan with it. Trim away the excess dough from the sides and reserve the scraps for another use.

2. Bake at 375°F (190°C) until baked halfway, about 10 minutes. Let cool.

3. Chop the candied orange peel and cherries to the size of currants and add them to the batter. Spread the mixture evenly over the dough in the pan. Return to the 375°F (190°C) oven and bake until the florentina has turned golden brown, about 15 minutes. Let the sheet cool.

4. Run the tip of a chef's knife around the inside perimeter of the pan, then invert to unmold the sheet. Remove the baking paper and turn the sheet right-side up onto a sheet of corrugated cardboard or the back of a sheet pan.

5. Spread the tempered chocolate approximately ¹/₁₆ inch (2 mm) thick into a rectangle measuring 12 x 16 inches (30 x 40 cm) on a sheet of baking paper. Carefully slide the Florentina–short dough sheet on top of the rectangle of chocolate. Place in the refrigerator to allow the chocolate to set.

6. Trim one long side to make it even. Starting from that side, cut the sheet lengthwise into 7 strips, each 1½ inches (3.7 cm) wide. Cut each strip across into 10 pieces. Store the cookies in an airtight container; do not refrigerate.

N O T E : Another solution is to use coating chocolate rather than tempered dark chocolate. In this case, you can spread it all out at once, as directed in Step 5, even if the weather is cool. If the coating chocolate sets up too quickly, you have the option of rewarming it, using a low setting on a hair dryer or heat gun.

Mexican Wedding Cookies   yield: 60 cookies, approximately 1¼ inches (3.1 cm) in diameter

These are known as *pastelitos de boda* ("small wedding pastries") in Mexico and, as you might have guessed, they are considered a must for inclusion among the treats served at a Mexican wedding. Just about the same melt-in-your-mouth pecan-butter cookies are known as *pecan butterballs* in the southern United States. As mentioned in the introduction to Butter Crescents on page 265, many variations on this theme are made throughout the world.

6 ounces (170 g) finely chopped pecans	3 ounces (85 g) powdered sugar
8 ounces (225 g) bread flour	1 tablespoon (15 ml) vanilla extract
8 ounces (225 g) cake flour	Powdered sugar
¾ teaspoon (3 g) salt	
12 ounces (340 g) unsalted butter, at room temperature	

1. Mix together the pecans, bread flour, cake flour, and salt.

2. Using the paddle attachment, cream the butter with the powdered sugar and the vanilla until light in color and texture. Incorporate the flour-nut mixture at low speed, mixing just until combined. Chill the dough until it is firm enough to work with.

3. Divide the dough into 3 equal pieces, about 12 ounces (360 g) each. Roll each piece into a rope 16 inches (40 cm) in length and cut 20 equal pieces from each rope.

4. Roll the pieces between your palms to make round balls and place them on sheet pans lined with baking paper or Silpats (see Note). Press down lightly to keep the balls of dough from rolling, but do not flatten. The cookies will not spread or change shape very much during baking, so you can space them fairly close.

5. Bake at 350°F (175°C) for about 20 minutes or until the cookies are firm to the touch and golden brown. While the cookies are still warm, roll them in powdered sugar to cover them heavily. The sugar will form something close to a glaze as it coats the warm, buttery cookies. Store in airtight containers.

N O T E : For a firmer crust on the cookies, roll the balls of dough in granulated sugar before baking. They should still be rolled in powdered sugar after they come out of the oven.

Moravian Spice Cookies

yield: approximately 325 to 375 very thin cookies, 2 inches (5 cm) in diameter or 2 inches (5 cm) square

If you are cutting these cookies as instructed in the recipe—directly on a Silpat after you bake them—be sure not to press too hard or you can damage the mat with the cutter. If you do not have any use for the scrap pieces (other than eating them, which is hard not to do), an alternative is to cut the cookies with a single- or multiple-blade pastry wheel, making 2-inch (5-cm) squares or rectangles. In this case, you cannot cut directly on the mat without causing damage, so you must invert the baked sheet quickly onto a sheet of cardboard. If you use a straightedge, such as a ruler or rolling pin, as a guide, don't press down too hard on the dough, or you will compress it and make the cookies tough.

A third way of cutting these cookies, and probably the most efficient, is to add a small amount of additional flour to the dough to make it more manageable, roll it out, cut the cookies, and transfer the cookies to sheet pans lined with Silpats or baking paper to bake. This way, you can reroll the scrap pieces of raw dough instead of wasting the baked scraps, and, in turn, produce more cookies.

You must keep the dough very cold as you work with it and attempt to roll only a small portion at a time. I have also had good success rolling out the dough between two Silpats, then placing them in the freezer for a few minutes or in the refrigerator a bit longer before pulling them apart.

1 pound 5 ounces (595 g) bread flour	2 teaspoons (10 g) salt
1 tablespoon (5 g) ground cinnamon	1½ cups (360 ml) molasses
1 tablespoon (6 g) ground ginger	8 ounces (225 g) dark brown sugar
1 teaspoon (2 g) ground allspice	4 ounces (115 g) vegetable shortening, melted
1 teaspoon (2 g) ground cloves	4 ounces (115 g) unsalted butter, melted
2 teaspoons (8 g) baking soda	9 ounces (255 g) cake flour

1. Sift together approximately one-fourth of the bread flour with the cinnamon, ginger, allspice, cloves, baking soda, and salt.

2. Beat the molasses and brown sugar together using the paddle attachment. Mix in the shortening and butter. Gradually add the sifted dry ingredients, the remaining bread flour, and the cake flour; mix to form a stiff dough. Press the dough flat and refrigerate overnight.

3. Weigh the dough into 8 equal pieces, approximately 7 ounces (200 g) each. Leave 1 piece out to work with and keep the remainder chilled.

About Moravian Spice Cookies

These spicy, paper-thin treats made their way to the United States with the immigrants who arrived during the 1800s from Moravia, at that time an independent country located in what is now the eastern part of the Czech Republic. Moravian Spice Cookies are very similar to Swedish Gingerbread Cookies, not only in the delightful mix of spices that fills the whole kitchen with an irresistible aroma as the cookies bake, but also because of their round, fluted shape and the fact that it is absolutely crucial that they are rolled very thin. Moravian cookies are actually even thinner than their Scandinavian cousins, and the addition of molasses gives them their own distinct flavor as well as a darker color.

4. Roll out the piece of dough onto a Silpat the size of a half-sheet pan (12 x 16 inches/30 x 40 cm), using the minimal amount of flour necessary to keep the dough from sticking. Roll the dough as thin as possible so it covers the entire mat; it will be almost translucent. Trim the edges even as necessary.

5. Place the mat with the dough on a sheet pan and bake at 325°F (163°C) for approximately 10 minutes. The dough should not darken, but it should feel firm and baked through. (It is a little hard to judge the color, as the dough is dark to begin with; however, it is likely you will have a few thinner spots on the dough sheet and when these brown, you will know it is ready.) Remove the pan from the oven and quickly cut out cookies in a staggered pattern to produce as few scrap pieces as possible, using a 2-inch (5-cm) round, fluted cutter. Transfer the cut cookies to a rack to cool as you cut them out. If the cookies curl after they are on the rack, flatten them with a flat-bottomed drinking glass. If the dough sheet becomes too hard to cut out cookies, return the pan to the oven for a few seconds. Repeat Steps 4 and 5 with the remaining dough pieces.

6. Store the cookies in an airtight container to preserve their crisp texture.

Oat Flakes yield: approximately 100 cookies, 2¹/₂ inches (6.2 cm) in diameter, or 60 cookies, 3³/₄ inches (9.4 cm) in diameter using Flexipan No. 1299 (Photo 51)

You might say that Oat Flakes are a peasant-style Florentina cookie, with less expensive oats replacing the almonds. They are, however, extremely crisp and delicious, plus they are fairly unusual. The batter can be kept in the refrigerator to be baked off as needed, just as with the Oat Flakes' more famous cousin. They taste great plain or dipped halfway into dark chocolate. Oat Flakes stay crisp if kept in airtight containers or on sheet pans tightly wrapped with plastic. Be careful in handling them, though, because part of their charm is that they are very fragile.

Another way to form these cookies is to pipe the batter on the bottom of small, buttered half-sphere forms, about 2 inches (5 cm) in diameter. The batter will climb up the sides of the forms as it bakes, as if you had lined the inside of the form. Mazarin forms or other shallow tartlet pans may also be used with this method. Serve the baked cookies inverted. Oak Flake batter should be made the day before it is used to allow the oats time to absorb moisture.

9 ounces (255 g) melted unsalted butter	1 ounce (30 g) bread flour
8 ounces (225 g) rolled oats	3 tablespoons (36 g) baking powder
3 eggs	Melted dark coating chocolate (optional)
12 ounces (340 g) granulated sugar	

1. Combine the melted butter and oats. Blend in the eggs and sugar. Mix the flour and baking powder together, then incorporate into the batter. Refrigerate at least 4 hours, or overnight.

2. Place the batter in a pastry bag with a No. 6 (12-mm) plain tip. Pipe into cherry-sized cookies on sheet pans lined with baking paper or Silpats (or into the indentations of a No. 1299 Flexipan); do not crowd the cookies if using sheet pans, as they will spread out quite a bit.

3. Bake at 375°F (190°C) about 8 minutes or until the whole surface of each cookie is golden brown, not just the edges.

4. When the cookies have cooled completely, dip them halfway into dark chocolate if desired. Store the cookies in an airtight container.

Palm Leaves yield: about 45 cookies, 3 inches (7.5 cm) in diameter

These are most often known by their French name, *palmiers*, which literally translates as "palm trees." The distinctive shape of the baked cookies resembles the leaves of a palm. It is not documented who first came up with the idea of rolling out puff pastry in sugar and giving it what amounts to a double-double turn in the wrong direction, but research shows the cookies were invented in the beginning of the twentieth century.

The granulated sugar not only takes the place of flour to prevent the dough from sticking, but also makes the Palm Leaves crisp, shiny, and sweet, as the sugar caramelizes while the cookies are baking. You may not use up all of the sugar in the recipe, but the more sugar you can roll into the puff pastry, the better. Should you fail to roll enough sugar into the dough, the cookies will not only be less sweet, they will spread out too far and lose their special shape.

2 pounds (910 g) Puff Pastry (page 74)   **8 ounces (225 g) granulated sugar**

I. Roll out the puff pastry in the granulated sugar to make a rectangle measuring 24 × 12 inches (60 × 30 cm) and about ⅛ inch (3 mm) thick. If the dough is uneven or too large on any side, trim it to the proper dimensions. Keep turning and moving the dough as you roll it out, spreading the sugar evenly underneath and on top of the puff pastry at the same time to keep the dough from sticking to the table.

2. Place the dough in front of you horizontally. Fold the long sides of the rectangle in to meet in the center. Fold in half in the opposite direction (crosswise) to bring the 2 short sides together at the right side.

3. Using a dowel about 1 inch (2.5 cm) in diameter, make a deep indentation horizontally down the center of the folded dough; fold in half again on this line (the indentation makes it possible to fold the dough again and still have the edges line up squarely). Do not press too hard with the dowel or the puff pastry will become too thin and the cookies will break apart as they expand in the oven. Refrigerate the strip until firm.

4. Cut the folded strip into slices ⅛ inch (3 mm) thick (Figure 6-18). Place the slices, cut-side up, on sheet pans lined with baking paper or Silpats. Keep in mind as you place them on the pans that they will spread to about 3 times as wide while baking.

5. Bake at 425°F (219°C) until the sugar starts to caramelize and turn golden on the bottoms, about 8 minutes.

6. Remove the pan from the oven and quickly turn each cookie over on the pan, using a spatula or metal scraper. Return the cookies to the oven and bake for a few minutes longer or until as much sugar as possible has caramelized on the tops. Let the cookies cool.

NOTE: Palm Leaves can be served as is, or you can dip the tip of each cookie into melted dark coating chocolate. Two cookies —with or without chocolate—can also be sandwiched together with Vanilla Buttercream (Swiss Method) (page 477).

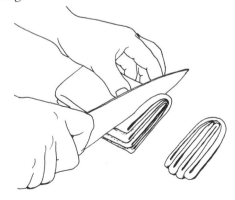

FIGURE 6-18 Slicing Palm Leaves

Tuiles yield: approximately 100 cookies, 3¼ inches (8.1 cm) in diameter

Tuile means "tile" in French; these thin, curved cookies are named after the clay roofing tiles that are made in a half-sphere shape. The same shape cookie is known as *tegolino* in Italian and *teja* in Spanish. This style of roofing construction is popular in the Mediterranean, where the curved ceramic tiles are laid on the roof in an alternating up-and-down pattern that locks them into place. Perhaps it is not so strange to name a cookie after a building material when you consider the following quote by the great Antoine Carême: "The fine arts are five in number: namely painting, sculpture, poetry, music, and architecture—the principal branch of the latter being pastry."

3 ounces (85 g) bread flour

3 ounces (85 g) cake flour

6 ounces (170 g) powdered sugar

6 egg whites (¾ cup/180 ml), at room temperature

4 ounces (115 g) melted unsalted butter

1 teaspoon (5 ml) vanilla extract

Sliced natural almonds (skin on) optional

1. Sift together the bread flour, cake flour, and powdered sugar; place in a mixer bowl with the paddle attachment. Incorporate the egg whites, scraping down the sides of the bowl once or twice, mixing just until the batter is smooth. Mix in the melted butter and the vanilla extract, scrape down the sides of the bowl again, and blend until fully incorporated. The batter can be stored in the refrigerator at this point for up to 1 week.

2. To form tuiles, you will need a template with a round opening 3¼ inches (8.1 cm) in diameter. To make one, copy the drawing in Figure 6-19, then cut the template out of ¹⁄₁₆-inch (2-mm) cardboard.

3. Spread the paste flat and even within the template, forming the cookies on Silpats or, if not available, on the back of sheet pans that have been lightly greased and floured (see Figures 10-30, page 482). If desired, sprinkle almonds over the tops of the cookies.

4. Bake one pan at a time at 375°F (190°C) until the cookies start to brown lightly, about 5 minutes.

5. Leave the pan in the oven with the oven door open. Immediately form the cookies into the classic tuile shape by draping them, almond-side up, over a rolling pin that is 3 to 4 inches (7.5 to 10 cm) in diameter. Another way to form the cookies is to lay them into a baguette baking pan, almond-side down, to form the curved shape (Figure 6-20). Lastly, you can roll them around a 1-inch (2.5-cm) dowel to make a pirouette shape. The latter must be done fairly quickly, or the cookies will start to cool and break.

FIGURE 6-20 Forming soft tuiles into a rounded shape by draping them, almond-side up, over a rolling pin as soon as they come out of the oven; forming the same shape by placing the soft cookies, almond-side down, in a baguette pan

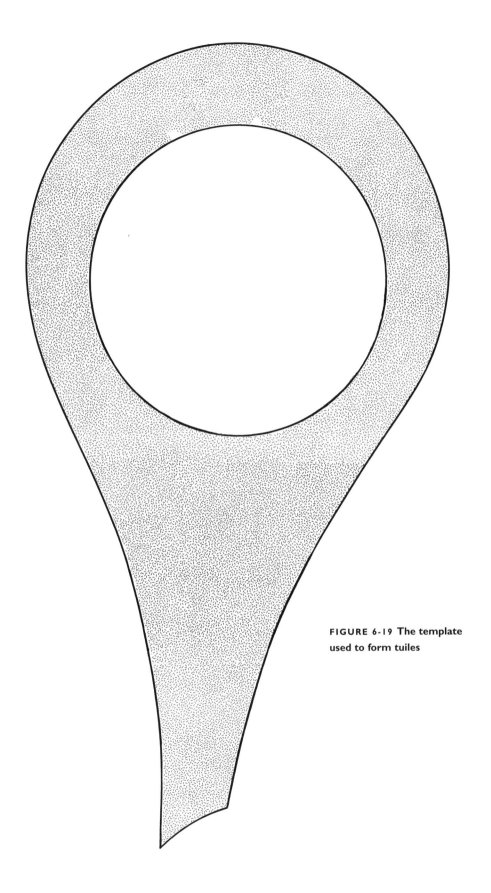

FIGURE 6-19 **The template used to form tuiles**

VARIATION

COCOA TUILES yield: approximately 100 cookies, 3¹/₄ inches (8.1 cm) in diameter

Replace 1 ounce (30 g) cake flour with an equal amount of sifted unsweetened cocoa powder.

Pirouettes yield: about 80 cookies, 3¹/₄ inches (8.1 cm) in diameter

Pirouette is a ballet term that means "a rapid spin of the body on the point of the toe." Here, it refers to the way the just-baked cookie wafers are curled around a dowel, which also must be done rapidly. Pirouettes can be served plain or with the ends dipped into melted coating chocolate. They may also be filled and served as a pastry. Additionally, a portion of the batter can be colored with unsweetened cocoa powder at the rate of 1 teaspoon (2.5 g) per 2 tablespoons (30 ml) batter. Use a piping bag with a very small opening to decorate the plain batter with spirals or parallel lines of cocoa-colored batter after you have spread the plain batter within the template. Bake as directed. Roll the striped cookies so that the lines run diagonally rather than horizontally or vertically.

8 ounces (225 g) granulated sugar	4 ounces (115 g) melted unsalted butter
5 ounces (140 g) cake flour	1 teaspoon (5 ml) vanilla extract
¹/₂ cup (120 ml) heavy cream	3 egg whites, at room temperature

1. Combine 2 ounces (55 g) sugar with the flour. Gradually stir in the cream, melted butter, and vanilla, and mix until smooth. Set aside to rest for about 30 minutes.

2. While the batter is resting, copy the drawing in Figure 6-19, page 315, and cut the template out of cardboard that is ¹/₁₆ inch (2 mm) thick. Grease and flour the inverted back of even sheet pans or use Silpats, which do not need to be greased and floured.

3. Whip the egg whites to a foam. Gradually add the remaining 6 ounces (170 g) sugar and whip to soft peaks. Gradually fold the meringue into the reserved batter.

4. Using the template, spread out thin wafers on the prepared sheet pans (see Figures 10-29 and 10-30, page 482).

5. Bake at 400°F (205°C) about 5 minutes, until light brown in a few spots; this ensures that the cookies are cooked enough to turn crisp when they cool.

6. Immediately roll the hot wafers around a dowel that is just large enough in diameter to allow the ends of the wafer to meet and overlap very slightly. Press the edges together to make them stick. Push each finished pirouette to the opposite end of the dowel and leave it there until it is firm. Continue forming the remaining wafers in the same way. If the cookies become too brittle to bend easily, reheat until soft. Store the pirouettes in airtight containers to keep them crisp and brittle.

Hamantaschen yield: approximately 100 cookies, 3 inches (7.5 cm) in diameter

Hamantaschen literally translates to "Haman's pockets," although these three-cornered filled cookies are also said to represent Haman's three-cornered hat. In either case, the cookies are named for Haman, whose story is told in the biblical Book of Esther. Haman was the prime minister of Persia and famous for his failed conspiracy to kill all of the Jews under his rule. His plan was prevented at the last moment due to the intervention of the Israelites Esther and Mordecai, and this victory is celebrated at the Jewish festival of Purim, during which these cookies are traditionally served. Esther, King Haman's wife and Mordecai's niece, had kept her Jewish heritage a secret but revealed it to her husband when she learned of his plot to kill her people.

Hamantaschen are made with poppy seed, prune, or apricot filling.

1 pound (455 g) unsalted butter, at room temperature	1 pound (455 g) bread flour
1 pound 4 ounces (570 g) granulated sugar	1 pound (455 g) cake flour
Finely grated zest of 2 oranges	2 tablespoons (24 g) baking powder
¼ cup (60 ml) fresh orange juice	1 teaspoon (5 g) salt
1 tablespoon (15 ml) vanilla extract	Egg wash
4 eggs	Apricot, Prune, and Poppy Seed Fillings (recipes follow)

1. Using the paddle attachment, cream the butter and sugar together until light and fluffy, 4 or 5 minutes. Add the orange zest, orange juice, and vanilla, and mix to incorporate. Beat in the eggs, one at a time.

2. Sift together the bread flour, cake flour, baking powder, and salt. Add the dry ingredients to the butter mixture and mix just until combined. Press the dough flat and chill until firm.

3. Divide the dough into 4 equal pieces approximately 1 pound 3 ounces (540 g) each. Roll the dough, one portion at a time, to ⅛-inch (3-mm) thickness. Cut circles from the dough, using a 3-inch (7.5-cm) fluted cutter. As you cut them, place the circles on sheet pans lined with baking paper or Silpats. Continue until you have used all the dough. Chill the circles until they are firm.

4. Brush egg wash over the dough circles.

5. If you are using the apricot and/or prune fillings, place them in pastry bags with No. 6 (12-mm) plain tips. If you are using the poppy seed filling, which has a doughlike consistency, divide it into 2 pieces, roll the pieces into ropes, using flour to prevent them from sticking, and cut each rope into 25 equal pieces.

6. Pipe about 2 teaspoons of apricot or prune filling in the center of each circle, or place a portion of poppy seed fill-

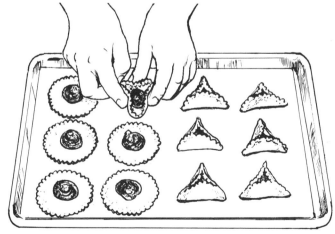

FIGURE 6-21 Folding in 3 sides of the cookie dough circle around the filling to make triangle-shaped Hamantaschen

ing in the center. Fold the sides of the dough in toward the filling to make three-cornered pastries with the filling exposed in the center (Figure 6-21). Pinch the corners to keep them from unfolding.

7. Bake at 350°F for approximately 12 minutes or until the dough is golden.

APRICOT FILLING yield: approximately 2 pounds 4 ounces (1 kg 25 g), or enough for 100 cookies

1 pound (455 g) pitted dried apricots	2 cups (480 ml) water
4 ounces (115 g) fresh pineapple, chopped	8 ounces (225 g) granulated sugar
2 cups (480 ml) fresh orange juice	

1. Place the apricots, pineapple, orange juice, and water in a saucepan. Bring to a boil, then reduce the heat. Cook over low heat, stirring occasionally, until approximately 1 cup (240 ml) of liquid remains, about 15 minutes. Stir in the sugar.

2. Process in a food processor to make a coarse paste. Chill before using.

PRUNE FILLING yield: approximately 1 pound 4 ounces (570 g), or enough for 50 cookies

12 ounces (340 g) soft pitted prunes	1 cinnamon stick
1 cup (240 ml) fresh orange juice	4 ounces (115 g) granulated sugar

1. Place the prunes, orange juice, and cinnamon stick in a saucepan. Bring to a boil, then reduce the heat. Cook over low heat, stirring from time to time, for about 15 minutes, or until approximately ½ cup (120 ml) of liquid remains. Remove the cinnamon stick. Stir in the sugar.

2. Process in a food processor to make a coarse paste. Chill before using.

POPPY SEED FILLING yield: approximately 1 pound 2 ounces (510 g), or enough for 50 cookies

5 ounces (140 g) poppy seeds	3 ounces (85 g) golden raisins
½ cup (120 ml) whole milk	Grated zest of 1 lemon
⅓ cup (80 ml) or 4 ounces (115 g) honey	6 ounces (170 g) soft almond paste (see Note)

1. Place the poppy seeds in a saucepan and add the milk and honey. Cook over low heat, stirring occasionally, until enough moisture has evaporated to thicken the mixture. Stir in the raisins and the lemon zest.

2. Remove from the heat and mix into the almond paste. Chill before using.

NOTE: If the almond paste is dry or hard, soften it by incorporating some water before mixing in the poppy seed mixture.

Cream Cheese Hamantaschen Cookies yield: 55 cookies, 3 inches (7.5 cm) in diameter

This rich version of Hamantaschen features a simple filling of apricot jam. Note that the dough for these cookies should be prepared in advance and allowed to rest in the refrigerator for at least 24 hours.

1 pound (455 g) cream cheese, at room temperature

1 pound (455 g) unsalted butter, at room temperature

3 ounces (85 g) vegetable shortening, at room temperature

12 ounces (340 g) bread flour

7 ounces (200 g) cake flour

1 teaspoon (5 g) salt

Egg wash

3 ounces (85 g) smooth apricot jam

Powdered sugar

1. Place the cream cheese, butter, and shortening in a mixer bowl. Using the paddle attachment at low speed, mix until smooth and fully combined. Incorporate the bread flour, cake flour, and salt. Scrape down the sides of the bowl and mix a few moments longer.

2. Roll out the dough, using flour to prevent it from sticking, to make a rectangle approximately ½ inch (1.2 cm) thick. Give the dough one single turn (see page 213). Place on a sheet pan lined with baking paper, cover, and refrigerate for a minimum of 24 hours.

3. Divide the dough into 2 equal pieces, 1 pound 11 ounces (765 g) each. Roll out one piece at a time to make it just slightly thicker than ⅛ inch (3 mm), using flour to prevent it from sticking. Cut out cookies, using a 3-inch (7.5-cm) plain round cutter. Place the cookies 1 inch (2.5 cm) apart on sheet pans lined with baking paper or a Silpat. Reroll the scrap dough as needed.

4. Brush egg wash over the dough circles. Fold 3 equal sides of each round in toward the center and pinch the corners. Use your thumb to make a small indentation in the middle.

5. Place the jam in a pastry bag with a small opening. Pipe a small dot of jam, about the size of a cranberry, in the indentation on each cookie.

6. Bake the cookies at 375°F (190°C) until light golden brown, about 15 minutes. Let the cookies cool; sift powdered sugar lightly over the tops. Store in an airtight container.

Chocolate-Orange Pillows yield: 72 cookies (Photo 18)

Rolling the cookies in two kinds of sugar is a bit unusual, but do not skip the granulated sugar step—it is there for a reason. Be sure that the dough is sticky so it will adhere. Without the granulated sugar coating, most of the powdered sugar will be absorbed into the dough during baking, and the desired two-tone finish will be lost.

1 pound 4 ounces (570 g) sweet dark chocolate, chopped

4 ounces (115 g) unsweetened chocolate, chopped

4 ounces (115 g) unsalted butter

7 ounces (200 g) bread flour

1½ teaspoons (6 g) baking powder

8 ounces (225 g) finely ground blanched almonds (almond meal)

6 eggs

7 ounces (200 g) granulated sugar

⅓ cup (80 ml) orange liqueur

Finely chopped zest of 4 oranges

Granulated sugar

Powdered sugar

1. Place the dark and unsweetened chocolates and the butter in a bowl. Melt together over simmering water. Set the mixture aside but keep warm.

2. Sift the bread flour and baking powder together. Stir in the ground almond meal and reserve.

3. Whip the eggs and granulated sugar to the ribbon stage. Stir in the orange liqueur and zest. Mixing with a spoon or with the paddle attachment, pour the melted chocolate mixture into the eggs and combine. Stir in the reserved dry ingredients. The dough will be soft, even runny. Refrigerate the dough for about 4 hours, or until firm.

4. Divide the dough into 6 equal pieces. Roll the pieces into 12-inch (30-cm) ropes, using flour to prevent the dough from sticking. Cut each rope into 12 equal pieces.

5. Roll the pieces into balls; then roll the balls first in granulated sugar and then twice in powdered sugar. The cookies must be thoroughly coated with powdered sugar in order to remain white after baking. Place the balls on sheet pans lined with baking paper or a Silpat. Press down on the top of each cookie just enough so that it will not roll.

6. Bake at 375°F (190°C) for approximately 20 minutes. The cookies will puff up, leaving a cracked white crust on the outside.

Raspberry Turnovers yield: 24 cookies, 3 × 1½ inches (7.5 × 3.7 cm) each

These little Swedish cookies can double as a simple pastry. Use fresh short dough that has not been rolled out previously; the dough will break as you fold it if too much flour has been mixed in. The jam should be fairly thick so it will not run when you pipe it. These turnovers taste best served the same day they are baked; the jam tends to dry out a little after a day or so. Raspberry Turnovers can be made up in large batches and stored in the refrigerator or freezer. Bake as needed directly from the freezer.

1 pound 2 ounces (510 g) Short Dough (page 67)	Crystal sugar
5 ounces (140 g) raspberry jam	Sliced almonds, crushed
Egg wash	

1. Roll out the dough to ⅛ inch (3 mm) thick. Cut out 24 cookies, using a 3-inch (7.5-cm) fluted cookie cutter.

2. Place the raspberry jam in a pastry bag. Pipe the jam onto each circle, slightly off center and toward you, dividing it evenly among the cookies.

3. Brush egg wash on the lower edge of the dough. Fold the top over the jam and onto the lower half. Press the edges together with your fingers.

4. Combine equal parts crystal sugar and almonds. Brush the tops of the turnovers with egg wash, then invert them into the almond-sugar mixture. Be sure not to get any egg wash or sugar on the bottom of the turnovers, as it will burn. Place the turnovers, right-side up, on sheet pans lined with baking paper or Silpats. Bake at 375°F (190°C) until golden brown, about 10 minutes.

Rugelach yield: 48 cookies, approximately 2¹/₂ inches (6.2 cm) each

Rugelach (also spelled *rugalach*) are cookies from eastern Europe whose name derives from the Yiddish word *rugel*, translating to "royal." Good rugelach are more chewy than flaky, so it is important that the dough not be too short. The cookies are made with several types of fillings, including various jams, poppy seed paste, and chocolate. To replace the apricot filling with chocolate filling in this recipe, combine 6 ounces (170 g) grated sweet dark chocolate, 2 ounces (55 g) grated unsweetened chocolate (or use a total of 8 ounces/225 g semisweet chocolate), 1 egg, 2 ounces (55 g) granulated sugar, and 8 ounces (225 g) crystal sugar, mixing to form a paste. If necessary, add 1 more egg (or part of one) to make the paste spreadable.

DOUGH	APRICOT-WALNUT FILLING
12 ounces (340 g) unsalted butter, at room temperature	3 ounces (85 g) walnuts
12 ounces (340 g) cream cheese, at room temperature	2 ounces (55 g) granulated sugar
6 ounces (170 g) granulated sugar	¹/₂ teaspoon (.75 g) ground cinnamon
1 teaspoon (5 g) salt	12 ounces (340 g) smooth apricot jam
2 teaspoons (10 ml) vanilla extract	Egg wash
4 egg yolks (¹/₃ cup/80 ml)	
1 pound (455 g) bread flour	

1. To make the dough, combine the butter, cream cheese, sugar, and salt in a mixing bowl. Beat until light and fluffy. Blend in the vanilla and egg yolks. Gradually add the flour and mix until just combined. Transfer the dough to a lightly floured baking table and knead gently until the dough is smooth.

2. Divide the dough into 3 equal pieces, approximately 17 ounces (485 g) each. Form the pieces into rounds, cover, and refrigerate for approximately 2 hours to relax the gluten.

3. To make the filling, place the walnuts, sugar, and cinnamon in a food processor and process until the walnuts are finely chopped.

4. Roll one of the dough rounds into a 14-inch (35-cm) circle, using flour to prevent the dough from sticking. Spread one-third of the jam over the dough. Sprinkle one-third of the nut mixture evenly over the jam.

5. Use a plain pastry wheel or a chef's knife to cut the circle into 16 equal wedges. Dip either tool into water from time to time to keep it from sticking. Starting at the wide end, roll up each wedge to the point as you would a croissant. Place the rugelach on sheet pans lined with baking paper or Silpats, placing them straight (do not bend them into half-circles like croissants).

6. Repeat Steps 4 and 5 with the remaining dough, jam, and nut mixture.

7. Brush egg wash lightly over the tops of the cookies. Bake, double-panned, at 350°F (175°C) for approximately 30 minutes or until golden brown and baked through.

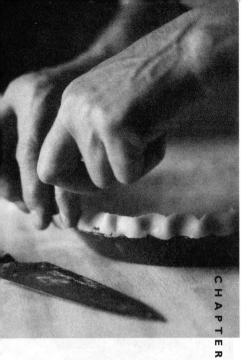

Tarts, Pies, Cobblers, and Crisps

It is a common misconception that a tart is a European type

of pie, or nothing more than a pie with a fancy name. Pies and

tarts do have some similarities. They are both made of a crust

and a filling, and they are usually baked in a metal tin.

However, the baking pan itself sets the two apart. Tart pans

are not as deep as pie pans, so they hold less filling, they have

almost straight sides, the sides are usually fluted, and the pans

do not have a lip. A tart is removed in one piece from the

baking pan. A pie, on the other hand, is cut and served from

the baking pan. Because of its fragile crust and large, mound-

ed filling, it cannot be unmolded. Because a pie will fall apart if

you try to take it out of the pan whole, pie pans have slanted

sides to make serving easier. In most cases, pies are made

with a double crust, and tarts with a single, but, actually, both can be made either way, and many of the tart and pie recipes in this chapter can be made in either style of pan. Some tarts are also made free-form and do not use a pan.

The tart pan most often used professionally is an 11-inch (27.5-cm) round, but tarts are also made in square or rectangular shapes. Tart pans can be one solid piece or two-piece false-bottomed pans; the latter make removing the baked tart easier. The tart pan is usually lined with short dough or a variation (pie dough and puff pastry are also used for some recipes). You will have a small piece of dough left over after lining the tart pans when using the amount called for in the individual recipes; it is unrealistic to work with precisely the amount of dough required, and some must be trimmed from the edges after it is fitted in the pans. In a professional kitchen, the doughs that are needed are kept as part of the regular mise en place, and the chef simply takes an approximate amount and returns the leftover to the supply.

Because a tart pan is only about 1 inch (2.5 cm) deep, it is important that the dough not be rolled out any thicker than $\frac{1}{8}$ inch (3 mm) to allow sufficient space for the filling. The shells are sometimes baked blind, which means the shell is lined with baking paper, aluminum foil, or commercial-grade plastic wrap; filled with dried beans or pie weights to prevent the dough from puffing or distorting; and fully or partially baked, depending on the filling used (directions follow). As a rule, the less time it takes to bake the filling, the longer the shells need to be prebaked. In the case of a custard filling, the shells must be completely baked through before the custard is added, even though they will go back in the oven later, because the custard is baked at such a low temperature. For tarts that are assembled and finished in a completely baked crust, you may want to waterproof the crust by coating the inside with a thin film of apricot glaze or melted coating chocolate. A thin layer of sponge cake or some leftover ladyfingers can also be placed in the bottom to absorb excess juices from fruits or moisture from the filling.

When making tarts with pie dough or puff pastry, allow a sufficient amount of resting time before baking the shells to keep the crust from shrinking. With short dough, the beans or weights are not used to prevent puffing, but to keep the sides straight. If you want the sides absolutely straight, place a circle of baking paper in the bottom of the pan only, so the beans come in contact with the dough on the sides. (The beans will stick to the crust; carefully pick them out with a fork.) Alternatively, use plastic wrap, as described on page 326. The wrap, being more flexible, will allow you to press the beans into the indentations on the sides of the fluted pan. Commercial-grade plastic wrap (the type sold for foodservice) must be used for this technique.

If you need to freeze unbaked tart shells, you can either store them frozen in the pans or remove the shells once they are frozen solid. In either case, if they are properly covered, they can be frozen for four to six weeks. If the pans are made of sheet metal (which they usually are), make sure the coating has not worn off as the metal will stain the dough if left too long.

To remove a tart from a false-bottomed tart pan, first make sure the sides are not stuck anywhere. Use the tip of a paring knife, if needed, to loosen the edge, but never run the knife around the sides. Remove the fluted ring by pushing the tart straight up from the bottom while holding on to the ring. Run a thin knife all around between the crust and the metal bottom, then slide the tart onto a serving platter or cardboard cake circle; do not attempt to lift it. If you use a one-piece pan, treat the sides in the same manner, then place a cardboard circle over the top, hold the tart with both hands, and invert it to unmold. Place your serving platter or a second cardboard circle on top (which is the bottom of the tart) and invert again. With either type of pan, the dough has a tendency to stick when cold, because the butter acts as a sort of glue. To remedy this, place a hot sheet pan or hot, damp towels on the outside of the pan to warm the butter and help loosen the crust.

In addition to being delicious, a freshly made tart looks beautiful, arranged, perhaps, with an assortment of fresh, colorful glazed fruit shining on top. A tart is elegant, which makes it appropriate for almost any occasion: as a luncheon dessert, as one of the selections on a buffet (where a fruit tart not only adds color, but offers a choice for the customer who wants something light), or even after dinner, perhaps dressed up with a sauce and decoration. With the exception of custard fillings, which should be chilled, a tart may be served warm or at room temperature but should never be served cold.

To Line a Tart Shell with Short Dough

You will need to start with 12 ounces (340 g) Short Dough (page 67) to line an 11-inch (27.5-cm) tart pan. (Instructions for lining individual tartlet shells are on page 69 and 70.)

1. Work the short dough smooth with your hands, shaping it to a thick disk in the process.

2. Start to roll out the dough to ⅛ inch (3 mm) thick and approximately 12 to 13 inches (30 to 32.5 cm) in diameter (an easy trick to check the size is to use a 12-inch (30-cm) cardboard cake circle for comparison). Sprinkle just enough bread flour on the board to keep the dough from sticking. Keep moving and turning the dough as you roll it, first with your hands and then, as the dough gets thinner, by rolling it up on a dowel. Look closely at the dough as you roll it out. If the edge of the dough is moving and not the middle, the middle is sticking to the table.

3. When the short dough is the correct size, roll the dough up on a dowel (not a rolling pin), place the tart pan in front of the dough, and, working as quickly as possible, unroll the dough over the pan (Figure 7-1).

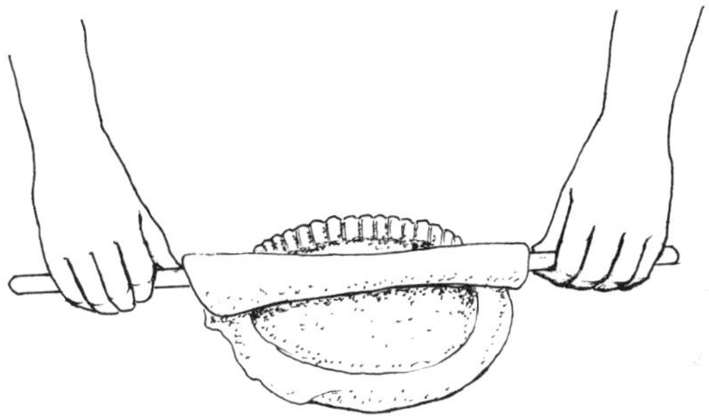

4. Pick up the edges of the dough all around to allow the dough to fall into the pan where the sides meet the bottom. Gently press the dough against the sides and bottom of the pan. Take care not to stretch the dough; when you have finished, it should still be ⅛ inch (3 mm) thick.

FIGURE 7-1 Lining a large tart shell with short dough by rolling up the dough sheet on a dowel and unrolling it over the pan

5. Roll your rolling pin over the top edge of the pan to trim away the excess dough.

6. Prick the dough lightly to be sure trapped air can escape.

Instructions for Prebaking or Blind Baking

1. After lining the pan as directed above, line the inside of the dough shell with a circle of baking paper or a sheet of commercial-grade plastic wrap that extends well up and over the sides.

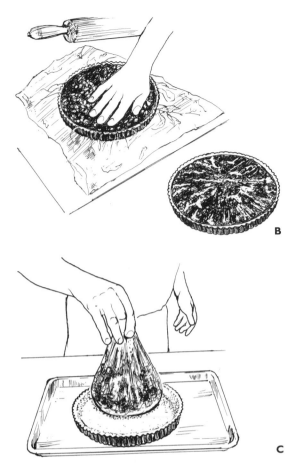

FIGURE 7-2A Pressing the beans or pie weights into the crevices on the fluted sides of a tart pan with baking paper between the weights and the uncooked dough

FIGURE 7-2B Pressing the beans or pie weights into the crevices on the fluted sides of a tart pan with a sheet of plastic wrap between the weights and the uncooked dough; the plastic folded back over the weights ensuring that it does not touch the sides of the metal pan

FIGURE 7-2C Removing the plastic wrap and pie weights after prebaking the tart shell. The plastic has softened enough to form a casing around the weights, creating a pouch that can be picked up easily and reused.

2. Fill the shell with dried beans or pie weights (see Note 1), pressing them gently into the crevices on the fluted sides of the pan (Figure 7-2A). If you use plastic wrap, which works much better than baking paper because it conforms more precisely to the shape of the fluted edges, fold the plastic back over the beans so that none of the plastic touches the metal pan (Figure 7-2B). Again, you must use commercial-grade plastic wrap for this technique (see Note 2).

3. Prebake the shell at 375°F (190°C) for about 15 minutes or until it is just starting to brown on the edges and is set (firm). Remove the beans or pie weights and the plastic or paper. If using plastic, the oven heat will have caused it to shrink into a pouch that is easy to pick up (Figure 7-2C) and can be reused two or three more times before the plastic begins to fall apart.

4. If the crust is to be baked fully (such as for a cream filling, where the tart will not be returned to the oven), return it to the oven and bake 7 to 8 minutes longer to brown the bottom and finish cooking the dough all the way through. Specific directions are given in the individual recipes.

NOTE 1: It is not necessary to use pie weights if it does not matter that the sides will settle slightly as the crust bakes. The dough settles because it is so thin and the sides of the form are almost completely straight. Lining the forms with a thicker layer of dough will prevent settling, but a thicker crust detracts from the taste of the filling in some recipes.

NOTE 2: I have used this method with several brands of commercial-grade plastic wrap with no problems. The same can not be said for some of the consumer brands which tend to melt when exposed to high heat.

To Prevent the Edges of the Tart Shell from Overbrowning

When prebaking a tart shell or when baking a tart with a filling, it is not uncommon for the top edge of the tart shell to become brown and baked through before the unfilled interior is fully set (this means you took the beans or pie weights out too late) or in the case of a filled shell, before the filling and bottom of the crust are baked. If you see this happening, use strips of aluminum foil to cover the edge of the crust, or invert the ring portion of the next larger size false-bottomed tart pan over the tart (Figure 7-3). For example, if you are baking an 11-inch (27.5-cm) tart, you would use the ring from a 12-inch (30-cm) pan; this is a quick and easy way to cover and protect the edges, provided you have several sizes of false-bottomed pans.

 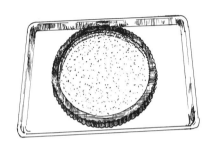

FIGURE 7-3 **Placing the metal ring from a false-bottomed tart pan over a partially baked tart or tart shell to protect the edges of the shell from becoming too dark before the base of the shell or filling are cooked through**

Apple Tart Parisienne yield: 2 tarts, 11 inches (27.5 cm) in diameter

A blowtorch can be used to brown the tarts, but be very careful in directing the flame and hold the torch far enough from the surface that you can control the browning process. Although it usually is not necessary to use dried beans or pie weights with short dough, in this recipe you want to make sure the sides do not settle during the prebaking, or you risk having the custard run between the crust and the rim of the pan.

1 pound 8 ounces (680 g) Short Dough (page 67)

3 pounds (1 kg 365 g) Granny Smith or Pippin apples (about 8 medium)

3 ounces (85 g) granulated sugar

2 ounces (55 g) unsalted butter

4 ounces (115 g) smooth apricot jam

Calvados Custard (recipe follows)

Cinnamon sugar

Powdered sugar

Crème Fraîche (page 821)

Fanned strawberry halves

1. Roll the short dough to ⅛ inch (3 mm) thick and use it to line 2 tart pans, 11 inches (27.5 cm) in diameter (see Figure 7-1, page 325). Line with baking paper or plastic wrap, then fill with dried beans or pie weights (see page 326).

2. Bake at 400°F (205°C) for about 12 minutes or until the dough is set but not colored. Do not use a double pan; place the pans directly on the oven rack. Set the shells aside to cool.

3. Peel and core the apples. Cut them into 10 wedges each.

4. Sauté the apples with the sugar and butter in a large skillet over medium heat until they begin to soften, about 10 minutes. If you do not have a skillet that is large enough to allow you to cook the apples no more than 2 layers deep in the pan, cook them in 2 batches. Set the cooked apples aside.

5. Remove the dried beans or pie weights from the cooled tart shells.

6. Divide the apricot jam between the shells and spread over the bottom. Arrange the apple wedges in concentric circles on top of the jam. Pour the Calvados custard over the apples. Sprinkle lightly with cinnamon sugar.

7. Bake the tarts at 350°F (175°C) for about 35 minutes or until the custard is set.

8. Let the tarts cool, then sift powdered sugar over the tops. Place the tarts under a salamander or hot broiler just long enough to caramelize the sugar on the apples. Be careful not to overbrown. Cut the tarts into the desired number of servings.

9. Presentation: Place a slice of tart off-center on a dessert plate. Spoon a small amount of crème fraîche in front of the slice and place a fanned strawberry on the plate behind the tart.

CALVADOS CUSTARD yield: about 5 cups (I L 200 ml)

3 ounces (85 g) bread flour

7 ounces (200 g) granulated sugar

6 eggs

1 vanilla bean *or* 1 teaspoon (5 ml) vanilla
    extract

2½ cups (600 ml) half-and-half

¼ cup (60 ml) Calvados

I. Combine the flour and sugar. Mix in the eggs and stir to make a smooth paste.

2. Cut the vanilla bean in half lengthwise and scrape out the seeds. Add the pod halves and the seeds to the half-and-half and bring the mixture to the scalding point. Remove the pod halves. Add the Calvados and vanilla extract, if used.

3. Gradually whisk the half-and-half into the egg mixture.

Caramel Toffee Almond Tart yield: 2 tarts, I I inches (27.5 cm) in diameter (Photo 2)

Like the Walnut-Caramel Tart (page 363), this dessert has a candylike filling; however, this one is more thin and crisp—closer to toffee in texture, whereas the other is chewy. Both are quite popular served unadorned or with a small scoop of ice cream or lightly whipped cream and fresh fruit.

To literally turn this into another dessert altogether, try this: Make the Soft Chocolate-Almond Glaze recipe that follows. After the tarts have cooled, unmold, invert, and place them on an icing rack. Pour the glaze over the back (bottom) of the tarts and decorate with concentric circles of small fresh raspberries. You will need about 8 ounces (225 g) per tart. You can also use the glaze to cover just the top of the tarts in the more conventional way; in that case, you will not need as much glaze.

1 pound 8 ounces (680 g) Short Dough (page 67)

3¼ cups (780 ml) heavy cream

1 pound 5 ounces (595 g) granulated sugar

2 tablespoons (30 ml) almond liqueur

2 tablespoons (30 ml) light corn syrup

13 ounces (370 g) sliced natural almonds, very lightly toasted

I. Roll out the short dough to ⅛ inch (3 mm) thick and use it to line 2 tart pans, 11 inches (27.5 cm) in diameter (see Figure 7-1, page 325).

2. Place a piece of baking paper or commercial-grade plastic wrap in each of the shells and fill with dried beans or pie weights. If using plastic wrap, fold it back over the beans to be certain it is not touching any of the metal pan.

3. Bake at 375°F (190°C) for approximately 10 to 15 minutes. Remove the plastic or paper and the weights and continue to bake about 5 to 8 minutes longer. The dough should be set and golden brown (other than on the top edge, the rest of the shell will not brown further during the time it bakes with the filling). Set the baked shells aside.

3. Combine the cream, sugar, almond liqueur, and corn syrup in an oversized saucepan (the mixture will bubble up considerably). Bring to a boil and cook to 230°F (110°C), stirring and scraping down the sides of the pan frequently; the mixture should be thickened and just beginning to caramelize. Remove from the heat and stir in the almonds.

4. Immediately divide the filling between the shells and spread it evenly using a metal spatula to flatten the surface and make sure the almonds are evenly distributed.

5. Bake at 375°F (190°C) for 20 to 25 minutes using a double pan. The tops of the tarts should be dark golden brown and the filling should be bubbling in the center as well as around the edges. Let cool to room temperature before serving.

> **CHEF'S TIP**
> Just in case you get the same idea that I had and consider making the filling ahead to save time, I can save you the trouble and tell you that it does not give a good result. The almonds become soggy and, instead of crisp almonds floating in toffee, you will end up with a one-dimensional, gummy filling.

SOFT CHOCOLATE-ALMOND GLAZE yield: about 3 cups (720 ml)

12 ounces (340 g) sweet dark chocolate, chopped

8 ounces (225 g) clarified butter

⅓ cup (80 ml) or 4 ounces (115 g) light corn syrup

1 tablespoon (15 ml) almond liqueur

I. Melt the chocolate over a bain-marie. Remove from the heat and add the butter, stirring until fully incorporated. Stir in the corn syrup and the almond liqueur.

2. Use immediately or cover and store until needed. If made ahead, reheat gently before using.

Cherry Meringue Tart with Rhubarb Sauce (Photo 45)

yield: 16 servings, 4¹/₂ × 2¹/₄ inches (11.2 × 5.6 cm) each

This is truly a case of the whole being greater than the sum of its parts—the relatively few ingredients come together delectably. If you serve this dessert in late spring or early summer, when the first fresh cherries become available, I guarantee rave reviews.

Preparing the tarts in 4½-inch (11.2-cm) forms and serving a half-tart per person allows you to expose the filling in the presentation, which would not be the case if you made individual tarts and served a whole tart to each guest. The other typical alternative, making standard 11-inch (27.5-cm) tarts and serving a wedge on each plate, shows off the filling but is more commonplace. See Chef's Tip for other presentation ideas.

1 pound 8 ounces (680 g) Short Dough (page 67)	Apricot Glaze (page 5)
3 ounces (85 g) smooth apricot jam	¼ recipe Italian Meringue (page 27) (see Note)
12 ounces (340 g) fresh cherries (10 ounces/285 g pitted)	Rhubarb Sauce (page 831)
Almond-Kirsch Filling (recipe follows)	70 fresh cherries, stems attached

CHEF'S TIP

The tarts can be prepared through Step 3 one or two days in advance and stored in the refrigerator. Bake and top with meringue the day they are to be served. Reserve at room temperature after browning the meringue. For a different presentation, bake the tarts in 16 fluted tart pans, 3½ inches (8.7 cm) in diameter, and use a whole tart for each serving. Present the tart cut in half and garnished with 5 or 6 fresh cherries (one cut to expose the pit) arranged between the pieces. The recipe can also be used to make a single tart, 11 inches (27.5 cm) in diameter. The larger tart will require about 15 minutes longer baking time. When cutting the large tart into the desired number of serving pieces, do not forget to dip your knife in hot water before each cut so as to be able to slice cleanly through the meringue.

1. Roll out the short dough to ⅛ inch (3 mm) thick and use it to line 8 tart pans, 4½ inches in diameter by ¾ inch high (11.2 × 2 cm) (see Figure 7-1, page 325). Pipe the apricot jam into the bottom of the shells, dividing it equally among them. Spread the jam out to cover the base of the shells.

2. Cut the cherries into halves and quarters. Divide them evenly over the bottom of the shells.

3. Place the almond kirsch filling in a pastry bag with a No. 4 (8-mm) plain tip. Pipe the filling on top of the cherries, dividing it evenly among the tarts.

4. Bake the tarts at 375°F (190°C) for approximately 25 minutes or until light brown and baked through. Let the tarts cool completely.

5. Remove the tarts from the forms. Brush the apricot glaze over the tops.

6. Place the meringue in a pastry bag with a No. 4 (8-mm) plain tip. Pipe a spiral of meringue covering the top of each tart. Start the first ring about ⅛ inch (3 mm) from the outside edge and overlap each previous ring halfway to mound the meringue slightly higher in the center. Brown the meringue under a hot broiler or salamander or by very carefully using a blowtorch.

7. Presentation: Cover the base of a dessert plate with rhubarb sauce. Cut a tart in half, using a serrated knife dipped in hot water to keep the meringue from sticking to the knife. Use a rocking motion as you cut to prevent the crust from breaking. Place one half in the center of the plate.

Place 4 or 5 fresh cherries next to the cut side of the tart. Serve immediately to prevent the bottom of the crust from becoming soft from the sauce.

NOTE: It is important to use a small pan when making only a quarter-recipe of Italian meringue, or it becomes almost impossible to get an accurate reading from the sugar thermometer because there is so little syrup in the pan. Easier still is to make ½ recipe and discard half of the finished meringue. The cost of the small amount of egg whites and sugar lost is not as valuable as your time.

ALMOND-KIRSCH FILLING yield: 1 pound 10 ounces (740 g)

8 ounces (225 g) Pastry Cream (page 845)

5 ounces (140 g) unsalted butter, at room temperature

4 ounces (115 g) granulated sugar

2 egg yolks

¼ cup (60 ml) kirschwasser

2 ounces (55 g) cornstarch

6 ounces (170 g) finely ground blanched almonds

1. If the pastry cream is cold (right out of the refrigerator), warm it gently over a bain-marie, stirring constantly, then pass it though a sieve. Set aside at room temperature. If you are making pastry cream fresh for this recipe and it is still warm, skip this step.

2. Mix the butter and sugar together. Incorporate the egg yolks and kirschwasser. Beat at medium speed until the mixture is light and fluffy.

3. Combine the cornstarch and ground almonds. Add to the butter mixture. Stir in the pastry cream.

Chocolate–Pine Nut Tart

yield: 2 tarts, 11 inches (27.5 cm) in diameter, or 60 miniature pastries, 1⅝ inches (4.2 cm) in diameter

Instead of making tarts, you can use this filling to make delicious, gooey, brownie-like bars. Pour the filling into a half-sheet pan lined with baking paper and spread it out evenly. Bake at 375°F (190°C) for about 35 minutes; let cool, then cut into pieces of the desired size. This offers a good alternative to and a change of pace from regular brownies.

1 pound 8 ounces (680 g) Short Dough (page 67)

12 ounces (340 g) sweet dark chocolate

3 ounces (85 g) unsweetened chocolate

8 ounces (225 g) unsalted butter

Grated zest of 2 oranges

6 ounces (170 g) toasted pine nuts

6 ounces (170 g) plus 2 teaspoons (10 g) granulated sugar

6 egg yolks (½ cup/120 ml)

¼ cup (60 ml) orange liqueur

6 egg whites (¾ cup/180 ml)

1 teaspoon (5 g) salt

4 ounces (115 g) smooth apricot jam

8 ounces (225 g) Ganache (page 842)

1 cup (240 ml) heavy cream

Orange Sauce (page 828)

Chocolate Sauce for Piping (page 820)

1. Roll out the short dough to ⅛ inch (3 mm) thick and use it to line 2 tart pans, 11 inches (27.5 cm) in diameter (see Figure 7-1, page 325). Reserve in the refrigerator.

2. Place the dark chocolate, unsweetened chocolate, butter, and orange zest in a bowl. Melt together over simmering water. Set aside but keep warm.

3. Reserve 2 ounces (55 g) pine nuts for garnish. Grind the remainder with 3 ounces (85 g) sugar to a fine flourlike consistency (be careful not to grind beyond this point or you will get an oily paste).

4. Whip the egg yolks to the ribbon stage. Add the orange liqueur.

5. Whip the egg whites and the salt to a foam. Gradually add another 3 ounces (85 g) sugar and whip to soft peaks. Do not overwhip, or the additional air will cause the tart to crack while baking.

6. Combine the nut mixture with the chocolate. Add the egg yolks, then carefully fold in the egg whites.

7. Spread the apricot jam over the bottom of the lined pans. Divide the chocolate filling between them.

8. Bake at 350°F (175°C) for approximately 35 minutes. Let the tarts cool.

9. Carefully remove the tarts from the pans. Warm the ganache until it is melted and liquid, then spread it quickly over the top of the tarts. Before it starts to set up, sprinkle the reserved pine nuts on top. Chill briefly to set the ganache.

10. Slice the tarts into the desired number of pieces. Whip the heavy cream with the 2 teaspoons (10 g) sugar to stiff peaks. Place in a pastry bag with a No. 7 (14-mm) star tip and reserve in the refrigerator.

11. Presentation: Pour a round pool of orange sauce on one side of a dessert plate. Pipe a pea-sized dot of whipped cream on the opposite side of the plate and set a tart slice on the whipped cream (to prevent it from sliding) so that the tip is in the sauce. Pipe a large rosette of whipped cream on the wide end of the tart. Decorate the orange sauce with chocolate sauce for piping, as shown on pages 809 to 814.

INSTRUCTIONS FOR USING FLEXIPAN NO. 1489 TO MAKE SMALL PASTRIES

1. Omit the short dough and Step 1 of the above instructions.

2. Follow the directions for making the filling in Steps 2 through 6.

3. Sprinkle a few of the reserved pine nuts in each indentation of the Flexipan (you will need additional pine nuts).

4. Place the filling in a pastry bag with a medium-size plain tip and pipe into the indentations of the pan (unless you have 2 pans, you will have batter left over to bake a second partial batch, as the pan has only 48 indentations).

5. Bake at 350°F (175°C) for about 15 minutes. Be careful not to overbake. Let cool, then place the Flexipan in the refrigerator or freezer before unmolding. Serve the pastries inverted to expose the pine nuts.

Clafoutis with Cherries yield: 2 tarts, 11 inches (27.5 cm) in diameter (Photo 10)

Clafoutis is a derivative of the French word *clafir*, which translates to "fill." The dessert is famous in the Limousin region of central France, where it originated. Clafoutis is actually a type of fruit pancake and does not normally have a short dough crust. I have added a crust to make it more practical to cut and serve, and to improve the taste by providing a contrasting texture. While cherries are the most commonly used fruit for clafoutis, other fruits that are suitable for baking, such as apricots, blueberries, and plums, can be substituted. Regardless, this tart should be served the same day it is baked, and there is really no reason not to because it is so simple and quick to make, especially if the shell is prepped ahead. Both cherries and blueberries will bleed and stain the custard around them if the tarts are left overnight.

1 pound 8 ounces (680 g) Short Dough (page 67)

1 ounce (30 g) flour

12 ounces (340 g) granulated sugar

6 eggs

1 cup (240 ml) heavy cream

1½ cups (360 ml) whole milk

1 pound 4 ounces (580 g) cherries, pitted and halved

Romanoff Sauce (page 831)

Whole cherries, stems attached

1. Roll out the short dough ⅛ inch (3 mm) thick and use it to line 2 tart pans, 11 inches (27.5 cm) in diameter (see Figure 7-1, page 325). Prick the dough lightly and place a piece of baking paper in each of the shells.

2. Fill the pastry shells with dried beans or pie weights and prebake at 375°F (190°C) for approximately 10 minutes. Remove the paper and the weights and continue to bake about 2 minutes longer. The dough should be set and golden but not browned.

3. Combine the flour and sugar. Mix in the eggs and cream with a whisk.

4. Scald the milk, then gradually whisk the hot milk into the first mixture. Reserve.

5. Divide the cherries between the two shells, arranging them, cut-side up, on top of the crust. Gently pour the custard over the cherries (see Note).

6. Bake the tarts at 350°F (175°C) for approximately 30 minutes or until the custard is set. Cool at room temperature.

7. Remove the tarts from the pans and cut into serving pieces of the desired size, using a serrated knife to cut through the cherries.

8. Presentation: Place a slice of clafoutis on a dessert plate. Pour Romanoff sauce over one-third of the tart on the narrow end. Set 2 or 3 whole cherries next to the slice. Serve at room temperature.

NOTE: It is best to place the tart shells next to the oven before you pour in the custard so you will be moving them as little as possible after filling. If the custard runs between the crust and the pan, the tarts will be difficult to remove later. One method that works well is to fill the shells only partway with custard, set them in the oven, then top off with the remaining custard. All custards shrink after they are baked, so the tarts should be filled as close to the top as practical without overflowing.

Italian Pear, Almond, and Cranberry Tart yield: 2 tarts, 11 inches (27.5 cm) in diameter (Photo 42)

A cornmeal crust gives this tart its distinctive taste and provides a nice contrast to the soft, juicy pears inside. If you do not plan to serve the tarts the same day they are baked, eliminate the top crust; the pears will cause it to become soggy if left overnight. Alternatively, you can prep the tarts ahead of time through Step 6, then bake them a few hours before they are to be served. If you opt to leave off the top crust, slice the pear halves lengthwise and fan them slightly as you place them on the filling. Sprinkle the cranberries between the pears. Let the baked tarts cool completely, then brush Apricot Glaze (page 5) or Pectin Glaze (page 30) over the tops before slicing.

12 medium pears (approximately 4 pounds/1 kg 820 g)

1 tablespoon (15 ml) whole black peppercorns

1½ recipes Spiced Poaching Syrup (page 31)

2 pounds 12 ounces (1 kg 250 g) Cornmeal Crust (page 71)

1 pound 12 ounces (795 g) Frangipane Filling (page 842)

3 ounces (85 g) dried cranberries

Powdered sugar

½ recipe Cranberry Coulis (page 821)

1 ounce (30 g) pistachios, blanched, skins removed, and coarsely chopped

Edible flowers

1. Peel the pears and cut them in half. Place the pears in acidulated water as you work to keep them from browning (oxidizing).

2. Crush the peppercorns and add them to the poaching syrup. Add the pear halves and poach until they begin to soften, but do not cook them all the way through. Remove from the heat and set aside to steep for at least 30 minutes.

3. Roll a portion of the cornmeal crust to ⅛ inch (3 mm) thick and use it to line 2 tart pans, 11 inches (27.5 cm) in diameter (they do not need to be false-bottomed; see Figure 7-1, page 325). Reserve the leftover dough. (See Note.)

4. Remove the pear halves from the poaching liquid. Remove the cores (I use a melon ball cutter for this). At the same time, look for and discard any peppercorns that are stuck to the pears. Blot the pears dry.

5. Divide the frangipane filling between the tart shells and spread it out evenly. Sprinkle the dried cranberries over the filling. Arrange 10 pear halves, cut-side down, in a circle on each tart. The stem end of the pears should point to the center of the circle, and the pears should be close, but don't force them together. Arrange the 4 remaining pear halves, 2 per tart, in the center of the circles, with the stem end of one half next to the bottom end of the other.

6. Roll the remaining cornmeal crust to ⅛ inch (3 mm) thick. Drape it over the top of the tarts and press the edges together to make them adhere firmly. Cut away any excess dough from the edges.

7. Bake the tarts at 375°F (190°C) directly on the hearth for about 30 minutes or until they are light brown on top. Let cool to room temperature. Remove from the pans, then cut into the desired number of pieces.

8. Presentation: Sift powdered sugar lightly over a tart slice and place in the center of a dessert plate. Pour a pool of cranberry coulis in front and sprinkle pistachios on top of the sauce. Place an edible flower on the plate next to the tip of tart.

NOTE: If your oven does not have a hearth, you should prebake the empty shells at this point. However, if you are using baking paper to line the shells, you may need to refrigerate them before placing the baking paper and adding the pie weights, depending on the texture of your dough. If you line the shells with plastic wrap they will not need to be chilled (see page 325 and 326). Do not overbake the dough; it should be just set and not yet beginning to brown. Bake the filled tart pans directly on the oven racks; do not set them on a sheet pan.

Linzer Tart yield: 2 tarts, 11 inches (27.5 cm) in diameter

The descent of this famous tart is somewhat obscure, but one can generally assume that it originated in the town of *Linz*, which is located in upper Austria on the banks of the river Danube. The Danube, which has inspired so many great pieces of music, majestically flows eastward, traveling through the birthplaces of two other well-known pastry creations: Vienna, home of the Sacher Torte, and Budapest, where the Dobos Torte was introduced.

Ground nuts, spices, citrus peels, and jam magically combine in the irresistible Linzer tart. I use hazelnuts, but almonds and even walnuts are featured in many recipes. Distinctly, the dough is piped into the pans, an eminently practical technique. Linzer tarts are great for making ahead and can be refrigerated or frozen either baked or before baking. It is actually preferable to bake the tarts the day before they are to be served, because the nuts in the crust, being hygroscopic, will not only absorb moisture from the air, but also from the jam, making the pastry more moist the next day.

If you experience the problem of the jam filling boiling over on the sides, burning, and looking messy, the best remedy (assuming you are not using too much jam) is to simply lower the heat so that the jam does not boil so vigorously. The most important thing, though, is to use a high-quality raspberry preserve to begin with.

1 pound 6 ounces (625 g) unsalted butter, at room temperature	1 pound 6 ounces (625 g) finely ground hazelnuts
1 pound 4 ounces (570 g) granulated sugar	1 tablespoon (18 g) grated lemon zest
3 eggs, at room temperature	1 pound 4 ounces (570 g) raspberry preserves
1 tablespoon (8 g) unsweetened cocoa powder	Powdered sugar
2 teaspoons (3 g) ground cinnamon	2 ounces (55 g) pistachios, blanched, skins removed, and finely chopped
1 teaspoon (2 g) ground cloves	
1 pound (455 g) plus 2 ounces (55 g) cake flour	

1. Cream the butter and granulated sugar together until light and fluffy. Add the eggs, 1 at a time.

2. Sift together the cocoa powder, cinnamon, cloves, and 1 pound (455 g) cake flour. Mix in the ground hazelnuts and the lemon zest, then incorporate this mixture into the butter mixture.

3. Weigh out 2 pounds 4 ounces (1 kg 25 g) dough; mix in the remaining 2 ounces (55 g) cake flour. Reserve this portion of the dough at room temperature.

4. Place the remaining dough in a pastry bag with a No. 3 (6-mm) plain tip. Pipe the dough over the bottom of 2 tart pans, 11 inches (27.5 cm) in diameter, starting at the outside edge and making concentric circles to cover the pans; use all of the paste (see Figure 1-5, page 29, as an example).

5. Bake at 375°F (190° C) for approximately 15 minutes, until the crust just starts to color. Remove from the oven and let cool slightly.

6. Divide the raspberry preserves evenly between the pans and spread over the crust, leaving a ¼-inch (6-mm) border uncovered around the outside.

7. Place the reserved dough in the pastry bag with the No. 3 (6-mm) plain tip. Pipe straight parallel lines, ½ inch (1.2 cm) apart, across each tart. Then pipe a second set of parallel lines at a 45-degree angle to the first set. Lastly, pipe a pearl pattern (see Figure 10-28, page 480) around the border of the tarts. Adjust the pattern to the amount of paste you have left; if necessary, stretch the piping a bit.

8. Bake at 375°F (190°F) for approximately 25 minutes or until the tarts have a pleasant brown color on top. Let cool.

9. Center a cardboard cake circle, 9 inches (22.5 cm) in diameter, on top of one tart. Sift powdered sugar over the exposed edge of the tart. Remove the cardboard and sprinkle the chopped pistachios around the inside edge of the powdered sugar. Repeat with the second tart.

VARIATION

LINZER BARS yield: I sheet, 12 × 16 inches (30 × 40 cm), or 48 bars, 4 × 1 inch (10 × 2.5 cm)

Follow the recipe and instructions above, making the following changes:

- Use only 1½ ounces (40 g) additional flour instead of 2 ounces (55 g) and add it to only 2 pounds (910 g) dough.

- Spread the remaining dough over the bottom of a half-sheet pan (12 × 16 inches/30 × 40 cm) lined with baking paper or a Silpat, evenly covering the entire pan.

- After baking the crust, spread the jam over the whole surface; do not leave a ¼-inch/6-mm border uncovered.

- Do not pipe a pearl pattern border around the edge.

- Bake the sheet 5 to 10 minutes longer than the tarts.

- Omit the pistachios.

- When cool, trim the edges and cut into 48 individual pieces.

Mandarin Tart with Armagnac yield: 2 tarts, 11 inches (27.5 cm) in diameter

This is a tart that I make during the winter months, when fresh berries are scarce and expensive but citrus fruits are plentiful, juicy, and reasonably priced. Because this recipe uses a thin layer of sponge cake, it is a sensible choice should you have leftover sponge from another project. But don't wait for that to try this refreshing combination.

The Almond Sponge Cake is very quick to make, so rather than just making the amount needed for the tarts, it is a good idea to make the full recipe and freeze the extra. It will keep for several weeks if properly covered, and it is always good to have handy. I have on many occasions found myself out of Armagnac and have substituted Cognac (or even brandy) without much noticeable difference in flavor, but perhaps the name should be changed.

½ recipe Almond Sponge Cake batter
(page 438)

1 pound 8 ounces (680 g) Hazelnut Short
Dough (page 68)

1 recipe Red Currant Glaze (page 33)

1 pound 8 ounces (680 g) Pastry Cream
(page 845)

¼ cup (60 ml) Armagnac

⅓ cup (80 ml) mandarin or orange juice

12 Satsuma mandarins (see Note)

Raspberry Sauce (page 830)

Sour Cream Mixture for Piping (page 832)

1. Line the bottom of a cake pan, 10 inches (25 cm) in diameter, with a circle of baking paper. Pour the sponge batter into the pan and spread it out evenly. (The diameter of the sponge will be a little smaller than that of the tarts, but this is insignificant.)

2. Bake at 400°F (205°C) for about 10 minutes. Set aside to cool.

3. Roll out the hazelnut short dough to ⅛ inch (3 mm) thick and use it to line 2 tart pans, 11 inches (27.5 cm) in diameter (see Figure 7-1, page 325). Cover the dough with baking paper or commercial-grade plastic wrap and fill with dried beans or pie weights.

4. Bake at 375°F (190°C) for approximately 18 minutes or until the edges are golden brown. Immediately remove the paper or plastic and the weights, then return to the oven to finish baking the bottom if necessary. Let the shells cool.

5. Brush red currant glaze over the base and slightly up the sides of the cooled shells; reserve the remaining glaze.

6. Place one-quarter of the pastry cream in each of the shells and spread it out over the glaze, covering the bottom of the shells.

7. Cut the top one-third of the cake, cutting it even at the same time, and reserve for another use. Slice the remaining cake into 2 layers horizontally. Place 1 sponge in each shell on top of the pastry cream.

8. Combine the Armagnac with the mandarin or orange juice. Brush the juice over the sponges. Spread the remaining pastry cream evenly on top.

9. Peel and section the mandarins, taking great care to remove all of the white membrane. Separate the segments by hand instead of cutting them out with a knife as you would oranges. Make concentric circles of fruit, starting at the edge of the tarts (see Chef's Tip).

10. Warm the reserved currant glaze (stir in a little water if it seems too thick) and brush on top of the mandarin segments. Cut the tarts into the desired number of slices.

11. Presentation: Place a slice of tart slightly off-center on a dessert plate. Pour a pool of raspberry sauce in front of the slice and decorate the sauce with the sour cream mixture for piping (see pages 809 to 814).

NOTE: If mandarins are not available, substitute seedless tangerines or oranges; you will need about 8 oranges. For a quick and colorful fruit tart, arrange other assorted fresh fruits (including some mandarins as desired) in concentric circles on top of the pastry cream; brush with glaze as directed.

CHEF'S TIP
If you know the number of servings you will be cutting the tarts into, mark the top of the custard accordingly, then arrange the fruit on top within the lines. This allows you to avoid having to cut through the fruit or possibly push it into the custard as you cut the tarts.

Mandarin Tarts with Cointreau Custard **yield: 12 tarts, 4¹/₂ inches (11.2 cm) in diameter**

These little mandarin tarts are irresistible and a great winter alternative to tarts using berries when they are out of season and so expensive. Satsuma mandarins are my favorite not only for eating out of hand, but also for pastries. They are virtually seedless and their distinctive "zipper skin" pulls away easily, revealing the easy-to-separate segments. There is no such thing as a mandarin that is always completely seedless, but Satsumas and clementines can have few or none. I have found, however, that clementines can be quite unreliable.

As good as mandarins are, try replacing the mandarin segments with a poached and fanned pear half (see Small Pear Tartlets with Caramel Sauce, page 680). The Cranberry Coulis is a fitting complement to the pears as well. When plums and apricots come into season, they are also a great choice. By substituting fresh cherries for the mandarin segments, you are basically making my version of clafouti.

Because of their small size, the tart shells do not need to be blind baked initially, but it is important that they receive proper bottom heat.

2 pounds (910 g) Short Dough (page 67)	Apricot Glaze (page 5)
6 medium Satsuma mandarins, peeled, seeded, and sectioned	Piping Chocolate (page 465), melted
½ recipe Cointreau Custard (page 344)	Cranberry Coulis (page 821)
12 fresh or frozen cranberries	Sour Cream Mixture for Piping (page 832)
	12 small mint leaves

1. Line 12 false-bottomed tart pans, 4½ inches (11.2 cm) in diameter, with short dough rolled ⅛ inch (3 mm) thick (see Figures 2-4 to 2-7, pages 69 and 70).

2. Arrange 5 mandarin segments in a fan shape in the bottom of each form. Skim the foam from the top of the Cointreau custard, then divide the custard among the forms, filling them almost to the top. Place a cranberry in the center of each tart.

3. Carefully place the tarts in a 350°F (175°C) oven and bake for approximately 35 minutes or until the custard is set and the short dough is light brown on the top and around the perimeter. Remove them from the oven and let cool.

4. Brush a thin layer of apricot glaze over the tops of the cooled tarts.

5. Decorate the number of dessert plates you anticipate needing by piping 4 straight lines of piping chocolate, ½ inch (1.2 cm) apart, across the center of each plate.

6. Presentation: Place the cranberry coulis in a piping bottle. Cover the lower half of one of the prepared plates with sauce, being careful not to get any sauce beyond the chocolate border (do not cover the chocolate lines with sauce). Place the sour cream mixture for piping in a piping bag and pipe 3 or 4 lines in the cranberry coulis parallel to the chocolate lines. Pull a small wooden skewer through the lines at a 90-degree angle to make a wavy pattern (see Figure 6-4, page 270). Place a tart above the sauce on the chocolate lines. Decorate with a mint leaf.

About Swiss Chard

Swiss chard is a member of the beet family but looks more like celery. There are three variations of chard, all of which are also called Swiss chard: the so-called rhubarb chard, which has reddish stalks; ruby chard, which has bright red stalks and leaves; and the type called for in this recipe (which is the one usually meant by "Swiss chard"), which has silvery white stalks and dark green, crunchy leaves. This last and best-known type also has a milder flavor than the other two varieties. Do not throw away the stalks; though they are not needed here, they can certainly be put to use in the hot kitchen.

Mediterranean Tart with Chard and Apples yield: 2 tarts, 11 inches (27.5 cm) in diameter

This is my version of a classic recipe from the south of France that I first tasted while working with François Payard at the Culinary Institute of America at Greystone a few years back. You might also want to try the more traditional French variation, substituting ricotta cheese for the pastry cream (or half of each). If you do, you will have to add some sugar to the recipe. Admittedly, it is not all that common to find a vegetable in a pastry filling, but when you think of the well-known and delicious pies and cakes made with rhubarb, pumpkins, butternut squash, carrots, and beets, perhaps this will not seem quite as unusual.

6 ounces (170 g) golden raisins, plumbed

¼ cup (60 ml) dark rum

1 pound 6 ounces (625 g) Cornmeal Crust (page 71)

10 ounces (285 g) Puff Pastry (page 74)

1 pound 8 ounces (680 g) fresh green-leaf Swiss chard

4 medium Granny Smith apples (about 1 pound 8 ounces/680 g total)

2 pounds 4 ounces (1 kg 25 g) Pastry Cream (page 845)

4 ounces (115 g) almond flour

4 ounces (115 g) pine nuts

Powdered sugar

1. Combine the raisins with the rum, cover, and allow to macerate for a minimum of 2 hours or, preferably, overnight.

2. Roll out a portion of the cornmeal dough to ⅛ inch (3 mm) thick, using flour to prevent the dough from sticking. Use the dough to line a tart pan, 11 inches (27.5 cm) in diameter. Repeat rolling the dough and lining a second pan.

3. Divide the puff pastry into 2 equal pieces. Roll out each piece to a rectangle measuring 12 x 6 inches (30 x 15 cm) and approximately ⅛ inch (3 mm) thick. Cover the dough pieces and refrigerate.

4. Using a paring knife, remove the stems and the large center vein in the leaves from the Swiss chard. Discard the veins and save the stems to use for another application. You should have 8 to 10 ounces (225 to 285 g) leaves remaining. Wash the leaves, blanch in boiling water for 3 minutes, shock in ice water, and squeeze out as much water as possible. Chop the chard coarsely and reserve.

5. Peel the apples, core, and cut into ¼-inch (6 mm) dice.

6. Place the pastry cream in a bowl and stir in the almond flour. Fold in the diced apples,

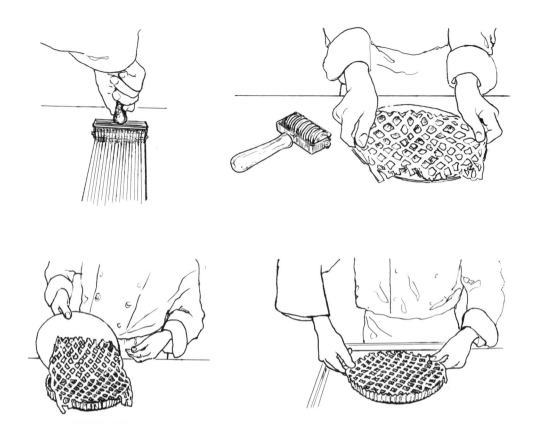

FIGURE 7-4 Using a lattice cutter: rolling the tool over a sheet of dough; stretching the perforated dough on top of a cardboard cake round; sliding the stretched dough sheet off of the cardboard and on top of the tart; sealing the edges of the lattice top to the sides of the tart and pinching off the excess dough

followed by the pine nuts, the raisins with rum, and the Swiss chard. Divide the filling evenly between the prepared tart shells.

7. Roll a lattice cutter lengthwise over the reserved puff pastry strips. Stretch them and use them to cover the tops of the tarts (Figure 7-4). Trim and reserve the scraps for another use.

8. Bake the tarts at 325°F (163°C) for approximately 45 minutes or until the filling has firmed somewhat and the dough has browned. Let cool.

9. Sift powdered sugar lightly over the tops and cut into the desired number of pieces.

NOTE: If you do not have a lattice cutter, follow the directions for making a lattice design on page 368.

Meyer Lemon Tarts with Lemon-Verbena Whipped Cream and Blood Orange Segments

yield: 16 tartlets, 4¹⁄₂ inches (11.2 cm) in diameter, or 3 tarts, 10 inches (25 cm) in diameter

These Mediterranean-inspired tarts can easily be transformed into plated desserts by serving them with a sauce or coulis made from blood oranges or raspberries and a crunchy garnish made from Hippen paste or Florentina batter. When serving the 4¹⁄₂-inch (11.2-cm) tarts as part of an assortment for afternoon tea or on a buffet display, cut them into 4 small wedges; decorate each wedge with whipped cream, using the Saint-Honoré tip as directed, and one small orange segment (do not use blood oranges for this type of display, because they will bleed into the whipped cream after a short time). As they say, "Necessity is the mother of invention," and as my students never seem to have enough tiny forms or enough time to make the required number of miniature pastries, this technique solves both problems. The tarts wedges should be cut, or at least plated or arranged, as close to serving time as possible because, unlike a tart baked in a tartlet form, the cut sides are exposed and will dry out easily.

Both Meyer lemons and blood oranges are plentiful and popular in the Mediterranean, especially in Spain, France, and Italy. Lemon verbena, as we usually refer to it in the United States, is also known simply as *verbena*. It is native to Chile and was brought back to Europe, like so many plants and spices, by early explorers returning from sea voyages. Its currently increasing popularity will, I hope, restore this fragrant, lemon-flavored herb to its former glory.

1 ounce (30 g) lemon verbena leaves	Meyer Lemon Filling (recipe follows)
3 cups (720 ml) heavy cream	Segments from 5 blood oranges
2 tablespoons (30 g) granulated sugar	
Brown Sugar Crust (recipe follows) *or* 1 recipe Cornmeal Crust (page 71), chilled	

1. Chop the lemon verbena leaves finely. Place in a saucepan with the cream and sugar. Bring to a quick boil while stirring. Pour the mixture into a container, cover, and cool to room temperature. Refrigerate for a minimum of 8 hours or, preferably, overnight.

2. Roll out the chilled brown sugar or cornmeal crust to slightly thicker than ¹⁄₈ inch (3 mm) and line the bottoms and sides of 16 round tart pans, 4¹⁄₂ inches in diameter by ³⁄₄ inch high (11.2 x 2 cm); lining 4 at a time works well. Prick the dough on the bottom of the pans. Place a small piece of commercial-grade plastic wrap in each pan, then fill the pans with dried beans or pie weights. Fold the excess plastic back toward the center of the pan on top of the beans or pie weights, making certain that the plastic does not touch the metal pan.

3. Bake the tarts shells at 375°F (190°C) until the crust is golden brown around the edges, approximately 12 minutes. Remove the beans or pie weights by picking up each plastic pouch. Return the shells to the oven to finish baking the crust on the bottoms, about 5 minutes longer.

4. Make the filling while the crust is baking. Divide the filling equally among the tart shells as soon as they come out of the oven. Return the tarts to the oven, lower the temperature to 350°F (175°C), and bake about 15 minutes longer or until the filling has thickened. Let cool completely.

5. Strain the leaves from the reserved cream by passing the mixture through a coarse strainer; small pieces of lemon verbena should be visible in the cream. Whip the cream to stiff peaks. Place in a pastry bag with a Saint-Honoré tip. Pipe a curved design in the center of each tart. Decorate each tart with 2 blood orange segments.

BROWN SUGAR CRUST yield: 2 pounds (910 g)

10 ounces (285 g) unsalted butter, at room
    temperature
8 ounces (225 g) light brown sugar

1 egg
13 ounces (370 g) bread flour

1. Place the butter, brown sugar, and egg in a mixing bowl. Mix at low speed, using the dough hook attachment, until the ingredients are just combined.

2. Add the flour and continue to mix until the dough is smooth, scraping down the sides of the mixing bowl once or twice. Do not mix any longer than necessary.

3. Refrigerate the dough until it is firm enough to work with.

MEYER LEMON FILLING yield: about 6 cups (1 L 440 ml)

4 tablespoons (32 g) cornstarch
1 pound 8 ounces (680 g) granulated sugar
12 whole eggs
4 egg yolks (1/3 cup/80 ml)

Finely grated zest of 4 Meyer or standard
    lemons
2 1/2 cups (600 ml) Meyer lemon juice

1. Stir the cornstarch into the sugar. Mix in the eggs, egg yolks, lemon zest, and lemon juice, stirring until the ingredients are well combined. Do not whip or beat the mixture.

2. Place the mixing bowl over a bain-marie and heat, stirring constantly, until the filling has thickened; do not overheat.

Nectarine Meringue Tart with Rhubarb

yield: 12 servings, 4 1/2 x 2 1/4 inches (11.2 x 5.6 cm) each (Photo 53)

Here the word *tart*, which has two meanings—a type of pie and a sour flavor—applies both ways. The slightly acidic, sour taste of rhubarb combines beautifully with sweet Italian meringue, providing the base for this refreshing dessert. Nectarines have a fairly short season; try replacing them with either plums or peaches when they are not available. My preference is to leave the skin on fruit whenever possible to provide color. Because most commercial peaches are gently scrubbed to remove their unwanted fuzz before they are shipped, chances are you will not have to blanch them and remove the skin. When none of the above are available, another excellent choice is strawberries, which are a classic accompaniment to rhubarb. If you do not have rectangular tart forms, use two 9-inch (22.5-cm) round false-bottomed pans instead.

1 pound 8 ounces (680 g) Hazelnut Short Dough (page 68)

½ recipe Apricot Glaze (page 5)

1 pound 12 ounces (795 g) fresh rhubarb stalks

1 ounce (30 g) cornstarch

¼ cup (60 ml) cold water

4 ounces (115 g) granulated sugar

½ recipe Italian Meringue (page 27)

6 medium-sized ripe nectarines (approximately 1 pound 12 ounces/ 795 g)

Piping Chocolate (page 465), melted

Raspberry Sauce (page 830) or Strawberry Sauce (page 832)

Edible flowers

1. Line 2 false-bottomed tart pans, 14 x 4½ inches (35 x 11.2 cm), with hazelnut short dough rolled to ⅛ inch (3 mm) thick (see Figure 7-1, page 325). Cover the bottom and sides of pans with baking paper or commercial-grade plastic wrap. Fill the pans with dried beans or pie weights.

2. Bake the tart shells at 375°F (190°C) until the dough starts to firm up and feel done, approximately 15 minutes. Remove the paper or plastic and the beans. If necessary, return the shells to the oven and continue baking until the bottoms of the shells are baked through.

3. Remove from the oven and let cool. Remove the shells from the pans. Brush apricot glaze over the insides of the shells. Reserve the leftover glaze.

4. Wash the rhubarb and trim both ends off each stalk. Chop the stalks into small pieces and place in a saucepan. Dissolve the cornstarch in the cold water and add it to the rhubarb along with the sugar. Cook over medium heat until the rhubarb falls apart and the mixture thickens to a jamlike consistency. This will take about 45 minutes; you should be left with 1¾ to 2 cups (420 to 480 ml) reduced rhubarb.

5. Divide the rhubarb mixture between the tart shells. Spread the Italian meringue in an even layer over the rhubarb. Use a serrated scraper or decorating comb to decorate the meringue, forming a wavy pattern.

6. Brown the meringue lightly under a broiler or salamander, or use a torch. Cut each tart across into 6 slices. Dip the knife in water before each cut to keep the meringue from sticking to the knife.

7. Cut the nectarines in half (see Note). Cut each half into 5 or 6 small, neat wedges. Arrange the wedges at an angle on top of each tart slice, using 1 nectarine half per serving. Adjust the consistency of the remaining apricot glaze and brush over the nectarine wedges.

8. Presentation: Place the piping chocolate in a piping bag and pipe chocolate in a zigzag pattern over half of the base of a dessert plate. Place a tart slice in the center of the plate so that half of it is on the piped lines. Pour a pool of raspberry or strawberry sauce on the undecorated part of the plate. Place edible flowers next to the sauce.

NOTE: Because in most cases nectarines are not a freestone fruit, cut them in the following manner to produce precise, attractive wedges with clean edges. Start by cutting the halves away from the center of the fruit by making 2 cuts about ¼ inch (6 mm) away from and parallel to the natural crease in the center. This will leave the stone and the surrounding fruit in a separate third piece. Trim the fruit away from the stone and use it for ice cream, sorbet, or nectarine-plum crisp. The half-rounds can then be set flat-side down and cut into attractive wedges (do not make slices).

Pear Tart with Cointreau Custard yield: 2 tarts, 11 inches (27.5 cm) in diameter

Because the filling in these tarts is quite fluid, it is important that the shells are prebaked correctly. Too much patching of the dough while lining the pans, or overbaking the shells, will make the dough susceptible to cracks where the thin custard can run out during baking. Refer to the blind baking instructions on page 325 and 326, and use commercial-grade plastic wrap rather than baking paper in the prebaking. If you do need to make repairs, dab a little egg white over the crack, then press some fresh short dough on top before you arrange the fruit or add the custard (see Note following Clafoutis with Cherries, page 333).

1 pound 8 ounces (680 g) Short Dough (page 67)

1 pound 8 ounces (680 g) pears (about 6 medium)

Cointreau Custard (recipe follows)

1 recipe Plain Poaching Syrup (page 31)

Cinnamon sugar

Apricot Glaze (page 5) or Pectin Glaze (page 30)

Whipped cream (optional)

1. Line 2 false-bottomed tart pans, 11 inches (27.5 cm) in diameter, with short dough rolled to ⅛ inch (3 mm) thick (see Figure 7-1, page 325). Prick the dough lightly with a fork. Line the bottom and sides of the shell with plastic wrap, fill with dried beans or pie weights, and fold the edges of the plastic back over the weights so the plastic does not touch the metal pan.

2. Bake at 375°F (190°C) just until golden, about 12 minutes. Let cool, then remove the plastic and the weights.

3. Peel and core the pears and cut them in half lengthwise; place them in acidulated water to prevent them from becoming brown (oxidizing). Poach the pear halves in the poaching syrup until they are tender (see page 32 for instructions).

4. When you are ready to assemble the tarts, slice the pears lengthwise, cutting them to about ½ inch (1.2 cm) from the stem end, leaving the stem intact. Fan the sliced pear halves and arrange them on top of the crust in each shell with the stem ends in the center.

5. Gently pour the Cointreau custard around the fruit, dividing it evenly between the shells.

6. Sprinkle cinnamon sugar over 2 or 3 circles of the fruit, creating alternating rings.

7. Bake at 350°F (175°C) until the custard is set, about 30 minutes.

8. When the tarts have cooled enough so that they will not break when you handle them, remove them from the pans and glaze with apricot or pectin glaze. Slice and serve at room temperature. If you like, pipe whipped cream at the edge of each slice.

COINTREAU CUSTARD yield: 4¾ cups (1 L 140 ml)

12 egg yolks (1 cup/240 ml)

7 ounces (200 g) granulated sugar

4 cups (960 ml) heavy cream

¼ cup (60 ml) Cointreau

1. Beat the egg yolks and sugar by hand for a few seconds, just to combine.

2. Add the cream and Cointreau and blend thoroughly.

APPLE TART WITH CALVADOS CUSTARD

Follow the directions in the main recipe, substituting apples for the pears and preparing the custard with Calvados instead of Cointreau. Slice the apple halves crosswise and cut all the way through. (Do not leave the slices attached at one end.) Fan the apple slices and arrange them in concentric circles within the shells, starting at the outside edge.

Pear-Frangipane Tart yield: 2 tarts, 11 inches (27.5 cm) in diameter (Photo 38)

The combination of poached pears or apples baked with creamy, almond-flavored frangipane filling in a short dough crust is a French classic. You will find some variation—sometimes the pears are poached in red wine, or the fruit might be sliced lengthwise instead of crosswise, for example—in just about every pâtisserie in France. The French versions are usually topped with an apricot glaze, but I place the apricot jam in the bottom of the tart instead to keep the crust from becoming soggy. This type of dessert originated in the Normandy region. A close relative is the classic Tarte Bourdaloue, which is itself a derivation of the dessert Bourdaloue, which contains poached pears in vanilla frangipane covered in crushed macaroons.

The tarts should be sold or presented to the table whole before they are sliced (just as with the Swedish Apple Tart, page 356), as quite a bit of the visual appeal is lost once the portions are cut. Although it would make for the most attractive servings, cutting the tart into 6 pieces, so that each slice contains a perfect pear half makes for a more than generous portion. I think going the other direction, cutting through the center of each pear half to make 12 servings, is a better idea.

6 Bartlett pears, stems intact	1 ounce (30 g) thinly sliced natural almonds
1 recipe Plain Poaching Syrup (page 31)	Cinnamon sugar
1 pound 8 ounces (680 g) Short Dough (page 67)	Simple syrup
5 ounces (140 g) apricot jam	Powdered sugar
2 pounds (910 g) Frangipane Filling (page 842)	

1. Peel the pears, cut in half lengthwise (including the stems), and place in a saucepan with the poaching syrup. Place a plate on top to keep the pears submerged and simmer until they are tender (see page 32 for more information on poaching fruit). Remove from the heat and let the pears cool in the syrup.

2. Line 2 false-bottomed tart pans, 11 inches (27.5 cm) in diameter, with short dough rolled to ⅛ inch (3 mm) thick (see Figure 7-1, page 325).

3. Divide the jam between the tart shells and spread it out evenly. Divide the frangipane on top and spread it out evenly over the jam.

4. Remove the pears from the poaching liquid and blot dry. Remove the cores and the inside portion of the stems with a

> **CHEF'S TIP**
>
> You cannot move the sliced pear halves once you set them down on the filling without making a mess, and spacing them evenly is sometimes more difficult than you might think. A little trick to help ensure that the pears are evenly spaced is to place the poached halves on top of the filling before slicing them, arranging them in their appropriate positions. Then, one at a time, pick up each pear half, slice and fan it, slide a palette knife underneath, and return it to its original spot.

melon ball tool, leaving the actual stems intact. Cut each pear half crosswise into thin slices and arrange the sliced halves, slightly fanned, within the tarts (6 halves per tart), evenly spacing them on the filling, flat-side down, alternating them stem-end up and stem-end down (see Chef's Tip). Sprinkle the sliced almonds around the pears and sprinkle a band of cinnamon sugar over each pear half.

5. Bake at 375°F (190°C) for 35 to 40 minutes. Cover the edges if they become too brown. Brush simple syrup over the pear halves and let cool. Remove the tarts from the pans. Lightly sift powdered sugar over the tops and brush the pears with syrup again if needed. Cut into the desired number of serving pieces.

Pecan-Whiskey Tart yield: 2 tarts, 11 inches (27.5 cm) in diameter

This is basically an American pecan pie dressed up a little for restaurant service. It is fabulous served warm with a scoop of vanilla ice cream, but as it is one of my favorites, I wouldn't turn a piece down at any temperature. If you prefer not to use alcohol, substitute orange juice for the whiskey.

1 pound 8 ounces (680 g) Short Dough (page 67)
Pecan Filling (recipe follows)
Dark coating chocolate, melted
1 pint (480 ml) heavy cream

1 tablespoon (15 g) granulated sugar
2 tablespoons (30 ml) whiskey
Pecan halves
Mint sprigs

1. Line 2 tart pans, 11 inches (27.5 cm) in diameter, with short dough rolled ⅛ inch (3 mm) thick (see Figure 7-1, page 325). Reserve the shells in the refrigerator while you make the filling.

2. Divide the pecan filling evenly between the shells.

3. Bake at 350°F (175°C) for approximately 35 minutes or until the filling is firmly set. Let cool completely.

4. Unmold the tarts. Place a small amount of melted coating chocolate in a piping bag (see page 56) and cut a very small opening. Decorate the tarts by streaking the chocolate across in thin parallel lines. Turn the tart 90 degrees and repeat the procedure to create lines going in the opposite direction (Figure 7-5). As you streak the chocolate across the tarts, move quickly, alternating left to right and right to left, overlapping the edge of the tart on both sides. Cut the tarts into the desired number of pieces.

5. Whip the cream, sugar, and whiskey to very soft peaks; reserve in the refrigerator.

6. Presentation: Place a tart slice on a dessert plate. Spoon a small mound of cream onto the plate next to the slice. Stand a pecan half in the cream and place a mint sprig next to it.

FIGURE 7-5 Streaking chocolate over Pecan-Whiskey Tart by quickly moving back and forth across the top in both directions, overlapping the edges, to create decorative lines

PECAN FILLING yield: enough for 2 tart shells, 11 inches (27.5 cm) in diameter

8 eggs, at room temperature

13 ounces (370 g) light brown sugar

½ cup (120 ml) or 6 ounces (170 g) light corn syrup

½ cup (120 ml) or 6 ounces (170 g) molasses

1 teaspoon (5 g) salt

1 teaspoon (5 ml) vanilla extract

¼ cup (60 ml) whiskey

3 ounces (85 g) melted unsalted butter

1 pound 4 ounces (570 g) pecans, roughly chopped

I. Whisk the eggs just to break them up, about 1 minute.

2. Mix in the brown sugar, corn syrup, molasses, salt, vanilla, and whiskey.

3. Stir in the melted butter and the pecans.

Pink Grapefruit and Orange Tart yield: 2 tarts, 11 inches (27.5 cm) in diameter

Citrus is an excellent (and often necessary) choice when making a fresh fruit tart during the early months of the year. In many establishments, strawberries are the only berry affordable (or available at all), and many times their quality is way below par. Pink grapefruit, which can be found in the market just about all year round, not only looks good but is very good for you, providing one of nature's best sources of vitamin C with very few calories. (I must point out, however, that to get the maximum amount of vitamins you must eat the whole grapefruit segment, including the membrane, which is removed in this recipe.) Look, or perhaps I should say feel, for grapefruit that are heavy and firm to the touch, with smooth-textured skin. I prefer the Star Ruby to the March Pink and Ruby Red. They are all pretty much free of seeds, but the Star has a deeper red (pink) flesh, and the reddish-gold peel is also very attractive. Bear in mind that, just as with blood oranges, the color of the peel is not an indication of the color or ripeness of the interior flesh in any of the grapefruit varieties.

Regular short dough can be used instead of the cornmeal crust and, if you have pastry cream sitting around with nowhere to go, stir orange liqueur into it and use it instead of the orange custard.

1 pound 8 ounces (680 g) Cornmeal Crust (page 71)

Orange Custard Filling (recipe follows)

4 pink grapefruits, in segments (see Figure 1-2, page 13)

6 oranges, in segments (see Figure 1-2, page 13)

Pectin Glaze (page 30) or Apricot Glaze (page 5)

Dark coating chocolate, melted

Lime Cream (page 845)

Long strips of lime zest

I. Line 2 false-bottomed tart pans, 11 inches (27.5 cm) in diameter, with cornmeal crust rolled to ⅛ inch (3 mm) thick (see Figure 7-1, page 325). Prick the dough lightly over the bottom of the pans. (If the dough has become soft at this point, place the shells in the freezer for a few minutes until firm.) Place a circle of baking paper in each one to cover the bottom and the sides of the crust (or use commercial-grade plastic wrap). Fill with dried beans or pie weights.

2. Bake the shells at 375°F (190°C) until the edges are golden, about 12 minutes. Remove the baking paper or plastic and the weights. Place the shells back in the oven and continue baking for approximately 10 minutes or until the bottom is set.

3. Divide the orange custard filling evenly between the shells. They should be about two-thirds full.

4. Bake at 350°F (175°C) until the custard is set, about 30 minutes. Let cool completely.

5. Remove the tarts from the pans and set them on cardboard cake circles. Cut or mark into the desired number of serving pieces. Arrange the grapefruit and orange segments on the tarts, placing the fruit at an angle within the marks for each slice. Brush pectin or apricot glaze over the fruit.

6. Presentation: Place melted dark coating chocolate in a piping bag and streak lines of chocolate over the upper half of a dessert plate. Place a tart slice on the other side of the plate at a 45-degree angle to the lines, with the tip of the tart on the first few lines. Pour a small pool of lime cream to the left of the tart. Twist a strip of lime zest into a spiral and set it on the cream.

ORANGE CUSTARD FILLING yield: 4¹/₂ cups (I L 80 ml)

12 egg yolks (1 cup/240 ml)	3¹/₃ cups (800 ml) heavy cream
6 ounces (170 g) granulated sugar	3 tablespoons (45 ml) orange liqueur

1. Beat the egg yolks and sugar together to combine.

2. Mix in the cream and liqueur.

Pizza-Style Apple Tart yield: 2 tarts, I I inches (27.5 cm) in diameter

This is basically a galette in disguise (see page 562 for more information), and a wonderful, simple treat that can be varied in many ways. You could, for example, substitute pears for the apples or spread a thin layer of Pastry Cream (page 845) or Almond Macaroons batter (page 292), or a combination of the two, over the dough before placing the fruit on top. To make individual pizzas, roll the puff pastry out to make a rectangle measuring 12 x 24 inches (30 x 60 cm). Let the dough relax; then, using a 6-inch (15-cm) cookie cutter or appropriately sized saucer as a guide, cut out 8 rounds. You will need a few extra apples and, preferably, you should use smaller apples for the small tarts, which will make it easier to arrange the slices attractively.

1 pound (455 g) Puff Pastry (page 74)	Granulated sugar
4 large Granny Smith apples, approximately 2 pounds 8 ounces (1 kg 135 g)	Cider Glaze (recipe follows)

1. Divide the puff pastry into 2 equal pieces. Using flour to prevent the dough from sticking, roll out one portion to make a 12-inch (30-cm) square, approximately ¹/₈ inch (3 mm) thick. Roll up the dough on a dowel and unroll on a sheet pan lined with baking paper or a Silpat (place the square on one side of the pan so the second piece will fit as well). Use the fluted edge of the ring from a false-bottomed tart pan, 11 inches (27.5 cm) in diameter to cut an 11-inch (27.5-cm) circle out of the dough. Remove the scraps and reserve for another use. Repeat with the remaining piece of dough so you have 2 circles on the pan. Prick the dough thoroughly and place the pan in the refrigerator or freezer until the dough is very cold.

2. Peel and core the apples. Using a mandoline, slice the apples as thinly as possible while still keeping the slices intact. Place the apple slices in acidulated water as you are working to prevent them from browning. When all the apples are sliced, place the slices on towels and quickly blot them dry.

3. Remove the puff pastry from the refrigerator or freezer. Beginning ½ inch (1.2 cm) from the outside edge of one pastry circle, arrange apple slices in concentric circles, overlapping each slice about halfway and just barely overlapping each row. Repeat with the second tart. Sprinkle granulated sugar over the top of each tart.

4. Bake immediately at 450°F (230°C) for 10 to 15 minutes. Remove from the oven and reduce the oven temperature to 375°F (190°C). Brush cider glaze lightly over the fruit; you will not use all of it. If the pastry is becoming too brown around the edges, cover it with foil or place an inverted ring from a false-bottomed tart pan on top to protect the edges.

5. Return the tarts to the oven and continue baking until the apples have caramelized on the edges and the pastry is baked through. Brush the remaining glaze over the tarts as soon as you remove them from the oven. Let cool at room temperature for 10 minutes. Cut into wedges to serve.

CIDER GLAZE yield: approximately ¾ cup (180 ml)

1 cup (240 ml) apple cider	1 vanilla bean
1 cinnamon stick, broken in half	4 ounces (115 g) granulated sugar

1. Place the cider and cinnamon stick pieces in a heavy saucepan. Split the vanilla bean lengthwise. Scrape out the seeds and thoroughly combine with the sugar to break up lumps of the seeds. Add the vanilla sugar and the pod to the cider mixture.

2. Cook over medium to low heat for 5 minutes, stirring frequently, or until the mixture thickens to a syrupy consistency. Remove the vanilla bean pod and cinnamon stick pieces.

3. Warm the glaze before brushing it on the tarts if it is made ahead of time. It will be too thick if it is at room temperature or chilled.

Quince Custard Tart yield: 2 tarts, 11 inches (27.5 cm) in diameter

It did not take me long to realize that most Americans do not care all that much for quince. Part of the reason, I think, is that they have never been exposed to this fruit. When I talk about quince at school, the majority of my students look somewhat bewildered, as if they are trying to figure out what it is I said (they probably think they missed something because of my accent). I am hoping that, if nothing else, your curiosity will tempt you to try this great dessert. The slightly tart custard filling contrasts perfectly with the sweet meringue and, if you are like me, a scoop of vanilla or caramel ice cream completes the picture beautifully.

As an alternative to a dressed-up tart, quince can also be enjoyed baked or caramelized as a simple country-style dessert. To make baked quince, peel, and core 2 quinces and cut each one into 6 wedges. Arrange in a single layer in a small baking dish. Add ½ cup (120 ml) orange juice and 1 ounce (30 g) melted butter. Sprinkle 5 ounces (140 g) granulated sugar on top. Bake at 375°F (190°C) for about 40 minutes or until tender. For caramelized quince, cut in half lengthwise after peeling and coring, then slice across ¼ inch (6 mm) thick. Place the slices in a skillet with 5 ounces (140 g) granulated sugar, 1 ounce (30 g) butter, and ½ cup (120 ml) heavy cream. Cook over medium heat, turning the fruit frequently, until the quince is tender and the liquid has been reduced to a caramel. Enjoy baked or caramelized quince with your favorite ice cream.

1 pound 8 ounces (680 g) Short Dough (page 67)

2 pounds 10 ounces (1 kg 195 g) quinces (about 6 medium)

1 recipe Plain Poaching Syrup (page 31)

½ teaspoon (1 g) grated nutmeg

½ teaspoon (.75 g) ground cinnamon

2 ounces (55 g) bread flour

2 ounces (55 g) melted unsalted butter

2 teaspoons (10 ml) lemon juice

6 egg yolks (½ cup/120 ml)

4 ounces (115 g) granulated sugar

2 cups (480 ml) half-and-half

¼ recipe Italian Meringue (page 27) (see Note, page 331)

1. Roll out the short dough to ⅛ inch (3 mm) thick and line 2 false-bottomed tart pans, 11 inches (27.5 cm) in diameter (see Figure 7-1, page 325).

2. Peel, core, and quarter the quinces. Poach in the poaching syrup until tender. Remove the fruit from the liquid and reserve the poaching liquid for another use, such as cake syrup. Puree the cooked quinces; you should have about 2 cups (480 ml). Add the nutmeg, cinnamon, bread flour, melted butter, and lemon juice to the puree.

3. Whip the egg yolks with the sugar until thick and foamy. Stir into the quince mixture together with the half-and-half. Divide the filling between the prepared tart shells.

4. Bake at 425°F (219°C) for 10 minutes. Reduce the heat to 350°F (175°C) and continue baking until the custard is set, approximately 30 minutes. Remove from the oven and set aside to cool.

5. Divide the Italian meringue evenly between the tarts. Spread it out to cover the filling, making swirls and tips by moving your spatula up and down. Brown the meringue using a salamander, broiler, or blowtorch.

6. Cut the tarts into the desired number of pieces, using a thin chef's knife. Dip the knife in hot water to keep the meringue from sticking.

Raspberry-Lemon Tart yield: 2 tarts, 11 inches (27.5 cm) in diameter

Do not miss out on trying this very pretty tart when fresh raspberries are plentiful and inexpensive. Fresh blueberries, ripe and bursting with flavor, make a great substitute. For a very colorful presentation, use a combination of the two. When using blueberries alone, reserve ¼ cup (60 ml) lemon cream and brush it over the top of the baked and cooled tarts before adding the blueberries, or they have a tendency to roll off.

1 pound 8 ounces (680 g) Short Dough (page 67)

½ recipe or 3½ cups (840 ml) Lemon Cream (page 844)

1 dry pint (480 ml) fresh raspberries

Softly whipped cream

Thin strips of lemon zest

1. Line 2 false-bottomed tart pans, 11 inches (27.5 cm) in diameter, with short dough rolled to ⅛ inch (3 mm) thick (see Figure 7-1, page 325). Place a circle of baking paper in each pan to cover the bottom and sides (or use a sheet of commercial-grade plastic wrap) and fill with dried beans or pie weights.

2. Bake at 375°F (190°C) to a light golden, not brown, color, about 12 minutes. Cool to room temperature.

3. Remove the paper or plastic and the weights from the cooled tart shells. Divide the lemon cream evenly between the shells.

4. Bake at 375°F (190°C) until the filling is just set, about 15 minutes; the filling will set a little more as it cools.

5. Let the tarts cool completely, then remove them from the pans and slide onto cake cardboards. Cut (or mark, if presenting whole) into the desired number of pieces.

6. Arrange the raspberries on the surface of each slice, placing them within the markings for each piece so that they will not be cut when the tart is sliced. To preserve the natural satin look of the raspberries, do not rinse or glaze them.

7. Presentation: Place a tart slice in the center of a dessert plate. Spoon softly whipped cream over the tip of the slice and onto the plate. Place 2 or 3 strips of lemon zest on the cream.

VARIATION

FIG TART yield: 2 tarts, 11 inches (27.5 cm) in diameter

1 pound 8 ounces (680 g) Short Dough (page 67)	24 fresh green or black figs, quartered lengthwise
¾ recipe or 5¼ cups (1 L 20 ml) Lemon Cream (page 844)	Softly whipped cream

1. Follow the preceding directions in Steps 1, 2, and 3.

2. Arrange the figs on top of the lemon cream, cut-side up, making concentric circles and spacing the fig quarters about ¼ inch (6 mm) apart.

3. Bake as instructed for Raspberry-Lemon Tart.

4. Presentation: Place a tart slice in the center of a dessert plate. Spoon softly whipped cream over the tip of the slice and onto the plate.

NOTE: You can also make 12 tarts, 4½ inches (11.2-cm) in diameter, using the same amount of dough and figs, but you will need only ½ recipe or 3½ cups (840 ml) lemon cream.

Rustic Plum and Blueberry Tart yield: 2 tarts, 10 inches (25 cm) in diameter

This rustic tart is basically another form of galette. It is a very quick-to-produce summer treat that you can make using just about any variety of fruit you have on hand. And don't be afraid to try another type of dough; the recipe works equally well with puff pastry or pie dough. If you decide to use short dough or cornmeal crust, you may want to skip chilling the dough circles in Step 1. If you must chill them because the dough is overly soft, allow the dough circles to soften partially before you fold the edge back against the fruit or the dough will break. In any event, it is important to bake the tarts (on the sheet pan) directly on the hearth of the oven or, if this is not possible, place the sheet pan where it will get the maximum amount of bottom heat. Do not over bake as this will cause the fruit to expand and the tart will crack.

1 recipe or 2 pounds 4 ounces (1 kg 25 g)
   Cream Cheese Pie Dough (page 64)

4 pounds (1 kg 820 g) firm, dark red plums,
   such as Santa Rosa

1 pound (455 g) fresh or frozen blueberries

3 ounces (85 g) bread flour

6 ounces (170 g) granulated sugar

½ teaspoon (1 g) grated nutmeg

Finely chopped zest of 2 lemons

3 tablespoons (45 ml) lemon juice

Seeds from 1 vanilla bean

2 ounces (55 g) unsalted butter, melted

Powdered sugar

1. Divide the pie dough into 2 equal pieces. Form the pieces into rounds and roll them out, 1 at a time, to make 2 circles, 14 inches (35 cm) in diameter and approximately ⅛ inch (3 mm) thick. Leave the edges rough rather than trimming them into perfect circles. Place the dough circles on a sheet pan lined with baking paper or a Silpat and place in the refrigerator.

2. Wash, pit, and quarter the plums (if you are using a particularly large variety, cut them into eighths). Combine the plum pieces, blueberries, flour, sugar, nutmeg, lemon zest, lemon juice, seeds from the vanilla bean, and the melted butter, mixing the filling thoroughly.

3. Remove the dough circles from the refrigerator. Allow to soften a bit if they are quite firm so that the dough will not break when you fold it over. Place a 10 x 2-inch (25 x 5-cm) cake ring in the center of one dough circle to serve as a guide. Mound half of the fruit filling in the ring, then remove the ring. Fold the edges of dough in toward the filling, pleating the edges and leaving the center uncovered. Repeat with the second dough circle and the remaining filling.

4. Bake at 400°F (205°C), preferably with the sheet pan directly on the hearth of the oven, for approximately 40 minutes. Let cool slightly.

5. Sift powdered sugar over the top of the tarts. Serve warm.

Strawberry-Kiwi Tart yield: 2 tarts, 11 inches (27.5 cm) in diameter

I made a version of this tart on the PBS series "Cooking at the Academy," using a rainbow of fresh seasonal fruit. I could have kicked myself later for not remembering to caution viewers about the different ways of arranging fruit on a tart, taking into consideration whether the tarts are to be cut and plated or presented whole. I often observe students arranging the fruit in a beautiful pattern without realizing what is going to happen to that carefully assembled creation once the tart is cut into 12 or more pieces, which is a typical buffet portion. Although cutting through the thin slices of kiwi in this tart may not pose a problem, it is always a good idea to plan ahead, and this extra step does not take much time or effort. It is especially important when working with fruit that should not be cut, such as raspberries, blackberries, and blueberries. First, mark the top of the custard into the number of slices desired. It is then easy to arrange the fruit within the marks so that you can later cut the tart without cutting into or ruining the design.

To mark 16 servings on an 11-inch (27.5-cm) round tart, begin by marking a circle in the center of the tart using a 5-inch (12.5-cm) plain cookie cutter. Next, mark the tart (including the center circle) into quarters. Lastly, mark each of the quarters around the outside ring (excluding the circle) into 3 equal pieces. You now have 16 pieces that, being short and wide, are easy to decorate. When you are ready to cut the tart, use the cookie cutter as a guide for your paring knife to cut the center.

1 pound 8 ounces (680 g) Short Dough (page 67)	**4 kiwis, peeled and thinly sliced crosswise (instructions follow)**
Apricot Glaze (page 5)	**20 strawberries, cut in half lengthwise**
3 pounds 14 ounces (1 kg 765 g) or ⅔ recipe Pastry Cream (page 845)	

1. Line 2 false-bottomed tart pans, 11 inches (27.5 cm) in diameter, with short dough rolled to ⅛ inch (3 mm) thick (see Figure 7-1, page 325). Line with circles of baking paper or sheets of commercial-grade plastic wrap to cover the bottom and sides, then fill with dried beans or pie weights.

2. Bake at 375°F (190°C) until light golden, about 12 minutes. Remove the paper or plastic and the weights. Place the shells back in the oven for about 6 to 8 minutes longer or until they are pale brown on the bottom. Let cool.

3. Brush apricot glaze over the bottom and sides of the cooled shells. Reserve the remaining glaze to use later.

4. Divide the pastry cream equally between the tart shells and spread it out evenly. If possible, it is best to make the pastry cream fresh so you can pour it into the shells while it is still warm (not hot). It will adhere to the sides of the crust nicely. If you do use it warm, let the pastry cream cool before adding the fruit.

5. Remove the tarts from the pans and place on serving platters or on cardboard rounds for support. Arrange sliced kiwis in the center and the strawberries around the edge. Reheat the apricot glaze (you may need to add a small amount of water). Brush the glaze over the top of the tarts. Cut the tarts into the desired number of slices.

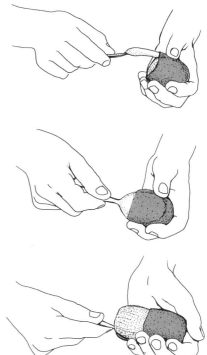

INSTRUCTIONS FOR PEELING KIWIFRUIT WITH A SPOON

A great way to peel kiwis and still retain their oval shape is to use an oval soupspoon, preferably one with a thin sharp edge. For this to work properly, the fruit must be ripe but not soft. Cut off the top and bottom of the kiwi. Carefully and gradually insert the spoon between the skin and the flesh. Hold the kiwi in your palm and gradually slide the spoon all the way around between the skin and the flesh, making 2 or 3 turns as you push the spoon through to the bottom of the kiwi. Pull the spoon out (Figure 7-6). You will have a perfectly smooth kiwi with its natural shape and a minimum of wasted fruit instead of a kiwi that resembles a potato peeled with a large knife.

FIGURE 7-6 Inserting a spoon between the skin and the flesh of a kiwi; gradually pushing the spoon to the bottom of the kiwi while turning the kiwi at the same time; after twisting the spoon all the way around inside the skin, pulling the spoon out to remove the peeled kiwi

Strawberry-Rhubarb Tart yield: 2 tarts, 11 inches (27.5 cm) in diameter

The combination of tangy rhubarb and sweet strawberries is not only delicious, but also looks pretty framed with dough strips in a diamond pattern. The cornmeal crust adds a robust flavor to this country-style tart. Short dough could be used as well, however, flaky pie dough lacks the sweetness needed. The use of cornstarch and pectin helps to keep the crust from getting soggy from the fruit juices, as does the almond meal (go ahead and use cake crumbs if necessary). It is of utmost importance that the filling is allowed to cool before adding it to the baked crust.

4 pounds (1 kg 820 g) rhubarb stalks

2 tablespoons (16 g) cornstarch

3 tablespoons (24 g) pectin powder

12 ounces (340 g) granulated sugar

2 pounds 8 ounces (1 kg 135 g) or ½ recipe Cornmeal Crust (page 71)

2 ounces (55 g) finely ground almonds or almond meal

20 medium strawberries

Pectin Glaze (page 30)

Romanoff Sauce (page 831) or Crème Fraîche (page 821)

1. Trim off the top and bottom of the rhubarb stalks and discard. You might want to peel the stalks at this point. I only feel this necessary if they are over 1 inch (2.5 cm) thick since I like the color the skin provides. Cut the stalks into ½-inch (1.2 cm) cubes.

2. Stir the cornstarch and pectin powder into the sugar. Add the rhubarb cubes and mix well. Set aside for about half an hour to drain some of the juice out of the rhubarb.

3. Cook the rhubarb mixture over low heat until soft but not falling apart. Strain off the liquid. You might want to save the liquid to make a sauce for a variation of this recipe (instructions follow), use it for cake syrup, or discard it. Set the rhubarb aside to cool.

4. Roll out a portion of the cornmeal crust ⅛ inch (3 mm) thick and use it to line 2 tart pans, 11 inches (27.5 cm) in diameter (see Figure 7-1, page 325). Reserve the remaining dough (see Note). Line the pans with baking paper or commercial-grade plastic film and fill with dried beans or pie weights. If using plastic, fold it back over the beans so that none of the plastic touches the metal pan.

5. Bake at 375°F (190°C) until the dough is set but has not yet started to brown, approximately 8 minutes.

6. Roll the remaining cornmeal crust into a rectangle measuring 11 inches (27.5 cm) wide and ⅛ inch (3 mm) thick. Transfer the dough to a sheet pan or a piece of corrugated cardboard and reserve in the refrigerator.

7. Remove the paper or plastic and the weights from the prebaked shells. Return the shells to the oven a bit longer to bake the bottom of the crust. Allow them to cool. Sprinkle the finely ground almonds over the bottom of the shells, then divide the rhubarb evenly on top.

8. Cut 24 strips, ⅜ inch (9 mm) wide, from the chilled refrigerated dough.

9. Arrange 12 strips, evenly spaced, on top of each tart, first placing 6 in one direction, then 6 on top at a 45-degree angle to the first set, to form a diamond pattern (see Figure 12-30, page 600). Brush egg wash on the first layer of strips before placing the second layer on top. Then brush additional egg wash on the second layer.

10. Return the tarts to the oven and bake at 375°F (190°C) until the cornmeal crust strips are golden brown, approximately 10 minutes. Let the tarts cool to room temperature.

11. Rinse the strawberries, trim off the tops (a melon ball tool is excellent for this), and slice them lengthwise into 6 pieces each. Place the strawberry slices in the diamonds between the cornmeal crust strips.

12. Brush the tops of the tarts with apricot glaze to preserve the fresh look of the berries. Cut the tarts into the desired number of serving pieces.

13. Presentation: Place a slice in the center of a dessert plate. Spoon Romanoff sauce or crème fraîche over the tip of the slice and let some run onto the plate. Serve at room temperature.

N O T E : If you have puff pastry available, try this variation for an even prettier finished look:

1. Roll 12 ounces (340 g) puff pastry out to the same size as specified for the remaining cornmeal crust in Step 6.

2. Brush egg wash on top of the cornmeal crust and place the puff pastry rectangle on top. Roll a dowel or rolling pin across the top to be certain the 2 sheets of dough are attached.

3. Continue as directed, cutting the decorative strips from the double layer of dough. Twist the strips as shown in Figure 12-17 (page 584), before placing them on the tarts.

VARIATION

STRAWBERRY-RHUBARB MERINGUE TART yield: 2 tarts, 11 inches (27.5 cm) in diameter (Photo 10)

Topping fruit desserts with Italian meringue is classic in Europe. The meringue gives the dessert a clean, finished look, and the sweet flavor contrasts beautifully with acidic fruits, especially rhubarb. Browning the meringue adds to the visual appeal. Do not pipe and brown the meringue more than 3 hours prior to serving; ideally, it should be done to order—à la minute. If you are presenting the tarts whole, glaze the rhubarb with pectin glaze, then pipe rosettes of meringue using a No. 6 (12-mm) star tip around the perimeter only. Or for a distinctive modern look, use a Saint-Honoré tip, piping the wedges in a curved pattern toward each other around the edge, so the rhubarb remains visible (see Photo 10). Serve the rhubarb meringue tart warm or at room temperature.

1. Follow the directions for Strawberry Rhubarb Tart (page 354) through Step 5, using only 1 pound 8 ounces (680 g) cornmeal crust.

2. Remove the paper or plastic and the weights from the prebaked shells. Return the shells to the oven a bit longer to bake the bottom of the crust. Allow them to cool.

3. Sprinkle the finely ground almonds over the bottom of the shells, then divide the rhubarb evenly on top of the almonds. Set aside to cool.

4. Make ½ recipe Italian Meringue (page 27).

5. Cut or mark the tarts into serving pieces.

6. Using a pastry bag with a No. 3 (6-mm) star tip, pipe the meringue on top of the rhubarb, within the markings for each slice, starting at the tip of the slice and piping the strips of meringue next to each other in a zigzag design (piping left to right then right to left) to the edge (see Figure 11-16, page 529, as an example, only the lines here should be piped straight across and touching).

7. Caramelize (brown) the meringue using a salamander, in a very hot oven (450°F/230°C), or with a propane torch.

8. Adjust the sweetness of the reserved rhubarb juice by adding either sugar or water as necessary. Thicken with 1 tablespoon (8 g) cornstarch per pint (480 ml) liquid.

9. Presentation: Place the tart slice off-center on a dessert plate. Pour a pool of sauce on the larger exposed part of the plate.

Swedish Apple Tart

yield: 2 tarts, 11 inches (27.5 cm) in diameter, or 16 individual tarts, 4¹/₂ inches (11.2 cm) in diameter

My mom made this popular Swedish country-style apple tart often enough when I was a kid that I should have remembered it (unfortunately, my excuse is that it has been quite a while since then), but I had forgotten this recipe until a few years back, when I was served a variation of it at *Operakällaren*, an old and well-known restaurant in Stockholm. Prepared lingonberries are a staple found in every Swedish pantry. You can substitute cranberry jam, if you wish, but if you use purchased cranberry jam, do not put any on top of the apples. The type of jam sold commercially dries out instead of soaking into the fruit. Another way to modify this recipe is to use poached pears instead of apples. They also taste great baked in the nut filling.

This recipe can be used to make 16 individual tarts by making the following changes: Use 8 small apples rather than 12 medium, double the amount of Short Dough, and increase the amount of lingonberry jam slightly. Follow the directions, using 4¹/₂-inch (11.2-cm) tart pans. The individual tarts take about 15 minutes to bake.

4 pounds 8 ounces (2 kg 45 g) Red Delicious apples (approximately 12 medium)	1 ounce (30 g) thinly sliced natural almonds
¹/₂ recipe Spiced Poaching Syrup (page 31)	Powdered sugar
1 pound 8 ounces (680 g) Short Dough (page 67)	1 cup (240 ml) heavy cream
1 cup (240 ml) lingonberry jam	1 teaspoon (5 ml) vanilla extract
¹/₂ recipe Swedish Hazelnut Filling (page 358)	Florentinas (page 305), cut in half
8 ounces (225 g) Pastry Cream (page 845)	Edible flowers

1. Peel, core, and cut the apples in half. Place the apples in a saucepan together with the poaching syrup and simmer until the apples are soft. Remove from the heat and reserve.

2. Line 2 false-bottomed tart pans, 11 inches (27.5 cm) in diameter, with short dough rolled to ¹/₈ inch (3 mm) thick (see Figure 7-1, page 325). Spread half of the lingonberry jam over the bottom of the tart shells.

3. Combine the Swedish hazelnut filling with the pastry cream. Divide between the shells.

4. Cut the apples into thin slices lengthwise, cutting from the round side without cutting all the way through (leave the slices attached on the flat sides). Divide the apples evenly between the tarts, placing them on the filling, flat-side down, leaving a ¹/₂-inch (1.2-cm) space between them. Press the apples down to fan the cuts out. Using all of the remaining jam, spoon a small dot of jam on each apple. Sprinkle sliced almonds around the apples.

5. Bake at 375°F (190°C) for 20 minutes. Remove from the oven and sift powdered sugar over the tops of the tarts. Place the tarts back in the oven and bake until cooked through, about 15 minutes longer. Let cool. Remove the tarts from the pans and cut into the desired number of serving pieces.

6. Whip the heavy cream and the vanilla until stiff peaks form. Place in a pastry bag with a No. 7 (14-mm) star tip. Reserve in the refrigerator.

7. Presentation: Place a tart slice in the center of a dessert plate. Pipe a rosette of cream on the plate next to the tart and stand a Florentina cookie in the cream. Place an edible flower next to the cookie.

Swedish Hazelnut Tart yield: 2 tarts, 11 inches (27.5 cm) in diameter (Photo 10)

You may substitute any other nut in place of the hazelnuts or use a combination of several varieties in this very adaptable recipe. I have even made the filling without the candied orange peel, substituting grated orange rind, pastry cream, and even apricot jam with excellent results. Another great thing about this recipe is that the baked tarts keep exceptionally well and taste even better, or I should say moister, after a few days in the refrigerator. (Nuts tend to absorb moisture in baked goods; many times this works to our disadvantage, as in cookies, but they are working with us here.) This tart has been a real lifesaver for large banquet functions. You can easily make small, pretty buffet-size pieces by covering the bottom only of a paper-lined sheet pan with short dough. Spread apricot jam over the short dough, then add the filling. The filling recipe makes enough for one half-sheet pan. Bake the sheet a little longer than the round tarts. Cool and cut into the desired size and shape pieces. Decorate each piece with a rosette of ganache and a small orange wedge or strip of orange peel.

1 pound 8 ounces (680 g) Short Dough (page 67)

5 ounces (140 g) apricot jam

Swedish Hazelnut Filling (recipe follows)

Powdered sugar

Ganache (page 842)

Fresh orange slices

I. Line 2 tart pans (false-bottomed or solid), 11 inches (27.5 cm) in diameter, with short dough rolled to ⅛ inch (3 mm) thick (see Figure 7-1, page 325). Place the lined pans in the refrigerator to firm the dough.

2. Soften the jam by working it in a bowl with a spoon until smooth. (You may need to add a small amount of water if the jam is too firm.) Divide the jam between the shells and spread out in a thin film on the bottom of each tart. Return the pans to the refrigerator while you make the filling.

3. Divide the filling between the tart shells and spread it out, mounding it just slightly higher in the center.

4. Bake the tarts at 350°F (175°C) until the filling is firm in the middle and the shells are golden brown, about 35 minutes. Let the tarts cool completely, then unmold.

5. Make a template that is ½ inch (1.2 cm) smaller than the tarts and has a 4-inch (10-cm) circle cut out of the center. Place the template on the tarts, 1 at a time, and sift powdered sugar on top. Slice the tarts into the desired number of servings.

6. Warm the ganache until it develops a slight shine. Place in a pastry bag with a No. 4 (8-mm) plain tip. Pipe the ganache in a heart design at the edge of each slice; decorate with a small slice of fresh orange. (Unfortunately, the oranges will look fresh for a few hours only, so do not decorate more tarts or slices than you will use within that time.)

NOTE: To get a precise and sharp contrast, use a plain cookie cutter as a guide for the center circle when you cut your template, then place the cutter in the opening to act as a seal while you sift the powdered sugar. Remove the cutter and the template carefully.

SWEDISH HAZELNUT FILLING yield: 3 pounds (1 kg 365 g)

12 ounces (340 g) hazelnuts

5 ounces (140 g) candied orange peel

12 ounces (340 g) granulated sugar

12 ounces (340 g) unsalted butter, at room temperature

3 whole eggs

4 egg yolks (⅓ cup/80 ml)

1½ teaspoons (7.5 ml) vanilla extract

1. Grind the hazelnuts, orange peel, and 6 ounces (170 g) sugar very finely, until almost a paste.

2. Cream the butter with the remaining 6 ounces (170 g) sugar. Gradually mix in the whole eggs, egg yolks, vanilla, and the nut mixture. Be careful not to overmix; if too much air is incorporated, the tarts will puff up while baking and then fall in the center, giving them an unattractive finished appearance.

Tart Hollandaise yield: 2 tarts, 11 inches (27.5 cm) in diameter

Puff pastry, short dough, and almonds, which combine so well and appear in many European pastries, are featured in this old-fashioned Dutch tart. You can easily adapt this recipe to make a wonderful apple or pear tart. Use a little less frangipane filling (make only ½ recipe or 2 pounds 5 ounces/1 kg 50 g) and press poached pears or apples halfway into the filling before baking. Sprinkle almonds over the fruit (plus some cinnamon sugar, if you like) and eliminate the short dough strips.

1 pound 12 ounces (795 g) Quick Puff Pastry (page 77) or Flaky Pie Dough (page 62)

5 ounces (140 g) apricot jam

3 pounds (1 kg 365 g) Frangipane Filling (page 842)

2 ounces (55 g) sliced almonds

1 pound 6 ounces (625 g) Short Dough (page 67)

Egg wash

Powdered sugar

1. Cut the puff pastry or pie dough in half. Roll out one piece at a time to ⅛ inch (3 mm) thick and line 2 tart pans (false-bottomed or solid), 11 inches (27.5 cm) in diameter. Using your thumbs, press the dough up about ¼ inch (6 mm) above the edge of the pans to allow for shrinkage. Place a circle of baking paper or a sheet of commercial-grade plastic wrap (see page 326) in each pan to cover the bottom and sides, fill with dried beans or pie weights, and let rest for at least 30 minutes in the refrigerator.

2. Bake the shells at 375°F (190°C) for about 10 minutes. Let them cool until they can be handled, then remove the paper or plastic wrap and the weights.

3. Spread the jam in a thin layer on the bottom of each shell. Place the frangipane filling in a pastry bag with a No. 6 (12-mm) plain tip. Pipe the filling into the tart shells in an even layer or just spread it out evenly using a metal spatula. Sprinkle sliced almonds evenly over the tops.

4. Roll out the short dough into a rectangle measuring 11 inches (27.5 cm) wide and ⅛ inch (3 mm) thick. Refrigerate the dough to make it easier to handle. Cut into strips, ¼ inch (6 mm) wide, using a fluted pastry wheel.

5. Arrange the dough strips ¼ inch (6 mm) apart over the almonds; then arrange strips on top in the other direction so they form a diamond pattern (see example in Figure 12-30, page 600). Press the strips lightly with your hand as you place them to make sure they stick together. Carefully brush the strips with egg wash.

6. Bake the tarts at 375°F (190°C) until golden brown, about 45 minutes. Let cool to room temperature.

7. Remove the tarts from the pans. Slice into the desired number of serving pieces and sift powdered sugar lightly over the tops. Serve warm or at room temperature.

NOTE: You may have noticed that it takes more puff pastry or pie dough than short dough, rolled out to the same thickness, to line the tart pans. The reason is this: After rolling out the short dough to line one pan, I can reroll the scraps to line the second pan; with puff pastry or pie dough, this is not practical, as the dough scraps would have to rest before being rolled out again.

Tarte Tatin yield: I tart, 9 inches (22.5 cm) in diameter

This fabulous French upside-down apple tart was first made by the Tatin sisters at their restaurant in the Loire Valley over 100 years ago. Still standing across from the station house in the little railroad junction of Lamotte-Beuvron is the Hotel Tatin, where you can enjoy a warm slice of their famous caramelized apple tart. I have seen many shortcuts in which baked puff pastry and cooked apples (and, in some extreme cases, even a separate caramel sauce) are individually prepared ahead of time, and the dessert (I cannot call it tarte Tatin) is assembled to order. This may taste good in some instances, but the result is an entirely different dessert from a genuine tarte Tatin. The only way you can achieve the true caramelized apple flavor is to cook the apples and sugar together. This creates a natural phenomenon in which the apple halves release their juice into the sugar and butter mixture, flavoring and diluting the liquid and, at the same time, keeping it from caramelizing too fast. This, in turn, allows the apples to become partially cooked before the liquid is reduced and caramelized. Your job is to oversee the process, making sure there are no hot spots and the heat is not too high.

The ingredients specify Red or Golden Delicious apples, and I mean it! I have not found any other apples that will not fall apart into applesauce using this cooking method. (Red and Golden Delicious have a higher starch content than other apples.) While I am sure some other varieties will work, do not try substituting any of the standard green cooking apple variations.

6 ounces (170 g) Puff Pastry (page 74), Quick Puff Pastry (page 77), or puff pastry scraps

6 pounds (2 kg 730 g) Red or Golden Delicious apples (approximately 12 medium)

5 ounces (140 g) unsalted butter

7 ounces (200 g) granulated sugar

1½ cups (360 ml) Crème Fraîche (page 821), approximately

Cinnamon sugar

Strawberry halves

1. Roll the puff pastry into a square approximately 10 x 10 inches (25 x 25 cm) and slightly thinner than ⅛ inch (3 mm) thick. Place on a sheet pan, prick well, and reserve in the refrigerator.

2. Peel, core, and cut the apples in half lengthwise.

3. Put the butter in a 9-inch (22.5-cm) skillet (see Chef's Tip) and melt over medium heat. Sprinkle the sugar evenly over the melted butter. Quickly arrange as many of the apples as possible in the skillet, standing them on their stem ends and packing them tightly. You will not be able to fit all of the pieces in the pan at the beginning, but, as the apples cook, release their juice, and shrink, you will be able to squeeze in the remainder. It is important that the apples form a tight layer in the pan or they will not hold together when the tart is inverted later.

4. Cook over medium heat, shaking the skillet gently to make sure the apples do not stick to the bottom and pressing lightly on the top to form a compact layer. As the apples in the skillet shrink, add the apple pieces that you were not able to fit in at the start. Continue cooking, still shaking the skillet and pressing the apples together, until the sugar turns a dark golden brown, about 30 minutes, depending on the type of skillet and the temperature of the stove. Remove from the heat and let cool for 10 minutes.

5. Cut a 10-inch (25-cm) circle from the reserved puff pastry square (save the scraps for another use). Cover the apples with the puff pastry, tucking the dough between the apples and the skillet (or the apples and the ring).

6. Bake at 375°F (190°C) for about 30 minutes or until the puff pastry is baked through. Let the tart cool until the caramelized sugar has thickened to a syrup. If it cools to the point that the apples are stuck on the bottom, place the skillet on the stove and warm slightly.

7. Invert a platter on top of the tart and flip both the platter and the tart over together to unmold the tart onto the platter. Be careful of the hot caramel as you do this. Cut the tart into the desired number of slices.

8. Presentation: Place a tart slice on a dessert plate, spoon crème fraîche over the tip, and sprinkle cinnamon sugar lightly over the top. Fan a strawberry half and set on the plate next to the crème fraîche.

CHEF'S TIP A skillet that measures 10 inches (25 cm) across the top with 2- to 2½-inch (5- to 6.2-cm) sides sloping down to 9 inches (22.5 cm) across the bottom is ideal. If you use a larger skillet, place an adjustable ring made of stainless steel (the anodized metal type will stain the apples) adjusted to 10 inches (25 cm) in the skillet, or use the ring from a 9-inch (22.5-cm) springform, unclamped. The ring will sit high on the sides of the skillet but, as the apples cook and compact, you can adjust it. I prefer to use a copper skillet lined with stainless steel (the French make one designed specifically for tarte Tatin), but any heavy skillet will do as long as the handle is heatproof so that the skillet can be placed in the oven.

NOTE: This tart is best served warm from the oven. If you must, serve it at room temperature, but never cold. Tarte Tatin should be served the same day it is made. Crème fraîche is the classic accompaniment to tarte Tatin, but Chantilly Cream (page 838) will do as well, if you sweeten it less than is called for in the recipe; there is plenty of sugar from the caramel in the tart. Alternatively, serve tarte Tatin the way I like it—with vanilla ice cream, either the old-fashioned version or a slightly acid yogurt-based ice cream.

Torta Ricotta yield: 2 tarts, 11 inches (27.5 cm) in diameter

Ricotta is a curd cheese traditionally prepared from the residual whey left after making other cheeses. It is quite easy to make your own ricotta, using the recipe on page 34. If you follow the recipe carefully, it will be well worth your time, as ricotta cheese purchased in the store often has a grainy feel in the mouth and can be lacking in flavor. Making the pastry cream called for in this recipe will set you back only slightly, and it gives the filling a lighter and more pleasant taste. But if you do not have any on hand and don't have time or want to make it, leave it out, increase the ricotta by 1 pound (455 g), double the amount of sugar, and use whole eggs rather than egg yolks.

The cornmeal-based short dough provides a wonderful, crisp crust. However, if this dessert is not to be eaten the same day it is made, it is better to use plain short dough. The cornmeal absorbs moisture more quickly and the crust becomes soft after one day.

1 pound 8 ounces (680 g) Cornmeal Crust (page 71)

2 pounds 4 ounces (1 kg 25 g) ricotta cheese (see Note)

12 ounces (340 g) cream cheese, at room temperature

3 egg yolks (¼ cup/60 ml)

6 ounces (170 g) granulated sugar

Grated zest of 2 lemons

2 teaspoons (10 ml) vanilla extract

⅓ recipe or 2 pounds (910 g) Pastry Cream (page 845)

1½ cups (360 ml) heavy cream

1 tablespoon (15 g) granulated sugar

Fresh fruit

1. Line 2 tart pans, 11 inches (27.5 cm) in diameter, with cornmeal crust rolled to ⅛ inch (3 mm) thick (see Figure 7-1, page 325). Save the scrap dough for another use.

2. Gradually mix the ricotta cheese into the soft cream cheese. Add the egg yolks, 6 ounces (170 g) granulated sugar, lemon zest, and vanilla. Avoid mixing air into the filling. Fold in the pastry cream. Divide the filling evenly between the prepared tart pans.

3. Bake at 350°F (175°C) for approximately 40 minutes or until the filling is set. To ensure that the crust will bake properly, place the tarts directly on the oven racks; do not set them on a sheet pan.

4. Whip the heavy cream with the remaining sugar until soft peaks form. Cut the tarts into the desired number of servings. Serve with a large dollop of whipped cream and sliced fresh fruit.

NOTE: When using commercial ricotta, which is homogenized, the liquid separates from the cheese during baking, leaking into the pastry shell and making it soggy. The solution is to first cook the ricotta in a skillet over medium heat for about 20 minutes, stirring frequently, forcing the liquid out and partially evaporating it. Then wrap the ricotta in cheesecloth and allow it to hang and drain for 20 minutes. This will produce an almost dry cheese.

CHESTNUT TORTA RICOTTA

Follow the directions in the main recipe, making these changes:

- Increase the ricotta cheese to 3 pounds 4 ounces (1 kg 480 g).

- Omit the pastry cream.

- Add:

1 pound (455 g) fresh chestnuts in the shell
   or 12 ounces (340 g) whole roasted
   shelled chestnuts

4 ounces (115 g) granulated sugar

½ cup (120 ml) dark rum

½ cup (120 ml) water

1 ounce (30 g) unsalted butter

2 tablespoons (30 ml) vanilla extract

1. If you are using fresh chestnuts, prepare them as directed for Chestnut Puree (page 12) but leave whole after cooking.

2. Chop the prepared or packaged chestnuts to about one-quarter of their original size. Combine with the granulated sugar, dark rum, water, and butter in a small saucepan. Cook over high heat, stirring frequently, until the liquid has thickened, about 5 minutes. Remove from the heat and stir in the vanilla.

3. Stir the chestnut mixture into the completed ricotta filling so it is marbled throughout. Do not overmix. Divide the filling between the shells.

Vanilla Custard Tart with Rhubarb   yield: 2 tarts, 11 inches (27.5 cm) in diameter

1 pound 8 ounces (680 g) Short Dough
   (page 67)

1 pound 8 ounces (680 g) rhubarb stalks

4 ounces (115 g) granulated sugar

Vanilla Custard Filling (recipe follows)

2 ounces (55 g) granulated sugar

Apricot Glaze (page 5) *or* Pectin Glaze
   (page 30)

Whipped cream (optional)

1. Line 2 false-bottomed tart pans, 11 inches (27.5 cm) in diameter, with short dough rolled to ⅛ inch (3 mm) thick (see Figure 7-1, page 325). Prick the dough lightly with a fork. Line the bottom and sides of the shell with commercial-grade plastic wrap, fill with dried beans or pie weights, and fold the edges of the plastic back over the weights so the plastic does not touch the metal pan.

2. Bake at 375°F (190°C) just until golden, about 12 minutes. Let cool, then remove the plastic and the weights.

3. Cut the rhubarb stalks into pieces measuring 2 x ½ inch (5 x 1.2 cm). Place them in a stainless steel or other nonreactive pan and sprinkle 4 ounces (115 g) granulated sugar on top to draw out some of the juice.

4. Bake covered at 375°F (190°C) until slightly softened, about 8 minutes. If overcooked, the rhubarb will turn into a puree. Arrange the rhubarb in the baked shells.

5. Gently pour the vanilla custard filling over the fruit, dividing it evenly between the shells. Sprinkle the remaining granulated sugar over the top of the tarts.

6. Bake at 350°F (175°C) until the custard is set, about 30 minutes.

7. When the tarts have cooled enough so that they will not break when you handle them, remove them from the pans and glaze with apricot or pectin glaze. Slice and serve at room temperature. If you like, pipe whipped cream at the edge of each slice.

VANILLA CUSTARD FILLING yield: 4³/₄ cups (1 L 140 ml)

2 vanilla beans

7 ounces (200 g) granulated sugar

12 egg yolks (1 cup/240)

4 cups (960 ml) heavy cream

1 teaspoon (5 ml) finely grated lemon zest

1. Split the vanilla beans lengthwise and scrape out the seeds. Rub the seeds into the sugar to distribute them evenly and break up any clumps. Save the pod halves for another use or discard.

2. Beat the egg yolks and the vanilla sugar by hand for a few seconds, just to combine.

3. Add the cream and lemon zest and blend thoroughly.

Walnut-Caramel Tart yield: 2 tarts, 11 inches (27.5 cm) in diameter (Photo 10)

You could argue that this is a candy disguised as a tart, but whatever you want to call it, it is a very rich, delicious combination of buttery, chewy caramel with walnuts in a crisp short dough crust. Who could resist?

Keep a watchful eye on the caramel when you make the filling, and have the cream ready. If you let the caramel get too dark, don't waste the cream and the butter—just start over. Not only will the filling be bitter if the caramel is overcooked, but it will set up hard enough to pull the fillings right out of your teeth! At the same time, keep in mind that if you play it too safe and do not caramelize the sugar enough, the filling will not harden sufficiently.

2 pounds 14 ounces (1 kg 310 g) Short Dough (page 67)

Caramel Filling (recipe follows)

Egg wash

10 ounces (285 g) Ganache (page 836)

5 ounces (140 g) walnuts, finely chopped

Orange Sauce (page 828)

Chocolate Sauce for Piping (page 820)

Raspberries

1. Roll out a portion of the short dough to ⅛ inch (3 mm) thick and use it to line 2 tart pans, 11 inches (27.5 cm) in diameter (see Figure 7-1, page 325). These do not have to be false-bottomed pans. Reserve the remaining dough. Place circles of baking paper or sheets of commercial-grade plastic wrap in the pans to cover the bottom and sides and fill with dried beans or pie weights.

2. Bake at 375°F (190°C) until set but not brown, about 12 minutes.

3. Remove the paper or plastic and the weights from the partially baked shells. Divide the caramel filling evenly between the shells.

4. Roll out the remaining short dough to ⅛ inch (3 mm) thick.

5. Brush the edge of the baked shells with egg wash, then cover with the dough. Press the edges together to seal and trim away any excess dough. Prick the top lightly to let air escape.

6. Bake the tarts at 350°F (175°C) until golden brown, about 30 minutes. If the pastry bubbles, press it down with the bottom of a cake pan or any other flat object while the tart is still hot from the oven. Let the tarts cool to room temperature. Remove the tarts from the pans.

7. Warm the ganache to a soft but not runny consistency; it should have a nice shine. Spread a thin, even layer of warm ganache on top of one tart. Place a plain cookie cutter, 5 to 6 inches (12.5 to 15 cm) in diameter (or anything with a rim around it so it will not damage the ganache), in the center of the tart. Sprinkle the chopped walnuts around the ring before the ganache hardens, taking care not to spill any in the middle. (Sprinkle the walnuts lightly; you should still be able to see as much uncovered ganache as you do nuts.) Remove the cookie cutter and refrigerate the tart to firm the ganache. Repeat with the remaining tart.

8. Cut the tarts into the desired number of slices, using a sharp knife dipped in hot water.

9. Presentation: Place a slice of tart slightly off-center on a dessert plate. Pour a pool of orange sauce in the larger space and decorate the sauce with chocolate sauce for piping (see pages 809 to 814). Place 3 raspberries on the opposite side of the plate.

NOTE: Walnut-Caramel Tart must be served at room temperature because the caramelized sugar becomes too hard if refrigerated.

CHEF'S TIP
Sift the chopped nuts to remove the small flakes and particles that are unavoidable when preparing chopped nuts as they detract from the appearance.

CARAMEL FILLING yield: 4 pounds 3 ounces (1 kg 905 g)

2 pounds (910 g) granulated sugar
4 teaspoons (20 ml) lemon juice
1 cup (240 ml) heavy cream, at room
  temperature

10 ounces (285 g) unsalted butter
1 pound (455 g) walnuts, coarsely chopped

1. Caramelize the sugar with the lemon juice in a heavy-bottomed saucepan (see page 10).

2. Cook, stirring constantly with a wooden spoon, until the mixture reaches a light brown color, 335°F (168°C). Remove from the heat.

3. Quickly add the cream and swirl it around to mix.

4. Stir in the butter, then the walnuts.

NOTE: If you make the filling ahead, you may need to warm it before spreading it in the tart shells.

Buttermilk Custard Pie

yield: 2 pies, 9 inches (22.5 cm) in diameter, or 2 tarts, 11 inches (27.5 cm) in diameter

Buttermilk has come a long way. In its natural form, it is the liquid that is forced out when cream is churned into butter. This liquid resembles nonfat milk and has a slightly tangy flavor. Buttermilk has been consumed for many centuries. It was especially popular during the Middle Ages, where at first it was enjoyed only by shepherds or those persons on a farm who were churning butter; but later, the aristocratic class came to look on it as a fashionable drink. The buttermilk you purchase today is likely to be cultured buttermilk, made from nonfat milk that has been fermented slightly, using a culture similar to the natural organism that coagulates heavy cream, allowing it to be churned into butter. The milk is then treated to kill any bacteria and stop the souring (fermentation) process. Buttermilk is a popular ingredient in cooking and is used to make pancakes, scones, and, of course, buttermilk pie, which is a classic of the American South.

1 recipe Pâte Brisée (page 64)

Buttermilk Pie Filling (recipe follows)

2 cups (480 ml) heavy cream (optional)

1 tablespoon (15 ml) granulated sugar (optional)

1. Roll out the dough to ⅛ inch (3 mm) thick. Line 2 pie pans, 9 inches (22.5 cm) in diameter, and flute the edges (see Figures 7-1, page 325, and 2-2 and 2-3, page 63; see Note). Place the pie shells on an even sheet pan and place in the refrigerator for about 30 minutes to firm the dough and relax the gluten. Cover the dough scraps and reserve for another use.

2. Divide the buttermilk pie filling between the chilled shells.

3. Bake at 425°F (219°C) placing the sheet pan directly on the hearth of the oven. If your oven does not have a hearth and you must place the pies on racks, do not set the pie pans on a sheet pan. Bake for 15 minutes, then lower the heat to 350°F (175°C) and continue baking approximately 35 minutes longer or until the filling is set. Remove from the oven and let cool to room temperature.

4. If desired, whip the heavy cream and the sugar until stiff peaks form. Place in a pastry bag with a No. 7 (14 mm) star tip. Pipe a shell border of cream around the inside edge of the pies and slice into servings of the desired size.

NOTE: As another option, you can use 2 tart pans, 11 x ¾ inches (27.5 x 2 cm). In this case, omit the instructions for fluting the edges of the dough. If you use tart pans, try piping the whipped cream as shown in Key Lime Chiffon Pie (Photo 39).

BUTTERMILK PIE FILLING

yield: enough for 2 pies, 9 inches (22.5 cm) in diameter, or 2 tarts, 11 inches (27.5 cm) in diameter

1 pound 4 ounces (570 g) granulated sugar

2 ounces (55 g) bread flour

1 teaspoon (5 g) salt

½ teaspoon (1 g) ground nutmeg

6 eggs, at room temperature

10 ounces (285 g) melted unsalted butter

3 cups (720 ml) buttermilk, at room temperature

Finely grated zest and juice of 1 lemon

2 teaspoons (10 ml) vanilla extract

1. Thoroughly combine the sugar, flour, salt, and nutmeg.

2. Beat the eggs lightly and stir into the sugar mixture. Stir in the butter, buttermilk, lemon zest and juice, and vanilla extract.

Caramelized Apple Pie with Lattice Crust yield: 1 pie, 10 inches (25 cm) in diameter

Although there is no question that apples were formed into tarts and baked between layers of dough as long ago as the Middle Ages, the first recorded use of the name *apple pie* was in late sixteenth-century England, with *pie* spelled "pye."

The United States is now the country most strongly associated with pies, apple in particular, as evidenced by the common phrase "as American as apple pie." My grandparents emigrated from Sweden to America (separately) at the end of the 1800s. They met here, married, worked hard and saved their money, and returned to southern Sweden, where they bought a small farm and, as was the norm, started a large family. As a kid, I loved spending part of each summer at my grandparents' house, where my two favorite activities were sitting on my Farfar's lap listening to stories about the big country of America and, second, eating Farmor's apple pies. The pies had a thick double crust (a trick she had no doubt picked up in the States) and, to a hungry kid, they were just as delicious a few days after they were baked as they were right out of the oven.

In this recipe, the apples are cooked in a rich caramel syrup flavored with bourbon and orange liqueur before they are enclosed in the pie crust. Some of this liquid is drained off and becomes an instant apple-flavored caramel sauce, the perfect accompaniment to the pie. If you do not have time to fuss with a lattice top, the pie dough is ample for a solid top crust. Regardless of the style of crust, if possible, serve this pie with a scoop of ice cream—Vanilla (page 734) or Cinnamon (page 720).

5 pounds (2 kg 275 g) cooking apples, such as Pippin, Granny Smith, or Golden Delicious (approximately 11 medium; see Note)

10 ounces (285 g) unsalted butter

2 teaspoons (3 g) ground cinnamon

1 pound (455 g) granulated sugar

1 pound 2 ounces (510 g) Pâte Brisée (page 64)

1 cup (240 ml) bourbon

½ cup (120 ml) orange liqueur

1 cup (240 ml) heavy cream

2 ounces (55 g) melted unsalted butter

1. Peel, core, and halve the apples. Cut the halves into ¼-inch (6-mm) slices. Melt the first measurement of butter in a large skillet or sauté pan. Add the apples and cook over medium heat, stirring frequently, for 5 minutes. Mix the ground cinnamon into the sugar. Add this to the apples, stirring until thoroughly combined. The juice released from the apples in combination with the melted sugar will cause a large amount of liquid to collect in the pan. Continue cooking the apples, still stirring frequently, until they are caramelized and translucent but still firm to the touch. Depending on the apples used and their stage of ripeness, it may be necessary to remove some of the liquid to expedite the caramelizing process and avoid overcooking the apples. If so, boil the liquid in a separate pan until it is reduced to a thick syrup, then add it back to the apples.

2. While the apples are cooking, roll out the pâte brisée to a rectangle measuring 11 inches (27.5 cm) wide and ⅛ inch (3 mm) thick, using flour to prevent the dough from sticking. Cut the dough in half across. Cover one piece and place in the refrigerator. Use the remaining piece to line a 10-inch (25-cm) pie pan. Reserve in the refrigerator.

3. Once the apples are caramelized, add the bourbon, orange liqueur, and cream. Continue cooking until the mixture has reduced and thickened again. Remove from the heat and strain the apples in a colander, reserving the liquid (see Chef's Tip). Let the apples cool before proceeding.

4. Brush some of the melted butter over the bottom of the lined pie pan. Fill the crust with the apples, shaping them into an even mound on the top. Cut the reserved pâte brisée into ⅜-inch (9-mm) strips and arrange on top of the apples in a lattice pattern (instructions follow). Pinch the ends of the strips against the edge of the bottom crust. Cover the dough scraps and save for another use. Brush the remainder of the melted butter (reheat if necessary) over the lattice strips.

5. Bake at 375°F (190°C) for approximately 1 hour. Let cool a bit, then serve with the reserved apple cooking liquid as a sauce. If the liquid has cooled substantially, it may need to be warmed to a pourable consistency.

NOTE: If you are in a hurry or making a fair number of pies, you can simplify things by using the Chunky Apple Filling (page 840) rather than cooking the apples and the other filling ingredients according to the lengthier procedure used here. It will not produce a pie as complex in flavor as this one, but certainly one with a great tart apple flavor. One recipe of filling is enough for 1 pie, 10 inches (25 cm) in diameter.

CHEF'S TIP
You will have 1 to 1½ cups (240 to 360 ml) of liquid from draining the apples. If you do not use all of it in serving the apple pie, it makes a great bourbon-apple flavored caramel sauce for ice cream. It pairs especially well with the ice cream flavors mentioned in this recipe introduction.

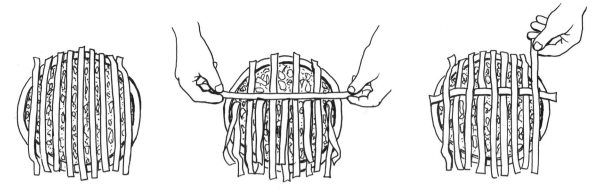

FIGURE 7-7 Strips of pie dough arranged vertically over the top of the filling; placing a strip of dough horizontally over the filling after folding back every other vertical strip halfway; unfolding the vertical strips to return them to their original position, now over and under the horizontal strip

TO MAKE A LATTICE CRUST

1. Evenly space strips of dough vertically across the pie, letting the ends hang over.

2. Starting with the strip on the left, lift up and fold back every other strip halfway.

3. Place a strip of dough horizontally across the center of the pie. Return the folded strips to their original position so they cross over the horizontal strip (Figure 7-7).

4. Starting with the second strip from the left this time, fold back every other strip. Place a second horizontal strip, evenly spaced, below the first. Return the folded strips to their original position.

5. Repeat this pattern until you have covered the bottom half of the pie, then turn the pie around and repeat with the other half (Figure 7-8).

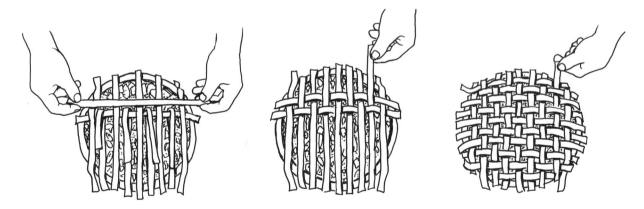

FIGURE 7-8 Adding a second horizontal strip after folding back every other vertical strip again, but beginning with the second strip from the left this time; unfolding the vertical strips to return them to their original position, now over and under the second horizontal strip; unfolding the last vertical strip to return it to its original position after repeating the pattern on both sides to cover the top of the pie

Traditional Key Lime Pie yield: 2 tarts, 11 inches (27.5 cm) in diameter

Both of the following pies can be made with Key lime juice or common lime juice with a good outcome, although if you do not use Key limes, don't call it Key Lime Pie. Whichever you use, the pies will be yellowish in color, not green. Please resist any temptation to add green food coloring, should such a thought occur to you. The zest of Key limes tends to be bitter and should not be used.

1 pound 8 ounces (680 g) Graham Cracker Crumbs (page 20)

8 ounces (225 g) melted unsalted butter

16 pasteurized egg yolks (1⅓ cups/320 ml; see "about Key lime pie," below)

4 cans (14 ounces/400 g each) sweetened condensed milk, or 5⅓ cups (1 L 280 ml)

2 cups (480 ml) freshly squeezed Key lime or common lime juice

1 tablespoon (15 ml) finely chopped grated lime zest (not from Key limes)

Softly whipped cream (optional)

1. Combine the graham cracker crumbs and the melted butter thoroughly. Divide evenly between 2 false-bottomed tart pans, 11 inches (27.5 cm) in diameter, and press the mixture against the sides and the bottoms of the pans to form an even crust in each. Use the back of a spoon to smooth the crust and help press it together tightly.

2. Bake the shells at 375°F (190°C) for 7 to 8 minutes until lightly browned and set. Set aside to cool.

About Key Lime Pie

The Key lime pie is an American classic that originated in Florida in the late 1800s as a result of two independent but concurrent events: the planting of the first Key lime groves in Florida and the invention of canned sweetened condensed milk, which was especially welcome in remote tropical areas. The Key lime is known botanically as *Citrus aurantifolia*. It is also known as *Mexican lime* and *West Indian lime*. Grown year round in many temperate climates all over the world, Key limes are more yellow in color than the common Persian lime (*Citrus latifolia*), they are smaller, and they have a rounder shape. They originated in Malaysia and were brought to North Africa, Europe, and the Caribbean by traders, explorers, and such. In 1835, a botanist named Henry Perrine planted the fruit trees in the Florida Keys, and the lime began to be known as the Key lime in the United States.

The classic Key lime pie is not cooked or baked (other than the crust) and contains only lime juice, sweetened condensed milk, and egg yolks. A chemical reaction between the egg yolks and the fresh lime juice causes the filling to set up (similar to the process of "cooking" raw fish in lime juice to make ceviche). Because raw eggs are frowned upon when cooking and serving food for the public, the traditional recipe above calls for pasteurized egg yolks. While the filling does thicken, it remains rather soft, whereas the chiffon variation holds up a bit better for restaurant service. Either can be garnished with whipped cream as desired.

The original Key lime pie was not served with whipped cream, of course, being that the whole point of the recipe was that it could be made even where fresh dairy products were unavailable. However, a dollop of cream on top provides a nice contrast to the sweet, rich filling, and serving it this way has become something of a tradition. Some sources say that a meringue topping was used at the start, and there are now many recipe variations with meringue folded into the filling and/or browned on the top.

3. Place the egg yolks in a mixer bowl. Whip for 3 or 4 minutes until they are lightened in color. Stir in the condensed milk, the lime juice, and the lime zest by hand, mixing just long enough to combine the ingredients.

4. Divide the filling evenly between the baked shells. Refrigerate for a minimum of 12 hours. The mixture will thicken to the consistency of a thin custard and can be sliced neatly, provided it is kept refrigerated. Serve with a dollop of whipped cream if desired (or follow the piping instructions in Step 9 for Key Lime Chiffon Pie).

Key Lime Chiffon Pie yield: 2 tarts, 11 inches (27.5 cm) in diameter (Photo 39)

1 pound 8 ounces (680 g) Graham Cracker Crumbs (page 20)

10 ounces (285 g) melted unsalted butter

8 egg yolks (²/₃ cup/160 ml)

½ cup (120 ml) simple syrup

¼ cup (60 ml) dark or light rum

2 tablespoons (30 ml) freshly squeezed orange juice

1 tablespoon (9 g) unflavored gelatin powder

2 cups (480 ml) plus 1½ cups (360 ml) heavy cream

3 tablespoons (45 g) plus 2 teaspoons (10 ml) granulated sugar

1 cup (240 ml) freshly squeezed Key lime or common lime juice

1 tablespoon (15 ml) finely chopped grated lime zest (not from Key limes)

2 cans (14 ounces/400 g each) sweetened condensed milk, or 2²/₃ cups (640 ml)

1. Combine the graham cracker crumbs and the melted butter thoroughly. Divide evenly between 2 false-bottomed tart pans, 11 inches (27.5 cm) in diameter, and press the mixture against the sides and the bottoms of the pans to form an even crust in each. Use the back of a spoon to smooth the crust and help press it together tightly.

2. Bake the shells at 375°F (190°C) for 7 to 8 minutes until lightly browned and set. Set aside to cool.

3. Place the egg yolks in a bowl and whip for 2 or 3 minutes. At the same time, bring the simple syrup to a boil. Gradually pour the hot simple syrup into the yolks while whipping constantly. Place the egg yolk mixture over a bain-marie and beat until it is thickened. Remove from the heat.

4. Combine the rum and the orange juice. Sprinkle the gelatin over the top and set aside to soften.

5. Whip the 2 cups (480 ml) heavy cream with the 3 tablespoons (45 g) granulated sugar to soft peaks.

6. Stir the lime juice and lime zest into the egg yolks, followed by the condensed milk.

7. Heat the gelatin mixture to dissolve the gelatin, then stir this into the milk mixture. Fold in the whipped cream.

8. Divide the filling evenly between the baked shells and refrigerate for at least 4 hours or overnight.

9. Whip 1½ cups (360 ml) heavy cream and the 2 teaspoons sugar to form stiff peaks. Place in a pastry bag with a Saint-Honoré tip and pipe a pattern of slightly curved lines around the perimeter of each tart (see Photo 39).

Lemon Meringue Pie yield: 2 pies, 10 inches (25 cm) in diameter

Like apple pie, lemon meringue pie is an American favorite and has been since the nineteenth century. The sweet, billowy meringue topping perfectly offsets the slightly tart lemon base, which seems by far to be the preferred portion of the pie, judging by the meringue often left on the dessert plate. The meringue topping is definitely the trouble spot in this dessert. I am constantly asked by my students (often prompted by the boss at their after-school jobs) how to prevent the meringue from weeping and separating from (sliding off) the filling. This really cannot be avoided in a pie that is more than 24 hours old, and this is a well-known and easy gauge used by consumers to judge if they are being served a pie that is not too fresh.

½ recipe Flaky Pie Dough (page 62)	5 ounces (140 g) unsalted butter
3 ounces (85 g) cornstarch	10 egg yolks (⅞ cup/200 ml)
1 pound 8 ounces (680 g) granulated sugar	¾ cup (180 ml) freshly squeezed lemon juice
1 teaspoon (5 g) salt	1 tablespoon (18 g) finely grated lemon zest
3 cups (720 ml) water	Meringue Pie Topping (recipe follows)

1. Roll out the pie dough to ⅛ inch (3 mm) thick, line 2 pie pans, 10 inches (25 cm) in diameter, and flute the edges (see Figure 7-1, page 325, and 2-2 and 2-3, page 63). Cover the dough scraps and save for another use. Place the shells in the refrigerator until firm.

2. Prick the bottom of the pie shells. Cover the dough with rounds of baking paper and fill with dried beans or pie weights. Bake at 375°F (190°C) until the dough begins to color around the edges, about 15 minutes. Remove the weights and the baking papers and continue baking until the shells are light brown and baked through, approximately 10 minutes longer. Set aside to cool.

About Meringue Topping

In making meringue, the baker must consider Mother Nature. Just as spun sugar is much more susceptible to breaking down or weeping in rainy weather or if the humidity is high, the sugar in the meringue will absorb moisture from the air and melt, releasing a liquid, under the same conditions. Some chefs emphasize that the lemon filling should be cold when the meringue is placed on it, and others specify just the opposite. Even though it does make sense to spread the meringue on a hot filling, as it has a better chance of adhering to a soft surface rather than a slick, firm filling that has been refrigerated, this is not always practical. In my experience, it is usually sufficient if the filling is no cooler than room temperature, as long as it has been covered to prevent a skin from forming.

A more important factor is the meringue itself. Proper procedure must be followed for whipping the meringue, placing it on the pie, and baking. Overwhipped egg whites or meringues prepared without enough sugar tend to break down and release moisture (weep) much faster after baking. Baking the topping at too high a temperature (which generally results in not baking long enough) makes the meringue brown too quickly before the structure of the egg whites has had time to fully gelatinize, which again will cause the meringue to release moisture after it has cooled. To keep the meringue from shrinking away from the pie shell, it is important to make certain that the meringue is touching the crust all around the edge, with no gaps. The meringue topping used here includes a small amount of cooked cornstarch, which helps stabilize the topping just as it does in the lemon filling. If it happens that your meringue still does not behave after following all of these rules, you can take consolation in the fact that you are by no means alone.

3. Place the cornstarch, granulated sugar, and salt in a saucepan and mix until thoroughly combined. Incorporate the water, stirring with a whisk. Cook over low heat, stirring constantly with the whisk, until the mixture comes to a boil. Boil gently for several minutes. Add the butter and stir until it is melted and incorporated. Remove from the heat.

4. Add a portion of the cornstarch mixture to the egg yolks to temper, then add this back to the remaining cornstarch mixture and stir until combined. Add the lemon juice and grated lemon zest. Place the saucepan back on the stove over low heat and cook the filling, stirring constantly, until it has boiled for about 2 minutes.

5. Immediately divide the hot filling between the prepared pie shells. Cover to prevent a skin from forming while you make the meringue pie topping. Evenly distribute the topping over the filling, spreading it into peaks and swirls and making sure it is attached to the pie crust all around the edges.

6. Place the pies on double sheet pans and bake at 375°F (190°C) for about 10 minutes or until the meringue is nicely browned. The pies must be refrigerated for several hours before serving to allow the filling to set.

MERINGUE PIE TOPPING yield: enough for 2 pies, 10 inches (25 cm) in diameter

It is important not to let the meringue mixture get to stiff peaks before you add the cornstarch mixture. You can cook the cornstarch mixture before you whip the egg whites if it is difficult for you to do both at the same time, but only just before (within a few minutes), and you must transfer the cornstarch mixture from the hot pan to a bowl or it will continue to cook and thicken from the residual heat.

1¼ cups (300 ml) egg whites (approximately 10)

2 or 3 drops lemon juice

10 ounces (285 g) granulated sugar

2 tablespoons (16 g) cornstarch

¾ cup (180 ml) water

2 teaspoons (10 ml) vanilla extract

1. With the mixer at high speed, whip the egg whites with the lemon juice until tripled in volume. Gradually add the sugar, lower the speed to medium, and continue whipping until soft peaks form.

2. While the egg whites are whipping (keep an eye on them), place the cornstarch in a small saucepan, gradually add the water, and stir until smooth. Bring to a simmer while stirring constantly. Once the mixture becomes translucent, continue cooking about 30 seconds longer. Remove from the heat and stir in the vanilla.

3. Immediately add the cornstarch mixture to the egg whites, turn the mixer back to high speed, and whip the meringue to stiff peaks. Be careful not to overwhip.

Pumpkin Pie yield: 2 pies, 10 inches (25 cm) in diameter

Although pumpkins are indigenous to North America, pumpkin pie, as with so many foods in this relatively young country, has an origin elsewhere as well. It is known to have existed in the early 1600s in England, where it was called *pompion* or *pompion pudding*. Pumpkin pies and other open-faced pies with soft fillings were referred to as *pumpkin puddings* early on in America. Even though it is easy enough to make your own pumpkin puree, the time involved makes it prohibitive for most people, who prefer to use canned, which in fact really tastes just about as good.

My first exposure to pumpkin was indeed making pumpkin pies, and it was certainly a memorable experience, if not a very funny one at the time. I was working on the cruise ship *MS Kungsholm*, and we were experiencing very rough weather in the Atlantic on our way from New York to the West Indies. Not only did neither I nor my two German colleagues know anything about pumpkin pies, but the tossing ship would have made it hard to prepare just about anything. The word from our executive chef was, "It is Thanksgiving and we must have pumpkin pies for the Americans, storm or no storm." He also cautioned us not to fill the pie shells more than halfway. Once we made the very liquid filling, we knew right away why that was and also that we were in for big trouble. The filling spilled out all over the ovens, causing smoke to pour out, the smell was horrible, and the portholes were all bolted shut due to the storm! I do not think we ever got the ovens completely clean again. The only consolation in this mess was that instead of needing dessert for 400 passengers, the storm caused a much smaller number to venture out of their cabins or, for that matter, to have dinner at all.

½ recipe Pâte Brisée (page 64)	2 teaspoons (3 g) ground cinnamon
5 eggs	1 teaspoon (2 g) ground ginger
3 cups (720 ml) cooked sugar pumpkin puree (directions follow) *or* canned pumpkin puree	½ teaspoon (1 g) ground cloves
	3½ cups (840 ml) half-and-half
12 ounces (340 g) granulated sugar	1 pint (480 ml) heavy cream
1 teaspoon (5 g) salt	1 tablespoon (15 g) granulated sugar

1. Roll the pâte brisée out to ⅛ inch (3 mm) thick. Line 2 pie pans, 10 inches (25 cm) in diameter, and flute the edges (see Figures 7-1, page 325, and 2-2 and 2-3, page 63). Cover the dough scraps and save for another use. Cover the dough in the pans with pieces of baking paper or commercial-grade plastic wrap and fill the shells with dried beans or pie weights. Bake the shells at 375°F (190°C) until the dough is set but has not yet started to color, about 12 minutes. Let the shells cool completely, then remove the paper or plastic and beans or pie weights.

2. Beat the eggs lightly to mix. Stir in the pumpkin puree. Mix together the first measure of granulated sugar, the salt, cinnamon, ginger, and cloves. Add this to the egg mixture. Stir in the half-and-half. Divide the filling evenly between the pie shells.

3. Bake at 375°F (190°C) for approximately 50 minutes or until the filling has puffed slightly and is firm around the edges. Let the pies cool.

4. Whip the heavy cream with the second measure of granulated sugar until stiff peaks form. Place the cream in a pastry bag with a No. 7 (14-mm) star tip. Pipe a shell border of cream around the edge of the pies (see Figure 10-28, page 480). Slice the pies into pieces of the desired size. Serve at room temperature.

You will need a 3-pound (1-kg, 365-g) sugar pumpkin. Bake the pumpkin at 375°F (190°C) until it feels soft when you press it with your thumb, about 1½ hours. Cool, peel or cut away the skin, cut the pumpkin in half, and remove the seeds (save them and toast them for snacks). Puree or mash the pumpkin flesh and pass it through a sieve.

Sweet Potato Pie yield: 2 pies, 10 inches (25 cm) in diameter

Sweet potatoes and sweet potato pie have deep ties to the American South and southern regional cooking. Sweet potatoes are also an important agricultural crop in the southern states, though they are also grown elsewhere in the country (New Jersey and California being the other top producers). The flesh is naturally sweet due to an enzyme in the potato that converts the majority of its starches to sugar as the potato matures. Still, most traditional American recipes call for generous quantities of additional sweeteners such as maple syrup, brown sugar, molasses, and, of course, marshmallows for the odd, but apparently essential, candied sweet potatoes served for Thanksgiving dinner. This strange combination was popularized in the 1920s, and though it is doubtful that anyone other than young children actually like it, is so ingrained in the holiday menu we will probably never be rid of it.

½ recipe Flaky Pie Dough (page 62)

5 eggs

3 cups (720 ml) cooked sweet potato puree (directions follow)

12 ounces (340 g) granulated sugar

1 teaspoon (5 g) salt

2 teaspoons (3 g) ground cinnamon

1 teaspoon (2 g) ground ginger

½ teaspoon (1 g) ground cloves

3½ cups (840 ml) half-and-half

1 pint (480 ml) heavy cream

1 tablespoon (15 g) granulated sugar

About Sweet Potatoes

The sweet potato is not related to the common white potato but is part of the morning glory family. Native to the Americas, it was brought back to Europe by Columbus in the late 1400s. By the middle of the sixteenth century, the sweet potato was cultivated in Spain and had been introduced to England, and sweet potato pie had became popular enough in England by the turn of the century to be mentioned by Shakespeare in *The Merry Wives of Windsor*. Sweet potatoes were so widely cultivated by the American colonists that this high-energy tuber was actually the main food source for some of the early settlers and soldiers in the Revolutionary War. (Sweet potatoes are, in fact, one of the most nutritious of all vegetables, containing only trace amounts of fat and approximately five times the recommended daily allowance of vitamin A in a single small potato, as well as substantial amounts of the vitamins B_6 and C.) The term *sweet potato* was not used in America until the mid-1700s, at which time it came about as a means to distinguish sweet potatoes from the white potatoes that had come to North America with the Irish immigrants.

There are two varieties of sweet potato. The moist orange-fleshed type has a darker skin and is longer and narrower in shape. The dry-fleshed variety has a slightly lighter skin, closer to the color of a russet potato, and is rounder, shaped something like a football. Darker moist-fleshed sweet potatoes are often erroneously called *yams*. Genuine yams are from a different botanical family and are much larger—growing up to 7 feet (2 m 10 cm) in length and up to 100 pounds (45 kg 500g)—and are found in Asia and Africa; they are seldom available in this country. Because of its widespread usage, this misnomer has become generally accepted.

1. Roll out the pie dough to ⅛ inch (3 mm) thick. Line 2 pie pans, 10 inches (25 cm) in diameter, and flute the edges (see Figures 7-1, page 325, and 2-2 and 2-3, page 63). Cover the dough scraps and save for another use. Cover the dough in the pans with rounds of baking paper or sheets of commercial-grade plastic wrap and fill the shells with dried beans or pie weights. Bake the shells at 375°F (190°C) until the dough is set but has not yet started to color, about 12 minutes. Let the shells cool completely, then remove the paper or plastic and beans or pie weights.

2. Beat the eggs lightly to mix. Stir in the sweet potato puree. Mix together the first measure of granulated sugar, the salt, cinnamon, ginger, and cloves. Add this to the egg mixture. Stir in the half-and-half. Divide the filling evenly between the pie shells.

3. Bake at 375°F (190°C) for approximately 50 minutes or until the filling has puffed slightly and is firm around the edges. Let the pies cool.

4. Whip the heavy cream with the second measure of granulated sugar until stiff peaks form. Slice the pies into pieces of the desired size. Serve at room temperature with a large dollop of whipped cream.

TO MAKE THE SWEET POTATO PUREE

Start with about 2 pounds (910 g) whole raw sweet potatoes (preferably the darker, moist-fleshed variety) with the skin on. Boil them gently until soft (do not let the skin break), peel, and puree or force through a fine sieve.

COBBLERS AND CRISPS

Cobblers are a very simple and quick way of using fresh seasonal fruit to create a delicious ending to a meal. Peach cobbler is an American favorite and is probably the best-known version; topped with homemade vanilla ice cream, it is almost synonymous with Fourth of July celebrations for some people. The only thing I do not like about cobblers made in the traditional form is that they really do not present very well and can often end up looking like a pie gone wrong! But then, a cobbler that does not look a little disheveled is not the genuine article. If the cobbler is not to be plated in the kitchen, use any presentable baking dish, such as an earthenware casserole, with a capacity of 2 quarts (1 L 920 ml). Cobblers are part of the "clump cake" category of desserts, which includes slumps, grunts, buckles, and betties. The French call them *poupeton*, which translates to "mess in the pan." Though none of these names may sound particularly appetizing, the continued popularity of these unaffected desserts after literally hundreds of years is ample proof of how good they are.

You could easily argue that a crisp is nothing but a cobbler with a different topping, and you would be absolutely right. Fruit crisps and cobblers are as traditional as the all-American fruit pie. Like a pie, they have a thick fruit filling, are easy and quick to make, and they're wonderful served warm with ice cream. But unlike a pie, neither has a bottom crust. Do not feel bound to use the exact types and proportions of fruit specified in fruit crisp recipes. These happen to be two of my favorites, but a fruit crisp (like a pie or a cobbler) is a great way to improvise and celebrate the abundant harvest of fresh ripe fruit.

Cobbler, crisp, crunch, crumble—what is the difference, you ask? Basically, not much, except for the topping. The biscuit-style topping of the cobbler is thick and soft. A crisp has a thin and crunchy topping, a crunch has almost the same topping except it is put on the bottom as well as the top, and a crumble is the name used more typically by the British for the same thing as a crisp. Does this make sense to you? It doesn't to me, but then, I did not grow up with these wonderful fruit treats.

Blueberry Cobbler yield: 2 cobblers, 10 inches (25 cm) in diameter, or 16 servings

1 pound 4 ounces (570 g) granulated sugar

2 ounces (55 g) cornstarch

1 teaspoon (1.5 g) ground cinnamon

1 teaspoon (2 g) ground nutmeg

1 cup (240 ml) water

2 quarts (1 L 920 ml) or 3 pounds (1 kg 365 g) blueberries

Cobbler Topping (recipe follows)

Crème Fraîche (page 821), sweetened whipped cream, or ice cream

1. In a saucepan, combine the sugar, cornstarch, cinnamon, and nutmeg. Gradually stir in the water. Bring the mixture to a full boil, stirring constantly. Remove from the heat.

2. Divide the berries between 2 cake pans, 10 inches (25 cm) in diameter. Pour the hot liquid over the fruit.

3. Bake uncovered at 400°F (205°C) for 10 minutes.

4. Remove from the oven and dollop the cobbler topping over the fruit.

5. Continue baking until the topping is golden brown and baked through, about 15 minutes longer. Serve warm with crème fraîche, whipped cream, or ice cream.

COBBLER TOPPING yield: 3 pounds 6 ounces (1 kg 535 g)

1 pound 6 ounces (625 g) bread flour

1 teaspoon (5 g) salt

3 tablespoons (36 g) baking powder

4 ounces (115 g) cold unsalted butter

3¼ cups (780 ml) heavy cream

1. Sift together the flour, salt, and baking powder. Cut the butter into small chunks, add, and cut into the flour mixture to the size of peas.

2. Pour in the cream all at once and stir rapidly with your hand to form a soft dough.

3. Place on a floured work surface and pat out to a rectangle 1½ inches (3.7 cm) thick. Make 2 rough single turns (see page 213), shaping the dough with your hands and not a rolling pin.

NOTE: Do not make the cobbler topping until you are ready to use it.

VARIATIONS

STRAWBERRY COBBLER

Follow the instructions for Blueberry Cobbler above substituting 3 pounds (1 kg 365 g), approximately 3 quarts (2L 880 ml), of strawberries. Wash the berries, remove the hulls, and cut the strawberries into quarters before weighing or measuring.

RASPBERRY COBBLER

Follow the instructions for Blueberry Cobbler above, but substitute 2 quarts (1 L 920 ml) or 4 pounds (1 kg 820 g) raspberries for the blueberries.

Cinnamon Peach Cobbler yield: 2 cobblers, 10 inches (25 cm) in diameter, or 16 servings

5 pounds (2 kg 275 g) ripe peaches (about 18 medium)

3 ounces (85 g) cinnamon sugar

1 recipe Cobbler Topping (page 376)

1 recipe Mascarpone-Amaretto Sauce (page 826)

Ground cinnamon

1. Wash the peaches, remove the pits, and cut each into about 8 wedges, leaving the skin on. Place in a bowl and toss with the cinnamon sugar. Divide between 2 cake pans, 10 inches (25 cm) in diameter, lightly pressing the fruit into the forms with your hands.

2. Use your hands or 2 spoons to place the cobbler topping on the peaches in random piles, leaving 1 inch (2.5 cm) of peaches uncovered around the rim of the pans to allow the batter to bake out. Do not smooth the batter top; it will not be an authentic cobbler if you do so.

3. Bake at 425°F (219°C) for approximately 40 minutes or until the topping is golden brown and baked through. Set the cobblers aside for at least 30 minutes before serving to allow the crust to absorb part of the liquid in the pan. Warm before serving, if necessary; cobbler should be served warm or hot, never chilled. Divide each pan into 8 portions.

4. Presentation: Place a portion of cobbler on a dessert plate. Spoon mascarpone sauce over one side of the cobbler, letting the sauce run onto the plate. Sprinkle cinnamon lightly on the sauce.

Gingered Apple Cobbler yield: 2 cobblers, 10 inches (25 cm) in diameter, or 16 servings

Try serving with Calvados Cream (page 698); it is much quicker to prepare than the bitter orange sauce, and it tastes great with the apples. Whipped cream flavored with bourbon is also good.

1½ ounces (40 g) Crystallized Ginger (page 15)

6 pounds 8 ounces (2 kg 955 g) tart cooking apples, such as Pippin or Granny Smith (approximately 15 medium)

¼ cup (60 ml) lemon juice

8 ounces (225 g) granulated sugar

4 ounces (115 g) unsalted butter

1 recipe Cobbler Topping (page 376)

Cinnamon sugar

1 recipe Bitter Orange Sauce (page 828)

Mint sprigs

1. Finely chop the crystallized ginger and reserve.

2. Peel, core, and cut the apples into ½-inch (1.2-cm) wedges. Place the wedges in a bowl with the lemon juice as you cut them, tossing them in the juice to coat.

3. Transfer the apples to a skillet or saucepan and add the sugar and butter. Cook over medium heat, stirring, until the apples are soft but not mushy. Mix in the ginger.

4. Divide the apples, including all of the liquid, between 2 cake pans, 10 inches (25 cm) in diameter and 2 inches (5 cm) high. Press the apples into the pans firmly.

5. Follow the instructions in Step 2 of Cinnamon Peach Cobbler (page 377) for adding the cobbler topping. Sprinkle cinnamon sugar lightly over the top.

6. Bake at 425°F (219°C) for approximately 40 minutes or until the topping is golden brown and baked through. Set the cobblers aside for at least 30 minutes before serving to allow the crust to absorb part of the liquid in the pan. Warm before serving if necessary. Divide each pan into 8 portions.

7. Presentation: Place a portion of cobbler on a dessert plate. Pour a pool of bitter orange sauce on the side and decorate with a sprig of mint.

Rhubarb Cobbler yield: 2 cobblers, 10 inches (25 cm) in diameter, or 16 servings

Rhubarb cobbler is excellent served with Honey-Vanilla Frozen Yogurt (page 740) instead of Romanoff sauce.

5 pounds (2 kg 275 g) rhubarb stalks	1 recipe Cobbler Topping (page 376) (see Step 3)
2 ounces (55 g) cornstarch	
12 ounces (340 g) granulated sugar	1 recipe Romanoff Sauce (page 831)
¾ cup (180 ml) or 9 ounces (225 g) honey	Mint sprigs
2 ounces (55 g) Crystallized Ginger (page 15)	

1. Wash and dry the rhubarb. Trim the top and bottom off each stalk and discard. If any stalks are wider than 1 inch (2.5 cm), cut them in half lengthwise. Cut the stalks into ½-inch (1.2-cm) slices.

2. Place a stainless steel bowl in the oven until it is hot. Stir the cornstarch and sugar together in the bowl, add the rhubarb pieces, and toss to coat them thoroughly. Mix in the honey and set aside at room temperature for about 30 minutes.

3. Chop the ginger and add it to the cobbler topping, mixed with the dry ingredients.

4. Transfer the rhubarb with all of the liquid to a saucepan. Cook over low heat, stirring constantly, until the rhubarb starts to turn a little soft. Do not overcook; the rhubarb will fall apart very quickly at this point.

5. Divide the rhubarb mixture between 2 cake pans, 10 inches (25 cm) in diameter, lightly pressing the fruit into the pans with your hands. Use 2 spoons or your hands to drop the cobbler topping over the rhubarb in random piles, leaving 1 inch (2.5 cm) of rhubarb uncovered around the outside of the pans to allow the topping to bake out. Do not smooth the batter over the top.

6. Bake at 425°F (219°C) for about 30 minutes or until the topping is golden brown and baked through. Set the cobblers aside for at least 30 minutes before serving to allow the crust to absorb part of the liquid in the pan. Warm before serving if necessary. Cobbler should be served warm or hot, never chilled. Divide into 16 portions.

7. Presentation: Place a portion of cobbler on a dessert plate. Pour a pool of Romanoff sauce on the side and decorate with a sprig of mint.

Fall Fruit Crisp with Cranberries yield: 1 crisp, 10 inches (25 cm) in diameter

This crisp makes a refreshing alternative to the pies that are traditionally served for Thanksgiving, and it is most appropriate because cranberries (like blueberries) are native to the United States. I use dried cranberries here to prevent the cranberry juice from staining the fruit filling, but if this is not a concern, replacing the dried cranberries with fresh will work fine: Use 8 ounces (225 g) fresh cranberries and add 4 ounces (115 g) granulated sugar. Place in a saucepan over medium heat and cook, stirring constantly, until the cranberries have popped open and the sugar is melted. Let cool a bit before combining with the apple and pear mixture.

For a delicious and unusual combination, try substituting domestic feijoas—which are inexpensive and available from late fall through the winter—for about 8 ounces (225 g) fruit mixture (1 pear or apple). Use 8 ounces (225 g) or 2 medium feijoas. Remove the skin from the feijoas with a vegetable peeler. Cut the flesh into ½-inch (1.2-cm) cubes and combine with the apple and pear chunks.

FILLING

2 pounds (910 g) cooking apples, such as Granny Smith or Pippin (approximately 5 medium)

2 pounds (910 g) Bartlett or Anjou pears (approximately 4 medium)

4 ounces (115 g) dried cranberries

2 tablespoons (16 g) bread flour

3 tablespoons (45 ml) lemon juice

¼ cup (80 ml) or 3 ounces (85 g) honey

TOPPING

5 ounces (140 g) bread flour

3 ounces (85 g) rolled oats

5 ounces (140 g) light brown sugar

1 teaspoon (1.5 g) ground cinnamon

6 ounces (170 g) cold unsalted butter

1. Peel, core, and cut the apples and pears in half, or cut them in half after peeling and use a melon ball cutter to cut out the core. Cut each half into ¾-inch (2-cm) chunks. Place the apples, pears, and dried cranberries in a bowl and toss to combine.

2. Combine the flour and lemon juice. Add the honey, then combine with the fruit cubes and cranberries, tossing to combine well. The lemon juice will help keep the fruit from turning brown and add a nice accent to the flavor as well.

3. Press the fruit pieces into a cake pan, 10 inches (25 cm) in diameter, including any liquid.

4. Prepare the topping by combining the remaining flour, rolled oats, brown sugar, and cinnamon. Cut the butter into small pieces and add to the flour mixture, mixing just until the topping starts to come together; it should still be lumpy. Sprinkle the topping evenly over the fruit mixture.

5. Bake at 375°F (190°C) for approximately 50 minutes. The apple and pear chunks should be soft, and the liquid released by the fruit during the initial cooking stage should be reduced to a small quantity of syrup. To check on the fruit and the amount of liquid, carefully lift off a small piece of the topping (it should be crisp and brown) and look inside. If the fruit needs to cook further and/or there is too much liquid, continue baking and check again. If the topping is already brown, cover the pan loosely to protect the topping from becoming too dark. Serve the crisp warm, accompanied by Bourbon Sauce (page 816) if desired.

Peach and Berry Crisp yield: 2 crisps, 10 inches (25 cm) in diameter, or 16 servings (Photo 14)

This unconventional way of serving a simple and humble fruit crisp transforms country-style fare into an elegant dessert. You can use the same treatment for fruit cobblers as well. If you do not want to be bothered with making handles for the Florentina baskets (I leave them out all the time for larger banquets), make a single recipe of Florentina Batter. In this case, you can achieve height in your presentation by piping the whipped cream rosette on the cookie that tops the dessert rather than on the plate in front. Place the sliced fruit on the rosette as directed.

Peach and Berry Filling (recipe follows)	Sour Cream Mixture for Piping (page 832)
1¼ recipes Florentina Batter (page 306)	Crisp Topping (recipe follows)
1 cup (240 ml) heavy cream	Powdered sugar
1 teaspoon (2 g) ground ginger	Berries and sliced peaches
1 recipe Raspberry Sauce (page 830)	

1. Divide the crisp filling evenly between 2 cake pans, 10 inches (25 cm) in diameter, or place it in 1 small hotel pan (see Note). Cover the pans with aluminum foil and puncture a few holes in the foil to allow steam to escape. Bake the filling at 375°F (190°C) until the fruit is soft and cooked through, approximately 1 hour. Set aside to cool to room temperature.

2. If you are making handles for the baskets, reserve a little less than one-quarter of the Florentina batter. Draw 16 circles, 5 inches (12.5 cm) in diameter, on a sheet of baking paper. Invert the paper on top of a sheet pan. Divide the remaining Florentina batter among the circles. Spread out, bake, and trim the cookies following the instructions on pages 305 and 306, using a 5-inch (12.5-cm) plain, round cookie cutter to trim them.

3. A few at a time, reheat the trimmed cookies to soften them. Using a shallow, round form approximately 4 inches (10 cm) in diameter with straight sides, shape the cookies into shallow bowls (see Figure 6-17, page 308). Reserve.

4. To make the handles, shape the reserved Florentina batter into a rectangle measuring 8 x 16 inches (20 x 40 cm) on a sheet pan lined with baking paper, patting it out with your hands. Bake as for the cookies; the rectangle will take a little longer. Cut across into 20 strips, ¾ inch (2 cm) wide (you only need 16, but chances are a few will break). The strips should be 7 to 8 inches (17.5 to 20 cm) long. Reheat the strips and form them into curved handles by draping them over a rolling pin when they come out of the oven.

5. Whip the heavy cream with the ground ginger until stiff peaks form. Place the whipped cream in a pastry bag with a No. 6 (12-mm) star tip. Reserve the cream in the refrigerator.

6. Presentation: Cover the base of a dessert plate with raspberry sauce. Place some of the sour cream mixture in a piping bag and cut a small opening. Pipe the mixture on top of the sauce in a spoke pattern, as if you were cutting a cake into 12 pieces. Drag a small wooden skewer through the lines in a spiral (see Figure 16-8, page 812). Using 2 soupspoons, lift about ⅓ cup (80 ml) fruit filling and place it in a prepared Florentina baskets. Place 1 crisp topping cookie in the center of the filling; the filling should be exposed around the sides. Sift powdered sugar lightly over the top. Place the dessert in the center of the plate on top of the sauce. Pipe a rosette of whipped cream in front of the dessert and decorate the cream with a slice of peach and a berry (use the same type of berry you used in the filling). If you are using handles, set a handle in place, pushing it gently into the filling to secure. Serve immediately.

NOTE: For a simple, traditional presentation, omit the Florentina cookie shells and bake the topping on top of the fruit filling, using 1 or 2 pans, as described in the recipe, or individual earthenware forms. Do not cover with foil when baking. Individual forms will take a shorter time.

PEACH AND BERRY FILLING yield: about 5 cups (1 L 200 ml) or 16 servings

3 pounds (1 kg 365 g) firm, ripe peaches

1 pound 6 ounces (625 g) fresh berries (blueberries and blackberries are best, but raspberries or strawberries also work)

2 tablespoons (16 g) cornstarch

1½ ounces (40 g) cake flour

4 ounces (115 g) granulated sugar

1. Wash, stone, and cut the peaches into ¼-inch (6-mm) slices. Place the sliced peaches in a mixing bowl and add the berries.

2. Sift together the cornstarch, cake flour, and sugar. Sprinkle on top of the fruit and combine gently, using your hands.

CRISP TOPPING yield: 1 pound 12 ounces (795 g) or 16 portions

8 ounces (225 g) light brown sugar

7 ounces (200 g) unsalted butter, at room temperature

7 ounces (200 g) cake flour

½ teaspoon (2 g) baking powder

½ teaspoon (2 g) baking soda

4 ounces (115 g) sliced almonds, lightly crushed

½ teaspoon (2.5 g) salt

1. Mix the brown sugar and the butter together until just combined. Sift the flour with the baking powder and baking soda. Stir the flour mixture into the butter and sugar mixture together with the sliced almonds and salt. The mixture should be the consistency of streusel.

2. Divide the topping into 16 equal portions and form them into mounds, 1½ inches (3.7 cm) in diameter, on a sheet pan lined with baking paper.

3. Bake at 375°F (190°C) until lightly browned, about 12 minutes. The cookies should be crisp throughout rather than soft and chewy.

Tea Cakes, Pound Cakes, Muffins, and Other Quick Breads

TEA CAKES

Tea cakes are generally made from a richer and heavier batter than sponge cakes. Therefore, they require a leavening agent, such as baking powder or baking soda. Rather than adding the filling after the cake is baked, a flavoring or filling is added directly to the batter. For example, chopped nuts, sliced apples, chocolate chips, raisins, bananas, and spices are used to flavor the tea cakes in this chapter. Because the cakes are heavier, they are baked in a tube pan, loaf pan, or other narrow form for even baking. The decoration, if any, on a tea cake is usually kept very simple, often just a sprinkling of powdered sugar or a plain glaze. This makes them quick and easy to prepare. Tea cakes will remain fresh for several days in the refrigerator and actually become moister after a few days. Sliced tea cakes are always included, along with an assortment of petits fours or cookies, at the traditional 3 o'clock coffee break in Sweden.

Apple Cinnamon Cake yield: 4 cakes, 1 pound 5 ounces (595 g) each

Try the following delicious variation on this classic tea cake: Instead of poaching the peeled and cored apples, cut them into wedges and set aside. Place 2 ounces (55 g) unsalted butter and 5 ounces (140 g) granulated sugar in a skillet. Heat, stirring constantly, until the mixture begins to bubble. Add the apple wedges and cook, stirring frequently, until the apples are soft. Add half of the batter to the tube pans, sprinkle cinnamon on top, arrange the apples over the batter, and top with the remaining batter.

Melted unsalted butter

Finely ground bread crumbs

2 pounds (910 g) Golden Delicious, Pippin, or Granny Smith apples (4 medium)

½ recipe Plain Poaching Syrup (page 31)

Cinnamon sugar

1 pound (455 g) granulated sugar

6 eggs, at room temperature

2 teaspoons (10 ml) vanilla extract

1 pound (455 g) bread flour

2 tablespoons (24 g) baking powder

1 teaspoon (1.5 g) ground cinnamon

1 teaspoon (2 g) ground cardamom

1 teaspoon (5 g) salt

12 ounces (340 g) melted unsalted butter

1¼ cups (300 ml) half-and-half, at room temperature

Small-Batch Apple Cinnamon Cake
yield: 2 cakes, 1 pound 5 ounces (595 g) each

Melted unsalted butter

Finely ground bread crumbs

1 pound (455 g) Golden Delicious, Pippin, or Granny Smith apples (about 2)

½ recipe Plain Poaching Syrup (page 31)

Cinnamon sugar

8 ounces (225 g) granulated sugar

3 eggs, at room temperature

1 teaspoon (5 ml) vanilla extract

8 ounces (225 g) bread flour

1 tablespoon (12 g) baking powder

1 teaspoon (1.5 g) ground cinnamon

½ teaspoon (1 g) ground cardamom

½ teaspoon (2.5 g) salt

7 ounces (200 g) melted unsalted butter

½ cup (120 ml) half-and-half, at room temperature

---

1. Brush melted butter on the inside of 4 tube-style cake pans, 1 quart (960 ml) in capacity (2 pans for the smaller recipe). Coat the pans with bread crumbs. Set aside.

2. Peel and core the apples. Poach them in the syrup until soft, about 15 minutes, remove from the liquid, and let cool. Slice the apples into ½-inch (1.2-cm) wedges. Toss the wedges in cinnamon sugar to coat and arrange them evenly over the bottoms of the forms.

3. Whip the sugar, eggs, and vanilla together until light and foamy.

4. Sift together the flour, baking powder, cinnamon, cardamom, and salt. Fold into the egg mixture.

5. Combine the melted butter with the half-and-half. Add to the batter slowly. Divide the batter among the prepared cake pans, filling them no more than halfway.

6. Bake at 350°F (175°C) for about 45 minutes or until baked through. Unmold the cakes and let them cool on a cake rack. When they are completely cool, cover the cakes and refrigerate.

Basque Cake yield: 2 cakes, 10 inches (25 cm) in diameter

Basque Cake comes from Spain. It is a type of pound cake, or tea cake, filled with a vanilla custard, which is certainly not all that unusual, except that here the filling is added before the cakes are baked. This step allows the vanilla and rum plenty of time to fully flavor the cake, and it makes the cakes very moist. Should the flavor seem too strong, adjust the amount of rum to suit your own taste. The custard layer in the center helps make this cake a great keeper. Stored, covered, in the refrigerator, it will keep fresh up to 1 week.

Butter and Flour Mixture (page 7) or pan spray

1 pound 8 ounces (680 g) unsalted butter, at room temperature

1 pound 8 ounces (680 g) granulated sugar

2 tablespoons (30 ml) vanilla extract

5 eggs, at room temperature

1 pound 4 ounces (570 g) cake flour

1 tablespoon (12 g) baking powder

1 teaspoon (5 g) salt

2 tablespoons (30 ml) dark rum

1 pound (455 g) Pastry Cream (page 845)

2 ounces (55 g) thinly sliced almonds

Powdered sugar

1. Grease the inside of 2 cake pans, 10 inches (25 cm) in diameter, using the butter and flour mixture or pan spray.

2. Cream together the butter, sugar, and vanilla until light and fluffy. Add the eggs, 1 at a time.

3. Sift together the flour, baking powder, and salt. Gradually incorporate the dry ingredients into the butter mixture.

4. Place the batter in a pastry bag with a No. 5 (10-mm) plain tip. Pipe the batter in a spiral over the bottom of a prepared cake pan, starting in the center. Pipe an additional ring of batter on top of the largest ring against the inside perimeter of the pan. Repeat with the second cake pan; you will not use all of the batter.

5. Stir the rum into the pastry cream. Divide the pastry cream between the pans on top of the batter and spread it out evenly within the frames made by the largest rings of batter so that the pastry cream does not touch the sides of the pans. Pipe the remaining batter in a spiral on top of the pastry cream in each pan. If needed, use a small spatula to spread the batter to the edge of the pan. Sprinkle the sliced almonds over the tops.

6. Bake at 350°F (175°C) for approximately 50 minutes. Allow to cool in the pans. Remove the cakes from the pans and dust powdered sugar lightly over the tops. Cut into the desired number of servings.

Butterless, Eggless, Milkless Spice Cake yield: 1 cake, 10 inches (25 cm) in diameter

This spice cake is based on a recipe from my wife's family, where it was known as Mrs. Ruby's Cake. The recipe is unusual in that, as evidenced by the title, it contains no dairy products. This type of dessert was popularized during World War I in part due to food shortages and also because it was very economical. This cake is composed of ingredients almost always in stock in the pantry, and at the same time it finds a use for leftovers—in this case, coffee. The batter can be put together in just a few minutes; the cake has a nice deep spice flavor, a moist texture, and it keeps well. Like many tea cakes, it actually improves after a day or two. This is a good choice for an afternoon snack.

Butter and Flour Mixture (page 7) or pan spray

1 cup (240 ml) strong brewed coffee (leftover is fine)

1 cup (240 ml) vegetable oil

8 ounces (225 g) granulated sugar

5 ounces (140 g) dark raisins

½ teaspoon (1 g) ground nutmeg

2 teaspoons (3 g) ground cinnamon

1 teaspoon (2 g) ground cloves

1 teaspoon (4 g) baking soda

1 tablespoon (15 ml) water

1 teaspoon (4 g) baking powder

6 ounces (170 g) bread flour

2 ounces (55 g) walnuts, coarsely chopped

1. Brush butter and flour mixture over the inside of a 10-inch (25-cm) tube pan, or coat with pan spray.

2. Pour the coffee and vegetable oil into a saucepan. Add the sugar, raisins, and the spices. Bring the mixture to a boil and boil 3 minutes. Remove from the heat and set aside to cool for about 10 minutes.

3. Stir the baking soda into the water. Stir this combination into the mixture in the saucepan; it will foam up.

4. Sift together the baking powder and flour. Stir into the batter. Stir in the walnuts. Spoon the batter into the prepared pan.

5. Bake at 350°F (175°C) for approximately 35 minutes or until baked through. Cool to room temperature, unmold, and store, tightly wrapped.

Chocolate Chip Cake yield: 4 cakes, I pound 5 ounces (595 g) each

Although this cake tastes great as is, especially if you age it a few days in the refrigerator, you can also dress it up a bit by first brushing Apricot Glaze (page 5) over the top and sides, then covering the glaze with a thin layer of melted coating chocolate. Place an icing rack on a sheet pan lined with baking paper, place the cakes on the rack, and slowly pour or spoon the melted chocolate over the top. Remove the cakes from the rack before the chocolate hardens. Slice the cakes, using a heated serrated knife in a sawing motion to avoid cracking the glaze.

Butter and Flour Mixture (page 7) or pan spray

12 ounces (340 g) unsalted butter, at room temperature

12 ounces (340 g) granulated sugar

8 eggs, at room temperature

2 teaspoons (10 ml) vanilla extract

1 pound 5 ounces (595 g) bread flour

1 tablespoon (12 g) baking powder

7 ounces (200 g) sweet dark chocolate, chopped into raisin-sized pieces

8 ounces (225 g) hazelnuts, toasted and crushed

Grated zest of 1 orange

1¼ cups (300 ml) whole milk, at room temperature

> **Small-Batch Chocolate Chip Cake**
> yield: 2 cakes, I pound 5 ounces (595 g) each
>
> Butter and Flour Mixture (page 7) or pan spray
>
> 6 ounces (170 g) unsalted butter, at room temperature
>
> 6 ounces (170 g) granulated sugar
>
> 4 eggs, at room temperature
>
> 1 teaspoon (5 ml) vanilla extract
>
> 11 ounces (310 g) bread flour
>
> 1½ teaspoons (6 g) baking powder
>
> 4 ounces (115 g) sweet dark chocolate, chopped into raisin-sized pieces
>
> 4 ounces (115 g) hazelnuts, toasted and crushed
>
> Grated zest of 1 small orange
>
> ¾ cup (180 ml) whole milk, at room temperature

1. Brush butter and flour mixture on the insides of 4 rectangular fluted forms, 1 quart (960 ml) in capacity (2 pans for the smaller recipe), or coat the pans with pan spray.

2. Beat the softened butter with the sugar until fluffy. Add the eggs, 1 at a time. Mix in the vanilla.

3. Sift the flour with the baking powder. Combine the chopped chocolate, hazelnuts, and orange zest with the flour. Mix into the butter mixture in 2 additions, alternating with the milk. Divide the batter between the prepared pans.

4. Bake at 350°F (175°C) for about 50 minutes or until baked through.

5. Unmold as soon as possible and let the cakes cool on a cake rack.

6. When cooled, wrap the cakes and store in the refrigerator.

Chocolate Gugelhupf *yield: 4 cakes, 1 pound 4 ounces (570 g) each*

This coffee cake version of the classic Gugelhupf (see page 244 for more information), gets an unusual flavor bonus from potatoes, which also add moisture and shelf life (although I don't think you will have to worry about leftovers). This batter can be used to make good muffins as well; they are especially nice with the addition of dried cranberries and/or pears. Reconstitute the fruit before adding it to the batter at the end of the recipe. Portion 4 ounces (115 g) batter for each muffin. Bake at 375°F (190°C) for approximately 25 minutes. You will get about 20 muffins.

Melted unsalted butter

Blanched almonds, finely ground (almond meal)

8 ounces (225 g) unsalted butter, at room temperature

1 pound 2 ounces (510 g) granulated sugar

2 teaspoons (10 ml) vanilla extract

6 eggs, at room temperature

12 ounces (340 g) russet potatoes, peeled, boiled, and mashed

15 ounces (430 g) cake flour

1½ ounces (40 g) unsweetened cocoa powder

1½ tablespoons (18 g) baking powder

1 teaspoon (5 g) salt

8 ounces (225 g) blanched almonds, finely ground (see Note, page 449)

1¼ cups (300 ml) heavy cream, at room temperature

Small-Batch Chocolate Gugelhupf
yield: 2 cakes, 1 pound 4 ounces (570 g) each

Melted unsalted butter

Blanched almonds, finely ground (almond meal)

4 ounces (115 g) unsalted butter, at room temperature

9 ounces (255 g) granulated sugar

1 teaspoon (5 ml) vanilla extract

3 eggs, at room temperature

6 ounces (170 g) russet potatoes, peeled, boiled, and mashed

7 ounces (200 g) cake flour

2½ tablespoons (20 g) unsweetened cocoa powder

1½ teaspoons (10 g) baking powder

½ teaspoon (3 g) salt

4 ounces (115 g) blanched almonds, finely ground (see Note, page 449)

½ cup (120 ml) heavy cream, at room temperature

---

1. Brush melted butter on the inside of 4 gugelhupf forms or other 1-quart (960-ml) tube pans. Coat with ground almonds.

2. Beat the soft butter with the sugar until light and fluffy. Add the vanilla to the eggs, then gradually add the eggs to the butter. Mix in the mashed potatoes.

3. Sift together the flour, cocoa powder, baking powder, and salt. Mix in the ground almonds. Add to the butter mixture in 2 additions, alternating with the cream. Divide the batter among the prepared forms. If you are using small forms, do not fill them more than two-thirds full.

4. Bake at 350°F (175°C) for about 50 minutes or until baked through.

5. Immediately unmold and let the cakes cool on a cake rack.

6. When the cakes are completely cold, wrap in plastic and refrigerate.

Cinnamon Lemon Cake yield: 2 cakes, baked in 1-quart (960-ml) gugelhupf or other ring-style pans (Photo 28)

If you bake the cakes in cake pans where the center is indented but not open all the way through to the bottom like a tube pan, try the following to add an unusual twist to the presentation. Sprinkle ½ teaspoon (1.5 g) unflavored gelatin powder on top of 1 tablespoon (15 ml) water in an oversized bowl and set aside to soften. Warm ¾ cup (180 ml) Lemon Curd (page 844) to room temperature over a bain-marie. Heat the gelatin to dissolve it, then quickly stir the warm lemon curd into the gelatin mixture. Divide the lemon curd between the two unmolded cakes, pouring it into the center openings on top of the inverted cakes. Place the cakes in the refrigerator for about 15 minutes to set the lemon curd. Decorate with a mint spring and sift powdered sugar over the tops.

If you use Flexipans, you will need to skip coating the pans with butter and almonds in Step 1. You can add the almonds to the batter instead, or just leave them out. The baking time will also increase by about 10 minutes. After the cakes have cooled a bit, place them in the refrigerator until they are completely chilled before pushing them out of the Flexipans.

The batter for these cakes can also be used to make muffins. A full recipe will yield approximately 32 muffins baked in Flexipan No. 3051.

Melted unsalted butter	2 tablespoons (30 ml) fresh lemon juice
2 ounces (55 g) sliced almonds, lightly crushed	5 eggs, at room temperature
14 ounces (400 g) granulated sugar	¾ cup whole milk, at room temperature
1 teaspoon (1.5 g) ground cinnamon	5 ounces (140 g) bread flour
10 ounces (285 g) unsalted butter, at room temperature	5 ounces (140 g) cake flour
3 tablespoons (45 ml) finely chopped lemon zest	1 tablespoon (12 g) baking powder

1. Brush the inside of 2 gugelhupf or other tube-style pans with melted butter (if using Flexipans, see introduction). Coat the butter with the crushed almonds (do not forget the center tube) and shake out the excess. Set the pans aside and reserve the leftover almonds.

2. Combine the sugar and the cinnamon. Add to the butter and cream together for a few minutes, scraping down the sides of the bowl as needed. Add the lemon zest and lemon juice.

3. Combine the eggs and the milk. Reserve.

4. Sift the bread flour, cake flour, and baking powder together. Mix into the batter in 2 portions, alternating with the milk-egg mixture. Divide the batter between the prepared pans and sprinkle the reserved almonds on top.

5. Bake at 350°F for approximately 30 minutes or until baked through. The cake should be well browned and completely set inside. Let cool at room temperature before inverting to unmold.

> **CHEF'S TIP**
> A typical gugelhupf pan is about twice the size of the pans called for here but can be used instead, with excellent results; they simply will not be filled with batter. Because the pattern is the same over the entire surface of the pans (top to bottom), the cakes will look just as if they were baked in the smaller pans.

Flourless Carrot Tea Cake yield: 2 cakes, 10 inches (25 cm) in diameter

Carrot cakes are probably the best-known survivor of the large group of cakes made with root vegetables—parsnips, potatoes, turnips, and, to a lesser extent, beets—which were popular throughout the eighteenth and nineteenth centuries. This recipe has a lighter composition than the more traditional Carrot Layer Cake (page 493). Here, finely ground almonds are used as a binding agent instead of flour. If you do not have ready-made almond flour (almond meal) and are grinding the blanched almonds in a food processor, add ¼ cup (60 ml) of the sugar to the almonds as you grind them to help absorb the oil released by the nuts and prevent the mixture from caking. The almonds should, ideally, be as fine as granulated sugar after processing. This cake is a great keeper; it may be stored in the refrigerator, well wrapped, for up to 1 week, and in the freezer for much longer.

12 egg yolks (1 cup/240 ml)

⅓ cup (80 ml) or 4 ounces (115 g) honey

12 ounces (340 g) carrots, peeled and finely grated (see Chef's Tip)

2 tablespoons (30 ml) dark rum

1 teaspoon (5 ml) vanilla extract

1 pound 3 ounces (540 g) blanched almonds, ground very fine, or almond meal

12 egg whites (1½ cups/360 ml)

10 ounces (285 g) granulated sugar

Powdered sugar

1. Line the bottom of 2 cake pans, 10 inches (25 cm) in diameter, with baking paper (see Figures 1-24 to 1-26, page 57).

2. Whip the egg yolks and honey to the ribbon stage. Fold in the carrots (including the juice), rum, and vanilla. Fold in the ground almonds.

3. Whip the egg whites to soft peaks while gradually adding the granulated sugar. Carefully fold this mixture into the carrot mixture. Divide the batter between the prepared pans.

4. Bake at 375°F (190°C) for 10 minutes. Lower the heat to 350°F (175°C) and continue baking approximately 30 minutes longer. Let the cakes cool for 10 to 15 minutes.

5. Run a knife around the inside perimeter of the cake pans and remove the cakes by inverting them onto cardboard; immediately turn them right-side up again. When the cakes are completely cool—or, better yet, the next day (wrap and refrigerate if leaving overnight)—place a lattice design template on top and sift powdered sugar over the cakes. Cut into the desired number of slices.

Lemon Verbena Scented Fruitcake yield: 2 loaves, 10 × 3 × 3 inches (25 × 7.5 × 7.5 cm) each

This recipe utilizes my latest favorite herb, lemon verbena, which gives the cakes a contemporary Mediterranean flavor, as does the candied angelica. If you have difficulty finding either the angelica or the verbena, you can substitute candied pineapple for the angelica and fresh mint for the verbena, or you can leave either one out; the cake will still have plenty of flavor.

Don't be scared off by the "fruitcake" part of this recipe title. Unlike some of those horrid holiday creations, this is a very light and great-tasting version that is actually meant to be eaten and enjoyed, not just given away as a gift. When it's done right, a buttery cake flavored with dried fruits and spices is really too good an idea to confine to just a few weeks out of the year, so I created this interpretation to enjoy year round.

2 ounces (55 g) candied angelica, diced

3 ounces (85 g) dried currants

3 ounces (85 g) light raisins

2 ounces (55 g) candied orange peel, diced

2 ounces (55 g) candied lemon peel, diced

¼ cup (60 ml) dark rum

12 ounces (340 g) unsalted butter, at room temperature

12 ounces (340 g) granulated sugar

6 egg yolks (½ cup/120 ml) at room temperature

1 ounce (30 g) fresh lemon verbena leaves, finely chopped

12 ounces (340 g) cake flour

2 teaspoons (8 g) baking powder

½ teaspoon (1 g) ground ginger

½ teaspoon (1 g) ground nutmeg

½ teaspoon (1 g) ground cloves

1 teaspoon (5 g) salt

3 ounces (85 g) poppy seeds

6 egg whites (¾ cup/180 ml), at room temperature

Powdered sugar

I. Line the loaf pans with baking paper and set aside.

2. Place the angelica, currants, raisins, candied orange peel, and candied lemon peel in a bowl. Add the rum and stir to combine. Cover and macerate at room temperature for 1 hour.

3. Place the butter, 6 ounces (170 g) granulated sugar, the egg yolks, and the lemon verbena in a bowl. Cream until light and fluffy.

4. Sift together the flour, baking powder, spices, and salt; mix in the poppy seeds. Combine with the fruit mixture, tossing to coat each piece of fruit with the flour mixture.

5. Beat the egg whites with the remaining granulated sugar until stiff peaks form. Stir half of the whipped egg whites into the butter mixture. Fold in the fruit mixture, followed by the remaining egg whites.

6. Divide the batter between the prepared pans and spread out evenly.

7. Bake at 375°F (190°C) for approximately 1 hour or until baked through; use a cake tester to check. Let the cakes cool in the pans for a few minutes before unmolding. Unmold and allow to cool completely.

8. Sift powdered sugar over the top of the loaves before serving.

Lingonberry Cake yield: 4 cakes, 1 pound 8 ounces (680 g) each

You can easily substitute cranberry jam if lingonberry jam is unavailable. Or you can substitute raw IQF lingonberries or cranberries, in which case you will need to cook them first, adding some sugar. This tea cake provides a nice change of pace, as the lingonberries add a special slightly tart flavor and also keep the cake moist. I have a passion for these small northern berries which grow wild in many sunny openings in the Scandinavian forest and other northern regions. I would probably love any recipe that featured them.

Melted unsalted butter

Finely ground bread crumbs or almond meal

12 ounces (340 g) walnuts

1 pound 2 ounces (510 g) granulated sugar

2 teaspoons (10 g) salt

8 ounces (225 g) unsalted butter, at room temperature

1 pound (455 g) cake flour

2 teaspoons (4 g) ground cardamom

1 teaspoon (2 g) ground nutmeg

1 teaspoon (4 g) baking soda

1 teaspoon (4 g) baking powder

1¼ cups (300 ml) heavy cream, at room temperature

1 cup (240 ml) buttermilk, at room temperature

5 eggs, at room temperature

1 pound (455 g) lingonberry jam

Small-Batch Lingonberry Cake
yield: 2 cakes, 1 pound 8 ounces (680 g) each

Melted unsalted butter

Finely ground bread crumbs or almond meal

6 ounces (170 g) walnuts

9 ounces (255 g) granulated sugar

1 teaspoon (5 g) salt

4 ounces (115 g) unsalted butter, at room temperature

8 ounces (225 g) cake flour

1 teaspoon (2 g) ground cardamom

½ teaspoon (1 g) ground nutmeg

½ teaspoon (2 g) baking soda

½ teaspoon (2 g) baking powder

½ cup (120 ml) heavy cream, at room temperature

½ cup (120 ml) buttermilk, at room temperature

3 eggs, at room temperature

8 ounces (225 g) lingonberry jam

---

1. Brush melted butter inside 4 rectangular fluted cake pans, 1 quart (960 ml) in capacity (2 pans for the smaller recipe). Coat the pans with bread crumbs or almond meal and set aside.

2. Chop the walnuts into raisin-sized pieces, toast them lightly, then set aside to cool.

3. Beat together the sugar, salt, and soft butter for a few minutes until well combined.

4. Sift together the flour, cardamom, nutmeg, baking soda, and baking powder.

5. Combine the heavy cream, buttermilk, and eggs.

6. Incorporate the dry ingredients into the butter mixture in 2 additions, alternating with the cream mixture. Mix at medium speed for 4 to 5 minutes. Stir the toasted walnuts and jam into the batter. Divide the batter between the prepared cake pans. If using smaller pans, do not fill them more than two-thirds full.

7. Bake at 375°F (190°C) for approximately 35 minutes or until the top springs back when pressed lightly in the center. Unmold immediately and let the cakes cool.

8. Store the cakes, wrapped in plastic, in the refrigerator for up to 1 week.

Meyer Lemon Semolina Cake yield: 2 cakes, 10 inches (25 cm) in diameter

This is a quick, easily made cake that can be served plain or with fresh berries. If you can get them, try Japanese wineberries, which are small and golden in color, ripening to a light red. These raspberry lookalikes are juicy and refreshing, with a flavor similar to grapes, and the plant that they grow on is particularly unusual and decorative.

For an even prettier plate presentation, make individual servings by piping the batter into cake rings instead. You will need 16 cake rings, 3 inches (7.5 cm) in diameter by 2 inches (5 cm) in height, placed on an even paper-lined sheet pan. These, of course, will require a much shorter baking time. In Step 7 pipe a rosette of whipped cream in the center of the small cakes and decorate with berries.

1 pound 6 ounces (625 g) unsalted butter, at room temperature	1 pound (455 g) sour cream, at room temperature
1 pound 10 ounces (740 g) granulated sugar	2 tablespoons (30 ml) vanilla extract
8 eggs, at room temperature	Meyer Lemon Syrup (recipe follows)
14 ounces (400 g) cake flour	1 cup (240 ml) heavy cream
6 ounces (170 g) fine semolina flour	1 teaspoon (5 g) granulated sugar
6 ounces (170 g) medium yellow cornmeal	Fresh berries
4 teaspoons (16 g) baking powder	

1. Line the bottom of 2 cake pans, 10 inches (25 cm) in diameter and 2 inches (5 cm) in height, with baking paper (see page 57). Set aside.

2. Using the paddle attachment, cream the butter and the first measurement of sugar together until light and fluffy in consistency. Gradually incorporate the eggs, scraping down the bowl once or twice, and continue to mix at medium speed for 5 to 10 minutes.

3. Meanwhile, sift together the cake flour, semolina flour, cornmeal, and baking powder. Mix the dry ingredients into the egg mixture in 2 portions, alternating with the sour cream. Add the vanilla extract. Divide the batter between the prepared caked pans.

4. Bake in a 325°F (163°C) oven for approximately 60 minutes or until the center springs back when pressed lightly. Let cool. Run a paring knife around the inside circumference of the cake pans. Unmold, peel the paper from the bottom of the cakes, and place them, right-side up, on a cake rack set over a sheet pan.

5. Brush or spray the Meyer lemon syrup heavily over the cakes, including the sides. Store, covered, in the refrigerator.

6. Presentation: Whip the heavy cream and remaining sugar to soft peaks. Cut the cake into serving pieces. Place 1 piece on a dessert plate and decorate with a dollop of cream and some fresh berries.

MEYER LEMON SYRUP yield: approximately 2½ cups (600 ml)

1½ cups (360 ml) Meyer lemon juice	½ cup (120 ml) water
12 ounces (340 g) granulated sugar	

Combine all of the ingredients in a saucepan and bring to a boil. Let cool, then store, covered, in the refrigerator.

Mom's Apple Cake yield: I cake, 10 inches (25 cm) in diameter

Mom's Apple Cake (*Mor's äppelkaka*), the traditional Swedish country-style variation of an apple pie, was standard at home and one of my favorites as a child. It was always served with a thick, rich vanilla sauce and, sometimes, whipped cream on the side. Because there was no pie tin to line, this dessert was quick and simple to prepare, and there was always a supply of stale bread either dried or already made into bread crumbs. Homemade apple jam was plentiful in the cellar after the harvest, so it was really just a question of layering the two ingredients together.

I have added the streusel topping for a little more finished look, but it can very well be left out. If you, as I often do, replace the vanilla sauce with ice cream—which can be purchased, as can the apple jam and bread crumbs—you have just run out of excuses for not trying this recipe. A word of caution: Do not leave the apple cake in the oven too long; although the jam will seem very loose when the cake first comes out of the oven, the natural pectin will set it as it cools.

3 pounds (1 kg 365 g) cooking apples, such as Golden Delicious or Granny Smith (approximately 7 medium)	10 ounces (285 g) finely ground white bread crumbs, toasted
12 ounces (340 g) granulated sugar	1 teaspoon (5 ml) vanilla extract
1¼ cups (300 ml) water	8 ounces (225 g) Streusel Topping (page 37)
Juice of ½ lemon	Powdered sugar
3 ounces (85 g) melted unsalted butter	½ recipe Crème Anglaise (page 817)
	Ground cinnamon (optional)

1. Peel and core the apples. Chop into large chunks. Place in a saucepan with the sugar, water, and lemon juice. If the apples are very sweet, decrease the sugar a bit; the filling should be tart and refreshing. Stir to combine and cook over medium heat, stirring from time to time, until the apple pieces are soft. Remove from the heat and process in a food processor until smooth.

2. Use some of the butter to coat the inside of a cake pan, 10 inches (25 cm) in diameter, or another ovenproof dish of approximately the same size. Add the remaining butter to the bread crumbs along with the vanilla. Mix to combine thoroughly. Sprinkle half of the bread crumb mixture evenly over the bottom of the pan. Press down to compact. Spread half of the apple filling over the top. Repeat with the remaining crumb mixture and remaining filling to make a total of 4 layers.

3. Sprinkle the streusel topping evenly over the second apple filling layer.

4. Bake at 400°F (205°C) for approximately 12 minutes or until the streusel begins to color. Let cool to room temperature.

5. Run a knife around the inside perimeter of the pan, invert onto a cake cardboard or platter, then invert again to turn right-side up. Sift powdered sugar lightly over the top. Cut into the desired number of servings. Serve with vanilla custard sauce and sprinkle cinnamon lightly over the sauce, if you like.

Mustard Gingerbread yield: 2 cakes, 8 × 4 inches (20 × 10 cm) each

Melted unsalted butter

8 ounces (225 g) unsalted butter, at room temperature

1 pound (455 g) granulated sugar

8 eggs, at room temperature

1 pound (455 g) bread flour

2 teaspoons (8 g) baking soda

2 teaspoons (8 g) baking powder

2 teaspoons (10 g) salt

1 tablespoon (6 g) ground ginger

4 teaspoons (8 g) dry mustard powder

1 teaspoon (1.5 g) ground cinnamon

½ teaspoon (1 g) ground cloves

1½ cups (360 ml) pumpkin puree

4 ounces (115 g) chopped pecans

1. Coat the inside of 2 loaf pans, approximately 8 × 4 inches (20 × 10 cm), with melted butter. Set aside.

2. Cream the soft butter and granulated sugar together until light and fluffy. Add the eggs and mix to combine.

3. Sift together the flour, baking soda, baking powder, salt, and spices. Add half of the dry ingredients to the creamed butter mixture. Mix in the pumpkin puree. Mix in the remaining dry ingredients and, last, the pecans. Pour the batter into the prepared pans.

4. Bake at 350°F (175°C) for about 1 hour or until baked through. Cool in the pans for 10 minutes, then remove and finish cooling on a cake rack.

About Mustard

Mustard plants, and mustard as a spice and a condiment, have been around since ancient times. The plants are known to have been cultivated as early as the fifth century B.C. Mustard has always been very popular throughout Europe, one reason being that it was one of the least expensive spices; the plants are indigenous to many areas, whereas most other spices are imported. Originally, the oily seeds (which are obtained from a number of species belonging to the cabbage family), were ground by hand, using a mortar and pestle, to produce a paste that varied in strength. It was not until the early part of the seventeenth century that a clever Englishman invented a process that allowed the seeds to be dried to the point where they could be ground into a powder. Powdered mustard can be potent, to say the least, and should given proper respect. Be sure to measure accurately. You may also want to consider adjusting the amount used in the recipe depending on the strength of the powder you are using.

Orange and Cranberry Gugelhupf

yield: enough for 2 gugelhupf pans, 5 cups (1 L 200 ml) in capacity

These turban-shaped cakes are extremely popular in the German-speaking countries of Europe. The configuration is said to have been modeled after the headdress of a sultan. Gugelhupf cakes were introduced by an inventive Viennese pastry chef in the seventeenth century. For more information see the traditional version on page 244, which is leavened with yeast, unlike this quickbread style, which uses chemical leaveners.

If you do not have a gugelhupf pan, a Bundt pan here will work just fine; however, if you must resort to using a loaf pan, you will need to increase the baking time slightly. The gugelhupf pan is designed not only to produce an attractive presentation that makes it look as if there is more than meets the eye, but as with any tube pan, the hole in the center allows the heat to penetrate and bake the cake evenly.

Butter and Flour Mixture (page 7)	½ teaspoon (2.5 g) salt
Grated zest of 3 oranges or 3 tablespoons (54 g)	1½ teaspoons (6 g) baking powder
Juice of 3 oranges or 1 cup (240 ml)	½ teaspoon (2 g) baking soda
½ cup (120 ml) or 3 ounces (85 g) dried cranberries	3 eggs
	8 ounces (225 g) granulated sugar
3 ounces (85 g) unsalted butter	1 cup (240 ml) buttermilk
8 ounces (225 g) cake flour	12 ounces (340 g) walnuts, chopped to raisin-sized pieces (see note)

1. Brush the butter and flour mixture over the inside of 2 gugelhupf pans, 5 cups (1 L 200 ml) in capacity, or other suitable tube pans.

2. Combine the orange juice, orange zest, cranberries, and butter in a saucepan. Bring to a boil. Remove from the heat and let stand for 30 minutes.

3. Sift together the flour, salt, baking powder, and baking soda. Reserve.

4. Beat the eggs with the granulated sugar at high speed until frothy, about 1 minute. Incorporate the orange mixture. Add the flour mixture in 2 additions, alternating with the buttermilk. Stir in the walnuts. Divide the batter between the prepared pans.

5. Bake at 375°F (190°C) for approximately 35 minutes or until a cake tester inserted into the cakes comes out dry. Unmold onto a cake rack and let cool.

NOTE: The nuts must be crushed as fine as rock salt; if too coarse, the batter will be to thin.

Pear Upside-Down Cake yield: 2 cakes, 10 inches (25 cm) in diameter

Upside-down cakes are also known as *skillet cakes* because they were originally baked in cast-iron skillets—something that was more useful to have in the old days than a cake pan. In addition, it was simple to melt the butter and sugar in the skillet and pour the batter on top instead of transferring the sugar mixture to another pan. The best-known version is the traditional pineapple upside-down cake, although just about any type of fruit can be used in this application. During the baking process, the sugar, butter, and fruit juices cook together into a light caramel underneath the cake batter. When the cake is inverted, the caramel glazes the fruit on top of the cake in much the same way as in a caramelized apple tart like tarte Tatin. It is important that the cake itself is dense enough to be able to absorb the juices and caramel without falling apart. For this reason, the batter is closer to the formula for a pound or tea cake than that of a sponge cake. Upside-down cakes should be served warm. As a dessert, serve with ice cream or whipped cream; offer as is for brunch or a coffee break.

12 ounces (340 g) unsalted butter

10 ounces (285 g) light brown sugar

6 pounds 12 ounces (3 kg 70 g) Bartlett or Anjou pears (approximately 12 medium)

2 recipes Plain Poaching Syrup (page 31)

7 ounces (200 g) unsalted butter, at room temperature

14 ounces (400 g) granulated sugar

3 eggs, at room temperature

1 tablespoon (15 ml) vanilla extract

1 pound (455 g) cake flour

2 tablespoons (24 g) baking powder

1¾ cups (420 ml) whole milk, at room temperature

Caramel Ice Cream (page 719)

1. Melt the first measurement of butter. Stir in the brown sugar. Spread the mixture evenly over the bottom of 2 cake pans, 10 inches (25 cm) in diameter. Set aside.

2. Peel, core, and halve the pears, placing them into acidulated water as you work. Transfer the pear halves to the poaching syrup and poach just until they begin to soften. Let cool in the liquid.

3. Remove the pears from the liquid. Cut each half into 3 wedges. Arrange the pear wedges, round-side down, in a spoke pattern on top of the sugar mixture in the cake pans. Reserve.

4. Cream the soft butter with the granulated sugar until light and fluffy. Beat in the eggs and vanilla and continue beating for 1 minute. Sift the flour and baking powder together and add to the batter in 2 additions, alternating with the milk.

5. Divide the cake batter between the prepared pans, spreading it out evenly on top of the pears.

6. Bake at 375°F (190°C) for approximately 45 minutes. Remove from the oven and let the cakes cool for 10 minutes. Run a knife around the sides of the pans to loosen the cakes. Invert the cakes onto serving platters or cake cardboards. Serve warm with caramel ice cream.

VARIATION

PINEAPPLE UPSIDE-DOWN CAKE

Prepare the pear upside-down cake as instructed above, but substitute 2 pounds (910 g) fresh pineapple for the pears. Cut off the crown and cut away the skin, cutting deep enough to remove all of the eyes. Cut the pineapple into ¼-inch (6-mm) slices. Cut out the core using a plain cookie cutter. Place 2 of the largest pineapple slices on top of the sugar mixture in the center of the pans. Cut the remaining slices across to make half-rings. Arrange the cut pieces side by side with the round edge against the pan, beginning at the edge and forming concentric circles around the center ring. Invert as soon as the cakes are removed from the oven and leave in this position for a few minutes before removing the baking pans.

Poppy Seed Coffee Cake with Orange Glaze

yield: 2 coffee cakes, 10 inches (25 cm) in diameter

As with most tea cakes and pound cakes, the batter for this cake can be used to make great muffins. Muffins should be baked at a slightly higher temperature—375°F (190°C)—for approximately 30 minutes. This recipe will yield 18 muffins baked in 4-ounce (120-ml) muffin pans. The quantity of poppy seeds can be adjusted up or down according to your own taste. Avoid overmixing the batter and incorporating too much air, which can result in an inferior texture in the baked cakes or muffins.

Butter and Flour Mixture (page 7) or pan spray

12 ounces (340 g) bread flour

8 ounces (225 g) cake flour

1½ teaspoons (6 g) baking soda

1 teaspoon (4 g) baking powder

5 ounces (140 g) poppy seeds

2 tablespoons (36 g) grated or finely chopped orange zest

1 pound (455 g) unsalted butter, at room temperature

1 pound 8 ounces (680 g) granulated sugar

10 egg yolks (7/8 cup/210 ml), at room temperature

1 tablespoon (15 ml) vanilla extract

12 ounces (340 g) sour cream

12 egg whites (1½ cups/360 ml)

½ teaspoon (2.5 g) salt

½ teaspoon (1 g) cream of tartar

2 recipes Orange Glaze (page 30)

1. Brush the butter and flour mixture over the inside of 2 tube-style cake pans, 10 inches (25 cm) in diameter by 4 inches (10 cm) in height, or coat the pans with pan spray.

2. Sift together the bread flour, cake flour, baking soda, and baking powder. Mix in the poppy seeds and orange zest.

3. Cream the butter. Add 1 pound 4 ounces (570 g) sugar and beat until light and fluffy. Add the egg yolks and vanilla. Mix for 2 minutes.

4. Mix in half of the dry ingredients at low speed. Add the sour cream and mix until just combined. Mix in the remaining dry ingredients.

5. Whip the egg whites, salt, and cream of tartar to a foam. Gradually add the remaining 4 ounces (115 g) sugar and whip to soft peaks. Fold the beaten egg whites into the batter one-quarter at a time.

6. Divide the batter between the reserved tube pans, they should be two-thirds full.

7. Bake at 350°F (175°C) for approximately 40 minutes or until baked through; the tops should spring back when pressed lightly in the center. Allow the cakes to cool in the pans before unmolding.

8. Place the cakes on an icing rack set over a sheet pan. Pour the orange glaze over the top of each cake, using just enough so that the glaze coats the top of the cakes and runs down the sides, leaving the base of the sides uncovered. Allow the glaze to set before slicing the cakes.

Raisin Cake yield: 4 cakes, 1 pound 7 ounces (655 g) each

You will love this Swedish version of traditional pound cake—unless, of course, you do not like raisins. Raisins are included in many Swedish recipes and, as you may have already noticed if you have used this book for a while, my recipes are no exception. Raisins not only add flavor and texture to the cakes, but also because of their moisture and sugar content, help to keep them fresh. Raisin cake is terrific right out of the oven, or it can be used to make a quick country-style dessert after the cakes have been in the refrigerator for a day or two, by serving the sliced cake with whipped cream and fresh strawberries.

Melted unsalted butter

Finely ground bread crumbs *or* almond meal

1 pound 8 ounces (680 g) unsalted butter, at room temperature

1 pound 8 ounces (680 g) granulated sugar

2 teaspoons (10 ml) vanilla extract

10 eggs, at room temperature

13 ounces (370 g) bread flour

10 ounces (285 g) cornstarch

1½ tablespoons (18 g) baking powder

8 ounces (225 g) dark raisins

Small-Batch Raisin Cake
yield: 2 cakes, 1 pound 7 ounces (655 g) each

Melted unsalted butter

Finely ground bread crumbs *or* almond meal

12 ounces (340 g) unsalted butter, at room temperature

12 ounces (340 g) granulated sugar

1 teaspoon (5 ml) vanilla extract

5 eggs, at room temperature

6 ounces (170 g) bread flour

6 ounces (170 g) cornstarch

2 teaspoons (10 g) baking powder

5 ounces (140 g) dark raisins

---

1. Brush melted butter inside of 4 gugelhupf forms or other tube pans, 1 quart (960 ml) in capacity (2 pans for the smaller recipe). Coat the forms thoroughly with the bread crumbs or almond meal.

2. Beat the butter, sugar, and vanilla together until creamy. Mix in the eggs, a few at a time.

3. Sift the flour with the cornstarch and baking powder. Add the raisins and mix to coat them with the flour. Stir the flour into the butter mixture, taking care not to incorporate too much air by overmixing. Divide the batter equally between the prepared pans. If you use small pans, do not fill them more than two-thirds full.

4. Bake at 375°F (190°C) until the cake springs back when pressed lightly, about 30 minutes. Unmold and cool the cakes on a cake rack.

5. When cool, wrap and store in the refrigerator.

NOTE: The batter can also be used to make muffins. If using Flexipans, pipe the batter into the indentations of Flexipan No. 3051, filling them to just below the rim. Then, use the back of a spoon to push the batter up against the sides of the forms, creating a concave surface. The muffins will then have nice, rounded tops rather than sides that rise straight up from the forms like a soufflé. Bake at 400°F (205°C) for about 25 minutes or until the cakes spring back when pressed lightly. This will yield 26 muffins.

Soft Gingerbread Cake yield: 4 cakes, 14 x 4 inches (35 x 10 cm) each

Mjuk Pepparkaka is one of the family recipes in this book; it was a standard coffee cake in my home. In Scandinavia, gingerbread cakes are a traditional must-have for the holidays, but this cake is really too good to ignore for a year at a time. My sister and I used to have big arguments over whose turn it was to scrape the last of the batter from the mixing bowl. It was, in our opinion, every bit as good raw as it would be when baked.

Butter and Flour Mixture (page 7) or pan spray

1 pound (455 g) light brown sugar

6 eggs, at room temperature

1 pound (455 g) bread flour

2 tablespoons (24 g) baking powder

1 teaspoon (4 g) baking soda

4 tablespoons (20 g) ground cinnamon

2 teaspoons (4 g) ground ginger

1 teaspoon (2 g) ground cloves

2 teaspoons (4 g) ground cardamom

1 teaspoon (5 g) salt

14 ounces (400 g) melted unsalted butter

1¼ cups (300 ml) half-and-half, at room temperature

Powdered sugar

1. Brush butter and flour mixture on the insides of 4 rectangular fluted cake pans, 14 inches (35 cm) long and 4 inches (10 cm) wide, or tube-style pans with a 1-quart (960-ml) capacity (if you use the taller gugelhupf or bundt-style pans, they will require an increased baking time).

2. Whip the brown sugar and eggs together to a thick foamy consistency.

3. Sift together the flour, baking powder, baking soda, cinnamon, ginger, cloves, cardamom, and salt. Add to the egg mixture.

4. Combine the melted butter with the half-and-half. Add to the batter slowly. Divide the batter among the prepared pans.

5. Bake at 350°F (175°C) for about 45 minutes or until the cakes spring back when pressed lightly in the center.

6. Unmold the cakes and cool on a cake rack.

7. When the cakes have cooled completely, wrap in plastic and refrigerate. When ready to serve, place a strip of baking paper, 1 inch (2.5 cm) wide, lengthwise on top of the cakes. Sift powdered sugar over the cakes. Remove the paper template and slice the cakes into the desired size pieces.

NOTE: This batter can also be baked in muffin tins. Line every other space of muffin pans with paper cups and grease the top of the pan around the cups with butter and flour mixture. Pipe the batter into the cups, using a No. 6 (12-mm) plain tip. Bake at 375°F (190°C) for about 30 minutes or until baked through. Makes about 16 muffins, 4 ounces (115 g) each.

Streusel Kuchen yield: 24 pieces, approximately 2 x 4 inches (5 x 10 cm) each

Streusel is a German word that means "sprinkled" or "strewn together." *Kuchen*, of course, translates to "cake" or "pastry." Streusel Kuchen is from the famous city of Leipzig—home of Johann Sebastian Bach—which is in the former kingdom of Saxony. The early Saxons were well known for their cakes and pastries.

Melted unsalted butter

⅔ ounce (20 g) fresh compressed yeast

1 cup (240 ml) warm whole milk (105° to 115°F/40° to 46°C; see Note)

2½ ounces (70 g) granulated sugar

½ teaspoon (3 g) salt

3 egg yolks (¼ cup/60 ml)

1 teaspoon (5 ml) vanilla extract

1 pound (455 g) bread flour

2 ounces (55 g) unsalted butter, at room temperature

Egg wash

14 ounces (400 g) or ⅓ recipe Streusel Topping (page 37)

Custard Filling (recipe follows)

Powdered sugar

1. Brush melted butter over the bottom and sides of a half-sheet pan, 16 x 12 inches (40 x 30 cm). Place a piece of baking paper in the bottom and reserve.

2. In a mixer bowl, dissolve the yeast in the warm milk. Add the sugar, salt, egg yolks, and vanilla. Incorporate approximately half of the flour, using the dough hook. Add the soft butter and the remaining flour and mix until you have a very soft, smooth dough, approximately 5 minutes. Incorporate additional flour if necessary while mixing. Place the dough in an oiled bowl, cover, and let rise in a warm place until doubled in volume.

3. Punch the dough down. Roll and stretch it to fit the prepared sheet pan. Place the dough in the pan. Let rise again until doubled in volume.

4. Brush the dough with egg wash. Sprinkle the streusel topping over the dough.

5. Bake at 400°F (205°C) for about 12 minutes or until baked through. Let cool.

6. Cut around the edges of the pan if necessary to loosen the cake. Invert the cake onto a sheet pan and peel away the baking paper. Invert again to turn the cake right-side up on an inverted sheet pan or cardboard. Slice horizontally into 2 equal layers. Spread custard filling on the bottom layer, then replace the top. Refrigerate 1 hour to set the custard.

7. Trim the sides of the cake. Cut lengthwise into 3 equal strips. Cut each strip into 8 equal pieces. Sift powdered sugar lightly over the cut pieces. Serve within 24 hours and refrigerate if not serving immediately.

NOTE: Be careful not to overheat the milk as this may damage the yeast.

About Streusel Kuchen

Streusel Kuchen is a staple German coffee cake, typical of good home cooking. It is traditionally served at an afternoon coffee break either with a cream-type filling, as in my version, or with various sweet toppings. One such variation is known as *bien stick* ("bee sting" in English). The baked cake is topped with a coarse Florentina batter, then returned to the oven to cook the topping, as is done with Tosca pastries. To make Streusel Kuchen without a filling, follow the instructions through Step 5, brushing 2 ounces (55 g) melted butter on the dough before applying the streusel. Let cool slightly before cutting into serving pieces.

CUSTARD FILLING yield: 1 pound 5 ounces (595 g)

1½ teaspoons (5 g) unflavored gelatin powder

1¼ cup (60 ml) cherry liqueur

½ cup (120 ml) heavy cream

1 pound (455 g) Pastry Cream (page 845)

1. Sprinkle the gelatin over the liqueur and set aside to soften.

2. Whip the heavy cream to soft peaks. Fold into the pastry cream.

3. Heat the gelatin to dissolve and quickly beat it into one-third of the cream mixture. Still working quickly, mix this into the remaining cream. Use immediately.

Swedish Jelly Roll yield: 2 roulades, 11 inches (27.5 cm) long

This is a simple and delicious tea cake that can be made in a very short amount of time and does not even require any particular cake pan. Rolled cakes (roulades) are popular all over Europe because, in addition to being quick to make, they can be made ahead and sliced to order, which keeps the servings from becoming dry. Roulades are made with various fillings, citrus and kirsch being two old flavor favorites. Roulades can also be iced and decorated to use as part of a pastry display. The following recipe is a typical Scandinavian version known as *Rull Tårta*.

Roulade Batter (recipe follows)

Granulated sugar

12 ounces (340 g) smooth strawberry or raspberry jam *or* strained preserves

1. Spread the roulade batter evenly over a sheet of baking paper measuring 16 x 24 inches (40 x 60 cm), leaving approximately ½ inch (1.2 cm) of paper uncovered along all 4 sides. Drag the paper onto a sheet pan (see Figure 9-4, page 443).

2. Bake immediately at 425°F (219°C) for about 10 minutes or until just done. Transfer the sponge to a second (cool) sheet pan after removing it from the oven so it will not dry out. Let the sponge sheet cool, then store it, covered, in the refrigerator if it is not to be rolled right away. If the sponge seems too dry to roll, follow the instructions given in the Note on page 438 to soften it.

3. Sprinkle granulated sugar over a sheet of baking paper. Invert the sponge sheet on top. Peel the paper off the back. Trim the sheet to 15 x 22 inches (37.5 x 55 cm).

4. Spread the jam evenly over the entire surface of the sponge.

5. Pick up the 2 upper corners of the paper and roll the cake into a tight log, starting from the top long edge and rolling toward you, using the paper underneath the help you form the roll (see Figure 13-11, page 621).

6. Leaving the paper in place around the cake, hold the bottom of the paper still with your left hand and push a dowel or ruler against the roll with your free hand. The paper will wrap around the roll and tighten it (Figure 8-1).

FIGURE 8-1 Pushing a ruler against a roulade with a sheet of baking paper between the roulade and the ruler while holding the opposite end of the baking paper steady to force the paper to wrap tightly around the roulade and compact it slightly

7. Cut the roll into 2 pieces, 11 inches (27.5 cm) long. Wrap them in plastic and place, seam-side down, on a sheet pan lined with baking paper. Refrigerate until ready to serve. The jelly rolls can be kept in the refrigerator up to 1 week at this point.

ROULADE BATTER yield: 1 sheet, 16 × 24 inches (40 × 60 cm), or 1 layer, 10 inches (25 cm) in diameter

1 egg white	5 ounces (140 g) granulated sugar
4 ounces (115 g) almond paste	Grated zest of ½ lemon
6 eggs, separated	3½ ounces (100 g) cake flour, sifted

1. Mix the egg white into the almond paste to soften the paste.

2. Whip the egg yolks with half of the sugar to the ribbon stage. Add the lemon zest. Gradually add the yolk mixture to the softened almond paste.

3. Whip the egg whites for a few seconds then gradually add the remaining sugar and continue to whip until stiff peaks form.

4. Fold the whipped egg whites then the cake flour into the yolk mixture by hand.

NOTE: To make a 10-inch (25-cm) layer, pour the batter into a prepared cake pan and bake at 375°F (190°C) for about 18 minutes.

Tiger Cake yield: 4 cakes, 17 ounces (485 g) each

This is the designer version of coffee cake—no two patterns of the light and dark batters ever turn out quite the same. Very popular all over Europe, these cakes are also known as *marble cakes*. Alternatively, if you leave out the cocoa powder altogether this recipe makes a very nice pound cake with a hint of lemon. If you would like to make 2 plain cakes and 2 tiger cakes, divide the batter in half and add the zest of 1 lemon and half of the vanilla to one portion of the batter. Divide the lemon batter evenly between 2 pans. Add ½ ounce (15 g) unsweetened cocoa powder to one-third of the remaining batter and the zest of 1 lemon plus the remaining vanilla to the remaining plain batter. Proceed as directed to make the tiger pattern. To make any variation of this (3 plain, 1 tiger, etc.), mix 1 tablespoon unsweetened cocoa powder per cake into one-third of the batter for 1 cake.

Melted unsalted butter	14 ounces (400 g) cake flour
Finely ground bread crumbs or almond meal	1 tablespoon (12 g) baking powder
8 egg yolks (⅔ cup/160 ml)	8 egg whites (1 cup/240 ml)
1 pound 2 ounces (510 g) granulated sugar	1 ounce (30 g) unsweetened cocoa powder
¾ cup (180 ml) whole milk, at room temperature	Grated zest of 2 lemons
1 pound 6 ounces (625 g) melted unsalted butter	1 teaspoon (5 ml) vanilla extract

1. Brush the inside of 4 gugelhupf forms, 1 quart (960 ml) in capacity, with melted butter and coat with the bread crumbs or the almond meal.

2. Whip the egg yolks with 9 ounces (255 g) sugar until light and fluffy. Add the milk and the melted butter (the butter should not be hot).

3. Sift the flour with the baking powder, then mix into the butter mixture.

4. Whip the egg whites until foamy; gradually add the remaining 9 ounces (255 g) sugar and whip to stiff peaks. Carefully fold the butter mixture into the whipped egg whites by hand.

5. Sift the cocoa powder into a bowl; gradually add one-third of the batter while mixing to combine. Mix the lemon zest and the vanilla into the remaining two-thirds of the batter.

6. Starting and finishing with the white batter, spoon 3 or 4 alternating layers of vanilla and chocolate batters into the prepared forms. If you are using small forms, fill each only two-thirds full.

7. Bake immediately at 375°F (190°C) for about 40 minutes or until the cake springs back when pressed lightly.

8. Unmold onto a cake rack to cool.

9. When the cakes have cooled completely, wrap in plastic and store in the refrigerator.

Walnut–Whipped Cream Cake

yield: 2 cakes, 10 inches (25 cm) in diameter, or enough for 4 gugelhupf pans, 1 quart (960 ml) in capacity, or 25 to 30 muffins

This recipe creates a very moist and delicious cake base that you can serve as is, with a sprinkling of powdered sugar, a dollop of whipped cream, and fresh fruit, or use to make a frosted and decorated cake. You could also use this recipe to replace one of the other cake bases called for in a recipe from the Decorated Cakes chapter, such as the Poppy Seed Layer Cake (page 529). Further, the walnut whipped cream cake batter also makes excellent pound cakes (baked in gugelhupf or Bundt-style pans) and muffins (for muffins, increase the oven temperature and decrease the baking time to about 30 minutes).

Like the poppy seed cake base, this cake gets its moist texture from a large amount of dairy in the batter—whipped cream in this recipe versus sour cream in the poppy seed cake. Because the moisture content of these cakes is higher than normal, they require a longer baking time and are baked at a lower temperature than, for example, a sponge cake. Be very sure the centers are done before removing the cakes from the oven. This cake is one of the few where I would recommend inserting a wooden skewer or cake tester to check for doneness rather than relying on the usual "springs back when pressed lightly" approach.

You can substitute another variety of nut for the walnuts. However, if you use a nut with a lower oil content, such as hazelnut or almond, add 2 tablespoons (30 ml) vegetable oil, mixed with the eggs, to make up the difference.

Butter and Flour Mixture (page 7) or pan spray	8 eggs
7 ounces (200 g) walnuts	1 tablespoon (15 ml) vanilla extract
2 ounces (55 g) powdered sugar	10 ounces (285 g) bread flour
3½ cups (840 ml) heavy cream	8 ounces (225 g) cake flour
1 pound 6 ounces (625 g) granulated sugar	1 tablespoon (12 g) baking powder
	1½ teaspoons (7.5 g) salt

1. Prepare 2 cake pans, 10 inches (25 cm) in diameter, or use gugelhupf pans (see Chef's Tip, page 389), by coating them with butter and flour mixture or pan spray. Reserve.

2. Place the walnuts and powdered sugar in a food processor and process the mixture to make it as fine as possible without caking. Spread in a thin layer over a sheet pan and toast lightly in a 375°F (190°C) oven for approximately 5 minutes. Reserve.

3. Whip the heavy cream to soft peaks and set aside.

4. Whip the granulated sugar and the eggs at high speed to a light and fluffy consistency. Add the vanilla.

5. Sift together the bread flour, cake flour, baking powder, and salt. Combine this with the reserved walnut mixture. Fold the flour mixture into the egg mixture in 2 portions, alternating with the whipped cream. Divide the batter between the reserved cake pans.

6. Bake at 325°F (163°C) for approximately 50 minutes.

White Spice Buttermilk Cake yield: 2 cakes, 8 × 4 × 3¹/₂ inches (20 × 10 × 8.7 cm)

This cake pairs very nicely with fruit poached in a wine syrup and Honey-Yogurt Sauce (page 822). For the presentation, trim away the crust from one short end of a buttermilk cake. Cut a ³/₄-inch (2-cm) slice and set it in the center of a dessert plate. Spoon the fruit and poaching liquid onto the plate all around the cake slice, arranging the fruit pieces attractively. Spoon a dollop of honey-yogurt sauce on top of the cake and sift powdered sugar over the entire plate, including the rim.

Butter and Flour Mixture (page 7) or pan spray	¹/₂ teaspoon (1 g) ground white pepper
10 ounces (285 g) bread flour	10 ounces (285 g) unsalted butter, at room temperature
4 ounces (115 g) cake flour	10 ounces (285 g) granulated sugar
1¹/₂ teaspoons (6 g) baking powder	4 eggs, at room temperature
1 teaspoon (4 g) baking soda	1 tablespoon (15 ml) vanilla extract
4 teaspoons (8 g) ground cardamom	2 teaspoons (10 ml) finely grated lemon zest
1 teaspoon (2 g) ground ginger	1¹/₂ cups (360 ml) buttermilk

1. Brush butter and flour mixture over the inside of 2 loaf pans measuring 8 × 4 × 3¹/₂ inches (20 × 10 × 8.7 cm) or coat the pans with pan spray.

2. Combine the bread flour, cake flour, baking powder, baking soda, cardamom, ginger, and white pepper. Reserve.

3. Beat the soft butter with the sugar until the mixture is light and fluffy. Mix in the eggs, 2 at a time. Add the vanilla and the lemon zest. Stir in the dry ingredients in 2 additions, alternating with the buttermilk. Divide the batter between the prepared pans.

4. Bake the cakes at 350°F (175°C) for approximately 50 minutes or until they are golden brown and baked through. Let the cakes cool in the pans for 10 minutes. Unmold onto a rack and let cool completely. Wrap the cakes in plastic and store in the refrigerator.

Pound cakes—cakes prepared with 1 pound each butter, sugar, eggs, and flour—were made in England beginning in the mid-1600s. At first, these cakes also contained dried and candied fruits, nuts, and spices, as was popular in most of the desserts of that era. These original pound cakes (although they were not known as such) were the first deviation from the yeast-leavened or bread-style cakes (similar to stollen or panettone) that had been made up to that point and were, in fact, the forerunners of the butter cakes and sponge cakes we know today. It was not until about a century later that the batter was baked plain without the extra flavorings, and the term *pound cake* came into fashion. Approximately 100 years after that (mid-1800s), pound cake really hit its stride; recipes were included in most of the cookbooks of the day. These often varied slightly from the 1-pound-each formula, using a little more flour or sugar to suit a particular cook's taste. These recipes generally included some liquid as well, such as brandy, sherry, or rose water, calling for about 8 ounces to the pound of each of the other ingredients. In *Mrs. Beeton's Book of Household Management* (1861), she states, "A glass of wine can sometimes be added to the mixture, but this is scarcely necessary as the cake will be found quite rich enough without it." In the twentieth century, bakers began to add leaveners to the basic mixture, along with additional flour and sugar to maintain the density associated with the original.

An authentic pound cake contains only butter, sugar, eggs, and flour in equal proportions. Salt and flavorings such as vanilla or almond extract, citrus rind, and spices are optional. Because classic pound cakes do not contain baking powder or baking soda, there is no residual flavor from a chemical leavener to mask the flavor of the ingredients, and, as the name of the Vanilla-Butter Pound Cake suggests, the taste of these ingredients really comes through. But as good as they are plain, pound cakes lend themselves quite well to flavorful additions and hybrids, as shown in the recipes for Almond Pound Cake, Basil and Tarragon Pound Cake, Lemon Buttermilk Pound Cake, Mustard Gingerbread, and White Spice Buttermilk Cake.

Almond Pound Cake yield: enough for 2 tube pans, 5 cups (1 L 200 ml) in capacity (Photo 28)

Second to the Vanilla-Butter Pound Cake, this recipe is closest of the group to the classic version. It may not look as if the ingredients are in line with the 1-pound-each formula at first glance, but when you consider that the almond paste is basically half fat and half sugar, this cake actually comes quite close to the original, except for the addition of a leavener and milk, which are not traditional. However, these added ingredients work well in this recipe to give the cake a rich almond flavor from the almond paste without becoming too heavy. Because almonds are hygroscopic—that is, they absorb moisture from the air—this cake is a great keeper.

Butter and Flour Mixture (page 7) or pan spray	1 tablespoon (12 g) baking powder
Sliced almonds, crushed	1 teaspoon (5 g) salt
8 ounces (225 g) almond paste	Grated zest of 1 lemon
6 ounces (170 g) granulated sugar	1 teaspoon (5 ml) vanilla extract
11 ounces (310 g) unsalted butter, at room temperature	¾ cup (180 ml) whole milk, at room temperature
6 whole eggs, at room temperature	4 egg whites (½ cup/120 ml)
7 ounces (200 g) bread flour	6 ounces (170 g) granulated sugar
7 ounces (200 g) cake flour	Powdered sugar

1. Coat the inside of 2 gugelhupf pans, 5 cups (1 L 200 ml) in capacity, or other suitable pans, with butter and flour mixture or pan spray. Coat the inside of the pans with the crushed almonds. Set the pans aside.

2. Combine the almond paste, the first measurement of granulated sugar, and the soft butter (add the butter gradually to avoid lumps). Cream until light and fluffy. Beat in the eggs.

3. Sift together both flours, the baking powder, and the salt. Add this to the almond paste mixture along with the lemon zest, vanilla, and milk.

4. Whip the egg whites until foamy. Gradually add the remaining sugar while whipping to stiff peaks. Fold the egg whites into the cake batter, one-third at a time. Divide the batter between the prepared cake pans.

5. Bake at 375°F (190°C) for approximately 35 minutes or until the cakes are baked through; they should spring back when pressed lightly on top. Unmold onto a cake rack and let cool.

6. Sift powdered sugar lightly over the top.

Basil and Tarragon Pound Cake yield: 2 cakes, 8 × 4 inches (20 × 10 cm) each

We see a great deal of crossover between the hot kitchen and the pastry shop these days with respect to ingredients, such as the herbs used in this recipe. Adding basil and tarragon to a pound cake may strike you as strange, but it is actually a surprisingly refreshing combination. You can, of course, vary the amount of herbs used or substitute another flavor, such as mint, lavender, or verbena, but be certain you use enough so that the flavor is vibrant and noticeable, or there is no point in making this recipe. When you measure the chopped basil and tarragon, pack the leaves firmly into the measuring spoon.

Butter and Flour Mixture (page 7) or pan spray	8 ounces (225 g) cake flour
1 pound (455 g) unsalted butter, at room temperature	½ teaspoon (2.5 g) salt
1 pound (455 g) granulated sugar	2 teaspoons (10 ml) very finely chopped fresh basil
9 eggs, at room temperature	¼ teaspoon (1.25 ml) very finely chopped fresh tarragon
7 ounces (200 g) bread flour	

1. Coat the inside of 2 loaf pans measuring 8 × 4 inches (20 × 10 cm) with butter and flour mixture or pan spray.

2. Cream the butter and sugar until light and fluffy. Beat in the eggs, 1 at a time.

3. Sift together the bread flour, cake flour, and salt. Add the basil and tarragon and combine well so there are no clumps of herbs. Add the flour mixture to the butter mixture and beat until thoroughly blended. Divide between the prepared pans.

4. Bake at 325°F (163°C) for approximately 1 hour or until baked through.

Lemon-Buttermilk Pound Cake yield: enough for 2 tube pans, 5 cups (1 L 200 ml) in capacity

Buttermilk is a very popular ingredient in cakes and quick breads whenever the creaming method is used. Its inherent acidity allows us to use baking soda in addition to or instead of baking powder as a leavening agent. If it is not combined with an acidic ingredient, baking soda alone becomes carbon dioxide gas and sodium carbonate when it is heated. The carbon dioxide gas is what we want to produce the air bubbles and leavening effect, but the sodium carbonate leaves behind a disagreeable, pungent, and unpleasant (some describe it as soapy) flavor that is moderately alkaline. However, when an acid is introduced (buttermilk, as used here, or chocolate, citrus juice, sour cream, brown sugar, honey, or molasses, to name some of the others commonly utilized), the carbon dioxide gas is produced more rapidly and leaves behind a much milder form of the sodium. In addition to its leavening properties, baking soda also helps darken the baked product, which can add to a more appetizing appearance.

Butter and Flour Mixture (page 7) or pan spray

10 ounces (285 g) unsalted butter, at room temperature

12 ounces (340 g) granulated sugar

6 eggs, at room temperature

6 ounces (170 g) cake flour

6 ounces (170 g) bread flour

4 teaspoons (15 g) baking powder

¼ teaspoon (1 g) baking soda

1 teaspoon (5 g) salt

¾ cup (180 ml) buttermilk, at room temperature

Finely grated zest of 2 lemons

Juice of 2 medium lemons

1. Coat the inside of 2 tube pans, 5 cups (1 L 200 ml) in capacity, with butter and flour mixture or pan spray.

2. Cream the butter and sugar together until the mixture is light and fluffy. Beat in the eggs, 1 at a time. Continue beating for 1 minute.

3. Sift together the flour, baking powder, baking soda, and salt. Combine the buttermilk, lemon zest, and lemon juice. Add the dry ingredients to the egg mixture in 2 parts, alternating with the buttermilk.

4. Divide the batter evenly between the prepared pans. They should not be more than three-quarters full.

5. Bake at 375°F (190°C) for approximately 35 minutes or until baked through. A wooden skewer inserted into the cake should come out clean. Let the cakes cool for a few minutes, then unmold and finish cooling on a rack. If left to cool in the pans, they will become wet from trapped steam.

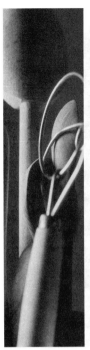

About Pound Cakes

Because authentic pound cakes, like classic sponge cakes, rely solely on the air that is incorporated into the batter for leavening, the mixing technique is critical. It is different from that used for sponge cake, however, because pound cakes contain such a large percentage of butter, which, though it contributes to their rich flavor, can make them too dense and heavy if they are not prepared correctly.

A common mixing method is to cream the butter, sugar, and egg yolks together, incorporate the flour, whip the egg whites to stiff peaks separately, then fold the whites into the batter. This makes a light pound cake, but one that is not as moist and rich as a classic pound cake should be. (Note, however, that this technique is used successfully with some of the pound cake hybrids in this section, which achieve the necessary body from the addition of other ingredients.) The method used for Vanilla-Butter Pound Cake incorporates whole eggs plus extra egg yolks and so does not benefit from the added air whipped into the whites. However, because the eggs are incorporated very slowly and because extra yolks, which are an excellent emulsifier, are used, an emulsion is created that is able to support the trapped air and moisture in the correct balance. The resulting cake is rich, moist, and buttery without being too airy and fluffy on one end or rubbery and heavy on the other. To create and maintain the emulsion, it is critical not only to add the eggs very gradually but also that all of the ingredients are at about 70°F (21°C). If the mixture is too cold, it will curdle and the trapped air will escape. Because of the dense batter, pound cakes are baked at a relatively low temperature.

Vanilla-Butter Pound Cake yield: 2 cakes, 8 × 4 inches (20 × 10 cm) each

As is true of many things that are very simple and comprise only a few components, if not prepared correctly, the desired outcome of this classic pound cake will be lost. Properly made pound cakes walk a fine line between rich and moist but not too heavy or compact.

This cake is wonderful with crème fraîche and fresh fruit; the acidity of both offsets the rich, sweet cake nicely. Slices of vanilla-butter pound cake are also very good toasted. Watch closely, however, as they brown quickly due to the high sugar content.

Melted unsalted butter	1 pound (455 g) unsalted butter, at room temperature
6 whole eggs, at room temperature	
6 egg yolks (½ cup/120 ml), at room temperature	1 pound 2 ounces (510 g) Vanilla Sugar (page 40) *or* granulated sugar
1 tablespoon (15 ml) vanilla extract	1 teaspoon (5 g) salt
1 tablespoon (15 ml) water	14 ounces (400 g) cake flour, sifted

1. Brush melted butter over the inside of 2 loaf pans measuring 8 × 4 inches (20 × 10 cm), then line the pans with baking paper as shown in Figures 1-22 and 1-23, page 56). Set aside.

2. Place the whole eggs, egg yolks, vanilla, and water in a small bowl. Mix to break up the eggs and combine the ingredients without beating in any air. If the mixture is cooler than approximately 70°F (21°C), place the bowl in a bain-marie and stir for a moment or two to warm it. Do not heat to the point of cooking the eggs. Set aside off the heat.

3. Place the soft butter in a mixer bowl and beat, using the paddle attachment, for about 2 minutes. Add the sugar gradually and continue beating for 4 to 5 minutes until the mixture is light in color (almost white) and fluffy. With the mixer running, pour the egg mixture in very gradually, taking about 5 minutes to add all of it. Beat in the salt. Fold in the sifted cake flour one-fourth at a time. Divide the batter between the prepared pans.

4. Bake at 350°F (175°C) for about 1 hour. A wooden skewer inserted in the top of the cakes should come out clean. Unmold from the baking pans and cool to room temperature. Wrap and store at room temperature for up to one week.

The word muffin is derived from the Germanic word *muffe*, which is the name for a type of cake. Muffins are always baked in forms and, like tea cakes, the batter almost always contains some type of addition, such as chopped fruit or nuts. Muffins are not iced or decorated in any way after they are baked.

Although really quite simple, muffins are finicky by nature—they can be extremely good or just plain bad. The secret to success lies in how you add and trap the moisture. If you overmix the batter or add too much leavening (both of which add air), overbake, or store the muffins improperly, you can end up with a dry product. When the recipe calls for beating or creaming the ingredients, always use the paddle attachment rather than the whip, which again can incorporate excess air. Mix at low to medium speed, depending on the variety and the amount of batter (a small batch can easily be mixed up with a spoon), and don't overdo it.

Lining the muffin tins with paper cups helps keep the muffins from drying out and tasting stale, but if you prefer your muffins with a crust all around, omit the paper cups and grease the inside of the tins instead. As soon as you remove the muffins from the oven, quickly turn them on their sides in the pans to allow air to circulate underneath.

The best way to store baked muffins is not to, which is to say that, ideally, muffins should be eaten the same day they are baked. You can keep muffin batter in the refrigerator for several days, or in the freezer for up to 2 weeks, with no loss in quality. Another solution is to freeze the batter preportioned in the muffin cups. Thaw overnight in the refrigerator and they are ready to bake in the morning; saving time when you often need it most.

About Baking Muffins in Flexipans

When using Flexipans to make any of the following recipes, you can, of course, omit the steps calling for brushing the pan with butter and flour mixture, using pan spray, or lining the pans with paper cups, as Flexipans do not require pretreatment. Pipe or scoop the batter into the indentations of Flexipan No. 3051, filling them to just below the rim. Then, if desired, use the back of a spoon to push the batter up against the sides in each form, creating a concave surface. This will result in more traditional-looking rounded tops on the baked muffins rather than the muffins rising straight up from the forms like a soufflé. Let the muffins cool in the Flexipans for about 10 to 15 minutes before unmolding; muffins baked in Flexipans are too soft to remove right out of the oven.

Apple-Pecan Buttermilk Muffins yield: 30 muffins, 4 ounces (115 g) each

These muffins combine the moist goodness of apples and buttermilk with a crunchy streusel topping. The recipe is very adaptable. You can use unflavored yogurt in place of the buttermilk, and you can substitute any other nuts you have on hand for the pecans. If you're in a hurry and don't have streusel topping, sprinkle additional chopped nuts on top instead.

Butter and Flour Mixture (page 7) or pan spray

1 pound (455 g) unsalted butter, at room temperature

1 pound (455 g) light brown sugar

1 cup (240 ml) or 12 ounces (340 g) honey

6 eggs

1 teaspoon (5 ml) vanilla extract

1 teaspoon (5 g) salt

4 teaspoons (16 g) baking powder

4 teaspoons (16 g) baking soda

1 pound 8 ounces (680 g) cake flour

1 tablespoon (5 g) ground cinnamon

1 teaspoon (2 g) ground nutmeg

6 ounces (170 g) whole wheat flour

1¼ cups (300 ml) buttermilk

¾ cup (180 ml) half-and-half

1 recipe Chunky Apple Filling (page 840)

8 ounces (225 g) pecans, coarsely chopped

Streusel Topping (page 37)

1. Line muffin pans with paper cups, skipping every other space because this amount of batter will make oversized muffins that mushroom out on top of the pan as they bake. Grease the top of the pan around each cup with butter and flour mixture or coat with pan spray; set aside (see Note).

2. Cream the soft butter with the brown sugar and honey to a light and fluffy consistency. Mix in the eggs and the vanilla.

3. Sift together the salt, baking powder, baking soda, cake flour, cinnamon, and nutmeg. Stir the whole wheat flour into the sifted ingredients. Add to the batter in 3 segments, alternating with the buttermilk and half-and-half.

4. Add the apple filling to the batter together with the pecans.

5. Use an ice cream scoop to portion 4 ounces (115 g) batter into each muffin cup, then sprinkle streusel topping lightly on top of the batter.

6. Bake at 400°F (205°C) for about 30 minutes or until the muffins spring back when pressed lightly in the middle. Remove from the pans as soon as they are cool enough to handle to prevent the muffins from becoming wet on the bottom.

NOTE: To make smaller muffins that stay within the paper cups, use 3 ounces (85 g) batter per muffin. It is not necessary, in this case, to skip any spaces or grease the top of the pan. To bake the muffins in Flexipans, see page 410.

VARIATION

RAISIN AND PEAR MUFFINS yield: 30 muffins, 4 ounces (115 g) each

Substitute 8 pears, poached and chopped into ½-inch (1.2-cm) chunks, for the Chunky Apple Filling. Replace the pecans with raisins.

Blue Corn Muffins yield: 28 muffins, 4¹/₂ ounces (130 g) each

Three of the ingredients in this recipe—blue corn, maple syrup, and pine nuts—are native to North America. When European explorers first came to what they then referred to as the New World, the Native Americans were already cultivating several varieties of corn, including black, red, white, yellow, and blue. Each type had a different primary usage; the blue variety was generally dried and ground into meal. While the corn kernels are truly a dark blue color, the pinkish lavender tint found in many of the foodstuffs that are so popular in today's Southwestern cooking comes about as a result of treating the cornmeal with an alkaline substance; you can achieve the same effect with baking soda. If you do not have or prefer not to use blue cornmeal, finely ground yellow can certainly be substituted. The pine nuts add a pleasant texture and crunch, but so will pecans or walnuts, should you prefer to use of those instead.

8 ounces (225 g) pine nuts	8 eggs, at room temperature
Butter and Flour Mixture (page 7) or pan spray	7 ounces (200 g) light brown sugar
10 ounces (285 g) blue cornmeal	12 ounces (340 g) melted unsalted butter
10 ounces (285 g) cake flour	1¹/₂ cups (360 ml) maple syrup, at room temperature
6 ounces (170 g) bread flour	2 cups (480 ml) half-and-half, at room temperature
3 tablespoons (36 g) baking powder	
2 teaspoons (10 g) salt	

1. Lightly toast the pine nuts and set aside.

2. Brush the butter and flour mixture over the insides of 28 muffin cups, or coat with pan spray (see Note).

3. Combine and sift together the cornmeal, cake flour, bread flour, baking powder, and salt. Mix in the pine nuts and set aside.

4. In a mixer bowl, beat the eggs and brown sugar until foamy, about 2 minutes. Stir in the butter, maple syrup, and half-and-half.

5. Gradually mix in the dry ingredients at low speed, scraping down the bowl once or twice and mixing only until just combined; do not overmix.

6. Divide the batter evenly among the prepared muffin tins; the cups should be filled to just below the rim.

7. Bake at 375°F (190°C) for approximately 30 minutes or until baked through. Carefully remove from the pans and allow to cool slightly on a rack before serving.

NOTE: To bake the muffins in Flexipans, see page 410.

Blueberry-Ginger Muffins yield: 30 muffins, 4 ounces (115 g) each

If you like blueberry muffins, these are the very best. The ginger adds an extra zing, but if it doesn't appeal to you, just leave it out. When using frozen blueberries, do not thaw them before adding to the batter. If thawed, they will break up, turn the batter light blue, and make the batter too thin as well. Also, do not fold them in until you are ready to portion the muffins; if left to stand, the batter will set up, making it very difficult to work with.

A former student of mine learned the hard way (if you will pardon the pun) that if you multiply the recipe and use frozen berries, you had better not be the only one with an ice cream scoop. He was working in a Seattle restaurant that did a brisk business in blueberry muffins each Sunday brunch, and he was making 10 times this recipe for each batch. This worked out fine until the fresh blueberry season was over; then he added 15 pounds of frozen blueberries to all of that batter, which caused it to set up just like cement.

Butter and Flour Mixture (page 7) or pan spray

14 ounces (400 g) light brown sugar

14 ounces (400 g) unsalted butter, at room temperature

½ cup (120 ml) or 6 ounces (170 g) molasses

⅔ cup (160 ml) or 8 ounces (225 g) honey

6 eggs, at room temperature

1 teaspoon (5 ml) vanilla extract

1 pound (455 g) cake flour

14 ounces (400 g) bread flour

1 tablespoon (12 g) baking powder

1 tablespoon (12 g) baking soda

2 teaspoons (10 g) salt

1 teaspoon (2 g) ground ginger

1 cup (240 ml) buttermilk, at room temperature

1 pound 8 ounces (680 g) fresh or frozen blueberries (if frozen, do not thaw)

1. Line muffin pans with paper cups, skipping every other space because the muffins will mushroom out on top as they bake. Grease the top of the pan around each cup with butter and flour mixture or coat with pan spray; set aside.

2. Cream together the brown sugar and butter until light and fluffy. Mix in the molasses, honey, eggs, and vanilla.

3. Combine the cake flour, bread flour, baking powder, baking soda, salt, and ginger. Blend into the sugar mixture in 3 segments, alternating with the buttermilk.

4. Stir in the blueberries gently so that the berries do not break and turn the batter blue.

5. Place the batter in a pastry bag with a large plain tip. Pipe the batter in a dome shape slightly above the rim of each cup, using 4 ounces (115 g) batter per muffin. If the batter is firm enough to allow you to do so, use an ice cream scoop to portion them out instead. (If you use frozen berries, you will have no choice but to use an ice-cream scoop.)

6. Bake at 375°F (190°C) until brown and baked through, about 35 minutes.

VARIATION

BANANA MUFFINS yield: 30 muffins, 4 ounces (115 g) each

Replace the blueberries with bananas chopped into ½-inch (1.2-cm) cubes. Increase the bread flour by 2 ounces (55 g) and omit the ground ginger. The bananas should be ripe but firm. If they are very soft they will fall apart and would be better suited for use in Banana Bread (page 422).

Chocolate-Cherry Muffins yield: 26 muffins, 4 ounces (115 g) each

These rich, dark muffins have a distinctive, slightly bitter chocolate taste that is sweetened by the cherries and honey. The beets too add sweetness to the muffins, and they contribute to the intense dark color, which could otherwise be achieved only by adding an overpowering amount of chocolate. These muffins are not only tasty, they are great keepers as well, as both the beets and the cherries are instrumental in retaining moisture. The batter for these, as for many muffins containing both baking powder and baking soda, can be prepared the day before baking without any ill effects and stored overnight, covered, in the refrigerator, either preportioned in muffin cups or in bulk. Freeze the batter for longer storage. If you have a craving for another fruit, or you just don't have cherries on hand, cubed poached pears or whole fresh raspberries would make a great substitute.

Butter and Flour Mixture (page 7) or pan spray

6 eggs, at room temperature

1 pound 6 ounces (625 g) granulated sugar

1½ cups (360 ml) buttermilk, at room temperature

1½ cups (360 ml) or 12 ounces (340 g) sour cream, at room temperature

⅓ cup (80 ml) or 4 ounces (115 g) honey

1 pound 8 ounces (680 g) bread flour

4 ounces (115 g) unsweetened cocoa powder

1 tablespoon (12 g) baking soda

1 tablespoon (12 g) baking powder

10 ounces (285 g) finely ground almonds

12 ounces (340 g) melted unsalted butter

3 ounces (85 g) or ½ cup (120 ml) grated fresh purple beets

1 pound (455 g) fresh cherries *or* canned cherries (see Note)

1. Brush butter and flour mixture over the inside of muffin pans or coat with pan spray. Skip every other space because the muffins will mushroom out on top as they bake. Grease the top of the pan around each cup as well (see Chef's Tip).

2. Beat the eggs and sugar together just long enough to break up the eggs; do not overmix. Stir in the buttermilk, sour cream, and honey.

3. Sift together the flour, cocoa powder, baking soda, and baking powder. Add to the batter, together with the ground almonds, and mix until completely incorporated. Stir in the melted butter, grated beets, and the cherries.

4. If necessary, refrigerate the batter until it is firm enough to scoop. Portion 4 ounces (115 g) batter into each of the greased muffin cups, using an ice cream scoop of the appropriate size. Alternatively, you can pipe the batter into the pans right away, using a pastry bag with a No. 8 (16-mm) plain tip.

5. Bake at 375°F (190°C) for approximately 25 minutes or until the tops of the muffins spring back when you press lightly with your finger.

NOTE: If you use fresh cherries, stem them, remove the pits, and quarter them. Drain canned cherries, pat dry, then cut into quarters as well.

> **CHEF'S TIP**
> It is a lot more convenient to line the pans with paper cups instead of using the butter and flour mixture; however, the latter contributes to a more attractive appearance and a better volume. The batter tends to stick to the paper cups, thereby inhibiting a proper rise from the eggs and the chemical leavening agents. This results in a cracked and peaked muffin, which is undesirable in a mushrooming-type muffin. Baking the muffins in Flexipan No. 3051 will produce an additional 10 (slightly smaller) muffins. To bake the muffins in Flexipans, see page 410.

CHOCOLATE-CHERRY COFFEE CAKE yield: 4 cakes, 1 pound 14 ounces (855 g) each

The batter can be made into coffee cakes without any alteration. You can use larger gugelhupf or bundt pans if you do not have the size specified here. The batter will not fill the forms, but as long as the pans have a pattern around the top, they will look just fine.

1. Butter 4 gugelhupf or tube pans, 1 quart (960 ml) in capacity, and coat the pans lightly with dry cake crumbs or finely ground almonds or hazelnuts.

2. Divide the batter among the pans and bake as directed, increasing the time by about 15 minutes.

Chocolate Chip Muffins yield: 28 muffins, 4 ounces (115 g) each

These are gooey and delicious and, like chocolate chip cookies, are especially so right out of the oven, when the chocolate chunks are still runny. Take care not to overbake, or they can go from fabulous to dry and boring.

Butter and Flour Mixture (page 7) or pan spray	1 tablespoon (12 g) baking powder
14 ounces (400 g) sweet dark chocolate	4 teaspoons (16 g) baking soda
8 ounces (225 g) walnuts	1 pound 12 ounces (795 g) bread flour
10 ounces (285 g) unsalted butter, at room temperature	2 ounces (55 g) unprocessed wheat bran
10 ounces (285 g) light brown sugar	1¼ cups (300 ml) buttermilk, at room temperature
¾ cup (180 ml) or 9 ounces (255 g) honey	1½ cups (360 ml) half-and-half, at room temperature
4 eggs, at room temperature	8 ounces (225 g) dark raisins
1 teaspoon (5 ml) vanilla extract	

1. Line muffin pans with paper cups, skipping every other space because the muffins will mushroom out on top as they bake. Grease the top of the pan around each cup with butter and flour mixture or use pan spray; set aside (see Note).

2. Chop the chocolate and walnuts into raisin-sized pieces; set aside.

3. Beat the butter and brown sugar until fluffy. Add the honey, eggs, and vanilla.

4. Sift the baking powder, baking soda, and flour together. Add the bran.

5. Add the dry ingredients to the butter mixture in 3 parts, alternating with the buttermilk and half-and-half. Stir in the raisins, chocolate, and walnuts.

6. Use an ice cream scoop to portion 4 ounces (115 g) batter into each muffin cup.

7. Bake at 375°F (190°C) for about 25 minutes or until brown and baked through. To check if the muffins are done, press down in the center; they should spring back. As soon as they can be handled, either remove the muffins from the pans or tilt them in the pans to allow air underneath; this will keep them from getting wet on the bottom.

NOTE: To make smaller muffins that stay within the paper cups, use 3 ounces (85 g) batter per muffin. It is not necessary, in this case, to skip any spaces or to grease the top of the pan. To bake the muffins in Flexipans, use No. 3051 and follow the directions on page 410.

Chocolate-Honey Muffins yield: 30 muffins, 4 ounces (115 g) each

These muffins are good-looking and great-tasting. Honey adds a round, deep flavor and contributes to the moist texture. Chunks of both dark and white chocolate give these muffins lots of visual appeal.

Butter and Flour Mixture (page 7) or pan spray

6 ounces (170 g) walnuts

7 ounces (200 g) sweet dark chocolate

7 ounces (200 g) white chocolate

10 ounces (285 g) unsalted butter, at room temperature

10 ounces (285 g) light brown sugar

1 cup (240 ml) or 12 ounces (340 g) honey

¼ cup (60 ml) or 3 ounces (85 g) molasses

6 eggs, at room temperature

1 teaspoon (5 ml) vanilla extract

1 teaspoon (5 g) salt

4 teaspoons (16 g) baking powder

2 teaspoons (8 g) baking soda

14 ounces (400 g) bread flour

10 ounces (285 g) cake flour

2 ounces (55 g) unsweetened cocoa powder

2¼ cups (540 ml) buttermilk, at room temperature

1¾ cups (420 ml) half-and-half, at room temperature

6 ounces (170 g) dark raisins

1. Line muffin pans with paper cups, skipping every other space because the muffins will mushroom out on top of the pan as they bake. Grease the top of the pan around each cup with butter and flour mixture or use pan spray; set aside (see Note).

2. Chop the walnuts, dark chocolate, and white chocolate into raisin-sized pieces; set aside.

3. Cream together the butter and brown sugar until light and fluffy. Add the honey, molasses, eggs, and vanilla.

4. Sift together the salt, baking powder, baking soda, bread flour, cake flour, and cocoa powder. Add to the butter mixture in 3 parts, alternating with the buttermilk and half-and-half. Add the raisins, walnuts, and chocolate.

5. Use an ice cream scoop to portion 4 ounces (115 g) batter into each muffin cup.

6. Bake at 400°F (205°C) for about 30 minutes or until the muffins spring back when pressed lightly in the center. Remove from the pans as soon as they are cool enough to handle to prevent the muffins from becoming wet on the bottom.

NOTE: To make smaller muffins that stay within the paper cups, use 3 ounces (85 g) batter per muffin. It is not necessary, in this case, to skip any spaces or to grease the top of the pan. To bake the muffins in Flexipans, see instructions on page 410.

Honey-Bran Muffins yield: 36 muffins, 4 ounces (115 g) each

This healthy muffin can stand in as a light breakfast all by itself. If the muffins seem heavy and do not mushroom out much as they bake, you may need to increase the water a little. The consistency of the batter will vary with the type of bran used; smaller pieces absorb more liquid.

1¾ cups (420 ml) water

1 pound 3 ounces (540 g) unprocessed wheat bran

4 ounces (115 g) wheat germ

Butter and Flour Mixture (page 7) or pan spray

12 ounces (340 g) unsalted butter, at room temperature

1 pound 5 ounces (595 g) light brown sugar

1 cup (240 ml) or 12 ounces (340 g) molasses

1 cup (240 ml) or 12 ounces (340 g) honey

6 eggs, at room temperature

1 teaspoon (5 ml) vanilla extract

1 pound 12 ounces (795 g) bread flour

2½ teaspoons (10 g) baking powder

2 tablespoons (24 g) baking soda

1 teaspoon (5 g) salt

1¾ cups (420 ml) half-and-half, at room temperature

2¼ cups (540 ml) buttermilk, at room temperature

6 ounces (170 g) dark raisins

1. Bring the water to a boil and pour over the bran and wheat germ. Mix to combine and set aside to cool.

2. Line muffin pans with paper cups, skipping every other space because this amount of batter will make the muffins mushroom out on top of the pan as they bake. Grease the top of the pans around each cup with butter and flour mixture or use pan spray; set aside (see Note).

3. Cream together the butter and brown sugar until fluffy. Combine the molasses, honey, eggs, and vanilla; add to the butter mixture. Fold in the soaked bran and wheat germ.

4. Sift together the bread flour, baking powder, baking soda, and salt. Add to the batter in 3 parts, alternating with the half-and-half and the buttermilk. Stir in the raisins.

5. Use an ice cream scoop to portion 4 ounces (115 g) batter into each muffin cup.

6. Bake at 375°F (190°C) for about 25 minutes or until dark brown and baked through. To check if the muffins are done, press down in the center, they should spring back. As soon as the muffins can be handled, either remove them from the pans or tilt them in the pans to allow air underneath; this will keep the muffins from getting wet on the bottom.

NOTE: To make smaller muffins that stay within the paper cups, use 3 ounces (85 g) batter per muffin. It is not necessary, in this case, to skip any spaces or to grease the top of the pan. To bake muffins in Flexipans, follow the instructions on page 410.

Nutmeg Muffins yield: 18 muffins, 4 ounces (115 g) each

This recipe was given to me by one of my students after she learned of my love for nutmeg. In the original version, the wonderful taste and aroma that is only obtained from freshly grated nutmeg was there all right, but the remaining ingredients needed some tender loving care. For one thing, the muffins were very plain-looking—pale yellow, like the type of muffin you find in a six-pack at your local supermarket. The addition of a little baking soda darkens them a bit, the cranberries give the muffins color and a slight tang without taking away from the nutmeg taste, and the nuts on top add visual appeal as well.

Due to my passion for nutmeg, you might find the flavor a little too strong for some tastes, in which case you may want to reduce the quantity accordingly. Please do not attempt this recipe with commercial ground nutmeg. The flavor simply isn't there, and increasing the amount does not help because the taste then becomes bitter. Instead, try substituting cardamom pods—another of my favorite spices—for the nutmeg. Crush the seeds fine in a mortar and use the same amount. The cranberries can be left out of either variation if you wish.

Butter and Flour Mixture (page 7) or pan spray

10 ounces (285 g) bread flour

12 ounces (340 g) cake flour

2 tablespoons (24 g) baking powder

1 teaspoon (4 g) baking soda

2 tablespoons (15 g) freshly grated nutmeg (see Note 1)

4 eggs, at room temperature

1½ teaspoons (7.5 g) salt

8 ounces (225 g) granulated sugar

½ cup (120 ml) or 6 ounces (170 g) honey

½ cup (120 ml) buttermilk, at room temperature

1½ cups (360 ml) half-and-half, at room temperature

8 ounces (225 g) melted unsalted butter

6 ounces (170 g) fresh or frozen cranberries

4 ounces (115 g) cashews, finely chopped

1. Line muffin pans with paper cups, skipping every other space to allow the batter to mushroom out on top of the pan as the muffins bake. Grease the top of the pans around each cup with butter and flour mixture or use pan spray (see Note 2); set aside.

2. Sift together the bread flour, cake flour, baking powder, and baking soda. Add the nutmeg and reserve.

3. Combine the eggs, salt, and granulated sugar. Beat rapidly for 2 minutes. Gradually stir the egg mixture into the reserved dry ingredients. Mix in the honey, buttermilk, and half-and-half, stirring until the batter is smooth. Stir in the melted butter, cranberries, and half of the cashews.

CHEF'S TIP

If using frozen cranberries, do not thaw; keep them in the freezer until you are ready to add them to the batter. If thawed, they may break and discolor the batter.

4. Use an ice cream scoop to portion the batter into the prepared pans. (If the batter seems too soft to use a scoop, you probably had the butter too hot. Refrigerate the batter until it firms up a bit.) Sprinkle the remaining cashews on top of the muffins.

5. Bake at 375°F (190°C) for approximately 20 minutes or until the muffins spring back when pressed lightly on top. Let cool slightly, then remove from the pans.

NOTE 1: Grate the nutmeg with a nutmeg grinder. Avoid using a box or sheet grater, as it is almost impossible to grate the end of the nut without including part of your fingers. Measure the nutmeg loosely packed; do not press it down.

NOTE 2: To bake the muffins in Flexipans, follow the instructions on page 410.

Oat Bran–Yogurt Muffins yield: 36 muffins, 4 ounces (115 g) each

This is a variation of the Honey-Bran Muffin recipe. Oat Bran–Yogurt Muffins provide an alternate way to enjoy the goodness of oats at breakfast instead of the usual oatmeal. For a long time, oats were used only as animal feed and were considered a weed when they sprouted up in wheat fields. Only recently have they received due credit for their high soluble fiber content as well as plenty of vitamins E and B. Oat bran does not contain any gluten and so, in baking, must be always be combined with another flour that does have gluten.

Butter and Flour Mixture (page 7) or pan spray

12 ounces (340 g) unsalted butter, at room temperature

1 pound 6 ounces (625 g) light brown sugar

1 cup (240 ml) or 12 ounces (340 g) molasses

1 cup (240 ml) or 12 ounces (340 g) honey

12 eggs, at room temperature

2 teaspoons (10 ml) vanilla extract

1 pound 12 ounces (795 g) bread flour

2 tablespoons (24 g) baking powder

4 teaspoons (16 g) baking soda

1 teaspoon (5 g) salt

1 pound 10 ounces (740 g) unprocessed oat bran

1½ cups (360 ml) half-and-half, at room temperature

2¼ cups (540 ml) unflavored low-fat yogurt, at room temperature

8 ounces (225 g) dark raisins

1. Line muffin pans with paper cups, skipping every other space because this amount of batter will make the muffins mushroom out on top of the pans as they bake. Grease the top of the pans around each cup with butter and flour mixture or use pan spray (see Note); set aside.

2. Cream the butter and brown sugar until fluffy. Combine the molasses, honey, eggs, and vanilla; add to the butter mixture.

3. Sift together the flour, baking powder, baking soda, and salt. Stir in the oat bran and reserve.

4. Stir the half-and-half into the yogurt. Add the dry ingredients to the batter in 3 parts, alternating with the yogurt mixture. Stir in the raisins.

5. Portion 4 ounces (115 g) batter per muffin into the muffin cups, using an ice cream scoop.

6. Bake at 375°F (190°C) for about 25 minutes or until brown and baked through (the muffins should spring back when pressed lightly in the center). As soon as they can be handled, either remove the muffins from the pans or tilt them in the pans to allow air underneath and prevent the muffins from getting wet on the bottom as they cool.

NOTE: To make smaller muffins that stay within the paper cups, use 3 ounces (85 g) batter per muffin. It is not necessary, in this case, to skip any spaces or to grease the tops of the pans. To bake the muffins in Flexipans, follow the instructions on page 410.

Pumpkin Muffins yield: 24 muffins, 4 ounces (115 g) each

This is a versatile recipe that can be made any time of the year, although we seem to associate pumpkin mostly with the holiday season. Many other types of cooked and pureed winter squash (except spaghetti squash), such as acorn, butternut, and Hubbard, can be substituted in equal amounts. Alternatively, try using cooked sweet potato puree instead of the pumpkin puree. The batter can also be baked in loaf pans or ring forms to create tea cakes, which are convenient to have on hand for a quick snack.

Butter and Flour Mixture (page 7) or pan
spray

1 pound (455 g) unsalted butter, at room
temperature

13 ounces (370 g) light brown sugar

4 eggs, at room temperature

½ cup (120 ml) or 6 ounces (170 g) molasses

½ cup (120 ml) or 6 ounces (170 g) honey

1 teaspoon (5 g) salt

1 teaspoon (2 g) ground ginger

1 teaspoon (1.5 g) ground cinnamon

1 teaspoon (2 g) ground allspice

½ teaspoon (1 g) grated nutmeg

1 tablespoon (12 g) baking powder

1 tablespoon (12 g) baking soda

2 pounds (910 g) bread flour

8 ounces (225 g) dark raisins

1 teaspoon (5 ml) vanilla extract

1½ cups (360 ml) buttermilk, at room
temperature

1½ cups (360 ml) pumpkin puree

1. Line muffin pans with paper cups, skipping every other space because this amount of batter will make the muffins mushroom out on top of the pans as they bake. Grease the tops of the pans around each cup with butter and flour mixture or use pan spray (see Note); set aside.

2. Cream together the butter and brown sugar. Mix in eggs, molasses, and honey; reserve.

3. Sift together the salt, ginger, cinnamon, allspice, nutmeg, baking powder, baking soda, and flour. Mix in the raisins, coating them with flour to keep them from sinking in the batter.

4. Combine the vanilla, buttermilk, and pumpkin. Add the pumpkin mixture to the butter mixture in 2 portions, alternating with the dry ingredients.

5. Place the batter in a pastry bag with a No. 8 (16-mm) plain tip. Pipe the batter into the prepared pans, slightly above the rim of each cup, using 4 ounces (115 g) batter per muffin. Alternatively, use an ice cream scoop to fill the pans.

6. Bake at 375°F (190°C) until the crust is brown, about 35 minutes. The muffins should spring back when pressed lightly in the center.

NOTE: To make smaller muffins that stay within the paper cups, use 3 ounces (85 g) batter per muffin. It is not necessary, in this case, to skip any spaces or to grease the tops of the pans. To bake the muffins in Flexipans, follow the instructions on page 410 but use No. 1269.

VARIATION

PERSIMMON MUFFINS yield: 24 muffins, 4 ounces (115 g) each

Omit the raisins and pumpkin puree. Add instead 8 ounces (225 g) dates chopped to the size of raisins, 1¼ cups (300 ml) persimmon puree, and 8 ounces (225 g) persimmon chunks, also chopped into raisin-sized pieces.

Zucchini-Walnut Muffins yield: 30 muffins, 4 ounces (115 g) each

As with pumpkin muffins, you can experiment here by substituting other summer squash varieties for the zucchini. However, the green zucchini skin really looks good and adds a nice texture to the finished product. You can certainly use whatever type of nuts you have on hand, and you can replace the wheat bran with oat bran. With all of that flexibility, there is just no excuse not to try this recipe. A particular type or brand of bran may absorb more moisture than is desirable, resulting in a heavy, dense muffin. If this happens, increase either the zucchini or the carrots a little.

Butter and Flour Mixture (page 7) or pan
spray

8 eggs

1 pound 12 ounces (795 g) granulated sugar

1 pound 4 ounces (570 g) grated zucchini
(skin on)

10 ounces (285 g) peeled, grated carrots

2 cups (480 ml) vegetable oil

1 teaspoon (5 g) salt

1 pound 12 ounces (795 g) bread flour

4 teaspoons (16 g) baking powder

1 tablespoon (12 g) baking soda

1 tablespoon (5 g) ground cinnamon

2 teaspoons (4 g) allspice

1 teaspoon (2 g) nutmeg

8 ounces (225 g) unprocessed wheat bran

10 ounces (285 g) chopped walnuts

Finely chopped walnuts

Light brown sugar

1. Line muffin pans with paper cups, skipping every other space because the muffins will
mushroom out on top of the pans as they bake. Grease the top of the pans around each cup
with butter and flour mixture or coat with pan spray (see Note); set aside.

2. Beat the eggs and sugar just to combine. Stir in the zucchini, carrots, oil, and salt.

3. Sift the flour with the baking powder, baking soda, and spices. Add to the egg mixture.

4. Stir in the bran and the 10 ounces (285 g) walnuts.

5. Use an ice cream scoop to portion 4 ounces (115 g) batter into each muffin cup.

6. Mix equal parts of finely chopped walnuts and brown sugar by volume and sprinkle on
top of the muffins.

7. Bake at 400°F (205°C) for approximately 35 minutes. Remove the muffins from the pans
as soon as they are cool enough to touch, to prevent them from becoming wet on the bottom.

NOTE: To make smaller muffins that stay within the paper cups, use 3 ounces (85 g) batter per
muffin. It is not necessary, in this case, to skip any spaces or to grease the tops of the pans. To
bake the muffins in Flexipans, follow the instructions on page 410.

VARIATION

ZUCCHINI-FIG MUFFINS yield: 30 muffins, 4 ounces (115 g) each

Reduce the amount of zucchini to 8 ounces (225 g). Soak 12 ounces (340 g) dried figs in hot
water for 30 minutes. Drain and chop into raisin-sized pieces. Add the figs to the batter together
with the walnuts.

OTHER QUICK BREADS, BISCUITS, AND SCONES

Although almost all of the recipes in this chapter fall under the quick bread heading, the recipes
that follow are those that are other than tea cakes, pound cakes, or muffins. Unlike yeast breads,
quick breads are leavened chemically with baking soda and/or baking powder. Chemical leavening agents work by producing carbon dioxide gas when they come into contact with moisture
and/or heat. This quick reaction, unlike that of yeast, which requires time to develop, gives quick
breads their name. Quick breads can be prepared from a dough (examples are soda breads, biscuits, and scones) or from a batter (as in muffins, pound cakes, banana bread, and others).

Banana Bread *yield: 3 cakes, 1 pound 5 ounces (595 g) each*

There's just one secret to great banana bread: really ripe fruit. Greenish yellow bananas will add little or no flavor. Even a bright yellow banana perfect for snacking or sautéeing will not do. Only a banana past its eating prime—light brown with darker brown spots—will yield the moisture and rich taste necessary for a fine quick bread like this one. So do not throw out those overripe bananas; just place them in the refrigerator to stop the ripening process until you are ready to make your banana bread.

Butter and Flour Mixture (page 7) or pan spray	1 pound 5 ounces (595 g) pureed bananas, somewhat overripe
10 ounces (285 g) unsalted butter	1 pound 2 ounces (510 g) bread flour
1 pound 2 ounces (510 g) granulated sugar	2 teaspoons (10 g) salt
3 eggs, at room temperature	2 teaspoons (8 g) baking soda
1 teaspoon (5 ml) vanilla extract	9 ounces (255 g) coarsely chopped walnuts

1. Brush butter and flour mixture over the inside of 3 gugelhupf forms, 1 quart (960 ml) in capacity, or other molds with the same capacity, or coat the forms with pan spray.

2. Melt the butter and add the sugar. Mix for a few minutes. Stir in the eggs, vanilla, and pureed bananas.

3. Combine the flour, salt, baking soda, and walnuts. Stir into the butter mixture.

4. Spoon the batter into the prepared forms. If you are using small forms, fill them only three-quarters full.

5. Bake at 350°F (175°C) for about 45 minutes or until baked through. You may need to use a second pan underneath to ensure that the cakes do not get too dark on the bottom while baking.

6. Unmold the cakes as soon as possible and let cool on a cake rack (they will get wet if left to cool in the pans).

Buttermilk-Cream Biscuits *yield: approximately 28 biscuits, 2½ inches (6.2 cm) in diameter*

Using both buttermilk and cream in this biscuit recipe gives you the best of both worlds. Buttermilk contributes to a light, airy texture as it assists the leavening agents, and cream adds richness and moisture. As with making pie dough, it is crucial that both the butter and the liquid ingredients are very cold and that the dough is mixed and handled gently. If the butter is soft to begin with, if it becomes warm (and therefore soft) when the liquid is added, or if the dough is overmixed, the baked biscuits will be heavy and compact instead of tall, light, and flaky. Ideally, small lumps of butter should be dispersed throughout the dough. As the biscuits bake, the pieces of butter melt and create layers in much the same way that puff pastry develops layers as it bakes. If the butter is worked into the dough instead, you not only lose the layer structure but also create gluten, which toughens the finished product.

9 ounces (255 g) cake flour	2 tablespoons (30 g) granulated sugar
8 ounces (225 g) bread flour	1 cup (240 ml) cold buttermilk
1 tablespoon plus 2 teaspoons (20 g) baking powder	½ cup (120 ml) cold heavy cream
1 teaspoon (4 g) baking soda	2 eggs
1 teaspoon (5 g) salt	5 ounces (140 g) very cold unsalted butter, cut into ½-inch (1.2-cm) cubes

1. Stir together the flours, baking powder, baking soda, salt, and sugar in a mixing bowl until well combined.

2. Combine the buttermilk, cream, and the eggs in a separate bowl and mix with a whisk to break up the eggs and incorporate the ingredients.

3. Add the cold butter chunks to the flour mixture and rub the butter into the flour, using your fingertips, until the butter is broken into tiny pieces about the size of kernels of corn.

4. Using a wooden spoon or your hand, quickly mix in the liquid ingredients, stirring just until the mixture forms a dough.

5. Very lightly flour your work surface and turn the dough out of the bowl. Knead very gently for just 1 minute or so until you have a smooth ball of dough. It is important not to overmix or handle the dough roughly. Pat the dough flat with your hands, then use a rolling pin to make it ¾ to 1 inch (2 to 2.5 cm) thick.

6. Dip a 2-inch (5-cm) round cutter in flour and cut out biscuits, placing the cuts close together to create the minimum amount of scrap pieces. You will have to gently knead the scrap pieces together once to cut out all 28 biscuits.

7. Arrange the biscuits on a sheet pan lined with baking paper, placing them in rows with their sides touching (see Note).

8. Bake at 450°F (230°C) for 15 to 18 minutes or until the biscuits are deep golden brown.

9. Carefully remove the biscuits and place on a cooling rack. Serve warm.

NOTE: Placing the biscuits close together on the pans (touching) results in a much higher biscuit. As they expand in the oven, the biscuits press against each other and, with nowhere else to go, they rise straight up instead of spreading out.

Cornbread yield: 2 breads, 9 inches (22.5 cm) in diameter

Cornbread is a quick bread that has been very popular all over the United States for many years, and it is made in endless variations. The best result is achieved by baking the bread in a very hot greased or buttered cast-iron skillet, so that the batter sizzles and starts to cook immediately when it is poured into the pan. I usually melt the butter needed for the recipe in the baking skillet, add the butter to the batter, put the skillet in the oven for a few minutes to get hot while finishing the batter, and have one less pan to clean up. If the batter is baked in cake pans, it is still good, but it does not have a crisp crust. The same batter can also be baked in muffin pans or in cast-iron pans specially made for corn sticks, should you have these. Corn stick pans have shallow indentations, each in the shape of an ear of corn. These should be buttered or oiled and heated until very hot before the batter is added.

5 ounces (140 g) cake flour

5 ounces (140 g) bread flour

11 ounces (310 g) yellow cornmeal

2 tablespoons (24 g) baking powder

2 teaspoons (10 g) salt

4 eggs

8 ounces (225 g) melted unsalted butter

2 cups (480 ml) whole milk, at room temperature

Diced onion (optional)

Blanched corn kernels (optional)

Cooked crumbled bacon (optional)

Chopped green chilies (optional)

1. Thoroughly combine the flours, cornmeal, baking powder, and salt.

2. Lightly beat the eggs, then whisk in the melted butter and the milk. Add the liquid to the dry ingredients; stir just until combined.

3. Stir in any of the optional ingredients, if using.

4. Divide the batter between 2 very hot greased cast-iron skillets, 9 inches (22.5 cm) in diameter, or 2 greased cake pans, 9 inches (22.5 cm) in diameter.

5. Bake at 375°F (190°C) for 20 to 25 minutes or until the top springs back when pressed lightly, the same as a sponge cake.

VARIATIONS

CORN MUFFINS yield: approximately 18 muffins

Divide the batter between 18 muffin cups, 4 ounces (120 ml) in capacity. Bake at 375°F (190°C) for approximately 15 minutes or until baked through.

CORN STICKS yield: approximately 24 sticks

Preheat the corn stick pans in the oven (while you make the batter) until they are very hot. Carefully add enough batter to fill each indentation and return the pans to the oven as quickly as possible. Bake at 375°F (190°C) until baked through; the time needed will depend on the size of the pans. When done, the tops will spring back when pressed lightly, the same as with a sponge cake.

Irish Soda Breads

Irish soda bread could be said to be nothing more than a large biscuit baked in a loaf shape and, really, the line is fairly thin between soda bread, scones, and biscuits. A typical Irish soda bread, as we have come to know it in the United States, contains raisins or dried currants and caraway seeds. These additions were not the norm in old Ireland, however, where they would have been very expensive and out of the reach of a peasant farmer. The traditions of shaping the loaves round, dusting them heavily with flour, and cutting a cross deep into the top so that it opens up as it bakes, on the other hand, seem to go back to the early days, when the breads were often baked in iron skillets or deep Dutch ovens.

If you talk to the patriotic Irish, they will tell you that Irish soda bread made from wheat grown in the Golden Vale, the fertile center of County Tipperary in southwest Ireland, simply can't be beat. In addition to national pride, there is a scientific reason for this opinion: This flat, lush area is known for its soft wheat flour. You could compare it to the soft wheat flour grown in the southern United States, which is renowned for producing the lightest biscuits.

About Hard and Soft Wheat and Gluten

The terms *hard flour* and *soft flour* refer to the flour's protein content. Hard flours have more protein and therefore produce more gluten; soft flours have less protein and produce less gluten. Remember, gluten is what gives a bread dough its elasticity and structure, and helps to produce a strong oven-spring. Gluten is created when the two proteins in the flour—glutenin and gliadin—are combined with water. As the mixture is blended (kneaded), the proteins bind with the water, and with each other, forming thin, stretchy sheets of gluten. These elastic sheets trap and hold the gases produced by yeast. Gluten is thus essential for yeast-leavened breads but disastrous for quick breads, such as soda bread, where a soft, moist dough without elasticity is desired.

Hard wheats, which are used for products such as pasta dough and yeast-leavened breads, require hot summers and freezing winters. Soft wheat grows in a warm climate, hence its popularity in the southern United States. Soft wheat flour is ideal for quick breads such as scones, muffins, and, of course, light-as-a-cloud biscuits.

Sweet Irish Soda Bread yield: 4 loaves, 1 pound (455 g) each

Even though this recipe contains no baking soda per se, it does contain a substantial amount of baking powder, and baking powder is one-third baking soda. So this is, technically, still a soda bread.

1 pound 10 ounces (740 g) cake flour

5 ounces (140 g) wheat or oat bran

4 ounces (115 g) granulated sugar

1½ ounces (40 g) baking powder

1 teaspoon (5 g) salt

4 ounces (115 g) firm unsalted butter

5 ounces (140 g) dried currants or raisins

1 tablespoon (7 g) caraway seeds

1¼ cups (300 ml) whole milk (see Note)

½ cup (120 ml) buttermilk

Bread flour

1. Thoroughly combine the cake flour, wheat or oat bran, sugar, baking powder, and salt.

2. Add the butter in small chunks and rub between your fingers until the butter is reduced to small pieces (about the size of raisins) and is evenly incorporated. Mix in the currants or raisins and the caraway seeds.

3. Combine the milk and buttermilk and add to the mixture, stirring with a wooden spoon or with your hand, just until the ingredients are incorporated and the mixture has formed a dough. Add more milk or more flour if necessary to make a soft dough, but avoid overmixing, as this will develop the gluten and compromise the texture of the final product.

4. Divide the dough into 4 equal pieces, approximately 1 pound (455 g) each, using enough bread flour to keep the dough from sticking to your hands and/or the worktable. Shape the pieces into round or oval loaves and place on sheet pans lined with baking paper.

5. Dust the tops of the loaves with bread flour. Using a sharp knife, cut a cross about ¾ inch (2 cm) deep on the top of each loaf.

6. Bake at 425° F (219°C) for approximately 20 minutes or until baked through.

NOTE: You may use all whole milk or all buttermilk (using 1¾ cups/420 ml total of either) if you prefer.

Savory Irish Soda Bread yield: 2 loaves, 2 pounds (910 g) each

Soda breads have a velvety, distinctive texture. This whole wheat savory variation makes for a wonderful breakfast treat, sliced thin and spread with butter (and it tastes even better toasted).

1 pound 4 ounces (570 g) cake flour	2 teaspoons (8 g) baking soda
12 ounces (340 g) whole wheat flour	6 ounces (170 g) firm unsalted butter
2 teaspoons (10 g) salt	3⅓ cups (800 ml) buttermilk
2 teaspoons (8 g) baking powder	Bread flour

1. Combine the cake flour, whole wheat flour, salt, baking powder, and baking soda in a mixer bowl. Add the butter cut into small, even chunks, and mix with the paddle attachment until the butter is reduced to the size of small peas.

2. Add the buttermilk all at once and mix at low speed just until the ingredients are combined and the mixture looks like a rough biscuit dough. If necessary, adjust with more flour or more buttermilk, but avoid overmixing.

3. Turn out the dough onto a floured surface and divide into 2 equal pieces. Form the pieces into round loaves. Place the loaves on sheet pans lined with baking paper. Dust the tops of the loaves with bread flour (dust it over the surface with your hand). Using a sharp knife, cut a cross ¾ inch (2 cm) deep on top of each loaf.

4. Bake at 375°F (190°C) for approximately 1 hour. The loaves should have a dark golden brown color, and a wooden skewer inserted into the center of the loaf should come out clean. Transfer to a rack to cool.

Pumpkin Quick Bread

yield: 2 loaves, 2 pounds 10 ounces (1 kg 195 g) each, or 20 muffins, 4 ounces (115 g) each

The only thing to remember with this simple no-fail pound cake is that you need to start plumping the raisins the day before to get the best result. In most professional bakeshops, soaked raisins are a standard mise en place item, so this is not an issue. If, for some reason, you have no choice, you can add regular dry raisins and ½ cup (120 ml) water to the batter instead of the full 1 cup (240 ml) used in Step 1.

If you use this batter for muffins, increase the baking temperature to 400°F (205°C) and decrease the time to approximately 25 minutes. To bake the muffins in Flexipans, see page 410.

10 ounces (285 g) dark raisins	10 ounces (285 g) bread flour
1 cup (240 ml) water	4 ounces (115 g) cake flour
Butter and Flour Mixture (page 7) or pan spray	2 teaspoons (4 g) ground cloves
	2 teaspoons (4 g) ground nutmeg
14 ounces (400 g) pumpkin puree	1 tablespoon (6 g) ground cinnamon
1 pound 2 ounces (510 g) granulated sugar	2 teaspoons (8 g) baking powder
4 eggs	1 teaspoon (4 g) baking soda
1½ teaspoons (7.5 g) salt	
¾ cup (180 ml) vegetable oil	

I. Combine the raisins and water and set aside the day before to plump the raisins. Be sure the container you choose will allow the water to completely cover the raisins.

2. Brush the butter and flour mixture over the insides of 2 loaf or Bundt-style pans (or the appropriate number of muffin pan indentations), or coat the forms with pan spray.

3. Using the paddle attachment, mix the pumpkin puree, sugar, eggs, and salt for approximately 8 minutes at medium speed. Gradually incorporate the oil, scraping down the sides of the bowl to produce a smooth, well-mixed batter.

4. Sift together the bread flour, cake flour, cloves, nutmeg, cinnamon, baking powder, and baking soda. Mix the dry ingredients into the batter, followed by the raisin and water mixture. Divide the batter between the prepared pans, filling cake pans halfway, muffin cups two-thirds full.

5. Bake at 350°F (175°C) for about 1 hour or until done (see introduction for instructions on baking the muffins). Let cool some before unmolding.

Scones yield: 16 wedges, 4 × 5 inches (10 × 12.5 cm) each

Use any combination of dried fruit you wish, such as cherries and apricots or cranberries and pears. The finished size suggested here gives you a rather large scone; you can certainly decrease the size for a larger yield. The scones can be made up ready-to-bake, then refrigerated overnight, with excellent results. The formed dough can also be frozen for longer storage. Thaw the scones before baking.

6 ounces (170 g) currants or dark raisins	3 tablespoons (36 g) baking powder
6 ounces (170 g) candied orange peel, cut into raisin-sized pieces	1 teaspoon (5 g) salt
1 pound 12 ounces (795 g) bread flour	3½ cups (840 ml) heavy cream
3 ounces (85 g) granulated sugar	⅓ cup (80 ml) or 4 ounces (115 g) honey
	Granulated sugar

I. Combine the currants or raisins and the orange peel. Add a handful of the flour and mix to coat the fruit pieces with flour and prevent them from sticking together. Set aside.

2. Combine the remaining flour, 3 ounces (85 g) granulated sugar, the baking powder, and the salt in a mixing bowl. Reserve approximately ¼ cup (60 ml) cream. Add the remainder of the cream, together with the honey and the reserved fruit, to the dry ingredients. Mix by hand only until the ingredients come together in a smooth dough. Do not overmix.

3. Gently form the dough (do not knead it) into a round disk. Cover the dough and set aside to relax for 5 minutes.

4. Cut the disk of dough in half horizontally (as you would a sponge cake) to form 2 equal pieces. Knead each piece of dough into a round loaf to tighten the gluten (see Figures 3-1 and 3-2, page 94). Press or pat the pieces out to form circles, 10 inches (25 cm) in diameter.

5. Cut each dough circle into 8 wedges. Brush the top of each wedge with some of the reserved cream. Invert the pieces in granulated sugar. Place, sugar-side up, on sheet pans lined with baking paper.

6. Bake at 425°F (219°C) for approximately 15 minutes.

Sponge Cakes and Cake Bases

Baking sponge cake and variations thereof is a basic skill every baker or pastry chef must master: These form the base for the majority of the cakes we create. Not having a properly made sponge to start with affects not only the taste of the cake but also the final appearance, as it will be harder to decorate attractively.

Sponge cakes are made from the three ingredients no baker can do without—eggs, sugar, and flour—although some sponges also contain butter. Classically made sponge cakes (genoise in French) do not contain baking powder or baking soda; their volume and light texture come solely from the air whipped into the eggs.

Formula Balance

An extremely heavy or rich sponge contains equal parts eggs, sugar, and flour. In other words, for every 8 ounces (225 g) eggs (approximately 4) there are 8 ounces (225 g) sugar and 8 ounces (225 g) flour. This ratio is actually the formula for a standard pound cake. A medium-bodied mixture will contain 5 ounces (140 g) each flour and sugar for the same 8 ounces (225 g) eggs. In the lighter and most common type of sponge cake, the sugar and flour weights are 4 ounces (115 g) each per 8 ounces (225 g) eggs. The sugar and flour ratio can be altered to a small degree in individual formulas, such as 3 ounces (85 g) sugar and 4 ounces (115 g) flour, or vice versa. If butter is used, the amount is generally about one-fourth of the weight of the sugar or flour, and it is added at the end.

Eggs

In any sponge formula, the weight of the eggs is always used as the basis for determining the quantity of the remaining ingredients. Whole eggs, entirely or in part, may be replaced with egg yolks or egg whites. More egg yolks will result in a denser sponge with finer pores. Increasing the amount of egg whites produces a lighter sponge with a larger pore structure. Increasing the yolk content in an already heavy sponge cake can have a detrimental effect. The yolks will reduce the available water content, making it difficult for all of the sugar to dissolve. The eggs should be shelled as close as possible to the time of making the sponge. Eggs that have been shelled and left overnight should not be used for sponges. Both egg whites and egg yolks are available in pasteurized form, ready-to-use and packaged in convenient refrigerator cartons (such as the type milk and juice come in). These are becoming increasingly popular in the industry not only from the health and sanitation standpoint but also because they are so efficient to use, reducing labor, spoilage, and breakage.

Sugar

Granulated sugar or, even better, the finer grade castor sugar, should always be used in a sponge cake to ensure that the sugar dissolves easily. The proper amount in relation to the other ingredients is also important, as discussed above. Too little sugar, in addition to affecting the taste and color, can make the cake tough by throwing the formula off balance; in actuality, you now have too much flour. This condition will also cause the crust to darken unfavorably and give the sponge a dense texture.

Flour

The flour used in a sponge cake must have a good ratio between starch and protein. Some gluten (a high percentage of which is found in bread flour, for instance), is necessary to bind and hold the structure, but too high a percentage makes the batter rubbery and hard to work with and results in a tough and chewy sponge. A flour with too much starch, such as cake flour, will produce a light and tender sponge, but the structure will collapse partially when baked. It is best to adjust this ratio yourself in individual recipes by combining both bread and cake flours in the proper proportions, as opposed to using premixed all-purpose flour.

Pure starches, such as potato starch and cornstarch, can be used to weaken the gluten, but no more than half of the weight of the flour should be replaced. Cocoa powder, which also does not contain any gluten, is usually added for flavor rather than as a means to reduce the gluten strength.

Flour for sponge cakes should always be sifted. If you use unsweetened cocoa powder or any other dry ingredient, sift it in with the flour. You must be very careful, when adding the flour to the batter, not to break the air bubbles that you just whipped in. Fold in the flour with a rubber spatula or your hand and turn the mixing bowl slowly with your other hand at the same time to combine the ingredients evenly. Never stir the flour into the batter or add it with the mixer.

Butter

Butter is added to a sponge cake not only for flavor but to improve the quality of the finished sponge. The cake will have a finer pore structure as the batter becomes heavier. Butter also extends shelf life.

Butter can be added to a sponge in an amount up to two-thirds the weight of the sugar. The butter should be melted but not hot. It is always added last, after the flour has been completely incorporated. Otherwise, the butter will surround any small lumps of flour and you won't be able to break them up without losing volume.

Nuts, Nut Paste, and Candied Fruit

Chopped nuts or chopped candied fruit may be added to a sponge cake without changing the formula, provided it is a fairly heavy sponge (the pieces will settle on the bottom in a very light sponge batter). Chopped nuts do not absorb much moisture and therefore do not have the same effect on the batter that ground nuts do. Almond or hazelnut paste may also be added without any reformulating; however, in this case, the butter is generally left out. The almond paste is first softened and worked free of lumps by incorporating egg white. The egg yolks are whipped as directed in the recipe and can then be folded into the almond paste mixture quickly and smoothly without causing lumps or losing volume.

Ideally, ground almonds and hazelnuts should be of such a fine consistency that they can be sifted with the flour. The flour must be reduced accordingly, as the fine structure of the nuts will absorb moisture. Decrease the weight of the flour by 1 ounce (30 g) for every 3 ounces (85 g) ground nuts added. Further, the quantity of ground nuts added cannot be higher than the weight of the sugar in the recipe.

Unsweetened Cocoa Powder, Unsweetened Chocolate, and Sweet Chocolate

Unsweetened cocoa powder may be substituted for cake flour in an equal weight. No more than 3 ounces (85 g) cocoa powder should be used for every 1 pound (455 g) flour. Sift in the cocoa powder with the flour. Unsweetened chocolate can be added (not substituted) at a ratio of no more than 5 ounces (140 g) per 1 pound (455 g) flour. Sweet chocolate may be added at the same rate, but the sugar should be decreased by 2 ounces (55 g) for this amount. Fold the chocolate into a small amount of the batter to temper it, then fold this into the remaining batter. Using this method, the best results are achieved with cakes containing a chemical leavening agent rather than with traditional egg-leavened sponges.

Sponge Methods

WARM-FOAMING-METHOD SPONGE

There are two basic ways to make a classic sponge cake: the warm foaming method and the cold foaming method. In the warm method, eggs and sugar are placed in a mixer bowl and stirred over simmering water (so that the eggs do not cook) to about 110°F (43°C) or until the sugar has dissolved completely. This improves the emulsifying properties of the eggs. Test to be certain that the sugar is completely dissolved by rubbing a little of the mixture between your thumb and forefinger. The mixture is removed from the heat and whipped at high speed until creamy and light in color and the foam has reached its maximum volume. When a large quantity is produced, it is recommended that the mixture be whipped at a lower speed for about 5 minutes longer to stabilize the batter. Sifted flour is folded in, followed by the melted butter, if used. The main objective in the foaming method is to create a batter with the maximum amount of air. This is most easily produced when the ingredients are balanced properly. The ratio should be 2 parts eggs, 1 part flour, and 1 part sugar by weight. For example: 12 whole eggs (approximately 24 ounces/680 g), 12 ounces (340 g) of flour, and 12 ounces (340 g) of sugar—12-12-12 is an easy way to remember the formula (a bit of salt and a few ounces of butter are generally added as well).

COLD-FOAMING-METHOD SPONGE

In the cold-foaming method, the eggs and sugar are placed directly in the mixer bowl and whipped at high speed until creamy and light in color and the foam has reached its maximum volume. Use the same formulas as for the warm-foaming method. The butter can be added as well, but is generally left out since this method is typically used when the sponge will be soaked with a liqueur or flavoring, as in tiramisu or trifle, for example.

Because part of the sugar melts in the oven rather than over the water bath as in the warm method, there are larger air bubbles in the finished sponge. These pockets are beneficial when the cake is used for the soaked-sponge desserts mentioned above.

OTHER FOAMING-METHOD SPONGE

In this method, the eggs are first separated; the yolks are whipped with part of the sugar to a light and fluffy consistency, and the whites and the remaining sugar are whipped to soft peaks. The yolks are gradually folded into the whites, followed by the sifted flour, part of which is replaced with finely ground nuts or almond paste, followed by any other ingredients, and, last, the melted butter, if used. If almond paste is used, it is folded into the yolks first and the mixture is then folded into the whites. Because this method produces a somewhat lighter sponge than the other two foaming methods, the sponge tends to shrink away from the sides of the pan more than is desirable. For this reason, it is best not to grease the sides of the cake pan. Instead, cut the baked sponge free using a sharp, thin knife.

Note that, in many recipes, this method is used with or without the addition of baking powder. Baking powder should be added to the sponge if you must use eggs that were shelled the previous day, or if for any other reason you are concerned about the outcome. Use 2 teaspoons (8 g) baking powder for every 12 eggs in the recipe, sifted in with the flour.

EMULSIFIER-METHOD SPONGE

Another method, and probably the most common in the baking industry today, is the emulsifier method; it is quick, convenient, and almost foolproof. Emulsifiers have been used by professional bakers for about 50 years. The emulsifier is basically a whipping agent that contains a molecule that preserves the emulsion of lipids (fat) and water. By keeping the ingredients suspended and preventing separation, emulsifiers allow the batter to hold the air that has been whipped in without falling. In the emulsifier-method sponge, all ingredients, including the flour, are whipped together with the emulsifier for a specified time. The emulsifier method uses baking powder and does not rely on air as a leavening agent, so the sponge does not need to be baked immediately but can wait its turn for the oven, just like any plain cookie—a big advantage in a busy bakery. Emulsifiers are available primarily through suppliers to the professional baking industry. They are used in recipes specifically formulated by the manufacturer, but these can be altered using the general guidelines outlined here.

LADYFINGER SPONGE

Another sponge variation is the ladyfinger sponge, also known as a *piped sponge*, which is used not only for cookies but also for several classic desserts, including tiramisu, charlotte Russe, and gâteau Malakoff. In this method, more air is whipped into the batter so that it can be piped into various shapes without running. Ladyfinger sponges are meant to be very dry after baking, but they easily absorb moisture from fillings or syrup.

OTHELLO SPONGE

Othello sponge is comparable to the ladyfinger sponge, and the two are easily interchangeable. The othello sponge has a lighter structure due to less flour and more egg white. The batter should immediately be piped out and baked as soon as it is finished, as the mixture becomes tough if left to stand too long.

Baking Pans

The batter should be divided into prepared pans and baked immediately or the air bubbles will start to break. Pans should be buttered and floured using a combination of 4 parts melted butter to 1 part flour by volume. By brushing this mixture on the pans, you need to handle them only once (pan spray may also be used). Lighter mixtures, such as two-way or chiffon, benefit from buttering and flouring only the bottom of the pan, or lining it with baking paper; this allows the sponge to stick to the sides, thereby preventing it from shrinking as it bakes.

FLEXIPANS

The latest tool for baking sponges and other cake bases is Flexipan cake molds. Just as with the Silpat baking mats made by the same company to replace baking paper, Flexipans are very convenient in that they do not require pretreatment, such as greasing and flouring. You do not need to adjust your oven temperature and baking time when using Flexipans; however, as is true in all situations, you may need to make alterations according to what type of oven you use, how full it is, and so on. The Flexipan will perform in the same way as a conventional pan, so if you know your oven tends to run hot, for example, make the your usual modifications. Flexipans should always be placed on top of a perforated sheet pan in an oven with grill-style racks or, when baking directly on the hearth in a deck oven, on a regular sheet pan. Sometimes it is necessary to double-pan when using a deck oven. To unmold the baked cakes, invert the cake in the pan, pick up two sides of the Flexipan, and gently peel the form away from the cake.

Baking

The oven should be around 400°F (205°C) for a typical cake pan or cake ring measuring 10 x 2 inches (25 x 5 cm). The deeper and wider your cake pan, the lower you should have the heat. On the other end of the scale, if you are baking a ¼-inch (6-mm) roulade, the oven should be at 425°F (219°C), or the roulade will dry out as it bakes and be difficult (or impossible) to roll. To test a sponge for doneness, gently press down in the center with your finger; the sponge should spring right back and not leave any indentation.

Storage

In most cases you should not unmold any sponge before it has cooled completely. Store it covered or wrapped in plastic. If you do not need to reuse the pans, leave the cakes in the pans, turn them upside down to store, and unmold as needed. When sponge cakes or sheets are refrigerated, the skin on top of the cakes becomes soft. It must be removed before the layers are used. Sponge cake freezes exceptionally well, even for weeks, if wrapped properly; both the professional baker and the home cook should always have some sponge cake in the freezer for creating a last-minute dessert.

Cake Mixtures Other Than Sponge Cakes

These mixtures are divided into two general groups: heavy mixtures, which include cakes made using the creaming method and the high-ratio method, and light mixtures, which include cakes made using the two-stage method, the angel-food method, and the chiffon method. Each of these employs a different technique to accomplish the same goal: combining the ingredients into a smooth and homogenous batter while developing and incorporating air pockets, or cells, which give the finished product its proper texture.

Two of these ingredients, fat and water (including the water in the eggs), are by nature incompatible; they will not mix together. A smooth and uniform substance made up of two unmixable foods is known as an *emulsion*. Cake batters that are properly mixed—emulsified —contain microscopic droplets of water surrounded by fat and other ingredients. The emulsion will break if the fat can no longer surround and hold the water.

One reason this can occur is if the wrong type of fat is used. Butter, although it contributes a superior flavor, has poor emulsifying abilities and also contains about 20 percent water. Butter, therefore, may not be substituted in a recipe that specifies shortening. It will be even less positive in a recipe that is designed to use high-ratio shortening, which contains an added emulsifier to enable it to hold a larger quantity of water without curdling.

If the ingredients are too cold, especially the fat and/or eggs, this can also affect the ability of the batter to form an emulsion; the ideal temperature is 70°F (21°C). If the fat is not soft, it cannot be creamed properly at the beginning and it will not develop the structure necessary to hold and contain the tiny water droplets. This factor is amplified if the liquid to be incorporated is added too quickly and not, as it should be, in several small portions.

CREAMING METHOD

This is the conventional method used for many cookie doughs, butter cakes, and pound cakes. In cake baking, the following rules must be observed for a good result:

- The ingredients should be at room temperature, approximately 70°F (21°C).

- The fat must be beaten until it is light and fluffy.

- The eggs must be added in small portions, with each one fully absorbed before the next is added.

- The dry and liquid ingredients should be added alternately, starting and finishing with the dry to ensure that the batter can absorb all of the liquid, which would be impossible without the assistance of the flour.

TWO-STAGE OR HIGH-RATIO METHOD

This is a simple, foolproof way of mixing a cake base, using very few steps in the process. Whole eggs, granulated sugar, cake flour, and baking powder are placed in a mixer and stirred at low speed to form a paste. Emulsified shortening is added and the mixture is whipped at high speed for two minutes. Milk or water is then added along with a flavoring, such as vanilla extract. The batter is whipped at high speed one minute longer.

This method is typically used when a recipe contains a higher portion of sugar than flour by weight. Emulsified shortening, such as the high-ratio variety, is used because the amount of liquid ingredients is also proportionally larger than, for example, in the foaming or creaming methods. This type of batter is always leavened with a chemical agent (baking soda and/or baking powder) rather than relying solely on the air incorporated with a whip. The same rules discussed in the creaming method should be followed. When using the two-stage method, it is important to pay attention to the length of time specified in the mixing steps and to scrape the sides and the bottom of the bowl several times during the mixing process to produce a smooth and homogenous batter.

SEPARATION-FOAMING METHOD

This method is used for both cold-method genoise-type sponge cakes and baking-powder cake bases. The eggs are separated and the yolks are first whipped with a small amount of the sugar. The egg whites are whipped separately. Because the fat (the egg yolks) has been removed, it is possible to whip the egg whites to stiff peaks, which produces a cake with a lighter texture and a greater volume. If the baked cake is going to be used to create a roulade or any type of rolled cake, the butter should be left out of the recipe, as it will cause the cake to become firmer when refrigerated, resulting in cracks when the sheet is rolled.

Sponge Cake Formulas Relative to 1 pound 8 ounce (12 Whole) Eggs

	Sponge Cake (Génoise)	Almond Sponge	Angel Food	Chiffon Sponge	Dobos Sponge	Othello Shells	High-Ratio Sponge	Ladyfingers
Eggs	12 whole plus 2 whites	12 separated	24 whites	12 separated	12 separated	12 separated	12 whole	12 separated
Granulated Sugar	12 ounces (340 grams)	10 ounces (285 grams)	24 ounces (680 grams)	21 ounces (595 grams)	12 ounces (340 grams)	6 ounces (170 grams)	15 ounces (430 grams)	12 ounces (340 grams)
Flour	12 ounces (340 grams)	7 ounces (200 grams)	8 ounces (225 grams)	21 ounces (595 grams)	8 ounces (225 grams)	5 ounces (140 grams)	13.5 ounces (385 grams)	8 ounces (225 grams)
Flour/Starch Type and Ratio	2:1 cake flour/ cornstarch	100% cake flour	100% cake flour	2:1 cake flour/ bread flour	100% cake flour	6:5 cornstarch/ bread flour	100% cake flour	4:3 bread flour/ cornstarch
Butter	5 ounces (140 grams)	0	0	0	12 ounces (340 g)	0	0	0
Other Ingredients	salt	almond paste, vanilla extract	cream of tartar, vanilla extract, lemon juice, lemon zest, salt	vegetable oil, water, salt, vanilla extract, baking powder	ground almonds, vanilla extract, salt, lemon zest	(cornstarch), cream of tartar	high-ratio shortening, milk, baking powder, vanilla extract	(cornstarch), lemon juice or tartaric acid
Production Method	Warm-Foaming Method	Cold-Foaming Method	Angel-Food Method	Chiffon Method	Creaming Method	Separation-Foaming Method	Two-Stage Method	Cold-Foaming Method
Characteristics	Somewhat crumbly, light and airy texture	Moist, flexible, not very crumbly	Light, moist; cholesterol- and fat-free	Few crumbs; moist; easy to prepare	Dense; little or no crumbs	Dry and crumbly; can be store for several weeks	Inflexible; breaks easily	Dry; holds its shape when piped or spread
Applications	Multipurpose cake base	Roulades and sheets	Light desserts	Multipurpose cake base	Petits fours; uses when crumbs are detrimental	Pastry shells and in desserts	General cake base	Alone as a cookie; in charlottes and other desserts

FIGURE 9-1 Comparison of sponge cake formulas relative to 1 pound 8 ounces (860 g) or 12 whole eggs

ANGEL FOOD METHOD

This type of cake contains neither fat nor chemical leaveners. It relies solely on stabilized egg-white foam for leavening. The foaming power of the egg whites results from a combined effort of various proteins to increase the thickness (viscosity) of the albumen and produce a fine mesh of foam (tiny bubbles) that will hold together for a time if properly combined with the sugar. Angel food batters have a much higher sugar content than any other sponge or butter cake. Although sugar has a mixed influence in the whipping stage, where it acts to delay the foaming of the whites, it stabilizes the foam once it is whipped, especially in the oven, where sugar is necessary to prevent a total collapse. Sugar does this by forming hydrogen bonds and delaying evaporation. Mixing and baking an angel food cake successfully is a delicate procedure.

CHIFFON METHOD

This method resembles the angel food method in that the light and airy texture is derived from whipped egg whites. Chiffon cakes are much easier to make, however, because they contain baking powder and do not depend exclusively on the air whipped into the egg whites for leavening. Also, here the whipped whites are folded into a batter containing yolks, oil, water, and flour, as opposed to the angel food cake, where part of the sugar is mixed with the flour and this is then folded into the whipped whites. Chiffon cakes using baking powder are the most common variety; some also use emulsifiers.

Sponge Cake yield: 2 cakes, 10 × 2 inches (25 × 5 cm)

Butter and Flour Mixture (page 7) or cake
   pan spray

12 eggs

12 ounces (340 g) granulated sugar

1 teaspoon (5 g) salt

8 ounces (225 g) cake flour

4 ounces (115 g) cornstarch

5 ounces (140 g) melted unsalted butter

1. Brush butter and flour mixture over the inside of 2 cake pans, 10 inches (25 cm) in diameter, or coat the pans with cake pan spray. Reserve.

2. Place the eggs, sugar, and salt in mixer bowl. Heat over simmering water to about 110°F (43°C), whipping continuously. Remove from the heat and whip at high speed until the mixture has cooled, is light and fluffy, and has reached its maximum volume.

3. Sift the flour and the cornstarch together and fold into the batter by hand (Figures 9-2 and 9-3). Fold in the melted butter. Divide the batter between the prepared pans.

4. Bake immediately at 400°F (205°C) for approximately 15 minutes. Let the sponges cool before removing them from the pans.

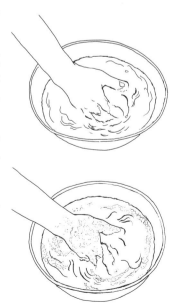

FIGURES 9-2 AND 9-3 Folding the flour into a sponge cake batter by moving the hand around the sides of the bowl and lifting the mixture from the bottom of the bowl to the top as the flour is incorporated

Chocolate Sponge Cake yield: 2 cakes, 10 x 2 inches (25 x 5 cm)

Butter and Flour Mixture (page 7) or cake
    pan spray

12 eggs

12 ounces (340 g) granulated sugar

1 teaspoon (5 g) salt

6 ounces (170 g) cake flour

4 ounces (115 g) cornstarch

2 ounces (55 g) unsweetened cocoa powder

4 ounces (115 g) melted unsalted butter

1. Brush butter and flour mixture over the inside of 2 cake pans, 10 inches (25 cm) in diameter, or use cake pan spray. Reserve.

2. Place the eggs, sugar, and salt in mixer bowl. Heat over simmering water to about 110°F (43°C), whipping continuously. Remove from the heat and whip at high speed until the mixture has cooled and is light and fluffy.

3. Sift the flour, cornstarch, and cocoa powder together and fold into the batter by hand. Fold in the melted butter. Divide the batter between the prepared pans.

4. Bake immediately at 400°F (205°C) for approximately 15 minutes. Let the sponges cool before removing them from the pans.

Almond Sponge

yield: 2 sheets, 14 x 24 inches (35 x 60 cm), or 2 layers, 10 x 2 inches (25 x 5 cm)

2 egg whites (¼ cup/60 ml)

10 ounces (285 g) almond paste

12 eggs, separated

10 ounces (285 g) granulated sugar

1 teaspoon (5 ml) vanilla extract

7 ounces (200 g) cake flour

1. Gradually mix the 2 egg whites into the almond paste to soften it.

2. Whip the egg yolks with 3 ounces (85 g) sugar to the ribbon stage. Add the vanilla. Very gradually, add the yolk mixture to the almond paste mixture; if you try to add it too fast, you are sure to get lumps.

3. Whip the egg whites to a foam. Gradually add the remaining 7 ounces (200 g) sugar and whip to stiff peaks.

4. Sift the flour (and the cocoa powder, if making the variation). Carefully fold the egg whites into the yolk mixture. Fold in the dry ingredients.

TO MAKE SHEETS

1. Immediately spread the batter on paper-lined sheet pans to 14 x 24 inches (35 x 60 cm), taking care not to overwork the sponge.

2. Bake at 425°F (219°C) for approximately 8 minutes or until just done.

NOTE: If the oven is not hot enough or if the sheets are overcooked (and therefore dried out), the sponge will not bend without breaking. To remedy this, place a damp towel on a sheet pan and place the sponge on top with the paper next to the towel. Invert a second sheet pan on top as a lid. Place in the oven (400°F/205°C) for 5 to 10 minutes to soften. If the sponge is to be used the next day, repeat the process as above, but soften in the refrigerator instead of in the oven.

TO MAKE LAYERS

1. Line the bottoms of 2 cake pans, 10 inches (25 cm) in diameter, with baking paper (see Figures 1-24 to 1-26, page 57), or grease and flour, but do not grease and flour the sides. Divide the batter between the pans.

2. Bake at 375°F (190°C) for about 25 minutes or until the sponge springs back when pressed lightly in the middle. When cold, cut the sponge away from the side of the pan with a thin, sharp knife.

VARIATION

COCOA-ALMOND SPONGE

yield: 2 sheets, 14 × 24 × ¹/₄ inches (35 × 60 cm × 6mm), or 2 layers, 10 × 2 inches (25 × 5 cm)

Delete 3 ounces (85 g) flour and substitute 3 ounces (85 g) unsweetened cocoa powder, sifted with the remaining flour.

Angel Food Cake yield: 1 tube pan, 10 inches (25 cm) in diameter

This feather-light sponge cake uses only the air incorporated into stiffly beaten egg whites as a leavener; it contains no egg yolks or other fat and no chemical leavening agent. The one complaint I used to have about this completely cholesterol-free cake was that I found it too sweet. Sugar is needed to support and stabilize the albumin in the whipped egg whites, in part due to the lack of fat. After some experimenting, I managed to decrease the sugar to a level that supports the egg whites without being cloying. Because of its sweet flavor, angel food cake is especially nice paired with fruit.

Due to the tender and light structure of this cake, it is of the utmost importance that the ingredients are measured precisely and the directions followed exactly. It is also essential to use a tube pan to produce the traditional look and light composition. (You can bake the cake in 2 regular cake pans, 9 inches/22.5 cm in diameter, with a fairly good result, but the cakes will not have the same airiness.) The tube pan can be false-bottomed or not, and it does not have to have legs. The legs allow you to invert the baked cake so that it cools without falling and, at the same time, they allow air to circulate around the entire cake. Hanging the inverted cake on the neck of a bottle works just as well.

4 ounces (115 g) cake flour, sifted	¹/₂ teaspoon (2.5 g) salt
12 ounces (340 g) granulated sugar	2 teaspoons (10 ml) vanilla extract
12 egg whites (1¹/₂ cups/360 ml)	Grated zest of 1 lemon
1 teaspoon (2 g) cream of tartar	2 teaspoons (10 ml) lemon juice

1. Line the bottom of a tube pan, 10 inches (25 cm) in diameter, with a ring of baking paper (see Figures 1-24 to 1-26, page 57; refold and use the same technique to cut out the center).

2. Combine the flour with half of the granulated sugar. Reserve.

3. Whip the egg whites with the cream of tartar and salt at high speed until they have tripled in volume. Gradually add the remaining sugar and continue whipping until the whites hold soft peaks. Remove from the mixer.

4. Place the flour and sugar mixture in a sifter. (Set the sifter on baking paper so you do not lose any of the mixture.) Sift the flour-sugar mixture over the whipped egg whites, a little at a time, and gently fold it in together with the vanilla, lemon zest, and lemon juice. Place the batter in the prepared tube pan. Tap the pan firmly against the table a couple of times to release any large air pockets.

5. Bake at 325°F (163°C) for approximately 55 minutes or until the cake is golden brown on top and springs back when pressed lightly. Invert the pan onto its legs or over the neck of a bottle to allow air to circulate underneath as it cools upside down.

6. Run a thin knife around the inside of the outer edge of the pan (do not do this to the center ring) to loosen the cake. Invert and tap firmly to release the cake.

Chiffon Sponge Cake I yield: 2 cakes, 10 × 2 inches (25 × 5 cm)

The leavening in a chiffon sponge comes from both a chemical agent, baking powder, and the air whipped into the egg whites. This can make it a more practical choice in certain situations than the genoise type of sponge, which does not use a chemical leavener. The vegetable oil contributes moisture and gives the cake a longer shelf life than one made with butter. Another plus is that chiffon cakes tolerate freezing (and thawing) without a significant loss of quality.

The popularity of the chiffon method lessened somewhat in the professional industry following the introduction of the emulsifier method, which is even more convenient and practical in a professional setting, although overall flavor is sacrificed to some extent. Additional information contrasting these and other methods of making sponge cakes is found in the chapter introduction.

In the following recipes, Chiffon Sponge Cake I is used to create round layers that are to be split and filled. Chiffon Sponge Cake II is preferable to use for sheets; it is moister, making it easier to roll when the batter has been spread in a thin layer, or to slice into two layers when the batter is baked in a half-sheet pan.

⅔ cup (160 ml) vegetable oil	14 ounces (400 g) granulated sugar
8 egg yolks (⅔ cup/160 ml)	4 teaspoons (16 g) baking powder
1 cup (240 ml) water, at room temperature	1 teaspoon (5 g) salt
1 tablespoon (15 ml) vanilla extract	8 egg whites (1 cup/240 ml)
14 ounces (400 g) cake flour	

I. Line 2 cake pans, 10 inches (25 cm) in diameter, with circles of baking paper, or grease and flour, but do not grease and flour the sides.

2. Whip the vegetable oil and the egg yolks together just until combined. Stir in the water and the vanilla extract.

3. Sift together the cake flour, one-third of the sugar, the baking powder, and the salt. Stir this into the egg yolk mixture, then whip at high speed for 1 minute. Reserve.

4. Whip the egg whites to a foam. Gradually add the remaining sugar and continue whipping until stiff peaks form. Carefully fold the meringue into the reserved batter. Divide the batter between the prepared pans.

5. Bake at 375°F (190°C) for approximately 25 minutes or until the cakes spring back when pressed lightly in the center.

6. Invert the pans on a rack and allow the cakes to cool in the pans before unmolding.

About Chiffon Cakes

In culinary lingo, the word *chiffon* suggests a light and fluffy texture. In addition to indicating a particular style of sponge cake, the term also describes certain fillings that utilize whipped cream, whipped egg whites, and/or whipped egg yolks to maximize the amount of air that is incorporated, which contributes to the desired delicate and airy consistency.

Chiffon sponge cakes are also known as *mayonnaise cakes* because vegetable oil, egg yolks, and water are used in the batter. There are a couple of stories as to how the recipe originated. One says that the chiffon cake was invented by a pastry chef at the famed Brown Derby restaurant in Los Angeles. Other sources say that the formula was devised by an insurance salesman named Henry Baker who, despite his name, baked only as a hobby. He did live in California and perhaps he shared the recipe with the Brown Derby chef. In any case, the inventor supposedly sold the formula to a large cake mix company. Betty Crocker and General Mills introduced chiffon cake mix in 1948, and it was an immediate hit with both professional bakers and homemakers.

VARIATIONS

CHOCOLATE CHIFFON SPONGE CAKE I yield: 2 cakes, 10 × 2 inches (25 × 5 cm)

Decrease the cake flour by 3 ounces (85 g) and replace with 3 ounces (85 g) unsweetened cocoa powder, sifted with the remaining flour.

LEMON CHIFFON SPONGE CAKE I yield: 2 cakes, 10 × 2 inches (25 × 5 cm)

Replace ½ cup (120 ml) water with ½ cup (120 ml) lemon juice. Add the grated zest of 3 lemons together with the water-juice mixture.

Chiffon Sponge Cake II yield: 1 half-sheet pan, 12 × 16 inches (30 × 40 cm)

7 ounces (200 g) cake flour

3 ounces (85 g) bread flour

1 tablespoon (12 g) baking powder

12 ounces (340 g) granulated sugar

½ cup (120 ml) vegetable oil

6 egg yolks (½ cup/120 ml)

1 cup (240 ml) water

1 tablespoon (15 ml) vanilla extract

10 egg whites (1¼ cups/300 ml)

4 ounces (115 g) granulated sugar

½ teaspoon (2.5 g) salt

1. Line a half-sheet pan with baking paper or a Silpat. Set aside.

2. Sift the cake flour, bread flour, baking powder, and the first measurement of sugar together. Reserve.

3. Combine the oil, egg yolks, water, and vanilla. Mix until well incorporated. Gradually add the dry ingredients and mix until smooth, about 1 minute. Set aside.

4. Whip the egg whites with the remaining sugar and salt until stiff peaks form. Take care not to overwhip. Fold the whipped egg whites into the yolk and flour mixture. Spread the batter evenly over the half-sheet pan.

5. Bake at 375°F (190°C) for approximately 25 minutes or until the cake springs back when pressed lightly in the center. Dust cake flour lightly over the top of the cake and invert onto a sheet pan lined with baking paper. When the cake has cooled slightly, remove from the pan by running a thin knife around the inside perimeter before unmolding.

VARIATIONS

CHOCOLATE CHIFFON SPONGE CAKE II

Decrease the cake flour by 2 ounces (55 g) and replace with 3 ounces (85 g) unsweetened cocoa powder, sifted together with the remaining flour.

LEMON CHIFFON SPONGE CAKE II

Replace ½ cup (120 ml) water with the juice and grated zest of 3 lemons (approximately ½ cup/120 ml juice; adjust as desired), combining the juice and zest with the remaining water.

ORANGE CHIFFON SPONGE CAKE II

Replace ½ cup (120 ml) water with the juice and grated zest of 2 small oranges (approximately ½ cup/120 ml juice; adjust as desired), combining the juice and zest with the remaining water.

Devil's Food Cake Layers yield: 2 layers, 10 inches (25 cm) in diameter

1 pound 4 ounces (570 g) granulated sugar	6 eggs
4 ounces (115 g) unsweetened cocoa powder	2 cups (480 ml) buttermilk
8 ounces (225 g) bread flour	2 cups (480 ml) sour cream
8 ounces (225 g) cake flour	12 ounces (340 g) melted unsalted butter
2 teaspoons (8 g) baking soda	8 ounces (225 g) finely grated raw purple beets
2 teaspoons (8 g) baking powder	

1. Cover the bottom of 2 cake pans, 10 inches (25 cm) in diameter, with rounds of baking paper. Reserve.

2. Sift together the granulated sugar, cocoa powder, bread flour, cake flour, baking soda, and baking powder. Set aside.

3. Beat the eggs for 1 minute. Stir in the buttermilk and the sour cream. Add the reserved dry ingredients, mixing until well combined and smooth. Mix in the melted butter and the grated beets.

4. Divide the batter between the prepared pans. Smooth the top of the cakes to make them level.

5. Bake at 350°F (175°C) for approximately 40 minutes or until the cakes spring back when pressed lightly in the center. Allow the cakes to cool completely before unmolding.

Dobos Sponge yield: I sheet, 16 x 24 inches (40 x 60 cm)

12 ounces (340 g) unsalted butter, at room temperature

12 ounces (340 g) granulated sugar

12 egg yolks (1 cup/240 ml), at room temperature

1 teaspoon (5 ml) vanilla extract

1 teaspoon (5 g) salt

Grated zest of 1 lemon

12 egg whites (1½ cups/360 ml), at room temperature

8 ounces (225 g) sifted cake flour

5 ounces (140 g) finely ground almonds (almond meal; see Note 1)

I. Cream the butter with half of the sugar to a light and fluffy consistency. Beat in the egg yolks, a few at a time. Mix in the vanilla, salt, and lemon zest (see Note 2).

2. Whip the egg whites until foamy. Gradually add the remaining sugar and whip until soft peaks form. Carefully fold the whipped egg whites into the yolk mixture.

3. Combine the sifted flour (and cocoa powder, if making the variation) with the ground almonds. Gently fold the flour and almond mixture into the egg mixture.

4. Immediately spread the batter evenly over a sheet of baking paper measuring 16 x 24 inches (40 x 60 cm). Drag the paper onto a sheet pan (Figure 9-4).

5. Bake at 425°F (219°C) for about 10 minutes or until baked through.

NOTE I: If you have neither almond meal nor the proper equipment to make it, add part of the granulated sugar from the recipe (taking it away from the amount used in Step 1) to blanched (dry) almonds and process to a fine consistency in a food processor. The sugar will absorb some of the oil released by the almonds and prevent the mixture from caking.

NOTE 2: If the egg yolks are not approximately the same temperature as the butter and sugar emulsion, the mixture will break when they are added. If this happens, warm the broken mixture over a bain-marie, stirring constantly, before folding in the egg whites.

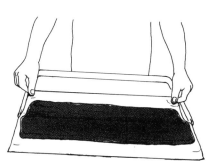

FIGURE 9-4 **Dragging a sheet of baking paper onto a sheet pan after spreading the cake batter over the paper. This technique is used instead of spreading the batter over the paper while it is in place on the pan, to prevent the sides of the pan from getting in the way as the batter is spread out. If an offset spatula is used, the batter can be spread directly over the lined pan.**

VARIATION

COCOA DOBOS SPONGE yield: I sheet, 16 x 24 inches (40 x 60 cm)

Delete 2 ounces (55 g) cake flour and replace with 2 ounces (55 g) unsweetened cocoa powder, sifted with the remaining flour.

Hazelnut-Chocolate Sponge yield: 2 cakes, 10 inches (25 cm) in diameter

Butter and Flour Mixture (page 7) or cake pan spray

14 eggs (3 cups/720 ml)

12 ounces (340 g) granulated sugar

1 teaspoon (5 ml) vanilla extract

1 teaspoon (5 g) salt

12 ounces (340 g) bread flour

1 teaspoon (4 g) baking powder

6 ounces (170 g) hazelnuts, toasted and finely ground (see Note)

3 ounces (85 g) sweetened dark chocolate, grated

4 ounces (115 g) melted unsalted butter

1. Brush butter and flour mixture inside 2 cake pans, 10 inches (25 cm) in diameter, or coat with cake pan spray. Reserve.

2. Combine the eggs, sugar, vanilla, and salt in a mixer bowl. Heat over simmering water until the mixture reaches about 110°F (43°C), whipping continuously. Remove from the heat and whip at high speed until the mixture has cooled and has a light and fluffy consistency.

3. Sift the flour and baking powder. Mix in the hazelnuts and chocolate, then carefully fold into the batter by hand. Fold in the melted butter. Divide the batter between the prepared pans.

4. Bake immediately at 400°F (205°C) until the cakes spring back when pressed lightly on top, approximately 25 minutes. Allow the sponges to cool completely before unmolding.

NOTE: Add about one-quarter of the sugar to the nuts if you are using a food processor to grind them. The sugar will absorb any oil that is released by the nuts due to the heat and friction.

High-Ratio Sponge Cake yield: 2 cakes, 10 × 2 inches (25 × 5 cm)

Butter and Flour Mixture (page 7) or cake pan spray

14 eggs, at room temperature

1 pound 2 ounces (510 g) granulated sugar

1 pound (455 g) cake flour

2 tablespoons (24 g) baking powder

10 ounces (285 g) emulsified shortening, at room temperature

1 cup (240 ml) whole milk, at room temperature

2 teaspoons (10 ml) vanilla extract

1. Brush butter and flour mixture over the inside of 2 cake pans, 10 inches (25 cm) in diameter, or coat with pan spray. Reserve.

2. Place the eggs, granulated sugar, cake flour, and baking powder in a mixer bowl. Stir at low speed, using the whip attachment, until the mixture forms a paste. Add the shortening and whip at high speed for 2 minutes, scraping down the sides of the bowl as needed. Lower the speed and incorporate the milk and vanilla. Continue whipping 1 minute longer.

3. Divide the batter evenly between the prepared pans. Bake at 375°F (190°C) for approximately 35 minutes or until the cake springs back when pressed lightly in the center.

CHOCOLATE HIGH-RATIO SPONGE CAKE yield: 2 cakes, 10 × 2 inches (25 × 5 cm)

Replace 4 ounces (115 g) cake flour with 4 ounces (115 g) unsweetened cocoa powder.

Ladyfingers yield: approximately 180 cookies, 2 inches (5 cm) long

This light and delicate sponge has many uses. Ladyfingers are served as an accompaniment to ice cream and are an integral part of several classic desserts, including tiramisu and gâteau Malakoff. The cookies are soaked in a liqueur or other flavoring before or after they are added to the dessert. Ladyfingers are also used to line the sides of many varieties of charlotte, including Royal and Charente. Ladyfinger sponge batter contains a little more flour in relation to sugar than the usual 50-50 ratio. This, combined with the method of whipping the egg yolks and whites separately, makes the batter thick enough to hold its shape. Ladyfinger cookies are similar in shape to cat's-tongue cookies (*langues-de-chat*) which are usually sandwiched together with nougat. The name *lady's fingers* is also used for the vegetable okra.

4 ounces (115 g) bread flour	Few drops Tartaric Acid Solution (page 38) or lemon juice
6 eggs, separated	3 ounces (85 g) cornstarch
6 ounces (170 g) granulated sugar	

1. Sift the flour (together with the cocoa powder if making the chocolate variation).

2. Whip the egg yolks and one-third of the sugar at high speed until light and creamy.

3. Add half of the remaining sugar, along with the tartaric acid or lemon juice, to the egg whites. Whip the egg white mixture at high speed until it is foamy and has tripled in volume, about 2 minutes.

4. Combine the remaining sugar and the cornstarch. Gradually add this to the egg white mixture and whip to stiff peaks.

5. Fold in the reserved egg yolk and sugar mixture, and then fold in the sifted flour. (Follow the instructions in a particular recipe if not making individual ladyfingers.)

6. Place the batter in a pastry bag with a No. 5 (10-mm) plain tip. Pipe cookies, 2 inches (5 cm) long, onto sheet pans lined with baking paper or Silpats (Figure 9-5).

7. Bake at 425°F (219°C) for about 8 minutes or until golden brown. Ladyfingers will keep for weeks if stored in a dry place.

FIGURE 9-5 **Piping ladyfingers onto a sheet pan lined with a Silpat; baked ladyfingers after removing them from the oven**

CHOCOLATE LADYFINGERS yield: approximately 180 cookies, 2 inches (5 cm) long

Delete 1 ounce (30 g) cornstarch and replace with 1 ounce (30 g) unsweetened cocoa powder.

Lemon Ladyfingers yield: approximately 50 cookies, 4 inches (10 cm) long

8 egg yolks (²⁄₃ cup/160 ml)	2 ounces (55 g) cornstarch
6 ounces (170 g) granulated sugar	5 ounces (140 g) cake flour
Finely grated zest of 1 lemon	Powdered sugar
8 egg whites (1 cup/240 ml)	

1. Whip the egg yolks with one-third of the sugar to a stiff ribbon stage; the mixture will be fluffy and light in color. Reserve.

2. Thoroughly combine the lemon zest and the remaining sugar. Whip the egg whites, gradually adding the lemon-sugar mixture, to soft peaks. Turn the mixer to low speed, add the cornstarch, then whip at high speed until stiff peaks form.

3. Fold the reserved yolk mixture into the egg whites, followed by the flour.

4. Place in a pastry bag with a No. 8 (16-mm) plain tip. Pipe into 4-inch (10-cm) fingers on sheet pans lined with baking paper. Sift powdered sugar lightly over the top.

5. Bake immediately at 400°F (205°C) until golden brown.

Othello Shells yield: approximately 100 pastry shells, 2 × ³⁄₄ inches (5 × 2 cm)

6 ounces (170 g) granulated sugar	12 egg yolks (1 cup/240 ml)
6 ounces (170 g) cornstarch	14 egg whites (1³⁄₄ cups/420 ml)
5 ounces (140 g) bread flour	1 teaspoon (2 g) cream of tartar

1. Combine half of the sugar with half of the cornstarch. Set aside.

2. Sift the remaining cornstarch with the flour. Set aside.

3. Whip the egg yolks with the remaining sugar until the consistency is light and fluffy.

4. Whip the egg whites and cream of tartar for a few minutes until they have quadrupled in volume, lower the mixer speed, and gradually add the sugar and cornstarch mixture. Increase the speed and whip to stiff but not dry peaks. Carefully fold half of the egg whites into the whipped egg yolks. Fold in the flour mixture, then fold in the remaining whites. Use immediately.

5. Place the batter in a pastry bag with a No. 7 (14-mm) plain tip. Pipe out mounds ³⁄₄ inch (2 cm) high and 2 inches (5 cm) in diameter on sheet pans lined with baking paper or Silpats.

6. Bake at 450°F (230°C) for approximately 10 minutes or until golden brown. Let cool completely.

Ribbon-Pattern Decorated Sponge Sheets yield: 2 sheets, 23 × 15 inches (57.5 × 37.5 cm)

Thin, ornate sponge sheets with striped patterns in various configurations can be made very easily using Silpats (imported French silicone baking mats) and a special scraper that is made to fit the mats. This tool, called a *decorating comb*, consists of a frame and interchangeable blades (typically made of rubber) that have notched edges and are available in different sizes and patterns. A similar but less expensive tool is a molded plastic comb with two patterns, one on each side. These are intended for chocolate work but can be used to create sponge sheets as well. Because the plastic combs are smaller, it is necessary to make two passes over a full sheet instead of one. For more information, see "Decorating Comb with Frame" (page 945).

The two recipes for Joconde Sponge Base that follow are fairly similar and can be used interchangeably. Sponge Base II takes a bit longer to make but is a better choice if you plan to add coloring to the base portion. With either recipe, be sure to keep the whipped egg whites and sugar very soft because a thinner batter will flow out and fill in much more tightly between the tuile paste lines. Being careful not to overwhip the egg whites will also help prevent air bubbles in the finished sponge sheets, which can detract from the appearance.

14 ounces (400 g) Chocolate Tuile Decorating Paste (page 482)

Joconde Sponge Base I or II (recipes follow)

4 ounces (115 g) cocoa butter, melted (see Note)

1. Spread the chocolate tuile paste evenly over 2 full-size Silpats, covering them completely; the paste should be approximately ¹/₁₆ inch (2 mm) thick. Use a decorating comb to remove half of the paste in straight lines lengthwise, crosswise, or diagonally on each sheet (Figure 9-6).

2. Lift up the Silpats by the edges (Figure 9-7) and set them on top of inverted sheet pans. Place in the freezer to firm the tuile paste while you make the Joconde sponge base. If you are not proceeding to the next step immediately, the prepped Silpats can be left at room temperature for several hours. When you are ready to resume, place them in the freezer for a few minutes to firm the paste.

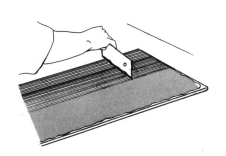  

FIGURE 9-6 **Using a decorating comb to remove tuile paste in stright lines for Ribbon-Pattern Decorated Sponge Sheets**

FIGURE 9-7 **Lifting the Silpat by the edges**

Both Silpats and plastic decorating combs are readily available and relatively inexpensive; both are tools that no professional—or serious amateur—should be without. In addition to making straight lines lengthwise, crosswise, and diagonally, try using the decorating comb to make curved or wavy lines. To create a colorful decorated sponge, substitute vanilla tuile decorating paste for the chocolate paste and color it as desired to create special effects. Or color the Joconde sponge base to contrast with either plain or chocolate lines. There are many possible combinations and the results can be stunning, but use restraint; colors that are too bright or combinations using too many colors can turn out garish.

You do not have to limit these impressive sponge sheet designs to ribbons. A wide variety of decorative metal templates made to fit the Silpats are available from Europe (although they are not cheap) in patterns such as diamond, herringbone, and polka dot, to name just a few. Plastic versions are also produced but are not recommended as they break easily. Other options are to use a silkscreen or photo transfer sheets to decorate the sponge sheet.

3. Leave the mats in place on the inverted pans. Divide the Joconde sponge base between the 2 mats, spreading it out evenly on top of the chocolate lines. Tap the pans quite firmly against the table to set the batter and remove air bubbles.

4. Bake immediately at 450° to 500°F (230° to 260°C) for approximately 4 minutes or until the sponge begins to color slightly.

FIGURE 9-8 Peeling the Silpat away from the baked Ribbon-Pattern Sponge Sheet

5. Dust flour lightly over the top of the sponge sheets. Invert them onto sheets of baking paper and let cool for 2 minutes. Carefully peel away the Silpats (Figure 9-8). Spray or brush melted cocoa butter over the patterned side of the sheets. The cocoa butter will help keep the sheets flexible and prevent them from sticking to the forms or rings when the sheets are used in assembling cakes or other desserts. Cover the decorated sponge sheets with plastic wrap and store in the refrigerator for up to 1 week or in the freezer for up to 1 month.

NOTE: The amount of cocoa butter specified in the ingredient list is far more than you will need if you use a brush to apply it. However, if you use a spray bottle, the additional liquid is required for the sprayer to work well.

JOCONDE SPONGE BASE I yield: 2 sheets, 23 × 15 × ⅛ inch (57.5 × 37.5 cm × 3 mm)

This version of Joconde will yield two quite thin (but very elegant-looking) sheets, which means you have very little leverage in spreading out the batter. Care must also be taken when baking the sheets because a hot oven is essential and, as thin as they are, they can become overdone quickly. You will need to watch them carefully while they are in the oven. If you do not mind that the sheets will be a bit thicker, use Joconde Base II, which is a bit easier to work with.

5 whole eggs

4 egg yolks (⅓ cup/80 ml)

7 ounces (200 g) granulated sugar

7 ounces (200 g) blanched almonds, finely ground (or almond meal; see Note)

2 ounces (55 g) bread flour, sifted

4 egg whites (½ cup/120 ml)

2 ounces (55 g) melted unsalted butter

I. Place the whole eggs, egg yolks, and half of the sugar in a bowl. Set the bowl over simmering water. Heat the mixture to 120°F (49°C) while stirring constantly. Remove from the heat and whip at high speed for 1 minute.

2. Thoroughly combine the ground almonds and flour.

3. Whip the egg whites with the remaining sugar until they have the appearance of snow; the egg whites should be very thick and foamy but should not hold a peak.

4. Carefully fold the reserved almond mixture into the whipped whole egg mixture. Stir in the melted butter. Gradually fold in the beaten egg whites. Use as directed in the individual recipes.

NOTE: The almonds should be ground as fine as granulated sugar. You can purchase almond flour or almond meal from bakery suppliers but if this is not available and you must use a food processor to grind the nuts, add most of the sugar used in Step 1 (saving a few tablespoons to whip with the eggs) to the almonds when you grind them. The sugar will prevent the mixture from caking.

JOCONDE SPONGE BASE II

yield: 1 full sheet, 16 × 24 × ¹/₄ inch (40 × 60 cm × 6mm) and 1 half sheet, 16 × 12 × ¹/₄ inch (40 × 30 cm × 6 mm), or 2 full sheets if made slightly thinner

As mentioned previously, this recipe will yield a thicker finished product than Joconde Sponge Base I, which is easier to manipulate and can be used for other purposes, such as Opera Cake and Opera Slices. Joconde Sponge Base II is also a good choice if you need to prepare the sheets ahead of time. The sheets can be kept, well wrapped, in the refrigerator for several days or in the freezer for up to 1 month.

9 ounces (255 g) blanched almonds, finely ground (or almond meal; see Note)

6 ounces (170 g) powdered sugar

3 ounces (85 g) bread flour

9 whole eggs

3 egg yolks (¹/₄ cup/60 ml)

6 egg whites (³/₄ cup/180 ml)

3 ounces (85 g) granulated sugar

3 ounces (85 g) melted unsalted butter

Small-Batch Recipe for Joconde Sponge Base II

yield: 1 half sheet, 16 × 12 inches (40 × 30 cm)

3 ounces (85 g) blanched almonds, finely ground (or almond meal; see Note)

2 ounces (55 g) powdered sugar

1 ounce (30 g) bread flour

3 whole eggs

1 egg yolk

2 egg whites (¹/₄ cup/60 ml)

1 ounce (30 g) granulated sugar

1 ounce (30 g) melted unsalted butter

---

1. Place the ground almonds, powdered sugar, and bread flour into a mixer bowl and gradually incorporate the whole eggs. Beat with the paddle attachment for 5 minutes at high speed, scraping down the sides of the bowl (the small recipe can be made by hand with a whisk).

2. Incorporate the egg yolks, mixing at medium speed until well combined. Set aside.

3. Whip the egg whites with the granulated sugar until they just barely hold a soft shape. Fold half of the meringue into the egg mixture. Stir in the melted butter, followed by the remaining meringue. Spread out and bake as directed in the individual recipes.

NOTE: If almond meal is not available and you must grind the almonds in a food processor, add 3 ounces (85 g) granulated sugar to the nuts when you grind them and decrease the amount of powdered sugar in the recipe by 3 ounces (85 g). The granulated sugar will absorb the oil released by the almonds during processing and prevent the mixture from caking. The almonds should be ground to a consistency as fine as granulated sugar.

Basic Chocolate Work and Introduction to Other Decorating Techniques

Candies

TRUFFLES

Truffles are among the best-known chocolate candies, and they can also be among the easiest to make, depending on how you finish them. For large-quantity production, most pastry chefs buy premade chocolate shells, pipe in a soft center ganache, seal the top, and dip the shells in chocolate. Although these do not have the classic spiked surface, they look just

CHEF'S TIP

If you can't make all three flavors, make just one kind of filling and divide it into three parts. Roll and coat each with the various types of chocolate—dark, milk, and white—and you will still have a nice assortment of truffles, in only half the time.

fine with nothing more than streaks of chocolate for decoration, as their size and shape are perfectly uniform.

The fastest way to finish or decorate any of the following three recipes is to roll them in chocolate a second time after precoating, then literally drop them into a pan filled with either cocoa powder or powdered sugar to coat the outside, instead of dipping them into tempered chocolate. Use a dipping fork to roll the candies around in the cocoa powder or powdered sugar so that they are coated evenly, then transfer them to a sheet pan lined with baking paper. When the truffles are set, use a brush to gently remove some of the excess cocoa powder or powdered sugar. This method does not require tempering the chocolate and, though the chocolate will take longer to harden, the powdered coating will hide the bloom.

Dark Chocolate Espresso Truffles yield: approximately 60 candies (Photo 4)

1 cup (240 ml) heavy cream	3 ounces (85 g) melted unsalted butter
1 pound (455 g) sweet dark chocolate, chopped	1 teaspoon (5 ml) mocha paste
2 ounces (55 g) unsweetened chocolate, chopped	Powdered sugar
1 teaspoon (5 ml) vanilla extract	Sweet dark chocolate, tempered (pages 468 to 471)

1. Heat the cream to the boiling point. Remove from the heat and add the chopped chocolate, stirring until it is completely melted. Let cool to body temperature, approximately 98°F (36°C), then stir in the vanilla, butter, and mocha paste.

2. Wait until the filling starts to thicken, then transfer it to a pastry bag with a No. 6 (12-mm) plain tip. Pipe out in small mounds the size of cherries, or a little less than $\frac{1}{2}$ ounce (15 g) each, on sheet pans lined with baking paper. Refrigerate for a few minutes to set.

3. Roll the centers into round balls between your hands, using powdered sugar to keep them from sticking. Let them firm up again, then precoat by rolling on a thin coat of tempered chocolate with your hands. When the coating has hardened and the interiors have reached room temperature, dip them into tempered chocolate, using a round dipping fork. As they are dipped, transfer to a fine wire rack and roll to produce the typical spiked surface.

Milk Chocolate Truffles yield: approximately 65 candies (Photo 4)

1 cup (240 ml) heavy cream	3 ounces (85 g) melted unsalted butter
1 pound 5 ounces (595 g) milk chocolate, chopped	Powdered sugar
1 teaspoon (5 ml) vanilla extract	Milk chocolate, tempered (pages 468 to 471)

1. Heat the cream to the boiling point. Remove from the heat and add the chopped chocolate and vanilla; stir until the chocolate is completely melted. Let cool to body temperature, approximately 98°F (36°C), then stir in the butter.

2. Wait until the filling starts to thicken, then transfer it to a pastry bag with a No. 6 (12-mm) plain tip. Pipe out in small mounds the size of cherries, or a little less than ½ ounce (15 g) each, on sheet pans lined with baking paper. Refrigerate for a few minutes to set.

3. Roll the centers into round balls between your hands, using powdered sugar to keep them from sticking. Let them firm up again, then precoat by rolling on a thin coat of tempered chocolate with your hands. When the coating has hardened and the interiors have reached room temperature, dip them into tempered chocolate, using a round dipping fork. As they are dipped, transfer to a fine wire rack and roll to produce the typical spiked surface.

VARIATION

SOFT-CENTER MILK CHOCOLATE TRUFFLE FILLING FOR PREMADE SHELLS
yield: enough filling for approximately 150 shells, 1 inch (2.5 cm) in diameter

1. Follow the directions above, making the following changes:

- Increase the heavy cream to 1⅓ cups (420 ml).

- Add ¼ cup (60 ml) orange liqueur with the vanilla.

- Add 3 ounces (85 g) melted cocoa butter with the regular melted butter.

2. Wait until the filling begins to thicken, then pipe it into the shells or fill using a fondant funnel, in which case you may fill the shells as soon as the filling has cooled to body temperature. Fill the shells to just below the rim so there will be room to seal the candies without the filling overflowing.

3. Pipe a small dot of chocolate on top of each truffle to seal the hole. If you have a stencil made to fit the shells you are using, place it on top of the filled shells, spread chocolate over the stencil to fill the holes, and remove the stencil. See page 969 for more information.

4. Finish the truffles by dipping them, streaking chocolate over the tops, piping a chocolate spiral on top, or creating a spiked surface, as directed in the main recipe.

White Chocolate Truffles with Praline   yield: approximately 75 candies

1 cup (240 ml) heavy cream	3 ounces (85 g) unsalted butter, at room temperature
1 pound 2 ounces (510 g) white chocolate, chopped	3 ounces (85 g) cocoa butter, melted
3 ounces (85 g) Praline Paste (page 33) *or* purchased praline paste	Powdered sugar
	White chocolate, tempered (pages 468 to 471)

1. Heat the cream to the boiling point. Remove from the heat and stir in the chopped chocolate. Keep stirring until the chocolate is completely melted. Set aside to cool to approximately room temperature.

2. Combine the praline paste and butter and beat to a creamy consistency. Stir into the chocolate mixture. Mix in the cocoa butter. Wait until the filling starts to thicken, then transfer it to a pastry bag with a No. 6 (12-mm) plain tip. Pipe out in small mounds the size of cherries, or a little less than ½ ounce (15 g) each, on sheet pans lined with baking paper. Refrigerate for a few minutes to set.

3. Roll the centers into round balls between your hands, using powdered sugar to keep them from sticking. Let them firm up again, then precoat by rolling on a thin coat of tempered white chocolate with your hands. When the coating has hardened and the interiors have reached the proper temperature, dip them into tempered white chocolate, using a round dipping fork. As they are dipped, transfer to a fine wire rack and roll to produce the typical spiked surface.

VARIATION
SOFT-CENTER WHITE CHOCOLATE TRUFFLE FILLING FOR PREMADE SHELLS
yield: enough filling for approximately 160 shells, 1 inch (2.5 cm) in diameter

1. Follow the directions above, making the following changes:

- Increase the heavy cream to 1⅓ cups (420 ml).

- Add 5 ounces (140 g) melted cocoa butter with the regular melted butter.

2. Wait until the filling begins to thicken, then pipe it into the shells (or fill, using a fondant funnel, in which case you may fill the shells as soon as the filling has cooled to body temperature). Fill the shells to just below the rim so there will be room to seal the candies without the filling overflowing.

3. Pipe a small dot of chocolate on top of each truffle to seal the hole. If you have a stencil made to fit the shells you are using, place it on top of the filled shells, spread chocolate over the stencil to fill the holes, and remove the stencil. See page 969 for more information.

4. Finish the truffles by dipping them, streaking chocolate over the tops, piping a chocolate spiral on top, or creating a spiked surface, as directed in the main recipe.

Chocolate Cobblestones **Yield: 60 candies, 1¼ inches (3.1 cm) in diameter (Photo 5)**

This is another candy that is easy to produce even if you do not have a candy kitchen, special equipment, or even much experience. As with the bark and the rochers, you can adapt the toppings to suit your own taste and/or what you have in the pantry, substituting other nuts and dried or candied fruit. Sliced or slivered almonds can be arranged to stand vertically for an unusual look.

Adding the decorations after piping the rounds requires some judgment in timing. If they are added too early, they will sink to the bottom and deform the round shape of the base, but if you wait too long, the toppings will not stick. You may need to experiment a little to achieve the desired look. How fast you work, the type of chocolate you use, and the temperature of the room where you are working are all contributing factors. In general, dark chocolate sets up more rapidly than milk chocolate, and a properly tempered chocolate will set up more quickly than one that was tempered less perfectly but is still usable.

60 whole pistachios, shelled

60 large whole cashews *or* cashew halves, toasted

60 large dark raisins

60 pecan *or* walnut quarters, toasted

1 pound (455 g) sweet dark *or* milk chocolate, tempered (pages 468 to 471)

1. Blanch the pistachios, adding a pinch of salt to the water to intensify the color. Remove the skins and dry the nuts. Do not toast them or you will lose the bright green hue.

2. Place the sorted pistachios, cashews, raisins, and pecans or walnuts in separate bowls where they will be easy to reach. Line a full sheet pan, 16 x 24 inches (40 x 60 cm), with baking paper.

3. Make a paper pastry bag (see page 54) and fill it with approximately one-third of the tempered chocolate. Pipe out 10 to 20 rounds of chocolate, 1¼ inches (3.1 cm) in diameter, evenly spaced in straight lines on the sheet pan. Don't move the bag while you pipe each round; hold it just above the pan where the round will be, press gently until you have the correct size, release the pressure to stop the flow, and move to the next spot.

4. Quickly arrange 1 pistachio, 1 cashew, 1 raisin, and 1 pecan or walnut quarter attractively on each round. Do not press the toppings into the chocolate or the round will become too large and/or misshapen. Repeat with the remaining chocolate and toppings.

Ginger-Almond Bark yield: approximately 3 pounds (1 kg 365 g) (Photo 5)

B ark is one of the fastest and easiest types of candy to make. It does not require any special equipment, the individual pieces are not dipped, and the recipe can be varied to suit the ingredients you have on hand. You may substitute other types of nuts, chocolate, and candied fruit, using the same quantities called for here, to create other flavors. One tasty and colorful combination is white chocolate with toasted cashews, pistachios, candied lemon peel, and candied cherries. Another is sweet dark chocolate with toasted hazelnuts and candied orange peel.

1 pound (455 g) whole blanched almonds, at room temperature	1 ounce (30 g) candied ginger, finely chopped
2 pounds (910 g) sweet dark chocolate, tempered (pages 468 to 471)	

1. Lightly toast the almonds and let them cool. You can either leave the almonds whole or chop them coarsely. Whole nuts will produce a more attractive sheet of bark if it is to be displayed intact or in large pieces, but chopping the nuts coarsely before mixing them into the chocolate will make it easier to break the bark into small pieces if you plan to serve that way. If you opt for chopping the nuts, sift out and discard the very fine nut particles instead of mixing them into the bark.

2. Line the bottom and sides of a half-sheet pan, 12 x 16 inches (30 x 40 cm), with aluminum foil or plastic wrap, smoothing out the wrinkles in either as much as possible.

3. Mix the candied ginger with the chopped nuts to break up any clumps of ginger and distribute it evenly. Add the nut mixture to the tempered chocolate and blend gently but quickly as the nuts will cause the chocolate to begin to set.

4. Pour the chocolate into the prepared sheet pan and spread out to ¼ inch (6 mm) thick.

5. Allow the chocolate to set or place the sheet pan in the refrigerator for approximately 10 minutes to expedite the process.

6. Invert the pan and peel the foil or plastic from the back of the chocolate sheet. Cut or break the sheet into pieces of the desired size.

Rochers yield: 60 candies, 1¼ inches (3.1 cm) in diamter (Photo 5)

Like the preceding recipe for almond-ginger bark, rochers, or rocks, are a classic, quick, and easy candy that is also quite versatile. You can replace the milk chocolate with sweet dark or white chocolate, or use a combination by making the rounds from one chocolate and coating the nuts with another. As with the bark candy, you can add chopped candied fruit to the rocher mixture; some chefs add dry breakfast cereal, such as Rice Krispies or granola. You can eliminate making the round bases to save time, but they do give the candy a more finished look, and it is easier to portion the almonds evenly to create uniform pieces. If you have small cylinder Flexipans (No. 2435), you can use them instead of making the bases. Either pipe a thin layer of chocolate on the bottoms of the forms, allow to set, and portion the mixture on top or simply portion the almond mixture in the indentations, let set, and then unmold.

Coating the almonds with sugar before toasting gives them a candied feel and adds a nice crunch. The following instructions specify mixing the almonds into the chocolate in two batches to make sure the mixture does not set up before you finish portioning it, as warming it will most likely ruin the temper. Once you have made these candies a few times and provided you are not working in a very cold room, you can probably mix all the ingredients in one batch.

1 pound (455 g) slivered almonds	6 ounces (170 g) milk chocolate, tempered (pages 468 to 471)
2 tablespoons (30 ml) orange or nut-flavored liqueur	8 ounces (225 g) milk chocolate, chopped
2 ounces (55 g) powdered sugar, sifted	2 ounces (55 g) cocoa butter, chopped

1. Place the slivered almonds and the liqueur in a bowl. Toss with your hands to completely coat all sides of the almonds with liqueur.

2. Place the powdered sugar in a second bowl and add the coated almonds. Toss the almonds in the powdered sugar to coat them evenly. Spread the almonds out in a single layer on a sheet pan lined with baking paper or a Silpat. Avoid leaving any powdered sugar on the pan around the nuts, as it can burn while the nuts are toasting. Toast at 350°F (175°C) until golden brown, turning and moving the nuts with a spatula so that they brown evenly. Let cool.

3. Spread the melted, tempered chocolate out over a sheet of baking paper into an even rectangle measuring approximately 16 x 14 inches (35 x 40 cm); the chocolate will be about ⅛ inch (3 mm) thick. Allow the chocolate to just set; do not refrigerate.

4. As soon as the chocolate is firm but not hard, cut out 60 rounds, using a 1¼-inch (3.1-cm) plain round cookie cutter. (If necessary, warm the cutter to avoid breaking the chocolate.) Place the chocolate rounds in straight rows on sheet pans lined with baking paper as you cut them. Reserve the chocolate scraps for another use.

5. Combine the chopped chocolate and the cocoa butter. Place over a bain-marie, melt, then temper (see page 468 to 471). Place half of the tempered chocolate mixture in a warm bowl (not hot). Keep the other half of the chocolate warm, but do not let it get too hot. Stir half of the almonds into the chocolate in the warm bowl.

6. Use 2 spoons to drop portions of the chocolate-covered almonds on top of the prepared chocolate rounds; the almonds should cover most of each round but should not stick out beyond the edges. Mix the remaining almonds and chocolate and repeat to cover the remaining rounds.

About Toffees and Brittles

Toffees and nut brittles in various forms have been made all over the world for hundreds if not thousands of years. Nut brittles made with pistachios, cashews, or almonds are found throughout the Middle East and Asia. In India, they make a very pretty thin brittle that contains all three—pistachios, cashews, and almonds—plus spices, including cinnamon and saffron threads. This candy, called *chikki*, is made in a perfectly even flat layer just thick enough to contain the nuts, giving it an appearance similar to stained glass. Brittles made with a combination of nuts and sesame seeds or sesame seeds alone are popular in parts of the Middle East and Asia.

Brittles are made by stirring toasted nuts into caramelized sugar or by cooking raw nuts in a sugar syrup until the mixture reaches the hard crack or caramel stage. If butter or cream is added, the candy becomes a toffee. In addition to the crisp version made here, toffees are also made in soft and chewy varieties by adding a larger percentage of cream. Because they do not contain dairy products, nut brittles have a very hard consistency. These are usually made thinner than toffees or they would be almost impossible to eat. The use of baking soda in addition to the butter in Macadamia Nut Toffee helps make the candy a little softer and easier both to break apart and to eat.

Macadamia Nut Toffee yield: approximately 2 pounds (910 g) (Photo 5)

This recipe can be made with any type of nut you have on hand, or you can use a combination; the macadamia version is my personal favorite. Chopping the nuts coarsely, as directed, makes the finished toffee easy to break into small pieces. If you leave the nuts whole, however, the candy has a more elegant appearance and is especially attractive for presenting in a whole slab. If you plan to present the candy this way, you may want to pour the mixture onto a full sheet pan rather than a half-sheet (or use a large marble slab) so that the candy can run out and form natural curved edges.

12 ounces (340 g) macadamia nuts

Vegetable oil

12 ounces (340 g) granulated sugar

½ cup (120 ml) water

⅓ cup (80 ml) or 4 ounces (115 g) light corn syrup

8 ounces (225 g) unsalted butter, at room temperature

½ teaspoon (2.5 g) salt

½ teaspoon (2 g) baking soda

1. Place the macadamia nuts on a sheet pan and toast them at 375°F (190°C), shaking the pan and/or stirring the nuts so that they cook evenly, until they are light golden brown. Let the nuts cool to room temperature, then chop them coarsely (or leave them whole if desired; see recipe introduction).

2. Line the inside of a half-sheet pan, 12 × 16 inches (30 × 40 cm) with aluminum foil. Smooth out any wrinkles in the foil to make an even surface. Brush vegetable oil over the foil.

3. Taking the usual precautions when boiling sugar, combine the sugar and water in a heavy-bottomed saucepan. Bring to a boil and add the corn syrup. Continue boiling the mixture over high heat, brushing down the sides of the pan occasionally with a brush dipped in water to wash down any sugar crystals. When the syrup reaches 250°F (122°C), gradually add the butter, but do not stir. Continue cooking until the syrup turns a light caramel color.

4. Remove the pan from the heat and quickly stir in the salt, baking soda, and toasted nuts. Pour the mixture onto the prepared sheet pan. Tilt the pan as needed to distribute the caramel and the nuts in an even layer or use a well-oiled spatula to spread the candy over the pan.

5. Allow the toffee to cool completely. Turn the slab of toffee out of the pan and peel the foil from the back. Break into pieces of the desired size. Store the candy in an airtight container.

CHOCOLATE CURLS (CIGARETTES)

Chocolate curls take a bit of practice to master. One thing to remember is that the ideal room temperature for chocolate work is approximately 68°F (20°C). The more the temperature varies from this figure in either direction, the harder it will be to work with the chocolate. Waiting until the chocolate is just the right consistency to curl is the key. If it is too soft, it will just smear and stick to the knife instead of curling. If this happens, wait a few seconds until it has set further. If that does not help—if the room and/or the surface are too warm—briefly place a chilled sheet pan on top. If it has set too hard, the chocolate will break when you try to curl it. Use a hair dryer to soften it (be careful when using this technique with tempered chocolate) or, provided you have spread the chocolate thin enough, you can warm it by rubbing your hand over the top as you work your way down the strip. If you are using a knife rather than a palette knife, a long slicing knife is preferable to a chef's knife because its width is uniform throughout a greater portion of its length. The blade of a chef's knife is more tapered, giving you a smaller area to work with. A caulking spatula or a bench scraper work well also.

Chocolate Curls Using Tempered or Coating Chocolate

I. Pour a strip of tempered or melted coating chocolate on a marble or perfectly smooth hardwood surface (see Note). Spread it as close to the edge as possible in a strip about $\frac{1}{16}$ inch (2 mm) thick, or as thin as possible without being able to see the surface through the chocolate. Make the strip a bit wider than the length you want the finished curls (Figure 10-1).

2. As soon as the chocolate has set up, make a cut lengthwise next to each edge to even the sides and make the strip as wide as the desired length of the finished curls (Figure 10-2).

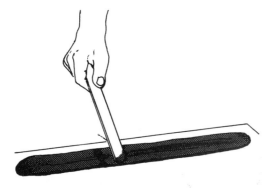

FIGURE 10-1 **The thin strip of chocolate for chocolate curls. The strip is made a bit wider than the desired length of the finished curls.**

FIGURE 10-2 **Cutting lengthwise next to each edge to make the center section of the chocolate strip as wide as the desired length of the finished curls**

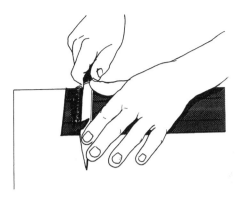

FIGURE 10-3 Making a chocolate curl using a slicing knife

FIGURE 10-4 Making a chocolate curl using a palette knife

3. Hold a long knife or palette knife at a 45-degree angle to the surface and push the knife away from you to cut off and curl about 1 inch (2.5 cm) of the strip (Figures 10-3 and 10-4).

NOTE: Working in a kitchen without temperature control during hot weather, it is just about impossible to produce chocolate curls without the use of a marble slab or table; even with it, this is a tricky procedure. Conversely, when the room temperature is cold, working on marble may be too much of a good thing, and a wooden surface can be preferable. Do not use a wooden cutting board, wooden workbench, or table that is worn, cracked, or splintered, or bits of wood will be scraped up into the curls. The wooden surface must be made of hardwood and must be smooth, with few or no cuts on it.

Chocolate Curls Using Quick-Method Tempered Chocolate

1. Cut chocolate into small pieces. Melt over a bain-marie and temper, using the cold water method described on page 470. Have one or two clean and perfectly even sheet pans ready.

2. Place the sheet pan in the oven for just a few seconds so it is just slightly warmer than body temperature (you should be able to remove the pan comfortably with your bare hands, but it should not feel cool to the touch). Invert the sheet pan.

3. Spread the tempered chocolate out in a strip approximately $\frac{1}{16}$ inch (2 mm) thick, or as thin as possible without being able to see the pan underneath. Let the chocolate set up. To speed up the process, you can place the pan in the refrigerator, but only for the amount of time it takes for the chocolate to become firm.

4. When the chocolate has set, immediately brace the pan between your body and the back of the table so it is held steady. Push the blade of a knife or caulking spatula against the chocolate to make the desired shape and size curl. By manipulating the angle and pressure of the blade, together with the length of the strip curled, it is possible to make either loose curls or tight and compact (cigarette-type) curls. Transfer the curls to a sheet pan lined with baking paper, taking care not to leave fingerprints.

CHEF'S TIP

If you need chocolate curls that are a specific length or all precisely the same length, follow the method described under "Chocolate Curls Using Tempered or Coating Chocolate," as you cannot make the lengthwise cuts to even the edges when using a sheet pan.

CHOCOLATE CUTOUTS: SQUARES, RECTANGLES, CIRCLES, HEARTS, AND TRIANGLES

This is a quick method for creating decorations that can be made up in advance. The assorted chocolate shapes can be used to decorate the sides of a cake or placed at an angle on top. They are used this way with Swedish Chocolate Cake and Meringue Black Forest Cake, for example. Finished chocolate cutouts can be enhanced with the streaking technique described on page 468, applying the same or a different color chocolate for contrast. Chocolate cutouts are good to have on hand to use as a finishing touch. They can be placed on top of virtually any dessert to give it a special finesse.

1. Place a sheet of baking paper on the table and pour coating or tempered chocolate on top. Spread it out very thin (¹⁄₁₆ inch/2 mm) and evenly, using a palette knife (Figure 10-5). Make sure the table around the paper is clean so you do not have to worry about spreading the chocolate beyond the paper onto the table.

2. Immediately pick up the paper by two diagonal corners (Figure 10-6) and place it on a cardboard or inverted sheet pan. Allow the chocolate to set partially. Do not refrigerate.

3. Cut squares or rectangles, using a sharp knife (Figure 10-7) or a multiple pastry wheel (Figure 10-8). Avoid cutting through the paper. Cut out circles, hearts, or other shapes with cookie cutters of the appropriate size and shape. If necessary, heat the cutter by dipping it in hot water; quickly shake off the water and dry the cutter on a towel before using. You can probably cut four or five pieces before reheating the cutter. Chocolate triangles can be cut using the same technique and pattern described in cutting croissants (see Figure 5-4, page 212), if you are making a full sheet. When only a few triangles are needed (to decorate a single Meringue Black Forest Cake, for example), simply cut them out from strips, using a knife.

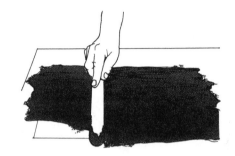

FIGURE 10-5 Spreading a thin coating of melted chocolate over a sheet of baking paper

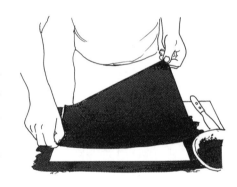

FIGURE 10-6 Lifting the chocolate-covered paper by 2 diagonal corners

FIGURE 10-7 Cutting square chocolate cutouts using a chef's knife

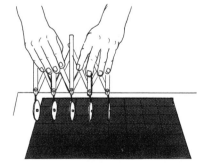

FIGURE 10-8 Cutting squares using a multiple pastry wheel

4. Store the chocolate cutouts (still attached to the paper) in a dark, cool place. Do not store them in the refrigerator. To remove them from the paper, place one hand underneath and push up gently to separate the decorations from the paper as you lift them off with your other hand (Figure 10-9). This technique is especially helpful when working with large, extra-thin, or unusual shapes.

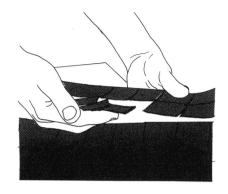

FIGURE 10-9 **Pressing gently underneath the paper to facilitate removing the hardened chocolate cutouts**

CHOCOLATE FIGURINES

In addition to being used to coat and dip pastries, cookies, or cakes, coating chocolate (dark, milk, or white) is very practical for piping various decorative ornaments. These can be piped either directly onto a cake or petit four freehand, or onto baking paper (sometimes with the help of a template) to place on the item after the decoration has hardened. Tempered chocolate may also be used. The latter method is an efficient way of making fancy decorations when you are not too busy, because they can be made up far in advance and stored in a dark cool place (but not in the refrigerator). If you want the chocolate to float out slightly, use it as is, but if it is important to the design that the chocolate stays in precise lines, use Piping Chocolate (page 465).

Some of the figurines look especially nice with a combination of dark, milk, and white chocolate in the same design. To create these, make the frame with piping chocolate and let it harden. Fill in the design with coating or tempered chocolate in the desired shade or shades. When the chocolate has set, place these two-tone designs on the cake or pastry, flat-side up. Different shades and colors can also be obtained by blending the dark, milk, and white chocolates, or by tinting white chocolate with fat-soluble coloring (see Note).

Although it may seem like only a small amount of chocolate is involved, piping bags with chocolate left inside (partially used bags or bags with chocolate that set up before it could be used) should not be discarded. Put the used bag in the refrigerator to harden, then open it up and the chocolate will fall right out and can be put back into the bowl to melt again.

NOTE: If you do not have milk chocolate colored coating chocolate you can create that shade by combining 3 to 4 parts white coating chocolate with 1 part dark coating chocolate.

CHEF'S TIP
Because the tip and the opening of the piping bag are so small, the chocolate will set up very quickly in that spot. When you pause while piping out the designs, hold the tip between your pinched fingers to keep it warm. If you forget and only the chocolate at the very tip of the bag has set up, hold the tip of the piping bag against the side of a warm pot on the stove, or on the oven door, to melt it quickly.

FIGURE 10-10 **Piping designs**

FIGURES 10-11 Piping designs

1. Trace onto a sheet of paper any of the small individual designs you would like to make from the examples shown in the bottom 3 rows of Figure 10-11, drawing as many as you need of each design. (The border designs in the top 3 rows of Figure 10-11 and the animals in Figure 10-10 are designs that can be piped directly onto a cake, pastry, or rolled sheet of marzipan.)

2. Attach the paper securely to a sheet of cardboard. Place a piece of baking or waxed paper on top; attach it securely so it will not shift as you pipe the designs.

3. Make a piping bag (see page 55) and fill it with a small amount of melted coating chocolate, tempered chocolate, or piping chocolate. Cut a small opening in the bag. Pipe the chocolate over the design, tracing it in one unbroken line as much as possible.

4. Let the chocolate harden, then store the figures attached to the paper. To remove them, place one hand under the paper and push up very gently to separate the chocolate from the paper as you lift the design off with the other hand. If they are very fragile, slide the blade of a thin knife underneath instead.

CHOCOLATE LEAVES
Method I

1. Spread tempered chocolate or melted coating chocolate over a sheet of baking paper, as described in the directions for Chocolate Cutouts (page 460).

2. When the chocolate has set partially, use the tip of a small knife to cut out leaves of the appropriate size and shape (short and wide for rose leaves, longer and narrower for pear leaves).

3. Carefully, without cutting all the way through, score the top to show the veins of the leaf. Let set, store, and remove as directed for Chocolate Cutouts.

Method II

1. A more eye-catching—but also more time-consuming—way to make chocolate leaves is to paint a thin layer of tempered chocolate or melted coating chocolate on the back of a real leaf, typically a rose leaf (Figure 10-12). Naturally, you want to make sure any leaves you use are non-toxic; citrus trees are safe, and small citrus leaves produce a good result.

2. Let the chocolate set, then carefully peel the real leaf away from the chocolate leaf (Figure 10-13). You should be able to use the same leaf three or four times before the chocolate begins to stick. Any type of leaf can be produced in this manner as long as it is thin enough to be bent and peeled from the chocolate leaf without the chocolate breaking.

FIGURE 10-12 **Brushing melted chocolate over the back of a real leaf to create a chocolate leaf**

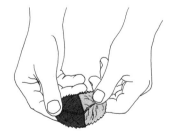

FIGURE 10-13 **Peeling the real leaf away from the chocolate leaf after the chocolate has hardened**

CHOCOLATE SHAVINGS AND SMALL CURLED SHAVINGS

Chocolate shavings are made by holding a small knife at a 90-degree angle to a piece of chocolate and scraping away from you, letting the shavings fall onto a paper-lined sheet pan (Figure 10-14). Small, elegant 180-degree curls can be created, using a sharp-edged melon ball cutter in the same way. Move the melon ball cutter away from you in short strokes (Figure 10-15).

As described in some of the other decorations, the chocolate for shavings must have the correct consistency to produce a good result. If it is too warm, chocolate will cake up on the tool; if too cold, it will break into small unattractive specks and pieces. Using milk or gianduja chocolate, which by nature is softer than dark or white chocolate, will make it much easier to create thin shavings or pretty curled shavings.

Store the shavings or curls covered in a cool, dry place to use as needed. Do not store in the refrigerator. You can refrigerate the shavings for just a few minutes right before using them, if it is necessary, to keep them from melting and sticking to your hand (if you are placing them on the side of a cake, for example). In most instances, where the shavings are to be sprinkled on top of the dessert, it is best to use a spoon to avoid contact with the heat of your hands.

FIGURE 10-14 **Making chocolate shavings by scraping the surface of the chocolate with a small sharp knife**

FIGURE 10-15 **Making curled chocolate shavings using a melon ball tool**

Chocolate Glaze yield: 4½ cups (1 L 80 ml)

1 pound (455 g) sweet dark chocolate

5 ounces (140 g) unsalted butter, at room temperature

5 tablespoons (1½ ounces/40 g) unsweetened cocoa powder, sifted

¼ cup (60 ml) dark rum

¾ cup (180 ml) or 9 ounces (255 g) light corn syrup

1. Cut the chocolate into small chunks and melt over hot water. Remove from the heat, add the butter, and stir until the butter is fully incorporated.

2. Stir the cocoa powder into the rum, mixing until smooth. Add the corn syrup, then stir into the chocolate mixture.

3. Let cool. Store in a covered container. The glaze does not need to be refrigerated. To use, heat the glaze to the consistency suitable for the recipe in which you are using it. If a skin forms on the surface during storage, pour a little hot water on top, wait a few seconds, then pour the water off.

> **CHEF'S TIP**
> If a fatty film develops on the top of the glaze once it has cooled, the chocolate you are using contains too much cocoa butter; it is probably semisweet or bittersweet instead of sweet. Decrease the amount of butter in the recipe to compensate. If you desire a firmer glaze, increase the amount of sweet dark chocolate in the recipe.

Piping Chocolate yield: 1 cup (240 ml)

Piping chocolate can be purchased from chocolate manufacturers, but the quality of the product is not commensurate with the price, considering that you can make the same thing for about one-eighth of the cost. For practical reasons, I prefer to use coating chocolate for piping chocolate decorations that will be moved after they have hardened because I can be certain the coating chocolate will set up firm.

If you do not have or do not want to use coating chocolate, real chocolate must be perfectly tempered to be utilized the same way. In cases where the decoration is not moved—when it is piped directly on to a pastry or is used for decorating a dessert plate, for example—real chocolate can be used without tempering, as the addition of a liquid will aid in setting the chocolate sufficiently. Keep in mind, however, that piping chocolate made from real untempered chocolate will not hold up as long and may start to bloom within a few hours.

12 ounces (340 g) dark coating chocolate

¼ to ½ teaspoon (1.25 to 2.5 ml) simple syrup *or* orange liqueur

1. Chop the chocolate into small pieces, place in a small bowl, and set over simmering water, stirring until melted. Do not overheat.

2. Using a drop bottle, add the simple syrup or orange liqueur gradually. The amount required varies depending on the brand of chocolate. Add enough for the chocolate to form soft peaks.

3. Piping chocolate will keep as long as any dark chocolate stored, covered, in a cool place. Melt over hot water to use.

Spraying with Chocolate

Most people associate power sprayers with house paint, wood stain, or plant insecticides. However, they have been used in our industry for quite some time, even as far back as when I was attending culinary school in Sweden. At that time, we were shown how to use power sprayers for applying egg wash to proofed doughs such as croissant, braided bread, and other delicate items. Using a power sprayer for egg wash has three advantages: speed, the production of a perfectly even coating, and no risk of deflating the item by using a heavy hand with a brush. Back then, it was only practical to use a technique like this in a high-volume shop, as besides being bulky, the sprayers were also expensive.

Today, one can buy a small electric paint sprayer in any hardware store for less than the cost of a set of good-quality pastry cutters, although you should get a sprayer that has an adjustable nozzle and the capability of controlling the air pressure. Sprayed chocolate can be utilized in many ways. Plates used for dessert presentations can be enhanced by spraying chocolate lightly and evenly over the whole surface, which is especially appropriate if the plates are solid white, or a portion of the plate can be highlighted by fanning the chocolate over one side. To decorate plates with chocolate using a template, place the template on the base of the plate and hold it steady by placing a small heavy object, such as a metal nut or bolt, on top. Using low air pressure, spray the solution over the plate. Remove the template and let the chocolate set. Fill in the exposed area with a sauce or leave it plain. For the reverse effect, place a stencil on the plate and spray the chocolate over it to create a chocolate silhouette of the shape. This is nice for a sea-sonal motif, such as a tree or star, on one side of the base of a plate.

Another option is to use a stencil with a design that will appear over the entire base of the plate, either protecting the rim of the plate to leave it without decoration or covering the rim with chocolate at the same time. If possible, set the spray gun on low whenever you are using a template or stencil to avoid disturbing the pattern as you spray. For a different look with any of these techniques, place the plates in the freezer for a few minutes before spraying; the chocolate will set up immediately, creating a velvet finish.

Molded chocolate figures can also be sprayed to give them an unusual look. Just like the plates, they can be placed in the freezer beforehand to alter the finish. Chocolate designs may also be sprayed onto chocolate cutouts and chocolate candies.

It may seem obvious, but it is worth stating that under no circumstance should you use the same equipment for food as for spraying paint or other nonfood items. At the minimum, one should have a complete set consisting of piston, housing pump, spray tip assembly, filter assembly, and, of course, the container, reserved for kitchen use only. The main portion, the gun assembly, can be used for any purpose, as liquid does not pass through it. However, the ideal solution is to have a sprayer dedicated to the pastry kitchen alone. (If you do not want to invest in a power sprayer, use the Cocoa Solution for Manual Spray Bottle instead).

Spraying the chocolate solution is really no different than spraying thick-viscosity paint, so read the instructions from the manufacturer before starting. Be sure to protect the immediate surrounding areas wherever you are spraying with sheets of plastic wrap or baking paper. When you are first learning, it is a good idea to practice with an inexpensive chocolate thinned with a commercial thinning agent, soybean oil, or vegetable shortening, as cocoa butter is expensive.

Chocolate Solution for Spraying yield: 1 quart (960 ml)

1 pound (455 g) sweet dark chocolate   1 pound (455 g) cocoa butter

1. Chop the chocolate and cocoa butter into small pieces, place together in a bowl, and melt over simmering water. Continue to heat the mixture to 130°F (54°C) and hold as close to this temperature as possible while spraying for the best result.

2. Have your plates ready—also the template or stencil, if you are using one. Warm the spray gun to ensure that the chocolate does not set up inside. Place the warm solution in the sprayer and spray the desired design over the serving plates with or without a template or stencil as desired. Let the plates dry. This should not take more than 10 minutes unless your work area is adversely warm; if so, place the plates in the refrigerator to expedite the process or use the velvet finish method discussed above. The plates can be decorated many hours ahead of service and reserved in a cool, dry area.

3. The sprayer should be disassembled and cleaned after you finish spraying unless you plan to use it again in the near future. To clean it, remove the container holding the chocolate solution. If needed warm the gun in a very low temperature oven, leaving the door open, to melt the chocolate that has hardened on the other parts. Be careful not to overheat the gun and damage it; the cocoa butter–rich chocolate requires very little heat to melt. Wash the parts using hot water. However, if you are using the spray gun more or less daily, just remove the chocolate container and store the rest of the gun intact, covered, on a sheet pan. It is necessary to clean the assembly thoroughly only every two weeks or so, depending on use. If the spray-gun container is made of plastic (which I highly recommend), the solution can be stored there until next time, then melted in a microwave oven or over a bain-marie. Regardless of the storage container, the leftover solution should be covered; it will keep for up to 1 year.

NOTE: The neutral 50-50 proportion of this mixture will produce a very fine texture. For a coarser and darker finish, a ratio of up to 2 parts chocolate to 1 part cocoa butter may be used. However, when using that much chocolate, the consistency of the solution may be too thick to produce a good result with some spray guns.

Cocoa Solution for Manual Spray Bottle yield: approximately 3¹/₂ cups (360 ml)

This will make a medium-dark spray. Add more cocoa powder if a darker color is desired.

¼ cup (60 ml) light corn syrup   2 ounces (55 g) cocoa powder
3 cups (720 ml) warm water

1. Stir the corn syrup into the water.

2. Place the cocoa powder in a bowl. Add just enough of the water mixture to make a smooth paste. Gradually mix in the remaining water. Store in the refrigerator.

Streaking Chocolate

A very simple and elegant way to decorate petits fours, pastries, candies, and serving plates is to pipe a series of very thin lines across them. The lines can be piped in just one direction or in opposite directions, as shown in Pecan Whiskey Tart (see Figure 7-5, page 346). It is important to use a small opening in the piping bag to keep the lines thin. Fill the bag with a small amount of tempered chocolate or melted coating chocolate. Pipe the chocolate, moving the bag very quickly over the item and alternating left to right and right to left. You need to extend the lines out just beyond the edge of the item and let them fall on a paper to get the desired effect.

Tempering Chocolate

To achieve the desired high gloss and hard, brittle texture, and to make the chocolate more resistant to warm temperatures, it is necessary to temper it. The cocoa butter in chocolate consists of many fat groups with melting points that vary between approximately 60° and 110°F (16° and 43°C). Cocoa butter actually melts a few degrees below this, but we warm it slightly higher to make sure. The fats that melt at the higher temperature are also the first ones to solidify as the melted chocolate cools. These fats, when distributed throughout, are what give the chocolate its gloss and solidity (a properly tempered chocolate should break with a crisp snap). One might say that these high-melting-point fats act as a starting point around which the remaining chocolate solidifies.

There are various methods used to temper chocolate by hand. They all consist of three basic steps: melting, cooling, and rewarming. The more commonly used methods are *tabliering* and *seeding*. Many busy chefs today prefer to speed up the process by cooling the chocolate over ice water, referred to in the following instructions as the *cold water method*.

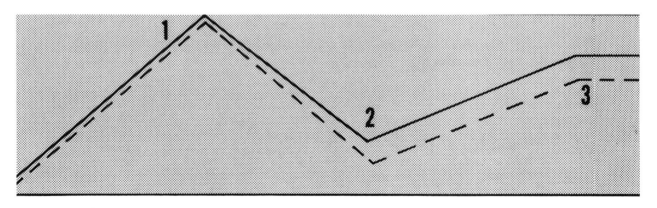

FIGURE 10-16 The 3 steps in tempering chocolate

Dark chocolate (solid line)
1. Melt and heat to 115° to 120°F (46° to 49°C)
2. Cool to 80° to 82°F (26° to 28°C)
3. Warm slowly to 87° to 90°F (30° to 32°C)

Milk or white chocolate (broken line)
1. Melt and heat to 110° to 115°F (43° to 46°C)
2. Cool to 78° to 80°F (25° to 26°C)
3. Warm slowly to 85° to 87°F (29° to 30°C)

TABLIERING METHOD

1. Cut the chocolate into small pieces (a serrated knife works great for this) and place it in a bowl over hot water to melt. Stir it constantly to avoid overheating or burning; this is especially important if you are working with milk chocolate, which tends to get lumpy if overheated. Stirring is essential when melting white chocolate, which can become grainy and useless very quickly. To completely melt all of the fats, heat the chocolate to between115° and 120°F (46° and 49°C) for dark chocolate or between 110 and 115°F (43 and 46°C) for milk or white chocolates.

2. Cool the melted chocolate to approximately 95°F (34°C) by removing it from the heat (continue to stir as you do this) and pour approximately one-third (or up to two-thirds, if you are more experienced) of it onto a marble slab. Using a metal spatula in combination with a metal scraper, spread the chocolate out and scrape it back together until it cools and shows signs of thickening (the high-melting-point fats are starting to crystallize). Before the chocolate sets completely, stir it back into the remaining melted chocolate, continuing to stir until it forms a homogeneous mass. Check the temperature. If it is near 80° to 82°F (26° to 28°C), just continue stirring until it reaches that temperature. If it is quite a bit warmer, pour a portion of the chocolate off and repeat the scraping together and cooling process, add this back, and test again. When the chocolate is smooth and homogeneous and the temperature registers between 80° and 82°F (26° and 28°C) for dark chocolate or 78° and 80°F (25° and 26°C) for milk or white chocolate, proceed to the next step.

The chocolate is now too thick to use and must be warmed before it can be utilized. However, there is no point in warming it to the working temperature before you test the temper. To test, dip the corner of a small piece of baking paper into the chocolate. Fold the dipped part of the paper back onto the clean area and let the chocolate cool at a room temperature of 64° to 68°F (18° to 20°C). Within 5 minutes, the chocolate should have set to the point that it is not sticky when you pull the folded paper apart and, if scraped with a knife, it should roll up like a chocolate curl (see page 458). You can expedite the test by placing the paper with chocolate in the refrigerator; the chocolate should break in half with a clean snap after 1 or 2 minutes. If the chocolate passes this test, proceed to warm it as follows. If not, repeat steps 1 and 2.

3. Warm the tempered chocolate slowly over hot water to the correct working temperature: 87° to 90°F (30° to 32°C) for dark chocolate and 85° to 87°F (29° to 30°C) for milk or white chocolate. If the chocolate is still too thick to use for a particular purpose at this temperature, thin it by adding a small amount of cocoa butter. Great care must be taken in this final (third) step. If you let the chocolate get just a few degrees above the recommended temperature, too much fat will melt and the chocolate will require a longer time to set. It also will not be as attractive, as part of the fat will separate and show on the surface in the whitish pattern known as *bloom*.

SEEDING

1. Cut the chocolate into pieces and melt over a water bath, as described in the tabliering method. Remove the bowl from the heat source and cool to 95°F (34°C), stirring frequently.

2. Stir in grated, shaved, or finely chopped chocolate at a rate of 5 to 10 percent of the total weight of the melted chocolate, stirring the seeding chocolate in gradually and waiting until each addition is completely incorporated before adding the next. Example regarding the amount of seeding chocolate to use: For 2 pounds 8 ounces or 40 ounces (1 kg 135 g) melted chocolate, use 2 to 4 ounces (55 to 115 g) seeding chocolate.

3. When the chocolate is perfectly smooth and the temperature has dropped to 88° to 90°F (30° to 32°C) for dark chocolate or 85° to 87°F (29° to 30°C) for white or milk chocolate, hold the chocolate at this temperature, stirring constantly, for at least 2 minutes. Test as described in Step 2 of the tabliering method. The tempered chocolate should be ready to use. When using this method, it is important that the seeding chocolate was originally tempered before it set up.

BLOCK METHOD

In this shortcut variation, appropriate for small batches, one solid piece of chocolate is added to the melted chocolate and stirred until the melted chocolate reaches the working temperature. The unmelted portion of the piece is removed. The chocolate is then ready to use after testing. This method will not produce the same long-lasting temper as tabliering.

COLD WATER METHOD

Cooling the chocolate by simply placing the bowl of melted chocolate over ice water is the quickest and most efficient method for tempering. You will find, however, that chocolate manufacturers do not recommend it because the quality of the temper is not high enough, and it is easy to accidentally get water in the chocolate and ruin it. Still, this is a good method to keep in mind for emergencies.

1. Chop the chocolate into pieces and melt over a water bath as directed for tabliering, using an oversized bowl.

2. Place the bowl over ice water and stir from time to time during the first few minutes. When the chocolate begins to set up on the sides and the bottom of the bowl, scrape down the sides and stir constantly until the chocolate is thick and pasty, around 80°F (26°C). Test the temper as described in Step 2 of the tabliering method.

3. Place the bowl over a bain-marie and warm the chocolate to 85° to 90°F (29° to 32°C), depending on the type of chocolate.

USING A MICROWAVE OVEN TO TEMPER CHOCOLATE

A microwave oven can be used to melt the chocolate, as described in "Using Pretempered Chocolate" below, or it can be used to melt or rewarm chocolate that has not set up completely after it has been tempered using any of the methods discussed in this section. It takes some trial and error to learn what power setting to use and the time required for the amount and type of chocolate you are working with. In all instances, you should start with a low power setting and be careful that the chocolate never exceeds the maximum temperature specified for the particular type of chocolate in each of the methods.

Tempering Tips

Testing the tempered chocolate—Before starting to work with the product, it is always a good idea to check whether or not the chocolate has been tempered correctly, regardless of the method used. See Step 2 of the tabliering method (page 469).

Warming tempered chocolate—If you are working with tempered chocolate and it starts to cool down and set up, heat it gently, using a hairdryer or a heat gun, or add warm melted and tempered chocolate to restabilize the cocoa butter and make the chocolate more fluid. Add the warm chocolate all at once (estimating what you consider will be enough), then stir the two together. A natural inclination might be to add a slow stream of chocolate while stirring and to continue to add chocolate until you reach the desired consistency, but adding chocolate slowly will actually destabilize the temper.

To use a microwave oven, melt the chocolate pellets to the point that approximately two-thirds of the chocolate pellets are melted. Stir the chocolate at room temperature until all the pellets have melted and the chocolate has reached the correct temperature.

USING PRETEMPERED CHOCOLATE

Because all commercial chocolate is tempered at the factory before packaging and shipping, it is possible to use it without going through any of the tempering procedures described here, provided that you are able to melt and warm the chocolate to its correct working temperature without allowing any part of it to exceed 90°F (32°C) for dark chocolate or 85° to 87°F (29° to 30°C) for white or milk chocolate. To achieve this, the water in the bain-marie should not exceed 140°F (60°C) and you must stir the chocolate constantly. Because the part closest to the heat source will always be hotter than the remainder, you must monitor the temperature very closely.

If you have a special thermostatically controlled bain-marie and no need to use the chocolate in a hurry (this process can take up to 12 hours), it is also possible to melt pretempered chocolate very slowly and omit the cooling process, provided that the temperature never exceeds the guidelines mentioned above at any time.

When melting pretempered chocolate in a microwave you should use chocolate that is produced by the manufacturer in small pellets or buttons (also known as pistoles or rondos), and the chocolate must be stirred frequently. It is impossible to chop the chocolate into perfectly even pieces by hand and smaller pieces will overheat before the larger pieces are melted.

CAKE DECORATION AND SPECIAL-OCCASION CAKES

Without question, the most special of all of the cakes made by the pastry chef is the wedding cake. Elaborate wedding cakes are truly works of art that often require days, even weeks, of advance planning and preparation, and may include the creation of fanciful decorations and ornaments made from royal icing, marzipan, chocolate, pulled sugar, or gum paste. While not as elaborate, other special-occasion cakes are made daily in many bakeshops for birthdays, anniversaries, graduations, bar and bat mitzvahs, and, of course, the many annual holidays, such as Easter, Christmas, New Year's, Independence Day, and so on. I am pleased to say I have made several 75th wedding anniversary cakes, as gratifying to me as the occasion that I wrote the highest number I have ever had the honor of placing on a birthday cake: "Happy 105!"

INSCRIPTIONS AND DECORATING PLAQUES

There are many ways to include an inscription on a cake, the most common and straightforward method being simply to write the message on the finished cake, using a pastry bag or piping bag filled with buttercream, piping chocolate, or piping gel. Another option is to make a plaque from marzipan or modeling chocolate, write the message on this, then place the inscribed marker on the cake. In some cases, if you are given the task of adding an inscription to a cake that has already been sliced, for example, or a cake that was decorated without leaving any space where the writing could be placed, you have no choice but to use a plaque. This happens in restaurant settings when a customer brings in a cake from a bakery and asks if the pastry department can write "Happy Birthday" on top. Similarly, a customer may select from a bakery display case a decorated cake whose top is covered with sliced fruit, for example, and ask that a message be added. Whatever the circumstances, a plaque is actually the easiest way of adding an inscription for two reasons: You are not as committed if you make a mistake— you can turn the plaque over or make a new one without damaging the cake—and you can make up extra plaques ahead of time, completely finished or with space left for adding a name or a number.

Making a Decorating Plaque from Marzipan or Modeling Chocolate

Roll out the marzipan or modeling chocolate no thicker than ⅛ inch (3 mm), using powdered sugar (or cocoa powder for dark chocolate) to prevent it from sticking to your work surface. Using a ruler as a guide, cut the sheet into strips measuring 2 x 6 inches (5 x 15 cm); cutting the short edges on an angle looks nice. This is a versatile size to keep on hand for last-minute decorating jobs. Other sizes may be more appropriate, depending on the size of the cake and the length of the message. You can decorate the edges of the plaque using a marzipan tool or pincers (see page 954), and/or you can use a torch to caramelize the edges on a marzipan strip to add interest or to give it an antique look. Another option is to roll both short edges in toward the center or to roll one edge over and one edge under to resemble a scroll. The plaques may be stored for up to 1 week at room temperature on a sheet pan placed on a speed rack or in a dry box; they do not need to be covered.

SYMMETRICAL AND ASYMMETRICAL DESIGNS

The two basic types of design used when decorating the top of a cake are symmetrical designs and asymmetrical designs. Symmetrical designs are more common, owing, no doubt, to the fact that they are both easier to produce if the chef is inexperienced and are almost always used for cakes that are to be portioned into individual slices. A symmetrical design is one in which each of the design elements is of equal size and shape relative to its position on either side of a central line (see Figure 10-17). This does not mean that there is actually a line down the center as part of the design but rather that if you were to draw a line, the elements would be evenly balanced on each side. A classic example of this type of arrangement is a ring of buttercream roses evenly spaced around the perimeter of a cake.

FIGURE 10-17 **A symmetrical design**

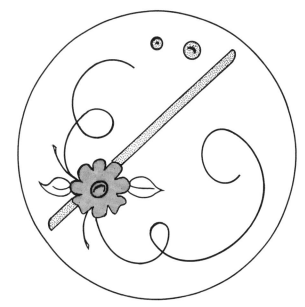

FIGURE 10-18 **An asymmetrical design**

Creating a symmetrical design on a cake that will later be portioned into individual slices can take longer to produce because it is crucial that the decorations are applied with accuracy. If the cake will be sliced before it is presented or displayed, then by all means cut or mark the cake into portions before applying the design. This will make it much easier to decorate each slice.

If the cake will be presented or displayed whole and you cannot use the markings as a guide, the easiest way to make sure the decorations are evenly spaced is to begin (as is done when portioning a cake; see pages 486 and 487) by dividing the cake into quarters. Rather than actually cutting or marking the four quarters of the cake, start by piping or placing your decorations at 12, 6, 3, and 9, as if the cake circle were the face of a clock. To complete placement for 12 portions (the most common division of a cake 10 inches/25 cm in diameter), add two more decorations between each of these first four, spacing them evenly. If you are placing premade marzipan or buttercream roses, for example, you will probably be able to set them down in the correct positions using this method. If you are piping buttercream rosettes from a pastry bag, to use another example, it is more difficult to judge the spacing because you are closer to the cake for piping. For a little extra help, begin by making small marks on the surface of the cake at 12, 6, 3, and 9, as directed above. Then make two small marks, evenly spaced, between each of these four. You can then use the marks as a guide as you are piping, centering the rosettes on the marks and hiding them at the same time.

Asymmetrical designs are rarely used for cakes that are to be portioned before presentation. This type of design is more difficult to execute and requires a more experienced hand to achieve a balanced appearance (see Figure 10-18, for example). If the idea is not well thought out or if the first steps of the design are placed incorrectly (see Figure 10-19), the result can easily end up looking off balance. Once the chef has some experience and practice, an asymmetrical design

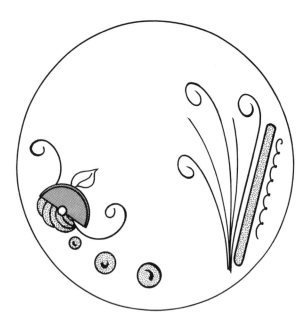

FIGURE 10-19 **An example of incorrect placement in an asymmetrical design**

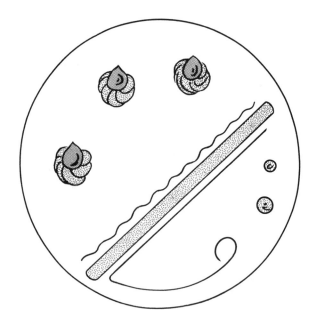

FIGURE 10-20 **An asymmetrical design using lines as a guide**

FIGURE 10-21 **A simple, well-balanced asymmetrical design**

FIGURE 10-22 **An asymmetrical design enhanced by piping dots of chocolate**

is actually faster to produce than a symmetrical one because it does not require the same degree of precision. An asymmetrical design is an ideal choice when several cakes are to be decorated identically since small inconsistencies will be less obvious.

A good way to get started when creating an asymmetrical pattern is to make several lines on the top of the cake, using the appropriate decorating media (chocolate, buttercream, etc.), then elaborate on the design using these lines as a guide or starting point. This type of design is shown in Figure 10-20; note that there is still room to add an inscription or a plaque without having the design become crowded or off balance. Figure 10-21 shows a simple, well-balanced design that can be enhanced by adding small mounds of buttercream or ganache or by piping dots of chocolate, as shown in Figure 10-22. In each, the plaque and the hearts are made from marzipan.

GENERAL DECORATING GUIDELINES

Before starting any decoration, consider the following points:

- Will the cake be portioned before or after decorating?

- Is a symmetrical or asymmetrical design more appropriate?

- Will the cake require an inscription and, if so, will this be written directly on the surface or on a plaque? (If there is to be writing directly on the cake, it is best to start with that portion, then fill in the rest of the design. A plaque, on the other hand, is generally added after the design is complete—although, of course, its position is planned in advance.)

- Will the design include a border? (The addition of a decorative border, piped around the entire perimeter of the cake or over just a portion, can be an excellent finishing touch that brings the design elements together, or it can end up making the design busy and crowded. If a border is to be part of the design, it should be added last.)

Buttercream

Buttercream is indispensable in the pastry kitchen. Its primary use is for filling, icing, and decorating cakes and pastries. Buttercream should be light and smooth and should always be made from a high-quality sweet butter. Icings made from all margarine or shortening can be unpleasant to eat—because of their higher melting point, they tend to leave a film of fat in your mouth—but a small amount of margarine or shortening added to the buttercream stabilizes it without detracting from the taste. On very hot days or in hot climates, you can increase the ratio of butter to margarine to equal amounts, but only if absolutely necessary to prevent the buttercream from melting.

If you prefer not to use margarine or shortening, another alternative for stabilizing the buttercream is to add white chocolate, which is firmer at room temperature than butter. Add 4 ounces (115 g) melted white chocolate for every 1 pound (455 g) butter in the recipe. Because many weddings take place in the summertime, it often becomes necessary to display a buttercream-iced cake for several hours in a warm room during the reception. Another trick, in this situation, is to freeze the cake layers (fully or partially) after icing and decorating with buttercream so that the cake will stay cold and prevent the buttercream from melting. If you use this method, it is important to be certain that there will be enough time for the cake to have thawed all the way through before it is served. This method should not be used with a filling that will suffer from freezing and thawing.

Buttercream can be stored at normal room temperature for three or four days and in the refrigerator for up to two weeks. It can also be frozen for longer storage. Buttercream that is kept in the refrigerator should be taken out in plenty of time to soften before using. If you need to soften it quickly, cut or break the firm buttercream into small pieces, in the same way that you would when you need to soften butter, place it in a warm location until partially softened, then warm it slightly over simmering water, stirring vigorously, until smooth and shiny. Be careful not to overheat and melt the buttercream; continue to stir after you take it off of the heat because the bowl will stay hot a little longer and can melt the buttercream on the sides. Use the same warming technique to repair buttercream that has broken, or place the broken buttercream in a mixer bowl and use a blowtorch to warm the outside of the bowl. When buttercream breaks, it is generally because the butter was too cold when it was added it to the meringue, but this can also occur when a cold ingredient, such as lemon curd from the refrigerator, is added. Softening buttercream on a low setting in the microwave is a technique you might want to try if it is more convenient for you.

Meringue-based buttercream—that is, soft butter beaten into whipped egg whites and sugar—is probably the most widely used. This is known as the *Swiss method*. It is quick and easy to make and has a very light and fluffy texture. French-method buttercream is made by whipping whole eggs or egg yolks to a thick foam with hot sugar syrup, then whipping in soft butter. Italian-method buttercream is made in the same way, except that egg whites are used instead of whole eggs and/or egg yolks. In Italian-method buttercream, you are essentially producing an Italian meringue, then whipping butter into it. Both the Italian and the French methods produce very rich yet light buttercreams.

The following buttercream recipes can easily be multiplied or scaled down with no loss of flavor or texture.

Chocolate Buttercream (Italian Method) yield: 4 pounds 6 ounces (1 kg 990 g)

To make white chocolate buttercream, substitute melted white chocolate for the sweet dark chocolate in equal amounts. Both white and dark chocolate buttercream can be flavored with hazelnut paste or praline paste. Dark chocolate buttercream is also nice with the addition of coffee reduction to create a mocha flavor.

2 pounds (910 g) unsalted butter, at room temperature

14 ounces (400 g) granulated sugar

⅓ cup (80 ml) water

1 tablespoon (15 ml) light corn syrup

4 whole eggs

2 egg whites (¼ cup/60 ml)

1 teaspoon (5 g) salt

1 teaspoon (5 ml) vanilla extract

1 pound 8 ounces (680 g) sweet dark chocolate, melted and at approximately 110°F (43°C)

1. Cream the butter until light and fluffy (soften it first if necessary). Reserve.

2. Combine the sugar, water, and corn syrup in a saucepan. Boil to 240°F (115°C), brushing down the sides of the pan. Do not stir.

3. While the syrup is boiling, whip the eggs, egg whites, salt, and vanilla for 1 minute, just to combine. Remove the syrup from the heat, wait about 10 seconds, then gradually pour the hot syrup into the egg mixture, adding it in a steady stream between the whip and the side of the bowl, with the mixer at medium speed. Increase to high speed and whip until cold.

4. Reduce to low speed and gradually mix in the reserved butter. Remove the mixing bowl from the machine. Place one-third of the buttercream in a separate bowl and quickly mix in the melted chocolate to temper. Still working quickly, add this to the remaining buttercream.

NOTE: A more convenient reverse-tempering method is to make a well in the center of the buttercream mixture in the mixer bowl (after taking it off of the machine) and pour the chocolate into the well. Mixing by hand with a whip, gradually, but still working quickly, mix a little of the buttercream from the sides into the chocolate before mixing this into the remaining buttercream.

Vanilla Buttercream (French Method) yield: 4 pounds 8 ounces (2 kg 45 g)

1 pound 8 ounces (680 g) granulated sugar

½ cup (120 ml) water

12 egg yolks (1 cup/240 ml)

2 pounds (910 g) unsalted butter, at room temperature

2 teaspoons (10 ml) vanilla extract

1. Place the sugar and water in a saucepan. Bring to a boil, stirring to dissolve the sugar. Reduce the heat and boil until the sugar syrup reaches 240°F (115°C).

2. While the syrup is boiling, whip the egg yolks until light and fluffy. Lower the speed on the mixer, then carefully pour the hot syrup into the egg yolks in a steady stream between the whip and the side of the bowl. Whip at high speed until the mixture is cool and light in texture.

3. Turn to low speed and gradually add the softened butter, adding it only as fast as it can be absorbed. Mix in the vanilla.

Vanilla Buttercream (Swiss Method) yield: 5 pounds 4 ounces (2 kg 390 g)

This recipe can be used as a starting point to create numerous other flavors. Vanilla buttercream can be flavored with lemon curd, coffee reduction, chestnut puree, hazelnut paste, praline paste, or liqueurs to use as both filling and icing. When used as a filling only, you can also add chopped toasted nuts or candied fruit. When using fresh fruit with a buttercream filling, it is best to arrange thin slices of fruit on top of a layer of buttercream, then cover with additional buttercream, rather than to mix the two together, both to make uniform level layers and because the moisture can cause the buttercream to break.

2 pounds (910 g) unsalted butter, at room
temperature

10 ounces (285 g) soft vegetable margarine
(see Note)

1 recipe Swiss Meringue (page 29)

2 teaspoons (10 ml) vanilla extract

I. Thoroughly combine the butter with the margarine. Reserve at room temperature.

2. When the meringue has been whipped to stiff peaks and is lukewarm, lower the speed on the mixer, add the vanilla, and gradually whip in the butter mixture. The butter mixture must not be too cold when it is added or the buttercream may break.

NOTE: If you replace the margarine with unsalted butter, add 1 teaspoon (5 g) salt to the recipe, whipped with the egg whites. To provide further stability when margarine is omitted, you can slowly blend 10 ounces (285 g) melted white chocolate into the finished buttercream.

Buttercream Decorations

Refer to pages 52 and 53 for information on filling, using, and caring for pastry bags.

BUTTERCREAM ROSES

It is easier than it looks to make a buttercream rose, but it does require practice. You also need a very smooth buttercream that is not too soft; a decorating nail, which looks like a nail with a very large head, about 1½ inches (3.7 cm) in diameter; and a special curved or straight rose-petal tip for the pastry bag. If you tint the buttercream for roses, keep the colors to pale shades.

I. Place the buttercream in the pastry bag with the rose-petal tip. Hold the stem of the decorating nail between the thumb and forefinger of your left hand (if you are right-handed). Hold the pastry bag so that the opening in the tip is perpendicular to the nail, with the wider end of the opening at the bottom.

FIGURE 10-23 **The center of a buttercream rose**

FIGURE 10-24 **After piping the first petal**

FIGURE 10-25 **After piping 3 petals evenly spaced around the center cone**

FIGURE 10-26 **After piping the second row of petals staggered between those in the first row**

2. Start by making the base of the rose. Place the bottom of the tip directly on the nail just outside the center. Angle the top of the tip just a bit toward the center and pipe while turning the nail one complete turn. You should now have a small cone in the center of the nail. Make a second cone on top of the first one, slightly smaller and coming to a point at the top (Figure 10-23).

3. To form the petals, pipe the buttercream in a clockwise direction while turning the nail counterclockwise. Hold the bag in the same way you did to make the cone—wide end at the bottom. For the first row of petals, place the bottom of the tip slightly above the base of the cone and the top of the tip angled out just a little (Figure 10-24). The first row of petals should look fairly closed. Pipe three petals, evenly spaced, around the cone, lifting the tip up and then down in an arc to make the rounded shape (Figure 10-25).

4. Make a second row of three petals in the same way. Start the bottom of these petals just below the first row, angling the top out a little further so the second row of petals opens a bit more than the first. Stagger the petals relative to those in the first row (Figure 10-26).

5. The third row should contain four or five petals. Using the same turning and piping method, start this row a little below the row before, angle the top out a bit more, and again stagger the petals so they fall between those in the second row. You can stop at this point, with three rows, or continue to add more rows to reach the desired size.

6. To remove the rose from the nail, cut it off with a thin knife and set it on the cake or other item. The roses are easier to cut off if you chill them first.

> **CHEF'S TIP**
>
> If you are making up buttercream roses in advance, cut squares of baking paper just slightly larger than the head of the decorating nail, attach a paper to the nail with a little buttercream, and form a rose on the paper square. Lift the paper off the nail and set the paper on a sheet pan in the refrigerator. To use, peel the rose off the paper with the tip of a knife and place on the cake or other item.

BUTTERCREAM LEAVES

Pipe buttercream leaves directly on the cake or pastry after you have set the rose in place, using buttercream tinted to a pale green shade if desired.

1. Use a leaf tip in the pastry bag. Hold the bag at a 45-degree angle with the base of the tip against the cake. Squeeze the bag with the palm of your hand while holding the tip in place for a split second to make the base of the leaf flow out. Gradually decrease the pressure as you pull the tip along, making the leaf narrower and bringing it to the length you want.

2. Stop pressing on the bag and pull the tip away to bring the end of the leaf to a point. If you have difficulty forming a point at the end, the buttercream is not soft enough.

BASKETWEAVE PATTERN

This design can be done with any type of tip, but it looks best made with a flat tip (plain or star). If you do not have one, you can flatten the end of a regular tip yourself.

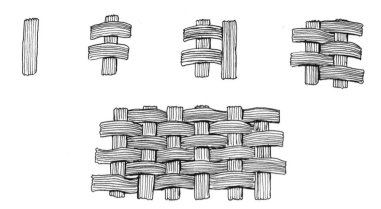

1. Start by piping a vertical line close to one edge of the item you are decorating. (In the case of a round cake, you can start anywhere on the side.)

2. Pipe horizontal lines on top of the vertical line, leaving a space between them the same size as the width of the lines. The length of the horizontal lines should be 3 times the width, and the ends must line up evenly.

3. Pipe a second vertical line, one line-width from the first one, just slightly overlapping the ends of the horizontal lines.

4. Pipe more horizontal lines between the first rows, going over the second vertical line. Repeat alternating vertical and horizontal lines until finished (Figure 10-27).

PEARL AND SHELL PATTERNS

The technique used to make these two patterns is the same. You simply use a plain tip to make the pearl pattern (also known as a *bead pattern*) and a star tip for the shell pattern. The same method is applied for any soft filling.

1. Hold the bag at approximately a 45-degree angle. The tip should just barely touch the surface you plan to pipe on.

2. Squeeze the bag with the palm of your hand, applying enough pressure to make the filling flow out to a wide base for the shell or pearl, then gradually relaxing the pressure as you slowly move the tip along to form the narrow point of the shell or pearl.

FIGURE 10-28 **The finished pearl pattern; piping a shell pattern**

3. Stop squeezing and pull the bag away to finish the design. This design is used individually or as part of a border design. For a border, start the next shell or bead just slightly overlapping the narrow tip of the last one (Figure 10-28).

ROSETTES

This technique applies to forming rosettes using other fillings—whipped cream, ganache, etc.—as well as buttercream.

1. Place a star tip in the pastry bag. Add the filling. Hold the bag almost straight up and down above the place you want the rosette.

2. As you apply pressure, simultaneously move the bag in a tight circle.

3. Stop the pressure, then lift the bag to finish the rosette.

Tuile Decorating Paste

This versatile decorating paste can be formed or made into almost any shape you like. Tuile decorating paste consists of only four ingredients, used in equal weights. Due to the gluten in the flour, the shapes may shrink just a little during baking, but they will do so evenly all around, so provided this is taken into consideration in cases where it will matter, the shrinkage does not cause a problem. The apparent solution to avoiding or reducing shrinkage would be to reduce the gluten strength of the flour, but this is not a viable option because by doing so, the baked pieces would become too fragile. Take care not to overmix the batter once the flour has been incorporated to avoid developing the gluten any more than necessary.

Tuile means "tile" in French. Thin, curved Tuiles (page 315) are said to resemble roof tiles that are made in a half-sphere shape. Tuile decorating paste is also called pâte à cigarette, from its use in making the familiar thin, tube-shaped cigarette cookies (also known as Pirouettes, page 316), which are usually decorated by dipping the ends in chocolate. Finally, it is also known as *tulip paste*, a name that no doubt comes from its well-known application whereby the paste is spread into circles, 7 to 8 inches (17.5 to 20 cm) in diameter, on greased and floured sheet pans, and the flexible, warm cookies are sandwiched between two bowls to form tulip-shaped cups after baking. These are typically used as containers for sorbet or ice cream.

The use of greased and floured sheet pans is yielding rapidly to the more convenient non-stick Silpats (silicone mats), and the classic tuile cookie and tulip-shaped containers are giving way to new, intricate modern designs.

In the recipes in this book that call for tuile decorating paste, you first need to trace and cut out a template from cardboard or plastic to use in creating the desired shape. Some of the templates in this book are specifically designed to coordinate with the presentation for a particular recipe, but many generic shapes may be purchased from suppliers. These templates are available in stainless steel, aluminum, or plastic, and while obviously more durable than a template made from cardboard (the metal templates will last forever), they are relatively expensive, as they are almost always imported from Europe.

FIGURE 10-29 Spreading tuile decorating paste flat and even with a template

FIGURE 10-30 Holding down the opposite side of the template as it is removed to prevent distortion

Tuile paste decorations are easiest to make using Silpats, if you have them. If not, grease the backs of even sheet pans very lightly, coat the pans with flour, then shake off as much flour as possible. Spread the paste onto the Silpats or prepared pans, spreading it flat and even within the template (Figure 10-29). Be careful when you pick up the template from the pan after spreading each one. Hold down the opposite end with your spatula as you lift off the template to avoid disturbing the paste (Figure 10-30). Specific templates and instructions are given in the individual recipes.

Vanilla Tuile Decorating Paste yield: 2 pounds (910 g) or 3¼ cups (780 ml)

8 ounces (225 g) unsalted butter, at room temperature

8 ounces (225 g) powdered sugar, sifted

1 cup (240 ml) egg whites, at room temperature

1 teaspoon (5 ml) vanilla extract

8 ounces (225 g) cake flour, sifted

I. Cream the butter and powdered sugar together. Incorporate the egg whites, a few at a time. Add the vanilla. Add the flour and mix just until incorporated; do not overmix.

2. Store, covered, in the refrigerator. Tuile decorating paste will keep for several weeks. Allow the paste to soften slightly after removing it from the refrigerator, then stir it smooth and into a spreadable consistency before using. If the paste is too soft, the edges of the tuile decorations will be ragged and unprofessional-looking. If this happens, chill the paste briefly.

Chocolate Tuile Decorating Paste yield: 2 pounds (910 g) or 3¼ cups (780 ml)

8 ounces (225 g) unsalted butter, at room temperature

8 ounces (225 g) powdered sugar, sifted

1 cup (240 ml) egg whites, at room temperature

1 teaspoon (5 ml) vanilla extract

6 ounces (170 g) bread flour, sifted

2½ ounces (70 g) unsweetened cocoa powder, sifted

Follow the procedure for Vanilla Tuile Decorating Paste except sift the flour with the cocoa powder in Step 1 before adding it to the paste. Store and use as directed in Step 2.

Dark Modeling Chocolate yield: I pound 8 ounces (680 g)

Yου cannot use coating chocolate here. The cocoa mass and large amount of cocoa butter found in real chocolate are what give modeling chocolate the pliability that is necessary to shape it and the stability to set up after it is formed. As the ratio of cocoa butter to cocoa mass varies in different brands of chocolate, you may have to adjust the recipe. If the paste is too hard, increase the corn syrup. If too soft, increase the chocolate. Ideally, make modeling chocolate two or three days ahead in case it requires more time to set. With some chocolates the cocoa butter can separate, causing the mixture to break. Use the back of a knife to work the cocoa butter back in after the paste has been left to set. Modeling chocolate can be used for many applications: It can replace marzipan or rolled fondant for covering cakes or pastries or for making ribbons; or it can be formed, much like marzipan, into decorations. To make thin sheets, roll it out with a rolling pin or use a dough sheeter. Use powdered sugar to prevent sticking.

> **CHEF'S TIP**
>
> If you are making dark, milk, and white modeling chocolates, or if you already have both white and dark modeling chocolate on hand, simply combine those two to create the desired milk chocolate shade.

14 ounces (400 g) sweet dark chocolate
2 ounces (55 g) unsweetened chocolate

⅔ cup (160 ml) or 8 ounces (225 g) light corn syrup

1. Chop both chocolates into small pieces. Place in a bowl and melt over simmering water while stirring constantly. Do not heat higher than about 110°F (43°C). Remove from the heat.

2. Heat the corn syrup to the same temperature. Pour into the melted chocolate and combine. Let cool. Cover and leave at room temperature for 24 hours.

3. Work the mixture into a smooth paste by forcing it against the table with the back of a knife and/or by using the warmth of your hands. If you are working with a substantial amount, using a manual pasta machine can accelerate this tedious and sometimes difficult step. Store the chocolate paste tightly covered in a cool place. It will keep for several weeks, but as it becomes older it will become harder and will require a little extra effort to soften.

VARIATION
MILK MODELING CHOCOLATE yield: I pound 8 ounces (680 g)

Follow the recipe for Dark Modeling Chocolate, substituting milk chocolate for both the sweet dark and unsweetened chocolates in the recipe.

VARIATION
WHITE MODELING CHOCOLATE yield: I pound I4 ounces (855 g)

1½ ounces (40 g) cocoa butter
1 pound 5 ounces (595 g) white chocolate

5 ounces (140 g) light corn syrup
½ cup (120 ml) simple syrup

Cut the cocoa butter and chocolate into small pieces. Place in a bowl set over simmering water. Heat, stirring constantly, just until melted. Do not overheat. Remove from the heat and stir in the corn syrup and simple syrup. Mix until smooth. Follow Step 3 in the main recipe.

Decorated Cakes

The term decorated cake is generally used to describe a cake that has been filled, iced, and has some type of finishing touch on the icing. Whether or not the cake is decorated attractively can influence your sales to a great degree. The decoration should tempt the customer to try the product and, at the same time, it should suggest the flavor and texture of the cake and filling. The decoration is the final wrapping, or packaging, designed to market your product.

Cutting or Marking Portions

Many of the cakes in this chapter are decorated after being marked or cut into serving pieces. This enables you to decorate each serving identically. If you are displaying the cakes in a pastry case, the servings will still look attractive even if only a few remain. Precut or marked slices can save time for the waitperson or retail clerk, and it is also a good way for the chef to designate the portion size from the standpoint of cost control. If you do choose to cut the pieces rather than simply mark them, you may want to cover the cut sides of each slice with small sheets of paper to prevent the cake from drying out. The slices should then be reassembled for display.

Figures 11-1 to 11-5 explain the techniques used to cut round cakes into equal portions, beginning with the standard division of 12 servings per 10-inch (25-cm) finished cake, to the more complicated uneven-numbered servings and tiny portions for buffets.

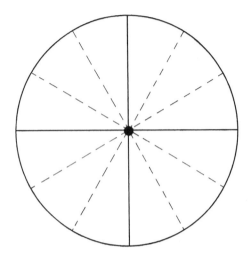

FIGURE 11-1 To cut 12 equal portions from a round cake:

- Cut a straight vertical line down the center to divide the cake in half (shown as a solid line).
- Turn the cake 90° and repeat (also shown as a solid line).
- Cut each quarter into 3 equal pieces (shown as dotted lines).

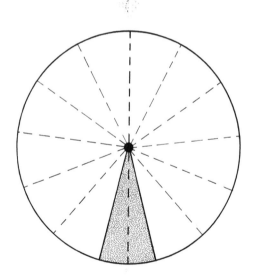

FIGURE 11-2 To cut 13 equal portions from a round cake:

- Lightly mark the top of the cake (do not cut through) with a straight vertical line down the center to divide it in half (shown as a bold dotted line).
- Cut out 1 serving (shown as a shaded area) using an equal amount of cake from either side of the marked line. Repair the surface of this portion to remove the initial mark.
- Turn the cake 180° and cut through the cake on the opposite side following the initial mark (bold dotted line).
- Turn the cake 90° and find the center point between the edge of the cut serving and the cut you just made to divide the cake in half, and slice through at this point to cut the section of the cake in front of you into 2 equal portions.
- Cut each of these portions into 3 equal servings.
- Turn the cake 180° and repeat on the other side.

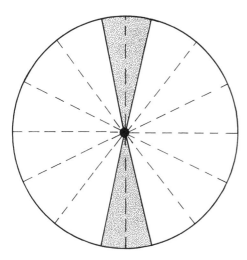

FIGURE 11-3 To cut 14 equal portions from a round cake:

- Lightly mark the top of the cake (do not cut through) with a straight vertical line down the center to divide it in half (shown as a bold dotted line within the shaded cake portions).
- Cut out the shaded serving closest to you using an equal amount of cake from either side of the marked line. Repair the surface of this serving to remove the initial mark.
- Turn the cake 180° and cut out the second shaded serving, again using an equal amount of cake from each side of your initial mark. Repair the surface.
- Turn the cake 90° and find the center point between the edges of the 2 cut servings and slice through at this point to cut the section of the cake in front of you into 2 equal portions.
- Cut each of these portions into 3 equal servings.
- Turn the cake 180° and repeat on the other side.

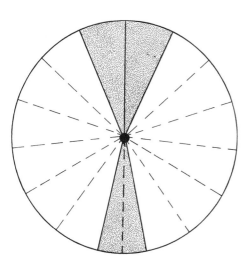

FIGURE 11-4 To cut 15 equal portions from a round cake:

- Lightly mark the top of the cake (do not cut through) with a straight vertical line down the center to divide it in half (shown as a bold dotted line on the lower half and a solid line on the upper half within the shaded cake portions).
- Cut out the shaded serving closest to you using an equal amount of cake from either side of the marked line. Repair the surface of this serving to remove the initial mark.
- Turn the cake 180° and slice through the cake on your initial mark, up to the middle of the cake. Cut out 2 servings, cutting 1 from each side of where you cut the cake in half (the bold solid line).
- Turn the cake 90° and find the center point between the edge of the serving you just cut and the serving cut initially, and slice through at this point to cut the section of the cake in front of you into 2 equal portions.
- Cut each of these portions into 3 equal servings.
- Turn the cake 180° and repeat on the other side.

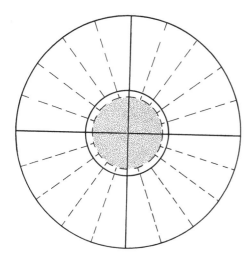

FIGURE 11-5 To cut 22 small portions for buffet service:

- Cut the cake in half from top to bottom (shown as a solid vertical line)
- Place a 2¾-inch (7-cm) round cookie cutter in the center of the cake (shaded area) and press it into the cake no more than ¼ inch (6mm). Leave the cutter in place and using a paring knife, and the cutter as a guide, cut around the inside perimeter of the cookie cutter to create 2 half circle-shaped servings.
- Turn the cake 90° and slice through the cake to divide the section in front of you into 2 equal portions cutting up to the half circle serving (shaded area).
- Turn the cake 180° and repeat on the other side.
- Cut each of the cake quarters into 5 equal servings.

To cut 24 small portions for buffet service:

- Cut the cake into 4 equal quarters (shown as solid vertical and horizontal lines).
- Place a 3-inch (7.5-cm) round cookie cutter in the center of the cake (shown as a solid line larger than the shaded area), and press it into the cake no more than ¼ inch (6 mm). Leave the cutter in place and using a paring knife and the cutter as a guide, cut around the inside perimeter of the cookie cutter to create 4 small wedge-shaped servings.
- Cut each of the cake quarters into 5 equal servings.

Cutting Sponge Layers

Before you can assemble and decorate the cake, it is usually necessary to cut a baked sponge into two or three layers and alternate these layers with the filling. Cutting and moving thin sponge layers is often a more challenging skill for students to master than some of the decorating procedures. Use a serrated knife to slice the layers and hold the blade of the knife parallel to the tabletop. Place your left hand flat on top of the cake (if you are right-handed) and turn the cake counterclockwise as you cut. Do not move the knife from side to side; hold it level and move it away and toward you as you turn the cake into the knife's path. Start by cutting the skin off the top of the cake and cutting the top flat at the same time if necessary. Then cut the desired number of layers, starting from the top and removing each layer before cutting the next. Assuming the sponge was made correctly, you should be able to move standard layers (10 x 2 inches/25 x 5 cm) with your hand or by lifting the cake with the knife used for slicing (Figure 11-6). However, with a more fragile sponge, or when working with a half- or full sheet of sponge, it is easier if you use a sheet of cardboard. After completing the cut for the first layer, leave the layer in place on the cake. Carefully slide a cardboard cake round into the cut, easing it in by wiggling it up and down a bit instead of just pushing it into the cut, which can break the cake, then simply pick up the cardboard to move the layer to the side. Repeat to cut the remaining layers. It becomes more difficult to cut thin, even layers as the size of the sponge increases in circumference, but use the same technique for all sizes.

When you are ready to stack the layers, pick up the cardboard and hold the layer just above the cake where you want to place it. Slide the layer off the cardboard and onto the cake, guiding it into place with your free hand as you pull the cardboard away from the bottom.

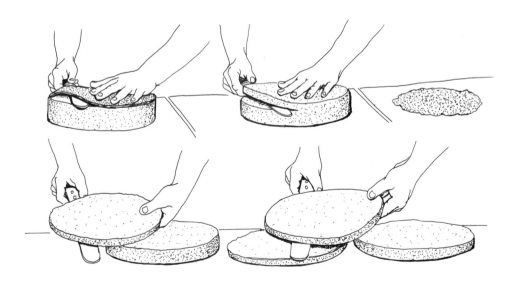

FIGURE 11-6 TOP: Cutting the skin from the top of a sponge cake and cutting the top level at the same time if necessary; cutting the first cake layer of the sponge cake. BOTTOM: Using the slicing knife to transfer the cut layers of sponge

Banana Layer Cake with Maple–Cream Cheese Frosting and Pecans

yield: 1 cake, 10 inches (25 cm) in diameter

This cake is a variation that starts with the Banana Bread quick bread recipe and dresses it up with crisp oven-dried banana chips, tangy rich cream cheese frosting infused with maple syrup, and crunchy toasted pecans. While the addition of fruits and vegetables to a cake batter generally helps retain moisture and makes the cakes suitable for longer storage, banana layer cake must be served the same day it is assembled or the sliced bananas between the layers will oxidize and turn dark.

½ recipe Banana Bread batter (page 422)

1 medium banana, firm

Simple syrup

½ cup (120 ml) Plain Cake Syrup (page 31) *or* orange juice

Maple–Cream Cheese Frosting (recipe follows)

2 medium bananas, ripe

4 ounces (115 g) lightly toasted pecan halves

1. Line the bottom of a cake pan, 10 inches (25 cm) in diameter, with baking paper. Pour the banana bread batter in the pan and spread it level on top. Bake at 375°F (190°C) for approximately 35 minutes or until baked through. Unmold by inverting on a cake rack and removing the pan.

2. Reduce the oven temperature to 175°F (80°C). Peel the firm banana and cut it diagonally into very thin slices. Dip each piece into hot simple syrup and arrange the pieces on a Silpat. Place in the oven and dry until crisp, turning the pieces from time to time to keep them from becoming brown (see Chef's Tip). Reserve the dried pieces at room temperature.

3. Cut the crust from the top of the banana cake, slicing it level at the same time. Slice the cake horizontally into 2 layers. Brush cake syrup or orange juice over the bottom layer. Spread one-quarter of the cream cheese frosting on top.

4. Remove the skin from the 2 ripe bananas and cut each into 4 pieces lengthwise. Arrange the banana quarters on top of the filling, covering the entire surface in an even layer. Spread one-third of the remaining frosting over the bananas. Top with the remaining cake layer. Brush cake syrup or orange juice over the top layer. Use the remaining cream cheese frosting to ice the top and sides of the cake.

5. Reserve 1 pecan half for each serving of cake. Coarsely chop the remaining nuts. Cover the sides of the cake with the chopped nuts (see Figure 11-12, page 520). Use a palette knife to press the nuts against the side of the cake for an even finish. Cut or mark the cake into the desired number of servings and decorate the top of each piece with a pecan half and some of the dried banana chips.

CHEF'S TIP

To test the banana chips to see if they are done (dried enough to remain crisp), take one out and place it on a chilled or frozen plate. It will become crisp immediately if it has baked long enough.

MAPLE–CREAM CHEESE FROSTING yield: 1 pound (455 g)

¾ cup (180 ml) heavy cream

6 ounces (170 g) cream cheese, at room temperature

2 ounces (55 g) unsalted butter, at room temperature

¼ cup (60 ml) pure maple syrup

1. Whip the heavy cream until stiff peaks form. Reserve.

2. Soften the cream cheese by stirring with the paddle attachment at low speed; do not incorporate air. Mix in the butter, then gradually incorporate the maple syrup, continuing to mix until smooth and spreadable.

3. Fold in the whipped cream. Store, covered, in the refrigerator no longer than 1 day. Bring to room temperature and mix until soft before using.

Black Forest Cake yield: 2 cakes, 10 inches (25 cm) in diameter

This is one of the Western World's most popular cakes, and for good reason. Schwartzwalder Kirsch Torte is as delicious as the Black Forest (located in the Swabia region of Germany) is beautiful. If you do not find one of these cakes in any pastry shop there (or anywhere in Germany, for that matter), it's a good bet that they have just run out. Each shop seems to make its own version; some add rum to the cherry filling, others use a light sponge cake instead of chocolate, and still others use chocolate whipped cream.

The four basic building blocks of a Black Forest cake are chocolate, cherries, kirsch liqueur or kirschwasser, and whipped cream. Sour cherries, such as Montmorency or Morello, are always used in the classic rendition. Whichever variety you use, do not skimp on the cherries. This exquisite cake should be moist and bursting with cherry flavor. I think you will also enjoy my own hybrid, the Meringue Black Forest Cake (page 526).

Butter and Flour Mixture (page 7) or pan spray

1 recipe Chocolate Sponge Cake batter (page 438)

¾ cup (180 ml) kirschwasser

½ cup (120 ml) simple syrup

1 quart (960 ml) heavy cream

Black Forest Cherry Filling (recipe follows)

2 cups (480 ml) heavy cream

1 tablespoon (15 g) granulated sugar

Dark Chocolate Squares (page 460)

Dark chocolate shavings

Powdered sugar

Fresh cherries (see Note)

1. Grease and flour 2 cake pans, 10 inches (25 cm) in diameter. Divide the chocolate sponge cake batter between the pans. Bake at 400°F (205°C) for approximately 12 minutes. Set aside to cool.

2. Combine the kirschwasser and simple syrup. Reserve.

3. Whip 1 quart (960 ml) heavy cream with about one-third of the kirschwasser mixture to stiff peaks. Reserve in the refrigerator.

4. Unmold the cooled sponge cakes and cut them into 3 layers each. Place the 2 bottom layers on your work surface, saving the 2 best sponges for the tops, if there seems to be any difference. Brush the bottom sponge layers with some of the remaining kirschwasser mixture.

5. Place a portion of the reserved whipped cream in a pastry bag with a large, plain tip. Pipe

2 concentric circles of cream on each of the bottom cake layers, placing the first ring next to the perimeter of each sponge and the second ring about 2 inches (5 cm) closer to the center. Finish by piping a 1-inch (2.5-cm) dot of cream in the center of each sponge. You should now have 2 rings of cake exposed on each layer. Using one-quarter of the cherry filling for each layer, spoon it between the rings of cream. Place the middle sponge layers on top and press lightly to make the tops level. Brush the kirschwasser mixture over the sponges. Repeat the same pattern of piping the cream rings and placing the cherry filling between them, using up the remaining cream mixture and filling. Place the third layers of sponge on top and again press gently to make sure they adhere and to make the tops level. Brush the remaining kirschwasser mixture over the sponges.

6. If you plan to precut the cakes into serving pieces, you should cover them at this point and place them in the freezer until they are frozen solid. This will enable you to cut cleanly through the cream and the cherries without dragging one into the other.

7. Remove the cakes from the freezer.

8. Whip the remaining heavy cream with the granulated sugar to stiff peaks. Spread enough of the cream over the top and sides of the cakes to cover the sponge.

9. When the cakes have thawed halfway (if the inside feels too hard, wait a little longer), cut them into the desired number of pieces. Put the remaining whipped cream in a pastry bag with a No. 6 (12-mm) star tip and pipe a rosette at the edge of each slice. Place a chocolate square on the side of each slice. Sprinkle the shaved chocolate over the top of the cake, inside the piped rosettes. Sift powdered sugar lightly over the shavings. Place a cherry on each whipped cream rosette. Be certain that the cake is fully thawed before serving.

NOTE: If fresh cherries are not available, substitute a chocolate figurine for decoration or leave the rosettes plain rather than using canned cherries—or, worse yet, the infamous maraschino.

BLACK FOREST CHERRY FILLING yield: 6 cups (1 L 440 ml)

2 pounds (910 g) well-drained canned sour cherries (see Note)

½ cup (120 ml) kirschwasser

2¼ cups (540 ml) juice from canned cherries

3 ounces (85 g) cornstarch

¼ cup (60 ml) water

2 tablespoons (18 g) pectin powder

10 ounces (285 g) granulated sugar

1 to 2 drops red food coloring

1. Macerate the cherries in the kirschwasser for at least 2 hours or, preferably, overnight.

2. Strain the kirschwasser from the cherries and add enough of the cherry juice to the kirschwasser to make 2½ cups (600 ml) liquid. Dissolve the cornstarch in the water. Mix the pectin powder into the granulated sugar. Add to the cherry liquid along with the red color and cornstarch-water mixture.

3. Bring to a boil and cook for a few seconds to eliminate the cornstarch flavor.

4. Remove from the heat and carefully stir in the cherries without breaking them. Cool completely before using the filling.

NOTE: If you must substitute sweet canned cherries, cut them in half before macerating (do not chop) and decrease the sugar in the recipe to 3 ounces (85 g).

Boston Cream Pie yield: 2 cakes, 10 inches (25 cm) in diameter

Boston cream pie is, of course, not a pie at all, but a cake disguised by a misnomer. The first reference to this dessert dates back to 1855, when a New York newspaper published a recipe for a "pudding pie cake." That recipe was similar to Boston cream pie as we know it, but it had a powdered sugar topping. A year later, Harvey D. Parker opened his Parker House Restaurant in Boston (this restaurant was also the birthplace of the famous Parker House rolls) and featured a version of the pudding pie cake on his menu. Parker's cake was topped with a chocolate glaze. How the cake became known as Boston cream pie is not entirely clear, but it seems likely that the name stems from the original title combined with the reference to Boston as the place where the cake became well known.

It was common for New England colonists to bake cakes in pie tins, as they were more likely to have a baking pan for a pie than for a cake, if they did not have both.

2 Boston Cream Pie Cake Bases (recipe follows)	¼ recipe or 1 pound 8 ounces (680 g) Pastry Cream (page 845; see Note)
Rum Syrup (recipe follows)	½ recipe Chocolate Glaze (page 465)
1 cup (240 ml) heavy cream	Unsweetened cocoa powder
2 tablespoons (30 ml) dark rum	Powdered sugar

1. Cut the skin and as much of the top as necessary off of the cake bases to make the tops level. Invert so that the wider end of each cake becomes the bottom and cut them into 2 layers each.

2. Brush rum syrup on both bottom layers, paying special attention to the edges.

3. Whip the heavy cream to stiff peaks.

4. Stir the rum into the pastry cream. Stir about ½ cup (120 ml) pastry cream mixture into the whipped cream. Divide the remainder evenly between the bottom layers and spread it out evenly. Place the top cake layers on the custard. Press down lightly to secure and to force the custard to the edges of the cake. Brush the remaining rum syrup over the top of the cake layers. Divide the whipped cream mixture between the cakes and spread it over the tops and sides.

5. Place the cakes on a cake rack set over a clean sheet pan. Pour half of the chocolate glaze on top of one cake (you may have to reheat the glaze to get it to a spreadable consistency). Use a spatula to carefully push some of the glaze from the top to the edges, letting it run down to cover the sides of the cake as well. Repeat the procedure with the second cake and the remaining glaze. Transfer the cakes to cardboard cake circles. Refrigerate until the glaze is set, then cut the cakes into the desired number of servings, using a knife dipped in hot water.

6. Presentation: Lightly sift cocoa powder over the base of a dessert plate, using a small, fine mesh strainer. Lightly sift powdered sugar on top of the cocoa powder. Place a slice of cake on top of the design.

NOTE: Replace the milk with half-and-half when preparing the pastry cream.

BOSTON CREAM PIE CAKE BASE yield: 2 cakes, 10 inches (25 cm) in diameter

Butter and Flour Mixture (page 7) or pan spray

4 egg whites (½ cup/120 ml)

1¼ cups (300 ml) half-and-half, at room temperature

1 pound (455 g) cake flour

1 pound (455 g) granulated sugar

4 teaspoons (16 g) baking powder

½ teaspoon (2.5 g) salt

2 teaspoons (10 ml) vanilla extract

12 ounces (340 g) melted unsalted butter

1 whole egg

1. Brush the butter and flour mixture over the inside of 2 pie pans, 10 inches (25 cm) in diameter (or use pan spray). Reserve.

2. Stir together the egg whites and one-third of the half-and-half. Reserve.

3. Sift together the cake flour, granulated sugar, baking powder, and salt. Add the vanilla, melted butter, the remaining half-and-half, and the whole egg. Beat at high speed for a few minutes. Gradually stir in the reserved egg white mixture and mix until combined. Divide between the prepared pie pans.

4. Bake at 350°F (175°C) for approximately 40 minutes or until the center springs back when you press the cakes lightly with your finger. Invert on a sheet pan lined with baking paper. Let cool.

RUM SYRUP yield: ¾ cup (180 ml)

¼ cup (60 ml) dark rum

¼ cup (60 ml) water

¼ cup (60 ml) simple syrup

1. Combine all ingredients.

2. Use as directed.

Carrot Layer Cake with Cream Cheese Filling

yield: 2 cakes, 10 inches (25 cm) in diameter

The carrot sponge recipe is very adaptable. It can be baked in a tube pan and served plain as a coffee cake; it makes great muffins; and it can also be baked in sheets, cut into small squares, and topped with a rosette of cream cheese filling to use as a simple buffet item or snack cake. When the sponges are made into decorated layer cakes, it is necessary to level the tops before assembling. Baking powder and baking soda stop working at approximately 170°F (77°C); the batter next to the side of the pan will reach that temperature first (in part due to the hot metal), so a heavy sponge like this one always bakes higher in the middle. This will not occur to the same extent when making sheets, as they are not as thick and the batter responds more evenly. I'm sure you will have plenty of help getting rid of the scraps!

The following is an elegant but also time-consuming finish. For a quick and easy alternative, follow the instructions through Step 3 only, icing the tops and sides of the cakes with cream cheese filling instead of buttercream.

Carrot Sponges (recipe follows)

Cream Cheese Filling (recipe follows)

8 ounces (225 g) Vanilla Buttercream (Swiss Method) (page 477)

Hazelnuts, toasted and finely crushed

10 ounces (285 g) Marzipan (page 21), untinted

Powdered sugar

Dark coating chocolate, melted

Marzipan Carrots (recipe follows)

1. Cut the tops off the carrot sponges to make them level. Cut both sponges in half to make 2 layers each.

2. Divide the cream cheese filling between the bottom sponge layers; spread it out evenly. Place the top layers on the filling.

3. Ice the tops and sides of the cakes with a thin layer of vanilla buttercream. Cover the sides of the cakes with the crushed hazelnuts (see Figure 11-12, page 520).

4. Roll out the marzipan, using powdered sugar to prevent it from sticking, to ⅛ inch (3 mm) thick. Cut out 2 circles the same size as the tops of the cakes. Place them on the cakes.

5. Place a cardboard circle on each cake and invert the cakes onto the cardboards. Place in the refrigerator upside down to flatten the tops and firm the filling. Do not leave the cakes like this for more than 2 hours or the moist air will make the marzipan wet.

6. Turn the cakes right-side up and cut them into the desired number of serving pieces. Sift powdered sugar very lightly over the cakes. Pipe a dime-sized dot of melted coating chocolate on each slice, ½ inch (1.2 cm) away from the edge. Before the chocolate hardens, place a marzipan carrot on top.

CARROT SPONGES yield: 2 cakes, 10 × 2 inches (25 × 5 cm)

Butter and Flour Mixture (page 7) or pan spray

8 eggs

1½ cups (360 ml) vegetable oil

1 pound 12 ounces (795 g) granulated sugar

1 teaspoon (5 g) salt

1 pound 2 ounces (510 g) bread flour

3 tablespoons (15 g) ground cinnamon

1½ teaspoons (6 g) baking soda

½ teaspoon (2 g) baking powder

2 pounds (910 g) peeled carrots, shredded or grated finely

5 ounces (140 g) walnuts, chopped

1. Brush the butter and flour mixture over the insides of 2 cake pans, 10 inches (25 cm) in diameter, or coat them with pan spray. Reserve.

2. Whip the eggs at high speed to a light and frothy consistency. Reduce the mixer speed to medium and gradually add the oil. Turn the mixer speed to low and mix in the sugar and salt.

3. Sift together the flour, cinnamon, baking soda, and baking powder. Add to the egg mixture. Fold in the carrots and walnuts, evenly distributing them in the batter.

4. Divide the batter between the prepared pans.

5. Bake at 375°F (190°C) for about 50 minutes or until the cakes spring back when pressed lightly in the center.

CREAM CHEESE FILLING yield: 1 pound 10 ounces (740 g)

14 ounces (400 g) cream cheese, at room temperature

4 ounces (115 g) unsalted butter, at room temperature

1 teaspoon (5 ml) vanilla extract

8 ounces (225 g) powdered sugar, sifted

Soften the cream cheese, using the paddle attachment of an electric mixer, without beating in any air. Add the butter gradually, blending until the mixture is smooth. Add the vanilla and powdered sugar. Mix until smooth and spreadable, but do not overmix.

MARZIPAN CARROTS yield: 24 carrot decorations

5 ounces (140 g) Marzipan (page 21), untinted   Green, red, and yellow food coloring

1. Color 1 ounce (30 g) marzipan green. Cover and reserve. Use red and yellow food coloring to tint the remainder orange.

2. Divide the orange marzipan into 2 equal pieces. Roll each one into a 9-inch (22.5-cm) rope. Place the ropes next to each other.

3. Roll the green marzipan into a rope the same length as the orange ropes and place it next to them. Cut through all 3 ropes together, cutting each one into 12 equal pieces. Cut each of the green pieces in half. You should now have 24 orange pieces and 24 smaller green pieces, 1 orange and 1 green for each carrot. Keep the pieces covered with plastic to prevent them from drying out.

4. Roll the orange pieces into round balls between your palms. Roll the balls into cone shapes, about 1 inch (2.5 cm) long, by rolling them back and forth against the table.

5. Mark the cones crosswise with the back of a knife to make them look ringed like a carrot. Starting at the wide end, turn them slowly and make random marks, crosswise, all around. Make a small round hole in the wide end of each carrot, using a marzipan modeling tool or the end of an instant-read thermometer.

6. One at a time, roll each of the small green pieces into a ½-inch (1.2-cm) string, tapered on both ends. Insert one end of the green stem into the hole in each carrot. Cut and fan the other end of each one to resemble a carrot top (Figure 11-7).

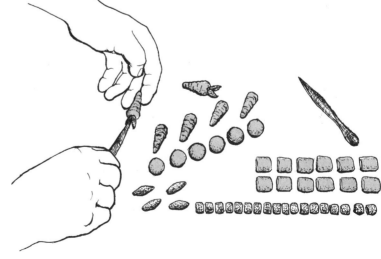

FIGURE 11-7 Sequence of steps in making marzipan carrot decorations

About Cheesecake

Cheesecakes have been made in Europe and other places around the world since the fifteenth century. They are created in many variations, from light and fluffy to dense and rich. Virtually any region that has a dairy industry will produce some version of cheesecake, using the local product. In the United States, the main ingredient is usually cream cheese, but ricotta and cottage cheese are used, in some cases, to produce a lighter-style or lower-fat alternative. Ricotta cheesecakes are very popular in Italy, and Germany uses a soft, fresh cheese called *quark* in their rendition. In parts of Sweden (especially so where I grew up in Småland), in addition to using quark, they make cheesecakes with milk that has been coagulated with a small amount of rennet. Actually, these are more of a tart. They are very special and always served with—you guessed it—lingonberries.

The cheesecake recipe that I call West Coast Cheesecake, for lack of a better name, is the type that many people are probably most familiar with. Here, the cream cheese is thickened with eggs (and heat) and topped with a sweetened sour cream mixture containing the desired flavoring. The cakes are baked again, just long enough to set the sour cream. In the case of a fresh fruit topping, the sour cream is sweetened but not flavored, and the fruit is added after the final baking.

The problem I see all too often when it comes to beginners making cheesecake is lumps in varying degrees of seriousness. Lumps occur when the eggs are added to the cream cheese mixture too fast, when the bottom of the mixing bowl is not scraped properly, or both. The problem is often exaggerated by using cream cheese straight out of the refrigerator (which can be done, but you must be even more careful). Unless there are only a few small lumps, the batter must be made smooth before it is poured into the forms. The best way to accomplish this is to use a food processor. You can't avoid incorporating more air than is desirable, but this is the lesser of the two evils.

Cheesecake is considered a plain, country-style dessert in Europe, but it can (as you will see by some of the recipes in this book) be presented in a very elegant manner. Each of the following cheesecakes has a graham cracker crust. Because some graham crackers contain more moisture than others, the measurement given for the melted butter in the crust is always approximate. Adjust the amount of butter you add accordingly so that the crumbs are moist enough to hold together well when the crust is pressed into place.

The cheesecake recipes given here were developed using block-style cream cheese, which contains gum and stabilizing agents. Substituting the softer product, usually sold in a log-shape and labeled *natural cream cheese*, will not produce a good result.

Cheesecake with Caramelized Apples

yield: 2 cakes, 10 inches (25 cm) in diameter, or 4 cakes, 7 inches (17.5 cm) in diameter

It seems entirely appropriate that this recipe that incorporates the method used in a traditional New York–style cheesecake should contain apples, as the city of New York is known as the Big Apple. This cake is so moist it does not require any sauce or garnish, but if you want to dress up the plate a little, Cranberry Coulis (page 821) would be an excellent choice.

1 pound 6 ounces (625 g) Graham Cracker Crumbs (page 20)	1 pound (455 g) cream cheese, at room temperature
8 ounces (225 g) melted unsalted butter, approximately	8 ounces (225 g) granulated sugar
4 ounces (115 g) walnuts, chopped fine	4 eggs, at room temperature
5 pounds (2 kg 275 g) Red Delicious apples (approximately 14 medium)	1 pound (455 g) sour cream
	1 tablespoon (15 ml) vanilla extract
8 ounces (225 g) unsalted butter, cut into chunks	1 pound 8 ounces (680 g) sour cream
12 ounces (340 g) granulated sugar	4 ounces (115 g) granulated sugar
1¼ cups (300 ml) heavy cream, at room temperature	4 ounces (115 g) dried cranberries, cut into small pieces
2 lemons	Marzipan Apples (recipe follows)

1. Combine the graham cracker crumbs and the melted butter. Mix in the walnuts and additional melted butter if necessary for the mixture to hold together. Divide the crumb mixture between 2 springform pans, 10 inches (25 cm) in diameter, or 4 springform pans, 7 inches (17.5 cm) in diameter. Press evenly over the bottoms and halfway up the sides of the pans, using your hands. Cut the top edge of the crumbs even. Reserve.

2. Peel and core the apples. Slice them into ¼-inch (6-mm) wedges.

3. Place the butter chunks and 12 ounces (340 g) granulated sugar in a large skillet over medium heat. Stir together and bring to a rapid boil. Add the apple wedges and cook, turning the apples frequently so that they cook evenly. (If you don't have a large enough skillet, you may need to start cooking in 2 batches. Once the apples start to soften and reduce in size, you can combine them.) When the liquid in the skillet has reduced and caramelized to light brown and the apples are soft but not mushy, remove the skillet from the heat. Add the room-temperature cream, stirring it in carefully so that it does not splatter. Set the apple mixture aside to cool.

4. Finely grate the zest from the lemons. Juice the lemons and combine the juice and zest.

5. Mix the cream cheese and 8 ounces (225 g) granulated sugar on low speed, using the paddle, just until smooth. Beat in the eggs, 1 at a time. Mix in 1 pound (455 g) sour cream, the lemon juice and zest, and the vanilla. Scrape the sides and bottom of the bowl frequently while mixing to avoid lumps.

6. Divide the apple mixture among the prepared pans in an even layer on top of the crumbs. Divide the cream cheese mixture among the pans on top of the apples. Spread the tops level.

7. Bake at 350°F (175°C) for about 35 minutes (a bit less for the smaller cakes) or until the filling is set. Let cool for at least 10 minutes.

8. Mix together the remaining 1 pound 8 ounces (680 g) sour cream and 4 ounces (115 g) granulated sugar. Divide the mixture evenly among the cooled cakes and spread the tops level. Sprinkle the dried cranberries on top of the sour cream.

9. Bake the cakes at 375°F (190°C) for 8 minutes (5 minutes for the small version). Let the cheesecakes cool for at least 6 hours or, preferably, refrigerate overnight.

10. Run a knife around the inside perimeter of the cakes where the cake touches the pan; do not disturb the crust. Release the springforms and remove the cakes. Cut into the desired number of servings and decorate each slice with a marzipan apple.

MARZIPAN APPLES yield: 24 decorations

If you make the apples more than a few days before they will be eaten, you can keep the outside of the marzipan from drying out by coating the apples lightly with hot, melted cocoa butter, using just the tip of a brush. This should be done after applying the red color. The cocoa butter also gives the marzipan a nice satin shine, so it always a good idea to apply it to marzipan decorations.

4 ounces (115 g) Marzipan (page 21), tinted pale green
Powdered sugar

24 whole cloves
Red food coloring

1. Take the usual precautions for working with marzipan by making certain that your hands and your work space are clean. Work the marzipan in your hands until it is soft and pliable. Roll it into a 12-inch (30-cm) rope, using powdered sugar if necessary to prevent it from sticking to your work surface. Cut the rope into 24 pieces, ½ inch (1.2 cm) long.

2. Roll each piece between your palms first into a round ball and then very slightly oblong. Use a marzipan tool to make a small dimple in each end.

3. Make a hole on top of each apple and carefully, without altering the shape, insert the clove end of a whole clove so only the stem is protruding.

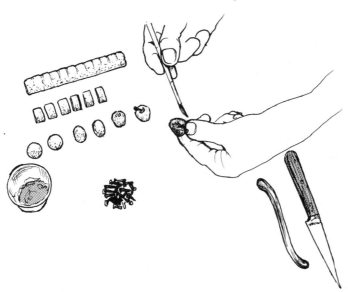

4. Put a tiny amount of red food coloring (1 drop) on a piece of paper and apply the color to the very tip of a coarse, flat brush. Holding each apple by the stem, streak the color from top to bottom (Figure 11-8).

FIGURE 11-8 Sequence of steps in making marzipan apple decorations

Chèvre Cheesecake with Vanilla Bean Topping

yield: 1 cake, 9 inches (22.5 cm) in diameter, or 12 servings for plated presentation (Photos 35 and 43)

Both this Chèvre Cheesecake and the Mascarpone Cheesecake on page 504 started out as individual plated desserts in which the cheesecakes were made in small ring forms. Naturally, one large cake takes less time to make than many small cakes and, although the results may not be as eye-catching, the unusual and delicious flavors are still there when you are pressed for time. The suggested plate presentation can be prepared any time of the year with orange slices and orange syrup. During the holiday season, you may want to substitute persimmon (the fuyu variation only); this version is shown in the color photo. If using persimmons, follow the same instructions for cutting out the rounds and serve the cake with Persimmon Sauce (page 828) and a sprinkling of pomegranate seeds. The method of serving the cake wedge standing on end can succeed only with a very dense or heavy cake such as a cheesecake.

This recipe can also be prepared in springform pans, 6 x 3 inches (15 x 7.5 cm) or 7 x 3 inches (17.5 x 7.5 cm). In this case, you may want to omit the graham cracker crumbs on the sides of the pans to be sure you have a thick enough layer on the bottom or increase the amount of crumbs and melted butter. To make a cake 10 inches (25 cm) in diameter, increase the sour cream in the topping to 1 pound 8 ounces (680 g) and increase the sugar to 4 ounces (115 g).

8 ounces (225 g) Graham Cracker Crumbs (page 20)

3 ounces (85 g) melted unsalted butter

Chèvre Cheesecake Batter (recipe follows)

1 vanilla bean

3 ounces (85 g) granulated sugar

1 pound (455 g) sour cream

1 teaspoon (5 ml) vanilla extract

INGREDIENTS FOR OPTIONAL PLATE PRESENTATION

1 firm orange, preferably navel, *or* 2 Fuyu persimmons

Pectin Glaze (page 30)

½ recipe Orange–Vanilla Bean Decorating Syrup (page 834)

Seasonal fruit

12 Rounded Tuile Leaves (recipe follows)

Powdered sugar

1. Prepare a springform pan, 9 x 3 inches (22.5 x 7.5 cm), by tightly covering the outside bottom and sides with a double layer of aluminum foil (see Note 1).

2. Combine the graham cracker crumbs with the melted butter. Press the crust firmly and evenly over the bottom and one-third of the way up the sides of the pan, using your hands. Use the rounded side of a bowl scraper to cut the top edge of the crumbs straight and even.

3. Pour the chèvre cheesecake batter into the pan and smooth the top to make it even. Set the pan in a hotel pan and add hot water around it to reach about halfway up the sides of the springform.

4. Bake at 325°F (163°C) for approximately 50 minutes (slightly less, if making the smaller version described in the introduction) or until the filling is set.

5. Remove the pan from the water bath and peel off the foil. Let the cake cool for 10 to 15 minutes (see Note 2).

6. Split the vanilla bean lengthwise and scrape out the seeds. Reserve the pod halves for another use. Rub the vanilla bean seeds into the granulated sugar to distribute them evenly and avoid having any clumps of the tiny seeds. Mix the sugar into the sour cream along with the vanilla extract. Pour the mixture over the cooled cheesecake and spread it out evenly.

7. Bake at 375°F (190°C) for 8 minutes to set the sour cream (5 minutes for the smaller cakes). The sour cream will still appear to be liquid, but it will set as it cools. Allow the cake to cool at room temperature, then refrigerate for at least 4 hours or, preferably, overnight before serving.

FOR THE OPTIONAL PLATE PRESENTATION

8. Cut the chilled cheesecake into 12 portions. Using a sharp knife, slice the orange cross-wise into thin slices. Using a 1½-inch (3.7-cm) plain round cookie cutter, cut out 12 rounds. Place 1 orange round at the wide end of each slice of cheesecake. Brush pectin glaze over the fruit. Place the orange decorating syrup in a piping bottle and reserve until time of service.

9. Presentation: Stand a wedge of cheesecake on end in the center of a dessert plate. Pipe orange decorating syrup in random dots or in a continuous irregular pattern around the cake. Decorate with seasonal fruit, arranging it on the plate around the syrup. Gently attach a tuile leaf to the top of the cake slice. Stand a vanilla bean pod against the side (see Chef's Tip). Sift powdered sugar lightly over the dessert and the plate. Serve immediately.

NOTE 1: Instead of covering the outside of the springform with foil, you can place the 9-inch (22.5-cm) springform inside a regular 10-inch (25-cm) cake pan, then set this assembly in the hotel pan. The foil or the double-panning are necessary to prevent water from seeping into the springform from the water bath.

NOTE 2: You can add the sour cream topping right away without waiting for the cake to cool, provided you pour it on gently and carefully to avoid making a hole in the very soft cake.

CHEVRE CHEESECAKE BATTER yield: enough for 1 cake, 9 inches (22.5 cm) in diameter

1 pound 2 ounces (510 g) mild, unripened
    goat's milk cheese, at room temperature

6 ounces (170 g) mascarpone cheese

6 ounces (170 g) granulated sugar

⅓ cup (80 ml) heavy cream

5 eggs, at room temperature

1. Cream the goat's-milk cheese, mascarpone cheese, and the sugar together.

2. Combine the cream and the eggs and beat for a few seconds to blend. Gradually add the egg mixture to the cheese mixture, blending until smooth and scraping down the sides of the bowl a few times to make sure that there are no lumps.

CHEF'S TIP
Since vanilla beans are an expensive commodity, using a whole fresh bean as part of the decoration for one serving might not always be practical. Many recipes in this text call for splitting the vanilla bean pod and scraping out the seeds, saving the pod halves for another use. Conversely, you can scrape out and save the seeds. They will always come in handy.

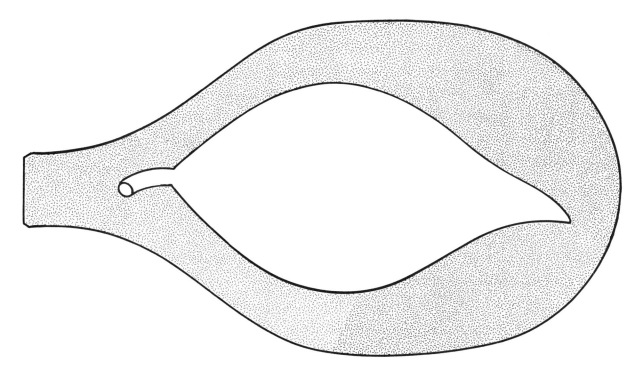

FIGURE 11-9 The template used to create rounded tuile leaves

ROUNDED TUILE LEAVES yield: approximately 35 decorations

> ¼ recipe or 8 ounces Vanilla Tuile Decorating
> Paste (page 482)

I. Trace the template shown in Figure 11-9. Cut it out of ¹⁄₁₆-inch (2-mm) sturdy cardboard such as the type used for cake boxes. The template shown is the correct size for use in this recipe. If you do not have Silpats, grease the backs of flat, even sheet pans, coat with flour, then shake off as much flour as possible.

2. Spread the tuile paste flat and even within the template on a Silpat or on one of the prepared sheet pans (see Figures 10-29 and 10-30, page 482). If you are going to curve the leaves while they are still warm, do not place more than 8 to 10 per pan or you will not have time to shape them before they become crisp.

3. Bake at 400°F (205°C) until you see a few brown spots on the cookies. You can leave them to cool flat on the pan or Silpat or immediately drape each cookie over a wide, round object about 6 inches (15 cm) in diameter (such as a No. 10 can) to give them a curved shape; a rolling pin is too narrow and will produce too tight a curve. As a third alternative, you can shape the leaves with your hands, making each one unique, just as in nature.

Individual Lingonberry-Topped Cheesecakes

yield: 16 servings, 5 ounces (150 ml) each (Photo 36)

While you will probably find that these pretty, individual-size cheesecakes take a bit longer to make than a traditional 10-inch (25-cm) cake, due to their small size they bake, cool, and are ready to serve much more quickly, so this is definitely the way to go if you need to prepare cheesecake on short notice. They can easily be completed from homemade graham cracker crumbs through plating in less than 3 hours.

For good reason, lingonberries are known in my native country as "the red gold of the forest." Although they are cultivated, to some extent, the majority are a product of nature growing wild all over Sweden, especially in the north. By the time they reach the United States, lingonberries demand a fairly steep price, so if they are too expensive or simply not available, try this variation. Bake the sour cream topping plain, let cool, then top with 5 thin strawberry slices, cut lengthwise and arranged in a fan shape with the points toward the center. You will need 1 medium-size attractive strawberry per serving. Glaze the fruit with pectin or apricot glaze and serve with strawberry sauce.

4 ounces (115 g) melted unsalted butter, approximately

8 ounces (225 g) Graham Cracker Crumbs (page 20)

2 pounds (910 g) cream cheese, at room temperature

4 eggs, at room temperature

10 ounces (285 g) granulated sugar

1 pound 14 ounces (855 g) sour cream

4 ounces (115 g) granulated sugar

1 cup (240 ml) lingonberries, pureed and strained (see Note)

Water

Sour Cream Mixture for Piping (page 832)

1. Cut out pieces of baking paper to line the forms, using Figure 11-10 as a guide. The drawing as shown is the correct size for typical soufflé ramekins, 3¼ inches (8.1 cm) in diameter. If this size form is not available, coffee cups close to the same size work well. Adjust the size of the cutout accordingly. Trace the drawing, then cut 16 shapes out of baking paper (see Chef's Tip). The flaps should extend about ¾ inch (2 cm) above the form on both sides so you can hold them to remove the dessert. Make a test before cutting all of the papers to be sure the flaps are long enough; adjust as needed. (See "Baking in Metal Rings," page 504.)

2. Grease the inside of 16 ramekins, 3¼ inches (8.1 cm) in diameter, with melted butter. Line the forms with the papers, pressing the flaps against the sides.

3. Mix the graham cracker crumbs with the remaining melted butter. If the crumbs are very dry, you may need additional butter to ensure that they bind together. Divide among the forms and press the crumbs evenly over the bottoms.

CHEF'S TIP
There are two grades of baking paper, or silicone paper, available in the United States. The thicker grade is preferable for this recipe because the thinner paper tends to break if the cakes are left in the cups overnight, which is usually the case.

4. Soften the cream cheese in a mixer at low speed, taking care not to incorporate too much air. Add the eggs to the 10 ounces (285 g) sugar and stir until well combined. Gradually add the mixture to the cream cheese, scraping the sides and bottom of the bowl frequently to avoid lumps.

5. Place the batter in a pastry bag with a No. 6 (12-mm) plain tip. Pipe the batter into the forms, dividing it equally among them. Be very careful not to get any batter on the sides at the top of the forms, as this will detract from the final presentation.

6. Bake the cheesecakes at 375°F (190°C) for approximately 20 minutes or until just done. Take into consideration that they will set further as they cool.

7. Mix the sour cream with the remaining 4 ounces (115 g) sugar. Place the mixture in a pastry bag with a No. 6 (12-mm) plain tip. Pipe the sour cream on top of the cakes. Flatten the top of the sour cream with the back of a spoon by moving it up and down a few times on top of the sour cream layer, or by tapping the forms against the table.

8. Place part of the lingonberry puree in a paper pastry bag (see page 52) and cut a small opening. Pipe a small amount of the puree in a spiral pattern on top of the sour cream layer in each of the forms, starting in the center. Reserve the remaining puree for the sauce. Pull a small wooden skewer from the center of the spiral to the outside to create a spiderweb pattern (see Figure 16-8, page 812).

9. Bake the cheesecakes for 4 minutes at 375°F (190°C) to set the sour cream. Let cool completely.

10. Thin the remaining lingonberry puree with water to a saucelike consistency. Reserve.

11. Unmold the cheesecakes by running the blade of a small knife around the inside of the ramekin; do not cut the flaps. Carefully lift the cake out by the paper flaps. If the cakes have been refrigerated, dip the bottom of the ramekins in hot water first.

12. Presentation: Place a cheesecake off-center on a dessert plate. Pour a small, round pool of sauce in front of the dessert. Decorate the sauce with the sour cream mixture for piping, making the same spiderweb design used on the cheesecake.

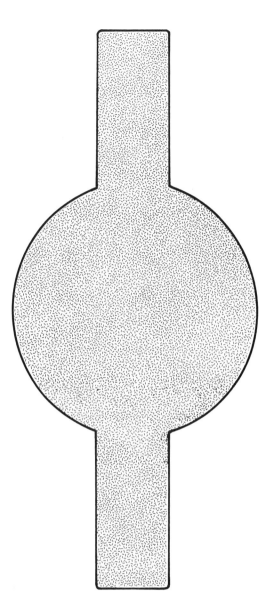

FIGURE 11-10 The template used to cut baking paper strips to line the forms for Individual Lingonberry-Topped Cheesecakes

NOTE: It is assumed that you are using canned and sweetened lingonberries for the puree. If you are fortunate enough to find fresh lingonberries, cook and sweeten them before pureeing. You will need approximately 1 pound 8 ounces (680 g) fresh berries to make the amount called for in the recipe.

Baking in Metal Rings

If you prefer, you can bake the Individual Ligonberry-Topped Cheesecakes (page 502) in individual metal rings rather than ceramic forms, using the following instructions:

- To replace Steps 1 and 2, prepare 12 metal rings, 3 inches (7.5 cm) in diameter and 2 inches (5 cm) in height, by
covering the bottom and outside of each with a square of aluminum foil. If the foil is particularly thin, use a double layer. Pleat the foil tightly around the sides because the cakes will be baked in a water bath.

- Follow the main recipe as directed. However, bake the cheesecakes in a water bath and take the forms out of the water bath once you remove them from the oven.

- To unmold the cakes, peel away the foil, run a small knife around the inside perimeter, and remove the rings from as many servings as you anticipate needing.

Mascarpone Cheesecake with Cassis Panna Cotta Topping

yield: 1 cake, 9 inches (22.5 cm) in diameter

8 ounces (225 g) Graham Cracker Crumbs
(page 20)

3 ounces (85 g) melted unsalted butter

Mascarpone Cheesecake Batter (recipe
follows)

Cassis Panna Cotta Topping (recipe follows)

Guinettes Cherry Sauce (page 822)

1. Prepare a springform pan, 9 x 3 inches (22.5 x 7.5), by lining the outside bottom and sides with a double layer of aluminum foil (see Note).

2. Combine the graham cracker crumbs with the melted butter. Press the crust firmly and evenly over the bottom of the pan with your hands.

3. Pour the mascarpone cheesecake batter into the pan and smooth the top to make it even (be careful not to get any of the filling on the sides of the pan above the cheesecake batter, as this will detract from the final appearance of the cake). Set the pan inside a hotel pan and add hot water around it to reach about halfway up the sides of the springform.

4. Bake at 325°F (163°C) for approximately 50 minutes or until the filling is set.

5. Remove the pan from the water bath and peel off the foil. Let the cake cool until it is just slightly warm; do not allow it to cool completely.

6. Place a strip of acetate, 1 to 2½ inches (2.5 to 6.2 cm) wide, around the inside perimeter of the cake pan, pressing it down ¼ inch (6 mm) between the baked cheesecake and the side of the pan. Pour the cassis panna cotta topping on top of the cake. Place the cake in the refrigerator for at least 4 hours or, preferably, overnight.

7. To unmold, run a thin knife around the inside of the pan before releasing the springform. Cut the cake into the desired number of portions. Serve with the cherry sauce if desired.

NOTE: Instead of covering the outside of the springform with foil, you can place the 9-inch (22.5-cm) springform inside a standard 10-inch (25-cm) cake pan, then set this assembly in the hotel pan. The foil or the double-panning is necessary to prevent water from seeping into the springform from the water bath.

If you do not have a springform pan, the cake can alternatively be prepared in a conventional cake pan, 9 x 2 inches (22.5 x 5 cm). In this case, line the bottom with a circle of baking paper before you press in the crust. To unmold, run a thin knife around the inside of the pan, pressing tightly against the side of the pan so you do not damage the cake, to loosen the sides. Place a piece of plastic wrap on top of the panna cotta topping (after it is well chilled and firm), place a cardboard cake circle on top of the pan, and invert the cake onto the cardboard. If it sticks on the bottom, warm the bottom of the pan to melt the butter in the crust slightly. Turn the cheesecake right-side up and remove the plastic wrap.

MASCARPONE CHEESECAKE BATTER yield: enough for 1 cake, 9 inches (22.5 cm) in diameter

12 ounces (340 g) mascarpone cheese, at room temperature

8 ounces (225 g) cream cheese, at room temperature

6 ounces (170 g) powdered sugar

1 vanilla bean

2 teaspoons (10 ml) vanilla extract

3 eggs, at room temperature

½ cup (120 ml) sweetened condensed milk

½ cup (120 ml) sour cream

½ cup (120 ml) heavy cream

1. Using the paddle attachment, blend the mascarpone cheese, cream cheese, and powdered sugar until fully combined, scraping down the sides of the bowl several times to make sure there are no lumps.

2. Split the vanilla bean lengthwise and scrape out the seeds. Blend the seeds into the batter by first mixing them into a small amount of the batter against the side of the bowl to break up any clumps of the tiny seeds, then mixing them with the remainder. Mix in the vanilla extract, then incorporate the eggs, 1 at time. Stir in the condensed milk, sour cream, and heavy cream.

CASSIS PANNA COTTA TOPPING yield: enough for 1 cake, 9 inches (22.5 cm) in diameter

1 cup (240 ml) whole milk

¼ cup (60 ml) crème de cassis

1½ tablespoons (14 g) unflavored gelatin powder

3 cups (720 ml) heavy cream

3 ounces (85 g) granulated sugar

1. Pour the milk into a bowl. Stir in the crème de cassis and sprinkle the gelatin powder over the surface. Set aside for 10 to 15 minutes, until the gelatin is softened.

2. In a saucepan, combine the cream and sugar. Warm over medium-low heat, stirring to dissolve the sugar.

3. Heat the cassis milk to dissolve the gelatin and stir into the cream mixture.

4. Let cool to room temperature before pouring on top of the cheesecake, but do not wait too long or the gelatin will begin to set up.

LEMON VERBENA PANNA COTTA TOPPING

Here, ½ ounce (15 g) fresh lemon verbena leaves, finely chopped, is substituted for the cassis, and the sugar is increased to 6 ounces (170 g).

1. Pour the cream into a saucepan. Add ½ ounce (15 g) lemon verbena leaves, finely chopped, and bring to the scalding point. Remove from the heat, cover, and let steep for 1 hour.

2. Pour the milk into a bowl and sprinkle the gelatin powder over the surface. Let stand until softened, 10 to 15 minutes.

3. Warm the lemon verbena cream with the 6 ounces (170 g) cream, stirring to dissolve the sugar. Strain through a chinois into a large bowl.

4. Heat the milk to dissolve the gelatin. Stir into the lemon verbena cream. Let cool before pouring on top of the cheesecake, but do not wait too long or the gelatin will set up.

New York–Style Cheesecake

yield: 2 cakes, 10 inches (25 cm) in diameter, or 4 cakes, 7 inches (17.5 cm) in diameter

One of the main differences between New York–style cheesecake and the West Coast version is that, here, the sour cream is part of the filling and is mixed with the other ingredients at the beginning. In the other cake, the sour cream is added as a topping after the cream cheese filling is baked. Secondly, in the West Coast recipe, the ratio of sour cream to cream cheese is just about equal, while here, a comparatively small amount of sour cream is used. Lastly, the New York cheesecake contains approximately half again as much egg.

1 pound 12 ounces (795 g) Graham Cracker Crumbs (page 20)

10 ounces (285 g) melted unsalted butter

5 pounds (2 kg 275 g) cream cheese, at room temperature

1 pound 8 ounces (680 g) granulated sugar

4 ounces (115 g) cornstarch

Finely grated zest of 1 lemon

4 teaspoons (20 ml) vanilla extract

10 whole eggs, at room temperature

4 egg yolks (⅓ cup/80 ml)

10 ounces (285 g) sour cream

1. Combine the graham cracker crumbs and the melted butter. Divide the crumb mixture between 2 springform pans, 10 inches (25 cm) in diameter, or 4 springform pans, 7 inches (17.5 cm) in diameter. Press evenly over the bottoms and sides of the pans using your hands. Reserve.

2. Mix the cream cheese and granulated sugar together at low speed, using the paddle attachment, until completely smooth. Mix in the cornstarch, lemon zest, and vanilla. Mix until smooth, scraping down the sides and the bottom of the bowl. Add the whole eggs and egg yolks, a few at a time, blending thoroughly after each addition. Incorporate the sour cream.

3. Divide the batter evenly between the prepared pans.

4. Bake at 350°F (175°C) until set, approximately 40 minutes (35 minutes for the small size). Cool completely, then chill before removing the cakes from the pans. Decorate the tops of the cakes with thinly sliced fresh fruit, serve fruit on the plate next to a slice of cake, or serve the cheesecake with a thick fruit sauce, such as Blueberry Sauce (page 815).

Pumpkin Cheesecake with White Chocolate

yield: 2 cakes, 10 inches (25 cm) in diameter, or 4 cakes, 7 inches (17.5 cm) in diameter

I make this cake all year round as a nice change of pace, but it is at the holidays that it really stands out as a welcome alternative to the more traditional offerings. The smaller 7-inch (17.5-cm) size often makes sense, as cheesecakes, being rich and filling, can be served in small portions.

CRUST

12 ounces (340 g) Graham Cracker Crumbs (page 20)

4 ounces (115 g) finely ground almonds

1 teaspoon (2 g) ground ginger

1 teaspoon (1.5 g) ground cinnamon

6 ounces (170 g) melted unsalted butter, approximately

FILLING

2 pounds 6 ounces (1 kg 80 g) cream cheese, at room temperature

1 pound (455 g) white chocolate, melted

6 eggs, at room temperature

¼ cup (60 ml) pure maple syrup

¼ cup (60 ml) brandy

2 teaspoons (4 g) ground ginger

2 teaspoons (3 g) ground cinnamon

1 teaspoon (2 g) ground nutmeg

1½ cups (360 ml) canned pumpkin puree *or* freshly cooked Pumpkin Puree (page 374)

TOPPING

2 pounds 8 ounces (1 kg 135 g) sour cream

6 ounces (170 g) granulated sugar

2 tablespoons (30 ml) pure maple syrup

2 tablespoons (30 ml) brandy

2 tablespoons (30 ml) canned pumpkin puree *or* freshly cooked Pumpkin Puree (page 374)

1. Combine all of the ingredients for the crust. Divide the mixture between 2 springform pans, 10 inches (25 cm) in diameter, or 4 springform pans, 7 inches (17.5 cm) in diameter. Use your hands to pat the crumbs in place, covering the bottom of the pans. Set the pans aside.

2. For the filling, place the cream cheese in a mixer bowl and soften it by stirring at low speed with the paddle. Be careful not to overmix and incorporate too much air, as this will result in a dry and crumbly cheesecake. Stir the white chocolate into the cream cheese, then add the eggs gradually. Scrape the sides and bottom of the mixing bowl frequently to avoid lumps. Combine the maple syrup, brandy, spices, and pumpkin puree. Add this mixture to the cream cheese mixture, stirring only long enough to combine. Divide the batter among the prepared pans and spread it out evenly.

3. Bake at 325°F (163°C) for approximately 40 minutes (slightly less for the small cakes) or until the filling is set. The filling should move in one mass inside the forms when shaken gently. If it moves more in the center than on the sides, continue baking. The cakes become firmer once they have cooled, so do not overbake or they will crack on the surface and taste dry.

4. Combine all of the topping ingredients except the pumpkin puree. Reserve ¼ cup (60 ml) of the mixture and divide the remainder among the baked cakes. This can be done as soon as they come out of the oven if necessary, but pour the topping gently around the outside edges of the cakes to avoid denting the softer centers.

CHEF'S TIP

For an elegant holiday presentation, make individual pumpkin cheesecakes using the template and instructions for Individual Lingonberry-Topped Cheesecakes (page 502). Bake at 375°F (190°C), as specified; the pumpkin cheesecakes will take slightly less time than the lingonberry version. Be careful not to overbake. Follow the presentation instructions in Step 12 (page 503), substituting Cranberry Coulis (page 821) for the lingonberry sauce.

5. Combine the reserved sour cream mixture with the remaining 2 tablespoons (30 ml) pumpkin puree and place in a pastry bag with a No. 2 (4-mm) plain tip. Pipe the decoration in a spiral pattern on the top of each cake, starting in the center. Run the back of a paring knife through the spiral starting in the center and pulling toward the edge of the pan to make a spiderweb pattern (see Figure 16-8, page 812).

6. Bake the cakes at 400°F (205°C) for 8 minutes to set the topping. The topping will still look liquid but will set as it cools.

VARIATION

CRANBERRY CHEESECAKE WITH WHITE CHOCOLATE

yield: 2 cakes, 10 inches (25 cm) in diameter, or 4 cakes, 7 inches (17.5 cm) in diameter

Follow the recipe and instructions for Pumpkin Cheesecake with White Chocolate, making the following changes:

- Omit the maple syrup.
- Substitute 2 cups (480 ml) canned pureed cranberry sauce (the thick type) for the pumpkin puree. Force ½ cup (120 ml) through a fine mesh strainer and stir into the reserved sour cream for the topping. Use the remaining 1½ cups (360 ml) in the cake filling.

West Coast Cheesecake

yield: 2 cakes, 10 inches (25 cm) in diameter, or 4 7 inches (17.5 cm) in diameter

This recipe, as simple as it is, has been highly praised for years by cheesecake lovers. It was given to me by default many years ago by a young woman who had a summer job in my kitchen. She kept asking me to make cheesecakes, saying that many customers had requested them. My consistent reply was that I didn't have time to add another item, and besides that, I didn't even have a good recipe. Not one to give up, she said her mother had a great recipe and she could even make the cheesecakes herself on Friday afternoons after I went home, so we would have them for the weekend. I finally decided it was worth a try and, sure enough, we began selling more and more of her cheesecakes as the summer went on. I must admit my feelings were hurt a few times when people would say to me (after learning of my association with their favorite pastry shop), "Oh, I just love that bakery; they have the best cheesecake!" So when the young woman went back to school in the fall, I had no choice but to continue making her cheesecake.

1 pound (455 g) Graham Cracker Crumbs (page 20)	7 eggs, at room temperature
6 ounces (170 g) melted unsalted butter, approximately	1 pound (455 g) granulated sugar
3 pounds 7 ounces (1 kg 565 g) cream cheese, at room temperature	3 pounds (1 kg 365 g) sour cream
	7 ounces (200 g) granulated sugar
	Flavoring (choices follow)

I. Mix the graham cracker crumbs with the melted butter. Divide the crumbs between 2 springform pans, 10 inches (25 cm) in diameter, or 4 springform pans, 7 inches (17.5 cm) in diameter, covering the bottom of the pans. Pat the crumbs even with your hands.

2. Soften the cream cheese in a mixer at low speed, using the paddle attachment, or stir by hand, until it has a smooth consistency. Take care not to incorporate too much air or you will end up with a dry and crumbly cheesecake.

3. Lightly mix the eggs and 1 pound (455 g) sugar, stirring them together by hand. Gradually add the egg mixture to the cream cheese, scraping the bottom and sides of the mixing bowl frequently to avoid lumps. Divide the batter among the prepared pans and spread out evenly.

4. Bake at 375°F (190°C) until just done, about 35 minutes (slightly less for the smaller version). The filling should move in one mass inside the forms when shaken gently. If it moves more in the center than on the sides, continue baking. The cakes will become firmer once they have cooled, so do not overbake them "just to play it safe" or the cakes will crack on the surface and taste dry and stale.

5. Mix the sour cream with the remaining 7 ounces (200 g) sugar. Divide the mixture between the baked cakes. (You can do this as soon as they are baked, but be careful not to damage the tops of the cakes when you pour on the sour cream mixture.)

6. Place the flavoring in a pastry bag with the piping tip indicated in the flavoring instructions. Pipe the flavoring in a spiral pattern on top of each cake, starting in the center. Drag the back of a paring knife through the spiral starting in the center and pulling toward the edge of the pan to make a spiderweb pattern. See the example in Figure 16-8, page 812.

7. Bake the cakes at 375°F (190°C) for 8 minutes to set the sour cream (5 minutes for the small size). The sour cream will still look liquid but will set as it cools.

FLAVORINGS

LINGONBERRY

Lingonberries are an expensive Scandinavian delicacy that look like small cranberries but taste sweeter. They are available as a preserve in most grocery stores. Pipe lingonberry jam in a spiral pattern using a No. 4 (8-mm) plain tip (you may need to crush the berries to ensure that they will go through the tip).

CHOCOLATE

Reserve ¼ cup (60 ml) sour cream mixture per cake. Flavor the remainder with 2 tablespoons (16 g) unsweetened cocoa powder per cake (add a little sour cream to the cocoa powder to make a paste before mixing with the remainder to avoid lumps). Top the baked cheesecake with the cocoa-flavored sour cream and use the reserved plain sour cream mixture to pipe the spiral pattern on top, using a No. 2 (4-mm) plain tip.

STRAWBERRY

Use good-quality strawberry preserves. If the preserves have large chunks of puree or fruit, break them up with a spoon. Pipe the preserves onto the cakes in a spiral pattern using a

No. 2 (4-mm) plain tip. For a fresh strawberry topping, bake the sour cream mixture plain. Top the cooled cakes with strawberries cut into thin slices lengthwise. Brush the strawberries with Apricot Glaze (page 5).

LEMON

Add 2 teaspoons (12 g) grated lemon zest per cake to the cream cheese batter (not the sour cream topping) before baking the cake. Pipe Lemon Curd (page 844) into a spiral pattern on top of the sour cream mixture, using a No. 2 (4-mm) plain tip.

Chocolate-Almond Cake with Hazelnut Cream

yield: 2 cakes, 10 inches (25 cm) in diameter

A few years ago, this cake was a regular feature on the dessert buffet prepared by my students. In addition to being much requested, it often aroused the curiosity of our guests, many of whom are very interested in cooking and know quite a bit about it. The puzzle was this: How is it possible to make a clean, precise cut through the whole hazelnuts in the middle of the soft cream filling? This type of little trick or mystery is an excellent way to get and keep the attention of your customers. When you create a pastry, cake, or plated dessert, what often stands out the most to the customer is an unusual decoration or presentation. It might be something that is actually quick and easy for the chef once he or she has learned a few tricks of the trade, but when it has the guests saying, "I wonder how they do that?" they are likely to remember their meal and also where they had it. The answer in this recipe is that the cakes are frozen, then finished and sliced when they are half thawed.

2 Cocoa-Almond Sponges (page 439), 10 inches (25 cm) in diameter

2 Short Dough Cake Bottoms (page 69), 10 inches (25 cm) in diameter

Nougat Butter (recipe follows)

½ cup (120 ml) Plain Cake Syrup (page 31)

Hazelnut Cream (recipe follows)

1½ cups (360 ml) heavy cream

1 tablespoon (15 g) granulated sugar

6 ounces (170 g) sliced almonds, toasted and lightly crushed

Unsweetened cocoa powder

Chocolate Crescent Cookies (recipe follows)

1. Cut the skin from the tops of the sponge cakes and trim the tops to make them even if necessary. Cut each sponge into 2 layers.

2. Place the short dough bottoms on cardboard cake circles for support. Divide the nougat butter between them and spread it out evenly. Place a sponge layer on top of each and brush the sponges lightly with the cake syrup.

3. Spread the hazelnut cream evenly over the first sponge layers. Place the second sponge layers on the hazelnut cream and press down lightly to even the tops. Brush again with cake syrup.

4. Place the cakes in the freezer, covered, until completely frozen (this is not necessary if you plan to present the cakes whole rather than cut into serving pieces).

5. Trim away any short dough that protrudes outside the sponge to make the sides even (Figure 11-11).

6. Whip the cream and the sugar to stiff peaks. Ice the tops and sides of the cakes with a thin layer of whipped cream. Reserve the remaining cream.

7. Cover the sides of the cakes with crushed almonds (see Figure 11-12, page 520).

8. Place a round template, 10 inches (25 cm) in diameter and with a 6-inch (15-cm) hole cut out of the center, on one of the cakes. Sift cocoa powder over the cake to cover the whipped cream. Remove the template carefully. Repeat with the second cake.

9. When the cakes have thawed halfway, cut them into the desired number of serving pieces. (Do not let the cakes thaw completely or you will push the nuts in the filling into the cake rather than slicing through them.)

FIGURE 11-11 Trimming the excess short dough from the base of the Chocolate-Almond Cake with Hazelnut Cream to make the sides even

10. Place the remaining whipped cream in a pastry bag with a No. 7 (14-mm) plain tip. Pipe a mound of whipped cream the size of a cherry at the edge of each slice. Place a Chocolate Crescent Cookie on each mound.

NOUGAT BUTTER yield: 4 ounces (115 g)

2 ounces (55 g) unsalted butter, at room temperature

2 ounces (55 g) Hazelnut Paste (page 20)

1. Gradually work the soft butter into the hazelnut paste to make a smooth, lump-free mixture. Use at room temperature.

HAZELNUT CREAM yield: approximately 2 quarts 1 pint (2 L 400 ml)

8 ounces (225 g) toasted hazelnuts
1 quart (960 ml) heavy cream

6 ounces (170 g) Hazelnut Paste (page 20)

1. Remove the skin from the hazelnuts (see page 6).

2. Very gradually, mix enough of the cream into the hazelnut paste to make it soft and similar in consistency to lightly whipped cream. Whip the remaining cream to soft peaks.

3. Fold the cream into the hazelnut paste together with the toasted nuts. If the cream is overwhipped, it can break when the rest of the ingredients are added. If it is not whipped enough and the filling seems too runny, just mix a little longer.

CHOCOLATE CRESCENT COOKIES yield: 24 cookies

> 5 ounces (140 g) Cocoa Short Dough
> (page 68) or Short Dough (page 67)
> flavored with unsweetened cocoa powder

I. Roll out the short dough to ⅛ inch (3 mm) thick.

2. Using a ¾-inch (2-cm) plain cookie cutter, cut out crescents as described in making Fleurons (see Figure 2-14, page 78).

3. Bake the cookies at 375°F (190°C). Let them cool completely before placing them on the whipped cream.

Chocolate Decadence yield: 2 cakes, 10 inches (25 cm) in diameter (Photo 40)

This sumptuous chocolate and cream combination is the ultimate chocolate-lover's dream cake—actually much closer to a baked chocolate truffle than to a cake. Some versions are known by the straight-to-the-point name of *Flourless Chocolate Cake*. Chocolate Decadence is a very easy cake to make—basically, it's a brownie without the flour and nuts—and it's quite practical, as it can be stored unfinished in the refrigerator for weeks, or in the freezer for many months, ready to complete quickly as needed. I always have some in the refrigerator to ice and use as a backup if we run out of any of the desserts on the menu. When the guests are offered Chocolate Decadence as an alternative to their first choice, they seldom decline.

The richness of this cake contrasts beautifully with a fresh fruit sauce. Raspberry sauce is traditional and the color looks great next to the dark chocolate, but don't miss trying either Bitter Orange Sauce or Bijou Coulis (a tangy combination of cranberry and raspberry).

Melted unsalted butter	6 ounces (170 g) sugar
12 ounces (340 g) sweet dark chocolate	3 cups (720 ml) heavy cream
14 ounces (400 g) unsweetened chocolate	2 tablespoons (30 g) granulated sugar
1¼ cups (300 ml) water	Milk chocolate shavings
12 ounces (340 g) granulated sugar	Raspberry Sauce (page 830)
1 pound 2 ounces (510 g) unsalted butter, at room temperature	Sour Cream Mixture for Piping (page 832)
	Raspberries
12 eggs	Mint leaves

I. Brush melted butter over the insides of 2 cake pans, 10 inches (25 cm) in diameter. Place rounds of baking paper in the bottoms and butter the papers. Set the pans aside. (See Chef's Tip.)

2. Cut the dark chocolate and unsweetened chocolate into small pieces.

3. Bring the water and 12 ounces (340 g) sugar to a boil. Remove from the heat and add the chocolate; stir until the chocolate is melted and completely incorporated. Add the butter, in chunks, and stir until melted. Set aside at room temperature.

4. Whip the eggs with the 6 ounces (170 g) sugar at high speed for about 3 minutes. The mixture should be light and fluffy. Do not whip to maximum volume as you would a sponge cake; incorporating too much air will make the finished cakes crumbly and difficult to work with. Very gently, fold the melted chocolate into the egg mixture. The chocolate may be warm, but it must not be hot.

5. Divide the batter between the prepared pans. Place the pans in a water bath.

6. Bake immediately at 350°F (175°C) for approximately 40 minutes or until the top feels firm. Refrigerate the cakes for at least 2 hours or, preferably, overnight. The chocolate must be completely set before you unmold or finish the cakes.

7. Unmold the cakes by briefly warming the outside bottom of the pans (moving them over a gas or electric burner just until the cake moves freely inside the pan), and invert them onto 10-inch (25-cm) cardboard circles (see Note). Peel the circles of baking paper off the tops of the cakes.

8. Whip the cream with the 2 tablespoons (30 g) sugar to just under stiff peaks. Place the whipped cream in a pastry bag with a No. 4 (8-mm) plain tip. Mark the top of the cakes into quarters to easily locate the exact center. Starting at this point, pipe a spiral of whipped cream, with each circle touching the last one, over the entire top of each cake. Cut the cakes into the desired number of servings, using a thin knife dipped in hot water. Sprinkle the chocolate shavings lightly over the top.

9. Presentation: Place a cake slice off-center on a prepared dessert plate. Pour a round pool of raspberry sauce in front of the slice. Decorate the sauce with sour cream mixture for piping. Place 3 raspberries with a mint leaf next to each on the left side of the plate.

NOTE: Chocolate Decadence must be cut when it is chilled, but it should be served at room temperature. Because of the fragile consistency of this cake (due, in part, to the absence of flour), it should be handled as little as possible. You cannot pick the cake up to move it as you would a sponge cake. Instead, leave it on the 10-inch (25-cm) cardboard cake circle and set this on a larger cake cardboard and/or doily, depending on the situation. If this is not appropriate, invert the cake onto a platter instead. Of course, if you have prepared the cakes ahead of time and they are frozen, you will be able to move them around quite easily before you decorate them.

CHEF'S TIP

This recipe made 1½ times will make 16 individual servings, 4 ounces (120 ml) each, using ramekins 3¼ inches (8.1 cm) in diameter. Omit the paper in the bottom and just brush with butter. The smaller servings will bake more quickly than the cakes.

Chocolate Hazelnut Cake yield: 2 cakes, 10 inches (25 cm) in diameter

This is another cake that features the classic combination of chocolate and nuts, and it is fast and easy to make. If you are really pressed for time, eliminate the decoration in Step 8 and instead, after you have cut or marked the cakes into slices, pipe a rosette of buttercream at the end of each slice, using a No. 6 (12-mm) star tip. Place a hazelnut on each rosette, then sprinkle milk chocolate shavings over the center of the cakes.

⅔ recipe Chiffon Sponge Cake I batter
   (page 440)

1 ounce (30 g) unsweetened cocoa powder

6 ounces (170 g) whole hazelnuts, toasted

3 pounds (1 kg 365 g) Vanilla Buttercream
   (Swiss Method) (page 477)

3 ounces (85 g) Hazelnut Paste (page 20)

4 ounces (115 g) sweet dark chocolate, melted

Dark coating chocolate, melted

Chocolate Rounds (page 460)

1. Cover the bottom of 2 cake pans, 10 inches (25 cm) in diameter, with rounds of baking paper. Add two-thirds of the batter to one of the pans. Spread the top level. Sift the cocoa powder over the remaining portion of batter and fold it in carefully. Place the cocoa batter in the other pan. Spread the top level. Bake the sponges at 375°F (190°C) for approximately 20 minutes or until they spring back when pressed lightly in the center; the cocoa sponge will be done a little sooner than the plain sponge. Allow the cakes to cool in the pans before unmolding.

2. Remove as much of the skin from the hazelnuts as possible (see page 6). Set aside enough of the best-looking nuts to place 1 on each slice of cake. Crush the remaining nuts.

3. Flavor 1 pound 8 ounces (680 g) vanilla buttercream with the hazelnut paste. Flavor the remaining buttercream with the melted sweet dark chocolate.

4. Cut the skin from the top of both sponge cakes, cutting the tops level at the same time. Cut the cocoa sponge into 2 layers. Cut the plain sponge into 4 thin layers.

5. Place the cocoa layers on cardboard cake rounds and spread a ⅛-inch (3-mm) layer of hazelnut buttercream on each. Place one of the plain layers on top of each and spread a layer of hazelnut buttercream on top.

6. Add the remaining plain layers, 1 to each cake, layering with hazelnut buttercream between each layer the same way. Use all of the hazelnut buttercream.

7. Reserve 6 ounces (170 g) chocolate buttercream. Divide the remainder between the cakes and spread it in a thin layer over the top and sides. Cover the sides of the cakes with the reserved crushed hazelnuts (see Figure 11-12, page 520). Refrigerate the cakes until the buttercream is set.

CHEF'S TIP

The decorating instructions assume that you will be cutting the cakes into a typical number of slices, about 12. If you will be cutting a significantly larger number of pieces (making the servings much smaller), pipe only 1 or 2 chocolate lines, omit the chocolate circles, and place the hazelnut directly on the buttercream line(s).

8. Place 1 reserved whole toasted hazelnut in the middle of each chocolate round, securing it with the melted coating chocolate. Make 1 decoration for each serving.

9. Cut or mark the cakes into the desired number of serving pieces. Place the reserved chocolate buttercream in a pastry bag with a No. 1 (2-mm) plain tip. Pipe 2 straight lines of buttercream, next to each other, in the center and down the length of each slice, starting about one-third from the center of the cake. Pipe a third line, slightly longer, in between and on top of the first two. Place a chocolate round at a slight angle on top of the 3 lines at the end of each slice.

Chocolate-Mint Torte with a Golden Touch

yield: 2 tortes, 10 inches (25 cm) in diameter, or 16 servings (Photo 11)

This dessert was born of necessity: I was trying to find something to do with the large outer mint leaves that are left once all of the small leaves and sprigs have been pinched off and used for garnish (another good use is Fresh Mint Ice Cream, page 724). This torte is also quite practical, as it can be stored, covered, in the refrigerator for 2 to 3 days. The glaze tends to become a bit dull, but it can be brought back to life by carefully applying indirect heat from above using a broiler or, better yet, a blowtorch. If you want to simplify the torte and/or the presentation, omit the gold leaf and the mint pesto. Decorate the slices instead with a small edible flower or a single petal from a larger one. Add 2 tablespoons (30 ml) mint liqueur to the mousseline sauce when the sauce is finished.

Butter and Flour Mixture (page 7) or pan spray

1 ounce (30 g) fresh mint leaves

⅓ cup (80 ml) water

10 ounces (285 g) sweet dark chocolate

6 ounces (170 g) almond paste

10 eggs, at room temperature

4 ounces (115 g) bread flour

2 ounces (55 g) unsweetened cocoa powder

4 ounces (115 g) finely ground almonds

10 ounces (285 g) unsalted butter, at room temperature

1 pound (455 g) granulated sugar

Chocolate-Mint Glaze (recipe follows)

½ recipe Mousseline Sauce (page 827)

Mint Pesto (recipe follows)

3 sheets gold leaf, 3½ × 3½ inches (8.7 × 8.7 cm)

Lavender or other edible flowers

1. Brush the butter and flour mixture over the inside of 2 cake pans, 10 inches (25 cm) in diameter, or use pan spray. Set aside.

2. Finely chop the mint and place it in a small pan with the water. Bring to a boil. Cover and set aside to steep for at least 30 minutes or, ideally, complete this step a day ahead.

3. Melt the chocolate in a bain-marie over simmering water. Add the mint-flavored water and mint leaves and stir to combine. Keep the chocolate warm.

4. Soften the almond paste by mixing in the white from one of the eggs. Reserve.

5. Sift the bread flour and cocoa powder together. Mix in the ground almonds. Set aside.

6. Beat the butter and sugar together until creamy. Add the soft almond paste and beat until smooth. Add the eggs in 4 additions. Blend in the chocolate mixture, then the flour mixture, mixing until thoroughly combined. Divide the batter between the prepared cake pans.

7. Bake at 350°F (175°C) until baked through but still moist, about 30 minutes. Let cool completely.

8. Remove the cracked skin from the top of the tortes as necessary. Carefully unmold by inverting the cakes onto cardboard cake circles. Slide onto a cake rack keeping the cakes inverted. Pour the Chocolate-Mint Glaze over the cakes and use a spatula in a back and forth motion to move the glaze to the edges of the cakes, coating the top and sides. Make sure the spatula leaves a wavy pattern on top. Allow the glaze to set up, refrigerating if necessary.

9. Using a warm thin, sharp knife, cut the tortes into 8 pieces each.

10. Presentation: Place a slice of torte off-center on a dessert plate. Pour a pool of mousseline sauce in front. Place 1 tablespoon (15 ml) mint pesto in the mousseline sauce. Transfer a small piece of gold leaf (about 1 inch/2.5 cm) in diameter) to each slice, placing it in the center at the wide end of each slice (see page 891 for more information). Place a second piece of gold leaf the same size on the pesto. Decorate the other side of the plate with lavender or other edible flowers.

CHOCOLATE-MINT GLAZE yield: 4 cups (960 ml)

1 pound (455 g) sweet dark chocolate, chopped

10 ounces (285 g) unsalted butter, at room temperature

½ cup (120 ml) or 6 ounces (170 g) light corn syrup

4 teaspoons (20 ml) mint liqueur

CHEF'S TIP
If the glaze breaks or looks broken, melt 4 ounces (115 g) sweet dark chocolate together with 3 tablespoons (45 ml) heavy cream and add to the glaze. Warm and stir until the glaze is thick and smooth.

1. Melt the chocolate over hot water. Remove from the heat, add the butter, and stir until fully incorporated.

2. Stir in the corn syrup and the liqueur. Cool until the glaze has a spreadable consistency, stirring occasionally (see Chef's Tip).

MINT PESTO yield: 1 cup (240 ml)

2½ ounces (70 g) fresh mint leaves, without stems

2 ounces (55 g) blanched almonds, finely ground

3 tablespoons (45 ml) simple syrup

1. Place the mint leaves and the almonds in a food processor with the metal blade. Process on and off until the mixture is pureed.

2. With the machine running, add enough simple syrup to make a loose paste. The pesto should be used immediately. If necessary, it may be stored in the refrigerator for several days; however, the outside will oxidize and turn dark and should not be used. The interior portion will still be bright green.

Chocolate Soufflé Cake yield: 2 cakes, 10 inches (25 cm) in diameter

This is another version of the very popular flourless chocolate cake, sometimes known as *chocolate silk cake* or *chocolate decadence cake*. This one, by design, is more rustic in appearance. It actually looks the way a decadence cake would if you made two major mistakes: whipping too much air into the eggs and baking the cake at too high a temperature. But both of these things are, of course, exactly what makes a soufflé rise, and are what gives this cake its name.

This is a good recipe to choose if you want to make a chocolate cake and you don't have a lot of time, as the only decorating requirements are the easy-to-make chocolate shavings and a sprinkling of powdered sugar. Because gianduja chocolate is soft in texture, it works especially well to make chocolate shavings, but if it is too soft, place it in the refrigerator from time to time to firm the surface. Use a large melon ball tool and short curved strokes to achieve the best result (see Figure 10-15, page 464).

Melted unsalted butter

1 pound 8 ounces (680 g) sweet dark chocolate

4 ounces (115 g) unsweetened chocolate (see Note)

12 ounces (340 g) unsalted butter

18 egg yolks (1½ cups (360 ml)

2 whole eggs

10 ounces (285 g) granulated sugar

½ cup (120 ml) hazelnut liqueur

18 egg whites (2¼ cups/540 ml)

Curled Chocolate Shavings (page 464), made with gianduja chocolate

Powdered sugar

1. Cut 2 strips of baking paper, 3½ inches (8.7 cm) wide and long enough to line the inside of 2 cake pans, 10 inches (25 cm) in diameter and 2 inches (5 cm) high. Brush melted butter over the inside of the pans, then fasten the paper collars to the insides over the butter. Place circles of baking paper in the bottom of the pans. Brush melted butter over the papers and reserve.

2. Melt the chocolates and butter together over a bain-marie. Set aside to cool slightly.

3. Whip the egg yolks and whole eggs with half of the granulated sugar until the mixture is light and fluffy and has reached its full volume. Mix in the hazelnut liqueur. Set aside.

4. Whip the egg whites with the remaining sugar to soft peaks. Fold one-third of the whites into the yolk mixture. Quickly stir the chocolate into the yolks (the chocolate should be warm, but not hot). Fold in the remaining whites.

5. Divide the batter between the prepared pans and place them in a bain-marie (see Chef's Tip). Bake at 350°F (175°C) for approximately 45 minutes. Remove the pans from the bain-marie and allow the cakes to cool at room temperature for 30 minutes; they will sink lightly in the center. Turn out of the pans and place on 10-inch (25-cm) cardboard rounds. Let cool completely. Cut into the desired number of servings. Fill the center with chocolate shavings and sift powdered sugar lightly over the top of the cakes.

NOTE: You may manipulate the ratio of unsweetened to sweet dark chocolate to suit your taste, provided that you keep the total to 1 pound 12 ounces (795 g). Keep in mind, however, that using more than 8 ounces (225 g) unsweetened chocolate will produce a somewhat strong flavor and a firmer, less pleasant texture.

CHEF'S TIP

A perfectly even full sheet pan (or two half sheet pans) filled two-thirds with water will work also. Better yet, place each 10-inch cake pan in the center of a 12-inch (30-cm) cake pan and carefully pour water into the two larger pans.

Chocolate Sponge Cake with Vanilla Buttercream and Strawberry Wreath yield: 2 cakes, 10 inches (25 cm) in diameter (Photo 41)

This cake has a very pretty and appetizing appearance, making it is a great choice to present whole in a showcase or as part of a buffet. The top layer of cake has a smaller diameter than the base, creating a riser something like the top of a wedding cake; however, in this case, it is not as tall. The elevated center is decorated with stripes of dark cocoa powder, and the empty space surrounding the top tier is filled in with a ring of strawberry halves arranged cut-side up. The strawberry wreath gives a burst of color that is set off nicely by the dark stripes on the white buttercream background, and the berries provide a refreshing flavor and textural contrast when enjoyed together with the cake and buttercream.

2 Cocoa-Almond Sponges (page 439), 10 inches (25 cm) in diameter, or 2 Chocolate Chiffon Sponge Cake I (page 441), 10 inches (25 cm) in diameter

3 pounds (1 kg 365 g) Vanilla Buttercream (Swiss Method) (page 477)

½ cup (120 ml) arrack or dark rum

⅓ cup (80 ml) Plain Cake Syrup (page 31)

6 ounces (170 g) sliced almonds, toasted and lightly crushed

Unsweetened cocoa powder

Small, ripe strawberries

1. Cut the sponge cakes into 3 layers each. Use a 6-inch (15-cm) round template or plain cookie cutter to cut the top layers from each cake into 6-inch (15-cm) circles. Cut them level and trim off the skins if necessary. Save the doughnut-shaped rings that are left for another use. (The middle and bottom layers remain whole.)

2. Flavor the buttercream with half of the arrack or rum. Add the remainder of the arrack or rum to the cake syrup. Brush the bottom sponge layers lightly with cake syrup. Spread a ¼-inch (6-mm) layer of buttercream on each of the 2 bottom sponge layers. Place the middle layers on top and brush again with cake syrup.

3. Ice the top and sides of both the 10-inch (25-cm) base cakes and the 6-inch (15-cm) sponge cakes with buttercream. Reserve the remaining buttercream for decoration. Cover the sides of both the larger and small cakes with the crushed almonds (see Figure 11-12, page 520).

4. Refrigerate the 4 iced sponges until the buttercream is firm.

5. Place a stencil with parallel striped openings, similar to a cake cooler or aspic rack, over the 6-inch (15-cm) layers. Sift cocoa powder through a fine sieve on top. Be very careful as you remove the stencil so that you do not disturb the pattern.

6. Set a 6-inch (15-cm) layer in the center of each of the 10-inch (25-cm) layers. Cut or mark the cakes into the desired number of pieces.

7. Place the remaining buttercream in a pastry bag with a No. 6 (12-mm) plain tip; pipe a mound of buttercream the size of a Bing cherry at the edge of each piece.

8. Remove the stems from the strawberries and cut them in half lengthwise. Place 1 half, cut-side up, on each buttercream mound. Although this cake looks best if cut while the buttercream is cold, it should be eaten when the buttercream is at room temperature.

Devil's Food Cake with Chocolate Whipped Cream Filling and Whipped Fudge Frosting

yield: 1 cake, approximately 10 inches (25 cm) in diameter and 4 inches (10 cm) tall

The word *devil*, or *deviled*, is applied to a number of savory culinary dishes, most notably stuffed eggs, fried oysters, and ham sandwich spread. It suggests that they have a spicy flavor, generally originating from such "devilish" ingredients as cayenne, Tabasco sauce, or paprika. Devil's food cake, however, has been spared this peppery fate. This dense, deeply chocolate American hallmark is found at the opposite end of the spectrum from the airy, white, nonfat, low-calorie, low-cholesterol angel food cake. Devil's food cake is dramatically dark, with a reddish tint that is produced from the alkalizing effect of the baking soda on cocoa and amplified by the red tint of the beets used in the cake layer recipe. A finished devil's food cake is traditionally assembled with a rich chocolate filling and frosted country-style with a fudge-type icing.

1 Devil's Food Cake Layer (page 442), 10 inches (25 cm) in diameter

½ recipe Crème Parisienne (page 841)

Whipped Fudge Frosting (recipe follows)

Curled Chocolate Shavings (page 464), made with gianduja chocolate

Powdered sugar

1. Slice the cake evenly into 3 horizontal layers.

2. Spread half of the crème Parisienne over the bottom cake layer. Place the middle layer on top and spread the remaining chocolate cream over the surface. Add the third (top) cake layer and press lightly to make the top level. (Place a cardboard cake circle on top first, then press gently and evenly on the cardboard.) Set the assembled cake aside.

3. Whip the fudge frosting as directed in the recipe. Quickly (before the fudge sets up), ice the top and sides of the cake. Move your palette knife back and forth over the top to make wavy lines in the frosting. Sprinkle chocolate shavings over the top. If the frosting has started to set before you are ready to add the shavings, soften it very slightly by carefully using a torch so that the shavings will stick. Sift powdered sugar lightly over the top of the cake.

WHIPPED FUDGE FROSTING

yield: enough to generously ice the top and sides of 1 cake, 10 x 4 inches (25 x 10 cm)

6 ounces (170 g) milk chocolate

4 ounces (115 g) sweet dark chocolate

1 cup (240 ml) heavy cream

½ cup (120 ml) glucose *or* light corn syrup

¼ cup (60 ml) hazelnut *or* chocolate-flavored liqueur

1 ounce (30 g) unsalted butter

1. Chop both types of chocolate into small pieces. Place in a mixing bowl and reserve.

2. Place the cream and the glucose or corn syrup in a saucepan and bring to a boil. Pour over the chopped chocolate in the bowl and stir until the chocolate is melted. Add the liqueur and the butter and continue stirring until all of the ingredients are incorporated and the mixture is smooth.

3. Allow the mixture to cool to room temperature; it should thicken to the consistency of soft butter. If you are making this ahead, cover and refrigerate, but bring back to room temperature before whipping.

4. When you are ready to ice the cake, place the frosting in a mixer bowl with the paddle attachment and cream at high speed for a few minutes; it should become lighter in color and fluffy in texture. Use immediately to frost the cake.

Diplomat Cake yield: 2 cakes, 10 inches (25 cm) in diameter (Photo 49)

The light, fresh taste of this traditional Swedish cake is always welcome, and its colorful appearance makes a great addition to a buffet table. I make Diplomat wedding cakes by piping the macaroon paste into four hearts on the top of each cake, with the points of the hearts meeting in the center. After the cakes are baked, the hearts are filled with fresh raspberries, which are very colorful. The French version of Diplomat cake, Gâteau Senator, is basically made the same way except that there, raspberry and apricot jams are piped within the macaroon paste rings before the cake is baked. The variation is also very pretty but is much sweeter than the Diplomat cake's fresh fruit topping. Truthfully, I do not know which cake is the original and which the variation.

2 Sponge Cakes (page 437), 10 inches (25 cm) in diameter, or 2 Chiffon Sponge Cake I (page 440), 10 inches in diameter

¾ cup (180 ml) Plain Cake Syrup (page 31)

6 ounces (170 g) smooth strawberry jam

2 pounds 7 ounces (1 kg 110 g) Pastry Cream (page 845)

6 ounces (170 g) sliced almonds, lightly crushed (untoasted)

1 pound (455 g) Macaroon Decorating Paste (page 293)

Almond paste as needed (see Step 4)

Fresh fruit

Apricot Glaze (page 5) or Pectin Glaze (page 30)

1. Slice the sponge cakes level, then into 3 layers each (see Figyre 11-6, page 488).

2. Brush the 2 bottom layers lightly with cake syrup. Divide the jam between the layers and spread it out evenly. Place the middle layers on the jam and brush them with cake syrup. Spread a ¼-inch (6-mm) layer of pastry cream on the middle layers. Place the top layers on the pastry cream and brush them with cake syrup. Spread another layer of pastry cream, ⅛ inch (3 mm) thick, on the top and sides of the cakes. Cover the sides of the cakes with crushed almonds (Figure 11-12).

3. Place the cakes on a sheet pan lined with baking paper. Mark the cakes into pieces of the desired size for serving (this design does not look good with more than 14 pieces per cake).

FIGURE 11-12 Pressing crushed almonds onto the side of the Diplomat Cake

4. Place the macaroon paste in a pastry bag with a No. 3 (6-mm) plain tip. The macaroon paste should be firm enough that it will not run when it is baked. Add a bit of almond paste if necessary; it should be somewhat difficult to pipe out. Pipe a flower design on the top of each cake, just inside the marks for the individual pieces, forming 1 petal on each slice (Figure 11-13).

5. Bake the cakes at 425°F (219°C), double-panned, for about 10 minutes or until the macaroon paste is light brown and the sliced almonds are toasted. Let the cakes cool completely.

6. Decorate the cakes with 2 or 3 kinds of fruit on each slice, using the macaroon paste as a frame. Use small, soft fruits that can be cut into thin slices, such as kiwi, strawberries, plums, and apricots (see "Decorating with Fruit" on page 564 for more information). Make the same design on each slice to create a uniform and elegant look. Brush apricot or pectin glaze over the fruit and the baked macaroon paste. Cut the cakes, following the marks between each flower petal.

FIGURE 11-13 Piping the macaroon decorating paste on the top of the Diplomat Cake

VARIATION

GATEAU SENATOR yield: 2 cakes, 10 inches (25 cm) in diameter

1. Omit the fresh fruit and apricot or pectin glaze. Replace with 4 ounces (115 g) raspberry jam, 4 ounces (115 g) apricot jam, and simple syrup. Follow Steps 1 and 2 in the main recipe.

2. Place the cakes on a sheet pan lined with baking paper. Place the macaroon paste in a pastry bag with a No. 3 (6-mm) plain tip. Starting at the edge of the cake, pipe 5 concentric rings, spaced about 1 inch (2.5 cm) apart, on the top of each cake. If you are making a large number of cakes, you can make this easier by marking the pastry cream with the appropriate sized rings first.

3. Put the 2 varieties of jam into disposable pastry bags made from baking paper (see Figures 1-15 and 1-16, page 54). Pipe the jam into the spaces between the macaroon paste rings, alternating raspberry and apricot. Do not overfill the rings; the jam will bubble up when the cakes are baked and can boil over the frame.

4. Bake at 425°F (219°C) for approximately 10 minutes or until the macaroon paste is light brown and the almonds on the sides are toasted. As soon as the cakes come out of the oven, carefully brush simple syrup over the macaroon paste without disturbing the jam. Let the cakes cool completely.

5. Cut the cakes into the desired number of servings, using a serrated knife to saw through the macaroon rings.

CHEF'S TIP

If the cakes will be cut the same day they are baked, press the back of a knife dipped in water through the macaroon paste to mark the slices before the cakes are baked. This will allow you to cut clean, precise slices without breaking the firm macaroon paste.

Gâteau Saint-Honoré yield: 2 cakes, 11 inches (27.5 cm) in diameter (Photo 34)

This cake is far more attractive than it is practical. It is named for Saint Honorius, the Bishop of Amiens in the sixth century and the French patron saint of pastry cooks. You will also find a street in Paris that bears his name; it is the Rue du Faubourg Saint-Honoré. Unfortunately, this absolutely delicious and unusual-looking cake must be served the same day it is finished. If not, two of its components—puff pastry and pâte à choux—become soggy and less appetizing. The cake can, however, be prepared through Step 4, then frozen for several weeks until needed. Place the sheet pan in the freezer for 10 minutes before wrapping in plastic to keep the plastic from sticking to the pâte à choux.

Gâteau Saint-Honoré was the "show-me-what-you-can-do" cake back when I was starting out. It was a good test of what a prospective employee could actually produce on the bench under a time constraint. Completing this cake successfully would prove you had mastered the three ps-puff pastry, pâte à choux, and pastry cream (obviously, because of the time involved, you could not actually make the puff pastry needed for the cake; this was given to you. But you had to make a new dough to replace what you used, showing the chef that you had planned your work so that all the turns were completed in the four hours or so you were usually given to finish the full project).

You then had to make Italian meringue for the Crème Chiboust and delicately combine it with the hot pastry cream, testing more of your skills. This mixture was piped on the cake in a symmetrical pattern using a special Saint-Honoré tip (the pattern looks very much as though you piped short V-shaped lines all over the cake), which would show how well you did with a pastry bag. But you were not finished yet; you still had to caramelize sugar and dip the top and sides of the small profiteroles in the hot sugar syrup before placing them around the perimeter of the Saint-Honoré. All in all, a rather exhaustive test in one dessert!

Today, with few exceptions, the somewhat tricky Crème Chiboust is no longer used for this cake.

1 pound (455 g) Puff Pastry (page 74)	1 cup (240 ml) heavy cream
½ recipe Pâte à Choux (page 83)	2 teaspoons (10 g) granulated sugar
1 recipe Diplomat Cream (page 841)	Milk Chocolate Shavings (page 464)
1 recipe Caramelized Sugar for Decorations (page 11)	

1. Roll out the puff pastry to ⅛ inch (3 mm) thick, 23 inches (57.5 cm) long, and 12 inches (30 cm) wide. Place on a sheet pan lined with baking paper. Refrigerate, covered, at least 20 minutes.

2. While the puff pastry is resting, make the pâte à choux and place it in a pastry bag with a No. 4 (8-mm) plain tip. Reserve.

3. Leaving the puff pastry in place on the sheet pan, cut from the dough 2 fluted circles, 11 inches (27.5 cm) in diameter, and remove the scraps. (An easy way to cut them is to use the rim of an appropriately sized tart pan as a cookie cutter.) Prick the circles lightly with a fork.

4. Pipe 4 concentric rings of pâte à choux on each circle. Pipe out 24 pâte à choux profiteroles the size of Bing cherries onto the paper around the cakes (Figure 11-14).

5. Bake the puff pastry circles and the profiteroles at 400°F (205°C) until the pâte à choux has puffed, about 10 minutes. Reduce the heat to 375°F (190°C) and bake until everything is dry enough to hold its shape, about 35 minutes longer for the cake and about 8 minutes longer for the profiteroles. (Just pick the profiteroles up and take them out as they are done.)

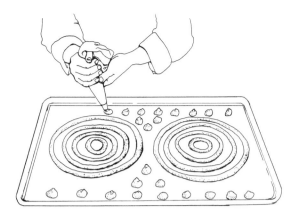

6. Place approximately 6 ounces (170 g) diplomat cream in a pastry bag with a No. 2 (4-mm) plain tip. Use the pastry bag tip or the tip of a paring knife to make a small hole in the bottom of each profiterole. Pipe the cream into the profiteroles to fill them. Refrigerate the filled profiteroles.

7. Divide the remaining filling evenly between the cakes, spreading it into a dome shape. Refrigerate the cakes for at least 2 hours to set the cream.

8. Prepare the caramelized sugar and let it cool slightly. Dip the filled profiteroles into the hot caramel, using 2 forks to avoid burning your fingers. Place them on a sheet pan. The caramel must be hot enough to go on in a thin layer. Reheat if necessary as you are dipping, stirring constantly to avoid darkening the caramel any more than necessary. Also, avoid mixing diplomat cream into the caramel while dipping, as the cream can cause the sugar to recrystallize.

9. Whip the heavy cream and remaining sugar to stiff peaks. Place the whipped cream in a pastry bag with a No. 5 (10-mm) star tip. Pipe a border of whipped cream around the top of the cakes. Arrange the profiteroles, evenly spaced, on top of the filling next to the cream. Sprinkle the chocolate shavings over the center of the cakes inside the profiteroles. If the cakes are to be sliced and not presented whole, slice them after piping the whipped cream and before adding the profiteroles.

VARIATION
GATEAU SAINT-HONORE NOUVELLE (Photo 24)

This contemporary variation of the well-known classic is a good choice when you want to present something special. If they happen to be in season, use fresh cherries with the stems left on to decorate the tops of the cakes. The cherries not only lend color to the presentation but their flavor also pairs nicely with the kirschwasser-flavored diplomat cream. When decorating with fresh cherries, I prefer also to leave them whole (unpitted) whenever possible because they lose a great deal of their attractiveness, and also their stems, when the pits are removed. I do, however, like to slice off a bit less than half of the flesh on one side of each cherry so the guest is made aware of the pit. The small portion that has been removed may be set, cut-side up, next to the cherry.

If you have caramelized sugar left over after dipping the profiteroles, another optional decoration that looks nice is a small mound of spun sugar placed in the center of each cake.

Change the ingredients for Gâteau Saint-Honoré as follows:

- Increase the heavy cream to 1½ cups (360 ml).

- Increase the granulated sugar to 1 tablespoon (15 g).

1. Follow the directions for Gâteau Saint-Honoré through Step 7.

2. After placing the cakes in the refrigerator (see Note), prepare your work area for making the spiked profiteroles that are used for decoration by placing a few sheets of baking paper on the floor in front of your worktable. Place a thin strip of wood or a long ruler at the edge of the table and secure it by placing a weight on each end (see Chef's Tip). Prepare the caramelized sugar and set it aside to cool for a few minutes.

3. While the sugar is cooling, insert a wooden skewer horizontally into each of the filled profiteroles, close to the base of the profiterole and just far enough in that the tip of the skewer shows through on the other side.

CHEF'S TIP

In addition to a strip of wood or a ruler, several other objects can be used to hold the skewers in place so that the profiteroles extend into the air to form the caramel tails. One device that works great is a block of Styrofoam, which, like the ruler or wood, must be weighed down on each end to hold it secure. Instead of inserting the skewers between the ruler and the table, insert them directly into the Styrofoam block. Because you will be inserting the blunt end of the skewers rather than the pointed end, it is easier if you first make series of small holes in the Styrofoam using a thin nail or an awl. The Styrofoam block can be reused many times, but as it will most likely appear to be something that should be thrown away to anyone who does not know what it is, I recommend that you label it before storing it for the next use. A quick solution for one-time use is to press a strip of cold short dough, marzipan, or almond paste along the edge of the table. The skewers can be inserted directly into any of these materials; it is not necessary to pierce the holes ahead of time.

4. Holding the skewer so that the top of the profiterole faces down, dip a profiterole into the sugar, coating the top and sides but not the base. There is often some cream filling on the base of the profiteroles where the filling was piped in; be careful not to get any of it into the sugar, as it can cause the sugar to crystallize. As you bring the profiterole out of the sugar, hold the skewer level so that the sugar runs away in a stream from the center on top of the profiterole, forming a long tail or spike. Secure the blunt end of the skewer under the ruler or wood on the table so that the profiterole extends over the paper on the floor (see Figure 13-12, page 630). Continue dipping the remaining profiteroles in the same manner. Place the first skewer under the ruler at the end farthest away from where you are working, then place each one in line working toward the dipping area to avoid dripping sugar on the profiteroles that have been dipped.

5. Allow the caramelized sugar to harden. Heat the blade of a knife by holding it over an open flame, then use it to cut (melt) through the caramelized tail on each profiterole, making each approximately 8 inches (20 cm) in length (shown in Figure 13-12, page 630, also referred to in Step 4 above). Transfer the profiteroles to a sheet pan lined with baking paper and reserve at room temperature—or, if possible, leave the profiteroles in place until needed.

6. Whip the heavy cream and the sugar to stiff peaks, but be careful not to overwhip. Place the cream in a pastry bag with a Saint-Honoré piping tip. Pipe 12 evenly spaced, curved lines of cream on each cake starting each line at the edge of the cake and curving it toward the center.

7. Remove the skewers from the dipped profiteroles by turning each skewer to separate it from the sugar. Place the profiteroles on the cakes, placing one next to each line of whipped cream around the edge of each cake. Sprinkle the chocolate shavings in the center of the cakes.

NOTE: Gâteau Saint-Honoré Nouvelle is ideally completed as close to serving time as possible; this is especially true for the profiteroles. They should not be dipped into the caramelized sugar more than 1 hour before being placed on the cake or the filling inside may begin to adversely effect the sugar coating. Once they are coated with sugar, they can not be refrigerated, so the filling (which contains dairy and must be kept cold) should not be piped in until just before you are ready to apply the sugar coating.

Lemon-Honey Cake with Raspberries and Italian Meringue

yield: 2 cakes, 10 inches (25 cm) in diameter (Photos 31 and 37)

This Mediterranean-influenced cake is iced and decorated with piped meringue that is torched to create an inviting golden brown exterior. The decoration can be simplified by spreading the meringue over the tops of the cakes only and forming it into swirls, as is typical for a lemon meringue pie, before browning it. Because this method leaves the sides of the cakes exposed, you should carefully place a row of berries all around the perimeter when you arrange them on top of the first layer of batter. Then, before inverting the cakes to unmold them, run a knife around the inside to loosen the berries, which will stick to the side. If you make this cake with IQF raspberries in the off-season, keep in mind that they tend to fall apart and bleed a bit, so it is best to ice both the sides and the top with the meringue before browning it.

Olive oil is a traditional ingredient for this cake, but it should be very mild-tasting to lend a subtle flavor. If you have only strongly flavored olive oil, it would be better to substitute vegetable oil.

Butter and Flour Mixture (page 7)

10 ounces (285 g) bread flour

1 tablespoon (12 g) baking powder

6 ounces (170 g) finely ground almonds (almond flour)

10 ounces (285 g) granulated sugar

Finely grated zest of 4 lemons

8 ounces (225 g) honey

8 eggs, at room temperature

½ cup (120 ml) whole milk, at room temperature

2 tablespoons (30 ml) lemon juice (approximately ½ lemon)

7 ounces (200 g) unsalted butter, melted

1½ cups (360 ml) mild olive oil *or* vegetable oil

2 dry pints or 1 pound (455 g) fresh raspberries

1 recipe Italian Meringue (page 27)

FOR PLATED PRESENTATION

Raspberries

Small mint sprigs

Seasonal fruit sauce

Piped Cookie Curly Cues (page 795)

Powdered sugar

1. Brush butter and flour mixture over the insides of 2 cake pans, 10 inches (25 cm) in diameter. Reserve.

2. Sift together the flour and baking powder, then thoroughly mix in the ground almonds. Reserve.

3. Place the sugar and the lemon zest in a food processor and process for 1 to 2 minutes to thoroughly mix the zest into the sugar. Place the sugar mixture in a mixer bowl and add the honey and the eggs. Whip at high speed to the ribbon stage. Turn to low speed and incorporate the milk.

4. Fold in the reserved flour mixture by hand, followed by the lemon juice, then the butter and olive oil.

5. Divide half of the batter between the pans. Arrange the raspberries over the batter. Top with the remaining batter.

6. Bake at 350°F (175°C) for approximately 40 minutes or until the center of the cake springs back when pressed lightly. Remove from the pans and cool on a rack.

7. Ice the tops and the sides of the cakes with the Italian meringue. Place a portion of the remaining meringue in a pastry bag with a large Saint-Honoré tip. Pipe curved lines of meringue in a fan or spoke pattern covering the top of each cake. Carefully brown (caramelize) the meringue, using a blowtorch.

8. Presentation: Place a slice of cake off-center on a dessert plate. Decorate the tip of the slice with raspberries and a mint sprig. Pipe fruit sauce on the plate in front of the cake. Lean a curly cue against the cake slice and sift powdered sugar over the dessert and the plate.

Meringue Black Forest Cake yield: 2 cakes, 10 inches (25 cm) in diameter

This cake is a variation combining the chocolate-flavored whipped cream and sponge cake of the traditional German Black Forest Cake with the meringue layers and kirsch flavoring of the Swiss specialty Swiss Kirsch Cake (*Zugar Kirsch Torte*).

The chocolate triangles make a spectacular decorative finish, but they can be a bit time-consuming to make. A much quicker and still perfectly acceptable method is simply to break the chocolate sheet into small pieces after it has hardened. Place the pieces on the whipped cream as directed for the triangles. This rustic version was born of necessity at the school when a young future chef decided to challenge nature and attempted (and would not give up) to cut the triangles out of a thin sheet of chocolate after first placing the sheet in the refrigerator for quite some time! A second option, which is very showy when the cake is to be presented whole, is to decorate the slices with chocolate fans. Place the fans in concentric circles starting at the perimeter of the cake.

⅔ recipe or 3 pounds (1 kg 365 g) Crème Parisienne (page 841; see Note)

⅓ cup (80 ml) kirschwasser

Dark coating chocolate, melted

4 Meringues Noisettes (page 29), 10 inches (25 cm) in diameter

1 Chocolate Chiffon Sponge Cake I (page 441), 10 inches (25 cm) in diameter

⅓ cup (80 ml) simple syrup

⅓ cup (80 ml) kirschwasser

1½ cups (360 ml) heavy cream

2 teaspoons (10 g) granulated sugar

Dark Chocolate Triangles (page 460), 1½ inches (3.7 cm) tall and ¾ inches (2 cm) wide at the base

Dark Chocolate Squares (page 460)

Unsweetened cocoa powder

1. Combine the crème Parisienne and ⅓ cup (80 ml) kirschwasser and whip to stiff peaks.

2. Brush a thin layer of melted coating chocolate on the top sides of the meringues noisettes. Place 2 of the meringues, chocolate-side up, on cardboard cake circles for support. Place one-quarter of the crème Parisienne on each and spread out flat.

3. Cut the skin from the top of the chocolate sponge, cutting it even at the same time. Cut the sponge into 2 layers and place them on top of the crème Parisienne, pressing down lightly.

Combine the simple syrup and the remaining ⅓ cup (80 ml) kirschwasser. Brush the mixture over the sponges, using all of it. Divide the remaining crème Parisienne on top of the sponges and spread out evenly. Place the remaining meringue bottoms, chocolate-side down, on top of the cream and press down lightly. Do not worry if the meringues stick out beyond the sponge; you will trim them later. If you plan to present the cakes in serving pieces rather than whole, place the cakes in the freezer until they are hard before finishing them. This will make them easier to cut.

4. Trim any meringue that protrudes outside the sponge so that the sides of the cakes are even (see Figure 11-11, page 511). Whip the heavy cream and sugar to stiff peaks. Divide the cream between the cakes and ice the tops and sides, spreading just a thin layer on the sides and the remainder on the tops.

5. Cut or mark the cakes into the desired number of serving pieces, making sure the cakes are still half frozen when you cut them to avoid smashing the layers.

6. Decorate the length of each slice with the dark chocolate triangles. Start by placing 1 triangle at the tip of the slice, then 2 behind it, and 3 behind those, continuing as the piece becomes wider. Stick the pointed ends into the cream so that the triangles stand up at a very slight angle. Fasten a chocolate square on the side of each slice. Sift cocoa powder lightly over the top.

NOTE: Crème Parisienne must be refrigerated for a minimum of 8 hours or, preferably, overnight before it can be whipped to stiff peaks. If this is not practical, substitute the full recipe of Chocolate Cream (page 839).

Pithiviers yield: 2 cakes, 10 inches (25 cm) in diameter

This very famous classic French almond cake takes its name from the small town of Pithivier (pronounced *pa-tiv-e-ay*) outside Orléans near Paris. If you are in the neighborhood and have a few days to spare, keep going southwest along the Loire River and, if at all possible, do not end your journey until you get to Tours. It is fabulous country there, and everywhere you go, at any time you want, they will be happy to serve you a slice of Pithiviers with your afternoon coffee or for dessert with caramel or vanilla ice cream.

The puff pastry on top of the cakes is always scored in a fan-shaped pattern with a small, sharp knife before the cakes are baked. They can be refrigerated at this point for a few days, or frozen for much longer, to bake as needed. This makes Pithiviers a practical (and not so commonplace) choice as an addition to a buffet table. If the cakes are to be presented whole, you may want to dress up the tops by glazing them in the following manner. Bake the cakes at 400°F (205°C) for the first 25 minutes (rather than 12 minutes at 450°F/230°C). Quickly sift a thin layer of powdered sugar on top, using a fine mesh sieve. Return the cakes to the oven, lower the oven temperature to 375°F (190°C) (leaving the oven door ajar while you sift the sugar will take care of this), and continue baking approximately 20 minutes longer or until the sugar has melted and beautifully glazed the tops. This cake is best served warm or at least at room temperature and should be enjoyed the same day it is baked. Any leftovers should be heated slightly before serving.

2 pounds 12 ounces (1 kg 250 g) Puff Pastry (page 74)

1 pound (455 g) Frangipane Filling (page 842)

6 ounces (170 g) Pastry Cream (page 845)

¼ cup (60 ml) light rum

Egg wash

1. Divide the puff pastry into 2 pieces, 1 pound 6 ounces (625 g) each. Divide these into 2 unequal pieces, making 1 piece in each pair 3 to 4 ounces (85 to 115 g) heavier than the other.

2. Roll out the smaller pieces of dough into 11-inch (27.5-cm) squares, approximately ¹⁄₁₆ inch (2 mm) thick. These squares will be used for the base of the cakes. Place the squares on a sheet pan brushed lightly with water. Place in the refrigerator.

3. Roll the remaining (larger) pieces of dough into squares the same size as the first two; these should be about ⅛ inch (3 mm) thick. Place these dough squares on a sheet pan lined with baking paper and refrigerate.

4. Combine the frangipane filling, the pastry cream, and the rum. Set aside.

5. When the puff pastry has relaxed for at least 30 minutes and is firm, cut all 4 squares into circles, 11 inches (27.5 cm) in diameter, leaving the dough in place on the pans.

6. Divide the filling evenly between the base circles (the circles on the sheet pan brushed with water), spreading it out to 1½ inches (3.7 cm) from the edge. Brush egg wash on the uncovered edges. Place the remaining dough circles on top of the filling, then use your thumbs to press the edges together and make a tight seal.

7. Choose a Pithivier ring, a 10-inch (25-cm) flan ring, or the frame of a 10-inch (25-cm) springform pan. Press the ring into the top of the cakes, 1 at a time, hard enough to mark a distinctive border 1 inch (2.5 cm) from the edge. Leave the ring in place and cut the border in scallop pattern (Figure 11-15). If the dough has become soft, refrigerate before proceeding.

8. Brush egg wash over the entire top of each cake. Score slightly curved, faint lines on top of the cakes, using the tip of a paring knife. Cut from the center to the edge of the cakes without cutting through the dough, as shown in the illustration.

9. Bake at 450°F (230°C) for 12 minutes. Lower the heat to 375°F (190°C) and continue baking approximately 35 minutes longer or until baked through. Cool to room temperature, then cut the cakes into the desired number of serving pieces.

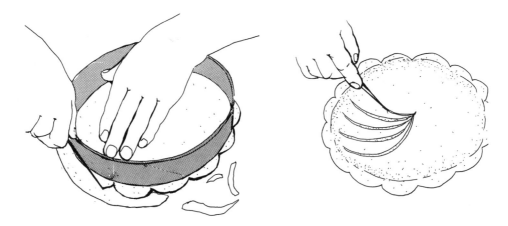

FIGURE 11-15 Using a cake ring as a guide while cutting the edge of the puff pastry in a scalloped pattern; scoring the puff pastry on top of Pithiviers in a fan pattern

Poppy Seed Layer Cake yield: 2 cakes, 10 inches (25 cm) in diameter

Speckled cake layers, dotted with orange zest and separated by white cream and red strawberries, make this cake as visually appealing as it is delicious. The ingredient list calls for thinly sliced strawberries, and as I have found that students interpret this as anywhere from paper-thin to ¼ inch (6mm), let me emphasize the importance of slicing the strawberries as thinly as possible without having them fall apart. The slices can be placed on the cake in overlapping rows, if needed, or even stacked in several layers, as long as they are very thin. If the strawberries are too thick, the servings will fall apart when the finished cake is portioned.

Be careful not to overmix the batter and incorporate excess air. Overmixing can cause what is known as a *tunnel effect*: long, worm-shaped holes found throughout the baked cake.

Poppy Seed Cake Base (recipe follows)

1 quart (960 ml) heavy cream

2 tablespoons (30 g) granulated sugar

12 ounces (340 g) medium strawberries, stemmed, thinly sliced (about 20)

6 ounces (170 g) sliced almonds, toasted and lightly crushed

Piping Chocolate (page 465), melted

Strawberry wedges

1. Cut the skin from the tops of the cakes and even the tops if necessary. Cut the cakes into 3 layers each (see Figure 11-6, page 488).

2. Whip the cream and sugar to stiff peaks. Spread a thin layer of cream, ⅛ inch (3 mm) thick, on the bottom cake layers. Cover the cream with a single layer of strawberry slices. Spread another thin layer of cream on top of the strawberries. Place the second cake layers on top of the cream and repeat the procedure. Add the top cake layers.

3. Ice the top and sides of the cakes with a thin layer of whipped cream. Use just enough to cover the sponge; you should have some left for decorating.

4. Cover the sides of the cakes with the crushed almonds (see Figure 11-12, page 520).

5. Cut or mark the cakes into the desired number of serving pieces. Decorate the top of each slice with the piping chocolate (Figure 11-16). Place the reserved whipped cream in a pastry bag with a No. 4 (8-mm) star tip. Pipe a rosette at the edge of each slice. Place a small strawberry wedge on each rosette.

NOTE: If you do not have time to pipe the chocolate design, pipe the rosettes and sprinkle dark chocolate shavings on top of the cakes within the rosettes.

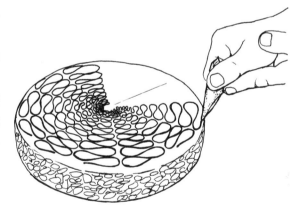

FIGURE 11-16 Decorating the top of the Poppy Seed Layer Cake with a design made from piping chocolate

POPPY SEED CAKE BASE yield: 2 layers, 10 inches (25 cm) in diameter

The quantity of poppy seeds here can be scaled up or down to suit your taste.

Butter and Flour Mixture (page 7) or pan spray

8 ounces (225 g) bread flour

8 ounces (225 g) cake flour

1½ teaspoons (6 g) baking soda

1 teaspoon (4 g) baking powder

5 ounces (140 g) poppy seeds

2 tablespoons (36 g) grated or finely chopped orange zest (about 2 medium oranges)

1 pound (455 g) unsalted butter, at room temperature

1 pound 8 ounces (680 g) granulated sugar

10 egg yolks (⅞ cup/210 ml), at room temperature

1 tablespoon (15 ml) vanilla extract

12 ounces (340 g) sour cream

12 egg whites (1½ cups/360 ml)

½ teaspoon (2.5 g) salt

½ teaspoon (1 g) cream of tartar

1. Brush the butter and flour mixture over the inside of 2 cake pans, 10 inches (25 cm) in diameter, or use pan spray.

2. Sift the flours, baking soda, and baking powder together. Mix in the poppy seeds and the orange zest.

3. Cream the butter. Add 1 pound 4 ounces (570 g) sugar and beat until light and fluffy. Add the egg yolks and vanilla. Mix for 2 minutes.

4. Mix in half of the dry ingredients at low speed. Add the sour cream and mix until just combined. Mix in the remaining dry ingredients.

5. Whip the egg whites, salt, and cream of tartar to a foam. Gradually add the remaining 4 ounces (115 g) sugar and whip to soft peaks. Fold the whites into the batter one-quarter at a time. Divide the batter between the reserved cake pans.

6. Bake at 350°F (175°C) for approximately 45 minutes or until the cake springs back when pressed lightly in the center.

Princess Cake yield: 2 cakes, 10 inches (25 cm) in diameter (Photo 52)

I am slightly embarrassed to admit that I do not have a definite answer as to why the marzipan on top of a Princess Cake is traditionally colored green. This is a question I have been asked time after time and, believe me, I have tried to find out. It would at least make more sense to me if the cake were flavored with mint or pistachio.

Princess Cakes are often made in other colors. The marzipan is left its natural off-white hue, and the cakes are sometimes made with pale pink marzipan for special occasions; however, pale green is the norm. Regrettably, not everyone remembers the pale part. Food colorings come in different strengths, and once you have added too much, it might be too late (unfortunately, there isn't a natural green coloring agent that can be added to marzipan).

The smooth marzipan covering on the Princess Cake makes an ideal surface on which to pipe a design in chocolate, such as "Happy Birthday" or a message to acknowledge a special occasion. Otherwise, the only decoration required is a light dusting of powdered sugar.

2 Sponge Cakes (page 437), 10 inches (25 cm) in diameter, or 2 Chiffon Sponge Cake I (page 440), 10 inches (25 cm) in diameter

¾ cup (120 ml) Plain Cake Syrup (page 31)

6 ounces (170 g) smooth strawberry jam

1 pound 4 ounces (570 g) Quick Bavarian Cream (page 846)

5 cups (1 L 200 ml) heavy cream

2 tablespoons (30 g) granulated sugar

1 pound 4 ounces (570 g) Marzipan (page 21), tinted light green

Powdered sugar

Strawberry Sauce (page 832)

Piping Chocolate (page 465)

1. Cut the skin from the top of the 2 cakes, cutting the tops level at the same time if necessary. Cut the cakes into 3 layers each.

2. Brush cake syrup over the 2 bottom layers. Divide the jam between them and spread out evenly. Place the middle cake layers on top of the jam. Brush with cake syrup. Divide the Bavarian cream between the middle layers and spread out evenly. Place the top cake layers on the Bavarian cream.

3. Whip the heavy cream and granulated sugar to stiff peaks. Divide the cream between the cakes. Spread just enough cream on the sides of the cakes to cover them. Spread the remaining cream into a dome shape on the tops, about ¾ inch (2 cm) thick in the center.

4. Divide the marzipan into 2 pieces. Roll them out, 1 at a time, into circles ⅛ inch (3 mm) thick and about 15 inches (37.5 cm) in diameter, using powdered sugar to prevent the marzipan from sticking.

5. Roll 1 circle onto a dowel and unroll over a cake. Smooth the marzipan onto the cake with your hands, keeping the dome shape on top. Pay special attention to the sides to be sure the marzipan is not wrinkled. Trim the marzipan around the base of the cake to make it even. Repeat the procedure to cover the second cake.

6. Cut or mark the cakes into the desired number of serving pieces. Cut from the edge of the cake toward the center to prevent the marzipan from being pushed into the whipped cream. If you have problems, cut through the marzipan layer first before cutting the cake. Sift powdered sugar lightly over the cakes.

7. Put a portion of the strawberry sauce into a piping bottle. Place a small amount of melted piping chocolate in a piping bag and decorate the base of as many dessert plates as you anticipate needing by piping a zigzag pattern of chocolate on the top half of the plates, ending with a large loop on the bottom half. Set the plates aside.

8. Presentation: Sift powdered sugar over the base of a prepared plate. Place 1 slice of cake crosswise on top of the chocolate lines. Pipe strawberry sauce inside the piped chocolate loop.

CHEF'S TIP

The marzipan may alternatively be textured with a tread roller or waffle roller before it is placed on the cake. If you plan to decorate the cakes, sift the powdered sugar over the top after adding the decoration. To protect the marzipan from becoming wet from the whipped cream if the cake is to be served the next day, brush or spread a thin film of vanilla buttercream on the bottom side of the marzipan before placing it on the cake. You then have to invert the marzipan onto the cake and will not be able to avoid getting some buttercream on your hands.

Sacher Torte yield: 2 cakes, 10 inches (25 cm) in diameter

In the nineteenth century, Vienna was the undisputed capital of the confectioner's art. Among all of the calorie-rich, cholesterol-saturated offerings, none was more famous than the Sacher Torte. Franz Sacher was the head pastry cook of Prince Metternich and part of the famous Viennese hotel and restaurant family. He invented the Sacher Torte for the Congress of Vienna (1814–1815). Long after Sacher's death, a great controversy about the torte divided many in Vienna into two groups: the descendants of Franz Sacher, who proclaimed that the cake must consist of two layers with jam in the center, and the contingent led by Edouard Demel of the famed Demel's Pâtisserie, who insisted on only one layer with jam spread on top (a recipe he claimed was authorized by Sacher's grandson). A court battle went on for six years before it was won by the Hotel Sacher family.

A slice of Sacher Torte *mit schlag*—which means "with cream"—and a good cup of coffee are a must during a visit to Vienna. If you have the opportunity to visit Vienna, you can still enjoy this treat on the terrace of the Sacher Hotel, across from the Opera. I have come across many recipes that specify raspberry jam rather than apricot. This recipe was given to me by an Austrian konditor named Manfred with whom I worked. Recently, this Sacher Torte was on the menu at school and received what the server described as "the ultimate accolade." One of his guests, a tourist from Vienna, told him to send word to the kitchen that this was the best Sacher Torte she had ever tasted.

Sacher Biscuits (recipe follows)
3 cups (720 ml) Apricot Glaze (page 5)
1½ cups (360 ml) Chocolate Glaze (page 465)

Dark or milk Piping Chocolate (page 465), melted

1. Cut the skins from the tops of the Sacher biscuits (even the tops, if necessary) and cut each cake into 2 layers.

2. Heat the apricot glaze until completely melted and smooth. Place one-quarter on each of the 2 bottom cake layers and spread it out quickly, forcing it into the cake before it has a chance to form a skin. Add the second cake layers and press them into the glaze. Use the remaining apricot glaze to ice the tops and sides of the cakes.

3. Move the cakes to a cake cooler or aspic rack with a sheet pan underneath. Be careful not to disturb the apricot glaze once it has started to form a skin. Spread a thin layer of chocolate glaze on the tops and sides of the cakes. It should be just thick enough to mask the apricot glaze underneath. Leave the cakes on the rack for a few minutes, then move them to cardboard cake circles before the glaze is completely set.

4. When the glaze is firm enough to be cut without running, mark or cut the cakes into the desired number of servings. Place milk or dark piping chocolate in a piping bag and pipe a large *S* on each slice.

SACHER BISCUIT yield: 2 biscuits, 10 inches (25 cm) in diameter

14 egg yolks (1¼ cups /300 ml)

12 ounces (340 g) granulated sugar

6 ounces (170 g) bread flour

3 ounces (85 g) cake flour

3 ounces (85 g) unsweetened cocoa powder

3 ounces (85 g) hazelnuts, finely ground

3 ounces (85 g) sweet dark chocolate

7 ounces (200 g) unsalted butter

14 egg whites (1¾ cups/420 ml)

1. Whip the egg yolks with 5 ounces (140 g) sugar until light and fluffy.

2. Sift the flours and cocoa powder together; mix in the ground hazelnuts.

3. Melt the chocolate and butter together. Keep warm.

4. Whip the egg whites to a foam. Gradually add the remaining 7 ounces (200 g) sugar and whip to stiff peaks. Fold the yolk mixture into the egg whites, then fold in the dry ingredients. Fold in the chocolate mixture. Divide the batter evenly between 2 greased and floured cake pans, 10 inches (25 cm) in diameter.

5. Bake at 375°F (190°C) for about 20 minutes. Let the cakes cool completely before using them in the recipe.

Strawberry Choux Cake yield: 2 cakes, 10 inches (25 cm) in diameter

This may strike you as an unusual use for pâte à choux, which most people think of as a base for creating individual pastries. But, as I have said before, it's always nice to offer something a bit different and, to tell you the truth, the flavor is very much like eating a giant strawberry cream puff.

All items prepared from pâte à choux are at their best served the same day they are made. If you do not have time to start early enough to do so here, make the pâte à choux sheet, bake it, allow it to cool, then store it, covered, in a dry box or a warm location overnight. On the other hand, if you did not think this far in advance and you suspect the cakes are not going to be set up on time and you are going to end up in the weeds, add a bit more gelatin than the recipe calls for, which accelerates the setting process. This trick comes in handy with any cake or dessert set with gelatin. Be careful here: There is an adverse side effect in that the item—the filling, in this case—will end up too firm, which can be unpleasant. However, this does not happen for several hours, so if you will be serving right way, you can increase the gelatin to 5 teaspoons (15 g) and the water to ½ cup (120 ml) to get yourself out of a tight spot. Do not do this if the cake (or other gelatin item) will not be served until the following day.

⅔ recipe Pâte à Choux (page 83)

Strawberry Compote Cream (recipe follows)

1 recipe Chantilly Cream (page 838)

Powdered sugar

8 small strawberries, stems attached

1. Line 2 full sheet pans, 16 x 24 inches (40 x 60 cm), with baking paper; secure the papers to the pans with a touch of pâte à choux in each corner. Divide the pâte à choux batter between the pans and spread it out to about ½ inch (1.2 ml) from the edge of the pan on each side.

2. Bake at 375°F (190°C) for approximately 40 minutes or until the pâte à choux is completely baked. Cool thoroughly.

3. Cut out 2 circles, 10 inches (25 cm) in diameter, from each pâte à choux sheet (4 total). Place the scraps left after cutting the circles onto a sheet pan lined with baking paper and set aside.

4. Place 2 cake rings, 10 inches (25 cm) in diameter, on top of 12-inch (30-cm) cardboard cake rounds. Place a choux paste circle inside each ring, right-side up. Reserve.

5. Finish the strawberry compote cream and divide it evenly between the cake rings, spreading it out level on top. Place the remaining choux circles on top inverting them so that the flat sides are facing up. Press the circles gently into the cream. Refrigerate for at least 2 hours to set the filling.

6. Tear the reserved pâte à choux scraps into small pieces measuring approximately ½ inch (1.2 cm) and place in a 250°F (122°C) oven to dry thoroughly. Reserve.

7. Run a knife around the inside perimeter of the cake rings and remove the rings. Ice the top and sides of the cakes with the Chantilly cream. Cover the cream with the pâte à choux crumbs. Sift powdered sugar lightly over the cakes. Decorate with the whole strawberries.

STRAWBERRY COMPOTE CREAM yield: 9 cups (2 L 160 ml)

Make the compote part of this recipe (Step 1) while the pâte à choux circles are baking and/or cooling, but do not finish the cream until you are ready to assemble the cakes in Step 5 of the main recipe. You may want to increase the amount of sugar if the strawberries are not at their peak.

If you do not have strawberries or prefer not to use them, you can substitute blueberries, blackberries, or raspberries with excellent results. You should, of course, change the name of the cake and garnish the finished cakes appropriately.

14 ounces (400 g) strawberries	4 teaspoons (12 g) unflavored gelatin powder
4 ounces (115 g) granulated sugar	⅓ cup (80 ml) water
Juice of 1 lime	3 cups (720 ml) heavy cream

1. Rinse, stem, and cut the strawberries into pieces. Place in a saucepan together with the sugar and lime juice. Bring to a boil while stirring constantly. Remove from the heat, transfer to a bowl, and set aside to chill in the refrigerator.

2. Sprinkle the gelatin over the water and set aside to soften. Heat to dissolve.

3. Warm ½ cup cream (it should be warm but not hot) and combine with the gelatin mixture. Begin whipping the remaining cream. Slowly pour the gelatin into the cream and continue whipping to soft peaks. Fold the berry compote into the cream and use immediately.

Swiss Kirsch Cake (Zuger Kirsch Torte) yield: 2 cakes, 10 inches (25 cm) in diameter (Photo 50)

This cake is as synonymous with Switzerland as the Black Forest Cake is with Germany, although both cakes are made and are quite popular in each country. Swiss Kirsch Cake is especially favored in the Black Forest region of Germany, which is on the Swiss border. The people there love cherries in everything!

Zuger Kirsch Torte, also known simply as *Zug Torte*, was named after the medieval Swiss town of Zug, located near the northern end of the Zuger Sea (perhaps a bit too near, as part of the town sank in 1435, 1594, and again in 1887). A wonderful time to visit this area is in the early spring, when the cherry trees are in bloom and the tourist season hasn't officially started. You can hardly find a konditorei in this region, or for that matter in Switzerland, that does not have some version of this diet-busting dessert, with its delicious combination of kirschwasser-soaked sponge, thin, crisp layers of meringue, and a covering of kirsch-flavored buttercream. Add to that the practicality of this cake, which can be made several days ahead and then finished quickly, and it is not hard to understand why Zuger Kirsch Torte is a hit with both the consumer and the konditor.

1 recipe Japonaise Meringue Batter (page 28)

1¼ cups (300 ml) simple syrup

¾ cup (180 ml) kirschwasser

½ teaspoon (2.5 ml) Beet Juice (page 5) or 1 drop red food coloring

½ recipe or 2 pounds 10 ounces (1 kg 195 g) Vanilla Buttercream (Swiss Method) (page 477)

1 Chiffon Sponge Cake I (page 440), 10 inches (25 cm) in diameter

Powdered sugar

Cherry Cookies (instructions follow)

Cherry Sauce (page 819)

I. Pipe the Japonaise meringue batter into 4 circles, 10 inches (25 cm) in diameter, following the instructions for Meringue Noisette (see Figure 1-5, page 29). Bake at 300°F (149°C) for approximately 30 minutes or until dry and golden. Set aside to cool.

2. Combine the simple syrup and kirschwasser. Add half of the mixture, together with the beet juice, to the buttercream. Stir until completely incorporated. Reserve the remaining syrup mixture.

3. Cut the skin from the top of the sponge cake and cut the top even at the same time. Cut the cake into 2 layers.

4. Place 2 of the Japonaise circles on cardboard cake rounds for support. Spread a ¼-inch (6-mm) layer of buttercream on each one. Brush some of the reserved syrup mixture over the sponge layers, then invert them, syrup-side down, onto the buttercream. Press down lightly so they adhere. Brush as much of the remaining syrup as needed over the top and sides of the sponges so that the syrup thoroughly penetrates the cake. Spread a ¼-inch (6-mm) layer of buttercream over the sponges. Place the remaining Japonaise circles on top of the buttercream layer, flat-side up. Refrigerate the cakes until the buttercream is firm.

5. Trim any Japonaise that protrudes from the sides of the cakes to make the sides even (see Figure 11-11, page 511). Ice the top and sides of the cakes with a thin layer of buttercream,

FIGURE 11-17 **Using a serrated cake-decorating comb to mark horizontal lines on the sides of Swiss Kirsch Cake by holding the comb against the cake while rotating the cake-decorating turntable**

using just enough to cover the sponge. You should have a small amount of buttercream left to use in decorating. Mark the sides of the cakes with horizontal lines, using a serrated cake-decorating comb (Figure 11-17). Mark the tops of the cakes in a diamond pattern, using either a diamond template or by marking parallel lines every ½ inch (1.2 cm), first in one direction, then again at a 45-degree angle, with the back of a long knife. Refrigerate the cakes to set the buttercream.

6. Sift powdered sugar lightly over the tops of the cakes. Cut or mark the cakes into the desired number of servings. Place the remaining buttercream in a pastry bag with a No. 4 (8-mm) plain tip. Pipe a small dot of buttercream at the wide end of each slice. Place a cherry cookie on each buttercream dot (see Note). Serve with cherry sauce if using as a plated dessert.

NOTE: This is an excellent cake to prepare ahead, as it can be stored covered in the refrigerator for up to 4 days. However, do not add the powdered sugar and cookie decorations until the day the cakes will be served.

CHERRY COOKIES yield: 24 cookies, 1¼ inch (3.1 cm) in diameter

2 ounces (55 g) Short Dough (page 67)

1 ounce (30 g) Marzipan (page 21), colored red

Piping Chocolate (page 465), melted

1. Roll out the short dough to ⅛ inch (3 mm) thick, using flour to keep it from sticking. Cut out 1 cookie for each serving of cake, using a 1¼-inch (3.1-cm) fluted round cookie cutter. Place the cookies on a sheet pan lined with baking paper or a Silpat.

2. Bake at 375°F (190°C) until golden brown, approximately 10 minutes. Let the cookies cool completely.

3. Roll the marzipan into a ¼-inch (6-mm) rope. Slice the rope into pea-sized pieces, making 2 for each cookie. Roll the pieces into round balls and set aside.

4. Place the piping chocolate in a piping bag and cut a small opening. Pipe 2 cherry stems on each cookie. Pipe the lines so that the stems are attached at the top, curve toward the outside, and are separate at the bottom (Figure 11-18). Place 1 reserved marzipan cherry at the end of each stem before the chocolate sets up. If you are making a large number of these decorations, pipe all of the stems, then go back and add a tiny drop of chocolate at the bottom to attach the cherries. Store the cookies covered in a dry place until needed.

FIGURE 11-18 Piping cherry stems on the short dough cookies to decorate the Swiss Kirsch Cake

Swedish Chocolate Cake yield: 2 cakes, 10 inches (25 cm) in diameter

This is one of the recipes from the konditori where I was an apprentice. It is simply the way a chocolate layer cake was made in my hometown—and for good reason, it would seem, because I have received compliments from customers and guests over the course of many years wherever I have made it. The main difference between this cake and the multitude of other chocolate cakes around to choose from is that this one is not overbearingly rich. The pastry cream, in addition to adding a pleasant, moist flavor, offsets the chocolate buttercream, making it less overwhelming.

Probably the ultimate praise I received for this cake came to me indirectly from the guests of a large hotel in Oslo, Norway. One of my former students, a Norwegian woman who apprenticed under me here in the United States and then moved back to Norway, returned for a visit and proudly told me that she was now in charge of the desserts in one of the hotel's restaurants. She said she was featuring, among other things, my Swedish Chocolate Cake and that it was a big hit. Taking into consideration the well-known, but not too serious, old feud between the two countries (Norway was part of Sweden from 1814 until it was given its independence in 1905), I said I was surprised she could sell even one slice. She responded with a sly smile, saying, "No offense, Chef Bo, but I left the Swedish part out of the title!"

2 Chocolate Sponge Cakes (page 438), 10 inches (25 cm) in diameter

¾ cup (180 ml) Plain Cake Syrup (page 31)

1 pound 12 ounces (795 g) Pastry Cream (page 845)

2 pounds 10 ounces (1 kg 195 g) Chocolate Buttercream (Italian Method) (page 476)

Curled Dark Chocolate Shavings (page 464)

Chocolate Rectangles, 4 × 1 inch (10 × 2.5 cm) (page 460)

Chocolate Squares (page 460)

1. Cut the skin off the chocolate sponges, cutting the tops even at the same time. Cut each into 3 layers. Use the bottom layers as the base for each cake.

2. Brush some of the cake syrup over the bottom cake layers. Place half of the pastry cream on each and spread out evenly. Place the second cake layers on the cream and brush with cake syrup. Spread a ¼-inch (6-mm) layer of chocolate buttercream on the second cake layers. Place the remaining cake layers on top and brush with cake syrup.

3. Ice the top and sides of the cakes with chocolate buttercream, spreading it just thick enough to cover the sponge. Reserve some buttercream for decoration. Refrigerate the cakes until the buttercream is firm so that the cakes will slice cleanly.

4. Put the reserved buttercream in a pastry bag with a No. 4 (8-mm) plain tip. Making 1 decoration for each serving of cake, pipe a small mound of buttercream, about the size of a cherry half, onto a sheet pan lined with baking paper. Cover the mounds with curled chocolate shavings. Refrigerate the decorations until they are firm.

5. Cut the cakes into the desired number of slices. Place a chocolate square on the side of each piece. Pipe a straight line of buttercream next to one cut side on the top of each piece (Figure 11-19). Stand a chocolate rectangle at an angle on each slice, supported by the buttercream lines and angled slightly toward the center of the cake, as shown in the illustration. Place 1 reserved decoration at the end of each slice.

FIGURE 11-19 **Piping chocolate buttercream lines on top of Swedish Chocolate Cake; placing the chocolate rectangle at an angle against the buttercream lines**

CHAPTER

TWELVE

some of the

most labor

intensive items

in the bakeshop

Individual Pastries

The term pastries includes small, decorated cuts of cakes or tarts, fancy individual pieces in numerous shapes, and the much larger classics, such as napoleons and chocolate éclairs. They are perhaps best known in the United States as *French pastries*, which is a bit misleading. In France, they are called *les petits gâteaux*, or "small cakes," but these individual sweets are tremendously popular all over Europe.

When you enter a European pastry shop—called a *konditori* in Scandinavia, a *konditorei* in Austria, Germany, and Switzerland, and a *pâtisserie* in France—you see an amazing selection of pastries. They range from simple mazarins and apple tartlets to the elegant petits fours glacé. Certain larger pastries are intended for a single serving and require a fork or spoon to eat; examples of these are babas, cream puffs, and apple strudel. Many in this category can be offered as plated desserts, in which case they are served with an appropriate sauce and garnish. Other pastries are small enough that you can consume two or three without guilt or calling attention to yourself. These are appropriately eaten with the fingers and include petits fours sec and petits fours glacé. In the same way that many petits fours can be made into larger single-portion pastries, many larger pastries can be made into petits fours simply by cutting them into smaller pieces and perhaps enhancing the decoration a bit. A petit four, by definition, is bite-sized and elegantly decorated.

Each country in Europe has pastry specialties that vary in flavor and style. The variations are influenced, to some degree, by the climate. It is much easier to work with chocolate and whipped cream—and more pleasant to eat them—in the cooler northern part of Europe than in the heat of the Mediterranean. In southern France or Italy, you will find a tendency (too often, in my opinion) to use fondant, candied fruits, and apricot glaze, which make the pastries very sweet. In the Scandinavian countries, many pastries are made from almond, chocolate, and/or fresh fruit. Pastries topped with fresh fruit are typically covered with pectin glaze, a sugar syrup that develops a pleasant tart flavor when tartaric acid is added to it, which complements the fruit nicely. A similar style is popular in Germany, Switzerland, and Austria.

The pastries in this chapter are quite varied. Some must be started a day in advance of serving, while others can be made on the spur of the moment. Some have a plain finish, although many others require a bit of artistic ability. All of these recipes have proven very popular in the United States, as I can attest from watching customers delight in my students' creations.

Portioning Pastry Strips

Figures 12-1 to 12-3 show 3 techniques for cutting pastry strips or rectangular cakes into individual servings.

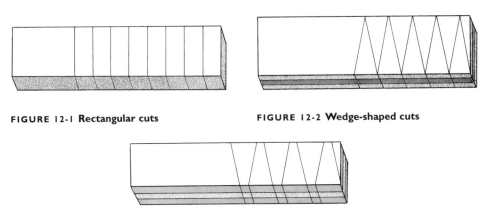

FIGURE 12-1 Rectangular cuts   **FIGURE 12-2 Wedge-shaped cuts**

FIGURE 12-3 Blunt-end triangle cuts

Final Steps

There is no question that individual pastries represent some of the most labor-intensive items in the bakeshop, and they tend to use primarily expensive ingredients, such as almond paste, chocolate, nuts, and candied fruits. This makes it all the more critical to finish and store the pastries properly. It is a shame to go through the necessary steps to create perfect Florentina Surprise pastries, for example, then dip them improperly so they end up with unprofessional-looking rings of chocolate all around the bottom, or to create lovely little petits fours and coat them with thick fondant so that the multiple layers are obscured. Another step during which it is important to pay close attention to the instructions is when pastries are sliced into individual pieces. Always use a sharp knife held at a 90-degree angle to achieve straight sides and uniform pieces. In some cases, the directions call for cutting the pastry upside-down, when it is topped with marzipan, for example. This allows you to cut cleanly through the topping without marring the edges. Always be certain you invert the sheet onto a clean surface.

TEMPERATURE FOR COATING CHOCOLATE

The final step in the majority of the following recipes calls for covering the finished pastries partially or completely with melted chocolate. Although in each case the instructions specify the use of coating chocolate, which simply has to be melted and does not require tempering, it is still critical to work with the chocolate at the proper temperature, or your efforts may be ruined. The chocolate should generally be between 100° and 110°F (38° and 43°C), depending on the brand you are using. If the melted chocolate is too cold and, therefore, too thick, the result will be a clumsy looking, heavy coating that will not drape and conform to the shape of the pastry as it should, and your cost will be higher because you will use more product. Conversely, coating chocolate that is too hot will lose its satin shine and set up with a dull, lackluster finish instead. If the chocolate is too hot when dipping a pastry topped with buttercream, such as chocolate macaroons, part of the buttercream will melt, ruining both the shape of the pastry and the supply of chocolate.

DIPPING PASTRIES IN CHOCOLATE

Whether you use coating chocolate or tempered chocolate to cover the pastries, you should create an organized and efficient workstation for dipping. If you are right-handed, always work from left to right: the undipped pastries on the left, followed by the melted chocolate, a sheet of baking paper, and, finally, a sheet pan lined with baking paper to hold the finished pastries. Your left hand should pick up an undipped pastry as your right hand sets a dipped item down on the tray. When using a dipping fork, as is done with Tosca and Angelica Points, the tool is inserted into the side of the pastry. After the item is dipped into the chocolate, it is moved up and down over the bowl of chocolate to force as much chocolate as possible off the pastry; this is to eliminate what are known as *feet*—excess chocolate drips that float out around the pastry after it has been placed on the pan. After being moved up and down, the bottom of the pastry is scraped against the side of the bowl, then blotted on the sheet of baking paper in a further effort to remove excess chocolate before finally setting it on the tray.

When you remove the dipping fork from either of the two pastries mentioned, you will leave a mark; this is unavoidable. However, as you remove the fork, you can use your free hand to hold the pastry in place if necessary, as there is no chocolate on the top. This is not possible when the entire pastry is covered with chocolate. Instead, press the bottom of the pastry firmly against the sheet pan as you pull the fork out. For Sarah Bernhardts and chocolate macaroons, a dipping fork is not needed because you can hold onto the bottom of the pastry with your fingers. These require just a few up and down motions and perhaps a small scrape against the side of the bowl; they are not blotted on the paper.

When the pastry is held with your fingers, it is very important not to leave fingerprints, which will happen if you grasp the pastry too close to the chocolate. This is even harder to avoid with small, thin pastries such as Citrons. If you have trouble holding the pastry with your fingers, try using a dipping fork, or even a paring knife, inserted into the bottom of the barquette at an angle. This will provide a convenient handle, making them easier to manage. Simply pull the knife or fork out after setting the Citron, chocolate-side up, on the tray. You may need to use a finger on your free hand to steady the pastry as you pull out the knife or dipping fork; do not press down to free the tool or you will break the crust.

Display

When preparing pastries to serve buffet-style, the items should be small enough that the guests can enjoy a variety. Most of the recipes in this chapter are portioned accordingly but, in some cases, you may want to make them a little smaller either by piping or rolling them smaller to begin with—in the case of chocolate macaroons and Rum Balls, for example—or simply by cutting the pieces smaller for pastries such as Meringue Landeck and Orange Truffle Cuts.

When creating a pastry display, it is important to give some thought to your design as you choose the pastries to be prepared. Consider contrast of color, texture, flavor, and shape. Secondly, plan your arrangement before you start to place the items on the trays or mirrors to avoid moving them, which mars both the item and the display surface. Start to arrange the items as close as possible to serving time. U.S. Public Health Service guidelines require that highly perishable foodstuffs, are not kept at a temperature above 45°F (6°C) or below 140°F (60°C) for more than 4 hours. Two hours is about the maximum time for most pastries that are filled with whipped cream or custard, before they start to deteriorate in quality. If your buffet service is longer than two hours, you should plan to replenish the pastries during service.

The pastries should be displayed in rows, one type per row, evenly spaced, on a clean mirror or tray. Cut slices look best displayed in an angled row rather than parallel to one another. When using a round or oval mirror or tray, consider that you will need much more of the item placed around the outside edge when arranging the items in concentric circles, or of the item used in the center row when making straight lines across the diameter. In both instances, this pastry will be the focal point of the platter, so plan to use something colorful and eye-catching. It is a good idea to wear food-handling latex gloves to avoid leaving fingerprints on chocolate-covered pastries as you move them. If you are creating a buffet for a small number of guests but

must use a large table (in other words, the table might hold three mirrors but you need to put out pastries for only two), it looks better to use more trays and space the pastries farther apart on each one than to have a lot of empty tablecloth showing. Use care when transporting the assembled trays from the kitchen to the dining room. It sometimes makes sense to have an extra person walk ahead of you as a lookout. The assembled trays or mirrors should be arranged on the table at varying heights and/or should be angled slightly by placing a few plates or another object under the edge farthest from the guest to avoid a flat table display.

FIGURE 12-4 Using a cookie cutter with the desired shape and diameter as a guide to mold paper petits fours cups

If the guests will be helping themselves, it is a good idea to place the pastries in small paper cups. Known as *petits fours cups*, these containers are usually round but should be altered to fit individual shapes for the most finished appearance. This can be done by pressing a stack of cups with the appropriate size and shape of cookie cutter to enlarge the bottom (Figure 12-4) or by bending the sides to create a new bottom edge with your hands. If there is a server at the buffet table or when a dessert tray is presented to the table after a meal, it is not necessary to use paper cups, as the server should place the selection on the plate using a cake spatula or tongs.

Storage

Pastries based on pâte à choux or puff pastry, or those with a dairy-based filling, must be made up fresh every day. Other varieties that are covered with chocolate, fondant, or marzipan will keep fresh much longer and can be made once or twice a week, provided you have a storage area with the proper conditions. Storing some of the following pastries can present a problem at times if you have no other choice than the refrigerator, because of hot climate or lack of an alternate cold storage area. The moist air in the refrigerator will leave tiny droplets or a moist film on top of chocolate if the item is refrigerated for more than a few hours and, when the moisture dries, it leaves an unpresentable finish. Pastries iced with fondant, dipped in caramelized sugar, or covered with marzipan do not develop the same unseemly spots that occur on chocolate, but the dampness causes the sugar or marzipan to melt and become soggy. If you cannot store these pastries at cool room temperature, they should be stored, unfinished, in the refrigerator or freezer to decorate as needed. If this is not feasible, placing the pastries in a box before refrigerating will protect them from the moist air; you will still have to contend with the condensation that occurs after they are removed, but the appearance will be acceptable.

Angelica Points yield: 45 pastries

Many small, simple pastries can be made up starting with the same base of frangipane filling baked on a short dough crust, each topped and decorated in its own way. If you do not need the full yield of this recipe, rather than dividing it in half, make the full amount and use the extra for another variation or freeze it to use next time.

If you have not cut this triangle shape before, I recommend that you measure, mark, and cut as directed to get the proper angle. Attempting it freehand is unlikely to produce precise, professional-looking pastries.

1 pound 5 ounces (595 g) Short Dough (page 67)	2 ounces (55 g) Vanilla Buttercream (Swiss Method) (page 477)
4½ ounces (130 g) smooth strawberry jam	1 pound (455 g) Marzipan (page 21), untinted
6 ounces (170 g) candied angelica	Dark coating chocolate, melted
Bread flour	Piping Chocolate (page 465), melted
4 pounds 10 ounces (2 kg 105 g) Frangipane Filling (page 842)	

1. Line the bottom of a half-sheet pan, 16 × 12 inches (40 × 30 cm), with baking paper or a Silpat. Roll out the short dough to ⅛ inch (3 mm) thick and slightly larger than the bottom of the pan; place in the pan. Trim the edges so only the bottom of the pan is covered. Cover and save the scraps for another use. Spread the jam over the short dough.

2. Reserve enough of the nicest-looking angelica pieces to make 45 small decorations. Chop the remainder into small pieces. Toss with a little bread flour to prevent the pieces from sticking together, then mix into the frangipane filling. Spread the filling out evenly over the jam.

3. Bake at 375°F (190°C) until baked through, about 40 minutes. Cool to room temperature; then refrigerate.

4. When the frangipane sheet is cold (preferably, the day after baking), cut off the skin and even the top of the sheet. To do this, leave the frangipane sheet in the pan and cut with a serrated knife held parallel to the top of the cake, using the edge of the pan as a guide for your knife. Run the tip of the knife around the inside edge of the pan, then invert the sheet to unmold. If the bottom of the sheet sticks to the pan, do not force it. Instead, place a hot sheet pan on the outside for a few seconds to soften the fat in the short dough, then try again. Remove the sheet pan and the baking paper or Silpat and turn the sheet right-side up. Spread a thin film of buttercream on top of the frangipane filling.

5. Roll out the marzipan to ⅛ inch (3 mm) thick; it should be slightly larger than the frangipane sheet. Texture the marzipan with a waffle roller. Roll it up on a dowel and unroll on top of the buttercream. Place a clean cardboard on top and invert. With the pastry upside down, trim away the excess marzipan. Refrigerate until the buttercream is firm, but no longer than a few hours or the marzipan will become sticky.

6. Still working with the pastry upside down, trim both long sides, then cut the sheet lengthwise into 5 strips, holding the knife at a 90-degree angle so that the edges are straight; a serrated knife or the very tip of a sharp chef's knife works best.

7. Trim the left short end of one strip to make it even. To achieve the correct angle in cutting the triangles, mark the strip in the following manner. Beginning ⅞ inch (2.1 cm) to the right of the top left corner, mark the strip, alternating every ¾ inch (2 cm) and 2½ inches (6.2 cm) for the length of the strip. Next, make a mark 2½ inches (6.2 cm) from the bottom left corner and then every ¾ inch (2 cm) and 2½ inches (6.2 cm) along the bottom. Cut 9 triangles from the strip, following your marks. The triangles will be ¾ inch (2 cm) wide at the top and 2½ inches (6.2 cm) wide along the bottom. The trimmings can be saved to use in rum ball filling. Repeat with the remaining strips.

8. Dip each triangle into melted dark coating chocolate, coating the bottom and sides up to the marzipan (see Figures 12-25 to 12-29, page 599).

9. Place the piping chocolate in a piping bag. Pipe a figurine on top of each pastry.

10. Cut the reserved angelica into decorations in the same shape as the pastries. The angelica may be sticky enough to adhere to the pastries as is; if not, attach on top with a tiny bit of simple syrup. Do not attach by piping a dot of chocolate underneath because it will show through. Angelica Points will remain fresh for up to 1 week, stored in a cool place, but should not be refrigerated. If you must refrigerate them, they should be boxed and well wrapped to prevent the marzipan from becoming wet.

Apple Mazarins yield: 35 pastries, 2¹/₂ inches (6.2 cm) in diameter

These are unpretentious, country-style pastries—a cross between Streusel Kuchen and, as the name suggests, Mazarins (page 571). This version tastes like a good, wholesome slice of Swedish-style pie. The tops of the pastries are misted with water before baking to keep the streusel from falling off as they are unmolded. Placing them in the refrigerator overnight will also help hold the topping in place.

1 pound 14 ounces (855 g) Short Dough (page 67)	1 pound 8 ounces (680 g) Streusel Topping (page 37)
2 tablespoons (30 ml) Calvados	Powdered sugar
¹/₃ recipe Chunky Apple Filling (page 840)	
1 pound (455 g) Frangipane Filling (page 842), soft	

1. Line mazarin forms with short dough rolled to ¹/₈ inch (3 mm) thick (see Figures 2-4 to 2-7, pages 69 and 70). Cover the dough scraps and save for another use.

2. Stir the Calvados into the apple filling and place in a pastry bag with a No. 6 (12-mm) plain tip. Pipe the apple filling into the forms, filling them halfway.

3. Place the frangipane filling in the same pastry bag used for the apple filling and pipe over the apple filling to the rim of the forms.

4. Top each pastry with a small mound of the streusel; it is a good idea to prepare the mazarins on one sheet pan and transfer them to another, because it is impossible not to spill the streusel around the forms, and the crumbs will burn in the oven. Spray the pastries with a fine mist of water.

5. Bake at 375°F (190°C) until golden brown, about 25 minutes. Let cool to room temperature.

6. When the pastries have cooled, carefully unmold each one while cupping your hand over the streusel to hold it in place. Sift powdered sugar very lightly over the tops.

Baked Potato Pastries yield: 30 oval pastries, 2¹/₂ × 2 inches (6.2 × 5 cm) each

When I delegate the students' assignments for a class on traditional individual pastries, the team that gets these whimsical Baked Potato Pastries, which look just like their name, always has confused smiles, as if they are thinking, "That Chef Bo sure is a funny guy." This seems to be a pastry that very few people have even heard of, much less seen or tasted, and this goes for professional chefs as well as the general public. Their obscurity is actually a good reason to make them. Everyone else makes éclairs, cream puffs, fresh fruit and lemon tarts, and so on, and while all of these are practical to produce and taste great if done properly, they don't really stand out or seem unique, as these do.

Although I use freshly baked sponge cake cut to size in my recipe for these pastries, the classic method, just as with rum balls, is to use leftovers. Typically, leftover sponge scraps are mixed with arrack- or rum-flavored buttercream and, in some recipes, a touch of pastry cream. If you prepare a mixture such as this, it is important to combine the ingredients lightly so that the customer can distinguish what it is they are eating. You don't want to make a paste, as is done with the rum ball mixture, for example. Baked Potato Pastries are sometimes made for St. Patrick's Day celebrations as a nod to the well-known link between the Irish and potatoes.

1 recipe Chiffon Sponge Cake II batter
(page 441)

¾ cup (180 ml) Plain Cake Syrup (page 31)

½ cup (120 ml) arrack or light rum

1 pound 8 ounces (680 g) Vanilla Buttercream
(Swiss Method) (page 477)

12 ounces (340 g) Pastry Cream (page 845)

1 pound 8 ounces (680 g) Marzipan (page 21),
untinted

Cocoa powder

I. Line the bottom of a half-sheet pan, 12 x 16 inches (30 x 40 cm), with baking paper or a Silpat. Fill the pan with the sponge cake batter and spread it out evenly. Bake immediately at 400°F (205°C) for about 15 minutes or until the cake springs back when pressed lightly in the center. Let cool completely.

2. Cut around the side of the pan and invert to remove the sponge. Peel the paper or Silpat from the back and turn right side up. Trim the skin and level the top at the same time.

3. Cut a ¼-inch (6-mm) horizontal layer through the top of the cake. Leaving the layers stacked together, cut out 30 ovals, using a plain oval cutter measuring approximately 2½ x 2 inches (6.2 x 5 cm). If you do not have an oval cutter, you can make one easily by bending a 2½-inch (6.2-cm) round cutter. Place the cake ovals on a paper-lined sheet pan as you cut them out, keeping the thicker and thinner pieces separate and stacking the thinner pieces in groups of 5. Wrap the scraps and save for another use if desired.

4. Flavor the cake syrup with approximately one-third of the arrack or rum. Flavor the buttercream with the remainder, softening it at the same time if necessary.

5. Brush the cake syrup over the thicker cake ovals.

6. Place the pastry cream in a pastry bag with a No. 3 (6-mm) plain tip. Pipe the cream over the cake ovals in an even layer, covering the entire surface.

7. Place the buttercream in pastry bag with a No. 7 (14-mm) plain tip. Pipe an oval mound of buttercream about 1 inch (2.5 cm) high on top of the pastry cream on each pastry. Make the mound higher in the center or the finished pastry will be too flat and will not resemble a potato.

8. Cut the thin sponge cake ovals in half diagonally; you can cut through a stack of 5 all at once. Place 2 halves on top of the buttercream on each pastry, leaving a gap in the center between the long sides (Figure 12-5).

9. Roll out a portion of the marzipan at a time to ¹⁄₁₆ inch (2 mm) thick. Cut out 4-inch (10-cm) rounds, then stretch each round to make it oval. The pieces should be large enough to drape over the pastries, covering the top and sides but not the bottom. Place a piece of marzipan on each pastry and, at the same time, make indentations with your fingers so that the surface is a little bumpy like a potato. Continue until all of the pastries are covered.

FIGURE 12-5 Placing the 2 halves of a cut oval of sponge cake at an angle on top of the partially assembled Baked Potato Pastries. The bottom row shows the thicker cake base ovals topped with pastry cream.

10. Use a torch to brown (caramelize) the marzipan in a few places on each potato pastry.

11. Use the pointed end of a skewer to make a few "eyes" on each potato. Sift cocoa powder lightly over the pastries, removing the excess with a pastry brush. (Another option is to push a few slivered almonds into each pastry to make the eyes.)

Caramel-Walnut Tartlets yield: 30 pastries, 2 to 2¹/₂ inches in diameter × 1 inch deep (5 to 6.2 cm × 2.5 cm), or 12 tartlets, 4 inches in diameter × ³/₄ inch deep (10 × 2 cm)

Be forewarned that these pastries—basically a piece of walnut toffee wrapped in short dough—are addictive. If you do not have ganache on hand, omit the powdered sugar, dip the top of the tartlets into melted dark coating chocolate instead, and place a walnut half in the center before the chocolate hardens. Lining the shells with hazelnut short dough amplifies the flavor of the walnuts.

This recipe is one that is easy to adapt to your needs. Because it is less time-consuming to line a smaller number of larger forms than vice versa, when you are in a hurry, make the 4-inch (10-cm) size, cut each one into quarters, and you can still use them as part of a *mignardise* assortment for tea or buffet service. They may not look quite as elegant as the individual version, but they will still be quite popular, I assure you.

1 pound 8 ounces (680 g) Short Dough (page 67) *or* **Hazelnut Short Dough (page 68)**

¹/₂ recipe Caramel Filling (page 364), walnuts chopped fine rather than coarse

Powdered sugar

6 ounces (170 g) Ganache (page 842), softened

30 small walnut quarters

1. Line 30 mazarin or other appropriately sized forms with short dough rolled to ¹/₁₆ inch (2 mm) thick (see Figures 2-4 to 2-7, pages 69 and 70). To make the larger size, see instructions. Reserve the leftover short dough to use later. Prick the bottom of the shells with a fork.

2. Bake the shells at 375°F (190°C) for approximately 12 minutes or until they start to brown lightly. Remove from the oven and let cool for a few minutes.

3. Warm the caramel filling if necessary to soften it. Place in a pastry bag with a No. 7 (14-mm) plain tip. Pipe the filling into the shells. Flatten the top of the filling if necessary. Push the forms as close together as possible.

4. Roll out the reserved short dough to ¹/₁₆ inch (2 mm) thick, roughly in the same shape as the forms on the sheet pan. Roll up the dough on a dowel and unroll over the top of the tartlets. Press down on the top of each one with the palm of your hand to trim the short dough around the sides of the forms. Cover the scrap dough and save for another use. Spread out the tartlets over the pan. Use a fork to prick the top of the dough.

5. Bake the tartlets at 325°F (163°C) for approximately 12 minutes or until the tops are baked (they should only have a very light golden color; see Note). Let the tartlets cool.

6. Unmold and sift powdered sugar lightly over the tops. Place the ganache in a pastry bag with a No. 5 (10-mm) star tip. Pipe a small rosette of ganache in the center of each pastry. Place a walnut quarter on the ganache.

NOTE: Do not bake the tartlets in a hotter oven or longer than necessary or you risk having the filling boil over, making it impossible to remove the tartlets from the forms.

1. After lining the shells as directed and reserving the extra short dough, rather than pricking the bottom of the shells, line them with plastic wrap, fill with dried beans or pie weights, and gather the edges of the plastic in the center so it does not touch the metal forms (see page 326). Bake until the short dough has set, about 8 minutes. Remove the plastic and the beans and return the partially baked shells to the oven. Continue baking until the shells begin to turn golden brown.

2. Divide the caramel filling evenly between the shells, as directed in the main recipe.

3. Roll out the reserved short dough to ⅛ inch (3 mm) thick, using flour to prevent sticking. Cut 48 strips of dough, ¼ inch wide × 4 inches long (6 mm × 10 cm); you need 4 per tart.

4. Place 2 strips on top of each tart, evenly spaced and parallel, then 2 more strips, also spaced the same distance from each other, at a 90-degree angle to the first set (so you end up with a square opening in the center). Pinch off the excess dough on the end of the strips as you attach them.

5. Bake at 325°F (163°C) for approximately 20 minutes or until the short dough strips have turned golden but not brown. Let cool before unmolding. If the dough sticks to the forms because of the caramel, chill the tartlets until the caramel is firm, which will make them easier to remove.

6. Cut each tart into quarters, as suggested in the introduction, or serve them whole as a plated dessert with Cinnamon Ice Cream (page 720) and Orange Sauce (page 828). Another option is to pipe a rosette of ganache in the center and decorate with a Chocolate Cutout (page 460).

Chocolate Eclairs yield: 30 pastries, 4½ inches (11.2 cm) long

Eclair literally means "lightning" in French. I don't know if this is a reference to the speed with which one will consume these irresistible filled choux pastries, or if it has to do with the reflection of light from the glaze on top. Unlike their equally well-known and popular close relative the cream puff, or profiterole, éclairs should always be topped with a sweet, shiny icing, typically fondant, corresponding to the flavor of the filling. In the case of the best-known variety, chocolate éclairs, the tops are usually decorated with a rich chocolate glaze. Other customary fillings are pastry cream and sweetened whipped cream.

The pâte à choux of the classic éclair is piped with a plain tip. I was taught to use a star tip and, being stubborn, continue to do so. I prefer the visual interest of the resulting ridges. Use either, according to your preference.

½ recipe Pâte à Choux (page 83)
Apricot Glaze (page 5)
Chocolate Glaze (page 465)

8 ounces (225 g) smooth strawberry jam
½ recipe Crème Parisienne (page 841) *or* Chocolate Cream (page 839)

1. Place the pâte à choux in a pastry bag with a No. 8 (16-mm) star tip. Pipe out 4½-inch (11.2-cm) strips onto sheet pans lined with baking paper. Do not put more than 20 éclairs on a pan because they need enough space around them to bake and color evenly (see Note).

2. Bake the éclairs at 425°F (219°C) until puffed and starting to color, about 10 minutes. Reduce the heat to 375°F (190°C) and continue baking until the éclairs are dry enough to hold their shape when you remove them from the oven, about 12 minutes longer. Let the éclairs cool.

3. Cut off the top third of each éclair and place on a separate sheet pan. Brush apricot glaze over the tops. Heat the chocolate glaze to make it fairly thin. When the apricot glaze has formed a skin (the one you brushed first should be ready by the time you finish the last one), dip the glazed side of the tops into the chocolate glaze. Reserve in the refrigerator.

4. Place the strawberry jam in a pastry bag with a No. 5 (10-mm) plain tip. Pipe a small ribbon of jam in the bottom of each éclair. Place the crème Parisienne or chocolate cream in a pastry bag with a No. 6 (12-mm) plain tip. Pipe a coil of cream on top of the jam (Figure 12-6). The coil shape makes the cream more visible in the final presentation. The cream should be at least a ½ inch (1.2 cm) higher than the base of the éclair.

5. Set the glazed tops on the cream at an angle so the filling shows nicely. Serve the éclairs as soon as possible, as the pâte à choux will become soggy and rubbery if left to stand too long. Try not to fill any more éclairs than you will serve within the next few hours.

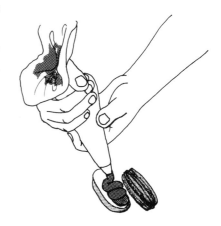

FIGURE 12-6 Piping chocolate filling in a coil shape over the base of an éclair shell

NOTE: If you are planning to freeze the éclairs before baking and are making a large quantity, pipe them as close together as possible to conserve freezer space. If well covered, they can be frozen for weeks without losing quality. Before baking as needed, respace them on the sheet pan as follows. Tap the pan firmly against the table to loosen the frozen éclairs. Place a second paper-lined pan next to you and quickly, using both hands, pick up every other éclair and transfer to the second pan. You must do this quickly because pâte à choux will become sticky very fast. This technique can also be used with frozen pâte à choux piped for profiteroles. Bake without thawing. The timing will be slightly longer.

Chocolate Hearts with Orange Cream and Cape Gooseberries

yield: 16 heart-shaped pastries using Flexipan No. 1340 (Photo 12)

You can certainly adjust this recipe to make the pastries in squares, rounds, or triangles instead of hearts, and can replace the cape gooseberries, which are admittedly hard to come by, with raspberries or small wedges of strawberry. The gooseberries are so decorative and unusual, though, I love to use them whenever I get the chance.

I first made these pastries to be included as part of a buffet assortment close to Valentine's Day, a time of the year when cape gooseberries are most definitely out of season in the United States. I was very fortunate, however, to be able to obtain a supply through a friend who imports produce internationally, and he went out of his way to get Colombian cape gooseberries for me so that I could use them in the photo of these pastries shown in the color insert.

Melted unsalted butter, if needed

Granulated sugar, if needed

1 recipe Chocolate Mousse for Baking (page 616)

1 cup (240 ml) heavy cream

3 tablespoons (45 ml) orange liqueur

16 cape gooseberries (physalis)

1. If you are using a Flexipan as specified, no pretreatment is needed. Place the Flexipan on a flat, even sheet pan with raised sides. If you are not using a Flexipan, use 16 individual heart-shaped ceramic or metal molds with a capacity of approximately ⅓ cup (80 ml); the molds must be suitable for baking in a water bath. Prepare the molds by brushing the insides with melted butter, then coating the butter with granulated sugar. Place the forms in a hotel pan or other appropriate pan that can be used as a water bath.

2. Place the chocolate mousse batter in a pastry bag with a large plain tip. Pipe the batter into 16 of the indentations in the Flexipan or into the prepared individual molds; either should be filled almost to the top.

3. Add hot water to the sheet pan so it flows around the indentations of the Flexipan, or to the hotel pan so that the water reaches approximately halfway up the sides of the forms.

4. Bake at 350°F (175°C) for approximately 30 minutes or until the batter is set.

5. Tilt the sheet pan to drain off as much water as possible without disturbing the pastries, leaving the Flexipan in place on the sheet pan. Place the Flexipan on the sheet pan in the refrigerator until the pastries are completely cold. If using individual forms, remove them from the water bath and set them aside to cool at room temperature.

6. Invert the chocolate hearts to unmold them and place them, still inverted, on a sheet pan lined with baking paper.

7. Whip the heavy cream and orange liqueur to stiff peaks. Place in a pastry bag with a No. 4 (8-mm) star tip. Pipe a rosette of cream on top of each pastry. Garnish with a cape gooseberry or with another berry, depending on the season. If not serving right away, wait to decorate with the whipped cream and berries until just before serving.

Chocolate Macaroon Pastries with Almond Paste and Chocolate Buttercream yield: 25 pastries, 2½ inches (6.2 cm) long

These pastries are easy to vary. For example, instead of chocolate buttercream, flavor an equal amount of vanilla buttercream with ¼ cup (60 ml) each Grand Marnier and kirsch. Mix in 2 ounces (55 g) chopped candied orange peel. Dip the finished pastries in light coating chocolate and decorate with a small piece of candied orange peel. There are many other possible variations. Chocolate-coated chocolate macaroons can be kept in a cool place (ideally, not the refrigerator) for up to 1 week. They must be well covered if they are refrigerated.

½ ounce (15 g) unsweetened cocoa powder

8 ounces (225 g) granulated sugar

12 ounces (340 g) almond paste

6 egg whites (¾ cup/180 ml)

1 pound 8 ounces (680 g) Chocolate Buttercream (Italian Method) (page 476)

Dark coating chocolate, melted

25 whole hazelnuts, toasted and skinned

1. Sift the cocoa powder into the sugar and mix to combine. Put this in a mixer bowl with the almond paste. Using the paddle attachment at low speed, incorporate 1 egg white at a time to avoid getting lumps in the batter. Add as many of the egg whites as the batter will absorb without becoming runny; this will vary quite a bit, depending on the moisture level of the almond paste and, to some degree, on the size of the egg whites. Beat for a few minutes at high speed to develop a creamy consistency.

2. Place the batter (paste) in a pastry bag with a No. 8 (16-mm) plain tip. Line a sheet pan with baking paper and fasten the paper to the pan, using a small dab of batter in the corners. Pipe the batter onto the paper, making cookies that are 2½ inches (6.2 cm) long. As you pipe the cookies, hold the tip of the pastry bag close enough to the pan that the batter flattens slightly (becomes wider and lower than the size of the tip) rather than making ropes.

3. Bake the cookies immediately, double-panned, at 410°F (210°C) for about 12 minutes or until baked through.

4. Let the cookies cool, then invert the paper and peel it away from the cookies. Arrange the cookies in rows on a sheet pan, flat-side up. Press down lightly if necessary to flatten the tops (now the bottoms) so that the cookies do not wobble.

5. Place the chocolate buttercream in a pastry bag with a No. 7 (14-mm) plain tip. Pipe 2 small pointed mounds on each cookie, wide enough to cover most of the surface and about ½ inch (1.2 cm) high (Figure 12-7). Refrigerate until the buttercream is firm.

6. Hold a cookie upside down, touching only the edges of the macaroon, and dip it into melted dark coating chocolate, covering the buttercream mounds and the flat side of the macaroon. Move the cookie up and down a few times over the bowl to allow as much of the excess chocolate as possible to drip off, then place it, chocolate-side up, on a sheet pan. Repeat with the remaining cookies. Set a hazelnut between the buttercream mounds before the chocolate hardens.

NOTE: Depending on the strength and color (brut) of the cocoa powder you are using, you may want to vary the amount.

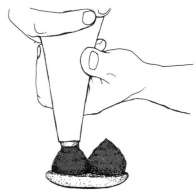

FIGURE 12-7 **Piping 2 pointed mounds of chocolate buttercream onto a macaroon cookie base for Chocolate Macaroon Pastries**

About Macaroons

History tells us that macaroons were made in France as early as the middle of the sixteenth century. They were probably introduced by Catherine de Médici of Italy, who, in 1533, when she was only 14 years old, married the French Duke of Orléans, who later (in 1547) became King Henry II.

The almond macaroon cookies used as a base for these simple little pastries are the most common type of macaroon among the dozens of variations. All types of macaroons are made up of three primary ingredients: finely ground almonds (or other nuts, including coconut), sugar, and egg whites. The ratio of almonds to sugar is usually 2:1, although a good quality and chewy texture can still be achieved with up to a 1:1 ratio. Macaroons made with a higher proportion of sugar will be lighter and will also be dry and crumbly, unless the oven temperature is high enough that they bake on the outside while remaining slightly underdone (chewy) inside. Macaroons can be made up, baked, and frozen, still attached to their baking papers, for several weeks. They should be well wrapped. Placing the cookies in the freezer for a few minutes is also a quick and easy way to remove them cleanly from the baking paper if they stick and this method is a lot less messy than brushing the back of the paper with water.

Citrons yield: 45 pastries, 3 inches (7.5 cm) long (Photos 20 and 21)

This is just one of the many small boat-shaped pastries that are made using barquette molds. In other variations, the buttercream may be flavored with rum or praline. The tops are then dipped in appropriately flavored fondant, and the pastries are decorated by artistically piping the name or flavor on top of the fondant, or by attaching chocolate figurines. The same writing technique can be applied to the Citrons instead of writing on the strips of marzipan. It is not as difficult as you might think to pipe directly on top of these crested pastries. Or do as one of my students did: He wrote the word *lemon* instead, explaining that it had one less letter to worry about!

There is a good chance that the buttercream will break when you incorporate the lemon curd. To repair it, stir the mixture over hot water just until it is smooth again; do not melt the buttercream. When glazing these pastries, either with chocolate or with fondant, it is easy to leave fingerprints. This can be avoided by inserting the tip of a paring knife into the bottom of the pastry at a 45-degree angle and using it as a handle.

1 pound 8 ounces (680 g) Short Dough (page 67)	12 ounces (340 g) Vanilla Buttercream (Swiss Method) (page 477)
4 ounces (115 g) smooth strawberry jam	3 ounces (85 g) Lemon Curd (page 844)
1 pound 2 ounces (510 g) Frangipane Filling (page 842), softened	Dark coating chocolate, melted
Granulated sugar	Marzipan (page 21), tinted pale yellow
	Piping Chocolate (page 465), melted

1. Line 45 barquette forms, 3 inches long x ¾ inch high (7.5 x 2 cm), with short dough rolled to ⅛ inch (3 mm) thick (see Figures 2-4 to 2-7, pages 69 and 70). Cover the scrap dough and reserve for another use.

2. Make a disposable pastry bag from baking paper (see page 54). Place the jam in the cone and pipe a ribbon of jam in each form.

3. Place the frangipane filling in a pastry bag with a No. 6 (12-mm) plain tip. Pipe the filling into the forms on top of the jam, filling each two-thirds full.

4. Bake at 400°F (205°C) until golden brown, about 10 minutes.

5. As soon as you remove the tartlets from the oven, immediately sprinkle sugar over the tops, then turn the forms upside-down on the pan so they will become flat on the top. Cool completely upside-down, then remove the forms.

6. Combine the buttercream and lemon curd. Place the mixture in a pastry bag with a No. 5 (10-mm) plain tip. Turn the barquettes right-side up and pipe a rope of buttercream straight down the center of each pastry. With a small metal spatula, spread both sides of the buttercream into a ridge in the center about ½ inch (1.2 cm) high (Figure 12-8). Refrigerate until the buttercream is firm.

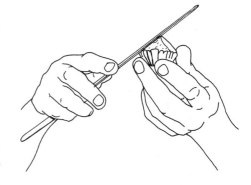

FIGURE 12-8 Using a small metal spatula to shape a piped rope of buttercream into a triangular ridge that will cover the top of a Citron pastry

7. Dip the tops of the pastries (the buttercream) into melted dark coating chocolate.

8. Roll out yellow marzipan to ¹⁄₁₆ inch (2 mm) thick. Cut out 45 strips, 1¾ × ⅜ inch (4.5 cm × 9 mm). Put the piping chocolate in a piping bag and use it to write the word *citron* on each strip. Pipe a thin diagonal line of chocolate on each pastry and place a marzipan strip on top.

NOTE: Citrons keep well for several days at normal room temperature; they should be well covered if refrigerated.

Conversations yield: 40 pastries (Photo 20)

These pastries have an interesting and unusual appearance and an equally peculiar name. I am sure we have all heard the expression conversation piece or we have heard something referred to as a real conversation starter. It's not too hard to imagine curiosity getting the better of a guest prompting them to stop and ask "What are those pastries?" And then, before you know it, you might be having a "conversation."

In actuality, the name comes from a play that was popular at the time the pastries were first created—*Les Conversations d'Emilie* by Madame d'Epinay. It is not known if the chef who created the pastries had any particular reason for naming them for the play or if the title held a particular significance.

If you do not have puff pastry on hand, substitute pie dough. The decorative strips on top will not have the same dramatic lift, but the overall effect is still good. The royal icing should be soft enough to spread easily but not at all runny. If it is too thin, it will run between the dough and the form, ruining the appearance of the crust and making it very difficult to remove the pastries.

1 pound 12 ounces (795 g) Puff Pastry (page 74)	**Conversation Filling (recipe follows)**
4 ounces (115 g) smooth apricot jam	**¼ recipe Royal Icing (page 34; see Note)**

1. Roll the puff pastry out to a rectangle measuring approximately 18 × 24 inches (45 × 60 cm); it should be slightly thinner than ⅛ inch (3 mm). Refrigerate the dough to relax and firm it.

2. Cut a strip, 6½ inches (16.2 cm) long, from 1 short end of the chilled dough. Reserve this piece in the refrigerator. Use the remaining dough to line 40 mazarin forms (see Figures 2-4 to 2-7, pages 69 and 70). Cover the scrap dough and reserve for another use.

3. Place the apricot jam in a disposable pastry bag made from baking paper (see page 54). Pipe the jam into the forms, dividing it evenly among them.

4. Place the conversation filling in a pastry bag with a No. 7 (14-mm) plain tip. Pipe the filling on top of the jam, filling the forms almost to the top. If the surface of the filling is not flat, use a small palette knife dipped in water to make it level. Place the forms in the freezer for 30 minutes to firm the top of the filling.

5. Cut the reserved puff pastry lengthwise into 3 strips, 2 inches (5 cm) wide. Leaving them in place on a sheet of cardboard, cut each strip across into ¼-inch (6-mm) pieces. You need a total of 160 pieces, 4 per pastry. Place the cut pieces in the refrigerator.

6. Spread a thin layer of royal icing on top of the chilled filling. Decorate with the puff pastry strips, placing 2 parallel strips across the top, close to the edges of the form, then 2 additional strips perpendicular to the first set, forming a square in the center. Let stand at room temperature until the royal icing has formed a crust.

7. Bake at 400°F (205°C) for approximately 15 minutes.

NOTE: Make the royal icing without lemon juice and add 1 teaspoon (2.5 g) cornstarch to the amount called for in the ¼ recipe. Avoid overmixing the icing when you add the cornstarch.

CONVERSATION FILLING yield: approximately 3 pounds (1 kg 365 g)

3 ounces (85 g) candied orange peel

3 ounces (85 g) candied angelica

Grated zest of 1 lemon

Bread flour

8 egg yolks (⅔ cup/160 ml)

2 pounds (910 g) almond paste

¼ cup (60 ml) water

1. Finely chop the orange peel and angelica. Combine with the lemon zest and toss with a small amount of bread flour to keep the pieces from sticking together.

2. Beat the egg yolks into the almond paste a few at a time to avoid lumps. Stir in the water and the chopped candied fruit. Adjust the consistency if needed by adding additional water; the filling should be just soft enough to become level when it is piped into the forms.

Cream Horns yield: 20 pastries, 5 inches (12.5 cm) long

Cream horns (also known as *lady locks*), together with cream puffs, chocolate éclairs, and napoleons, have been standard fare in pastry shops throughout Europe for many years. The ability to produce a properly baked and formed cream horn was one of the skills that had to be mastered before a young apprentice could even think about passing the all-so-important konditor's test when I was learning.

Puff pastry scraps work particularly well for cream horns. A dough with too much rise accentuates the problems described in the Note below. If you do not have any dough scraps on hand, be sure to prick the dough you use well.

In addition to sometimes having to literally glue the puff pastry strips to the forms, as discussed in the Note at right, it is important to roll the tip of the strips fairly loose. If too tight, they will crack and break along the side. The same thing can happen if the dough is not allowed to rest sufficiently before baking. Be certain the oven is hot enough so the sugar will melt and caramelize on top. Unfilled baked shells can be stored, covered, in a dry place for several days. Reheating the shells (then cooling them before adding the filling) will ensure a fresh-tasting pastry.

1 pound 8 ounces (680 g) Puff Pastry (page 74)

Melted unsalted butter

Egg wash

Granulated sugar

5 ounces (140 g) strawberry jam

1½ cups (360 ml) heavy cream

1 tablespoon (15 g) granulated sugar

Powdered sugar

1. Roll out the puff pastry to ⅛-inch (3-mm) thick and just slightly larger than 16 x 18 inches (40 x 45 cm). Cover the dough and place it in the refrigerator to rest for a few minutes.

2. Brush melted butter over the outside of 20 larger-size cream horn cones, 5 inches (12.5 cm) long with a 2-inch (5-cm) opening. Set aside.

3. Trim the edges of the dough sheet to make them even. Prick the dough well, then cut the puff pastry lengthwise into 20 strips, ¾ inch (2 cm) wide. Brush the strips lightly with egg wash. Wind the dough strips around the prepared cones, placing the egg-washed side against the form, starting at the narrow end and over-lapping each previous strip halfway as you go (Figure 12-9). Line them up next to each other on the table as you cover the remaining molds.

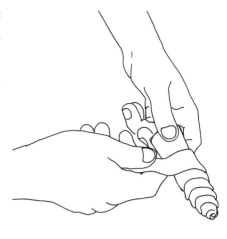

FIGURE 12-9 **Winding a strip of puff pastry around a cone-shaped mold for Cream Horns**

4. Brush the top and sides of the pastries with egg wash. Invert onto granulated sugar to coat the top and sides. Roll them back and forth to get sugar on the sides, but do not get any on the bottom. Place, sugar-side up, on sheet pans lined with baking paper.

5. Bake at 400°F (205°C) for about 45 minutes (removing the forms, as described in the Note). Let cool completely.

6. Place the strawberry jam in a disposable pastry bag made from baking paper (see page 54). Pipe a thin string of jam along the inside of each horn.

7. Whip the cream and 1 tablespoon (15 g) sugar to stiff peaks. Place the cream in a pastry bag with a No. 5 (10-mm) star tip and pipe into the horns, filling them completely.

8. Lightly sift powdered sugar over the pastries. Ideally, serve within 3 hours after filling.

NOTE: The coiled puff pastry strips have a tendency to slide off of the forms during baking, curling into various interesting but not very presentable shapes. There are a number of tricks for keeping the puff pastry on the molds. Freezing them before baking or brushing the strips (the side that goes against the form) with egg wash both work well. If you use egg wash, you must remove the forms just before the pastries have finished baking, as soon as you can handle them after removing from the oven. Stick a chef's knife (one you are not too fond of) into the opening of the metal cone and twist to remove the cone. Return the pastries to the oven to dry the inside as needed. If you let them cool completely before removing the cones, the pastries will break into little pieces. This will also happen if the cones are not cleaned properly or if too much egg wash is used. The best way I have found to prevent the strips from sliding off the cones is to place the tip of the cones against the edge of the baking sheet so that the dough has nowhere to go.

Diplomats yield: 45 pastries, 2 inches (5 cm) in diameter

This individual version of the cake by the same name will make a refreshing and colorful addition to your pastry display; so many displays tend to be top-heavy with chocolate and/or fondant-glazed pastries. The macaroon paste must be soft enough to stick to the sponge when it is piped on top. However, if the paste is too soft it will change shape when it bakes, creating a less attractive finished pastry. This can also occur if the oven temperature is too low.

For something a little more distinctive, make the Diplomats in a teardrop shape. If you do not have a tear-shaped cutter, use an oval cutter, 2 inches (5 cm) wide, and cut one end of each pastry into a point. This method, or using an oval cutter, will create fewer pastries than the round version. While both the round and teardrop pastries are appealing, they take longer to produce and create more scrap pieces than the traditional rectangles cut from strips (see the variations below).

1 recipe Chiffon Sponge Cake II batter (page 441)	Sliced almonds, lightly crushed
¾ cup (180 ml) Plain Cake Syrup (page 31)	¼ recipe or 14 ounces (400 g) Macaroon Decorating Paste (page 293)
7 ounces (200 g) smooth strawberry jam	Strawberries
1 pound 6 ounces (625 g) Pastry Cream (page 845)	Pectin Glaze (page 30) or Apricot Glaze (page 5)

I. Line the bottom of a half-sheet pan, 16 × 12 inches (40 × 30 cm) with baking paper. Fill the pan with the sponge batter, spreading it evenly.

2. Bake immediately at 400°F (205°C) for about 15 minutes or until the cake springs back when pressed lightly in the center. Let cool completely.

3. Cut around the inside edge of the pan and invert to remove the sponge. Peel the paper from the back and turn right-side up. Cut away the skin and, at the same time, even the top to make it level if necessary. Cut into 2 layers horizontally.

4. Brush half of the cake syrup over the bottom cake layer. Spread the strawberry jam evenly on top. Place the top layer on the jam. Brush the remaining cake syrup over the top layer.

5. Cut out 45 rounds, 2 inches (5 cm) in diameter, using a plain cookie cutter. You will need to keep the cuts close together and stagger the rows to get 45 pieces. Reserve the leftover cake scraps for another use, such as Rum Balls (page 586).

6. Spread a thin layer of pastry cream on the sides of each pastry; there will be extra. Roll the sides of the pastries in crushed almonds. Place the cakes on a sheet pan lined with baking paper.

7. Place the macaroon decorating paste in a pastry bag with a No. 3 (6-mm) plain tip. Pipe a ring of paste at the edge of each cake.

8. Place the remaining pastry cream in a pastry bag with a No. 4 (8-mm) plain tip. Pipe the pastry cream in a spiral, inside the macaroon paste border, to cover the sponge on the top of each cake.

9. Bake the cakes, double-panned, at 425°F (219°C) for about 8 minutes or until the macaroon paste is light brown. Let the cakes cool completely.

10. Cut the strawberries across to get round slices. Place a slice in the center of each cake. Glaze the tops of the cakes with apricot or pectin glaze.

SENATOR CUTS yield: 36 pastries, 3¹/₂ × 1¹/₄ inches (8.7 × 3.1 cm) each (Photo 21)

These are great production pastries with a minimum of scrap pieces. Both Diplomat Pastries and the Diplomat Cake are known as *Senator* when jam is substituted for the fresh fruit topping. You will need 2 ounces (55 g) strained apricot preserves and 4 ounces (115 g) strained strawberry preserves instead of the fresh strawberries, only 12 ounces (340 g) macaroon decorating paste, and a small amount of simple syrup.

1. Follow the instructions in the main recipe through Step 4.

2. Trim 1 long side of the sheet. Measure and cut lengthwise into 3 strips, 3½ inches (8.7 cm) wide. Save the trimmings for another use. Ice the top and long sides of each strip with pastry cream. Cover the long sides with crushed almonds and transfer the strips to a sheet pan lined with baking paper.

3. Place the macaroon paste in a pastry bag with a No. 3 (6-mm) star tip. Pipe 4 evenly spaced lines of paste lengthwise on each strip, starting and ending at the long edges. Pipe apricot preserves between the 2 center lines of paste and strawberry preserves between the frames on either side. Use a knife dipped in water to cut through the macaroon paste borders, marking the top of the strips crosswise in 1¼-inch (3.1-cm) pieces. This will make it easier to cut the pastries after baking (see Note). Do not disturb the jam.

4. Bake as directed for diplomat pastries. Brush simple syrup over the macaroon borders as soon as the pastries come out of the oven. Let cool completely.

5. Cut each strip into 12 slices, following the markings.

NOTE: It is not necessary to mark the tops before baking if the pastries will not be cut until the following day. The macaroon paste will soften sufficiently after being refrigerated overnight.

DIPLOMAT CUTS

Follow the directions for Senator Cuts, but omit the preserves in Step 3. Decorate with fresh fruit between the macaroon borders when cold. Glaze before slicing.

Financiers with a Soft Chocolate Filling yield: 25 pastries, 2¹/₂ inches (6.2 cm) in diameter
using Flexipan No. 1476, or 120 pastries, 1¹/₂ inches (3.7 cm) in diameter using Flexipan no. 1586 (Photo 13)

I got the idea for these little pastries during a trip to Caracas, Venezuela, where I had been invited to visit the St. Honoré bakery and the El Rey chocolate plantation. Although St. Honoré's overall excellence and their attention to detail can certainly rival any pastry shop I have seen, I was particularly impressed by their rendition of the always-popular financier pastry for two reasons, both of which are crucial in today's retail market. First, they are very simple to make and can prepped ahead, either through making the batter or baking off and storing in the refrigerator to fill as needed over several days. Second, the flavor combination of the buttery almond cake and the soft chocolate center is irresistible, and the filling keeps its shine even if refrigerated. At the St Honoré bakery, they called these *tigres* ("tigers") in reference to their chocolate stripes, which are produced by adding chocolate flakes.

Chocolate flakes are produced for the baking industry. They are approximately the same thickness as a breakfast cereal cornflake but much smaller. If you are not able to purchase them ready-made, the closest you can come to creating a similar product is to use the following method. Use a semisweet or bittersweet dark chocolate. The chocolate must be very firm, so refrigerate it first if necessary. Using a serrated knife, shave off slices of chocolate as thin as possible. The thin slices will fall apart as you cut them. Sift the broken pieces through a fine mesh strainer to remove any small crumbs and use the larger pieces in the recipe.

Butter and Flour Mixture (page 7) or pan spray	Soft Chocolate-Orange Filling (recipe follows)
Financier Batter (recipe follows)	1 ounce (30 g) Glazed Pistachios, optional (see below)

1. If not using Flexipans, prepare savarin molds (see Note) of the appropriate size by coating with butter and flour mixture or pan spray. If you are using Flexipans, this step is, of course, not necessary.

2. Place the financier batter in a pastry bag with a medium-sized plain tip. Pipe the batter into the prepared forms, filling them almost to the top.

3. Bake at 375°F for approximately 12 minutes or until the tops of the pastries become light brown. Let cool slightly, then invert to unmold.

4. To add the soft chocolate center, warm the filling until it becomes soft and shiny and has a thick liquid consistency. Place it in a pastry bag with a small plain tip and pipe into the center of the cooled pastries, filling them just to the rim. Place 1 prepared pistachio garnish, if using, at an angle in the center of the filling.

5. If the pastries are well wrapped, you may store them in the refrigerator for up to 4 days.

N O T E : You must use the type of savarin (ring) molds that have a closed center tube so that when the baked pastries are inverted, there will be a (closed) indentation in which to put the filling.

Glazed Pistachios

You will need approximately 50 whole pistachios with a good color and attractive shape. Blanch the nuts in boiling water with a pinch of salt added to enhance the green color. Refresh under cold water, blot dry, and remove the outer skin. Cut each nut lengthwise into quarters. Toss the nuts in a small amount of simple syrup to give them a nice shine. Spread the nuts out in a single layer on a Silpat and place in a 375°F (190°C) oven for just 1 minute to dry the glaze; do not brown the nuts. If you do not have simple syrup on hand and need only enough for this task, mix ¼ cup (60 ml) granulated sugar with an equal amount of water and bring to a boil.

FINANCIER BATTER

You must complete Steps 1 and 2 of the recipe at least 6 hours or, preferably, the day before finishing the batter, or it may separate during baking.

1 pound (455 g) finely ground blanched almond meal (see Note)

10 ounces (285 g) granulated sugar

3 ounces (85 g) cake flour

12 egg whites (1½ cups/360 ml), at room temperature

3 ounces (85 g) or ¼ cup (60 ml) glucose *or* light corn syrup

14 ounces (400 g) clarified unsalted butter *or* approximately 1 pound 4 ounces (570g) unsalted butter, clarified

3 ounces (85 g) chocolate flakes, optional

1. Combine the almond meal, granulated sugar, and cake flour in a mixing bowl. Stir in the egg whites, followed by the glucose or light corn syrup.

2. Cover the bowl and refrigerate for at least 6 hours or, preferably, overnight, to allow the almond meal to absorb moisture from the egg whites.

3. Heat the clarified butter to make it fairly warm and liquid, but do not bring it to the boiling point. Stir the butter into the almond mixture. Let cool completely.

4. Stir in the chocolate flakes. The batter may be refrigerated at this point and used over several days as needed.

NOTE: If almond meal is unavailable, you can make your own by substituting 1 pound (455 g) blanched almonds (whole, slivered, or sliced) and grinding them in a high-speed food processor with approximately half of the sugar used in the recipe. Process until the mixture is as fine as possible. The sugar is added to keep the almonds from turning into a paste. Subtract the amount of sugar used in grinding the almonds from the amount you add to the batter.

SOFT CHOCOLATE-ORANGE FILLING yield: approximately 1⅔ cups (400 ml)

This soft filling can be used as a glaze. The mixture retains a pretty shine for many hours once it is applied, even if the item on which it is used is refrigerated. This feature makes the glaze an excellent choice for cakes or pastries displayed in a refrigerated display case.

6 ounces (170 g) milk chocolate

4 ounces (115 g) sweet dark chocolate

1 cup (240 ml) heavy cream

⅓ cup (80 ml) glucose *or* light corn syrup

¼ cup (60 ml) orange liqueur

1 ounce (30 g) unsalted butter

1. Chop both types of chocolate into small pieces. Place in a mixing bowl and reserve.

2. Place the cream and the glucose or corn syrup in a saucepan and bring to a boil. Pour over the chopped chocolate and stir until the chocolate is melted. Add the orange liqueur and the butter and continue stirring until the ingredients are incorporated and the mixture is smooth.

3. Let the filling cool to room temperature before using. If not using right away, cover and store at room temperature for a few days, or refrigerate for longer storage.

Florentina Noisettes

yield: 30 pastries, 3¹⁄₂ inches (8.7 cm) in diameter, or 35 pastries using Flexipan No. 1299

Florentinas, in one form or another, should be a standard component of a dessert buffet. These small pastries and the variations that follow, which demonstrate the versatility of Florentina batter, are ideally suited for a buffet or other assorted pastry display. It seems almost impossible to make enough of these popular pastries; one reason is that nobody takes just one. Their popularity is evident beginning in the kitchen: The scrap pieces left after trimming the cookies make a great addition to rum ball filling but, mysteriously, they rarely make it that far. (In fact, sometimes my students are able to produce perfectly trimmed cookies with no scrap pieces whatsoever!) I must admit this is one sweet I have trouble staying away from myself.

I enjoy Florentina pastries most once they start to get a little soft and chewy; however, they are a bit difficult to handle and serve at that point. Although planning ahead usually makes this a moot point, the one drawback to Florentinas in a production kitchen is that they will not keep to the following day once filled with a moist filling such as the cream filling used here. Shells filled with a ganache or flavored buttercream mixture will keep longer. Unfilled shells, on the other hand, can be stored for several weeks, well covered, in a dry location.

The shapes and fillings used in the variations are all interchangeable; you can fill the cones with the noisette or coconut filling, pipe Chantilly cream in the tube shapes, and so on. If you use the coconut filling in the cone shape, dip the entire opening into coating chocolate to cover the filling.

1 pound 10 ounces (740 g) or 1 recipe Florentina Batter (page 306)	¹⁄₂ recipe Hazelnut Paste (page 20) *or* 2 ounces (55 g) commercial hazelnut paste
Dark coating chocolate, melted	Hazelnut Cookies (recipe follows)
1 pint (480 ml) heavy cream	
1 tablespoon (15 g) granulated sugar	

1. Draw 30 circles, 3¹⁄₂ inches (8.7 cm) in diameter, on baking paper. Invert the papers and place on sheet pans. Divide the Florentina batter between the circles; spread out, bake, and trim as instructed in the recipe for Florentinas. If you are using a Flexipan, follow the directions given on page 307 for making Florentinas in Flexipans. The cookies do not need to be trimmed in this case.

2. Return the cookies to the oven, a portion at a time, for a few minutes until soft. Immediately roll each cookie, top-side out, around a ³⁄₄-inch (2-cm) dowel so that the ends of the cookie overlap slightly. Push the ends together between the dowel and the table to make sure they stick. Turn the cookie a half-turn so it will not stick to the dowel as it cools. Let each Florentina roll cool completely before sliding it off the dowel (Figure 12-10).

3. Dip both ends of each Florentina ¹⁄₈ inch (3 mm) into melted coating chocolate and immediately place, seam-side up, on a sheet pan lined with baking paper.

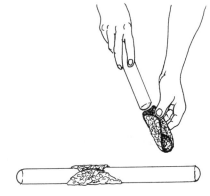

FIGURE 12-10 A Florentina cookie wrapped around a dowel to form a tube; sliding a Florentina off the dowel after it has hardened

4. Whip the cream and sugar to soft peaks. Add a small amount of the cream to the hazelnut paste and mix until softened; add to the remaining cream and whip to stiff peaks.

5. Place the cream in a pastry bag with a No. 4 (8-mm) star tip. Fill each Florentina with the cream mixture by piping it into both ends. Attach a hazelnut cookie to the top with a dot of coating chocolate. Do not fill any more Florentinas than you plan to serve the same day; they will become soft because they must be stored in the refrigerator once filled.

HAZELNUT COOKIES yield: 30 cookies, ³/₄ inch (2 cm) in diameter

3 ounces (85 g) Short Dough (page 67)
Dark coating chocolate, melted

30 whole hazelnuts, toasted and skins removed

1. Roll out the short dough to ¹/₁₆ inch (2 mm) thick. Cut out 30 cookies, ³/₄ inches (2 cm) in diameter, using a fluted cutter. Cover the dough scraps and reserve for another use. Place the cookies on a sheet pan lined with baking paper and bake at 375°F (190°C) for approximately 8 minutes or until golden brown. Let cool.

2. Pipe a pea-sized dot of coating chocolate in the center of each cookie. Place a hazelnut, pointed end up, on each chocolate dot. The chocolate should spread out a little to show all around the nut on the top of the cookies.

VARIATIONS

FLORENTINA CONES WITH CHANTILLY CREAM

yield: 30 pastries, 3¹/₂ inches (8.7 cm) long, or 35 pastries using Flexipan No. 1299 (Photo 21)

1 pound 10 ounces (740 g) or 1 recipe
    Florentina Batter (page 306)
Dark coating chocolate, melted
1 recipe Chantilly Cream (page 838)

Small edible flowers, such as borage or
    johnny-jump-ups, or fresh raspberries
    or blueberries

1. Draw 30 circles, 3¹/₂ inches (8.7 cm) in diameter, on baking paper. Invert the papers on sheet pans. Divide the Florentina batter among the circles; spread out, bake, and trim as directed in the recipe for Florentinas. If you are using a Flexipan, follow the directions on page 307 for making Florentinas in a Flexipan.

2. Place the trimmed cookies, a few at a time, back in the oven for a few minutes to soften. Place the cookies, top-side down, on the table and immediately roll around cream horn molds or other cone-shaped molds (see Figure 13-20, page 649); you should have 3 or 4 molds to work efficiently. Press the seam together between the mold and the table to be sure they stick. Allow to cool sufficiently before removing the forms so the Florentina cones do not collapse.

3. Dip the open end of each cone ¼ inch (6 mm) into melted coating chocolate. Place, seam-side up, on a sheet pan lined with baking paper (see Chef's Tip, page 561).

4. Whip the Chantilly cream to stiff peaks and place in a pastry bag with a No. 7 (14-mm) star tip. Pipe the cream into the cones, filling them just to the edge. Place an edible flower or a berry on the cream. Store in the refrigerator. The filled pastries will stay crisp for a few hours but should not be left overnight.

COCONUT-FILLED FLORENTINAS yield: 30 pastries, 3½ inches (8.7 cm) long

1 pound 10 ounces (740 g) or 1 recipe
Florentina Batter (page 306)

10 ounces (285 g) Vanilla Buttercream
(Swiss Method) (page 477)

½ recipe Coconut Haystack Cookies batter
(page 294)

Dark coating chocolate, melted

I. Follow the Florentina Noisettes recipe through Step 2.

2. Stir the buttercream into the cooled coconut batter. Place the filling in a pastry bag with a No. 6 (12-mm) plain tip. Pipe the filling into both ends of the Florentina shells, piping it flush with the opening on each end; do not fill the entire shell.

3. Dip both ends of each pastry into melted chocolate just deep enough to cover the coconut filling. Store in a cool, dry place; do not refrigerate. Although these pastries have a much longer shelf life than the noisettes, you should still try to fill only as many as will be needed within 1 day. The empty shells can be kept for weeks if stored in an airtight container.

Fresh Fruit Galettes yield: 8 pastries, 6 inches (15 cm) in diameter

The French word *galette* refers to a small round pastry or cake. The word derives from *galet*, a term for a smooth pebble that has been worn flat over the years by running water, making it into a perfect skipping stone. Many variations are found using everything from buckwheat crepes to shortbread and biscuits, but the basic ingredients usually present are sugar, butter, eggs, and flour. The French equivalent of the American expression "flat as a pancake" is *plat comme une galette*.

1 pound 14 ounces (855 g) Quick Puff Pastry
(page 77)

Egg wash

12 ounces (340 g) Pastry Cream (page 845)

Powdered sugar

1 pound 12 ounces (795g) fresh fruit and/or
berries

Apricot Glaze (page 5) or Pectin Glaze
(page 30)

I. Roll out the puff pastry to ⅛ inch (3 mm) thick and approximately 16 x 24 inches (40 x 60 cm); it is important that the dough is not any thinner than this. Let the dough relax for a few minutes, then cut out 8 rounds, 6 inches (15 cm) in diameter. Reroll the scraps if necessary. Place the rounds on a sheet pan lined with baking paper. Dock each round well.

2. Brush egg wash lightly over the top of each dough round. Crimp the edges of each piece, folding the dough in approximately ½ inch all around (see Figures 2-2 and 2-3, page 63).

3. Bake at 400°F (205°C) for approximately 15 minutes or until the dough is thoroughly baked. Let cool completely at room temperature.

4. Divide the pastry cream between the rounds of dough and spread it out to cover the dough inside the crimped edges. Sift powdered sugar lightly over the pastries.

5. Decorate each pastry with fresh fruit, completely covering the pastry cream. Glaze with apricot or pectin glaze.

Florentina Surprise yield: 45 pastries, 2 inches (5 cm) in diameter

Florentina Surprise pastries contain a medley of flavors—chocolate, nuts, rum, and caramelized sugar—that blend together well, and these pastries give my students an opportunity to work with a broad range of techniques in their preparation. The surprise part of the name refers to the ganache, which is hidden underneath the Florentina cookie. The name is also fitting when, as happens from time to time, someone forgets to include the filling, leaving the inside hollow.

1 pound 8 ounces (680 g) Short Dough (page 67)

½ recipe Florentina Batter (page 306)

1 pound 5 ounces (595 g) Vanilla Buttercream (Swiss Method) (page 477)

5 ounces (140 g) Hazelnut Paste (page 20) *or* 2½ ounces (70 g) commercial hazelnut paste

10 ounces (285 g) Ganache (page 842)

¼ cup (60 ml) light rum

Dark coating chocolate, melted

I. Roll out the short dough to ⅛ inch (3 mm) thick. Cut out 45 cookies, 2 inches (5 cm) in diameter, using a plain cutter. Cover the dough scraps and reserve for another use. Bake the cookies at 375°F (190°C) for about 10 minutes or until light brown. Set aside to cool.

2. Draw 45 circles, 2 inches (5 cm) in diameter, on baking papers, using a cookie cutter as a guide. Invert the papers and place them on sheet pans. Divide the Florentina batter among the circles, spread out, bake, and trim the cookies according to the instructions on page 305.

3. Flavor the buttercream with the hazelnut paste; place in a pastry bag with a No. 5 (10-mm) plain tip. Pipe a ring of buttercream on each of the short dough cookies inside the edge.

4. Flavor the ganache with rum. Place it in a pastry bag with a No. 4 (8-mm) plain tip. Pipe a small mound of ganache inside the buttercream rings. Refrigerate until the buttercream is firm.

5. Holding a cookie upside-down, dip the buttercream, ganache, and the top part of the short dough cookie into melted coating chocolate. Shake off as much excess chocolate as possible by moving the cookie up and down a few times over the bowl so that the chocolate does not run out around the pastries as it hardens. Place the cookies on paper-lined sheet pans.

6. Before the chocolate hardens, place a Florentina on top of each pastry and press gently to make it level. Do not refrigerate Florentina Surprise pastries.

Decorating with Fruit

Choose fruit that is in season. Use small fruits if possible, such as raspberries, blackberries, strawberries, kiwis, figs, plums, and blueberries. Leave the skin on when it is edible and adds to the appearance (figs and plums, for example). While small berries should be left whole, larger fruit should be cut into small pieces or thin slices to make it look more appealing; a whole or half strawberry may look good on a large tart, but on a small tartlet, it looks clumsy and is too plain. The same is true for an apricot half or a single round slice of kiwifruit covering the top. Including slices of banana, kiwi, and/or mango adds color, and these fruits are generally available year round. A nice idea is to use a very small melon ball cutter to cut out balls of honeydew melon. These, arranged with thin slices of mango and strawberry, for example, make for a nice color contrast. The entire top of the tartlet should be covered with fruit in a simple pattern. The height of the arrangement and the kind of fruit or berries used will, to some extent, determine the amount needed. Do not get too complicated.

Fruit Tartlets yield: 30 pastries, 2 inches (5 cm) in diameter (Photo 20)

No pastry tray or pastry display should be without some form of fruit pastry. Fruit adds color and offers an alternative for the customer or guest who cannot or prefers not to eat rich desserts or pastries containing chocolate and/or nuts. The tart shells can be baked several days in advance, then coated, filled, and decorated as needed. I brush the inside with melted chocolate, but apricot glaze will suffice as well. Both are used to protect the crust against absorbing moisture from the custard and becoming soft. I feel the dark color of the chocolate provides a better contrast as a background for the fruit.

1 pound (455 g) Short Dough (page 67)

Melted dark coating chocolate or Apricot Glaze (page 5)

14 ounces (400 g) Quick Bavarian Cream (page 846)

1 to 1½ pounds (455 to 680 g) fresh fruit

Apricot Glaze (page 5) or Pectin Glaze (page 30)

1. Line 30 tart pans, 2 inches (5 cm) in diameter, with short dough rolled to ⅛ inch (3 mm) thick (see Figures 2-4 to 2-7, pages 69 and 70). Cover and reserve the dough scraps for another use. Prick the shells lightly with a fork and bake at 375°F (190°C) until light golden brown. Unmold while still warm, then cool the shells completely.

2. Brush melted dark coating chocolate or apricot glaze on the inside of each shell.

3. Place the Bavarian cream in a pastry bag with a No. 6 (12-mm) plain tip. Pipe the cream into each shell, up to the rim, in a nice mound.

4. Decorate the tartlets with the fresh fruit.

5. Brush apricot or pectin glaze over the fruit. Refrigerate if not serving immediately. Use these tarts the day they are made; the fruit tends to bleed into the filling, and they usually look a bit wilted the second day. If they are not refrigerated, as when displayed on a buffet, the tarts must be served within 1 to 2 hours.

Japonaise yield: 40 pastries, approximately 2¼ inches (5.6 cm) in diameter

Japonaise can be found in virtually every pastry shop in central Europe. These familiar, classic pastries never seem to go out of style—and for good reason, as they are both practical and delicious. In addition, the Japonaise bases can be used to make a number of variations by changing the filling and/or the decoration. Try filling them with coffee-flavored buttercream instead of hazelnut and replacing the fondant dot on top with a candy coffee bean or one made out of marzipan.

1 recipe Japonaise Meringue Batter (page 28)

2 pounds (910 g) Vanilla Buttercream (Swiss Method) (page 477)

6 ounces (170 g) Hazelnut Paste (page 20) *or* 3 ounces (85 g) commercial hazelnut paste

Fondant (page 18), tinted pink

1. The fastest and most efficient way to make Japonaise shells is to spread the batter over rubber templates made expressly for this purpose (see Note). If these are not available, you can make a pattern by drawing circles, 2¼ inches (5.6 cm) in diameter and spaced 1 inch (2.5 cm) apart, on baking paper, using a heavy pen. You can fit about 35 circles on a full sheet of baking paper (16 × 24 inches/40 × 60 cm). Draw the circles before you make the Japonaise meringue batter. Fasten the pattern to the table with a dab of butter in each corner. Place a second sheet of baking paper on top.

2. Place the meringue batter in a pastry bag with a No. 2 (4-mm) plain tip. Pipe the batter, following the pattern under the paper, starting in the center of the circles and working to the outside, to fill in the circles completely, as in Meringue Noisette (see Figure 1-5, page 29). Drag the filled paper onto a sheet pan (see Figure 9-4, page 443). Repeat, using a new sheet of baking paper to make the remaining shells; you should get about 50. If you are making just a few shells, invert the paper with the pattern and pipe the shells directly on the back of the paper. After you have had some practice, you can eliminate using the guide completely and just pipe the batter into circles, keeping the shells the same size by piping an equal number of rings for each one.

3. Bake immediately at 300°F (149°C) until the meringues are completely dry, about 30 minutes. Make sure that the oven is not too hot; too high a temperature will cause the shells to puff up, become brittle, and be very hard to work with.

4. Set aside about 10 of the least attractive shells. Trim any of the remaining shells as needed so that they are round and about 2¼ inches (5.6 cm) in diameter. Reserve the trimmings.

5. Flavor the vanilla buttercream with the hazelnut paste. Place it in a pastry bag with a No. 3 (6-mm) plain tip. Pipe a layer of buttercream on half of the shells, using the same piping technique that you used to make the shells. Invert the remaining shells on top and press down lightly, making sure the sides are lined up evenly. Refrigerate until the buttercream is firm.

6. Crush the reserved shells, as well as any trimmings from the others, to very fine crumbs. Pass the crumbs through a coarse sifter.

7. Spread a very thin layer of buttercream on the sides of the chilled pastries. (You can do this faster by holding 2 pastries together while you ice the sides.) Roll the sides in the reserved crumbs. Ice the tops, being careful not to mar the sides, then sprinkle crumbs over the tops to completely cover the buttercream. Pipe a small dot of melted pink fondant, about ½ inch (1.2

cm) in diameter, in the center of each Japonaise. Store, covered, at room temperature for up to 4 days.

NOTE: You can make templates for Japonaise from food-grade rubber, ⅛ inch (3-mm) thick, by cutting out the desired size circles with a utility knife.

VARIATION

ZUGER KIRSCH PASTRIES yield: 40 pastries, approximately 2½ inches (6.2 cm) in diameter

1 recipe Japonaise Meringue Batter (page 28)

½ recipe Almond Sponge batter (page 438)

2 pounds (910 g) Vanilla Buttercream (Swiss Method) (page 477)

⅓ cup (80 ml) plus ¾ cup (180 ml) kirsch liqueur

¼ cup (60 ml) water

Powdered sugar

Chopped blanched pistachios

1. Prepare the meringue shells as directed in Steps 1 through 4 in the main recipe.

2. Spread the almond sponge batter evenly over a half sheet pan (12 × 16 inches/30 × 40 cm) lined with baking paper or a Silpat. Bake at 400°F (205°C) for approximately 6 to 8 minutes or until the top springs back when pressed lightly. Set aside to cool.

3. Flavor the buttercream with ⅓ cup (80 ml) kirsch liqueur.

4. Combine the remaining kirsch liqueur with the water.

5. Unmold the sponge, remove the paper or the Silpat, and cut out 40 rounds, 2¼ inches (5.6 cm) in diameter, using a plain cookie cutter. Brush the sponge circles generously with the kirsch and water mixture.

6. To assemble each pastry, spread cherry-flavored buttercream on the top of 2 Japonaise circles and sandwich them together, placing a soaked sponge circle inside. Refrigerate until firm.

7. Crush the reserved shells, as well as any trimmings from the others, to very fine crumbs. Pass the crumbs through a coarse sifter.

8. Spread a very thin layer of buttercream on the sides of the chilled pastries. (You can do this faster by holding 2 pastries together while you ice the sides.) Roll the sides in the reserved crumbs to coat them completely, leaving the tops exposed.

9. Sift powdered sugar over the tops of the pastries, using enough to cover them completely. Use the back of a paring knife or the wire of a hard-boiled-egg slicer to mark the sugar, first in one direction and then at a 45-degree angle, to create a diamond pattern.

10. Place a small amount of chopped blanched pistachios in the center of each pastry. Store, covered, at room temperature for up to 4 days.

Kirschwasser Rings yield: 25 pastries, 3¹/₂ inches (8.7 cm) in diameter

You can create a quick and delicious light dessert from these tasty almond rings by serving them with a fresh fruit sauce and a dollop of Italian Cream (page 844) or a scoop of frozen yogurt. For buffet service, cut the rings in half and dip ¼ inch (6 mm) of each end into melted dark coating chocolate. This gives the pastries some color contrast and at the same time keeps the cut edges from drying out.

Melted unsalted butter	3 eggs, at room temperature
Sliced almonds, lightly crushed	¼ cup (60 ml) kirschwasser
4 ounces (115 g) granulated sugar	4 ounces (115 g) bread flour
11 ounces (310 g) almond paste	¼ teaspoon (1 g) baking powder
6 ounces (170 g) unsalted butter, at room temperature	Flour
	Powdered sugar

I. Grease 25 savarin forms, 3½ inches (8.7 cm) in diameter, with melted butter. Coat with crushed almonds and place the forms on a sheet pan.

2. Place the sugar and almond paste in a mixing bowl. Blend in the butter gradually, making sure there are no lumps. Add the eggs, 1 at a time, then the kirschwasser.

3. Sift the flour and baking powder together and stir it into the batter. Take care not to overwhip the mixture at this time or you will incorporate too much air and the finished product will be dry and crumbly.

4. Place the batter in a pastry bag with a No. 6 (12-mm) plain tip. Pipe the batter into the forms, filling each two-thirds full.

5. Bake at 400°F (205°C) for about 20 minutes or until baked through and golden brown on the bottom as well as the top; unmold one first to check. Dust flour lightly over the pastries in their forms, then invert and let cool completely.

6. Remove the forms from the pastries. Sift a small amount of powdered sugar over the tops. Kirschwasser Rings will keep for 1 week if covered and stored in the refrigerator. Allow them to reach room temperature before dusting with powdered sugar, or the sugar will quickly disappear.

PETIT GUINETTES CHERRY OCTAGONS yield: 70 pastries using Flexipan No. 1560

Guinettes are a special type of brandied cherries imported from France. They are labeled as semi-confit, meaning they are partially cooked or preserved. The pitted cherries are packed in bottles with sugar and brandy and, sometimes, kirsch (cherry liqueur) as well. Both the cherries themselves and the liquid in the bottle are wonderfully delicious. Simply serving them over vanilla ice cream makes an excellent, simple treat and, of course, because they are packed in alcohol, they are perfect for flambéed dishes like Cherries Jubilee. The word *guinettes* is actually the name of a small red cherry varietal grown in France. However, the term has come to refer to the finished brandied cherry product in the same way, for example, that most people use the word cabernet to refer to the wine, not the cabernet grape. Another popular label is Griottines.

1. Omit the melted butter, sliced almonds, and kirschwasser from the ingredient list. Instead, you will need 70 small brandied cherries plus ¼ cup (60 ml) of the juice they are packed in.

2. Omit Step 1 in the recipe above. Place the Flexipan on a suitable baking pan (see Note).

3. Follow Steps 2 and 3 to make the batter, substituting the cherry juice for the kirschwasser. Place a portion of the batter in a pastry bag with a medium-size plain tip. Pipe the batter into the indentations in the pan, filling them three-quarters full. Because this pan has only 40 indentations, you will have to make these in two batches (unless you have more than one pan).

4. Place a brandied cherry on each pastry, pushing it into the batter so only the top half is visible.

5. Bake at 375°F (190°C) for approximately 12 minutes or until the pastries are golden brown on the top as well as the bottom (you may need to push one out of the pan to check).

6. Allow the pastries to cool in the pan. Unmold by pressing the pastries out of the molds. If they do not unmold easily, refrigerate them until they are cold.

7. Sift powdered sugar lightly over the tops of the pastries. Stored, covered, in the refrigerator, they will stay fresh for 3 to 4 days (freeze for longer storage).

NOTE: Place the Flexipan on a screened or perforated sheet pan if you are baking the pastries in a conventional rack oven. If you have a deck oven and can place the support pan directly on the hearth, a regular sheet pan is fine.

Lemon-Almond Tartlets yield: 45 tartlets, 2½ inches (6.2 cm) in diameter

When I was in the retail end of the business, we used to line and fill a week's worth of mazarin forms for both Lemon-Almond Tartlets and Mazarins at the same time. After baking, we would store them in the freezer and/or refrigerator to remove each morning and finish with either toasted almonds and lemon curd or apricot glaze and fondant. It was an easy and productive way to quickly have two pastries, similar in shape but distinctively different in taste, ready to display and sell.

2 pounds (910 g) Short Dough (page 67)

1 pound 10 ounces (740 g) Frangipane Filling (page 842), softened

Bread flour

Apricot Glaze (page 5)

Sliced almonds, toasted and crushed

½ recipe Lemon Curd (page 844)

Powdered sugar

1. Line 45 mazarin forms (see page 571) with short dough rolled to ⅛ inch (3 mm) thick (see Figures 2-4 to 2-7, pages 69 and 70). Cover the leftover dough and reserve for another use.

2. Place the frangipane filling in a pastry bag with a No. 6 (12-mm) plain tip. Pipe the filling into the lined pans, filling them two-thirds full.

3. Bake at 400°F (205°C) until golden brown, about 12 minutes.

4. As soon as you remove the tartlets from the oven, dust the tops lightly with bread flour and immediately turn them upside down on the pan to make the tops flat and even.

5. When the tartlets have cooled, brush apricot glaze over the tops and dip the tartlets into the almonds to coat.

6. Cut out the center of each tartlet, using a 1-inch (2.5-cm) plain cookie cutter. Do not cut through the crust. Reserve the centers.

7. Place the lemon curd in a pastry bag made from baking paper (see page 54). Pipe the curd into the holes, filling them to the top. Sift powdered sugar lightly over the pastries. Replace the cutouts on top of the lemon curd. Store the pastries, covered, in the refrigerator.

Lemon-Fig Wedges yield: 24 pastries (Photo 8)

Figs are a very interesting and attractive variety of fruit with an ancient history. Their unique flavor is particularly enhanced by pairing them with the lemon-orange cream that is used in this recipe and also in the plated dessert variation found on page 646, where the baked tarts are served with a port wine reduction. A third fig tart recipe can be found on page 351. That recipe makes a large tart in which the sliced figs are baked in the tart shell together with a lemon-flavored cream, and the whole is cut into wedges for serving.

Using pectin glaze on Lemon-Fig Wedges rather than mirror glaze gives the pastries a whole new dimension in flavor that comes from the puckery taste of the tartaric acid which is used to set the pectin glaze.

If you are blind-baking the shells in a rack oven (as opposed to one where you can place the sheet pan directly on the hearth), place the pan as close to the bottom of the oven as possible. If you are unable to do this, you may have to remove the bean pouches halfway through baking to ensure that the short dough crust is evenly baked throughout.

12 ounces (340 g) Short Dough (page 67)

1 recipe Lemon-Orange Cream (page 647)

8 fresh Black Mission or Dakota figs (also known as green figs)

Pectin Glaze (page 30) or Mirror Glaze (page 31)

1. Roll out the short dough to ⅛ inch (3 mm) thick and use it to line 6 fluted tartlet forms, 4½ inches (11.2 cm) in diameter and ¾ inch (2 cm) high.

2. Place a small square of commercial-grade plastic wrap inside each shell and fill the shells with dried beans or pie weights. Gather the plastic in the center and press it together (see Figure 7-1, page 325). Bake the shells at 375°F (190°C) until light golden, but not brown, around the edges. Remove the plastic pouches and save to use another time. Let the shells cool to room temperature.

3. Divide the lemon-orange cream evenly between the shells and bake at 375°F (190°C) for approximately 10 minutes or until the filling is just set. The filling will not be firm at this point but will set further as it cools. Allow the tartlets to cool completely.

4. Remove the tarts from the forms. Cut the figs crosswise into ¼-inch (6-mm) slices and arrange the slices close together on top of the cream. Glaze with pectin glaze or mirror glaze. Using a serrated knife dipped in hot water, carefully cut through the top of the short dough crust and the fig rounds, using a sawing motion, then push the knife straight down to cut the tartlets in half. Use the same technique to cut each half into 2 pieces, creating 4 wedge-shaped pastries per tartlet.

Linzer Tartlets yield: 45 pastries, 2 inches (5 cm) in diameter, or I tart, I I inches (27.5 cm) in diameter

The dough used here is very soft. To make it easier to work with, prepare it at least one day in advance and be certain that the nuts are ground very finely. The nuts will absorb moisture, making the dough firmer and more pliable. However, if the dough feels crumbly and is difficult to manage, which often happens if too much flour is worked in as you roll it out, adjust the consistency by working in a small amount of butter.

Due to the softness and composition of the dough, the forms must be lined one at a time; however, the tender and fragile crust is one of the things that makes this specialty from the Austrian town of Linz so delicious. They should be made with only the highest-quality raspberry jam.

1 recipe Linzer Dough (page 65)	1 pound 4 ounces (570 g) smooth raspberry jam
Butter and Flour Mixture (page 7)	Powdered sugar

I. Roll out 10 ounces (285 g) Linzer dough to ⅛ inch (3 mm) thick and as square as possible. Reserve in the refrigerator.

2. Brush butter and flour mixture on the inside of 45 shallow tartlet forms, about 2 inches (5 cm) in diameter and ½ inch (1.2 cm) high.

3. Roll out the remaining Linzer dough to ¼ inch (6 mm) thick. Cut out 2½-inch (6.2-cm) cookies. Gently press the cookies into the buttered forms, then cut away any excess on the tops to make them even.

4. Place the raspberry jam in a pastry bag with a No. 5 (10-mm) plain tip. Pipe the jam into the forms, filling them halfway.

5. Using a fluted pastry wheel, cut the reserved piece of dough into ¼-inch (6-mm) strips. Place 2 strips on top of each tartlet in an X, pressing the ends into the dough on the sides.

6. Bake at 350°F (175°C) for about 15 minutes or until golden brown on top. Let cool completely before unmolding (see Note). Sift powdered sugar lightly over the tartlets. Linzer tartlets taste best if they are served the same day they are baked; the jam tends to get dry and rubbery after that.

NOTE: To remove the forms, tap them gently against the table. If this does not work (or if you forgot to grease them), invert the forms, place a damp towel on top, and put into a hot oven for a few minutes.

Mazarins yield: 50 pastries, 2¹/₂ inches (6.2 cm) in diameter

Mazarins are popular in most Scandinavian pastry shops—especially in Sweden, where they are referred to as "a man's pastry" because they are not too fancy or fussy. When I was in the retail pastry business, there was a woman working behind the counter who always mentioned the mazarin pastries whenever a male customer asked for a suggestion, explaining, "The chef refers to these as a man's pastry." I learned that the typical response upon hearing this was (with a smile and a bit of bravado), "In that case, I'll take two." Traditional mazarin pans are small, round, plain (not fluted) forms, about 1¼ inches (3.1 cm) high and 2½ inches (6.2 cm) across the top, sloping down to about 1½ inches (3.7 cm) across the bottom. They look like miniature pie tins.

2 pounds (910 g) Short Dough (page 67)	**Apricot Glaze (page 5)**
2 pounds (910 g) Frangipane Filling (page 842), softened	**Simple Icing (page 35)**
Bread flour	

1. Line mazarin forms with short dough rolled to ⅛ inch (3 mm) thick (see Figures 2-4 to 2-7, pages 69 and 70). Cover the leftover dough and reserve for another use.

2. Place the frangipane filling in a pastry bag with a No. 7 (14-mm) plain tip. Pipe the filling into the shells almost to the top of the forms.

3. Bake at 400°F (205°C) for about 20 minutes or until filling springs back when pressed gently.

4. As soon as you remove the mazarins from the oven, dust flour lightly over the tops, then quickly invert them on the sheet pan to make the tops flat and even. A fast way to do this is to place an inverted sheet pan on top of the pastries and flip the whole thing at once. Allow them to cool upside down.

5. When cold, remove the forms and turn the pastries right-side up on a paper-lined sheet pan. Refrigerate briefly until firm.

6. Glaze the tops of the mazarins with a thin layer of apricot glaze, applying it with a brush. Ice with a thin layer of simple icing by dipping the top surface of the pastries into the icing and removing the excess with a spatula.

NOTE: Before they are glazed, mazarins will keep fresh for up to 1 week stored, covered, in the refrigerator. Glaze and ice as needed.

Meringue Landeck yield: 24 pastries, 3 × 2¼ inches (7.5 × 5.6 cm) each

I borrowed the idea for this pastry many years ago during my first visit to Landeck, a quaint little town high in the Austrian Alps that I highly recommend you visit if you are traveling in that area. I have been back a few times and the same pastry shop is still there, most likely passed along to the next generation —a tradition that, happily, is still common in Europe. This recipe has been altered somewhat from the original to lighten the flavor and texture.

The method used to create this eye-catching and tasty pastry is both simple and distinctive. Two very different batters are piped out next to one another in alternating ropes to create two-tone strips. Because both the meringue and the ladyfinger batter are actually dried in the oven and not really baked, they can successfully "cook" together. The baked strips are layered with a liqueur-flavored cream for a multitude of flavors and textures in the finished dessert—cool, creamy, crunchy, and chewy. Although the pastries can be kept overnight if covered and refrigerated, ideally, they should be assembled and served the same day.

¼ recipe French Meringue (page 27)   Dark coating chocolate, melted
½ recipe Ladyfingers batter (page 445)   Powdered sugar
Sambuca Cream (recipe follows)

1. Draw 6 strips, 2½ inches (6.2 cm) wide, evenly spaced across the width (16 inches/40 cm) of a sheet of baking paper. Invert the paper on a sheet pan. Place the French meringue in a pastry bag with a No. 8 (16-mm) plain tip. Pipe a rope of meringue lengthwise along both marked edges of 4 strips. Pipe the ropes a little flatter than they come out of the tip of the bag, leaving just enough room between the meringue ropes for a rope of ladyfinger batter. Pipe a single rope of meringue down the center of the remaining 2 strips (Figure 12-11). A small amount of meringue will be left over. Pipe out a few cookies on another pan or discard the meringue.

2. Place the ladyfinger batter in the pastry bag. Pipe 1 rope between the meringue ropes on the first 4 strips and 1 rope on either side of the meringue ropes on the last 2 strips.

3. Bake at 210° to 220°F (99° to 104°C) until the strips are dry and the ladyfinger batter has turned golden brown, approximately 2 hours. Set aside to cool.

4. Trim the strips as needed so they are all the same width. Reserve the 2 best-looking of the strips with 2 meringue ropes. Place the other 2 on cardboard strips for support. Spread a little less than half of the Sambuca cream over the strips on the cardboards. Place the 2 strips composed in the opposite pattern (2 ladyfinger, 1 meringue) on top of the cream. Ice the tops and

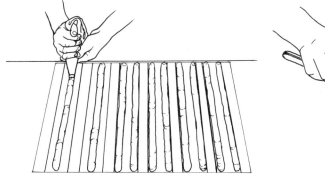

FIGURE 12-11 (left) Piping ropes of meringue within the marked lines on a sheet of baking paper for Meringue Landeck

FIGURE 12-12 (right) Adding the second layer of filling in assembling Meringue Landeck, using crème Parisienne to make the recipe variation

the long sides of the strips, using all of the remaining Sambuca cream (Figure 12-12). Top with the reserved strips. Brush melted chocolate lightly over the 2 meringue ropes on each assembled strip. Refrigerate for a minimum of 2 hours to set the cream.

5. Cut each strip into 12 slices, 2¼ inches (5.6 cm) wide, using a serrated knife dipped in hot water. Sift powdered sugar over the tops of the pastries. Store covered in the refrigerator.

SAMBUCA CREAM yield: approximately 3 cups (720 ml)

Do not make this cream until you are ready to use it.

2 teaspoons (6 g) unflavored gelatin powder	¼ cup (60 ml) Sambuca liqueur
¼ cup (60 ml) cold water	¼ recipe Italian Meringue (page 27; see Note, page 331)
1½ cups (360 ml) heavy cream	

1. Sprinkle the gelatin over the water to soften.

2. Whip the heavy cream to soft peaks. Add the liqueur and combine with the Italian meringue.

3. Heat the gelatin mixture over a bain-marie to dissolve. Do not overheat. Working quickly, add the gelatin to a small part of the cream mixture to temper, then quickly mix this into the remaining cream.

VARIATION

CHOCOLATE MERINGUE LANDECK yield: 24 pastries, 3 x 2¼ inches (7.5 x 5.6 cm) each

Follow the directions as given, replacing the Sambuca Cream with ½ recipe or 2 pounds 4 ounces (1 kg 25 g) Crème Parisienne (page 841).

Mocha Meringues yield: about 50 pastries, 1¾ inches (4.5 cm) in diameter

You might say the name *Mocha Meringues* is little misleading, as the mocha flavoring is not in the meringue component, but in the buttercream filling. However, this is part of the charm of these little pastries, as it allows you to change the flavor as needed to suit a special occasion or request, or to provide a greater variety if you are already offering several selections with coffee flavoring. If stored properly and under ideal conditions, the meringue shells can be made up to several weeks in advance, allowing you to fill and finish the pastries as required.

One of my favorite alterations is to flavor the buttercream with either orange liqueur or kirsch (use ⅓ to ½ cup/80 to 120 ml, depending on the strength). You can decorate the fruit-flavored meringues with chocolate curls, as described in the original recipe, or garnish the orange liqueur version with a marzipan orange and the kirsch-flavored pastries with a marzipan and chocolate decoration, as shown in Figure 11-18, page 536. Pipe the chocolate stems directly on the buttercream lines on top of each pastry, with the lines for the stems perpendicular to the buttercream lines. Regardless of which option you choose, these pastries easily enhance a typical assortment. They are a breath of fresh air compared to the usual rectangular, square, or piped selections.

½ recipe French Meringue (page 27)

1 pound 8 ounces (680 g) Vanilla Buttercream (Swiss Method) (page 477)

½ teaspoon (2 g) mocha paste *or* 2 tablespoons (30 ml) Coffee Reduction (page 14)

Sliced almonds, toasted and lightly crushed

100 Chocolate Curls (page 458), 1½ inches (3.7 cm) long

Powdered sugar

1. Place the meringue in a pastry bag with a No. 8 (16-mm) plain tip. Pipe it onto sheet pans lined with baking paper or Silpats in 1½-inch (3.7-cm) wide domes. Leave the tops as flat as possible as you pipe, without tails sticking up; in other words, the mounds should not be shaped like chocolate kisses.

2. Bake at 210° to 220°F (99° to 104°C) until completely dry, 3 to 4 hours.

3. Flavor the buttercream with the mocha paste or coffee reduction, mixing until soft and smooth. Place in a pastry bag with a No. 2 (4-mm) plain tip. Pipe a mound of buttercream the size of a cherry on top of half of the meringues. Invert the remaining meringues on top of the buttercream and press down lightly to level the tops.

4. Spread enough buttercream on the sides of the stacked meringues to completely fill in the gap between them and make the sides straight. Roll the sides in the crushed almonds to coat. Using the same tip as before, cover the tops of the meringues with parallel lines of buttercream, piping back and forth in a zigzag pattern with the lines touching.

5. Set 2 chocolate curls on top of each pastry, arranging them diagonally across the buttercream lines.

6. Place 6 to 8 pastries next to each other. Place on top a strip of cardboard, ¾ inch (2 cm) wide, perpendicular to the curls. Sift powdered sugar over the pastries. Remove the cardboard and repeat with the remaining pastries. Mocha meringues can be stored at room temperature for 1 or 2 days under normal conditions. Refrigerate if the weather is very warm.

NOTE: If you do not have time to make the chocolate curls, substitute small Chocolate Rectangles (page 460).

Napoleon Hats yield: 40 pastries, 2¾ inches (7 cm) in diameter

The word *pastry* is a generic term used for a multitude of sweets—from simple cookies to ornate filled, layered, and decorated creations, with these Napoleon Hats falling in that gray area between dressed-up cookies and modest individual pastries. Several European languages have a word for this type of sweet, which roughly translates to mean a filled or fancy cookie. These items are larger than a petit four and not as intricate or complex as what is often called a French pastry. Some examples of this type of not-so-showy pastry in this text are the various items that start by baking frangipane filling in a short dough crust, such as Tosca and Angelica Points. These should not be confused with petits fours sec, which can also rightly be described as elaborate cookies, the difference being that petits fours sec are miniature and much more elegant.

14 ounces (400 g) almond paste

6 ounces (170 g) granulated sugar

1 teaspoon (5 ml) pistachio extract

Green food coloring

1 or 2 egg whites

1 pound 10 ounces (740 g) Short Dough (page 67)

Egg wash

Simple syrup

I. Combine the almond paste, sugar, pistachio extract, and just enough green food color for a very light tint. Incorporate 1 to 2 egg whites, depending on the consistency of the almond paste. You want a soft paste that is just firm enough to shape with your hands.

2. Divide the paste into 2 pieces. Using flour to prevent it from sticking, roll each piece into a 12-inch (30-cm) rope, then cut each rope into 20 pieces.

3. Roll out the short dough to ⅛ (3 mm) inch thick. Cut out 40 cookies, 2¾ inches (7 cm) in diameter, using a fluted cutter. Place the cookies on sheet pans lined with baking paper. Lightly roll the almond paste pieces into balls. Brush egg wash over the tops of half of the short dough cookies. Place a ball of almond paste mixture in the center of each cookie. Pick up each cookie from 3 sides and press the sides of the short dough into the ball of filling to create a 3-cornered hat (see Figure 6-21, page 317, as an example). Repeat with the remaining 20 pastries.

4. Bake at 375°F for approximately 15 minutes or until light brown. Brush simple syrup over the pastries as soon as you remove them from the oven.

NOTE: For a slightly larger pastry, use 1 pound (455 g) almond paste, 8 ounces (225 g) granulated sugar, and 2 pounds 4 ounces (1 kg 25 g) short dough. Cut out the cookies with a 3-inch (7.5-cm) fluted cutter.

Orange Truffle Cuts yield: 60 pastries, 3 x I inches (7.5 x 2.5 cm) each (Photo 20)

You will need to start these rich, creamy, and crunchy chocolate cuts the day before serving them to give yourself enough time to assemble, ice, cut, and finish them in a practical manner. Should 60 pastries be too many, rather than going through all of the steps to make a small yield, follow the instructions for the full recipe through Step 6, cut the assembled sheet in half or quarters, then cover and place the portion you do not need in the freezer. It will keep for up to four weeks.

Upon occasion, to save time, I have been forced to omit either the marzipan oranges or icing the long sides of the cut strips. The pastries still look great with the meringue and ganache layers exposed all around, but by covering the sides with ganache, the unsliced strips can be left, covered, in the refrigerator for many days. When needed, sift cocoa powder over the top, mark the pattern, and cut them into slices.

½ recipe Japonaise Meringue Batter (page 28)

½ recipe Chocolate Chiffon Sponge Cake I batter (page 441)

⅓ cup (80 ml) simple syrup

½ cup (120 ml) Grand Marnier

3 pounds (1 kg 365 g) soft Ganache (page 842)

Unsweetened cocoa powder

60 Marzipan Oranges (recipe follows)

1 large stalk candied angelica

I. Spread the Japonaise meringue batter into a rectangle measuring 16 x 12 inches (40 x 30 cm) on a sheet of baking paper. Slide the paper onto a sheet pan (see Figure 9-4, page 443) and bake at 300°F (149°C) until golden brown and dry, about 30 minutes. Set aside to cool.

2. Line the bottom of a half-sheet pan, 16 x 12 inches (40 x 30 cm), with baking paper. Spread the chocolate sponge batter evenly on top. Bake immediately at 400°F (205°C) for about 12 minutes or until the cake springs back when pressed lightly in the center.

3. Flavor the simple syrup with about one-quarter of the Grand Marnier. Add the remaining Grand Marnier to the ganache.

4. Remove the chocolate sponge from the pan by cutting around the edge and inverting. Peel the paper from the back and turn right-side up again. Slice horizontally into 2 layers. Place the bottom layer on a cardboard or inverted sheet pan. Brush some of the Grand Marnier–flavored simple syrup mixture on top.

5. Reserve 1 pound 8 ounces (680 g) ganache. Spread half of the remaining ganache on top of the sponge. Place the Japonaise layer upside down on the ganache; peel the paper from the back. Spread the other half of the ganache over the Japonaise.

6. Top with the second sponge layer and press down to even the sheet. Brush the remaining simple syrup over the sponge. Refrigerate until the ganache is firm.

7. Trim the 2 long sides of the assembled sheet. Cut the sheet lengthwise into 4 strips. Ice the top and long sides of each strip with the reserved ganache (soften first to spread easily, if necessary), dividing it equally between the strips.

8. Sift cocoa powder over the top of the strips to cover the ganache. Using the back of a chef's knife, lightly press straight down to mark the cocoa powder with diagonal lines in both directions, creating a diamond pattern.

9. Cut each strip into 15 pieces, 1 inch (2.5 cm) each, using a thin knife dipped in hot water. Drill a small hole in the center of each pastry with the tip of a paring knife. Place a marzipan orange on the hole.

10. Select a good-looking stalk of angelica and cut it lengthwise into strips, ½ inch (1.2 cm) wide. Trim the strips at the thicker (bottom) end of the stalk. Cut ½-inch (1.2-cm) pieces at a 45-degree angle to make diamond shapes. Make a small cut next to each marzipan orange and place an angelica "leaf" in the cut.

MARZIPAN ORANGES yield: 60 decorations

5 ounces (140 g) marzipan, tinted orange   Melted cocoa butter (optional)

1. Divide the marzipan into 2 equal pieces and roll the pieces into ropes. Cut the ropes into 30 pieces each.

2. Roll the small pieces into balls, keeping them covered until you form them to prevent them from drying out.

3. Roll the balls lightly over a fine grater (a nutmeg grater is ideal) to give them an orange-peel texture. Use a small wooden skewer to make a small indentation in one end where the stem would be.

4. The finished oranges can be stored for weeks. To keep them looking fresh, coat them with a thin film of cocoa butter. Place a small amount of cocoa butter in the palm of one hand and gently, without altering the shape or texture on the outside, roll a few marzipan oranges at a time between your palms.

Paris-Brest

yield: 30 individual pastries, 3¹/₄ inches (8.1 cm) in diameter, or 2 rings, 11 inches (27.5 cm) in diameter

This delightful pâte à choux dessert was created by a French pastry chef named Pierre Gateau (no kidding). His shop was located in a suburb of Paris on the route of the famous bicycle race from Paris to Brest (a town in Brittany) and back. In 1891, he decided to honor the race and at the same time try to increase his business a little by creating a cake that resembled the wheel of a bicycle.

Paris-Brest is traditionally filled with a very rich praline-flavored mixture of pastry cream, buttercream, and Italian meringue. A variation of the dessert called Paris-Nice is filled with Crème Chiboust. In this version, I use Italian cream to lighten the filling. The crushed praline can be left out if you wish.

½ recipe Pâte à Choux (page 83)

Water

2 ounces (55 g) sliced almonds

¼ recipe or 4 ounces (115 g) Praline (page 33), finely crushed

1 recipe Italian Cream (page 844)

Powdered sugar

1. Draw 30 circles, 3 inches (7.5 cm) in diameter, on sheets of baking paper. Invert the papers on sheet pans. Alternatively, butter and flour the sheet pans and use a cake ring or cookie cutter, 3 inches (7.5 cm) in diameter, to mark outlines on the pan.

2. Place the pâte à choux in a pastry bag with a No. 6 (12-mm) star tip. Pipe the paste into rings centered on top of the outlines. Spray water lightly over the rings and sprinkle sliced almonds on top.

3. Bake at 400°F (205°C) until the pâte à choux is puffed, then reduce the heat to 375°F (190°C) and continue baking approximately 25 minutes or until the pastry is baked through. Let cool completely.

4. Slice each ring horizontally, removing about one-third to be used as a lid.

5. Combine the praline and Italian cream. Place in a pastry bag with a No. 6 (12-mm) star tip. Pipe a ring of filling on top of each pâte à choux bottom ring. Place the lids on top of the filling. Sift powdered sugar lightly over the tops. These pastries and the larger rings, as is true for all filled pâte à choux items, should be served within a few hours of assembly. While this is not always possible or practical, they must without exception be served the same day they are filled.

TO MAKE 2 RINGS, 11 INCHES (27.5 CM) IN DIAMETER

Follow the directions above, making the following changes:

- Draw or mark 2 circles, 10 inches (25 cm) in diameter.

- Instead of piping the paste into rings on top of the lines, pipe it in a corkscrew pattern, letting the paste fall within the circles (Figure 12-13). Another

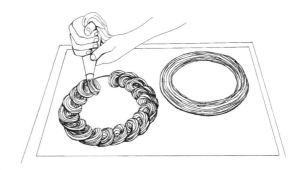

FIGURE 12-13 Two methods of piping the pâte à choux to make the larger version of Paris-Brest

method is to pipe 2 rings, one on either side of the lines, then finish with a third ring piped on top of the other two, as shown in the second example in the illustration. If you choose this method, use a slightly larger pastry tip and start each ring in a different place to avoid a noticeable seam and to make the rings stronger.

- Bake at 375°F (190°C) until golden brown and cooked through, 45 to 50 minutes. If necessary, tent the top with foil to prevent the almonds from burning. Be certain the rings are baked through; if they start to fall after being removed from the oven, it will be too late.

- Use the same corkscrew pattern when piping the filling onto the bottom rings.

- If the rings are to be cut into serving pieces within a few hours, cut the tops into pieces of the appropriate size and reassemble them on top of the filling. This will allow you to cut the pastry cleanly and avoid mashing the top and forcing the filling out. Several hours after assembly, the pâte à choux will have softened sufficiently to make precutting unnecessary.

Polynées yield: 40 pastries, 2¹⁄₂ inches (6.2 cm) in diameter

How these rather plain and typically Scandinavian pastries came to be named after such an exotic place as tropical Polynesia is unclear. Perhaps the French, who were responsible for naming so many culinary creations, had something to do with these as well. Polynées are basically almond macaroon cookies wrapped in short dough. They are similar to the pastry known as Conversation, the main differences being that there the forms are lined with puff pastry instead of short dough and the almond paste is thinned with egg yolks. The Polynée filling should puff up around the short dough cross. If it does not, the batter was too firm or the oven wasn't hot enough.

2 pounds (910 g) Short Dough (page 67)	1 recipe Almond Macaroons batter (page 292)
6 ounces (170 g) smooth strawberry jam	Powdered sugar
3 egg whites (³⁄₈ cup/90 ml)	

1. Roll out one-third of the short dough to ¹⁄₈ inch (3 mm) thick and reserve in the refrigerator. Roll out the remaining dough to ¹⁄₈ inch (3 mm) thick and use it to line 40 mazarin forms (see page 571) or other forms of similar size (see Figures 2-4 to 2-7, pages 69 and 70). Cover the scrap dough and save for another use.

2. Make a pastry bag from a half-sheet of baking paper (see page 54) and fill it with the strawberry jam. Pipe the jam into the forms, dividing it evenly.

3. Add 1 to 3 egg whites to the macaroon batter, beating it to a soft, creamy, yet still pipeable consistency. It should be liquid enough to flatten when piped. Place the batter in a pastry bag with a No. 4 (8-mm) plain tip. Pipe the batter into the forms on top of the jam, almost filling the forms.

4. Cut the reserved short dough into strips, ¹⁄₄ inch (6 mm) wide. Place 2 strips on top of each form, crossing them at a 90-degree angle and pinching the ends to the dough lining the sides. Add the scraps to the others reserved earlier.

5. Bake the pastries at 400°F (205°C) until golden brown, about 20 minutes. Let cool slightly, then remove the forms. Very lightly sift powdered sugar over the tops. Polynées will keep fresh for up to 1 week if stored, covered, in the refrigerator.

Porcupines yield: 30 pastries, 2¼ inches (5.6 cm) long (Photo 21)

Porcupine pastries always bring a smile. Although they are not a particularly sophisticated pastry when judged by today's standards, they can, if properly prepared, hold their own even when displayed with the nouvelle generation of pastries made using transfer sheets and decorated Joconde sponge, some of which actually look too precise and perfect to be real. Porcupine pastries are unusual and can be given a very cute, whimsical appearance by piping the eyes in various configurations—looking up, down, cross-eyed, and so on.

Judging from the reaction of the majority of customers and students at the school, it seems most people immediately recognize these as porcupines, with their pointed heads and big rounded quill-covered bodies, even if they have never seen a real one. However, a few years back, one of my students brought me a finished pastry on which he had inserted the almonds into the narrow end and piped the eyes on the rounded (rear) end! I guess his classmates were giving him a bit of a hard time because when he brought it to me, he said, "I have been told that I have done something wrong." I told him there was indeed a problem and that I would show him the proper way to finish the remaining pastries. With a bit of hesitation, he then told me they were all done. Because this was a popular pastry and, being a school, we always had plenty of material for the filling, this amounted to about 300 backward animals ready for the buffet. There was nothing really to do at that point but serve them, so I told the student just put them out as they were. The embarrassed young man replied, "I am so sorry, chef, but I have never seen one of these animals. I'm a city slicker, not a country boy!"

½ recipe or 2 pounds 12 ounces (1 kg 250 g) Rum Ball filling (page 588)

Powdered sugar

2 ounces (55 g) blanched, slivered (not sliced) almonds

Dark coating chocolate, melted

Royal Icing (page 34)

1. Divide the rum ball filling into 2 equal pieces, about 1 pound 6 ounces (625 g) each. Roll each piece into a 15-inch (37.5-cm) rope, using powdered sugar to prevent the filling from sticking to the table. Cut each rope into 15 equal pieces.

2. Roll the small pieces into round balls. One at a time, keeping the ball between your palms, taper one end to make a small cone, rounded at the wide end. To be sure the pastries will resemble porcupines (and not some other strange rodent instead), make the cones only about 2 inches (5 cm) long, with a definite point at the narrow end. Place the cones on sheet pans lined with baking paper and press lightly, just enough to keep them from rolling. Refrigerate until firm.

3. Push 7 almond slivers into the top of the wide portion of each rum ball cone (Figure 12-14).

4. Bring the porcupines close to room temperature if they have been chilled. One at a time, set the porcupines on a dipping fork and dip into melted coating chocolate, covering them completely. As you remove each porcupine, move it up and down over the bowl of chocolate a few times to remove as much excess chocolate as possible (see Figures 12-25 to 12-29, page 599). Place the porcupines on sheet pans lined with baking paper.

FIGURE 12-14 Pushing slivered almonds into shaped rum ball filling to make Porcupines

5. Check the royal icing to be sure it is thick enough not to run after it is piped. Put the icing in a piping bag and cut a very small opening. Pipe 2 dots (the size of white peppercorns) on each porcupine for eyes. Place a small amount of melted dark coating chocolate in a second piping bag and pipe a smaller dot of chocolate on the icing, making pupils in the eyes. Store the finished porcupines in a dry box or, well covered, in the refrigerator.

Pretzel Pastries yield: 36 pastries

The combination of two completely different doughs twisted into an interesting pretzel shape brings a smile of pleasant surprise to everyone who bites into one of these pastries; the flaky, unsweetened puff pastry and sweet, crumbly short dough complement each other perfectly. I teach this recipe in a class on basic doughs, and I have yet to come across a student who had either heard of or tasted these simple pastries previously.

Perhaps instead of pastries I should call these dressed-up cookies, as they really straddle the fence between the two. Pretzel Pastries can be made up very quickly anytime you have puff pastry and short dough handy; they are a good way to utilize scraps of either. The step that seems to present problems more times than not is the baking. Because short dough will normally bake faster than puff pastry, it is important to heed the instruction to bake double-panned and at the specified temperature, or the short dough portion will become overbaked.

1 pound (455 g) Puff Pastry (page 74)	Crystal sugar
1 pound (455 g) Short Dough (page 67)	Sliced almonds, crushed
Egg wash	Simple syrup

1. Roll the puff pastry into a rectangle measuring 9 x 14 inches (22.5 x 35 cm), using the smallest possible amount of flour to prevent the dough from sticking. The dough should be about ⅛ inch (3 mm) thick. Place the dough on a sheet of cardboard or on an inverted sheet pan.

2. Roll the short dough to the same size as the puff pastry, again using as little flour as possible to prevent the dough from sticking. It will be slightly thicker.

3. Brush egg wash on the puff pastry. Carefully, so you do not alter the shape, roll up the short dough on a dowel and unroll it on top of the puff pastry. Press the pieces together by rolling the dowel over them. Refrigerate until firm.

4. Mix equal amounts of crystal sugar and crushed almonds (by volume). Spread the mixture on a sheet pan and reserve.

5. With a dowel or ruler as a guide, use a sharp knife or pastry wheel to cut the sheet lengthwise into ¼-inch (6-mm) strips.

6. Twist each strip into a corkscrew by rolling the ends in opposite directions against the table (Figure 12-15), then form the corkscrew into a pretzel shape (Figure 12-16). Do not use any flour while forming the pretzels or the sugar-nut topping will not stick. Set the pretzel on the sugar and almond mixture and press gently to make sure the mixture adheres. Continue forming pretzels in the same way.

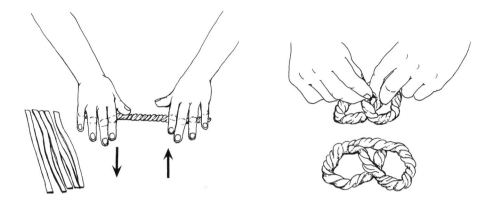

FIGURE 12-15 (left) **Twisting the layered strip of puff pastry and short dough into a corkscrew shape by rolling it against the table, moving the hands in opposite directions**
FIGURE 12-16 (right) **Forming the twisted strip into a pretzel shape**

7. When the pan of sugar mixture is full, transfer the pretzels, sugar-side up, to a sheet pan lined with baking paper or a Silpat. Repeat with the remaining strips. If the strips get soft or sticky and hard to work with, refrigerate for a short time.

8. Bake the pastries, double-panned, at 375°F (190°C) for 15 minutes or until golden brown. As soon as you remove the pretzels from the oven, brush simple syrup lightly over the tops.

CHEF'S TIP
Anything made with puff pastry is best the day it is baked, so bake only as many Pretzel Pastries as you will use that day. The formed pretzels can be frozen and baked as needed.

Puff Pastry Apple Points yield: 16 pastries (Photos 22 and 25)

This is another version of the classic mille-feuille, or Napoleon, but an unusual one because of its configuration and the addition of the apple flavor. The flavor and texture of this pastry could also be compared to an apple turnover with a serving of Calvados-flavored whipped cream, always an unbeatable combination. The most common fault found in an apple turnover—unbaked dough next to the filling—is eliminated here because the puff pastry and the filling are cooked separately. Even so, it is still of the utmost importance to use high-quality puff pastry dough and to make certain that the dough is completely baked through and dry.

Because Apple Points are taller than a typical Napoleon and are sliced after they are assembled, a tough or improperly baked sheet of dough will produce a pastry strip that is impossible to slice without making a mess. If prepared correctly, however, these pastries are guaranteed to earn you plenty of kudos, not only because of their unusual shape and the attractive exposed sides but also because of their delicious flavor. Puff Pastry Apple Points can also be served as a plated dessert. See page 607 for presentation instructions.

1 pound 8 ounces (680 g) Puff Pastry
(page 74) *or* Quick Puff Pastry (page 77)

Calvados-Apple Filling (recipe follows)

1½ cups (360 ml) heavy cream

2 teaspoons (10 g) granulated sugar

Calvados Cream (recipe follows)

1. Roll out the puff pastry dough to a rectangle measuring 14 x 20 inches (35 x 50 cm) and approximately ⅛ inch (3 mm) thick. Place the dough on an even sheet pan lined with baking paper. Prick the dough well and let it rest in the refrigerator for at least 30 minutes.

2. Cover the dough with a second sheet of baking paper and place a second flat, even sheet pan on top. Bake at 375°F (190°C) for 15 minutes. Remove the top sheet pan and the top piece of baking paper. Continue baking approximately 15 minutes longer or until the dough is golden brown and completely baked through. Let cool.

3. Whip the heavy cream with the sugar until stiff peaks form. Reserve in the refrigerator.

4. Cut the puff pastry sheet in half crosswise to make 2 strips, 10 inches (25 cm) wide. Starting from the evenly cut long edge, cut 3 strips lengthwise from each of the 2 pieces, making the strips 4, 3, and 2 inches (10, 7.5, and 5 cm) wide. Reserve the scraps pieces left on the ends. You should now have 6 strips of puff pastry, 2 of each size.

5. Place the 4-inch (10-cm) strips of puff pastry on opposite sides of an inverted sheet pan. Spread a layer of apple filling ½ inch (1.2 cm) thick over each of the strips, covering the full length. Spread a layer of Calvados cream just less than ½ inch (1.2 cm) thick on top of the apple filling. Place the 3-inch (7.5-cm) strips of puff pastry on top and repeat layering the apple filling and the cream. You should use up the entire amount of apple filling in assembling the pastries; however, there should be cream left over. Place the remaining 2-inch (5-cm) pastry strips on top and spread the remaining Calvados cream over the strips.

6. Ice the top and sides of the triangular pastry strips with the reserved whipped cream, shaping the cream so that there is a flat surface on the top approximately 1 inch (2.5 cm) wide.

7. Crush the reserved puff pastry scraps with your hands to make small crumblike pieces. Sprinkle the pieces over the top and sides of the strips.

8. Place the sheet pan in the refrigerator until the cream has set, approximately 2 hours.

9. Carefully cut each strip into 8 equal pieces, 1½ inches (3.7 cm) wide, using a serrated knife and holding a metal table scraper behind and against the pastry strip for support. Cutting with a sawing motion through the pastry layers, then pushing straight down through the filling layers works best.

CALVADOS APPLE FILLING yield: approximately 1 pound 12 ounces (795 g)

3 pounds (1 kg 365 g) cooking apples
7 ounces (200 g) granulated sugar
3 ounces (85 g) unsalted butter

1 tablespoon (15 ml) lemon juice
¼ cup (60 ml) water
⅓ cup (80 ml) Calvados

1. Peel and core the apples. Chop them into small pieces and set one-third of the pieces aside.

2. Place the remaining chopped apples in a skillet together with the sugar, butter, lemon juice, and water. If the apples are tart, you may want to add a little more sugar. Cook over low heat, stirring frequently, until the mixture starts to soften and thicken. Add a little extra water if needed to keep the filling from scorching.

3. Stir in the reserved chopped apples. Continue cooking until the added apple chunks have softened but still hold their shape and the remainder of the filling has reached a jamlike consistency. Add the Calvados and stir to combine. Let cool completely before using.

CALVADOS CREAM yield: approximately 6 cups (1 L 440 ml)

Calvados Cream must be used immediately and should therefore not be made until it is needed.

2½ teaspoons (18 g) unflavored gelatin powder
⅓ cup (80 ml) Calvados
2 cups (480 ml) heavy cream

1 tablespoon (15 g) cinnamon sugar
8 ounces (225 g) Pastry Cream (page 845; see Note)

1. Sprinkle the gelatin over the Calvados and set aside to soften.

2. Whip the heavy cream with the cinnamon sugar until soft peaks form. Reserve in the refrigerator.

3. Heat the gelatin mixture to dissolve.

4. Warm the pastry cream over a bain-marie until it reaches body temperature. Working quickly, stir in the gelatin mixture. Still working rapidly, incorporate the whipped cream.

NOTE: If pastry cream is not available, increase the heavy cream to 3¾ cups (900 ml). Temper the gelatin mixture into one-quarter of the softly whipped cream before adding it to the remainder.

Puff Pastry Strip Fruit Tart

yield: 4 strips, 8 × 4 inches (20 × 10 cm), or 16 individual servings, 4 × 2 inches (10 × 5 cm) each

The technique used here is a classic and very attractive way to combine fresh fruit with a pastry crust and a filling, but you might say that this is a version with a twist. The more commonly used method is simply to attach a narrow strip of puff pastry to each of the two long sides of a dough rectangle, producing a raised edge like a vol-au-vent (because the center of the dough has been docked, the border rises higher). Here, each side of the rectangle is made from two narrow strips of dough twisted together, as is done when making cheese straws. Using two pieces shaped together rather than one thicker piece not only produces a more attractive finish, it is practical because you use pieces cut from the same thickness of dough you have already rolled out for the base. It also provides an opportunity to sprinkle cinnamon sugar between the two pieces before you cut them into narrow strips and twist them together. This is especially appropriate if you bake the dough topped with pastry cream and thinly sliced apples (see Pizza-Style Apple Tart, page 348) instead of baking the shells blind, as directed in the recipe. If you make this variation, don't use the apricot jam.

Before you arrange the fruit on top of the baked shells, you should decide if you will be presenting the tart strips whole or making individual servings. The second option requires that you be more careful when arranging the fruit. I find it helpful to mark the pastry cream to indicate where the cuts will be and arrange the fruit within the lines. This way, you can avoid damaging the fruit when slicing the tarts later.

1 pound 2 ounces (510 g) Quick Puff Pastry (page 77)

Egg wash

4 ounces (115 g) apricot jam

8 ounces (225 g) Pastry Cream (page 845)

1 pound 8 ounces (680g) assorted fresh fruit and berries (see "Decorating with Fruit," page 564)

Apricot Glaze (page 5) or Pectin Glaze (page 30)

1. Roll out the puff pastry dough to a rectangle measuring 16 × 12 inches (40 × 30 cm) and approximately ⅛ inch (3 mm) thick. Let the dough rest in the refrigerator until it is completely firm. Trim 1 long edge of the dough, then cut 2 strips, 4 inches wide, lengthwise starting from the trimmed edge. Place the pieces on a sheet pan lined with baking paper or a Silpat. Cut 8 strips, ¼ inch (6 mm) wide, from the remaining dough, using a ruler or other straightedge as a guide.

2. Dock the wide strips thoroughly. Brush egg wash along the long sides of both strips. Twist 2 narrow strips together and place along 1 long edge, pressing in place gently. Repeat to place twisted strips along the remaining long edges (Figure 12-17). Let the assembled strips rest for 15 minutes.

FIGURE 12-17 Twisting the layered puff pastry strip by rolling it against the table, moving the hands in opposite directions; placing the twisted strip on the edge of the puff pastry rectangle to form a border

3. Bake at 375°F (190°F) until the puff pastry is golden brown and baked through. Let cool.

4. Spread the jam thinly and evenly over the strips between the raised borders. Place the pastry cream in a paper pastry bag. Cut a small opening and pipe it on top of the jam, dividing it evenly among the strips. Avoid getting cream on the borders.

5. Trim the short edges of the strips to make them even. Cut assorted fruit into decorative shapes and arrange on top of the tarts together with the berries. Glaze with apricot or pectin glaze. Cut each strip in half to make 4 tarts, 8 x 4 inches (20 x 10 cm) each, or cut each strip into 8 pieces, approximately 2 inches (5 cm) wide, to produce individual servings.

Rainbow Pastries yield: 40 pastries, approximately 2¹/₄ x 1¹/₄ inches (5.6 x 3.1 cm) each (Photo 20)

This old-fashioned recipe is more elegant than practical. Although Rainbow Pastries can be prepared through Step 5 and kept, covered, in the refrigerator for a few days to be completed as needed, once they are iced and cut, they are easily smeared and damaged. On a positive note, they add a nice splash of color to your pastry selection. You can use this basic idea and instructions to create other combinations. Try replacing the lemon buttercream with buttercream flavored with praline or coffee and the strawberry with buttercream flavored with rum or arrack. These flavors complement the chocolate nicely.

The glazed pastries must be refrigerated before they can be cut; however, chilling the pastries will cause the chocolate glaze to become dull and unattractive. To remedy this, the pastries should always be left at room temperature long enough for the shine to return before they are served. The buttercream is also more pleasant to eat when it is soft and creamy rather than cold and hard.

1 pound 13 ounces (825 g) or ¹/₃ recipe Frangipane Filling (page 842)	1 teaspoon (5 ml) Beet Juice (page 5; see Note)
1 pound 8 ounces (680 g) Vanilla Buttercream (Swiss Method) (page 477)	2 ounces (55 g) Lemon Cream *or* Lemon Curd (page 844)
2 ounces (55 g) strawberry jam or preserves, strained	2 ounces (55 g) sweet dark chocolate, melted
	1 recipe Chocolate Glaze (page 465)

1. Spread the frangipane filling over the bottom of a quarter-sheet pan, 8 x 12 inches (20 x 30 cm), lined with baking paper. If you do not have a pan this size, use a half-sheet pan and place a strip of cardboard, wrapped in foil, across the width of the pan and against the exposed long side of the filling to prevent it from spreading.

2. Bake at 400°F (205°C) for about 15 minutes or until the cake is baked through. Allow to cool completely, preferably overnight in the refrigerator, covered.

3. Run a knife along the edge of the cake to loosen it from the pan. Invert, then peel the baking paper from the back. Turn right-side up and level the top, if necessary. Cut the cake lengthwise into 4 strips, 2 inches (5 cm) each. Place each strip on a rectangular piece of cardboard.

4. Divide the buttercream into 3 equal portions. Flavor 1 portion with the strawberry jam or preserves and add the beet juice for color. Flavor 1 portion of buttercream with the lemon cream or curd. Flavor the remaining portion of buttercream with the melted chocolate.

5. Place the lemon-flavored buttercream in a pastry bag with a No. 8 (16-mm) plain tip. Pipe a rope of buttercream ¼ inch (6 mm) from the edge along one long side on all 4 frangipane strips. Squeeze out any buttercream left in the bag and refill it with the strawberry-flavored buttercream. Pipe a rope of strawberry-flavored buttercream next to the lemon buttercream on each frangipane strip. This should leave an equal amount of space on the opposite long side (the ropes should be centered on the frangipane strip). Squeeze out any leftover strawberry buttercream and refill the bag with the chocolate buttercream. Pipe a rope of chocolate buttercream in the center on the top of the first two buttercream ropes (Figure 12-18). Refrigerate the strips until the buttercream is firm.

FIGURE 12-18 **Piping a rope of chocolate-flavored buttercream on top of the lemon- and strawberry-flavored buttercream ropes for Rainbow Pastries**

6. Place the strips on an icing rack or a cake cooling rack set over a sheet pan lined with baking paper. Warm the chocolate glaze to the proper temperature so that it will easily coat the pastries (see Chef's Tip). Use a spoon to apply the glaze to 1 strip at a time in smooth, even strokes. Immediately go back and cover any bare spots on the sides before moving on. Waiting even a minute will leave a mark after the glaze has hardened. Wait until the glaze has run off completely so that none is dripping from the sides, then carefully transfer the strips to a sheet pan lined with baking paper. Refrigerate until the glaze is firm to the touch.

CHEF'S TIP

When coating Rainbow Pastries with chocolate glaze, the temperature of the glaze is critical. If the glaze is too cool and thick, the chilled surface of the buttercream will cause it to set up before it has floated down to cover the pastry. On the other hand, if the glaze is too warm, it can melt the buttercream on contact. Anything above body temperature is considered too warm. Make a test before you attempt to glaze an entire strip.

7. Trim the short ends. Using a sharp chef's knife dipped in hot water to heat and clean the knife between each cut, slice each strip into 10 pieces at a 45-degree angle. The warm knife will smear the different colors of buttercream into one another as you slice. To repair this, gently run the edge of the knife from the bottom up to the top immediately after making each cut. Store, covered, in the refrigerator.

N O T E : You may want to adjust the amount of beet juice used or omit it all together, depending on the jam or preserves you are using.

Rum Balls yield: 60 pastries, 1³/₄ inches (4.5 cm) in diameter

Rum balls are an excellent way of recycling good leftover pastries, end pieces, scraps, and other preparations, just as vegetable trimmings, bones, and some types of leftover sauce go into the stockpot in the hot kitchen. However, the rum ball bucket should not be mistaken for a garbage can; only those scraps that will not spoil within a week or so should be added. No pastry cream or whipped cream should be used, and buttercream or buttercream-filled items should be used only if they are no more than one day old. The best kinds of scraps to use are slightly stale cookies, meringues and macaroons, Florentinas, ladyfingers, pastries such as Tosca and Polynées that do not contain buttercream, light and dark sponge cake, and baked short dough cookies and cake bottoms. Danish or other yeast-dough pastries should not be used in a high-quality rum ball mixture but can be recycled as part of a Bear Claw filling.

The technique used for coating rum balls with chocolate is a little more complicated than the dipping technique used in many of the other recipes. However, because rum balls are so simple and inexpensive to make, there is no need to speed up the finishing process by simply dipping them or, worse yet, rolling them in chocolate sprinkles. I prefer to use light coating chocolate for rum balls, as so many of the other pastries in this chapter are finished with dark chocolate, but of course the two are interchangeable.

Rum Ball Filling (recipe follows)

Powdered sugar

2 pounds (910 g) melted light coating chocolate (see Note)

4 teaspoons (20 ml) simple syrup

1. Divide the rum ball filling into 5 pieces, a little over 1 pound (455 g) each. Roll each piece into a 12-inch (30-cm) rope, using powdered sugar to prevent the filling from sticking to the table. Cut each rope into 12 equal pieces. Roll the small pieces into round balls and place the balls on sheet pans lined with baking paper. Refrigerate until firm.

2. The temperature of the coating chocolate should be between 100° and 110°F (38° to 43°C). Cover the rum balls with a thin layer of melted chocolate by picking up some melted chocolate with your fingers and rolling a rum ball between your palms to coat. Place them back on the pans and reserve at room temperature.

3. Weigh out 1 pound 8 ounces (680 g) of the remaining chocolate; add more chocolate if necessary, depending on the amount used to coat the rum balls the first time. Return the chocolate to the proper working temperature. Stir in the simple syrup. You may need to increase the amount of syrup added, depending on the brand of chocolate you are using. The chocolate should thicken to the consistency of mayonnaise.

FIGURE 12-19 **Coating Rum Balls with thickened melted chocolate by rolling them between the palms to produce a spiked surface**

4. Pick up some of the thickened chocolate with your fingers and roll each rum ball between your palms as before, but this time cover them with a thick layer of chocolate, with spikes and tails of chocolate standing up (Figure 12-19). You must work quickly or the heat from your hands will melt the chocolate and you will not be able to achieve the rough texture. The finished pastry should be full of ridges and points, like a properly rolled truffle.

5. Replace the rum balls on the pans and store in a dry box or covered in the refrigerator.

NOTE: I generally do not specify the amount of melted chocolate where the item is simply to be dipped in or decorated with chocolate, but here I do because a fairly large amount is needed. If you'd rather cover these truffle look-alike pastries with milk chocolate, temper the chocolate (see page 468) but keep it on the thick side. Follow the instructions given here, but do not add the simple syrup.

CHEF'S TIP
The first coating is necessary to seal the surface of the rum balls before they are rolled in thick chocolate. This makes it possible to roll the rum balls in thick chocolate at room temperature without having them fall apart. Simply firming them in the refrigerator will produce small cracks in the chocolate coating, as the filling will expand when it reaches room temperature.

RUM BALL FILLING yield: about 5 pounds 10 ounces (2 kg 560 g)

¾ cup (180 ml) dark rum

6 ounces (170 g) dark raisins

4 pounds (1 kg 820 g) baked pastry or cake scraps

¼ cup (60 ml) water

5 ounces (140 g) nuts, any variety, crushed fine

12 ounces (340 g) sweet dark chocolate *or* milk chocolate, melted

1. Heat the rum and raisins slightly. Macerate for a few hours.

2. Place the pastry scraps and water in a mixer bowl and mix with a paddle to a smooth consistency. You may have to adjust the amount of water, depending on how many dry items you are using. Mix until you have a very firm, smooth dough, approximately 10 minutes. Add the crushed nuts and the chocolate and mix until combined. Incorporate the rum and raisins.

3. Place on a sheet pan lined with baking paper. Refrigerate until the filling is firm before shaping. If the mixture is too soft to work with, add more scraps from dry items, finely ground, to absorb moisture. If the filling is dry and crumbly, mix in enough buttercream or ganache to bring it to a workable consistency.

Rum-Chocolate Spools yield: 40 pastries, 2¼ inches (5.6 cm) in length

The combination of marzipan, chocolate, and rum is found in many desserts and pastries, and for good reason. These ingredients complement and play off one another well. A candy that features the same flavors and is also prepared in a similar way is called *branchli* (meaning "small branches" in the Swiss-German language). These are made by piping rum-flavored ganache into thin ropes, rolling each rope in a sheet of marzipan to cover, and then brushing melted chocolate over the marzipan to resemble the bark on a tree.

Rum-Chocolate Spools have been well known in Scandinavia for a long time. They are particularly popular in Sweden, where they are also known as *damsugare*, which translates to "vacuum cleaner." This name came about because the earliest vacuum cleaner canisters had a rounded tube shape, just like these pastries. At least I hope that is the reason and that the nickname is not a reference to the fact that rum ball filling and vacuum cleaners are both used to clean up scraps!

Although it is true enough, let me remind you again that the items used in the filling are perfectly good. Throughout the day in a professional bakeshop, sponge cakes are being trimmed to use for decorated cakes, perfectly good cookies and meringues become broken and cannot be sold, the ends of various assembled pastry strips must be trimmed even before they can be sliced into neat portions, and so on. Rather than throwing these scraps away (although a fair share do get eaten, especially by students who have not yet become as jaded to these treats as professionals who have been in the business for a few years), using them to create a moist chocolate and rum-flavored paste that can be made into a variety of pastries is a much more sensible and cost-effective alternative.

2 pounds 12 ounces (1 kg 250 g) *or* ½ recipe
   Rum Ball Filling (page 588)

2 ounces (55 g) Vanilla Buttercream (Swiss
   Method) (page 477)

Powdered sugar

Dark coating chocolate, melted

1 pound 2 ounces (510 g) Marzipan (page 21),
   untinted

1. Divide the rum ball filling into 4 equal pieces, about 11 ounces (310 g) each. Roll each piece into a rope 20 inches (50 cm) long, using powdered sugar to prevent the filling from sticking to the table. Set the ropes aside on a sheet pan lined with baking paper.

2. Using powdered sugar to keep it from sticking, roll out a portion of the marzipan to ⅛ inch (3 mm) thick; the width of the strips should be the same as the length of the ropes. Trim 1 short side to make it even and straight. Turn the marzipan upside down and spread a thin film of buttercream over it.

3. Set 1 rum ball rope at the trimmed edge of the marzipan sheet and roll up 1 full turn to encase it completely; the edges should line up, not overlap. Cut the rope away from the marzipan sheet (Figure 12-20).

4. Roll the covered rope against the table until it is 24 inches (60 cm) long, making it even at the same time. Carefully transfer the rope back to the sheet pan. Cover the remaining ropes, rolling out additional marzipan as needed. Refrigerate the ropes, covered, until they are firm.

5. Trim the ends, then cut each rope into 10 equal pieces, about 2¼ inches (5.6 cm) long.

6. Dip ⅛ inch (3 mm) of both ends of each pastry into melted dark coating chocolate. Place the rum-chocolate spools back on sheet pans with paper, arranging them, seam-side down, in straight rows.

7. Place a small amount of the melted chocolate in a piping bag (see page 55). Pipe a small dot of chocolate, the size of a pea, in the center of each pastry. Store as directed for Rum Balls.

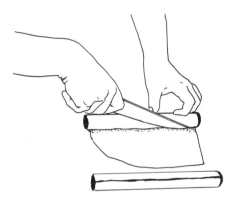

FIGURE 12-20 Cutting away the excess marzipan sheet after rolling the marzipan around a rope of rum ball filling for Rum-Chocolate Spools. The edges of the marzipan just meet but do not overlap.

Sarah Bernhardts yield: 30 pastries, approximately 2 inches (5 cm) in diameter

My version of this classic pastry, named after the famous nineteenth-century actress, uses a macaroon base topped with mocha-flavored buttercream, but Japonaise crowned with ganache and iced with either chocolate glaze or mocha-flavored fondant is also very common. In any case, Sarah Bernhardts should be small, simple, and elegant, just like their namesake.

30 Almond Macaroons (page 292)

Dark coating chocolate, melted

1 pound (455 g) Vanilla Buttercream (Swiss
   Method, page 477) (see Note)

30 chocolate candy or Marzipan Coffee Beans
   (directions follow)

½ teaspoon (2.5 ml) mocha paste *or* 2
   tablespoons (30 ml) Coffee Reduction
   (page 14)

I. Remove the macaroons from the baking paper as instructed and shown in Figure 6-14, page 292. Arrange them in rows, flat-side up. Press down lightly to flatten the cookies so they do not wobble.

2. Soften the buttercream as needed and flavor it with the mocha paste or coffee reduction. Place the buttercream in a pastry bag with a No. 6 (12-mm) plain tip. Pipe a mound of buttercream, the size of a large egg yolk, onto each cookie. Use a soupspoon to smooth and shape the butter-

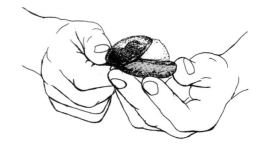

FIGURE 12-21 **Using a spoon to mold the buttercream in a smooth mound that covers the flat side of macaroon cookie for Sarah Bernhardts**

cream into an even mound about ½ inch (1.2 cm) thick in the center, tapering down to the sides of the cookie (Figure 12-21). Refrigerate until the buttercream is firm.

3. Holding a pastry upside down, insert a dipping fork at an angle into the base. Dip the buttercream mound into the melted dark coating chocolate. Hold the dipped pastry over the bowl of chocolate for a few moments, moving it up and down to allow as much excess chocolate as possible to fall back into the bowl. Place the cookies on a sheet pan in straight rows, chocolate-side up.

4. Put a small amount of melted coating chocolate in a piping bag. Cut a small opening in the tip. Use the chocolate to attach a coffee bean in the center on top of each pastry. Sarah Bernhardts will keep for up to 1 week stored in a cool location. If you must store them in the refrigerator, they should be boxed to protect the chocolate.

NOTE: An equal amount of ganache, flavored with coffee reduction or mocha paste, can be substituted for the buttercream. Spread the ganache into a point rather than a dome.

MARZIPAN COFFEE BEANS yield: 30 decorations, ³⁄₄ inch (2 cm) long

2¼ ounces (62 g) Marzipan (page 21), untinted   Unsweetened cocoa powder

I. Color the marzipan dark brown by kneading in a small amount of cocoa powder.

2. Roll the marzipan into a rope, 13½ inches (33.7 cm) long. Cut the rope into 30 equal pieces.

3. Roll 1 piece at a time between your palms to make it soft, then roll into a ball. Roll the ball into an oval. Place the oval in the palm of your hand and use a marzipan tool or the back of a chef's knife to make a mark lengthwise in the center, pushing the tool halfway into the "bean." Make the remaining decorations in the same way.

23. Crème Brûlée

24. Gâteau Saint-Honoré Nouvelle

25. Puff Pastry Apple Points

26. Cookie-Crusted Profiteroles with Nougat Sauce

27. Ciabatta

28. (above, clockwise from top) **Cinnamon Lemon Cake, Cream-Filled Coffee Cake Square, Almond Pound Cake**

29. (center left) **Trio of Cannolis**

30. (center right) **Tiramisu with Fresh Fruit**

31. (bottom) **Lemon-Honey Cake with Raspberries and Italian Meringue (as a plated dessert)**

(clockwise from top left) **32. Mint-Scented Chocolate Silk Cake   33. Blackberry Meringue Tartlet   34. Gâteau Saint-Honoré 35. Chèvre Cheesecake with Vanilla Bean Topping   36. Individual Lingonberry-Topped Cheesecake**

(clockwise from top left) **37. Lemon-Honey Cake with Raspberries and Italian Meringue 38. Pear-Frangipane Tart 39. Key Lime Chiffon Pie 40. Chocolate Decadence 41. Chocolate Sponge Cake with Vanilla Buttercream and Strawberry Wreath 42. Italian Pear, Almond, and Cranberry Tart**

**43. Chèvre Cheesecake with Vanilla Bean Topping
(as a plated dessert)**

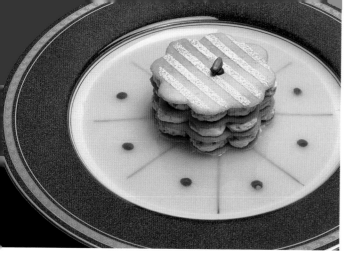

(clockwise from top left) **44. Almond Crisp Towers with Pistachio-Walnut Cream   45. Cherry Meringue Tart with Rhubarb Sauce   46. Mille-Feuille   47. Raspberry Choux Strips   48. Individual Baked Alaska Beehives**

(clockwise from top left) **49. Diplomat Cake 50. Swiss Kirsch Cake 51. Oat Flakes 52. Princess Cake
53. Nectarine Meringue Tart with Rhubarb**

Small Saint-Honoré yield: 45 pastries, approximately 2½ inches (6.2 cm) in diameter (Photos 20 and 21)

These pastries, topped with small, caramel-dipped profiteroles, stand out on a dessert tray amid the typical assortment of French pastries, such as Napoleons, éclairs, and the many variations of chocolate pastries, which are cut into different shapes from layered sheets of cake. Of course, we need all of those, especially as many are easily done way ahead, but the following are a sure bet when you or your customer are looking for something out of the ordinary. The profiterole decorations make the whole pastry tray shine and come alive.

3 pounds (1 kg 365 g) Puff Pastry (page 74) or puff pastry scraps, *or* 1 pound 10 ounces (740 g) Pâte Brisée (page 64) or Flaky Pie Dough (page 62)

¼ recipe Pâte à Choux (page 83)

1 recipe Diplomat Cream (page 841)

½ recipe Caramelized Sugar with Water *or* Caramelized Sugar for Decorations (page 11), cooked just to light brown

1⅓ cups (320 ml) heavy cream

1 teaspoon (5 g) granulated sugar

1. Roll out the puff pastry or pie dough to ¹⁄₁₆ inch (2 mm) thick. Prick well, then let the dough rest for a minimum of 30 minutes in the refrigerator.

2. Line 45 mazarin forms (or other forms of approximately the same size) with the dough (see Figures 2-4 to 2-7, pages 69 and 70). Reroll the pie dough scraps as needed to line all the forms. Cover any leftover dough and save for another use. Fill the forms with dried beans or pie weights.

3. Bake at 375°F (190°C) for approximately 15 minutes or until they are golden brown and baked through. Let the shells cool.

4. Using a fork, scrape all of the beans out of the shells and at the same time remove the shells from the forms.

5. Place the pâte à choux in a pastry bag with a No. 5 (10-mm) plain tip. Pipe out small mounds, about 1 inch (2.5 cm) in diameter on a sheet pan lined with baking paper. Use up all the choux paste; you should get about 50 to 60 mounds, which gives you a few extra for insurance. Bake at 425°F (219°C) until light brown and baked through, about 10 minutes. Set aside to cool.

6. Using the tip of a paring knife, make a small hole in the bottom of each profiterole. Place a small amount of the Bavarian rum cream in a pastry bag with a No. 2 (4-mm) plain tip. Pipe the cream into the profiteroles and reserve them in the refrigerator. Place the remaining rum cream in a pastry bag with a No. 5 (10-mm) plain tip. Pipe the cream into the puff pastry or pie dough shells, dividing it evenly and forming a smooth mound on each, just slightly above the rim. Place the pastries in the refrigerator to allow the filling to set.

7. Dip the tops and sides—do not dip the bottom—of each filled profiterole into the hot caramel, using a 2- or 3-pronged dipping fork or a table fork inserted into the side. Use a second

CHEF'S TIP

If you are short on time, you can simplify Small Saint-Honorés without sacrificing taste or appeal. Lining small forms with puff pastry can be time-consuming. By substituting pie dough, although not faithful to the classical rendition, lining the forms becomes quick and effortless. You need only about half as much pie dough as the scraps can be rerolled right away. Another shortcut is to eliminate filling the profiteroles and simply divide the Bavarian rum cream among the shells; the small profiteroles do not hold very much filling anyway. However, do not in any case omit dipping the profiteroles in caramel, which is what makes these pastries so unusual and pretty.

fork to push the profiterole off onto a Silpat or a sheet pan lined with baking paper, caramel-side up. Return to the refrigerator.

8. Whip the heavy cream and granulated sugar until stiff peaks form. Place in a pastry bag with a No. 5 (10-mm) plain tip. Pipe a cross of cream on the top of each pastry. Place a reserved caramelized profiterole on the top in the center. These pastries should be stored in the refrigerator and served the same day they are assembled.

Sugar-Glazed Puff Pastry Waffles with Apple

yield: 30 pastries, 4 × 2 inches (10 × 5 cm) each

The waffle part of this title derives from the traditional method of making these pastries, which left a waffle-like pattern on top of the puff pastry. This was done either by rolling the dough against a waffle board, an aluminum board with a small raised waffle pattern, or by using a studded rolling pin. The latter is a tool that looks very much like the waffle roller used to texture marzipan, but with a larger pattern.

The waffles can also be baked without the apples, in which case reduce the baking time to 15 minutes. After they have cooled completely, decorate the waffles by placing seasonal fresh fruit on top of the pastry cream, then glaze as directed.

3 pounds (1 kg 365 g) Pippin or Granny Smith apples (approximately 7 medium)	Granulated sugar
1 recipe Plain Poaching Syrup (page 31)	8 ounces (225 g) Pastry Cream (page 845)
1 pound (455 g) Puff Pastry (page 74)	Cinnamon sugar
Flour	1 recipe Apricot Glaze (page 5) or Pectin Glaze (page 30)

1. Peel and core the apples, cut them in half, and poach in the poaching syrup until soft. Remove from the heat and set aside to cool in the syrup. Cut the apples into small wedges and reserve.

2. Roll the puff pastry out to a rectangle measuring 9 × 11 inches (22.5 × 27.5 cm); it will be about ¼ inch (6 mm) thick. Cut out 30 circles, using a fluted cookie cutter approximately 1¾ inches (4.5 cm) in diameter. Stagger the cuts to get the full amount of circles. Press the scrap pieces together, cover, and reserve in the refrigerator or freezer for another use. Place the cut circles in the refrigerator to firm up if necessary.

3. Set up your workstation efficiently. If you are right-handed, place some flour in a pie tin on your left, granulated sugar directly on the table in front of you, and sheet pans lined with baking paper or Silpats on your right.

4. Place a few of the puff pastry circles on top of the flour. Pick up 1 circle at a time, invert it (flour-side up) onto the sugar in front of you, and use a dowel to roll it in the sugar, making an oval about 4 × 2 inches (10 × 5 cm), and, at the same time, rolling sugar into the dough on one side. If the dough sticks to the dowel, turn the puff pastry back over in the flour again, but do not get any sugar on the flour side or it will burn when the pastries bake. Place each rolled pastry, sugar-side up, on the sheet pan.

5. Place the pastry cream in a pastry bag with a No. 3 (6-mm) plain tip. Pipe a small oval of cream in the center of each pastry oval, leaving a ¼-inch (6-mm) border of puff pastry uncovered.

6. Arrange 5 or 6 apple wedges at an angle in the pastry cream. Sprinkle cinnamon sugar over the apples.

7. Bake at 400°F (205°C) just until the sugar caramelizes, about 20 minutes. Cool completely.

8. When the pastries have cooled, brush apricot or pectin glaze over the tops. The waffles should be served the same day they are made.

CHEF'S TIP
Because these waffles, like all puff pastry goods, should be baked fresh every day, it is a good idea to make a large number to freeze and bake as needed. You can stack 6 layers of waffles, rolled in sugar and separated with baking paper, per sheet pan.

VARIATION
PARISIAN SUGAR-GLAZED WAFFLES yield: 15 pastries, 4 × 2 inches (10 × 5 cm) each

These golden puff pastry ovals, sandwiched together with various flavors of buttercream, are also known as Parisian Tongues—a name, no doubt, that has to do with their long oval shape. Parisian waffles are a good illustration of the principle that one should not judge a book by its cover. Though rather plain and humble-looking, they have a wonderful crisp texture and unusual taste, and they are somewhat of a novelty today among showier and fancier pastry selections.

1 pound (455 g) Puff Pastry (page 74)

Flour

Granulated sugar

1 tablespoon (15 ml) arrack *or* rum

7 ounces (200 g) Vanilla Buttercream (Swiss Method) (page 477)

2 ounces (55 g) strawberry jam

1. Follow the directions in Steps 2, 3, and 4 of the main recipe.

2. Make 3 angled cuts, ¼ inch (6 mm) long, lengthwise down the center of the ovals. Let the dough rest for at least 30 minutes. Bake at 425°F (219°C) until the ovals are golden and the sugar begins to caramelize, about 12 minutes. After they have cooled completely, turn half of the ovals upside down and set the remaining ovals aside to use as the tops.

3. Flavor the buttercream with arrack or rum and pipe a border around each bottom waffle, using a No. 3 (6-mm) plain tip in your pastry bag. Pipe a small ribbon of strawberry jam lengthwise in the center.

4. Place the reserved waffles on top and press lightly into the buttercream so they adhere.

Swans yield: approximately 50 pastries, 3¼ × 2 inches (8.1 × 5 cm) each

Swans are a natural for buffet displays. They are light and delicious, and they look very elegant presented on mirrors. There is something magical about these winged pastries that makes people fall in love with them. I have occasionally run out of swans at the end of service and have had customers expressing their disappointment close to the point of crying or wanting their money back! It doesn't seem to matter to the untrained eye that there are times when the student's creations more closely resemble scavenger birds or pelicans (from piping the beak too large) than swans. Depending on the other pastries you are offering, you may want to place a small wedge of strawberry on top of the whipped cream at the back end of each swan to add some color.

1 recipe Pâte à Choux (page 83)

6 ounces (170 g) smooth strawberry jam

2 recipes Chantilly Cream (page 838)

Dark coating chocolate, melted

Powdered sugar

I. Reserve about 1 cup (240 ml) pâte à choux to make the swan necks; cover tightly so it doesn't form a skin. Place the remaining paste, 1 portion at a time, in a pastry bag with a No. 7 (14-mm) star tip. Pipe the paste in cone shapes, 3 inches (7.5 cm) long and 1¾ inches (4.5 cm) wide, on sheet pans lined with baking paper. Start by making the wide end of the cone, piping in an up-and-over motion (Figure 12-22), then relax the pressure on the bag and end in a narrow point. It is important that the wide end be quite a bit higher than the narrow end for nice-looking swans.

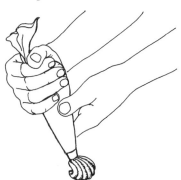

FIGURE 12-22 **Starting to pipe the bodies for Swans, using an up-and-over motion to make the wide end of the pâte à choux cones higher than the narrow end**

2. Place the reserved pâte à choux in a pastry bag with a No. 1 (2-mm) plain tip. To pipe out the head and neck pieces, start by piping a ¼-inch (6-mm) strip for the beak, moving quickly so the flow of paste is actually thinner than the pastry tip. Pause for a second so you get a lump for the head, then continue in the shape of a question mark, forming the long, curved neck with the flow of paste the same thickness as the pastry tip for this section (Figure 12-23). You should make quite a few extra head and neck pieces so you will be able to pick and choose during the assembly and to allow for breakage.

3. Bake the bodies and the head and neck pieces at 400°F (205°C). The bodies will take about 20 minutes and the neck pieces about half as long. Let cool completely.

FIGURE 12-23 **The piped pâte à choux Swan bodies and head-neck pieces before baking**

4. Cut the top third off the bodies; then cut the top piece in half lengthwise to create 2 wings (scissors work best). Place the wings on either side of each body, lining the pastries up for assembly.

5. Pipe a thin ribbon of strawberry jam in the bottom of each shell.

6. Whip the Chantilly cream to stiff peaks and place in a pastry bag with a No. 6 (12-mm) star tip. Pipe the cream into the shells, using the same up-and-over motion you used to pipe the shells and coming to a point at the narrow end, which will be the tail.

7. Arrange the wings in the whipped cream pointing upward and meeting at the top. Dip the bottom of each neck in coating chocolate to prevent the whipped cream from softening it and causing it to fall (this is not necessary if you assemble the swans to order). Push the necks into the whipped cream so they lean back slightly between the wings.

8. Sift a little powdered sugar over the top of the pastries. Place in the refrigerator. As with all pâte à choux products, swans should be served the same day they are assembled.

CHEF'S TIP

If you are making a small batch of swans, or if it just makes more sense, spacewise, it is fine to pipe both the bodies and the necks on the same sheet pan. If you do, simply remove the necks individually as they are done baking.

Swedish Napoleons yield: 15 pastries, 4 × 1¹/₂ inches (10 × 3.7 cm) each (Photo 57)

A good production method for napoleons, or any time you need thin baked sheets of puff pastry, is to roll out the dough sheets and place them, well wrapped, in the freezer to bake as needed. When I was in the retail business, we always rolled out a week's worth at one time, then baked the sheets fresh every morning. Alternatively, storing baked sheets overnight, covered tightly, is certainly acceptable. It is very important that the puff pastry sheets are baked properly to be dry and crisp. This not only makes the napoleons taste better but also makes them much easier to cut after they are assembled.

Napoleon is the adopted name for the classic French pastry mille-feuille, or "thousand leaves," which refers to the composition of the pastry. My version, Swedish Napoleon, is a little different in that it does not contain pastry cream and has colorful pink icing on top. Instructions for Mille-Feuille follow this recipe.

The name napoleon is a little confusing. People widely assume an association with the famous French general Napoleon Bonaparte, who proclaimed himself Napoleon I in 1804. Although he stands out as one of the most brilliant military leaders in history, he has nothing to do with this pastry other than the fact that both he and it are from France. The name *napoleon* is instead a reference to the layer structure stemming from the Neapolitan style of making pastries. This is also where the name for layered Neapolitan ice cream comes from.

1 pound 8 ounces (680 g) Puff Pastry (page 74) or scrap puff pastry

5 ounces (140 g) smooth red currant jelly

3 ounces (85 g) Fondant (page 18) or Simple Icing (page 35)

Simple syrup

2 cups (480 ml) heavy cream

1 tablespoon (15 g) granulated sugar

1. Roll out the puff pastry to a rectangle measuring 24 × 14 inches (60 × 35 cm); it should be approximately ⅛ inch (3 mm) thick. Place the dough on an even sheet pan lined with baking paper. Prick the dough well and let it rest in the refrigerator for at least 30 minutes.

2. Cover the dough with a second sheet of baking paper and place a second flat and even sheet pan on top. Bake at 375°F (190°C) for 15 minutes; the sheet should be golden brown around the edges. Remove the top sheet pan and baking paper and continue baking approximately 15 minutes longer or until golden brown and completely baked through. Let cool.

3. Cut 3 strips from the pastry sheet, the full length of the sheet and 4 inches (10 cm) wide for regular servings or 3 inches (7.5 cm) wide for buffet servings.

4. Select the nicest strip for the top and turn it upside down. Spread a very thin film of red currant jelly, just enough to color it, over the top of this strip. Spread a slightly thicker layer of jelly on one of the remaining strips, which will become the bottom.

5. Thin the fondant or simple icing to an easy-to-spread consistency with simple syrup. Carefully spread a thin film on top of the jelly on the top strip, blending the two together just enough to produce a pretty marbled surface. Set the top strip aside for about 30 minutes or until a crust has formed on the top of the icing. If you are in hurry, you can speed this up by placing the iced strip in a warm oven for 30 seconds; take care not to melt the icing.

6. Whip the heavy cream and sugar to stiff peaks; place in a pastry bag with a large plain tip. Place the middle strip on the bottom strip. Pipe the whipped cream on top of the middle strip in a 1-inch (2.5-cm) layer.

7. Cut the glazed top layer crosswise into 1½-inch (3.7-cm) pieces. Reassemble the top strip on top of the whipped cream. Using the top pieces as a guide, cut through the other layers. Napoleons must be served the same day they are made.

VARIATION

MILLE-FEUILLE yield: 15 pastries, 4 × 1½ inches (10 × 3.7 cm) each (Photo 46)

Mille-feuille means "a thousand leaves" and refers to the multiple strata of the classic French puff pastry dough, which is given a greater number of turns (six single turns, preferably over a three-day period) than the more practical, and more commonly used, dough included in this text. It is something of a misnomer to call these pastries by their French name when using this puff pastry recipe, as the dough falls short of 1000 layers. A way to make up for it is to take finished puff pastry made according to the directions in this book and give the dough a half-turn; roll out the dough as you would to make a double turn, then fold it in half. The dough will then have just over 1000 layers. However, if you are not such a stickler for accuracy, don't worry.

This version of napoleons, like the one that precedes it, contains three strips of puff pastry. Because of this, you may want to increase the cornstarch in the pastry cream by 1 ounce (30 g) per full recipe. The firmer pastry cream will make it easier to slice and handle the assembled napoleons.

1 pound 8 ounces (680 g) Puff Pastry (page 74) or scrap puff pastry

4 ounces (115 g) Fondant (page 18) or Simple Icing (page 35)

Simple syrup

2 tablespoons (16 g) cocoa powder (see Note)

2 pounds (910 g) Pastry Cream (page 845)

1 tablespoon (15 ml) kirschwasser

1. Follow the instructions in the recipe for Swedish Napoleons through Step 3. Select the best of the strips and turn it upside down.

2. If you are using fondant, soften it to a spreadable consistency by adding simple syrup.

3. Remove 1 tablespoon (15 ml) fondant or simple icing and thoroughly mix the cocoa powder into it. Add enough simple syrup to this cocoa icing to bring it to the same consistency as the white icing, approximately 2 tablespoons (30 ml). Place the cocoa icing in a piping bag.

4. Spread the white icing over the inverted strip. Immediately pipe 8 to 10 thin, straight lines of cocoa icing lengthwise on top. Draw a knife across every ¾ inch (2 cm) in one direction, then go back and draw a line in the opposite direction between each of the first lines to create a herringbone pattern (Figure 12-24). Set the strip aside.

5. Flavor the pastry cream with the kirschwasser. Spread half of it on top of one of the remaining puff pastry strips. Top with the second strip and spread the remaining pastry cream on top.

6. Cut the glazed top layer crosswise into 1½-inch (3.7-cm) pieces (check first to be sure a skin has formed on the icing). Reassemble the top strip on top of the pastry cream. Using the top pieces as a guide, cut through the other layers. Mille-feuille must be served the same day they are assembled.

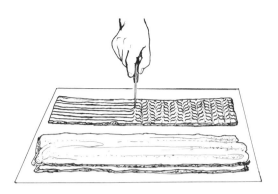

FIGURE 12-24 Dragging a thin knife through the chocolate lines piped in the fondant to create the herringbone pattern on mille-feuille

NOTE: If using simple icing instead of fondant, you will need only half as much cocoa powder. Also, it is not necessary to use simple syrup to thin the cocoa icing in this case; water will do. However, with either type of icing it is of the utmost importance that the icing is kept as firm as possible or the contrasting color (the cocoa lines) will bleed into the white icing when applied.

Swedish Profiteroles yield: 35 pastries

The Swedish Profiteroles recipe evolved from a popular Swedish pastry known as *Maria Bollar*, or "Maria Balls," strictly translated. One of the many pastries made with pâte à choux, Maria Bollar are not as well known as éclairs, cream puffs, profiteroles, and Paris-Brest. The unusual-looking cracked surface on top makes people want to try them, and then it's too late—they're hooked. The soft filling coupled with the sweet, crunchy topping makes an irresistible combination.

1½ ounces (40 g) granulated sugar

4 ounces (140 g) Short Dough (page 67)

½ recipe Pâte à Choux (page 83)

1 recipe Quick Bavarian Cream (page 846)

Powdered sugar

1. Mix the granulated sugar into the short dough. Roll the dough to ¹⁄₁₆ inch (2 mm) thick and cut out 35 circles, using a 1½-inch (3.7-cm) plain or fluted cookie cutter. Set aside. Discard the scrap pieces.

2. Place the pâte à choux in a pastry bag with a No. 6 (12-mm) plain tip. Pipe out 35 mounds of pâte à choux making them slightly larger than the cookies. Immediately place a short dough circle on each mound and press lightly with your fingers to be sure they stick (see Note).

3. Bake the profiteroles at 400°F (205°C) until puffed, about 10 minutes. Reduce the heat to 375°F (190°C) and bake until they will hold their shape, about 10 minutes longer. Let the puffs cool completely.

4. No longer than 1 hour before serving, make a small slit in the bottom of each puff just large enough to insert a small pastry tip. Put the Bavarian cream in a pastry bag with a No. 3 (6-

mm) plain tip and pipe into the profiteroles. Dust lightly with powdered sugar and reserve the profiteroles in the refrigerator. Swedish profiteroles are best eaten as soon as possible after they are filled and should not be served the following day.

NOTE: The profiteroles can be frozen after they have been piped out and topped with the cookies. Bake straight from the freezer without thawing. I try to place them in the freezer long enough to harden even when they are to be baked right away because they seem to puff up better if baked frozen.

Tosca yield: 48 pastries, 2³/₄ × 1¹/₄ inches (7 × 3.1 cm) each

Puccini's famous opera by the same name, which was first performed in Rome in 1900, probably has nothing to do with these pastries other than it is very Italian and so is the Florentina topping. The combination of short dough, frangipane, and chocolate, on the other hand, is as Swedish as the Princess Cake (page 530) and, like princess pastries, Tosca pastries are an adaptation of a celebrated cake. Tosca cake (or, more literally translated, Tosca tart) has always been popular. The traditional finish includes brushing melted chocolate over the sides and around the edge on the top, a step that once saved a young apprentice a lot of grief when he happened to bake the tarts just a little too dark! The base for Tosca can be used to make any number of pastries, so it is a good idea to keep a baked sheet on hand in the freezer.

1 pound 5 ounces (595 g) Short Dough (page 67)	¹/₂ recipe or 13 ounces (370 g) Florentina Batter (page 306)
4¹/₂ ounces (130 g) smooth strawberry jam	Dark coating chocolate, melted
4 pounds 10 ounces (2 kg 105 g) Frangipane Filling (page 842)	

1. Line the bottom of a half-sheet pan, 16 × 12 inches (40 × 30 cm) with baking paper. Roll out the short dough to ¹/₈ inch (3 mm) thick and place in the pan. Trim the edges so only the bottom of the pan is covered with dough. Cover the dough scraps and reserve for another use. Spread the jam in a thin layer over the dough. Spread the frangipane filling evenly on top.

2. Bake at 375°F (190°C) until baked through, about 45 minutes (keep in mind that the pastry will be baked an additional 5 minutes with the topping). Let cool to room temperature, then refrigerate.

3. When the frangipane sheet is cold (preferably the day after baking), cut off the skin and even the top. To do this, leave the frangipane sheet in the pan and cut with a serrated knife held parallel to the top of the cake, using the edge of the pan as a guide for your knife.

4. Spread the Florentina batter over the frangipane, using a spatula dipped into hot water to make it slide more easily. Place the frangipane sheet, still in its original pan, onto a second pan the same size (double-panning).

5. Bake at 425°F (219°C) until the Florentina topping begins to bubble and turn golden brown, about 5 minutes. Let cool to room temperature.

6. Cut the sheet loose from the sides of the pan; place a cake cardboard on top, invert, and unmold onto the cardboard. Refrigerate (upside down) until cool.

7. While the sheet is still upside down, trim both long sides, then cut lengthwise into 4 equal

FIGURE 12-25 **Inserting a dipping fork partway into the side of a Tosca pastry**

FIGURE 12-26 **Letting the excess chocolate drip back into the bowl after dipping the bottom and sides of the pastry into the melted chocolate**

FIGURE 12-27 **Scraping the pastry against the side of the bowl to remove excess chocolate from the bottom**

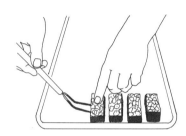

FIGURE 12-28 **Blotting the pastry on a piece of baking paper**

FIGURE 12-29 **Removing the dipping fork after placing the dipped pastry on a paper-lined sheet pan, touching the Florentina topping rather than the chocolate coating if needed to steady the pastry**

strips, approximately 2¾ inches (7 cm) wide. Cut each strip across into 12 pieces, 1¾ inches (3.1 cm) wide. Hold the knife at a 90-degree angle so that the edges are straight. Turn the cut pieces over so that the Florentina faces up.

8. Dip the bottom and sides, but not the top, of each pastry into dark coating chocolate, using a dipping fork inserted partway into the pastry. Carefully move the pastry up and down over the bowl a few times to allow as much excess chocolate as possible to fall back into the bowl. Drag the bottom against the side of the bowl. Blot the pastry on a piece of baking paper to remove more chocolate. Place the slices in straight rows on sheet pans lined with baking paper (Figures 12-25 to 12-29). Store the finished pastries in a cool place; they will keep for up to 1 week.

NOTE: If you must refrigerate Tosca, they should be boxed and well wrapped to prevent the Florentina topping from getting wet and sticky.

Trier Squares yield: 48 pastries, 2 inches (5 cm) square

These pastries are named for the ancient town of Trier, located on the banks of the Mosel River in southwestern Germany. I based my version on a recipe I found in a German cookbook from the turn of the century. Trier Squares are another one of my personal favorites; I can't keep myself from eating the scraps when the baked sheets are trimmed and cut in class.

These pastries are very easy to make, they taste great, and they keep quite well after baking. Trier Squares can also be stored in the refrigerator (up to one week) or in the freezer (for several weeks), finished through Step 4. They make a good choice for beginning students because their preparation offers an opportunity to practice rolling out short dough, lining pans, cutting thin dough strips, and arranging them in a precise pattern. Because these pastries are also pretty much foolproof, they also provide a good morale boost.

2 pounds 3 ounces (1 kg) Short Dough (page 67)

4½ ounces (130 g) smooth apricot jam

Trier Filling (recipe follows)

Egg wash

I. Line the bottom of a half-sheet pan, 16 x 12 inches (40 x 30 cm), with baking paper. Roll a portion of the short dough out to ⅛ inch (3 mm) thick, roll it up on a dowel, and unroll over the pan. Trim the edges to cover just the bottom of the pan and place the pan in the refrigerator. Add the scraps to the remaining short dough and roll to the same thickness and about 16 inches (40 cm) in length. Place on a sheet of cardboard or on an inverted sheet pan and place in the refrigerator until firm as well.

2. Spread the jam in a thin layer over the short dough in the pan. Top with the Trier filling and use a palette knife to spread it out evenly.

3. Cut the reserved dough lengthwise into strips, ¼ inch (6-mm) wide, using a fluted or plain pastry wheel.

4. Brush the top of the Trier filling with egg wash. Arrange the dough strips diagonally, ¼ inch (6 mm) apart, over the filling. Then arrange strips diagonally in the other direction so they form a diamond pattern (Figure 12-30). Press the strips lightly with your hand as you place them to make sure they stick. Trim the edges around the pan and cover the dough trimmings to save for another use. Brush the strips with egg wash.

5. Bake at 375°F (190°C) until golden brown and baked through, about 40 minutes. Let the pastry cool completely, preferably overnight. Cut around the inside edge of the pan and invert the sheet. Remove the pan and the baking paper. Turn right-

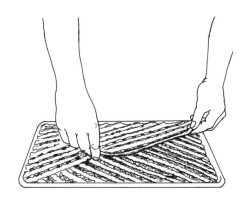

FIGURE 12-30 Arranging strips of short dough diagonally to form a diamond lattice pattern on the top of Trier Squares

side up. Trim the long edges. Measure and cut into 6 equal strips the long way and cut each strip into 8 equal pieces. Use a serrated knife with a sawing action to minimize breaking the short dough.

TRIER FILLING yield: 2 pounds 13 ounces (1 kg 280 g)

15 ounces (430 g) sliced almonds

14 ounces (400 g) granulated sugar

½ cup (120 ml) whole milk

5 ounces (140 g) Beurre Noisette (see page 7)

6 ounces (170 g) golden raisins

¼ cup (60 ml) lemon juice

Grated zest of 1 lemon

1 tablespoon (5 g) ground cinnamon

1. Combine the almonds, sugar, and milk. Add the beurre noisette.

2. Mix in the raisins, lemon juice, lemon zest, and cinnamon.

FROZEN PLATED DESSERTS

Plated Desserts

For many hundreds of years, sweet and elegant desserts have been a favorite way to reward ourselves and those who are special to us. They are a small luxury that, even though not an essential part of the everyday diet, has played an important role in cultural history. From the first sweets, which were probably nothing more than a plate of fruit topped with honey, cooking and baking have developed into a creative and sophisticated art. This is especially evident in dessert presentations, which are often a meaningful part of celebrations and special occasions.

Some of the more elaborate recipes in this chapter require time and patience, but they yield breathtaking results. However, any of these desserts, even the quickest and most humble, should be presented in its own elegant way, served on an attractive plate, and accompanied by an appropriate sauce and/or garnish. Remember: We eat with our eyes as well as our mouths. Even the simple and homey-looking Rum Baba can be dressed up with a little effort, although this type of dessert is not meant to compete with the artistry and complexity of the more architectural dessert presentations.

The size of the serving plate alone can make a big difference in a dessert's appearance. The dessert should not touch the rim of the plate, so, for most items, it is essential to use a plate 10 to 12 inches (25 to 30 cm) in diameter to display the pastry, sauce, and garnish without crowding. All of the presentation instructions in this chapter are based on using plates of this size, with a minimum base of 7 inches (17.5 cm) in diameter. So as not to detract from the dessert, it is best to use plates with little or no pattern on the surface and with just a simple design on the rim. This is especially important if decorating with two or more sauces, or the result can look like a bad example of modern art. Keep in mind that the serving plate, sauce, and garnish are there to enhance the dessert, not to compete with it. Strive for a well-balanced presentation.

With small adjustments—often just leaving off the sauce and garnish—many of the selections in this chapter can be adapted for the showcase in a pastry shop or for a dessert buffet, instead of plate service. Tiramisu, Cookie-Crusted Profiteroles, German-Style Apple Strudel, Small Pear Tartlets, and White Chocolate Citrus Roulade are examples. Conversely, some of the pastries found in the Individual Pastries chapter can easily be turned into elegant plated desserts by serving them with an appropriate sauce and decoration.

In either case, whether you serve an elegant petits fours tray or a dessert that is artistically embellished with tuile paste, sugar, or chocolate decorations, when your customers are finished eating, they should agree that it was worth every calorie.

Almond Crisp Towers with Pistachio-Walnut Cream yield: 16 servings (Photo 67)

This elegant and delicious dessert was born over a cup of coffee with a colleague who needed a nutty dessert for a special function. The original name on the menu was Trio of Nuts, but I have since decided on a more conservative title. I'm using slightly modified versions of the Crisp Hazelnut Wafers batter and template.

The fragile wafers literally fall apart in your mouth and also, unfortunately, in your hands if you are not careful during the assembly. The recipe will give you about ten extra wafers, and you will probably need some of them. If any are left over, they can be stored in an airtight container for up to one week. If you must start assembly ahead of time, heed the warning in Step 5: The wafers will absorb moisture very quickly and become soggy. Part of the appeal of this dessert comes from the contrast in textures between the crisp wafers and the rich cream filling.

You can easily simplify and reduce the calories in this dessert by eliminating both types of nuts, the heavy cream, and the sugar from the ingredients. Instead, substitute Italian Cream (page 844) flavored with Amaretto di Saronno, Frangelico, or another nut-flavored liqueur.

Butter and Flour Mixture (page 7)	4 cups (960 ml) heavy cream
Toasted Almond Crisp Batter (recipe follows)	2 tablespoons (30 g) granulated sugar
4 ounces (115 g) pistachios	¼ recipe Raspberry Sauce (page 830)
3 ounces (85 g) walnuts	1 recipe Orange Sauce (page 828)
Powdered sugar	
Dark coating chocolate, melted	

1. Make the template shown in Figure 13-1. The template as shown is the correct size required for this recipe. Trace the drawing, then cut the template out of ¹⁄₁₆-inch (2-mm) cardboard (cake boxes work fine for this). Make a second template, using Figure 13-2 as a guide, and reserve this template for the presentation. If you do not have Silpats, brush the butter and flour mixture on the back of clean, even sheet pans.

2. Spread the Almond Crisp batter onto Silpats or the prepared sheet pans, spreading it flat and even within the template (see Figures 10-29 and 10-30, page 482). You will need 4 wafers per serving, but make a few extra, as they break easily.

3. Bake at 400°F (205°C) for approximately 5 minutes or until slightly brown in places. Allow the wafers to cool before removing them from the pans.

4. Blanch the pistachios, using a pinch of salt in the blanching water to bring out the green color. Remove the skin and set the nuts aside to dry. (You can speed up the drying process by placing the nuts in a very low oven. Do not toast them, however.) Reserve 16 good-looking pistachios or pistachio halves to use for garnish. Crush the remainder finely and set aside. Finely chop the walnuts.

5. Select the 16 best-looking wafers to use as the tops of the desserts. One at a time, set the presentation template on top of these wafers and sift powdered sugar over the template. Remove the template very carefully so you do not disturb the powdered sugar. Place a small amount of melted chocolate in a piping bag. Pipe a small dot of chocolate in the center of each decorated wafer and place 1 reserved pistachio on top. Do not decorate more tops than you expect to use the same day. Set the tops aside. Pipe lines of melted chocolate in a spoke pattern over the entire base of as many dessert plates as you made tops.

6. Whip the heavy cream with the granulated sugar to soft peaks. Divide the cream into 2 portions, one almost twice the size of the other. Flavor the smaller portion with the chopped walnuts and place in a pastry bag with a No. 6 (12-mm) plain tip. Flavor the larger portion with the crushed pistachios and place in a second pastry bag with a No. 6 (12-mm) plain tip.

7. The desserts should be assembled to order or no more than 15 minutes prior to serving. Pipe small mounds of pistachio cream on each of the petals on 1 wafer. Top with a second wafer and press down very lightly. Pipe mounds of walnut cream on the second wafer in the same manner. Top with the third wafer, press down lightly, and pipe mounds of pistachio cream on top. Place the raspberry sauce in a piping bottle with a small opening and reserve.

8. Presentation: Pour a pool of orange sauce in the center of a decorated plate, then tilt the plate to cover the base entirely. Pipe 4 small dots of walnut cream in the center of the plate. Place an assembled dessert on top. Carefully top with 1 decorated top wafer. Pipe small dots of raspberry sauce in the orange sauce between the chocolate lines all around the dessert. Serve immediately.

NOTE: If you do not have time to make the presentation template, dust powdered sugar over the entire top wafer.

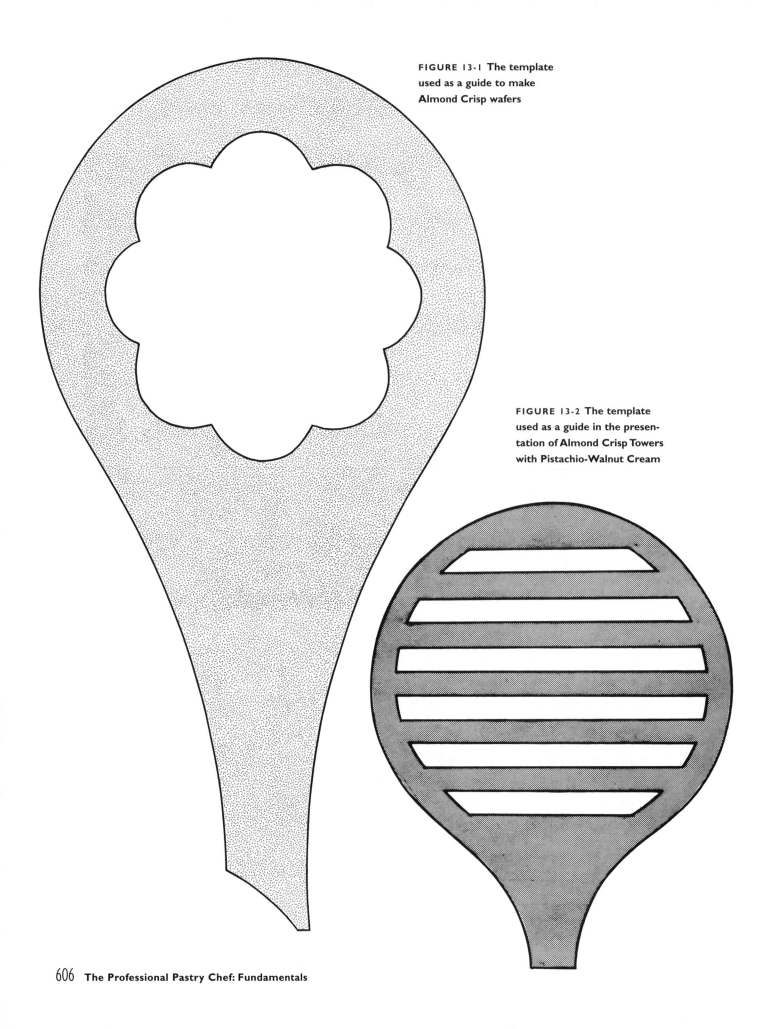

FIGURE 13-1 The template used as a guide to make Almond Crisp wafers

FIGURE 13-2 The template used as a guide in the presentation of Almond Crisp Towers with Pistachio-Walnut Cream

TOASTED ALMOND CRISP BATTER yield: 2 cups (240 ml)

5 ounces (140 g) lightly toasted blanched almonds or lightly toasted almond meal (see Note)

5 ounces (140 g) granulated sugar

4 ounces (115 g) unsalted butter, at room temperature

½ teaspoon (3 g) salt

⅓ cup (80 ml) heavy cream

2 egg whites (¼ cup/60 ml)

1 tablespoon (15 ml) amaretto liqueur

3 ounces (85 g) bread flour

I. Grind the almonds with half of the sugar to a fine consistency. Cream the butter with the remainder of the sugar, then mix in the ground nuts, salt, and heavy cream.

2. Add the egg whites and amaretto. Sift the flour and incorporate it into the batter. Let the batter rest for 1 hour.

NOTE: To substitute toasted almond meal, cream the butter and sugar, mix in the almond meal, and continue as directed.

Apple–Puff Pastry Pyramids with Almond Ice Cream and Caramel Sauce yield: 16 servings (Photo 22)

This variation of the French classic *mille-feuille* is the result of an effort to utilize the crumbs and trimmings inevitably produced whenever a sheet of baked puff pastry is cut into strips to make Napoleons or any of that dessert's hybrids. One way to minimize the scraps and also speed up the assembly is to use what I call the production method for making Napoleons. Here, three full sheets of baked puff pastry are layered with the filling, glazed, trimmed, then cut into four lengthwise strips. All four strips are cut across simultaneously to produce 60 or more individual pastries, quickly and with a minimum of scraps.

The production method cannot be applied to these pastries because of their triangular shape; however, crushing the scrap pieces yields crumbs that can be put to use as an attractive, buttery-tasting decoration. A part of this dessert that always catches the eye is the square portion of ice cream served in a tuile cup. (Who says you can't put a square peg in a round hole?) If you have a square ice-cream scoop, you might want to use that instead of forming the ice cream squares as directed in the recipe. The squares produced by the scoop will not be as clearly defined but, in a pinch or when making a large number of servings, the scoop can come in handy.

1 recipe Almond Ice Cream (page 717)

4 small apples, preferably Fuji

½ recipe Fortified Caramel Sauce (page 821)

1 cup (240 ml) heavy cream

1 teaspoon (5 g) granulated sugar

16 Puff Pastry Apple Points (page 581)

16 Miniature Tulips (page 664)

16 seasonal small berries

16 mint sprigs

Powdered sugar

1. If the almond ice cream has been made ahead and is frozen very hard, soften it before proceeding. If the ice cream is freshly made and soft, you may skip this step. Place the softened ice cream in a frame or pan, 1½ inches (3.7 cm) or more in height. Spread the ice cream inside to form an even layer with straight sides, 1½ inches (3.7 cm) thick. Cover and place in the freezer.

2. Cut 2 sides from each apple, slicing down vertically and leaving the center of each apple intact (save the centers for another use, such as an apple filling). Place each apple half cut-side down and slice crosswise to make thin, even slices. Keep each group of slices together. Cover and reserve (see Note).

3. Adjust the consistency of the caramel sauce if necessary then place it in a piping bottle and set aside at room temperature.

4. Cut the frozen ice cream into 1½-inch (3.7-cm) cubes. If it is too difficult to do so easily, soften the ice cream for a short time in the refrigerator. Cut a few more squares than the 16 you will need for this recipe.

5. Whip the heavy cream with the sugar to stiff peaks. Place in a pastry bag with a small Saint-Honoré pastry tip. Reserve in the refrigerator.

6. Presentation: Place an Apple Point pastry off-center on a dessert plate. Fan the slices from half of 1 group of apple slices and place the slices on the plate to the left of the pastry, arranging them so that the fan curves away from the pastry. Carefully transfer an ice cream square to a small tuile shell. Pipe a small dot of caramel sauce next to the apple fan and place the shell on top. Pipe dots of caramel sauce in a curved line from the shell to the pastry, making the dots increasingly larger in size as you approach the pastry. Pipe an *S*-shaped wedge of whipped cream on top of the ice cream and decorate with a berry and a mint sprig. Sift powdered sugar lightly over the center of the plate. Serve immediately.

NOTE: Cut the apples as close to service as possible or, ideally, cut them to order. If this is not possible, use a bit of lemon or lime juice on the cut sides to prevent the slices from turning brown.

Apple Strudel, Austrian Style yield: about 16 servings

Paper-thin strudel dough is stretched rather than rolled to achieve its almost transparent composition. Strudel dough has been described as being "so thin that you must look twice to see it," or, as a German colleague of mine says, "You should be able to read a newspaper through the dough." Successfully producing a properly stretched strudel dough requires time, patience, and a large work space. For these reasons, many people purchase the dough already prepared.

If strudel dough is not available, phyllo dough makes a fine substitute. To use phyllo dough in this recipe, overlap the edges of the sheets and glue them together with melted butter on top of a tablecloth to create a large rectangle, the same size specified for the strudel dough. Use two layers of phyllo with melted butter brushed between them; brush butter on top of the second layer as well. You will not be able to lift the rolled strudel onto a sheet pan as directed if it is made with phyllo dough. Instead, cut the rope into two pieces and roll them, one at a time, onto a sheet of baking paper, then lift the paper onto the sheet pan.

4 ounces (115 g) tiny white-bread croutons, ¼ inch (6 mm) cubes

6 ounces (170 g) melted unsalted butter, approximately

2 pounds 10 ounces (1 kg 195 g) Granny Smith, Pippin, or other cooking apples (approximately 6 medium)

3 ounces (85 g) granulated sugar

6 ounces (170 g) dark raisins

6 ounces (170 g) coarsely crushed nuts

1 teaspoon (1.5 g) ground cinnamon

4 ounces (115 g) firm unsalted butter

12 ounces (340 g) bread flour

1 egg

2 ounces (55 g) unsalted butter, at room temperature

½ teaspoon (2.5 g) salt

¾ cup (180 ml) cold water

Vegetable oil

Bread flour

Crème Anglaise (page 817) or Chantilly Cream (page 838)

1. Sauté the croutons in 2 ounces (55g) melted butter over medium heat until they are golden brown and crisp, 5 to 7 minutes. Reserve the croutons and the remaining melted butter separately.

2. Peel and core the apples. Cut them in half lengthwise from the stem end. Cut each half crosswise into thin slices.

3. Combine the sliced apples, granulated sugar, raisins, nuts, cinnamon, and about half of the croutons. Cut the firm butter into small chunks and gently toss together with the apple mixture. Set aside.

4. Place the flour, egg, soft butter, and salt in a mixer bowl. Mixing with the dough hook at low speed, add enough of the cold water to make a soft dough. Knead the dough at medium speed until it is smooth and elastic, about 5 minutes. Form the dough into a ball and coat it with oil. Cover and let rest at room temperature for about 1 hour.

5. Cover a work surface measuring approximately 3 × 4 feet (90 cm × 1 m 20 cm) with a clean tablecloth. The cloth is used to facilitate stretching and rolling the dough. To prevent the cloth from sliding, fasten it under the table with thumbtacks. Sprinkle bread flour lightly and evenly

About Strudel

To many people, apple strudel is the most famous of all Austrian pastries; it has always been closely associated with Vienna in particular. However, it is generally accepted that the dessert did not originate in Austria at all. The Hungarians, who call their strudel *retes*, first adopted the incredibly thin strudel dough from the Turkish pastry baklava. The Hungarians filled the dough with apples, nuts, raisins, and whatever cake or bread crumbs were at hand. Accounts differ on exactly how this Hungarian strudel arrived in Vienna, but the general theory begins with the departure of the Ottoman invaders. The now unemployed Turkish and Hungarian cooks took their skills and specialties (strudel among them) to the kitchens of the Viennese aristocrats in the new Austro-Hungarian empire. On another note, the Turks (although they lost) certainly deserve additional recognition for the coffee addiction they left behind in Vienna, which in turn gave birth to the many great coffeehouses that are so renowned in Austria today.

Strudel is a German word that literally translates to "whirlpool," "eddy," or "vortex"—in this case, a swirling mass of pastry dough and filling. Although apple is by far the best-known variety, the number of strudel fillings is almost limitless and includes both sweet and savory fare. The savory varieties were especially popular among Eastern Europeans and, in fact, were a staple food for the majority in places such as Hungary, Turkey, and Greece at one time.

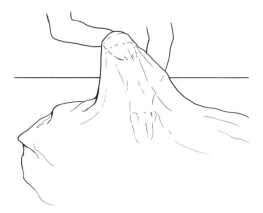

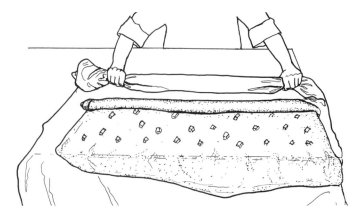

FIGURE 13-3 Using the top part of the hands to pull and stretch strudel dough into a thin membrane

FIGURE 13-4 Using a tablecloth under the dough to help guide the filled strudel as it is rolled into a spiral

over the cloth. Place the relaxed dough in the center of the cloth. Using a rolling pin, roll out the dough to make a small rectangle. Then, using first your fingertips and then the top part of your hands, gradually and evenly lift and pull the dough into a thin membrane approximately 40 inches long x 30 inches wide (1 m x 75 cm) (Figure 13-3). Let the dough relax and dry on the table for 2 to 3 minutes.

6. Trim away the thick edge all around as well as any dough that hangs over the edge of the table. Distribute the apple filling next to the long edge of the dough closest to you. Form the filling into a thick rope with your hands. Brush some of the reserved melted butter (heat if necessary) generously over the remainder of the dough. Sprinkle the remaining croutons over the dough.

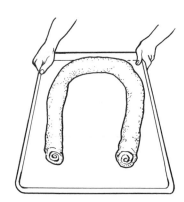

FIGURE 13-5 The assembled Apple Strudel, Austrian Style, arranged in a horseshoe shape on the baking pan

7. Remove the thumbtacks to free the cloth. Using the cloth to help lift the dough, roll the strudel, starting from the filling side, into a fairly loose spiral (Figure 13-4). Place the strudel, seam-side down, in a horseshoe shape on a sheet pan lined with baking paper (Figure 13-5).

8. Bake at 375°F (190°C) about 35 minutes, brushing several times with the remaining melted butter and any juices that run out of the pastry. Let the strudel cool slightly, trim the ends, and slice into 16 servings, approximately 2¼ inches (5.6 cm) wide. Sift powdered sugar over the slices. Serve hot or cold with Crème Anglaise or Chantilly cream.

Apple Strudel, German Style yield: 16 servings (Photo 7)

You can find this appetizing pastry for sale in many German konditoreis, both in individual portions and in larger pieces that serve 10 to 12 people (something like buying a rectangular apple pie). German Apple Strudel is refreshing and not too filling as a luncheon dessert, served perhaps with your favorite ice cream instead of the custard sauce in warm weather. If you do not have pastry cream already made up and do not need it for anything else, you can easily substitute apricot jam. Along the same lines, this is a good recipe in which to use up leftover sponges and sponge pieces. If they feel a bit dry, dab some poaching liquid on top before using.

12 ounces (340 g) Short Dough (page 67)	1 ounce (30 g) cinnamon sugar
1 pound (455 g) Puff Pastry (page 74) *or* Quick Puff Pastry (page 77)	3 ounces (85 g) Pastry Cream (page 845)
1 Almond Sponge (page 438), ¼ × 14 × 24 inches (6 mm × 35 × 60 cm)	3 ounces (85 g) apricot jam
	Egg wash
2 pounds (910 g) Granny Smith, Pippin, or, when available, Gravenstein apples, peeled and cored (approximately 5 medium)	Apricot Glaze (page 5)
	Simple Icing (page 35)
	Simple syrup
Spiced Poaching Syrup (page 31)	½ recipe Crème Anglaise (page 817; see Note)
6 ounces (170 g) walnuts	16 medium strawberries
8 ounces (225 g) dark raisins	

1. Roll out the short dough into a strip ⅛ inch (3 mm) thick and 24 inches (60 cm) long. Trim the edges to make the dough strip 4 inches (10 cm) wide. Refrigerate.

2. Roll out the puff pastry to ⅛ inch (3 mm) thick, 8 inches (20 cm) wide, and as long as the short dough. Refrigerate. Cover and reserve the scraps from both doughs for another use.

3. Cut a strip from the sponge sheet, 3½ inches (8.7 cm) wide and as long as the short dough. Tear the remainder of the sponge sheet into small pieces.

4. Poach the apples in the spiced poaching syrup for 10 to 15 minutes. They should give when pressed lightly. Remove from the liquid, let cool, then cut the apples into ½-inch (1.2-cm) slices.

5. Chop the walnuts to the size of the raisins. Mix thoroughly with the apple slices, raisins, cinnamon sugar, and pastry cream. Add the reserved sponge cake pieces.

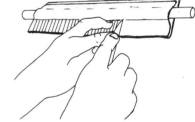

FIGURE 13-6 Cutting slits on the folded side of the puff pastry sheet with a dowel between the top and bottom layers to create the top for Apple Strudel, German Style

6. Spread the apricot jam on the short dough, leaving ¼ inch (6 mm) of the dough exposed on the long sides. Place the sponge cake strip on top of the jam. Use your hands to place the filling on top of the sponge cake, shaping the apple mixture so that it is slightly rounded and leaving a ¼-inch (6-mm) edge of short dough exposed on each long side.

7. Place a 1-inch (2.5-cm) dowel lengthwise in the center of the reserved puff pastry sheet. Fold the dough over the dowel so that fold is facing you. Move the dowel so that it is positioned 2 inches (5 cm) away from the fold. With the back of a chef's knife and using the dowel as a guide, lightly mark (do not cut) a line parallel to the fold and approximately 1½ inches (3.7 cm) away from it toward the dowel. Cut through the fold, up to the mark, at ¼-inch (6-mm) intervals (Figure 13-6).

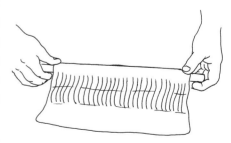

FIGURE 13-7 Using the dowel to lift the dough and unfold it over the strudel filling

8. Brush egg wash on the exposed short dough borders. Move the dowel to the fold of the puff pastry and use the dowel to lift the puff pastry and unfold it over the strudel (Figure 13-7). Position the dough so that the slits are centered over the filling. Fasten the puff pastry to the short dough with your thumbs. Trim the excess from the sides (do not worry about sealing the short ends). Brush with egg wash.

9. Bake at 375°F (190°C) until golden brown, about 45 minutes. You may need to place a second pan underneath to prevent the bottom from becoming too dark. Let cool.

10. Glaze the strudel with apricot glaze, then brush with simple icing that has been thinned enough with simple syrup to look transparent. Do not just warm the icing to make it thin enough to use or the glaze will be too thick when it sets. Cut the strudel into 16 slices, approximately 1½ inches (3.7 cm) wide. Wash the strawberries, pat dry, and reserve.

11. Presentation: Pour 1½ ounces (45 ml) Crème Anglaise on a dessert plate, making a round pool off-center. Place a slice of strudel in the middle of the plate next to the sauce. Fan a strawberry and place the berry behind the strudel on the opposite side. The strudel can be served hot or cold.

NOTE: You can omit the Crème Anglaise and serve the warm strudel with vanilla ice cream instead. As the ice cream melts, you actually get to enjoy both accompaniments.

Apple Sacks yield: 16 servings (Photo 73)

Wrapping a filling in dough or a thin pancake is a fairly common but nevertheless appealing presentation used for both savory dishes and sweets. When wrapped in the fashion described here, the assembled items are also known as *pouches* or *purses*. Perhaps the best known of the savory dishes utilizing this technique is the Beggar's Purse. This is made by topping a thin crepe with the highest-quality caviar and a little crème fraîche, then gathering up the edges, pleating them into a purse shape, and securing the package by tying it tightly closed with a strip of blanched chive. In preparing the Apple Sacks, however, you want to make sure that the top of the sacks are not fastened because they should open up as they bake to reveal the filling inside. The surface of the filling also provides a flat space on which to place the ice cream and the decoration.

The semolina dough used here is a type of pie dough and, as such, it is of the utmost importance that you start with cold butter and that the butter remain cold and in small chunks as the dough is being mixed. If prepared improperly, the dough can become tough and hard and no matter how decorative the preparation, the finished product will be unappealing. While the Cookie Tumbleweeds definitely dress up what is really a fairly simple dessert, they can easily be eliminated without compromising the great flavor combination of apples, dates, pecans, maple syrup, buttery crust, and ice cream. The crust itself should provide plenty of crunchy contrast.

Semolina Dough (page 71)

Egg wash

Apple and Pear Filling (recipe follows)

Maple Poaching Syrup (recipe follows)

1 vanilla bean

Lemon Verbena Ice Cream (page 725)

16 Cookie Tumbleweeds (recipe follows)

Pomegranate seeds or chopped blanched pistachios (optional)

Powdered sugar

1. Roll out the semolina dough to ⅛ inch (3 mm) thick and cut out rounds, 6 inches (15 cm) in diameter. Place the rounds on sheet pans lined with baking paper. If necessary, layer the pieces of scrap dough on top of each other and let rest before rerolling; continue until you have cut 16 rounds.

2. Brush egg wash over the rounds. Divide the apple filling evenly among them, using approximately ⅓ cup (80 ml) for each and mounding it high in the center. Fold in the edges, making an overlapping pattern all the way around each circle and leaving the filling exposed in the center (Figure 13-8). Pinch lightly to secure, but do not press too hard; you want the sacks to open up as they bake. Brush egg wash over the outside of the packages.

3. Bake at 375°F (190°C) until golden brown and baked through, approximately 40 minutes. Set aside to cool slightly.

4. While the Apple Sacks are baking, measure 2 cups (480 ml) reserved poaching syrup into a saucepan; save the remainder for another use. Split the vanilla bean lengthwise in half and scrape out the seeds, adding them to the measured syrup. Discard the outside of the bean or save for another use. Boil the syrup until it is reduced by two-thirds to about ⅔ cup (160 ml); let cool to room temperature. The syrup should have a consistency similar to maple syrup once it has cooled. If necessary, thin it by adding some of the remaining poaching liquid. Place the vanilla-flavored syrup in a piping bottle.

5. Presentation: Place a warm Apple Sack in the center of a dessert plate. Pipe syrup in a thin layer on the plate around the dessert. Place a scoop of lemon verbena ice cream on the sack and top with a Cookie Tumbleweed. Sprinkle pomegranate seeds or chopped pistachios around the dessert, if desired. Sift powdered sugar lightly over the top of the dessert and the plate and serve immediately.

FIGURE 13-8 Pleating the dough around the filling to make Apple Sacks; pinching the sides while leaving the filling exposed on the top; an Apple Sack after baking

APPLE AND PEAR FILLING yield: approximately 3 pounds (1 kg 365 g)

2 pounds (910 g) cooking apples, such as Granny Smith, Pippin, or Fuji

1 pound (455 g) pears, such as Bartlett

Maple Poaching Syrup (recipe follows)

4 ounces (115 g) dates, chopped to raisin-size

4 ounces (115 g) pecans, coarsely chopped

1. Peel and core the apples and pears; cut them into chunks, ½ inch (1.2 cm) in size.

2. Bring the maple poaching syrup to a boil, add the fruit, and poach until tender but not falling apart; do not overcook. Strain and save the syrup to use in the Apple Sacks recipe. Place the drained fruit in a bowl and mix in the dates and pecans. Let cool, then cover and refrigerate until needed.

MAPLE POACHING SYRUP yield: 5 cups (1 L 200 ml) syrup

1 quart (960 ml) water

8 ounces (225 g) granulated sugar

1 cup (240 ml) maple syrup

1. Place the water, sugar and maple syrup in a saucepan. Bring the syrup to a boil, stirring to dissolve the sugar.

2. Use as directed in the apple filling recipe.

COOKIE TUMBLEWEEDS yield: approximately 20 decorations

These are easy to make and can be used to add a contemporary look to many desserts. Adding the extra butter to the tuile paste makes the decorations a bit thinner and more elegant-looking. Pipe the lines thin and not too close together so that the loops and circles do not bake together in the oven; the paste will flow out slightly during baking.

1 ounce (30 g) unsalted butter, melted

½ recipe Vanilla Tuile Decorating Paste (page 482)

1. Place a sheet of plastic wrap over an empty cardboard egg carton to create a place in which to store the fragile decorations. If you do not have Silpats, grease the backs of inverted sheet pans, coat with flour and shake off as much flour as possible.

2. Stir the melted butter into the tuile paste. Place a portion of the mixture into a paper pastry bag and cut a small opening.

3. To make each tumbleweed, pipe the mixture out onto a Silpat; make overlapping small loops and circles, starting from the center and piping in an unbroken line moving outward, until you have gradually formed a lacy decoration approximately 8 inches (20 cm) in diameter (Figure 13-9; the illustration is much smaller than the actual decoration). There should be approximately as much uncovered space as there is tuile paste. Place 4 tumbleweeds per sheet pan.

4. Bake at 400°F (205°C) until golden brown spots appear on 1 cookie, about 4 minutes. Leave the pan in the oven with the door open.

5. Using a palette knife, pick up the cookie with the most brown color and quickly gather it into a loose ball in your hands to form a tumbleweed. Place in the plastic-covered egg carton. Quickly repeat with the remaining cookies on the pan.

6. Pipe, bake, and form the remaining cookies in the same way. Store in airtight containers so the decorations remain crisp.

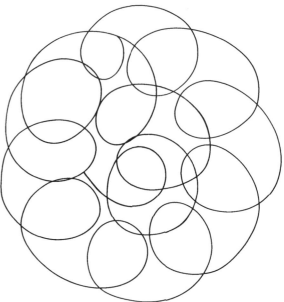

FIGURE 13-9 The pattern of tuile paste lines piped out to produce Cookie Tumbleweeds

Berries with Baked Chocolate Mousse and Mint Syrup yield: 16 servings (Photo 54)

I admit the title "Baked Chocolate Mousse" is a bit awkward, as a classic dessert mousse is never baked. The texture of the mousse and the technique used to produce it are comparable to a flourless chocolate cake (see Chocolate Decadence Cake, page 512); however, here the portions are baked individually. The recipe could also be described as a ganache that is thickened by the addition of eggs and heat. The moose head decorations are intended as a whimsical play on words but, at the same time, they provide another textural dimension to offset the soft chocolate inside the shell.

You can simplify the presentation and still enjoy the combination of flavors from the various components used here by leaving out the tuile moose heads and what is certainly the most challenging and time-consuming step in this recipe, the Translucent Chocolate Shells. By serving the mousse and berries with a simple, tasteful garnish, you can produce a lovely dessert in very little time.

1 pound 6 ounces (625 g) fresh, ripe strawberries	Dark coating chocolate, melted
¼ cup (60 ml) orange liqueur	Tuile Moose Head Decorations (instructions follow)
¼ cup (60 ml) simple syrup	16 mint sprigs
Melted unsalted butter	1 recipe Mint Decorating Syrup (page 835)
Granulated sugar	Powdered sugar
Chocolate Mousse for Baking (recipe follows)	
Translucent Chocolate Shells (instructions follow)	

1. Cut the strawberries into small, raspberry-sized pieces. Combine the orange liqueur and the simple syrup in a nonreactive saucepan. Add the strawberries and mix well. Heat gently and cook just until the strawberries begin to soften, stirring constantly. Transfer to a bowl and reserve.

2. Prepare 16 forms, 4 ounces (120 ml) in capacity, by brushing melted butter over the insides, then coating the butter with granulated sugar. Set the forms aside.

3. Make the chocolate mousse and divide it among the prepared forms, filling them approximately three-quarters full.

4. Place the forms in a baking pan and add hot water to reach three-quarters of the way up the sides of the forms. Bake at 325°F (163°C) for approximately 40 minutes or until the tops of the mousses feel firm to the touch. Remove the desserts from the oven. Immediately remove each dessert from the water bath, invert it onto a paper-lined sheet pan, and remove the baking form.

5. Pour the mint syrup into a piping bottle.

6. Place as many chocolate shells as you anticipate needing for service in the refrigerator (see Note).

7. Presentation: Pipe (or dab with a spoon) a small amount of melted chocolate onto the center of a serving plate. Place a

CHEF'S TIP

When it comes to making Translucent Chocolate Shells, as is true of many things that take time and effort, practice makes perfect. If you are producing the shells in any real quantity, you need to work with at least two Silpats, as you cannot spread the paste on a warm mat. This holds true for all of the decorating pastes, including Tuile Paste. If you do not have ladles available in the correct size, bowls or cups with a similar size and shape will do, or you can simply drape the baked paper over the citrus fruit and shape it with your hands. This last technique, however, will not produce a perfectly round shell.

chilled Translucent Chocolate Shell on top and hold it in place at a slight angle leaning toward you for a few seconds until the chocolate has hardened (or spray the chocolate with food-grade coolant). Place a baked mousse inside the shell. Spoon approximately ⅓ cup (80 ml) reserved strawberries with syrup on top. Decorate with a mint sprig. Place a tuile moose head cookie behind the mousse. Randomly pipe mint syrup around the dessert. Lightly sift powdered sugar over the dessert and the plate. Serve at once.

NOTE: Chilling the Translucent Chocolate Shells causes them to act as a catalyst so that the chocolate on the plate will harden in just a few seconds (catalyst: a substance that alters the rate of a chemical reaction while itself remaining unchanged by the process). However, be sure you do not chill the shells too long or they will soften from condensation that will form when they are returned to the warm kitchen. Assuming you have the space, you can attach the shells to the plates far in advance of service. If you have food-grade spray coolant, use that to set the chocolate and omit chilling the shells.

CHOCOLATE MOUSSE FOR BAKING yield: approximately 1½ quarts (1 L 440 ml)

1 pound (455 g) sweet dark chocolate	7 eggs
4 ounces (115 g) unsweetened chocolate	2 ounces (55 g) granulated sugar
3 cups (720 ml) heavy cream	

1. Chop both types of chocolate into small pieces. Combine in a bowl and set over a bain-marie to melt. When the chocolate has melted, remove the bowl from the heat but keep the chocolate warm.

2. Whip the cream to soft peaks; reserve.

3. Whip the eggs with the sugar until they are light and fluffy and have reached maximum volume. Gradually incorporate the egg mixture into the chocolate. Fold in the whipped cream.

4. Use as directed in the main recipe.

TRANSLUCENT CHOCOLATE SHELLS yield: 16 shells

Because these shells are rather fragile, you may want to make a full recipe of the chocolate paste to allow for breakage and to give yourself some extra to experiment with.

½ recipe Chocolate Paste (recipe follows)

1. Have ready 1 or, preferably, 2 ladles, 6 to 8 ounces (180 to 240 ml) in capacity, 1 or 2 oranges or small grapefruits that will fit loosely inside the ladles (see Note), and a container that is close to the same height as the length of the ladle handles; a round bain-marie insert usually works great. Hook the ladles to the top of the container so that the bowls of the ladles are resting on the table as level as possible (see Figure 6-16, page 308). Set aside.

2. Spread out the chocolate paste in thin rounds, about 5½ inches (13.7 cm) in diameter, on a Silpat or on sheet pans lined with baking paper (see Chef's Tip, page 617).

3. Bake at 375°F (190°C) for approximately 4 minutes. Because chocolate paste is such a dark color to begin with, it can be difficult to tell when it is finished baking. To help you judge, place a few sliced natural almonds on the pan next to the paste. When the almonds are golden brown, you can be certain that the paste is baked.

4. As soon as the first decoration is firm enough to be picked up with a spatula, place it over the bowl of a ladle and, working as fast as you can, press the paper into the ladle, using the orange or grapefruit to form a round shell (see Figure 6-16, page 308). The shells will harden almost immediately. Continue until you have made enough shells to allow for a few extra in the event that some break.

NOTE: Chilling the orange or grapefruit will help the shells harden more quickly.

CHOCOLATE PASTE yield: 1 pound 7 ounces (655 g)

Decorations made from this paste acquire a craterlike texture that gives them an interesting and stylish appearance, but this happens only if the paste is spread out in a very thin layer. Chocolate paste is best suited for free-form shapes. It can be used with a template, but it will not stay in its precise original shape as tuile paste does. While the edges will become ragged, this too can add interest, depending on the look desired. Chocolate paste can be used to form dessert containers and can be cut into shapes after baking; these can be left flat or molded into curves, spirals, etc., or the baked sheet can simply be broken into random pieces. Because decorations made from chocolate paste are so thin, they harden very quickly once removed from the heat of the sheet pan.

Due to the flour in the recipe as well as the cornstarch in the powdered sugar, decorations made from chocolate paste can be made days in advance without having to worry about keeping them in an airtight container. If appropriate to the shape you are making, simply placing them on a sheet pan at room temperature will do.

3 ounces (85 g) cake flour
11 ounces (310 g) powdered sugar
1¾ ounces (50 g) unsweetened cocoa powder
⅓ cup (80 ml) water, at room temperature
4½ ounces (130 g) unsalted butter, melted

1. Sift the flour, sugar, and cocoa powder together. Gradually stir in the water, then the butter. Continue to stir until you have a smooth, pliable paste.

2. Use as directed in the individual recipes.

CHEF'S TIP
Chocolate paste may be stored at room temperature, covered, for 3 to 4 days. If it becomes too firm to spread out in a thin layer, incorporate a small amount of water. If it is refrigerated, allow the paste to soften at room temperature before using. Do not warm the hard paste over hot water. You may soften the paste in the microwave for just a few seconds at a time so that none of the paste melts. If the paste is warmed to the point of melting, it will drastically change in appearance and flexibility after it has baked.

TUILE MOOSE HEAD DECORATIONS yield: 34 decorations

¼ recipe or 8 ounces (225 g) Vanilla Tuile
Decorating Paste (page 482)

½ teaspoon (1 g) unsweetened cocoa powder

1. Trace the moose head in Figure 13-10, then cut the template out of cardboard that is ¹⁄₁₆ inch (2 mm) thick. The template as shown is the correct size for use in this recipe.

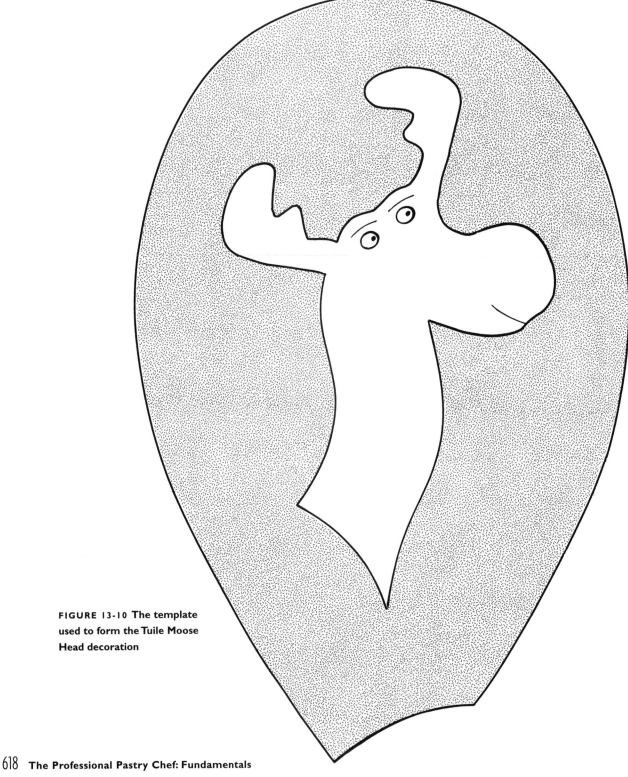

FIGURE 13-10 The template used to form the Tuile Moose Head decoration

2. If you do not have Silpats, grease the back of flat, even sheet pans, coat with flour, then shake off as much flour as possible.

3. Mix the cocoa powder into 1 tablespoon (15 ml) tuile paste. Place in a piping bag and reserve.

4. Spread the plain tuile paste out flat and even within the template on Silpats or on the prepared sheet pans (see Figures 10-29 and 10-30, page 482), making as many decorations as needed. Cut a small opening in the piping bag and use the cocoa-colored tuile paste to make the eyes and mouth of the moose, as shown in the template. You can also decorate the antlers or the neck if desired.

5. Bake at 400°F (205°C) for approximately 4 minutes or until you begin to see some golden brown spots on the moose heads (they should be a healthy-looking golden-brown color, but not so dark as to suggest the animal survived a forest fire). Remove from the oven and set aside to cool. To create a more 3-dimensional look, you can shape the warm cookies as soon as they come out of the oven. In this case, bake just 1 pan at a time and, when the cookies are ready, leave the pan in the oven with the door open. Quickly pick up one moose head and shape the head and/or the antlers as desired, keeping the neck straight.

6. Store the tuile decorations in an airtight container, preferably with a desiccant to keep them from becoming soft. Stored this way, they will stay crisp for up to 2 weeks.

Blackberry Meringue Tartlets yield: 16 servings (Photo 33)

Make this quick and delightfully refreshing dessert when blackberries are perfectly ripe and sweet so their flavor will offset the slightly tangy lemon curd. Any of the blackberry hybrids, such as boysenberries, loganberries, or olallie blackberries, may be substituted, but I prefer blackberries because they are smaller and make a more attractive arrangement on top of the meringue shell. The other components of this dessert can be made in advance. The meringue shells can be stored, airtight, in a warm place ready to be filled as needed, and lemon curd is always handy to have around. It can be kept, well covered, in the refrigerator for up to a month.

Blackberry Meringue Tartlets could very well be classified as a light dessert, but when no one is counting the calories, try serving them with a scoop of vanilla ice cream. The combination is delicious, though it does upset the presentation.

½ recipe **French Meringue (page 27)**
½ recipe **Blackberry Sauce (page 830)**
2½ **cups (600 ml) or** ½ recipe **Lemon Curd (page 844)**

1 pound (455 g) fresh ripe blackberries, approximately
Sour Cream Mixture for Piping (page 832)

1. Draw 16 circles, 4 inches (10 cm) in diameter, properly spaced, on sheets of baking paper. Invert the papers and place on sheet pans.

2. Place the meringue in a pastry bag with a No. 4 (8-mm) plain tip. Pipe a ring of pointed dots (kisses) next to each other all around the insides of the circles. For a perfectly clean look, use your finger or a small spoon to straighten the points. To make the bottom of the cases, pipe rings of meringue inside the dots, using the same technique used for Meringue Noisette (see Figure 1-5, page 29) but holding the tip closer to the sheet pan to make the bottom thinner. Allow enough space for the filling later.

3. Bake immediately at 210° to 220°F (99° to 104°C) for approximately 2 hours or until the meringue has dried all the way through.

4. Place the blackberry sauce in a piping bottle; reserve.

5. Presentation: Fill a meringue shell with just over 2 tablespoons (30 ml) lemon curd. Place the shell off-center on a dessert plate (put a dab of curd underneath to prevent it from sliding). Arrange whole fresh blackberries on top of the filling. Pipe a half-circle of blackberry sauce to the right of the dessert and decorate with the sour cream mixture for piping (see pages 809 to 814).

Budapest Swirls yield: 16 servings (Photo 88)

Budapest Swirls are a good example of a pastry transformed into a plated dessert by the addition of a sauce and garnish. In a European pastry shop, they would more typically be offered like the selections in the Individual Pastries chapter—eaten as is with your fingers, or served on a plate to enjoy with coffee. Although the filled roulade is not a good keeper, the baked sheet before it is filled can be kept, well wrapped, in a cool place for several days. If the sheet becomes too hard to roll without cracking, try placing it (with the baking paper still attached) on a hot sheet pan lined with a damp towel. To simplify the presentation, omit the chocolate sauce and serve a Budapest Swirl with a pool of bitter orange sauce placed in front of the dessert; decorate the plate with orange segments.

Butter and Flour Mixture (page 7)	Bitter Orange Sauce (page 828)
1½ recipes Japonaise Meringue Batter (page 28)	Chocolate Sauce (page 820), at room temperature
2 teaspoons (6 g) unflavored gelatin powder	Powdered sugar
¼ cup (60 ml) cold water	Strips of orange zest
¾ recipe Quick Bavarian Cream (page 846)	Edible flowers, such as borage or johnny-jump-ups
Segments of 6 medium oranges (see page 13)	

1. Place a Silpat on a baking sheet or line a full sheet pan, 16 x 24 inches (40 x 60 cm), with baking paper. Lightly grease the paper with butter and flour mixture. Place the Japonaise meringue batter in a pastry bag with a No. 5 (10-mm) plain tip. Pipe the batter into 15-inch (37.5-cm) strings, side by side and touching, across the width of the pan. Continue piping down the full length of the pan.

2. Bake the sheet at 300°F (149°C) for about 15 to 20 minutes. It should begin to color and have a crust on top, but it should not be dry all the way through. (To put it in another way, remove the sheet from the oven when it is only half-baked compared to regular Japonaise sheets.) Slide onto a cold sheet pan and let cool completely (see Chef's Tip).

3. Sprinkle the gelatin over the cold water and set aside to soften.

4. Invert the Japonaise sheet onto a baking paper and peel the Silpat or the other sheet of paper from the back.

5. Place the softened gelatin mixture over a bain-marie and heat to dissolve. Do not overheat. Working quickly, add the gelatin to a small portion of the Bavarian cream to temper it. Still working quickly, add this to the remaining Bavarian cream. Spread out the Bavarian cream evenly over the Japonaise sheet.

6. Reserve 48 good-looking orange segments to use for decorating. Arrange the remaining orange segments in a straight line, lengthwise, approximately 1 inch (2.5 cm) from the top long edge of the sheet. Refrigerate for about 15 minutes to partially set the cream.

7. Roll up the sheet as for a roulade by lifting the back of the paper and letting the pastry roll toward you (Figure 13-11). Refrigerate until the cream is completely set, approximately 1 hour.

8. Holding the knife straight up and down so that the width of the slices is even, cut the roll into 1½-inch (3.7-cm) slices at a slight angle. Place the orange sauce and the chocolate sauce in separate piping bottles.

9. Presentation: Sift powdered sugar lightly over the rim of a dessert plate and on top of a Budapest Swirl. Decorate the rim of the plate with small curls of orange zest. Pipe a large backward S design (like a question mark without the dot) of chocolate sauce in the center of the dessert plate, covering the base. Place the pastry in the center of the design. Pipe ½-inch (1.2-cm) dots of orange sauce on each side. Arrange 3 orange segments on the right side in front, then decorate with edible flowers.

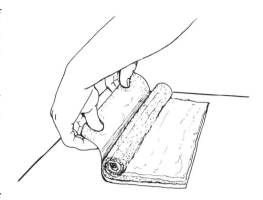

FIGURE 13-11 Using the baking paper underneath to facilitate rolling the Japonaise sheet into a roulade for Budapest Swirls

CHEF'S TIP
Ideally, the Japonaise sheet is baked the day before assembly and placed in the refrigerator overnight to ensure that it will be soft enough to roll. If necessary, follow the directions for softening sponge sheets given in the Note on page xx. While it is preferable to bake the sheet 1 day ahead of time, the Budapest Swirls should be assembled the day they are to be served; if left too long, the meringue will absorb moisture from the filling and become soggy.

Caramelized Upside-Down Apple and Almond Cakes

yield: 16 servings, 3¼ inches in diameter × 1½ inches high (8.1 × 3.7 cm)

This simple and foolproof combination of almond cake and caramelized apples can be made, start to finish, in about 2 hours You can substitute frangipane filling for the vanilla bean–almond filling, should you have some frangipane left over. You will need ½ recipe or 2 pounds 5 ounces (1 kg 50 g) frangipane. Because frangipane does not contain any baking powder, the crumb will be slightly dense but very moist. Cinnamon Ice Cream (page 720) and Vanilla Ice Cream (page 734) are also nice paired with this dessert.

12 ounces (340 g) dark brown sugar

8 ounces (225 g) unsalted butter, at room temperature, plus 2 to 3 tablespoons to grease the forms

3 pounds 8 ounces (1 kg 590 g) Golden Delicious or small Granny Smith apples (approximately 8 apples)

Vanilla Bean–Almond Filling (recipe follows)

½ recipe Fortified Caramel Sauce (page 821)

Lemon Verbena Ice Cream (page 725)

16 vanilla bean pod halves (split lengthwise)

1. Cream the brown sugar and 8 ounces (225 g) butter until smooth and lightened in color. Brush the remaining soft butter over the inside of 16 ramekins, 3¼ x 1½ inches (8.1 x 3.7 cm). Divide the brown sugar mixture evenly among the ramekins and spread over the bottom and sides of the forms, using your fingers. Place the forms on a sheet pan and reserve.

2. Peel, core, and halve the apples, placing them in acidulated water as you work to prevent discoloration. Cut the apple halves across into thin slices. Layer the slices in the prepared molds, filling the molds to the top and making sure that the center of the mold is covered as well as the sides. Avoid using the end pieces of the apples. Cover the ramekins with aluminum foil.

3. Bake at 375°F (190°C) until the apples feel soft and tender, approximately 30 minutes. The apples will have cooked down to about half of their original volume. Remove the foil and set the forms aside to let the apple mixture cool for at least 30 minutes.

4. Place the vanilla bean–almond filling in a pastry bag with a large plain tip. Pipe the filling on top of the baked apples, dividing it evenly among the forms. If necessary, spread the tops of the filling flat.

5. Bake at 375°F (190°C) for approximately 20 minutes or until the filling is just baked through; be careful not to overbake the cakes, which will cause them to become dry. Let the apple cakes cool at room temperature until the forms are cool enough to pick up with your bare hands. If you need to bake off the cakes several hours before service, heat each serving as needed. This is done not only because the cake tastes better warm but also to make it easier to unmold.

6. Adjust the consistency of the caramel sauce as needed so it can be piped into smooth rounds that will hold their shape. Place in a piping bottle and reserve at room temperature or keep warm.

7. Presentation: Run a knife around the inside edge of a warm cake and unmold in the center of a dessert plate. Pipe caramel sauce on the plate around the dessert in random dots. Place a scoop of lemon verbena ice cream on top of the cake, lean a vanilla bean pod against the ice cream, and serve immediately.

VANILLA BEAN–ALMOND FILLING yield: I pound 14 ounces (855 g)

1 vanilla bean

4 ounces (115 g) granulated sugar

6 ounces (170 g) almond paste

6 ounces (170 g) unsalted butter, at room temperature

4 eggs, at room temperature

6 ounces 170 g) bread flour

1 teaspoon (4 g) baking powder

1. Split the vanilla bean lengthwise and scrape out the seeds. Rub the seeds into a portion of the granulated sugar to separate and distribute them evenly. Set the pod aside for another use.

2. Place the vanilla-infused sugar and the remainder of the sugar in a mixer bowl together with the almond paste. Using the paddle attachment, add the butter gradually to avoid getting lumps in the batter. Cream the mixture together for a few minutes until it is smooth and light in color. Add the eggs, 1 at a time, scraping down the bowl as needed.

3. Sift the flour with the baking powder. Add the flour mixture to the batter on low speed, mixing just until it is incorporated.

Cheesecake Soufflé with Summer Strawberries

yield: 12 servings, 3¹/₄ inches (8.1 cm) in diameter (Photo 69)

This soufflé is not as temperamental as the classic dessert soufflé that is usually flavored with fruit or liqueur. Not only can the batter for these be made ahead of time and the forms filled and set aside in the refrigerator before baking, the baked soufflés do not need to rushed to the table after plating; they will hold up well for five minutes or so after the cake rings have been removed. These factors make this recipe a more practical choice for a large party or banquet.

Something else that sets this type of soufflé apart is that the baked desserts are unmolded for service, something that is never done with the classic version, which is always served (very quickly) still in its baking ramekin. If you do not have cake rings, you can bake these soufflés in traditional 3¹/₄ -inch (8.1-cm) soufflé ramekins as well, but you will not be able to unmold them. Coat the ramekins with melted butter and granulated sugar as directed below. If using ramekins, you will need 16, and they should be filled all the way to the top.

The plate presentation described here and shown in the photograph is suitable for à la carte service only, although it is not too complicated if you already have the sauces on hand. If you need to simplify the presentation, eliminate the piped flower design and serve the soufflés with strawberry sauce or another fruit sauce piped attractively on the plate.

Piping Chocolate (page 465)	Strawberry Sauce (page 832)
Melted unsalted butter	Orange Sauce (page 828)
Granulated sugar	Kiwi Sauce (page 823)
8 eggs, separated	12 strawberries, stems on
2 ounces (55 g) granulated sugar	12 Pâte à Choux Ornaments (recipe follows)
1 vanilla bean	Powdered sugar
7 ounces (200 g) quark cheese or baker's cheese, drained and pureed until smooth	

1. Prepare as many dessert plates as you anticipate needing for service by piping a hollow flower design made from piping chocolate on one side of each plate (see photograph in the color insert). Set the plates aside where they will not be disturbed.

2. Cut out 12 squares of aluminum foil measuring 6¹/₂ inches (16.2 cm). Set a cake ring, 3 inches (7.5 cm) in diameter and 2 inches (5 cm) in height, in the center of each square. Fold and pleat the edges of the foil up around the rings to make a tight seal. Because the cakes will be baked in a water bath, be certain that the foil reaches at least three-quarters of the way up the side of the rings. Brush melted butter over the inside of the rings as well as over the foil on the base, then coat the butter with granulated sugar. Set the forms aside.

3. Whip the egg yolks with 1 ounce (30 g) sugar until light and fluffy. Cut the vanilla bean in half lengthwise and scrape out the seeds. Stir the seeds into the cheese and mix until thoroughly combined; save the pod halves for another use. Whip the egg whites with the remaining 1 ounce (30 g) sugar until stiff peaks form; be careful not to overwhip. Combine the egg yolk mixture and the cheese, then gradually fold in the whipped egg whites.

4. Place the batter in a pastry bag with a No. 8 (16-mm) plain tip. Pipe the batter into the prepared forms, filling them to just below the rim. The soufflés may be refrigerated for up to 30 minutes at this point before proceeding.

5. Place as many soufflés as desired in a hotel pan. Add enough hot water to the pan so that it reaches halfway up the sides of the forms. Bake at 400°F (205°C) for approximately 15 minutes or until the soufflés are dark golden brown on top and baked through.

6. While the soufflés are baking, finish decorating the dessert plates by piping the sauces within the piped chocolate lines. If you are baking a large number, finish decorating the plates before baking.

7. Slice the strawberries crosswise, leaving the stems attached to the end slices. Keep each group of slices together.

8. Presentation: Remove a soufflé from the pan and peel the foil away from the cake ring. Slide a spatula under the cake ring and transfer the dessert to the decorated plate, placing it opposite the flower design. Lift away the cake ring. Fan 1 sliced strawberry and arrange in front of the soufflé. Lean a pâte à choux ornament against the soufflé. Sift powdered sugar lightly over the dessert as well as the plate and serve immediately.

PÂTE À CHOUX ORNAMENTS yield: variable

¼ cup (60 ml) whole milk

½ ounce (15 g) unsalted butter

3 tablespoons (22.5 g) bread flour

2 egg yolks

Whole milk as needed

1. Follow the directions for making pâte à choux on page 66. Force the finished paste through a fine strainer and cover tightly.

2. Draw 5 circles, 3½ inches (8.7 cm) in diameter, on each of 3 half sheets of baking paper. Invert each paper on a half-sheet pan securing the papers to the pans with a small dab of pâte à choux in each corner.

3. Have ready a plain cookie cutter, 3½ inches (8.7 cm) in diameter, and place a small amount of vegetable oil on a saucer.

4. Make a piping bag that is slightly larger than normal (see page 56) and place a portion of the pâte à choux inside. Pipe the paste over the drawn circles in parallel lines spaced ¼ inch apart, overlapping the circle at the end of each line. Pipe a second set of lines in the same manner pacing these at a 45-degree angle to the first set. Each line must extend beyond the drawn circle. The finished patter should consist of diamond-shaped openings between the lines.

5. Bake 1 pan of ornaments at a time at 375°F (190°C) until the paste is set but has not yet started to brown. This will take only about 4 minutes so you need to watch carefully. Remove the pan from the oven and, working quickly, dip the cookie cutter in oil and use it to firmly cut out the center of each ornament. Place the pan back in the oven and continue baking until the ornaments are light golden brown. Repeat baking and cutting the remaining ornaments in the same way. When the ornaments have cooled, store the round centers in airtight containers and discard the trimmed scraps. The ornaments may be stored for up to 2 weeks.

Chestnut-Rum Cream Cakes yield: 16 servings (Photo 87)

In this recipe, the pureed chestnuts are delicious mixed with cream, flavored with a hint of rum, and paired with chocolate. If you use canned chestnut puree, which you must do most of the year, be very careful to work it completely smooth before mixing in the mascarpone cheese. Because of the high starch content, the puree is quite firm and will give new meaning to the word lumpy if you fail to do so.

⅓ recipe Chocolate Chiffon Sponge Cake I
   batter (page 441)

½ cup (120 ml) Plain Cake Syrup (page 31)

Chocolate-Rum Cream (recipe follows)

Chestnut-Mascarpone Cream (recipe follows)

1 recipe Mousseline Sauce (page 827)

¼ cup (60 ml) dark rum

1 cup (240 ml) heavy cream

2 teaspoons (10 g) granulated sugar

Milk chocolate shavings

Chocolate Sauce for Piping (page 820)

16 Candied Chestnuts (page 8)

3 sheets gold leaf (optional; see Note)

1. Line the bottom of a cake pan, 10 inches (25 cm) in diameter, with baking paper. Add the sponge batter and spread the top even. Bake at 425°F (219°C) for approximately 15 minutes or until baked through. The cake should spring back when pressed lightly in the center. Set aside to cool.

2. Place 16 cake rings, 3 inches (7.5 cm) in diameter, on a sheet pan lined with baking paper. If you do not have cake rings, cut 16 strips from acetate, 10 x 1½ inches (25 x 3.7 cm), overlap the short ends, and tape them together to make rings that are 3 inches (7.5 cm) in diameter. Line the rings with strips of acetate.

3. Run a knife around the edge of the pan to release the cooled sponge cake and unmold the sponge. Remove the skin from the top of the cake. Slice the cake horizontally to make 2 layers. Brush the layers with cake syrup, using it all up. Cut 16 circles from the 2 layers, using a 3-inch (7.5-cm) plain cookie cutter; you will have to piece the last 2 together. Place a sponge circle in the bottom of each ring.

4. Place the chocolate-rum cream in a pastry bag with a No. 3 (6-mm) plain tip. Pipe the filling on top of the sponge circles, dividing it evenly. Be careful not to get any filling on the sides of the ring above the cream. Refrigerate while making the chestnut-mascarpone cream.

About Chestnuts

Chestnuts are actually classified as a fruit rather than a nut because they contain a greater amount of starch than oil. The spectacular European sweet chestnut tree (not to be confused with the American variety, which produces a much smaller nut) is a great ornamental shade tree, growing up to 100 feet tall. These trees are part of the landscape all over Northern Europe. In the springtime, the trees are covered with clusters of yellowish flowers, which later become spiny burrs, each containing up to three nuts. The chestnuts that are sold for cooking, either fresh in the fall and winter or canned in sugar syrup or water throughout the year, are the European variety. For some reason, chestnuts are utilized much more in cooking all across Europe than in the United States, where they still seem a bit underrated, except around Thanksgiving and Christmas, when they enjoy a brief burst of popularity.

5. Place the chestnut-mascarpone cream in a pastry bag with a No. 5 (10-mm) plain tip. Pipe the filling on top of the chocolate cream, dividing it evenly among the rings. Use a spatula to even the tops. Refrigerate the desserts until set, at least 2 hours or, preferably, overnight.

6. Flavor the mousseline sauce with the rum. Reserve in the refrigerator.

7. Whip the heavy cream with the sugar until stiff peaks form. Place in a pastry bag with a No. 6 (12-mm) star tip.

8. No more than 1 hour before serving, remove the metal rings or acetate strips from as many desserts as you plan to serve. Pipe a whipped cream rosette in the center on top of each one. Cover the top around the whipped cream with shaved chocolate. Place the decorated servings back in the refrigerator. The undecorated servings can be kept in the refrigerator, covered and left in the rings, for several days.

9. Presentation: Pour approximately ⅓ cup (80 ml) mousseline sauce off-center on a dessert plate. Use the back of a spoon to shape the sauce into a round pool about 5 inches (12.5 cm) in diameter. Place a small amount of chocolate sauce for piping in a piping bag. Pipe a rounded zigzag pattern, about 1 inch (2.5 cm) wide, around the perimeter of the sauce. Pull a small wooden skewer through the center of the zigzag (see Figure 16-2, page 814). Place a serving of cake behind the sauce with about one-quarter of the cake in the sauce pool. Decorate with a candied chestnut on top of the whipped cream rosette.

NOTE: To use the optional gold leaf decoration, cover half of each candied chestnut with ⅙ of a gold leaf sheet. See page 891 for more information on working with gold leaf.

CHOCOLATE-RUM CREAM yield: 3½ cups (840 ml)

3 ounces (85 g) unsweetened chocolate	3 egg yolks (¼ cup/60 ml)
7 ounces (200 g) sweet dark chocolate	¼ cup (60 ml) or 3 ounces (85 g) honey
1¾ cups (420 ml) heavy cream	2 tablespoons (30 ml) dark rum

1. Chop both chocolates into small pieces. Melt in a bowl set over simmering water. Set aside but keep warm.

2. Whip the heavy cream until soft peaks form.

3. Whip the egg yolks by hand until light and fluffy, about 2 or 3 minutes. Bring the honey to a boil and gradually add it to the egg yolks. Add the dark rum and continue to whip rapidly until the mixture has cooled completely.

4. Mix in the melted chocolate. Quickly fold in the whipped cream.

NOTE: If the filling thickens too much before you are ready to use it, soften it by warming very slightly over a bain-marie, stirring constantly with a whisk or a spoon.

CHESTNUT-MASCARPONE CREAM yield: 4½ cups (1 L 80 ml)

Do not make this filling before you are ready to use it or it will set up, causing lumps when it is applied to the top of the chocolate-rum cream.

10 ounces (285 g) Chestnut Puree (page 12) *or* unsweetened canned chestnut puree

8 ounces (225 g) Mascarpone Cheese (page 22), softened

1½ cups (360 ml) heavy cream

5 teaspoons (15 g) unflavored gelatin powder

⅓ cup (80 ml) cold water

6 ounces (170 g) granulated sugar

4 egg whites (½ cup/120 ml)

1. Work the chestnut puree until it is smooth. Mix in the mascarpone cheese gradually.

2. Whip the heavy cream until soft peaks form; do not overwhip. Fold the cream into the chestnut mixture. Reserve in the refrigerator.

3. Sprinkle the gelatin over the cold water and set aside to soften.

4. Combine the sugar and egg whites in a mixer bowl. Set the bowl over simmering water and heat, stirring constantly with a whisk, to 140°F (60°C). Remove from the heat and whip immediately until the meringue has formed stiff peaks, set aside.

5. Place the softened gelatin over a bain-marie and heat to dissolve; do not overheat. Place a small amount of the chestnut mixture in a bowl. Quickly stir in the gelatin. Continuing to work quickly, add this to the remaining chestnut cream. Stir the meringue to make it smooth, then quickly fold it into the cream mixture.

Chèvre Coeur à la Crème with Pistachio Crust

yield: 2 heart molds, 3 cups (720 ml) in capacity, or 12 individual heart molds, ⅓ cup (80 ml) in capacity (Photo 86)

Coeur à la crème—"heart of cream," in English—can be made from any combination of fresh cheeses, such as farmer's cheese, cottage cheese, or cream cheese. It is a very simple dish with only a few ingredients the cheese, sugar, cream (or meringue, to make a lighter version), and fruit. The flavor varies according to the proportion of whipped cream and/or meringue added. This recipe is not too sweet and has a little bite, which comes from the addition of chèvre, or fresh goat's milk cheese. Coeur à la crème is traditionally served with sweetened fresh strawberries and strawberry sauce. Although the cheese dessert is the classic interpretation, the word *coeur* is sometimes applied to a heart-shaped frozen mousse.

Heart-shaped wicker baskets and heart-shaped porcelain molds with small holes in the bottom are made especially for this dessert in sizes that make individual servings and larger ones that can hold up to eight servings. Before the forms are filled, they are lined with slightly dampened cheesecloth. The cheese filling is placed in the forms, and they are left overnight in the refrigerator to allow the whey to drain off, leaving a smooth, creamy mixture. I prefer the porcelain molds, as the little drainage holes can be taped over, allowing the use of the molds for other purposes.

If you do not have coeur à la crème molds (or you do not have enough molds for the number of servings you are making), leave the cheese mixture to drain in a fine mesh strainer or a colander lined with cheesecloth. The next day, you can pack the mixture into a heart-shaped metal form lined with cheesecloth or, for individual servings, a heart-shaped cookie cutter (or a coeur à la crème mold, provided you have at least one—it does create a much more attractive shape). Press the cheese in tightly, using a spoon or a small palette knife. Place in the freezer for 10 minutes, remove, unmold, and repeat until you have made the desired number of servings.

1½ cups (360 ml) heavy cream

7 ounces (200 g) granulated sugar

8 ounces (225 g) cream cheese, softened

3½ ounces (100 g) soft mild chèvre, such as Montrachet

1 pound 8 ounces (680 g) farmer's cheese *or* cottage cheese

½ recipe Strawberry Sauce (page 832)

5 ounces (140 g) pistachios, blanched, skins removed, and coarsely crushed

12 medium, fresh strawberries

12 large mint leaves, cut into julienne (see Chef's Tip)

12 Piped Curly Cues (page 795)

1. Line 12 individual coeur à la crème molds or 2 larger coeur à la crème molds, 3 cups (720 ml) in capacity, with damp cheesecloth, using enough to overhang the edges. Set the molds aside.

2. Whip the heavy cream and granulated sugar until soft peaks form. Reserve in the refrigerator.

3. Place the cream cheese and chèvre in a mixer bowl. Using the paddle attachment, beat until the mixture is smooth, scraping down the sides of the bowl a few times to make sure there are no lumps.

4. Place the farmer's or cottage cheese in a food processor and blend until completely smooth. Blend this into the cream cheese mixture. Fold the reserved whipped cream in by hand.

5. Pipe or pour the mixture into the lined molds, dividing it equally. Fold the cheesecloth over the top to cover. Place the molds in the refrigerator overnight, setting them on a sheet pan or tray to catch the whey as it drains off.

6. Adjust the consistency of the strawberry sauce, if needed, to make it thin enough to flow out but still hold its shape when piped. Place a portion of the sauce in a piping bottle. Reserve in the refrigerator together with the remaining sauce.

7. Spread the crushed pistachios out in a flat layer in a shallow dish.

8. Presentation: Lift a coeur à la crème out of the mold. Peel away the cheesecloth and place the heart, flat-side down, on top of the pistachios so that the nuts adhere to the bottom of the dessert (the side that was exposed when it was in the mold). Press some of the nuts into the side of the heart around the bottom edge as well. Place the heart, nut-side down, slightly above the center of a dessert plate. Slice the stem end off 1 strawberry, cutting the end flat and removing the hull. Cut 1 thin, round slice from this end, then cut the remainder of the strawberry into thin slices lengthwise. Arrange 3 of the larger lengthwise slices on the base of the plate around the top half of the heart with the points toward the rim of the plate. Place the round slice on top of the sliced strawberries next to the heart. Pipe teardrops of strawberry sauce on the base of the plate on both sides and around the bottom of the coeur à la crème. Sprinkle julienned mint leaves over the sauce. Place a piped curly cue leaning against the point of the heart with the tip angled toward the strawberries.

CHEF'S TIP

To cut the mint into julienne strips, stack 3 or 4 leaves together and use a chef's knife to slice across the width into ⅛-inch (3-mm) pieces. Discard the pieces from the tip and stem ends.

Chianti-Poached Figs with Lavender Mascarpone yield: 12 servings (Photo 66)

Brown Turkey figs, also known as Black Spanish figs, are large, beautiful fruits with an exceptional mahogany brown skin tinged with purple. The first crop of the year is always particularly eye-catching. (Figs, which produce fruit without flowering, are also unusual in that they provide two crops annually.)

This recipe utilizes the classic technique of poaching figs in wine and reducing the liquid to use as a sauce. The lightly cooked fruit is paired with mascarpone cheese and caramel sauce—a traditional and fabulous combination. The only time-consuming step here is caramelizing the figs, which can easily be omitted if necessary. Instead, poach the reserved figs lightly (less than 5 minutes) after removing the first 18 from the poaching liquid. Stand the second group of figs on end and allow them to drain thoroughly. Cut a cross on top of each one, cutting halfway through the fruit, so that the figs open up like flowers. Place in the center of the sauce when serving. With either presentation, you may wish to include a small dish of caramel ice cream on the side.

30 Brown Turkey figs, ripe but firm	Lavender petals
5 cups (1 L 200 ml) Chianti wine	Fortified Caramel Sauce (page 821)
4 ounces (115 g) granulated sugar	Crushed toasted hazelnuts
1 recipe Caramelized Sugar for Decorations (page 11)	Caramel Ice Cream (page 719), optional
8 ounces (225 g) Mascarpone Cheese (page 22)	

1. Select 12 of the nicest figs and reserve for decoration.

2. Combine the Chianti and the granulated sugar in a large saucepan. Bring to a boil and add the remaining 18 figs. Adjust the heat so that the liquid is just simmering and poach the figs for 5 minutes. Depending on the size of your pan, you may need to poach the figs in 2 batches. Gently remove the figs and stand them upright on a sheet pan lined with baking paper. Boil the poaching liquid until it is reduced to a thick syrup. You should have approximately 1¾ cups (420 ml) left. Set aside to cool.

3. Caramelize the 12 reserved figs in the caramelized sugar (see instructions that follow).

4. Cut the poached figs lengthwise in half, cutting evenly through the stem as well. Place them back on the sheet pan, cut-side up. Soften the mascarpone cheese and place in a pastry bag with a No. 4 (8-mm) plain tip. Pipe the cheese in a pearl pattern down the center of each fig. Sprinkle lavender petals on top of the mascarpone. Reserve the decorated fig halves in the refrigerator for up to 1 hour.

5. Place the caramel sauce in a piping bottle and set aside. Carefully twist the caramelized figs off the skewers; wear a latex glove on the hand that touches the fruit to avoid fingerprints on the caramel. Stand the figs upright on a sheet pan (see Chef's Tip).

6. Presentation: Pour a small pool of the reduced poaching syrup into the center of a dessert plate. Place a caramelized fig in the center of the sauce. Sprinkle crushed hazelnuts on the syrup

CHEF'S TIP

If the caramelized figs do not stand straight or steady enough, they can be fixed easily. Place a sheet pan lined with baking paper in the freezer while you melt a small amount of piping or coating chocolate. One at a time, pipe a dime-sized dot of chocolate on the chilled pan, set a fig on top, and hold it straight for a few seconds until the chocolate hardens.

around the fig. Place 3 prepared fig halves, evenly spaced, around the sauce with the stem ends pointing out. Pipe random teardrops of caramel sauce around the fig halves. Serve the ice cream in a small dish on the side if used.

CARAMEL-DIPPED FIGS

1. Let the caramelized sugar cool until it has the consistency of a thick syrup.

2. Prepare your work area by placing sheets of baking paper on the floor in front of your worktable. Place a ruler or thin strip of wood at the edge of the table and set a heavy can on top at each end to hold it in place. You can also use a block of Styrofoam to secure the skewers (see Chef's Tip page 574). Have ready as many wooden skewers as you have figs to caramelize.

3. Insert the pointed end of a skewer horizontally through the base of a fig, about ⅓ inch (8 mm) from the bottom, without pushing the skewer all the way through. As you move the figs while holding them by the skewers, be very careful that you do not tilt the skewers down, or the figs can slip off. Dip the whole fig into the caramel syrup, lift it out holding it so that the stem end is pointing down; secure the blunt end of the skewer under the ruler. The fig should extend out from the table over the floor above the baking papers, which can catch any excess caramel, with the stem end of the fig pointing straight down. Dip the remaining figs in the same manner, working from left to right if the sugar pot is on your right or right to left if the sugar pot is on your left, so that you will not drip across any figs after they are dipped.

4. When the caramel on the figs has hardened, heat the blade of a knife and use it to melt through the caramel tail at the desired length, anywhere from 4 to 8 inches (10 to 20 cm) from the fig (Figure 13-12).

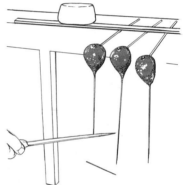

5. Transfer the figs to a sheet pan, holding them up by the wooden skewer. (If it is possible, leave them hanging in place until needed; see Note.) When you are ready to remove the skewers, wear a latex glove on the hand that touches the caramel, hold the fruit securely, and twist out the skewer with the other hand. Touching the caramel with your hands will leave fingerprints.

NOTE: It is crucial that the fruit be dipped in caramel as close to the serving time as possible. The hot caramel will start to cook the surface of the fruit, softening it and causing the juice to leak out. By leaving the skewer inserted in the fruit until the last moment, it will hold up a little better.

FIGURE 13-12 Using a hot knife to cut the tail of a Caramel-Dipped Fig to the desired length, in this case approximately 8 inches (20 cm)

CARAMEL-DIPPED MACADAMIA NUTS OR HAZELNUTS

1. Follow the instructions for Caramel-Dipped Figs. The trick here is inserting the skewers into the sides of the nuts. If you push them in too far and/or from the wrong side you will divide the nut into 2 halves. If you do not push them in far enough, the nuts will fall off the skewers into the caramel.

2. Arrange the dipped nuts so that the tiny point on the nut faces straight down, creating a tail in a straight line from that point.

Chilled Red Fruit Soup with Lemon Thyme and Mascarpone Sherbet

yield: 12 servings (Photo 89)

Chilled fruit soup is a refreshing dessert alternative on hot summer days. It has an intense flavor without being overly rich, and it's a great choice for guests who cannot eat chocolate. While I have seen more and more cold soups offered on dessert menus lately, they are certainly nothing new. As a kid, I used to love cold rosehip soup, which was served for dessert with toasted bread croutons and, if we were lucky, whipped cream. The technique used to make the soup is essentially the same as for preparing a poached fruit compote. Whatever you name it, this dish makes for a truly unusual presentation for sorbets, sherbets, and ice creams.

1 tablespoon (15 ml) finely chopped orange zest

½ cup (120 ml) fresh orange juice

2 cups (480 ml) Riesling wine

1 pound (455 g) firm red plums (about 10), cut into wedges, pits removed

1 pound (455 g) Bing cherries, stems removed, pitted if desired

1 large stem fresh basil (6 to 8 leaves)

1 pound (455 g) red Flame grapes, removed from the stems

1 pound (455 g) blueberries

1 pound (455 g) strawberries, hulled and cut into wedges

Lemon Thyme and Mascarpone Sherbet (page 750)

Zested orange peel

24 Wavy Tuile Strips (directions follow)

Small berries

Small sprigs fresh lemon thyme

1. Place the chopped orange zest, orange juice, and wine in a saucepan. Bring to a boil and boil for 1 minute. Add the plum wedges and whole cherries to the liquid. Add the basil sprig, return to a boil, and cook for 1 minute.

2. With a slotted spoon or a skimmer, remove the fruit from the cooking liquid and transfer it to a shallow bowl or a hotel pan (do not crush the fruit).

3. Return the basil to the cooking pan, add the grapes, return the mixture to a boil, and cook for 30 seconds. Transfer the grapes to the bowl or pan with the plums and cherries, leaving the basil in the liquid.

4. Add the blueberries and the strawberry wedges to the cooking liquid. Return the mixture just to the boiling point, then skim off the fruit, adding it to the bowl or pan. Pour all of the liquid that has collected in the bowl back into the cooking pan. Boil the cooking liquid until reduced by about one-third. Pour the reduced liquid over the fruit and chill several hours to develop the flavors. Remove the basil sprig before serving.

5. Presentation: Spoon a portion of the fruit and juice into the center of a dessert bowl, arranging the pieces attractively. Place a quenelle-shaped scoop of lemon thyme and mascarpone sherbet in the center of the soup. Sprinkle zested orange peel on top of the soup all around the scoop. Place 2 Wavy Tuile Strips parallel to one another with their opposite ends resting on the sherbet and the side of the bowl (see picture in color insert). Decorate with a few berries and a sprig of lemon thyme.

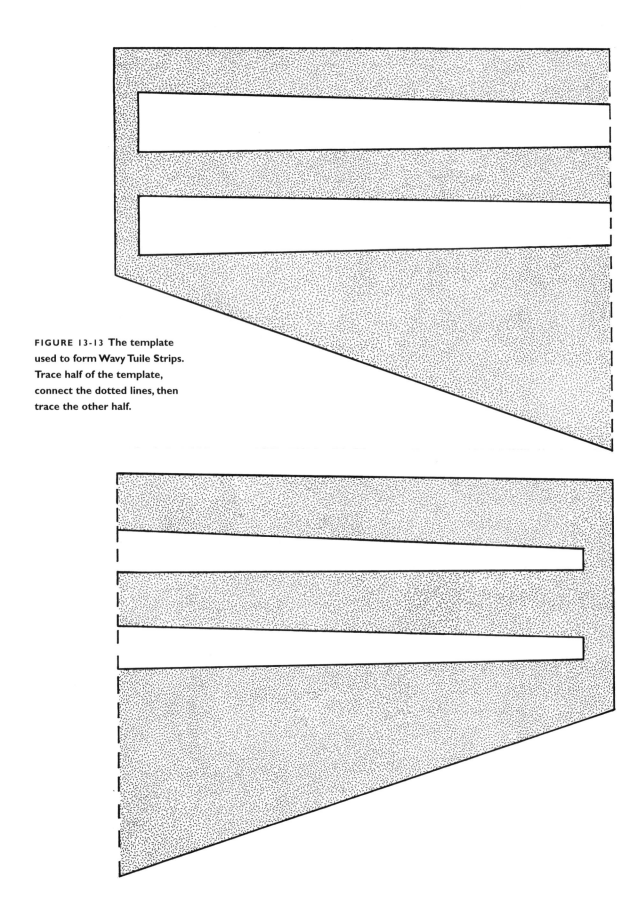

FIGURE 13-13 The template used to form Wavy Tuile Strips. Trace half of the template, connect the dotted lines, then trace the other half.

WAVY TUILE STRIPS yield: approximately 70 decorations

½ recipe Vanilla Tuile Decorating Paste
(page 482)

1½ teaspoons (4 g) unsweetened cocoa
powder

I. Trace the template shown in Figure 13-13. The template as shown is the correct size for use in this recipe; however, to fit the page, it is shown cut in half. Cut the template out of ¹⁄₁₆-inch (2-mm) cardboard such as the type used for cake boxes.

2. If you do not have Silpats, lightly grease the backs of flat, even sheet pans, then coat with flour. Shake off as much flour as possible.

3. Have ready a wavy molding tool to shape the warm cookies (instructions follow).

4. Thoroughly mix the cocoa powder into 3 tablespoons (45 ml) tuile paste. Place a small portion of the cocoa-colored paste in a piping bag and cut a small opening.

5. Spread the plain tuile paste flat and even within the template (see Figures 10-29 and 10-30, page 482), making 6 to 8 cookies per Silpat or sheet pan. Pipe a wavy line of the cocoa-colored paste down the full length of each cookie.

6. Bake, 1 pan at a time, at 400°F (205°C) for approximately 2 minutes or until a few brown spots appear on 1 cookie. It may take some trial and error to judge the baking time: If the cookies are too brown, they will break as you try to form them; if they are not brown enough, they will not become crisp after they cool.

7. Remove the pan from the oven. Quickly and carefully transfer the cookies, 1 at a time, to the wavy molding tool, being certain that the cookies fall into the grooves of the mold and that they are placed on the mold in a straight line. Press down with your fingertips to shape them (Figure 13-14); the cookies will become crisp very quickly. Move the wavy cookies to the side and continue shaping the remaining cookies. If the cookies become too firm to bend, soften them in the oven. Repeat Steps 5, 6, and 7 to form the remaining decorations.

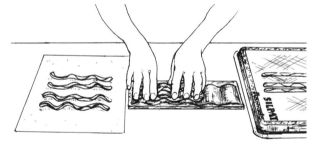

FIGURE 13-14 **Shaping the warm tuile strips as soon as they come out of the oven**

To Make a Tool for Molding Tuile Strips

As with some of the other unusual hand tools used in the pastry kitchen these days—PVC pipe, plastic scrapers, aluminum, and plastic screening—the material used to make this molding tool comes from the hardware store. It is important to note that not all of these materials are considered food grade and some should be used only for showpieces. In some cases, as when using PVC pipe to mold a filling as it sets, the item must be lined with food-grade plastic wrap. For this molding tool, the material used is aluminum, which is safe for contact with food.

Buy a piece of aluminum corrugated flashing, the type that is used in combination with corrugated roof panels. Using metal shears, cut off the flat part of the flashing and discard. You need a piece about 10 inches (25 cm) long x 4 inches (10 cm) wide, but there will be enough material to make 2 tools of this size. You can simply use them as is or, to create a more secure base, attach the aluminum to a piece of clear plastic or plywood, ¼ inch (6 mm) thick and the same length and width as the aluminum flashing.

Chocolate Marquise **yield: 16 servings** (Photo 85)

his is a classic recipe that I dusted off and dressed up a little. (The term *Marquise*, if not specified as *Chocolate Marquise*, refers to a fruit ice and cream combination.) Either marquise can be made in many shapes and forms. The following is a very elegant presentation. If necessary, it can be simplified by omitting certain steps or making a few changes. For example, if you do not have a Silpat to make the decorated sponge, substitute a half-recipe of Cocoa Dobos Sponge batter (page 443). Spread the batter into a 16-inch (40-cm) square and bake as directed. Another way to save time is to use fresh fruit as a garnish rather than the marzipan flowers and tuile leaves. It is best to serve the scaled-down version in one slice rather than cutting it on the diagonal as described below.

1 Ribbon-Pattern Decorated Sponge Sheet, 23 × 15 inches (57.5 × 37.5 cm) (page 447)	1 cup (240 ml) heavy cream, whipped
¼ cup (60 ml) light rum	16 Marzipan Forget-Me-Not Flowers (recipe follows)
¼ cup (60 ml) Plain Cake Syrup (page 31)	16 Elongated Tuile Leaves (page 690)
Chocolate Marquise Filling (recipe follows)	½ recipe Raspberry Sauce (page 830)
Piping Chocolate (page 465), melted	16 mint sprigs

I. Line the bottom and the long sides of 2 bread pans, 3½ × 3½ × 8 inches (8.7 × 8.7 × 20 cm), with baking paper. Set the forms aside.

2. Trim 1 short end of the sponge sheet to make it even, if necessary. Cut crosswise to make 2 strips, 8 × 14 inches (20 × 35 cm), with the ribbons now running across (Figure 13-15). (You will have a little less than one-third of the sheet left over for another use). Combine the rum with the cake syrup. Carefully brush some of the mixture on the back (plain side) of the sponge sheets. Do not soak the sponge sheets or they will fall apart.

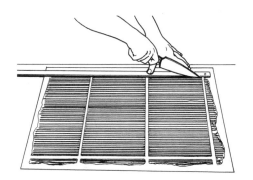

FIGURE 13-15 **Cutting the ribbon-pattern sponge sheet to create 2 pieces for lining the forms. The piece on the left side will be reserved for another use.**

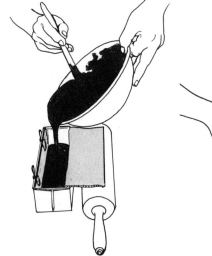

FIGURE 13-16 **Adding the filling to the form after lining the form with the decorated sponge. The portion of sponge that extends beyond the form is supported by a rolling pin.**

FIGURE 13-17 **Folding the extended portion of decorated sponge over the filling**

3. Place the sponge sheets in the forms with the striped side against the baking paper and 1 short side of each sponge flush with 1 long top edge of each form so that the stripes run lengthwise. Support the pieces that extend outside each form with a rolling pin or more bread pans. If the top edge that is flush with the pan falls in, hold it in place against the form with 2 paper clips until you add the filling.

4. Divide the marquise filling evenly between the pans (Figure 13-16). Tap the forms sharply to settle the filling, then smooth the tops to make them level. Fold the sponges over the top of the filling (Figure 13-17). Press lightly to make sure they stick. Trim away any excess sponge.

5. Place the forms in the refrigerator for at least 4 hours or, preferably, overnight.

6. Decorate the number of dessert plates you will be needing with piping chocolate by first piping 3 parallel lines in the center of the base of the plate, then 3 more at a 90-degree angle to the first set. Set the plates aside. Place the whipped cream in a pastry bag with a No. 6 (12-mm) star tip. Reserve in the refrigerator.

7. Remove each chocolate marquise from its form. Trim the short ends, then use a thin, sharp knife, heated in either hot water or on the stove, to cut each into 8 slices (if you will not be serving the full amount right away, cut only the number required). The slices will be slightly wider than ¾ inch (2 cm). Do not force the knife as you cut but instead let it melt through the chocolate. Wipe the knife clean and reheat it for each cut so you do not mar the sponge. Place the slices back in the refrigerator.

8. Adjust the consistency of the raspberry sauce if needed. Place the sauce in a piping bottle and set aside.

9. Presentation: Cut a slice of chocolate marquise in half diagonally, cutting from the corner with the seam to the opposite diagonal corner so the seam does not show. Arrange the wedges in the center of a prepared dessert plate with one piece leaning against the other and the sponge facing out. Pipe a rosette of whipped cream on the plate to the right of the dessert. Set a marzipan flower and a tuile leaf on the cream. Pipe a small pool of raspberry sauce on the left side of the marquise. Place a mint sprig next to the sauce and serve immediately.

CHOCOLATE MARQUISE FILLING yield: 9 cups (2 L 160 ml)

1 pound 8 ounces (680 g) sweet dark chocolate

4 ounces (115 g) unsweetened chocolate

3 cups (720 ml) heavy cream

6 egg yolks (½ cup/120 ml)

3 whole eggs

1 ounce (30 g) granulated sugar

⅓ cup (80 ml) or 4 ounces (115 g) honey

¼ cup (60 ml) chartreuse liqueur

1. Chop the sweet and unsweetened chocolates into small chunks. Place in a bowl set over simmering water and melt together. Set aside, but keep warm.

2. Whip the heavy cream until soft peaks form. Reserve.

3. Whip the egg yolks, eggs, and sugar for about 3 minutes at high speed; the mixture should be light and fluffy. Bring the honey to a boil and gradually pour it into the egg mixture while whipping. Continue whipping until cold.

4. Fold in the reserved chocolate and the chartreuse. Quickly stir in the whipped cream.

MARZIPAN FORGET-ME-NOT FLOWERS yield: 20 flowers, 1 inch (2.5 cm) in diameter

Crystal sugar	Granulated sugar
3 ounces (85 g) Marzipan (page 21), tinted light pink	½ ounce (15 g) Marzipan (page 21), tinted yellow
Powdered sugar	Piping Chocolate (page 465), melted

1. Fill a cake pan, 10 inches (25 cm) in diameter, with a 1-inch (2.5-cm) layer of crystal sugar. Smooth the top even.

2. Roll the pink marzipan out to slightly thinner than ⅛ inch (3 mm), using powdered sugar to prevent it from sticking. Cut out circles, using a 1-inch (2.5-cm) fluted cookie cutter. Place the circles on top of the decorating sugar in the baking pan.

3. Press down in the center of each circle, pushing it into the sugar to make it concave.

4. Gather the scrap pieces of marzipan, roll them out again to the same thickness, and continue cutting circles and placing them in the sugar in the same manner until you have made 20.

5. Put a small amount of granulated sugar in a saucer or any small form. Set aside.

6. Roll the yellow marzipan into a rope, ¼ inch (6 mm) in diameter. Cut the rope into 20 equal pea-sized pieces. Two at a time, roll the pieces into round balls between your thumbs and index fingers, using both hands, then drop them into the granulated sugar on the saucer. Roll the balls in the sugar so it sticks to the marzipan. Reserve.

7. Place the piping chocolate in a piping bag and cut a small opening. Pipe a small dot of chocolate in the center of each of the pink marzipan circles. Place a yellow marzipan ball on top.

8. Let the flowers dry for 1 day in a warm place. Do not cover them.

9. Brush off any crystal sugar that sticks to the back of the marzipan as you remove the flowers from the sugar. Store, covered, in a dry place.

Chocolate Refrigerator Soufflés

yield: 12 servings made in ramekins, 3½ inches (8.7 cm) in diameter and 5 ounces (150 ml) in capacity

Many restaurants are simply not equipped to prepare and serve traditional soufflés, which must be ordered, fired, and picked up at precisely the right times, either because of the way the front-of-the-house service is set up or, more likely, because the pastry kitchen does not have the time or space. (In some operations, the so-called pastry kitchen is nothing more than the corner of the main kitchen where they happen to keep the mixer!)

Whatever the situation, if you cannot prepare soufflés the classic way, this recipe and the Cheesecake Soufflé on page 623, are the next best thing. The soufflé batter can be made up and stored, covered, in the refrigerator (either ready to bake in ramekins or in a container) for up to 4 days. As you would expect, this type of convenience has its price; these do not rise to the same height as conventional soufflés, but they definitely rise high enough to be regarded as such.

Melted unsalted butter

Granulated sugar

4 ounces (115 g) unsalted butter

12 ounces (340 g) sweet dark chocolate, chopped coarsely

4 ounces (115 g) unsweetened chocolate, chopped coarsely

12 egg yolks (1 cup/240 ml)

¼ cup (60 ml) water

12 ounces (340 g) granulated sugar

12 egg whites (1½ cups/360 ml)

¼ cup (60 ml) chocolate liqueur

1 teaspoon (2 g) cream of tartar

Powdered sugar

½ recipe Crème Anglaise (page 817)

1. Brush melted butter over the insides of 12 ramekins, 3¼ inches (8.1 cm) in diameter. Fill 1 form halfway with granulated sugar. Twist the form so that the sugar coats the entire inside, then pour the sugar into the next form. Repeat until all the forms are coated, adding more sugar as necessary. Place the forms on a sheet pan and reserve in the refrigerator.

2. Combine the butter and both chocolates in a bowl. Set the bowl over a bain-marie and melt the chocolate and butter together, stirring from time to time. Do not overheat.

3. Start whipping the egg yolks. As the yolks are whipping, combine the water with a little less than half of the granulated sugar in a saucepan and bring to a boil. Pour the boiling sugar syrup into the yolks as they are beating at medium speed. After the syrup has been added, turn the speed to high and continue whipping until the yolks are light and fluffy; they should be approximately tripled in volume.

4. Fold the whipped yolks into the reserved chocolate mixture together with the chocolate liqueur.

5. Whip the egg whites with the remaining sugar and the cream of tartar to stiff peaks. Gradually fold the chocolate mixture into the whipped whites.

6. Fill the prepared ramekins with the batter. Wipe the rims clean, cover, and refrigerate for at least 2 hours or, preferably, overnight. The batter must be chilled all the way through before baking.

7. Bake the soufflés at 350°F (175°C) for about 15 minutes. The tops should feel firm and the insides should be soft but not liquid.

8. Presentation: Quickly remove the soufflés from the oven. Sift powdered sugar lightly over the tops. Place each soufflé ramekin on a dessert plate lined with a folded napkin or a doily. Serve immediately with crème anglaise in a small pitcher or serving bowl on the side.

Cookie-Crusted Profiteroles with Nougat Sauce

yield: 16 servings; about 55 profiteroles (Photo 26)

This recipe serves as a prime example of the old adage that one should never judge a book by its cover. The appearance of the profiteroles may be somewhat plain, but if you factor in the degrees of difficulty, practicality, and popularity as you evaluate them, you will rank these with the most elaborately decorated desserts. As the profiteroles bake, the expanding pâte à choux forces the short dough cookie stuck on top to break into tiny pieces. The sweet, crunchy cookie makes a perfect match to the Bavarian cream inside. I always keep cookie-topped profiteroles on hand in the freezer for an emergency. They are a cinch to bake, cool, fill, and dust with powdered sugar, and then they're ready to serve.

About Profiteroles

The French word *profiterole* derives from the word *profit* and means "small profit" or "gain." One theory is that the name may stem from these pastries being something extra the chef or servant could make for himself from leftover batter as he prepared food for his employer. Profiteroles are simply miniature cream puffs, usually piped out using a plain tip in the pastry bag, filled with either a savory or a sweet mixture after baking. Savory profiteroles are used as hors d'oeuvres or appetizers, and the dessert types are most commonly filled with Bavarian cream and served with chocolate sauce. The most ambitious and famous dessert prepared with these diminutive pastries is the Croquembouche. Here, the top and sides of each profiterole are dipped into caramel and the pieces are compiled into a large conical *pièce monté*.

1½ ounces (40 g) granulated sugar

4 ounces (115 g) Short Dough (page 67)

½ recipe Pâte à Choux (page 83)

1 recipe Quick Bavarian Cream (page 846)

Piping Chocolate (page 465), melted

3 tablespoons (45 ml) strained strawberry preserves, approximately

1 cup (240 ml) heavy cream

1 teaspoon (5 g) granulated sugar

1 recipe Nougat Sauce (page 827)

Powdered sugar

16 Piped Curly Cues (page 790)

1. Mix the first measurement of granulated sugar into the short dough. Roll the dough to ¹⁄₁₆ inch (2 mm) thick and cut out about 55 circles, using a 1½-inch (3.7-cm) plain or fluted cookie cutter. Set aside. Discard the scrap pieces.

2. Place the pâte à choux in a pastry bag with a No. 4 (8-mm) plain tip. Pipe out 55 mounds onto sheet pans lined with baking paper, making them the same diameter as the cookies. The profiteroles should be about the size of golf balls when baked. Immediately place a short dough circle on each mound and press lightly with your fingers to be sure they stick (see Note).

3. Bake the profiteroles at 400°F (205°C) until puffed, about 10 minutes. Reduce the heat to 375°F (190°C) and bake until they will hold their shape, about 10 minutes longer. Let the puffs cool completely.

4. No more than 1 hour before serving, make a small slit in the bottom of each puff just large enough to insert the pastry tip. Put the Bavarian cream in a pastry bag with a No. 3 (6-mm) plain tip and pipe into the profiteroles. Reserve the profiteroles in the refrigerator.

5. Place the piping chocolate and the strained preserves into piping bags and cut small openings in the bags. Pipe 3 chocolate figurines on the base of as many dessert plates as you anticipate needing. Pipe the designs so that the figurines begin in the center of the plate and end next to the edge of the base, are evenly spaced, and provide enough room to place a profiterole between them (see photo in color insert). Fill the loops of the chocolate figurines with the strained preserves. Set the plates aside.

6. Whip the heavy cream and the remaining sugar to stiff peaks. Place in a pastry bag with a No. 7 (14-mm) star tip and reserve in the refrigerator. Place a portion of the nougat sauce in a piping bottle and reserve in the refrigerator with the remaining sauce.

7. Presentation: Pipe 3 small, round pools of nougat sauce between the chocolate figurines on one of the prepared plates. Sift powdered sugar over 3 filled profiteroles and place 1 on each pool of sauce. Pipe a rosette of whipped cream in the center of the plate. Stand a curly cue upright in the cream. Serve immediately.

NOTE: The profiteroles can be frozen after they have been piped out and topped with the cookies. Bake straight from the freezer without thawing. I try to place them in the freezer long enough to harden even when they are to be baked right away because they seem to puff up better if baked frozen.

Courting Swans yield: 16 servings (Photo 6)

Ever-elegant swans really make this very simple plated dessert stand out. Courting swans make a good choice when you need a dessert that can be served without a lot of finishing touches, or for a very large party, as they can be assembled hours ahead—and it takes a minimum of time to complete the presentation. Do keep in mind that the swans should be small. If either the head and neck portion or the bodies are piped out too large, or if they are misshapen, you will end up with ugly ducklings instead.

This amount of pâte à choux will make a few more swans than you need for 16 servings, which allows you to pick and choose a bit during the assembly.

½ recipe Pâte à Choux (page 83)

3 ounces (85 g) smooth strawberry jam

1 recipe Chantilly Cream (page 838)

Dark coating chocolate, melted

½ recipe Chocolate Sauce (page 820)

½ recipe Raspberry Sauce (page 830)

Sour Cream Mixture for Piping (page 832)

Powdered sugar

1. Place 1 cup (240 ml) pâte à choux in a separate bowl. Cover and reserve.

2. Place the remaining paste in a pastry bag with a No. 6 (12-mm) star tip. Pipe the paste in small cone shapes (the wide end should be about the size of an unshelled walnut) onto sheet pans lined with baking paper, following the instructions in the recipe for Swans (page 593). You are making them the correct size if you have used half of the paste after making about 20; there are 2 swans per serving.

3. After piping the bodies, replace the star tip with a No. 1 (2-mm) plain tip and place the reserved pâte à choux in the bag. Pipe out the head and neck shapes (see illustration and instructions, page 594). You should be able to pipe out quite a few extras, so you will have a choice and not have to worry about breakage.

4. Bake the bodies and the head and neck pieces at 400°F (205°C). The head and neck pieces will take about 10 minutes and the bodies will take about 20 minutes. Let cool completely.

5. Cut the top third off the bodies; then cut the top piece in half lengthwise to create 2 wings (scissors work best). Place a wing on both sides of each body, lining the pastries up for assembly.

6. Pipe a thin ribbon of strawberry jam in the bottom of each shell.

7. Whip the Chantilly cream to stiff peaks and place in a pastry bag with a No. 6 (12-mm) star tip. Pipe the cream into the shells, using the same up-and-over motion you used to pipe the shells and coming to a point at the narrow end, which will be the tail.

8. Arrange the wings in the whipped cream pointing upward and meeting at the top. Dip the bottom of each neck in coating chocolate to prevent the whipped cream from softening it and causing it to fall. (This is not necessary if you assemble the swans to order.) Push the necks into the whipped cream so they lean back slightly between the wings.

9. Presentation: Adjust the consistency of the chocolate and raspberry sauces, if necessary, so they are thick enough not to run on the plate when piped out. Place a portion of each sauce in a piping bottle. Pipe the sauces onto the base of a dessert plate in a yin-yang pattern, covering the base of the plate. Hold the plate in one hand and tap it with the palm of your other hand to flatten and smooth the surface of the sauces. Place the sour cream mixture in a piping bag and pipe a line following the border where the sauces come together in the center. Use a wooden skewer to blend the sour cream with the 2 sauces (see photo in color insert). Sift powdered sugar lightly over 2 swans. Place 1 in each pool of sauce, arranging them so they face each other. Serve immediately.

Crepe Soufflé yield: 16 servings

A crepe soufflé is a classic French dessert made by baking soufflé batter inside a folded crepe. When prepared in the traditional fashion, the finished dessert looks something like a pancake—a bit too flat on the plate for my taste, as the first thing that comes to mind when you hear the word soufflé is the height of the dessert. This variation, in which the crepe is supported by a soufflé ramekin during baking, is much more appealing; the technique produces a dessert more in keeping with the traditional soufflé appearance.

4 ounces (115 g) granulated sugar	½ teaspoon (2.5 ml) vanilla extract
1½ ounces (40 g) cornstarch	⅓ cup (80 ml) orange liqueur
1½ ounces (40 g) bread flour	16 Crepes (page 14; see Note)
1½ ounces (40 g) unsalted butter, at room temperature	6 egg whites (¾ cup/180 ml)
1½ cups (360 ml) whole milk	1½ recipes Strawberry Sauce (page 832)
6 egg yolks (½ cup/120 ml)	Sour Cream Mixture for Piping (page 832)
	Powdered sugar

1. Combine about one-third of the sugar with the cornstarch. Reserve.

2. Mix the flour and butter to form a paste. Heat the milk to the scalding point in a heavy saucepan. Add the butter and flour mixture and stir with a whisk; it will melt into the milk. Quickly mix in one-third of the egg yolks. Bring to a boil over low heat, stirring constantly. Cook the mixture until it thickens, about 1 minute. Remove from the heat but continue to stir for 10 to 15 seconds.

3. Add the remaining egg yolks, vanilla, liqueur, and the sugar and cornstarch mixture. Cover the custard mixture and reserve. It will keep for up to 2 days if refrigerated.

4. Thirty minutes before the crepe soufflés are to be served, place 1 crepe for each serving you are firing, browned-side down, on top of a 5-ounce (150-ml) soufflé ramekin that is 3¼ inches (8.1 cm) in diameter. Push the crepes halfway into the forms.

5. Whip the egg whites until they have quadrupled in volume and have a thick and foamy consistency. Gradually whip in the reserved two-thirds of the sugar, then whip a few seconds longer until the egg whites are stiff but not dry. Fold the egg whites into the reserved custard mixture.

6. Pipe the soufflé batter into the ramekins on top of the crepes so that the crepes are pushed to the bottom and line the sides and bottom of the ramekins. Fill the forms even with the rim of the ramekins.

7. Bake immediately at 400°F (205°C) for approximately 20 minutes. These do not puff up as high as a regular soufflé; instead they will stick to the crepe and crack on the top.

8. Presentation: Cover the base of as many dessert plates as you have soufflés in the oven with strawberry sauce. A few minutes before the soufflés are finished baking, pipe 5 evenly spaced dots of sour cream mixture, about ¾ inch (2 cm) in diameter, in the strawberry sauce on each plate close to the perimeter of the strawberry sauce. Use the tip of a small wooden skewer to shape the sour cream dots into hearts with tails (see Figure 16-10, page 813). Remove the soufflés from the oven. Quickly but gently remove them from the ramekins by inverting each into your hand. Place the soufflés, right-side up, in the center of the prepared plates. Sift powdered sugar lightly over the tops. Serve immediately.

NOTE: Use the typical 6-inch (15-cm) crepe or a slightly smaller size. The outer edge of a larger crepe will not be supported by the ramekin and will fall over during baking.

Crisp Hazelnut Wafers with Raspberries and Cream yield: 16 servings (Photo 44)

The technique used to create and present Crisp Hazelnut Wafers is one of the quickest and easiest ways of making an impressive dessert. This ideal summer offering can be assembled in just a few minutes provided the components are at hand: whipped cream in a pastry bag, sorted raspberries, and sauce in a piping bottle. The batter will yield a few extra wafers, so you can afford to break some during the assembly. This is almost unavoidable because they are so fragile, but their delicacy is part of the dessert's appeal.

If it is not possible to assemble each serving à la minute, the assembly should be completed no more than 15 minutes prior to serving or the wafers will become soft and unappetizing. It is also important to keep in mind that, just as with other fruits and berries, there are small, medium, and large raspberries. Mixing them up within the same serving will probably result in the layers leaning to one side.

Butter and Flour Mixture (page 7)	2 cups (480 ml) heavy cream
Hazelnut Wafer Batter (recipe follows)	2 teaspoons (10 g) granulated sugar
Powdered sugar	2 dry pints (960 ml) raspberries, approximately (see Note)
5 ounces (140 g) strained strawberry jam *or* preserves	16 small mint leaves
1 recipe Raspberry Sauce (page 830)	Sour Cream Mixture for Piping (page 832)

I. Make the template shown in Figure 13-18. The template as shown is the correct size required for this recipe. Trace the drawing, then cut the template out of ¹⁄₁₆-inch (2-mm) cardboard (cake boxes work fine for this). Make a second solid template that is 2 inches (5 cm) larger than the first one (1 inch/2.5 cm on each of the 8 sides) and reserve this template for the presentation. If you do not have Silpats, brush the butter and flour mixture on the back of clean, even sheet pans.

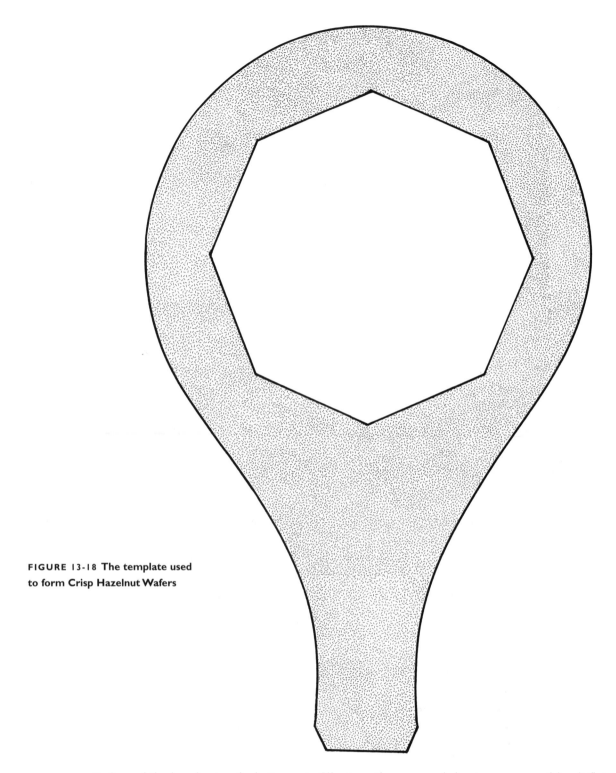

FIGURE 13-18 The template used to form Crisp Hazelnut Wafers

2. Spread the hazelnut wafer batter onto Silpats or the prepared sheet pans, smoothing it flat and even within the template (see Figures 10-29 and 10-30, pages 482). You will need 3 wafers per serving.

3. Bake at 400°F (205°C) until slightly brown in places, approximately 5 minutes. Allow the wafers to cool before removing them from the pans.

4. Place the reserved solid template in the center of a dessert plate. Sift powdered sugar over the exposed portion of the plate. Remove the template (make a handle from a piece of tape and attach it to the template, or, for a more permanent solution, glue the cork from a wine bottle in the center on top of the template). Remove any sugar from the rim of the plate. Place strawberry jam or preserves in a piping bag and cut a larger than normal opening. Pipe a line of jam, following the perimeter of the powdered sugar octagon. Prepare as many remaining plates as you expect to need in the same way. Set the plates aside. If needed, strain and/or adjust the consistency of the raspberry sauce. Place a portion of the raspberry sauce in a piping bottle and reserve.

5. Whip the heavy cream with the granulated sugar to stiff peaks. Place in a pastry bag with a No. 6 (12-mm) plain tip. Reserve in the refrigerator.

6. Presentation: Pipe raspberry sauce within the octagonal jam outline, filling in all but a space in the center that is slightly smaller than the size of the wafers. Pipe a small mound of whipped cream at every other point on each of 2 wafers. Place 5 raspberries on top of each, arranging 4 of them between the mounds of cream and 1 in the center. Stack the wafers on top of one another, placing the second wafer so that the cream and berries that are visible on the sides alternate. Top the stack with a plain wafer. Hold a No. 4 (8-mm) star tip in place over the plain tip on the pastry bag with whipped cream. Pipe a small rosette of cream in the center of the top wafer. Sift powdered sugar lightly over the top wafer. Place a raspberry and a small mint leaf on the cream.

Place the assembled stack of wafers in the center of the sauce with the edges of the sauce and wafer parallel. Pipe dots of sour cream mixture in the sauce around the wafers at each point of the octagon. Drag a wooden skewer through the dots toward the dessert to create teardrops. Clean the tip of the skewer, then dip it into raspberry sauce and decorate each sour cream teardrop with a tiny dot of raspberry sauce. Serve immediately.

NOTE: If at all possible, try to work with a few extra pints of raspberries so you can choose the best-looking and most evenly sized berries to use in the desserts. Leftover raspberries can be used in part to make the sauce.

HAZELNUT WAFER BATTER yield: 2 cups (240 ml)

5 ounces (140 g) toasted hazelnuts or finely ground hazelnuts (see Note)

5 ounces (140 g) granulated sugar

4 ounces (115 g) unsalted butter, at room temperature

½ teaspoon (3 g) salt

⅓ cup (80 ml) heavy cream

2 egg whites (¼ cup/60 ml)

1 tablespoon (15 ml) Frangelico liqueur

3 ounces (85 g) bread flour

1. Rub the toasted hazelnuts between your hands to remove some, but not all, of the brown skin. Grind them with half of the sugar to a fine consistency. Cream the butter with the remainder of the sugar, then mix in the ground nuts, salt, and heavy cream.

2. Add the egg whites and Frangelico. Sift the flour and incorporate it into the batter. Let the batter rest for 1 hour.

NOTE: If you have finely ground hazelnuts on hand, these can be used instead to save time. Toast the ground hazelnuts and let cool. Cream the butter and sugar together, mix in the ground nuts, and continue as directed.

Date-Stuffed Poached Pears in Phyllo Crowns with Brandied Mousseline Sauce yield: 12 servings (Photo 62)

Pears have been popular with epicures for a very long time. The Romans had pear trees in virtually every garden and tended them with the utmost of care. In fact, during the time of the Roman Empire, the number of pear varieties cultivated grew from as few as 6 to nearly 60. The pear recipes in this text in no way begin to cover the possibilities; one could easily write a cookbook on this fruit alone. An excellent pear dessert that certainly doesn't require a recipe is simply a perfectly ripe pear served with blue cheese or mascarpone cheese, toasted pecans or hazelnuts, and a glass of port-fabulous!

12 small Bosc pears, stems on	Almond Filling (recipe follows)
2 recipes Spiced Poaching Syrup (page 31)	1 recipe Mousseline Sauce (page 827)
16 sheets phyllo dough (approximately 10 ounces/285 g)	¼ cup (60 ml) brandy
4 ounces (115 g) melted unsalted butter	Raspberry Sauce (page 830) or another red fruit sauce
12 fresh dates	Powdered sugar

1. Peel the pears, keeping the stems intact, and place them into acidulated water to prevent oxidation as you are working. Poach the pears in the poaching syrup, following the instructions on page 32, until they are just soft to the touch. Be especially careful not to overcook the pears because they are presented later standing on end. Let the pears cool in the liquid. Ideally, to absorb as much flavor as possible from the spices, let stand overnight.

2. Trace the template (Figure 13-19) and cut it out of thin cardboard, such as a cake box.

3. Layer 8 sheets of phyllo dough, brushing each with some of the melted butter as you stack them. With the template as a guide and using a sharp paring knife, cut out 6 stars from the layered sheets.

4. Gently push the phyllo stars into 7-ounce (210-ml) individual pie forms measuring 4½ inches (11.2 cm) in diameter across the top, 2¾ inches (6.8 cm) in diameter across the bottom, and 1½ inches (3.7 cm) in height. Repeat with the remaining 8 sheets of phyllo to make 6 more crowns. The phyllo shells can be refrigerated in the forms for several days, provided they are well covered.

5. Remove the pears from the poaching liquid and pat them dry with paper towels. Reserve the liquid. Using the tip of a paring knife, make a horizontal cut beginning no more than ½ inch (1.2 cm) below the stem, cutting three-quarters of the way through each pear and leaving the stems attached. Cut just enough from the bottom of each pear so it will stand straight up. Push an apple corer up through the bottom of each pear to the horizontal cut and remove the core. If you do not have a corer, this step can be completed with a melon ball cutter. In this case, omit the horizontal cut and proceed with care.

6. Make a cut lengthwise in each date and remove the pit. Push a date into each pear from the bottom. Stand the pears straight up. Using a paring knife, score vertical lines, about ⅜ inch (9 mm) apart; cut from the bottom to the top of the pears, making softly curved cuts without cutting all the way through to the date. Wrap aluminum foil around the pear stems to keep them from getting too dark while they bake.

FIGURE 13-19 **The template used as a guide in cutting the stacked phyllo sheets for Date-Stuffed Poached Pears**

7. Place the almond filling in a pastry bag. Pipe the filling into the phyllo shells, dividing it evenly. Place a pear in each shell and press it down firmly into the filling.

8. Bake at 400°F (205°C) until the phyllo dough and the almond filling are dark golden brown, approximately 15 minutes. Allow the pastries to cool slightly before unmolding and unwrapping the stems.

9. Presentation: Flavor the mousseline sauce with the brandy. Cover the base of a dessert plate with some of the sauce. Place a small amount of raspberry sauce in a piping bag. Pipe a ring of raspberry sauce about ¾ inch (2 cm) away from the perimeter of the mousseline sauce. Use the blunt edge of a small wooden skewer to blend the sauces together by moving the skewer back and forth in a wavy pattern, as shown in Figure 16-9, page 813. Brush a little poaching syrup over a pear (do not brush the stem). Sift powdered sugar over the entire pastry, then set in the center of the decorated plate. Serve at once.

NOTE: This dessert should be served while it is still warm from the oven. It may be served at room temperature but should never be served chilled.

ALMOND FILLING yield: approximately 1 pound 2 ounces (510 g)

6 ounces (170 g) almond paste

8 ounces (225 g) granulated sugar

4 egg whites (½ cup/120 ml)

1. Place the almond paste, granulated sugar, and 1 egg white in a mixer bowl. Combine using the paddle attachment of a mixer or by hand with a spoon.

2. When completely smooth, add the remaining egg whites, 1 at a time, again mixing until smooth after each addition to avoid lumps. The mixture should be fairly thin, almost runny. It is not possible to specify the exact number of egg whites needed, as this varies with the texture of the almond paste.

Fig Tart with Citrus Cream and Port Wine Reduction yield: 12 servings (back cover)

This dessert is one of many that illustrate how easy it can be to transform a slice of cake, a tartlet, or an individual pastry into a plated dessert with an elegant presentation. In this case, the dessert utilizes fresh summer figs. Because several varieties are generally available whenever figs are fresh and plentiful in the marketplace, you may want to use a combination of Black Mission and Dakota figs—which are also simply known as green figs, a reference to the color of their skin, not their flesh—for added visual interest. You could, for example, use one variety on top of the tarts and the other for garnish, as is shown in Photo 68.

Other attractive ways to vary the presentation include using both the reduced poaching syrup as well as Orange Sauce (page 828) and/or using an additional whole fig as part of the garnish placed next to the sliced fig. Try it if you have orange sauce on hand or if you have extra figs; I think it adds a great deal to this already pretty plate.

12 ounces (340 g) Short Dough (page 67)

Lemon-Orange Cream (recipe follows)

20 fresh Dakota or Black Mission figs

Pectin Glaze (page 30) or Mirror Glaze (page 31)

1 cup (240 ml) heavy cream

1 teaspoon (5 g) granulated sugar

Port Wine Reduction (recipe follows)

Piping Chocolate, melted (page 465)

Orange Sauce (page 828), optional

1. Roll out the short dough to ⅛ inch (3 mm) thick. Use it to line 6 fluted tartlet forms that measure 4½ inches (11.2 cm) in diameter and ¾ inch (2 cm) in height.

2. Place a small square of commercial-grade plastic wrap inside each shell and then fill the shells with dried beans or pie weights. Gather the plastic in the center and press it together (see Figure 7-1, page 325). Bake the shells at 375°F (190°C) until light golden but not brown around the edges (see Note). Remove the plastic pouches and save to use another time. Let the shells cool to room temperature.

3. Divide the lemon-orange cream evenly between the shells and bake at 375°F (190°C) for 10 minutes or until the filling just starts to set. The filling will not be firm at this point but will set further as it cools. Allow the tartlets to cool completely.

4. Remove the tarts from the forms. Select the 12 best-looking figs for garnish; set them aside. Cut the remaining figs crosswise into ¼-inch (6-mm) slices and arrange them on top of the filling on each tart. Glaze with pectin glaze or mirror glaze; let stand at room temperature, if using pectin glaze, or chill if using mirror glaze, until the glaze sets.

5. To slice each tartlet in half, use a serrated knife dipped in hot water; using a sawing motion, carefully cut through the top of the short dough crust and the sliced figs, then push the knife straight down.

6. Whip the heavy cream and the sugar to stiff peaks. Place in a pastry bag with a small Saint-Honoré pastry tip. Reserve in the refrigerator. Place the port wine reduction in a piping bottle; reserve. If using the optional orange sauce, as described in the introduction, place it in a second piping bottle and set aside with the reduction. Place a small portion of piping chocolate in a piping bag and cut a small opening. Pipe a curved design with 4 loops on the lower (front) area of a dessert plate. If space permits, you can pipe the chocolate on as many plates as you anticipate needing for service; set the plates aside.

7. Presentation: Place a fig tart opposite the piped design on the back portion of a prepared plate securing it with a dab of whipped cream. Pipe a whipped cream design between the tart and the chocolate design. Cut 1 reserved fig crosswise into slices; fan them out and place next to the cream. Fill the piped chocolate loops with port wine reduction (and orange sauce, if using).

NOTE: If you are blind-baking the shells in a rack oven (rather than directly on the hearth of a deck oven), place the pan as close as possible to the bottom of the oven. If you are not able to do so, you may need to remove the bean pouches halfway through prebaking to ensure that the short dough is evenly baked through.

CHEF'S TIP
If you are preparing other fig desserts and happen to have syrup left over from poaching either Black Mission or Brown Turkey figs, you can use that instead of making the port wine reduction. Reduce about 1 cup (240 ml) leftover syrup until it is thick enough to coat a spoon; you will have a great-tasting decorating syrup with a stunning blue-violet color.

LEMON-ORANGE CREAM yield: 2 cups (480 ml)

¾ cup (180 ml) lemon juice

¼ cup (60 ml) orange juice (see Note)

Finely grated zest of 2 lemons

Finely grated zest of 1 orange

2 teaspoons (6 g) cornstarch

6 ounces (170 g) granulated sugar

3 eggs

1 ounce (30 g) unsalted butter

¼ cup (60 ml) heavy cream

1. Combine the lemon juice, orange juice, lemon zest, and orange zest. Set aside.

2. In a heavy nonreactive saucepan, mix the cornstarch into the sugar. Add the eggs and whisk the mixture for a few seconds just to combine. Add the juice and zest mixture, then the butter and heavy cream.

3. Bring to the scalding point over medium heat, stirring constantly; do not boil. Strain immediately through a fine-meshed sieve.

4. Use the cream hot, as directed in individual recipes, or let cool and store, covered, in the refrigerator. The filling can be refrigerated for up to for 2 weeks.

NOTE: If you would like the filling to be a little more tangy, eliminate the orange juice and zest and increase the lemon juice and zest by the same amounts. This will produce a lemon cream, so you should change the title of the recipe if necessary.

PORT WINE REDUCTION yield: approximately ¹⁄₂ cup (120 ml)

1¹⁄₂ cups (360 ml) ruby port wine

1. Bring the wine to a boil in a heavy nonreactive saucepan. Lower the heat and simmer until the wine is reduced by approximately two-thirds, or until thickened.

2. Because you cannot determine its final consistency before the syrup has cooled completely, check by removing the syrup from the heat and placing a small amount in the refrigerator. If necessary, put the remaining syrup back on the stove and reduce further.

Florentina Cones with Seasonal Fruit yield: 16 servings (Photo 82)

This colorful dessert is an excellent choice when you need to do most of the work ahead and you want a minimum of last-minute finishing touches to worry about at serving time. You can pipe the Bavarian cream into the cones and set them aside in the refrigerator for up to four hours. With the sauces and the fruit mixture ready, the final assembly and presentation will go quickly.

For a vibrant presentation, use four or five kinds of fruit. Cut the fruit into raspberry-sized chunks. If you use peaches or apricots, leave the skin on. Take care to make nice uniform cuts rather than just chopping the fruit up. Do not use apples or pears unless they have been poached. Apricots, peaches, blueberries, raspberries, and strawberries work well. Add either kiwi or honeydew melon for contrasting color. Leave the varieties separate, waiting to combine them until serving, to protect the fruits from bleeding and staining each other.

1 recipe Florentina Batter (page 306)

1 pound 6 ounces (625 g) or ²⁄₃ recipe Quick Bavarian Cream (page 846)

¹⁄₂ cup (120 ml) heavy cream, whipped to stiff peaks

2 recipes Bitter Orange Sauce (page 828)

2 pounds 8 ounces (1 kg 135 g) prepared fresh fruit, approximately

Strawberry Sauce (page 832) or Raspberry Sauce (page 830)

Sour Cream Mixture for Piping (page 832)

I. Make the Florentina batter; pour it into a bowl and refrigerate. If you have a No. 2452 Flexipan (the indentations are approximately 5¹⁄₂ inches/13.7 cm), follow the directions for making the cookie shells on page 307. If not, proceed as follows.

2. Make a template by drawing 9 circles, 5¹⁄₂ inches (13.7 cm) in diameter, on sheet of baking paper with a black marking pen. Space the circles evenly and arrange them in a staggered pattern. The template can be reused many times.

3. Place a second sheet of baking paper on top of your template; tape the edges to the table if necessary to keep the papers from sliding.

4. Divide the chilled and thickened Florentina batter into 2 equal pieces. Using a small amount of flour if necessary to keep the dough from sticking to your hands and the table, roll out each piece into a rope, then cut each rope into 9 equal pieces.

5. Place 9 of the small slices inside the circles on the baking paper set over the template. Press each piece with your fingers to flatten it and bring it to ½ inch (1.2 cm) from the edge of the drawn circle. Remove the paper from the template and place it, with the flattened slices, on a perfectly flat sheet pan.

6. Place a new sheet of baking paper over your template and repeat Step 5 with the remaining 9 slices of Florentina dough. This will give you 2 extra cookies in case of breakage.

7. Bake 1 sheet pan of Florentinas at a time at 350°F (175°C) for approximately 10 minutes or until they are golden brown.

8. Transfer the baking paper with the baked cookies on it to a piece of cardboard or an even tabletop. Use a 5½-inch (13.7-cm) cookie cutter to cut out the center of the cookie to the correct size. Pull the baking paper back on the pan, let the cookies cool, then break off the excess from the outside (see Figure 6-15, page 306).

9. Reheat the trimmed cookies until they are soft enough to bend. Immediately form them into cones by wrapping them, top-side out, around a cone-shaped object. Press the edges together where they meet so the cone will hold together (Figure 13-20). If you do not have an appropriate form, you can make one by cutting it out of Styrofoam and covering it with aluminum foil. The cone should be about 4 inches (10 cm) long and 2½ inches (6.2 cm) across at the base. If the cookies become too firm to bend easily, just reheat them. Reserve the finished cones, covered, in a dry place. They can be kept for several days at this point.

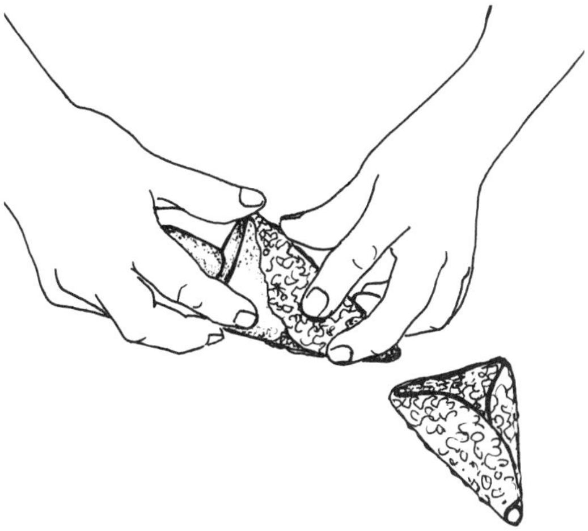

FIGURE 13-20 **Wrapping a soft Florentina cookie around a cone-shaped object and pressing the edges together where they overlap**

10. Place the Bavarian cream in a pastry bag with a No. 5 (10-mm) star tip. Fill as many cones as you expect to serve within a few hours halfway with the filling. Place the filled cones and any remaining Bavarian cream in the refrigerator. Place the whipped cream in a pastry bag with a No. 4 (8-mm) star tip. Reserve in the refrigerator. Place a portion of the orange sauce in a piping bottle and reserve.

11. Presentation: Pipe a rosette of whipped cream in the center of a dessert plate. Pipe bitter orange sauce on the lower part of the plate. Combine about ½ cup (120 ml) fruit mixture. Hold 1 filled cone vertically and fill with the fruit on top of the Bavarian cream. Gently place the cone on its side on the whipped cream rosette with the wide end in the orange sauce. Part of the fruit should fall out onto the orange sauce naturally. Decorate the sauce with strawberry or raspberry sauce and the sour cream mixture (see pages 809 to 814). Serve immediately.

Fresh Peaches in Puff Pastry yield: 12 servings

There are few combinations I can think of creating in my kitchen that are as natural together as fresh ripe peaches, buttery puff pastry, rich caramel sauce, and cinnamon—especially when the cinnamon flavor comes in the form of cinnamon ice cream, as it does here. Nectarines work just as well as peaches for this dessert, although you should try to avoid the larger size and, because most nectarines are clingstone, a different technique is required to remove the pits. Cut the nectarines in half crosswise (at a 90-degree angle to the fruit seam), cutting down to the pit all around. Twist the halves apart carefully, then remove the pit. Fill the cavity with the amaretto filling, reassemble the two halves, and continue as directed for using fresh peaches.

12 medium freestone peaches, ripe	1 recipe Fortified Caramel Sauce (page 821)
2 pounds 8 ounces (1 kg 135 g) Puff Pastry (page 74)	Sour Cream Mixture for Piping (page 832)
	Strawberry Sauce (page 832)
Amaretto Filling (recipe follows)	Powdered sugar
Egg wash	Cinnamon Ice Cream (page 720)
Cinnamon sugar	

1. Remove the peach pits by using a ¾-inch (2-cm) plain cookie cutter to cut a hole down from the stem end of each peach to the pit, then use a paring knife to remove it.

2. Cut the puff pastry dough in half. Roll each piece into a rectangle measuring 14 x 20 inches (35 x 50 cm) in 2 or 3 phases, alternating the pieces and letting 1 piece rest in the refrigerator as you work on the other. Refrigerate both finished pieces for 30 minutes to allow the dough to relax and become firm.

3. Make the template shown in Figure 13-26, page 670. The template as shown is the correct size to use in this recipe, but it can be sized up or down if the peaches you are using are particularly large or small. Trace the drawing; cut out 2 templates from thick or corrugated cardboard, making 1 a solid round and cutting the wedges indicated by the dotted lines out of the other.

4. Place the amaretto filling in a pastry bag with a No. 6 (12-mm) plain tip. Set aside.

5. Using the tip of a paring knife and the solid template as a guide, cut out 6 circles from each of the chilled puff pastry sheets for a total of 12 circles. Place the circles back into the refrigerator. Use a ¾-inch (2-cm) fluted cutter to cut 12 cookies from the scrap pieces (refrigerate the scrap pieces before cutting the cookies if the dough seems soft). Also cut out 12 leaves, using a leaf cutter or cutting freehand with the tip of a paring knife. Place the cookies and leaves in the refrigerator. Cover the remaining scrap pieces and reserve for another use.

6. Remove 2 circles at a time from the refrigerator. Place the template with the cutouts on the circles, 1 at a time, and cut out the 4 wedges. Cover the dough scraps and reserve for another use. Brush egg wash over the cross-shaped pieces of dough. Sprinkle cinnamon sugar lightly over the entire surface of 2 peaches, then place a peach in the center of each cross. Pipe amaretto filling into the cavity where the pit was removed in each peach. Bring 2 opposite flaps of the puff pastry dough together and press to secure; you will have to stretch the dough slightly as you do this. Bring the remaining 2 flaps together in the same way. Invert the peaches on a sheet pan lined with baking paper. Repeat to fill and wrap the remaining peaches in the same way. Brush egg wash over the top and sides of each peach, then set a puff pastry cookie on top of each. Attach the leaves next to the cookies on top of the peaches. Brush egg wash over the cookies and the leaves. Refrigerate the peaches (see Note).

7. Approximately 1 hour before the desserts are to be served, bake the peaches at 375°F (190°C) for about 40 minutes or until both the puff pastry and the peaches are baked through. Remove from the oven and reserve in a warm spot.

8. Presentation: Cover the base of a dessert plate with caramel sauce. Pipe a ring of sour cream mixture close to the perimeter of the sauce. Pipe a ring of strawberry sauce ½ inch (1.2 cm) away from the sour cream mixture toward the center of the plate. Blend the sauces together, using a small wooden skewer (see Figure 16-6, page 812). Sift powdered sugar lightly over the top of a baked peach. Place in the center of the plate, securing it to prevent it from sliding by gently pressing it down to the plate. Serve immediately with cinnamon ice cream in a separate bowl.

N O T E : The wrapped peaches should be refrigerated for a minimum of 30 minutes before they are baked. If they are wrapped more than 2 hours in advance of baking, use egg wash only on the inside and to attach the puff pastry cookies and leaves; do not brush egg wash over the outside of the dough. Cover the peaches with plastic wrap in the refrigerator. Brush egg wash over the outside of the peaches just before baking.

AMARETTO FILLING yield: 12 ounces (340 g)

1 ounce (30 g) dry currants

½ cup (120 ml) amaretto liqueur

4 ounces (115 g) almond paste

3 ounces (85 g) blanched almonds, finely ground

½ teaspoon (.75 g) ground cinnamon

2 tablespoons (30 g) granulated sugar

1. Combine the currants and amaretto liqueur in a saucepan. Heat to approximately 120°F (49°C). Remove from the heat and set aside to macerate for at least 30 minutes.

2. Gradually add the currant mixture to the almond paste. Add the ground almonds. Mix the cinnamon and granulated sugar together, then stir into the filling.

Fruit and Coconut Tapioca Pudding Maui yield: 16 servings (Photo 61)

Tapioca pearls must be soaked before cooking. If you buy them at your local grocer, it is best to follow the instructions on the individual packages. If you have access to an Asian market, tapioca can usually be obtained in bulk for less than one-tenth the cost, although the label will usually be in a foreign language.

To prepare the fresh coconut shavings for the garnish, refer to page 875 for instructions on cracking a fresh coconut, then use a vegetable peeler to shave the meat. Do not prepare the shavings too far ahead of service and keep them, covered, in the refrigerator to prevent their drying out.

½ teaspoon (1.25 g) cocoa powder

1 recipe Vanilla Tuile Decorating Paste (page 482)

Green food coloring

Piping Chocolate (page 465), melted

2 medium papayas, preferably Hawaiian rather than Mexican, *or* 2 medium mangoes

1 pineapple, about 4 pounds (1 kg 820 g)

16 finger bananas *or* 4 red bananas

4 star fruit *or* 4 kiwis

Tapioca Pudding (recipe follows)

Fresh coconut shavings

4 ounces (115 g) lightly toasted macadamia nut halves

Seeds of ½ pomegranate

I. Make the templates for the palm trees (Figure 13-21). The templates as shown are the correct size for this recipe. Trace the drawings, creating a frame and handle around each one, then cut the templates out of ¹⁄₁₆-inch (2-mm) cardboard. Combine the cocoa powder with 1 tablespoon (15 ml) tuile paste, stirring until smooth. Place in a piping bag. Color half of the remaining paste pale green. Reserve the plain and the tinted paste separately.

2. Place a Silpat on a flat, even sheet pan. If you do not have Silpats, lightly grease the backs of clean, even sheet pans, coat them with flour, then shake off as much flour as possible. Spread the green tuile paste over the Silpat or sheet pan, flat and even within the template, to make the palm tree crowns (see Figures 10-29 and 10-30, page 482). Bake the crowns at 400°F (205°C) for approximately 6 minutes or until light brown in a few spots. Before they cool completely, transfer the crowns to a sheet pan lined with baking paper and reserve.

3. Using the same procedure as for the crowns, spread the plain tuile paste within the template for the trunk. Do not place more than 5 or 6 on each mat or sheet pan or you will not have enough time to form them. Beginning 1 inch (2.5 cm) from the top, pipe 3 large X shapes of cocoa-colored tuile paste along the length of each trunk. Bake the trunks as directed for the crowns.

4. Leave the pan in the oven and remove the trunks, 1 at a time. Bend the pointed wide base of the trunk back lengthwise 90 degrees or more to allow it to stand upright. You may use a V- or L-shaped form to help you in shaping the trunks and a small, square piece of wood to push against the trunk to aid in forming. Set the trunks aside with the crowns (see Note).

5. To assemble the palm trees, invert the crowns and arrange in a line. Pipe a small dot of melted piping chocolate in the center toward the bottom of a crown. Place an inverted trunk on top and press down lightly to secure. Repeat with the remaining trees. Refrigerate the palm trees for a few minutes to set the chocolate. Do not refrigerate too long or they will soften.

6. Carefully turn the assembled palm trees right-side up. Use piping chocolate to pipe 2 groups of 3 coconuts each in the center of each crown.

7. Prepare the tropical fruit as directed on page 654.

8. Presentation: Spoon tapioca pudding across the center of a dessert plate. Stand a palm tree up in the center of the pudding. Arrange

CHEF'S TIP

As a variation, try substituting unsweetened coconut milk for the half-and-half and large tapioca pearls for the small. Large pearls require longer soaking. Cover the tapioca with water by about 2 inches (5 cm) and let soak overnight. Drain, place in a saucepan, and cover with fresh water to the same level. Bring to a boil and let simmer for 15 to 20 minutes or until the pearls have turned soft and translucent. Drain the water and add the coconut milk.

FIGURE 13-21 The template used to make the palm trees for Fruit and Coconut Tapioca Pudding Maui

tropical fruit around and partially on top of the pudding. Sprinkle fresh coconut shavings, macadamia nuts, and pomegranate seeds on top. Serve immediately.

NOTE: If you use finger bananas, it is not necessary to bend the base of the trunk back to make it stand up. Instead, leave the trunks flat and make a cut halfway through the finger banana. Stand the palm tree upright by sliding the trunk into the cut.

To Prepare the Tropical Fruit

Although dependent on seasonal availability, price, and, perhaps, personal taste, there is now an immense variety of new tropical and subtropical fruits on the market from which to choose. That is not to say that these fruits are newly discovered but that they are now receiving wide retail distribution. It was not long ago that both papaya and kiwi were unavailable or unknown in many markets. Today they are available almost year round, together with pineapple and mangoes. We do not even think of yellow bananas as a tropical fruit any longer, and there are always plenty of citrus varieties to be had. Both finger and red bananas are offered not only in ethnic food stores but in the produce section of the local supermarket as well.

The combination of fruit suggested for this dessert both looks and tastes good together, but feel free to use your imagination. I use pomegranate seeds to add color and a crunchy texture in the fall. When they are not available, small strawberry halves may be used instead. While strawberries are not a true tropical fruit, they do grow on the Hawaiian Islands. Feijoas are a small aromatic fruit with the appearance of a shaved kiwi. The whole fruit is edible, including the dark green skin, and makes a good addition or substitution if desired.

To prepare the tropical fruit:

1. Peel the papaya and cut in half. Remove the seeds and slice lengthwise. If using mango, peel and cut all around down to the stone on the pointed side of the fruit (so you are cutting down to the pointed edge of the flat stone). Insert a small knife into the cut and cut around the stone to remove the half in one piece. Repeat with the other half. Slice the halves crosswise.

2. Peel the pineapple, core, and cut into half circles (see page 913).

3. Peel the finger bananas. Slice in half lengthwise or leave whole. If using red bananas, peel and slice diagonally.

4. Use a vegetable peeler to remove the skin from the five ridges if the starfruit. Slice the fruit across. Remove the skin from the kiwis using a spoon (see Figure 7-6, page 353). Slice crosswise.

TAPIOCA PUDDING yield: 12 servings, 4 ounces (120 ml) each

¾ cup (180 ml) small- or medium-pearl tapioca

2 cups (480 ml) cold water

6 cups (1 L 440 ml) half-and-half

8 ounces (225 g) granulated sugar

4 eggs

1 teaspoon (5 ml) vanilla extract

1. Place the tapioca in a bowl and pour the cold water on top. Set aside to soak for 1 to 2 hours.

2. Strain the tapioca and combine with the half-and-half. Place the mixture in a bowl set over simmering water. Whisk the sugar and eggs together in a separate bowl, just enough to blend. Add this to the tapioca mixture along with the vanilla. Heat, stirring constantly, until the custard thickens, approximately 20 minutes.

3. Remove from the heat, cover, and set aside to cool. Store, covered, in the refrigerator.

NOTE: If you are filling individual forms, pour or spoon into the molds while the pudding is hot.

Italian Cranberry Cheesecake Strudel with Candied Chestnuts and Caramel Sauce yield: 12 servings (Photo 83)

This recipe is not in the low-fat category, but the phyllo crust may allow you to feel a bit more virtuous as you enjoy the creamy, rich filling. The strudel should be served warm or, at the least, room temperature; it should not be served cold. For another tasty presentation, omit the caramel sauce and cranberry coulis and serve the strudel country-style with a scoop of vanilla ice cream or a ladle of crème anglaise.

4 ounces (115 g) granulated sugar

4 ounces (115 g) unsalted butter, at room temperature

8 ounces (225 g) Mascarpone Cheese (page 22), at room temperature

4 egg yolks (⅓ cup 80 ml), at room temperature

6 ounces (170 g) Ricotta Cheese (page 34)

1½ teaspoons (7.5 ml) vanilla extract

2 ounces (55 g) dried cranberries

Grated zest of 1 orange

Grated zest of 1 lemon

4 egg whites (½ cup/120 ml), at room temperature

3 ounces (85 g) cake flour, sifted

4 ounces (115 g) finely ground almonds (almond meal)

12 sheets phyllo dough (see "About Phyllo Dough")

4 ounces (115 g) melted unsalted butter

½ recipe Fortified Caramel Sauce (page 821)

½ recipe Cranberry Coulis (page 821)

1 pound 4 ounces (570 g) Candied Chestnuts (page 8) (about 24 halves)

Powdered sugar

1. Combine one-third of the granulated sugar with the soft butter and mascarpone. Beat until light and fluffy, about 5 minutes. Beat in the egg yolks, 1 at a time. Stir in the ricotta cheese. Add the vanilla, dried cranberries, and grated citrus zests. Set aside.

2. Whip the egg whites at high speed until foamy. Gradually add the remaining sugar and whip to stiff peaks. Fold the reserved cheese mixture into the meringue. Combine the flour and ground almonds, then carefully fold into the filling. Reserve.

3. Unwrap and unroll the phyllo dough. Keep the stack of dough from drying out by covering it with a piece of plastic wrap and a slightly damp (not wet) towel as much as possible while you are working. Cut 3 sheets of baking paper to approximately the same size as the sheets of phyllo dough.

4. Place a baking paper sheet on the table in front of you with a short side closest to you. Place a sheet of phyllo dough on top. Brush the sheet lightly with melted butter. Top with a second phyllo sheet, brush butter on top, and continue until you have a stack of 4 sheets with butter between each layer. Lightly brush the top of the stack with butter.

5. Place one-third of the filling horizontally, starting about 1½ inches (3.7 cm) from the bottom (short) end of the stack and leaving about the same amount of dough uncovered on both sides. Fold the sides in toward the center (Figure 13-22).

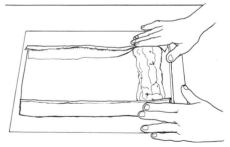

FIGURE 13-22 **Folding the long sides of the phyllo dough in toward the center before enclosing the filling in the dough**

About Phyllo Dough

Phyllo dough, or *fillo* (which, appropriately enough, is the Greek word for "leaf"), has been used in the Mediterranean since ancient times. It is an interesting concept: Paper-thin sheets of pastry are layered with fat to bake up crisp and fragile. The multiple leaves provide a layer structure very similar to puff pastry, but phyllo dough itself is virtually fat-free, making it suitable for the preparation of low-fat or low-cholesterol desserts. Naturally, you must take into consideration the butter that is brushed onto the leaves of dough, but this can be cut down if desired, and vegetable oil can be used if cholesterol is a concern. One option is to spray the melted butter (you must use clarified butter for this) or oil onto the dough instead of using a brush. Some people spray the sheets with a pan coating instead of butter to reduce the fat.

Phyllo sheets vary in size from 12 x 14 inches (30 x 35 cm) to 16 x 18 inches (40 x 45 cm), depending on the brand used. Each 1-pound (455-g) package typically contains about 24 sheets. Frozen phyllo dough must be allowed to defrost slowly in the refrigerator overnight before it is used. If it is thawed too quickly, the thin sheets tend to break.

Roll the stack into a strudel shape by picking up the short end of the baking paper next to the filling and, using your hands to guide the dough, gently fold it over 4 times (Figure 13-23). If necessary, turn the strudel so that the seam is underneath. Leaving the strudel in place on the baking paper, pick up the paper and place the strudel on a sheet pan. Brush butter over the top and sides.

6. Repeat Steps 4 and 5 twice to form 2 more strudels with the remaining dough, filling, and butter.

7. Use a serrated knife to score the dough on top of each strudel diagonally, marking 4 servings. This will make it possible to cut cleanly through the dough after baking.

8. Bake at 375°F (190°C) for approximately 25 minutes or until golden brown. Let cool for 10 to 15 minutes. Cut into serving pieces at the scored lines, using a serrated knife with a sawing motion until you cut through to the filling all around, then cut straight down. Reserve at room temperature for up to 1 hour or refrigerate until needed.

9. Place the caramel sauce and cranberry coulis in separate piping bottles. The sauces should be thick enough to allow you to pipe them out without running or changing shape more than slightly.

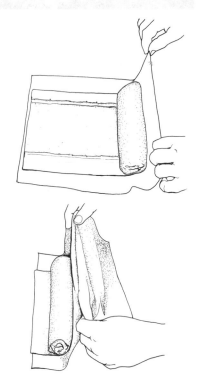

FIGURE 13-23 **Using the baking paper underneath to lift and roll the phyllo dough and filling into a spiral**

10. Slice the candied chestnuts into small chunks, 4 from each half.

11. Presentation: Warm a serving of strudel if necessary. Sift powdered sugar over the slice. Pipe a small dot of caramel sauce in the center of the plate to keep the strudel from sliding and set the slice on top. Pipe 6 small pools of caramel sauce around the dessert on the base of the plate. Pipe a dot of cranberry coulis in the center of each caramel sauce pool. Use a small wooden skewer to swirl the sauces together (see Photo 83). Arrange approximately 6 to 8 chestnut pieces evenly around the plate between the sauce pools. Serve immediately.

Mint-Scented Chocolate Silk Cake yield 16 servings (Photo 32)

This hybrid belongs to the large family of flourless chocolate cakes. These cakes are often given names such as Velvet Cake, Decadence Cake, and, as in this recipe, Silk Cake. All are references to the luxurious smooth texture and the rich chocolate flavor. The absence of flour in the batter eliminates the gluten that would make the texture tough rather than smooth and would take away the desirable melt-in-your-mouth feel.

Finely ground almonds, also known as *almond meal*, are used as a substitute for flour. The almonds add flavor and stability to the cake without compromising the texture. If you prefer a flavoring other than mint, you can very easily modify this recipe by replacing the crème de menthe and water with orange liqueur, rum, or another spirit. Of course, if you do so, change the name of the desert and the accompanying syrup and sauces accordingly.

Mint-Chocolate Silk Cakes (recipe follows)	1 pound (455 g) fresh raspberries
Chocolate-Mint Glaze (page 516)	16 Tuile Screens (recipe follows)
½ recipe Mint Decorating Syrup (page 835)	16 chocolate fans *or* Chocolate Figurines (page 461)
½ recipe Raspberry Sauce (page 830)	16 small edible leaves, such as fig leaves or mint leaves
1 cup (240 ml) heavy cream	
1 teaspoon (5 g) granulated sugar	Powdered sugar

1. Unmold the baked chocolate silk cakes and place them, crust-side down, on an aspic or cake cooling rack, allowing plenty of room between them. Set the rack on a sheet pan and pour or pipe the chocolate-mint glaze over the cakes. Make sure the glaze runs down the sides and covers each cake completely; if necessary, adjust the consistency of the glaze for an even coat.

2. Wait until the glaze has formed a skin, then carefully remove the cakes from the rack, using a palette knife. Set the cakes aside at room temperature until serving time (see Note).

3. Adjust the consistency of the mint syrup and the raspberry sauce as needed, then place them in separate piping bottles; reserve at room temperature. Whip the heavy cream with the sugar to stiff peaks and place in a piping bag with a No. 7 (14-mm) tip; reserve in the refrigerator.

4. Presentation: Pipe a rosette of whipped cream in the center of one silk cake. (If the glaze on the cake has lost its gloss, carefully warm with a torch first; this will definitely be necessary if the cakes have been refrigerated.) Place raspberries around the top perimeter of the cake; transfer to the center of a serving plate. Place a Tuile Screen directly behind the cake. Pipe mint syrup in a narrow uneven curved band in front of the cake parallel to the rim of the plate. Pipe dots of raspberry sauce in gradually decreasing size from left to right behind the mint syrup. Decorate the top of the cake with a chocolate fan or Chocolate Figurine and a small edible leaf, such as a fig leaf or mint sprig. Sift powdered sugar lightly over the dessert and the front portion of the plate.

NOTE: Before plating and decorating, the glazed cakes can be left at room temperature for up to 4 hours; they taste best at that temperature. If necessary, they can be stored, covered, in the refrigerator for a few days.

MINT-CHOCOLATE SILK CAKES yield: 16 cakes, 3 inches (7.5 cm) in diameter

Melted unsalted butter

6 ounces (170 g) unsweetened chocolate

12 ounces (340 g) sweet dark chocolate

¼ cup (60 ml) crème de menthe

½ cup (120 ml) water

12 ounces (340 g) granulated sugar

12 ounces (340 g) melted unsalted butter

8 eggs

10 ounces (285 g) blanched almonds, finely ground

1. Cut out 16 squares of aluminum foil measuring 6½ inches (16.2 cm). Set a cake ring, 3 inches (7.5 cm) in diameter and 2 inches (5 cm) tall in the center of each square. Fold and pleat the edges of the foil up around the rings to make a tight seal. Because the cakes will be baked in a water bath, be certain that the foil reaches at least three-quarters of the way up the side of the rings. Brush melted butter inside the rings and over the bottom of the foil inside. Place the foil-covered rings on an even sheet pan or inside flat, even hotel pans. Set aside. To use a Flexipan, see "Directions for Using a Flexipan."

2. Cut the unsweetened and sweet chocolate into small pieces. In an oversized pan, bring the crème de menthe, water, and 8 ounces (225 g) sugar to the scalding point. Remove from the heat and stir in the chocolate, mixing until all of the pieces are melted and thoroughly incorporated. Gradually add the butter, stirring until completely smooth. Set aside at room temperature.

3. Whip the eggs and the remaining 4 ounces (115 g) sugar at high speed until light and fluffy, about 3 minutes. Do not incorporate too much air or the finished cakes will be crumbly and difficult to work with. Gently fold the melted chocolate mixture into the egg mixture. Fold in the ground almonds.

4. Pour the batter into the prepared cake rings, dividing it evenly among them. Pour enough hot water into the pan around the rings to reach about ½ inch (6 mm) up the sides.

5. Bake immediately at 350°F (175°C) for approximately 30 minutes or until the tops of the cakes feel firm. Allow to cool slightly then refrigerate for at least 1 hour or, preferably, overnight before glazing.

Directions for Using a Flexipan

The cakes can alternatively be baked in Flexipan No. 1897, in which case skip Step 1 and simply place the Flexipan on a flat, even sheet pan. Divide the filling evenly among the 16 indentations and place the pan in the oven. Add hot water to the sheet pan under the Flexipan to fill the sheet pan halfway. Bake as directed. Take care not to spill the water as you remove the pan from the oven. Allow the pans to cool a bit, then tilt the sheet pan to pour out as much of the water as possible without disturbing the structure of the cakes. After the cakes have cooled completely, transfer the Flexipan to another sheet pan and place in the freezer. To unmold the cakes, turn the indentations of the Flexipan inside out. Let the cakes thaw completely before glazing or serving.

TUILE SCREENS yield: 18 to 20

½ recipe Vanilla Tuile Decorating Paste
(page 482)

1 teaspoon (2.5 g) unsweetened cocoa powder

I. Trace the drawing in Figure 13-24 then cut the template out of cardboard that is ¹⁄₁₆ inch (2 mm) thick. The template as shown is the correct size to make these decorations, however, because of its size, the template is shown cut in half. Trace one half, match the dotted lines in the center, and then trace the other half.

FIGURE 13-24 **The
template used as a
guide when forming
Tuile Screens**

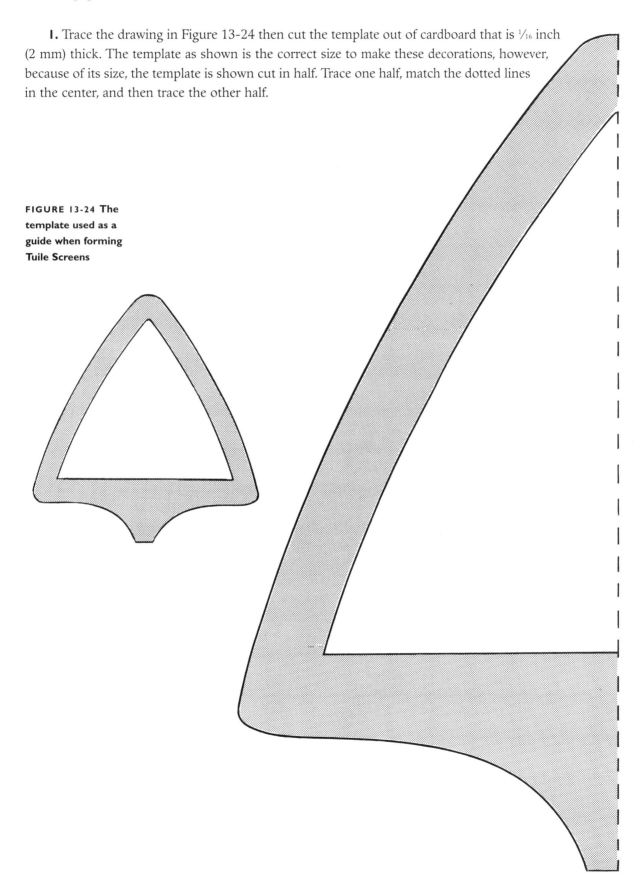

2. If you do not have Silpats, grease the back of flat, even sheet pans, coat with flour, and shake off as much flour as possible.

3. Add the cocoa powder to 2 tablespoons (30 ml) tuile paste and stir until well blended. Cover and set aside. Have ready a rolling pin or 1 to 2 wine bottles to use in shaping the decorations. Attach them to a sheet pan with a small piece of leftover dough or almond paste, or use a damp towel to keep them from rolling.

4. Spread tuile paste onto the Silpat or sheet pan, spreading it flat and even within the template as shown in Figures 10-29 and 10-30, page 482. Do not place more than 6 decorations per pan. Place a portion of the cocoa-colored tuile paste in a piping bag and cut a small opening. Pipe dots of cocoa tuile paste, evenly spaced, along the curved edges of the screens.

5. Bake 1 pan of decorations at a time at 400°F (205°C) for approximately 6 minutes or until the screens start to turn golden brown. Remove the pan from the oven and immediately drape each screen lengthwise, dotted side down, over a rolling pin or wine bottle. Store the decoration in an airtight container; they will remain crisp for 2 to 3 days.

Pavlova yield: 1 dessert, 10 inches (25 cm) in diameter, or 12 individual servings approximately 3½ inches (8.7 cm) in diameter (Photo 81)

While there is a great controversy as to whether Australia or New Zealand invented the Pavlova, one thing is known for certain: The famous Russian ballerina Anna Pavlova never tasted the creation subsequent to its being "officially" named for her, as that occurred three years after her death.

In 1934, Mrs. Elizabeth Paxton, owner of the Hotel Esplanade, where Anna had stayed during her Australian tour, asked her chef, Bert Sachse, to create a new dessert for afternoon tea. The story goes that Chef Sachse spent a month creating the new dessert and, when it was first presented, either Mrs. Paxton or the hotel manager was said to exclaim, "it is as light as Pavlova!" and the name was set.

The controversy as to who really created the Pavlova stems from the fact that a recipe for a very similar dessert with practically the same name—Pavlova Cakes—had previously been published in New Zealand in 1929, the year of Anna Pavlova's Australian tour. The only difference was that Pavlova Cakes were made as individual servings, while Chef Sachse's dessert served several guests. In a diplomatic effort, the following recipe makes both the individual New Zealand version and the larger one created by Chef Sachse.

A properly prepared Pavlova features crisp meringue on the outside and a soft, chewy, marshmallow-like center. The vinegar and cornstarch both contribute to this effect, but it is also important that the meringue is refrigerated for several hours after being topped with the whipped cream to ensure the correct texture. While strawberries and kiwis are the classic choices for Pavlova, don't let this stop you from using any ripe seasonal berry or stone fruit, especially if you are making the large version.

4 egg whites (½ cup/120 ml)

Several drops lemon juice

8 ounces (225 g) granulated sugar

1 ounce (30 g) cornstarch

1 teaspoon (5 ml) white vinegar

1¼ cups (300 ml) heavy cream

1 teaspoon (5 g) granulated sugar

½ teaspoon (2.5 ml) vanilla extract

Strawberries, kiwis, and/or other seasonal fruit and berries

Pectin Glaze (page 30) or Red Currant Glaze (page 33), optional

Mint sprigs

Powdered sugar

FOR INDIVIDUAL SERVINGS

½ recipe Orange–Vanilla Bean Decorating Syrup (page 829)

12 Wavy Tuile Strips (page 632)

1. Draw a circle, 10 inches (25 cm) in diameter—or, for individual servings, 12 circles, 3½ inches (8.7 cm) in diameter—on a sheet of baking paper. Invert and place on a sheet pan.

2. In a stainless steel or copper bowl, whip the egg whites with the lemon juice until the mixture has increased 3 to 4 times in volume. Stir approximately 2 ounces (55 g) granulated sugar into the cornstarch and set aside. Gradually incorporate the remainder of the 8-ounce (225-g) measurement of sugar into the egg whites while whipping; continue to whip until stiff peaks form. Lower the mixer speed and add the cornstarch mixture and the vinegar.

3. Spread the meringue within the large circle. It should be about 1 inch (2.5 cm) thick, so you may not need to use the full amount. For the individual shells, place a portion of the meringue in a pastry bag with a No. 8 (16-mm) plain tip. Pipe the meringue, following the inside perimeter of each of the drawn circles. Spoon the remaining meringue within the piped rings and spread it out evenly. Use the back of a wet spoon to shape the meringue (either the large circle or the individual shells) so that the circle(s) are slightly concave.

4. Bake at 210° to 220°F (99° to 104°C), approximately 1 hour and 15 minutes for the large circle and about 1 hour for the individual circles. The meringue should feel crisp and dry; however, be careful not to overbake—if anything, it is preferable to have it a little soft in the center.

5. A minimum of 3 to 4 hours before serving, whip the heavy cream with the remaining 1 teaspoon (5 g) sugar and the vanilla to stiff peaks.

6. Spread the cream over the center of the Pavlova; use all of the cream for the large ring or about ⅓ cup (80 ml) per individual serving. Cover the Pavlova(s) loosely with plastic and place in the refrigerator (see Note). If, for practical reasons, you must finish assembling the dessert(s) before refrigerating, brush pectin or red currant glaze over the fruit to keep it looking fresh.

7. Presentation for the large Pavlova: Place the cream-topped shell on an appropriate serving platter. Arrange the fruit and berries on top of the cream in a decorative manner. Garnish with mint sprigs. Sift powdered sugar lightly over the top and present whole. Serve in wedges.

8. Presentation for the individual servings: Arrange fruit and berries on top of the cream within the shell on each serving. Peel 6 additional kiwis (see page 353) and cut crosswise into very thin slices. Place a dab of whipped cream in the center of a dessert plate and set a decorated Pavlova on top. Arrange 4 or 5 overlapping kiwi slices on the plate to the right of the dessert. Pipe dots of orange syrup, in decreasing sizes, on the opposite side of the plate. Lean a Wavy Tuile Strip against the dessert, decorate with a sprig of mint, and serve.

NOTE: If you do not mind that all of the meringue will be crisp, you can skip the refrigerating step. However, the dessert tastes best when the meringue around the edge is crisp and the center is soft and chewy; refrigerating the shell(s) with the cream produces this effect.

Pears Belle Hélène yield:16 servings (Photo 84)

In classic French cooking, a savory dish proclaimed *Belle Hélène*, or Hélène style, always includes asparagus and truffles in some form. As you might expect, the truffles and asparagus have been left out in the dessert interpretations, of which Poire Belle Hélène is the most famous. The dish instead consists of a poached pear or pear half—typically French Butter or Anjou—served on a scoop of vanilla ice cream and accompanied by chocolate sauce. I use Bosc pears in my version of this simple and delightful old-timer because of the pear's elegant stretched neck and the long stems that seem to stay on better than other varieties. Be certain that the pears are fully poached not only because the flavor is improved but also because an underpoached pear will be hard and brittle and may break when being prepared for this presentation.

16 Bosc pears, stems attached	1 recipe Chocolate Sauce (page 820)
3 recipes Plain Poaching Syrup (page 31)	½ recipe Crème Anglaise (page 817)
Sponge Cake (page 437) or Joconde Sponge Base (see Note)	1 recipe Vanilla Ice Cream (page 734)

1. Peel the pears and place them in the poaching syrup as they are peeled. Poach the pears in the syrup until they are tender (see page 32). Remove from the heat and set aside to cool in the liquid.

2. Use a 1½-inch (3.7-cm) plain cookie cutter to cut out 16 rounds from the sponge cake. Cover the rounds and reserve.

3. Remove the cooled pears from the syrup and pat as dry as possible. Hold a pear upside down in your hand and make a cut in the center from the bottom about two-thirds of the length to the top. Make a second cut, the same length as the first, at a 90-degree angle. The stem and neck of the pear should remain intact, and the bottom two-thirds should be cut into quarters. Keeping the pear in your cupped hand, carefully use a melon ball cutter to remove the core and, at the same time, hollow out the base of the pear slightly. Repeat with the remaining pears. Pat the pears dry again. Reserve in the refrigerator.

4. Check the consistency of both sauces to be sure they are thick enough to hold their shape when piped; however, they should still level out and create a smooth surface. Place the sauces in piping bottles.

5. Presentation: Place a sponge round in the center of a dessert plate. Pipe chocolate sauce in a circle, 4 inches (10 cm) in diameter, around the sponge. Pipe a ring of crème anglaise, 1 inch (2.5 cm) in diameter, around the chocolate sauce (or to the edge of the base of the plate). Use a wooden skewer to blend the sauces together decoratively where they meet (see Figure 6-11, page 814). Place a scoop of vanilla ice cream on top of the sponge cake. Working quickly, stand a pear on top, arranging the quarters evenly around the ice cream. Pipe chocolate sauce on each quarter of the pear, starting close to the stem and letting it run down into the chocolate sauce pool on the plate. Serve immediately.

NOTE: You need a layer only ⅛ to ¼ inch (3 to 6 mm) thick from a joconde sheet, or a 10-inch (25-cm) sponge cake, either plain or chocolate. If you don't have it on hand, you can make a sheet of joconde sponge or a full cake and save the unused portion for another use. Alternatively, you can make a half-recipe of Roulade Batter (page 403) and spread it into a 12-inch (30-cm) square, in which case you will not have any left over.

Pineapple Fritters with Gingered Pineapple Frozen Yogurt

yield: 12 servings (Photo 80)

This is a very pretty, healthier-than-many dessert that I hope you will try. It is not a good choice for preparing ahead of time because the fritters must be served while they are still warm from frying to taste their best. If you would rather leave out the tulip cups, serve a larger scoop of pineapple yogurt. In that case, set the yogurt scoop on a thin round of sponge cake (see Note, page 662), cut slightly smaller than the scoop size, to keep the yogurt from sliding on the plate. You will still have a very pretty presentation—not quite as elegant, but the important thing is that the shortcut doesn't alter the taste.

2 medium pineapples, approximately 3 pounds 12 ounces (1 kg 705 g) each before trimming

1 recipe Spiced Poaching Syrup (page 31)

Vegetable oil for deep-frying

Bread flour

1 recipe Fritter Batter (page 667)

½ recipe Gingered Pineapple Frozen Yogurt (page 739)

Dark coating chocolate, melted

½ recipe Raspberry Sauce (page 830)

Powdered sugar

12 Miniature Tulips (instructions follow)

1 ounce (30 g) Crystallized Ginger (page 15), approximately, cut into 48 julienne strips

1. Cut the top and bottom off of each pineapple. Trim off the skin, making certain that you remove all of the eyes. Cut the pineapple into ½-inch (1.2-cm) slices, then remove the core, using an appropriately sized plain round cookie cutter. Reserve the trimmings and the core (see recipe, page 665). Cut each pineapple ring in quarters.

2. Poach the pineapple pieces in simmering poaching syrup for about 5 minutes. The pieces should yield easily to pressure. Set aside and let cool in the liquid for at least 30 minutes to infuse. Remove the pieces and drain on paper towels.

3. Heat the oil to 375°F (190°C). Pat the poached pineapple pieces dry if necessary, then coat with bread flour to help the batter adhere. Dip them into the fritter batter and carefully drop them into the oil. Do not add too many pieces at one time or the fat will cool rapidly and the fritters will become greasy and heavy from absorbing the oil. Fry for about 5 minutes or until golden brown, turning the fritters in the oil so that they brown evenly.

4. Remove the fritters with a slotted spoon or skimmer and place them on paper towels to drain. Keep the fritters warm as you fry the remaining pieces.

5. Use a 1½-ounce (45-ml) ice cream scoop (size 20 in the United States) to portion out 12 servings of gingered pineapple frozen yogurt onto a chilled paper-lined sheet pan. Streak fine lines of melted dark coating chocolate in one direction over the scoops. Reserve in the freezer. Place a portion of the raspberry sauce in a piping bottle.

6. Presentation: Pipe a circle of raspberry sauce, 3 inches (7.5 cm) in diameter, in the center of a dessert plate. Dust 4 warm fritters generously with powdered sugar. Arrange them on the plate, evenly spaced around the sauce. Place a scoop of yogurt in a miniature tulip and place this in the center of the sauce. Place a strip of ginger between each of the fritters. Serve immediately.

MINIATURE TULIPS yield: about 40 cookie shells

For a different look, try replacing the dots of cocoa-colored paste with lines piped from the center of the cookie through the center of each flower petal. To save time, the cookies may also be left undecorated.

¼ recipe Vanilla Tuile Decorating Paste
    page 482)

1 teaspoon (5 g) unsweetened cocoa powder

1. Make the template shown in Figure 13-25. The template as shown is the correct size for this recipe. Trace the drawing, then cut the template out of ¹⁄₁₆-inch (2-mm) cardboard (cake boxes work fine for this).

2. If you do not have Silpats, lightly grease the backs of clean, even sheet pans, coat with flour, then shake off as much flour as possible.

FIGURE 13-25 The template
used to form Miniature Tulips

2. Color 2 tablespoons (30 ml) tuile paste with the cocoa powder. Place the cocoa-colored paste in a piping bag. Spread the plain tuile paste onto the Silpats or prepared sheet pans, spreading it flat and even within the template (see Figures 10-29 and 10-30, page 482).

3. Pipe a small dot of the cocoa-colored paste in each petal of the tuile flowers.

4. Bake, 1 pan at a time, at 425°F (219°C) for approximately 5 minutes or until there are a few light brown spots on the cookies.

5. Leave the pan in the oven and remove the cookie shells, 1 at a time. Working quickly, shape them by pressing each cookie gently between 2 small forms, as shown in Figure 6-17, page 308, example on the left. Center the cookie over the form, center a smaller form on top, and press the center of the cookie into the form to make a tiny cup. It is easiest to work with 2 sets of forms at a time. As you finish shaping the second cup, the first should be firm enough to remove and set aside. Repeat to shape the remaining tulips. Reserve until time of service. The cookie shells can be kept for several days at this point if stored in an airtight container at room temperature.

Pineapple Drink

I mentioned to one of my students, who was doing her externship with me and on this particular day was working the pineapple fritters station, that she might need go to the storeroom for more pineapple juice. She indicated that we had plenty, explaining that she had made some from the pineapple skin and core that "you throw out anyway, Chef." She said this with a slightly guilty look of "sorry for not checking with you first" on her face. Well, shame on me! All this time, I had simply discarded the pineapple skin and core. This young lady, from the island of Trinidad, went on to explain that she had been taught never to waste anything, and besides, it gets very hot where she lives and the pineapple skin makes a refreshing drink. Here is her recipe for Pineapple Drink. Thank you, Alana.

I. Wash the pineapple, cut away the skin, and place the peel in a saucepan along with any other trimmings, such as the core. Add enough water to just cover the peel.

2. Bring to a boil and simmer until the liquid is reduced by half. Strain. Adjust by adding sugar or water to taste.

3. Store in the refrigerator and serve chilled. This procedure can be used with other tropical fruits, such as papaya and mango, as well.

About Fritters

The French words *fritter* and *beignet* refer to food, both savory and sweet, that is coated with a batter and deep-fried, either whole or in portions, depending on the item. In Japan, the equivalent is known as *tempura*. In the savory renditions of fritters, various kinds of seafood are most commonly used (fish-and-chips is probably the best-known example, with soft-shell crabs among the more exclusive offerings), but all kinds of vegetables, as well as certain cheeses, are prepared this way as well. In the United States, fritters are often associated with New Orleans, where they are most definitely called *beignets* and where the dessert version is invariably paired with that city's dark, rich café au lait. The most famous spot to enjoy a serving of warm bignets in New Orleans is Café du Monde. Their version is prepared by frying dollops of a rich, thick yeast-leavened batter and topping the small fried cakes with plenty of powdered sugar.

Fruits, and even flowers, fried in a batter coating make an especially delicious and very common sweet, from a simple quarter-inch apple ring sprinkled with cinnamon sugar after frying to fresh cherries, pitted and fried on the stem in pairs or trios. The flowering heads of the elderberry shrub can also be dipped into batter and deep-fried. They should not be washed first because this will remove most of their fragrance. Instead, check them carefully for insects that might lurk inside. The fried clusters of flowers are absolutely spectacular. Served with cream, they are a delicious specialty of the Bavarian region of Germany, where elderberries seem to grow in almost every garden. The pretty white flowers are available only in the beginning of summer, when the shrubs are in full bloom. Elderberry shrubs are also found in the western part of the United States, where the small black berries are used in pies and breads and for making wine and jelly.

Plum Fritters yield: 16 servings

Depending on the time of year and the variety of plums used, you may need to adjust the number, cutting a smaller variety into halves rather than quarters for frying. Conversely, use only a quarter-plum to make each garnish if the plums are large. Be sure to use a sharp knife that will cut through the skin cleanly, allowing you to make thin, elegant slices. Instead of using fanned plums as a decoration, try making a rose out of plum peel, which looks very nice. This is often done in the garde-manger department with tomato peel.

24 medium whole plums	Bread flour
1 recipe Spiced Poaching Syrup (page 31)	Fritter Batter (recipe follows)
1½ recipes Apricot Sauce (page 814)	Cinnamon sugar
Vegetable oil for deep-frying	Powdered sugar

1. Select and reserve 8 good-looking plums for the garnish. Cut the remaining plums into quarters and remove the pits. Poach the plum quarters gently in the poaching syrup for about 5 minutes. They should be soft but not mushy. Remove and set aside to drain on paper towels. Place a portion of the apricot sauce in a piping bottle. Reserve it and the remaining sauce at room temperature.

2. Heat the frying oil to 375°F (190°C). Coat the poached plums with bread flour to help the batter adhere. Dip them into the fritter batter and carefully drop them into the oil. Do not add too many pieces at one time or the fat will cool rapidly and the fritters will become greasy and heavy from absorbing the oil. Fry for about 5 minutes or until golden brown, turning the fritters in the oil so they will color evenly.

3. Remove the fritters with a slotted spoon or skimmer and place them on paper towels or napkins to drain. Sprinkle cinnamon sugar lightly over the fritters and keep them warm as you fry the remaining pieces.

4. Presentation: Cut a reserved plum in half, fan it quickly, and place it in the center of a dessert plate. Pipe apricot sauce to cover the lower half of the base of the plate in front of the plum (be sure the sauce is at room temperature or it will cool off the fritters as they are eaten together). Sift powdered sugar over 4 warm fritters and arrange them on the opposite side of the plate. Serve immediately.

FRITTER BATTER yield: 2¾ cups (660 ml)

5 ounces (140 g) bread flour	Finely grated zest of 1 lemon
½ teaspoon (3 g) salt	1 cup (240 ml) sweet white wine
2 egg yolks	1 teaspoon (5 ml) vanilla extract
4 ounces (115 g) granulated sugar	2 egg whites (¼ cup/60 ml)

I. Sift the flour and salt together.

2. Beat the egg yolks, 2 ounces (55 g) sugar, and the lemon zest just to combine. Add the wine and vanilla. Gradually stir this mixture into the dry ingredients and mix until completely smooth. Refrigerate for about 30 minutes.

3. Just before the batter is to be used, whip the egg whites with the remaining 2 ounces (55 g) sugar until stiff peaks form. Gradually fold the reserved batter into the egg whites. For the best result, the batter should be used within 30 minutes. If you know you will not be able to use all of the batter right away, whip just 1 egg white with 1 ounce (30 g) sugar and add this to half of the reserved batter.

VARIATION
FRITTERS WITH FRESH BLACKBERRY SAUCE

Try this delicious combination when fresh blackberries or any of the hybrids, such as boysenberries and loganberries, are available.

I. Follow the recipe and instructions for Plum Fritters, using fresh peaches or nectarines instead of plums. Cut the fruit into ¾-inch (2-cm) wedges and allow 5 pieces per serving. Substitute Blackberry Sauce (page 830) for the Apricot Sauce.

2. Presentation: Arrange 5 warm fritters in a half-circle on one side of a dessert plate. Pour a small pool of blackberry sauce in front and decorate the sauce with Sour Cream Mixture for Piping (see page 832 for the recipe and pages 809 to 814 for decorating instructions). Serve immediately.

Puff Pastry with Fruit and Champagne Sabayon yield: 16 servings (Photo 64)

It is crucial to use well-made, rested, and chilled puff pastry. The dough should never be cut with a pastry wheel or a dull knife; either will press the layers near the edge together, reducing the dough's ability to expand in the oven. The puff pastry shells, ideally, should be assembled to order. If this is not possible, assemble them no more than 30 minutes ahead or the puff pastry will start to become soggy.

2 pounds (910 g) Puff Pastry (page 74)

Egg wash

2 pounds (910 g) prepared fresh fruit (see page 694)

½ cup (120 ml) orange liquer

Powdered sugar

1½ recipes Cold Sabayon (recipe follows), made with champagne

½ recipe Italian Cream (page 844)

16 mint sprigs

Chocolate Sauce for Piping (page 820)

1. Roll out the puff pastry to a square slightly larger than 14 inches (35 cm); it will be about ¼ inch (6 mm) thick. Refrigerate the dough for 30 minutes to firm and relax it.

2. Trim the edges to make an even 14-inch (35-cm) square. Cover the scraps and reserve for another use. Cut the puff pastry into 16 squares, 3½ inches (8.7 cm) each. Brush the squares with egg wash, being careful not to let any egg wash drip down the sides, which can keep the dough from puffing. Lightly score the tops with parallel lines, marking diagonally in both directions.

3. Place the squares on sheet pans lined with baking paper. Bake at 425°F (219°C) for 12 minutes. Lower the heat to 375°F (190°C) and continue baking until dark golden brown and dried all the way through. Set aside to cool.

4. Cut off the top third of the baked pastry squares. Place the resulting lids next to the bottoms and sift powdered sugar lightly over the lids.

5. Place the Italian cream in a pastry bag with a No. 4 (8-mm) plain tip; refrigerate.

6. Presentation: Pour approximately ⅓ cup (80 ml) sabayon in the center of a dessert plate. Use the back of a spoon to gently shape the sauce into a large, even circle without covering the entire base of the plate. Pipe lines of Italian cream back and forth next to one another on a bottom puff pastry square. Pipe a small dot of cream on the plate next to the sauce circle at the top of the plate. Using approximately ½ cup (120 ml) fruit mixture per serving, arrange a portion of it on the cream on top of the puff pastry. Place the puff pastry square on the plate on top of the dot of cream, arranging it diagonally so that the bottom corner of the square is in the center of the sabayon pool. Drizzle a little additional sabayon over the fruit inside the pastry. Sprinkle additional fruit on the sauce in front of the pastry. Place the lid on top at an angle so you can see the fruit inside. Place a mint sprig so that it sticks out from under the lid. Place the chocolate sauce in a piping bag. Pipe 2 lines of chocolate near the edge of the sauce extending from one edge of the pastry square to the other to form two half-circles. Drag a skewer through the lines toward the edge of the sauce every ½ inch (1.2 cm). Serve immediately.

SABAYON yield: about 4 cups (960 ml)

Sabayon is the French name for the Italian dessert *zabaglione*. To make zabaglione, substitute sweet marsala for the wine and use only 4 ounces (115 g) of sugar.

Used as a sauce, sabayon is the classic companion to many hot soufflés, especially liqueur-flavored soufflés. Sabayon is often poured over fresh strawberries or other fruits, but it can also be served by itself as a light dessert, either plain or garnished with a sprinkling of nutmeg. Make the sabayon as close to serving time as possible; it tends to lose some of its fluffiness and will separate if it stands too long.

6 egg yolks (½ cup/120 ml)

6 ounces (170 g) granulated sugar

1½ cups (360 ml) dry white wine or champagne

Beat the egg yolks and sugar in a stainless steel bowl until light and fluffy. Add the wine or champagne. Place over simmering water and continue to whip constantly until the mixture is hot and thick enough to coat a spoon. Serve hot as soon as possible.

VARIATION

COLD SABAYON

Soften ½ teaspoon (1.5 g) unflavored gelatin powder in 1 tablespoon (15 ml) of the wine or champagne. Stir into the remaining liquid and continue as for hot sabayon, removing the mixture from the heat and placing over ice water once the mixture has thickened. Whip slowly until cold. Refrigerate no longer than 30 minutes. Adjust the consistency by adding more wine or champagne as needed, depending on use.

Queen's Apple yield: 12 servings (Photo 65)

Queen's Apple is so named because the baked pastry-wrapped apple becomes round on the top with a fairly flat bottom and, when the slits on the sides bake open, it resembles a crown. It is a more elegant presentation than the conventional method of encasing the apples, commonly called apple dumplings, but a bit more time-consuming. You can, of course, skip using the template, cut the rounds of puff pastry using any round guide of the appropriate size, such as a plate, then cut out the wedges free-hand, but you will still have to deal with leftover scrap dough. The dumpling method leaves virtually no scrap pieces and is much easier to make. For this technique, prepare the apples as instructed but use only 2 pounds (910 g) puff pastry. Roll out the dough to a rectangle measuring 18 x 24 inches (45 x 60 cm); it should be approximately ⅛ inch (3 mm) thick. Place the dough on a full sheet of cardboard, or fold in half and place on a large sheet pan, and refrigerate to relax and firm the dough.

Remove from the refrigerator and adjust as needed to make the dough even and the same size as before. Cut the dough into 12 squares, 6 inches (15 cm) each. Follow the instructions in the main recipe for assembling, baking, and serving the apples (except you will not have any cookies to decorate the tops with).

12 medium cooking apples, such as Pippin or Granny Smith

Plain Poaching Syrup (page 31)

2 pounds 8 ounces (1 kg 135 g) Puff Pastry (page 74)

Calvados Apple Filling (recipe follows)

Egg wash

Cinnamon sugar

½ recipe Strawberry Sauce (page 832)

1 recipe Mousseline Sauce (page 827)

Ground cinnamon

Powdered sugar

Vanilla Ice Cream (page 734) or Cinnamon Ice Cream (page 720), optional

1. Peel, core, and poach the apples in the poaching syrup until they give when pressed lightly. Do not overcook the apples at this stage or they will fall apart when they are baked later. Remove the apples from the syrup and set aside to cool.

2. Cut the puff pastry dough in half. In 2 or 3 phases, roll each piece into a rectangle measuring 14 x 20 inches (35 x 50 cm), alternating the pieces and letting 1 piece rest in the refrigerator as you work on the other. Refrigerate both finished pieces for 30 minutes to allow the dough to relax and become firm.

3. Make the template shown in Figure 13-26. The template is the correct size to use in this recipe, but it can be sized up or down if the apples you are using are particularly large or small. Trace the drawing, then cut out 2 templates from thick or corrugated cardboard, making 1 template a solid round and cutting the wedges indicated by the dotted lines out of the other.

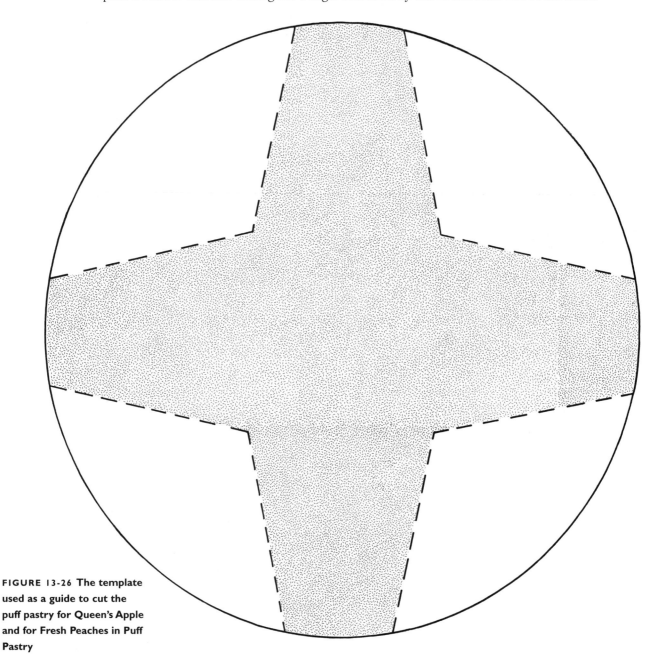

FIGURE 13-26 The template used as a guide to cut the puff pastry for Queen's Apple and for Fresh Peaches in Puff Pastry

4. Place the Calvados apple filling in a pastry bag with a No. 6 (12-mm) plain tip. Set aside.

5. Using the tip of a paring knife and the solid template as a guide, cut out 6 circles from each of the chilled puff pastry sheets for 12 total. Place the circles back into the refrigerator. Use a fluted cookie cutter, about 1¼ inches (3.1 cm) in diameter, to cut 12 cookies from the scrap pieces (refrigerate the scraps before cutting the cookies if the dough seems soft). Place the cookies in the refrigerator. Cover the remaining scrap pieces and reserve for another use.

6. Remove 2 circles at a time from the refrigerator. Place the template with the cutouts on the circles, 1 at a time, and cut out the 4 wedges. Cover the dough scraps and reserve for another use. Brush egg wash over the cross-shaped pieces of dough. Sprinkle cinnamon sugar lightly over the entire surface of 2 apples, then place 1 apple in the center of each cross. Pipe Calvados filling into the cavity where the core was removed in each apple. Bring 2 opposite flaps of the puff pastry dough together and press to secure; you will have to stretch the dough slightly as you do this. Bring the remaining 2 flaps together in the same way. Invert the apples on a sheet pan lined with baking paper. Repeat to fill and wrap the remaining apples in the same way. Brush egg wash over the top and sides of each apple and set a puff pastry cookie on top of each. Brush egg wash over the cookies. Refrigerate the apples (see Note).

7. Approximately 1 hour before the desserts are to be served, bake the apples at 375°F (190°C) for about 40 minutes or until both the puff pastry and the apples are baked through. Remove from the oven and reserve in a warm spot. Fill a piping bottle with strawberry sauce and a second bottle with mousseline sauce.

8. Presentation: Pipe a circle of strawberry sauce, 5 inches (12.5 cm) in diameter, in the center of the base of a dessert plate. Pipe a ring of mousseline sauce, filling in the space between the strawberry sauce and the perimeter of the base of the plate. Using a small, fine mesh strainer, lightly sift ground cinnamon over the mousseline sauce. Sift powdered sugar over a baked apple and set in the center of the strawberry sauce, securing it so it will not slide by gently pressing down to the plate. Serve immediately.

When serving Queen's Apple with vanilla or cinnamon ice cream, omit the mousseline sauce. Place a baked apple in the center of the plate and pipe 3 irregularly shaped pools of strawberry sauce around the apple. Place a small scoop of ice cream between each of the sauce pools.

NOTE: The wrapped apples should be refrigerated for a minimum of 30 minutes before they are baked. If they are wrapped more than 2 hours in advance of baking, use egg wash only on the inside and to attach the puff pastry cookies; do not brush egg wash over the outside of the dough. Cover the apples with plastic wrap in the refrigerator. Brush egg wash over the outside of the apples just before baking.

CALVADOS APPLE FILLING yield: 14 ounces (400 g)

1 ounce (30 g) dry currants	2 ounces (55 g) finely ground hazelnuts
½ cup (120 ml) Calvados	½ teaspoon (.75 g) ground cinnamon
6 ounces (170 g) almond paste	2 tablespoons (30 g) granulated sugar

1. Combine the currants and Calvados in a saucepan and heat to approximately 120°F (49°C). Remove from the heat and set aside to macerate for a minimum of 30 minutes.

2. Gradually, to avoid lumps, combine the currant mixture with the almond paste. Add the ground hazelnuts. Mix the cinnamon and sugar together and stir into the filling.

Red Bananas Foster with Marshmallow and Spice Cake yield: 16 servings (Photo 77)

First off, this is not a recipe for traditional Bananas Foster, but it shares some of the same elements and was inspired by the original. The true Bananas Foster was invented in New Orleans at Brennan's Restaurant in the 1950s. It was named for a regular patron, Richard Foster, whom one would have to assume was quite fond of the preparation. The original dish was (and still is) prepared tableside by the waiter or captain and is most often made for two or more persons. Directions to make the classic version follow this recipe. I added gingerbread spice cake to my banana creation both for contrasting texture and flavor and to reflect the spiciness of New Orleans cuisine. This presentation is also plated in the kitchen, as few restaurants today are able to offer tableside service. The red bananas are a good choice because they are smaller than yellow bananas and fit the plate better, the color is pleasing, and they add an unusual touch; the more common type could certainly be substituted. The color of the flesh of a red banana is actually a deeper yellow than that of a yellow banana. The red and yellow classifications refer to the skin rather than the flesh.

½ recipe Soft Gingerbread Cake batter (page 400)

2 tablespoons (30 ml) dark rum

¼ cup (60 ml) Plain Cake Syrup (page 31)

Rum Decorating Syrup (page 836)

8 red bananas

Granulated sugar

16 Marshmallows (recipe follows)

½ recipe Vanilla Ice Cream (page 734)

16 Red Pepper Sails (recipe follows)

1. Make the gingerbread cake batter and spread it out evenly within a quarter-sheet pan, 12 x 8 inches (30 x 20 cm), lined with baking paper. Bake at 350°F (175°C) for about 30 minutes or until the cake springs back when pressed lightly in the center. Allow the cake to cool completely. If time permits, wrap well after cooling and let the cake sit overnight.

2. Combine the rum and the cake syrup. Unmold the cake and trim both long edges. Cut in half lengthwise to make 2 strips, 4 inches (10 cm) wide. Brush the cake syrup over the strips, then cut each into 2¼-inch (5.6-cm) wedges. Cover the cake wedges and reserve.

3. Pour the rum decorating syrup into a piping bottle and reserve.

4. Presentation: Place a wedge of spice cake on the left side of a dessert plate with the wide end in back. Peel a banana and cut in half lengthwise. Sprinkle granulated sugar over the cut side of one half. Use a torch to caramelize the sugar on the banana and also to toast the top and sides of one of the marshmallow squares. Place the marshmallow on the plate next to the wide end of the spice cake. Top the cake with a scoop of ice cream. Make a small slit in the ice cream using a paring knife and insert a red pepper sail decoration arranging it so it stands straight up. Lean the caramelized banana half at an angle on the cake and the marshmallow. Pipe rum syrup in an irregular curved design on the plate around half of the dessert and serve immediately.

MARSHMALLOWS

yield: 1 quarter-sheet pan (12 × 8 inches/ 30 × 20 cm), approximately ³/₄ inch (2 cm) thick

Cornstarch

3 tablespoons (18 g) unflavored gelatin
    powder

½ cup (120 ml) cold water

1 pound (455 g) granulated sugar

2 ounces (5 g) glucose *or* light corn syrup

½ cup water

4 egg whites (½ cup/120 ml)

1. Prepare a quarter-sheet pan, 12 x 8 inches (30 x 20 cm), or other suitable pan of approximately the same size, by lining the bottom with baking paper and dusting lightly with cornstarch.

2. Sprinkle the gelatin over the first measurement of water (be sure to pour the water in a wide enough bowl so that all of the gelatin will be moist) and set aside to soften.

3. Combine the sugar, glucose or corn syrup, and the second measurement of water in a saucepan. Start cooking the mixture over medium heat.

4. Place the egg whites in a mixer bowl with the whip attachment.

5. Heat the gelatin mixture to dissolve. Reserve, but keep warm.

6. When the sugar has reached 230°F (110°C), start whipping the egg whites at high speed. Watch the sugar syrup closely; it will reach 245°F (118°C) very quickly. When the syrup reaches this temperature, remove it from the heat. Lower the speed of the mixer and gradually, but in a steady stream, pour the sugar syrup into the egg whites, taking care to pour it between the whip and the side of the bowl. Add the reserved gelatin in the same way, making certain all of it is added (use a small spatula or your thumb to scrape out the last bit). Turn the mixer back to high speed. As soon as the meringue has a smooth, light, and fluffy consistency, pour the mixture into the prepared sheet pan and spread out to even the top. The sheet should be about ³/₄ inch (2 cm) thick. Lightly sift cornstarch over the top and set aside to cool completely. (If needed, the cooling process can be accelerated by placing the marshmallows in the refrigerator).

7. The marshmallow sheet can be stored, covered, for 1 week. Use a knife dipped in hot water to cut the marshmallow sheet away from the sheet pan. Invert the sheet and peel off the paper. Brush away the cornstarch and cut into pieces of the desired size, again using a knife dipped into hot water. For the Red Bananas Foster recipe, cut the sheet into 18 rectangles, 2 x 2 ¼ inches (5 x 6.8 cm). For other uses, coat the marshmallows with powdered sugar to prevent them from sticking together.

RED PEPPER SAILS   **yield: variable**

2 medium red bell peppers

Vegetable oil

2 ounces (55 g) powdered sugar, sifted

2 teaspoons (5 g) bread flour

1. Coat the peppers with vegetable oil and place them on a sheet pan. Use a propane torch to blacken the skin, turning the peppers to cook all sides. If you are making more than a single recipe, bake the peppers at 450°F (230°C) until blackened, turning them once or twice. Wrap the peppers in a moist towel or place them in a plastic bag and set aside to cool to room temperature.

2. Peel the peppers and remove the seeds and stems. Puree the roasted pepper flesh in a food processor then force the puree through a fine strainer.

3. Stir the powdered sugar and flour into the puree.

4. Spread the batter out thinly and evenly on Silpats in freeform shapes, approximately 2 × 3 inches (5 × 7.5 cm) each.

5. Bake at 200° to 250°F (94° to 108°C) until the decorations are dry and have started to brown slightly at the edges. Use a thin spatula to remove them from the Silpat as soon as possible and place the decorations on a flat surface to cool; be very careful, they are quite fragile. If desired, the warm decorations can be molded in the same way as tuile paste. Store in airtight containers.

VARIATION
CLASSIC BANANAS FOSTER

INGREDIENTS PER SERVING TO PREPARE TABLESIDE

1 tablespoon (15 g) unsalted butter

2 ounces (55 g) brown sugar

1 tablespoon (15 ml) banana liqueur

1 whole yellow banana, peeled and split lengthwise

2 tablespoon (30 ml) dark rum

2 scoops Vanilla Ice Cream (page 734)

Ground cinnamon

1. Arrange all of the ingredients on a tray, with the ice cream resting on a bed of ice so it will not melt during the preparation.

2. Melt the butter in a sauté pan or the skillet of the guéridon. Add the brown sugar and stir until the sugar is melted. Add the banana liqueur and the cut banana halves, placing them cut-side down in the pan. Cook, shaking the pan, stirring the caramel, and occasionally basting the banana halves with the caramel syrup, until the banana is soft and the sugar-butter mixture has formed a caramel sauce.

3. Pour the rum on top of the bananas; do not stir it in. Let the rum heat for approximately 30 seconds, then ignite with a match or by tilting the skillet to allow the flames from the guéridon to set the rum on fire.

4. Place the ice cream in a serving dish, top with the banana halves, and pour the caramel sauce from the skillet on top. Sprinkle a little ground cinnamon on top and serve immediately.

Rhubarb-Meringue Napoleons yield: 16 servings (Photo 78)

I have wondered lately what the great Carême would make of the current trend in the food industry to borrow the name of his famous dessert and use it for all manner of layered creations. His original pastry was not named Napoleon out of respect for the notorious general but in reference to the Neapolitan way of making sweets and glazes with layers of varying colors and textures. The title does seem to be a good way to indicate that a dish has more than one layer, but I can't help but feel the rationale is being stretched too far when I see a dish of layered vegetables or fish labeled Napoleon of this or that. Perhaps I'm prejudiced, but I feel the name belongs to the original dessert, or at least to the pastry department! Having said all that, my justification for applying it here is that at least I am using it for a dessert containing puff pastry.

1 pound 8 ounces (680 g) Puff Pastry
(page 74)

1 pound 8 ounces (680 g) granulated sugar

2 pounds (910 g) fresh rhubarb stalks

2 cups (480 ml) water

Cornstarch

¼ recipe Italian Meringue (page 27) (see
Note, page 331)

16 small strawberries, stemmed

I. Divide the puff pastry into 2 equal pieces. Roll out each piece in part of the sugar (about one-third of the sugar will be sufficient to work with at this point) to a rectangle measuring 13 x 19 inches (32.5 x 47.5 cm) (see Note). The sheets should be about ⅛ inch (3 mm) thick. As you roll the sheets, sprinkle sugar on top of the dough and turn it over frequently so that the sugar prevents the dough from sticking and, at the same time, is rolled into the puff pastry. Add the leftover rolling sugar to the rest of the sugar.

2. Place the puff pastry sheets on perfectly flat, even, paper-lined sheet pans. Prick the dough well. Refrigerate for at least 30 minutes so the dough can relax.

3. Place a sheet of baking paper on top of each puff pastry sheet. Top each with another flat, even sheet pan to prevent the pastry from puffing too much, which would make it difficult to cut into neat squares. Bake the sheets at 400°F (205°C) for 12 minutes. Remove the top sheet pans and the sheets of baking paper. Continue baking until the sugar in the dough begins to caramelize and the sheets are deep golden brown, approximately 10 minutes longer. Let the sheets cool.

4. Using a serrated knife and a ruler as a guide, trim the edges of the puff pastry sheets as necessary to make them straight and even. Measure and carefully cut each sheet into 24 squares, 3 inches (7.5 cm) each. Set the squares aside. Discard the scrap pieces.

5. Trim the top and bottom of the rhubarb stalks (do not peel them). Cut the stalks into pieces, 3 inches (7.5 cm) long. Cut these pieces lengthwise so they are about ½ inch (1.2 cm) wide. Arrange the pieces in a single layer in a hotel pan or on a half-sheet pan. Sprinkle the reserved sugar over the rhubarb pieces, then pour the water over the sugar. Set the rhubarb aside for about 30 minutes.

6. Cover the rhubarb with foil or with an inverted sheet pan. Bake at 400°F (205°C) for about 8 minutes or until the rhubarb is just soft. (Watch carefully here; rhubarb will go from soft to mushy, then literally disintegrate, in about 1 minute. If this happens, save it to make sauce and start over.) Let the rhubarb cool in the liquid.

7. Remove the rhubarb pieces from the liquid and set them aside. Strain the rhubarb cooking liquid. Thicken it with cornstarch, using 2 teaspoons (5 g) cornstarch per pint (480 ml) liquid. Place a portion of the sauce in a piping bottle and reserve.

8. Reserve the 16 best-looking puff pastry squares to use for the top layers.

9. Place the Italian meringue in a pastry bag with a No. 3 (6-mm) plain tip.

10. Presentation: Arrange 4 or 5 pieces of rhubarb on top of a puff pastry square. Place a second square on top. Pipe meringue back and forth diagonally over the second square, each line

CHEF'S TIP
The napoleons should be assembled to order. If you need to expedite several orders together, the meringue can be piped onto the middle and top layers up to 30 minutes ahead of time, then each dessert can be assembled with the rhubarb as you are ready to serve.

touching the previous one, and also over half of 1 reserved puff pastry square in the same pattern (do not place the top piece on the pastry). Lightly brown the meringue on both pieces by placing them under a salamander or by using a blowtorch very carefully. Pipe a small dot of meringue in the center of a dessert plate. Place the assembled dessert on top. Pipe just enough rhubarb sauce around the napoleon to cover the base of the plate. Place the top puff pastry square leaning against the side of the pastry. Place a strawberry on top of the napoleon.

NOTE: If you increase or decrease the size of this recipe, always roll out the sheet(s) to a size that is slightly larger than a multiple of 3 inches (7.5 cm) so that, after trimming the sheets, you can cut 3-inch (7.5-cm) squares.

Rum Babas yield: 16 servings

This light yeast cake, studded with raisins and soaked in rum syrup, originated in seventeenth-century Poland—where, as the story goes, King Stanislas Leczyinski, finding his gugelhupf too dry, moistened it with syrup. He named his invention Ali Baba after the character in his favorite story, the classic "Thousand and One Nights." When the dessert was later introduced to the West, apparently by a French pâtissier who came across it among members of the Polish court who were visiting France, it became especially popular and was dubbed simply Baba.

The classic baba is baked in a tall cylindrical mold, but the cake is also typically made into individual pastries in timbales about 3 inches (7.5 cm) deep and 1¾ inches (4.5 cm) wide. A variety of other shapes and sizes can also be tried, including the brioche mold used in my version. When the baba dough is baked in a ring mold, the dessert is known as *Savarin*.

Babas are still very popular in France, and it seems they are part of almost every pastry assortment—sumptuous, soaked in rum syrup, glazed with apricot, and decorated with the infamous maraschino cherry. If you like to enjoy a baba handheld on the go, as I often do, be sure to lean forward as you bite into it or the syrup will run down your front, the same as if you were eating a fresh ripe peach.

Butter and Flour Mixture (page 7)
Baba Dough (recipe follows)
Rum Baba Syrup (recipe follows)
Apricot Glaze (page 5)

1 recipe Cold Sabayon (page 669)
1 pound 8 ounces (680 g) fresh cherries (see Note)

1. Brush the butter and flour mixture on the inside of 16 standard-size brioche molds, 3¼ x 1½ inches (8.1 x 3.7 cm). Reserve.

2. Place the baba dough in a pastry bag with a No. 7 (14-mm) plain tip. Pipe the batter into the forms, dividing it evenly; they will be about half full. Let the babas rise until they fill the forms. Make sure they have proofed enough or the baked babas will not be able to absorb enough syrup.

3. Bake at 400°F (205°C) until golden brown and baked through, about 20 minutes. Remove from the forms as soon as possible and let cool.

4. Cut the crust from the top of the babas, making them flat at the same time.

5. Heat the rum baba syrup to scalding and remove from the heat. Place a few babas at a time in the hot syrup. Push them down and let them soak long enough to absorb as much of the syrup as they can. The air bubbles rising to the top of the syrup should disappear completely, indicating that all of the air pockets in the pastries have filled with syrup. (The babas will also increase in size as they absorb the syrup.) The time needed will vary depending on the size of the pastry and whether or not they were proofed correctly. Soaking can take 20 seconds for a small pastry to 1 or 2 minutes for a large, multiple-serving size. To be certain, cut partway into 1 pastry to see if the syrup has soaked all the way through. Carefully remove the babas from the syrup and place them inverted (cut-side down) on a cooling rack set over a sheet pan to drain. Reheat the syrup, if necessary, while you soak the remaining babas.

6. Brush the sides and the top of each baba with apricot glaze. Reserve in the refrigerator until time of service.

7. Presentation: Place a rum baba off-center on a dessert plate. Spoon sabayon over part of the cake and let it flow into a pool on the base of the plate. Place a few fresh cherries next to the sauce. Cut 1 cherry in half to expose the pit (which will let the guest know that the cherries are not pitted).

NOTE: Pick out nice-looking cherries with the stems attached. When cherries are out of season, substitute raspberries.

BABA DOUGH yield: 2 pounds (910 g)

1 tablespoon (15 ml) fresh compressed yeast	½ teaspoon (3 g) salt
½ cup (120 ml) warm whole milk (105° to 115°F/40° to 46°C; see Note, page 210)	6 ounces (170 g) unsalted butter, at room temperature
4 ounces (115 g) bread flour	8 ounces (225 g) cake flour
4 eggs	2 ounces (55 g) dark raisins
1 teaspoon (5 ml) vanilla extract	

1. Dissolve the yeast in the warm milk. Stir in the bread flour and mix until you have a smooth, soft sponge. Let rise, covered, in a warm place until the sponge starts to bubble and fall.

2. Mix the eggs, vanilla, salt, and butter into the sponge. Add the cake flour and mix until it becomes a soft, smooth paste. Incorporate the raisins.

RUM BABA SYRUP yield: 6 cups (1 L 440 ml)

4 cups (960 ml) water	1 unpeeled orange, quartered
1 pound 8 ounces (680 g) granulated sugar	¾ cup (180 ml) light rum

1. Place the water, sugar, and orange pieces in a saucepan. Bring to a boil and cook for about 2 minutes or until all of the sugar has dissolved.

2. Remove from the heat, strain, and add the rum.

Savarin yield: 16 individual pastries, or 2 Savarin rings, 8 to 10 servings each

Savarins are simply babas made in a different shape and without raisins. They are formed as either a large ring-shaped cake serving eight to ten people or as individual doughnut-like pastries. In both cases, the dessert is moistened with maraschino or another cherry-flavored syrup. Savarin is named after the French gourmet and writer Antoine Brillat-Savarin, who, in 1825, just a year before his death, authored *The Physiology of Taste*, which became a classic culinary text.

Butter and Flour Mixture (page 7)

1½ recipes Baba Dough (page 677), made without raisins

Maraschino Syrup (recipe follows)

Apricot Glaze (page 5)

½ cup (120 ml) heavy cream

1 teaspoon (5 g) granulated sugar

1 pound 4 ounces (570 g) fresh red currants (see Note)

1. Brush the butter and flour mixture on the inside of 16 ring molds, 3¼ inches (8.1 cm) in diameter and 1½ inches (3.7 cm) in height, or 2 ring molds, 10 inches (25 cm) in diameter.

2. Place the baba dough in a pastry bag with a No. 7 (14-mm) plain tip. Pipe the dough into the forms, dividing it equally; the forms will be about half full. Let the savarins rise until they have doubled in volume. Do not take a shortcut here. A savarin that has not been left to proof properly will not be able to absorb enough syrup and will be dense and unpleasant to eat.

3. Bake at 400°F (205°C) until golden brown and baked through, about 20 minutes (40 minutes for the larger size). Remove from the forms as soon as possible and cool on a rack.

4. Cut the crust from the top of the savarins, making them flat at the same time.

5. Heat the maraschino syrup to scalding and remove from the heat. Place a few savarins at a time in the hot syrup, push them down into the syrup, and let them soak long enough to absorb as much of the syrup as they can before carefully removing them (see Step 5 in the Rum Baba recipe, page 676). Place them, cut-side down, on a cooling rack set over a sheet pan to drain. Reheat the syrup, if necessary, while you soak the remaining savarins. (If you are making the larger savarin, place it directly on the cooling rack after trimming the crust and spoon the hot syrup evenly over the top until you are sure it has penetrated all the way through. Let the savarin drain, then use 2 metal spatulas to carefully place it on a serving platter.) Strain the remaining syrup through cheesecloth. Place a portion of the syrup in a piping bottle and reserve for the presentation. Brush apricot glaze over the top and sides of both the large and individual-size savarins.

6. Whip the heavy cream and sugar to stiff peaks. Place in a pastry bag with a No. 7 (14-mm) star tip. Reserve in the refrigerator.

7. Presentation: Place an individual savarin, flat-side down, slightly off-center on a dessert plate. Pipe a rosette of whipped cream on the plate next to the pastry. Fill the center of the savarin with loose red currants and decorate the cream with one of the reserved clusters of berries. Pipe a small amount of syrup on top of the savarin and onto the plate. Serve the large-size ring from the serving tray in the dining room or at the buffet table, cutting 8 to 10 portions from each ring, spooning currants in front of the slice on each plate and adding whipped cream and reserved syrup.

NOTE: Reserve 16 attractive clusters of red currants on the stem to use in the presentation. Remove the stems from the remainder and reserve the individual currants separately. If red currants are unavailable, try using wild strawberries or other small berries instead.

MARASCHINO SYRUP yield: 6 cups (1 L 440 ml)

4 cups (960 ml) water

1 pound 8 ounces (680 g) granulated sugar

1 unpeeled orange, quartered

¾ cup (180 ml) maraschino liqueur

1. Place the water, sugar, and orange pieces in a saucepan. Bring to a boil and cook for about 2 minutes or until all of the sugar has dissolved.

2. Remove from the heat, strain, and add the maraschino liqueur.

Small Pear Tartlets with Caramel Sauce yield: 12 to 16 servings (Photo 76)

There are many ways to make and present these tarts, which have the unbeatable flavor combination of crisp, flaky puff pastry, creamy almond filling, and refreshing poached pear, plus a rich caramel sauce that tastes like liquid candy. As if that were not enough, serving the tarts with ice cream really brings on the accolades! The three versions presented here all stand out in their own way. Both the round and pear-shaped patterns lend themselves to elegant presentations. The drawbacks are that these take longer to cut out if you do not have an appropriate cutter, and you end up with fewer tarts and a lot more scrap pieces of dough left over. The latter is no problem, provided you have a use for the scraps. If not, or if you need to make a large quantity of tarts, you will appreciate the simplicity and speed of the rectangular version, which leaves close to zero scraps. Small Pear Tartlets make a practical banquet dessert because they can be made ahead and baked just before serving, but they should be served warm.

6 small to medium pears (see Step 1)

1 recipe Spiced Poaching Syrup (page 31)

2 pounds 12 ounces (1 kg 250 g) or Small-Batch Puff Pastry (page 74)

5 ounces (140 g) Pastry Cream (page 845)

4 ounces (115 g) almond paste

Cinnamon sugar

Apricot Glaze (page 5)

1 to 1½ recipes Fortified Caramel Sauce (page 821), at room temperature

Chocolate Sauce (page 820)

Sour Cream Mixture for Piping (page 832)

Raspberry Sauce (page 830)

12 or 16 fresh edible flowers

1. Ideally, use French Butter or Anjou pears. If the pears are too large, try to peel them to size or use the round tart presentation. If using the pear-shaped presentation, choose pears that have the stem intact. Use a vegetable peeler to peel the pears, then cut them in half lengthwise, leaving the stem intact on 1 pear half. Place the pears in acidulated water as you work to prevent them from browning.

2. Poach the pear halves in poaching syrup until soft. Take care not to overcook or they will become difficult to work with. If time permits, allow the pears to cool in the syrup.

PEAR-SHAPED TARTS yield: 12 servings

1. Make the solid pear-shaped template (Figure 13-27). The template as shown is the correct size for use in this recipe. Trace the drawing, then cut the template out of ¹⁄₁₆-inch (2-mm) cardboard (cake boxes are ideal for this purpose).

2. Roll out the puff pastry to a rectangle measuring 22 x 16 inches (55 x 40 cm). Place the dough in the refrigerator or freezer long enough for it to become completely relaxed and firm.

3. Using a sharp knife and the template as your guide, cut out 12 pear-shaped pieces of puff pastry (Figure 13-28). Place them on a sheet pan lined with baking paper as you cut. Gather the scrap pieces, cover, and reserve for another use in the refrigerator or freezer. Make certain that the dough is still firm and cool; if not, place in the refrigerator before proceeding. Using the tip

FIGURE 13-28 **Cutting around the template to make pear-shaped pieces of puff pastry**

FIGURE 13-27 **The template used as a guide to cut the puff pastry when making the pear-shaped version of Small Pear Tartlets with Caramel Sauce**

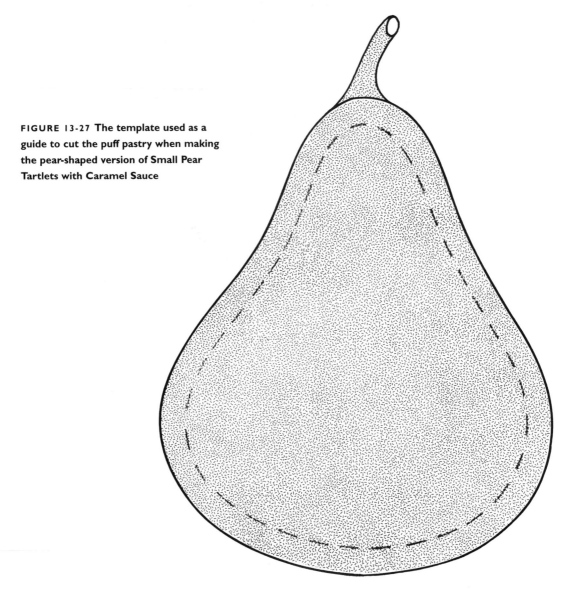

of a sharp paring knife, cut a border halfway through the dough all around the perimeter of each pear, ¼ inch (6 mm) from the edge (shown as a broken line in Figure 13-27). Prick the dough well inside the frame.

4. Add a small amount of pastry cream to the almond paste to soften it, then gradually mix in the remainder of the custard. (If you try to add all the pastry cream at once, the mixture will form lumps.) Place in a paper pastry bag (see page 53). Cut a small opening in the bag and pipe a layer of filling over the pricked part of the puff pastry pieces.

5. Remove the pear halves from the poaching liquid. Remove the stems and reserve (see Note). Core the pears, using a melon ball cutter. Slice the pears lengthwise, starting just below the neck of the pear, keeping the slices attached at the top. Fan the slices slightly and place on top of the cream (Figure 13-29). Sprinkle cinnamon sugar lightly over the pears.

FIGURE 13-29 **Placing a fanned pear half on top of the filling**

6. Bake at 375°F (190°C) for about 35 minutes or until the puff pastry is golden brown. Melt the apricot glaze and brush lightly on top of the fruit and the crust.

7. Place a portion of the caramel sauce in a piping bottle (adjust the consistency first if necessary) and set aside at room temperature. Place a portion of each of the chocolate sauce, sour cream mixture, and raspberry sauce into 3 piping bags. Reserve.

8. Presentation: Pipe caramel sauce in a thin layer to cover the base of a dessert plate. Hold the plate in one hand and tap the rim sharply with your other hand to even the surface of the sauce. Place a tart in the center of the plate. Pipe a ring of chocolate sauce on top of the caramel sauce close to the edge of the caramel sauce. Pipe a ring of sour cream mixture just inside the chocolate sauce ring. Pipe dots of raspberry sauce, spaced 1 inch (2.5 cm) apart, in a circle about halfway between the other sauce rings and the tart. Drag a small wooden skewer through each dot in a clockwise direction to form teardrops. Then drag the skewer through the other 2 sauce rings every 1 inch (2.5 cm), from the edge toward the center of the plate. Place an edible flower on the tart and push a reserved pear stem into the pear neck. Serve immediately.

NOTE: If you want to present the tarts with a pear stem (which looks nice), you will have to do a little pirating in your pear supply, as you get only 1 stem per pear but 2 servings.

ROUND TARTS yield: 12 servings

1. Poach pears as directed above. Trace and cut out the solid fluted circle shown in Figure 13-30. Follow the procedure for rolling out and cutting the dough under Pear-Shaped Tarts, using the fluted circle template as your guide. Cover the scrap pieces and reserve in the refrigerator or freezer for another use.

2. Make sure the puff pastry circles are still firm. If not, refrigerate before proceeding. Use a smaller plain cookie cutter, approximately 4 inches (10 cm) in diameter, to cut halfway through the dough, making a border as you would to make a production-style Bouchée. Prick the dough well inside the circle.

FIGURE 13-30 The template used as a guide to cut the puff pastry when making the round version of Small Pear Tartlets with Caramel Sauce

3. Pipe the almond paste mixture over the inside circle. Slice the cored pear halves across into thin slices and arrange in overlapping concentric circles, starting at the outside edge and building slightly higher in the center. Use 1 pear half per serving. Sprinkle cinnamon sugar over the fruit; bake and glaze as directed above.

4. Follow the presentation directions above, omitting the raspberry dots and the pear stem. Place an edible flower in the center of the tart.

RECTANGULAR TARTS yield: 16 servings

1. Use 8 pears, 1½ recipes poaching liquid, half as much almond paste—pastry cream mixture, and 2 pounds (910 g) puff pastry. Poach the pears as directed above.

2. Roll the puff pastry to a rectangle slightly larger than 14 x 20 inches (35 x 50 cm). Refrigerate to relax and firm the dough.

3. Use a ruler as a guide and trim 1 long and 1 short side of the dough to make them even. Measure and cut 4 strips, 5 inches (12.5 cm) long, starting at the even short side. Measure and cut these into rectangles, 3½ inches (8.7 cm) wide, starting from the even long side. Place the pieces, now measuring 3½ x 5 inches (8.7 x 12.5 cm), on sheet pans lined with baking paper.

4. Use a plain, oval cookie cutter that will leave an approximately ½-inch (1.2-cm) border to cut halfway through the dough pieces. If you do not have an oval cutter, you can bend a round cutter to the correct size. Prick the dough well inside the oval.

5. Pipe the almond paste mixture over the ovals. Slice and arrange the pear halves as directed in the pear-shaped version, using 1 pear half per serving. Sprinkle cinnamon sugar over the fruit; bake and glaze as directed above.

6. Follow the presentation directions for the pear-shaped tarts, omitting the raspberry dots and the pear stem. You might want to use only 1 type of sauce for the decoration and/or swirl the circles into the sauce instead (see Figure 16-6, page 812). Place an edible flower in the center of the tart.

Small Swedish Pancakes (Plättar) yield: 16 servings

These delicious little pancakes are so tender that they seem to just dissolve on your tongue as you eat them. Being so delicate, they would be impossible to handle if they were made the same size as regular pancakes. *Plättar* are traditionally enjoyed in Sweden after yellow pea soup on Thursdays. Served warm, dusted with powdered sugar and topped with cloudberries, they make an unusual light dessert, or try them on your breakfast or brunch table.

I remember how the American passengers fell in love with Swedish pancakes when I was working on the Swedish American Lines cruise ships in the 1960s. One woman in particular was so enamored that she asked the kitchen to make her a special order so she could attach them to her dress and go to the masquerade ball as a Small Swedish Pancake!

Plättar should, if at all possible, be made to order. If you must make them ahead, you can keep them covered in a low oven (200°F/94°C) for a short time.

¾ cup (180 ml) heavy cream	Powdered sugar
1 teaspoon (5 g) granulated sugar	8 ounces (225 g) cloudberry jam (see Note)
Small Swedish Pancakes Batter (recipe follows)	16 edible fresh flowers

1. Whip the heavy cream and the sugar to stiff peaks. Place in a pastry bag with a No. 6 (12-mm) star tip. Reserve in the refrigerator.

2. Heat the plättiron (the traditional Swedish sectional pancake pan; see page 964), a pancake griddle, or a cast-iron skillet large enough to accommodate at least 6 pancakes, 3 inches (7.5 cm) in diameter, until it is hot enough that a small drop of water evaporates instantly when it touches the surface.

3. Stir the rested pancake batter thoroughly. Pour 1 ounce (30 ml) batter into each depression in the pan. The iron does not need to be greased because of the large amount of butter in the batter (if you are using a skillet, it may need to be greased for the first batch). Turn the pancakes, using a narrow metal spatula, as soon as they become light brown on the bottom, about 1 minute. Cook for approximately 1 minute longer to brown the other side. Turning the pancakes takes some practice; it has to be done very rapidly, as the batter is not completely set at this point and the pancakes are very tender.

4. Quickly transfer the pancakes to a warm plate and keep them warm if it is necessary to make additional Plättar. Make sure the iron does not get too hot or you will risk burning the last few pancakes. This recipe requires quick action, even with the iron at the correct temperature. Try the technique of stacking 2 or 3 pancakes before removing them from the pan.

5. Presentation: Arrange 6 Plättar in a circle on a warm dessert plate, overlapping them just enough to leave a small opening in the center. Sift powdered sugar on top of the pancakes and over the exposed part of the plate. Spoon a small dot of cloudberry jam, the size of a hazelnut, in the center of each pancake. Pipe a rosette of whipped cream in the center of the plate. Decorate with an edible flower and serve immediately.

NOTE: If cloudberry jam is unavailable, lingonberry jam makes an excellent substitute.

SMALL SWEDISH PANCAKES BATTER yield: about 100 pancakes

8 eggs, at room temperature	1½ teaspoons (7.5 g) salt
2 ounces (55 g) granulated sugar	1½ teaspoons (7.5 ml) vanilla extract
4½ cups (1 L 80 ml) whole milk	8 ounces (225 g) clarified unsalted butter, melted
10 ounces (285 g) cake flour, sifted	
1⅓ cups (320 ml) heavy cream	

1. Place the eggs and sugar in a mixer bowl and whisk by hand for 2 minutes to blend well.

2. Warm the milk to body temperature and stir half of it into the egg mixture.

3. Place the mixer bowl on the machine with the whip attachment. With the mixer running at medium speed, gradually incorporate the flour. Mix in the heavy cream, scrape down the sides of the bowl as needed, and continue mixing until you have a smooth paste.

4. On low speed, gradually add the remaining milk along with the salt, vanilla, and butter. The batter will be quite thin. Let the batter rest at room temperature for 1 hour.

NOTE: Be sure to stir the batter every few minutes as you cook the pancakes, and also before you start, to prevent the flour from sinking to the bottom of the thin batter.

Soufflé Pancakes with Gooseberry Ice Cream yield: 12 servings

This is a variation of a recipe I have had in my files for many years called Pancakes Johann Strauss. In the original, the soufflé pancakes are cooked on both sides, then sandwiched together with orange segments and served with orange sauce.

If you do not have a small Swedish pancakes pan, or plättiron, it is best to use a 6-inch (15-cm) crepe pan instead and portion only one pancake per serving (two sandwiched together). In this case, cut the pancake into four wedges before putting it into the hot oven to "soufflé." The pancakes will spread out too far if you attempt to make the small size in a standard skillet, reducing their height during the final baking. Either way, whole or sliced into quarters, the pancakes should be served just like a bona fide soufflé—immediately after they are removed from the oven. The precooked, sandwiched pancakes, however, can be stored in the refrigerator, well wrapped, for up to two days before the final baking, with excellent results. Please do not serve these cold; though the result is fairly acceptable, your guests will unfortunately never know what they are missing.

Soufflé Pancake Batter (recipe follows)	Edible flowers
Melted unsalted butter	Powdered sugar
⅓ recipe Gooseberry Ice Cream (page 725)	Gooseberry preserves (see Note 2)
12 sponge cake rounds (see Note 1)	

I. Heat a plättiron (see page 964), large skillet, or other suitable cooking vessel until medium hot. Grease lightly with melted butter and pour approximately 2 tablespoons (30 ml) batter into each depression in the pan (or about ⅓ cup/80 ml for each pancake, if using a 6-inch/15-cm skillet). Cook the pancakes for about 3 minutes, adjusting the heat as necessary. They should be light brown on the bottom but still liquid on top. Remove the pan from the stove and let the pancakes finish cooking for 1 minute off the heat. The top will thicken to a sticky consistency. Use a narrow palette knife to remove the pancakes, being very careful not to damage the sides. Place them, brown side down, on a sheet pan lined with baking paper. Make a second batch and invert these on top of the first set so that the raw sides are sandwiched together. Before they cool completely, transfer the pancakes to another area of the pan to keep them from sticking. Repeat with the remaining batter. You need 72 pancakes for this recipe (36 after sandwiching). The batter will make about 12 extra single pancakes. Cover the pancakes and reserve in the refrigerator until serving time.

2. Arrange the pancakes in groups of 3 (or 4 quarters, if making the larger size) on small pieces of baking paper. Preheat 2 sheet pans, stacked together (double-panned), in a 400°F (205°C) oven.

3. Use a No. 20 (1¾-ounce/50-ml) ice cream scoop to portion a scoop of gooseberry ice cream on top of each sponge circle. Reserve in the freezer.

4. Remove the petals from edible flowers of 2 or 3 colors and reserve on a damp paper towel.

5. Presentation: Place a set of 3 double pancakes on the hot sheet pans in the oven. Bake until they are puffed, about 4 minutes. Sift powdered sugar over the base of a dessert plate. Place a sponge round with ice cream in the center of the plate. Use the bottom of a false-bottomed tart pan or a similar tool to remove the puffed pancakes from the oven. Place them around the ice cream. Quickly sift powdered sugar on top, place a small dollop of gooseberry preserves on each pancake, decorate with flower petals between each pancake, and serve at once.

NOTE 1: Use any type of sponge or pound cake you have on hand. Either light or chocolate would be fine. Slice the cake thin and cut out 12 rounds, using a 1½-inch (3.7-cm) plain cookie cutter. Cover and reserve.

NOTE 2: Use commercial gooseberry preserves or make one-third of the gooseberry mixture in the Gooseberry Ice Cream recipe (page 725), but reduce and thicken it further.

CHEF'S TIP
Soufflé pancakes are wonderful as a brunch offering. Try sandwiching sliced peaches or bananas between the pancakes in Step 1. The banana version is fabulous served with maple syrup and toasted pecans, and the peach-stuffed pancakes are great with cinnamon butter.

SOUFFLÉ PANCAKE BATTER yield: approximately 85 pancakes, 3 inches (7.5 cm) in diameter

6 ounces (170 g) bread flour

4 ounces (115 g) cake flour

2 cups (480 ml) water

1 teaspoon (5 g) salt

5 ounces (140 g) unsalted butter

10 eggs, separated

Grated zest of 3 lemons

1¼ cups (300 ml) heavy cream

6 ounces (170 g) granulated sugar

I. Sift the flours together and set aside.

2. Combine the water, salt, and butter in a saucepan and bring to a boil. Stir in two-thirds of the flour mixture (1¾ cups/420 ml), reserving the remainder. Continue to cook, stirring constantly, until the paste is smooth and comes away from the sides of the pan, approximately 2 minutes. Remove from the heat.

3. Mix in the egg yolks, 1 or 2 at a time, together with the lemon zest. Cover and set aside to cool.

4. Whip the heavy cream to soft peaks. Reserve in the refrigerator.

5. When the batter is cold, whip the egg whites and granulated sugar to stiff peaks. Set aside briefly. Gradually fold the reserved whipped cream into the batter. Add the reserved flour to a small portion of the batter, then mix this into the remaining batter, followed by the egg whites. Use immediately.

Sour Apple and Cheese Turnovers yield: 16 servings (Photo 15)

I came upon the idea for this dessert as a result of having a leftover sheet of puff pastry dough that had been prepared for cheese straws. I made it into apple turnovers on a whim and thought the combination was great. After a few adjustments to the cheese and the apple filling, this recipe, which has a nice tangy bite, was born. You may want to vary the amount of cheddar, use a different aged cheese, and/or decrease the amount of Parmesan if it is particularly strong or salty. The Apple-Rum Filling (page 800) used for the Apple-Rum Charlotte can be used here as well. You will need one-half recipe made without brown sugar or pectin powder and with Calvados or another brandy instead of rum.

2 pounds (910 g) Puff Pastry (page 74)

5 ounces (140 g) sharp cheddar cheese, finely chopped

3 ounces (85 g) Parmesan cheese, ground

Egg wash

Chunky Sour Apple Filling (recipe follows)

½ recipe Fortified Caramel Sauce (page 821)

Ground cinnamon

Cinnamon Custard Sauce (see Note)

Apricots or other seasonal fruit for decoration

16 mint sprigs

I. Roll the puff pastry dough into a 20-inch (50-cm) square. The dough should be about ⅛ inch (3 mm) thick. Let the dough rest in the refrigerator for 30 minutes to firm up and relax and to help minimize shrinking.

2. Cut the sheet into 4 rows in each direction to make 16 squares, 5 inches (12.5 cm) each. Leave the squares in place.

3. Combine the cheddar and Parmesan cheeses. Brush egg wash over the puff pastry squares. Place 1 tablespoon (15 ml) cheese mixture in the center of each square. Spread out the cheese a little and press it into the dough. Pipe or spoon a mound of sour apple filling in the center of each square on top of the cheese, dividing it evenly. Fold the top of each square over diagonally to form a triangle. Press the edges together firmly with your fingers.

4. Brush egg wash on top of the turnovers and invert them into the remaining cheese mixture. Place, cheese-side up, on a sheet pan lined with baking paper. Make a small cut in the center of each turnover.

5. Bake the turnovers at 375°F (190°C) until completely baked through, about 45 minutes. Cover the turnovers with baking paper or aluminum foil as needed to keep the cheese from getting too dark. You may need a second pan underneath as well to prevent overbrowning on the bottom. Place the caramel sauce in a piping bottle with a small opening and reserve.

6. Presentation: Sift ground cinnamon lightly over the rim and base of a dessert plate. Place a warm turnover in the center of the plate. Pour a round pool of cinnamon custard sauce in front of the turnover. Pipe caramel sauce in a ring near the perimeter of the sauce pool. Use a small wooden skewer to swirl the sauces together (see Figure 16-1, page 810). Decorate with fresh apricot slices or other seasonal fruit. Place a mint sprig in the center of the sauce. Serve immediately.

NOTE: To make the cinnamon custard sauce, follow the recipe and instructions for 1 recipe Crème Anglaise (page 817), adding 1 teaspoon (1.5 g) ground cinnamon at the end of the recipe.

CHUNKY SOUR APPLE FILLING

Make ½ recipe or 1 pound 4 ounces (570 g) Chunky Apple Filling (page 840), omitting the sugar.

Strawberry Shortcake yield: 16 servings (Photo 55)

Shortcakes are an American classic. They are made from a quick bread dough that is baked, split, filled with fruit (most commonly, strawberries), and topped with whipped cream or ice cream. The application of shortcake differs from place to place, although the name derives—as it does for short dough—from the use of shortening, butter, or other fat in the dough for a crisp and crumbly texture. Having never made or even heard of this dish before I came to the United States (and I certainly did not want to ask any of the customers who requested it what it was), for many years I made strawberry shortcake using a sponge cake base. Little did I know that this was probably not what most of the guests had in mind, as no one complained.

For a purist, shortcake should be made from biscuit dough. It can be prepared using one large, round, cakelike biscuit for several servings or with individual biscuits. The dish most likely began as a way to create a dessert using leftover biscuits or rolls from the dinner table. Strawberry shortcake is mentioned in writings from England as far back as the 1500s. It was not before the 1830s, however, that it became so loved and well known in America as the popularity of strawberries increased; in fact, by 1850 there was talk of "strawberry fever."

I got the idea of adding poppy seeds to the dough from my Strawberry Poppy Seed Cake recipe, where the flavors complement each other nicely; they add a pleasant bite and crunch here as well.

Biscuit Dough for Strawberry Shortcake
(recipe follows)

Egg wash

Granulated sugar

1 pound 8 ounces (680 g) strawberries
(approximately 2 dry pint baskets)

3 cups (720 ml) heavy cream

4 teaspoons (20 g) granulated sugar

1 teaspoon (5 ml) vanilla extract

Powdered sugar

2 recipes Sabayon (page 669), made with
white wine

16 mint sprigs

1. Roll out the biscuit dough to a 12-inch (30-cm) square and give the dough a second single turn. Roll the dough into a rectangle measuring 7 x 18 inches (17.5 x 45 cm) and about ¾ inch (2 cm) thick. Cut the strip in half lengthwise. Cut each half into 8 triangles. (You can reshape the end pieces and cut 2 more triangles if necessary to make 16 pieces.)

2. Brush the tops of the triangles with egg wash, then invert them in granulated sugar. Place, sugar-side up, on a sheet pan lined with baking paper. Score the top of each piece with 3 parallel lines, then repeat at a 45-degree angle to form a diamond pattern.

3. Bake the biscuits at 400°F (205°C) for about 15 minutes. Set aside to cool.

4. Rinse the strawberries and remove the hulls. Cut the strawberries into thin slices lengthwise (from the point). Cover and reserve.

5. Whip the heavy cream, 4 teaspoons (20 g) sugar, and vanilla until stiff peaks form. Place in a pastry bag with a No. 4 (8-mm) plain tip.

6. Presentation: Cut a biscuit in half horizontally. Pipe whipped cream onto the bottom half of the biscuit, covering it in a zigzag pattern. Cover the cream with sliced strawberries, reserving the best-looking slices for garnish. Pipe a second layer of cream on top of the berries in the same way. Make a second layer of strawberries. Place the top of the biscuit on the strawberries at an angle. Sift powdered sugar lightly over the top. Cover the base of a serving plate with sabayon. Brown (gratinée) the sauce under a salamander or broiler. Line up the reserved (best-looking) strawberry slices next to each other, points toward the outside, next to the rim of the serving plate on top of the sauce. Place the assembled shortcake on top of the sauce in the center of the plate. Decorate with a mint sprig and serve immediately.

NOTE: For a simplified presentation, replace the sabayon with Strawberry Sauce (page 832) (do not gratinée the strawberry sauce) or serve the shortcakes with Vanilla Ice Cream (page 734).

CHEF'S TIP

To make the more traditional round biscuits rather than the triangular shape used in the recipe, roll the dough as directed and cut out biscuits using a 3¼-inch (8.1-cm) plain or fluted cookie cutter. Gather the scrap dough, pat it out gently, and cut the remainder. You will get only 12 round biscuits rather than 16 triangles. Instead of forming the remaining scraps again, just bake them alongside the biscuits for a snack.

BISCUIT DOUGH FOR STRAWBERRY SHORTCAKE yield: 16 triangles, 3½ inches (8.7 cm) each

1 pound 6 ounces (625 g) bread flour

1 teaspoon (5 g) salt

3 tablespoons (36 g) baking powder

2 ounces (55 g) poppy seeds

4 ounces (115 g) cold unsalted butter

Grated zest of 1 orange

3¼ cups (780 ml) heavy cream

1. Sift together the flour, salt, and baking powder. Mix in the poppy seeds. Cut the butter into small chunks and add it to the flour mixture. Cut the butter into the flour mixture until it is the size of peas.

2. Stir the orange zest into the cream. Pour the cream into the flour mixture all at once and stir rapidly with your hand to form a soft dough. Take care not to overmix.

3. Place on a floured work surface and pat out to a rectangle 1½ inches (3.7 cm) thick. Make 1 rough single turn (see Figures 5-6 and 5-7, page 213), shaping the dough with your hands and not a rolling pin. The biscuit dough can be covered and refrigerated for 1 day at this point, if desired.

Swedish Pancakes Filled with Apples yield: 12 servings (Photo 79)

I'm not sure what my mom would say if she could see what I have done to her pancake recipe! But because they are so flat on the plate ("flat as a pancake," as the saying goes) and rather uninteresting visually (even after folding), adding height to the presentation could possibly be used to justify what I think she would consider a lot of unnecessary fuss.

Pancakes (which fall under the heading of flatbreads) can be defined as flat, round cakes of varying thickness that are cooked on both sides—which implies, of course, that they must be turned. Any chef worth his or her title will accomplish this by flipping the pancakes in the air and catching them in the pan on the way down—especially if someone is watching. Pancakes date back to the 1500s; countless variations, from sweet to savory and from tiny and petite to big and thick, can be found served with different toppings and fillings. Pancakes are offered as a main course for breakfast, as an appetizer at lunch or dinner, and, obviously, for dessert. Each region has its own specialty when it comes to this popular country fare. The Swedish make small *plättar*, the French have paper-thin *crepes*, you can find Hungarian *palatschinken* (*palacsinta*), which are sort of a large crepe, the Germans make a soufflé or omelette pancake, the Russians are famous for *blini*, and let's not forget American hot cakes or flapjacks, thick breakfast pancakes often enjoyed with maple syrup.

5 pounds (2 kg 275 g) cooking apples, such as Pippin or Granny Smith (approximately 12 medium)

6 ounces (170 g) unsalted butter

8 ounces (225 g) granulated sugar

½ cup (120 ml) Calvados

1 recipe Small Swedish Pancakes Batter (page 684; see Note)

1 cup (240 ml) heavy cream

1 teaspoon (5 g) granulated sugar

¼ recipe Raspberry Sauce (page 830)

½ recipe Fortified Caramel Sauce (page 821)

Powdered sugar

12 Elongated Tuile Leaves (instructions follow)

12 edible fresh flowers

1. Peel, core, and halve the apples. Cut each half into ¼-inch (6-mm) wedges.

2. Melt the butter in a skillet and stir in the first measurement of sugar and the apple wedges. Cook over medium heat, stirring occasionally, until the apples are soft and the sugar is close to caramelizing (just starting to turn light brown). As the apples cook, they will release more juice than will be evaporated. Pour or spoon the liquid off as it accumulates and discard or use as cake syrup. Deglaze the pan with the Calvados. Set the apple mixture aside but keep very warm.

3. Once the pancake batter has rested, stir well, then make at least 36 pancakes, using a crepe pan (you can make the pancakes while the apple filling is cooking). Make them just slightly thicker than a standard crepe (see page 14).

4. Whip the heavy cream with the remaining sugar until stiff peaks form. Place in a pastry bag with a No. 6 (12-mm) star tip. Reserve in the refrigerator.

5. Presentation: Place a small amount of the warm apple filling on the lower half of 3 pancakes. Fold the tops over the filling, then fold in half again, making quarters. Using plastic piping bottles, pipe the raspberry and caramel sauces randomly in small dots and teardrops on the base of a dessert plate. Brush a thick layer of caramel sauce on top of the filled pancakes. Quickly place the pancakes in a hot skillet, sauce-side down, to crisp and caramelize the tops. Place the filled pancakes on top of the sauce on the prepared plate, arranging them sauce-side up, evenly spaced, with the points toward the center of the plate. Sift powdered sugar lightly over the entire plate, including the rim. Pipe a large rosette of whipped cream in the center of the plate. Place a tuile leaf standing upright in the cream, then set an edible flower next to the leaf. Serve immediately.

NOTE: Make the pancake batter using ½ cup (120 ml) less milk than called for in the recipe. This will make it possible to turn the larger pancakes.

ELONGATED TUILE LEAVES yield: approximately 35 decorations

¼ recipe Plain Tuile Decorating Paste (page 482)

1 teaspoon (2.5 g) unsweetened cocoa powder

1. Trace the drawing shown Figure 13-31 and cut the template out of ¹⁄₁₆-inch (2-mm) cardboard (cake boxes work great for this). The template as shown is the correct size for use in this recipe.

2. If you do not have Silpats, lightly grease the backs of even sheet pans, coat the pans with flour, then shake off as much flour as possible.

3. Color 2 tablespoons (30 ml) tuile paste with the cocoa powder, mixing it until completely smooth. Place a portion in a piping bag and cut a small opening.

4. Spread the plain tuile paste flat and even within the template on the prepared pans or silicone mats (see Figures 10-29 and 10-30, page 482). Do not spread too many per pan or the last few will be too dark when you get to them. Pipe a straight line of cocoa-colored paste, in the center, down the full length of each cookie.

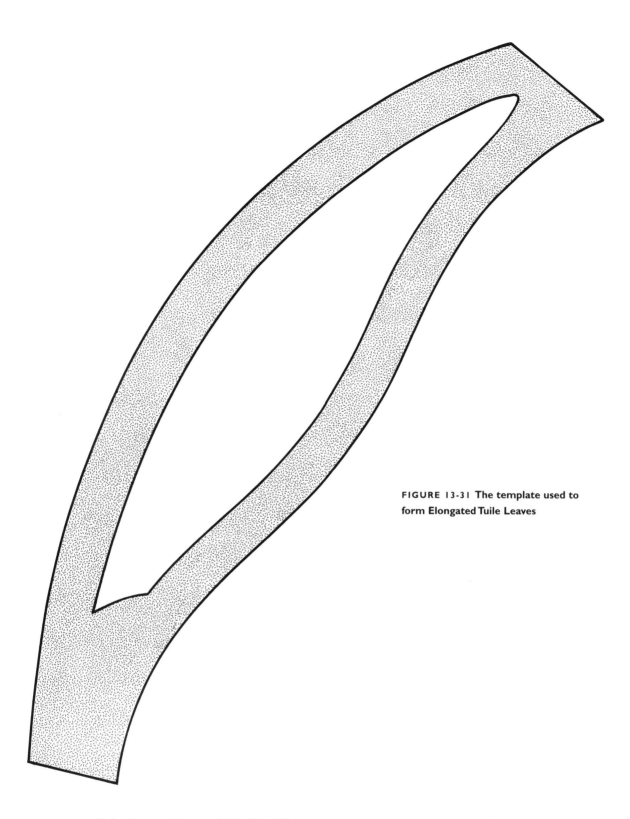

FIGURE 13-31 **The template used to form Elongated Tuile Leaves**

5. Bake the cookies at 400°F (205°C) for approximately 4 minutes or until they just begin to turn brown in a few spots and around the edges. Keep the pan in the oven with the door open and remove the cookies, 1 at a time. Quickly twist each leaf to make it curved. Hold it for 1 or 2 seconds, and it will be firm enough to keep its shape. For a slightly different look and a faster way to form them, place the leaves on top of a rolling pin at an angle almost parallel to the bias.

Tiramisu with Fresh Fruit yield: 16 servings (Photo 30)

Tiramisu literally means "pick-me-up." The name is a reference to the espresso coffee in the dessert, which not only gives it a little flavor lift but also just might keep you from getting drowsy. Tiramisu is also known as *Mascarpone à la Venetian*, in honor of the Italian city where it is a popular favorite. Tiramisu was invented only about 25 years ago at El Touga, a restaurant in Treviso. It has become a regular feature on many restaurant menus in the last few years. My interpretation, in which the servings are put together individually, is a little time-consuming but much more elegant than the conventional way of assembling and presenting this dessert.

To convert the recipe to the traditional tiramisu presentation, see the instructions following the recipe. The fabulous—and expensive—mascarpone cheese from Lombardo can be replaced with a combination of 3 parts soft cream cheese to 1 part sour cream by weight, or you can make the cheese yourself with the recipe on page 22.

2 recipes Ladyfingers batter (page 445)	16 Marzipan Coffee Beans (page 590)
6 cups (1 L 440 ml) strong coffee (use good-quality coffee brewed double strength)	1 pound (455 g) prepared fresh fruit, approximately (instructions follow)
Mascarpone Filling (recipe follows)	¼ cup (60 ml) orange liqueur
Unsweetened cocoa powder	Small mint sprigs
Dark chocolate shavings	

1. Place the ladyfinger batter in a pastry bag with a No. 3 (6-mm) plain tip. Pipe out circles 2½ inches (6.2 cm) in diameter on sheet pans lined with baking paper, making at least 64 (see Figure 1-5, page 29).

2. Bake the cookies at 400°F (205°C) for approximately 10 minutes or until they are golden brown. Set aside to cool.

3. If necessary, use a 2½-inch (6.2-cm) plain cookie cutter to trim the baked cookies and make them uniform.

4. Dip 16 cookies in the strong coffee, then place them on a sheet pan lined with baking paper. Test a couple first to be sure the coffee has soaked all the way through, then place the mascarpone mixture in a pastry bag with a No. 3 (6-mm) plain tip. Pipe a spiral of mascarpone filling on top of the dipped cookies, using the same technique as before. Sift cocoa powder over the filling. Dip 16 additional cookies in the coffee, placing them on top of the filling after you dip each. Pipe mascarpone filling onto the cookies, then sift cocoa powder over the top. Repeat 2 more times, making stacks of 4 coffee-dipped cookies separated by mascarpone filling topped with cocoa powder. Do not sift cocoa powder on the top (mascarpone) layer. Refrigerate the desserts for a minimum of 30 minutes or, preferably, overnight to ensure that the coffee has fully penetrated the cookies (see Note).

5. Make the template shown in Figure 13-32. The design as shown is the correct size for use in the presentation; however, make the overall size the same as the base of your dessert plates so the template will sit flat and protect the entire surface. Trace the drawing, then cut the template out of ¹⁄₁₆-inch (2-mm) cardboard; cake boxes work well for this.

6. Presentation: Place the template so the design (exposed portion) is on the left side of the dessert plate. Sift cocoa powder over the template. Remove the template carefully. Sift cocoa

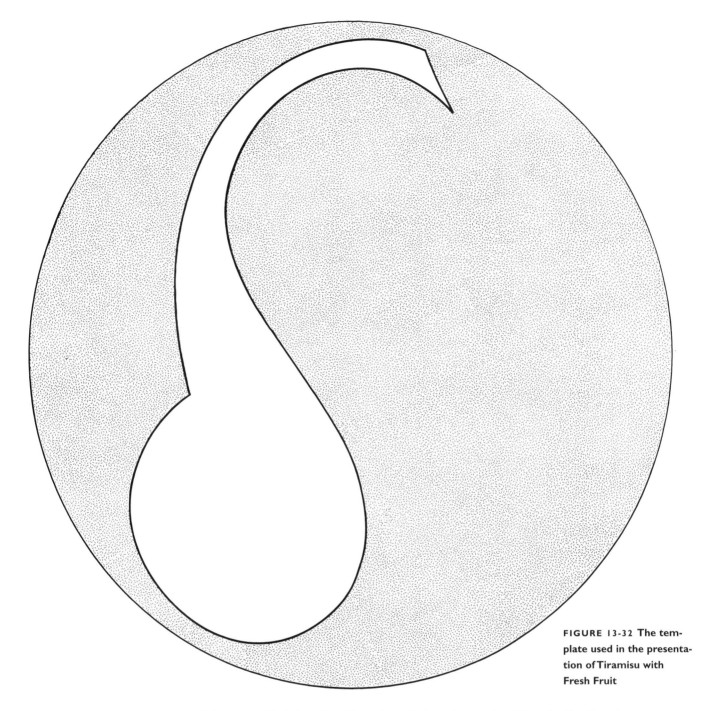

FIGURE 13-32 The template used in the presentation of Tiramisu with Fresh Fruit

powder over one of the assembled tiramisu. Place shaved chocolate on top. Transfer the tiramisu to the dessert plate, placing it within the curve of the cocoa powder design. Place a marzipan coffee bean in the center of the round part of the cocoa powder design. Arrange 8 to 10 pieces of fresh fruit on the bottom right side of the plate. Decorate with a few small mint sprigs. Serve immediately.

NOTE: If you are preparing the desserts with the intention of serving them the following day, reserve one-quarter of the mascarpone filling and leave the top cookies bare. Just before serving, pipe the reserved mascarpone over the assembled desserts and decorate with cocoa powder as directed. If the mascarpone layer and the cocoa powder sit overnight the cocoa dissolves into the cream and becomes unattractive. The cream also dries up and does not look appealing.

MASCARPONE FILLING yield: 2 quarts (1 L 920 ml)

1½ teaspoons (5 g) unflavored gelatin powder

1¼ cups (300 ml) sweet marsala

6 egg yolks (½ cup/120 ml)

6 ounces (170 g) granulated sugar

2 cups (480 ml) heavy cream

1 pound (455 g) Mascarpone Cheese (page 22), at room temperature

1. Sprinkle the gelatin powder on top of ¼ cup (60 ml) marsala; reserve.

2. Combine the egg yolks, sugar, and remaining wine in a mixer bowl. Set over a bain-marie and, whisking constantly by hand, heat the mixture until it has thickened to a sabayon consistency. Remove from the heat and place on the mixer with the whip attachment. Continue to whip at medium speed until cool to the touch. Refrigerate.

3. Whip the heavy cream to stiff peaks, reserve. Gradually stir the egg mixture into the soft mascarpone cheese, followed by the whipped cream. Heat the gelatin mixture to dissolve. Quickly stir the gelatin into a small portion of the cream mixture to temper. Still working rapidly, add this to the remaining mixture. Use immediately.

TO PREPARE THE FRESH FRUIT

Although you are limited, of course, to whatever fresh fruit is in season in your area, try to use 3 or 4 kinds for a nice color contrast. Cut the fruit into equal-sized pieces about the size of a raspberry, keeping each variety separate until serving time. Then combine the fruit gently and add the orange liqueur. Fold the liqueur in carefully so you do not bruise the fruit. If you are using a red fruit or any fruit that tends to bleed, add it at the last moment and only to the amount you are serving right away.

VARIATION

TRADITIONAL TIRAMISU PRESENTATION yield: 16 servings

Due to the thicker sponge layer in this version and the fact that you cannot dip the sponge in the coffee, it is a good idea to brush the bottom of the sponge with coffee before placing it in the sheet pan and to brush the bottom of the second sheet before placing it on the filling as well.

1½ recipes Ladyfingers batter (page 445)

3 cups (720 ml) strong coffee

1 recipe Mascarpone Filling (above)

Unsweetened cocoa powder

1. Spread out the ladyfinger batter evenly forming a rectangle 11 x 21 inches (27.5 x 55 cm) on a full sheet pan lined with baking paper. Bake at 400°F (205°C) for about 30 minutes or until baked through and dry. Let cool.

2. Invert the baked sheet and remove the baking paper from the back. Cut to make 2 pieces. Turn the sheets right-side up. Place 1 sheet on a full-sheet pan.

3. Brush strong coffee heavily over the sheet (see introduction). Spread half of the mascarpone filling on top (you might have to refrigerate, stirring often or, stir over ice cold water to thicken the filling a little). Sift cocoa powder over the filling. Top with the second sheet. Brush strong coffee generously on top. Spread the remaining mascarpone filling on top. Cover the cake and refrigerate for at least 3 hours or, preferably, overnight.

4. Sift cocoa powder over the sheet. Trim 1 long and 1 short side, using a sharp knife dipped in hot water. Starting from the trimmed sides, measure and cut 16 square pieces measuring aproximately 2½ x 2½ inches (6.2 x 6.2 cm).

Trio of Cannolis yield: 16 servings (Photo 29)

Most Italian grandmothers would probably scoff at this filling and my updated presentation of this traditional Italian cheese-filled pastry. But they would have to agree that it is refreshingly different. As long as the shells are cooked through and crisp, they can be prepared one day ahead and stored, covered, in a dry place. Any unfilled leftover shells also make great and unusual cookies. Instead of the Jasmine Rice Pudding, try filling the cannoli shells with Classic Bavarian Cream mixed with chopped candied fruit and chocolate. You will come very close to the original cannoli filling.

2 cups (480 ml) warm white wine
    (110°F/43°C)
2 tablespoons (30 g) granulated sugar
3 ounces (85 g) fresh compressed yeast
¼ cup (60 ml) olive oil
1 teaspoon (2 g) ground anise seed
½ teaspoon (2.5 g) salt
1 pound 8 ounces (680 g) bread flour
Egg wash

Vegetable oil for deep-frying
Granulated sugar
1 cup (240 ml) heavy cream
1 teaspoon (5 ml) vanilla extract
½ recipe Jasmine Rice Pudding (page 772)
1 recipe Cranberry Coulis (page 821)
2 ounces (55 g) pistachios, blanched, skins
    removed, dried, and coarsely chopped

I. Combine the wine and granulated sugar. Dissolve the yeast in the liquid. Add the oil, anise seed, and salt. Incorporate two-thirds of the flour and mix, using the dough hook, for 3 minutes. Add the remaining flour and continue mixing until the dough forms a smooth ball.

2. Place the dough in a lightly oiled bowl and turn it to coat the entire dough with oil. Cover and let rise in a warm place until doubled in volume.

3. Punch the dough down and divide it into 2 equal pieces. Form the pieces into round loaves (see Figures 3-1 and 3-2, page 94). Cut an *X* in the top of each loaf, then leave the dough to relax for about 5 minutes. Pull the corners of the cut *X* out to form squares (see Figure 2-4, page 73). Roll the pieces, 1 at a time, into rectangles the size of a full sheet pan, 16 x 24 inches (40 x 60 cm), and ⅛ inch (3 mm) thick. Should the dough shrink too much as you work with it, roll each piece halfway, allow it to relax in the refrigerator for 30 minutes, then finish rolling. Refrigerate the rectangles for 30 minutes.

4. Trim 1 long and 1 short side of each sheet of dough. Cut each sheet into 4 lengthwise strips, 3½ inches (8.7 cm) wide, starting at the trimmed side. Cut across to make a total of at least 16 strips, 4 inches long; 16 strips, 3 inches long; and 16 strips, 2 inches long (you should get about 9 of each size from each piece of dough, giving you a few extras) (Figure 13-33).

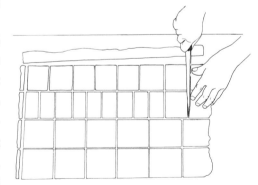

FIGURE 13-33 Cutting half of the dough for Trio of Cannolis to produce small, medium, and large rectangles for the different finished sizes

5. Wrap the dough sheets around cannoli tubes. Brush egg wash on 1 edge of the dough and press the edges together to seal. (Do not get egg wash on the tubes.) Place the cannoli in the refrigerator until you are ready to fry them.

6. Heat the vegetable oil to 375°F (190°C). Fry the cannolis, a few at a time, until they start to brown. Remove the tubes from the oil with a slotted spoon or by inserting a metal skewer into the tube. Pull the cannoli shells off the metal tubes. Place the shells back in the oil and continue frying until the shells are golden brown and crisp. Remove from the oil with a slotted spoon and drain on paper towels. Gently roll the cannoli shells in granulated sugar.

7. Use a serrated knife to trim one end of each cannoli shell as necessary so that the tubes will stand straight on end. As you trim them, place 1 of each size in 16 groups of 3 to facilitate serving.

8. Whip the heavy cream with the vanilla until it forms stiff peaks. Fold the cream into the rice pudding. Place the rice pudding mixture in a pastry bag with a No. 6 (12-mm) plain tip. Place the cranberry coulis in a piping bottle and reserve.

9. Presentation: Pipe the pudding into 1 group of cannoli shells, filling them to the top. Sprinkle pistachio nuts over the top of the pudding. Pipe cranberry coulis in an uneven pool in the center of a dessert plate. Place the filled cannolis, standing on end, in the center of the coulis. Sprinkle pistachios lightly on the plate around the coulis. Serve immediately.

NOTE: The characteristic bubbles found on fried cannoli shells (and also on fritters) are a result of the wine in the dough (or batter). The wine ferments and produces a small amount of carbon dioxide as the pastry cooks.

Whipped Cream Waffles with Apple Jam and Calvados Cream

yield: about 16 servings

To many people, waffles are associated only with breakfast, but I think you will find that this crisp, light waffle paired with cream and apple jam makes a tempting dessert. That is, unless you have to face the combination every day for two weeks in a row, as my colleagues at the lunch table did when I first starting making this waffle recipe again. It is one I have had since my days as an apprentice and, when I dug it up a few years ago, it was clear right away that something was amiss. Back then, it was a common practice to write down your special recipes using a protective code of some sort to sabotage anyone who copied your recipes without permission. For example, you might add 100 grams to all of the dry ingredient weights and/or delete a set percentage of all liquid quantities. Well, you guessed it—I had forgotten my code, and I had to start from scratch, using my colleagues as guinea pigs.

The waffles should be served as soon as they are made, while still warm, to taste their best. If it is necessary to make them ahead of time, reserve them on a cake rack in a single layer in a low oven (220°F/104°C). This will keep the waffles crisp; however, they must not be kept this way longer than about 15 minutes or they will start to dry all the way through. The waffle batter can be made ahead of time and kept in the refrigerator for three or four days, or in the freezer for several weeks with no loss in quality. I keep it on hand at all times.

1 pound 8 ounces (680 g) bread flour

10 ounces (285 g) cornstarch

2 ounces (55 g) granulated sugar (see Chef's Tip)

1 teaspoon (5 g) salt

1 quart (960 ml) warm water

6 eggs, at room temperature

6 ounces (170 g) melted unsalted butter

Finely grated zest of ½ lemon (optional)

2 teaspoons (10 ml) vanilla extract

1 quart (960 ml) heavy cream

Apple Jam (recipe follows)

Powdered sugar

Calvados Cream (recipe follows)

1. Sift the flour and cornstarch into an oversized mixing bowl. Stir in the sugar and salt.

2. Gradually incorporate the water, mixing with a whisk. Whisk in the eggs, then the butter and lemon zest, if used. Mix until you have a smooth paste, about 3 minutes longer. Stir in the vanilla.

3. Cover the batter and let it rest for 30 minutes.

4. Whip the heavy cream to stiff peaks. Fold the cream into the waffle batter.

5. Heat a waffle iron (grease if not using a nonstick iron). Portion 1 to 2 cups (240 to 480 ml) batter onto the iron and quickly spread it out a little (see Note). Close the lid and bake approximately 3 minutes per side if using a stovetop iron, about 5 minutes total if using an electric iron. Warm the apple jam.

6. Presentation: Place 2 or 3 waffle sections, depending on size, off-center on a dessert plate, leaning 1 against the other(s). Sift powdered sugar lightly over the tops of the waffles and over the plate. Spoon a large dollop of warm apple jam on the plate next to the waffles. Pour a pool of Calvados cream in front of the dessert and over a corner of the waffles. Serve immediately.

NOTE: The amount of batter needed for each waffle will vary depending on the type of iron used. Belgian waffle irons use more batter because of the deep grooves.

APPLE JAM yield: approximately 4 cups (960 ml)

3 ounces (85 g) dark raisins

¼ cup (60 ml) Calvados

3 pounds 8 ounces (1 kg 590 g) cooking apples, such as Granny Smith or Golden Delicious

5 cups (1 L 200 ml) or 1 recipe Plain Poaching Syrup (page 31)

4 ounces (115 g) light brown sugar

3 tablespoons (45 ml) lemon juice

1 teaspoon (1.5 g) ground cinnamon

1. Combine the raisins and Calvados. Set aside to macerate for at least 30 minutes.

2. Peel and core the apples and cut them into quarters. Cook in the poaching syrup until soft. Drain, reserving ½ cup (120 ml) liquid. Use the remainder for cake syrup. Chop the apples into small pieces.

3. Combine the apples, half of the sugar, the reserved poaching liquid, and the lemon juice in a saucepan. Cook over medium heat until the apples start to fall apart. Mix the cinnamon with the remaining sugar and add this to the apple mixture. Continue cooking over low heat until the mixture is reduced to a pastelike consistency. Don't overreduce, however; there should still be a few chunks of apple left. Remove from the heat and stir in the raisin and Calvados mixture.

CALVADOS CREAM yield: 2¼ cups (540 ml)

1 pint (480 ml) heavy cream

1 tablespoon (15 g) granulated sugar

¼ cup (60 ml) Calvados

1 teaspoon (5 ml) vanilla extract

I. Whip the cream and sugar until the mixture is fairly thick yet still pourable. Stir in the Calvados and vanilla.

2. Reserve, covered, in the refrigerator. If necessary, adjust the consistency of the sauce at serving time by adding additional cream to thin it or by whipping it a little longer to thicken. The sauce should be thick enough not to run on the plate.

VARIATION

WHIPPED CREAM WAFFLES WITH STRAWBERRY-LIME SAUCE

Try serving these waffles for brunch with the following Strawberry-Lime Sauce and whipped cream flavored with vanilla. You will need 1 cup (240 ml) heavy cream whipped with ½ teaspoon (2.5 ml) vanilla extract.

STRAWBERRY-LIME SAUCE yield: 2½ cups (600 ml)

2 pounds (910 g) fresh strawberries

6 ounces (170 g) granulated sugar

3 tablespoons (45 ml) or 2 ounces (55 g) honey

½ cup (120 ml) lime juice

2 tablespoons (16 g) cornstarch

2 tablespoons (30 ml) strained raspberry puree (optional)

I. Remove the hulls from the strawberries (a small melon ball cutter works well for this). Wash, puree, and strain the berries.

2. Add the sugar, honey, and lime juice. Stir the cornstarch into a small part of the liquid, then mix into the remainder.

3. Bring the sauce to a boil and cook for 2 minutes over low heat to eliminate any aftertaste from the cornstarch.

NOTE: If the sauce is pale from using strawberries that were not perfectly ripe, adding the raspberry puree will give the sauce a more attractive color.

White-Chocolate–Citrus Roulade yield: 16 servings (Photo 75)

This would make a light and refreshing dessert to prepare for a summer luncheon. All of the preparation steps can be completed ahead of time, making the presentation quick and easy. Fill and roll the sponge sheets as soon as possible after they are baked, certainly the same day. If they are made ahead and refrigerated before filling, the skin becomes moist and parts of it will come off as you fill and roll the sheets, making the roulade very unattractive, if not unusable in a quality establishment. To prevent this, place the sheets in the oven for a minute or so to dry the skin, but don't overdo it.

Granulated sugar	1 recipe Raspberry Sauce (page 830)
Citrus-Almond Sponge (recipe follows)	Sour Cream Mixture for Piping (page 832)
White Chocolate Bavarian Cream (recipe follows)	80 small pink grapefruit segments (see Note 1)

1. Sprinkle a little granulated sugar over 2 sheets of baking paper (see Note 2). Invert the citrus-almond sponge sheets on top. Peel the baking paper off the back of the sponges. Do this by tearing the top long side of the paper; then, using both hands, pull down and toward the short ends at the same time (Figure 13-34). This will prevent the thin sponge sheets from breaking as you remove the paper. An alternate method is to hold a dowel against the paper and sponge with one hand as you pull the paper away with your other hand; move both hands together in an even speed, working from one end of the sponge to the other (Figure 13-35). The dowel prevents the sponge from pulling up with the paper and tearing. Trim the long edges if necessary and cut the sheets in half lengthwise to make 4 narrow pieces.

2. Divide the Bavarian cream filling equally between the sponge sheets and spread it out evenly. The filling should be just starting to thicken when you use it. Place the sheets in the refrigerator until the filling feels firm but still sticky, 5 to 10 minutes.

3. Roll each sheet into a roulade. Start by folding the top edge into the filling, then pick up the paper underneath and use it to guide the sponge sheet as you roll it toward you (see Figure 13-11, page 621). Place the roulades, seam-side down, on a sheet pan lined with baking paper and refrigerate for 1 to 2 hours.

FIGURE 13-34 **Using both hands to remove the baking paper from a thin sponge sheet by starting in the center and working toward each end to prevent tearing the sponge**

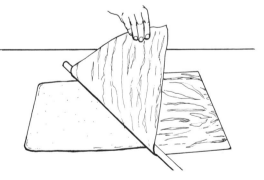

FIGURE 13-35 **A second method of removing the baking paper; holding a dowel against the baking paper and sponge to prevent the sponge from pulling up with the baking paper and tearing as the paper is pulled away with the other hand**

4. Trim the ends of the roulades. Cut each roulade into 4 slices, approximately 4 inches (10 cm) long (see Notes). Use a hot metal skewer to brand each serving, marking 4 parallel lines at an angle on the top of each pastry. Fill a piping bottle with a portion of the raspberry sauce and reserve.

5. Presentation: Pipe a large circle of raspberry sauce, approximately 6 inches (15 cm) in diameter, in the center of a dessert plate. Place a roulade serving in the center of the sauce. Pipe small dots of sour cream mixture 1 inch (2.5 cm) apart all around the perimeter of the sauce. Drag a wooden skewer through the dots in one motion, without lifting the skewer, to make a string of hearts (see Figure 16-2, page 810). Place 5 thin grapefruit segments on the plate between the sauce and the edge of the plate. Serve immediately.

NOTE 1: You will need about 5 medium grapefruit. Cut large segments into 2 or 3 slices if they are too thick. See text and Figures 1-1 and 1-2 (page 13) for instructions on cutting citrus segments.

NOTE 2: The granulated sugar is used to prevent the skin on the sponge from sticking to the paper. The sugar also adds a nice color as it caramelizes when the roulades are decorated with the hot skewer.

NOTE 3: For a different presentation, slice the cut roulades in Step 4 on the bias and arrange the pieces on top of the sauce, leaning against each other. If you are making quite a few of these or just want them all to look the same in the presentation, cut a circle of cardboard, 6 inches (15 cm) in diameter, and attach a looped piece of tape in the center that will act as a handle and allow you to lift the template straight up. Place a small amount of strained strawberry jam, about 5 ounces (140 g) total, in a piping bag. Place the template in the center of a dessert plate (large enough that the template lies flat). Sift powdered sugar over the exposed part of the plate, including the rim. Remove the template carefully by pulling it straight up, using the tape handle. Pipe a thin string of jam on the plate next to the powdered sugar, following the outside edge of the template. Fill the inside of the jam pattern with the raspberry sauce.

CITRUS-ALMOND SPONGE yield: 2 sheets, 15 × 18 inches (37.5 × 45 cm)

2 egg whites (¼ cup/60 ml)

8 ounces (225 g) almond paste

8 whole eggs, separated

8 ounces (225 g) granulated sugar

1 teaspoon (5 ml) vanilla extract

Finely grated zest of 2 lemons (see Note)

5 ounces (140 g) cake flour

1. Gradually mix the 2 egg whites into the almond paste to soften it.

2. Whip the egg yolks with 2 ounces (55 g) sugar to the ribbon stage. Add the vanilla. Very gradually blend the yolk mixture into the almond paste. Do not try to do this too fast or the mixture will become lumpy.

3. Whip the 8 egg whites until foamy. Gradually add the remaining 6 ounces (170 g) sugar and continue whipping until stiff peaks form.

4. Sift the cake flour. Carefully fold the reserved egg yolk mixture into the whipped egg whites together with the lemon zest. Fold in the flour. Divide the batter between 2 sheets of baking paper and spread it out evenly into sheets measuring 15 × 18 inches (37.5 × 45 cm); they should be about ¼ inch (6 mm) thick. Drag the papers onto sheet pans (see Figure 9-4, page 443).

5. Bake immediately at 425°F (219°C) for approximately 8 minutes or until just baked through.

NOTE: After grating the zest, juice the lemons for the White Chocolate Bavarian Cream.

WHITE CHOCOLATE BAVARIAN CREAM yield: 6 cups (1 L 440 ml)

Do not make this filling until you are ready to use it.

1½ cups (360 ml) heavy cream

4 teaspoons (12 g) unflavored gelatin powder

⅓ cup (80 ml) cold water

5 ounces (140 g) granulated sugar

6 egg whites (¾ cup/180 ml)

Grated zest of 1 lemon

Grated zest of 2 oranges

½ cup (120 ml) lemon juice (see Note from previous recipe)

5 ounces (140 g) white chocolate, melted

1. Whip the cream to soft peaks. Reserve in the refrigerator.

2. Sprinkle the gelatin over the cold water and set aside to soften.

3. Combine the sugar and egg whites in a mixer bowl. Heat over simmering water, stirring constantly to prevent the egg whites from cooking, until the mixture reaches 140°F (60°C). Remove from the heat while continuing to stir. Put the bowl on the mixer and whip at high speed until the mixture is cold and has formed stiff peaks. Reserve the meringue.

4. Add both grated citrus zests and the lemon juice to the softened gelatin. Place the mixture over a bain-marie and heat until the gelatin is dissolved. Do not overheat. Quickly stir in the white chocolate. Combine the reserved whipped cream with the meringue. Gradually, to avoid lumps, add the white chocolate mixture.

FROZEN PLATED DESSERTS

Frozen Apple Towers with Warm Sautéed Apples and Raisins yield: 12 servings

This presentation incorporates a theme that is quite prevalent today, that of stacking or layering the components of a dish before serving it to the guest. This idea is illustrated in numerous trend-setting offerings by pastry and hot kitchen chefs alike, often with the title of "napoleon of this" or "napoleon of that." Unfortunately, many of the creations pictured in magazines and cookbooks are simply unservable—they are designed purely for the camera and would never survive if they actually had to be carried across the dining room by a waiter in the real world. Other ill-fated concepts may at best (or at worst, depending on who is the victim) actually make it to the table standing upright, but the poor customer is often afraid to touch the precarious assembly for fear of it falling in the wrong direction. In some cases, you can't help but wonder if the chefs that come up with these ideas may have a vested interest in the dry cleaning business!

Your guests will not have to worry about any of the above problems with the following recipe because it keeps the size and number of layers within reason. And even if they should for some reason sit and stare at it too long, it will simply melt before their eyes and their problem of determining a course of attack will be over.

Any small, low forms would be suitable for the financier, such as tartlet or barquette molds, ½ inch deep. The recipe will make enough extra financier that you can serve two or three per person on a separate small side plate. A nice touch is to offer enough for the table, if possible, serving four pieces to a party of two, etc. Keep in mind that the financiers should bite-sized.

⅓ cup (80 ml) Calvados	5 ounces (140 g) unsalted butter
3 ounces (85 g) golden raisins	Apple Chips (instructions follow)
6 Granny Smith apples	Almond Financiers (recipe follows)
Juice of 1 lemon	Apple Cider-Calvados Sorbet (page 746)
5 ounces (140 g) granulated sugar	Powdered sugar
1 teaspoon (2 g) ground cinnamon	

I. Warm the Calvados and add the raisins. Remove from the heat, cover, and macerate for several hours (or, better yet, overnight) until most or all of the Calvados is absorbed.

2. Peel and core the apples. Slice very thin, using a mandoline, then cut across the slices to make a fine julienne. Squeeze the lemon juice over the apple pieces and toss to coat the pieces with juice.

3. Combine the sugar and the cinnamon. Melt the butter in a sauté pan. Add the sugar mixture and the apples. Sauté for just a few minutes so that the apples stay crunchy; do not cook them too long. Add the raisins and Calvados and keep the mixture warm.

4. Presentation: Set aside the 12 best-looking apple chips to use for garnish. Place some of the sautéed apple mixture on the lower half of a dessert plate. Place an unmolded almond financier centered on top of the apple mixture. Working quickly, place an apple chip on your work surface. Top with a small scoop of apple cider-Calvados sorbet. Layer a second chip and a second scoop of sorbet, and garnish by standing a reserved chip upright in the sorbet. Set the assembled stack on the plate opposite the cake and apples. Sift powdered sugar over the entire plate and serve immediately.

APPLE CHIPS yield: variable

Juice of 1 lemon	4 large green apples
1 cup (240 ml) simple syrup	

I. Add the lemon juice to the simple syrup.

2. Place an apple lengthwise on an electric slicer so that the fruit stem is parallel to the blade. Cut off slices, making them as thin as possible without having them break or tear. Repeat with the other apples.

3. Discard the end pieces that do not have a complete apple outline. One or two at a time, dip the remaining apple slices into simple syrup, letting all of the excess run back into the bowl, and place the slices on Silpats.

4. Bake (dry) the slices at 250°F (122°C) until dried through. The time needed will vary depending on the fruit itself and the oven. When you think the chips are ready, test by removing 1 or 2 chips and placing them on a cold surface, such as marble or metal. Let sit for about a minute, then lift up to see if they are crisp. If not, return them to the tray and keep baking the chips a bit longer. It is necessary to test in this manner because the fruit chips will always be soft and flexible while they are still warm even if they have dried all the way. Do not allow the fruit chips to brown at all. If this happens, your oven is too hot.

5. Remove the sheet pans from the oven, and transfer the chips to an airtight container as soon as possible. This is especially important in humid weather, in which case you should also use some type of desiccant, such as limestone or silica gel. Should the chips soften, however, they can always be dried again.

NOTE: The method described here can be used to make fruit chips using any similar firm fruit such as pears, quince, or Asian pears.

ALMOND FINANCIERS yield: 20 to 30 small cakes

Melted unsalted butter	3 eggs, at room temperature
Sliced almonds, lightly crushed	1 tablespoon (15 ml) Calvados
4 ounces (115 g) granulated sugar	3 ounces (85 g) bread flour
11 ounces (310 g) almond paste	¼ teaspoon (1 g) baking powder
6 ounces (170 g) Beurre Noisette (page 7)	Powdered sugar

1. Brush melted butter over the inside of 20 to 30 small madeleine baking forms, coat with crushed almonds, and place the forms on a sheet pan.

2. Place the sugar and almond paste in a mixing bowl. Blend the butter in gradually, making sure there are no lumps. Add the eggs, 1 at a time, then the Calvados.

3. Sift the flour and baking powder together and stir into the batter. Take care not to over-whip the mixture at this time or the excess air will make the finished product dry and crumbly.

4. Place the batter in a pastry bag with a medium plain tip. Pipe into the prepared forms, dividing it evenly.

5. Bake at 400°F (190°C) for about 20 minutes or until baked through and golden brown on the bottom as well as the top (unmold one to check). Dust a sheet of baking paper with powdered sugar. Invert the forms onto the paper and let them cool. After the cakes have cooled, remove the forms.

Frozen Mint Mousse with a Frosty Chocolate Shell yield: 16 servings (Photo 1)

The great chef Antoine Carême would probably turn over in his grave if he found out that many recipes for his classic Soufflé Glacé are prepared with a small amount of gelatin, even though the freezing process alone firms the filling sufficiently. The same trick has been applied to this mint-flavored frozen mousse to give you the option of serving the desserts frozen or thawed. In either case, the desserts are coated with sprayed chocolate to form a thin, hard crust on the exterior while they are still frozen.

To thaw the desserts before serving, transfer them from the freezer to the refrigerator (or to room temperature) just long enough for the filling to thaw all the way through but remain cold. Even though the filling becomes quite soft, thanks to the gelatin—and, to a lesser degree, the hard chocolate crust—the desserts still hold their shape. The contrasting flavors and textures of the crisp chocolate shell and the creamy mint filling play off one another quite well. The photograph of this dessert features a presentation in which the serving plate has been partially covered with sprayed chocolate. If this is not practical, sift cocoa powder very lightly over one side of each dessert plate instead.

1 sheet Joconde Sponge Base II (page 449)	1 teaspoon (5 g) granulated sugar
Frozen Mint Mousse Filling (recipe follows)	1 recipe Mint Decorating Syrup (page 835)
1 recipe Chocolate Solution for Spraying (page 467)	16 Tuile Spoons (recipe follows)
1 cup (240 ml) heavy cream	16 fresh cherries or other small berries
	1 recipe Spun Sugar (recipe follows)

I. Line 16 cake rings, 3 inches (7.5 cm) in diameter and 2 inches (5 cm) in height, with acetate strips (see Chef's Tip). Place the rings on an even sheet pan lined with baking paper.

2. Using a plain cookie cutter, 3 inches (7.5 cm) in diameter, cut 16 rounds from the Joconde sponge sheet. Place the cake rings in the bottom of the prepared cake rings and set them aside while you make the filling.

3. Place the mint filling in a pastry bag with a No. 8 (16-mm) plain tip. Pipe the filling into the prepared rings on top of the sponge rounds. Smooth the tops even with a spatula or by tapping the sheet pan firmly against the table. Cover the rings and place the pan in the freezer for at least 4 hours or, preferably, overnight.

4. Have a spray gun clean and ready, melt the chocolate solution, and be sure to read the instructions for spraying with chocolate (page 466) if you are not familiar with this technique. Set up a workstation for spraying in the following manner. If possible, choose a corner area and line the work surface and the lower wall area with baking paper or plastic wrap. Cover the base and the top of a cake-decorating turntable with plastic wrap; place this in your prepared area (see Note). Remove the cake rings from the frozen desserts and peel off the acetate strips. Place 4 to 6 desserts at a time around the perimeter on top of the cake-decorating stand, spacing them well apart. Spray them with the chocolate solution until they are just evenly covered; do not spray a thick coating of chocolate. Place these desserts back in the freezer and repeat with the remaining servings. As necessary, reheat the chocolate spray and change the plastic on top of the cake-decorating stand. If desired, also spray one side of each serving plate lightly with the chocolate solution; set the plates aside where they will not be disturbed.

5. If you plan to serve the desserts thawed, as discussed in the introduction, transfer them to the refrigerator for 1 to 2 hours or leave them at room temperature for 30 to 45 minutes.

CHEF'S TIP

If you do not have cake rings in the size called for, you can certainly use another size as long as it is fairly close. In the case that you do not have enough of any one size (for a large party, for example), it is quite simple to make rings from strips of acetate of the proper width and length by taping the over-lapping short ends. To be sure that the rings will stand straight when placed on end, wrap the acetate strips around a metal ring or plastic tube of the appropriate diameter with the ring set on an even surface. Position the long side of the acetate strip that will become the bottom part of the ring so that it is pressed evenly against the work surface all around before securing the end with tape. When using this method, keep in mind that the size of your new rings will increase by the thickness of the ring or tube you use to form them. If you are using these standalone plastic rings, instead of using a cookie cutter to cut the sponge rounds, simply push the plastic through the sponge to create an instant base. This technique works well provided the plastic is thick enough to pierce the sponge.

6. Whip the heavy cream and sugar together until stiff peaks form. Place in a pastry bag with a No. 8 (16-mm) French-Style star tip (see page 959) and reserve in the refrigerator. Place the mint syrup in a piping bottle and set aside at room temperature.

7. Presentation: Place a serving of mousse off-center on a prepared dessert plate. Heat a small spoon by holding it under hot water or over a flame (it does not need to be very hot) and use the spoon to remove a small portion from the front of the mousse. Set this piece on the plate next to the dessert. Pipe a rosette of whipped cream on top of the mousse. Stand a tuile spoon straight up next to the rosette. Place a cherry (or other small fruit) by the spoon, then arrange a small portion of spun sugar behind the mousse and pipe mint syrup in an uneven circular band in front. Serve immediately.

NOTE: A cake-decorating turntable is convenient because it can easily be rotated for even coverage as you spray. If one is not available, use the next best thing that you have on hand. For example, you could use an inverted cake pan, 10 inches (25 cm) in diameter, set on top of a saucepan or another utensil to raise it to the proper height.

FROZEN MINT MOUSSE FILLING yield: 3 quarts (2 L 860 ml)

¾ cup (180 ml) crème de menthe

¼ cup (60 ml) water

4 teaspoons (12 g) unflavored gelatin powder

6 eggs, separated

8 ounces (225 g) granulated sugar

1 cup (240 ml) orange juice

⅓ cup (80 ml) water

2½ cups (600 ml) heavy cream

1. Combine the crème de menthe and ¼ cup (60 ml) water. Sprinkle the gelatin on top and set aside to soften.

2. Whip the egg yolks with half of the sugar to a light and fluffy consistency. Stir in the orange juice. Place over a bain-marie and, whisking constantly, heat the mixture until it is thick enough to coat a spoon. Set aside to cool to room temperature.

3. Combine the remaining half of the sugar with ⅓ cup (80 ml) water in a saucepan, bring to a boil and cook to 230°F (110°C). Beat the egg whites until soft peaks form. Gradually add the sugar syrup and whip until the meringue is cool.

4. Whip the heavy cream to soft peaks. Heat the gelatin until dissolved. Gradually fold the yolk mixture into the whipped cream. Stir this into the meringue. Transfer about one-quarter of the mixture into another bowl and, working quickly, stir in the warm gelatin mixture. Still working quickly, stir this into the remaining filling. Use immediately.

> **CHEF'S TIP**
> Unless you use a very small saucepan (1 cup/240 ml capacity), it is virtually impossible to cook and accurately measure the small amount of sugar syrup called for here. Often it is easier to simply double the amounts and pour half the syrup into the egg whites; you can approximate the quantity. Discard the remaining syrup. The few cents wasted on the sugar is a small price to pay for efficiency and precision.

TUILE COOKIE SPOONS yield: about 60 spoon decorations

Butter and Flour Mixture (page 7)

¼ recipe or 8 ounces (225 g) Vanilla Tuile Decorating Paste (page 482)

½ teaspoon (1.25 g) unsweetened cocoa powder, sifted

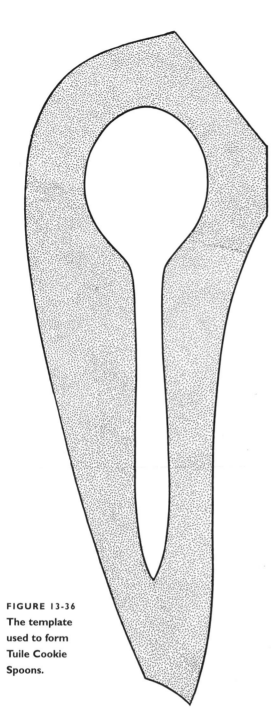

FIGURE 13-36
The template used to form Tuile Cookie Spoons.

1. Make the cookie spoon template (Figure 13-36). The template as shown is the correct size required for this recipe. Trace the drawing, then cut the template out of ¹⁄₁₆-inch (2-mm) cardboard (cake boxes work fine for this).

2. Brush the butter and flour mixture on the backs of clean, even sheet pans; if you have Silpats, which do not need to be greased and floured, use them instead. Have ready at least 2 or, better yet, 4 identical small metal spoons approximately the same size as the template.

3. Color 1 tablespoon (15 ml) tuile paste with the cocoa powder, mixing until completely smooth. Place the cocoa-colored paste in a piping bag.

4. Spread the plain tuile paste onto the prepared sheet pans (or Silpats), spreading it flat and even within the template (see Figures 10-29 and 10-30, page 482). Do not spread more than 8 to 10 spoons on each pan or mat or you will not have time to form them before the small cookies get too dark.

5. Pipe 3 small dots of the cocoa-colored paste in the handle of each spoon.

6. Bake at 400°F (205°C) for approximately 4 minutes or until there are a few light brown spots on the cookies.

7. Leave the pan in the oven and remove the cookie spoons, 1 at a time. Working quickly, form them by pressing each cookie gently between 2 metal spoons: Center the cookie over 1 spoon, place a second spoon on top, and press together to shape the bowl of the spoon. Repeat to bake and form the remaining spoons. Reserve until time of service. The cookie spoons can be kept for several days at this point if stored in an airtight container at room temperature.

SPUN SUGAR yield: variable

Spun sugar is traditionally used to decorate ice cream desserts, but it can be used to dress up many others as well. It looks very showy but is actually easy to make. The mass of thin, hairlike sugar threads is also used to decorate *pièces montées*, such as Croquembouche. Gâteau Saint-Honoré is also decorated with spun sugar on some occasions.

Unless the weather is dry, it is best to make spun sugar immediately before serving. Moisture is gradually absorbed by the thin threads, which become sticky and eventually dissolve. When spun sugar is used as part of a plate presentation, it should not come in contact with a sauce or it will melt.

As with any sugar work, you should prepare everything you will need before you begin to boil the sugar. Cover two wooden dowels or yardsticks with plastic wrap. Place them, parallel, about 18 inches

(45 cm) apart and extending over the edge of the table. Set a heavy cutting board on top at the back to hold them in place. Place a couple of sheet pans on the floor beneath the dowels to catch any drips. You will need a metal balloon whisk with the end cut off and the wires slightly spead apart (Figure 13-37, see Chef's Tip). Have an airtight container handy in which to put the sugar as it is ready. If you are adding color, keep in mind that the color will appear much lighter after the sugar is spun into thin threads, so a darker shade than is normally used is called for here.

Caramelized Sugar with Water (page 11)   **Food coloring (optional)**

1. Following the recipe and directions for Caramelized Sugar with Water, boil the syrup only to 310°F (155°C), the hard crack stage; add the coloring, if using, at 265°F (130°C). Immediately remove from the heat and plunge the bottom of the pan into cold water for a few seconds to stop the cooking process. Remove the pan from the water and let the syrup stand until slightly thickened before you start to spin to prevent too many drops falling off the whisk during the spinning process. Do not stir the sugar.

2. Dip the cut whisk about ½ inch (1.2 cm) into the sugar. Gently shake off excess by moving the whisk in an up-and-down motion just above the surface of the sugar syrup. Do not hold the whisk up too high when you do this or the sugar drops will cool down too much as they fall back into the pan, which can cause the sugar to recrystallize.

3. Spin the sugar by flicking the whisk back and forth in a rapid motion between the two dowels (Figure 13-38). Continue dipping and spinning the sugar until a reasonable amount has accumulated on the dowels.

4. Gather the sugar threads off the dowels and place in the airtight container. Continue spinning the remaining sugar. If the syrup cools down too much, warm it over low heat, stirring constantly to prevent the sugar from becoming any darker than necessary.

NOTE 1: It is impossible to predict a precise yield when spinning sugar. On a rainy or humid day, you will get a much smaller volume. Also, depending on how many times you have to reheat the sugar, you may not be able to use all of the syrup.

NOTE 2: If you spin the sugar in a dry place, you can store it for up to 2 days by lining the bottom of an airtight container with a dehumidifying agent covered with a sheet of foil.

CHEF'S TIP
If you are spinning only a small amount of sugar for 1 or 2 desserts, a quick and easy method is to hold a prepared dowel in front of you horizontally and flick the whisk back and forth with your other hand. When you are making a large quantity of spun sugar, it is helpful to work with 2 cut-off whisks so that you can set 1 aside to let the sugar cool when the wires become clogged with sugar, and continue spinning using the second whisk. To clean the sugar-coated whisks, let the sugar cool and harden, then place the bottom of the whisk in a small plastic bag. Hit the whisk hard against the edge of a table and the sugar will fall off the wires into the bag.

FIGURE 13-37 A metal whisk before and after removing the round end and spreading the wires apart slightly to use in making spun sugar

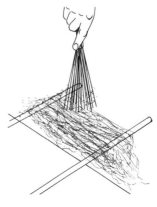

FIGURE 13-38 Making spun sugar by flicking the hot sugar syrup back and forth between 2 dowels extended over the edge of a table

Individual Baked Alaska Beehives yield: 16 servings (Photo 48)

This is one of my desserts that appeared in the original PBS television series "Cooking at the Academy." For the program, we had planned a flambéed presentation. When the show was filmed, the beehives were the last item I was to prepare in the day's shoot, and it was to be very simple, or so I thought—until I discovered that there wasn't any 151-proof rum available; this rum is convenient because it can be ignited cold.

At this point, we had to change the format to use the more conventional method of heating the spirit or liqueur first before burning. Easy enough; however, when poured on a frozen dessert like this one, the alcohol cools down and stops burning very rapidly. I piped meringue beehives and poured hot brandy on top a half-dozen times, but when I got to the flambé part, it always ended with a resounding "Cut!" from the director, who could not see enough of the flames before the brandy had cooled and stopped burning. I then decided to apply some Hollywood-type special effects and use pure alcohol (as no one was actually going to eat the dessert; it was just for the film), which resulted in a spectacular fire show and, unfortunately, a beehive resembling the charred black remains of a forest fire! Finally, after trial and error (on a plate instead of a beehive), we came up with the right combination of pure alcohol and brandy so that the flames showed up on film but didn't burn so long that the dessert was ruined. By the time we finished filming this "simple" dessert, it was 4 o'clock in the morning!

You now may have trouble believing that the beehives are really very easy to execute, but it's true. They can be prepped long in advance and held in the freezer ready to brown and serve. The bees can even be left out if time does not allow you to make them; they could just as well be inside their hives as sitting on top.

½ recipe Dobos Sponge batter (page 443)

Orange liqueur

1 recipe Rhubarb Ice Cream (page 732) or Strawberry Ice Cream (page 733)

½ recipe Italian Meringue (page 27)

1 recipe Rhubarb Sauce (page 831)

Powdered sugar

16 edible fresh flowers

16 Marzipan Bumblebees (directions follow)

1. Spread the Dobos batter into a rectangle measuring 16 x 14 inches (40 x 35 cm) on a sheet of baking paper. Drag the paper onto a sheet pan (see Figure 9-4, page 443). Bake as directed in the sponge recipe. Let cool.

2. Cut 16 circles, 2¾ to 3 inches (7 to 7.5 cm) in diameter, from the sponge sheet. Brush orange liqueur over the circles. Place a scoop of ice cream, 2½ to 3 ounces (75 to 90 ml), on each circle. Cover and reserve in the freezer.

3. Presentation: Place the meringue in a pastry bag with a No. 4 (8-mm) plain tip. Place a frozen sponge circle with ice cream in the center of an ovenproof dessert plate. Working quickly, completely cover the sponge and ice cream with meringue by piping circles of meringue on top of each other, starting on the plate around the dessert (Figure 13-39) Pour just enough rhubarb sauce around the beehive to cover the base of the plate. Lightly sift powdered sugar over the meringue and the rim of the plate. Brown the meringue by placing the dessert under a broiler or salamander, or by very carefully using a blowtorch. Place a flower and a marzipan bumblebee on top

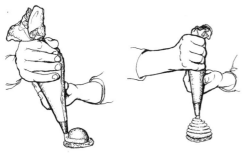

FIGURE 13-39 **Starting on the sponge base (as described in the Note), piping meringue in a circular fashion to completely cover the ice cream scoop for Individual Baked Alaska Beehives**

of the beehive and a second flower next to the hive in the sauce. Serve immediately.

NOTE: If you are expecting to serve a lot of these, you know you have a large order coming up, or you just want to prep ahead, you can place the sponge circles with ice cream 3 inches (7.5 cm) apart on sheet pans lined with baking paper. Make sure that the ice cream scoops are small enough that you have room to pipe the first row of meringue on the sponge and not on the sheet pan. Pipe the meringue as directed. Reserve in the freezer until needed. (They can be left this way for up to 24 hours.) Sift powdered sugar on top just before browning.

CHEF'S TIP
For a dramatic dining room presentation, pour 151-proof rum on the dessert, ignite, and quickly present to the guest. This technique is really more practical for the larger classic version of baked Alaska because you don't want to flambé the marzipan bee and you must either place it in the sauce (which is not as appealing), add it after the flames go out (which is a little awkward), or risk being reported to the Society for the Prevention of Cruelty to Animals.

MARZIPAN BUMBLEBEES yield: 16 decorations

Though it can be a bit more difficult to work with very small pieces of marzipan, as is done here, do not be tempted to plump up the bumblebees; they can easily begin to take the shape of a small hummingbird, and while the two may share the same interest in flowers, the larger creatures look quite out of place on a beehive. Following these instructions produces life-size bees, admittedly rather simplified.

½ ounce (15 g) plus 3 ounces (85 g) Marzipan (page 21), untinted	Yellow food coloring
Unsweetened cocoa powder	Egg white
	Sliced almonds

1. Be certain that your work area and your hands are absolutely clean. Color the ½-ounce (15-g) piece of marzipan dark brown by mixing cocoa powder into it. Roll it out to a rope 6 inches (15 cm) long and cut the rope into 16 equal pieces. Cover the pieces and set them aside.

2. Color the remaining piece of marzipan pale yellow. Roll this piece out to make a 16-inch (40-cm) rope and cut it into 16 equal pieces. Roll a yellow piece between the palms of your hands to make it soft and pliable, then roll it into a round ball. Roll the ball against the work surface to make it oblong, about 1 inch (2.5 cm) in length, and slightly tapered at both ends. Repeat with the remaining yellow pieces of marzipan to form the bodies of the bees.

3. Roll a reserved cocoa-colored piece of marzipan between your thumb and forefinger to make it soft and pliable. Divide the piece in half. Roll each half into a smooth, round ball.

4. Slightly flatten one end of a bee body and attach a cocoa-colored ball, using egg white as glue. This will be the bee's head. It should be slightly larger than the end of the bee where it is attached. Cut the body of the bee in half across the width, flatten the second cocoa-colored ball, and attach it between the two body halves with egg white. Place the bee on top of a dowel, 2 inches (5 cm) in diameter, set on a sheet pan lined with baking paper (secure the dowel with a little marzipan so it will not roll) so the bee will dry in a slightly curved position. Assemble the remaining marzipan bumblebees in the same way.

5. For the wings, select 32 unbroken almond slices. Pair them so that the wings on each bee will be the same size. Use a paring knife to make a small insertion point on both sides of each bee just behind the head, then carefully push the narrow end of an almond slice into the cuts. If necessary, allow the bees to remain on the dowel until they will hold their shape.

Ice Cream, Sorbets, and Sherbets

Ice creams and other frozen desserts in different shapes and combinations have always been favorites of guests and chefs alike. Ice cream seems to bring out the child in us, making it almost impossible to resist. Ice cream and many ice cream desserts are very practical for the chef because they can be made days in advance. Today, with small electric ice cream freezers available at a reasonable cost, home cooks can make wonderful ice creams as effortlessly as professionals. Churning ice cream by hand has become almost obsolete. Many of the ice creams that follow are used as part of another recipe or in a plate presentation elsewhere in this book. In some cases, a particular accompaniment such as a sauce, a type of fresh fruit, or a tuile shell is suggested with the ice cream recipe, when it goes particularly well with a certain flavor.

Custard-Based Ice Cream

The term *ice cream* generally refers to the custard-based variety, which is a confection made from cream and/or whole milk, sugar, and egg yolks. These ingredients are cooked over a bain-marie until the custard thickens sufficiently to coat a spoon—when you pull a wooden spoon out of the mixture, you will not be able to see the wood—which is also referred to as the *ribbon* or *nappe stage*. It is important not to overheat and coagulate the eggs. After this minimal cooking, the custard base is first chilled, then placed in an ice cream freezer together with the desired flavorings, and the mixture is frozen to a temperature below 32°F (0°C) while being churned to incorporate air and produce the desired texture and overrun. The result should be smooth, airy, and creamy.

Vanilla ice cream is the forerunner of this type with the French vanilla method being the most common flavor produced. The flavor of vanilla ice cream mixes and blends well with a wide range of other desserts, and the cooked custard itself serves as the base for many other flavors of ice cream, as you will see in the recipes that follow. There are all kinds of hybrids and variations of custard-based ice creams. Three examples are: Philadelphia-style ice creams, which do not contain egg products (although sometimes a relatively small amount is added to improve mouth feel); French vanilla ice cream, which has a high ratio of milkfat to egg yolks; and Italian-style gelato, which is made using whole milk (no cream) and a larger proportion of egg yolks than the French vanilla type. The large quantity of egg yolks produces almost no overrun, which in turn gives gelato its distinctive dense texture and intense flavor.

COMPOSITION

Ice cream is composed of milk products, sweeteners, eggs, flavorings, and stabilizers or emulsifiers. The U.S. Food and Drug Administration (FDA) requires that commercial products labeled *ice cream* must contain no less than 10 percent milkfat (butterfat) and must have at least 20 percent MSNF (milk solids no fat). A good-quality ice cream should have a minimum of 40 percent total solids (fat, sweetener, and MSNF). Milk solids contribute to the whipping capability of the custard; however, if the custard contains too large a percentage of milk solids without enough fat from egg yolks to balance, the lactose, or milk sugar, can crystallize, making the custard feel gritty; this is known as *sanding*.

Judging the Quality of an Ice Cream

Ice creams are judged and rated on the following points:

- Texture and smoothness—This is determined primarily by the size of the ice crystals and the emulsifying or whipping ability of the custard combined with the amount of milk sugar (lactose) that is added.

- Mouth feel or body—This is established by the total solids in the custard in conjunction with the overrun, which is the amount of air incorporated while freezing.

- Richness and flavor—These factors are produced from the composition of the custard. The fat and MSNF contained in premium ice cream should come from a mixture of whole milk and cream. Evaporated, condensed, or dried milk should not be used, as these products adversely affect the fresh taste of the finished ice cream.

FAT CONTENT

The fat content of the cream and milk blend, and the proportions of cream and milk required to achieve the desired percentage in the finished product, can be calculated using the following method. Draw a rectangle with two lines crossing diagonally. In the upper left corner, write the fat percentage of the cream you are using. Write the fat percentage of the milk you are using in the lower left corner. In the center, write the desired fat content for the finished ice cream. Subtract the desired fat percentage from the cream fat percentage and write the result in the opposite diagonal corner. Subtract the milk fat percentage from the desired fat percentage and write this figure in the remaining corner. The resulting figures are the proportions of milk and cream you should use in order to achieve the desired fat content. The example (Figure 14-1) shows

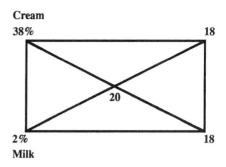

FIGURE 14-1 The formula used to calculate the proportions of milk and cream required to achieve the desired fat content in the finished ice cream

the fat content in an ice cream using half-and-half. In other words, because both figures are 18, you would use equal parts of milk and cream; if the cream figure were 10 and the milk figure 30, you would use 1 part cream to 3 parts milk.

While it is true that milk fat (this term denotes the fat from either the milk or the cream, as cream comes from milk) is responsible for most of the rich, creamy flavor we associate with superior ice cream, too much milk fat—using too much heavy cream—will not only affect the whipping ability but also cause the finished product to be more compact; the overrun (yield) will also be impaired. Another problem that can occur is that the milkfat can be churned into tiny lumps of butter, causing a grainy finished ice cream. This often happens with custards composed of whole cream, or when using mascarpone or white chocolate as part of the base.

SWEETENERS

Sucrose (cane sugar or beet sugar) is the typical sweetener used in ice cream, but maple syrup, molasses, and honey are also common. When substituting honey for granulated sugar in an ice cream custard, the amount should be reduced about 20 percent. Keep in mind also that once it has been frozen, the ice cream will not taste as sweet, as freezing dulls the intensity of the sweet flavor. Even though the sugar content of the total solids in a custard is typically close to 15 percent, particular flavors will require a sweeter custard than others. While a relatively high proportion of sugar can be beneficial in keeping an ice cream smooth and pliable after freezing, too much sugar can prevent the ice cream from becoming firm enough to use.

EGGS

Egg yolks enhance both the smoothness and color of the custard. Due to their emulsifying properties, they also greatly improve the body of the ice cream, although they have almost no effect on the freezing process in the way that sugar does. Egg yolks and whole eggs must be pasteurized by heating the custard to a specific temperature (the scalding point is more than sufficient). Uncooked ice creams, such as Philadelphia-style, which do not contain any egg products, benefit from the use of mono- and diglycerides as emulsifiers and gelatin or gums as stabilizers.

AGING

A warm ice cream custard should never be poured directly into the ice cream freezer. It should be cooled slowly, then refrigerated several hours or overnight. The texture of the finished churned ice cream is greatly improved by this process, which is known in the industry as *aging*. Chilling the custard enhances smoothness, body, and texture in the final product because, as it rests, the proteins in the custard swell and bind with the water. It is not the process of making the custard colder that is doing the work; refrigeration is necessary simply so that the product does not spoil during the aging process. At least 4 hours are necessary, but refrigerating the custard base 12 hours or overnight is ideal.

CHURNING

When the ice cream has churned to the desired consistency, turn off the freezer unit of the ice cream maker but keep the churner on for a few minutes longer, if your machine has this option, before removing the finished ice cream. This will cause a minimum amount of ice cream to stick to the sides of the container.

The amount of air churned into the ice cream during freezing determines the volume and lightness of the finished product. As a rule, the higher the fat content, the lower the finished volume when compared by weight. Because an ice cream made with heavy cream is more compact in its composition, it yields less than an ice cream made with milk or half-and-half and is richer and smoother.

OVERRUN

Overrun is the amount or volume of ice cream obtained after churning that is in excess of the volume of the base. It is actually the amount of air incorporated into the mix during the freezing and churning process. Overrun is discussed as the percentage of overrun. A 100 percent overrun would describe a custard that has doubled in volume during freezing. This is the maximum overrun allowed by the FDA. While some overrun is necessary for a smooth and light texture, too much will give the ice cream an airiness and a less intense flavor. For example, a dense ice cream, such as gelato, has a lower percentage of overrun than French vanilla ice cream. Overrun is determined by:

- the freezing equipment.

- the length of time the ice cream spends in the ice cream freezer. It should be removed as soon as it is frozen.

- the amount of custard in relation to the freezer size. For maximum overrun, the freezer should be filled only halfway.

- the ingredients in the mixture that affect its ability to increase—for example, eggs.

- the total solid content of the base. A custard that has a total solid content of 40 percent (fat, sweetener, and MSNF combined) can produce an overrun of up to 100 percent without diminishing in quality.

ADDITIONS TO ICE CREAM

Many of the recipes in this chapter can be enhanced and varied with the addition to the finished product of specialty ingredients such as chunks of white, milk, or dark chocolate, toasted nuts, candy (for Christmas, try adding crushed peppermint candy to vanilla ice cream), dried or candied fruit, crushed cookies, chopped brownies, caramel sauce (use the recipe for Fortified Caramel Sauce), and/or chocolate sauce. Some classic combinations are vanilla ice cream with candied pecans and swirls of caramel, chocolate ice cream with chips or chunks of dark chocolate, and vanilla ice cream marbleized with fruit preserves. Do not use fresh pureed fruit for this; it must first be sweetened and reduced by cooking or it will not produce the desired marble look and will also adversely effect the texture, freezing hard and icy.

In order to avoid breaking or mashing the pieces, most additions should be incorporated after the ice cream has been churned. Stir the flavoring in while the ice cream is still soft before placing it in the freezer, taking care to distribute the pieces evenly. Fresh or dried fruit should first be macerated in a spirit or liqueur, a sugar syrup, or a combination of the two, so that the fruit will not freeze so hard that it becomes unpleasant to eat. To create a marbleized or swirled pattern of sauce or fruit preserves, alternate layers of freshly churned soft ice cream with much thinner layers of the desired flavor as you place the ice cream in the storage container. (With ice cream machines that extrude the finished product through a spigot, add the fruit preserve or sauce layers as the ice cream flows into the container.) Then, insert a wooden spoon or spatula straight down through the center of the layered mixture after the container is full. Pull from side to side—left to right and back to front—once in each direction, then pull straight out. It is important not to mix the layers too much or instead of ripples you will simply incorporate the flavoring into the base. The swirled pattern will be accentuated as you scoop out the frozen ice cream.

STORAGE AND SERVING

It is possible to store ice cream for 3 to 4 weeks without any loss of volume or quality, provided it is stored in airtight containers. Ice cream should be frozen at 6°F (-15°C) so it will harden quickly. It should then be stored at a temperature between 6° and 14°F (-15° to -9°C). However, ice cream should be served at a higher temperature so that it is pleasant to eat and easy to scoop and work with. The ideal temperature for serving varies by flavor and type. Ice cream and other frozen desserts can be unmolded or scooped into serving glasses 1 to 2 hours in advance and held in the freezer, but final touches and garnishes must be applied at the last moment.

SANITATION

To achieve a finished product of the highest quality, it is immensely important that ice cream is made using only fresh and pure first-rate raw materials that have been properly pasteurized to kill bacteria. The equipment and utensils that come into contact with ice cream must not only be made of stainless steel or another noncorrosive material but also must be properly cleaned and sterilized after each use. The importance of this cannot be overstated. Absolute cleanliness is essential because the ice cream mixture provides a perfect breeding ground for bacteria. Bacteria are unicellular microscopic organisms belonging to the plant kingdom—either cocci, which are spherical in shape; the rod-shaped bacilli; or spirilla, which are formed in a spiral. All reproduce by division and fusion. The factors that accelerate or eliminate their growth are temperature, oxygen, moisture, food particles, chemicals, and light.

Sanitizing Agents

Soap is not a good cleaning agent for ice cream equipment because it leaves a film that can be difficult to rinse away. Heat is the most common and reliable source for sanitizing food equipment; it can offer the added advantage of speeding up the drying time, provided the temperature is high enough. For proper water sanitizing, however, the equipment must be submerged in water with a temperature between 180° and 212°F (82° to 100°C) for at least 10 minutes. Obviously, this is not practical for the ice cream maker itself, so a chemical agent must be applied to that piece of equipment. For the chemical to be completely effective, the item must be thoroughly clean so that its surface comes in direct contact with the chemical. It is also critical that the solution has the proper concentration of the active chemical and, most importantly, that the sanitizing agent is in contact with the equipment for a sufficient time to kill the bacteria. The time will vary with the type of chemical used. A quick, inexpensive, and effective solution can be made from regular laundry bleach. Use 1 to 2 tablespoons (15 to 30 ml) bleach per gallon (3L 840 ml) of warm water. The water should not exceed 110°F (43°C). This solution must be in contact with the surface for a minimum of 1 minute and, of course, it should be thoroughly rinsed to remove all traces of bleach.

About Other Frozen Desserts

In addition to ice creams and sorbets, other popular frozen creations include classical parfaits, frozen soufflés (soufflés glacés), frozen mousses, and desserts composed of several items, such as coupes and bombes. All of these have at least one thing in common: they must be served immediately once they are plated.

- **Parfaits,** made from a mixture of egg yolks and sugar syrup whipped to the ribbon stage, with the addition of whipped cream and flavoring, are usually lighter and less sweet than ice cream. The parfait mixture is poured into tall slender molds, still frozen, and unmolded before serving.

- **Soufflés glacés,** or frozen soufflés, fold Italian meringue into a parfait or bombe mixture flavored with liqueur or fruit, to give the dish a hint of the lightness found in a hot soufflé. The filling is then piled high above the rim of a soufflé mold and served frozen still in the form.

- **Frozen mousses** are closely related to both parfaits and soufflés glacés. Although each of these desserts is classically made using a different formula, in actual practice the bases are interchangeable. All achieve volume from air that is whipped into either cream, eggs, or meringue, all are still frozen, and all require little or no stabilizers, such as gelatin or pectin. What distinguishes a frozen mousse from a parfait is the inclusion of whipped egg whites, which are never used in a true classical parfait mixture.

- **Coupes** are popular and practical individual ice cream or sorbet servings decorated with liqueurs, sauces, fruits, nuts, and/or whipped cream. Some coupes are elaborately decorated with cookies and marzipan or chocolate figures; others are plain and simple. Either way, they look very elegant if served in suitable dishes. Coupes always must be assembled and decorated to order.

- **Bombes** are made by lining a chilled mold with ice cream, sorbet, or sherbet and filling it with a mixture made from egg yolks, sugar, and cream flavored according to the individual recipe. The mold is covered with a clamped lid and then frozen. After unmolding, the bombe reveals its dome shape.

Almond Ice Cream yield: 5 cups (1 L 200 ml)

If you flip through the pages of the text, my love for almonds should become quite obvious. They are used extensively in and on many desserts and other baked goods, from the classic frangipane to the ultimate almond lover's delicacy, marzipan.

If you like, you can substitute almond meal for the blanched almonds called for in this recipe. Use a few ounces less and add the almond meal and the sugar directly to the milk; there is no need to grind them together.

1 pound (455 g) blanched almonds (see
   Chef's Tip)

12 ounces (340 g) granulated sugar

3 cups (720 ml) whole milk

8 egg yolks (⅔ cup/160 ml)

½ cup (120 ml) amaretto liqueur

2 cups (480 ml) heavy cream

1. Place the almonds and sugar in a food processor and process until the mixture has a very fine, even consistency, but do not grind the mixture so fine that it begins to cake. Place in a saucepan and add the milk. Bring to scalding, remove from the heat, and set aside at room temperature to infuse until the milk has cooled completely.

2. Strain the almond milk through a piece of cheesecloth, squeezing the cloth to remove as much of the liquid as possible. You should have close to 3 cups (720 ml) almond-flavored milk. Discard the ground almonds.

3. Place the egg yolks and amaretto in a bowl. Set the bowl over simmering water and heat, whipping constantly, until the mixture is thick enough to coat a spoon. Add the heavy cream and heat until close to scalding, stirring with a wooden spoon or heat-proof spatula; do not let the mixture boil. Remove from the heat and stir the cream mixture into the almond milk. Let cool to room temperature, then cover and refrigerate until thoroughly chilled or, preferably, overnight.

4. Process in an ice cream freezer following the manufacturer's directions. Store the finished ice cream, covered, in the freezer.

CHEF'S TIP
Use any variety of blanched almonds here—sliced, slivered, or whole. If you blanch the nuts yourself, soak them in cold water for 1 hour after you remove the skins; this will whiten the nuts. Allow the almonds to dry at room temperature, preferably until the next day, before you grind them. If you do not have time to wait, dry the almonds in a low oven, but be very careful not to brown them.

About Almonds

Almonds made their way to Europe from the Middle East during the early part of the Middle Ages. As the Moors' rule swept to the west, almonds were introduced to Sicily, Spain, and Portugal, which are today, together with Italy and Turkey, the top almond-producing countries in Europe. Spain generates two of the world's most prized almond varieties: the elongated almonds that grow in the Málaga region (known as Jordan almonds) and the broad Valencia nuts.

Avocado-Mango Ice Cream yield: 2 quarts (1 L 920 ml)

I first tasted avocado ice cream on a trip to Mexico. It was a great surprise to me, and a very pleasant one at that. In this recipe, I have substituted mangoes for half of the avocados, but you can actually go either way: all avocados or all mangoes. (If you use all avocados you will most likely need additional simple syrup.) Combining the two fruits produces a wonderful flavor and texture; the color remains a delicate pale green. Because the sweet mangoes are high in fiber and avocados can contain up to 30 percent oil, it is possible to achieve a soft, smooth creamy texture without adding fat from egg yolks or as large a proportion of dairy fat in the form of heavy cream, as is typical.

1 pound 6 ounces (625 g) perfectly ripe avocados (approximately 3 small)

1 pound 8 ounces (680 g) perfectly ripe mangoes (approximately 2 medium)

⅓ cup (80 ml) lime juice (3 to 4 limes)

1½ cups (360 ml) simple syrup, approximately

1 cup (240 ml) half-and-half

2 cups (480 ml) whole milk

1. Peel and pit the avocados and mangoes. Discard the pits and place the pulp in a food processor or blender. Process to a smooth consistency.

2. Stir in the lime juice and about two-thirds of the simple syrup. Strain the mixture to remove any stringy fibers from the mango. Stir in the half-and-half and the milk.

3. Adjust the sweetness by adding the remaining simple syrup as needed.

4. Process in an ice cream freezer following the manufacturer's instructions.

5. Store, covered, in the freezer.

Banana–Poppy Seed Ice Cream yield: approximately 6 cups (1 L 440 ml)

I am surprised that this flavor combination has not made its way into the commercial marketplace. Many years ago, a friend gave me this recipe; he said it had been in his family for quite some time. This ice cream goes with just about any dessert, but I particularly like it served with fresh strawberries or strawberry sauce. Like mangoes and papayas, pureed ripe bananas have a creamy, full-bodied texture that gives the ice cream a silky-smooth consistency. The crunchy poppy seeds contrast wonderfully. Any nut-flavored liqueur may be substituted for the Frangelico if you want to experiment. Macadamia nut liqueur is especially nice if you can find it.

8 ounces (225 g) granulated sugar

10 egg yolks (⅞ cup/210 ml)

3 cups (720 ml) whole milk

2 cups (480 ml) heavy cream

2 pounds (910 g) ripe bananas (4 medium)

Juice of ¼ lime

2 ounces (55 g) poppy seeds

⅓ cup (80 ml) Frangelico (hazelnut liqueur)

I. Beat the sugar and egg yolks together lightly to combine. Heat the milk and cream to the scalding point. Stirring constantly, gradually pour the hot liquid into the egg mixture. Place over simmering water and, continuing to stir with a whisk or wooden spoon, heat until the custard thickens enough to coat the spoon. Be careful not to overcook and break the custard. Set aside to cool at room temperature, then cover and refrigerate until thoroughly chilled.

2. Peel the bananas and puree with the lime juice. (If you use fruit that is not fully ripe, it may not puree smoothly, making it necessary to pass the pulp through a fine mesh strainer before proceeding.) Stir the banana puree, poppy seeds, and liqueur into the custard.

3. Process immediately in an ice cream freezer according to the manufacturer's directions. Place a bowl in the freezer at the same time so it will be chilled to hold the finished product. Store the ice cream, covered, in the freezer.

NOTE: As with any custard-based ice cream, Banana–Poppy Seed Ice Cream will have a smoother texture if you rest the custard in the refrigerator for about 8 hours before freezing. Do not prepare, or stir in, the banana puree until you are ready to process the ice cream in the freezer, as the puree will darken as it sits.

Caramel Ice Cream yield: approximately 5 cups (1 L 200 ml)

Due to the addition of caramel sauce, this ice cream remains creamy and malleable without the necessity of softening or smoothing, even after days in the freezer. Be careful, nonetheless, not to add more caramel than specified in the recipe, because too much sugar will keep the ice cream from freezing, leaving you with a product pliable to the point of being unmanageable. Caramel ice cream, like vanilla, has a neutral flavor that goes well with many desserts.

½ recipe Clear Caramel Sauce (page 817)	2 cups (480 ml) heavy cream
1 quart (960 ml) half-and-half	½ recipe Praline (page 33)
10 egg yolks (⅞ cup/210 ml)	

I. Reserve ⅓ cup (80 ml) of the caramel sauce. Place the remaining caramel sauce and the half-and-half in a saucepan and heat the mixture to the scalding point.

2. Whip the egg yolks and the reserved caramel sauce until fluffy. Gradually add the scalded milk mixture to the egg yolks while whipping rapidly. Heat the mixture over simmering water, stirring constantly with a whisk or wooden spoon, until it is thick enough to coat the spoon. Remove from the heat and blend in the heavy cream. Let the custard cool slightly at room temperature, then cover and refrigerate until thoroughly chilled.

3. Process in an ice cream freezer according to the manufacturer's directions.

4. Crush the praline into currant-sized pieces using a heavy dowel or rolling pin. Stir the praline into the finished ice cream and store, covered, in the freezer.

Cashew Ice Cream yield: approximately 5 cups (1 L 200 ml)

Raw unsalted cashews are not only quite expensive, they can be difficult to find in the retail market. Often a health food or natural foods store is a good place to look. If you must settle for roasted and salted nuts, blanch and dry them to rid them of the salt, and omit toasting the nuts in Step 1. The distinctive buttery, rich flavor of cashews is delightful in combination with fresh ripe fruits, such as peaches, nectarines, and especially mangoes.

1 pound (455 g) unsalted cashews, whole or in pieces	12 egg yolks (1 cup/240 ml)
3 cups (720 ml) whole milk	10 ounces (280 g) granulated sugar
1 vanilla bean, split lengthwise, or 1 teaspoon (5 ml) vanilla extract	2 cups (480 ml) heavy cream

1. Toast the cashews, let cool, then crush coarsely. Reserve 2 ounces (55 g) or about ½ cup (120 ml) nuts.

2. Place the remaining nuts in a food processor with ½ cup (120 ml) milk and process to a pastelike consistency. Set the nut paste aside.

3. Pour the remaining milk into a heavy saucepan. If using the vanilla bean, scrape out the seeds and add both the seeds and the pod halves to the milk. Bring to a boil, then remove from the heat and stir in the nut paste. Cover the pan and set the mixture aside to steep for a minimum of 30 minutes.

4. Whip the egg yolks and sugar together until light in color. Return the milk mixture to boiling, then strain through a fine mesh strainer or a cheesecloth (see Note). Remove the vanilla bean pods and discard. Gradually stir the hot milk into the yolk mixture.

5. Set the bowl over simmering water and, stirring constantly with a whisk or wooden spoon, heat the custard until it is thick enough to coat the spoon. Remove from the heat. Stir in the heavy cream, the vanilla extract, if using, and the reserved crushed cashews. Let cool to room temperature, then cover and refrigerate the custard until it is completely cold.

6. Process in an ice cream freezer according to the manufacturer's instructions. Transfer the finished ice cream to a chilled container. Cover and store in the freezer.

NOTE: Rather than discarding these expensive nuts, try to find a use for them in cookies, a torte, or even Bear Claw filling. Rinse to remove the milk, then spread out on a sheet pan to dry. Use within a few days.

Cinnamon Ice Cream yield: approximately 5 cups (1 L 200 ml)

Cinnamon ice cream makes a wonderful accompaniment to many types of fruit desserts and, because of the natural affinity of the two flavors, especially any containing apple. Warm apple desserts, such as apple pie, turnovers, crisp, and apples en croûte, are particularly pleasing, as the cold, creamy ice cream provides a delicious contrast to the crisp crust and tart apple filling and melts into a cinnamon-flavored custard sauce.

1 quart (960 ml) half-and-half

2 cinnamon sticks, approximately 3 inches (7.5 ml) long

1 vanilla bean, split lengthwise, or 2 teaspoons (10 ml) vanilla extract

2 teaspoons (3 g) ground cinnamon

10 ounces (285 g) granulated sugar

10 egg yolks (⅞ cup/210 ml)

1. Heat the half-and-half with the cinnamon sticks and the split vanilla bean, if using, to scalding. Remove from the heat, cover, and set aside to infuse for 30 minutes.

2. Thoroughly combine the ground cinnamon and the granulated sugar. Add to the egg yolks and beat until light and fluffy.

3. Remove the vanilla bean halves from the half-and-half and use the back of a paring knife to scrape the seeds into the half-and-half. Discard the empty pods or rinse and save for another use if desired. Gradually pour the half-and-half into the whipped egg yolk mixture while whisking rapidly. (Place a towel under the bowl to keep it from turning with your whisk.)

4. Heat the mixture over simmering water, stirring constantly with a whisk or wooden spoon, until it thickens enough to coat the spoon. Be careful not to overheat and break the custard. Remove from the heat and continue to stir for a few seconds to keep the mixture from overcooking where it touches the hot bowl. Stir in the vanilla extract, if using. Let cool to room temperature, then refrigerate, covered, until completely cold, several hours or, preferably, overnight.

5. Remove the cinnamon sticks. Process the mixture in an ice cream freezer following the manufacturer's instructions. Transfer to a chilled container and store, covered, in the freezer.

NOTE: Cinnamon ice cream will improve in texture if the custard is made the day before churning and left to rest in the refrigerator.

VARIATION

LOW-FAT CINNAMON-MAPLE ICE CREAM yield: approximately 1 quart (960 ml)

1½ cups (360 ml) part-skim ricotta cheese

1 pint (480 ml) Unflavored Yogurt (page 38), made with low-fat milk

½ cup (120 ml) pure maple syrup

1 vanilla bean, split lengthwise

2 teaspoons (3 g) ground cinnamon

1. Puree the ricotta cheese. Stir in the yogurt and maple syrup.

2. Scrape the seeds from the vanilla bean halves into the ricotta mixture along with the cinnamon. Discard the empty pods or rinse and save for another use if desired.

3. Process in an ice cream freezer according to the manufacturer's directions.

Cocoa Nib–White Chocolate Ice Cream yield: 9 cups (2 L 160 ml)

Cocoa nibs are produced in one of the first stages of chocolate manufacturing. After whole cocoa beans have been roasted, they are crushed, the shells or husks are removed, and the small roasted kernels of cocoa bean that remain are called *nibs*. Many more steps must be completed to transform these into finished chocolate, but added to ice cream, a cake batter, or a decorating paste, cocoa nibs contribute an intense roasted chocolate flavor and a pleasant crunchy texture. Cocoa nibs can be purchased from most large chocolate purveyors.

Because of the white chocolate in the recipe, it is very important not to overchurn or the texture can become gritty and the ice cream will be unusable.

4½ cups (1 L 80 ml) half-and-half

3 cups (720 ml) heavy cream

12 egg yolks (1 cup/240 ml)

4 ounces (115 g) granulated sugar

12 ounces (340 g) white chocolate, cut into small chunks

4 ounces (115 g) cocoa nibs

1. Combine the half-and-half and cream and heat to scalding.

2. Beat the egg yolks with the sugar until light and fluffy. Whisk the hot cream into the egg yolk mixture.

3. Place over simmering water and heat, stirring constantly with a whisk or wooden spoon (do not whip), until the custard is thick enough to coat the spoon.

4. Remove from the heat and add the white chocolate, continuing to stir until all of the chunks are melted. Let cool to room temperature, then refrigerate until completely cold.

5. Process in an ice cream freezer according to the manufacturer's directions. Remove the ice cream from the ice cream freezer just before it is fully churned and thickened; it should be too soft to scoop out. Transfer to a chilled bowl, stir in the cocoa nibs, cover, and place in the freezer. The ice cream will become firmer once frozen. If allowed to freeze completely while churning, the texture will be compromised.

Coffee-Scented Chocolate Ice Cream yield: approximately 6 cups (1 L 440 ml)

If you are a chocolate lover, you will not be able to stop eating this rich chocolate ice cream. It has just a hint of coffee flavor, which, if you prefer, can easily be left out. I recommend you do so rather than use instant coffee if espresso is not available. Try serving this ice cream with a splash of Grand Marnier or Cointreau on top and one or two Florentina cookies on the side.

1 quart (960 ml) half-and-half

4 ounces (115 g) unsweetened cocoa powder

½ cup (120 ml) brewed espresso coffee

1 vanilla bean, split lengthwise, or 1 teaspoon (5 ml) vanilla extract

4 ounces (115 g) sweet dark chocolate

8 egg yolks (⅔ cup/160 ml)

6 ounces (170 g) granulated sugar

1. Gradually mix enough half-and-half into the cocoa powder to dissolve it and make a smooth paste. Stir in the remaining half-and-half and the espresso. Bring to the scalding point with the vanilla bean, if using.

2. Chop the chocolate into small pieces. Remove the cream mixture from the heat, add the chopped chocolate, and stir until completely melted.

3. Whip the egg yolks with the sugar until light and fluffy. Remove the vanilla bean from the half-and-half; scrape the seeds back into the half-and-half for a more intense flavor. Discard the pod halves or rinse and reserve for another use. Add the vanilla extract if using that instead. Gradually pour the hot half-and-half into the yolk mixture while stirring rapidly. Place over simmering water and heat, stirring constantly with a whisk or wooden spoon, until the mixture is thick enough to coat the spoon. Set aside to cool. Cover and refrigerate until thoroughly chilled, preferably overnight.

4. Process in an ice cream freezer according to the manufacturer's directions. Store, covered, in the freezer.

Fresh Coconut Ice Cream yield: approximately 6 cups (1 L 440 ml)

The value of the coconut palm to the native inhabitants wherever it flourishes cannot be described better than in the old native proverb, "He who plants a coconut tree plants vessel and clothing, food and drink, a habitat for himself and a heritage for his children." I am using only a small portion of the "tree of life" in this recipe—the coconut milk and meat. Using a fresh coconut here, rather than desiccated, makes all the difference in flavor. When choosing fresh coconuts, test for freshness by weighing them in your hand; they should feel heavy and, when shaken, should have plenty of milk inside. Coconut ice cream is ideal paired with fresh tropical fruit and a macadamia nut cookie.

2 medium, fresh coconuts, about 2 pounds (910 g) each

Whole milk, as needed

1 vanilla bean, split lengthwise, or 1 teaspoon (5 ml) vanilla extract

2 cups (480 ml) heavy cream

10 egg yolks (⅞ cup/210 ml)

3 ounces (85 g) granulated sugar

1. Puncture the 3 eyes on each coconut with an ice pick and drain out the coconut milk, reserving 3 cups (720 ml). If the coconuts do not contain that much liquid, add enough regular milk to make the amount needed.

2. Tap the coconuts all around with a hammer or heavy cleaver to help loosen the meat from the shell. Crack the coconuts open, using the same tool. Remove the meat from the shell, then use a vegetable peeler to remove the brown skin from the meat. (If some pieces do not separate from the shell, place them on a sheet pan and bake at 350°F/175°C for about 30 minutes to loosen.) Chop the coconut meat finely in a food processor.

3. Combine the coconut meat, coconut milk, and vanilla bean, if using, in a nonreactive saucepan. Heat to scalding, remove from the heat, cover, and let infuse for at least 30 minutes.

4. Strain the mixture, pressing with a spoon to remove as much liquid as possible from the coconut meat. Remove the vanilla bean, rinse, and save it for another use. Discard the coconut meat. Add enough heavy cream to the strained coconut milk to make 5 cups (1 L 200 ml) liquid. Return to the saucepan and heat to scalding.

5. Beat the egg yolks and sugar together for a few minutes. Gradually pour the hot liquid into the yolk mixture, whisking continuously. Heat the mixture over simmering water, stirring constantly with a whisk or wooden spoon until it thickens enough to coat the back of the spoon. Remove from the heat and continue to stir for 1 minute to prevent overcooking on the bottom or sides. Add the vanilla extract, if using. Let cool to room temperature, then cover and refrigerate until completely cold.

6. Process in an ice cream freezer according to the manufacturer's directions. Store, covered, in the freezer.

VARIATION

QUICK COCONUT ICE CREAM yield: approximately 5 cups (1 L 200 ml)

If you just can't live with yourself if you use anything but fresh coconut to make your coconut ice cream—and I agree there is a difference—use the preceding recipe. However, if you are short on time, this is a very good quick compromise. Use the recipe for Vanilla Ice Cream (page 734), replacing 2 cups (480 ml) half-and-half with unsweetened, canned coconut milk, and use only 4 ounces (115 g) sugar.

Fresh Mint Ice Cream yield: approximately 6 cups (1 L 440 ml)

You will find that numerous recipes in this book use mint in the presentation. I generally use peppermint, although spearmint or lemon mint can be used as well. Because in most cases only the smaller top leaves or sprigs are suitable for garnish, I am naturally left with a steady and abundant supply of large leaves, which are perfect for making mint ice cream or sorbet. It makes sense even if you have no immediate use for the ice cream, as once it is frozen it will keep for several weeks, provided it is stored properly. (The same cannot be said for the picked-over fresh leaves, which don't keep very long and cannot be frozen without turning black.) Although mint leaves are a very pretty dark green color, they do not produce much color when mixed with other ingredients. For this reason, I use parsley stems to tint the ice cream light green. It is only a little extra work, you really don't taste it, and I feel it is more worthwhile than using the commercial shortcut of green dye.

4 ounces (115 g) fresh mint leaves	8 ounces (225 g) granulated sugar
12 Italian parsley stems (½ ounce/15 g)	12 egg yolks (1 cup/240 ml)
2 cups (480 ml) whole milk	1 cup (240 ml) Crème Fraîche (page 821)
2 cups (480 ml) heavy cream	⅓ cup (80 ml) crème de menthe

1. Finely chop the mint leaves and parsley stems.

2. Place the milk in a saucepan, add the mint and the parsley, and bring the mixture to a boil. Remove from the heat and set aside to steep for 1 hour.

3. Add the heavy cream to the milk mixture. Return to the heat and bring to the scalding point.

4. While the milk is heating, beat the sugar and egg yolks together just to combine. Strain the milk and cream mixture into the egg and sugar mixture while whisking rapidly.

5. Place the custard over a hot water bath and heat, stirring constantly with a whisk or wooden spoon, until it thickens to the ribbon stage; do not overheat. Let cool to room temperature, then cover and refrigerate until completely cold, preferably overnight.

6. Stir the crème fraîche and crème de menthe into the custard.

7. Process in an ice cream freezer following the manufacturer's instructions. Store, covered, in the freezer.

Gooseberry Ice Cream yield: approximately 2 quarts (1 L 920 ml)

Gooseberries are so popular and common in Sweden that not having gooseberry bushes growing in your yard is practically considered unpatriotic! They also grow wild in much of the United States. This is a wonderful, tart ice cream with a distinctive flavor. It is particularly nice teamed with an apple or pear dessert, such as Apple Sacks (page 612) or Pear-Frangipane Tart (page 345), or enjoy it topped with caramel sauce alongside a slice of gugelhupf.

1 pound 8 ounces (680 g) green or yellow gooseberries (see Note)	6 ounces (170 g) granulated sugar
¼ cup (60 ml) water	1 recipe Vanilla Ice Cream Custard (page 734)

1. Rinse the gooseberries and trim both the flower and stem ends. Place in a saucepan with the water and sugar. Bring to a boil and cook over medium heat until the berries pop open and fall apart. Lower the heat and continue cooking until the mixture has been reduced by half. Watch carefully during this time and stir as needed to prevent the mixture from burning.

2. Stir the fruit into the ice cream custard, cover, and place in the refrigerator to chill, preferably overnight.

3. Process in an ice cream freezer following the manufacturer's directions. Store, covered, in the freezer.

NOTE: Green and yellow gooseberries turn amber or white when they are fully ripe, and they also lose most of their tartness at this point, becoming rather bland. You may want to leave out part or even all of the sugar when cooking the fruit, depending on the stage of ripeness. It is necessary to trim the berries because the fruit is not strained after cooking. The easiest way to remove both the blossom portion and the stem from the berries is to use small pointed scissors.

Lemon Verbena Ice Cream yield: approximately 5 cups (1 L 200 ml)

Lemon verbena is also known simply as *verbena*. It is a small, shrublike herb that has become especially popular with chefs in recent years. Its long, slender green leaves are used to flavor both sweet and savory dishes, to make tea, and to add fragrance to sachets. If the lemony flavor is too strong for your liking, it can be decreased either by using a smaller amount of verbena and/or by infusing the leaves for a shorter period. Should you need to use dried lemon verbena, however, you will need to increase the amount in order to obtain a satisfactory result.

1 ounce (30 g) fresh lemon verbena leaves

1 pint (480 ml) whole milk

1 pint (480 ml) heavy cream

10 egg yolks (⅞ cup/210 ml)

10 ounces (285 g) granulated sugar

1 tablespoon (15 ml) vanilla extract

1. Chop the lemon verbena leaves finely. Combine with the milk and heat to scalding. Cover and set aside to infuse for at least 4 hours or, preferably, overnight.

2. Strain through a coarse strainer so that some specks of lemon verbena are visible in the milk. Add the heavy cream to the milk mixture. Heat to scalding.

3. Beat the egg yolks and sugar until light and fluffy. Gradually pour the cream mixture into the egg yolks while whisking rapidly. Heat the mixture over simmering water, stirring—not whipping—constantly with a whip, until it thickens enough to coat a spoon.

4. Stir in the vanilla extract and let cool to room temperature. Refrigerate, covered, until thoroughly chilled.

5. Process the custard in an ice cream freezer. Transfer to a chilled container and store, covered, in the freezer.

Macadamia Nut Ice Cream yield: approximately 2 quarts (1 L 920 ml)

If you think it is a shame to grind up these expensive nuts and put them to soak in some milk, please wait and pass judgment after you have tasted the finished product. I first had macadamia nut ice cream on a trip to Maui a few years back and set about right away to try to duplicate the rich and creamy yet delicate flavor. If you have macadamia nut liqueur, try pouring a little over the top just before serving. Accompany with a sweet tropical fruit.

1 pound (455 g) unsalted macadamia nuts

1 quart (960 ml) whole milk

1 vanilla bean

1 teaspoon (5 ml) vanilla extract

12 egg yolks (1 cup/240 ml)

14 ounces (400 g) granulated sugar

2 cups (480 ml) heavy cream

1. Toast the macadamia nuts and set aside until cool. Grind or crush the nuts coarsely, combine with ½ cup (120 ml) milk, and grind to a paste in a food processor.

2. Add the vanilla bean to the remaining 3½ cups (840 ml) milk and bring to a boil. Mix in the nut paste. Remove the pan from the heat, cover, and set aside to steep for at least 30 minutes.

3. Whip the egg yolks and sugar until they are light and fluffy and form a slowly dissolving ribbon. Reheat the milk mixture to boiling, then strain through a fine mesh strainer or cheesecloth (see Note). Remove the vanilla bean, cut it in half lengthwise, and scrape the seeds back into the strained mixture, using the back of a paring knife. Discard the pod, or rinse and save for another use. Gradually add the hot milk to the beaten yolks while stirring constantly.

4. Cook the custard over hot water, stirring with a whisk or wooden spoon, until it thickens enough to coat the spoon. Stir in the heavy cream and the vanilla extract. Let cool to room temperature, then cover and chill the mixture until it is completely cold.

5. Process in an ice cream freezer according to the manufacturer's directions. Transfer to a chilled container and store, covered, in the freezer.

NOTE: Do not discard these costly nuts. Dry the fine pieces and use them in cookies or in a nut torte. The nuts will not keep very long, however, after being soaked in milk.

Mango Ice Cream yield: approximately 6 cups (1 L 440 ml)

The mango has been described as the world's most sensuous fruit. In tropical areas, it is the fruit most commonly eaten out of hand, the way you might think of eating an apple in the United States. In fact, the mango is one of the most popular fruits in the world.

Mangoes are one of the most difficult fruits when it comes to removing the peel and stone, if you're hoping to keep the flesh intact for decoration. To serve mango with the peel on, simply cut the two halves free of the stone lengthwise and use a small, sharp knife to cut through the flesh down to the peel in both directions on each cut half. Then turn the halves inside-out to raise the scored flesh in a hedgehog pattern (Figure 14-2).

3 cups (720 ml) whole milk

1 cup (240 ml) heavy cream

2 eggs

10 ounces (285 g) granulated sugar

2 pounds (910 g) fresh whole ripe mangoes (approximately 3 medium)

⅓ cup (80 ml) lime juice

1. Combine the milk and cream in a saucepan and heat to scalding. Whip the eggs and sugar in a mixing bowl until well combined. Gradually whisk the hot milk mixture into the eggs. Place the bowl over a bain-marie and cook, stirring with a whisk or a wooden spoon, until the custard has thickened slightly (nappe stage). Set aside to cool.

2. Slice each mango into halves by cutting through vertically on both sides of the large flat stone. Use a spoon to scrape the flesh away from the skin and the stones. Puree the mango and pass through a strainer. Stir the mango puree and the lime juice into the cooled custard. Cover and place in the refrigerator until completely cold, preferably overnight.

CHEF'S TIP
If you use fruit that is not fully ripe, it is better to first peel the mangoes and then cut the flesh away from the stones.

3. Transfer the custard to an ice cream freezer and process following the manufacturer's directions. Store, covered, in the freezer.

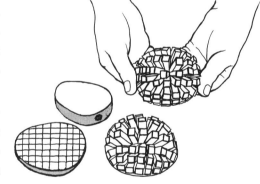

FIGURE 14-2 Making a mango hedgehog. The 2 halves cut away from the center stone and surrounding flesh, leaving the peel on the fruit; the flat cut sides of each half scored in both directions down to but not through the skin; turning the halves inside-out to raise the cut flesh

Papaya Ice Cream yield: approximately 7 cups (1 L 680 ml)

For a special and festive presentation, serve papaya ice cream in a chocolate tulip with kiwi sauce and fresh tropical fruit. The presentation is as colorful as the Hawaiian Islands.

4 pounds (1 kg 820 g) papaya (4 small)

1 recipe Vanilla Ice Cream Custard (page 734)

¾ cup (180 ml) lime juice (from about 5 limes)

1. Peel the papayas, cut in half, and remove the seeds. Puree the fruit and measure. You should have approximately 3 cups (720 ml) papaya puree. (If you use fruit that is not fully ripe, it may not puree smoothly, making it necessary to pass the pulp through a fine mesh strainer before proceeding.)

2. Combine the vanilla ice cream custard, papaya puree, and lime juice. Let cool to room temperature, then refrigerate, covered, until completely cold, preferably overnight.

3. Process in an ice cream freezer following the manufacturer's instructions. Chill a container to hold the finished product.

4. Store the ice cream, covered, in the freezer.

Passion Fruit Ice Cream yield 9 cups (2 L 160 ml)

1 recipe Vanilla Ice Cream Custard (page 734)   1 cup (240 ml) passion fruit pulp (from approximately 20 passion fruit)

1. Combine the ice cream custard with the passion fruit pulp. If the custard has been made ahead and refrigerated, proceed to the next step. If not, chill the custard several hours or, preferably, overnight before proceeding.

2. Process the cold custard in an ice cream freezer, following the manufacturer's directions.

3. Store the finished ice cream, covered, in the freezer.

CHEF'S TIP

The black seeds contained in passion fruit pulp are edible, and I prefer to leave them in the ice cream for two reasons. I feel that the seeds contribute to the appearance of the final product, and their visibility also lets the consumer know that fresh passion fruits were used to make the ice cream. If you do not care for the seeds in the passion fruit, an easy way to remove them without losing the pulp that clings to them is to warm the pulp without boiling until the seeds loosen. Then pass the pulp through a strainer and discard the seeds. However, if you are going to strain out the seeds, you might as well use the popular and convenient ready-to-use passion fruit puree, which is sold with the seeds removed.

Peach Ice Cream yield: approximately 6 cups (1 L 440 ml)

If this ice cream will be eaten the same day it is made—and it will be, if it is made as peach ice cream so often is, as part of a backyard barbecue party in the summertime—skip the macerating step. If the peaches are tree-ripened or perfectly ripe, you can omit pureeing them as well. But do include the amaretto if you have some. Peaches and almonds are made for each other. Peach ice cream is great for topping many pies and tarts à la mode, especially those that contain nuts.

2 pounds (910 g) fresh peaches, ripe but firm   1 quart (960 ml) half-and-half

⅓ cup (80 ml) amaretto liqueur   2½ cups (600 ml) Plain Poaching Syrup (page 31)

5 ounces (140 g) granulated sugar

10 egg yolks (⅞ cup/210 ml)

1. Pick out one-third of the firmest peaches, wash, cut in half, and discard the pits. Cut into pea-sized chunks and macerate the peach chunks in the amaretto for 4 to 5 hours or, preferably, overnight.

2. Whip the sugar and egg yolks to the ribbon stage. Scald the half-and-half and gradually combine with the egg mixture while stirring rapidly. Set over simmering water, stirring constantly with a whisk or wooden spoon, and thicken the custard until it coats the spoon. Be careful not to overheat or you will coagulate the yolks. Remove the custard from the heat and let it cool to room temperature. Cover and refrigerate until completely cold, preferably overnight.

3. Wash the remaining peaches, cut in half, discard the pits, and remove the skin. If you lose too much pulp as you do this, add another peach. Place the peaches in a saucepan with the poaching syrup. Simmer until the fruit starts to fall apart. Remove the fruit from the syrup. Puree the peaches and set the mixture aside to cool. (If you use fruit that is not fully ripe, it may not puree smoothly, making it necessary to pass the pulp through a fine mesh strainer before proceeding.) Discard the poaching syrup.

4. Add the macerated peach chunks and peach puree to the custard. Process the mixture in an ice cream freezer. Place in a chilled container and store, covered, in the freezer.

Pistachio Ice Cream yield: approximately 2 quarts (1 L 920 ml)

Contrary to the impression you might get from some of the commercial pistachio ice creams on the market, pistachios have a very mild flavor and are not nearly green enough to color the ice cream to the bright shade often seen. This recipe makes an ice cream with a delicious, subtle taste and just a hint of green color, which comes naturally from the nuts.

10 ounces (285 g) pistachios

3 cups (720 ml) whole milk

1 recipe Vanilla Ice Cream Custard (page 734; see Step 3 below)

1. Boil the pistachios in lightly salted water for 1 minute. Drain, cool, and remove the skin with your fingers. Dry the nuts at 325°F (163°C) without toasting. Reserve 2 ounces (55 g) nuts and grind the remainder finely.

2. Combine the ground pistachios with the milk in a saucepan. Heat to scalding, then remove from the heat, cover, and allow to steep for 30 minutes. Strain through a fine mesh strainer or cheesecloth, forcing all of the liquid from the nuts. (Because they are fairly expensive, try to use the nuts for another project, such as a torte or Bear Claw filling, instead of discarding them at this point.)

3. Prepare the vanilla ice cream custard, using only half the amount of sugar called for in the recipe. Stir the strained pistachio liquid into the custard. Crush the reserved pistachios coarsely and add. Let cool to room temperature, then cover and refrigerate until completely cold.

4. Process in an ice cream freezer following the manufacturer's directions. Store, covered, in the freezer.

Plum Ice Cream yield: approximately 6 cups (1 L 440 ml)

While I generally try to get the Laroda or Casselman variety of plum for cooking, the tart skin of the Santa Rosa plum gives this ice cream a wonderful color and a tart, puckery taste. It is a wonderful companion to many sweet desserts, particularly any based on meringue.

2 pounds (910 g) tart plums (see Note)	5 ounces (140 g) granulated sugar
¼ cup (60 ml) simple syrup	10 egg yolks (⅞ cup/210 ml)
¼ cup (60 ml) plum brandy *or* liqueur	1 quart (960 ml) half-and-half
1 recipe Spiced Poaching Syrup (page 31)	

1. Wash the plums, cut in half, and discard the pits. Cut one-third of the fruit into pea-sized chunks. Combine the chunks with the simple syrup and brandy or liqueur. Set aside to macerate for a few hours or, preferably, overnight.

2. Place the remaining plums in a saucepan with the poaching syrup. Cook until the plums are soft and begin to fall apart. Remove from the heat and strain off the poaching liquid, reserving 1 quart (960 ml) to use as a sauce for the ice cream if desired, or discard. (To use the poaching liquid as a sauce, reduce it by approximately half or until it has thickened to a nappe consistency.)

3. Whip the sugar and egg yolks to the ribbon stage. Heat the half-and-half to scalding. Gradually pour the hot cream into the egg yolk and sugar mixture while whisking rapidly. Place over simmering water and heat, stirring constantly with a whisk or wooden spoon, until the custard is thick enough to coat the spoon. Remove from the heat and stir in the reserved poached plums and the macerated plum chunks. Let cool at room temperature, then cover and refrigerate until completely cold.

4. Process in an ice cream freezer following the manufacturer's directions. Place the finished ice cream in a chilled container and store, covered, in the freezer.

NOTE: When the season for fresh local plums is over, canned tart plums may be a better choice than the sometimes tasteless imported varieties. Drain; use the liquid as part of the poaching syrup, adjusting the sweetness and amount as needed. Canned plums require only about 5 minutes of poaching.

Pomegranate Ice Cream yield: approximately 2 quarts (1 L 920 ml)

A vibrant red color makes this tart-sweet ice cream a valuable addition to many dessert plates. The season for pomegranates lasts only from September to December. This is much too short a time to be able to take advantage of this decorative, juicy fruit. Luckily, whole pomegranates can be kept in the refrigerator for up to 3 months, and the seeds can be frozen indefinitely. To simplify the tedious task of separating the edible seeds from the spongy, bitter membrane that surrounds them, freeze and thaw the fruit, then slice in half. This will dislodge the kernels, allowing you to pull them apart quite easily.

2 pounds (910 g) pomegranate seeds (about 7 medium pomegranates)

1½ cups (360 ml) water

8 ounces (225 g) granulated sugar

2 teaspoons (10 ml) Beet Juice (page 5; see Chef's Tip with Rhubarb Ice Cream below)

1 recipe Vanilla Ice Cream Custard (page 734; see Step 2 below)

CHEF'S TIP
If you have extra seeds or pomegranates, try making a pomegranate drink: Add 3 cups (720 ml) water and one-quarter of a lemon to every 6 ounces (170 g) of pomegranate seeds (one large fruit). Boil about 15 minutes to release the color and flavor from the seeds. Add 4 ounces (115 g) of granulated sugar and bring the liquid back to boiling. Strain through a cheese-cloth and chill. Makes 4 servings.

I. Place the pomegranate seeds, water, and granulated sugar in a saucepan. Bring to a boil and cook over medium heat until reduced by half. Stir in the beet juice.

2. Make the vanilla ice cream custard, using only half the amount of sugar specified. Stir the pomegranate mixture into the vanilla custard. Cool to room temperature, then cover and refrigerate until completely cold, preferably several hours or overnight.

3. Process in an ice cream freezer following the manufacturer's directions and store, covered, in the freezer.

Rhubarb Ice Cream yield: approximately 5 cups (1 L 200 ml)

In botanical terms, rhubarb is a vegetable, but we tend to use this "pink-hued celery" more as a fruit. It is great in tarts and pies that are topped with meringue and, in fact, was traditionally referred to by country farmers as *pie plant*. It is also pleasing as a cool, refreshing ice cream. When trimming the rhubarb, be sure to remove all the leaves, which are potentially toxic in excessive amounts, because their oxalic acid content is high enough that it can interfere with calcium and iron absorption.

2 pounds 8 ounces (1 kg 135 g) fresh rhubarb stalks

⅓ cup (80 ml) water

5 ounces (140 g) granulated sugar

½ recipe Vanilla Ice Cream Custard (page 734)

½ teaspoon (2.5 ml) Tartaric Acid Solution (page 38)

2 teaspoons (10 ml) Beet Juice (page 5)

CHEF'S TIP
Because rhubarb does not produce enough color on its own and I do not want to use artificial coloring, I add beet juice to enhance the appearance of the ice cream. Due to its intense color, beet juice makes a great natural food coloring. Raspberry juice also works well, but it is not as strong.

I. Wash the rhubarb and trim both ends of each stalk. Chop the rhubarb stalks into small pieces. Place in a saucepan with the water and granulated sugar and mix to combine. Cook over medium heat until the rhubarb falls apart and the mixture has thickened to a jamlike consistency, approximately 20 minutes. Remove from the heat and set aside to cool.

2. Stir the rhubarb mixture into the vanilla ice cream custard together with the tartaric acid solution and the beet juice. Cover and refrigerate until completely cold, preferably several hours or overnight.

3. Process in an ice cream freezer following the manufacturer's instructions. Store, covered, in the freezer.

Rum-Raisin Ice Cream yield: approximately 5 cups (1 L 200 ml)

Using dark rum in this ice cream would generate a more pronounced rum flavor, but I don't care for the muddled color it produces. Don't skip macerating the raisins in the rum. It is a necessary step, not only to prevent them from freezing into little rocks but also because it gives the raisins a wonderful rum flavor that comes across the instant you bite into them. The alcohol also keeps the ice cream itself soft and pliable, even when stored overnight.

1 cup (240 ml) light rum

8 ounces (225 g) dark raisins

1 recipe Vanilla Ice Cream Custard (page 734; see Step 2 below)

1. Heat the rum to around 150°F (65°C), then add the raisins. Cover and let macerate at room temperature overnight.

2. Make the vanilla ice cream custard, using only half the amount of sugar specified in the recipe. Let cool a bit, then cover and refrigerate overnight.

3. Pour the custard into an ice cream freezer and process following the manufacturer's directions until the ice cream begins to thicken. Add the raisins and any rum that has not been absorbed. Finish churning. Transfer the ice cream to a chilled container. If necessary, stir gently to distribute the raisins. Cover and store in the freezer.

Strawberry Ice Cream yield: approximately 7 cups (1 L 680 ml)

Like peach, this ice cream is traditionally made at home in the summertime. As mentioned in the Peach Ice Cream recipe, the fruit must be prepared with sugar before it is added, unless the ice cream is to be eaten the same day it is made. This is necessary because both peaches and strawberries contain a large amount of juice, which is not always as sweet as needed to create a soft rather than icy texture. Try serving strawberry ice cream with Strawberry-Rhubarb Meringue Tart (page 355).

1 recipe Vanilla Ice Cream Custard (page 734; see Step 1 below)

1 pound (455 g) fresh ripe strawberries

4 ounces (115 g) granulated sugar, approximately (see Note)

½ cup (120 ml) strained raspberry puree (see Note)

1. Make the ice cream custard, using only half the amount of sugar specified in the recipe.

2. Clean and stem the strawberries. Chop into small pieces. Place in a saucepan with the sugar and cook over medium heat, stirring from time to time, until the mixture starts to thicken, about 10 minutes.

3. Add to the ice cream custard together with the raspberry puree. Let cool to room temperature, then cover and refrigerate until completely cold.

4. Process in an ice cream freezer according to the manufacturer's instructions. Transfer the ice cream to a chilled container and store, covered, in the freezer.

NOTE: Because this recipe does not use any artificial ingredients, the color may not be as bright as you are used to seeing in commercial strawberry ice creams. The raspberry juice is added to intensify the hue. Adjust the amounts of sugar and raspberry juice according to the ripeness (and sweetness) of the strawberries.

Sun-Brewed Jasmine Tea Ice Cream yield: approximately 5 cups (1 L 200 ml)

For a less calorie-charged alternative, add the strained tea to the base for Honey-Vanilla Frozen Yogurt (page 740), omitting the lemon juice and vanilla extract from that recipe. If you wish, customize the tea infusion according to your own taste, using either a green tea, as suggested here, or a black tea. Possible black tea choices are darjeeling and assam, a blend such as orange spice, and a scented tea such as Earl Grey.

1 ounce (30 g) jasmine tea leaves	1 recipe Vanilla Ice Cream Custard (page 734;
½ cup (120 ml) cold water	see Step 2)

1. Combine the tea leaves and water in a glass jar. Cover with cheesecloth and leave to brew outside in the sun or in a warm place in the kitchen for 2 to 3 hours.

2. Make the ice cream custard, substituting heavy cream for the half-and-half.

3. Strain the tea mixture and add it to the custard. Cover and place the mixture in the refrigerator overnight or for at least 8 hours to mature.

4. Process in an ice cream freezer following the manufacturer's directions. Remove the ice cream from the ice cream freezer just before it is fully churned and thickened. Transfer to a chilled container and store, covered, in the freezer. The ice cream will become firmer once frozen.

Vanilla Ice Cream yield: approximately 5 cups (1 L 200 ml)

This is the old granddad of custard ice creams. The base is used to make numerous variations; it is simple to prepare; and vanilla ice cream makes an excellent companion to just about any dessert you can think of. In an emergency, frozen vanilla ice cream can be melted back down to a liquid and used as crème anglaise, which is basically what it starts out as. Any leftover melted ice cream should not be saved, however. This fabulous ice cream can be kept in the freezer for several days and still remain soft, creamy, and easy to serve.

Vanilla Ice Cream Custard (recipe follows)

1. Process the chilled vanilla ice cream custard in an ice cream freezer following the manufacturer's instructions.

2. Transfer to a chilled container and store, covered, in the freezer.

VANILLA ICE CREAM CUSTARD

1 quart (960 ml) half-and-half	10 egg yolks (⅞ cup/210 ml)
1 vanilla bean, split lengthwise	10 ounces (285 g) granulated sugar
2 teaspoons (10 ml) vanilla extract	

1. Heat the half-and-half with the vanilla bean to scalding.

2. Beat the egg yolks and sugar until light and fluffy. Remove the vanilla bean halves and use the back of a paring knife to scrape out the seeds (Figure14-3). Stir the seeds into the half-and-half. Discard the vanilla bean pods. Gradually pour the half-and-half into the whipped egg yolk mixture while whisking rapidly. (Place a towel under the bowl to keep it from turning with your whisk.)

3. Heat the mixture over simmering water, stirring constantly with a whisk or wooden spoon, until it thickens enough to coat the spoon. Be careful not to overheat and break the custard. Remove from the heat and continue to stir for a few seconds to keep the mixture from overcooking where it touches the hot bowl. Stir in the vanilla extract. Let cool to room temperature, then refrigerate, covered, until completely cold, for several hours or, preferably, overnight (see "Aging," page 714).

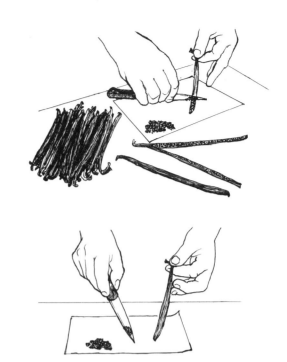

FIGURE 14-3 Using the back side of a paring knife to scrape the seeds out of a vanilla bean that has been split lengthwise; a pile of the tiny seeds and an empty pod half

White Chocolate Ice Cream with Ginger yield: approximately 6 cups (1 L 440 ml)

This ice cream is incredibly rich, dense, and luxurious—there is basically zero overrun—but you do have to baby it a little. By adding the white chocolate to the hot custard and stirring until it is melted, you do not risk overheating this sensitive ingredient, as you can so easily do when melting it over heat. Also be careful not to overchurn the ice cream. The added fat from the cocoa butter in the chocolate can make the ice cream gritty very readily.

1 ounce (30 g) fresh ginger, sliced

3 cups (720 ml) half-and-half

2 cups (480 ml) heavy cream

8 egg yolks (²⁄₃ cup/160 ml)

3 ounces (85 g) granulated sugar

8 ounces (225 g) white chocolate, cut into small chunks

½ ounce (15 g) Crystallized Ginger (page 15), finely chopped

1. Combine the fresh ginger, half-and-half, and cream in a saucepan. Heat to scalding. Set aside to steep for 30 minutes.

2. Beat the egg yolks with the sugar until light and fluffy. Strain the ginger from the cream mixture and reheat to the scalding point. Gradually whisk the hot cream into the egg yolk mixture.

3. Place over simmering water and heat, stirring constantly with a whisk or wooden spoon (do not whip), until the custard is thick enough to coat the spoon.

4. Remove from the heat and add the white chocolate, continuing to stir until all of the chunks are melted. Stir in the crystallized ginger. Let cool to room temperature, then refrigerate until completely cold, preferably overnight.

5. Process in an ice cream freezer according to the manufacturer's directions. Remove the ice cream from the ice cream freezer just before it is fully churned and thickened (it should be too soft to scoop out). Transfer to a chilled container, cover, and place in the freezer. The ice cream will become firmer once frozen. If allowed to freeze completely while churning, the texture will be compromised, as explained in the introduction.

VARIATION
WHITE CHOCOLATE ICE CREAM

Prepare the main recipe as directed above, but omit the fresh ginger and candied ginger and increase the white chocolate by 2 ounces (55 g) for a total of 10 ounces (285 g). After scalding the half-and-half and cream in Step 1, proceed directly to Step 2; it is not necessary to wait 30 minutes or to scald the cream mixture again in Step 2.

PHILADELPHIA-STYLE ICE CREAMS

Philadelphia-style ice creams are completely uncooked. Though they are frozen in the same way as a custard-based ice cream, they contain little or no egg, which makes them fairly close to sherbet in their composition. Because they lack the emulsifying properties of eggs—which act to keep the water molecules separate during freezing—this type of ice cream, although quicker to make and for some people a healthier choice than the classic custard-based version, tends to have a slightly grainy consistency. Using a thick fruit pulp, such as mango, papaya, or banana, which provides its own emulsifying action, will significantly improve the texture. Chocolate also acts as a smoothing agent, enhancing the appeal of the finished product to the largest degree.

Philadelphia-Style Ice Cream yield: approximately 7 cups (1 L 680 ml)

2 cups (480 ml) heavy cream	1 vanilla bean, split lengthwise
3 cups (720 ml) half-and-half	1 teaspoon (5 ml) vanilla extract
12 ounces (340 g) granulated sugar	12 ounces (340 g) thick fruit pulp (optional)

1. Combine the heavy cream, half-and-half, and sugar and stir until the sugar is dissolved. Scrape the seeds from the vanilla bean into the cream mixture and stir in the vanilla extract (save the vanilla bean pod for another use). Add the fruit pulp, if using.

2. Process in an ice cream freezer following the manufacturer's instructions. Store, covered, in the freezer.

Philadelphia-Style Chocolate Ice Cream yield: approximately 7 cups (1 L 680 ml)

12 ounces (340 g) sweet dark chocolate (see Note)

5 cups (1 L 200 ml) half-and-half

8 ounces (225 g) granulated sugar

1 vanilla bean, split lengthwise

1 teaspoon (5 ml) vanilla extract

1. Melt the chocolate in an oversized bowl set over simmering water. Remove from the heat and quickly stir in the half-and-half. Add the sugar, stirring until completely dissolved. Scrape the seeds from the vanilla bean into the chocolate mixture and stir in the vanilla extract (save the vanilla bean pod for another use). Let cool to room temperature.

2. Process in an ice cream freezer following the manufacturer's directions. Store, covered, in the freezer.

NOTE: You may want to adjust the amount of sugar depending on the sweetness of the brand of chocolate you are using.

Low-Fat Philadelphia-Style Ice Cream yield: approximately 7 cups (1 L 680 ml)

This recipe is a low-fat variation that uses yogurt and ricotta cheese in place of cream and fruit, and adds fruit pulp to improve the texture. In the traditional Philadelphia-style ice cream recipe on page 736, fruit pulp is listed as an option to add flavor and improve texture however the bona fide version of this old favorite consisted simply of sweetened cream flavored with vanilla.

1½ cups (360 ml) part-skim ricotta cheese

4½ cups (1 L 80 ml) Unflavored Yogurt (page 38), made with low-fat milk

2 cups (480 ml) pure maple syrup (do not use imitation)

10 ounces (285 g) mango or papaya puree, strained

1 vanilla bean, split lengthwise

1 teaspoon (5 ml) vanilla extract

1. Process the ricotta cheese in a food processor until smooth. Transfer to a bowl and stir in the yogurt, maple syrup, and fruit puree. Scrape the seeds from the vanilla bean into the yogurt and stir in the vanilla extract (save the vanilla bean pod for another use).

2. Process the mixture in an ice cream freezer following the manufacturer's directions. Store, covered, in the freezer.

Frozen yogurts are churned and frozen in an ice cream maker. They contain cultured milk with varying percentages of fat; flavorings; sweeteners (usually honey or sucrose); emulsifiers, such as vegetable oil and pasteurized eggs or egg yolks (in a much smaller amount than a custard-based ice cream); and they can be made with or without a stabilizer. The final product has a tangy, refreshing flavor. Due to the typically low percentages of milkfat and egg yolk, frozen yogurt is often very low in calories and cholesterol.

Banana-Tofu Frozen Yogurt yield: approximately 6 cups (1 L 440 ml)

The first reaction my students always seem to have to this recipe title is a frown, but that changes when they taste the finished product. The flavor is great—slightly tart and very refreshing—and it has a smooth texture that would normally require a considerable quantity of cream and eggs to achieve. Try serving this with Banana Layer Cake with Maple Cream Cheese Frosting (page 489).

12 ounces (340 g) soft tofu

2 pounds (910 g) ripe bananas (about 4 medium)

4 teaspoons (20 ml) lime juice

½ cup (120 ml) vegetable oil

1½ cups (360 ml) Unflavored Yogurt (page 38)

¾ cup (180 ml) or 9 ounces (255 g) honey

2 teaspoons (10 ml) vanilla extract

1. Blend the tofu, peeled bananas, and lime juice in a food processor until smooth. Transfer to a bowl. Stir in the oil, yogurt, honey, and vanilla.

2. Process in an ice cream freezer following the manufacturer's instructions. Transfer to a chilled container and store, covered, in the freezer.

Calvados-Tofu Frozen Yogurt yield: approximately 2 quarts (1 L 920 ml)

1 pound 8 ounces (680 g) cooking apples, such as Pippin or Granny Smith, *or* 1 pound (455 g) unsweetened apple puree

1 pound 8 ounces (680 g) soft tofu

¾ cup (180 ml) vegetable oil

1 pound (455 g) Unflavored Yogurt (page 38)

¼ cup (60 ml) Calvados

1 tablespoon (15 ml) vanilla extract

1 cup (240 ml) or 12 ounces (340 g) honey

1. If you are using fresh apples, peel them, core, and cut each one in half. Poach the apples in Plain Poaching Syrup (page 31) until soft.

2. In a food processor, blend the poached apples or apple puree, the tofu, and the vegetable oil until smooth.

3. Transfer the apple mixture to a mixing bowl and stir in the yogurt, Calvados, vanilla, and honey.

4. Process the mixture in an ice cream freezer according to the manufacturer's directions. Transfer to a chilled container and store, covered, in the freezer.

Black Pepper–Honey Frozen Yogurt yield: 5 cups (1 L 200 ml)

Don't expect a sharp bite here. The pepper just adds a hint of spiciness that contrasts nicely with the sweet coolness of the frozen yogurt. This yogurt pairs especially well with cherry sauce and/or cherry desserts.

6 ounces (170 g) granulated sugar

4 ounces (115 g) honey

2 teaspoons (10 ml) lemon juice

2 teaspoons (10 ml) vanilla extract

2 eggs, separated

4 cups (960 ml) Unflavored Yogurt (page 38)

1 teaspoon (5 ml) coarsely ground black pepper

1. Place half of the sugar, the honey, and the lemon juice in a saucepan. Bring to a boil and cook for 1 minute. Remove from the heat and add the vanilla.

2. Beat the egg yolks, stir in some of the hot sugar syrup to temper, then stir in the remaining syrup. Let cool to room temperature.

3. Whip the egg whites until foamy. Gradually add the remaining sugar and whip to stiff peaks.

4. Place the yogurt in a bowl and stir smooth with a whisk. Stir in the pepper. Fold in the sugar syrup and yolk mixture. Fold in the whipped egg whites.

5. Process in an ice cream freezer following the manufacturer's directions. Store, covered, in the freezer.

Gingered Pineapple Frozen Yogurt yield: approximately 2 quarts (1 L 920 ml)

1 pound (455 g) granulated sugar (see Note 1)

1 cup (240 ml) pineapple juice

1 ounce (30 g) fresh ginger, thinly sliced

3 eggs, separated

1 tablespoon (15 ml) vanilla extract

5 cups (1 L 200 ml) Unflavored Yogurt (page 38)

6 ounces (170 g) fresh pineapple puree (see Note 2)

1. Place half of the sugar, the pineapple juice, and the ginger in a nonreactive saucepan. Bring to a boil, stirring to dissolve the sugar. Boil for 1 minute. Remove from the heat and let steep in the saucepan for at least 30 minutes.

2. Reheat the syrup to about 150°F (65°C). Beat the egg yolks for a few seconds to combine, then gradually strain the hot syrup into the yolks while whipping rapidly. Discard the ginger. Add the vanilla to the yolk mixture and set aside to cool to room temperature.

3. Whip the egg whites until foamy. Gradually add the remaining sugar and continue whipping until stiff peaks form.

4. Place the yogurt in a bowl and stir with a whisk until smooth. Stir in the cooled yolk mixture and the pineapple puree. Fold in the whipped egg whites.

5. Process in an ice cream freezer following the manufacturer's directions. Store, covered, in the freezer.

NOTE 1: You may need to adjust the amount of sugar depending on the ripeness (sweetness) of the pineapple.

NOTE 2: If you are making this recipe to accompany Pineapple Fritters, the end slices from the pineapple, which are often too small to cut into proper-sized pieces for fritters, are ideal to use here.

Honey-Scented Pear Frozen Yogurt yield: approximately 6 cups (1 L 440 ml)

2 pounds (910 g) Bosc pears (about 5 medium)

1 recipe Plain Poaching Syrup (page 31)

¼ cup (60 ml) or 3 ounces (85 g) honey

2 eggs

4 ounces (115 g) granulated sugar

4 cups (960 ml) Unflavored Yogurt (page 38)

1. Peel, and core the pears. Cut them in half, placing them in acidulated water as you work to prevent oxidation. Remove from the water and place the pear halves in a saucepan with the poaching syrup. Poach until soft. Drain. Puree the pears until smooth; set aside to cool. Discard the syrup or save for another use.

2. Bring the honey to a boil in a small saucepan. At the same time, whisk the eggs and sugar together until frothy, about 1 minute. Add the honey to the egg and sugar mixture while whipping constantly. Continue to whip until the mixture has cooled to room temperature.

3. Stir the egg mixture into the yogurt together with the cool pear puree.

4. Process in an ice cream freezer following the manufacturer's directions. Store, covered, in the freezer.

Honey-Vanilla Frozen Yogurt yield: approximately 5 cups (1 L 200 ml)

6 ounces (170 g) granulated sugar

⅓ cup (80 ml) or 4 ounces (115 g) honey

1 tablespoon (15 ml) lemon juice

1 tablespoon (15 ml) vanilla extract

2 eggs, separated

4 cups (960 ml) Unflavored Yogurt (page 38)

1. Place half of the sugar, the honey, and the lemon juice in a saucepan. Bring to a boil, stirring to dissolve the sugar. Boil for 1 minute, then remove from the heat and add the vanilla.

2. Beat the egg yolks lightly. Stir in some of the sugar syrup to temper, then add remaining syrup. Let cool to room temperature.

3. Whip the egg whites until they are foamy. Gradually add the remaining sugar and whip to stiff peaks.

4. Place the yogurt in a bowl and stir smooth with a whisk. Fold in the syrup and egg yolk mixture, then the whipped egg whites.

5. Process in an ice cream freezer according to the manufacturer's directions. Store, covered, in the freezer.

Strawberry-Rhubarb Frozen Yogurt with Ginger

yield: approximately 2 quarts (1 L 920 ml)

The amount of sugar called for will produce a tangy, refreshing flavor. Adjust the sugar as needed, depending on the sweetness of the strawberries and your own taste.

8 ounces (225 g) rhubarb stalks	8 ounces (225 g) granulated sugar
5 slices fresh ginger, about 1 inch (2.5 cm) in diameter	⅓ cup (80 ml) or 4 ounces (115 g) light corn syrup
1 cup (240 ml) water	2 eggs
1 pound (455 g) ripe fresh strawberries	4 cups (960 ml) Unflavored Yogurt (page 38)

1. Wash the rhubarb and trim the top and bottom of each stalk. Cut the stalks into small pieces and place in a saucepan with the ginger and the water. Cook over medium heat until the rhubarb is soft and begins to fall apart. Remove the ginger slices and discard. Strain the remaining mixture, then return the pulp to the saucepan. Discard the liquid.

2. Clean and stem the strawberries. Chop them into small pieces and add to the rhubarb in the saucepan. Stir in the sugar. Cook over medium heat, stirring from time to time, until the strawberries fall apart and the mixture begins to thicken. Remove from the heat and set aside.

3. In a separate small saucepan, bring the corn syrup to a boil. At the same time, whip the eggs until they are foamy. Whisk the corn syrup into the eggs and continue to whip until the mixture is cold. Stir the egg mixture and reserved strawberries and rhubarb into the yogurt. Cover and refrigerate until cold.

4. Process in an ice cream freezer following the manufacturer's instructions. Store, covered, in the freezer.

SORBETS AND SHERBETS

There is often confusion between sorbets, which are also called *fruit ices* or *water ices*, and sherbets—and for good reason. In some books, they are considered to be the same thing, distinguished only by *sorbet* being the French word for *sherbet*. Actually, it is the other way around—*sherbet* is an American word derived from the French *sorbet*, which came first, though in recent years the term *sorbet* has become more fashionable in the United States. There is, however, a difference between the two products, albeit a rather confusing one.

In America, a small portion of dairy product (milk or cream and, sometimes, egg) is typically added to the basic mixture, and this is called *sherbet*. A classic sorbet never contains milk, cream, or egg. In some sorbet recipes, a very small amount of lightly beaten pasteurized egg whites or Italian meringue is sometimes added during churning to lighten the texture and improve over-run (yield). Although meringue does contribute to a smooth mouth feel, at the same time it dulls the flavor and color and, technically, the product is then a sherbet. So, as you can see, a sorbet can always become a sherbet, but a sherbet can not be made into a sorbet.

As compared to ice creams, sorbets and sherbets have a lower percentage of solids, generally contain no emulsifiers, and therefore have a less creamy texture and a lower melting point. This is also due to the fact that they have a higher water and sugar content than the richer ice cream. Stabilizers are sometimes added to ensure that the finished product holds together, especially in the case of sorbets. It is also critical that the sugar content is adjusted properly to control over-run and to prevent the finished product from bleeding (separating). Sorbets taste best when freshly made and still soft. Sorbets and sherbets should not be kept longer than 1 or 2 weeks at the most, because the texture will deteriorate.

SORBETS

Sorbets are made from a wide variety of fruit juices or purees. Recently, the addition of spices and herbs such as thyme, rosemary, and basil have been popularized by some adventurous chefs, along with savory sorbet variations made from tomato or cucumber for example. These are served as refreshing first courses or as intermezzos (between courses) to cleanse the palate.

The flavor of the sorbet base is adjusted to the proper level of sweetness by the addition of water or sugar syrup. This is most easily done using a saccharometer, also known as a *syrup density meter*, *hydrometer*, or *Baumé hydrometer*, which measures the sugar content in a liquid. A saccharometer is a hollow glass tube weighted at the bottom, which will read 0° in tepid water. The mixture, therefore, must be at room temperature for the reading to be accurate. The calibration on the scale, usually from 0° to 50°, refers to degrees of Baumé, named for the Frenchman Antoine Baumé, who invented both the Baumé scale and the Baumé hydrometer. The reading for sorbet and ices is generally between 12° and 20°, depending on their use (by comparison, icy granitàs typically have a Baumé reading around 8° to 12°). In some instances, the mixture may be too thick for the saccharometer to float freely, which is also necessary in order to give an accurate reading. In such cases, a small amount of the mixture can be diluted with an equal amount of measured water, and the "diluted" reading on the saccharometer is then doubled to determine the Baumé level for the remaining mixture.

If you do not have a saccharometer, use trial and error to determine the proper sugar level. Use the amounts of water and/or simple syrup specified in the recipes that follow and freeze the sorbet as directed. If necessary, thaw, adjust the mixture by adding simple syrup or water, and refreeze. Unlike ice creams and sherbets, which contain dairy, sorbets are not adversely affected by thawing and refreezing. When sorbets are based on a spirit, wine, or liqueur, it is not necessary to check and adjust their Baumé level because with these ingredients, unlike fresh fruits, the sugar and alcohol contents are predetermined.

The level of sweetness for a sorbet depends on its use. If it is served as a dessert or as a component thereof, it is made a bit sweeter, usually between 16° and 20° Baumé. If it is served between courses as a palate cleanser, it should be crisp and refreshing, with a reading around 12° Baumé. The majority of the sorbets in this section can be used for an intermezzo ("between the work") or at the end of a large meal before dessert by lowering the sugar content appropriately—although granitàs (coarse, flaked ices) are the classic choice for this purpose.

Stabilizers in Sorbets

There is generally some liquid, such as sugar and/or alcohol in both sorbets and sherbets, which does not freeze solid. This liquid can bleed, or separate from the ice crystals, in the finished product, especially in the case of sorbets. A stabilizer or thickening agent is used to prevent this and to improve the texture. The stabilizer also allows the finished product to be stored in the freezer for a longer period.

When a sorbet is based on an ingredient that is rich in fiber and pulp, such as mango, papaya, peach, or nectarine, it does not require a stabilizer, or it requires a much smaller amount of stabilizer relative to other varieties. The same is true for sorbets based on ingredients that are naturally high in pectin—citrus fruits, apples, and blueberries are examples—so, ideally, you should not strain these mixtures, apart from removing skin and seeds. However, when using fruit that is not fully ripe, it can be difficult to achieve a smooth puree. In that instance, it may be necessary to pass the pulp through a fine mesh strainer.

Stabilizers are used primarily in the commercial manufacturing of sorbets, sherbets, and ice creams; they are much less commonly used in today's restaurants. In the case of sorbets, the process of freezing the base is, in itself, a method of stabilizing the juice mixture. Melting and reprocessing a stored sorbet (spinning it in an ice cream freezer) each day, or at least every other day, and/or making small batches frequently to avoid long storage, are options preferable to the use of stabilizers.

General Information Regarding Stabilizers

- Stabilizers are used to increase emulsification, prevent separation, improve body (texture), and retard or reduce ice crystals in storage by binding water and increase resistance to melting.

- Stabilizers are more important in sorbet and sherbet than in ice cream because sorbet and sherbet have less total solids than ice cream mixtures.

- A stabilizer will affect body (make it less crumbly), syrup drainage, and overrun in the finished product. Gum-type stabilizers retard whipping, so overrun is less.

- Using a combination of two or more stabilizers will often give a better result.

- Enough stabilizer should be used in a sorbet or sherbet mixture that the base gels very slightly at cold room temperature.

- Stickiness can be a sign of too much stabilizer.

- A crumbly texture can indicate insufficient stabilizer.

- A product that does not melt indicates too much stabilizer.

Types of Stabilizers

- Eggs—Eggs act as a stabilizer in ice creams. For the most part, egg yolks are used rather than whole eggs. When the yolks are whipped with the sugar before adding them to the milk or cream, they help to emulsify and homogenize the base mixture.

- Gums—Gum karaya, oat gum, guar seed gum, gum acacia, India gum, gum tragacanth, and cellulose gum are all used as stabilizers.

- Carrageen; salts of carrageen—A vegetable stabilizer; carrageen (also known as *Irish moss*) is a seaweed found growing off the coast of Ireland (also France and Massachusetts). It is comparable to gelatin in strength and added in the same way.

- Locust bean gum; carob flour—Locust bean is another name for carob.

- CMC (sodium carboxmethylcellulose)—Widely used by commercial ice cream makers, it has the qualities of both a stabilizer and an emulsifier. It does not set as firmly as gelatin.

- Psyllium seed husk—A vegetable-based stabilizer; psyllium is a plant.

- Lecithin—A fatty substance found in egg yolks.

- Gelatin—The amount required per quart (960 ml) of sorbet mixture is approximately 2 teaspoons (6 g) unflavored powdered gelatin. Soften on the surface of a cold liquid (use about $^1/_3$ cup/80 ml for this amount, taking it from part of the recipe) and heat to dissolve as usual. Quickly whisk into the sorbet mixture while it is still warm or at room temperature. Age a minimum of 4 hours before processing. Gelatin can be advantageous because of its ability to gel the mixture at various temperatures and stages of production. However, it is better suited to ice cream than sherbets or sorbets because it tends to produce an increased overrun in the latter.

- Agar-agar—An expensive vegetable stabilizer extracted from red algae (seaweed) found off the Pacific coast. Generally used in combination with gums and/or gelatin.

- Pectin—Obtained primarily from citrus fruits but also from sugar beets. It is best used in combination with gum tragacanth in the amount of 1 teaspoon (3 g) pectin powder and 1 teaspoon (3 g) gum tragacanth per quart of sorbet mixture. Combine the powders with 3 ounces (85 g) granulated sugar (for this amount of stabilizer), stir this into part of the sorbet mixture, heat to dissolve, then stir back into the remainder.

- Propylene glycol alginate—Propylene is an inflammable gaseous hydrocarbon obtained by breaking down petroleum hydrocarbons. Glycol is a chemical in the form of a sweet liquid obtained as a byproduct in manufacturing. Alginate is explained below.

- Algin (sodium alginate)—A vegetable stabilizer extracted from kelp. The commercial products combine sodium alginate mixed with sugar and sodium citrate. Algin is added to the base mixture with the base at 155° to 160°F (68° to 71°C) to dissolve.

Amount of Stabilizer Required

Slightly less is required for sherbets than for sorbets.

- Gelatin (200 bloom) — .45 percent of total ingredient weight

- CMC gum — .20 percent of total ingredient weight

- Pectin — .18 percent of total ingredient weight

- Algin products — .20 percent of total ingredient weight

- Locust bean gum — .25 percent of total ingredient weight

SHERBETS

Sherbets, although close to sorbets in character, are always served as a dessert. They contain milk or cream and, sometimes, a small amount of egg, giving them a smoother and richer texture than sorbets. When made without eggs, they compare very closely to Philadelphia-style ice creams; however, sherbets lack the richness associated with a traditional custard-based ice cream.

SPOOMS

When Italian meringue is added to a sorbet (approximately 25 percent), the product becomes known as a *spoom*. Spooms should placed in the freezer for several hours to set further after churning.

GRANITÀ AND GRANITÉ

Granità and *granité* are the Italian and French names, respectively, for a type of coarse dessert ice. They use basically the same ingredients as sorbets; however, they have a lower sugar content and are still frozen without churning. The name *granità* is taken from the Italian word *grana*, meaning "grainy," which refers both to the coarse texture of the ice crystals in the finished product and its resemblance to the grainy pattern of the Italian rock slabs known as granite. Granitàs are said to have become popular in Paris in the late nineteenth century and were mentioned by Mark Twain in his book *The Innocents Abroad* (1869), in which he described "people at small tables in Venice smoking and taking granità." Granitàs quickly became favored in the United States, where they are usually known by the French name *granité*.

Granitàs or granités are made by combining simple syrup or water with various fruit purees, liqueurs, wines, or brewed coffee or tea. In general, a granité or granità has less sugar than a sorbet; the ratio is typically 4 parts liquid to 1 part sugar, resulting in a Baumé level of 8° to 12°. The mixture is frozen in a shallow pan, preferably stainless steel, without churning. Sometimes the base is stirred with a fork from time to time as it hardens, but it is commonly placed in the freezer to still freeze. The mixture is then scraped into flakes and granules at serving time. Granités and granitàs may be served for dessert accompanied by fresh fruit or other garnishes, or plain as a palate cleanser between courses. In either case, they benefit from being presented in a well-chilled glass, because even though they should be served slightly thawed and slushy, they melt and return to liquid very quickly due to their delicate structure.

Apple Cider–Calvados Sorbet yield: 6 cups (1 L 420 ml)

5½ cups (1 L 320 ml) apple cider

14 ounces (400 g) granulated sugar

Juice of 1 lemon

1 cinnamon stick

½ cup (120 ml) Calvados

1. Combine the apple cider, sugar, lemon juice, and cinnamon stick in a nonreactive saucepan. Bring to a boil and cook for 2 minutes.

2. Remove from the heat and add the Calvados. Set aside to steep until cooled to room temperature, then refrigerate until well chilled.

3. Remove the cinnamon stick and process in an ice cream freezer following the manufacturer's directions. Transfer to a chilled container and store, covered, in the freezer.

Blood Orange Sorbet yield: approximately 6 cups (1 L 440 ml)

2 pounds 12 ounces (1 kg 250 g) blood oranges (approximately 10)

2 cups (480 ml) simple syrup, at room temperature

1 cup (240 ml) water

Few drops Tartaric Acid Solution (page 38) or lemon juice

1. Juice the oranges. Strain the juice; there should be approximately 2 cups (480 ml). Proceed as long as you have reasonably close to this amount.

2. Combine the orange juice and simple syrup. Add enough water to bring the mixture to between 16 and 20° Baumé (see page 742). Add the tartaric acid or lemon juice.

3. Process in an ice cream freezer following the manufacturer's directions. Transfer to a chilled container and store, covered, in the freezer.

Blueberry Sorbet yield: approximately 5 cups (1 L 200 ml)

2 pounds 8 ounces (1 kg 135 g) fresh blueberries

1 cup (240 ml) water

2 cups (480 ml) simple syrup, at room temperature

Few drops Tartaric Acid Solution (page 38) or lemon juice

1. Place the blueberries and water in a saucepan and cook over medium heat for about 10 minutes or until the blueberries pop open and begin to fall apart. Strain, pressing firmly on the contents of the strainer; discard the pulp.

2. Add enough simple syrup to the blueberry juice to bring the mixture to between 16° and 20° Baumé (see page 742). Add the tartaric acid or lemon juice.

3. Process in an ice cream freezer following the manufacturer's instructions. Transfer to a chilled bowl and store, covered, in the freezer.

Champagne Sorbet yield: approximately 2 quarts (1 L 920 ml)

When making ice from wine, spirits, or liqueur, it is not necessary to test the Baumé level prior to freezing because, as compared to fruits and berries, the sugar content of the alcoholic beverages does not vary to the same extent. When serving champagne sorbet as an intermezzo, reduce the simple syrup by half.

3½ cups (840 ml) dry champagne

2½ cups (600 ml) simple syrup, at room temperature

1½ cups (360 ml) water

⅓ cup (80 ml) lemon juice

1. Combine the champagne, simple syrup, water, and lemon juice.

2. Process in an ice cream freezer following the manufacturer's instructions. Place in a chilled container and store, covered, in the freezer.

Double Cherry Sorbet yield: approximately 6 cups (1 L 440 ml)

2 pounds (910 g) fresh Bing cherries

2 pounds (910 g) fresh Royal Anne cherries

4 ounces (115 g) granulated sugar

1 cup (240 ml) water

1½ cups (360 ml) simple syrup, at room temperature

Few drops Tartaric Acid Solution (page 38) or lemon juice

1. Rinse, stem, and pit the cherries. Place in a saucepan with the sugar and water. Stir to combine and bring to a boil. Cook over medium heat, stirring from time to time, until the cherries start to soften, about 10 minutes. Puree the mixture in a food processor. Force through a fine mesh strainer and discard the solids.

2. Combine the cherry juice with most of the simple syrup. Test the Baumé level (sugar content) using a saccharometer and, if needed, add additional simple syrup to bring the mixture to between 16° and 20° Baumé. Add the tartaric acid or lemon juice.

3. Process in an ice cream freezer following the manufacturer's instructions. Transfer to a chilled container and store, covered, in the freezer.

Feijoa Sorbet yield: approximately 5 cups (1 L 200 ml)

Feijoa is a fragrant tropical fruit often called *pineapple guava*. It is important that the strainer and other utensils used here are made of a noncorrosive material or the acid will discolor the fruit.

3 pounds (1 kg 365 g) feijoas

½ cup (120 ml) lime juice

1½ cups (360 ml) unsweetened pineapple juice

2 cups (480 ml) simple syrup, at room temperature

½ cup (120 ml) water

1. Use a vegetable peeler to remove the skin from the feijoas. You should have approximately 2 pounds (910 g) fruit left. Cut the fruit into small pieces.

2. Place the fruit pieces in a food processor with the lime juice. Process to a smooth puree. Force the mixture through a fine mesh strainer; discard the seeds and solids.

3. Add the pineapple juice and simple syrup to the puree. Add enough of the water (or additional simple syrup, depending on the ripeness of the fruit) to bring the mixture to between 16° and 20° Baumé (see page 742).

4. Process in an ice cream freezer according to the manufacturer's instructions. Transfer the finished sorbet to a chilled container and store, covered, in the freezer.

Gooseberry Sorbet yield: approximately 6 cups (1 L 440 ml)

This sorbet can be prepared with canned gooseberries if you cannot obtain fresh or it is the off-season. Canned gooseberries require only about 5 minutes of cooking. Because they are usually sold in sugar syrup, adjust the amount of granulated sugar accordingly or leave it out altogether. The flavor of canned gooseberries is usually a bit bland, so it is a good idea to add a few drops of Tartaric Acid Solution (page 38) or lemon juice.

3 pounds 8 ounces (1 kg 590 g) fresh gooseberries

12 ounces (340 g) granulated sugar

½ cup (120 ml) water

1½ cups (360 ml) simple syrup, at room temperature

1. Rinse the gooseberries. Place in a saucepan with the sugar and water and stir to combine. Cook over medium heat, stirring from time to time, until the gooseberries burst, about 10 minutes. Force the mixture through a fine mesh strainer; discard the seeds and solids.

2. Add most of the simple syrup to the gooseberry juice. Test the sugar content with a saccharometer (Baumé thermometer) and add enough additional simple syrup to bring the mixture to between 16° and 20° Baumé (see page 742).

3. Process in an ice cream freezer following the manufacturer's directions. Transfer to a chilled container and store, covered, in the freezer.

Honey Mandarin Sorbet yield: approximately 6 cups (1 L 440 ml)

To make other citrus sorbets, such as orange, tangerine, or tangelo, simply substitute the desired juice for the mandarin juice in the recipe.

3 pounds 8 ounces (1 kg 590 g) honey mandarins (approximately 8 medium)

2 cups (480 ml) simple syrup, at room temperature

2½ cups (600 ml) water

Few drops Tartaric Acid Solution (page 38) or lemon juice

1. Juice the mandarins. Strain the juice and discard the seeds and solids. You should have approximately 2 cups (480 ml) juice. Proceed as long as you have reasonably close to this amount; the measurement need not be exact.

2. Combine the mandarin juice and simple syrup. Add enough water to bring the mixture to between 16 and 20° Baumé (see page 742). Add the tartaric acid or lemon juice.

3. Process in an ice cream freezer following the manufacturer's instructions. Transfer to a chilled bowl, cover, and store in the freezer.

Honeydew Melon Sorbet yield: approximately 6 cups (1 L 440 ml)

The amount of water required in this recipe can vary quite a bit depending on the sugar content of the melon, which fluctuates with the time of year. It is important that the melons are fully ripe, not just for the flavor but so you will get enough juice out of the pulp when you puree them.

4 pounds (1 kg 820 g) honeydew melon (1 medium or 2 small)

3 cups (720 ml) simple syrup, at room temperature

½ teaspoon (1.5 g) gum tragacanth powder

½ teaspoon (1.5 g) powdered pectin

1½ cups (360 ml) water

Few drops Tartaric Acid Solution (page 38) or lemon juice

1. Cut the melons into sections, scoop out the seeds, and cut the meat away from the rind. Puree to a smooth pulp. You should have approximately 3 cups (720 ml). Proceed as long as you have reasonably close to this amount; the measurement need not be exact. Stir in the simple syrup.

2. Combine the gum tragacanth and pectin powder with a small amount of the water. Heat to dissolve, then stir into the fruit juice mixture. Add enough of the remaining water to bring the mixture to between 16° and 20° Baumé (see page 742). Add the tartaric acid or lemon juice.

3. Process in an ice cream freezer following the manufacturer's directions. Transfer the finished sorbet to a chilled bowl and store, covered, in the freezer.

Kiwi Sorbet yield: approximately 6 cups (1 L 440 ml)

4 pounds (1 kg 820 g) kiwis (about 10 medium)

½ cup (120 ml) lime juice

2 cups (480 ml) simple syrup, at room temperature

2 cups (480 ml) water

1. Peel the kiwis (see Figures 7-6, page 353). Cut in half lengthwise and remove the small hard section at the bottom. Place the fruit in a food processor, add the lime juice, and puree just until the mixture is smooth. Be careful not to overprocess the fruit; too many broken seeds will turn the mixture a grayish color. The seeds are also what give this sorbet its distinctive look, so do not strain the pulp.

2. Stir in the simple syrup and enough of the water to bring the mixture to between 16° and 20° Baumé (see page 742).

3. Process in an ice cream freezer following the manufacturer's instructions. Transfer to a chilled container and store, covered, in the freezer.

Lemon-Lime Sherbet yield: approximately 2 quarts (1 L 920 ml)

1 cup (240 ml) strained lemon juice

1 cup (240 ml) strained lime juice

Finely grated zest of 8 lemons

Finely grated zest of 6 limes

2 cups (480 ml) Unflavored Yogurt (page 38)

4 cups (960 ml) simple syrup, at room temperature

1. Combine the lemon juice, lime juice, lemon zest, and lime zest. Stir into the yogurt. Add enough of the simple syrup to bring the mixture to between 16° and 20° Baumé (see page 742).

2. Process in a ice cream freezer according to the manufacturer's directions. Transfer to a chilled bowl and store, covered, in the freezer.

Lemon Thyme and Mascarpone Sherbet yield: approximately 7 cups (1 L 680 ml)

Mascarpone makes a smooth, rich sherbet. If you are not making your own mascarpone, be certain to use only a very high-quality product, or the cheese may separate in Step 2.

3 cups (720 ml) water

1 tablespoon (30 ml) chopped lemon thyme leaves

8 ounces (225 g) granulated sugar

⅓ cup (80 ml) lemon juice

4 egg yolks (80 ml)

½ cup (120 ml) or 6 ounces (170 g) honey

12 ounces (225 g) Mascarpone Cheese (page 22)

1½ cups (360 ml) sour cream

1. Place the water, lemon thyme, sugar, and lemon juice in a saucepan. Bring to a boil. Remove from the heat, cover, and set aside to steep for 1 hour.

2. Whip the egg yolks for 1 minute. In a saucepan, bring the honey to a boil. In a slow steady stream, add the honey to the egg yolks, beating constantly, until cooled.

3. Beat the mascarpone cheese for 1 or 2 minutes or until smooth. Add the sour cream and the honey-yolk mixture and mix to combine. Strain the reserved infusion to remove the lemon thyme. Gradually incorporate the liquid into the cheese mixture.

4. Process in an ice cream freezer following the manufacturer's directions. Store, covered, in the freezer.

Mango Sorbet yield: approximately 6 cups (1 L 440 ml)

If the mangoes are not fully ripe, they will contain more stringy fibers, reducing the yield. Mangoes that are somewhat unripe are easier to work with if you peel them before cutting the flesh from the stones.

4 pounds (1 kg 820 g) ripe mangoes (about 5 medium)

½ cup (120 ml) lime juice

2 cups (480 ml) simple syrup

2 cups (480 ml) water

1. Slice each mango in half by making a cut on either side of the large flat stone. Use a spoon to scrape the flesh away from the skin and the stones. Place the flesh in a food processor. Add the lime juice and puree the fruit until smooth. Strain through a chinois and discard the solids.

2. Stir in the simple syrup and enough of the water to bring the mixture to between 16° and 20° Baumé (see page 742).

3. Process in an ice cream freezer according to the manufacturer's directions. Transfer the sorbet to a chilled container, cover, and store in the freezer.

Prickly Pear Sorbet yield: approximately 3 cups (720 ml)

2 pounds 8 ounces (1 kg 135 g) prickly pears (about 8) (see Chef's Tip)

½ cup (120 ml) simple syrup, at room temperature

⅓ cup (80 ml) water

¼ cup (60 ml) kirschwasser

Juice of 1 lime

1. Cut the prickly pears in half crosswise and scoop out the pulp using a small spoon. Save the shells to use in serving or discard them. Place the fruit pulp in a food processor and process to a smooth consistency (see Note).

2. Strain the mixture and discard the solids; you should have about 3 cups (720 ml) of juice. Add the simple syrup, water, kirschwasser, and lime juice to the fruit juice. Let cool.

3. Adjust the Baumé level of the liquid to between 16° and 20° by adding additional water if it is too high or simple syrup if it is too low (see page 742).

4. Process in an ice cream freezer following the manufacturer's instructions. Transfer to a chilled container, cover, and store in the freezer.

> **CHEF'S TIP**
> A quick and perfectly acceptable substitute for the fresh prickly pears in this recipe is the frozen prickly pear juice now readily available through commercial distributors. Most juices are sold unsweetened or with only a minimal amount of sugar added. Check the label and adjust the amount of simple syrup accordingly. You need 3 cups (720 ml) of juice for this recipe.

NOTE: If the prickly pears are not totally ripe, place the fruit pulp, simple syrup, and water in a nonreactive saucepan and heat, stirring, until the fruit falls apart. Do not boil. Process the cooked mixture and continue.

Raspberry Sorbet yield: approximately 6 cups (1 L 440 ml)

It is important to use a chilled container for storage or the sorbet will start to liquefy immediately. The amount of water needed in the recipe can vary quite a bit depending on the time of year and the sweetness of the particular variety of raspberry.

1 pound 4 ounces (570 g) fresh raspberries (approximately 5 cups/1 L 200 ml, loosely packed)

2 cups (480 ml) simple syrup, at room temperature

2 cups (480 ml) water

Few drops Tartaric Acid Solution (page 38) or lemon juice

1. Puree the raspberries in a food processor; strain. There should be about 2 cups (480 ml) juice. Proceed as long as you have reasonably close to this amount; the measurement need not be exact.

2. Combine the raspberry juice and simple syrup. Add enough water to bring the mixture to between 16° and 20° Baumé (see page 742). Add the tartaric acid or lemon juice.

3. Process in an ice cream freezer according to the manufacturer's directions. When finished, transfer to a chilled bowl, cover, and store in the freezer.

Red Currant Sorbet yield: approximately 4 cups (960 ml)

2 pounds (910 g) fresh red currants (see Chef's Tip)

¾ cup (180 ml) water

1¼ cups (300 ml) ruby port wine

5 ounces (140 g) granulated sugar

Few drops Tartaric Acid Solution (page 38) or lemon juice

Water or simple syrup, at room temperature

CHEF'S TIP

Because fresh red currants are not readily available in the United States, using unsweetened frozen berries (IQF type) is an excellent alternative. While the flavor of the frozen fruit is good, in my experience frozen berries do not produce the same intense red color that the fresh currants provide, so adding a bit of Beet Juice (page 5), raspberry juice, or 1 to 2 drops red food coloring may be necessary. Another easy substitution is to use readymade frozen juice. Many common and exotic or tropical juice flavors are now readily available through produce companies and baking suppliers. In most cases these juices are available unsweetened but if you purchase sweetened juice, reduce the amount of simple syrup used accordingly. You need 2 cups (480 ml) of juice for this recipe.

1. Wash the currants and remove the berries from the stems. Place the currants in a saucepan with the water, port wine, and granulated sugar. Stir to combine and bring the mixture to a boil.

2. Puree the mixture and strain through a fine mesh strainer; discard the solids. Add the tartaric acid or lemon juice to the liquid.

3. Add additional water or simple syrup as needed so that the sugar content measures between 16° and 20° Baumé (see page 742).

4. Process in an ice cream freezer following the manufacturer's instructions. Place the sorbet in a chilled bowl, cover, and freeze.

White Nectarine Sorbet yield: approximately 6 cups (1 L 440 ml)

2 pounds 8 ounces (1 kg, 135 g) ripe white nectarines (see Variation)

2 cups (480 ml) water

2 cups (480 ml) simple syrup, at room temperature

Few drops Tartaric Acid Solution (page 38) or lemon juice

1. Wash, stone, and cut the nectarines into small pieces. Place in a saucepan with the water and half of the simple syrup. Bring to a boil and cook, stirring occasionally, until the fruit falls apart, about 10 minutes. Remove from the heat and force through a fine mesh strainer.

2. Let cool to room temperature. Add enough of the remaining simple syrup to bring the mixture to between 16° and 20° Baumé (see page 742). Add the tartaric acid or lemon juice.

3. Process in an ice cream freezer according to the manufacturer's directions. Transfer the finished sorbet to a chilled container, cover, and store in the freezer.

VARIATION
NECTARINE OR PEACH SORBET

If you can not obtain white nectarines, you can easily substitute regular nectarines or peaches. The color of the sorbet will be golden rather than ivory—unless, of course, you use white peaches.

Custards, Puddings, Mousses, Charlottes, and Bavarian Creams

At first glance, you may wonder why the desserts in this chapter are grouped together. As you read the definitions that follow, you will see what these formulas have in common and how several desserts are actually hybrids of two or more elements.

Custards

Simply stated, a custard is a liquid—milk, cream, or a combination of the two—that is thickened using a combination of eggs and heat. The coagulation of the egg protein sets the custard. Custards are easy to prepare, they can be made one to two days in advance, and they need little or no finishing touch.

The most basic custard formula contains simply eggs and sugar plus milk or cream. The consistency of the finished product is determined by the fat content of the milk or cream used and the ratio of whole eggs and/or egg yolks to that liquid.

The three best-known baked custards are crème caramel, pots de crème, and crème brûlée. All are baked in a bain-marie, or water bath, to protect the custard from a high heat. Heating the custard above 185°F (85°C) will cause it to become curdled and watery because the moisture will separate from the toughened protein. Custards are generally baked in individual earthenware cups, but they can be made in larger ovenproof dishes to serve on a buffet.

- Crème caramel uses the least rich mixture of the three custards, 1¾ whole eggs to 1 cup whole milk. This custard is firm enough to unmold after baking and chilling.

- Pots de crème contain ¾ whole egg plus 1 egg yolk per 1 cup of half-and-half. This custard is softer than the crème caramel because of the additional fat in the half-and-half and because less egg white is present. It is too soft to unmold and is baked and served in individual ramekins or custard cups.

- Crème brûlée is the softest and richest of the three custards. Its formula contains 2 egg yolks per 1 cup heavy cream, with 1 whole egg added for stability for every 7 cups of cream. Like pots de crème, crème brûlée is served in its baking form.

Some custards are cooked and thickened on top of the stove; these are called *stirred custards*. Pastry cream and vanilla custard sauce, also known as *crème anglaise*, are examples of stirred custards. Some stirred custards are cooked over direct heat, others must be cooked over a water bath. A trifle is made from freshly prepared warm pastry cream that is layered with various types of liqueur-soaked cake and fruit. As the pastry cream cools, it sets up much like a baked custard, holding the other ingredients together.

Puddings

Puddings are made in much the same way as custards, but in place of or in addition to the eggs, they contain a starch thickener, such as cornstarch or flour. Puddings are, for the most part, cooked on the stovetop, and they are cooked to a higher temperature than custards. The starch allows you to do this without curdling any egg that may be present. An example of a pudding-custard hybrid is pastry cream, which is basically a stirred custard. However, due to the addition of a starch thickener, with its inherent stabilizing properties, it can brought to the boiling point.

- Rice puddings and bread puddings are essentially baked custards with the addition of other ingredients and flavorings.

- Pudding cakes are another hybrid. These are egg custards with the addition of flour and whipped egg whites. During baking, the egg whites rise, causing the top of the dessert to develop a sponge cake–like texture, while the creamy bottom settles into a moist pudding.

- Panna cotta and blanc mange are made with sweetened milk or cream, like custards and puddings, but they are set using gelatin rather than starch or eggs thickened with heat. They are always served cold.

- Summer pudding is prepared in a similar way to a hot charlotte in that it contains a fruit filling in a bread-lined mold; however, summer puddings are always served cold. While summer pudding is the well-known and accepted name of a particular dessert, it is not actually related to starch-thickened cooked puddings.

Mousses

A classic mousse is made up of whipped cream, beaten egg whites and/or yolks, sugar, and the desired flavoring. The word *mousse* means "foam" or "froth" in French. A chocolate mousse, which seems to be synonymous with the word *mousse*, should not require any thickener other than the chocolate itself. A fruit or liqueur mousse must usually be fortified with pectin or gelatin. When using either thickener, take care not to get it too hot or you may melt and deflate the whipped cream. Fruit mousses are a snap to make—especially these days, with so many high-quality fresh fruit purees available to the industry. In some recipes, the egg whites are incorporated before the cream to prevent overmixing the cream as the egg whites are added, which could result in a loss of volume. However, by whipping the cream to soft peaks only, it can be added prior to the egg whites with no ill effect.

Mousses are extremely versatile and can be elaborately presented in edible containers made of tuile paste, Florentina paste, or chocolate, or they can be served simply in a pretty ramekin or a stemmed glass. Whatever the interpretation, mousses are very popular with consumers and also with busy chefs, because they are easy to make and can be prepared well in advance.

Charlottes

Charlottes fall into two categories: hot and cold. Bavarian cream, which is an excellent dessert in and of itself and is defined in detail below, provides the filling for cold charlottes. Charlottes are always made in molds, which are traditionally pail-shaped, with straight sides, but many modern versions are made in other shapes. Charlottes may be made in individual serving sizes or in forms that will serve up to ten. For both hot and cold charlottes, the molds are always lined before the filling is added. In the case of the well-known versions Charlotte Royal and Charlotte Russe, the molds are lined with jelly rolls and ladyfingers, respectively. In other recipes, the molds are lined with different sponge or meringue products, or with sliced fruit.

Classic hot charlottes are made with a fruit filling, typically apple, which is baked in a form lined with buttered bread slices. Hot charlottes came first and were the inspiration for the cold versions, but the only points these desserts have in common is that they are made in the same molds, and the molds are always lined. Hot charlottes do not contain gelatin. Instead, the filling is cooked until the proper thickness is achieved. Occasionally, pectin is added as a further thickening agent.

Bavarian Creams

These are also known as Bavarians, or by the French term *bavarois*. A classic Bavarian cream is made by adding gelatin and whipped cream to a stirred custard sauce made with whole eggs (see

Figure 16-13, page 818). The mixture is then flavored with fruit puree, liqueur, chocolate, or nuts and poured into molds or used as a filling for cakes or pastries. Many modified versions are created by using egg yolks alone in the custard base, or by adding whipped egg whites instead of—or in addition to—the whipped cream. A Bavarian is always unmolded before it is served.

Because Bavarian creams are set up by chilling the gelatin-strengthened mixture, the chef does not have the same control as when making a cooked product, where the cooking time can be adjusted to achieve a desired texture. Therefore, precise measurement and proper incorporation of the gelatin are musts. If too little gelatin is used, or if the gelatin is added improperly so that part of it starts to set up and forms lumps before it can be fully incorporated, the dessert will not hold its shape and will be impossible to unmold. On the other hand, if too much gelatin is used, the Bavarian cream will be tough and rubbery.

It is also important to remember that unless they are first poached or pureed and brought to a boil to destroy the active enzyme (see page 889), many tropical fruits inhibit the gelatinization process if you are using a protein (that is, animal-based) gelatin. The acid content of the fruit will also affect the ability of the gelatin to set. A higher acid content requires less gelatin. Keep this in mind when you substitute a different variety of fruit in a recipe.

Like other gelatin-based desserts, Bavarian creams can be made up and used over two to three days if they are kept properly covered and refrigerated in their original molds. To unmold, dip the outside of the form into hot water for a few seconds, wipe the bottom, and invert onto a serving plate or paper-lined sheet pan. Repeat the procedure if the dessert does not unmold easily. With experience, you will learn how long to hold the form in the water. Take care not to immerse the form too long or you will melt the filling. A Bavarian can also be helped out of its mold by using the back of a spoon to gently push the filling away from the side of the mold, thereby breaking the suction.

When the desserts are made in metal rings, gently heating the outside of the rings with a blow torch will allow you to simply lift the rings off. To unmold Bavarian creams made in Flexipans, place the desserts in the freezer to allow the desserts to freeze solid. Turn the Flexipan indentations inside out and push the desserts out of the mold. Let the Bavarian creams thaw completely (either in the refrigerator or at room temperature) before decorating and serving.

Crème Brûlée yield: 12 servings, 6 ounces (180 ml) each (Photo 23)

One could easily argue that even though they have many similarities, crème brûlée is, in several ways, the opposite of crème caramel. These small cholesterol bombs use all heavy cream and additional egg yolks (as opposed to milk and whole eggs in the other); the sugar goes on the top instead of the bottom; and the sugar is caramelized after the custards are baked—unlike crème caramel, where the sugar is caramelized first, then poured on the bottom of the molds before the custard is added and the desserts are baked. Finally, crème brûlée is served in its baking dish, while crème caramel is unmolded onto a serving plate.

This rich, smooth-textured dessert is known as *Burnt Cream* in England, where it has been popular since the seventeenth century. It was not, however, until late in the nineteenth century that the French term *crème brûlée*, which means precisely the same thing, became popular and the dessert became standard fare in many American restaurants.

The richness of the custard lends itself extremely well to being paired with fresh fruit, either as part of the presentation, as a flavoring for the custard itself, or as a container for the custard. In some variations, the custard is cooked on the stovetop instead of being thickened the traditional way by baking in a water bath. This method is particularly useful when the custard is presented in a hollowed-out fruit shell.

The caramelized sugar crust on a fine crème brûlée should be thin and crisp, so the spoon can go right through. Too much sugar on top will make the crust too hard. If made ahead, the crust will melt, so it should be caramelized to order.

1 vanilla bean	1 teaspoon (5 ml) vanilla extract
12 ounces (340 g) granulated sugar	Granulated sugar
14 egg yolks (1¼ cups/300 ml)	Seasonal berries or other fresh fruit
1 whole egg	Sugar decorations (optional)
7 cups (1 L 680 ml) heavy cream	Mint sprigs *or* edible fresh flowers
1½ teaspoons (7.5 g) salt	Piped Cookie Curly Cues (page 795)

1. Cut the vanilla bean in half lengthwise and scrape out the seeds; save the pods halves for another use. Mix the vanilla bean seeds with the measured sugar, rubbing the mixture lightly with your fingertips to combine. Set aside.

2. Mix—do not whip—the egg yolks, whole egg, and vanilla-flavored sugar until well combined. Heat the cream to the scalding point, then gradually pour into the egg mixture while stirring constantly. Add the salt and the vanilla.

3. Place crème brûlée forms (see Note) or ovenproof forms such as soufflé ramekins, 3¼ inches (8.1 cm) in diameter, in hotel pans or other suitable pans and fill them close to the top with the custard. Add hot water around the forms to reach about three-fourths of the way up the sides. Move the pan to the oven, then top off each form with the remaining custard. Be sure to fill the forms all the way to the top because crème brûlée—like any custard—will settle slightly while it is cooking.

4. Bake at 350°F (175°C) for about 25 minutes or until the custards are set. If using soufflé

If you are not certain your oven
temperature is accurate, test it
with an oven thermometer. If you
do not have a removable thermometer, start cooking the custards at 325°F (163°C). If after 30
minutes the custard is still as liquid
as when you started, your thermostat is incorrect and you should
increase the temperature. Wasting
a half hour is better than overcooking the custard due to a
poorly calibrated oven.

ramekins, the baking time will be a few minutes longer. Do not overcook, or the custard may break and have an unpleasant texture. Remove the custards from the water bath and let them cool slightly at room temperature, then refrigerate until thoroughly chilled. The custards may be stored in the refrigerator for 4 to 5 days at this point, left in their baking forms and covered tightly.

5. Presentation: Sprinkle just enough granulated sugar on top of a custard to cover the surface. Clean off any sugar on the edge or the outside of the form. Caramelize the sugar using a salamander or a blowtorch, or by placing the dish under a broiler. Decorate one side of the top of the crème brûlée with a few berries or small slices of fruit, sugar decoration, if desired, and a mint sprig or edible flower. Place the custard dish on a plate lined with a napkin and serve with a cookie curly cue next to the dessert.

NOTE: Traditional crème brûlée dishes are made of ceramic and are 4½ inches (11.2 cm) in diameter and ¾ inch (2 cm) deep.

VARIATIONS
PASSION FRUIT CREME BRULEE

1. Add ½ cup passion fruit pulp, including the seeds (from about 8 passion fruit), to the custard base after incorporating the cream in Step 2.

2. Clean the outside of passion fruit shell halves.

3. Immediately after caramelizing the sugar, stand a shell half at the back edge of the dish, tilted so that the opening of the shell faces forward—the side that will be presented to the customer; the soft sugar will glue the shell in place.

4. Fill the shell with sliced fruit or berries, letting one or two spill out onto the top of the dessert.

LEMON CREME BRULEE

1. Add the finely chopped zest of 2 lemons to the custard.

2. Place 2 tablespoons Lemon Curd (page 844) in each baking form and spread it out to cover the bottom of the dish.

3. Add the lemon-flavored custard and proceed as directed.

4. Garnish with candied lemon peel after caramelizing the sugar on top.

5. This variation will give you a slightly higher crème brûlée, or you can make 2 additional servings, as each form will use less custard.

TWO-TONE CHOCOLATE AND VANILLA CREME BRULEE

1. Place 2 tablespoons Ganache (page 842) in each baking form and spread it out to cover the bottom of the dish. If the ganache is very firm, warm it before you do this so that you can make an even layer.

2. Add the custard and proceed as directed in the main recipe. Adding a few cocoa nibs to the custard will enhance the chocolate flavor; they can also be sprinkled on top after the custard is poured into the molds.

3. Garnish with raspberries and a Chocolate Cutout (page 460).

4. This variation will give you a slightly higher crème brûlée, or you can make 2 additional servings, as each form will use less custard.

Crème Caramel yield: 16 servings, 3¼ inches (8.1 cm) in diameter

Crème caramel is titled *crème renversé* in French, which literally means "cream reversed," referring to the fact that the desserts are unmolded and served upside-down. Crème caramel is made by coating the bottom of baking forms with a layer of caramelized sugar, filling them with a raw custard mixture, and baking in a water bath. The caramel coating colors and flavors the bottom of the custard during baking. When the cold custard is inverted onto a serving plate, a portion of the caramel, which has become liquefied (it takes about 48 hours in the refrigerator for all of the caramel to melt) runs over and around the dessert, doubling as a sauce. The Spanish equivalent is called *flan*. All three are the same dessert, although flan is made in both individual forms as well as larger sizes to provide multiple servings, whereas crème caramel is traditionally made only in single servings. Crème caramel is one of several desserts that fall under the heading of baked custards. These are grouped separately from stovetop thickened or stirred custards, examples of which are pastry cream and crème anglaise.

A quick glance at this recipe's few ingredients and its short list of instructions will tell you it is a fairly simple dessert to produce and, while that is true, there are still a few crucial points you need to pay attention to. The water in the bain-marie must never be brought to a full boil, at the most, it can simmer gently, but ideally the water should just quiver in the pan without any bubbles rising to the surface. The caramelized sugar should have a healthy brown color so that the custard is not only flavored by the caramel, but also picks up an appetizing color. However, the caramel must not be cooked too dark or it will be taste bitter. Pay close attention once the sugar reaches an amber color, as it will darken quite quickly after that point, and have a cold water bath ready so you can shock the sugar and stop the cooking process.

An alternative method to placing the bottom of the pan in cold water once the sugar reaches the desired color is to pour in a small amount of hot water, ¼ cup (60 ml) for this amount of caramel. Stand back as you add the water because the mixture may splatter. Stir the water in and warm the sugar if necessary to eliminate any lumps. This technique works particularly well if the caramel was accidentally cooked just a bit too dark, but if it has become very dark, you should throw it out and start over.

1 pound 8 ounces (680 g) granulated sugar

¼ teaspoon (1.25 ml) lemon juice

2 quarts (1 l 920 ml) whole milk

1 pound (455 g) granulated sugar

3½ cups (840 ml) eggs (approximately 14)

1 recipe Clear Caramel Sauce (page 817)

Whipped cream (optional)

Fresh fruit (optional)

Cookies such as Pirouettes (page 314) or
Butter Crescents (page 265) (optional)

1. Place the first measurement of sugar and the lemon juice in a thick-bottomed saucepan. Place over medium heat and stir constantly with a wooden spoon until the sugar melts and caramelizes to a rich brown color. Immediately plunge the bottom of the pan into cold water to stop the caramelization.

2. Pour a ⅛-inch (3-mm) layer of caramel on the bottom of 16 soufflé ramekins, 3¼ inches (8.1 cm) in diameter, or in coffee cups with straight sides. Set the forms aside.

3. Heat the milk to the scalding point. Whisk together the remaining sugar and eggs. Gradually add the hot milk to the sugar mixture while whisking constantly. Strain the custard.

CHEF'S TIP

The best serving method is to first unmold the custard onto a separate unmolding plate, as directed here, rather than to unmold directly onto the serving plate. Another option is to use a spoon to gently press the skin away from the sides and then, holding the custard about 1 inch (2.5 cm) above the plate, use the back of the spoon to lightly push part of the custard away from the side of the form to release the suction; the custard should drop right out. This is the traditional method, and it is quick and easy; however, the caramel that will run out onto the plate may be a bit dark and can be bitter. I prefer to serve a separately made caramel sauce.

4. Place the forms in a hotel pan or another suitable pan. Fill the forms almost to the top with custard. Add hot water to the larger pan to reach about three-fourths of the way up the sides of the forms. Move the pan to the oven. Fill each form to the top with custard.

5. Bake at 350°F (175°C) for approximately 35 minutes or until the custard is set. Let cool completely, then refrigerate for a minimum of 4 hours.

6. To unmold, run a thin knife around the inside of the form without cutting down into the custard; you only need to loosen the top skin from the sides of the form. Invert the form on top of a plate (not the serving plate) and, holding the form and plate together, shake vigorously up and down a few times until the custard falls out onto the plate. Transfer the crème caramel to a serving plate with a small spatula or palette knife; discard the caramel sauce from the unmolding plate. Using a piping bottle, pipe just enough caramel sauce around the custard to cover the base of the plate. Serve with whipped cream, fresh fruit, and/or a crisp cookie as desired. The remaining custards can be stored, refrigerated in their baking forms, for several days.

FLAN yield: 3 flans, 9 inches (22.5 cm) in diameter

Crème caramel can be baked in pie pans to create a larger dessert with the traditional round flan shape and sloping sides.

1. Follow the instructions in the main recipe, dividing both the caramel and the custard evenly among 3 glass or ceramic pie pans, 9 inches (22.5 cm) in diameter.

2. Bake these in a bain-marie as directed; the baking time will be slightly longer. Refrigerate for a minimum of 4 hours.

3. Unmold each flan (see Step 6, page 762) onto a serving platter large enough to accommodate it and the caramelized sugar sauce that will run out around the sides. Serve cut into wedges and accompanied by whipped cream, fresh berries, and Mexican Wedding Cookies (page 310).

Gingered Caramel Custards yield: 16 servings, 3¼ inches (8.1 cm) in diameter

2 tablespoons (30 ml) finely chopped fresh ginger	¼ teaspoon (1.25 ml) lemon juice
2 quarts (1 L 920 ml) milk	3½ cups (840 ml) eggs (approximately 14)
1 pound 8 ounces (680 g) plus 1 pound (455 g) granulated sugar	1 recipe Clear Caramel Sauce (page 817)

1. Combine the ginger and milk in a saucepan. Bring to the scalding point, then remove from the heat and set aside to infuse while preparing the caramel.

2. Place the first measurement of sugar and the lemon juice in a thick-bottomed saucepan. Place over medium heat and stir constantly with a wooden spoon until the sugar melts and caramelizes to a rich brown color. Immediately plunge the bottom of the pan into cold water to stop the caramelization.

3. Pour a ⅛-inch (3-mm) layer of caramel on the bottom of 16 soufflé ramekins, 3¼ inches (8.1 cm) in diameter, or in coffee cups with straight sides. Set the forms aside.

4. Reheat the milk to the scalding point. Whisk together the remaining sugar and eggs. Gradually add the hot milk to the sugar mixture while whisking constantly. Strain the custard and discard the ginger.

5. Place the forms in a hotel pan or in another suitable pan. Fill the forms almost to the top with custard. Add hot water to the larger pan to reach about three-fourths of the way up the sides of the forms. Move the pan to the oven. Fill each form to the top with custard.

6. Bake at 350°F (175°C) for approximately 35 minutes or until the custard is set. Let cool completely, then refrigerate for a minimum of 4 hours.

7. Unmold and serve as directed in Step 6, page 762. Tropical fruits and Layered Florentina Squares (page 309) make nice accompaniments to these custards.

Cardamom Custards yield: 16 servings, 3¼ inches (8.1 cm) in diameter

16 Gingered Caramel Custards (page 763; see
Step 1)

1 cup (240 ml) heavy cream

1 tablespoon (15 g) granulated sugar

Piping Chocolate (page 465), melted

1 recipe Clear Caramel Sauce (page 817)

16 Chocolate Cutouts (page 460)

Fresh fruit

1. Follow the recipe and instructions for Gingered Caramel Custards, substituting an equal amount of ground cardamom for the fresh ginger. Do not strain in Step 4.

2. Whip the heavy cream and sugar until stiff peaks form. Place in a pastry bag with a No. 4 (8-mm) star tip. Reserve in the refrigerator.

3. Unmold as many custards as you anticipate serving (see Step 6, page 762) and reserve in the refrigerator. Any remaining can be refrigerated in their molds for up to 3 days.

4. Decorate as many dessert plates as you will need with the piping chocolate.

5. Presentation: Place a custard in the center of a prepared dessert plate. Use a piping bottle to pipe just enough caramel sauce around the custard to cover the base of the plate. Pipe a rosette of whipped cream on top of the custard. Decorate with a chocolate cutout and a small piece of fresh fruit.

Trifle with Fresh Fruit yield: 12 servings

During Elizabethan times, a trifle was a simple syllabub—that is to say, a dessert consisting of whipped cream flavored with sugar, sherry or Madeira wine, lemon, and cinnamon. Gradually, macaroons soaked in wine, ratafias (macaroons with the addition of butter), and biscuits were added. This variation became extremely popular in eighteenth-century England. Eventually, custard was used between the layers of macaroons and biscuits, and the dessert was then topped with the syllabub. This evolved into the trifle we know today. The Italian version of this dessert is called *Zuppa Inglese* ("English Soup"), created by an Italian chef who was inspired by the spirit-laden English specialty.

Trifle should be assembled in and served from a large glass bowl so that all of the layers can be seen. It is therefore better suited to buffet service or use on a pastry cart than as a dessert served directly from the kitchen. Trifle is an excellent way of using dry or leftover sponge pieces. Instead of the traditional raspberry jam, I prefer to use seasonal fresh fruit. However, the variations of this dessert are endless. Here are two of my favorites.

4 cups (960 ml) or about 1½ pounds (680 g)
prepared fresh fruit (see Step 1)

1 teaspoon (3 g) unflavored gelatin powder

2 tablespoons (30 ml) cold water

1 Sponge Cake (page 437), 10 inches (25 cm)
in diameter, *or* about the same amount of
leftover sponge pieces

¾ cup (180 ml) orange liqueur

½ recipe Pastry Cream (page 845), freshly
made (see Note)

1½ cups (360 ml) heavy cream

2 teaspoons (10 g) granulated sugar

1 teaspoon (5 ml) vanilla extract

Dark chocolate shavings

1. Prepare the fruit. Although you are, of course, limited to the available fresh fruit in season, a good combination is peaches, oranges, kiwis, and strawberries (the flavor of peaches and strawberries goes very nicely with the orange liqueur). To prepare 1 cup (240 ml) of each variety, you will need 1 medium peach, pitted; 2 oranges, peeled and sectioned (see Figures 1-1 and 1-2, page 13); and ½ basket strawberries (6 ounces/170 g), stems removed. Cut the fruit into pieces about the size of a raspberry. If you use small berries, such as raspberries or blueberries, leave them whole. Set aside approximately ½ cup (120 ml) fruit to use in decorating.

2. Sprinkle the gelatin over the water and set aside to soften.

3. Cut the skin from the top of the sponge cake and slice the cake into 2 layers. Use bite-sized chunks from half of the cake to cover the bottom of a glass serving bowl approximately 10 inches (25 cm) in diameter. Sprinkle 6 tablespoons (90 ml) orange liqueur generously over the sponge pieces. You may need to use more liqueur, depending on how dry the sponge is. The pieces should be well saturated—after all, trifle is not known as tipsy pudding for nothing!

4. Place the gelatin mixture over a bain-marie and heat to dissolve. Do not overheat. Whisk the gelatin into the warm pastry cream. Spoon half of the custard over the sponge and spread it out to the edge of the bowl.

5. Sprinkle half of the fruit on top of the custard. Layer the reserved sponge (in chunks), remaining orange liqueur, custard, and fruit in the same manner. Place the trifle in the refrigerator to chill.

6. Whip the heavy cream to stiff peaks with the sugar and vanilla. Spread enough cream on top of the trifle to cover the fruit. Place the remaining whipped cream in a pastry bag with a No. 6 (12-mm) star tip. Pipe a border around the edge. Sprinkle shaved chocolate in the center and decorate around the chocolate with the reserved fruit.

NOTE: Although in a pinch you can use a chilled custard that is already made (providing it is smooth and soft), the trifle will look much nicer if warm custard is draped over the sponge, filling all the crevices and holding the sponge chunks together when set.

VARIATION

AMARETTO-CHOCOLATE TRIFLE yield: 12 servings

Replace the sponge cake with Cocoa Almond Sponge (page 439) and use amaretto rather than orange liqueur. If they are in season, try using cherries instead of mixed fresh fruit.

Vanilla Pots de Crème yield: 16 servings, 5 ounces (150 ml) each

The formula for pots de crème is comparable to both crème caramel and crème brûlée. What sets this dessert apart from the other two is that it does not include caramelized sugar, which is placed on the bottom of the custard before baking in crème caramel and on top as part of the presentation in crème brûlée. Of course, the main distinction of this dessert is that pots de crème are baked and served in distinctive covered forms known as *pots de crème cups*.

The surface of the baked custard should have an even, glossy appearance. It is therefore important to skim off any foam that accumulates on top before placing the forms in the oven. If you do not have the proper covered cups, you must cover the forms you are using with a lid or sheet of foil, leaving only a tiny hole to allow steam to escape.

Chocolate mousse served in pots de crème cups is often erroneously labeled *Chocolate Pots de Crème*. All French dessert crèmes—crème brûlée, crème caramel, pots de crème, as well as the variations of all three—are custards, which by definition means they are thickened by heat rather than chilled until set.

8 egg yolks (⅔ cup/160 ml)	1 vanilla bean, split lengthwise, or 1 teaspoon (5 ml) vanilla extract
6 whole eggs	
10 ounces (285 g) granulated sugar	Whipped cream (optional)
2 quarts (1 L 920 ml) half-and-half	Candied violets (optional)

1. Whisk the egg yolks, whole eggs, and sugar just until combined. Heat the half-and-half to the scalding point with the vanilla bean, if used. Remove the bean and reserve for another use. Gradually stir the half-and-half into the egg mixture. Add the vanilla extract, if used.

2. Strain the mixture into a pitcher and pour into pots de crème cups, filling them all the way to the top (see Chef's Tip). If these forms are not available, use individual ovenproof pudding cups, ramekins, or other small dessert dishes with an approximate capacity of 5 ounces (150 ml). Skim off any foam that forms on the top of the custards. Place the forms in a larger pan and add hot water around the forms to reach about 1 inch (2.5 cm) up the sides. Place the lids on the pots de crème cups or cover the pan with aluminum foil.

3. Bake at 350°F (175°C) for about 30 minutes or until the custard is set. Be careful not to overcook (see the Chef's Tip at Crème Brûlée, page 760). Transfer the custards to a sheet pan. Let cool slightly at room temperature, then refrigerate, covered, until needed.

4. Presentation: Traditionally, pots de crème are served just as they are. If you are not using pots de crème forms, however, you may want to dress them up a bit. Pipe a rosette of whipped cream on the top using a No. 4 (8-mm) star tip in your pastry bag. Place a small piece of candied violet in the cream.

VARIATIONS

CHOCOLATE POTS DE CREME yield: 16 servings, 5½ ounces (165 ml) each

1. Cut 6 ounces (170 g) unsweetened chocolate and 6 ounces (170 g) sweet dark chocolate into very small pieces.

2. Stir into the hot half-and-half (off the heat) and keep stirring until all of the chocolate is melted before stirring into the egg mixture.

CARAMEL POTS DE CREME yield: 16 servings, 5 ounces (150 ml) each

1. Replace 1 cup (240 ml) half-and-half with 1 cup (240 ml) Fortified Caramel Sauce (page 821).

2. Stir the caramel sauce into the half-and-half after removing it from the heat.

Brandy Bread and Butter Pudding yield: 1 pan, 11 x 9 inches (27.5 x 22.5 cm), or 12 servings

Brandy bread and butter pudding is very rich; it must be left to soak long enough before baking for the cream mixture to thoroughly penetrate the bread. If you are in a hurry, or want a less rich pudding, replace the cream with half-and-half or milk, adding it all at once, and omit the soaking step. This express-method pudding should be served with plenty of the brandy-flavored whipped cream.

3 ounces (85 g) melted unsalted butter

1 pound 8 ounces (680 g) unsliced white or egg bread, approximately 2 loaves (see Note, page 768)

6 ounces (170 g) unsalted butter, at room temperature

5 ounces (140 g) granulated sugar

8 eggs, at room temperature

1¼ cups (300 ml) warm milk

⅓ cup (80 ml) brandy

1 teaspoon (5 ml) vanilla extract

½ teaspoon (.75 g) ground cinnamon

6 ounces (170 g) golden raisins

2 cups (480 ml) heavy cream

8 ounces (225 g) Streusel Topping (page 37)

Brandied Cinnamon Whipped Cream (recipe follows)

Cinnamon sugar

Fruit

1. Use some of the melted butter to butter a hotel pan or other baking dish approximately 11 x 9 x 2 inches (27.5 x 22.5 x 5 cm). Set aside.

2. Trim the crust from the bread and cut the bread into ½-inch thick (1.2-cm) slices. Place on a sheet pan. Brush the slices with the remainder of the melted butter. Toast in a 400°F (205°C) oven for approximately 10 minutes or until golden brown.

3. Beat the softened butter and sugar together. Beat in the eggs. Add the warm milk, brandy, vanilla, and cinnamon.

4. Place a level single layer of bread in the buttered baking pan. The sides of the bread should touch so that the pan is completely covered. Sprinkle the raisins evenly on top of the bread. Pour half of the custard slowly and evenly over the bread. Cover with a second bread layer and press down with your hands to make the top level. Pour the remaining custard evenly over the second layer; press down again. Pour 1 cup (240 ml) cream over the top. Cover with baking paper and place another pan, just slightly smaller, over the paper, then weigh down the top with cans. Let sit at room temperature for 2 hours or, preferably, refrigerate overnight.

5. Remove the weights, pan, and baking paper. Pour the remaining 1 cup (240 ml) cream evenly over the pudding. Sprinkle the streusel over the top.

6. Bake, covered, at 350°F (175°C) for 30 minutes. Uncover and bake approximately 30 minutes longer or until the pudding is set and the top is golden brown. Let cool to room temperature. Cut into 12 servings.

7. Presentation: Set a piece of bread pudding in the center of a dessert plate. Spoon brandy-flavored whipped cream in front of the pudding. Sprinkle cinnamon sugar lightly over the cream. Decorate the opposite side of the plate with fresh seasonal fruit for color. Serve warm or at room temperature, do not serve chilled.

About Bread Puddings

Bread puddings have been popular in England since the thirteenth century, at which time virtually every kitchen had a deep bowl called the *pudding basin* that was used to gradually collect stale bread. This dessert was once known as *poor man's pudding* because instead of being moistened with the rich milk or cream custard we are used to, the stale bread was first soaked in hot water, then squeezed dry before it was mixed with sugar, spices, and other ingredients. The early settlers brought the pudding to America, but because wheat was not readily available in the Colonies, they at first made their *hasty puddings*, as they were known, with cornmeal. From such modest beginnings, delicious bread puddings have become popular throughout the industrialized world, certainly so in the United States and especially in New Orleans, where you can find some type of bread pudding on virtually every restaurant menu.

Bread puddings in today's restaurants are often made with trendy breads, such as panettone, brioche, croissant, and yes, even biscotti. This, of course, invalidates the original intention of the dish—to use up plain stale bread—but at least these use bread, unlike some recipes I have seen which call for sponge cake or, worse yet, cake crumbs! These desserts, in my opinion, have nothing to do with bread pudding.

Some of the old-fashioned recipes specify removing the bread crust; in others it is left on. There are recipes that use sliced bread and some where the bread is cubed. However, almost all stipulate that the bread should be stale or fairly dry. The reason for this is to allow the bread to absorb the maximum amount of milk and/or cream. In the Brandy Bread and Butter Pudding recipe, the fresh bread is toasted to achieve the same effect. When the bread slices are buttered and toasted before the pudding is assembled, the dish is termed a *bread and butter pudding*. Bread puddings are best served hot or warm, but some can be acceptable cold. They are always accompanied by a sauce or ice cream.

NOTE: Any type of leftover plain white bread can be used. Although, in a way, it defeats the purpose of bread puddings, there may be times when you have no choice but to bake a batch of bread especially for this use. I prefer either Brioche (page 210) or Challah (page 117), formed into loaves. You might as well make the full recipe of either, even though you only need half. Any leftover makes great toast (or more bread pudding).

BRANDIED CINNAMON WHIPPED CREAM yield: 6 cups (1 L 440 ml)

3 cups (720 ml) heavy cream

2 tablespoons (30 g) granulated sugar

⅓ cup (80 ml) brandy

½ teaspoon (.75 g) ground cinnamon

1 teaspoon (5 ml) vanilla extract

1. Whip the cream and sugar until the mixture is quite thick but still pourable. Stir in the brandy, cinnamon, and vanilla.

2. Cover and reserve in the refrigerator. Adjust the consistency of the sauce at serving time; it should be thick enough so that it will not run on the plate.

Chocolate Bread and Butter Pudding Kungsholm

yield: 1 pan, 11 x 9 inches (27.5 x 22.5 cm), or 12 servings

In the 1960s and 1970s there were dozens of passenger ships that plowed the Atlantic route between the United States and Europe from June to September, after which time they would switch to warmer climates and less hostile waters as winter approached. Back when passengers still had a choice of transatlantic cruise ships, travel books not only gave recommendations for hotels and sightseeing once in Europe but also on how to get there, reviewing and rating the various ships from five stars on down. I was proud to see in the 1967 Fodor's Guide that both of the ships I had worked on had received five-star ratings. More than that, of all the descriptions that could have been applied to the ship I was working on before moving to the United States—the brand-new (in 1966), gorgeous *MS Kungsholm*—the reviewer wrote, "she is 660 feet and 26½ thousand tons of delightful Swedish pastry!" The writer obviously had a sweet tooth, but money being no object (or so it seemed), we did put together some very impressive desserts and baked goods.

Chocolate Bread and Butter Pudding Kungsholm was mainly served during the transatlantic crossing, when we would have around 1100 passengers rather than the 450 that was the ship's cruising capacity (for cruising, there was no such thing as tourist class, only first). This dessert was quick and easy for mass production and we always had plenty of dark bread on hand, as it was part of the bread basket on the dining tables. Because this type of bread is not always readily available, you may need to bake your own. If you are going to the extra step of making Chocolate Apricot Bread or Black Forest Bread just for the pudding, make the full recipe of either. They are both great-tasting breads that keep well and can be frozen for several weeks.

This recipe can easily be stretched to serve 16 rather than 12; you will need to increase the amount of raspberries to decorate 16 servings.

3 ounces (85 g) melted unsalted butter	1½ cups (360 ml) warm whole milk
1 loaf Chocolate Apricot Bread (page 118) *or* Black Forest Bread with Cocoa and Dried Cherries (page 113), *or* 1 pound 8 ounces (680 g) black or dark bread	⅓ cup (80 ml) brandy
	1 teaspoon (5 ml) vanilla extract
	1 tablespoon (5 g) ground cinnamon
2 ounces (55 g) unsweetened cocoa powder	2¾ cups (660 ml) heavy cream
6 ounces (170 g) granulated sugar	½ recipe Bourbon Sauce (page 816)
6 ounces (170 g) unsalted butter, at room temperature	Dark coating chocolate, melted
	Powdered sugar
8 eggs, at room temperature	½ dry pint fresh raspberries

1. Use some of the melted butter to butter an 11-x-9-inch (27.5-x-22.5-cm) baking pan.

2. Trim the crust from the bread, cut into ¼-inch (6-mm) slices, and place on a sheet pan. Brush with the remainder of the melted butter and toast in a 400°F (205°C) oven for approximately 10 minutes or until lightly crisp on top.

3. Sift the cocoa powder on top of the sugar. Combine the two well. Beat the softened butter and the sugar mixture together. Beat in the eggs, then add the warm milk, brandy, vanilla, and cinnamon. If the mixture appears separated at this point, it means the milk was not warm enough and the butter has solidified. Warm the custard over a bain-marie, stirring constantly, until the butter melts and the mixture is smooth. Do not allow it to become hot enough to cook the eggs.

4. Make a level single layer of bread in the buttered baking pan. The sides of the bread should touch so that the bread completely covers the bottom of the pan. Pour half of the custard slowly and evenly over the bread. Cover with a second bread layer and press down with your hands to make the top level. Pour the remaining custard evenly over the second layer; press down again. Pour 2 cups (480 ml) cream over the top. Cover with baking paper and place another pan, just slightly smaller, over the paper to weigh down the top. Let sit at room temperature for 1 hour.

5. Remove the pan and the baking paper. Pour the remaining ¾ cup (180 ml) cream evenly over the pudding.

6. Bake at 350°F (175°C) for approximately 40 minutes. Let cool to room temperature, then cut into 12 servings.

7. Place a portion of the bourbon sauce in a piping bottle and reserve in the refrigerator with the remainder of the sauce. Place melted coating chocolate in a piping bag and cut a small opening. Decorate dessert plates, including the rims, by piping the chocolate over the plates in a series of large figure eights (see Note). Reserve the plates.

8. Presentation: Sift powdered sugar lightly over 1 serving of bread pudding. Place the pudding in the center of a prepared plate. Pipe bourbon sauce in large dots and teardrops randomly around the dessert. Sprinkle a few raspberries on top.

NOTE: This looks great, provided you are using plates that have little or no pattern on the rim. If your plates have a pattern, either omit the piping or pipe only over the base to avoid a look that is too busy.

Pumpkin Bread Pudding with Dried Cranberries and Maple Whipped Cream yield: I pan, II x 9 inches (27.5 x 22.5 cm), or 12 servings

The only thing the following pumpkin bread pudding has in common with any of the ancient steaming cannonballs of suet, raisins, bread, and spices is that it, too, is made for the holidays, although this recipe is actually equally appropriate for Thanksgiving and Christmas. If egg bread is not available, any white bread will do, but avoid using a dense or underproofed bread, as the custard may not penetrate all the way through.

Melted unsalted butter

1 pound 8 ounces to 2 pounds (680 to 910 g) white or egg bread, preferably Brioche (page 210)

6 ounces (170 g) unsalted butter, at room temperature

6 ounces (170 g) granulated sugar

8 eggs, at room temperature

2 teaspoons (3 g) ground cinnamon

2 teaspoons (4 g) ground ginger

1 teaspoon (2 g) ground cloves

1 teaspoon (5 g) salt

1½ cups (360 ml) Pumpkin Puree (page 374) or purchased pumpkin puree

3 cups (720 ml) half-and-half, scalded

6 ounces (170 g) dried cranberries

1 cup (240 ml) heavy cream

4 ounces (115 g) Streusel Topping (page 37)

1 recipe Cranberry Coulis (page 821)

Powdered sugar

Maple Whipped Cream (recipe follows)

About Steamed Puddings

As discussed elsewhere in this book, the term *pudding* covers a wide range of both sweet and savory dishes. Although many of these hail from England, and in British English, the word *pudding* is used as the word *dessert* is used in the United States, the British by no means have a monopoly on puddings; there are several famous French and American interpretations as well. The old-fashioned steamed or boiled puddings that were made in England and Colonial America were typical of the rustic homespun desserts of that era. Unfortunately, many of these were known to play havoc with the digestive system due to the abundance of suet or suet made into mincemeat that they contained. The more common holiday dishes included suet pudding, pumpkin pudding, mincemeat pudding, and, of course, the well-known plum pudding. These did not contain plums but were given this title because raisins were known as plums (spelled *ploms*) in old English. This pudding also became known as *plum duff* (still without plums, however), and it later evolved into the celebrated flaming Christmas pudding now synonymous with English Christmas celebrations.

1. Brush melted butter over the inside of a baking pan or hotel pan measuring approximately 11 x 9 inches (27.5 x 22.5 cm). The sides of the pan should be at least 2 inches (5 cm) high. Set the pan aside.

2. Trim the crust from the bread, then cut it into ½-inch (1.2-cm) thick slices.

3. Beat the softened butter and granulated sugar together. Beat in the eggs.

4. Mix the spices and salt into the pumpkin puree. Stir in the half-and-half. Add this to the butter mixture (see Note).

5. Place a single, even layer of bread in the prepared pan. Trim the bread slices as needed so that each piece fits tight against the others and the entire pan is covered. Reserve ½ cup (120 ml) of the best-looking dried cranberries to use for the presentation. Sprinkle half of the remaining cranberries over the bread. Slowly pour half of the custard evenly over the bread. Do not pour it all in one spot but instead work your way from one side to the other, back to front, so that all of the bread will absorb the mixture.

6. Add a second layer of bread slices, covering the entire pan in the same manner as before. Pour the remaining custard mixture over the bread, using the same method as before.

7. Place a sheet of baking paper on top of the pudding. Place a pan on top (just slightly smaller than the baking pan so it will fit against the top of the pudding) and weigh down the top with cans. Let sit at room temperature for 2 hours or, better yet, refrigerate overnight.

8. Remove the weights, pan, and baking paper. Pour the heavy cream evenly over the pudding. Sprinkle the remaining cranberries over the top (still reserving ½ cup/120 ml to use in serving). Distribute the streusel topping evenly over the pudding.

9. Bake covered at 350°F (175°C) for 30 minutes. Uncover and continue baking approximately 30 minutes longer or until the custard is set and the pudding is a pleasant golden brown on top. Let cool to room temperature. Cut into 12 servings. Place a portion of the cranberry coulis in a piping bottle, adjusting the consistency first if necessary.

10. Presentation: Place a serving of pumpkin bread pudding in the center of a dessert plate. Pipe cranberry coulis on the base of the plate around the dessert. Sprinkle some of the reserved dried cranberries in the sauce. Sift powdered sugar lightly over the cranberries and the pudding. Place a dollop of maple whipped cream on top of the pudding.

NOTE: The mixture may appear broken at this point if the eggs were very cold or if the half-and-half was not warm enough. Do not be concerned; this will not adversely effect the outcome of the dessert in any way.

MAPLE WHIPPED CREAM yield: approximately 2 cups (480 ml)

This also makes a nice topping for pumpkin pie.

2 tablespoons (30 ml) pure maple syrup

1¼ cups (300 ml) heavy cream

1. Add the syrup to the heavy cream and whip until very soft peaks form.
2. Refrigerate until needed.

Jasmine Rice Pudding with Coconut Milk and Caramelized Coconut Chips yield: 12 servings, 5 ounces (150 ml) each

Rice is the grain grown most extensively throughout the world, and it is a principal food for more than one-third of the world's population. More than two dozen types of rice are available in the marketplace. Short- or medium-grain varieties are generally used for puddings because their starch breaks down and aids in the thickening process. Long-grain types (such as the jasmine rice used here) will work as well, provided they are cooked long enough.

It is easy to draw a parallel between rice puddings and bread puddings, for throughout many countries both are typically made from rice or bread left over from a previous meal, with the addition of sugar, honey, eggs, and milk or cream. In this recipe, the pudding is molded into individual servings to give the dessert a better dining room appearance. For a more country-style presentation, it can also be spooned directly into serving dishes with the sauce drizzled over the top. Although the cherry compote is really delicious with this dessert, either Cherry Sauce (page 819) or Fortified Caramel Sauce (page 821) go almost as well. Any of the three can be made well in advance and will keep for weeks stored, covered, in the refrigerator.

8 ounces (225 g) jasmine rice

3 cups (720 ml) whole milk

Peel from 1 orange, removed in a long strip

10 ounces (285 g) granulated sugar

2½ cups (600 ml) heavy cream, at room temperature

3 cups (720 ml) canned unsweetened coconut milk, at room temperature

1 tablespoon (15 ml) vanilla extract

Vegetable oil

Cherry Compote (recipe follows)

Caramelized Coconut Chips (directions follow)

1. Rinse the rice in a colander, then parboil in water for 5 minutes. Drain and reserve.

2. In a heavy-bottomed saucepan, bring the milk to scalding. Add the orange peel, sugar, and the drained rice. Cook over very low heat, stirring frequently, until the rice is tender. Remove from the heat and discard the orange peel.

3. Mix the cream and coconut milk into the cooked rice.

4. Transfer the mixture to a hotel pan or other ovenproof dish. Cover and continue cooking in a 375°F (190°C) oven, stirring from time to time to prevent overcooking on the sides and bottom, for approximately 1 hour and 15 minutes or until the rice is very soft and the mixture has thickened. (If you are in a hurry, this process can be accelerated by leaving the rice mixture in the saucepan and cooking it over low heat for about 30 minutes, stirring constantly. You will need to increase the milk by 1 cup/240 ml to compensate for the evaporation that will occur when the mixture is cooked on the stove.) Remove from the heat and stir in the vanilla.

5. Very lightly coat with vegetable oil the inside of 12 soufflé ramekins, 3¼ inches (8.1 cm) in diameter and 5 ounces (150 ml) in capacity, or other suitable molds. Divide the rice pudding among them, cover, and refrigerate until the puddings are firm enough to unmold.

6. Presentation: Unmold 1 serving and invert in the center of a dessert plate. Spoon cherry compote on the base of the plate around the dessert. Arrange a pile of coconut chips on top of the pudding.

CHERRY COMPOTE yield: about 3 cups (720 ml), including the juice

2 pounds (910 g) Bing cherries	2 tablespoons (18 g) pectin powder
½ cup (120 ml) port wine	6 ounces (170 g) granulated sugar
1 tablespoon (15 ml) lemon juice	

1. Wash, stem, and pit the cherries.

2. Combine the port and lemon juice in a saucepan. Thoroughly mix the pectin powder and granulated sugar then add to the mixture in the saucepan. Bring to a boil, add the cherries, and simmer, stirring frequently for 10 to 12 minutes or until the cherries are very soft but have not fallen apart.

3. Remove from the heat and allow to cool to room temperature. If the liquid seems too thin, strain the cherries and reduce it further. The compote will thicken further if refrigerated.

CARAMELIZED COCONUT CHIPS yield: variable

1 whole coconut	Simple syrup

1. Puncture the eyes on the end of the coconut and drain the liquid inside. Save the liquid (known as *coconut milk*) for another use if desired.

2. Using a mallet or hammer, tap the shell all around to loosen the meat inside. Break the coconut open, using the same tool. Remove the meat from the shell by inserting a table knife between the meat and shell. Use a vegetable peeler or a sharp knife to remove the brown skin from the meat, leaving it in large pieces. Rinse the coconut pieces.

3. Using a mandoline, slice the coconut pieces against the grain into strips $\frac{1}{16}$ inch (2 mm) thick and as long as possible. They break fairly easily, so you will most likely have shavings about 1 to 2 inches (2.5 to 5 cm) long. Cutting against the grain will make for curved strips, which hold together better and are more attractive. Do not mix slices of differing thickness on the same baking pan, as it makes it very hard to bake them evenly. If it takes a few tries to adjust the mandoline to the proper thickness, discard the trial slices.

4. Place the slices in a bowl and add enough simple syrup to coat the pieces with syrup, mixing them with your fingers. Place the slices on Silpats in a single layer.

5. Bake at 325°F (163°C) for 15 to 20 minutes or until the slices are golden. If they appear dry during the baking process, brush additional simple syrup on top to keep them moist. Remove from the oven and use 2 forks to transfer the chips to a cold nonstick surface, keeping them separate so they don't stick together. The chips will cool and become crisp almost immediately and can then be stored in an airtight container.

Old-Fashioned Vanilla Rice Pudding with Meringue

yield: 16 servings, 5 ounces (150 ml) each

This is a real home-style rice pudding with a creamy texture that contrasts nicely with the browned meringue on top. It should be served warm or at least at room temperature. If this presents a problem for restaurant service, you can make the "batter" through Step 3 and keep it in the refrigerator for 3 or 4 hours. Do not store it any longer than that before baking or the rice will absorb too much moisture. Bake the puddings no more than 2 hours before service and reserve them at room temperature after browning the meringue. Alternatively, omit the meringue, chill the baked custards, and serve them garnished with whipped cream on top.

12 ounces (340 g) long-grain rice, such as jasmine	1 teaspoon (5 g) salt
6 cups (1 L 440 ml) whole milk	Finely grated zest of 3 lemons
2 vanilla beans	1 cup (240 ml) heavy cream
Melted unsalted butter	12 egg yolks (1 cup/240 ml)
12 ounces (340 g) granulated sugar	12 egg whites (1½ cups/360 ml)
4 ounces (115 g) unsalted butter	½ teaspoon (2.5 g) salt
	7 ounces (140 g) granulated sugar

1. Place the rice and the milk in a saucepan. Split the vanilla beans in half lengthwise, scrape out the seeds, and add the seeds and pods to the saucepan. Bring the mixture to a simmer over medium heat, stirring constantly. Place the saucepan over a bain-marie, cover the saucepan, and cook, stirring 3 or 4 times, until the rice is completely tender; approximately 20 to 30 minutes. Keep the pan covered between stirrings and do not allow the water in the bain-marie to boil. The rice will not become any more tender during the baking period, so be certain it is very tender before proceeding or the finished dessert will be chewy.

2. While the rice is cooking, brush melted butter over the insides of 16 ramekins, 3¼ inches (8.1 cm) in diameter and 5 ounces (150 ml) in capacity.

3. Transfer the cooked rice mixture to a mixing bowl. Remove the vanilla bean pods and discard them. Stir in 12 ounces (340 g) sugar, the butter, 1 teaspoon salt, and the lemon zest, continuing to stir until the butter is melted and the mixture is fully combined. Stir in the cream. Add a portion of the rice mixture to the egg yolks to temper, then mix this back into the remaining rice mixture.

4. Divide the rice pudding evenly among the prepared forms, taking care to include an equal amount of rice in each form by stirring the mixture as you portion it. If you simply pour off the top, all of the rice will sink to the bottom and end up in only the last few desserts.

5. Place the ramekins in a hotel pan or other suitable baking dish and add hot water around the forms to reach halfway up the sides (use the water from the bain-marie that was used to cook the rice).

6. Bake the puddings at 325°F (163°C) for approximately 20 minutes; the custard should be set around the edges but still wobbly in the center. Transfer the forms from the water bath to a sheet pan and let them cool at room temperature for 10 to 15 minutes.

7. Whip the egg whites and the remaining salt until frothy. Gradually beat in the final measurement of sugar and whip to stiff peaks. Divide the meringue between the puddings and spread it over the tops, using the back of a soup spoon to make peaks and swirls and to seal it to the edge of the ramekins all around.

8. Place under a broiler or salamander, or use a torch to brown the meringue. Let sit at room temperature for a minimum of 15 minutes before serving; the desserts will still be warm but need this time to solidify slightly.

Riz à la Malta yield: 16 servings, 4 ounces (120 ml) each

The pretty island of Malta (actually part of a group of three islands, including the much smaller Gozo and Comino) is located about 60 miles south of Sicily and is an independent member of the British Commonwealth. In French culinary parlance, the word *Maltaise* almost always signifies orange flavoring of some kind. Typically, "Rice Maltaise Style" refers to a sweet rice pudding served with blood orange sauce and blood orange segments.

A simple, lightly sweetened rice pudding is traditionally served for dessert after Christmas Eve dinner in Sweden, and it is also customary to serve Riz à la Malta on Christmas Day. Usually, enough rice pudding is prepared for the first batch so that the busy cook on Christmas has only to fold in sweetened whipped cream and make some type of red sauce to accompany the pudding, most often cherry.

Typically, the soft pudding is simply spooned onto serving plates. I have added a little gelatin and molded the rice in this version to make the presentation a bit more stylish. If you prefer, omit the gelatin and the cherry aspic and serve the pudding the old-fashioned way.

1¼ teaspoons (4 g) unflavored gelatin powder	2 tablespoons (30 ml) Grand Marnier liqueur
4 teaspoons (20 ml) cold water	Grated zest of 1 orange
1 recipe Cherry Sauce (page 819)	¼ cup (60 ml) cold water
2½ cups (600 ml) milk	4 teaspoons (12 g) unflavored gelatin powder
1 vanilla bean, split lengthwise	2 cups (480 ml) heavy cream
5 ounces (140 g) long-grain rice, blanched (see "Cooking Rice for Rice Puddings")	6 ounces (170 g) granulated sugar
	Sour Cream Mixture for Piping (page 832)

Cooking Rice for Rice Puddings

Blanching the rice before cooking it in milk will speed up the cooking process and reduce your chances of burning the rice. Before adding the rice to the milk, wash it in cold water, drain, and cover with fresh water, using approximately 3 times the amount of the rice. Bring to a boil and cook over low heat for 5 minutes. Drain the rice and proceed with the recipe.

As an alternative to cooking the rice on the stove in Step 2, you can cook it, covered, in a shallow pan in a 400°F (205°C) oven, stirring from time to time. With either method, avoid stirring the rice with a whip and be careful not to break or smash the grains as the rice becomes tender. Remove from the heat when the grains flatten easily when pressed gently between your fingers. Converted rice should not be used in this recipe.

1. Sprinkle 1¼ teaspoons (4 g) gelatin over 4 teaspoons (20 ml) cold water and set aside to soften. Stir into ¾ cup (180 ml) cherry sauce (reserve the remaining sauce). Place the softened gelatin mixture over a bain-marie and heat to dissolve the gelatin. Do not overheat. Pour on the bottom of 16 brioche forms, 4 ounces (120 ml) in capacity, and place in the refrigerator to set.

2. Scrape the vanilla bean seeds into the milk and include the pod halves. Bring the milk to scalding point. Add the rice and cook over medium heat, stirring from time to time, until the rice is tender and the mixture has started to thicken (see "Cooking Rice for Rice Puddings"). Remove from the heat and remove the vanilla bean halves; rinse and save them for another use.

3. Add the Grand Marnier liqueur and the grated orange zest to the remaining ¼ cup (60 ml) cold water. Sprinkle the remaining 4 teaspoons (12 g) gelatin on top and set aside to soften. Place the mixture over a bain-marie and heat until the gelatin is dissolved. Stir into the rice mixture and set aside to cool to room temperature. Do not refrigerate.

4. Whip the heavy cream and sugar to soft peaks. Gently fold the cream into the rice. Fill the prepared forms and return to the refrigerator until the pudding has set up, about 2 hours.

5. Dip the bottom and sides of the forms into hot water very briefly and unmold on a paper-lined sheet pan. Reserve in the refrigerator until needed. Place a portion of the cherry sauce in a piping bottle and reserve.

6. Presentation: Place a rice pudding in the center of a dessert plate. Pipe cherry sauce around the dessert, using just enough to cover the base of the plate. Place the sour cream mixture in a piping bag and pipe a ring around the pudding halfway between it and the edge of the sauce. Use a wooden skewer to swirl the sour cream mixture into the sauce (see Figure 16-1, page 810).

Riz l'Impératrice yield: 16 servings, 4 ounces (120 ml) each

In keeping with its royal name, this is probably the finest and most elegant of all rice puddings. Rice in the Style of the Empress is said to have been inspired by Empress Eugénie, the Spanish wife of Napoleon III. You don't see this one-time champion much anymore; I suppose it has had to yield to the modern, "high-tech," elaborately garnished desserts popular in most restaurants today. If you're looking for a classic rice dessert, think of this old aristocrat.

1¼ teaspoons (4 g) unflavored gelatin powder

4 teaspoons (20 ml) cold water

1 recipe Melba Sauce (page 826)

2½ cups (600 ml) milk

1 vanilla bean, split lengthwise

1 teaspoon (5 ml) vanilla extract

5 ounces (140 g) long-grain rice, blanched (see "Cooking Rice for Rice Puddings," page 776)

2 tablespoons (30 ml) Grand Marnier liqueur

Grated zest of 1 orange

¼ cup (60 ml) cold water

4 teaspoons (12 g) unflavored gelatin powder

⅓ cup (80 ml) light corn syrup

6 egg yolks (½ cup/120 ml)

1½ cups (360 ml) heavy cream

6 ounces (170 g) chopped mixed candied fruit

Sour Cream Mixture for Piping (page 832)

1. Sprinkle 1¼ teaspoons (4 g) gelatin over 4 teaspoons (20 ml) cold water to soften. Stir into ¾ cup (180 ml) Melba sauce; reserve the remaining sauce. Place the mixture over a bain-marie and heat to dissolve the gelatin. Do not overheat. Pour on the bottom of 16 timbale molds, 4 ounces (120 ml) in capacity, and place in the refrigerator to set.

2. Scrape the vanilla bean seeds into the milk and add the pod as well. Bring the milk to the scalding point. Add the rice and cook over medium heat, stirring from time to time, until the rice is tender and the mixture has started to thicken. Remove from the heat, add the vanilla extract. Remove the vanilla bean pod and discard.

3. Add the Grand Marnier liqueur and the grated orange zest to the remaining ¼ cup (60 ml) cold water. Sprinkle the remaining 4 teaspoons (12 g) gelatin on top to soften. Place the mixture over a bain-marie and heat until the gelatin is dissolved. Stir into the rice mixture and set aside to cool to room temperature. Do not refrigerate.

4. Bring the corn syrup to a boil. At the same time, start whipping the egg yolks. Gradually, while continuing to whip, pour the hot syrup into the yolks and continue to whip until the mixture is cold and is light and fluffy in consistency. Whip the heavy cream to soft peaks separately. Add the whipped yolk mixture to the rice together with the cream. Stir in the candied fruit.

5. Fill the prepared forms and return to the refrigerator until the pudding has set up, about 2 hours.

6. Dip the bottom and sides of the forms into hot water very briefly and unmold on a paper-lined sheet pan. Reserve in the refrigerator until needed. Place a portion of the Melba sauce in a piping bottle and reserve.

7. Presentation: Place a dessert in the center of a dessert plate. Pipe Melba sauce around the dessert, using just enough to cover the base of the plate. Place the sour cream mixture in a piping bag and pipe a ring around the dessert halfway between it and the edge of the sauce. Use a wooden skewer to swirl the sour cream mixture into the sauce (see Figure 16-1, page 810).

Blancmange with Florentina Halos, Dried Kumquats, and Kumquat and Pear Sauces yield: 12 servings (Photo 72)

The following recipe produces a pure white custard. The slight tang from the bitter almonds and the yogurt is balanced nicely by the sweet pear sauce and very colorful kumquat sauce. When kumquats are out of season or unavailable, use pear sauce alone or substitute orange sauce. Save the cutouts from making the Florentina Halos and use these instead of the whole kumquats specified in the presentation; arrange a cutout either on the rosette behind the Halo or standing inside the halo, turned so the edges of the cutout are perpendicular to the edges of the Halo. If bitter almonds are not available, just leave them out.

2 tablespoons plus 2 teaspoons (24 g)
   unflavored gelatin powder

1 cup (240 ml) cold water

1 pound 8 ounces (680 g) blanched almonds
   (see Note)

20 blanched bitter almonds

1 pound 8 ounces (680 g) granulated sugar

3 cups (720 ml) whole milk

2 cups (480 ml) heavy cream

2 cups (480 ml) Unflavored Yogurt (page 38)

½ cup (120 ml) kirschwasser

½ recipe Chantilly Cream (page 838)

½ recipe Kumquat Sauce (page 824)

¼ recipe Cointreau-Pear Sauce (page 820)

Oven-Dried Kumquat Slices (recipe follows)

12 Florentina Halos (instructions follow)

12 whole kumquats

1. Sprinkle the gelatin over the cold water and set aside to soften.

2. Place both types of almonds in a food processor with the sugar and grind to the consistency of crystal sugar. Do not grind too fine.

3. Place the almond mixture in a saucepan with the milk. Heat to scalding. Set aside to infuse until cool to the touch. Strain (squeeze) through a cheesecloth. You should have 3 cups (720 ml) almond-flavored milk. If not, add milk to reach this measurement. Save the almonds for another use, such as Bear Claw filling, or discard. Reserve the almond-flavored milk.

4. Whip the heavy cream to soft peaks. Mix the whipped cream into the yogurt. Add the reserved almond milk and the kirschwasser.

5. Place the gelatin mixture over a bain-marie and heat until dissolved. Take care not to overheat. Quickly whisk the gelatin into a small amount of the milk and cream mixture to temper, then, still working quickly, add this to the remaining mixture.

6. Pour into 12 soufflé ramekins, 3¼ inches (8.1 cm) in diameter and 5 ounces (150 ml) in capacity, or into other suitable molds such as Flexipan No. 1897. Refrigerate for at least 2 hours or, preferably, overnight.

7. Unmold by dipping each form briefly into hot water, then inverting it onto a tray or sheet pan lined with baking paper. Cover and place in the refrigerator until time of service.

8. Place the Chantilly cream in a pastry bag with a No. 8 (16-mm) star tip. Reserve in the refrigerator. Place the kumquat sauce and the pear sauce into separate piping bottles.

About Blancmange

Blancmange dates all the way back to the Middle Ages. As the word *blanc* ("white") in the title implies, it is a dish that is made from all white ingredients. The original blancmange was a savory dish made of chicken (usually capon) or, less often, veal, pounded into a paste and thickened with grated stag's horn. Later, beef and mutton juice were used as thickening agents before gelatin eventually took their place. Some recipes call for thickening with cornstarch instead of gelatin. Blancmange gradually transformed into a dish made with a combination of both savory and sweet ingredients and eventually became the molded almond-flavored dessert custard we know today. The earlier spelling, blancmanger, translates to "eat white." The *r* at the end disappeared in the 1800s.

In earlier years, this dessert required a great deal of manual labor because not only did the almonds have to be blanched and the skins removed by hand but they also had to be ground with a mortar—an even bigger job. Blancmange was regarded as a difficult dish and was judged perfect only if it was snow-white and smooth as silk.

9. Presentation: Place a blancmange (inverted) in the center of a dessert plate. Pipe an irregularly shaped ring of kumquat sauce centered between the dessert and the edge of the base of the plate. Pipe dots of pear sauce on the base of the plate on either side of the kumquat sauce. Place approximately 8 dried kumquat slices randomly on top of the sauces. Pipe a rosette of Chantilly cream on top of the blancmange. Stand a Florentina Halo in the rosette, pushing it partially into the blancmange. Place a whole kumquat on top of the cream rosette centered in the opening of the Halo. Serve immediately.

NOTE: Use any type of blanched almonds (sliced, slivered, or whole). If you blanch them yourself, soak in cold water for 1 hour after blanching and removing the skins to whiten them. Then allow to dry thoroughly at room temperature, preferably overnight, before grinding. If you must speed this up by drying the almonds in a low oven, be very careful not to let them color at all.

OVEN-DRIED KUMQUAT SLICES yield: approximately 100

The method used here to dry the kumquat slices may be applied to a variety of other fruits as well. The time required for drying will vary with different varieties. Prepare the fruit as necessary, removing hulls, peel, pits, and cores as appropriate. Cut into slices ¹⁄₁₆-inch (2-mm) thick (cut cherries in half). When using bananas, rub the cut sides with a little lemon juice.

20 kumquats   **Simple syrup**

1. Remove the stems if present and wash the kumquats. Slice across into ¹⁄₁₆-inch (2-mm) round slices. Do not use the rounded end pieces.

2. Bring the simple syrup to a boil, then remove it from the heat. Dip each kumquat slice into the hot syrup and place the slices on Silpats.

3. Dry the slices in a 180° to 200°F (82° to 94°C) oven for approximately 1½ hours or until dried all the way through, turning the slices over halfway through the process.

NOTE: Because the fruit has not been treated with sulfur, as is done with commercially prepared dried fruit, it will darken from oxidation. This is a small price to pay, however, for a healthier and more economical product.

FLORENTINA HALOS yield: 20 decorations, 4 inches (10 cm) in diameter

This amount of Florentina batter will make more Halos than you need, but some will inevitably break (or be eaten).

½ recipe or 12 ounces (340 g) Florentina
  Batter (page 306)

1. Draw 20 circles, 4 inches (10 cm) in diameter, on a sheet of baking paper, using a plain cookie cutter as a guide. Invert the paper on a sheet pan. Divide the Florentina batter evenly between the circles, using 2 spoons, then flatten it and spread it out within the circles. Wet your fingers or the spoons to keep the batter from sticking.

2. Bake at 375°F (190°C) until golden brown, approximately 10 minutes. Let the cookies cool just a little, then use the same cutter used to draw the circles to cut the cookies round. Let the cookies cool completely, then break off the uneven edges. Techniques for trimming the edges even are described in more detail in the recipe for Florentinas (page 305).

3. Warm the trimmed cookies slightly. Using a 1¾-inch (4.5-cm) plain round cookie cutter, cut the centers out of the cookies to create halos (rings). Save the centers if desired to use in the presentation as described in the blancmange introduction.

Lemon Pudding Cake yield: 12 servings (Photo 74)

In this recipe, I use individual cake rings to create a presentation more suited to restaurant service. However, pudding cakes are meant to be served very simply and are great with just about any fresh fruit or fruit sauce and/or a dollop of whipped cream or a scoop of ice cream. For the more traditional method of baking and presenting the pudding cake, which is in a single large casserole dish, bake the batter in a buttered 10-inch (25-cm) pan (at least 2 inches/5 cm deep) lined with a buttered round of baking paper in the bottom, and increase the baking time by about 10 minutes. Use two large spoons to remove the portions, being careful to include some of each layer. If you plan to unmold the larger pudding cake, let it cool at room temperature first, then refrigerate for at least 4 hours or, preferably, overnight. Before unmolding, place the cake in the oven for a few minutes to warm it slightly or the custard will stick.

Melted unsalted butter

5 ounces (140 g) unsalted butter, at room
  temperature

14 ounces (400 g) granulated sugar

10 eggs, separated and at room temperature

Grated zest of 2 medium lemons
  (2 tablespoons/36 g)

3½ ounces (100 g) bread flour

2½ cups (600 ml) whole milk, at room
  temperature

1¼ cups (300 ml) lemon juice

Dark coating chocolate, melted

½ recipe Strawberry Sauce (page 832) *or*
  Raspberry Sauce (page 830)

Sliced fresh fruit (see Note 1)

Powdered sugar

12 mint sprigs

About Pudding Cakes

Pudding cakes date all the way back to Colonial times, originating from what were called flour or plain puddings; today they are also known as sponge custards. Pudding cakes are basically egg custards with the addition of a small amount of flour and a large amount of air—the air whipped into the separated egg whites. Lemon and orange pudding cakes are the most common and seem to work best due to the acidity of the citrus juice, which both aids in setting the cake layer and keeps the bottom layer from becoming too compact. Just like other custards, pudding cakes must be protected from extreme heat that would cause them to curdle. Therefore, they are baked in a bain-marie (because water can never reach a higher temperature than the boiling point—212°F/100°C—the surrounding water equalizes the temperature and acts as an insulator to protect from overcooking). The puddings should be left in the bain-marie for 10 minutes after they are removed from the oven to allow them to stabilize.

1. Cut 12 squares of aluminum foil, 6½ inches (16.2 cm) each. (If you are using a thin grade of foil, use a double layer.) Set metal cake rings 3 inches (7.5 cm) in diameter and 2 inches (5 cm) high in the center of the squares. Pleat and fold the edges of the foil up tightly against the rings all around to form a tight seal. (Be sure the seal reaches at least three-quarters of the way up the sides of the rings because the puddings are to be baked in a water bath.) Brush melted butter over the inside and bottoms of the rings. Place the rings in a hotel pan and set aside (see Note 2).

2. Cream the soft butter with one-third of the sugar. Beat in the egg yolks, a few at a time. Stir in the lemon zest, flour, milk, and lemon juice. Continue stirring until all of the ingredients are completely incorporated. If the eggs—and, even more so, the milk—were cooler than specified (they should be around 70°F/21°C), the emulsion will break. This can be corrected by warming the mixture slightly, but the finished puddings will be dense and not as high.

3. Whip the egg whites until they have tripled in volume. Gradually add the remaining sugar and whip until soft peaks form. Carefully stir the whipped whites into the lemon mixture. Pour or spoon the batter into the prepared cake rings, dividing it equally. Add ¾ inch (2 cm) hot water to the hotel pan.

4. Bake at 350°F (175°C) for approximately 40 minutes or until set. The sponge on top of the desserts will develop a light brown color. Set aside, still in the water bath, for 10 minutes. Remove the puddings from the water bath, allow them to cool to room temperature, then refrigerate for a minimum of 3 hours to allow the custard to set. The puddings may be stored in the baking rings, covered and in the refrigerator, for up to 3 days.

5. Place melted coating chocolate in a piping bag. Pipe a design of 4 intersecting lines over the base and rim of 12 dessert plates, forming an open diamond-shaped box in the center of the lines and placing the lines so that the diamond is positioned slightly off-center toward the lower part of the plate. Set the plates aside.

6. Place the strawberry or raspberry sauce in a piping bottle. Reserve.

7. Presentation: Peel the aluminum foil away from the sides of 1 dessert. Place one hand underneath the foil on the bottom and hold onto the cake ring with the other hand. Tilt the dessert (so it doesn't slide out) and peel the foil away from the bottom. Carefully set the pudding (with the cake ring still attached) on the upper part of the base on a prepared dessert plate, next to the diamond-shaped box. Remove the cake ring. Pipe strawberry or raspberry sauce inside the chocolate lines of the center diamond. Arrange fresh fruit around the pudding. Sift powdered sugar over the pudding and the plate. Garnish with a mint sprig and serve immediately.

NOTE 1: Use 4 or 5 varieties of fruit or berries. Slice the fruit into precise pieces; leave berries whole. Try to cut the fruit as close to serving time as possible so the pieces do not become dry.

NOTE 2: If cake rings are not available, you can use 16 soufflé ramekins, 5 ounces (150 ml) in capacity and 3¼ inches (8.1 cm) in diameter. This will make slightly smaller portions, which can be served in the forms or unmolded to display the pudding on top.

Panna Cotta with Warm Strawberry-Mango Salsa, Hazelnut Cookie Wafer, Prickly Pear Sorbet, and a Caramel Halo yield: 16 servings (jacket spine)

This modern-looking creation was invented to illustrate the concept of a properly prepared composed dessert. *Compose* is a verb meaning to arrange, create, devise, fashion, form, or shape. In the case of a composed dessert, or dessert composition, several elements are arranged together on a serving plate in a way that is appealing both to the eye and the palate. I teach my students that any plated dessert must contain a minimum of three components. The individual elements should harmonize and also contrast at the same time. In choosing and arranging the elements of the dish, the chef should consider height, color, shape, texture, flavor, and temperature.

This version of panna cotta demonstrates all these ideas. It contains a refreshing, colorful fruit salsa that is served slightly warm; a sweet, transparent strawberry-orange syrup; a crisp and crunchy nut cookie; cold, creamy, snow-white panna cotta; a vibrant purple-toned icy sorbet; and, finally, a fragile, buttery caramel halo and a caramelized macadamia nut—both of which provide height as well as additional taste and texture.

The fact that this dessert has so many components means that you have a lot of options, should you wish to simplify the presentation. For large parties or banquets, consider eliminating both the caramel halo and the caramelized macadamia nut. Instead, place the sorbet directly on top of the panna cotta, using a small, thin round of sponge cake underneath to keep the sorbet from sliding. You will still have the wonderful crisp texture of the hazelnut cookie. Another option is to substitute Florentina Halos from the Blancmange recipe (page 780) for the Caramel Halos called for here. Blancmange is, as a matter of fact, very closely related to panna cotta.

16 Vanilla Panna Cottas (page 793)

Strawberry-Mango Salsa (recipe follows)

2 teaspoons (8 g) cornstarch

16 Hazelnut Cookie Wafers (recipe follows)

1 recipe Prickly Pear Sorbet (page 751)

16 Caramel Halos (instructions follow)

16 Caramelized Macadamia Nuts (page 630) (optional)

16 small fig leaves or mint sprigs

1. Unmold as many servings of panna cotta as you anticipate needing for service by very gently warming the exterior of the ramekins. You may do this either with a torch or by briefly immersing the outside of the ramekins in hot water. To unmold the desserts from Flexipans, place the panna cotta in the freezer either directly after filling the forms or transfer them from the refrigerator to the freezer 30 to 60 minutes before serving. Push the frozen desserts out of the Flexipans, 1 at a time (pushing from the reverse side to turn each indentation inside out), and place on a sheet pan lined with baking paper. Set aside at room temperature or in the refrigerator to thaw. Be certain that the desserts are cold but not frozen before plating.

2. Strain the syrup from the macerated strawberries that are part of the salsa recipe and place the syrup in a saucepan. Remove a small amount of the syrup and mix it with the cornstarch to make a slurry. Stir this into the remaining syrup and bring to a boil while stirring. Remove from the heat and allow the syrup to cool. Strain the syrup, place in a piping bottle, and reserve at room temperature.

3. In a small bowl set over a warm water bath, combine approximately 2 parts prepared strawberries to 1 part prepared mango chunks to make just enough salsa for the number of desserts that you will be serving right away. If the 2 types of fruit are mixed together and left to sit, the red juice from the strawberries will stain the mango.

4. Presentation: Place a 5-inch (12.5-cm) plain cookie cutter or ring in the center of a dessert plate. Spoon approximately ½ cup (120 ml) warm fruit salsa inside the ring and lightly press the top of the fruit to press it into the shape of the ring and create an even surface on which to place the hazelnut wafer. Remove the ring. Pipe approximately 2 tablespoons (30 ml) strawberry syrup over the fruit. Place a reserved panna cotta serving in the center of a hazelnut cookie wafer and carefully place the wafer on top of the fruit disk on the dessert plate. Gently place a small scoop of prickly pear sorbet on top of the seam inside a caramel halo. Use a palette knife to transfer the halo and sorbet to the top of the panna cotta. Carefully thread the pointed tail of a caramelized macadamia nut through an opening in the top of the halo, or simply lean the tail against the halo, and let the nut rest on the panna cotta in front of the halo. Decorate the sorbet with a small fig leaf or mint sprig. Serve immediately.

STRAWBERRY-MANGO SALSA yield: approximately 2 quarts (1 L 920 ml)

2 pounds 8 ounces (1 kg 135 g) strawberries
(approximately 3 dry pints/1 L 440 ml)

½ cup (120 ml) orange liqueur

½ cup (120 ml) simple syrup

¼ cup (60 ml) water

2 medium, ripe mangoes, approximately
1 pound 8 ounces (680 g)

I. Wash and hull the strawberries. Cut the fruit into small, evenly sized wedges or cubes.

2. Place the strawberries in a bowl and add the liqueur, simple syrup, and water. Toss to combine and coat the fruit pieces with the liquid. Set aside to macerate for 1 to 2 hours (see Chef's Tip).

3. Peel the mangoes and cut the flesh away from the stones. Cut the fruit into small attractive cubes, not slices. Place the mango cubes in a bowl (not with the strawberries); cover and reserve.

4. At serving time, combine the strawberries and mangoes to order as directed in the main recipe.

HAZELNUT COOKIE WAFERS

yield: approximately 20 cookies, 4 inches (10 cm) in diameter, plus scrap dough

These wonderfully crisp cookies are very tender because a minimal amount of flour is used in the dough. Although this gives a delightful texture to the baked cookies, it makes the dough difficult to roll out as thinly as required. Therefore, instead of using the conventional method of rolling the dough on the table with flour, the dough is rolled out between two Silpats.

You will have some scrap dough left after cutting out the 20 cookies specified in the yield. Wrap the dough scraps and reserve for another use. If you have the time and inclination, this recipe can be made into smaller cookies for a cookie platter or to serve with tea. The cookies are attractive and taste great, but the manufacturing method makes them rather time-consuming to produce in large numbers.

2 ounces (55 g) almond paste, softened

3½ ounces (100 g) granulated sugar

3½ ounces (100 g) unsalted butter, at room temperature

1 egg, at room temperature

2 ounces (55 g) bread flour

2 ounces (55 g) cake flour

1 teaspoon (1.5 g) ground cinnamon

½ teaspoon (1 g) ground cloves

½ teaspoon (1 g) ground nutmeg

3 ounces (85 g) finely ground hazelnuts

1 ounce (30 g) dry white cake crumbs or bread crumbs (see Note)

I. In a mixer bowl and using the paddle attachment, combine the almond paste and sugar, mixing until smooth. Gradually add the butter, scraping down the sides of the bowl as needed (if you add all of the butter at once, it will form lumps). Incorporate the egg, again mixing until smooth and scraping down the bowl.

2. Sift together the bread flour, cake flour, cinnamon, cloves, and nutmeg. Stir in the ground nuts and the cake or bread crumbs. Add the dry ingredients to the dough and mix until just combined. Place the dough on a sheet pan lined with baking paper. Flatten the dough to help it chill more rapidly, cover, and refrigerate until firm.

3. Remove the dough from the refrigerator and knead it against the table until it is pliable but still cool and firm. Form the dough into a flat rectangle and place it in the center of a full-size Silpat, 16 × 24 inches (40 × 60 cm). Place a second Silpat on top and roll the dough between the mats until it is thin enough to completely cover the bottom mat (there will be some places where the dough oozes out between the edges of the mats). The dough should be just slightly thicker than ¹⁄₁₆ inch (2 mm). Place the dough, still between the mats, on a perfectly even sheet pan and freeze until firm, about 30 minutes.

4. Remove the sheet pan from the freezer. Remove the dough and the mats from the pan, keeping them together. Peel away the top mat and return it to the sheet pan. Invert the second mat (with the dough attached) on top of the mat on the pan, then peel the top mat away from the dough. Working quickly (with the dough still on top of the cool sheet pan), cut out 20 cookies, using a 4-inch (10-cm) plain round cookie cutter and place the rounds on a sheet pan lined with baking paper.

5. Bake the cookies at 375°F (190°C) for approximately 12 minutes or until golden brown.

NOTE: If you do not have cake or bread crumbs on hand, use an additional 1 ounce (30 g) ground hazelnuts instead.

CARAMEL HALOS yield: approximately 20 decorations

Before you begin, have ready a ruler, 15 to 18 inches (37.5 to 45 cm) long; a sharp chef's knife; and at least 2 round objects that have an approximate circumference of 4 inches (10 cm). Plain round cookie cutters are one option or cans may also be used; however, I have found that plastic tubes, 4 inches (10 cm) in diameter, cut into rounds, 1 inch (2.5 cm) in height, make the easiest tool to work with for this application. Because you are able to lay the tube sections flat against the table as you wrap and shape the caramel strips, you can be sure that the halos will stand straight and even and the ends will align. The tubes can also be reused for creating molded desserts.

¼ **recipe or 8 ounces (225 g) Caramel Glass Paste (page 791)**

1. Spread half of the paste (4 ounces/115 g) evenly into a rectangle measuring 15 × 9 inches (37.5 × 22.5 cm) on a sheet of baking paper; make sure that the corners are square (see Note). Transfer the paper to a perfectly even sheet pan. Repeat with the remaining paste.

2. Bake 1 sheet at a time at 350°F (175°C) until light golden brown. Remove the pan from the oven carefully; any jarring or tilting movements will cause ripples in the soft, thin surface. Place the sheet pan on a flat wooden table or work surface. Let the caramel cool for a few seconds until the paste stabilizes. Lift the baking paper and caramel off the sheet pan and place it on the warm spot on the table where the sheet pan had been resting or onto a sheet of corrugated cardboard.

3. Place the ruler on top of the sheet of caramel along 1 short end; do not push down too hard or you will flatten and disfigure the pattern. Measure and trim the short ends on each sheet to make each of the rectangles 14 inches (35 cm) long. Again without pressing too hard on the ruler, cut the rectangles lengthwise into strips, ¾ inch (2 cm) wide. Reheat the caramel sheets as necessary to avoid breaking them as you cut, but be very careful not to overheat the paste and let it change shape. After all the strips have been cut on 1 sheet, transfer them to a rack to cool (do not attempt to separate them at this point). Repeat with the remaining sheet.

4. To shape the halos, carefully separate the cut strips and place them, 3 or 4 per pan, on sheet pans lined with baking paper; be sure that the strips do not touch each other. Reheat 1 pan at a time just until the strips become soft enough that they can be picked up and formed into the round shape.

5. Place one of the reserved 4-inch (10-cm) round objects flat on the table and wrap a strip horizontally around the outside, pinching the overlapping ends so that they stick together. Allow this ring to cool as you shape the next one. Remove the first halo and repeat with the remaining strips. If you have more than 2 rings or molding tools, you can, of course, let them set a bit longer and do not have to keep alternating. Store the halos in an airtight container. They will keep for up to 1 week. In wet or humid environments, it is advisable to use a desiccant.

NOTE: If you are using very thin baking paper, you may have to bake each sheet of paste immediately after spreading it out. Thinner paper will sometimes wrinkle as it sits with the paste on it, which makes the paste unusable for this purpose.

Summer Pudding yield: 12 servings (Photo 63)

This is a traditional English country-style dessert. It can be prepared using many types of berries, but either raspberries or strawberries are a must to provide the glorious crimson color. Just as bread puddings are often made from whatever leftover bread is available, the flavor of summer puddings is determined by the variety of berries. If you do not have a wide assortment of fresh berries to choose from, frozen berries can be used, preferably the IQF variety. No matter how carefully you handle them, thawed frozen berries will fall apart, but on the plus side, this provides plenty of juice to moisten and flavor the bread.

The white bread used to line the forms must be dense and stale to prevent it from falling apart when it becomes saturated with fruit juice. Typically, summer puddings are made in large forms, often in a loaf shape, that provide 8 to 10 servings.

The following version is created in individual molds and features a curved wedge of caramel to add height, contrasting texture, and a more contemporary plate presentation. To simplify a bit, you can omit curving the wedges and attaching them to the plates with chocolate; instead, just lean a straight caramel wedge against the pudding. Alternatively, you can serve the puddings as is in the old-fashioned way. In any case, be sure they are well chilled and that you serve plenty of whipped cream as an accompaniment.

Melted unsalted butter *or* pan spray

2 loaves of any dense, day-old white bread, such as Sicilian White Bread (page 103) *or* Pullman Loaves (page 127), approximately 2 pounds (910 g) total

Summer Fruit Mixture (recipe follows)

Raspberry juice *or* Raspberry Sauce (page 830), as needed

1 cup (240 ml) heavy cream

1 tablespoon (15 g) granulated sugar

12 Fluted Caramel Wedges (recipe follows)

Powdered sugar

4 ounces (115 g) strained strawberry jam *or* preserves

1 recipe Blueberry Sauce (page 815)

Dark coating chocolate, melted

12 small fig leaves *or* mint sprigs

1. Cut out 12 rounds of baking paper to fit in the bottom of ramekins, 3¼ inches (8.1 cm) in diameter and 1½ inches (3.7 cm) in height. Brush melted butter over the insides of 12 ramekins or coat with pan spray. Place a paper round in the bottom of each ramekin, then brush melted butter over the papers or spray the papers with pan spray. Place the ramekins on a sheet pan.

2. Cut the bread into ¼-inch (6-mm) slices. Using a plain cookie cutter, cut out 24 rounds of bread that will just fit inside the molds you are using; each serving will use 1 for the top and 1 for the bottom. Place the bottom rounds in the forms and reserve the other 12.

3. Cut small squares or rectangles of appropriate size from the remaining bread to create pieces that can be used to line the sides of the forms, making the top edge even with the rim of the ramekins. You can place the pieces pushed tightly next to one another or overlap them slightly; in either case, press them firmly against the sides so they stay in place.

4. Divide the fruit mixture among the forms, packing it in tightly and filling the forms to the top. Place 1 reserved bread round on top of the fruit in each form and press down firmly.

5. Cover the tops of the ramekins with a sheet of plastic wrap. Place a sheet pan on the plastic and distribute some weights evenly over the pan to compact the desserts and force the fruit juices into the bread. Place the assembly in the refrigerator and chill for at least 12 hours.

6. Remove the weights, the top sheet pan, and the plastic wrap. If there are any spots of white on the top bread rounds where the bread was not saturated with fruit juice, brush raspberry juice or sauce on these places to make the color uniform.

7. Unmold the desserts, using the following method. One at a time, dip the ramekins into a piping hot water bath for just a few seconds. Run a knife around the inside perimeter without disturbing the bread on the sides and invert onto a sheet pan lined with baking paper. Remove the mold and peel the circle of baking paper off the top. After all of the desserts have been unmolded, brush raspberry sauce or raspberry juice over any white spots on the bread on the tops or sides, as in Step 6, to make the color even.

8. Whip the heavy cream and granulated sugar to stiff peaks. Chill as many caramel wedges as you will need within 1 hour; do not refrigerate them longer than that (see Note, page 616).

9. Copy the inside (white portion) of the template shown in Figure 13-30 (page 682). Cut the shape out of $^1/_{16}$-inch (2-mm) cardboard. Make a handle for the fluted circle by attaching a loop of tape to the center; another easy way to make a handle is to glue a leftover wine cork vertically in the center of the template. Place the template in the center of a dessert plate. The base of the plate must be large enough so that the template lies flat on the plate with space around it. Sift powdered sugar over the exposed potion of the plate, including the rim. Carefully remove the template by lifting it straight up so as not to disturb the sugar pattern. Place the strawberry jam or preserves in a piping bag and cut a larger-than-usual opening. Pipe the jam onto the plate in an unbroken line, following the fluted inside perimeter of the powdered sugar pattern. Repeat with as many plates as you anticipate needing for service or that you have room to set aside.

10. Presentation: Place a pudding off-center on a prepared plate so that it is sitting on the jam outline at the back of the plate. Spoon blueberry sauce in front of the pudding within the jam circle and gently push it out toward the jam so that the sauce fills in the circle completely. Make an oval scoop of whipped cream and set it on the pudding. Pipe some coating chocolate behind the pudding and place the wide edge of a chilled caramel wedge in the chocolate so that it curves over the pudding. Because the wedge is cold, the chocolate will set up quickly and hold it in place. Decorate with a small fig leaf or a mint sprig.

SUMMER FRUIT MIXTURE

yield: enough to fill 12 molds, 3$^1/_4$ inches (8.1 cm) in diameter and 1$^1/_2$ inches in height

1 tablespoon (9 g) unflavored gelatin powder

1½ cups (360 ml) water

4 teaspoons (12 g) commercial canning pectin powder *or* 2 teaspoons (6 g) 100 percent pure pectin powder

6 ounces (170 g) granulated sugar

10 ounces (285 g) strawberries

2 cups (480 ml) or 10 ounces (285 g) raspberries

2 cups (480 ml) or 10 ounces (285 g) blackberries

2 cups (480 ml) or 10 ounces (285 g) red currants *or* 1 pound (455 g) Black Mission figs, preferably a bit overripe (see Note)

2 cups (480 ml) or 10 ounces (285 g) blueberries

1. Sprinkle the gelatin powder over ¼ cup (60 ml) water and set aside to soften.

2. Place the remaining water in a nonreactive saucepan large enough to hold all of the fruit. Combine the pectin powder with the sugar and stir this into the water in the pan.

3. Rinse and stem the strawberries and cut them into quarters. Add to the saucepan together with the raspberries, blackberries, red currants or figs, and blueberries. Stir gently to combine.

4. Heat the berry mixture until the juices begin to flow out of the fruit, but do not let it boil and do not cook until the fruit begins to fall apart. Remove from the heat and pour the fruit into a strainer set over a bowl to hold the juice. Allow the fruit to drain naturally; do not press. When most of the liquid has drained off the fruit (give it a few minutes), taste the juice and add sugar if needed; stir until the sugar is dissolved.

5. Heat the gelatin mixture to dissolve the gelatin.

7. Stir the gelatin into the fruit juice, then gently combine the juice mixture with the drained fruit. Fill the molds while the fruit mixture is still warm.

NOTE: Red currants have a short season in the United States; figs make a nice substitute. However, if you are unable to get either fruit, simply substitute another berry or use twice the amount of one of the varieties already included.

FLUTED CARAMEL WEDGES yield: approximately 16 to 20 decorations

½ recipe Caramel Glass Paste (recipe
    follows)

1. Trace the template in Figure 15-1. Cut the shape out of ¹⁄₁₆-inch (2-mm) cardboard.

2. Place half of the caramel glass paste (8 ounces/225 g) in the center of a full sheet of baking paper and spread it out to form a rectangle measuring 8½ x 20 inches (21.2 x 50 cm). Transfer the paper and the paste to a perfectly flat sheet pan. Repeat with the other half of the paste.

3. Bake 1 sheet at a time at 350°F (175°C) for approximately 12 minutes or until the paste has turned a light caramel color. Carefully remove the sheet pan from the oven without shaking or jarring it, which would cause the soft surface to ripple.

4. Let the sheet cool for just a few seconds, then transfer the baking paper and paste to the table top or to a full-size sheet of heavy corrugated cardboard that is set on the table.

5. Place the fluted template on top of the paste at the left edge and cut around it with a paring knife while holding the template in place with your other hand. Work your way across the sheet, cutting around the template and reheating the caramel if it becomes to firm to cut. Do not overheat, however, or the paste will change shape and the lines that were previously cut will melt back together. You should get 8 to 10 decorations from the sheet if you position your template to the best advantage by inverting it with every other cut. Set aside to cool. Repeat Steps 3, 4, and 5 to bake and cut the second sheet of decorations.

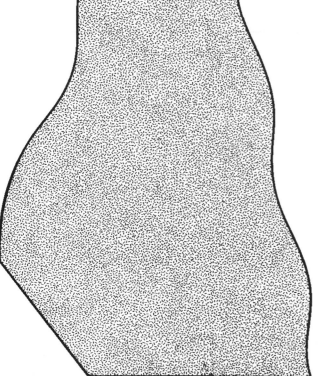

6. When the cut caramel sheets have cooled and hardened, carefully separate the decorations from the scrap pieces. Discard the scraps or save them for another use if desired. The decorations can be stored at this point, or you may curve them; instructions follow.

7. To curve the fluted wedges, reheat a few at a time just until they become soft; as before, do not heat them to the point where they change shape. Invert each soft caramel wedge (top-side down) over a metal round, 8 to 10 inches (20 to 25 cm) in diameter, such as a bain-marie insert, bucket, or cake ring; the wedges will harden and hold the curve almost immediately. Store the decorations, covered, at room temperature; they do not require an airtight container.

FIGURE 15-1 **The template used as a guide to cut out Fluted Caramel Wedges**

CARAMEL GLASS PASTE yield: approximately 2 pounds (910 g)

This versatile paste can be used to make containers for serving ice cream or sherbets. However, unlike tuile decorating paste, this batter will not stay in the precise shape you create but instead will float out slightly as it bakes.

If you use the common thin grade of baking paper, spread the caramel glass paste out as soon as you portion it onto the paper. Portioning all of the paste out, then going back to spread it into the desired shape, will cause the paper to become wet and wrinkled and make the paste difficult to shape. The paste should be soft enough to spread easily. If it has been stored, even at room temperature, you may need to warm it gently over a bain-marie to soften the butter and make it workable.

11 ounces (310 g) unsalted butter, at room temperature	¼ cup (60 ml) or 3 ounces (85 g) glucose *or* light corn syrup
11 ounces (310 g) powdered sugar, sifted	6 ounces (170 g) bread flour

1. Cream the soft butter with the sugar. Add the glucose or corn syrup and mix to combine, scraping the sides of the bowl. Incorporate the flour.

2. Use as directed in the individual recipes. The paste can be stored at room temperature for 2 or 3 days. Refrigerate for longer storage.

VARIATION

SIMPLE CARAMEL GLASS PASTE WEDGES yield: approximately 16 decorations

If you need to produce a large number of wedge-shaped decorations or you simply want to speed things up a bit, don't use the template. Instead, cut the baked sheet into wedges (triangles); you should get 7 or 8 from each sheet.

1. Follow the directions for Fluted Wedges from Step 2 through Step 4.

2. Trim both long sides of the sheet to create a strip, 8 inches (20 cm) wide. Cut the strip into 2½-inch (6.2-cm) wedges.

3. Bake and cut the second sheet in the same manner and store as directed in the main recipe for fluted wedges.

Vanilla Bean–Infused Panna Cotta with a Caramel Wedge and Orange Syrup yield: 16 servings (Photo 56)

Depending on the proportions of milk and cream in a particular recipe, panna cotta can be made to be fairly light (in calories) or as rich as desired. Many variations add ingredients like nuts, mascarpone cheese, and other flavor enhancers, which contribute further to creating a luxurious dessert.

Do not divide the cream among the ramekins until it begins to thicken. This will ensure that the vanilla bean seeds will be evenly distributed throughout the mixture instead of the majority settling on the bottom of the forms. Waiting for the cream to thicken before portioning is even more important in a recipe that uses a larger ratio of milk to cream than this one does, as it prevents the mixture from separating. The milk, because it contains less fat, will settle on the bottom and the cream will float on top, resulting in an undesireable two-tone finished dessert.

About Panna Cotta

Panna cotta is an ancient dessert said to have originated in the Piedmont region of northern Italy, an area that is perhaps better known for its Barolo and Barbaresco wines. Panna cotta, called Italy's comfort food by some, has grown immensely in popularity on dessert menus in the United States in the past few years. Literally translated, *panna cotta* means "cooked cream," but the dessert is not really cooked in the conventional sense. Instead, the cream in the recipe is simply brought to a boil to dissolve the sugar and to bring out the essence of the lemon and vanilla flavorings.

Adding to the confusion, menu descriptions often compare panna cotta to some other dessert, never seeming to really tell you what it is. For instance, I have seen panna cotta characterized as "an eggless Bavarian," but if the customer does not know that a Bavarian can be something other than a person living in the south of Germany, this description is not really going to get them too far! It could be said that panna cotta is Italy's answer to the Spanish flan, using gelatin and refrigeration instead of eggs and heat to set the cream. But again, this doesn't really work as a menu description, nor does simply translating the name, because the idea of eating cooked heavy cream for dessert does not appeal to most people.

The name *cooked cream* most likely stems from a time when the dish was indeed prepared in the same way as a traditional custard—thickened with eggs and cooked on the stove. Later, as gelatin became more convenient (around the mid-1800s) and refrigeration became more widespread, chefs began to prepare the dish as we know it today.

---

4 ounces (115 g) pistachios

1 cup (240 ml) heavy cream

2 teaspoons (10 g) granulated sugar

½ recipe Orange–Vanilla Bean Decorating Syrup (page 835)

16 Vanilla Panna Cottas (recipe follows)

16 Simple Caramel Glass Paste Wedges (page 791)

2 or 3 small strawberries

16 small mint sprigs

Powdered sugar

I. In a small saucepan of salted boiling water, blanch the pistachio nuts; the salt in the water will intensify the green color. Remove the skins and dry the nuts (do not toast them). Crush the pistachios coarsely. Remove half of the larger pieces and set aside. Crush the remaining nuts to a very fine consistency. Reserve the 2 groups separately.

2. Whip the heavy cream with the sugar to stiff peaks. Place in a pastry bag with a large French-Style Star tip or a No. 8 (16-mm) star tip. Reserve in the refrigerator.

3. Place the orange decorating syrup in a piping bottle.

4. Unmold as many of the panna cottas as you anticipate serving by very gently warming the exterior of the ramekins with a torch or by briefly immersing the outside of the ramekins in hot water. To unmold from Flexipans, place the desserts in the freezer either directly after filling the forms or transfer them from the refrigerator to the freezer several hours before serving time. Push the frozen desserts out of the Flexipans, 1 at a time, and set them aside at room temperature or in the refrigerator to thaw. Be certain they are cold but not frozen before plating.

5. After unmolding, cover the bottom third of the sides of each dessert with the finely crushed pistachios.

6. Presentation: Place a panna cotta in the center of a dessert plate. Drizzle orange syrup around the dessert. Pipe a rosette of whipped cream on top of the panna cotta. Lean a caramel wedge at an angle so that it rests against the dessert. Place a small wedge of strawberry and a small mint sprig next to the whipped cream. Sprinkle a few of the reserved larger pistachio pieces in the orange syrup. Lightly sift powdered sugar over the dessert and the plate.

VANILLA PANNA COTTA

yield: 16 servings, 3¼ inches (8.1 cm) in diameter and 5 ounces (150 ml) each, or 16 servings made in Flexipan No. 1897

2 vanilla beans

12 ounces (340 g) granulated sugar

7 cups (1 L 680 ml) heavy cream

Finely grated zest of 1 orange

2 cups (480 ml) whole milk

2 tablespoons (18 g) unflavored gelatin powder

1. Split the vanilla beans lengthwise and scrape out the seeds. Rub the seeds into a small potion of the sugar to distribute them evenly and break up any clumps.

2. Combine the heavy cream, vanilla bean–sugar mixture, remaining sugar, vanilla bean pods, and orange zest in a saucepan. Heat to scalding, then remove from the heat and let infuse for about 30 minutes.

3. Pour the milk into a bowl and sprinkle the gelatin over the surface. Set aside to soften.

4. Heat the milk mixture to dissolve the gelatin, then stir into the cream mixture. Heat to scalding while stirring constantly. Remove from the heat; remove and discard the vanilla bean pod halves. Let the cream mixture cool until it just begins to thicken and set, then stir gently without incorporating any air before pouring it into the forms. If you skip this step, the vanilla bean seeds will sink to the bottom of the forms instead of being dispersed throughout the dessert.

5. Divide the cream among 16 ramekins, 3¼ inches (8.1 cm) in diameter, or use the Flexipan specified in the yield (see Note). Cover and refrigerate at least 4 hours or, preferably, overnight.

NOTE: The Flexipan specified only has 15 indentations. Either divide the mixture evenly among them or, if you need 16 servings, form the last serving in a ramekin.

Lemon Mousse yield: 12 servings, 5 ounces (150 ml) each

This is a versatile recipe that can be served chilled or frozen. To make a lime or orange mousse, simply substitute ¾ cup (180 ml) lime or orange juice for the lemon juice, using the zest from those fruits as well. The rum blends well with both the lemon and lime flavors, but if you decide to make orange mousse, use an orange liqueur instead.

Serve the mousse as is with whipped cream and fresh berries for a simple presentation, or borrow the presentation instructions from other recipes in this book and serve the mousse, chilled or frozen, in a Florentina Cup (page 307), or in a tuile cookie shell, as described on page 615.

1 tablespoon (9 g) unflavored gelatin powder
¼ (60 ml) cup light rum
5 lemons
6 eggs, separated

8 ounces (225 g) granulated sugar
⅓ cup (80 ml) water
1¾ cups (420 ml) heavy cream

1. Sprinkle the gelatin over the rum. Set aside to soften.

2. Finely grate the zest from 3 of the lemons. Juice all of the lemons and measure the juice. You should have approximately ¾ cup (180 ml); adjust if necessary. Add the grated zest to the juice. Reserve.

3. Beat the egg yolks with 4 ounces (115 g) sugar to the ribbon stage. Add the lemon juice and zest. Place over a bain-marie and whip constantly until the mixture thickens. Add the rum and gelatin mixture. Set aside but keep warm.

4. Combine the remaining 4 ounces (115 g) sugar with the water in a saucepan. Bring to a boil and cook to 230°F (110°C). Beat the egg whites until soft peaks form. Gradually add the sugar syrup and whip until the mixture has cooled.

5. Whip the heavy cream to soft peaks.

6. Fold the meringue into the warm yolk mixture, followed by the whipped cream. Quickly pipe the mousse into serving dishes or glasses, or into ramekins, 5 ounces (150 ml) in capacity.

Milk Chocolate–Coffee Mousse in a Cocoa Nib Florentina Cup

yield: 12 servings, 5 ounces (150 ml) each

Milk Chocolate–Coffee Mousse (recipe follows)
12 Cocoa Nib Florentina Cups (page 309)
1 cup (240 ml) heavy cream
2 tablespoons (30 ml) coffee liqueur

½ recipe Fortified Caramel Sauce (page 821)
12 Piped Cookie Curly Cues (recipe follows)
12 small raspberries
12 mint leaves *or* small sprigs

1. Place the freshly made mousse (before it has set up) in a pastry bag with a No. 8 (16-mm) plain tip and pipe it into the Florentina cups. Reserve the filled cups in the refrigerator no longer than 4 hours. The Florentina shells will deteriorate if refrigerated any longer, so if you do not anticipate needing the full recipe during one service, fill only as many shells as you estimate you will need and pipe the remain mousse into other suitable serving dishes.

2. Whip the heavy cream with the coffee liqueur to stiff peaks and place it in a pastry bag with a No. 8 star tip. Reserve in the refrigerator.

3. If the caramel sauce has been refrigerated, warm it to make it liquid enough to pipe. Place the sauce in a piping bottle and reserve at room temperature.

4. Presentation: Pipe a small dot of whipped cream off-center on a dessert plate and set a filled Florentina cup on top (the cream is just to keep the cup from sliding; it should not be visible). Pipe a large rosette of cream on top of the mousse in the cup. Pipe dots of caramel sauce around the cup on one side of the plate, starting with a larger dot next to the cup and decreasing the size as you reach the other side of the plate. Arrange a piped cookie curly cue at an angle, leaning against the cup with the opposite end placed next to the last (smallest) dot of sauce. Place a raspberry and a mint leaf next to the whipped cream on top of the mousse and serve immediately.

MILK CHOCOLATE–COFFEE MOUSSE yield: 8 cups (1 L 920 ml)

3 cups (720 ml) heavy cream	¼ cup (60 ml) coffee liqueur
6 egg yolks (½ cup/120 ml)	10 ounces (225 g) milk chocolate
⅓ cup (80 ml) or 4 ounces (115 g) honey	4 ounces (115 g) sweet dark chocolate

1. Whip the heavy cream to soft peaks. Set aside.

2. Whip the egg yolks to the ribbon stage.

3. Heat the honey just until it starts to boil, then immediately whip it into the egg yolks (because it is a small amount, be certain to scrape all of the honey out of the pan). Continue whipping the yolks until the mixture is fluffy and no longer warm. Stir in the liqueur.

4. Chop the chocolates into small pieces and place in a bowl. Set the bowl over a bain-marie and heat the chocolate until just melted, stirring frequently; do not overheat.

5. Quickly incorporate the warm chocolate into the egg yolk mixture. Fold in the cream.

PIPED COOKIE CURLY CUES yield: approximately 25 decorations

This recipe involves winding a soft strip of baked tuile paste around a dowel to create an attractive crisp cookie spiral. Though they look like they are difficult to produce, my beginning-level students, some of whom have no prior pastry experience, find they are able to make piped curly cues they can be proud of with only a little practice. Because the paste is piped rather than spread out in a thin layer within a template (like the version on page 663), the finished spirals are not always precise and elegant but, on the plus side, you have more time to form them and they are not prone to breakage.

¼ recipe Vanilla Tuile Decorating Paste
   (page 482)

1. Have ready 2 dowels, ½ inch in diameter and approximately 16 inches long; in some cases, the handle of a wooden spoon is the correct size.

2. Place a Silpat on top of a flat, even sheet pan, or grease and flour the backs of 3 flat sheet pans, shaking off as much flour as possible.

3. Place the tuile paste in a pastry bag with a No. 1 (2-mm) plain tip. Pipe 8 to 10 straight lines across the width of the Silpat or sheet pan, making them 9 inches (22.5 cm) long and spacing them 1 inch (2.5 cm) apart. There is no point in piping any more lines than this on one mat or pan because you have only a limited window of time in which to form the cookies before they become crisp. However, you can pipe the paste out on all 3 pans or on 3 Silpats if you like. The piped paste does not have to be baked immediately.

4. Bake, 1 pan at a time, at 400°F (205°C) for approximately 4 minutes or until 1 cookie begins to show a few brown spots. It takes a little experience to judge when to begin with the first cookie, and you have to move quickly at this point. If the cookies are overbrowned, it is impossible to form them without breaking. However, if they are removed before they show any color at all, the cookies will not become crisp after they cool. Leave the pan in the oven with the door open.

5. Hold the dowel in one hand and quickly pick up the darkest cookie strip. Place the strip at a 45-degree angle to the dowel and quickly turn the dowel as you allow the cookie to wrap around the dowel and form a spiral (Figure 15-2). You can adjust the length and shape of the finished cookie by adjusting the angle at which the cookie falls on the dowel. For example, placing the cookie at close to a 90-degree angle to the dowel will produce a short, tightly wound cookie, similar to a telephone cord. Leave the cookie on the dowel for about 5 seconds, holding both ends tightly against the dowel, then slide it off. If you are working with more than 1 dowel, place the dowel on the table with the ends of the cookie underneath and start to form the next cookie right away.

6. Form and bake the remaining cookies. The finished decorations will keep for weeks if stored in a dry place.

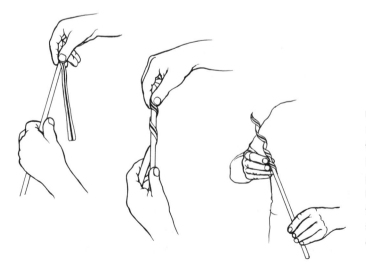

FIGURE 15-2 **Wrapping a soft Piped Curly Cue around a dowel to form it into a spiral as soon as it is removed from the oven, then pulling it off the dowel once it has become crisp. The drawing shows the Curly Cues with the optional stripe of cocoa tuile paste, as described on page 633.**

Raspberry–White Chocolate Mousse yield: 16 servings, 4 ounces (120 ml) each

Like the lemon mousse recipe, this recipe can be altered to produce a number of different flavors. White chocolate complements any slightly acidic berry or other fruit, so try substituting blueberries, blackberries, or strawberries for the raspberries, or use an equal amount of pureed mango, kiwi, or papaya for a tropical feel. Because these tropical fruits contain an enzyme that inhibits gelatin from setting, bring the puree to a boil, then chill it before using if you are making your own puree from fresh fruit. The good-quality frozen fruit purees and juices sold to the baking industry are already pasteurized. Both blueberries and blackberries not only create a delicious flavor but also produce a very vivid color when mixed with the white chocolate and cream.

When you double the amount of gelatin and increase the water to ½ cup (120 ml), the filling will set up firmly enough to be sliced. This allows you to chill it in a loaf pan and serve the mousse in a slice, nicely garnished with a sauce, some compatible fruit, and perhaps a tuile or chocolate decoration. Alternatively, cut a slice in half diagonally to form two triangles and arrange these on the dessert plate, slightly overlapping.

The serving presentation suggested here is just as quick and simple as making the mousse filling; it is an ideal dessert when you don't want to have (or don't have time for) any last-minute details. The mousse can be prepared up to 2 days in advance if it is kept, covered, in the refrigerator.

2 cups (480 ml) heavy cream

3 tablespoons (27 g) powdered pectin for canning fruit *or* 1 tablespoon (9 g) pure pectin powder

6 ounces (170 g) granulated sugar

1 cup (240 ml) egg whites

1 tablespoon (9 g) unflavored gelatin powder

⅓ cup (80 ml) cold water

8 ounces (225 g) white chocolate, melted

2½ cups (600 ml) strained raspberry puree, at room temperature (see Note)

⅓ cup (80 ml) lemon juice

½ cup (120 ml) heavy cream

½ teaspoon (2.5 g) granulated sugar

Dark chocolate shavings (page 464)

Fresh raspberries

16 Almond Macaroons (page 292)

1. Whip the 2 cups (480 ml) heavy cream to soft peaks. Reserve in the refrigerator.

2. Combine the pectin powder with 6 ounces (170 g) granulated sugar. Add the egg whites. Heat the mixture over simmering water until it reaches 140°F (60°C), stirring constantly to make sure that the egg whites on the bottom do not get too hot and cook. Remove from the heat and whip until the mixture is cold and has formed stiff peaks. Reserve the meringue.

3. Sprinkle the gelatin over the cold water and set aside to soften.

4. Stir the melted white chocolate into the raspberry puree (make sure that the raspberry puree is not colder than room temperature). Add the lemon juice.

5. Place the gelatin mixture over a bain-marie and heat until dissolved. Do not overheat. Quickly add the gelatin to the raspberry mixture. Gradually (to avoid lumps) fold this mixture into the reserved meringue. Fold into the reserved whipped cream. Pipe into dessert glasses or cups. Refrigerate for about 2 hours to set.

6. Whip the remaining ½ cup (120 ml) heavy cream with ½ teaspoon (2.5 g) granulated sugar to stiff peaks. Place in a pastry bag with a No. 7 (14-mm) star tip. Reserve in the refrigerator.

7. Presentation: Pipe a rosette of whipped cream in the center of a mousse. Decorate the cream with a small amount of the shaved dark chocolate. Arrange a ring of raspberries circling the rosette. Place the glass on a dessert plate lined with a doily and serve with an almond macaroon on the plate.

NOTE: You will need approximately 2 pounds (910 g) fresh or frozen raspberries to make the puree. If fresh raspberries are out of season or are too expensive, substitute frozen berries and omit them from the decoration. If the berries are frozen in sugar or sugar syrup, use only half the amount of sugar called for in the recipe.

CHARLOTTES AND BAVARIAN CREAMS

Apple-Rum Charlotte yield: 12 servings, 3 inches (7.5 cm) in diameter (Photo 71)

This is an old classic that will never lose its popularity. An apple charlotte is a hot pudding that can be made in individual forms or in larger sizes that serve eight to ten people. They are assembled and baked in characteristically deep, rounded molds. The dish originated in England around the beginning of the eighteenth century. History speculates that apple charlotte was named for Queen Charlotte, the wife of George III, who had a particular liking for apples.

Mrs. Beeton suggests in the Apple Charlotte recipe in her *Guide to Household Management* (1861), that "if a pretty dish is desired," one can line the molds with overlapping disks of bread dipped into "oiled" butter. She cautions, however, that "this method occupies considerable time."

I suggest that you make the full recipe of brioche loaves. The leftover can be reserved (frozen if necessary) for use in bread pudding, together with the scrap pieces left from lining the forms. I prefer to use brioche for this purpose whenever possible, not just for the taste but also because this somewhat sweet dough gives the baked charlottes a beautiful rich color. The fine texture of the bread is also helpful when lining the molds. An egg bread such as challah or Braided White Bread baked in a loaf pan (see page 147) can also be used with great results. Avoid the temptation to use finely textured store-bought bread for toasting; it tends to fall apart when buttered.

The melted butter must be thin, and therefore hot, when you apply it to the brioche slices. If the butter is cold and thick, too much will stick to the bread. The excess butter accumulates on the bottom of the forms, soaking the bread slices instead of toasting them. You will not have this problem if you use cake rings because the excess butter will simply run out onto the sheet pan. In this case, you must be careful not to overtoast the bread on the bottom.

2 Brioche Loaves (page 210)	½ teaspoon (2.5 g) granulated sugar
12 ounces (340 g) melted unsalted butter, hot	Chocolate Sauce for Piping (page 820)
Apple-Rum Filling (recipe follows)	12 tiny lady apples, stems attached, or other small, sweet crab apples (see Note)
¼ cup (60 ml) dark rum	
1 recipe Mousseline Sauce (page 827)	12 small mint leaves
½ cup (120 ml) heavy cream	

I. Trim the crust from the brioche (or other bread) and slice to ⅛ inch (3 mm) thick (do not cut it any thinner; a little thicker is okay if it happens). Cut 24 circles, 3 inches (7.5 cm) in diameter, from the sliced bread. Brush both sides of 12 circles with melted butter (or dip them in butter) and place in the bottom of 3-inch (7.5-cm) round forms, cake rings, or coffee cups with straight sides. Cut 1½-inch (3.7-cm) strips from the remaining bread slices, brush butter on both sides, and use to line the sides of the forms. You will need to miter the ends to go all the way around the inside. Reserve the scraps for bread pudding or bread crumbs.

2. Fill the forms with the apple-rum filling up to the top of the brioche on the sides. Mound the filling slightly so it will not become concave as it bakes. Brush the remaining bread circles with butter on both sides and put in place over the filling to enclose it completely.

3. Bake the charlottes at 400°F (205°C) for approximately 30 minutes or until the brioche is golden brown (invert one to check). Let the charlottes cool to room temperature before attempting to unmold them. If you wait until they are completely cold, you will have to reheat them slightly or the butter will cause them to stick to the forms. (This dessert should be served at warm or at room temperature, never chilled.)

4. Stir the rum into the mousseline sauce. Reserve in the refrigerator until time of service.

5. Whip the heavy cream and the granulated sugar until stiff peaks form. Place in a pastry bag with a No. 7 (14-mm) star tip. Reserve in the refrigerator.

6. Presentation: Pour enough mousseline sauce on a dessert plate to cover the base in a thin layer. Hold the plate with one hand and lightly tap the edge with the palm of your other hand to make the surface of the sauce smooth. Place the chocolate sauce for piping in a piping bag and cut a very small opening. Pipe 2 concentric circles, ½ inch (1.2 cm) apart, next to the edge of the sauce. Drag a small wooden skewer through the lines in a series of small circles (see Figure 16-6, page 812). Place an inverted apple charlotte in the center of the plate. Pipe a rosette of whipped cream on top and decorate with half of a lady apple and a mint leaf.

NOTE: Cut each apple in half from the top, leaving the stem attached to one half. Rub lemon juice on the cut sides of the apples with stems and reserve these for decoration. Use the stemless apple halves in the filling.

> **CHEF'S TIP**
>
> If you use cups with a different diameter, cut the bread circles accordingly. With standard ramekins, 3¼ inches (8.1 cm) in diameter, which are a little wider and lower than most coffee cups, cut the bread slices a little narrower. For a more elegant but also slightly more time-consuming presentation, cut the bread strips across into 1-inch (2.5-cm) pieces and use these pieces to line the sides (you will need 7 pieces for each 3-inch/7.5-cm diameter mold). The small pieces are easy to attach to the sides once they are dipped in butter. This version is shown in the color insert.

APPLE-RUM FILLING yield: approximately 4 cups (960 ml)

This is my Mom's favorite apple tart and pie filling, to which I have added rum and raisins. This amount of filling will make 2 pies, 9 inches (22.5 cm) in diameter. You may also use this filling instead of Chunky Apple Filling in turnovers or other puff pastry treats.

3 ounces (85 g) dark raisins

¼ cup (60 ml) dark rum

3 pounds 8 ounces (1 kg 590 g) cooking apples, such as Granny Smith *or* Golden Delicious

5 cups (1 L 200 ml) or 1 recipe Plain Poaching Syrup (page 31)

4 ounces (115 g) light brown sugar

½ cup (120 ml) reserved poaching liquid

3 tablespoons (45 ml) lemon juice

1 tablespoon (9 g) pectin powder for canning fruit *or* 1½ teaspoons (5 g) pure pectin powder

1 teaspoon (1.5 g) ground cinnamon

1. Combine the raisins and rum. Set aside to macerate for at least 30 minutes.

2. Peel, core, and quarter the apples. Cook in the poaching syrup until soft. Drain, reserving ½ cup (120 ml) liquid. Use the remainder for cake syrup. Chop the apples into small pieces.

3. Combine the apples, half of the sugar, the reserved poaching liquid, and the lemon juice in a saucepan. Cook over medium heat until the apples start to fall apart. Mix the pectin powder and cinnamon with the remaining sugar and add this to the apple mixture. Continue cooking over low heat until the mixture is reduced to a pastelike consistency (don't overreduce, however; there should still be a few chunks of apple left). Remove from the heat and stir in the raisin and rum mixture.

Apricot Bavarois yield: 16 servings, 5 ounces (150 ml) each

It is not known how the simple, quickly prepared Bavarian cream, also known as *bavarois*, got its name, but one would assume that it was originally connected to Bavaria, in the south of Germany. These versatile fillings are used in a wide variety of desserts, cakes, and pastries and in scores of hybrids and variations, such as this one, with its slightly tangy apricot flavor. This particular dessert differs a great deal from the classic Bavarian cream in its preparation. It does not contain milk, and the eggs are separated, heated, and whipped independently to produce a lighter texture. Be sure to check that the apricot puree has cooled sufficiently before incorporating the other ingredients or the bavarois will have a grainy texture. This can also occur if the gelatin is overheated. In addition to adversely affecting the texture, if either of these ingredients are too hot, the whipped cream will melt, creating less volume but leaving the same amount of gelatin to stabilize the bavarois. This results in an overly firm, dense product. (Approximately 1 tablespoon gelatin is generally sufficient for every pound of filling. However, the air whipped into the filling is also taken into consideration and it, of course, does not weigh anything.)

2 pounds (910 g) fresh apricots, pitted, *or* 1 pound 8 ounces (680 g) strained canned apricots

1 recipe Plain Poaching Syrup (page 31)

5 teaspoons (15 g) unflavored gelatin powder

⅓ cup (80 ml) cold water

⅓ cup (80 ml) or 4 ounces (115 g) honey

4 eggs, separated

4 ounces (115 g) granulated sugar

3 cups (720 ml) heavy cream

1 recipe Apricot Sauce (page 814)

Raspberry Sauce (page 830) *or* Strawberry Sauce (page 832)

8 small apricots

1. Lightly poach the fresh apricots in poaching syrup (if you substitute canned apricots, do not poach them). Puree the apricots and strain the puree. Cook the puree over low heat, stirring from time to time, until it has been reduced by one-third. You should have about 1 cup (240 ml) reduced puree.

2. Sprinkle the gelatin over the cold water and set aside to soften.

3. Place the honey in a small saucepan and bring to a boil. At the same time, start whipping the egg yolks. Gradually pour the honey into the yolks while whipping. Continue whipping until the mixture has cooled and has a light and fluffy consistency. Reserve.

4. Place the egg whites and sugar in a bowl set over simmering water and heat, stirring constantly, until the mixture reaches 140°F (60°C). Remove from the heat and whip until stiff peaks form and the mixture has cooled completely.

5. Heat the gelatin mixture to dissolve. Working quickly, add the gelatin and the yolk mixture to the apricot puree. Cool to about 110°F (43°C), or just warmer than body temperature.

6. Whip the heavy cream to soft peaks and fold into the meringue (be certain the meringue is cool). Gradually fold the cooled apricot mixture into the cream mixture.

7. Divide the filling among 16 molds, such as ramekins 3¼ inches (8.1 cm) in diameter and 5 ounces (150 ml) in capacity, or use Flexipan No. 1897, and refrigerate until set, about 2 hours or, preferably, overnight.

8. Unmold the number of bavarois you anticipate serving by briefly dipping the forms into hot water, or by heating the outside with a blow torch, and inverting on a sheet pan lined with baking paper. Be careful not to heat the forms too much or you will melt the filling. If you are using Flexipans, see Chef's Tip, page 804, for unmolding instructions. Reserve in the refrigerator.

9. Presentation: Place a bavarois in the center of a dessert plate. Pour an oval pool of apricot sauce in front of the dessert. Use a piping bag to decorate the sauce with either raspberry or strawberry sauce. Cut a small apricot in half and slice thinly. Place the slices in a half-circle behind the bavarois.

Pear Charlotte with Golden Caramel Sauce yield: 16 servings, 5 ounces (150 ml) each

The term *charlotte* is used to describe two significantly different desserts: hot charlottes, which are baked with a fruit filling, and cold charlottes, which have a bavarois or custard filling. The two characteristics these desserts share is that the charlotte molds are lined before the filling is added (with buttered bread, sponge cake, or thinly sliced fruit) and, after the filling has set up, the desserts are unmolded before they are served. The first well-known chilled charlotte was Charlotte Russe, which was invented by Antoine Carême at the beginning of the nineteenth century and was derived from the original classic, apple charlotte.

I first tasted the inspiration for the following pear charlotte in a small, elegant restaurant located on l'Ile Saint-Louis (an island in the River Seine, just a stone's throw away from Notre Dame). I was immediately impressed by the light texture and flavor of the filling. After I ordered and carefully tasted a second Charlotte aux Poires Sauce Caramel Blond, it become quite evident that part of the whipped cream in the filling had been replaced with meringue (a sure way of cutting fat and calories in many desserts). Although I'm sure my version does not quite measure up to the original, I think I have come very close.

I have occasionally prepared this dessert by substituting peaches or nectarines for the pears. When substituting, use firm but ripe fruit. Poach and remove the skin, but do not macerate the fruit in caramel. Replace the pear brandy in the filling with amaretto liqueur (and, of course, change the name).

5 medium pears	Pear Bavarois (recipe follows)
1 recipe Plain Poaching Syrup (page 31)	¾ cup (180 ml) heavy cream
1 pound 4 ounces (570 g) granulated sugar	1 teaspoon (5 g) granulated sugar
4 drops lemon juice	1 recipe Clear Caramel Sauce (page 817)
2½ cups (600 ml) water, approximately	

1. Peel the pears. Poach in poaching syrup until they are soft (see page 32). Set aside to cool.

2. Place the sugar in a small, thick-bottomed saucepan. Add the lemon juice. Stir the sugar constantly over medium heat until it melts and caramelizes to a dark brown color. Immediately add the water and cook out any lumps that form. Remove from the heat and let cool. Thin the caramel, if necessary, by adding additional water; it should be the consistency of simple syrup.

3. Remove the pears from the poaching liquid, core, and cut in half lengthwise. (If you do not have a corer handy, slice the pears in half first and then use a melon ball cutter to remove the core from each half.) Slice the pear halves into thin slices crosswise, using just the wider part of the pears. Save the leftover pieces for fruit salad or pear sauce. Put the pear slices in the thinned caramel, cover, and set aside to macerate at room temperature. Start macerating the pears at least 4 hours before you assemble the desserts or, preferably, the day before, to ensure that the pear slices absorb the color and flavor of the caramel.

4. Remove the pear slices from the liquid and pat dry with paper towels.

5. Line the sides of 16 charlotte cups, 5 ounces (150 ml) in capacity, with 4 or 5 pear slices each, evenly spaced in a tulip pattern (Figure 15-3). If charlotte

FIGURE 15-3 The form for a Pear Charlotte lined with slices of poached pear

cups are not available, any form that has a similar shape and is smooth inside, such as pots de crème cups, or even coffee cups, can be used.

6. Divide the pear bavarois between the cups. Refrigerate for at least 2 hours.

7. Whip the heavy cream with the remaining sugar until stiff peaks form. Place in a pastry bag with a No. 7 (14-mm) star tip. Reserve in the refrigerator.

8. To unmold the charlottes, dip them in hot water just long enough so that they can be removed from the forms (not too long or you will melt the bavarois) and invert onto a paper-lined sheet pan (see Note). Place a portion of the caramel sauce in a piping bottle and reserve.

9. Presentation: Place a charlotte in the center of a dessert plate. Pipe just enough caramel sauce around the sides to cover the base of the plate. Pipe a rosette of whipped cream on top of the dessert, and serve.

NOTE: Unmold only as many charlottes as you are planning to serve. If kept in the forms, covered and refrigerated, they will stay fresh for up to 3 days.

PEAR BAVAROIS yield: 2¹/₂ quarts (2 L 400 ml) bavarois, or 16 servings, 5 ounces (150 ml) each

Do not make this recipe until you are ready to use it.

3 tablespoons (27 g) unflavored gelatin powder	1 vanilla bean, split lengthwise, *or* 1 teaspoon (5 ml) vanilla extract
¾ cup (180 ml) cold water	½ cup (120 ml) pear brandy
8 egg yolks (²/₃ cup/160 ml)	3 cups (720 ml) heavy cream
2 ounces (55 g) granulated sugar	¼ recipe Italian Meringue (page 27) (see Note 1, page 331)
3 cups (720 ml) whole milk	

1. Sprinkle the gelatin over the cold water and set aside to soften.

2. Beat the egg yolks and sugar just enough to combine. Heat the milk with the vanilla bean, if using, to the scalding point. Remove the bean, rinse, and reserve for another use. Gradually pour the milk into the egg mixture, beating constantly.

3. Heat the gelatin mixture to dissolve. Stir into the milk mixture. Add the vanilla extract, if using, and the pear brandy. Set aside to cool, stirring occasionally. If you want to speed up the cooling process, place the mixture over ice water and stir until it is slightly warmer than body temperature. (Should it get too firm, or lumpy, reheat the mixture and start again.)

4. Whip the cream until soft peaks form. Gradually fold the milk mixture into the cream. Fold that combination into the Italian meringue. Do not incorporate the bavarois into the Italian meringue until the bavarois has started to thicken or the mixture may separate.

VARIATION

Pear bavarois makes an excellent quick dessert by itself. Instead of lining forms with the macerated pear slices, just pour the bavarois directly into small, fluted forms. Unmold when set and serve with Clear Caramel Sauce (page 817).

White Chocolate Bavarian with Macadamia and Pistachio Nuts

yield: 16 servings, 5 ounces (130 ml) each; may be prepared using Flexipan No. 1897 (Photo 3)

This dessert is a converted blancmange recipe in which the macadamia nuts and white chocolate replace the almonds. It came about after I had taken a trip to Hawaii—hence the tropical garnish. The Bavarian is just as good, however, served with a seasonal fruit salad and presented with the sauce surrounding the dessert. Do not be afraid to experiment with a different sauce. Pineapple sauce, for example, provides an excellent contrast to the sweet Bavarian and makes a good canvas for the fruit.

4 ounces (115 g) macadamia nuts

1¼ cups (300 ml) milk

1 vanilla bean, split, *or* 1 teaspoon (5 ml) vanilla extract

2 ounces (55 g) pistachios

2½ tablespoons (23 g) unflavored gelatin powder

½ cup (120 ml) cold water

6 eggs, separated

6 ounces (170 g) granulated sugar

10 ounces (285 g) white chocolate, finely chopped

2½ cups (600 ml) heavy cream

¼ cup (60 ml) macadamia nut liqueur

½ cup (120 ml) heavy cream

½ teaspoon (2.5 g) granulated sugar

1 recipe Kiwi Sauce (page 823)

Mango or papaya slices

1. Toast the macadamia nuts. Grind to a paste with ¼ cup (60 ml) milk. Mix into the remaining milk and add the vanilla bean if using. Bring to a boil, remove from heat, and set aside to steep for 15 minutes.

2. Blanch the pistachios and remove the skins (a pinch of salt added to the blanching water helps to bring out the green color). Reserve 16 of the best-looking nuts for the garnish. Chop the remaining nuts coarsely; large pieces make the dessert look more attractive and also prevent a grainy texture.

3. Sprinkle the gelatin over the cold water and set aside to soften.

4. Mix the egg yolks with half of the sugar until well combined. Reheat the milk mixture to boiling, remove the vanilla bean if used, and gradually pour the milk into the egg yolk mixture while stirring rapidly. Strain through a fine mesh strainer. Stir in the white chocolate and continue to stir until all of the chocolate has melted.

5. Heat the gelatin and water mixture to dissolve the gelatin. Add to the warm white chocolate mixture. Add the vanilla extract if using. Let cool to about 100°F (38°C).

6. Whip the 2½ cups (600 ml) heavy cream to soft peaks and reserve in the refrigerator.

7. Place the egg whites and remaining 3 ounces (85 g) sugar in a bowl and set over a bain-marie. Heat to 140°F (60°C), stirring constantly. Remove from the heat and whip until the mixture holds soft peaks. Gradually add the white chocolate custard mixture to the whipped cream, then fold this into the whipped egg whites. Fold in the chopped pistachios and the liqueur. Divide the mixture between 16 ramekins, 3¼ inches (8.1 cm) in diameter, or use Flexipan No. 1897 (see Note). If you

CHEF'S TIP

To unmold the desserts from the Flexipan, they must be frozen. Place the pan directly into the freezer after filling it with the mixture or transfer the filled pan from the refrigerator to the freezer a few hours before serving. One at a time, push the frozen desserts out of the Flexipan from the reverse side (you will actually turn the form inside out) and set them aside at room temperature or in the refrigerator to thaw. They should be cold but not frozen when they are served.

About White Chocolate

White chocolate is not, as the name may suggest, made from some rare albino cocoa bean. Instead, it is simply a form of flavored cocoa butter—a "chocolate" that does not contain any chocolate (chocolate liquor) and therefore has very little chocolate flavor. The white chocolate fad in this country started several years ago with white chocolate mousse, and white chocolate quickly became a popular confectionery ingredient in many dessert preparations.

do not have ramekins or the specified Flexipan, you can use other forms or even coffee cups of the appropriate shape and size. Refrigerate to set, at least 2 hours.

8. Whip the remaining ½ cup (120 ml) heavy cream and ½ teaspoon (2.5 g) sugar to stiff peaks. Place in a pastry bag with a No. 4 (8-mm) tip; reserve in the refrigerator. Place a portion of the kiwi sauce in a piping bottle and reserve.

9. Presentation: Unmold a Bavarian by dipping the outside of the form briefly into hot water (if using Flexipan, see Chef's Tip for unmolding instructions). Place in the center of a dessert plate. Pipe an oval pool of kiwi sauce in front of the dessert. Place 3 thin slices of mango or papaya fanned in the space behind the dessert. Pipe a rosette of whipped cream on top and place a reserved pistachio on the rosette.

NOTE: Flexipan No. 1897 has only 15 indentations. You may either divide the mixture evenly among them to produce 15 servings or, if you need to make 16 servings, place the extra serving in a separate ramekin.

Sauces, Syrups, and Fillings

S I X T E E N

The old saying that a cook is judged by his or her sauces, albeit originally said with savory sauces in mind, can be just as true in the pastry kitchen and equally true of fillings. The sauce and filling can be as important as a pretty decoration on a cake. A refreshing red raspberry sauce with a dense slice of chocolate cake, rich caramel sauce on a warm apple tart, gooey hot fudge sauce on poached pears and vanilla ice cream, sabayon with a liqueur soufflé, or strawberry sauce with cream hearts to garnish a Valentine's dessert are all touches that really make the dessert memorable.

Served on the side in a sauceboat or presented on the plate and enhanced with a piped design, the sauce can add a tremendous amount to the presentation as well as to the flavor of the dessert. The current fashion of making elaborate paintings using sauces and drizzling flavored syrups and oils on the serving plate is extremely popular for desserts. A sauce can also be used to change the feeling of a traditional dessert presentation and add variety to your menu. For an exotic tropical presentation and a sophisticated tone, try serving mango or papaya sauce with a chocolate cake instead of the more mundane whipped cream or crème anglaise, whenever these fruits are plentiful and inexpensive.

Although many sauces, especially those made with pureed fruit, are quickly prepared, it is much better to have a little left over than to run out in the middle of the service. Many sauces and fillings should always be on hand as part of your general mise en place. The majority of the following sauces may be stretched by adding a little fruit juice, simple syrup, or even borrowing from another similar sauce, as long as this is done early enough and not excessively. The most common and perfectly acceptable rescue technique is the old trick of reliquefying vanilla ice cream to make a quick crème anglaise; when this is done, any leftover sauce should be discarded. Of course, there is another old saying to keep in mind (paraphrased slightly): "As long as there is water in the tap, there is sauce on the menu."

Decorating syrups are used in a similar way to sauces—to add flavor and contrast and to enhance the presentation. These are typically more concentrated and just a small amount is used, usually piped in small puddles or in a few random lines on the dessert plate.

As for fillings, what would a profiterole be without the Bavarian cream inside, or a bear claw without its nutty filling? A layer of ganache or lemon curd can go a long way toward dressing up and flavoring many other pastries and petits fours. A rich, moist filling can also come to your rescue in saving a slightly overbaked or stale sponge.

Just like sauces, different fillings can be used with the same shell to create a greater selection without increasing the work proportionately. Fill an assortment of tartlet shells with frangipane filling, ganache, pastry cream topped with fresh fruit, and caramel walnut filling. Garnish them appropriately, and you have four entirely different pastries. If these fillings are kept on hand, along with a supply of short dough, this can be done with very little effort.

TYPES OF DESSERT SAUCES

Dessert sauces can be generally categorized as follows, although there are many variations of each, as well as hybrids that combine two or more types:

CARAMEL SAUCES

Caramel sauces are prepared by melting and caramelizing sugar to the desired color, then adding a liquid (in most cases water) to thin it to a saucelike consistency. For the most basic caramel sauce nothing else is added. For a richer caramel sauce, cream and/or butter are incorporated. Other flavorings are sometimes added—for example, a spirit, such as Calvados.

CHOCOLATE SAUCES

Chocolate sauces are, of course, used extensively. They may be either hot or cold, and either thin for masking a plate or very rich and thick, as in a fudge sauce. A basic chocolate sauce is made from chocolate and/or cocoa powder, sugar, and water cooked together. Richer versions contain the addition of cream and/or butter.

COULIS

In the pastry kitchen, the term *coulis* is used for berry juices and fruit purees that are sweetened as needed, usually strained, then served as sauces. These are neither thickened nor bound. Though the title has gained popularity only in the last ten years or so, it is actually very old and was used as long as 600 years ago to refer to strained gravy or broth served with savory dishes. It comes from the Old French word *coleis*, an adjective used for "straining, pouring, flowing, or sliding," which in turn came from the same Latin source as the English word *colander*. Fruit coulis may be prepared using raw or cooked fruits; the best-known is raspberry coulis.

CUSTARD SAUCES

The foundational custard sauce is crème anglaise, also known as *vanilla custard sauce*. I refer to it as the mother sauce of the pastry kitchen. Not only can many other custard sauces, such as chocolate or coffee-flavored sauce, be prepared from this base, but the ingredients and method of preparation for crème anglaise are the starting point for many other dessert preparations as well (see Figure 16-13, page 818). Custard sauces are made by thickening milk, cream, or half-and-half with eggs. The desired flavoring is added—always vanilla, in the case of crème anglaise.

FRESH CREAM OR SOUR CREAM SAUCES

Crème fraîche, Devonshire cream, clotted cream, and sour cream are all used as dessert sauces and toppings, sometimes thinned and/or sweetened. They most frequently accompany fresh fruit but are also served with warm baked fruit desserts, such as an apple tart. These may be flavored with vanilla or a spice—for example, cinnamon. Fresh cream is used as a sauce both in the form of heavy cream that is lightly thickened by whipping and whipped cream, or Chantilly cream, which is really more of a topping.

SABAYON SAUCES

Sabayon sauces can be hot or cold and are made by thickening wine by whipping it over heat together with egg yolks and sugar. Sabayon sauces are served with fruit and with soufflés. Sabayon is also served as a dessert by itself. The Italian version of sabayon, zabaglione, is made with marsala.

STARCH-THICKENED SAUCES

Most fruit sauces are thickened with starch. In my recipes, I generally use cornstarch, but some recipes call for arrowroot instead. Starch-thickened sauces are cooked quickly to allow the starch to gelatinize and to eliminate the raw starch taste. Starches are also used to thicken sauces made of cream or milk and sauces based on spirits or liqueurs.

DECORATING WITH SAUCES

These are general decorating ideas for sauces. They can, of course, be combined or changed to suit a particular taste or occasion. The designs shown in a small pool of sauce can be made on the entire surface of the plate instead, and vice versa. Keep in mind that the more complicated the design, the less suitable it is for serving a large number of guests. Even though, in some cases, the sauce can be poured on the plates in advance, piping on the decoration must be done just before the desserts are served or it will start to deteriorate.

It is essential that the piping mixture or contrasting sauce and the sauce on the plate be the same consistency, or you will not get a good result. In most cases, the base sauce should be applied using a piping bottle with a fairly large opening, the exception being when the base sauce is piped as a frame (such as a hollow teardrop design) to be filled in with the contrasting sauce. The piping mixture or contrasting sauce should be applied using a piping bottle with a small opening or with a piping bag. The exception to this is when the contrasting sauce is piped directly onto the plate next to the other sauce, as in the Feathered Two-Tone Pool Pattern on page 813. I use small plastic squeeze bottles with a capacity of approximately 2 cups (480 ml). If you store leftover sauce in the bottles, be sure to check the consistency before using again and shake, strain, thin, thicken, etc., as necessary, as the consistency often changes during storage.

CORKSCREW PATTERN

This decoration is quick and looks especially good with a round dessert such as a charlotte or bavarois, or whenever the sauce is served encircling the dessert.

1. Place the dessert in the center of the plate and pipe sauce all around to cover the base of the plate in a thin layer.

2. Pipe a ring of the contrasting sauce between the dessert and the edge of the plate.

3. Use a small wooden skewer to draw a corkscrew pattern through the two sauces (Figure 16-1).

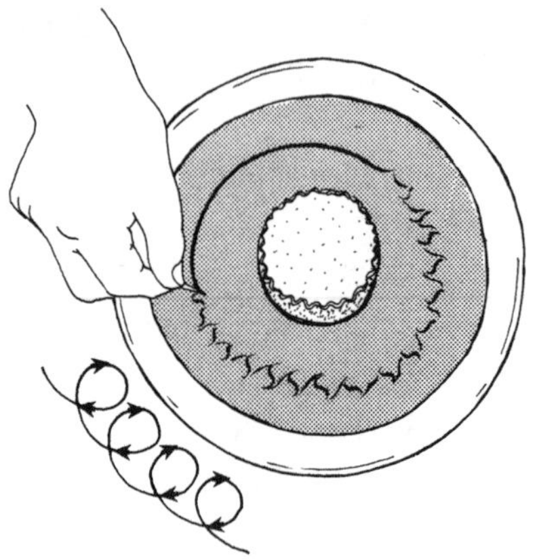

FIGURE 16-1 Making a corkscrew pattern

STRING OF HEARTS PATTERN

This design takes a little longer to complete. It is especially elegant when you do not have too much space between the dessert and the edge of the plate.

1. Place the dessert in the center of the plate and pipe sauce all around to cover the base of the plate in a thin layer.

2. Pipe small dots about 1 inch (2.5 cm) apart, forming a ring between the dessert and the edge of the plate.

FIGURE 16-2 Making a string of hearts pattern

3. Drag a small wooden skewer through the center of the circles in one continuous motion to create a string of hearts (Figure 16-2). You can also pick the skewer up and wipe it off between each heart to get a different effect.

CURVED STRING OF HEARTS PATTERN

This is a variation of the string of hearts pattern.

1. Place the dessert in the center of the upper half of the plate. Using a piping bottle, pipe a small oval or round pool of sauce in front (the side that will be facing the customer).

2. Pipe the contrasting sauce on top in a random series of dots.

3. Drag a small wooden skewer through the dots, making a succession of smooth turns, to create curved hearts (Figure 16-3).

FIGURE 16-3 Making a curved string of hearts pattern

WEAVE PATTERNS

1. Place the dessert in the center of the upper half of the plate. Using a piping bottle, pipe a small oval pool of sauce in front (the side that will be facing the customer).

2. Pipe three or four horizontal lines of the contrasting sauce across the pool.

3. Drag a small wooden skewer through the lines toward the edge of the plate. You can also alternate directions to make a herringbone pattern (Figure 16-4), or drag the lines through on the diagonal.

FIGURE 16-4 Making a herringbone-style weave pattern

SPIDERWEB PATTERN

1. Place the dessert in the center of the upper half of the plate. Using a piping bottle, pipe a small oval or round pool of sauce in front (the side that will be facing the customer).

2. Pipe a thin spiral of the contrasting sauce on top, making it oval or round to correspond with the pool.

3. Drag a small wooden skewer from the center to the outside in evenly spaced lines (Figure 16-5), or from the outside toward the center, or in alternating directions.

RIPPLE PATTERN

This design is very fast to make and is especially useful when there is a limited amount of space on the plate.

1. Place a slice of cake in the center of the dessert plate. Using a piping bottle, pipe a small oval pool of sauce at the tip of the slice, letting the sauce float out on both sides of the slice.

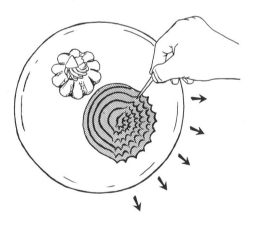

FIGURE 16-5 Making a spiderweb pattern

2. Pipe two lines of the contrasting sauce, close to each other, at the edge of the pool.

3. Drag a small wooden skewer through the lines, making connected circles, as for the Corkscrew Pattern (Figure 16-6).

HEARTS WITH WEAVE PATTERN

This design creates both hearts and a herringbone pattern.

1. Place the dessert in the center of the upper half of the plate. Using a piping bottle, pipe a teardrop-shaped pool of sauce on the plate so that the narrow end of the pool wraps halfway around the dessert.

2. Using the contrasting sauce, pipe a line of small dots, spaced about ½ inch (1.2 cm) apart, then 2 parallel solid lines under the dots, centered across the width of the pool.

3. Drag a small wooden skewer up and down through the pattern without picking it up, dragging through both the dots and the solid lines when moving toward the edge of the plate and through the solid lines between each dot when moving toward the dessert (Figure 16-7).

SPIRAL SPIDERWEB PATTERN

This pattern creates a spiderweb pattern using the reverse of the technique for the plain spiderweb pattern: Instead of piping the sauce in a spiral and dragging the skewer in radiating lines, the sauce is piped in a spoke pattern and then the skewer is dragged through in a spiral. Place the dessert in the center of the sauce after the pattern is completed.

1. Cover the base of the plate with a thin layer of sauce. Pipe the contrasting sauce on top in a spoke pattern.

2. Starting at the edge of the sauce pool, drag a small wooden skewer through the sauces in a spiral, ending in the center of the plate (Figure 16-8).

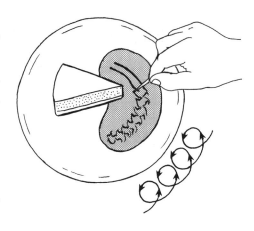

FIGURE 16-6 Making a ripple pattern

FIGURE 16-7 Making a hearts with weave pattern

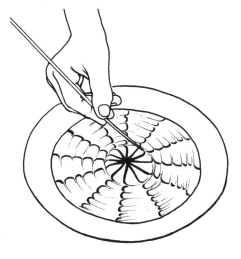

FIGURE 16-8 Making a spiral spiderweb pattern

TWO-TONE STRING OF HEARTS PATTERN

This is another variation on the string of hearts pattern. You can use just two sauces or use a third type (and color) for the center dots (hearts).

I. Cover the base of a plate with a thin layer of sauce. Pipe dots of the contrasting sauce fairly close together around the perimeter of the sauce, making them about 1 inch (2.5 cm) in diameter. Pipe smaller dots of the first sauce in the center of each 1-inch (2.5-cm) dot.

2. Drag a small wooden skewer in a curved side-to-side pattern through the center of the small dots, moving all the way around the plate in one continuous line (Figure 16-9). Place the dessert in the center of the plate.

FIGURE 16-9 Making a two-tone string of hearts pattern

HEARTS WITH STEMS PATTERN

This design makes a more elaborate heart shape.

I. Cover the base of the plate with a thin layer of sauce. Pipe five 1-inch (2.5-cm) dots of the contrasting sauce, evenly spaced and centered in the area that will be left between the dessert serving and the edge of the base sauce.

2. Dip the tip of a small wooden skewer into one of the dots of contrasting sauce to pick up a little bit on the skewer. Place the tip of the skewer into the sauce on the plate about ½ inch (1.2 cm) away from the dot, then drag it

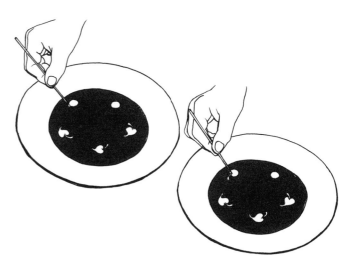

FIGURE 16-10 Making a hearts with stems pattern

through the dot and out the other side in a slightly curved motion, creating a heart with a stem (Figure 16-10). Repeat with the remaining dots. Place the dessert in the center of the plate.

FEATHERED TWO-TONE POOL PATTERN

I. Using a piping bottle, pipe a pool of sauce in the center of the plate that is large enough to accommodate the dessert serving and leave a border of sauce visible. Using a second piping bottle, cover the base of the plate around the pool with a layer of the contrasting sauce.

2. Drag a wooden skewer in a series of connecting circles through both sauces where they meet (Figure 16-11). Place the dessert in the center of the plate.

NOTE: Depending on the sauces used and/or the amount of con-

FIGURE 16-11 Making a feathered two-tone pool pattern

trast desired, use either the pointed or the blunt end of the skewer. This pattern can also be used by piping the sauces in two half-circles that cover the base of the plate side by side, meeting in the center.

SWIRLED ZIGZAG PATTERN

This looks best with a round dessert.

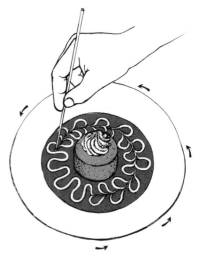

I. Place the dessert in the center of the plate and use a piping bottle to pipe sauce all around to cover the base of the plate. Pipe a continuous, curved zigzag line of the contrasting sauce between the dessert and the edge of the sauce on the plate.

2. Drag a small wooden skewer through the center of the line all the way around the plate in one continuous motion (Figure 16-12).

FIGURE 16-12 Making a swirled zigzag pattern

Apricot Sauce yield: approximately 4 cups (960 ml)

2 pounds 8 ounces (1 kg 135 g) pitted fresh apricots

3 cups (720 ml) water

3 ounces (85 g) granulated sugar

2 tablespoons (16 g) cornstarch

2 tablespoons (30 ml) water

I. Cut the apricots into quarters. Place in a saucepan with the first measurement of water and the sugar. Bring to a boil, then cook over medium heat until the fruit is soft. This will take approximately 10 minutes, depending on the ripeness of the fruit.

2. Strain the mixture, forcing as much of the fruit as possible through the strainer with the back of a spoon or ladle. Discard the solids. Pour the sauce back into the saucepan.

3. Dissolve the cornstarch in the remaining water. Stir into the sauce. Bring the sauce back to a boil and cook for about 1 minute to remove the flavor of the cornstarch. Store the sauce, covered, in the refrigerator. If the sauce is too thick, thin it with water to the desired consistency.

NOTE: The yield of this recipe will vary with the ripeness of the apricots.

(clockwise from top left) **54. Berries with Baked Chocolate Mousse and Mint Syrup**

55. Strawberry Shortcake

56. Vanilla Bean–Infused Panna Cotta with a Caramel Wedge and Orange Syrup

57. Swedish Napoleons

58. Assorted Breads and Rolls

59. Assorted Breads

60. Winter Dough Figures

61. Fruit and Coconut Tapioca Pudding Maui

62. Date-Stuffed Poached Pears in Phyllo Crowns

63. Summer Pudding

(clockwise from top left)

64. Puff Pastry with Fruit and Champagne Sabayon

65. Queen's Apple

66. Chianti-Poached Figs with Lavendar Mascarpone

67. Crisp Hazelnut Wafers with Raspberries and Cream

68. Fig Tart with Citrus Cream and Port Wine Reduction

69. Cheesecake Souffle with Summer Strawberries

(clockwise from top)

70. Panna Cotta with Warm Strawberry-Mango Salsa, Hazelnut Cookie Wafer, Prickly Pear Sorbet, and a Caramel Halo

71. Apple-Rum Charlotte

72. Blancmange with Florentina Halos, Dried Kumquats, and Kumquat and Pear Sauces

73. Apple Sack

(clockwise from top left) **74. Lemon Pudding Cake 75. White Chocolate–Citrus Roulade 76. Small Pear Tartlet with Caramel Sauce 77. Red Bananas Foster with Marshmallow and Spice Cake 78. Rhubarb-Meringue Napoleons 79. Swedish Pancakes Filled with Apples**

(clockwise from top) **80. Pineapple Fritters with Gingered Pineapple Frozen Yogurt 81. Pavlova 82. Florentina Cones with Seasonal Fruit 83. Italian Cranberry Cheesecake Strudel with Candied Chestnuts and Caramel Sauce 84. Pears Belle Hélène**

(clockwise from top left) **85. Chocolate Marquise**
86. Chèvre Coeur à la Crème with Pistachio Crust
87. Chestnut-Rum Cream Cake 88. Budapest Swirls
89. Chilled Red Fruit Soup with Lemon Thyme and
Mascarpone Sherbet 90. Assorted Breads

APRICOT SAUCE FROM CANNED APRICOTS yield: 4 cups (960 ml)

With such a variety of fresh fruit available from all over the world today, I am opposed to using fruit from a can just because a particular fruit is out of season. However, apricots are one of the few exceptions. Their season is too short to take full advantage of this delicious fruit, and because apricot sauce complements so many desserts, it is welcome all year round.

2 pounds 8 ounces (1 kg, 135 g) strained apricots canned in syrup

2 cups (480 ml) syrup reserved from canned apricots

2 tablespoons (16 g) cornstarch

2 tablespoons (30 ml) water

Follow the directions in the preceding recipe, replacing the first measurement of water and the sugar with the syrup from the canned apricots and reducing the cooking time in Step 1 to 1 minute.

Bijou Coulis yield: approximately 4 cups (960 ml)

Use the IQF type if you use frozen raspberries. (IQF stands for individually quick-frozen. Frozen fruit given this designation does not have any added sugar.) If you must use raspberries frozen in sugar syrup, you may want to decrease the sugar in the recipe. The coulis should be tangy.

1 pound (455 g) fresh or frozen raw cranberries

8 ounces (225 g) granulated sugar

½ cup (120 ml) water

1 pound (455 g) fresh or frozen raspberries

1. Combine the cranberries, sugar, and water in a saucepan. Bring to a boil, then reduce the heat and simmer for approximately 10 minutes or until the cranberries begin to pop open. Remove from the heat.

2. Transfer the cranberries to a food processor. Add the raspberries and puree. Strain through a fine mesh strainer. Discard the pulp and seeds. If the coulis is too thick, thin with water. Store in the refrigerator.

Blueberry Sauce yield: approximately 3 cups (720 ml)

Due to the large amount of pectin in blueberries, the sauce may set up too much. Reheat, stirring, until liquid and smooth again, then adjust with water or simple syrup, depending on the level of sweetness.

If cranberry juice is not available, apple juice makes a good substitute; add a small amount of beet juice or raspberry juice to enhance the color.

7 ounces (200 g) granulated sugar

1½ cups (360 ml) cranberry juice *or* apple juice

1 tablespoon (15 ml) lime juice

3 tablespoons (45 ml) rum

2 tablespoons (16 g) cornstarch

1 dry pint (480 ml) or 12 ounces (340 g) blueberries

Beet Juice (page 5) or raspberry juice, optional

1. Place the sugar and the cranberry or apple juice in a saucepan.

2. Combine the lime juice and rum. Add the cornstarch and stir to dissolve. Mix this into the juice mixture in the saucepan. Bring to a boil and cook for a few minutes.

3. Remove from the heat and stir in the blueberries as well as the coloring, if using apple juice. Let cool. Store, covered, in the refrigerator.

Bourbon Sauce yield: approximately 4 cups (960 ml)

6 egg yolks (½ cup/120 ml)

4 ounces (115 g) granulated sugar

¾ cup (180 ml) bourbon whiskey

1 tablespoon (15 ml) vanilla extract

1½ cups (360 ml) heavy cream

1. Whip the egg yolks and sugar together just to combine. Whisk in the bourbon. Place over simmering water and whisk constantly until the mixture has thickened to the ribbon stage. Remove from the heat and whip until cold. Add the vanilla.

2. Whip the heavy cream until thickened to a very soft consistency. Stir into the yolk mixture. Adjust the consistency as desired by adding more heavy cream to thin it or more whipped cream to make it thicker. Serve cold or at room temperature. Bourbon sauce may be stored covered in the refrigerator for 3 or 4 days. If the sauce separates, whisk it to bring it back together.

Calvados Sauce yield: approximately 3 cups (720 ml)

2 pounds (910 g) tart cooking apples

2½ cups (600 ml) unsweetened apple juice

1 cup (240 ml) white wine

12 ounces (340 g) granulated sugar

1 cinnamon stick

⅓ cup (80 ml) lemon juice

2 tablespoons (16 g) cornstarch

½ cup (120 ml) Calvados

1. Peel and core the apples; cut them into thin slices. Place in a heavy-bottomed saucepan with the apple juice, white wine, sugar, cinnamon stick, and lemon juice. Bring to a boil, then reduce the heat and cook slowly until the apples are very soft and beginning to fall apart. Do not allow any more of the liquid to evaporate than is necessary.

2. Remove the cinnamon stick and puree the apple mixture. Strain through a fine mesh strainer. Reserve the solids for another use (see Note).

3. Dissolve the cornstarch in a few tablespoons of the apple liquid and add this mixture to the remaining apple liquid. Bring to a boil and cook for a few seconds to eliminate the cornstarch taste.

4. Remove from the heat and pour into a storage container. Stir in the Calvados, adjusting the amount in accordance with the consistency and flavor desired.

NOTE: Leftover apple puree can be refrigerated or frozen and used in apple pie filling or served as applesauce.

Clear Caramel Sauce yield: approximately 4 cups (960 ml)

Making a clear caramel sauce is about as easy as making sweetened whipped cream. Typically, you do not measure with either "recipe"; you just do it, making the amount you need and adding sugar to taste. In this recipe, the proportion of sugar to water is just over 2:1. Once you get the procedure down, you can just caramelize the amount of sugar you need and add half as much water. Adjust the consistency as directed in Step 4.

2 pounds (910 g) granulated sugar	1½ cups (360 ml) water
1 teaspoon (5 ml) lemon juice	

1. Place the sugar and lemon juice in a small, heavy-bottomed saucepan. Cook over medium heat, stirring constantly with a wooden spoon, until all of the sugar has melted. Continue to cook the sugar until it reaches the color desired.

2. Immediately remove the pan from the heat and carefully pour in the water. Stand back a little as you do this because the syrup may splatter.

3. Return to the heat and cook, stirring constantly, to melt any lumps if necessary.

4. Let the sauce cool completely, then add additional water as needed to thin to the proper consistency. You must wait until the sauce has cooled before judging the thickness, because it will vary depending on the degree to which you caramelized the sugar.

Crème Anglaise yield: approximately 6 cups (1 L 440 ml)

This classic vanilla custard sauce is prepared using the same basic method and recipe that are used to make the custard for vanilla ice cream. I use half-and-half rather than the traditional milk so that the chilled sauce can be frozen in an emergency to make ice cream. The resulting ice cream will not be quite as rich as usual but, as they say, "Any port in a storm will do." If you run out of vanilla custard sauce, you can do the opposite and thaw vanilla ice cream. Depending on the richness of the ice cream, you will need to either thin it a bit with milk or half-and-half or thicken it with lightly whipped heavy cream.

This sauce tastes especially nice with apple or pear tarts, and though vanilla is classic, the custard can be flavored to complement many desserts. Like any heated mixture containing eggs, vanilla custard sauce is a perfect breeding ground for bacteria, so follow strict sanitary guidelines.

The ingredients and technique used to make crème anglaise are the beginning of many classic dessert preparations, as shown in Figure 16-13.

12 egg yolks (1 cup/240 ml)	1 quart (960 ml) half-and-half
10 ounces (285 g) granulated sugar	1 teaspoon (5 ml) vanilla extract
1 vanilla bean, split lengthwise	

1. Combine the egg yolks and sugar in a mixing bowl. Whip until light and fluffy.

2. Scrape the seeds out of the vanilla bean and add them, along with the pod halves, to the half-and-half. Bring to the scalding point. Gradually pour the hot cream into the yolk mixture while stirring rapidly.

CHEF'S TIP

The sauce can be made up much more quickly if you cook it directly over low heat rather than in a bain-marie. Of course, this is a little trickier. Should you overheat and curdle the sauce, you can usually save it by adding 2 tablespoons (30 ml) heavy cream and processing in a blender, providing the sauce has only curdled and not scorched.

3. Place the mixture over simmering water and heat slowly, stirring constantly, until it is thick enough to coat the back of a spoon. Be very careful not to get it hotter than 190°F (88°C) or it will start to curdle.

4. Immediately pour the custard into another container and continue stirring for a minute or so. Remove the vanilla bean halves and discard. Stir in the vanilla extract. Set the sauce aside to cool, stirring from time to time. When cold, store, covered, in the refrigerator. The sauce will keep this way for up to 1 week.

Crème Anglaise (Vanilla Custard Sauce)

INGREDIENTS: **Egg yolks, granulated sugar and half-and-half**

PREPARATION METHOD: **The egg yolks and sugar are whipped together until light and fluffy. Scalded half-and-half is added, and the mixture is thickened by stirring over simmering water.**

If Crème Anglaise is chilled at this stage, then churned and frozen, it becomes Vanilla Ice Cream

IN MAKING

Crème Brûlée	Pots de Crème	Crème Caramel	Pastry Cream	Bavarian Cream	Sabayon Sauce	Mousseline Sauce
The half-and-half is replaced with heavy cream. The mixture is thickened further by baking in a water bath in the oven.	Whole eggs are added. The mixture is thickened further by baking in a water bath in the oven.	The egg yolks are replaced with whole eggs. The half-and-half is replaced with milk. The mixture is thickened further by baking in a water bath in the oven.	The egg yolks are replaced with whole eggs. The half-and-half is replaced with milk. Starch is added for further thickening.	One third fewer egg yolks are used. Gelatin and whipped cream are added after thickening. The mixture is chilled to set the gelatin.	The half-and-half is replaced with wine or champagne and the mixture is whisked rather than stirred. If Marsala is used it becomes *Zabaglione.*	The half-and-half is replaced with water. Whipped cream and liqueur are added after cooking. If frozen, this becomes *Basic Bombe Mixture.*

FIGURE 16-13 A comparison of desserts and their prepartion as they relate to crème anglaise

Chardonnay Wine Sauce **yield: approximately 2 cups (480 ml)**

This sauce can also be made by replacing the chardonnay with champagne. To add to both the flavor and appearance, split a vanilla bean lengthwise, scrape out the seeds, and stir them into the finished sauce (save the pod for another use).

2 cups (480 ml) chardonnay wine
4 teaspoons (10 g) cornstarch
6 ounces (170 g) small green grapes, stemmed (see Note)
6 ounces (170 g) granulated sugar
¼ (60 ml) cup orange liqueur

1. Make a slurry by mixing ¼ cup (60 ml) wine with the cornstarch; reserve.

2. Rinse the grapes. Reserve half of them, choosing the smaller ones, depending on the variety (see Note). Place the remaining wine, the remaining grapes, the sugar, and the orange liqueur in a saucepan. Bring to a boil and cook over medium heat until the grapes split open, about 5 minutes.

3. Strain the mixture through a fine mesh strainer, using a spoon to force as much juice out of the grapes as possible. Discard the solids in the strainer.

4. Stir the reserved cornstarch slurry into the grape juice-wine mixture. Return to the heat and bring to a quick boil. You can, if you wish, test the viscosity at this point by placing a teaspoon of sauce in the refrigerator to chill, then bringing it back to room temperature; the puddle should hold its shape at room temperature. Adjust the consistency if necessary by cooking the sauce further to reduce it, or by adding more liquid—wine or simple syrup—if it is too thick.

5. Stir in the reserved whole or sliced grapes (see Chef's Tip). Let cool, then store in the refrigerator.

NOTE: Preferably, try to use Chardonnay grapes, as they are smaller than the more readily available table grapes. If you must use large grapes, cut the reserved grapes into slices before adding them to the syrup.

> **CHEF'S TIP**
>
> If you do not plan to use up the sauce by the following day, add grapes only to the part you are using at the time. The sliced grapes, not being cooked to preserve their green color and sugar acidity, will start to make the sauce deteriorate.

Cherry Sauce yield: 2 cups (480 ml)

I like to use Bing cherries here when I can get them, because their dark skin gives the sauce a rich color. If you use canned cherries, strain out the syrup and reserve for another use, such as Black Forest Cake, or discard. You may want to adjust the amount of sugar depending on the type of cherries and wine used.

1 pound (455 g) fresh cherries *or* sweet canned cherries

1½ cups (360 ml) red wine

8 ounces (225 g) granulated sugar

Grated zest of 1 lemon

2 tablespoons (16 g) cornstarch

1 teaspoon (5 ml) vanilla extract

1. Wash the cherries, pit them, and place in a saucepan.

2. Reserve ¼ cup (60 ml) wine. Add the remaining 1¼ cups (300 ml) to the cherries in the pan. Stir in the sugar and lemon zest. Bring to a boil and cook over medium heat until the cherries are soft; canned cherries will need to cook only about 5 minutes. Puree the mixture, then strain. Discard the solids in the strainer. Return the juice to the cleaned saucepan.

3. Dissolve the cornstarch in the reserved wine. Stir into the strained cherry liquid. Bring to a boil and cook for a few seconds. Remove from the heat and add the vanilla. Cherry sauce can be served hot or cold.

Chocolate Sauce yield: approximately 4½ cups (1 L 80 ml)

This is a versatile recipe that can be kept on hand to serve either hot or cold. It is best suited to garnish a dessert—a slice of cake, a pastry, or poached fruit, for example. If you serve a chocolate sauce as one of the main components of the dessert, most notably with ice cream, use Hot Fudge Sauce (page 823) instead.

Chocolate sauce is much thinner when it is hot. If you plan to serve the chocolate sauce cold, let it cool to room temperature then add water if it is too thick. The recipe as is makes a fairly thick sauce when cold—ideal to cover a pear, for example—but it is too thick to mask a plate without adding water. On the other hand, to thicken the sauce, incorporate additional melted chocolate after first warming the sauce.

2 cups (480 ml) water

10 ounces (285 g) granulated sugar

½ cup (120 ml) glucose or light corn syrup

4 ounces (115 g) unsweetened cocoa powder, sifted

1 pound (455 g) sweet dark chocolate, melted

1. Combine the water, sugar, and glucose or corn syrup in a saucepan. Bring to a boil, then remove from the heat.

2. Add enough of the syrup to the cocoa powder to make a soft paste, stirring until the mixture is completely smooth. Gradually add the remaining syrup to the paste.

3. Remove from the heat, add the melted chocolate, and stir until combined. If necessary, strain the sauce before serving.

VARIATIONS
BITTER CHOCOLATE SAUCE

Replace 3 ounces (85 g) melted sweet dark chocolate with an equal amount of melted unsweetened chocolate. Increase the water by ½ cup (120 ml).

CHOCOLATE SAUCE FOR PIPING

This sauce is used to pipe designs and decorate other sauces as part of many dessert presentations. To create attractive designs and prevent the sauces from bleeding together, make the chocolate sauce the same consistency as the other sauce you are using. Add water to make the chocolate sauce thinner or melted chocolate to make it thicker (warm the sauce first to prevent lumps).

Cointreau-Pear Sauce yield: approximately 4 cups (960 ml)

5 pounds (2 kg 275 g) ripe flavorful pears, preferably Bartlett or Anjou (approximately 9 medium)

2 recipes Spiced Poaching Syrup (page 31)

2 tablespoons (30 ml) lemon juice

½ cup (120 ml) water

1 ounce (30 g) cornstarch

¼ cup (60 ml) Cointreau liqueur

Granulated sugar, as needed

1. Peel the pears, cut in half, and poach in the poaching syrup until very soft but not falling apart. Drain, reserving 1 cup (240 ml) syrup. Save the remaining syrup for another use or discard.

2. Remove the pear cores and stems. Place the pears in a food processor together with the reserved syrup and puree until smooth. Strain the puree then discard the contents of the strainer. Add the lemon juice to the puree.

3. Stir enough of the water into the cornstarch to dissolve it. Add the cornstarch mixture and the remaining water to the pear puree. Bring to a boil. Remove from the heat and stir in the Cointreau. Let cool. Add sugar to sweeten as needed. Thin with water if the sauce is too thick.

Cranberry Coulis yield: 3 cups (720 ml)

12 ounces (340 g) fresh *or* frozen cranberries

8 ounces (225 g) granulated sugar

2 cups (480 ml) water

1. Combine the cranberries, sugar, and water in a saucepan. Bring to a boil, then reduce the heat and simmer for 10 minutes. The cranberries should be soft and have popped open.

2. Remove from the heat. Puree immediately and strain. Return to a quick boil, then let cool.

3. Skim off any foam that has formed on the surface. Store the cranberry coulis, covered, in the refrigerator, but serve at room temperature. If the coulis is too thick after it has cooled, thin it with water.

Crème Fraîche yield: 2 cups (480 ml)

1 ounce (30 g) sour cream

2 cups (480 ml) heavy cream

1. Stir the sour cream into the heavy cream. Cover and let stand at 80° to 90°F (26° to 32°C) for 24 hours. An oven with a pilot light, or the top of a stove with pilots, are possible places to maintain this temperature. Store, covered, in the refrigerator.

2. To thicken the cream, whip until you achieve the desired consistency.

Fortified Caramel Sauce yield: approximately 3 cups (720 ml)

This is a rich caramel sauce that is meant to be served hot. It will be quite thick when it has cooled, even just to room temperature. If the sauce is to be used to mask a plate, for example, you should thin it with water to the desired consistency, or you can use the Clear Caramel Sauce on page 817. Fortified caramel sauce is perfect for serving with ice cream or apple or pear tarts.

1 pound (455 g) granulated sugar

⅓ cup (80 ml) water

½ teaspoon (2.5 ml) lemon juice

2 tablespoons (30 ml) glucose *or* light corn syrup

1½ cups (360 ml) heavy cream

2 ounces (55 g) unsalted butter

1. Place the sugar, water, and lemon juice in a small saucepan. Bring to a boil. Brush down the sides of the pan with a clean brush dipped in water. Add the glucose or corn syrup. Cook over medium heat until the syrup reaches a golden amber color.

2. Remove the pan from the heat and add the heavy cream carefully. Stand back as you pour in the cream, as the mixture may splatter. Stir to mix in the cream. If the sauce is not smooth, return the pan to the heat and cook, stirring constantly, to melt any lumps.

3. With the pan off the heat, add the butter. Keep stirring until the butter has melted and the sauce is smooth.

Guinettes Cherry Sauce yield: 2 cups (240 ml)

Guinettes are a special type of brandied cherry imported from France. They are labeled as "semi-confit" meaning they are partially cooked or preserved. The pitted cherries are packed in bottles with sugar and brandy and sometimes kirsch (cherry liqueur) as well. Both the cherries themselves and the liquid in the bottle are wonderfully delicious. Simply serving them over vanilla ice cream makes an excellent, simple treat. Of course, because they are packed in alcohol, they are perfect for flambéed dishes, such as Cherries Jubilee. The word *guinettes* is actually the name of a small red cherry varietal grown in France. However, guinettes has come to refer to the finished brandied cherry product in the same way, for example, that most people use the word *cabernet* to refer to the wine, not the Cabernet grape. Another popular label used for French brandied cherries is *Griottines*.

1 pound 2 ounces (510 g) Guinettes cherries, including syrup
Simple syrup

2 tablespoons (16 g) cornstarch
¼ cup (60 ml) cold water

1. Strain the cherries, using the back of a spoon to gently press out as much of the syrup as possible. Measure the syrup and add simple syrup to make a total of 1 cup (240 ml). Reserve the cherries.

2. Dissolve the cornstarch in the cold water. Place in a saucepan along with the 1 cup (240 ml) syrup. Stir together and bring to a boil. Boil for 30 seconds. Remove from the heat.

3. Add the reserved cherries. Stored, covered, in the refrigerator.

Honey-Yogurt Sauce yield: approximately 1¼ cups (300 ml)

1 cup (240 ml) Unflavored Yogurt (page 38)
3 tablespoons (45 ml) honey

1 teaspoon (5 ml) vanilla extract

1. Combine the yogurt, honey, and vanilla.

2. Cover and sore in the refrigerator.

Hot Fudge Sauce yield: 4 cups (960 ml)

This sauce must be served warm because it becomes much too thick when cold or even at room temperature. It is particularly good over ice cream. Reheat leftover sauce over simmering water.

5 ounces (140 g) unsweetened cocoa powder, sifted

6 ounces (170 g) light brown sugar

6 ounces (170 g) granulated sugar

1¼ cups (300 ml) heavy cream

8 ounces (225 g) unsalted butter

½ teaspoon (3 g) salt

1. Thoroughly combine the cocoa powder, brown sugar, and granulated sugar.

2. Place the cream, butter, and salt in a saucepan over low heat. Melt the butter in the cream and bring the mixture to scalding.

3. Whisk in the sugar and cocoa mixture gradually to avoid lumps. Cook over low heat, stirring constantly with the whisk, until the sugar has dissolved and the mixture is smooth. Serve immediately or keep warm over a bain-marie.

Kiwi Sauce yield: approximately 4 cups (960 ml)

Kiwi, like most subtropical fruits, contain an enzyme that inhibits gelatin from setting up. In this recipe, because the fruit juice need only set up to the consistency of a pourable sauce, the problem is not as great as it would be if one were preparing a molded dessert, for example. Cooking the fruit, or puree in this case, would kill the enzyme, but the brilliant green color would be compromised. Kiwi goes from bright green to yellowish at about 140°F (60°C). The fact that the color is damaged at a high temperature is the reason that this sauce is not thickened with cornstarch, as many of the other fruit sauces in this book are, since cornstarch must be brought to a boil. Protecting the color is the reason you need to be careful not to overheat the sauce in Step 4. If you do not mind using a bit of green food coloring, and you want to have more control over the thickness of the sauce, omit the gelatin and water and use 2 tablespoons (16 g) cornstarch instead. Add enough kiwi juice to the cornstarch to make a slurry, stir in the remaining juice and the sugar, and bring to a boil. Add the food coloring to the finished sauce.

4 tablespoons (36 g) unflavored gelatin powder

½ cup (120 ml) cold water

1 pound 12 ounces (795 g) ripe kiwis (approximately 12) *or* 3 cups (720 ml) strained kiwi puree

6 ounces (170 g) granulated sugar

1. Sprinkle the gelatin over the cold water and set aside to soften.

2. Peel the kiwis. Process in a food processor just to puree. If the fruit is processed for too long, many of the black seeds will break and give the sauce a muddy appearance. Strain the puree through a fine mesh strainer; you should have about 3 cups (720 ml) juice (see Note). Adjust as necessary.

3. Heat the gelatin mixture over a water bath to dissolve.

4. Add the sugar and dissolved gelatin mixture to the strained kiwi juice. Heat the mixture to approximately 110°F (43°C), stirring constantly. Be careful not to overheat. Remove from the heat and, if necessary, continue stirring until all of the gelatin is dissolved. Store, covered, in the refrigerator. If the sauce sets or becomes too thick during storage, carefully warm it, stirring constantly, until it reaches the desired consistency.

NOTE: If you would like to include some of the distinctive black seeds in the sauce, strain the puree through a coarse strainer. Some of the pulp will come through as well, making the sauce less smooth. You can get around this, to some extent, by first straining all of the seeds through a piece of cheesecloth, then adding a few back in without adding any pulp. The cheesecloth works well because the pulp tends to stick to the fabric.

Kumquat Sauce yield: approximately 4 cups (960 ml)

Kumquats have a unique distinction among citrus fruits in that you eat the pleasant-tasting sweet peel and discard the fruit pulp. Peeling a kumquat and saving the flesh would be the equivalent of the classic kitchen joke where the young apprentice, after being told to strain the stock, returned to the chef proudly holding a bowl full of bones and vegetables! The kumquat peel produces an intense and vibrant orange color; it makes regular orange sauce look quite pale by comparison.

1 pound (455 g) kumquats

1½ cups (360 ml) water

2 tablespoons (16 g) cornstarch

2 cups (480 ml) fresh orange juice (from about 6 oranges), strained

8 ounces (225 g) granulated sugar

1. Slice the kumquats without peeling them. Place the fruit and the water in a saucepan and bring to a boil. Cook until the kumquat slices have softened, about 5 minutes. Remove from the heat.

2. Add the cornstarch to a small amount of the orange juice and mix to dissolve the cornstarch. Mix this back into the remaining orange juice. Pour the mixture into a noncorrosive saucepan.

3. Puree the kumquat mixture and strain it into the orange juice, pressing as much of the liquid as possible through the strainer. Discard the contents of the strainer. Add the granulated sugar (see Note). Bring the sauce to a boil, lower the heat, and cook for 30 seconds, stirring constantly. Remove from the heat and let the sauce cool completely before using. If the sauce is too thick, thin it with water. Store, covered, in the refrigerator.

NOTE: Adjust the amount of sugar to taste depending on the sweetness of the citrus.

Mandarin Sauce yield: approximately 3 cups (720 ml)

Y ou can use any of the mandarin varieties or, if mandarins are not available, make the sauce using orange juice instead. If you prefer to use presqueezed fresh juice, go ahead and leave out the zest; the sauce will still have a very nice flavor. You might want to include the juice from one or two blood oranges, if they are in season, to give the sauce a wonderful vibrant color. Adjust the amount of cornstarch used for thickening depending on whether you plan to use the sauce hot, cold, or at room temperature.

2 teaspoons (5 g) cornstarch

¼ cup (60 ml) cold water

1 vanilla bean

2 cups (480 ml) mandarin juice

½ cup (120 ml) chablis wine

4 ounces (115 g) honey

1 cinnamon stick

Zest of 3 mandarins, blanched

¼ cup (60 ml) orange liqueur

1. Make a slurry by combining the cornstarch and water. Reserve.

2. Cut the vanilla bean in half lengthwise and scrape out the seeds.

3. Place the mandarin juice, chablis, honey, cinnamon stick, mandarin zest, vanilla bean seeds, and the vanilla bean pod halves in a saucepan. Stir to combine and bring to a boil. Lower the heat and simmer for 5 minutes. Remove the vanilla bean pods halves, rinse, and save for another use if desired. Remove the cinnamon stick and discard.

4. Whisk in the cornstarch mixture quickly and return the sauce to a boil. Boil for 1 minute, stirring constantly.

5. Remove from the heat and stir in the orange liqueur.

Mango Coulis yield: 4 cups (960 ml)

U se only perfectly ripe mangoes for this sauce. They should yield easily to light pressure and have a pleasant, sweet smell. Unfortunately, the ripe fruits are extremely difficult to peel. I have found the best way to overcome this is to slice off the two broader sides as close to the large flat seed as possible, then scoop out the flesh from these halves and discard the skin. Cut and scrape the remaining flesh away from the seed. A quicker method is to use 3½ cups (840 ml) thawed, frozen mango puree, instead of fresh fruit. However, most brands of puree need to be thickened by adding 1 tablespoon (8 g) cornstarch and bringing the mixture to a boil. If you add the thickener, you will create a sauce rather than a coulis.

3 pounds 8 ounces (1 kg 590 g) ripe mangoes (5 or 6 medium) (see introduction)

¼ cup (60 ml) lime juice

¼ cup (60 ml) orange juice

1. Peel the mangoes and cut the flesh away from the skin and seed.

2. Place the mango pulp in a food processor with the lime and orange juices. Puree, then strain out the stringy fibers using a fine mesh strainer. Bring the puree to a quick boil. Adjust the flavor and consistency with additional lime or orange juice as desired. Store, covered, in the refrigerator.

Mascarpone-Amaretto Sauce yield: about 4 cups (960 ml)

1 pound 5 ounces (595 g) Mascarpone Cheese (page 22), at room temperature

3 tablespoons (45 ml) amaretto liqueur

1¼ cups (300 ml) half-and-half

CHEF'S TIP
In a pinch, you can make a quick version of mascarpone cheese by combining 3 parts soft cream cheese with 1 part sour cream, mixing just until smooth.

1. Thoroughly combine the cheese, liqueur, and half-and-half, mixing until completely smooth.

2. Incorporate additional half-and-half as necessary to make the sauce thin enough to flow out when poured. Store, covered, in the refrigerator, but serve at room temperature.

Melba Sauce yield: approximately 4 cups (960 ml)

There are many versions of this classic sauce. The original was invented by Auguste Escoffier to complement Peach Melba, a dessert he created for Dame Nellie Melba at a dinner given by the Duke of Orléans in 1892 to celebrate her success in the opera Lohengrin. Actually, Melba sauce was not used the first time Peach Melba was served. On the occasion of the special dinner, Escoffier presented the ice cream and peaches inside a swan made of ice and topped the creation with spun sugar. It was not until the opening of the Carlton Hotel some eight years later that the dessert made it onto one of his menus, where it was served with raspberry puree. The modern versions of Melba sauce usually include either red currant jelly and/or kirsch liqueur.

1 pound 12 ounces (795 g) fresh, ripe red raspberries *or* thawed IQF frozen raspberries

4 ounces (115 g) red currant jelly

3 tablespoons (24 g) cornstarch

Granulated sugar, as needed

2 tablespoons (30 ml) kirschwasser

1. Puree the raspberries with the red currant jelly. Strain through a fine mesh strainer and discard the seeds. Measure and add water, if necessary, to make 4 cups (960 ml) juice.

2. Place the cornstarch in a saucepan. Add enough of the raspberry juice to liquefy the cornstarch. Stir in the remaining raspberry juice. Bring the sauce to a boil and sweeten with sugar if necessary. Remove from the heat and stir in the kirschwasser. Let cool, then thin with water if the sauce is too thick. Store, covered, in the refrigerator.

Mousseline Sauce yield: approximately 4 cups (960 ml)

In the recipes in this book, creamy mousseline sauce is usually flavored with a spirit or liqueur that complements a particular dessert. If you are serving this sauce with a dessert that does not specify a flavoring, you may want to add ¼ cup (60 ml) of the liqueur or spirit of your choice.

3 ounces (85 g) granulated sugar

6 egg yolks (½ cup/120 ml)

⅓ cup (80 ml) boiling water

1 teaspoon (5 ml) vanilla extract

1½ cups (360 ml) heavy cream

1. Whip the sugar and egg yolks together just to combine. Whisk in the boiling water. Place the bowl over simmering water and thicken to the ribbon stage, whipping constantly. Remove from the heat and whip until cool. Add the vanilla.

2. Whip the heavy cream until thickened to a saucelike consistency. Combine with the yolk mixture. If needed, thin the sauce with a little heavy cream. If the sauce is too thin for your particular use, thicken by mixing in additional softly whipped cream. Store the mousseline sauce, covered, in the refrigerator for 3 to 4 days. If the sauce should separate, whisking will bring it back together.

Nougat Sauce yield: 4 cups (960 ml)

3 ounces (85 g) granulated sugar

6 egg yolks (½ cup/120 ml)

⅓ cup (80 ml) boiling water

½ cup (120 ml) Nougat Flavoring (recipe follows)

1¼ cups (300 ml) heavy cream

1. Whip the sugar and egg yolks just to combine. Whisk in the boiling water. Place the mixture over simmering water and heat, whipping constantly, until thickened to the ribbon stage. Add the nougat flavoring and remove from the heat.

2. Whip the heavy cream until it forms soft peaks. Combine with the egg yolk mixture. If the sauce is too thick, thin with a little additional water. Store, covered, in the refrigerator.

NOUGAT FLAVORING yield: 1½ cups (360 ml)

1 pound (455 g) granulated sugar

1 teaspoon (5 ml) lemon juice

1 cup (240 ml) water

3 tablespoons (45 ml) amaretto liqueur

1 tablespoon (15 ml) hazelnut liqueur

1. Place the sugar and lemon juice in a heavy-bottomed saucepan. Cook, stirring constantly, until the sugar reaches the light caramel stage.

2. Remove the pan from the heat and add the water. Be very careful; the hot caramel might splatter, so stand back. Place the pan back on the stove. Heat, stirring out any lumps, until the caramel is smooth. Let cool.

3. Add the liqueurs. Cover and store at room temperature.

Orange Sauce yield: approximately 4 cups (960 ml)

When refrigerated overnight, this sauce will set to a jellylike consistency. The gelling occurs because of the large amount of natural pectin present in oranges. Forcing the sauce through a fine mesh strainer is usually all that is needed to make it smooth again but, if necessary, reheat to thin it out.

4 cups (960 ml) strained fresh orange juice
(from 10 to 12 oranges)

5 tablespoons (40 g) cornstarch

2 tablespoons (30 ml) lemon juice

6 ounces (170 g) granulated sugar

1. Add enough orange juice to the cornstarch to make it liquid. Stir this into the remaining orange juice. Add the lemon juice and sugar, adjusting the taste by adding more or less sugar as needed, depending on the sweetness of the orange juice.

2. Heat to boiling in a stainless-steel or other noncorrosive pan. Lower the heat and cook for 1 minute, stirring constantly. Let cool completely. If the sauce is too thick, thin with water. Store covered in the refrigerator.

VARIATION
BITTER ORANGE SAUCE

Follow the recipe for Orange Sauce, with the following changes:

1. Cut the peel of half of the oranges into about 6 pieces each and add these to the juice. It is not necessary to strain the juice now as directed. Follow the procedure for making orange sauce, including the peels with the juice.

2. Set the sauce aside to allow the peels to macerate for 30 minutes. Strain to remove the orange peel as well as any pits or sediment.

Persimmon Sauce yield: about 2 cups (480 ml)

Hachiya persimmons have a slightly oblong shape and are pointed at the bottom end. They are very high in tannin and can be eaten raw only when fully ripe (the fruit should be almost jellylike throughout). The smaller Fuyu persimmon is shaped like a tomato. It has very little tannin and can therefore be eaten raw before it is completely ripe and soft. For this sauce, however, either variety should be very ripe and soft to the point of falling apart.

1 pound 8 ounces (680 g) ripe persimmons,
preferably Hachiya or 1¾ cups (420 ml)
strained persimmon pulp

3 tablespoons (45 ml) lime juice

2 tablespoons (30 ml) orange juice

2 tablespoons (30 ml) honey

2 teaspoons (5 g) cornstarch

1. Remove the stems from the persimmons. Puree the entire fruit with the skin on, then force the puree through a fine strainer.

2. Combine the persimmon pulp, lime juice, orange juice, and honey.

3. Add just enough water to the cornstarch to make it liquid. Add to the persimmon mixture and bring to a boil. Remove from the heat and thin with additional orange juice if desired.

Pineapple Sauce yield: about 3½ cups (840 ml)

2 medium fresh, ripe pineapples (about 2 pounds/910 g each, unpeeled and including the crown)

3 tablespoons (24 g) cornstarch

8 ounces (225 g) granulated sugar

1 tablespoon (15 ml) lime juice

1 tablespoon (15 ml) light rum

1. Rinse, remove the crowns, peel the pineapples, and cut away the cores. You may save the cores for use in Pineapple Drink (page 665) if desired.

2. Dice 5 ounces (140 g) pineapple flesh into ¼-inch (6-mm) pieces; reserve. Puree the remaining pineapple as smooth as possible in a food processor. Strain through a fine mesh strainer, pressing on the solids with a spoon or the back of a ladle to force out as much of the juice as possible. Discard the solids.

3. In a nonreactive saucepan, dissolve the cornstarch in a small amount of the pineapple juice, then stir back into the remainder together with the sugar.

4. Bring the mixture to a boil and cook over medium heat, stirring constantly, for about 1 minute. Remove from the heat, stir in the diced pineapple, lime juice, and rum. Let cool, then store, covered, in the refrigerator.

Plum Sauce yield: 4 cups (960 ml)

Santa Rosa or Casselman plums are good choices when in season, but in any case, use a red or purple variety of plum, which will give the sauce a pleasant pastel red color.

2 pounds 8 ounces (1 kg 135 g) pitted fresh plums *or* 2 pounds (910 g) drained canned pitted plums

3 cups (720 ml) water *or* liquid from canned plums

6 ounces (170 g) granulated sugar

3 tablespoons (24 g) cornstarch

1. If using fresh plums, cut them into quarters.

2. Reserve ¼ cup (60 ml) water or canning liquid and place the plums in a saucepan with the remaining liquid and the sugar; if you are using canned plums packed in syrup, omit the sugar. Bring to a boil and cook over medium heat until the fruit is soft enough to fall apart, approximately 15 minutes for fresh plums, 1 minute for canned.

3. Remove from the heat and strain, forcing as much of the pulp as possible through the strainer, using the back of a spoon or ladle. Discard the contents of the strainer.

4. Dissolve the cornstarch in the reserved liquid. Add to the sauce. Return the mixture to the saucepan and bring to a boil. Cook for 1 minute to remove the taste of the cornstarch. Serve hot or cold. When served cold, the sauce may need to be thinned with water. Store, covered, in the refrigerator.

Pomegranate Sauce yield: approximately 4 cups (960 ml)

3 pounds (1 kg 365 g) pomegranate seeds *or* 3 cups (720 ml) pomegranate juice (see Note)

3 tablespoons (24 g) cornstarch

6 ounces (170 g) granulated sugar

¾ cup (180 ml) grenadine

1. Place the pomegranate seeds in a food processor and process for just a few seconds to break open the seeds and release the juice; do not crack or pulverize the tiny white pits inside each seed. Force the mixture through a fine mesh strainer pressing hard on the solids to extract as much juice as possible (see Figure 1-10, page 51). Discard the solids. You should have close to 3 cups (720 ml) of juice; adjust as needed.

2. Add enough of the juice to the cornstarch to dissolve the starch. Place the remaining juice, the cornstarch mixture, sugar, and grenadine in a nonreactive saucepan. Bring to a boil while stirring. Let cool to room temperature then store, covered, in the refrigerator.

NOTE: You will need approximately 10 pomegranates, 8 to 10 ounces (225 to 285 g) each. For a more rustic looking sauce, reserve ½ cup (120 ml) of the seeds before processing and add these seeds to the finished sauce.

Raspberry Sauce yield: approximately 4 cups (960 ml)

2 pounds (910 g) fresh ripe raspberries *or* thawed IQF raspberries (see introduction to Bijou Coulis, page 815)

3 tablespoons (24 g) cornstarch

2 ounces (55 g) granulated sugar

1. Puree the berries. Strain out the seeds using a fine mesh strainer. Measure and add water, if necessary, to make 4 cups (960 ml) juice.

2. Place the cornstarch in a saucepan. Mix enough of the juice into the cornstarch to liquefy it, then stir in the remaining juice.

3. Heat the sauce to simmering. Add the granulated sugar, adjusting the amount as needed, depending on the sweetness of the berries.

4. Simmer the sauce for 1 minute. Cool and thin with water, if necessary. Store, covered, in the refrigerator.

VARIATION

BLACKBERRY SAUCE

Substitute blackberries for the raspberries.

Red Currant Sauce yield: 4 cups (960 ml)

If you use fresh currants here, remove the stems before weighing the berries. If fresh are not available, use IQF frozen berries, which are stemless and do not contain sugar, and do not thaw before weighing, unless you will be using the entire package. Once thawed, the juice separates from the berries and collects at the bottom.

2 pounds (910 g) fresh or frozen red currants

1 tablespoon (8 g) cornstarch

¾ cup (180 ml) dry white wine

10 ounces (285 g) granulated sugar

1. Puree the currants, strain through a fine mesh strainer, and discard the solids. You should have close to 2¼ cups (540 ml) of juice; adjust as necessary.

2. Dissolve the cornstarch in the wine. Place the currant juice and the cornstarch mixture in a nonreactive saucepan, add the sugar, bring to a boil and then remove from the heat.

3. Let the sauce cool then adjust the consistency as needed. Cover and refrigerate.

Rhubarb Sauce yield: 4 cups (960 ml)

3 pounds (1 kg 365 g) fresh rhubarb stalks

1½ cups (360 ml) water

1 pound 8 ounces (680 g) granulated sugar

¼ cup (32 g) cornstarch

1. Wash the rhubarb. Trim both ends off each stalk, then cut across into ½-inch (1.2-cm) pieces. Place the rhubarb pieces in a saucepan together with the water and sugar. Cook over medium heat just until the rhubarb falls apart.

2. Place a strainer over a second saucepan. Strain the rhubarb mixture into the pan, pressing hard on the contents of the strainer with the back of a wooden spoon to force as much of the juice as possible into the pan. Discard the rhubarb in the strainer.

3. Stir enough cold water into the cornstarch to dissolve it, then stir into the rhubarb liquid. Bring the sauce to a boil and cook for about 1 minute to eliminate any cornstarch flavor. Let cool to room temperature, then store, covered, in the refrigerator. If necessary, thin with water before serving.

Romanoff Sauce yield: approximately 4 cups (960 ml)

3 cups (720 ml) heavy cream

1 cup (240 ml) sour cream

1. Mix the heavy cream with the sour cream and whip them together until the mixture has thickened to the consistency of molasses.

2. If the sauce is not to be used immediately, adjust the consistency at serving time by whipping the sauce to thicken it or adding additional heavy cream to thin it. Store the sauce, covered, in the refrigerator.

Strawberry Sauce yield: approximately 4¹/₂ cups (1 L 80 ml)

When strawberries have white shoulders around the hull together with a little white on the tip (or nose), they are called cat-faced. This usually occurs once a year when one of the growing regions gets hit with rain, forcing a cooler area to pick its berries before they are fully ripe. These immature berries are inexpensive but bland and without much color. If you have no choice but to use them, add a small amount of raspberry juice or Beet Juice (page 5), or as a last resort 1 or 2 drops of red food coloring, to make the sauce more appealing.

3 pounds (1 kg 365 g) fresh ripe strawberries   4 ounces (115 g) granulated sugar

2 tablespoons (16 g) cornstarch

1. Puree the strawberries. Strain through a fine mesh strainer. Measure and add water if necessary to make 4 cups (960 ml) juice.

2. Place the cornstarch in a saucepan. Mix enough of the juice into the cornstarch to liquefy it, then stir in the remaining juice.

3. Heat the sauce to simmering. Add the sugar, adjusting the amount as needed, depending on the sweetness of the strawberries.

4. Simmer the sauce for a few minutes. Let cool, then thin with water, if necessary. Store, covered, in the refrigerator.

Sour Cream Mixture for Piping

This is a much easier and quicker method than thickening the cream by whipping and, because such a small amount is actually eaten, the flavor of the sour cream is not noticeable. Instructions for using sour cream mixture in decorating are given on pages 809 to 814.

Heavy cream   Sour cream

> **CHEF'S TIP**
> The sour cream mixture and the sauce to be decorated must have the same consistency. If the sour cream is too thick, it will not blend with the sauce but break up into pieces instead. If it is too thin, it will run into the sauce, and you will not get clearly defined lines. The sauce, too, must be of the proper consistency to begin with; if it is too thin, it cannot be decorated at all.

1. Gradually stir enough heavy cream into sour cream until the mixture is approximately the same consistency as the sauce you are decorating.

2. Use as directed in the individual recipes. This mixture will keep for days in the refrigerator, but it may have to be thinned.

White Chocolate Sauce yield: approximately 4 cups (960 ml)

1 cup (240 ml) water

10 ounces (285 g) granulated sugar

½ cup (120 ml) glucose *or* light corn syrup

1 pound 2 ounces (510 g) white chocolate

1. Combine the water, sugar, and glucose or corn syrup in a saucepan and bring the syrup to a boil. Remove from the heat and set aside to cool a bit.

2. Cut the white chocolate into small pieces so that it will melt quickly and evenly. Place in a bowl over a bain-marie and make sure the water is only simmering, not boiling. Stir the chocolate constantly until it is melted, never letting the bottom and sides of the bowl get too warm. It is very important to follow the instructions for stirring the chocolate constantly during melting. Because white chocolate does not contain any cocoa mass, only the cocoa butter that has been extracted from it, this type of "chocolate" will become gritty and unusable if it is overheated.

3. Add the melted chocolate to the warm sugar syrup and stir until combined.

4. Before serving, adjust the consistency as needed. To thicken, warm the sauce lightly and add more melted chocolate. To thin the sauce, add tepid water. White chocolate sauce may be served hot or cold. Store, covered, at room temperature for a few days, or refrigerate for longer storage.

DECORATING SYRUPS

Black Currant Decorating Syrup yield: approximately 2 cups (480 ml)

12 ounces (340 g) fresh *or* IQF black currants

2 cups (480 ml) simple syrup

1. Wash and stem the currants if using fresh. Select and reserve ½ cup (120 ml) small good-looking currants (see Note).

2. Place the remaining currants in a small saucepan together with the simple syrup. Bring the mixture to a boil and cook for 2 to 3 minutes, until the berries start to crack open.

3. Strain through a fine mesh sieve and discard the solids. Return the liquid to the heat and reduce to approximately 2 cups (480 ml) or to the particular viscosity you desire. (Test the consistency by placing a small amount in the refrigerator to chill, then bringing it back to room temperature.)

4. Remove from the heat and immediately stir in the reserved berries. Let cool to room temperature before using.

NOTE: Omit this step if you are using IQF berries because, like most fruit, once thawed, the berries will become soft and fall apart. Even when you leave out the decorative berries, the syrup will still have a radiant color and unusual taste.

Green Tea Decorating Syrup yield: approximately 2¹/₂ cups (540 ml)

2 teaspoons (6 g) unflavored gelatin powder

¹/₄ cup (60 ml) cold water

2 teaspoons (5 g) Japanese green tea powder (*maccha*)

2 tablespoons (30 ml) hot water

2 cups (480 ml) simple syrup

1. Sprinkle the gelatin powder over the cold water and set aside to soften.

2. Combine the green tea powder with the hot water and stir to dissolve.

3. In a heavy saucepan, bring the simple syrup to a boil and boil for 3 minutes to reduce it slightly. Pour the syrup into a bowl.

4. Heat the gelatin mixture to dissolve the gelatin.

5. Stir the dissolved gelatin and the tea mixture into the reduced simple syrup. Let the syrup cool to room temperature. It should be thick enough to hold its shape when piped into a puddle. If needed to bring the sauce to the desired consistency, reduce it to make it thicker or add a small amount of water to thin it.

6. Store in a piping bottle.

Lemon–Vanilla Bean Decorating Syrup yield: approximately 2 cups (480 ml)

2 teaspoons (6 g) unflavored gelatin powder

3 tablespoons (45 ml) cold water

2 lemons

2 vanilla beans

2¹/₂ ounces (70 g) granulated sugar

1¹/₂ cups (360 ml) simple syrup

1. Sprinkle the gelatin over the surface of the cold water and set aside to soften.

2. Using a citrus zester, remove the zest from 1 lemon (see page 40). Chop the zest finely. Extract the juice from both lemons and strain it. Combine the strained juice and the chopped zest; set aside.

3. Split the vanilla beans lengthwise. Scrape out the seeds and rub the seeds into the sugar. Stir the sugar into the simple syrup together with the reserved lemon juice and zest. Reserve the vanilla bean pods for another use. Bring the syrup to a boil.

4. Heat the gelatin mixture to dissolve the softened gelatin. Stir into the hot syrup. Place 1 teaspoon (5 ml) syrup in the refrigerator to test the consistency. After it has chilled and been brought back to room temperature, the puddle should hold its shape. Adjust as needed by reducing the syrup to thicken or adding a small amount of water if it is too thick.

5. Store in a piping bottle.

Licorice Decorating Syrup yield: approximately 1¼ cups (300 ml)

½ teaspoon (1.5 g) unflavored gelatin powder

⅓ cup (80 ml) water

1½ cups (360 ml) simple syrup

⅓ cup (80 ml) sambuca liqueur

1. Sprinkle the gelatin over the water and set aside to soften.

2. Combine the simple syrup and the sambuca in a saucepan and bring to a boil. Remove from the heat and stir in the softened gelatin, continue to stir until the gelatin is dissolved.

3. Return the pan to the stove and boil the mixture until it thickens. Test the consistency by refrigerating a few drops, then returning them to room temperature. The syrup should hold its shape at room temperature without running.

4. Store in a piping bottle.

Mint Decorating Syrup yield: approximately 1¼ cups (300 ml)

⅓ ounce (10 g) fresh peppermint leaves

1½ cups (360 ml) simple syrup

1 tablespoon (15 ml) green mint liqueur

1. Coarsely chop the mint leaves. Reserve 1 tablespoon (loosely measured) and place the remainder in a saucepan with the simple syrup and mint liqueur.

2. Bring to a boil and reduce by one-quarter. Test the consistency by placing 1 teaspoon (5 ml) syrup in the refrigerator until chilled. Bring it to room temperature; the puddle should hold its shape. Adjust as needed by reducing the syrup further if necessary.

3. Chop the reserved mint leaves very finely; set aside.

4. Strain the syrup. Discard the solids and stir in the finely chopped mint. Store, refrigerated, in a piping bottle.

Orange–Vanilla Bean Decorating Syrup yield: approximately 1¼ cups (300 ml)

½ teaspoon (1.5 g) unflavored gelatin powder

⅓ cup (80 ml) water

1 vanilla bean

1 cup (240 ml) simple syrup

½ cup (120 ml) orange juice

⅓ cup (80 ml) orange liqueur

1. Sprinkle the gelatin over the water and set aside to soften.

2. Split the vanilla bean lengthwise and scrape out the seeds. Save the empty pod halves for another use. Thoroughly mix the vanilla bean seeds in a small portion of the simple syrup to distribute them and break up any clumps. Mix this into the remaining simple syrup.

3. Combine the vanilla simple syrup, orange juice, and the orange liqueur in a saucepan and bring to a boil. Remove from the heat and stir in the softened gelatin, continuing to stir until the gelatin is dissolved.

4. Return the pan to the stove and boil the mixture for a few minutes until it thickens. Test the consistency by refrigerating a few drops, then returning them to room temperature. The syrup should hold its shape at room temperature without running.

5. Store in a piping bottle.

Raspberry Decorating Syrup yield: approximately 1³/₄ cups (420 ml)

1 pound (455 g) raspberries, fresh or IQF	1 cup (240 ml) simple syrup
1 cup (240 ml) water, if needed	3 tablespoons (45 ml) raspberry liqueur

1. Puree the raspberries. Strain the puree through a fine mesh strainer to remove the seeds; there should be approximately 1 cup (240 ml) raspberry juice. If not, add water as needed.

2. Place the raspberry juice, simple syrup, and raspberry liqueur in a saucepan. Bring to a boil and cook over medium heat until the liquid has been reduce to a viscosity that will hold when cold and spooned into a puddle; test by placing a small amount in the refrigerator. The puddle should hold its shape when returned to room temperature.

3. Store, refrigerated, in a piping bottle.

Red Currant Decorating Syrup or Glaze

yield: approximately 2 cups (480 ml) syrup or 1 cup (240 ml) glaze

14 ounces (400 g) stemless fresh or IQF red currants	1 cup (240 ml) simple syrup

1. Combine the currants with the simple syrup in a saucepan and cook over medium heat until berries start to burst, about 3 minutes.

2. Strain, using the back of a spoon or a ladle to extract as much juice as possible (see Figure 1-10, page 51). Discard the solids and return the liquid to the saucepan.

3. Bring to a boil and reduce to the thickness you desire—thicker for a glaze or thinner for a decorating syrup; test by placing a small pool in the refrigerator and then bringing it back to room temperature. To use, allow to cool to room temperature.

4. To use as a glaze, force the amount needed through a fine mesh strainer and brush or spread on the cake or pastry immediately. For a decorating syrup, store in a piping bottle.

Rum Decorating Syrup yield: approximately 1 cup (240 ml)

1¹/₂ cups (360 ml) simple syrup	1 vanilla bean
¹/₂ cup (120 ml) dark rum	

1. Combine the simple syrup and rum in a saucepan. Split the vanilla bean lengthwise and scrape the seeds into the syrup. Reserve the vanilla bean pod halves for another use.

2. Bring to a boil and reduce by one-quarter. The syrup should stay in puddles without running when cooled to room temperature and spooned onto the plate; test by placing 1 teaspoon syrup in the refrigerator, then returning it to room temperature.

3. Store the syrup in a piping bottle.

Calvados Diplomat Cream yield: 9 cups (2 L 160 ml)

2 teaspoons (6 g) unflavored gelatin powder

¼ cup (60 ml) cold water

½ teaspoon (1 g) ground cinnamon

1 tablespoon (15 g) granulated sugar

2 cups (480 ml) heavy cream

1 recipe Calvados Pastry Cream (recipe follows)

1. In a bowl large enough to hold the finished filling, sprinkle the gelatin over the cold water and set aside to soften.

2. Combine the cinnamon and sugar. Add to the heavy cream and whip to soft peaks. Set aside in the refrigerator.

3. Stir the Calvados pastry cream until smooth, straining first if necessary.

4. Heat the gelatin mixture over a bain-marie to dissolve. Quickly stir in about one-quarter of the pastry cream, continuing to stir until the mixture reaches body temperature. Rapidly combine this with the remaining pastry cream, then fold in the whipped cream. Use immediately.

Calvados Pastry Cream yield: approximately 2 pounds (910 g)

1 pint (480 ml) whole milk

1 vanilla bean

3 ounces (85 g) granulated sugar

1½ ounces (40 g) cornstarch

3 eggs

⅓ cup (80 ml) Calvados

2 ounces (55 g) unsalted butter

1. Place the milk in a thick-bottomed saucepan. Cut the vanilla bean in half lengthwise and scrape out the seeds. Add the seeds and the pod halves to the milk. Bring to the scalding point.

2. Keeping an eye on the milk, whisk together the sugar and cornstarch in a bowl. Gradually whisk in the eggs, followed by the Calvados; continue mixing until smooth.

3. Slowly pour about one-third of the hot milk into the egg mixture while whisking rapidly. Pour the tempered egg mixture back into the remaining milk.

4. Return the pan to the stove and bring to a boil, stirring constantly. Cook for a few seconds once the mixture reaches the boiling point.

5. Remove the vanilla bean pod halves. Stir in the butter. Pour the custard into a bowl, cover, and let cool slightly, then refrigerate.

Chantilly Cream yield: 6 cups (1 L 440 ml)

Chantilly cream takes its name from the château of Chantilly outside Paris, where the famous chef Vatel worked in the mid-1800s. The only difference between Chantilly cream and sweetened whipped cream is the addition of vanilla in the form of sugar, powder, or extract. Chantilly cream should have a light and fluffy texture and therefore should be made with heavy whipping cream rather than manufacturing cream, which has a higher fat content.

1 vanilla bean	2 cups (480 ml) well-chilled heavy cream
1 tablespoon (15 g) granulated sugar	1 teaspoon (5 ml) vanilla extract

1. Cut the vanilla bean in half lengthwise. Scrape the seeds out of each pod half and thoroughly mix the seeds into the granulated sugar. Save the empty pods for another use.

2. Chill the bowl and the whip attachment of an electric mixer. Pour the cream and the vanilla into the bowl. Start whipping at high speed. Add the vanilla sugar mixture.

3. Keeping a watchful eye on its progress, continue whipping until stiff peaks form or to the consistency specified in the individual recipes. Use as soon as possible.

NOTE: Chantilly cream must be refrigerated. It will break if left at room temperature for more than a short period.

Cherry Filling yield: approximately 4 pounds (1 kg 820 g)

Because cornstarch will break down, making the filling watery after a few days of storage, pectin powder is used here in addition to cornstarch. Be sure to choose regular fruit-canning pectin rather than pure pectin for this recipe.

2 pounds (910 g) drained sweet canned cherries (see Step 1)	2 tablespoons (30 ml) raspberry juice
3 cups (720 ml) liquid from canned cherries	2 ounces (55 g) cornstarch
Simple syrup, if needed	2 ounces (55 g) pectin powder for fruit canning
	2 ounces (55 g) granulated sugar

1. When you drain the juice from the cherries, press the cherries firmly without crushing them. The liquid must be completely drained off or the filling will be too runny. Measure the liquid; if there is not enough, add simple syrup to make up the difference.

2. Add the raspberry juice to the cherry liquid. Dissolve the cornstarch in a small amount of the mixture before stirring into the remainder. Mix the pectin powder with the sugar. Blend into the cherry liquid mixture.

3. Bring the sauce to a boil, stirring constantly. Cook over medium heat for about 5 minutes, continuing to stir constantly to reduce and thicken the filling.

4. Remove from the heat and add the drained cherries. Place a piece of baking paper directly on the surface to prevent a skin from forming as the filling cools. Store the filling, covered, in the refrigerator.

FRESH CHERRY FILLING yield: approximately 3 pounds 8 ounces (1 kg 590 g)

2 pounds (910 g) Bing or Lambert cherries

3 ounces (85 g) cornstarch

2½ cups (600 ml) water

1 pound 4 ounces (570 g) granulated sugar

2 ounces (55 g) pectin powder for fruit canning

2 tablespoons (30 ml) raspberry juice

¼ cup (60 ml) lemon juice

1. Wash the cherries and remove the stems. Pit the cherries.

2. Mix the cornstarch with just enough of the water to make a slurry.

3. Combine the sugar and pectin powder. Place this, together with the remaining water, in a saucepan and bring to a boil. Add the cherries and cook gently until tender, 4 to 5 minutes. Strain, reserving the cherries and the syrup separately.

4. Stir the raspberry juice and lemon juice into the reserved cornstarch slurry. Quickly and in a steady stream stir this into the reserved syrup. Bring the mixture to a boil, stirring constantly. Cook over medium heat until completely thickened, about 3 minutes.

5. Remove from the heat and add the drained cherries. Place a piece of baking paper directly on the surface to prevent a skin from forming as the filling cools. Store the filling, covered, in the refrigerator.

Chocolate Cream yield: 4 pounds 6 ounces (1 kg 990 g), or 9½ cups (2 L 280 ml)

Chocolate cream is likely to break if the chocolate mixture is too hot; it should be approximately 110°F (43°C). The filling can also break if the cream does not contain at least 36 percent butterfat, but unfortunately this is somewhat harder to control.

5 ounces (140 g) sweet dark chocolate

2 ounces (55 g) unsweetened chocolate

½ cup (120 ml) simple syrup

3 pints (1 L 440 ml) heavy cream

1. Cut the chocolates into small pieces. Place in a bowl and melt over simmering water. Remove from the heat and stir in the simple syrup.

2. Whip the cream until is becomes slightly thickened. Be careful: If you overwhip the cream, it will break when you add the chocolate.

3. Place a small amount of the whipped cream in a bowl and quickly fold in the chocolate mixture; do not whisk it in. Add the rest of the cream and mix in. If the chocolate cream seems runny, stir it until the consistency becomes firmer.

Chunky Apple Filling
yield: 2 pounds 12 ounces (1 kg 250 g), or 5 cups (1 L 200 ml)

3 pounds (1 kg 365 g) Granny Smith or
    Pippin apples (about 7; see Chef's Tip)

10 ounces (285 g) granulated sugar

¼ cup (60 ml) water

4 teaspoons (20 ml) lemon juice

1. Peel and core the apples. Chop approximately two-thirds of the apples into ½-inch (1.2-cm) pieces.

2. Place the chopped apples in a saucepan with the sugar, water, and lemon juice. Adjust the amount of sugar according to the tartness of the apples and your own taste. Stir to combine and cook over medium heat, stirring from time to time, until the apples have broken down and the mixture starts to thicken.

> **CHEF'S TIP**
> If neither of the apples called for is available, other good choices are Jonathan and Gravenstein. Varieties that should be avoided here are Red Delicious and Fuji as they are difficult or even impossible to cook down to a sauce-like consistency.

3. Chop the remaining apples into ¼-inch (6-mm) pieces and add to the mixture on the stove

4. Continue cooking the filling until the apple chunks are soft and the filling has reached a jamlike consistency, adding a bit more water if it seems necessary. Let cool at room temperature, then store, covered, in the refrigerator.

Classic Bavarian Cream
yield: 2 quarts (1 L 920 ml)

8 egg yolks (⅔ cup/160 ml)

8 ounces (225 g) granulated sugar

2 tablespoons (18 g) unflavored gelatin
    powder

½ cup (120 ml) cold water

1 vanilla bean

2 cups (480 ml) whole milk

2 cups (480 ml) heavy cream

1 teaspoon (5 ml) vanilla extract

1. Whip the egg yolks and sugar until light and fluffy.

2. Sprinkle the gelatin over the cold water and set aside to soften.

3. Split the vanilla bean lengthwise and scrape out the seeds. Add the seeds and the pod halves to the milk. Bring the milk to the scalding point. Gradually pour the hot milk, including the vanilla bean pods, into the yolk mixture while whipping rapidly. Return the mixture to the heat and bring back to the scalding point, stirring constantly. Do not boil.

4. Remove from the heat and remove the pod halves; stir in the softened gelatin. Set aside to cool at room temperature, stirring from time to time.

5. Whip the cream to soft peaks. Add the vanilla extract to the custard. When the custard has cooled to body temperature, slowly stir it into the cream.

6. Pour into molds or use as directed in the individual recipes.

CLASSIC CHOCOLATE BAVARIAN CREAM

Decrease the gelatin to 4 teaspoons (12 g) and add 8 ounces (225 g) melted sweet dark chocolate when you stir in the gelatin.

Crème Parisienne yield: 2 quarts (1 L 920 ml), or 4 pounds 8 ounces (2 kg 45 g)

This simple chocolate cream can be used for most of the recipes in this book that call for chocolate added to whipping cream, either as is or, if applicable, with gelatin added. This cream will not break, which can happen when you add warm melted chocolate to whipped cream that is too low in butterfat, because its fat content has been increased by whipping the cream with the chocolate already added. If prepared using regular heavy cream (35 percent butterfat), it should be made the day before (or at least 6 hours before) it is to be used to ensure that it will whip up to its maximum volume and thicken sufficiently. However, if it is made with manufacturing cream, which contains 40 percent butterfat, it only needs to be thoroughly chilled before whipping. Either way, crème Parisienne can be stored in the refrigerator unwhipped for up to 1 week and used as needed. This can be a real timesaver if, for example, you are filling chocolate éclairs or a similar pastry every day.

10 ounces (285 g) sweet dark chocolate

1 quart (960 ml) heavy cream

¾ cup (180 ml) whole milk

3 ounces (85 g) granulated sugar

1. Chop the chocolate into small pieces and reserve.

2. Bring the cream, milk, and sugar to a boil in a saucepan. Remove from the heat and use a whisk to stir in the chopped chocolate. Continue to stir until the chocolate is completely dissolved. Cool and refrigerate before whipping (see introduction).

3. To use, whip as you would whipping cream.

Diplomat Cream yield: 2 quarts (1 L 920 ml)

Diplomat Cream can be made with or without gelatin, depending on its intended use. In Sweden, when we leave out the gelatin and simply combine pastry cream and sweetened whipped cream, we call it *Quick Bavarian Cream*. If the gelatin is omitted, the cream should be whipped to stiff peaks rather than soft peaks, as in this recipe. It is also very important, in that case, that the pastry cream is not only completely smooth but quite firm to compensate for the missing gelatin. Diplomat Cream made without gelatin is limited in its applications, as it can be used only to fill a premade pastry or shell that will hold it in place. It is perfect for Swedish Profiteroles and for fruit tartlets, for example, but if it needs to stand alone in a molded cake or pastry—for instance, on the top of a gâteau Saint-Honoré—the addition of gelatin is a must.

1 tablespoon (9 g) unflavored gelatin powder

⅓ cup (80 ml) kirschwasser

1 Small-Batch recipe *or* 1 pound 8 ounces (680 g) Pastry Cream (page 845)

1 vanilla bean

2½ cups (600 ml) heavy cream

1 teaspoon (5 ml) vanilla extract

1. Sprinkle the gelatin powder over the kirschwasser and set aside to soften.

2. Stir the pastry cream to make it perfectly smooth or, if necessary, force it through a sieve then set it aside.

3. Split the vanilla bean lengthwise and scrape out the seeds. Add the seeds to the heavy cream and reserve the pod halves for another use. Add the vanilla extract.

4. Whip the cream to soft peaks. Gradually fold the whipped cream into the pastry cream.

5. Heat the gelatin mixture over a water bath to dissolve.

6. Place one-third of the cream mixture in a separate bowl. Rapidly stir in the warm gelatin and kirschwasser. Still working quickly, stir this into the remaining cream mixture.

N O T E : If the pastry cream is freshly made for this recipe, make sure it has cooled sufficiently before combining it with the whipped cream or the mixture may break. Also, heat the gelatin a bit hotter than you normally would because the cream and custard mixture will be very cool. If the gelatin is not hot, it may set up before you can thoroughly mix it in.

Frangipane Filling yield: 4 pounds 10 ounces (2 kg 105 g)

Frangipane is an almond-based filling used in numerous European pastries and tarts. In addition to giving the paste a delicious flavor, the almonds absorb moisture, which helps baked goods made with this filling stay fresh longer than average.

1 pound 14 ounces (855 g) almond paste	2½ cups (600 ml) eggs
6 ounces (170 g) granulated sugar	3 ounces (85 g) bread flour
14 ounces (400 g) unsalted butter, at room temperature	

1. Place the almond paste and sugar in a mixer bowl. Add the soft butter gradually while mixing at low speed, using a paddle.

2. After all of the butter has been incorporated and the mixture is smooth, mix in the eggs, a few at a time, then mix in the flour. Store the frangipane filling in the refrigerator. Bring to room temperature to soften, then stir until smooth before using. Use as directed in the individual recipes.

N O T E : As with any uncooked filling that contains a large number of eggs, frangipane filling should be used right away to ensure the maximum volume in baked pastries.

Ganache yield: 6 pounds 4 ounces (2 kg 845 g), or 9½ cups (2 L 280 ml)

In its most basic form, ganache is simply equal parts chocolate and cream by weight. Other ingredients, such as butter and egg yolks, can be included together with flavorings, if desired. It is a very rich mixture that has many uses in the pastry kitchen. It can be used warm as a glaze, for filling and decorating cakes and pastries, and as the filling for a basic truffle. The ratio of chocolate to cream determines the consistency of the product after it cools, in both Ganache and Quick Ganache (page 843), the ratio is approximately 2:1.

The formula here is ideal if you are adding flavorings containing a high level of moisture (such as spirits and liqueurs), as the additional fat from the egg yolks, in addition to the fat in the cocoa butter, helps stabilize the mixture. Ganache can easily be adjusted to individual needs. For a firmer ganache, add more chocolate; for a softer ganache, decrease the amount. By not overworking the ganache when adding flavorings or when softening it, you will preserve the rich, dark color. If you do want a lighter and fluffier ganache, incorporate air by first softening the ganache over simmering water; then, using the paddle attachment, cream for a few minutes.

8 egg yolks (⅔ cup/160 ml)

8 ounces (225 g) granulated sugar

2 teaspoons (10 ml) vanilla extract

3 pounds 8 ounces (1 kg 590 g) sweet dark chocolate

1 quart (960 ml) heavy cream

1. Whip the egg yolks, sugar, and vanilla until light and fluffy.

2. Cut the chocolate into small pieces, place in a saucepan, and add the cream. Heat to 150°F (65°C), stirring constantly.

3. Stir the hot cream mixture into the egg yolk mixture and keep stirring for a minute or so to make sure the sugar is melted. If you plan to whip air into the ganache, keep stirring at low speed until it is cold, then whip it for a few minutes until it is light and fluffy.

4. Let the ganache cool and store it in airtight containers to use as needed. Ganache can be stored at room temperature for up to 1 week; it should be refrigerated for longer storage.

NOTE: If a skin or crust forms on the top during storage, pour hot water on top of the ganache, let it stand for 1 minute, then pour the water off. If needed, ganache can be stored in the freezer for months. If the sugar has recrystallized, or if all of the sugar was not dissolved in the first place, heat the ganache in a saucepan over low heat, stirring constantly, until all of the sugar crystals have dissolved, around 150°F (65°C).

Quick Ganache yield: 6 cups (I L 440 ml)

This is my version of what is known in the industry as *basic ganache* or *2:1 ratio ganache*, meaning it is made with 2 parts dark chocolate to 1 part heavy cream by weight. If you are in a real hurry, you can leave out both the invert sugar and the butter. I use them to improve the shine when the ganache has cooled and set, making it suitable to use as a glaze, which is frequently done in a pinch.

2 cups (480 ml) heavy cream

2 ounces (55 g) glucose *or* light corn syrup

2 ounces (55 g) unsalted butter

2 pounds (910 g) sweet dark chocolate, chopped into fine pieces

1. Place the cream, glucose or corn syrup, and the butter in a saucepan and bring the mixture to a boil.

2. Remove from the heat and add the chopped chocolate, stirring constantly until the chocolate is completely melted and the mixture is homogenous.

NOTE: To make a slightly softer basic ganache, one particularly well suited to use as a glaze, increase the amount of cream by 1 cup (240 ml)—3 cups/720 ml total—the glucose or corn syrup by 1 ounce (30 g)—3 ounces/85 g total—and the butter by 1 ounce (30 g)—3 ounces/85 g total.

Italian Cream yield: 7 cups (I L 680 ml)

This is a great rich-looking and rich-tasting cream filling that you can enjoy while saving yourself some calories and cholesterol at the same time. Italian cream can be used as a substitute for Quick Bavarian Cream in any of the recipes in this book.

2 cups (480 ml) heavy cream

2 teaspoons (10 ml) vanilla extract

¼ recipe Italian Meringue (page 27) (see Note, page 331)

1. Whip the heavy cream and vanilla to soft peaks.

2. Fold the cream into the Italian meringue. Refrigerate until needed. This filling should be used the same day it is made.

Lemon Cream yield: 7 cups (I L 680 ml)

3 cups (720 ml) lemon juice

½ cup (120 ml) orange juice

Finely grated zest of 6 lemons

Finely grated zest of 2 oranges

2 tablespoons (16 g) cornstarch

1 pound 8 ounces (680 g) granulated sugar

12 eggs

6 ounces (170 g) unsalted butter

¾ cup (180 ml) heavy cream

1. Combine the lemon juice, orange juice, lemon zest, and orange zest. Set aside.

2. Mix the cornstarch into the sugar. Beat the eggs and the sugar mixture for a few seconds (just to combine) in a heavy saucepan made of stainless steel or another noncorrosive material; do not use aluminum. Add the juice and zest mixture, then the butter and heavy cream.

3. Bring to the scalding point, stirring constantly, over medium heat; do not boil. Strain immediately. Use hot, as directed in individual recipes, or cool. Store, covered, in the refrigerator for up to 3 weeks.

Lemon Curd yield: 5 cups (I L 200 ml)

Lemon curd makes an excellent flavoring or filling and can also be used as a sauce by thinning with lemon juice or simple syrup. You will need approximately 8 medium lemons for the juice in the recipe.

1½ cups (360 ml) lemon juice

Finely grated zest of 8 lemons

8 eggs

1 pound 8 ounces (680 g) granulated sugar

12 ounces (340 g) unsalted butter

1. Combine the lemon juice and zest.

2. Beat the eggs and sugar together in a heavy saucepan made of stainless steel or other noncorrosive material; do not use aluminum. Add the lemon juice and zest and the butter.

3. Heat to boiling over low heat. Cook for a few seconds, stirring constantly, until the curd thickens. Strain immediately. Cool and use as needed. Lemon curd will keep for weeks stored, covered, in the refrigerator.

Lime Cream yield: 2 cups (480 ml)

1¾ cups (420 ml) freshly squeezed lime juice (from approximately 7 limes)

Finely grated zest of 3 limes

3 eggs

8 ounces (225 g) granulated sugar

2 ounces (55 g) unsalted butter

¼ cup (60 ml) heavy cream

1. Combine the lime juice and the grated zest. Set aside.

2. Beat the eggs and sugar together in a heavy noncorrosive saucepan, just long enough to combine (do not use an aluminum pan). Add the juice and zest mixture, the butter, and the heavy cream. Bring the mixture to the scalding point, stirring constantly over medium heat. Do not boil.

3. Remove from the heat and strain immediately. Set aside to cool.

4. Stored, covered, in the refrigerator, the lime cream can be kept for 2 to 3 weeks. Thin with water if necessary before using.

Pastry Cream yield: 6 pounds (2 kg 730 g)

Making pastry cream is one of the basic techniques that anyone involved with cooking (pastry shop or otherwise) should master, because pastry cream has so many applications. In an emergency, it can be thinned and used as a sauce; it is a base for soufflés; it is a filling and flavoring for cakes and fruit tarts; and it can be used as a topping for Danish or other pastries. In the pastry kitchen, a supply of pastry cream should always be in the refrigerator.

Because pastry cream is made with cornstarch to stabilize the eggs, it is in no danger of overheating and curdling, as can happen, for example, with crème anglaise. Of course, you must still watch the heat and stir constantly to avoid burning the custard or having it lump.

2 quarts (1 L 920 ml) whole milk

2 vanilla beans *or* 2 teaspoons (10 ml) vanilla extract

5 ounces (140 g) cornstarch

1 pound (455 g) granulated sugar

1 teaspoon (5 g) salt

6 eggs

6 ounces (170 g) unsalted butter

Small-Batch Recipe Pastry Cream
yield: 1 pound 8 ounces (680 g)

1 pint (480 ml) whole milk

½ vanilla bean *or* ½ teaspoon (2.5 ml) vanilla extract

1 ounce (30 g) cornstarch

4 ounces (115 g) granulated sugar

¼ teaspoon (1 g) salt

2 eggs

2 ounces (55 g) unsalted butter

---

1. Place the milk in a heavy-bottomed saucepan. If using the vanilla bean(s), split lengthwise and scrape out the seeds. Add the seeds and the pod halves to the milk. Bring to a boil.

2. Keeping an eye on the milk, whisk the cornstarch, sugar, and salt together in a bowl. Gradually add the eggs and mix until smooth.

3. Slowly add about one-third of the hot milk to the egg mixture while whisking rapidly. Pour the tempered egg mixture back into the remaining milk.

4. Place over medium heat and cook, stirring constantly, until the mixture comes to a boil and thickens. Boil for a few seconds longer to make sure the raw starch taste has disappeared. Remove the vanilla bean(s), rinse, and save for another use. Stir in the vanilla extract, if using. Stir in the butter continuing to stir until it is completely incorporated.

5. Pour the custard into a bowl and cover with a piece of baking paper. When cooled, store in the refrigerator. If made and stored properly, pastry cream will keep fresh for up to 4 days. However, when it is that old, it should be used only for pastries in which it will be baked.

NOTE: If the heat is too high or you are stirring too slowly at the point when the pastry cream reaches a boil, it will lump. If this happens, pass it through a strainer immediately, before it cools.

Quick Bavarian Cream yield: approximately 3 pounds 12 ounces (1 kg 705 g), or 9 cups (2 L 160 ml)

This is not a classic Bavarian cream. In fact, it is closer to a Diplomat cream, but it can be used for many of the same applications and it is a real timesaver because it uses pastry cream, a stock item in most pastry kitchens, as a prefabricated base. This eliminates the need for making a custard and waiting for it cool. If you do not have pastry cream on hand, you might want to make the Classic Bavarian Cream instead (page 840). If you are making pastry cream specifically to use in this recipe, make it far enough in advance so that it is thoroughly chilled before you combine it with the whipped cream or you risk breaking the cream.

1½ cups (360 ml) heavy cream
½ teaspoon (2.5 ml) vanilla extract

½ recipe Pastry Cream made with vanilla bean (page 845)

1. Whip the heavy cream and vanilla to stiff peaks.

2. Fold the whipped cream into the pastry cream. Use as directed in the individual recipes.

Ingredients

A

Absinthe—Absinthe has a fascinating history; in fact, entire books have been written about this legendary emerald-green liquor. It is made from the plant wormwood (so named because it is used to kill intestinal parasites) and flavored with a multitude of herbs. The original recipe was created by Dr. Ordinaire, a Frenchman living in Switzerland at the time, and is said to have contained anise, hyssop, dittany, sweet flag, coriander, veronica, chamomile, and parsley. It is very potent (136 proof) and has been called everything from a powerful aphrodisiac to addictive and deadly. Dr. Ordinaire sold his recipe to a Swiss man named Henri-Louis Pernod (see **Pernod**), who was the first to produce absinthe commercially. Although made in Switzerland, absinthe has always been associated with France and the decadent artists of Paris in the late 1800s. Famous advocates and partakers of absinthe include Vincent van Gogh, Oscar Wilde, Henri de Toulouse-Lautrec, and Pablo Picasso. During its heyday in France, it was known as the Green Fairy and the Green One. Because the flavor alone is very bitter, absinthe was usually served with sugar and water. As the water was added, the mixture would turn an opalescent green, a fact mentioned often in poems applauding its virtues. In addition to poetry describing absinthe's supposed wondrous ability to eliminate all cares, the drink inspired hundreds of French paintings depicting every conceivable related image, from the drinkers themselves to the bottles absinthe was distilled in, the decanters and glasses used for service, the cafés where it was served, and so on. At the same time, cartoons and posters warned the public of its ill effects. In France during the 1880s, a slang name for absinthe was *une correspondance,* a shortened version of the phrase *une correspondance pour Charenton,* which translates to "a ticket to Charenton," Charenton being an insane asylum just outside of Paris. Doctors claimed it caused damage to the central nervous system and digestive system, caused amnesia, and produced convulsions, hallucinations, violence, epileptic seizures, tuberculosis, criminal behavior, and insanity! Scientific studies conducted in the 1970s concluded that absinthe produced similar psychological effects to those induced by the use of marijuana.

While many, if not most, countries have gone through a general prohibition phase, absinthe is the only alcoholic beverage that has ever been banned individually. By the time World War I began, absinthe had already been banished everywhere other than England, Spain, and France (the Department of Agriculture declared absinthe illegal in the Unites States on 25 July 1912). Following tremendous debate and political pressure from both sides that lasted many years, it was finally the war that brought about the end of absinthe in France. When the Germans declared war on France on 3 August 1914, the government ordered the police to prohibit the sale of absinthe by declaring a state of emergency. Two weeks later, the minister of the interior gave the same order and included any drinks that were at all similar to absinthe. With this support behind them, the Chamber of Deputies voted on 4 March 1915 to ban the production, circulation, and sale of absinthe in France. The party was over, but the legend lives on.

Acerola—This is both the name of a shrublike tree of the Caribbean and that of its fruit. The name *acerola* refers to the tree's resemblance to the Mediterranean tree *azarole*. The acerola fruit resembles a small cherry; it is dark red and sweet, yet tart; some say it is closer in flavor to a raspberry. Acerola is also known by the names *West Indies cherry, Puerto Rican cherry,* and *Barbados cherry;* scientifically, it is classified as *Malpighia punicifolia*. The trees grow, for the most part, in the West Indies but have been adapted for cultivation in the United States. Acerola cherries are extremely high in vitamin C (having 20 times that of oranges when compared by weight) and are used for juice and in preserves.

Aceto dolce—From Italy, *aceto dolce* is a fruit spread, served like jam, made from fruit preserved in vinegar that is then cooked with grape juice and honey. *Aceto* means "vinegar" in Italian, and *dolce* means "sweet."

Acetomel—A mixture of honey and vinegar that was used prevalently many years ago for the preservation of hard fruits such as pears, apples, and quinces. The name comes from two Latin words—*acetum,* meaning "vinegar," and *mel,* meaning "honey." See also **Aceto dolce** and **Hydromel**.

Acid—An acid produces the sour flavor found in various foods; the term also denotes a chemical intensity. If hydrogen is produced when a substance is submerged in a water solution, that substance is acid to some degree. The degree of acidity is expressed by the hydrogen concentration, commonly known as *pH*. The pH scale goes from 0 to 14, with

0 being very acid and 14 being very alkaline (the opposite of acid). At the center of the scale, with a reading of 7, is pure water, which is neutral. The word *acid* comes from the Latin *acidus,* meaning "sour." Some naturally occurring acids are found in vinegar (acetic acid), wine (tartaric acid), lemon juice (citric acid), sour milk (lactic acid), and apples (malic acid). Acids can be used as tenderizers because they break down connective tissue and cell walls. They are also used to give foods a tart taste and, in wine, they make the flavor more interesting and complex. The citric acid in lemon juice is used to prevent cut fruit from oxidizing (see **Acidulated water**), and acids help to coagulate proteins, which is why lemon juice or vinegar is added to the water used when poaching eggs. A small amount of acid such as lemon juice, tartaric acid, or cream of tartar is used in making meringue in order to lower the pH level in the albumen (the egg white). Citric acid is also added to both the dough and the butter block in the production of puff pastry to make the dough more pliable.

Acidophilus—*Lactobacillus acidophilus* is a bacterium found in fresh milk. The bacterium is destroyed during pasteurization, but it is possible to isolate this element and return it to milk or yogurt. The advantage of acidophilus milk and acidophilus yogurt is their ability to help those who have a low tolerance to the milk sugar lactose (making it difficult or impossible for them to digest milk without dietary upset) in that the bacteria help consume the lactose during the digestive process.

Acidulate; Acidulated water—To acidulate a food item means to make it slightly acid, most often by adding lemon juice or vinegar. Acidulated water (water that has been mixed with an acid, typically lemon juice) is commonly used to prevent cut pieces of fresh fruit from becoming brown from exposure to air. The fruit may be placed in enough acidulated water to cover it completely, or it may simply be tossed with enough to coat the cut surfaces. Approximately 1 tablespoon (15 ml) lemon juice per 1 quart (960 ml) of water is sufficient.

Acorn—Acorns are the nut of the oak tree. All acorns are edible, although most varieties are more suitable for animal consumption than for humans. White oak acorns may be eaten raw; other varieties must be cooked or leached to remove tannic acids. Along with hickory nuts, acorns were a staple food among many Native American tribes, particularly those in what is now northern California. Both nutmeats were used in soups and stews and were ground to form a paste used to thicken the same. The nuts were also dried and ground, then cooked in much the same way as cornmeal mush. The Hupa, Karok, Miwok, Pomo, and Yurok tribes were famous for the large conical baskets that were woven specifically to hold the harvested acorns.

Additives—Food additives are used to enhance flavor, improve nutritional quality, prolong shelf life, assist in preparation or manufacture, and to add visual appeal to food products. The food additives that would likely be used in the average restaurant pastry kitchen are generally limited to those already present in purchased ingredients. A high quality operation selling freshly prepared goods every day is unlikely to have a shelf full of chemicals and preservatives. This is not to say, however, that all items classified as food additives are artificial or unfavorable. Anti-caking agents are found in powdered cake or custard mixes and some flours, and preservatives may be present in purchased "halfway-products" such as candy fillings and nut pastes. Probably the only food additives used in preparation on any regular basis are food colorings, flavoring extracts, and thickening agents.

Agar-agar—Today, agar-agar, which is a Malaysian word for jelly, is simply known as *agar*. This natural vegetable-based substance is extracted from a type of Japanese seaweed and is used in the pastry kitchen to thicken and jell products in the same way as gelatin. It can be purchased in its natural form—greenish strips that look something like dried noodles—or in a more convenient fine powder. The strips must be soaked for a minimum of 12 hours prior to use. Imported powders can vary tremendously in both strength and quality, depending on the brand, so it is best to test and determine the gel strength before using it in your final product. In this text, I use agar powder classified as U.S.P.N.F. This is a pharmaceutical-grade product (which means it is approved for use in or on the body) that can be purchased from a chemical laboratory or by special order from your drugstore. The pharmaceutical-grade product is 8 to 12 times stronger than gelatin (brands and types of gelatin vary in strength as well). When using pharmaceutical-grade agar powder, it is not necessary to soften it before dissolving but it must be heated close or all the way to the boiling point to dissolve fully. Although enzymes do not affect agar, acids do, so when making jellies, for example, it is important to add a flavoring, such as a fruit puree, after the agar and the other ingredients are cooked, or the jelly will not set completely.

Agar is used when a very strong thickening agent is required—in certain meringues, pastries, jellies, and ice creams, for example. Because agar is not protein based like gelatin, it can be used as a thickening agent with raw tropical fruits that contain an enzyme such as bromelin or papain without the necessity of boiling the fruit first, as must be done when using gelatin. A product set with agar can also withstand a very high temperature without melting, making it popular in hot tropical climates. Because it comes from a vegetable rather than animal source, agar-agar is also suitable for consumption by vegetarians and in kosher preparations.

Albumen—The white portion of an egg.

Albumin—The protein found in egg whites. Albumin is one of a group of heat-coagulating proteins that are soluble in water. Albumin is also found in blood plasma, milk, and most animal tissues, as well as vegetable tissues including peas, wheat, and soybean. In addition to coagulating (thickening) when heated, albumin coagulates, to a lesser extent, when whipped, the obvious example being the whipping of egg whites.

Alchermes—A vibrant red liqueur from Italy. It has a spicy flavor and is used as both a flavoring and coloring agent in miscellaneous Italian confections.

Algin (sodium alginate)—Algin is extracted from kelp. Algin and sodium alginate are used as stabilizers in the commercial production of ice creams and sorbets. Some algin products made for the industry combine sodium alginate with sugar and sodium citrate. The base mixture must be at 155° to 160°F (68° to 71°C) when the algin is added in order for it to dissolve.

Alkali—Any of several chemical compounds that react when combined with an acid product or ingredient to form a salt, thereby neutralizing the acidic property of the ingredient. The most common example in the pastry kitchen is the use of baking soda (an alkali) to neutralize the acid when using dairy products such as sour cream or buttermilk in a cake batter. As the baking soda neutralizes the acid, the result is the release of carbon dioxide gas, which, in turn, forms air bubbles, causing the cake to rise.

Alligator pear—A name sometimes used for the avocado, it is, for the most part, out of date. See **Avocado.**

All-purpose flour—See **Flour.**

Allspice—Many people mistakenly believe allspice to be a manufactured combination of spices. It is actually the berry of the *Pimenta dioica* tree, an evergreen belonging to the myrtle family that is indigenous to Central and South America and the West Indies. (This pimento tree is not the same as the sweet red-fleshed pepper known as *pimientó,* familiar to many as the stuffing in green martini olives and as the source of paprika.) The name *allspice* is a consequence of its flavor being similar to a combination of cinnamon, nutmeg, and cloves. The pea-sized dried berries are reddish brown and are available both whole and ground. The flavor is superior if stored in the whole form and ground just before use. Jamaica currently produces most of the world's supply, so allspice is sometimes called *Jamaican pepper.* Allspice is used in cookies, cakes, and pies and is often an ingredient in pumpkin pie recipes. It is also used in savory cooking.

Almond—The name *almond* is used both to identify a type of tree (a member of the rose family) and the kernel of its fruit. Almonds are native to western Asia; they now grow wild and are commercially cultivated throughout southern Europe and are grown commercially in the United States. Almond wood is a reddish color and is used for furniture. There are two types of almonds: sweet almonds, which are available in markets and are used for cooking and eating, and bitter almonds, which contain prussic acid (toxic except in small amounts) and are used for flavorings and extracts. Almonds are widely used in the pastry shop as an ingredient in breads and cookies as well as to decorate many cakes, pastries, and Danish pastries. Almonds are available in a variety of forms—whole, sliced, slivered, and ground—and all of these, except slivered, can be purchased natural (skin on) or

blanched (skin off). Almond extracts and flavorings are also widely used, and almonds are, of course, used to make almond paste and marzipan, two other important products in professional baking. The elongated almonds grown in Málaga, Spain, are known as *Jordan almonds* (not to be confused with the candy by the same name). These and the wider almonds of Valencia, Spain, are favored by connoisseurs and command the highest commercial prices. The almonds grown in Sicily are also considered to be very fine.

Almond extract—A potent flavoring made from either sweet or bitter almond oil and alcohol. Because its flavor is so intense, especially when made from bitter almonds, care should be taken not to use too much.

Almond meal; Almond flour—Both terms are used to describe blanched almonds that have been ground very finely; the finished consistency is similar to granulated sugar. This product can be purchased already prepared. To make it yourself, you need a high-power food processor in order to achieve the same consistency of the commercial product. If you are making your own almond flour for use in a recipe that contains granulated sugar, add a portion of the sugar to the almonds when you process them to help prevent caking. In any case, be very careful not to allow the almond oil to extrude and form a paste, which will happen if the mixture becomes too warm and/or is overprocessed.

Almond paste—A moist mixture of finely ground blanched almonds and sugar (generally 50-50 by weight) that has a doughlike consistency. Almond paste has many applications in the pastry kitchen. It is the primary ingredient in macaroons, marzipan, Hippen decorating paste, and frangipane filling, and is used to flavor cake and cookie batters and numerous pastry and cookie fillings.

Amande—French for "almond."

Amande amère—French for "bitter almonds."

Amaretto; Amaretto di Saronno—An almond-flavored liqueur from northern Italy. The primary flavor comes from both sweet and bitter almonds, and the name comes from the Italian word *amaro,* meaning "bitter."

Amino acid—Amino acids are the main components of proteins. Twenty types are classified scientifically as "important" and, of those, half are considered "essential" for human survival (see below). A living cell creates protein when two amino acids link to form a bond. This first group is then linked to a third, and so on, until a long chain is produced. This chainlike molecule may contain up to several hundred amino acid subgroups or links. A protein may be formed of a single chain, or it may consist of several chains held together by molecular bonds. Most plants are able to make all the amino acids they require for growth. Humans, however, must obtain some of the standard amino acids from their diet; these amino acids are called "essential" and include lysine, tryptophan, valine, histidine, leucine, isoleucine, phenylalanine, threonine, methionine, and arginine. They are found in protein-rich foods from animal sources (such as meat and dairy products) and in some plant proteins. The process of breaking down these bonded proteins is a large part of both cooking and digesting food.

Ammonium carbonate—Ammonium carbonate (or bicarbonate) was once known by the name *hartshorn* because it was originally produced from harts' horns and hooves (a hart is a male deer). Today's commercial product is a chemical, specifically the ammonium salt of carbonic acid. Ammonium carbonate is used mainly in cookies and short dough to produce a longer-lasting crisp texture; it can also be used in pâte à choux to give it an extra puff. Ammonium carbonate can be used as a substitute for baking soda and baking powder, but only in cookies or doughs with very little moisture or in pastries that are baked at a high temperature. Unlike baking soda and baking powder, ammonium carbonate must be dissolved in water before it is added to a dry product. Ammonium carbonate reacts to heat, producing water, ammonia, and dioxide gas. It has a very strong odor that completely disappears above 140°F (60°C). It must always be stored in an airtight container or it will quickly evaporate. Ammonium carbonate can be difficult to find from bakery suppliers, but can be ordered from a chemist or local laboratory.

Amylose—One of the elements of starch, amylose is characterized by its straight chains of glucose units. This is the soluble component in the starch that forms a gel; to simplify, amylose is the part of starch that dissolves and later sets up.

Ananas—French, German, and Swedish for "pineapple."

Angelica—Angelica is an impressive plant, often growing to 6 feet (1 m 80 cm) and taller. It is a member of the parsley and carrot family and is native to northern Europe. The Vikings introduced it to France, where it was cultivated by monks, but today angelica can be found, both cultivated and growing wild, along the Mediterranean and in North America. All parts of this strongly aromatic plant are edible; the leaves and roots are used for infusions such as tea and to flavor sweet wines and liqueurs, and both the stalk and roots are boiled in some countries and eaten as a vegetable. In the seventeenth and eighteenth centuries, so-called angel water, derived from angelica, was a popular beauty treatment used for washing the face.

In the pastry kitchen, it is the celerylike stalks of candied angelica (unfortunately, often spiked with too much green food coloring) that we know best. These are used to decorate cakes and pastries, and even though a bit old-fashioned today, their color makes a nice addition to fruitcakes and other holiday treats. Candied angelica will keep indefinitely if stored, well wrapped, in the refrigerator to prevent it from drying out. The essential oil obtained from the roots of the plant is used to flavor **Chartreuse** and **Bénédictine** liqueurs.

Anise seed—Like so many other aromatic herbs, anise is native to the Middle East. It is botanically related to caraway, cumin, fennel, and dill, and the proper name for the anise plant is *Pimpinella anisum*. The greenish-brown comma-shaped seeds of this tall annual plant are used to flavor many confectionery dishes as well as savory and are an important flavoring for liqueurs, such as the French anisette, and apéritifs, like Greek **ouzo** and the French **pastis**. Anise is also used to flavor **Pernod**. Anise oil has an antiseptic quality and is used in toothpaste and to repel insects. Anise oil is also the traditional flavoring agent for springerle cookies. An infusion made of anise seeds sweetened with honey is said to be a good digestive aid. Anise seeds should be bought whole and ground as needed. The seeds should be stored in a cool, dark place but, even so, they do not retain their scent very well, and it is best to purchase a small quantity at a time. Anise is used to flavor gingerbreads, pretzels, biscotti, and crackerbreads.

Anisette—A liqueur made from anise. It is clear, very sweet, and tastes like licorice.

Anjou pear—See **Pear**.

Annatto—Used as a colorant in cheese, shortening, and margarine, annatto comes from the seeds of the tree *Bixa orellanna*, commonly called the *annatto tree*. The seeds themselves are called *achiote seeds*, and the substance called *annatto* or *annatto extract* is the coloring agent derived from the seeds. The main component is bizin, known chemically as $C_{25}H_{30}0_4$. Annatto can be used to produce a tint from light yellow to deep orange. The ground seeds can be purchased as a paste, generally labeled *achiote*. Annatto was used as a food coloring, primarily for cheeses, as long ago as the 1600s.

Annonae—The fruits of certain tropical tree species called *Annona*. The best known in this group is the cherimoya, also known as a *custard apple*. See **Cherimoya**.

Applejack—Brandy made from apple cider. Applejack varies from 80 to 100 proof. In France, apple brandy is known as **Calvados**, which is also the area of Normandy famous for both its apples and its cream. Apple brandy is most often used in desserts that contain apples as a primary ingredient. Deglazing sautéed apples with apple brandy, for instance, is a great way to intensify the apple flavor and add another dimension to the taste at the same time.

Apple—The word *apple* is used to identify many varieties of trees (all of which are related to the rose family) as well as the fruit that the trees bear, which varies considerably in size, shape, and color. Apple tree blossoms are particularly pretty and can be white or striped with pink or red. The wood of the apple tree is used in making fine furniture and for wooden casks used to age brandy, and apple wood is utilized for smoking pork products such as ham and bacon. Most of us can remember a particular variety of apple that we enjoyed eating in childhood, or climbing on the moss-covered branches of an old gnarled apple tree that looked as though it had been there forever. In fact, it is not uncommon for apple trees to live a century or more. The longest-lived apple tree in the United States was reportedly planted in Manhattan in 1647 and was still bearing fruit when it was, unfortunately, struck down by a derailed train in 1866.

Apples grow in temperate climates worldwide. They do not do well in areas with very hot weather, as they require a long dormant period each year that takes place only when the temperature is very cold or reaches freezing. The atmospheric conditions of most northern European countries are excellent for apple cultivation, with Sweden, located in the far north, perhaps topping the list. Even though the Normandy region of France is quite well known for its apples and its famous apple brandy, and Austria, of course, is celebrated for its apple strudel, it still seems that much of Europe closely associates apples with Sweden. This took me by surprise as I began to travel outside of Sweden and found many apple desserts, cakes, and pastries—in Austria, Switzerland, and Germany, for example—with *Sweden* or *Swedish* (*Schweden* or *Schwedisch*) as part of their title, meant to convey that the dish contained apples.

More than 20,000 varieties of apple are grown throughout the world but, of course, far fewer are sold commercially in the United States. Apples are generally classified as eating apples, cooking apples, or all-purpose apples. They are used in breakfast breads and pastries, tea cakes, apple strudel, apple charlotte, apple pies and tarts, and applesauce. Many apples are also commercially preserved by canning and drying and are manufactured into pasteurized juice, cider, and apple vinegar. In some recipes where the apples will be cooked into a filling, canned apples may be substituted for fresh. Apples are also used to make fermented cider and brandy. For long storage, apples should be kept in a cool place or in the refrigerator. They will keep for many months this way, especially the winter varieties. It is important however, to check them frequently and remove any that have gone bad—for, as the saying goes, one rotten apple can indeed spoil the whole lot.

History and Cultivation of Apples

The native home of the apple is not known for certain, but it *is* known that apples were enjoyed by the ancient Greeks and Romans. Apples came to America with European settlers and were brought toward the west by travelers. One famous historical figure is John Chapman, known as Johnny Appleseed, who was responsible for planting a multitude of apple trees throughout the Midwest. He is said to have been an eccentric but very smart businessman (and a student of Swedenborgian religious philosophy, no less). Another individual who gained his fame from the apple was Wilhelm Tell of Switzerland. While the story of his extraordinary marksmanship is legendary, few people seem to know that he was not attempting to show off his skill (nor was he simply being incredibly foolish) when he successfully shot through an apple placed on top of his son's head, using a bow and arrow. He had been sentenced to do so for refusing to pay homage to a symbol of the German emperor.

It is generally accepted that modern apple varieties are the result of natural cross-pollination involving many ancestors; these varieties are heterozygous, meaning that they do not reproduce authentically to type. For example, when growers set out to create hybrids, each tree (seedling) is selected to contribute half of the heritage. There is still an unknown element, however, because characteristics eventually may be produced by the new tree that were hidden in one of the parent trees. So the result—either improvement as hoped for, or the cultivation of an inferior species—is not known until the tree matures to fruit-bearing size. Apple trees are propagated by grafting; a bud from the desired varietal, called a *scion*, is inserted into the base of the seedling tree, known as the *rootstock*. The stock itself may be from a propagated (hybrid) tree but, in most cases, buds are developed on seedling trees. For home gardeners as well as large commercial operations, rootstocks are selected not only in an attempt to create a certain improvement or change in the fruit but also to control the size of the trees. Uniform tree height is important for commercial orchards, and dwarf rootstocks are popular where space is an issue. Certain apple varieties are heads of large groups or families. The descendants of these families are "born" in one of two ways: either as a direct result of planned breeding and cultivation or as a natural genetic change or mutation. Unplanned genetic alterations can occur at any time and without obvious reason. Suddenly, one tree branch is different from the others and produces a variation in bud and fruit; these are referred to in the fruit-growing industry as *sports*. In the majority of cases, sports have no value but, just as many inventions throughout history have come about as a result of an accident, here too, once in a while, a sport develops into a significant new strain.

The Three Primary Apple Varieties

Delicious is the best-known apple variety of modern times. These apples were first grown in an Iowa orchard in 1870. The original tree is thought to have been a seedling of a bellflower tree that was growing close by. History tells us that the owner, Jessie Hiatt, cut down the tree not once but twice, but it continued to sprout anew, and he finally let it be. Ten years later, when the tree had reached maturity, it produced some of the best apples Mr. Hiatt had ever tasted. Naturally occurring sports produced redder apples, including Red Queen, Royal Red, and Hi Early. Grafting spurs from the Delicious include Oregon Spur, Wellspur, and Starkrimson. Delicious is also a parent of the Melrose.

McIntosh, the oldest of the three primary apple varieties, was discovered by John McIntosh at his Canadian nursery around 1810. The strain did not become available until 1835, however, when the grafting technique was fully developed. McIntosh apples were widely known by the beginning of the 1900s. Macintosh trees produce the best-known spurs (used for grafting), known as *Macspurs.* Very popular in breeding, some of the better-known descendants are Macoun, Empire, Cortland, Summer Red, and Spartan.

Jonathon was first planted in Kingston, New York, from seeds from a Spitzenberg variety. The story goes that a judge from Albany, New York, liked the apple well enough to introduce it to the horticultural society, and he named the variety Jonathon after the person who had given him the first of these apples that he had tasted. Jonathon was the most popular apple variety in the United States until it was surpassed by Delicious. Sports of Jonathon are Jon-a-Red and Jonnee (also a red variety). Hybrids include Jonagold, Idared, Melrose, and Monroe.

Common Apple Varieties

Baldwin—A small red apple, sometimes featuring yellow stripes, with a slight acid taste; a good choice for baking and juicing. Season: Late fall.

Cortland—An American apple, born in New York in 1906 by crossing the Ben Franklin and McIntosh varieties. Cortlands are mostly dark red with yellow patches. The skin is shiny and slightly oily to the touch. They have a slightly tart flavor and the flesh has excellent resistance to browning when cut. Season: Late fall, but its good keeping quality makes it available most of the year.

Empire—This crisp, tasty all-purpose American apple was created by crossing McIntosh with Red Delicious, which produced its green skin with large red spots and/or streaks. Its flavor is similar to McIntosh, but it keeps longer and does not bruise as easily. Season: Generally available year round.

Fuji—An attractive medium apple. Its skin is a beautiful combination of orange and red over a pale yellow background, sprinkled here and there with dark brown to black dots. The flesh is firm and pale yellow. Fuji apples are great for baking and poaching but not a good choice to cook all the way down to a puree for applesauce or a filling. Their good looks make them popular for fruit baskets and displays. Season: Generally year round.

Gala—This apple originated in New Zealand as a result of crossing the English Cox Orange Pippin with both of the Delicious varieties, Red and Golden. The apples are a soft yellow color with pinkish streaks. They are very attractive and good for eating out of hand, but only fair for cooking. Season: Year round in most markets.

Golden Delicious—Born in West Virginia at the end of the nineteenth century, this is now one of the most popular apples in many countries. Its distinctive elongated shape ends in five small points. The flavor and texture can vary with the climate where the apples are grown. Golden Delicious apples have a pale green to yellow skin and are excellent for eating out of hand, but they are also great for baking because they keep retain their shape well when cooked. For this reason, I specify Delicious in my recipe for Tarte Tatin. Season: Early fall, but available year round.

Granny Smith—These apples originated in the mid-1800s in Australia, where they were developed—believe it or not—by a grandmother with the family name of Smith! Granny Smith apples have been cultivated in the United States for only about 30 years. If left to ripen properly, they are among the best all-around apples on the market and an excellent choice for your garden. They are slightly squat, usually fairly large, and have a dark green skin that, surprisingly, stays dark even when the apples are fully ripe. Season: Year round.

Gravenstein—This pretty summer apple was first produced at the Danish castle Graasten, which is located in the mostly German-speaking area of the Slesvig countryside (near the border of Germany and Denmark), so the Germans lay claim to the Gravenstein as well as the Danes. It was transplanted to the United States in the 1820s and today is very popular, especially in California, where we mostly see the variety with yellowish, pink to red streaks against a green background. In Europe, and especially in Scandinavia, yellow and deep red Gravensteins are also quite popular. Rounded and plump, with a crisp texture and distinct acid flavor, they are good for both cooking and eating out of hand. Season: Early summer to early fall. Not a good keeper.

Greening—Also known as Rhode Island Greening, this apple was introduced in the mid 1700s by—you guessed it—a fellow named Green, who also happened to live at Green's End, Rhode Island—and yes, the apple itself is green! Greenings are good for eating but even better for cooking and baking. Season: Mid-fall to spring.

Ida Red—Also spelled *Idared,* this American apple was crossbred in the 1940s using the Jonathon and Wagener varieties. It is one of the largest of our common apples and, as the name implies, is red in color, but it does have a touch of yellow. Although these make a fair eating apple, they really excel for baking due to their firm texture and medium acidity. Season: Fall through spring. This is a great keeper.

Jonagold—As its name reveals, this is a cross between the two better-known apple varieties, Jonathon and Golden Delicious, and it has characteristics of both. Firm and sweet, these are good for cooking and baking. Season: Early fall to late winter.

Jonathon—One of the apple ancestors (see history above), the Jonathon is a good all-around apple, very crisp, medium acid, with a light red skin. It is not a good keeper. Season: Very short; early fall to Thanksgiving.

Macoun—A large red apple developed from crossbreeding with the McIntosh but originating in America. Great for eating out of hand and also cooks well. Season: Short; early fall to the end of the year.

McIntosh—Originally from Canada and developed at the start of the 1800s, the apple is named for the man who discovered it, John McIntosh (see history above). It is medium in size and greenish yellow with red streaks. McIntosh apples have a nice, tart, juicy bite but are not a good choice for cooking. Season: Year round.

Northern Spy—A red American apple, large to medium in

size. It resembles the Baldwin, but with some green flecks and, more importantly, a better flavor. An excellent all-purpose apple that is a favorite of many apple connoisseurs. Season: Fall to late winter.

Pippin—This green to golden apple dates back to the sixteenth century, when it originated in France. It has many hybrids, the most common, in the United States, being the Newton Pippin and, more recently, the Ribston. The Cox Orange Pippin is very popular in Europe. Season: Fall to early spring, but one variety or another can often be found all year.

Red Delicious—Also known simply as *Delicious,* this apple was born in Iowa in the late 1800s (see history above). It is the most popular apple in America, large and handsome, and a must for decorative fruit baskets and displays. The apple's flesh is crisp but the flavor somewhat bland, lacking the acidity and bite that make some of the others more refreshing. It has a very distinctive shape, with well-defined ridges at the base, and although it is the wrong color for a traditional cooking apple, I recommend it (or the Golden Delicious) as the best choice for Tarte Tatin because it holds its shape well after baking. Red Delicious apples tend to develop an unappetizing mushy texture and flavor when they are overripe. Season: Available all year.

Rome Beauty—This American variety was discovered in Rome, Ohio, in the first decades of the 1800s. It is a large, firm red apple best used for baking because it keeps its shape well. Season: Rome Beauty is a good keeper, so its season lasts from mid-fall through the spring.

Stayman—A fine-textured juice apple with a light, tart flavor and firm, crisp skin that is red with green highlights. It is a good all-purpose apple. Season: Late fall through late winter.

Winesap—An American-born apple, dark red with a touch of yellow color, and elongated in shape. It has a firm bite, a great aroma, and, as its name implies, a somewhat fermented winey flavor. Winesaps are good for cooking. Season: Late fall to late winter.

York Imperial—An American apple with a splotchy dark red skin and excellent keeping qualities. It has tart, firm flesh, a very aromatic flavor, and is a good cooking apple to boot. York Imperials are not commonly found in grocery stores; they are mainly used in the food-processing industry. Season: Mid-fall to April.

Antique and Heirloom Apple Varieties

Lady—This beautiful, small, brightly colored apple (which is part of the crab apple family, as any apple tree that produces fruit 2 inches/5 cm or less in diameter is classified as such) is one of many in a distinguished group known as *old apples.* Lady apples originated in France and date all the way back to the Middle Ages. Their gorgeous red color (although you will also find them with a touch of green) and perfectly formed miniature proportions give them a storybook charm that makes them very popular for decorative use, especially around the holidays. The white flesh is sweet, and Lady apples are excellent for use, fresh, on desserts. Season: Late fall to early winter.

Caville Blanc d'Hiver—One of the most famous of all dessert apples in France, this variety is said to have thrived in the gardens of Louis XIII in Orleans, France. Excellent for eating as is, this apple has more than twice as much vitamin C as an orange, and it is a perfect choice for a classic French *tarte aux pommes.* Season: Mid-fall through spring, but you are unlikely to find this variety in the market; it is almost exclusively a home garden apple.

Chenango—Also known as Chenango Strawberry, this variety comes from New York, where it originated in the mid-eighteenth century. The fruit is medium in size, with yellow and white skin heavily striped in red. The flesh is unusual: white with random red and pink marbling throughout. This pretty apple is a good choice for eating fresh or for cooking. Season: Mid- to late fall; does not keep well.

Cox Orange—Also known as Cox Orange Pippin in the United States, where it is probably the best known of the Pippin family, it is also very popular in northern Europe. I can remember the large Cox Orange tree I used to climb in order to reach the apples on the highest branches, which had been left on the tree for the time being. Unfortunately for me, this was something I was not supposed to do, because in addition to being a delicious eating apple, Cox Orange apples were considered *the* apple to keep for long winter storage when I was growing up in Sweden. The origin of this apple, as I learned it in Sweden, is that an English brewmaster by the name of R. Cox planted nine seeds of the old English variety Ribston. Two seeds developed into trees and became the mothers of Cox Orange and its close cousin, Cox Pomona. Cox Orange is one of the best all-around apples; it is deliciously aromatic, with crisp, juicy yellow flesh. It is medium in size and has a golden skin with a pretty dull brownish-green overlay. One of the distinct characteristics of this apple is that its stem always grows at a discernible angle rather than straight up and down. Season: Late fall to early spring.

Pink Pearl—These apples were first cultivated in the 1940s and have only recently regained their popularity. This medium-sized fruit has an unusually colored pink flesh and light green skin, with occasional steaks of red. The flavor varies from quite tart to sweet-tart, depending on climate and, of course, the time of harvest. This apple is a great choice for making decorative apple chips. Season: Early fall to late winter; stores well.

Transparent Blanche—Despite the French word *blanche* in its title (signifying the light color of the apple's skin), this apple originated in Russia and the Baltic states. It is one of the first apples of the season in northern Europe. It has a pleasantly tart flavor and crisp flesh and is good for eating raw and for cooking. This is strictly a gardener's apple rather than a commercial variety because of its poor keeping quality.

White Astrachan—This apple originated in Russia and is one that I grew up eating in Sweden. It is a great apple for all culinary uses. It has a tart flavor, a crisp bite, and firm white flesh. The skin is green and yellow, with blush to darker pink stripes. The Red Astrachan apple has similar characteristics. Season: Early to late fall. Not a good keeper.

Apricot kernel—The soft innermost part of the apricot pit, which is used to make a paste similar to almond paste. Although it has an almondlike flavor, apricot kernel paste has a strong, bitter aftertaste.

Apricot—There are few sights prettier to look at in an orchard or in the home garden than an apricot tree in full bloom in the springtime. These magnificent trees are grown not only for their delicious fruit but also for ornamental purposes and as shade trees. A blooming apricot tree is one of the first signs that spring is on its way (the only tree keeping it out of first place is the almond).

Apricots are a **stone fruit** (drupe) and are part of the rose family, which includes, not surprisingly, peaches, plums, and nectarines. But it is surprising to note that this branch of the family also includes cherries, almonds, and coconuts. All have one seed (the kernel), which is enclosed in a stony endocarp called a *pit*. As is true of the other well-known drupes (plums, nectarines, and peaches in particular), there are both cling-free and clingstone varieties. Apricots are thought to have originated in China, and the Chinese are known to have cultivated apricots as far back as 2000 B.C. From China, the apricot made its way to Iran and then, eventually, to Rome and Greece in the first century A.D. The Greeks gave the apricot its botanical name *prunus armeniaca;* however, this was due to their mistaken belief that the fruit had originated in Armenia. The Romans named the fruit *praecocium,* meaning precocious (advanced), because apricots ripened earlier than other stone fruits. This is the origin of the word *apricot.* Apricot trees were taken to England and Italy in the mid-1500s, but they did not prosper in those climates. The fruit made its way to Virginia in the early eighteenth century, where again the climate was too cool. Finally, apricots arrived in California, via Mexico and the Spanish; there they flourished and continue to do so today.

Nearly all apricots sold in the United States are grown in California. In most areas (and certainly in California), apricots are available fresh throughout the summer. Unfortunately, apricots are picked and shipped before they are ripe (as are peaches and plums) to protect them during transport. Ripe, plump, and juicy apricots simply would not travel very far without ending up bruised and damaged. Ripe apricots are not good keepers. They should be stored in the refrigerator but will only last up to a week, depending on how carefully they were handled when they were picked.

Apricots are used in cakes, mousses, and fruit salads as well as in savory dishes. Both apricot jam and apricot glaze are used extensively in the pastry shop. Dried apricots are often found in fruitcakes and tea breads. Apricot seeds are made into a kernel paste that is similar to almond paste, but with a bitter aftertaste.

Apricot Varieties

Early Gold—Originated in Oregon. Medium-sized round fruit with intense golden skin and rich and juicy flesh. Best for canning and eating out of hand. Season: Early summer.

Perfection—Originated in Washington. Large oval to oblong fruit with light orange-yellow, pebbled, non-blushed skin. It has yellow to bright orange flesh of good quality, and is best used fresh for salads or eating out of hand. Season: Early summer.

Royal—Also known as Royal Blenheim. Originated in France. This is a large fruit with yellow to orange skin and firm, aromatic, juicy flesh. One of the main commercial apricot varieties, it is excellent for any application. A great keeper (if not bruised). Season: Midsummer.

Blenheim—See **Royal.** Identical to Royal except that it originated in England.

Tilton—First established in California. Similar to Royal in color, but the flavor is somewhat inferior. The fruit is larger, though, and ripens a little later. It is best for eating out of hand and cooking. Season: Midsummer.

Moorpark—Originated in England and hailed by many as the rival to Royal and the standard of excellence for the species. The skin of this attractive, large, oval fruit is orange, deeply blushed, and speckled with dots of brown and red. The orange flesh has a great aromatic flavor, but its drawbacks are a tendency toward halves of uneven size and staggered ripening. This is a good all-around fruit. Season: Midsummer.

Golden Amber—Developed in California. This large, uniform, and symmetrical fruit has, as the name implies, yellow skin. The yellow flesh is firm, with a touch of acid. This is an excellent all-around fruit. Season: Late summer.

Aquavit—The name of this potent Scandinavian spirit means "water of life." It is often flavored with anise seed, cucumber, caraway, and fennel. Aquavit is served very cold (usually right out of the freezer) and traditionally consumed in a straight shot while, according to Scandinavian custom, maintaining eye contact with your drinking partner. Aquavit has been made in Scandinavia since the 1400s. It can be distilled from grain or potatoes.

Armagnac—A type of brandy that, like **Cognac,** has an *appellation d'origine contrôlée,* meaning it cannot be labeled as such unless it comes from a specified area and is produced under certain controls. Armagnac is made only from wine produced in a region in Gascony. There are several production subareas, including Haut-Armagnac, but Bas-Armagnac is the main producer. The criteria specifying the area where the grapes may be grown, the method used in production, and the system for labeling have been in force since 1909; however, the name *Armagnac* was recorded as early as the 1400s. Armagnac is aged in oak and is given one of the following classifications: XXX, meaning it is aged 3 years; VO, meaning 5 to 10 years; VSOP, up to 15 years; or Hors d'Age, meaning that the Armagnac is at least 25 years old. See **Brandy**.

Arrack—The fermented and distilled product of palm juice, raisins, and dates. Arrack has a very strong and distinctive aroma, somewhat similar to rum, and is used in desserts and candies. It is made with different ingredients depending on the country in which it is produced. Some recipes include fermented rice, molasses, anise seed, and palm sap.

Arrowroot—The powdered root of a plant called *Maranta arundinacea,* grown in the Caribbean. It is used to thicken glazes, fruit fillings, and puddings. The acids found in fresh fruits do not have the same detrimental effect on products thickened with arrowroot as they do when the same products are thickened with cornstarch. Arrowroot thickens at a lower temperature than either cornstarch or flour, which is beneficial when you need to thicken a product that should not boil. The name came from the American Indian practice of using a paste made from the roots of the plant to treat arrow wounds.

Artificial sweetener—Artificial sweeteners are not used to a large extent in the majority of restaurant dessert kitchens or pastry shops other than those specializing in sugar-free or diabetic products. There are occasions, however, when the pastry department is asked to produce something for a special occasion or for a particular customer with dietary restrictions, where, for one reason or another, the instructions preclude the use of sugar. Certainly some recipes are much easier to modify than others. If the item will not be cooked, aspartame, which is readily available, can be used to sweeten a sauce, a finished custard or a whipped topping, but it cannot be used for baking. Aspartame is anywhere from 150 to 200 times sweeter than granulated sugar, so obviously a much smaller amount is used when substituting it for granulated sugar. Many new sugar substitutes have become available in the last few years due in part to the recent interest in low-carbohydrate diets. Many of these substitutes can be used for cooking and baking with very good results. Other artificial sweeteners, some of which are no longer used, include saccharin, cyclamates, and stevioside.

> **Aspartame**—Aspartame, discovered in 1965, is the most widely known artificial sweetener on the market. It is sold under the brand names NutraSweet and Equal and is familiar to most people in the individual serving-size paper packets generally offered with coffee and tea. It is an amino acid compound that is approximately 150 to 200 times as sweet as sugar. Aspartame cannot be used in cooking because its sweetening power is destroyed once the product reaches the boiling point. As with saccharin and cyclamates, many people are concerned about possible long-term health problems from aspartame use.

> **Saccharin**—Saccharin is a derivative of coal tar. It is a white, crystalline, aromatic compound that is 300 times as sweet as sugar. It was discovered accidentally by I. Remsen and C. Fahlberg in 1879. It is not soluble in water, but its sodium salt, which is the product sold commercially, dissolves readily. Saccharin has no nutritional value and passes through the body unchanged. Despite the fact that saccharin causes cancer in laboratory rats and was banned from the market for a time, the ban was rescinded due to public demand. In 1984, the World Health Organization suggested an intake limit of 2.5 mg/day per kg bodyweight.

> **Cyclamates**—Cyclamates were approved for consumer use in 1951; they are 30 times sweeter than sugar and, unlike saccharin, have no bitter aftertaste at high concentration. They were banned in 1969 because of suspected carcinogenic properties.

Asian pear—Asian pears are rapidly growing in popularity. Most varieties have a roundish shape very similar to that of an apple, which has led to the often used and misleading name of apple-pear, but these are true pears. They are also known as *Oriental pears, Chinese pears,* and *sand pears.* This delicious and very juicy fruit was first brought to the United States by Chinese gold miners during the gold rush of the mid-1800s. The trees are exceptionally attractive, producing bright white flowers in the spring that contrast with its then leathery green leaves; the leaves also give a cascade of fall colors later in the year. The cultivation of Asian pears is much the same as for European pear varieties, with the exception that Asian pears should be left to ripen on the tree. When ripe, the fruit is still quite firm to the touch and will not yield to slight pressure. The best indicator of ripeness is a sweet aroma. Asian pears are available on the market from late summer through the holiday season. They can be stored at room temperature for up to two weeks and in the refrigerator for much longer. Asian pears are excellent for cooking and poaching; however, they take much longer to cook than European pears. Asian pear trees are commonly used as rootstock in commercial pear orchards.

Asian Pear Varieties

Hosui—Medium-sized fruit with a golden russet skin. These have a crisp, refreshing apple flavor and keep exceptionally well. Hosui ripen in early August.

Nijisseiki—These pears come from Japan and are the most common commercial Asian pear variety. They are also called *Twentieth Century.* The fruit is roundish but squat and often lopsided, with a greenish-yellow skin that is tender and smooth. The flesh is pure white and slightly tart. These ripen in early September.

Shinseiki—Also known as *New Century,* these are similar to the Nijisseiki, with the same flattened, roundish shape; however, these are more uniform. The skin is yellow and slightly tough. The flesh is white, crisp, and sweet. Shinseiki pears ripen in mid-August.

Yali—This hardy variety is the exception to the usual roundish apple shape found in most Asian pears; it is instead *pyriform,* meaning pear-shaped. This pear basically looks like an overripe Bartlett with a white to yellow skin. The flesh is aromatic, with a mild, sweet taste. These pears ripen in early October.

Aspartame—See **Artificial sweetener.**

Aspic—A firm, clear jelly, usually applied in a thin layer for decorative purposes. In the savory kitchen, aspics are made from meat or fish stocks (which often have enough natural gelatin to cause them to set without adding gelatin) or from vegetable or fruit juices, sometimes with the addition of wine; these are thickened using gelatin. Aspics are used to glaze and decorate terrines, cold poached fish, and canapes. When used as a glaze, the aspic adds shine, making the food more attractive; it also seals the food from the air, which keeps it fresh longer. Its name comes form the Greek word *aspis,* meaning "shield." Aspic is also served cut into small cubes. These are used as a garnish and to provide a contrast in flavors and textures, as when the cool, smooth jelly is eaten together with a rich pâté, for example. Aspics do not play a large role in the pastry kitchen but when they are used, they are made from fruit juices or wine and set with gelatin. For example, a layer of fruit aspic is applied to the inside of a mold before filling it with a rice pudding set with gelatin for the classic Riz l'Impératrice. When unmolded for service, the aspic becomes the outer layer.

Average flour value—Grade given to qualify flour based on the following four characteristics: color, number of loaves that can be produced per barrel, loaf size, and overall quality.

Avocado—Avocado fruit, also known as *alligator pear,* is scientifically classified as *Persea americana.* Avocado is both the name of the tree itself (a type of laurel) and the fruit it produces. Avocado trees have been cultivated for thousands of years. The fruit is pear shaped, light to dark green, and with thinner or thicker skin, depending on the variety. Avocados are a **drupe fruit**, meaning they have a single stone or pit. When ripe, the flesh has the consistency of firm butter and a buttery, nutlike flavor. Avocados have both the highest protein and highest oil content of all fruits.

B

B&B. See **Bénédictine.**

Bacteria—A large class of microscopic unicellular organisms occurring in three main forms: spiral (spirilla), spherical (coccus), and rod-shaped (bacillus). Bacteria are found in soil, water, and organic matter as well as in living plants and animals. Bacterial growth causes a chemical effect that is significant in food production in ways that are both beneficial and harmful. As they reproduce, bacteria cause fermentation, which is necessary and desirable in yeast development and in the transformation of milk into yogurt, for example, but bacteria are also responsible for food spoilage and food-borne illness.

Bagasse—The material resulting after sugarcane has been passed through and pressed under a series of heavy rollers that extract the cane juice. This waste product is used as fuel to run the sugar refinement mills and is also processed into paper. See Figure A-4, page 921.

Baker's cheese—See **Cheese.**

Baker's chocolate—See **Chocolate.**

Baking chocolate—See **Chocolate.**

Baking powder—Baking powder is a leavener composed of one part sodium bicarbonate and two parts baking acid (generally cream of tartar, although phosphates are used in the case of single-acting baking powder), plus a small amount of starch to keep the product from caking. When baking powder comes into contact with liquid and heat, it releases carbon dioxide gas, which, in the case of a cake batter, for example, causes the batter to expand and rise as it fills with the gas bubbles. Single-acting baking powders react and release gas only when they come in contact with a liquid, which makes them impractical for use in some recipes. Double-acting baking powders, the type more commonly used and the type used in the recipes in *The Professional Pastry Chef,* react to both liquid and heat. Double-acting baking powder gives you the advantage of being able to delay baking the product. Provided the correct amount is used, baking powder will not cause an aftertaste and should leave only small, even holes inside the baked dessert rather than large air pockets. Generally speaking, the softer and more fluid the batter is, the more the baking powder will react. At high altitudes, the amount of baking powder called for in a recipe must be decreased. See "High-Altitude Baking" in Appendix C. Store baking powder, tightly covered, in a cool place.

Baking soda; Sodium bicarbonate—Baking soda, or sodium bicarbonate, produces carbon dioxide gas to inflate batters in the same way as baking powder (baking soda is an ingredient of baking powder). Baking soda starts to release gas as soon as it comes into contact with moisture, so products in which it is used should be baked as soon as possible after mixing. (This is especially true if baking soda is used alone and not used in combination with baking powder.) Recipes that use baking soda for leavening must contain an acid ingredient because without an acid, baking soda will produce a pungent and unpleasant flavor when the product is baked. Baking soda alone (without an acid) becomes carbon dioxide gas and sodium carbonate when it is heated. The carbon dioxide gas is desirable for producing air bubbles and the leavening effect, but the sodium carbonate has a disagreeable soapy taste and is moderately alkaline. When an acid is introduced (buttermilk, chocolate, citrus juice, sour cream, brown sugar, honey, or molasses, to name some of the ingredients commonly utilized), the gas is produced more rapidly, which leaves behind a milder form of the sodium. In addition to its leavening properties, baking soda also helps darken the baked product to some degree, which can add to a more appetizing appearance. Store sodium bicarbonate in an airtight container.

Baldwin—See Apple.

Banana—Few plants suggest the tropics as strongly as the banana and, indeed, the plant thrives in the heat and humidity of this region. The banana plant's appearance is something like a palm; its giant leaves sweep out to 12 feet (3 m 60 cm) in length from what looks like a trunk but is actually the tightly wrapped, overlapping long stalks of its branches. Banana trees are so called because their height can reach 30 feet (9 m). However, the banana is, in fact, the largest plant in the world without a woody trunk or stem; to be more precise, it is actually the world's largest herb.

Although we usually picture bunches of bananas hanging down, they grow with the ends of the fruit pointing up toward the sun in layer upon layer of semicircles, known as *hands*. Each hand contains 10 to 15 bananas, or "fingers"; a standard-size bunch has approximately nine hands. Bananas develop without pollination. Each plant produces one flower stalk with multiple rows of female flowers (which will become the hands). The fruits (the fingers) begin to develop at the base, close to where the flowers started to grow out of the plant. Interestingly enough, when the embryonic fruit starts to develop, it is covered by a protective sheet, and the tiny bananas point down toward the ground. As the fruit matures, the sheet falls away, the fingers begin to take shape, and they grow toward the sun, producing the typical curved shape. At this point, the male flower appears and, although the flowers (large pods on a thin, curved stalk) are attractive to the eye and are used in some types of Asian cooking, they rob the plant of energy, so on a commercial banana plantation, they are always removed.

The yellow banana was one of the first plants to be cultivated, and one could easily argue that bananas are an ideal food in many ways: They are in plentiful supply and inexpensive all year long; they are no trouble to transport, as they are shipped, still hard, before they are ripe; they are easy to peel and can be digested by just about all ages; nutritionally, they have more carbohydrate than any other fruit except the avocado; and, unlike avocados, which are very high in fat and calories, bananas have only a trace amount of fat and are low in calories. A ripe medium banana, 6 to 7 inches (15 to 17.5 cm) in length, has only about 80 calories (and, like all fruits and vegetables, no cholesterol) and is an excellent source of potassium. Bananas are composed of about 75 percent water and 20 percent sugar; the remaining 5 percent is a combination of starch, fiber, protein, and ash.

The existence of bananas is documented as far back as 327 B.C., when Alexander the Great happened upon well-established plants in India. Traders brought bananas across the Indian Ocean to Eastern Africa, and Chinese traders transplanted the banana to the Polynesian Islands, all before the second century A.D. However, many hundred years went by before bananas became an everyday treat for the American consumer. Bananas of one variety or another, including the plantain, are a staple food throughout many parts of the world.

Although there are hundreds of bananas species, the type we know today was developed by crossing and recrossing the two species *Musa acuminata* and *Musa balbisiana*. The varieties sold commercially are seedless hybrids of these two parents; some are closer to one parent than another. The common yellow banana, called the Cavendish, resembles the *Musa acuminata,* while the starchier types, such as the plantain, are more closely related to the *Musa balbisiana*.

If a recipe simply specifies "bananas," you can assume it is referring to the sweet type we eat out of hand, the yellow banana, also known as a *dessert banana,* of which the Cavendish is the most common.

Bananas are one of two fruits (pears are the other) that taste better when allowed to ripen off the tree. Therefore, bananas are shipped green, then ripened domestically in specially equipped warehouses. Costa Rica and Honduras are the two largest exporters of bananas to the United States. It is interesting to note, however, that bananas are among the top three exports from a most unlikely place: Iceland. There, they are grown in greenhouses heated naturally by geysers that produce the ideal humidity for the plants to thrive. Once bananas have ripened, store them in a cool place. Refrigerate only if absolutely necessary; the skin will turn brown, but the flesh will not be affected.

Yellow Banana Varieties

Chinese Dwarf Cavendish—The fingers are 6 to 8 inches (15 to 20 cm) in length; the fruit is sweet tasting, with a creamy yellow skin. These do not store as well as some of the other Cavendish varieties, such as giant Cavendish. Although these require a great deal of care to prevent bruising during shipping, the fruit's immunity to Panamanian wilting disease has made it the most popular commercial variety today.

Gros Michel—This was the first species imported to the United States but, because of its susceptibility to Panamanian wilting disease, it has been replaced, for the most part, by the Cavendish. Gros Michel is one of the most delicious bananas and is still a favorite of many when the fruit can be found. The fingers are 7 to 9 inches (17.5 to 22.5 cm) long and the peel is bright yellow.

Golden Aromatic—This banana is known in Chinese as *go san heong,* which I have been told translates roughly to "you can smell the fragrance from the next mountain." These closely resemble the Gros Michel in taste; however, their flavor is even sweeter. Like the Gros Michel, these are hard to come by. The fingers are 6 to 9 inches (15 to 22.5 cm) long, with golden yellow skin.

Red Bananas—Red bananas are becoming increasingly more available. They have the unpopular distinction (at least for commercial cultivation) of being the banana that is slowest to grow to maturity and the slowest to ripen; their price certainly reflects this. Be careful about buying a very unripe, hard hand of red bananas because they will most likely never ripen in your kitchen due to improper storage at the outset before shipping. Instead of becoming soft and ripe, they will simply turn even harder and dry, virtually petrified. Different varieties come in slender, plump, and stubby shapes. Red Cuban (also known as Cuban Red), Spanish Red, and the Costa Rican variety, Macaboo, are the three most commonly found. They are all fairly comparable. Fingers are 5 to 6 inches (12.5 to 15 cm) in length, with thick, dark purple skin that turns red when the fruit is perfectly ripe. The flesh of red bananas is a peachy dark yellow color and has a very distinctive, wonderfully sweet flavor. These are great keepers(up to two weeks after ripening, but heed the warning above.

Finger Bananas—Also known as *lady fingers,* these are the most esteemed bananas in tropical countries. They are very small, only 3 to 4 inches (7.5 to 8 cm) in length, with a thin yellow skin; their flesh is soft and sweet. Unfortunately, we do not get to enjoy this delicacy as frequently as we do yellow bananas because the thin-skinned finger bananas do not transport as well.

Finger Banana Varieties

Apple—Also known as *manzano* or *apple banana (manzano* is Spanish for "apple"). The fingers are 4 to 5 inches (10 to 12.5 cm) in length, with thin yellow skin. The flesh has a good flavor, with a hint of apple. The bananas must be fully ripe before they can be eaten, or they tend to have an astringent taste.

Ladyfinger—Also known as *ney poovan.* The fingers are 4 to 5 inches (10 to 12.5 cm) long. The skin is thin and pale and the flavor is similar to the apple finger banana.

Nino—This is the ultimate finger or baby banana, and the most common. You can find these bananas from time to time in the produce departments of most major grocery stores. They should be eaten when the skin is just yellow and starting to develop a few brown flecks. They are great keepers, once ripe. The fingers are 3 to 4 inches (7.5 to 10 cm) long. The skin is thin and pale yellow.

Plantains—Plantains are closely related to yellow bananas, but these ugly relations are considerably larger, averaging about 12 inches (30 cm) in length and weighing as much as 1 pound (455 g). Though they are indeed a fruit, plantains are sometimes referred to as *vegetable bananas* because they are cooked like a vegetable rather than being enjoyable raw, as are most types of fruit. Plantains require cooking because the ripening process, like that of the potato, does not convert all of the starch to sugar. Another name for plantains is *cooking bananas.* They are used in Latin American countries in a way that is similar to the use of potatoes in the United States. Plantains are left to ripen on the tree and change color from all green to all black (and become slightly wrinkled) when fully ripe. We usually see them in the market somewhere in between, when their thick, slightly blemished skin has started to turn a reddish brown. Plantains have distinctive ridges along their length, causing the fruit to have three or four flat sides.

Removing the peel from a raw plantain is quite a bit harder than removing the skin from a banana, especially if the fruit is not ripe. If the recipe calls for boiling or baking plantains, do so with the skin on, and it will slip right off after cooking. Otherwise, use a sharp knife to cut off both ends so that part of the flesh is exposed, then cut lengthwise along the edge of one of the ridges without cutting into the pulp. Repeat with the adjacent ridge and use the edge of the knife to lift up the cut section of peel and pull it away in one piece. Repeat this procedure with each remaining segment of peel or until the remaining skin can be removed in one piece.

Plantains should be refrigerated only if overripe. The exposure to cold interrupts their ripening cycle, and it will never resume, even if the fruit is returned to room temperature. A rock-hard green plantain can take up to two weeks to ripen. If the fruit was stored improperly during shipping (if it became too cold, as mentioned above), it may never ripen and instead will just dry to a petrified consistency. Several varieties of plantain are available in most grocery stores today; it is no longer necessary to go to Latin or Asian markets to find them, at least in large coastal cities. The giant plantain, also known as the *Puerto Rican,* and the horse plantain are the two most commonly found in the market.

Barbadine—A plant indigenous to South America and related to the passion flower. It was introduced to the West Indies in the nineteenth century. The white-fleshed fruit is used for jams and sorbet. The bark is used to make jelly.

Barbados cherry—See Acerola.

Barberry—A very sour berry that is almost never eaten fresh but instead is used for preserves. Barberries grow throughout Europe, Asia, and the United States. Varieties range in color from blue to red, coral, and almost black.

Barley; Barley flour—Barley is the oldest cultivated cereal grain, but it does not play a large role in baking as it has a very low gluten content. It was an important ancient food source, used to make porridge and griddled, unleavened breads, but when methods improving the cultivation of wheat were introduced, barley became less popular. Bread made from barley flour is darker and denser than bread made from wheat; it was generally considered peasant food for many centuries, although the higher classes of European society did use it as trenchers, which were edible plates or bowls used to serve stews and thick soups. Leavened breads made with a combination of barley and wheat have historically been met with greater enthusiasm; nevertheless, barley alone is still popular for use in making cracker-type flatbreads in Scandinavia.

Barm—(1) The yeast that is drawn off from fermented malt; (2) An English term for a sourdough starter.

Bartlett pear—Named for Enoch Bartlett, who introduced this variety to America, Bartlett pears are available in the late summer and early fall and are good for both cooking and eating plain. They were developed in England in the eighteenth century. See **Pear.**

Bean curd—See **Tofu.**

Bénédictine—A sweet liqueur first made in the sixteen century by the Benedictine monks of the Abbey of Fecamp in the Normandy region of France. Dom Bernardo Vincelli is the monk credited with creating the original recipe. Commercial production began in 1863, when Alexandre Le Grand found this recipe in some old family papers. He made some changes and began selling the product, with immediate success. He named it Bénédictine in honor of the monks who first made it. The labels on the bottles are printed with the initials D.O.M., for the Latin phrase *deo optimo maximo,* which means "to God, most good, most great." Bénédictine is based on **Cognac** and is said to be flavored with 27 spices and plants; however, the exact recipe is a highly guarded secret. Bénédictine is traditionally served after coffee, straight or on the rocks, as a digestive. B&B, or Bénédictine and brandy, a combination of the two, is also produced and bottled in Fecamp. It is drier than Bénédictine and is served in the same way.

Benne seed—See **Sesame seed.**

Bergamot orange—See **Orange.**

Berry—Any of many small fruits from a variety of plants, often bushes. All berries have seeds—never a pit—embedded in their pulp. See **Blackberry, Blueberry, Boysenberry, Cranberry, Gooseberry, Olallieberry, Raspberry,** and **Strawberry.**

Beurre—French for "butter."

Beurre composé—French for "compound butter." See **Compound butter.**

Beurre fondu—French for "melted butter."

Beurre manié—A paste made of soft butter mixed with flour in equal proportions. The French term translates to "kneaded butter." Beurre manié is used to thicken a hot liquid, such as a sauce, by whisking it in, then bringing the mixture to a boil. A beurre manié works in the same way as a roux except that here the thickening agent is added to the liquid and, with a roux, the liquid is added to the mixture of flour and fat. Also, a roux is cooked before use as a thickening agent, and a beurre manié is not.

Beurre noir—French for "black butter." Butter is cooked very slowly so that the milk solids caramelize and darken. It is not actually cooked long enough to become black. Beurre noir is used more in savory cooking than in the pastry kitchen; it is often combined with an acid ingredient, such as vinegar, lemon juice, or pickled capers, and served with sautéed fish or liver.

Beurre noisette—Also known simply as *brown butter.* The French term literally translates to "hazelnut butter." Noisette, or hazelnut, refers to both the color and the fragrance of the butter after browning. The butter is cooked over low heat to caramelize the milk solids, as in beurre noir, but is not darkened quite as much. The browning process gives the butter a nutty flavor and aroma; hence the name.

Bicarbonate of soda—See **Baking soda.**

Bigarade—A type of orange; also, a classic French sauce served with roasted duck. The sauce is made from reduced duck stock and pan drippings combined with orange and lemon juice and zest and thickened with butter.

Bilberry—Somewhat similar to blueberries, these berries grow wild in parts of Europe. A bilberry is smaller and less sweet than a blueberry but is utilized in many of the same ways, such as in pie filling, jams, and syrups.

Binding agent—Also known as a *binder* or *thickening agent,* a binding agent is the medium used to connect two or more ingredients to keep a mixture from separating and/or to thicken the mixture. Examples of binding agents are whole eggs, egg yolks, roux, beurre manié, flour-and-water paste, cornstarch, arrowroot, and cream. The liquid is cooked or at least heated so the binder has the desired effect. In some cases, the binding ingredient is added to a very hot liquid off the heat and no further cooking is necessary.

Bing cherry—See **Cherry.**

Bitter almond—Some sources erroneously use this term to refer to the bitter inner kernel of the apricot pit (see **Apricot kernel**), but bitter almonds are, in fact, a type of almond. The common almond is found in both sweet and bitter varieties. See **Almond.**

Bitter chocolate—See **Chocolate; Unsweetened chocolate.**

Bitter melon—Also known as *balsam pear.* Although bitter melons are technically classified as a fruit, they are prepared, for the most part, as a vegetable, mainly in Chinese cooking. They are in season from April through September and can be found in most Asian markets.

Bitters—A concentrated distilled bitter to bittersweet flavoring agent with a high alcohol content that is used in mixed drinks. Bitters, usually made with herbs and roots, are reputed to act as a potent digestive aid and to stimulate appetite. Angostura, Fernet-Branca, and Underberg are several common brand names.

Bittersweet chocolate—See **Chocolate.**

Blackberry—Blackberries are available fresh through the summer and are also sold frozen or canned. Loganberries, boysenberries, and olallieberries are all hybrids of blackberries. Fresh berries are excellent for decorating and for use in fruit salads, tarts, and pies. Dewberries are the "other" blackberry; they are not as common, but they look and taste so much like blackberries that, after harvest, they are really indistinguishable. It is easy to tell the difference before the berries are picked, however, because dewberries grow on trailing brambles along the ground, whereas the common blackberry grows on an erect woody plant that looks very similar to its close relation, the **raspberry.** The various crossbreeds and hybrids can be very confusing, and not just among the blackberry varieties but also because blackberries (*rubus fruticous*) are themselves a hybrid of raspberries (*rubus idaeus*). All of these berries belong, botanically, to the rose family. To add to the confusion (and interest), there are also black-colored raspberries and red-colored blackberries! One sure way of distinguishing between blackberries and raspberries is to look very closely at their skin; raspberries have a slightly hairy exterior (the word *rasp* can be used as a verb to mean "to rub with something rough"), while the surface of blackberries is shiny and smooth. Another difference is that, when harvested, blackberries retain the part of the stem that connected them to the plant, whereas raspberries have a hollow end because their center stem remains attached to the end of the branch. (This is not an absolute rule, and it applies more to homegrown fruit, as commercially grown blackberries have their centers removed before they are packaged and shipped.)

Blackberries are very juicy, and they make a delicious and attractive sauce when pureed. They are also made into jam. To keep fresh berries from becoming crushed and from molding prematurely, store them in the refrigerator, spread out in a single layer on sheet pans. To freeze fresh berries, spread them out in a single layer, without crowding, and place in the freezer until frozen solid. Package the frozen berries in airtight bags or storage containers.

The two most common growing regions for both wild and cultivated blackberries are North America and Europe. Serious commercial cultivation did not begin until around 1825. In general, the berries do best where the summers are fairly temperate, or on the cool side. In the United States, Washington, Oregon, and northern California are the primary growing areas. Many berry hybrids have been created or have developed naturally to adapt to different climates. Following are some of the most common:

Boysenberry—Named for Rudolph Boysen, who created this hybrid by crossing a blackberry, a loganberry, and a raspberry. This trailing dewberry variety is grown in California. The berries are large and long—up to 1¼ inches (3.1 cm)—and they turn reddish black when they are ripe. Boysenberries have an excellent flavor but are not quite as sweet as youngberries. Midsummer.

Loganberry—It is generally accepted that these are a cross between red raspberries and wild blackberries, although some say loganberries are a separate species altogether. They take their name from the man who first discovered or recognized them, a California judge named J. H. Logan. They are one of the oldest of the blackberry hybrids. The fruit is long, large, and dark red when mature. Late summer.

Olallieberry—This variety is grown mostly in California, although it was first developed in Oregon. Olallieberries are a cross between blackberries, loganberries, and youngberries. The berries are blunt in shape, medium in size, and bright black. Midsummer.

Youngberries—Similar to boysenberries; somewhat sweeter but not as productive. The fruit is large and shiny, with a color like red wine. Although originally from Louisiana, youngberries have adapted well to southern California. Midsummer.

Black currants—These very small berries should not be confused with **dried currants** (which are made from a variety of grape). Black currants are rarely available fresh in the United States; however, they are very popular in Scandinavia and other parts of Europe, including Germany and France. Black currants are always cooked before they are eaten because they are too bitter to eat raw. They are typically used in jams and to make the French liqueur **crème de cassis**. Their dark color, which turns almost purple when mixed with other ingredients, gives cakes, mousses, and other desserts a very special look.

Black pepper—See **Peppercorn**.

Black tea—See **Tea**.

Blackjack—See **Caramel coloring**.

Blackstrap molasses—See **Molasses**.

Blanched almonds—Almonds with the outer brown skin removed. They can be purchased whole, sliced, ground, or slivered. To remove the brown skin from whole (shelled) almonds, pour boiling water over them, cover, and let them soak for 5 minutes. Drain the water and immediately pinch the nuts between your fingers to remove the skin.

Blood orange—See **Orange**.

Blueberry—Blueberries grow wild in both Scandinavia and the United States. They are available fresh in the late spring and through the summer; they are also sold frozen and canned. Fresh blueberries are wonderful for adding color to fruit tarts and fruit salads. While not as desirable, frozen berries give a good result when used in muffins, tea cakes, pancakes, and other cooked products. Store or freeze blueberries as directed for **blackberries**. Do not thaw frozen blueberries before adding them to batters. Blueberries contain a large amount of pectin.

Borage—An herb with very pretty small, bright blue, star-shaped edible flowers that are often used for decorative purposes. See **Flowers, edible**.

Bosc pear—See **Pear**.

Bounceberry—Slang term for cranberry. See **Cranberry**.

Bourbon—American-made whiskey produced from a distilled mixture containing at least 51 percent corn (to be labeled *corn whiskey*, the mash must contain a minimum of 80 percent corn). The name *bourbon* comes from Bourbon County, Kentucky, which is well-known for its whiskey production.

Bourbon vanilla—See **Vanilla**.

Boysenberry—See **Blackberry**.

Bran—The outer husk of any type of grain. This husk is removed when the grain is milled into flour. In the case of whole wheat and graham flours, the bran is added back in at the end of the milling process. Bran has a high nutritional value due to its significant fiber content and the presence of B vitamins, although it should be noted that bran does limit, to some extent, the absorption of other food and nutrients during the digestive process. Bran flakes are often added to bread, cereals, and muffins for the benefits listed above. Care must be taken, however, not to use too much, as bran weakens the gluten strength of wheat flour.

Brandy—Distilled from wine (fermented grape juice) or other fermented fruit juices, brandy is classified by these labels: E—extra special, F—fine, M—mellow, O—old, P—

pale, S—superior, V—very, and X—extra. V.S.O.P. stands for "very superior old pale." These letters refer to the degree of aging, and the designations are regulated differently for American-produced brandy than for the famous regionally produced brandies of France, such as **Armagnac** and **Cognac** (see entries). The word *brandy* derives from original terms for the procedure used to distill it. The fermented juice is heated to separate the alcohol; this process is known as *burning*. The Dutch first named it *brandewijn,* meaning "burnt wine," which was adapted by the English to *brandewine* and later shortened to *brandy* as early as the mid-1600s. See **Applejack, Armagnac, Calvados, Cognac, Fraise des bois, Framboise, Grappa, Kirschwasser, Metaxa, Mirabelle, Pisco,** and **Poire Williams.**

Brazil nut—Brazil nuts are technically a seed rather than a nut. About 20 seeds grow packaged tightly together in large round pods on the South American tree *Bertholletia excelsa,* which is found only in Brazil (hence the name). The shells are dark brown, very hard, and triangular in shape, with three flat sides. Shelled Brazil nuts are comparatively large—about 3 times the size of a shelled almond—and ivory colored, with a very thin brown skin. They have a high oil content and a pleasing crunchy texture.

Bread flour—See **Flour.**

Breadfruit—A large green fruit from a tropical tree found in India, the South Pacific, and the West Indies. The name originates in the impression that the flesh of the fruit is similar in texture to baked bread. Breadfruit most likely originated in Malaysia, although New Guinea is also a possibility. The fruit has reportedly been consumed for over 2000 years in some parts of the world. Its existence was first recorded by European explorers in the late 1500s in the Marquesas Islands (a group of 12 islands located in the South Pacific, now a part of French Polynesia). It was successfully brought to Jamaica in the West Indies two centuries later and is still cultivated there today. Other places of cultivation are Central America and parts of South America. Legend has it that the breadfruit tree made its way to Kualoa, Hawaii, many centuries ago thanks to inhabitants of the Polynesian islands, who brought it as an offering to an important Hawaiian chief. Most of the breadfruit grown in Hawaii today is the seedless variety, so it is cultivated from offshoots of roots rather than planted from seed. Breadfruit is related to the fig and the mulberry. The tree itself is lush and elegant and can grow up to 60 feet (18 m) tall. Early Hawaiians used the lightweight wood from the trunks of the trees to make drums and canoes, among other things. The green, rounded fruit is approximately 8 inches (20 cm) in diameter and weighs an average of 3 pounds (1 kg 365 g). The flowers and subsequent fruit pods grow together in a group like grapefruit.

Breadfruit is not left to ripen on the tree; it is picked while the rind is still green and the fruit is firm to the touch. When the fruit is not fully ripe, the flesh is bland, starchy, and very white. As the fruit ripens, it becomes light yellow and much sweeter. Breadfruit has approximately the same quantities of sugar and starch as the sweet potato, and it can be utilized in many of the same ways as a white or sweet potato. Breadfruit has better flavor retention if it is cooked whole either in the microwave or baked in the oven, although cut pieces may be boiled in water. If slices or chunks are cooked in a sauce, keep in mind that they will absorb a great deal of liquid. When handling raw, cut fruit, you should wear latex gloves to protect your hands from the sticky sap. Lightly oiling your knife is also helpful in cutting through the gluey flesh and makes the job a bit less messy.

Brewer's yeast—Although a member of the same genus, *Saccharomyces,* or sugar fungi, as the yeast used in baking bread, brewer's yeast serves a much different function, and the two are not interchangeable. Baker's yeast produces little alcohol but a substantial amount of carbon dioxide for the rising of bread. Brewer's yeast produces more alcohol and is therefore instrumental in the brewing of beer. Due to its high content of B vitamins and protein, brewer's yeast is also taken as a dietary supplement.

Brik; Brek—These are paper-thin sheets of pastry dough sold packaged and ready for use, similar to phyllo dough or spring roll wrappers. *Brik* (also spelled *brek*) is actually the name of a savory pastry from Tunisia (comparable to the Moroccan pastilla, which is made with phyllo dough) that is filled with ground meat and a soft-boiled egg and wrapped in thin sheets of dough called *malsouqa.* These dough sheets are now sold under the name *brik,* taking their title from the end product for which they were originally used. The sheets are very thin, like phyllo dough, but they have a bit of elasticity. They are traditionally made by boiling semolina, then cooking the batter in a frying pan coated with olive oil, spreading it by hand with a practiced circular motion to produce the very delicate sheets. Sheets manufactured for commercial sale are, for the most part, produced using machines. In a pastry application, brik can be used like phyllo dough: brushed with butter and layered to enclose a filling. After baking, the crust becomes crisp and golden brown.

Brown sugar—See **Sugar.**

Buckwheat—A herbaceous plant (genus *fagopyrum*) with small, black, seedlike triangular fruits, and the seeds themselves, which are often ground into flour. Buckwheat is native to the shores of the Caspian Sea and those of southeast Asia. It is not related to true wheat, which belongs to the grass family. Buckwheat comes from the same family of plants as rhubarb and sorrel. The name *buckwheat* comes from the German word *buchweinen,* meaning "beech wheat," which refers to the buckwheat seed's resemblance to the beech nut. Its French name is *blé sarrasin.* Whole buckwheat grains (seeds) must be hulled before they can be cooked and eaten. Because of their unique triangular shape, special machinery is used to remove the hard outer shell without altering the triangular shape. Buckwheat is sold raw or roasted. Whole buckwheat grains can be cooked in the same way as rice; in Japan, noodles made from buckwheat are very popular; and the Brittany region of France is famous for buckwheat crepes.

Buckwheat flour—Buckwheat flour is made from the roasted seeds of the plant. It does not contain any useful gluten and has somewhat less protein and starch than wheat. The flour is grayish in color, with small flecks of black and white. Buckwheat flour is used most often in pancakes, especially for the popular buckwheat blini of eastern Europe.

Buckwheat groats—Hulled, crushed buckwheat grains.

Buckwheat kasha—Roasted and cracked buckwheat grains used to make a Russian porridge of the same name.

Buddha's hand—See **Citron**.

Bulgar wheat; Bulgur wheat—Bulgar wheat is made by cooking whole wheat grains, drying them, then grinding them coarsely into a cereal. The same product is also known as *cracked wheat*. Bulgar wheat is often used to add substance to meatless dishes and is used in Middle Eastern salads such as tabbouleh.

Burnt sugar—See **Caramel coloring**.

Butter—Butter is solidified milk fat. Years ago, and for those who still make it by hand, butter was made by skimming the cream off the top of a container of fresh milk and churning it by hand. In the commercial manufacture of butter, the cream is skimmed from the milk or separated by machine. It is then placed in a mechanical churn, and the butter is solidified by agitation. The process is basically the same, simply performed by machines and in greater quantity. The butter is then kneaded and simultaneously washed with water to remove as much of the milk solids as possible. Color and vitamins may be added, as well as salt. In the United States, federal regulations require that finished butter contain not more than 16 percent water and not less than 82.5 percent butterfat. The remaining percentage is mineral matter, such as salt and milk solids.

Because of its low melting point and wonderful aroma, butter is indispensable in the making of first-rate pastries, especially those made with buttercream and puff pastry. In hot climates, a small amount of margarine must be added to the butter to make it workable. Two types of butter are used in cooking and baking: salted and unsalted, or sweet. All of the recipes in *The Professional Pastry Chef* use sweet butter, but salted butter can be substituted if the salt called for in the recipe is reduced by approximately ⅕ ounce (6 g) for every 1 pound (455 g) butter. You cannot substitute salted butter, however, if there is little or no salt in the recipe or if the main ingredient is butter. Sweet butter should not be kept at room temperature for more than a day; it should be stored in the refrigerator or freezer.

Many high-end butters with a high fat content, often described as European-style butters, have become popular in the last few years, with manufacturers directing marketing efforts toward both the professional and the consumer. These high-fat butters naturally also command a high price. Their lower moisture content gives excellent results in any laminated dough, such as croissant and puff pastry, and

makes for a more stable buttercream. In a cookie dough or in other general baking, the difference is negligible.

Butterfat—The saturated fat found in butter. It is rich in the fat-soluble vitamins A and D and in phosphorus.

Buttermilk—Buttermilk is the liquid that remains after sweet (or sour) milk is churned to remove the fat. Commercially produced buttermilk, called *cultured buttermilk,* is made by adding a bacterial culture to pasteurized skim milk; this converts the milk sugar to lactic acid and gives the buttermilk its characteristic slightly tart taste. Because of its acidity, buttermilk is often used in pastry recipes containing baking soda. See **Baking soda**.

Butyric acid—A short-chained fatty acid that can be found in some fruits but is primarily found in butter. This substance is responsible for both for the characteristic pleasant flavor of butter and the unpleasant odor and flavor of rancid butter. When produced synthetically, it is called *butanoic acid* and is used as a flavoring agent in food and as an acidulant in soy milk beverages.

C

Cacao—The tree whose botanical name is *Theobroma cacao,* and its seeds, from which cocoa and chocolate are made. See **Chocolate; Chocolate production**.

Cactus pear—See **Prickly pear**.

Cake flour—See **Flour**.

Cake syrup—A sugar syrup used to moisten and flavor cake layers. It can be flavored with liqueur, vanilla, fruit juice, coffee, and so on. Plain cake syrup is important to have as part of your regular mise en place for use in assembling many cakes and pastries.

Calcium—This mineral is essential in the development and functioning of the human body by maintaining bone mass, nerve conduction, muscle contraction, and blood clotting. It is an important component of the bones and teeth and is the most abundant mineral found in the human body. The primary dietary sources of calcium include milk, yogurt, and cheese as well as sardines, broccoli, kale, and calcium-fortified foods. The recommended daily allowance is 800 milligrams for adults.

Calvados—Apple brandy from France, originating in the Normandy region. Known in the United States as applejack.

Camomile—See **Chamomile**.

Candied Fruit—See **Crystallized Fruit** and **Glacé fruit**.

Candlenut—Candlenuts come from the tree *Aleurites moluccana*. They play a big role in Indonesia cookery, where the roasted and ground nuts are cooked with other ingredients to make a frequently used seasoning paste. A whole candlenut is round, about 2 inches (5 cm) in diameter, with a very hard shell that is covered by a papery brown skin. The unshelled nuts bear some resemblance to walnuts and are thus sometimes referred to as *Indian* or *Tahitian walnuts*. The edible portion inside can be made up of either one or two kernels. Candlenuts contain a toxin that makes them inedible raw. The typical method of preparation is to roast the whole nuts until the shells crack open, then extract the kernels. The kernels are then cooked further before they become pleasant to eat. Because the nuts contain so much oil, they were, at one time, used to make candles, hence the name.

Cane syrup—A thick, very sweet syrup made from an intermediate step in the sugarcane refining process when the syrup is reduced. It is used primarily in Caribbean and Creole cookery. See also **Sugar; Sugar production,** and Figure A-4 (page 927).

Canola oil—A free-flowing oil extracted from a special form of rapeseed; also known as *rapeseed oil.* The popularity of canola oil is growing in the United States due, in large part, to the discovery that it is lower in saturated fat (about 6 percent) than any other oil. By comparison, peanut oil contains approximately 18 percent saturated fat, and palm oil, one of the highest, contains 79 percent. Another benefit of canola oil is that it contains more cholesterol-balancing monounsaturated fat than any oil except olive oil and a high proportion of omega-3 fatty acids, which some studies indicate can help to lower cholesterol and triglyceride counts. Canola oil is virtually flavorless and is used as an ingredient in desserts, pastries, and confections. It can be substituted for other vegetable oils that are higher in saturated fat. Because it has a high smoking point, it is an ideal choice for frying. It is best stored, tightly sealed, in the refrigerator.

Cantaloupe—Cantaloupes are named for the small Italian village of Cantalupo, which is located just outside of Rome. They were first grown there in the 1700s. This sweet, fragrant melon is spherical in shape, and the skin is covered with rough netting. The flesh is pale green to dark orange and very sweet and juicy when fully ripe. In Europe, the most commonly cultivated variety is the charentais.

The cantaloupe variety sold in the United States is a member of the **muskmelon** family. Cantaloupes are available all year, as they are imported from Mexico throughout the winter. Store ripe and/or cut melons in the refrigerator for no more than two to three days. Uncut melons may be left to ripen at room temperature. They will become softer and juicier, but their sweetness will not improve.

Cape gooseberry—See **Physalis.**

Carambola—More commonly known as *star fruit,* this incredibly showy and unusual-looking fruit originated in Malaysia but now grows throughout the tropics and, more rarely, in southern California and Florida. The carambola grows on small trees. The fruit is oblong in shape, varying in size from that of a small hen's egg to that of a medium mango (2 to 5 inches/5 to 12.5 cm), depending on where it is grown. Each fruit has five prominent ridges (you can find rebels that have four or six) that, when sliced crosswise, reveal a striking star shape. This has given the fruit its alternate and, in the United States, more common name. The fruit has a glossy skin that turns from green to golden yellow when ripe. The interior flesh is a matching golden color and is rich in vitamins. Unfortunately, the fruit grown in the United States generally has a somewhat nondescript, dull

flavor. The varieties grown in the tropics are eaten out of hand—skin, seeds, and all. They range in flavor from very sweet to refreshingly tart. In the United States, carambolas are used mostly for decorative purposes, as a garnish for desserts, salads, or beverages, often to give an exotic feel. The fruit will keep for up to two weeks in the refrigerator. The top of the ridges will turn brown, but this is not a problem because it will be removed. To use star fruit, wash, remove the skin on the very top of each ridge, using a vegetable peeler, then slice across.

Caramel coloring—A coloring agent made by cooking (caramelizing) sugar to the point (392°F/200°C) that it burns and turns black. It is also known as *blackjack* and *burnt sugar.* Once the mixture has cooled, it is used in small amounts to color baked goods, mainly breads. Caramel coloring lasts indefinitely and does not need to be refrigerated.

Caraway—This old spice originated in the temperate areas of Turkey and Iran and got its name from the Arabic word *karawyä.* In botanical terms, it is classified as a member of the parsley family, and caraway does look very much like fennel, anise, and dill, with its umbrella-like flower clusters and long, feathery bright green leaves. Each small, dark seed has five lighter ridges. Caraway seeds have a strong, aromatic, warm taste. Their flavor is essential to many bread recipes and sweet dishes, and they are used for savory dishes as well in many European countries, especially in the German-speaking areas and in Scandinavia. The seeds are high in protein and are well known for their digestive properties. They are good in combination with heavy dishes or those high in fat. Caraway has been used medicinally since early times, and the oil from the seeds is used in making the liqueur kümmel. Store the seeds in a dark, cool place to prevent them from losing their scent too soon. Legend has it that caraway seed was once added to chicken feed, supposedly because it would keep the chickens from wandering away.

Carbohydrate—One of a group of organic nutrients that contain only carbon, hydrogen, and oxygen. The group includes sugars, glycogen, starches, dextrin, and cellulose. The body eventually converts them into glucose, the body's primary source for energy. Carbohydrates are generally divided into two groups: simple sugars and compound sugars. Simple sugars are found in fruits and vegetables, beet or cane juice, and milk, and are absorbed by the body very quickly. Compound sugars comprise two or more molecules of simple sugar and are found in whole grains and legumes. Most compound sugars are tasteless and difficult for the body to digest, but they provide more nutrients than simple sugars. Carbohydrates occur naturally in plants and milk and are used by the body principally for energy.

Carbonate of ammonia—See **Ammonium carbonate.**

Cardamom—Cardamom ranks as the third most expensive flavoring in the world, following saffron and vanilla. It is also one that you can hardly be faulted for misspelling, as the name of this ancient spice has had many variations—one dictionary lists seven, including "cardamony."

Cardamom is a perennial shrub native to the Malabar Coast of India. The short flowering stems carry small, yellowish-green pods, each containing about 20 small seeds, which are black on the outside. Cardamom should be purchased in the pod and the seeds ground as needed, as they start to lose their essential oil as soon as they are removed from the pod. In addition to ground seeds and whole pods, ground pods are also available as a cost-saving commercial alternative. Store any of these in a cool, dry place. Avoid using brown cardamom, an imposter that, though related to cardamom, has an inferior and overpowering flavor.

Carob—Cultivated from the pulp of the pods that grow on the evergreen tree *Ceratonia silqua.* The pods have a brown, leathery skin that fill with a sweet gum when they are ripe. The pods are also known as *locust beans* because they supposedly resemble these large insects. The endosperm of the seeds is ground to produce locust bean gum, which is used as a stabilizer in commercial food production. Both locust beans (carob pods) and a candy made from carob are known as *St. John's bread,* stemming from the biblical story describing how St. John the Baptist survived in the desert by eating locusts and honey. However, it is not known whether the locusts referred to were carob pods or the actual insects.

Carob pods are roasted and ground to produce a powder with a flavor similar to chocolate. Because carob is much lower in fat, calories, and caffeine than chocolate, it is used as a chocolate substitute in various health food products.

The ancient Greeks cultivated carob, highly prizing it as a form of candy, and they also used carob seeds as weights for their balance scales. The Greek word for the carob seed, *keration,* is the root of the modern word *carat,* used by jewelers to specify the weight of gemstones.

Carrageen; Salts of carrageenan—A vegetable-based stabilizer; carrageenan (also known as *Irish moss*) is a seaweed found growing off the coast of Ireland, as well as the coasts of France and Massachusetts. It is comparable to gelatin in strength and added in the same way when used in ice creams and sorbets.

Carrot—A root vegetable and member of the parsley family. Carrots have a leafy green foliage top attached to a long, orange edible taproot that has a sweet, mild flavor and a crisp, crunchy texture. Carrots are found in a variety of shapes and sizes. They should be stored in the refrigerator and the green tops removed after purchase, as they rob the root of some of its moisture and vitamins. Carrots have always enjoyed popularity due to their highly beneficial health properties, including large quantities of vitamin A. Carrots also contain a great deal of sugar. In the Middle Ages, when sweeteners were a rare commodity, carrots were often used in cakes and desserts. In Britain, carrot puddings started appearing in recipe books in the 1700s and 1800s, and the use of carrots in this fashion was revived in Britain during the World War II, when sugar was in short supply.

Carrot cake is a popular American invention. It contains grated raw carrots, raisins, chopped walnuts, and spices in the batter. It is traditionally filled and iced with cream cheese frosting.

Casaba melon—A member of the **muskmelon** family, the casaba melon is a large, globe-shaped melon with a thick golden yellow to pale green rind and deep, rough furrows. The creamy-white flesh is extremely juicy and has a mild flavor similar to that of a cucumber. It can be used like cantaloupe as an ingredient in fruit salads, ice creams, sorbets, and parfaits. Although it originated in Persia thousands of years ago, it was not introduced to the United States until the nineteenth century, when it was imported from Kasaba, Turkey. Casabas are grown in California and are most readily available from September through November. The ideal fruit to choose is fresh smelling and has a deep, even-colored yellow rind with a slightly wrinkled appearance; it should give slightly when gently pressed at the blossom end. Avoid melons with soft spots or mold. Store underripe melons at room temperature until completely ripe, then refrigerate.

Cashew—The cashew tree is native to Brazil. The Portuguese introduced the tree to Africa and India. It belongs to the same family as the **mango** and the **pistachio.** The tree produces fleshy applelike fruits, each with a single seed—the cashew nut—growing from the bottom as a hard protuberance. The nut is protected by a double shell (or actually three shells, if you count the skin on the nut itself). The space between the inner and outer shells is filled with a toxic oily brown liquid called, appropriately enough, *cashew nut shell oil.* This oil is used to make resins and alkali-resistant flexible materials. Because small amounts of the oil are found on the inner shell and the kernel itself, the nuts are always heated before shelling to destroy the toxicity and avoid burns on the skin of the workers. Cashew nuts contain almost 50 percent fat and should therefore be stored, covered, in the refrigerator or freezer to prevent them from becoming rancid.

As with all nuts, toasting greatly enhances their flavor. Although the pear-shaped apple itself is consumed in the areas where trees grow, it is not favored as a fruit to eat out of hand, for the most part. Instead, the rather tart, almost astringent, apples are used to make vinegar and a liqueur called *Kajü.* This name comes from the word *caju,* the Brazilian name for the cashew; the old Brazilian name, *acaju,* was changed to *caju* by the Portuguese. Raw unsalted cashew nuts (whole or in pieces) are not only quite expensive, they can be difficult to find in the retail market. Often a health or natural foods store is a good place to look. If you must settle for roasted and salted nuts in a recipe calling for toasted cashews, blanch and dry them to rid them of the salt, and omit toasting the nuts. The distinctive buttery-rich flavor of cashews is delightful in combination with fresh ripe fruits such as peaches, nectarines, and, especially, mangoes.

Cashew apple—See **Cashew.**

Cassava—Although this starchy root is native to South America, it is now cultivated in Africa, where it is an important staple. The root ranges from 6 to 12 inches (15 to 30 cm) in length and from 2 to 3 inches (5 to 7.5 cm) in diameter. It has a tough brown skin that, when peeled, reveals a crisp white flesh. Cassava roots are cigar shaped, with a brown, often pinkish rind, which is usually hairy, and ivory white flesh. They vary in size but average about 10 inches (25 cm) long and 2 inches (5 cm) in diameter. There are many varieties of cassava but only two main categories: sweet and bitter. The sweet variety is eaten as a vegetable. The bitter version is poisonous unless cooked and is used to make cassava bread, starch, and, most frequently, for tapioca. It is also known as *manioc* and *yuca*. Either variety should be stored in the refrigerator for no more than four days.

Cassia—The dried bark of the Asian tree *Cinnamonum cassia*, used primarily as a substitute for **cinnamon**. While this spice resembles and is related to cinnamon, it is inferior in comparison (hence it is also referred to as *false* or *bastard cinnamon*). Cassia, which is reddish brown in color, is marketed and used like cinnamon in powdered form and in cured and curled quills of bark. Cassia buds—the dried, unripe fruits—are also used in China and elsewhere much in the manner of cloves, to lend their powerful aroma to confections and other items such as pickles. Cassia is also used in curries.

Cassis—A European **black currant** used mainly to make black currant syrup and **crème de cassis** liqueur. Crème de cassis can be used alone or mixed to make apéritifs such as *Kir* and *Kir Royale*. Cassis can be used as a garnish for fruit-flavored ice cream. The name can also refer to a wine produced in Provence.

Castor sugar—See Sugar.

Catawba grape—See Grape.

Cereal grains—From the Latin word *ceralis*, "of grain." Cereal grains range from **wheat, barley, corn**, and **oats** to quinoa, **rice**, rye, and **sorghum**. Some of these, when processed, make what are commonly known as breakfast cereals. Many cereal grains are used in baking bread.

Chalazae—The thick, white cordlike cluster of egg white that attaches to both ends of the yolk, thereby holding the yolk in the center of the egg white. A prominent chalazae means the egg is very fresh. It is not detrimental in most recipes but it cannot be whisked or cooked out. It must be strained out if a very smooth consistency is desired, like that of dessert custard.

Chambord—A liqueur made from black raspberries and other fruits, with herbs and honey.

Chamomile—A perennial plant (*Chamaemelum nobile*) whose daisylike flower heads have a soft aroma of lemon and pineapple. The flowers are used to make tea to calm the nerves. The European plant (*Anthemis nobilis*) was used by ladies of the Victorian era to brew a tea thought to restore failing health and vigor. Herb gardeners sometimes also grow German or sweet chamomile, which is similar, but slightly stronger.

Champagne—While the term has been inappropriately applied to any variety of sparkling wine, true champagne is produced in the designated Champagne region of northeast France using only three grape varieties: Chardonnay, Pinot Noir, and Pinot Meumier, and made with the traditional method, *méthode champenoise*. This traditional method requires a second fermentation in which the sparkle is fermented in the wine in the bottle and originally required some 100 manual operations (some of which are mechanized today). Champagnes can range in color from pale gold to apricot blush. Their flavors can range from toasty to yeasty and from dry (no sugar added) to sweet. A sugar-wine mixture called a *dosage*, added just before final corking, determines how sweet the particular champagne will be.

Champagne grape—See Grape.

Chartreuse—A very potent liqueur, made only by the Carthusian monks of La Grande Chartreuse, near Grenoble, France. Chartreuse is made from 130 alpine herbs following a secret formula developed in 1605. This recipe is known only to the monks, who protect it by their vow of silence. Chartreuse is imported in America in three flavors, or colors, which also signify the strength of the liqueur. Green is 110 proof, yellow is 80 proof, and a third style, known as *V.E.P.*, is 108 proof, but this is not readily available. The color chartreuse is named for the green variety of the liqueur.

Cheese—Cheese is one of the oldest manufactured foods and, as is true of other fermented products, the first curdled or spoiled milk that was enjoyed in this fashion was most likely discovered accidentally. Most researchers seem to agree that the discovery of utilizing **rennet** to curdle milk first occurred as a result of fresh milk being stored in pouches made from the stomachs of animals. It is assumed that producing cheese by way of bacterial milk fermentation was an unplanned invention as well. Once it was discovered that these products had a pleasing flavor and—possibly more important, in ancient times—that both curdling and fermenting were ways of preserving milk, these process were duplicated intentionally, and cheese making began.

All cheeses are made from milk but come in thousands of varieties. Cheeses are classified in several ways, the two main distinctions being the type of milk used (cow's milk, goat's milk, and sheep's milk are the most common) and the method used to make the cheese. All methods of cheese making begin by adding a bacterial culture and/or rennet (either animal or vegetable) to milk to cause the milk proteins to coagulate and form curds. Following are the main production classifications; however, within each of these categories are again a multitude of differences in the end product. These distinctions are influenced by location (not only the country but also the region within the country), length and method of aging, the type of milk used, and the cheese maker's own style.

Fresh cheeses are uncooked and are not ripened. The curds may or may not be drained from the whey, and the cheeses may be shaped into individual forms or simply placed in a storage container to scoop out as needed.

Fresh cheeses include **farmer's cheese, baker's cheese, cottage cheese, mascarpone, goat's milk cheeses** that are not aged, and the French *fromage blanc*.

Soft-ripened cheeses are shaped, and the surface of the cheese is treated with or exposed to mold so that the cheese ripens from the outside inward. These have a thin white crust. Familiar examples are Brie and Camembert.

Washed-rind cheeses are ripened cheeses that have been treated with a brine or alcohol solution (these include salt water, brandy, and beer) at some point during the ripening process. The term *washing* can refer to actually immersing the cheese in the liquid or simply rubbing it into the rind. The purpose of washing is to create mold on the exterior of the cheese. These cheeses usually have an orange to tan-colored rind. Italian Taleggio and French Pont l'Evêque fall into this category.

Natural-rind cheeses, as the name implies, are cheeses that are allowed to form a rind naturally as they age; they are not treated with mold, nor are their washed. Cheeses in this group are aged for a longer period than those discussed up to this point. Natural-rind cheeses include English Stilton and the two French cheeses Cantal and Tomme de Savoie.

Blue-veined cheeses are those that contain ribbons of mold throughout their interior, as opposed to cheeses that show mold on the exterior. Blue veined cheeses are made all over the world and include Italian Gorgonzola, French Roquefort, English Stilton (also a natural-rind cheese), and American Maytag Blue.

Pressed cheeses are divided into those that are uncooked and those that are cooked. *Cooking* refers to heating the curds before pressing them to produce a firm texture. Uncooked pressed cheeses include English Cheddar and French Morbier. Cooked pressed cheeses include Dutch Gouda, French Gruyère, Swiss Emmentaler and Appenzeller, and Italian Parmigiano-Reggiano.

Cheeses Commonly Used in Baking and Pastry

Baker's cheese—A fresh (unripened) cheese with a low fat content. It is similar to **cottage cheese,** but it does not have curds and its flavor is a bit sourer. Baker's cheese is used in cheesecakes and cheese fillings for pastries. It can be frozen.

Cottage cheese—Originating as a homemade cheese (the name probably reflects the cheese's development in farm cottage kitchens), this lumpy, soft white cheese can be purchased with small or large curds. The standard base for cottage cheese is skimmed pasteurized cow's milk, although sometimes whole milk or even cream is added to enrich the cheese. Commercial production of cottage cheese began in the United States in the early twentieth century. Processed cottage cheese is sometimes used as a low-fat alternative to cream cheese. Cottage cheese is also used in making pancake and crepe fillings. Also known as

curd cheese and *pot cheese.*

Cream cheese—Developed in the United States in 1872, cream cheese is a mildly tangy, spreadable cheese with a smooth, creamy texture. This soft, unripened cheese is made from cow's milk cultured with bacteria. There are specialty varieties, such as low fat and whipped, and cream cheese made with or without a stabilizer. The recipes in this text use whole-milk, block-style cream cheese made with a stabilizing agent. Cream cheese is a popular ingredient for many types of cheesecakes, pastry dough, tarts, and cookies.

Devonshire cheese—See **Cream.**

Double-crème—The French term for soft ripened cheeses made by enriching the fresh cheese curds with extra cream to increase the butterfat content to 60 to 74 percent. The first double-crème cheese was Petit-Suisse, made in Normandy in 1850. The cheese was named for the *fromager* (cheese maker) who invented it, who just happened to be a rather short man of Swiss nationality. Double-crème cheeses are often served with fruit as part of a dessert course.

Farmer's cheese—A form of **cottage cheese,** made from pasteurized cow's milk, from which the majority of the liquid has been forced out. It is typically used for cooking, eaten with fresh fruit, or seasoned and made into a spread or dip. This fresh cheese has a mild, slightly tangy flavor. It is dry and firm enough to slice or crumble; it is usually sold in a solid loaf. The terms *cottage cheese, farmer's cheese,* and *pot* or *potted cheese* are sometimes used interchangeably, depending on the manufacturer

Goat's milk cheese—Known as *chèvre* in French, goat's-milk cheese can range in texture from very dry and crumbly to moist and creamy. There are also both fresh and ripened varieties. Goat's-milk cheeses are made into many shapes, such as pyramids, disks, and cones.

Mascarpone cheese—This is a very rich cheese is made from fresh cream derived from cow's milk. The cream is reduced to near **triple-crème** consistency to give the cheese its soft, smooth, rich texture. It is Italian, originating in the Lombardy region, but is now made throughout the country. The flavor of mascarpone blends beautifully with other food, especially fruit. Fresh figs with mascarpone is a classic, although Tiramisu is probably the dessert that most people think of first when it comes to mascarpone. Mascarpone also makes a wonderfully rich cheesecake.

Pot cheese—See **Farmer's cheese.**

Quark cheese—Quark is a fresh dairy product loosely classified as a cheese. Its origins are in Austria and Germany. It is a bit like a cross between **yogurt** and **cottage cheese.**

Ricotta cheese—Ricotta is from Italy. The word means "recooked," and its origins are in Rome and connected to the making of Romano and mozzarella. Ricotta was first made from the whey that was left after the curds from these cheeses had been strained. Until about a century ago, this whey was discarded. At that time, it was discovered that the protein-rich whey could itself form curds if it were reheated. That product, after draining, was named *ricotta*. Ricotta is now produced commercially starting with whole or skim milk rather than with whey. Italian ricotta is primarily made from sheep's milk or water buffalo milk, and is more flavorful than the American version made from cow's milk.

Topfen—A fresh dairy product similar to **quark,** but slightly drier. It is used in cooking and baking in the same way as **cottage cheese.**

Triple-crème—The French term for soft ripened cheeses made by enriching the fresh cheese curds with extra cream to increase the fat content to a minimum of 75 percent. The first of these cheeses was called Le Magnum and was made around 1925 by the Dubuc family in Normandy; this evolved into the cheese known as Brillat-Savarin, one of the most famous of all dessert cheeses.

Cherimoya—The cherimoya is the fruit of the annona tree and is native to the mountain regions of Peru and Ecuador. Today it is grown in many temperate climates including, within the United States, southern California, Florida, and, to a lesser extent, Maui. This delicious fruit is sometimes referred to as a *custard apple* because the consistency of the pulp is soft and custardy; the ivory flesh also contains black seeds, which are not eaten. Other names for the cherimoya include *sugar apple* and *sweetsop*. Cherimoyas are sure to amaze anyone experiencing this fruit for the first time. They are almost heart-shaped; their skin looks very much like a cross between an artichoke and a pineapple; and their flavor is a wonderful tropical combination of pineapple, mango, and banana. Cherimoyas are best eaten chilled, either cut into halves or quarters with the pulp scooped out using a spoon, or juiced and strained to make sorbet or ice cream. They should be purchased when they are still firm and left at room temperature to ripen. They can then be stored, covered, in the refrigerator for up to four days.

Chéri-Suisse—A Swiss liqueur with the flavors of cherries and chocolate.

Cherry—Cherries come in four distinct groups. Altogether, some 1200 varieties are grown around the world. There are two main groups of sweet cherries, although hybridization and cross-pollination has made the distinction a little fuzzy. The first type of sweet cherry is the soft but extremely juicy variety classified as Guigne; of these, **Black Tartarian** is one of the more common. Guigne sweet cherries are not popular commercially because they are too delicate to ship. The second sweet variety is the Bigarreau. These cherries are firm, with a slightly dry flesh that is better suited to shipping. This category includes the well-known **Bing** cherry and the so-called white cherries, which actually have closer to light red and yellow skin and amber flesh; **Royal Ann** is one of the better known of these.

The third group of cherries is the sour cherries or sour morello; in the United States, they are also known as *pie cherries*. These are essential for making classic desserts such as Black Forest cake and cherry strudel. The Black Morello is the most popular of the sour varieties, especially in Europe. **Montmorency** is another that is well known and well liked. Sour cherries also include the small French **Guinettes** we can buy in this country macerated in **kirsch,** and the Marasca cherry, better known as the *Maraschino cherry*. The latter are used to make Maraschino liqueur, maraschino cherries preserved in a sweet syrup, and, of course, the candied (and brightly colored) maraschino cherries used in cocktails.

The fourth and last variety, known as *Duke cherries,* is a hybrid of the sweet and sour varieties. These are a good choice to use for cooking and preserving. The most common ones in the United States are the May Duke and the Late Duke.

Cherries do not keep well and should always be stored in the refrigerator and left whole (with stem and pit). Once pitted, they will oxidize, start to deteriorate, and spoil very quickly.

Sweet Cherries

Black Tartarian—Originated in Russia. They are medium in size and bright purplish-black in color. They soften quickly after picking for commercial shipping. Variety: Guigne (soft); early season.

Bing—Originated in Oregon. These large, mahogany-red cherries are probably the most popular red sweet cherry. They have a firm and juicy flesh. Variety: Bigarreau; mid-season.

Lambert—Originated in Oregon. The fruit is large and dark colored. They are similar in taste to Bing, but they ripen later. Variety: Bigarreau; late season.

Royal Ann (Napoleon)—Originated in France. These are a very large, yellow blushed red fruit. They are the best known of the so-called *white cherries*. The flesh is firm and juicy, and it is one of the best cherries for preserving. Variety: Bigarreau; early season.

Rainier—Originated in Washington. These are known as the *yellow Bing* because the shape is similar. However, these are a blushed-red yellow cherry with a firm and juicy flesh. Variety: Bigarreau; early season.

Sour Cherries

Montmorency—Originated in France. These are the standard sour cherry. They are round in shape and semi-tart in flavor, with a bright red color and firm yellow flesh. Variety: Sour Morello; season varies depending on the strain and fruit characteristics.

Guinette—Originated in France. These small semi-sour cherries are red, with unusually long stems. They are very popular for macerating in kirsch brandy. Variety: Sour Morello; midseason.

Morello—Origin unknown. This fruit is deep, actually black red in color, and large in size, with a tender and juicy flesh. The flavor is only slightly tart. Variety: Sour Morello; late season.

Cherry Heering—A dark red, cherry-flavored liqueur from Denmark, made by distilling brandy from cherries.

Cherry plum—Also know as *mirabelle,* this small plum is grown in Great Britain and other parts of Europe. It has a sweet flavor and ranges in color from golden yellow to red. The cherry plum is used primarily in tarts and preserves.

Chestnut—Chestnuts are the seed of the chestnut tree, of which there are quite a few varieties. Chestnut trees are found in many temperate regions and grow wild in much of Europe, where their name, from the Greek word *kastanéa,* changes depending on location; it is *kastanjer* in Sweden and *castagne* in Italy. The spectacular European sweet chestnut tree (not to be confused with the American variety, which produces a much smaller nut) is a great ornamental and shade tree growing up to 100 feet (30 m) tall. These trees are part of the landscape all over northern Europe. In the springtime, they are covered with clusters of yellowish flowers, which later become spiny burrs, each containing up to three nuts. The chestnuts that are sold for cooking, either fresh in the fall and winter or canned in sugar syrup or water throughout the year, are the European variety. For some reason, chestnuts are utilized much more in cooking all across Europe than in the United States, where they still seem a bit underrated (with the exception of a brief burst of popularity around the holidays).

Botanically, chestnuts are classified as a fruit rather than a nut because they contain a greater amount of starch than oil. The chestnuts (typically two or three) develop inside a prickly green husk and generally ripen with the first frost around October. Each golden nut is enclosed in a thin brown membrane and covered by a smooth mahogany-colored, leathery shell. The nuts are found fresh in the markets during the winter months; they must be cooked and peeled before they are eaten. Just as they are in Europe today, chestnuts were once plentiful in the United States until a blight, transferred from a newly planted Far East variety, destroyed most of the trees early in the twentieth century. Though slowly recovering, the chestnuts produced by the American variety of chestnut tree are much smaller, although sweeter, than the better-known European variety. Consequently, most of the fresh chestnuts available are imported from Europe and, for the most part, these come from Italy. Mount Olympus, home of the ancient Greek gods, was said to have an abundance of chestnut trees.

The chestnut harvest is one of the biggest events of the year in the mountain districts of southern Europe, from the Pyrenees to the alpine regions of France and Italy. Because cereal grains cannot be grown in these areas, chestnuts take the place of grain, to a large extent, as they are mostly starch.

In addition to fresh in the shell or fresh vacuum-packed, chestnuts can be purchased dried, either whole or ground into flour; canned in brine; frozen; dehydrated; as a puree, either sweetened or unsweetened; and last, but certainly not when it comes to flavor, are the wonderful and luxurious marrons glacés, which are outrageously expensive but sensationally delicious—the ultimate in candied fruits and nuts. Fresh or cooked chestnuts should be kept in the refrigerator. The unsweetened puree should not be stored longer than a week, but marrons glacés will keep just about indefinitely. Nutritionally, chestnuts are a world apart from other actual nuts, as they are mostly starch (carbohydrate) and relatively low in fat and calories.

Because fresh chestnuts are available in the winter months, they play a big role in holiday creations both savory and sweet. The most simple of all chestnut preparations are the whole nuts roasted over an open fire, made famous by a popular Christmas carol and sold by street vendors in some cities in the winter. These are prepared using a special skillet-type of roasting pan that has a long handle and a perforated bottom. For all other uses, there is no way to avoid the tedious task of removing the shell and skin.

Sweetened chestnut puree is used alone as a filling and to flavor buttercream. Whole candied chestnuts can be used to decorate cakes; chopped candied chestnuts can be added to candies and ice creams.

Chèvre—French for "goat"; used to refer to goat's milk cheeses. See **Cheese.**

Chinese date—The yellow flesh of this olive-sized fruit is encased by a leathery red, off-white, or black skin. Its flavor is similar to that of a prune. It is usually stewed with a sweetener. It can be used in both savory and sweet items or simply eaten alone. While the Chinese date is primarily imported from China, a small amount is harvested on the west coast of the United States. Also known as *Chinese jujube* and *red date.*

Chinese gooseberry—See **Kiwi.**

Chinese grapefruit—See **Pomelo.**

Chinese pear—See **Asian pear.**

Chocolate

Chocolate History

Many describe chocolate as the world's most perfect food, some consider it to have mystical properties, and around the world, with the exception of Asia, it is probably the best-loved flavor. Certainly no one can argue that life would be very different for anyone in our profession without this most wondrous ingredient. The transformation of the bitter cocoa bean into a delicious piece of smooth creamy chocolate candy or an elegant chocolate dessert is not only a lengthy and complex process but the evolution of the production technique itself covers hundreds of years and much of the globe.

Chocolate is derived from the fruit of the cocoa tree, which the Swedish botanist Carl von Linné designated *Theobroma* (Greek for "food of the gods") *cacao* in 1728. But long before that time, chocolate was enjoyed as a beverage by the people of ancient civilizations, including the Mayans, Aztecs, and Toltecs. The cocoa tree originated in South America and was brought north to Mexico by the Mayans prior to the seventh century A.D. The Aztecs, too, subscribed to the theory that chocolate was heaven sent, believing it to be a gift from their god Quetzalcóatl.

The word *chocolate* comes by way of the Spanish from the Aztec Indian word *xocolatl*, meaning "bitter water" or "cocoa water," referring to the beverage made by the Aztecs using ground cocoa beans. The Aztecs placed such a high value on cocoa beans that they were used as a form of currency. They flavored their chocolate drink with spices (even chilies) but did not add any sweetener (I'm sure anyone who has tasted unsweetened baking chocolate can understand the "bitter" designation). Columbus brought cocoa beans to Spain at the end of his fourth and final voyage (1502–1504). But it is the explorer Hernán Cortés who is given credit for popularizing and making the importance and great potential of cocoa understood by introducing the drink known as *chocolate* to Spain after returning from his Mexican expedition in 1519. Cortés first tasted chocolate at a ceremony with the Aztec emperor Montezuma. One of the Spanish lieutenants, Bernal Díaz del Castillo, in writing about their journey, said that Montezuma believed the chocolate to have powers as an aphrodisiac. His report went on to say that though Montezuma "ate very little," he drank more than 50 golden cups a day that were "filled with foaming chocolate."

The Spanish added sugar to the beverage, resulting in something vaguely similar to today's hot chocolate (although it was prepared with water rather than milk), and the popularity of the drink spread from Spain through Europe and then to England. Chocolate became a fashionable drink, and chocolate houses, like coffeehouses, were important social meeting places in the seventeenth and eighteenth centuries. The Dutch sent cocoa beans to New Amsterdam and, by the early 1700s, chocolate (in a beverage form) was being offered by pharmacists in Boston, who touted it as the latest cure-all. Dr. James Baker founded America's first chocolate company in 1765.

At that time, there was still no hard form of chocolate comparable to the candy we know today. That development did not occur until 1828, when the Dutchman Conrad J. Van Houten, whose family had a chocolate business in Amsterdam, produced chocolate powder with the invention of a screw press that removed the majority of the cocoa butter from the finely ground cocoa beans. His intention was to use the chocolate powder to make the chocolate drink less rich and oily. However, the extracted pure cocoa butter proved the key ingredient that led to hardened eating chocolate: By adding extra cocoa butter to the chocolate powder, a paste was developed that was smoother, more malleable, and more easily combined with sugar. Though it was still a far less refined product than we are familiar with, this forerunner of modern chocolate candy caught on in a big way. (Cocoa butter, because it melts at a temperature just under body temperature, is the ingredient that gives chocolate candy its melt-in-the-mouth consistency.)

Attempting to further improve the chocolate beverage, Van Houten also invented the process known as *Dutching*. This involves treating either the chocolate nibs (the crushed cocoa beans) or the chocolate liquor (the paste produced during the initial step in chocolate production) with an alkaline solution to raise its pH level. This produces cocoa powder that is darker in color, sometimes reddish, and milder in taste. The terms *Dutch-process* and *Dutch cocoa* are both used today for unsweetened cocoa powder that has been treated with an alkali, usually potassium carbonate.

With the process of making chocolate candy using additional cocoa butter established, two English companies, the Cadbury Company and Fry and Sons, were selling the product by the mid-1800s. The next significant development occurred in 1875, when the Swiss manufacturer Daniel Peter added the newly discovered product *condensed milk*, producing the first milk chocolate. The person responsible for the invention of condensed milk was none other than Henri Nestlé of Switzerland, who was, at that time, manufacturing baby foods. (Nestlé Brands, to this day, is one of the largest producers of food products in the world. In 1939, it created the first chocolate chip made for cookies.) Closely following the milk chocolate breakthrough, Rodolphe Lindt invented the technique known as *conching* in 1879. This process, named for the shell-shaped trough that Lindt used to hold the mixture, consists of slowly kneading the chocolate to develop a smooth texture and incorporate a still greater ratio of cocoa butter; conching elevated chocolate standards considerably. Jules Suchard created the first molded and filled chocolate shells in 1913.

None of these European companies set up shop to mass-produce milk chocolate in the United States, however. That distinction belongs to American-born Milton Snaveley Hershey (1857–1945), whose candy career started over a century ago in 1894. In 1903, after a few years of attempting to manufacturer several candies, Hershey decided to specialize in chocolate and opened a factory in a town known at that time as Derry Church. What started as housing for the Hershey factory employees ultimately became the city of Hershey, Pennsylvania. The Hershey Bar was a phenomenal success, and the Hershey factory eventually became the world's largest chocolate manufacturing plant. Today, Hershey Park is located at the site of the original factory. It attracts millions of visitors per year and includes a 23-acre rose garden, amusement park rides, and the Hotel Hershey (which features a circular dining room, because Mr. Hershey is said to have disliked restaurants where "they put you in a corner"). Hershey was the first manufacturer of powdered hot chocolate or hot cocoa mix and, of course, invented the ever-popular foil-wrapped candy, the Hershey Kiss.

Two other chocolate companies, Ghirardelli and Guittard, were started in California after the gold rush, and both are still major U.S. producers. Italian immigrant Domingo Ghirardelli founded his eponymous company in 1852. The site of the original Ghirardelli chocolate plant in San Francisco is now a popular tourist spot called Ghirardelli Square and features restaurants, art galleries, and specialty shops. In the late 1990s, the Lindt chocolate company purchased Ghirardelli, but the factory continues to produce under the Ghirardelli name. The Guittard Chocolate Company is located just south of San Francisco.

During World War II, chocolate bars were included in the rations issued to American soldiers, resulting in a shortage of chocolate in the stores back home. The Nestlé Company capitalized on this in their marketing efforts, proclaiming that "chocolate is a fighting food; it supplies the greatest amount of nourishment in the smallest possible bulk." Scientist Alexander Von Humbolt (1769–1859) had previously expressed an almost identical sentiment when he stated, "Nature has nowhere else concentrated such an abundance of the most valuable foods in such a limited space as in the cocoa bean." Although some nutritionists today may not endorse this assessment, the popularity of chocolate is more widespread than ever, and besides being a pleasure for the palate, chocolate is still a favorite source of quick energy, used by some athletes to prevent fatigue and gain stamina during sporting events.

In recent years, the public's devotion to chocolate has generated thousands of books and magazines devoted to the subject. It has inspired chefs to try to surpass each other at creating the richest, most intensely chocolate, most decadent desserts. Large numbers of people go so far as to say they are addicted to chocolate, referring to themselves as *chocoholics*.

Modern scientific research has been conducted to study the possibility of medicinal properties in chocolate, which has long had a place in folk medicine, and many people strongly believe in chocolate's mood-lifting ability. There is some scientific basis for this theory. Chocolate is rich in phenylethylamine, a naturally occurring substance that acts similarly to amphetamines. Two American psychiatrists have introduced a hypothesis that people who go on chocolate-eating binges as a result of depression are actually trying (perhaps unknowingly) to stabilize their body chemistry by ingesting phenylethylamine. An article in the San Francisco *Examiner* newspaper, dated February 2000, reports on a Washington State research project that found compounds in chocolate to have cardiovascular benefits. Responding to this study and describing his own research, Carl Keen, chairman of the nutrition department at The University of California at Davis, stated that "Our data would suggest that chocolate can be part of a healthy diet." Keen conducted a study in which healthy adults ingested water mixed with cocoa powder and sugar, then had their blood levels tested over the following six hours. He found their blood platelets became less active and less likely to clump, meaning the blood was less likely to clot, when compared to the test subjects who drank a mixture of water, caffeine, and sugar. This test was a follow-up to other research conducted in the laboratory that showed that compounds in chocolate known as *flavonoids* have a positive effect on the formation of nitric oxide, a chemical that relaxes the blood vessels. Flavonoids are also found in vegetables, fruits, tea, and red wine. They act as antioxidants, destroying free radicals, which are associated with disease and aging. Chocolate also contains caffeine, although a significant amount is not consumed unless one eats a large quantity of straight chocolate liquor or unsweetened baking chocolate—which is unlikely. Commercial chocolate products contain about 0.1 percent caffeine, and an average serving of chocolate candy contains far less caffeine than a cup of coffee.

Taste or flavor is the most subjective element and can be a matter of individual opinion. In judging chocolate, you should look for:

- **Temper**—The temper of chocolate has to do with its structure and is largely based on the crystallization of the cocoa butter particles. The grain structure should be tight and even throughout. The chocolate should break sharply rather than bend or crumble (naturally, the chocolate must be at the appropriate temperature to judge this accurately).
- **Texture**—The texture of chocolate when it is eaten should always be smooth, with no gritty or sandy feel. Chocolate should melt readily as soon as it is in your mouth.
- **Color**—Chocolate should have an even color throughout, with no gray streaking.
- **Aroma**—Chocolate can easily pick up foreign odors. It should smell only of chocolate and deliberately added flavorings, such as nut paste.

Chocolate Production

The cocoa or cacao tree is an evergreen that can be found all through the equatorial belt (within 20 degrees north or south) where the average temperature is 80°F (26°C) and humidity is high, in areas including Costa Rica, Guatemala, Nicaragua, Nigeria, Panama, Trinidad, and the Ivory Coast. The trees can grow taller but in most plantations are kept to about 25 feet (7 m 50 cm) in height. Like the trees of the citrus family, cocoa trees bear buds, blossoms, and fruit all at the same time. Each tree produces about 30 oblong fruits or pods, which, unlike other types of fruit, grow directly on the trunk and branches. Each pod is 6 to 10 inches (15 to 25 cm) long, 3 to 4 inches (7.5 to 10 cm) in diameter, and contains anywhere from 20 to 50 beans, 1 inch (2.5 cm) in length, embedded in the fleshy interior. The majority of the world crop of cocoa beans (which averages 2 million tons annually) comes from Africa. The largest African producer is by far is Côte d'Ivoire, where the Forastero bean is cultivated; Ghana is a distant second.

Chocolate Production

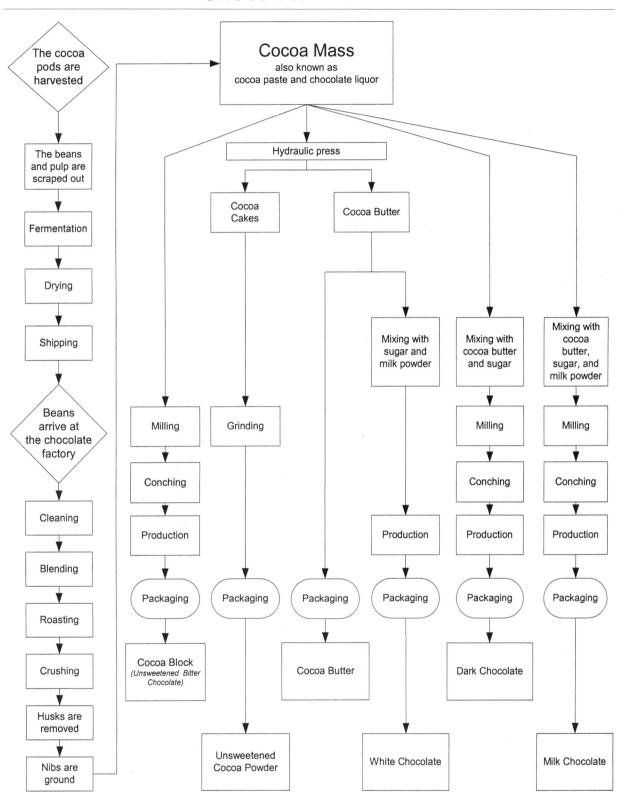

FIGURE A-1 The production process for chocolate

The cocoa fruits are harvested year round, although the first few months are generally a slower time and the main harvests take place twice a year following the rainy seasons. The seeds, along with the white flesh or pulp, are scraped out of the pods by hand and placed in heaps covered with banana leaves or left in boxes with slatted bottoms to allow the liquid to drain. The beans are then left to ferment, a process that is crucial to developing the flavor. This takes from as little as a few days to three weeks, depending on the climate. During the fermentation process, the pulp breaks down and the temperature rises, biochemical changes take place, the cell walls in the beans are broken down, and some of the bitterness is eliminated.

The fermented beans are spread out on mats and dried in the sun to remove most of the water content. After drying, the beans develop a more pronounced cocoa aroma. At this stage, the beans are ready to be packed into jute sacks and shipped.

When the beans arrive at the chocolate factories, they are thoroughly cleaned. Generally, several types of beans are blended at this point to create the desired flavor and to ensure a consistent finished product. The beans are then roasted at a fairly low temperature (250°F/122°C) to develop a richer flavor and aroma. After cooling, the whole beans are crushed, then the shells or husks are separated, using an air current to blow the lighter husk away; this process is known as *winnowing.* The husks are used for both fertilizer and animal feed. The roasted, crushed kernels of cocoa bean are called *cocoa nibs.*

The nibs are milled very fine, producing a thick liquid known as *cocoa paste, cocoa mass,* or *chocolate liquor,* which contains 53 to 55 percent cocoa butter (the term *chocolate liquor* has no reference to alcohol and should not be confused with spirits known as *chocolate liqueurs*). This is the main ingredient for a variety of chocolate products. All processing, after this point, is additional refinement to create individual products. Part of the cocoa mass is placed under high hydraulic pressure to extract the cocoa butter, a valuable aromatic fat that is an essential part of every chocolate recipe and the ingredient that gives chocolate a fine texture and attractive glaze. The cocoa cakes that are left after the fat has been removed are crushed, ground into a fine powder, and sifted to produce pure unsweetened cocoa powder.

Cocoa butter, sugar, and milk powder, in the case of milk chocolate, are added to the cocoa mass to make chocolate. The combination is kneaded together in large mixers with *S*-shaped blades until a smooth, homogeneous mixture has developed. This can now be called *chocolate,* but it is not yet the smooth confection we think of when we use that word.

To remove the gritty taste still present at this stage, the chocolate is conveyed to large refiners, heavy machines with rollers 40 to 60 inches (1 to 1.5 m) long and 12 to 16 inches (30 to 40 cm) in diameter. The mixture is passed through the rollers, each set of rollers becoming progressively more narrow (like rolling out pasta dough using a manual machine), until the particles are so fine as to be undetectable on the palate.

The chocolate is now ready for the final refining process, called *conching.* Chemical changes take place during conching that further develop chocolate's characteristic flavor. In conching, the chocolate is placed in machines that knead and roll it on rotary bases continuously for two to three days; the microscopic sugar and fat particles do not become any smaller, but the sharp edges become rounded. During this process, the mixture is typically warmed to between 70° and 160°F (21° and 71°C)—although the temperature can be as high as 200°F (90°C) for some dark chocolate varieties; this allows excess moisture to evaporate. At the same time, the chocolate is exposed to blasts of fresh air. For the highest-quality chocolate, additional cocoa butter is added and, if liquid flavorings such as vanilla or emulsifiers such as **lecithin** are used, they are added at this time as well. Lecithin (derived from soybeans), besides being less expensive than cocoa butter, brings out the chocolate flavor (which might otherwise be overpowered by excess cocoa butter) and is used to establish the appropriate viscosity necessary for smooth flow in coating and molding. The end result is a velvety-smooth chocolate product. The chocolate is poured and formed into blocks, wrapped, and stored in a cool, well-ventilated room. Dark chocolate will keep this way (if unopened) for up to one year, milk and white chocolates for slightly less time.

Chocolate Terminology and Definitions of Chocolate Products

Baker's chocolate—Another name for **coating chocolate.** Baker's is also the brand name of a chocolate manufacturer that happens to sell unsweetened baking chocolate, so the name can be rather confusing. In a professional text or setting, the term *baker's chocolate* means coating chocolate.

Baking chocolate—In this text, baking chocolate is called *unsweetened chocolate.* Other names are *cocoa block* and *bitter chocolate.* See **Unsweetened chocolate.**

Bittersweet chocolate—Chocolate containing approximately 70 percent cocoa mass and 30 percent sugar. The ratio varies according to the manufacturer.

Chocolate liquor—Another name for **cocoa mass.**

Coating chocolate—Coating chocolate can be dark, light, or white. The light variety is the color of milk chocolate but does not have the same flavor. Coating chocolate is also referred to as *confectionery coating, non-temp chocolate, compound chocolate,* and *baker's chocolate.* Because there is no cocoa butter in coating chocolate (it has been replaced with other fats), it does not need to be tempered like real chocolate, so it is very convenient to use. Coating chocolate is used for ornaments and for decorating many items in the pastry shop. Products made entirely of coating chocolate may not be labeled *chocolate.*

Cocoa block—Another name for **unsweetened chocolate.**

Cocoa butter—The fat extracted from **cocoa mass** with a hydraulic press. Its uses include thinning chocolate, candy production, coating marzipan figures for shine and to prevent them from drying out rapidly, plus noncooking uses, including the manufacture of cosmetic creams and lotions.

Cocoa mass—The thick liquid produced in the first stage of chocolate production. Made from finely milled cocoa nibs. Cocoa mass contains 53 to 55 percent **cocoa butter** and is the basis for all refined chocolate products.

Cocoa nibs—Roasted and crushed cocoa beans.

Cocoa paste—Another name for **cocoa mass**.

Couverture—A term used by some chocolate manufacturers for their product. Although *couverture* is French for "coating," this is not the same as **coating chocolate**. Couverture can be dark, light (milk), or white, and it often has a high ratio of cocoa butter.

Dutch-process cocoa powder—See **Unsweetened cocoa powder**.

Milk chocolate—Also known as *light chocolate*, milk chocolate is made in the same way as dark chocolate, with the addition of milk powder. Milk chocolate must contain at least 15 percent milk solids, 3 to 4 percent of which should be milk fat. The total fat content must be at least 25 percent, and the maximum sugar content is 50 percent.

Light chocolate—Another name for **milk chocolate**.

Semisweet chocolate—Chocolate containing approximately 60 percent cocoa mass and 40 percent sugar. The ratio varies according to the manufacturer.

Sweet dark chocolate—Sweet dark chocolate is cocoa paste finely ground and conched, with the addition of extra cocoa butter, sugar, and vanilla. Sweet dark chocolate generally contains 50 percent cocoa mass and 50 percent sugar. Included in that makeup should be a minimum of 20 percent total cocoa butter. Dark chocolate is used in fillings, such as ganache, and in a multitude of chocolate desserts. Tempered dark chocolate is used for decorations and coating candies and pastries.

Tempered chocolate—Refined chocolate that has been stabilized using the process known as *tempering*. Many methods are used to temper chocolate, but the majority consist of three basic steps: melting, cooling, and rewarming. The purpose of tempering is to achieve the desired high gloss and hard, brittle texture, and to make the chocolate more resistant to warm temperatures. When chocolate has been tempered, the fat groups within the cocoa butter in the chocolate become evenly distributed throughout. See pages 468 to 471.

Unsweetened chocolate—Also known as **cocoa block,** *bitter chocolate,* and **baking chocolate.** Unsweetened chocolate is made from cocoa paste that has been finely ground and conched; the **cocoa butter** content should be at least 50 percent. Unsweetened chocolate is used as a flavoring and coloring agent for fillings, marzipan, mousses, and many other products; it is not eaten plain.

Unsweetened cocoa powder—Unsweetened cocoa powder is the finely ground product of the pressed cake that remains after the **cocoa butter** is extracted from the **cocoa mass.** It should contain a minimum of 20 percent fat. There are two types of unsweetened cocoa powder: Dutch-process cocoa powder and natural cocoa powder, which is referred to throughout this text simply as *unsweetened cocoa powder.* Dutch-process powder is processed with an alkali, usually potassium carbonate, to raise its pH level. This produces cocoa powder that is darker in color, sometimes reddish, and milder in taste. It was invented by a Dutchman, Conrad J. Van Houten, who also invented the process used to separate cocoa butter and cocoa powder from finely ground cocoa beans that contributed significantly to the improvement of chocolate refinement. Natural unsweetened cocoa powder has not been treated and it has a slight acid taste. Dutch-process cocoa is easier to dissolve in liquid. Unsweetened cocoa powder is used in candy production, decorating pastries and cakes, and flavoring and coloring cake batters and cookies. Note: Baking soda is commonly used as part of the leavening agent in cakes and other batters that contain unsweetened cocoa powder because baking soda reacts with acid. If you are using Dutch-process unsweetened cocoa powder, which is neutral and will not react with baking soda, and the recipe does not contain any other acidic ingredient, substitute baking powder and double the measurement.

White chocolate—The term *white chocolate* is a misnomer. It is not a true chocolate because it does not contain any cocoa solids. In addition it is not white but an ivory color that is produced by the cocoa butter. White chocolate is made up of at least 15 percent milk solids (3 to 4 percent of which should be milk fat), a minimum of 20 percent cocoa butter, and a maximum of 55 percent sugar. The milk solids and fats make white chocolate very sensitive to heat. It is essential to use a low temperature in the bain-marie when melting it, watching closely and stirring frequently to prevent the white chocolate from overheating, which can cause it to thicken and develop a gritty texture.

Chocolate chip—Small piece of chocolate in a drop shape, sold in quantity for baking. The primary use for chocolate chips is as an ingredient in chocolate chip cookies. Chocolate chips are produced in various sizes known as *counts,* referring to the number of chips per pound.

Chokecherry—The name *chokecherry* is given to a number of varieties of wild cherry native to North America that are so named because of their intense sourness and astringency when unripe. The skin of this small, tart cherry turns red to almost black when mature. The dark red flesh is unpleasant raw but is an excellent ingredient for jams and jellies.

Christmas melon—The shape and skin of this melon, a member of the **muskmelon** family, looks similar to a small watermelon with a long, oval body and a splotchy green and yellow skin. Inside, however, the flesh is yellowish green, with a flavor much like a honeydew melon. It can grow up to 12 inches (30 cm) in length and weigh up to 10 pounds

(4 kg 550 g). Also known as *Santa Claus melon,* Christmas melon is so named because its peak season is in December.

Chufa; Chufa nut—This small wrinkled tuberous root of a plant native to Africa (*Cyerus esculentus*) has bumpy brown skin, white flesh, and a sweet, nutty flavor similar to that of an almond or a chestnut. They can be dried and eaten in a variety of ways—alone as a snack, candied, ground into flour, pressed for a milky liquid, and roasted as the base for a coffee beverage. They are widely popular in Spain and Mexico, primarily as a base for the drink *horchata.* Also known as *tiger nuts, earth almonds,* and *earth nuts.*

Chutney—A sweet and sour condiment, created to accompany Indian fruit and spice curries, it was a favorite of the English in India, who anglicized the original name, *chatni,* into *chutney.* Fruit and vegetables, or sometimes a combination of the two, are cooked in vinegar with sugar and spices until the mixture has the consistency of jam. Chutney can be reduced to a puree, or it can retain a chunky texture with recognizable pieces of ingredients. Their flavor can range from mild to spicy. All chutneys can be characterized by a syrupy juice that is usually highly spiced.

Cider—A popular beverage in early America, cider is produced from pressing the juice from fruit (usually apples). It can be drunk straight or diluted with water. Both still and sparkling ciders are produced. In North America, the term *cider* generally refers to unfermented pressed apple juice. In England, the term is associated with the fermented alcoholic beverage. Cider is referred to as *sweet cider* before fermentation. After fermentation, it becomes known as **hard cider.** Apple cider can be used to make vinegar, **brandy,** and **applejack** (a distilled spirit made from hard cider), and its many varieties are often used in cooking. The production of cider dates to ancient times.

Cider vinegar—Vinegar made from **cider,** usually apple, fermented to hard cider, then exposed to air. It has a strong, somewhat harsh flavor and a clear, pale brown color.

Cinnamon—Cinnamon was once a commodity of great value and, together with two other important spices—nutmeg and clove—has been the reason for much human bloodshed over time. The Arabs kept their source of cinnamon a highly guarded secret for many centuries and tried to discourage anyone from finding an alternate source by telling stories of monsters inhabiting countries they suspected of containing the spice. That cinnamon grows wild throughout Ceylon did not come to be known before the fourteenth century. The most widely used cinnamon today is the *Cinnamomum cassia* variety, which originated in Burma. The other type, *Cinnamomum zeylanicum,* is native to Ceylon, now called Sri Lanka. Both are derived from the bark of an evergreen laurel tree. The two types of cinnamon are often confused and have been since ancient times. The French word *cannelle* refers to either variety, as does the Swedish word *kanel. Cinnamomum zeylanicum,* which is the true cinnamon, is considered by many to have a superior flavor and aroma. However, the majority of the cinnamon sold in the

United States is the cassia variety. Either may legally be sold labeled as cinnamon.

Cinnamon made its way to Europe via the ancient and dangerous spice route. Because of a then poorly prepared Chinese product, cassia was once known as an inferior imitation of *Cinnamomum zeylanicum,* but today you would be hard put in most cases to tell the difference between the two, especially in ground form, which often contains a blend of both. Ceylon cinnamon has a slightly milder aroma and is lighter in color; the quills (the curled strips of bark) are easy to distinguish, being thin and having a smooth, round appearance. Preparation and marketing of both kinds is simple. Thin shoots or young branches are cut when the bark is easy to separate from the wood. These are trimmed to about 4 inches (10 cm) long. A slit is cut on two sides of the bark, and the piece is carefully separated into two long strips, which are immediately placed back on the stick so that they will retain their shape. The pieces are then set aside for about 6 hours to let the bark ferment. In the next step, the thin outer skin is scraped off to expose the inner bark, which is the part we call *cinnamon.* The strips are dried for a short time, then formed into quills, which, as they dry and contract, tighten into hard sticks. Cinnamon sticks keep indefinitely in a dry place where they are not exposed to sunlight.

The flavor of cinnamon makes a wonderful addition to many types of desserts—because of the natural affinity of the two flavors, especially fruit desserts containing apple. Warm apple desserts, such as apple pie, turnovers, crisp, or apples *en croûte,* are particularly pleasing with an accompaniment of cinnamon-flavored custard sauce or cinnamon ice cream. Cinnamon is used in many recipes for cookies, spice cakes, and poaching syrups, and cinnamon sugar is widely used in topping breakfast and Danish pastries.

Citric acid—A water-soluble acid extracted from the juice of citrus fruits—lemons, limes, and grapefruits—as well as other acid fruits, such as pineapples. It can also be produced by the fermentation of glucose. It is sold in both dry crystal form (as a white powder) and in liquid form. It is added to sugar syrups to prevent crystallization. With its strong, tart taste, it is also used to add flavoring to foods and beverages and to produce jams, jellies, and cordials. Additionally, it can be used as a food additive, acting as a pH control agent, preservative, or antioxidant in processed and canned foods.

Citron—(1) Dutch, French, and Swedish for "lemon." (2) A citrus fruit (*Citrus medica*), native to China and dating from the sixteenth century, that appears similar to a huge (it ranges from 6 to 9 inches/15 to 22.5 cm long) yellowish-green lemon. Although the citron resembles a lemon in many respects, a substantial difference is that the citron yields almost no juice. The bulk of the fruit is made up of dense rind. It has a hard, thick, lumpy peel and very tart flesh. Because its dry pulp is extremely sour and bitter, it cannot be eaten raw. The citron is thus cultivated for its peel, which is either pressed or candied and used in baking desserts, pastries, confections, and fruitcakes. Before the peel is candied, it is processed in brine and pressed to extract citron oil, which is used to flavor liqueurs, to scent cosmetic products, and in medicine. Additionally, the term *citron* is also the name for a preserve or pickle made from the rind of a variety of watermelon.

Buddha's Hand—A variety of citron also known as the *fingered citron*. It is used more for ornamental purposes than in cooking, but its highly unusual, almost scary, formation makes it an entertaining choice for a fruit display, as it always attracts attention. The tentacles of this unusual citron variety are used in same way as the main citron crop, in mixtures for fruitcakes and the like.

Citronella—Also known as *lemongrass* and *sereh*. A tropical perennial grass (*Cymbopogon nardus*), this herb with long, thin gray-green leaves and a scallionlike base is widely used in southeast Asian cuisine, especially in recipes from Thailand. The pale white inner stalks have a strong lemon flavor. The peel contains citral, an essential oil that gives citronella a sour-lemon flavor and fragrance. It is used as a flavoring, in salads, and as an insect repellant. Citronella grows abundantly in the tropical parts of Asia.

Citrus fruit—Fruits of the genus *Citrus*, native to Southeast Asia. Botanists have estimated that the history of the citrus tree dates back 20 million years. The trees arrived in the New World shortly after Columbus's first voyage and, from then on, they spread rapidly throughout the Americas. They thrive in tropical to temperate climates and are now grown in warm regions all over the world. Noted for its fruits' skin and juicy, pulpy flesh, the citrus family includes **citron, clementine, grapefruit, lemon, lime, mandarin, orange, pomelo, tangelo, tangerine,** and **ugli fruit.**

Citrus fruits have a slightly acidic tart flavor and are rich in vitamin C. They constitute the third most important group of fruits; with only the apple and pear group and the banana and plantain group surpassing them in production and consumption. They are used both raw and cooked and are among the most popular flavors used in confections. However, citrus is most important to the foodservice industry for its juice. Citrus fruits are also used to make jams, jellies, and a variety of liqueurs.

Claret; Clairet—The term *claret* is often used by the English in reference to red wine from France's Bordeaux region. The word is used broadly in the United States and continental Europe to refer to light red table wine made from any red wine grapes from any region.

Clarified butter—Butter with the milk solids removed. Clarified butter has a higher burning point than whole butter, which makes it preferable for frying.

Clementine—A spherical citrus fruit developed by Father Clément in North Africa by crossing the **tangerine** and the **Seville orange.** Clementines are reddish orange in color, with a thin, firm, easily removable skin and juicy, sweet, and usually seedless flesh. They are eaten out of hand and utilized like oranges in many desserts and pastries. They are grown in Mediterranean countries and are in season from November to April, with their peak in December and January.

Clingstone—Describes a fruit in which the flesh stubbornly clings to the pit, the most famous being the cling or clingstone peach.

Clotted cream—See Cream.

Clove—Cloves are the dried, unopened flower buds of the clove tree, a handsome tropical evergreen related to the eucalyptus family. The tree grows to a height of approximately 40 feet (12 m). It takes seven years before the trees develop the flower buds, which grow in small clusters and turn into beautiful purple flowers if they are not picked, unopened, to be used as a spice. Cloves take their name from the Latin *clavus,* meaning "nail," and it is easy to see why, as they have a rounded head set atop a thinner, straight body. This very important spice is widely used to flavor desserts and confections. It originated in the Spice Islands (the Moluccas), a few small islands that had a monopoly on the world's clove supply for many years. In an effort to protect this standing, the Dutch, after driving the Portuguese from the region in the mid-seventeenth century, destroyed every clove tree except those on a single island. Clove was a popular flavoring across Europe at this time, in savory dishes as well as sweet. The price, however, was considerable, due to the long and risky journey and the monopoly, as no sales were permitted unless the price reached a level set by the Dutch government. Today, clove trees flourish in many tropical maritime climates and are grown as close to the United States as the island of Grenada in the West Indies. Store cloves in an airtight container away from light.

The word *clove* is also used to refer to a unit of **garlic,** a single segment of the garlic bulb.

CMC (sodium carboxmethylcellulose)—Widely used as a stabilizer by commercial ice cream makers, CMC has the qualities of a stabilizer as well as an emulsifier. It does not set as firmly as gelatin.

Cloudberry—A wild berry that grows in cool northern climates such as New England, Canada, and Scandinavia. Related to the **blackberry,** it is similar to the **raspberry** in appearance. It starts out pink but turns a yellow-amber shade. Because they are tart, cloudberries are not suitable to eat raw but are primarily used for jams. They are favored for baking in Scandinavia. The cloudberry is also referred to as *bake-apple berry, yellow berry,* and *mountain berry*.

Cobnut—See Hazelnut.

Cocoa block—See Chocolate.

Cocoa butter—See Chocolate.

Cocoa mass—See Chocolate.

Cocoa nib—See Chocolate.

Cocoa paste—See Chocolate.

Cocoa powder—See Chocolate.

Coconut—The coconut palm grows throughout the temperate part of the globe. Its value to the indigenous inhabitants wherever it flourishes cannot be described better than in the old native proverb, "He who plants a coconut tree plants vessel and clothing, food and drink, a habitat for himself, and a heritage for his children." The coconut has, in fact, been called the tree of life, as it produces everything that is needed to sustain life. Ropes and fishing nets are made from the fibers surrounding the shell; the leaves are made into mats and used as roofing material; the trunk is used as timber; the coconut flesh and liquid are very nourishing; the shells can be used to make bowls; and the tiny shoots of the palm can be prepared and eaten as a vegetable.

Although the name suggests otherwise, the coconut is not a nut but a **drupe** (**stone fruit**), belonging to the same family as plums, apricots, and peaches. Actually, the word *coconut* comes from a Portuguese word, *coco,* meaning "goblin" or "frightening spirit," in reference to the three indentations on the bottom of the coconut shell, which are said resemble a small face. Each coconut palm carries about 20 nuts, which take approximately one year to ripen. Because the trees flower and bear fruit continuously, the fruits can be harvested all year.

Fresh coconuts are relatively inexpensive and are available year round. In most grocery stores in the United States, fresh coconuts are almost exclusively marketed with their thick, leathery skin and fibrous coating removed. In choosing a whole coconut, pick one that feels heavy for its size. You should be able to hear a sloshing sound from the liquid inside when you shake the coconut. To extract the meat, first puncture one or all three of the eyes on the end. Drain the liquid; then, using a mallet or hammer, firmly tap the shell all around to loosen the meat inside. Break the coconut open, using the same tool. Pry the meat away from the shell, then use a vegetable peeler or a sharp knife to remove the brown skin from the meat.

Before they have been opened, coconuts will keep in the refrigerator for up to a month, depending on how fresh they were at the time they were purchased. Once opened, the meat and the coconut milk should be used within a week's time or frozen for longer storage. Packaged coconut meat is available in many forms: flaked, shredded, grated, and ground.

Coconut cream—(1) Sweetened coconut cream is a liquid distilled from coconut, sugar, and various thickeners. Originating in Puerto Rico, coconut cream was first known as *Coco Lopez,* named after its creator, Don Ramon Lopez-Irizarry, and it is still produced under this brand name. Coconut cream is often used in cocktails like the piña colada. (2) The thicker portion of canned coconut milk that, being higher in fat content, naturally rises to the top of the liquid.

Coconut milk—(1) The name used for the liquid found inside a coconut. It is also called *coconut water.* (2) Unsweetened coconut milk, exported mainly from Thailand, is sold frozen and canned. It is usually found in grocery stores specializing in Asian food products or in the Asian food section of the supermarket. Coconut milk is made by grating fresh coconut meat and covering it with warm water. The mixture is left to sit and the liquid is then forced out through cheesecloth.

Coconut oil—Oil made by processing the dried meat of a coconut after it has been sweetened and shredded.

Desiccated coconut—Ground dried coconut. Desiccated means "dried up." A desiccant is a drying agent. Dried coconut is made from the white portion of the coconut kernel after the brown skin has been removed. After the coconut has been processed and dried, it is sorted into various grades of coarseness, the finest of which is labeled *macaroon coconut.* My experience, over the years, using desiccated coconut in various countries and many brands/suppliers in the United States is that the amount of moisture the coconut will absorb can vary greatly depending on how fine the coconut was ground and how dry it is. In many recipes, that factor affects the consistency of the dough or paste. It is often necessary to adjust the amount of moisture in the recipe until you have achieved a satisfactory result.

Coffee—Most of the world is indebted to northern Africa as the birthplace of the coffee bean, though the early history of coffee is clouded to the point where it is hard to say which appeared first, the coffee plant or humankind. The first coffee plants were discovered close to Kaffa in southwestern Ethiopia (coffee plants are still found growing wild in many countries today). The small, red, seed-bearing coffee cherries are sweet and pleasant tasting and were eaten raw long before they were used to make the popular beverage we know today. Around 1000 A.D., the Arabs began making a drink by boiling the raw berries. Through experimentation, they discovered that not only did extracting the seeds, or beans, from the cherries and using these alone make an improved drink but also that by roasting and grinding the beans before immersing them in boiling water, the flavor was dramatically different and decidedly popular. Once this technique was in place, the consumption of coffee soon became widespread throughout the Islamic countries. Coffee bars, known in Arabic as *gahneh khaneh,* soon sprang up in increasing numbers, providing men (women were not allowed) with a place to enjoy the stimulating effect of the drink, listen to music, play games, and, in general, discuss important matters. Coffee played an important role in family life as well once women began to enjoy the brew. Coffee was, in fact, regarded with such high esteem that a husband's failure to provide coffee for his wife was legal grounds (no pun intended) for divorce.

The word *coffee* does not, as one might assume, derive from the place-name *Kaffa,* where the plant was first discovered, but from the Arabic word *gahwah,* which was used for any beverage made from plant material, such as wine, for example. When coffee first reached Europe it was, in fact, known as *the wine of Arabia.* Arabia served as a stepping-stone for coffee's universal popularity. In the sixteenth century, coffee crossed from Egypt to Constantinople. History has it that the Turks brought to the Western world the first high-quality coffee, a great deal of which they left behind after they were defeated in the siege of Vienna during the war of 1683–1699. The enterprising Austrians not only quickly learned how to prepare the aromatic brew but they also invented the croissant to go with it in celebration of their victory.

Until a little more than 200 years ago, the world was completely dependent on the Arabian region for its coffee supply. But, despite being fiercely protected, plants and fertile beans slipped out, first to the Dutch East Indies, producing the famous Java blend, and then, little by little, to the West Indies and parts of Central and South America. Today, Brazil is by far the largest coffee producer in the world.

Coffee is the world's most prized agricultural commodity and an important ingredient in the baking industry. Not only is it used as a flavoring agent in baked goods but it is the beverage that is most often consumed with our products, from breakfast pastries to mid-afternoon cakes or cookies, through after-dinner plated desserts.

Growing the beans and preparing them for market is, in many ways, similar to the production of chocolate. Not only do the flavors of coffee and chocolate marry wonderfully in many dessert preparations but also wherever cocoa trees thrive, so does the coffee plant or tree, as it too requires a moist, hot climate.

There are typically two coffee beans in each fleshy coffee cherry, or berry. Occasionally there is only one, in which case it is slightly larger and called a *peaberry*. Among the many varieties of the genus *Coffea* that are known, only two species have a significant commercial importance in today's market: The Arabian coffee plant, *Coffea arabica,* and *Coffea robusta*. Arabica trees produce fruit six to eight weeks after flowering, while robusta takes up to one month longer. However, as its name suggests, robusta is heartier, being able to withstand extreme temperatures better, and robusta cherries stay on the tree after they ripen. The arabica cherries fall to the ground when ripe, making their cultivation more labor-intensive, as the trees must be monitored and picked over several times.

Coffee trees produce bright white flowers with a wonderful fragrance much like jasmine. Like many members of the citrus family, and again like cocoa trees, the plants produce all of the growth stages simultaneously, from buds to ripe berries. During the last part of their development, the berries change from green to amber, then become bright red. That the berries ripen at different times on the same tree means that growers must pick the ripe berries at regular intervals every few weeks—an expensive undertaking—or take the approach known as *stripping,* which means waiting until all of the berries on the tree are ripe before harvesting. This second method can produce contaminated fruit pulp.

Because only the small nuts (the coffee beans) are used, the outer layers, consisting of skin, pulp, mucilage, and parchment, must be removed once the berries are harvested. In what is known as the *old method,* the whole berries are allowed to dry out as the first step of their preparation,

which can take up to 20 days, before the dry pulp is removed. This is not practical in climates with frequent rainfalls or high humidity. In the new method, known as the *West Indian process,* the berries are moved through a series of water tanks first to separate the ripe and unripe berries. They are then drawn into a pulping machine that crushes the flesh but leaves the parchment skin intact. The pulp is washed off in the next tank, but because the mucilage is not water-soluble, the beans are allowed to ferment slightly at this stage to dissolve the mucilage. The fermentation occurs in shallow water tanks, and the beans are stirred frequently during this time. The unwanted mucilage is then washed away in yet another series of water tanks. After the final washing is completed, the beans, still in their parchment, must be dried (the beans contain over 50 percent moisture). This can be done naturally by spreading the beans out on wickerwork racks, or in special drying machines. The natural drying process is considered to produce a superior finished product. After drying, the beans are bagged and transported to processing centers, where they go through one final step to remove the parchment. The beans are then passed through a separator that removes any sand or dust and sorts them according to size. This is followed by careful hand sorting of the better grades to pick out any undesirable beans. The beans are then packed into sacks.

Before they are ready to compete on the market, the coffee beans are roasted, a process that produces profound changes. The beans become larger and lighter, and they turn from gray-green to brown in color. This last change occurs as a result of the conversion of the sugar in the bean to caramel as the beans are heated to between 400° and 450°F (205° and 230°C). The length of time for roasting varies and is determined by the desired color of the roast; around 30 to 35 minutes is the norm. The beans are turned constantly during roasting to prevent scorching. After roasting, they are cooled rapidly. The roasting process develops caffeol, a volatile oil that is the main source of the distinctive aroma and flavor of the coffee beverage. The roasted beans are then blended, which is an important part of the coffee industry. The formulas for various brands and companies are highly guarded secrets. Different beans are mixed to balance flavors. For example, pure mocha beans are a little too acid, while java are typically not acid enough. Just as a winemaker produces a desired product by blending grape varietals and varying the amount of time allowed for aging, the coffee producer carefully blends beans, combining several with various degrees of roasting, thus producing the desired strength and flavor of the coffee beverage.

Cognac—A type of brandy made in the vicinity of Cognac, a town in the Charente region of France.

Cointreau—A colorless French liqueur flavored with the peel of curaçao oranges and other oranges. In most cases, it is interchangeable with **Grand Marnier.**

Comice pear—See **Pear.**

Compound butter—Softened butter flavored with other

ingredients. It is used more often in the hot kitchen, where the best-known compound butters are flavored with shallots, fresh herbs, wine, etc. In the pastry kitchen, compound butters can be made by combining softened butter with chopped dried fruit, citrus zest, maple syrup, or brandy, for example, to use as a topping for scones, muffins, pancakes, or tea cakes.

Compressed yeast—See **Yeast.**

Concord grape—See **Grape.**

Condensed milk—See **Evaporated milk** and **Sweetened condensed milk.**

Confectioners' sugar—See **Sugar.**

Cordial—Derived from the Latin word *cor,* meaning "heart," cordial, as a noun, once commonly referred to a medicine or a medicinal beverage that invigorates the heart, and stimulates circulation. Today, the term has come to mean a fruit syrup or a concentrated fruit-based beverage, presumably because it was thought such a concoction would have the affect of arousing the functions of the heart. Use of the term *cordial* dates back to medieval times and has altered slightly over the years. Cordials are made by three methods: infusion, in which the flavorings steep in the alcohol; percolation, in which the alcohol is percolated with the flavors; and distillation, in which ingredients are distilled directly from their extracted flavors. Most American cordials are quite sweet, with up to 35 percent sugar. They are made from various fruits, herbs, beans, etc. A dry cordial must have less than 10 percent sugar. No cordial can have less than 2.5 percent sugar by weight. One of the most common cordials today is the French **cassis,** a spirit derived from black currant juice. Cordials are also known as **liqueurs,** the term is more popular in England and France.

Coriander seed—Native to the Far and Middle East, the coriander plant, also known as *cilantro,* is a member of the parsley family. The tiny yellow-tan seeds of the plant are dried and can be used whole or finely ground as an aromatic spice; however, once ground, they lose their taste rather quickly. Their aromatic flavor has been likened to a combination of **lemon, sage,** and **caraway.** With their sweet, pungent, almost orange-peel flavor, they are used to flavor desserts, baked goods (especially Scandinavian), and cordials. Whole coriander can be stored for an indefinite period in a tightly sealed jar in a cool, dark place. Ground coriander should be tightly sealed and stored in dark place; for maximum flavor, it should be replaced every four to six months.

Corn flour—Corn flour, not to be confused with **cornstarch** or **cornmeal,** is milled from either white, yellow, or blue corn. It is also produced as a byproduct in the making of cornmeal. This flour does not contain any **gluten.**

Corn oil—A refined pale yellow oil produced from dried, crushed corn kernels, corn oil is an odorless, flavorless oil that can be used virtually interchangeably with other vegetable oils such as canola, peanut, and soybean. Due to its high smoke point, it is a good choice for frying and sautéing. It is used as an ingredient in many desserts, pastries, and confections. It is low in saturated fats. Polyunsaturated corn oil is cholesterol free and is a major component of most margarines.

Corn syrup—Corn syrup is made from **cornstarch** that has been treated with enzymes to convert it to simpler compounds. It is used mostly in making candies and for sugar boiling because it keeps other sugars from recrystallizing. Corn syrup is also valuable for its ability to retain moisture in baked goods, and it is added to marzipan to improve elasticity. Corn syrup is available in both light and dark forms; the dark syrup contains added caramel color and flavorings and is not used as extensively. Although it is a liquid, a large amount of corn syrup or glucose is more easily (and less messily) measured by weight; weigh it on top of another ingredient in the recipe. Unless only a very small amount is required, measurements for corn syrup are given in both volume and weight throughout this book.

Cornmeal—Cornmeal is made from coarsely ground dried white, yellow, or blue corn. If a recipe calls for cornmeal, the yellow variety is usually what is meant. Cornmeal is sprinkled on top of English muffins, sourdough breads, and bread sticks to give them a crunchy crust. It is also the base for cornbread and corn muffins.

Cornstarch—Cornstarch is a fine white powder derived from the endosperm of the corn kernel. It is used to thicken fruit fillings, glazes, and sauces. It becomes almost transparent once it has been dissolved and brought to a boil, making it more desirable for maintaining bright colors and giving an attractive appearance to foods than thickeners that become cloudy. To keep cornstarch from lumping, you must dissolve it in a cold liquid before adding it to any hot mixture. It will gelatinize at temperatures above 170°F (77°C) and will leave an unpleasant taste if it is not brought to a boil. Cornstarch is also added to cake batters to dilute the **gluten** strength of the flour because it is close to 100 percent starch and does not contain any gluten. Foods thickened with cornstarch will start to soften and become more liquid after three to four days as the starch breaks down.

Cottage cheese—See **Cheese.**

Cottonseed oil—Up until the late 1800s, the seeds of the cotton plant were discarded once the fibers for which the plant was produced were removed. However, once it was discovered that a choice oil could be contrived by crushing the seed of the cotton plant, cottonseed oil became an important byproduct of the cotton industry. At its first stage in the mill, the oil that is extracted from the cotton seed is dull and impure and must be refined before consumption. Once it undergoes the rigorous refining process, a light, flavorless oil, high in polyunsaturates, is obtained. It can be used as a salad or cooking oil; however, upon exposure to air, it quickly becomes rancid. It is most commonly used as an ingredient in the production of vegetable margarine or blended with other oils to create highly refined vegetable or cooking oils. It is also used commercially to fry products.

Couverture—See Chocolate.

Cowberry—A member of the **cranberry** family (*Vacccinium vitis-ideae*), this red tart berry grows in mountain regions and pastures in the northern United States, northern Europe, and Canada. It is used in preserves, jams, and sauces. Also know as *mountain cranberry* and *red whortleberry*.

Crab apple—See Apple.

Cracked wheat—See Bulgar wheat.

Cranberry—Wild cranberry vines are indigenous to North America. Today, most of commercially grown cranberries come from Massachusetts. Cranberries are very tart and are almost always sweetened. They are used in tea cakes, muffins, sauces, and preserves. Their bright red color adds a festive touch to many holiday desserts. Fresh cranberries keep for weeks in the refrigerator and freeze very well with little loss of flavor or texture.

Cream—The fat contained in whole milk. When fresh milk is allowed to sit for several hours the fat (cream) rises to the top where it can be skimmed off. However, in modern dairies, instead of letting it rise to the surface on its own, it is skimmed off using a centrifugal method. Cream is produced and sold under many names, mostly based on the fat content of the product.

Cream Products

Clabbered cream—Obtained from unpasteurized whole milk that has thickened and soured naturally. The milk develops a layer of yellow cream on top, with a white, semi-firm liquid on the bottom. Pasteurized milk will not clabber the way old-fashioned fresh whole milk did in the past because it spoils first. Depending on the consistency, ice-cold clabbered milk was and sometimes still is enjoyed as a beverage. When it is very sour (and thick), it is usually enjoyed with fruit, topped with black pepper and cream, or sweetened with sugar. The term *clabber* means to curdle.

Clotted cream—Clotted cream is made by heating unpasteurized whole milk gently in a shallow pan and allowing it to cool. The cream portion rises in clots or coagulated clumps, forming a thick yellowish, crusty top, which is strained from the surface. This treatment improves the keeping qualities of the cream by destroying the bacteria that would cause it to sour. Clotted cream is thick enough to spread or spoon and does not require whipping. It is used as a filling and/or accompaniment to dessert scones. The traditional English cream tea consists of clotted cream and jam served with scones and tea. Clotted cream contains 55 percent butterfat. When produced in the west of England, specifically Devon and Cornwall, clotted cream is also known as *Devon cream* and *Devonshire cream.*

Crème fraîche—A cultured cream made by adding an acid-producing bacteria to pasteurized heavy cream. This produces a smooth, thick, yet pourable texture and a slightly tangy taste.

Devon cream—See Clotted cream.

Devonshire cheese—A soft, creamy, rich cheese made by draining all the whey from Devonshire cream (**clotted cream**).

Devonshire cream—See Clotted cream.

Half-and-half—A mixture of cream and whole milk in equal proportions, containing between 10 and 18 percent butterfat.

Heavy cream—Also called *heavy whipping cream,* this product should have at least 36 percent butterfat.

Light cream—The butterfat content of light cream should be between 18 and 30 percent. This product is also known as *coffee cream.*

Manufacturing cream—Manufacturing cream is produced especially for the food industry. It is made with or without a stabilizer. Manufacturing cream should contain 40 percent butterfat, which, together with the stabilizer, should make it possible to add a slightly warm mixture, such as melted chocolate, to the cream without having it separate. In many of the recipes where whipped cream is added to a warm ingredient, I add some egg white as a stabilizer for an extra precaution against separation (pasteurized egg whites should be used for this application).

Sour cream—In the past, sour cream simply developed from fresh cream that soured naturally. Nowadays, however, it is fermented with the bacteria *Streptococcus lactis,* which adds to its characteristic tangy (or sour) taste. Sour cream is pasteurized, homogenized light cream containing 18 to 20 percent fat with a creamy, gel-like white body. Its thick consistency derives not only from the culturing, but from the addition of such ingredients as gelatin, rennin, and vegetable enzymes. Regular sour cream is thicker than fresh cream of the same fat content due to the partial coagulation that develops during the souring process. Sour cream is often used as a condiment and in cooking and baking. Sour cream can also be made by adding vinegar to pasteurized cream and allowing it to curdle. This produces an acidified sour cream instead of the usual cultured product.

Whipped cream—See main entry **Whipped cream**.

Whipping cream—This form of cream should have between 30 and 36 percent butterfat. It is sometimes called *light whipping cream.*

Cream of tartar—Commercial cream of tartar, used in baking, is the acid potassium salt of **tartaric acid** that has been refined, bleached, and turned into a powder. Cream of tartar is used in manufacturing chemical leavening agents, such as **baking powder,** to release carbon dioxide; it is also used to inhibit recrystallization in candies and syrups and to help stiffen egg whites for meringues.

Crème d'abricots—A sweet apricot-flavored liqueur.

Crème d'amande—A pink almond-flavored liqueur.

Crème d'ananas—A pineapple-flavored liqueur.

Crème de banane—A banana-flavored liqueur.

Crème de cacao—A clear or brown liqueur from France, flavored with cocoa beans and vanilla beans.

Crème de cassis—A reddish-purplish liqueur made from black currants. It is used alone or mixed to make apèritifs such as *Kir* or *Kir Royale*.

Crème de cerise—A cherry-flavored French liqueur.

Crème de menthe—A syrupy mint-flavored liqueur. Available in green, gold, and colorless varieties.

Crème de noyaux—A nut-flavored liqueur. Occasionally called *crème d'amande*.

Crème de rose—A liqueur flavored with vanilla, spices, and the essential oil of rose petals.

Crème de violette—As its name implies, this Dutch liqueur flavored and perfumed with the essence of violets is a pale violet color.

Crème fraîche—See Cream.

Crenshaw melon—This hybrid of the **muskmelon** is one of the sweetest and most succulent of all of the melons. It is surrounded in a gold-green, netless, slightly furrowed, ribbed skin and has a moist pinkish-orange flesh with a spicy aroma. Crenshaw melons are used in desserts and pastries just like **cantaloupes**. The melon varies in size from 5 to 9 pounds (2 kg 295 g to 4 kg 95 g) and is almost pear-shaped, with a slightly pointed end at the stem. While they are available from July to October, their peak season is August to mid-September. A ripe melon should yield to gentle pressure. Also known as *Cranshaw*.

Crystal sugar—See Sugar.

Crystallized flower—A fresh edible flower that has been coated with egg white and dipped in superfine sugar, or cooked in sugar syrup and dried. Violets, roses, and rose petals are among the most commonly used. They are used as garnish for desserts, pastries, and other confections.

Crystallized fruit—A fresh or dried fruit that has been coated with egg white and dipped into superfine sugar, or cooked in sugar syrup and dried. When the latter method is used, the product is also known as **candied fruit** and **glacé fruit**. Pineapple, cherries, ginger, angelica, and citrus rind are among the most common fruits used.

Cube sugar—See Sugar.

Cumin seed—The seeds from this small annual look much like and are often confused with caraway seeds. Cumin, however, has a very distinctive warm and nutty flavor. The name comes from the Greek word *küminon*. Cumin is widely used in Greece as well as throughout the Middle East. The spice is also popular in Europe, especially in Scandinavia and the German-speaking countries, where it is often used to flavor breads. Kümmel, the caraway and/or cumin-scented liqueur, takes its name from the German word for cumin. The seeds come in three colors; the most common is amber, but white and black cumin seeds are also available. The latter have a peppery, more complex flavor. All are sold in seed or ground form. It is best to keep both products on hand, as the seeds are difficult to grind finely. Store both in airtight containers away from light. Cumin will keep fresh for up to six months.

Curaçao—A Dutch liqueur with the flavor of dried orange peel, garnered from sour and bitter oranges found on the Caribbean island of Curaçao. **Cointreau, triple sec,** and **Grand Marnier** are similar to curaçao. While it is often clear, it can be colored golden or blue. This orange-flavored liqueur is used to flavor various desserts and pastries.

Currant—See **Black currant**, **Dried currant**, and **Red currant**.

Custard apple—See Cherimoya.

Damson plum—See Plum.

Danziger Goldwasser—See Goldwasser.

Date—Dates are the fruit of the date palm, previously grown mostly in Iraq for commercial purposes but more recently grown in California. Dates are very sweet—almost half sugar. They are most often sold dried and are available whole or pitted. Whole dates are generally of higher quality. Dates can be stuffed with fondant or marzipan and glazed with sugar to serve on a petits fours tray. They are also used in nut breads and muffins. Fresh dates are very perishable and must be kept refrigerated, although the dried variety may be stored at room temperature if well covered. Dates have a pleasanter texture if stored in the refrigerator.

Decorating sugar—See Sugar.

Dehumidifying agent—See Appendix B.

Delaware grape—See Grape.

Delicious apple—See Apple.

Demerara sugar—See Sugar.

Desiccated coconut—See Coconut.

Devon cream; Devonshire cream—See Cream.

Devonshire cheese—See Cream.

Dewberry—See Blackberry.

Dextrose—(1) Naturally occurring **glucose**, also known as *grape sugar* and *corn sugar*. (2) An additive used to sweeten beverages, in particular fruit juices. It is also used as a binding agent in processed foods such as sausages.

Diastatic malt—See Malt extract.

Dill—A member of the parsley family (*Anethum graveolens*) grown primarily in India, this annual plant has a parsley flavor with undertones of anise. It grows to a height of about 3 feet (90 cm). The feathery leaves, known as *dill weed,* are used fresh or dried as an herb, although there is a vast difference in the flavor of the fresh and dried variety. The small brown seeds, with a flavor similar to **anise**, are used as a spice. The most popular use for dill seeds is in the brine mixture used to cure dill pickles. In the bakeshop, dill is used to flavor breads and rolls. The word *dill* derives from the old Norse word *dilla,* meaning "to lull," as in "to lull to sleep." In ancient Scandinavia, dill tea was used as sedative to calm the nerves and induce sleep.

Double-acting baking powder—See Baking powder.

Double-crème—See Cheese.

Dragée—(1) Tiny silver or gold balls used for decorating. Although edible, these hard decorations should be limited to showpieces. (2) Dragée almonds are sugar-coated almonds served with cookie or petits fours assortments.

Drambuie—Arguably the oldest Scotch liqueur, this secret formula is made using fine old Highland malt Scotch whisky, heather honey, and herbs. The name of this pale golden colored liqueur comes from a Gaelic expression, *an dram buidheach,* meaning "the liqueur that satisfies." With its slightly sweet flavor from the honey, Drambuie is often used as a flavoring for desserts, pastries, and confections.

Drawn butter—A purified butterfat that is obtained by melting butter, allowing the curd and salt (unless unsalted is used) to settle, then carefully removing the water and milk solids. The clear golden liquid that remains is the drawn butter, also known as **clarified butter.** Because none of the milk solids (which cause butter to burn when frying) remain in drawn butter, it has a higher smoke point and therefore may be used to cook at higher temperatures. In addition, the removal of the milk solids prevents the drawn butter from turning rancid as quickly as regular butter. **Ghee** is an Indian form of highly clarified butter.

Dried currant—Also called *currant raisins* and, sometimes, simply *currants,* dried currants are not, as you might expect, made from drying fresh black or red currants. Currants are miniature raisins, produced by drying a very small grape of the Zante variety. Zante grapes originated in the eastern part of the Mediterranean in Corinth, Greece (the word *currant* comes from the name *Corinth*), and dried currants are known as *Corinth raisins* in Europe. Currants are frequently used in baking and are often used to decorate cookies, especially gingerbread figures. Because currant raisins have their own distinct flavor, black raisins (although aside from being much larger may otherwise look the same) should not be used as a substitute. Currants, like other dried fruits, are often macerated in a spirit or liqueur, or plumped in boiling water, before they are combined with the other ingredients in a recipe, to impart a particular flavor and/or to soften them. Dried currants may be stored at room temperature for many months.

Dried fruit—The result of a natural or artificial dehydration process used to remove most of the moisture from fruit. The final moisture content of dried fruit ranges from 15 to 25 percent. The fruit can be sun dried naturally or commercially, using mechanical dehydrators. Sun drying the fruit can take up to three to four days, allowing a loss of nutrients, most notably vitamins A and C, through heat and time. Mechanically dried fruits can be completed in 24 hours. Before drying, many fruits are treated with sulfur dioxide, which preserves both color and nutrients. Drying fruits generally changes their flavor, producing a sweeter, more concentrated taste. The process also preserves the fruit for a longer shelf life. Dried fruit, which is available year round, is usually sold under five basic designations based on size, color, condition, and moisture content: extra fancy, fancy, extra choice, choice, and standard. Dried fruit can be eaten out of hand and is used as an ingredient in numerous baked goods and fruit compotes either as is or reconstituted or flavored by macerating it. Dried fruit can be stored for up to one year.

Drupe fruit—Stone fruit; any fruit with a thin skin, soft flesh, and a hard pit in the center. See **Stone fruit.**

Dry milk—Dry milk is produced when milk is rapidly evaporated by being forced through heated cylinders. Dry milk is usually made with skim milk, which gives it a very long shelf life and makes it an ideal substitute where it is impractical or impossible to get the fresh product. It is also used, in some instances, purely for the sake of convenience.

Dry yeast—See **Yeast.**

Dubonnet—A bittersweet French apéritif derived from red wine and flavored with quinine and bitter herbs. It is usually served over ice with lemon. Dubonnet is also referred to as *Dubonnet rouge.* A drier version, distilled from white wine, is also available and is known as *Dubonnet blanc.*

Durian—This very unusual fruit, native to Southeast Asia, provides a good opportunity to heed the old saying "Don't judge a book by its cover." Durians, an expensive delicacy in many parts of the Pacific Rim, are most certainly an acquired taste. The fruit has thickly spiked green to brown skin, can weigh up to 10 pounds (4 kg 550 g), and is slightly larger than a football. The flesh inside is pale yellow, aromatic, and sugary sweet, with a creamy texture and numerous seeds. What makes it so unusual is its pungent, very foul aroma. The durian's odor is so bad, in fact, that in some parts of Asia, it is actually outlawed on public transportation!

Durum wheat—A very hard wheat with high glutenin and gliadin contents. Due to its composition, it is not good for baking. It is usually ground into **semolina** and used for a variety of purposes, the most common being pasta. See **Semolina.**

Dutch-process cocoa powder—See **Chocolate.**

E

Earthnut—See **Chufa.**

Eau-de-vie—A strong, clear brandy or other fragrant liqueur distilled from fermented fruit juice. It is made by distillers in the Alsace region of France, with a proof level ranging from 80 to 90. The term is French for "water of life." Two of the most popular varieties are **kirsch** (distilled from cherries) and **framboise** (distilled from raspberries). Eau-de-vie is used to lend flavor to a variety of desserts, pastries, and candies.

Egg—When eggs are called for in a recipe, eggs laid by domestic hens are usually meant. However, eggs from turkeys, ostriches, or ducks can theoretically be used in baking; they are larger, but the basic composition is the same. Another variety of egg that is widely used is quail; the eggs taste very much like chicken eggs, and their petite size makes them popular for hors d'oeuvre preparations.

There is no nutritional or flavor difference between white

and brown eggs; the color variations come from different breeds of hens, and the choice is a matter of personal preference.

Eggs are one of the two structural materials in baking (flour is the other) that are indispensable in a pastry shop. The list of uses for eggs is endless. When eggs are combined with flour, they create a framework that supports and traps the air in cake batters; egg whites are needed for meringues, mousses, and soufflés; eggs are used to thicken custards; egg wash is used to glaze breads and pastries; and so on. Eggs also contain a natural emulsifier that contributes to smoother batters and creams.

Eggs require very gentle cooking; they start to thicken at just 145°F (63°C). In desserts where eggs are the main ingredient, such as crème caramel, crème anglaise, and zabaglione, the mixture is cooked over or in a water bath to protect the eggs from too high a heat.

The average hen egg weighs about 2 ounces (55 g); the white is 1 ounce (30 g), the yolk is ⅔ ounce (20 g), and the shell is ⅙ ounce (5 g). All of the recipes in this book use 2-ounce (55-g) eggs (graded as large). If you use eggs of a different size, adjust the number in the recipe accordingly. Eggs are graded for freshness and quality as AA, A, or B; and by size as jumbo, extra large, large, medium, small, and peewee.

Eggs are most commonly sold in the shell. The only reason for not buying eggs in this form is to save the time it takes to crack and empty the shell, which can be significant in a busy bakery. Eggs are sold freshly cracked for the culinary industry in many countries today. Once cracked, however, whole eggs start to deteriorate and lose their whipping power if not used the same day. When cracked and separated, egg yolks start to form a skin almost immediately, so they must always be kept covered. Egg whites may be stored, covered, in the refrigerator for several days with no loss in quality.

The shell of the egg is very porous, allowing the egg to absorb odors or flavors and to lose moisture even before it has been cracked. Many commercially packaged eggs are coated with mineral oil to decrease moisture loss. It is essential to buy fresh eggs and keep them refrigerated; only those eggs needed for the day's work should be left at room temperature. Conversely, although fresh eggs are desirable, eggs less than three days old will not whip as high or increase sufficiently in volume during baking. If you are lucky enough to have a source for just-laid eggs, save them for your breakfast. You can determine the freshness of an egg by placing it in water mixed with 12 percent salt (for example, 1 pint/480 ml water combined with 2 ounces/55 g salt). If the egg is not more than a few days old, it will sink to the bottom; if the egg floats to the top, it has spoiled.

Bad eggs are very rare these days due to improved methods of storage and inspection, but it is still a good idea, when cracking a large number of eggs, to crack a half dozen or so into a small container before emptying them into the big batch. In this way, should you encounter a rotten egg, the entire batch will not be wasted. (On a similar note, you should never crack and add eggs directly over the mixer with the machine running, because if a piece of shell falls in, it will be impossible to retrieve it before it is broken and mixed into the other ingredients.) An egg that is merely sour can be used as long as it is to be baked. Although it will not contribute as much to volume, the smell and taste of the sour egg will disappear with the heat.

Because eggs contain a large amount of protein, they are an ideal breeding ground for bacteria, especially salmonella. Inadequate cooking or unsanitary use or storage of eggs can lead to food-borne illnesses. U.S. Department of Agriculture (USDA) guidelines state that pasteurization is complete when the egg is heated to 140°F (60°C) and, ideally, held there for 2 to 3 minutes. (Pasteurization is defined as heating a liquid to a preset temperature for a specified period in order to destroy pathogenic bacteria.) Only fresh and freshly cracked eggs should be used in uncooked dishes. Frozen and precracked egg products should be reserved for use in dishes where they will be completely cooked, such as for baked items.

Proper storage of eggs is of the utmost importance. Eggs will keep for up to four weeks in their shells if held at a temperature below 40°F (4°C). They will lose quality rapidly if left at room temperature; in fact, eggs will age more in one day left at room temperature than in one week of refrigerated storage. Due to the porous nature of the shell, eggs should be stored away from strongly scented foods that might contaminate them.

Frozen egg—Shelled frozen eggs are an excellent substitute for fresh and are very convenient to use. Thaw them slowly in the refrigerator one or two days before you plan to use them (although you can place them under cold running water to thaw in an emergency). Frozen egg whites and yolks can be purchased separately. It is important to stir any thawed egg product thoroughly before using it.

Dehydrated egg—Eggs with the water removed are available in powdered form. They are used primarily by cake-mix and candy manufacturers and are not practical for use in batters that need volume, such as yeast doughs, cakes, and some pastries. Dried egg whites are more widely used in the pastry shop, with excellent results. These are especially useful and convenient for making meringue. Dried egg yolks can be used to make egg wash. Dried eggs, unlike most dehydrated products, are perishable and must be stored in the refrigerator or freezer, tightly sealed.

Egg substitute—A liquid made of egg whites, processed with corn oil, tofu, powdered skim milk, food coloring, and other additives. While egg substitutes contain no cholesterol and only a trace amount of fat, they still contain relatively the same amount of sodium as real whole eggs. Egg substitutes are sold in cartons, frozen or refrigerated, and can be scrambled and used in many baking and savory items calling for whole eggs.

Egg wash—Egg wash is made from whole eggs, egg yolks, or (less often) egg whites, beaten together with milk, cream, or water. Egg wash is brushed on top of breads or pastry products before baking to enhance browning. Egg wash is also used as a glue to hold toppings in place—sliced almonds or poppy seeds, for example.

Elderberry—Elderberries grow on bushes that are nevertheless often referred to as *elderberry trees*. They grow wild all over Europe, the western part of Asia, and in North America. Unlike some other berries, such as blueberries, blackberries, and raspberries, which are also typically found growing wild at the edge of a wood or by roadsides, elderberries must be cooked before they are eaten to have a pleasant flavor. Elderberries are also cultivated commercially in Europe, mainly in Austria and Scandinavia. The small, round black berries grow on umbrellalike stalks and are used in a variety of sweets, such as pancakes, muffins, and a mixed fruit soup that is quite popular in Sweden. In addition, the berries are used to make elderberry brandy, wine, and juice. The pretty, little white blossoms of the elderberry bush are used to flavor poached fruit, and clusters of the flowers, dipped in fritter batter and deep-fried, were eaten by the Native Americans and are still popular today in Europe, especially in Austria.

Emulsifier—An ingredient added to bind together two items that do not combine naturally, such as oil and water. Both natural and commercial emulsifiers are available. Natural emulsifiers, in the form of the lecithin in egg yolks, are used to thicken and bind sauces such as hollandaise. The commercial emulsifying agent **xanthan gum** is used in numerous items as well. As an additional benefit, emulsifiers inhibit baked goods from staling.

Emulsion—An emulsion is formed when two products that would not normally combine, such as oil and water, are forced together. A well-known example is mayonnaise. In the pastry kitchen, ganache and buttercream are examples of emulsions.

English walnut—See **Walnut.**

Essence—Also known as an **extract,** an essence is a flavoring agent. This concentrated liquid is usually made from a flower, spice, or herb.

Essential oil—Used as aromatics and flavorings in cooking and in producing alcoholic beverages. Essential oils are usually extracted from roots, seeds, flowers, and leaves of plants. Examples are peppermint oil, almond oil, and citrus oils. Essential oils are also used in the perfume industry because of their long-lasting scent.

Espresso powder—A powder made by grinding dried roasted espresso beans. This powder dissolves instantly in water and is often added to hot water to make an instant espresso beverage. Due to its strong, robust coffee flavor and aroma, it is a wonderful means to adding coffee flavor to desserts and pastries.

Evaporated milk—Evaporated milk is produced by heating whole milk to remove approximately 60 percent of the water content. It is then sterilized and canned. It can be reconstituted—made into whole milk again—by mixing it with an equal amount of water by volume. Condensed milk starts the same way, although it is usually not sterilized. Evaporated milk is also available as sweetened condensed milk, which contains 50 percent sugar. See **Sweetened condensed milk.**

Extract—A concentrated natural **essence** from a single element. When a concentration (such as a flavoring) is made from two or more components, it is called a *compound* rather than an *extract* or *essence.*

F

Farina—Italian for "flour." Farina is a granular meal made from hard wheat, other grains, potatoes, or tubers. Commonly used for puddings and as a breakfast cereal, farina can be also used as a thickener. It is rich in protein.

Farmer's cheese—See **Cheese.**

Fat

  Saturated fat—A fatty acid that is composed of hydrogen-saturated carbon single bonds. This type of fatty acid increases the amount of low-density lipoprotein (LDL) cholesterol in the blood. Generally, saturated fats come from animal meat, such as beef, pork, and lamb (fish is the exception), and from dairy fats. They hold their shape at room temperature in a solid form. The most common saturated fats are butter, coconut oil, lard, palm oil, suet, and hydrogenated vegetable oil.

  Hydrogenated fat—Hydrogenated fat is made through a process that involves adding hydrogen atoms to a polyunsaturated vegetable oil. It basically turns an unsaturated oil into a semisolid saturated fat. This procedure eliminates the beneficial qualities of the polyunsaturated fat but allows one to use a solid as an ingredient where a liquid would not work. Additionally, hydrogenation prevents or retards the spoilage of polyunsaturated oils. Hydrogenation also creates trans fatty acids, which may increase blood cholesterol levels. Many scientists agree that hydrogenated oil is more detrimental than saturated fat for those with cholesterol concerns.

  Unsaturated fat—Unsaturated fats are derived from plants and remain liquid at room temperature (approximately 70°F/21°C). The most common exception is coconut oil, which is a saturated fat of plant origin that remains solid at room temperature. Unsaturated fats are further broken down into the subcategories of monounsaturated and polyunsaturated fats, both of which are thought to reduce cholesterol in the blood.

  Monounsaturated fat—A fatty acid carbon chain, with one double bond taking the place of one hydrogen atom. Many scientists believe that monounsaturated fats can lower the level of cholesterol in the blood. While they may decrease the amount of low-density lipoprotein (LDL) cholesterol, they do not have any affect on reducing the high-density lipoprotein (HDL). The most common examples are olive oil, peanut oil, and cottonseed oil. The

American Heart Association recommends that 10 to 15 percent of total calorie intake per day be monounsaturated fatty acids.

Polyunsaturated fat—A fatty acid carbon chain, with two or more double bonds taking the place of two or more hydrogen atoms. Many scientists believe that polyunsaturated fats can actually lower the levels of cholesterol in the blood when they are substituted for saturated fat. Unlike monounsaturated fats, polyunsaturates actually lower both low-density lipoprotein (LDL) cholesterol and high-density lipoprotein (HDL) cholesterol. But studies have also proven that an intense amount of polyunsaturates in the diet can increase the risk of cancer. Some oils high in polyunsaturated fat include safflower, soybean, and corn oil.

Omega-3 oil—A special polyunsaturated oil found in the tissues of oily fish, such as salmon, sardines, herring, tuna, mackerel, and bluefish, and in some plants, such as flaxseed. These fatty acids are believed to be beneficial to coronary health in addition to stimulating brain growth and development. However, they do not actually lower cholesterol; they directly affect the blood vessels and the heart muscle to lessen the risk of heart disease. A number of health researchers also feel that omega-3 fatty acids also aid in lowering blood sugar levels and help in controlling immune-system disorders. While high heat can destroy up to half of the omega-3 oil in food, it is interesting to note that these oils maintain their integrity when cooked in a microwave.

Fat substitute—A substance designed and created to replace traditional fat in food. These substitutes attempt to mimic the mouth feel, flavor, and purpose of fat in food, with reduced calories and fewer grams of fat. While many substitutes have been developed and tested over time, no single replacement works with all food. Instead, the replacement is tailored to a specific food type. Carbohydrate-based fat substitutes, work in formulated foods and baked goods; however, they cannot be used for frying. Protein-based fat substitutes are used for refrigerated and frozen goods. Fat-based replacements are used for frying.

Fatty acid—A molecule composed of a long chain of carbon atoms that have hydrogen attached to them. Their relationship to fat is akin to the role of amino acids as the building blocks of protein.

Feijoa—Feijoas, also referred to as *pineapple guavas* and often confused with guavas, belong to the myrtle family and were named for the botanist Don da Silva Feijoa. The plants are native to South America, but today New Zealand is the largest supplier; California and Hawaii each produce a small crop as well. New Zealand feijoas are available from spring to early summer; those grown in the United States can be found in the market from late fall through January and February.

Feijoas have a delicious and very distinctive flavor—unusual and complex, with hints of pineapple, guava, and eucalyptus; it is unquestionably tropical. Just picking up the fruit and smelling its perfume tells you this is something out of the ordinary. The feijoa not only bears delicious fruit but it is an attractive addition to the garden. The leaves are dark green on top, with a silvery hue underneath. In spring, the shrub is full of flowers that have scarlet stamens. The petals of the feijoa flower measure up to 1½ inches (3.7 cm) across. They are pinkish white on the outside and deep pink within. These somewhat fleshy petals have an incredibly sweet tropical flavor all their own. They can be used as a dessert garnish and make a handsome addition to a fruit salad. Provided the petals are removed with care, the remaining flower may still develop into a fruit.

Mature, ripe feijoas are shaped like an elongated egg. Although the slightly acidic green skin is edible, it is generally peeled away and discarded. The feijoa is excellent in cream-based desserts, is a natural in salads, and can be enjoyed fresh eaten out of hand. Cut the fruit in halves or quarters and scoop out the flesh, including the small seeds (contained in the clover-shaped center and surrounded by a jellylike substance), which are edible as well. The ripe fruit should be stored in the refrigerator, where it will keep for several weeks.

Fennel; Fennel seed—Fennel is a tall, hardy plant with feathery leaves. It is native to the Mediterranean but has been used as an herb, spice, and vegetable throughout much of Europe since the time of the Roman Empire. Fennel was introduced to America by early European immigrants and today grows wild in many temperate climates along roads and in sunny meadows. There are two main types of fennel. The perennial (common fennel), also known as *Roman fennel,* is the source of the small, oval, greenish-brown seeds sold whole or in ground form. Fennel seeds are used in many ethnic breads, crackers, sausages, and savory dishes. The Florence fennel, also called *finocchio,* is an annual that looks very much like the common type but is smaller in size. It contains a swollen bulblike base and is cultivated throughout southern Europe and in the United States. This type is used as a vegetable, both raw and cooked, and its feathery foliage is used as a garnish much like fresh dill. Florence fennel has a light, sweet anise flavor and is sometimes erroneously labeled *sweet anise.* As is true of most spices and herbs, both ground fennel and fennel seeds should be stored in airtight containers in a cool, dry location.

Fenugreek—An herb (*Trigonella foenumgraecum*) native to Asia and southern Europe. Its bittersweet seeds are sold whole and ground. Fenugreek is used in Indian and Persian cooking—specifically in the preparation of spice blends and teas. Ground fenugreek seeds are also used to produce an artificial maple syrup flavor for candies and ice cream.

Fiber—Nutritionally, the indigestible portion of plants that contributes to a well-balanced diet and aids in digestion. Fibrous foods include beans, bran, fruit, oatmeal, and whole wheat. Bran and whole wheat are often added to baked goods to increase their fiber content.

Fig—The fig tree, a type of ficus, is an ancient species. Like grapevines, fig trees were held in high regard by the Greeks and Romans of the classical world. The Greeks, believing the tree was a gift to Athens from Ceres (the goddess of grain and agriculture), planted a grove of fig trees in the main public square. The Romans also honored the fig, recalling that their founding princes, Romulus and Remus, were born under its sheltering branches. They offered a sacrifice each year in the fig grove planted in the Forum. Since these noble beginnings, figs have been a predominant fruit along the Mediterranean seaboard. Today they are also widely cultivated in California.

Figs are classified in botanical terms as a fruit receptacle, which means an inside-out flower. In addition to the fact that the fruit grows right where the leaves are attached to the branches without any visible flowering having taken place, figs are also unique in that they yield two crops annually. Several hundred varieties exist in a wide range of colors and shapes, from small, squat, and round to large and pear-shaped, and from almost white to dark purple or black. One of the most common commercial figs is the Brown Turkey variety, also referred to as *Black Spanish.* These are quite large, with mahogany purple skin and juicy red flesh, and are the first figs on the market each year. Mission or Black Mission figs (brought to California by the Spanish, who came to establish missions—hence the name) are the most readily available and are the best overall for cooking. These have a dark pink interior. Kadota, the principal fig used for canning, are quite large, with yellowish-green skin and white to purple flesh inside. Smyrna figs from Turkey (known as *Calimyrna* when grown in California) are large, greenish, squat, extremely sweet figs that are available fresh but are mostly used for drying; these are the only figs that are not self-pollinating. Smyrna figs instead rely on a unique pollination method provided by a tiny wasp known as *blastophaga,* which lives inside the inedible figs that grow on the Capri fig tree. When the wasp larvae mature, they leave the Capri fig tree and look for another tree to serve as a nest in order to reproduce. Growers of Smyrna figs intervene just before this happens, placing baskets of Capri figs, complete with wasp larvae, throughout their orchards. The female wasps work their way through the bottom of the Smyrna figs, carrying pollen on their wings and bodies. Once they discover that the inside of the Smyrna fig is not suitable for laying their eggs, they retreat, leaving pollen behind.

Unripe figs can be ripened at room temperature; they should be placed away from direct sunlight and turned from time to time. Ripe figs may be stored in the refrigerator for up to three days. They bruise easily and should be arranged in a single layer, covered with plastic.

Filbert—See **Hazelnut.**

Fillo—See **Phyllo.**

Finger banana—See **Banana.**

Fino—A Spanish dry cocktail sherry. Fino is usually pungent, with a medium body and pale gold coloring. Considered by many to be the world's finest sherry, it is best served when young, as it does not age well. In addition to being served as an apéritif, sherries are used in the pastry kitchen to moisten cake layers and flavor sauces.

Finocchio—See **Fennel.**

Fiori di sicilia—See **Orange flower water.**

Flame Tokay grape—See **Grape.**

Flaxseed—A tiny seed containing several essential nutrients, including calcium, iron, niacin, phosphorus, and vitamin E. It is most commonly used to produce linseed oil (a component of paints, varnishes, and inks). However, due to its health benefits, it is available at most health foods stores and some supermarkets and can be used in a variety of foods. In its seed form, it has a mild nutty flavor and can be used as a topping on hot cereal. The seed can also be sprouted and used in salads and sandwiches. Flaxseed is mucilaginous, meaning that when it is ground and a liquid is added, it forms a gelatinous mixture, similar to egg whites. This mixture can be used as a replacement for eggs in baked goods. However, it does not have the same leavening ability as eggs. Flaxseed has a high fat content and should be stored, covered, in the refrigerator no longer than six months.

Fleur de sel—See **Salt.**

Flour—(1) Finely ground and sieved dried food matter, generally vegetables and grasses. When identified simply as "flour," the term generally refers to wheat flour. (2) The term *flour* is also used as a verb. "To flour the work surface" means to coat the surface lightly with flour.

Flour is one of the two structural materials used in baking (eggs are the other), and, like eggs, flour is a vital ingredient in the bakery; it simply would be impossible to make breads or pastries without it. Besides providing backbone and structure in baked goods, flour has four other important functions: generating a characteristic texture and appearance that is derived from the various strengths and types available; contributing to flavor, which comes from the grains used; providing nutrition (flour contains proteins, carbohydrates, fats, minerals, and vitamins); and acting as a binding and absorbing agent (flour absorbs liquid rather than dissolving in it). By law, flour must contain no more than 15 percent moisture when it is sold, but it can absorb more moisture if it is not stored properly. (Wheat flour with a high water content does not keep well and will also lose some of its baking ability.) It is also possible for flour to dry out in high altitudes. These two factors are the reason you will often see instructions to add more or less flour as needed to achieve the correct consistency in many of the dough recipes in this book, as the amount of flour required to reach a particular texture will vary with the amount of moisture in the flour.

Wheat Flour

Wheat flour, in a variety of forms, is the flour used most often in the bakery. There are both hard and soft wheats. The hard wheats have a lower starch content and contain more of the proteins that will form gluten when the flour comes in contact with water and is kneaded. Flours made from hard wheat (bread flour) are used most often in making breads and in other yeast doughs. Soft wheat flour (cake flour) has a higher starch content and less protein; it is used alone or in combination with other flours in many recipes where a weaker gluten structure is desirable.

Processing Wheat into Wheat Flour

Wheat is a very important cereal crop of the genus *Triticum*, belonging to the grass family, *Gramineae*. Wheat was probably first cultivated in the Euphrates Valley nearly 9000 years ago and has, ever since, played a significant role in the feeding of both people and animals. The most important species of wheat include common wheat, *Triticum vulgare*, used in bread; durum wheat, *Triticum durum*, used in pasta products; club wheat, *Triticum compactum*, used in cakes and pastries; and Polish wheat, *Triticum polonicum*, grown in warmer climates such as Spain and southern Europe. Most species of wheat have hollow stems and long, narrow leaves. The heads of the plants contain 20 to 100 flowers. Fertilization of the flowers produces the grain. The wheat plant can be grown in a wide range of environmental conditions but is best cultivated in temperate areas. Wheat cultivation has spread throughout the world through trade. The Spanish brought wheat to the Americas in 1519.

For thousands of years, the sickle was the most common tool used to harvest wheat, and the kernels were separated from the hulls by threshing (beating). Mechanical inventions greatly advanced these processes in the nineteenth century. Wheat is usually stored on the farm after harvest in anything from simple pits and earthen containers to more sophisticated wood, steel, or cement storage structures. The wheat is next moved to the local elevator, then shipped to terminal elevators, which, in turn, supply the processors or ship to export locations. Because many kinds of flour are made, wheat of different qualities is separated for delivery to mills that manufacture particular products.

The production process used to turn the grain into flour is called *milling*. The wheat kernel is made up of 83 percent endosperm, 14 percent bran, and 3 percent germ, which is the seed. The bran provides cover for the germ and endosperm and would serve as food for the seed if it were to grow into a strand of wheat. The process of milling is not done merely to pulverize the kernel but also to separate these three parts. If the kernel were simply to be finely crushed, it would produce a very crude form of whole wheat flour that, although very uncomplicated to make, would not store well because it would still contain the germ, which has a small percentage of fat and could therefore turn rancid. In the first step of the milling process, the wheat is cleaned and tempered (warmed), then ground and broken before it is passed through a series of rollers to be ground into a finer consistency. The crushed wheat is then sifted through a series of screens with increasingly fine mesh. This product then goes through the pulverizer, which, using a series of sifters, separates the bran from the endosperm. The endosperm, still containing the germ, is then passed through more reducing rollers, which press the germ into flakes (possible because of its fat content) and small particles. The flattened germ and the endosperm can now be separated by sifting. Wheat germ oil is extracted from the wheat germ flakes, and the flakes are marketed separately from the flour. The resulting flour now has a greater shelf life because the germ has been removed. (In the commercial production of whole wheat flour, some of the germ and the bran are ultimately recombined with the flour, bringing the composition close to that of the original wheat kernel.) The flour is then bleached and stored to mature; at this stage, it is known as *straight flour*. Some manufacturers use potassium bromate to increase the yield (called *bromating* the flour), a controversial procedure that is banned in some areas.

There is no nutritional difference between bleached and unbleached flour, although unbleached flour has a higher market value. It is more expensive because it takes longer (about two weeks) to mature. U.S. law requires that all flours not containing wheat germ must have niacin, riboflavin, thiamin, and iron added. After this is done, the flour is labeled *enriched*. Eight ounces of wheat-based flour must contain 50 percent of the recommended daily allowance of the aforementioned additives. From this base, various qualities of refined flour are produced, such as short patent flour, more commonly known as *cake flour*, which is high in starch and low in protein or gluten; medium patent flour, which uses about 90 percent straight flour, making it slightly higher in protein and lower in starch (this flour is known as *all-purpose flour*); and long patent flour, which yields a higher protein content and is known as *bread flour*.

Types of Flour

All-purpose flour—All-purpose flour is a mixture of approximately equal parts hard and soft wheat flours. It is used in the kitchen rather than the bakeshop.

Bread flour—Bread flour is a hard wheat (or hard patent) flour. It is very easy to dust into a thin film, making it ideal to use when rolling out and working with doughs. Bread flour is milled from wheat that is rich in protein. The wheat must be grown in areas with the appropriate amount of rainfall and in soil rich in nitrogen. Bread flour is pale yellow when first milled and turns off-white with aging. It feels slightly granular when rubbed between your fingers.

Cake flour—Cake flour (soft patent) is made from soft wheat. The flour is chlorinated to further break down the strength of the gluten. It feels very smooth and can be pressed into a lump in your hand. The color is much whiter than bread flour. Because it contains less of the gluten-producing proteins, cake flour yields a more crumbly but lighter texture. It is used in making sponge cakes and other baked goods where a weaker gluten structure is preferable.

Graham flour—A whole wheat flour, slightly more coarse

than regular ground flour, produced from unbolted wheat. Like the graham cracker, graham flour is named for Dr. Sylvester Graham.

High gluten flour—Higher in protein than bread flour, this is often used in hard-crusted breads. See page xvii for more information.

Pastry flour—Pastry flour is another of the soft wheat flours. It is closer in color to bread flour, being off-white rather than true white like cake flour. It is close to all-purpose flour in gluten strength.

Whole wheat flour—Also known as graham flour, whole wheat flour is milled from the entire wheat kernel, including the germ and the bran; for this reason, it is very nutritious. Whole wheat flour does not keep as long as white flour because of the fat contained in the wheat germ. Bread made from whole wheat flour is heavier than bread made with white flour, so most of the time, a combination is used. Whole wheat bread dough takes less time to knead than bread made with white flour.

Nonwheat flour—In addition to wheat flour, we also use flours milled from other plants. Each contributes its own distinctive taste, texture, and nutritional benefit; however, because these flours are lower in gluten content, they are combined with a percentage of wheat flour to assure proper leavening. See **Barley flour, Buckwheat flour, Corn flour, Potato flour, Rye flour,** and **Soy flour.**

Flowers, edible—Decorating with edible fresh flowers and/or using them in cooking is nothing new. Flowers have been used in food preparation since the Middle Ages; in fact, many flowers that we now grow for ornamental purposes, such as roses and lavender, were originally cultivated for their flavor.

It is safe to say that most of us have eaten flowers without realizing it. Artichokes and broccoli are basically the bud or immature flower of the plant; dried daylily petals are used in Chinese hot and sour soup; and herbal teas often include chamomile flowers or hibiscus, rose, or jasmine petals. When I was a kid, I used to enjoy sucking the sweet moisture out of clover flowers, which grew wild in the meadows, without regarding it as anything unusual.

When using edible flowers in food or as a decoration (unless you grow them yourself), it is crucial to be sure of how they have been cared for. Most flowers that are purchased at a nursery or florist shop have been sprayed with pesticide and should not be eaten. Produce companies and farmer's markets that offer organically grown edible flowers are a better choice for a supplier.

In many countries, including my native country, Sweden, and our neighbor, Canada, it is against the law to put anything on a plate of food or use any decoration on food intended for consumption unless it is edible. And yet in the United States—and I have been guilty of this myself—we think nothing of decorating a wedding cake with any type of beautiful fresh flower because we know it will be removed before the cake is served. (When using inedible flowers on a cake, make sure they are nontoxic, even though they will not be consumed, and cover the stems with plastic wrap if they are inserted into the cake.)

In some flowers, both the stamen and styles can be bitter and unpleasant to eat, even though they are not poisonous. In addition, the pollen of some edible flowers can cause an allergic reaction in certain individuals. Therefore the sepals should be removed in all flowers except johnny-jump-ups, lavender sprigs, violas, and pansies. With others, only the petals are edible; this applies to tulips, roses, chrysanthemums, and calendula. The petals should be separated from the remainder of the flower just before they are used. Additionally, roses, chrysanthemums, and marigolds have a white portion at the end of the petal that is bitter and should be broken off before they are used. You can use the entire flower of borage, violet, johnny-jump-up, marigold, and honeysuckle. Two tropical varieties that are edible and are also grown in parts of the United States are the flowers from passion fruit and feijoa. Both have a perfumed scent, are very pretty, and are something of a rarity.

Unfortunately, some of nature's prettiest creations are not edible, either because they have an unpleasant flavor or because they contain toxins in varying degrees that can make you sick and can even be fatal; lily of the valley, clematis, sweet pea, and foxglove fall into this category. So please remember: Just because you may have seen a flower served with food does not mean that it is safe to eat. As with wild mushrooms, if you cannot positively identify the flower as edible and be certain of its source, do not eat it and, moreover, do not place it on your customer's plate.

Edible flowers are used in many culinary creations in addition to desserts—for example, as a garnish for beverages or mixed with salad greens—and some larger varieties, such as zucchini and squash blossoms, are stuffed and deep-fried. Flowers from rosemary, oregano, chives, and some other herbs have a scent that makes them unsuitable for the pastry kitchen. The table in Figure A-2 provides a partial list of the flowers that are both edible and appropriate for use with sweets.

Fondant—A liquid icing that is widely used in the pastry shop for glazing and decorating. If properly applied, it dries to form a silky-smooth shell that not only enhances the appearance of a pastry but preserves it as well by sealing it from the air. Fondant is a sugar syrup that is recrystallized to a creamy white paste. **Glucose** and **cream of tartar** are used to invert part of the sugar to achieve the proper amount of recrystallization. Without these ingredients, the cooked sugar would harden and be impossible to work with. Conversely, if too much glucose or cream of tartar is used, there will not be enough recrystallization, and the fondant will be soft and runny.

Although fondant is inexpensive and relatively easy to make (once you get the hang of it), it is almost always purchased in a professional kitchen, either ready to use or as a

Edible Flowers

Name	Appearance	Usable Portion	Flavor	Notes
BORAGE	Small, star-shaped, sky blue flowers tinged with light pink.	The whole flower may be eaten.	Bittersweet	Wilts quickly once removed from the stem. Can have a diuretic effect and should not be consumed in large quantities.
CALENDULA (POT MARIGOLD)	Yellow or orange fluffy round flowers; petals are similar in appearance to those of a daisy.	Use the petals only.	Bitter	No fragrance. The petals are used more for color than for flavor.
ELDERBERRY	White or off-white. Dramatic clusters of small flowers are called *elderbow*.	Flowers only. They must be cooked. The leaves, bark, branches, and even the stems are poisonous.	Exceptionally sweet flavor and fragrance.	The berries are used to make wine, jam, and tea. Like the flowers, the berries must never be eaten raw.
HONEYSUCKLE	Small trumpet-shaped flowers are first white and then pale yellow.	Petals only. Only the *Lonicera japonica* variety is edible.	Perfumed flavor; wonderful sweet scent.	Each flower contains a drop of sweet nectar, which is the source of their flavor.
JASMINE (ARABIAN JASMINE)	Small, tubular, star-shaped white flowers,	The whole flower may be eaten. Do not use Carolina jasmine or jessamine, which are poisonous.	Sweet perfumed flavor.	Part of the olive family. Jasmine flowers are widely used to flavor tea.
JOHNNY-JUMP-UP	Small, multi-colored, purple, yellow, and white flowers, each with five flat, triangular petals.	The whole flower may be eaten.	Petals have almost no flavor. If the whole flower is eaten, including the sepal, it has a mint flavor.	A member of the viola family; related to pansies. Contains saponins and can be toxic in large amounts.
LAVENDER	Clusters of tiny light to dark purple flowers growing in a tight cylinder at the end of a thin stalk.	Use only the flowering sprig.	Perfumed flavor with a faint lemon taste.	From the mint family. Used extensively in perfumes, soaps, and sachets.
PANSY	Purple, blue, pink, yellow, and maroon. Flowers may be single or multicolored.	The whole flower may be eaten.	Grassy, vegetable flavor.	Same as the Johnny-jump-up, but about twice as large.
ROSE	Grows in virtually all colors and in many sizes.	The petals only are used.	Perfumed flavor.	Used to scent soaps and perfumes. Dried roses are included in sachets, potpourri, and tea.
TUBEROUS BEGONIA	White, red, yellow, orange, and combinations. Thick, fleshy petals.	Use the petals only. Do not eat other begonias. Only hybrid tuberous begonias are edible.	Citrus flavor.	Should be eaten sparingly since they contain oxalic acid.
TULIP	All colors; large oval flowers.	Use the petals only.	Flavor similar to a green bean.	Part of the lily family. Some people have an allergic reaction in the form of a rash from eating tulips.
VIOLET	Colors range from deep violet to white and rose. Very small flowers.	The whole flower may be eaten.	Perfumed flavor.	Leaves are also edible and may be used in salads.

FIGURE A-2 Edible flowers suitable for use in the pastry kitchen

powder to which you add water. In addition to its use as a glaze, fondant is used to create ornaments in the same way as royal icing is.

Food additive—See **Additive**.

Food coloring—Dye of various colors used to tint cakes, frostings, and candies. In addition to liquid food coloring, food coloring paste and powder are also available. Powdered food coloring is suitable for use with foods that do not blend well with liquid, such as fats and chocolate. To use, the powder is first dissolved in cocoa butter. Food coloring is very potent and, generally, a little goes a long way. It is best to begin with a small quantity and continue to add the coloring slowly until the desired shade is achieved.

Fortified wine—A wine to which **brandy** has been added to increase the alcoholic content or to stop the fermentation process. Such wines include **port, sherry, Madeira, Marsala,** and many dessert wines.

Fraise—French for "strawberry."

Fraise des bois—*Fraise des bois* is French for "strawberry of the woods." Wild strawberries are also known as *alpine strawberries* and, though these names may suggest that they are native only to the mountain regions of France, in fact, wild strawberries grow in the open patches and meadows of woodlands all over Europe, from Italy in the south to Lapland in the north. These small, intensely sweet strawberries are, for good reason, considered the queen of all strawberries. They produce a bounty of fruit from early July until the first frost. Commercially, wild strawberries are fairly expensive, mainly because they are time-consuming to pick and the fruit is quite susceptible to hot spells. There are both red and white (actually a pale yellow) varieties. Unlike their larger counterparts, red wild strawberries are still pale white inside even when they are fully ripe.

Framboise—(1) Raspberry brandy; a spirit distilled from fermented raspberry juice. Framboise is colorless and very strong. It is classified as an **eau-de-vie**, as is any colorless spirit or brandy made from fruit juice. (2) French for "raspberry."

Frangelico—An Italian liqueur derived primarily from hazelnuts but flavored with berries and flowers as well.

Freestone—A **drupe fruit** that contains a pit that separates easily from the flesh; the opposite of **clingstone**.

Fromage—French for "cheese."

Fructose—A natural byproduct of fruit and honey, this sweet substance is available in granulated and liquid forms. It is more water soluble than **glucose**, sweeter than glucose, and twice as sweet as **sucrose**, yet when heated, fructose loses some of its sweetening flavor. Fructose is a classified as a simple sugar because it is composed of only half of the sucrose molecule. It should not be substituted for regular sugar in recipes. Because of its makeup and the way it is digested by the body, it is an acceptable sweetener for diabetics. Also referred to as *fruit sugar* and *levulose.*

Fuyu persimmon—See **Persimmon**.

Fuzzy melon—Also known as *hairy melon* and *fuzzy squash.* Native to China, this cylindrical melon can grow to 10 inches (25 cm) in length and 3 inches (7.5 cm) in diameter. It has a medium green fuzzy skin (which must be peeled before the melon is used). The firm flesh has a bland flavor and is primarily used in Chinese cooking.

G

Galangal; Galanga root—This member of the **ginger** family is a common ingredient in the foods of southeast Asia, primarily in Malaysian and Indonesian cooking. It has a hot ginger-pepper flavor and is used mostly as a seasoning. There are two types of galangal: greater and lesser. Greater, also known as *Laos ginger, Siamese ginger,* and *Thai ginger* is more commonly known and easily available. It grows throughout southeast Asia and is most popular in Thai food. It can be used as a substitute for ginger. A powdered form, under the name *Laos,* is more intense in flavor. The lesser variety has an orange flesh and is much stronger in flavor. It is not as popular as the greater galangal.

Galliano—A sweet, anise-flavored liqueur from Italy, pale yellow in color.

Garlic—A member of the lily family, garlic is a pungent cousin of onions, chives, leeks, and shallots. The edible garlic bulb grows beneath the ground. Each bulb is made up of sections called *cloves.* Each clove is encased in a papery covering that is removed before cooking. There are several varieties of garlic: the white skinned, strongly favored American garlic; the Mexican and Italian garlic, both of which are purplish and pinkish in skin coloring and milder in flavor; elephant garlic, the most mild flavored of the three but certainly the largest in size (more closely related to the leek); and green garlic, which is young garlic that is harvested before it matures into cloves.

Gelatin—Type B gelatin is derived from beef bones and/or calf skins. Culinary gelatin, known as *type A,* is made primarily from pig skins. When dissolved, heated, and chilled, gelatin has the ability to turn a liquid into solid. This process is thermally reversible: The liquid will set at 68°F (20°C) and melt at 86°F (30°C). Unflavored gelatin is available in both powder and sheet (leaf) form. Either can be substituted in equal weights. When a recipe calls for powdered gelatin, the amount of liquid used to soften and dissolve the gelatin is generally specified. The liquid is usually cold water but might also be wine or milk, for example. The gelatin is sprinkled over the liquid and left for a few minutes to soften; it is then possible to heat the mixture in order to dissolve the granules.

Some nonprofessional recipes specify the amount of gelatin in units called *envelope* or *packet.* A consumer packet of gelatin weighs ¼ ounce (just over 7 grams) and is equivalent to 3 teaspoons (15 ml) when measuring by volume.

Most brands of sheet gelatin weigh $\frac{1}{10}$ ounce (3 g) per sheet. Gelatin sheets, like the powder, must be softened in a cold liquid before they can be dissolved. However, sheets can be softened in virtually any amount of liquid as long as they are submerged. The amount of liquid need not be specified because, as they soften, the sheets will always absorb the same amount: approximately 2 teaspoons (10 ml) per sheet. The sheets are removed once they are soft, without squeezing out the absorbed liquid. To use sheet gelatin in a recipe that calls for powdered, substitute an equal amount by weight remembering that each sheet weighs ¹⁄₁₀ ounce (3 g), or calculate the exchange based on 1 sheet replacing each 1 teaspoon (3 g) powdered gelatin. Submerge the sheet(s) in water and leave to soften. Lift the softened sheets out of the water without squeezing out the water that has been absorbed. Place the sheets in a pan or bain-marie and melt. Add the melted gelatin to the recipe as directed, omitting the water that was to be used for softening the powdered gelatin. If the recipe calls for softening the gelatin in a liquid other than water—wine, fruit juice, or milk, for example—this liquid should be used instead of water to soften the gelatin sheets. If necessary, add enough water to the liquid so that the sheets are just covered. Instead of lifting the sheets out of the liquid once they are soft, melt the sheets in the flavored liquid and add the mixture to the recipe.

It is not necessary to make adjustments in the water added to the recipe to offset the water absorbed by the sheet gelatin unless you are using as much as 3 ounces (85 g) or 28 sheets (84 g) or more in a single recipe. When using such a large amount of sheet gelatin in a recipe specifying powdered, calculate the total amount of water absorbed by the sheets and compare that to the water specified for softening the powdered gelatin. Add the additional amount of water needed to make up the difference instead of omitting the water as directed above. For example, if the recipe instructs you to soften 3 ounces (85 g) of powdered gelatin in 2½ cups (20 ounces) of water, substitute 28 gelatin sheets (28 sheets at 3 g each = 84 g) softened in enough water to cover. You would then calculate that 28 sheets absorbing 2 teaspoons each have absorbed a total of 54 teaspoons or 9 ounces. This means you need to add an additional 11 ounces of water (instead of leaving out the 2½ cups/20 ounces) originally called for in the recipe. Again, if the liquid called for was a flavoring agent, use that instead of water, but at this level use only the additional amount calculated as above, rather than the full quantity.

To substitute powdered gelatin in a recipe that calls for gelatin sheets, use an equal weight of powder dissolved in as much water as the sheets would have absorbed. For example: If the recipe uses 6 sheets (18 g) of softened gelatin, you would substitute 2 tablespoons (18 g) powdered gelatin, softened in the same amount of water that the sheets would have absorbed—in this case, 2 ounces (60 ml).

After they are softened, both types of gelatin must be heated until completely dissolved. However, they must never be boiled, as boiling reduces the strength of the gelatin and causes a skin to form on the top, which is impossible to incorporate without creating lumps.

Certain raw fruits—papayas, pineapples, guavas, kiwis, mangoes, passion fruit, and figs, to list the best known—contain an enzyme that inhibits gelatin from setting by breaking down or dissolving the protein structure; their presence in a recipe can adversely effect the outcome when gelatin is used. However, the enzyme is destroyed if the fruit is heated to at least 175°F (80°C), so these fruits will set normally if they are cooked first.

The strength or firmness of the set gelatin is measured using a tool called a *Bloom Gellometer* (see Appendix B).

The term *bloom* is also used, in some cases, to describe the process of softening the gelatin in a liquid before it is dissolved. This most likely has to do with the expansion of the gelatin as it absorbs the liquid. These two distinct meanings should not be confused.

Gewürztraminer—A grape that produces a dry white wine with a crisp, spicy, and refreshing flavor. It is available in various levels of sweetness and dryness. It has a perfumelike yet crisp aroma. This grape variety is grown primarily in Alsace, France, as well as in Germany, the Tyrol, and in California. It is best enjoyed when it is young, as it does not age well past five years. The name is derived from the German word *gewurz,* which means spicy.

Ghee—This Indian version of **clarified butter** is prepared in the same way as other clarified butter, however, instead of spooning off the clear fat once the milk solids have separated, it is simmered so that the moisture evaporates. At this point, the milk solids brown and, as a result, give the remaining butter a nutty caramel flavor and aroma. Ghee is, in a way, a combination of clarified butter and **buerre noisette.** With its higher smoke point than regular clarified butter, ghee can be used with good results for frying and sautéing. In India, it is usually made of butter made from buffalo milk, but it can be produced from any unsalted butter. While ghee originated in India and is used frequently in Indian cuisine, it is widely found commercially in the Netherlands as well as in Scandinavia and Australia.

Gianduja—This confection, chocolate with hazelnut paste, originated in Switzerland. It is very smooth and creamy and is used in preparing desserts and candies, and can be eaten plain. The basic proportions are equal amounts of prepared chocolate, sugar, and roasted hazelnut paste. It is generally purchased in blocks from chocolate manufacturers rather than prepared in the pastry shop. Gianduja is available in both milk and dark varieties; the milk chocolate version is more traditional. *Gianduja* is also the name of a candy made with chocolate and hazelnuts.

Ginger—Often erroneously called *ginger root,* ginger is the underground rhizome of an attractive perennial plant that produces leafy stems and pretty pink flowers. Ginger has a peppery sweet flavor and spicy aroma. It grows freely in most tropical and subtropical regions. It was first cultivated in Asia and slowly made its way to Europe via the old spice route. The Spanish conquistadors introduced ginger to the West Indies, where today its production is a flourishing industry, especially on the island of Jamaica, which is currently one of the two biggest producers of fresh ginger in the world, the other being the Malabar coast of India.

Mature ginger is harvested when the stalks begin to whiten by simply unearthing the large sections. The rhizomes are then washed and scraped, leaving them a natural light taupe color. Mature ginger is peeled before it is used. Immature or *spring ginger,* as it is sometimes called, as it is obtainable only in spring, can be used without peeling because its skin is more tender; it also has a milder flavor and aroma than mature ginger. Fresh ginger should have smooth shiny skin; dull and/or wrinkled skin indicates that the ginger is past its prime. Whole pieces of ginger can be stored in the refrigerator for a week or so and frozen for much longer; ginger should be tightly wrapped once peeled. Fresh ginger is used in Asian cooking, where candied, preserved, and pickled forms are also utilized. Thin slices of pink pickled ginger, known as *gari* in Japan, are always served as an accompaniment to sushi. Dried ground ginger has a much less pungent bite than the fresh, and it should not be substituted if fresh ginger is specified in a recipe. However, ground ginger is the type mostly widely used in the bakeshop, where it is employed to flavor cookies, spice breads, and a variety of sweets. Ginger, fresh or dried, tastes wonderful paired with many fruits and berries, including apples, pears, rhubarb, blueberries, and strawberries.

Ginko nut; Ginkgo nut—A delicacy in the Far East, this buff-colored, delicately sweet seed or nut is found on the ginkgo tree, native to China. The nut, available during the fall and winter, has a hard shell that must be removed before the nutmeats can be extracted and soaked in hot water to loosen the skins. It is sold canned in brine or dried but can be enjoyed raw or cooked. Dried ginkgo nuts must be shelled and blanched before being eaten or added to recipes. The nut, which turns bright green when cooked, is high in starch and primarily used in Chinese recipes for poultry, soup, and vegetables. It is also used in some Japanese cookies.

Glacé fruit—Glacé or **candied fruit** is made by boiling or dipping the fruit in sugar syrup or simple syrup; it is sometimes tossed in granulated sugar once it has dried. The fruits most commonly glacéed are cherries, pineapple, and citrus rinds. Glacé fruit is used in fruitcakes, breads, pastries, desserts, and other sweets. It is available for purchase ready made and should be stored in an airtight container.

Glayva—A Scottish liqueur made from Scotch whisky, honey, and a secret herbal formula.

Glazed fruit—Small, whole fresh fruits or berries, or pieces of dried fruit, coated with a thin layer of sugar syrup cooked to the hard crack stage, which forms a shiny transparent shell. Glazed fruits are used as a garnish or as part of a petits fours tray served after a meal. A whole stemmed strawberry may be glazed and used to decorate a strawberrry soufflé, just as orange, apple, or pear wedges can be glazed and used to enhance the presentation of desserts made with those fruits, such as a pear or apple charlotte or a Grand Marnier soufflé. Because the juices released when fresh fruits are

dipped into hot caramel will eventually penetrate and melt the sugar shell, glazed fruits should be prepared as close as possible to serving time. Glazed dried fruits, on the other hand, hold up better and can be kept in an airtight container for a few days if needed. They are generally used as a colorful addition to a candy or petits fours tray rather than to garnish a dessert.

Glazing sugar—See Sugar.

Glucose—Glucose, as it is used in the pastry kitchen, is a viscous, colorless syrup (about 44° Baumé) produced by partial hydrolytic decomposition, known as *hydrolysis,* which can be explained as the splitting of chemical bonds using water. The most common type is dextroglycose, mostly just called **dextrose**. It is made from the starch in potatoes, wheat, rice, or corn. Glucose plays an important role in the confectionery industry, where its stabilizing effect is used to help prevent recrystallization when sugar is boiled to high temperatures, such as for cast, pulled, and blown sugar; glucose also makes boiled sugar more elastic. More than half of the glucose manufactured is used by the confectionery industry. Glucose should not be stored at temperatures above 68°F (20°C) because it will change from transparent to pale yellow in color. In most instances, glucose can be replaced with light corn syrup.

Gluten—Gluten is what gives bread dough its elasticity, structure, and oven-spring. Gluten is created when the two proteins in the flour—glutenin and gliadin—are combined with water. As the mixture is blended (kneaded), the two proteins bind with the water, and with each other, forming thin, stretchy sheets of gluten. These elastic sheets trap and hold the gases produced by **yeast,** making gluten essential for yeast-leavened breads but disastrous for quick breads and cakes, where a dough or batter without elasticity is desired. **Hard flours** have more protein and therefore produce more gluten; **soft flours** have less protein and produce less gluten.

Glycerin—Also called *glycerol,* glycerin is an odorless, colorless, syrupy liquid that is chemically an alcohol and is obtained from fats and oils. Typically, glycerin is used to prevent crystallization of sugars in candies as well as to add sweetness and retain moisture in foods to preserve them longer. Glycerin is used commonly as a food additive in confectionery products such as cake icing and candies.

Goat's milk cheese—See Cheese.

Gold leaf—For a spectacular and elegant effect to salute a special occasion, gold leaf can be applied to many desserts, but it is shown to its best advantage against a background of rich, dark chocolate. Wrapping the gold leaf around a whole strawberry or other suitably sized fruit can also produce a stunning decoration. The thin (this is a major understatement) 22-karat gold leaf, also known as *patent gold,* is sold in sheets separated by tissue paper. The gold leaf I use comes in sheets that are 3¼ inches (8.1 cm) square; smaller sizes such as this are the easiest to work with. The sheets can be purchased at art supply stores, through some bakery suppliers, and often in Indian grocery stores, where it is known as *vark*. In India, gold leaf and gold dust are widely used to decorate desserts and other foods, including soup, where the thin leaves are floated on the surface. While completely edible (although I wouldn't make it a habit, as the craving can be rather expensive), gold is not absorbed by the body.

Working with gold leaf can be very frustrating—all the more so considering the expense—because the sheets turn to powder or clump into an unusable mass if the following rules are not observed. Be sure there is absolutely no draft whatsoever, including people working or walking near by. The slightest shift in the air is enough to make the thin sheets fly up somewhere other than where you are trying to place them. To transfer a whole sheet of gold leaf to any object, slide it off the nonstick tissue paper it comes on onto the desired food or area. Never touch the gold leaf with your fingers or try to pick up the sheet with your hands. It will stick immediately, and you will have lovely gold-covered fingertips—but no more gold leaf to use for decoration. To transfer a small piece of gold leaf, use a dry artist's brush. Simply touch the tip of the brush to the gold leaf (a small piece will stick to the brush), then touch the brush to the pastry. Some people use tweezers, but I find the brush to be easier and work better.

Gold powder—22- to 24-karat gold that is ground into an edible dust and used as decorations for desserts, pastries, and confections. This tasteless powder is very lightweight and should be handled carefully, as it has a tendency to fly. Gold powder will last indefinitely if stored in a cool, dry place in a well-covered container.

Gold spray—An aerosol spray containing 22-karat gold flecks. The spray is used to decorate desserts and pastries in the same way as gold leaf and gold powder. The spray version is very convenient as the product can be applied exactly where it is desired.

Golden Delicious apple—See Apple.

Golden sugar—See Sugar.

Golden syrup—Golden syrup is a byproduct of sugar manufacturing that is refined to a greater extent than **molasses**. When the sugar, after many boilings, stops yielding crystals, the remaining syrup is clarified by filtering, then reduced. Golden syrup also goes through a decolorizing process, which gives it a milder flavor. It is composed of **sucrose, dextrose, fructose,** and a small amount of water. It is used in breads, cookies, and cakes.

Goldwasser—German for "gold water." This full-bodied liqueur is pale yellow in color and flavored with caraway seed, orange peel, and spices. It has flecks of edible gold leaf suspended throughout; these are harmless to drink. The best-known brand is Danziger Goldwasser, made in Germany. Goldsläge, made in Switzerland, is another brand and is flavored with cinnamon.

Goma—Japanese for "sesame seed." Variations include *shiro goma*, unhulled white sesame seed; *muki goma*, hulled white sesame seed; *kuro goma*, black sesame seed; and *goma abura*, sesame seed oil.

Goober; Goober pea—A slang term for **peanut**, used in the southern United States.

Gooseberry—Gooseberries have never gained a foothold in the United States, partially due to the fact that native varieties are rather tart, small, and not as juicy as the European fruit but also because federal and state laws regulate both interstate shipping and the areas where gooseberries can be grown because the plants can serve as a host to white pine blister rust (red and black currants are likewise regulated). Gooseberries flourish in the northern parts of Europe, where you would be hard put to find a garden without some variety growing in it. In fact, they are so popular and common in Sweden that not having gooseberry bushes growing in your yard is considered practically unpatriotic!

The gooseberry shrub is an attractive plant with beautiful spring flowers, colorful fruit, and bright green, rounded foliage. Dozens of varieties produce different colors of fruit, including white, yellow (amber), green, and red berries. The berries are translucent, revealing the veins and seeds inside. These juicy fruits have been developed to perfection in England, where the berries of some types reach 1½ inches (3.7 cm) in size.

Gooseberries are excellent for use in jams, jellies, tarts, and pies. They also make a wonderful puckery ice cream. Gooseberries can be stored in the refrigerator for one week and frozen for many months. Green and yellow gooseberries turn amber or white when they are fully ripe; they also lose most of their tartness at this point, becoming rather bland. You may want to adjust the amount of sugar used when cooking the fruit in some recipes depending on the stage of ripeness. It is necessary to trim the small, hard stem from gooseberries before cooking, unless the mixture will be strained later. The easiest way to remove both the blossom portion and the stem from the berries is to use small, pointed scissors.

Graham flour—See Flour.

Grain—An edible seed yielded from any plant of the grass family. More commonly referred to as **cereal grain**.

Gram flour—A pale straw-colored flour produced from ground dried chickpeas. It is a nutritious, high-protein flour that is mainly used in East Indian cooking for dough, dumplings, noodles, as a sauce thickener, and to make a batter for deep-frying. Also known as *besan*.

Grand Marnier—A French liqueur made with oranges and aged **Cognac**.

Granny Smith apple—See Apple.

Granulated sugar—See Sugar.

Grape sugar—A naturally occurring form of **glucose**. Also referred to as **dextrose** and typically available in powdered form.

Grapefruit—Grapefruit are divided into two groups: the pigmented or pink varieties, and the common grapefruit, also called *white grapefruit* (although they are actually yellow).

The fruit of both varieties grow in grapelike clusters, which explains the name. The grapefruit tree is one of the largest in the **citrus** family, which makes sense, as grapefruit is the largest fruit of the commercially important citrus crops. The only citrus fruit that is larger than the grapefruit is the thick-skinned **pummelo,** which is the parent of the grapefruit we know today.

The majority of the commercial U.S. grapefruit crop is grown in the Indian River area of Florida. The grapefruits grown there are known to be of higher quality and larger size than those grown in the other principal growing areas of Texas, Arizona, and California. The popularity of grapefruit has held fast for many years due to their health value and tangy, refreshing flavor. Grapefruit are rich in vitamin C (1 cup/240 ml freshly squeezed juice supplies the average daily requirement), and they are also low in calories. Grapefruit require a hotter climate than other citrus varieties and, even so, they take from one to one and one-half years to ripen fully. Grapefruit are available almost year round. They can be left at room temperature for about one week. The fruit is juicier when served or used warm rather than cool. Grapefruits will keep in the refrigerator for up to two months.

Grape—Grapes are one of the oldest cultivated fruits. As we have all seen in drawings and on canvas, the ancient Greeks and Romans cultivated grapes and enjoyed them just as we do today—eaten fresh and used to make wine. After spreading throughout the Roman Empire, grape cultivation soon advanced to Asia, northern Europe, and south Africa. The European grape (*vitus vinifera*) made its way to the New World following Columbus's expeditions. European settlers also encountered the American type of grapevine (*vitus lambrusca*). American grapes differ from the European varieties in that they are classified as *slipskin grapes* (the pulp slides out of the skin with ease), the flesh is soft, and they have a distinct sort of musty flavor. American grapes are also very hardy and resistant to disease. The European varieties, besides being less resistant, have a firmer flesh and do not have the slipskin that characterizes the American grape. Hybrids that produce table grapes are still ranked for the most part as *vitus vinifera,* the European type.

Other grape varieties are grown especially for the production of currants, sultanas (blond raisins), dark raisins, and the large muscatel raisins. In the United States, most of the commercial grape crop is grown in California, including grapes produced for wine making. Grapes range in color from pale green to dark red, almost black. They are used in fruit salads and on fruit tarts. Grapes will keep for about one week stored, covered, in the refrigerator.

Grape Varietals

Cabernet Sauvignon—Best known for use in making wine, these small black grapes are also enjoyed fresh. Available early fall.

Catawba—This purplish-red grape is a medium in size and oval in shape. It has seeds and an intense sweet flavor. The Catawba grape is available from September to November but is mainly used commercially for jams, jellies, and white wines.

Champagne—This grape is very small, purplish-black or reddish brown, with a very sweet flavor. It is used primarily for snacking and for garnish but not for wine, as its name suggests.

Concord—The principal and typical American grape, basically because it grows well here, as it is resistant to the cold climate. This grape is a very large oblong shape with a blue-black skin. It is seedless and sweet in flavor. It is popular for juice and is also used for wine and during table grape season. It ripens in midseason.

Delaware—American hybrid whose berries are small, round, and have a soft, light red skin. It has a sweet flavor and is used for wine making as well as a table grape. Available early to midseason.

Emperor—A European grape with large berries that have a thick light red to red-purple skin. Its texture is firm and crisp. This is probably the second most popular grape (after the Thompson) in the United States, to a large extent due to its durability in transportation and storage. Available late in the season.

Flame—Also known as the *Flame Seedless* and *Red Flame European* grape. It is medium in size and light to dark pink in color. The flavor is excellent, and the flesh has a crisp texture. It grows in pretty cone shaped clusters, making them great for display purposes. Available early in the season.

Muscadine—American grape grown mainly in the southeast United States. It is famous as one of the first grapes used for wine making in this country. One of its varieties, the scuppernong grape, is still used to produce wine in the South. Available midseason.

Muscat—An American hybrid whose name actually refers to a whole group of varieties ranging in color from a light yellow to an almost black. This is one of the best table grapes. The flavor, as the name implies, is musky and rich. Muscat grapes are also made into a sweet wine that pairs wonderfully with desserts. Varieties include the American Golden Muscat and the European Muscat of Alexandria. Available early to midseason.

Niagara—An American hybrid, this large grape has light green skin. It is one of the most widely planted white varieties in this country, as the grape is excellent for wine, juice, and eating fresh. Available midseason.

Perlette—A European grape with white to pale yellow berries in compact translucent clusters. It is seedless, with a thin and very tender skin. Perlette grapes are juicy, with a mild pleasing flavor. Season is very early.

Ribier—A beautiful-looking, loosely clustered European dessert grape. It is deep purple to black, large in size, juicy, round, and mild in flavor, with no acidity and very few seeds. Although it is one of the best-selling grapes, known for its tough blue-black skin, it tends to soften quickly when stored. Available early to midseason.

Scuppernong—See **Muscadine.**

Thompson Seedless—This European grape is also known as *Sultana.* This is the top seedless green grape for commercial use in the United States. It is the leading table grape and also the grape grown for making sultanas, also known as blond or golden raisins. They grow in well-filled, long, attractive clusters. The berries are small to medium, green and golden in color, with crisp juicy flesh. Available midseason.

Tokay—A European grape also known as *Pinot Gris* (a popular wine grape) and, in California, as *Flame Tokay.* This grape has large, firm, brilliant red berries that grow in large clusters. Mostly grown as a table grape. Available late midseason.

Zante—A small, bright purple European grape that is grown mainly to produce **dried currant** raisins. Zante grapes originated in the eastern part of the Mediterranean in Corinth, Greece (the word *currant* comes from the name *Corinth*). California leads the nation in the production of the seedless sweet Zante variety, which grows in small, pretty clusters attached to the main cone. Zante grapes are also used fresh as a garnish for desserts, salads, and cheese displays, and small clusters on the stem make a very attractive decoration on fruit tarts and whole cakes. Available midseason.

Zinfandel—A reddish to black grape grown primarily for the wine industry. The grapes contain seeds and are very tightly clustered. Available early fall.

Grapeseed oil—Extracted from grape seeds, this oil usually has a slight grape flavor and fragrance. The majority comes from France, Italy, and Switzerland; it is also made in the United States. It has a relatively high smoke point and, as such, is a good choice for sautéing. With its relatively light flavor, it can be used in salad dressings.

Grappa—An Italian **eau-de-vie.** Grappa has been produced commercially since the eighteenth century. It is distilled from wine press residue (grape skins and seeds) once the juice of the grapes has been extracted. This colorless, robust brandy has a high alcohol content. Aged grappas are also available with such complex additions as being aged in a variety of woods.

Gravenstein apple—See **Apple.**

Greengage plum—See **Plum.**

Grenadine—A sweet, deep red, thick syrup made from **pomegranates**, it is sometimes alcoholic and most commonly used to color and flavor beverages, cocktails, and desserts.

Groundnut—A vine (*apios tuberosa*), native to North America, with an edible tuber that is boiled and eaten hot. Groundnut is also the British term for **peanut.**

Guar gum—A gum substance obtained from the legume family of plants. It is used in commercially produced items as a thickener and a stabilizer. Equivalent to **gum arabic, gum tragacanth,** and **xanthan gum.**

Guava—The tree *Psidium guajava* produces this highly aromatic berrylike tropical fruit. While the tree is native to Brazil, it is now grown throughout South America and the Caribbean as well as in many other tropical and semitropical climates throughout the world, including California, Florida, and Hawaii. While they can range in size from a small egg to a large pear, guavas are usually oval or round in shape and about 2 inches (5 cm) wide. The thin, yellowish-greenish skin covers a pinkish-orange, sweet flesh. The flavor of the guava has been equated with a mixture of banana, strawberry, and pineapple. Some varieties are seedless, while others have tiny black seeds in the center. Guavas are delicate and prone to infestation by fruit flies; as such, they do not travel well and are usually enjoyed fresh only in the region where they grow. They can be eaten fresh, either alone or with sugar for additional sweetening. They can be added as a raw ingredient to desserts and pastries. Guavas can also be made into a stew or paste, or mashed and flavored with spices or liqueur, then used as a topping. Guavas are also frequently made into preserves, jams, jellies, and sauces.

Guinettes preserved cherry—*Guinettes* are a special type of brandied cherries imported from France. They are labeled *semi-confit,* meaning they are partially cooked or preserved. The pitted cherries are packed in bottles with sugar and brandy and, sometimes, kirsch (cherry liqueur) as well. Both the cherries themselves and the liquid in the bottle are wonderfully delicious. Simply serving them over vanilla ice cream makes an excellent, simple treat and, of course, because they are packed in alcohol, Guinettes are perfect for flambéed dishes such as Cherries Jubilee. The word *Guinettes* is actually the name of a variety of small red cherry grown in France (see **Cherry**). However, it has come to refer to the finished brandied cherry product in the same way, for example, that most people use the word *cabernet* to refer to the wine, not the cabernet grape. Another popular label is *Griottines.*

Gum arabic—Similar to **gum tragacanth.** This substance is produced from the bark of various species of the acacia tree (the most common is the Senegal variety) and is used as a jelling agent in a variety of confections. It is also used as an emulsifier, stabilizer, and thickener in many processed foods such as ice cream, candy, sweet syrups, and commercial sauces. It is tasteless, colorless, and odorless.

Gum tragacanth—This jelling substance comes from the shrub *Astralagus gummifier,* which is native to the Middle East. It is collected and dried into a powder form, which is then reconstituted with water to form a gooey, gelatinous substance. This is an essential ingredient of gum paste. It is flavorless, colorless, and odorless. Used in the same fashion as **Gum arabic,** this vegetable gum is also used as an emulsifier, thickener, and stabilizer, and to help prevent crystallization in many processed foods such as ice cream, candy, jam, and commercial sauces.

H

Hachiya persimmon—See **Persimmon**.

Half-and-half—See **Cream**.

Hard cider—Fermented fruit juice. The terms *cider* and *hard cider* almost always refer to a product made with apples but, technically, other fruit can be used. A cider becomes hard after fermentation. Fermentation occurs naturally, without yeast or sugar, and takes about a month; the alcohol content in the finished product can vary greatly.

Hard flour; Hard wheat—Hard wheats are used for products such as pasta dough and yeast-leavened breads. The terms *hard flour* and *soft flour* refer to the flour's protein content. Hard flours have more protein and therefore produce more gluten; soft flours have less protein and produce less gluten. See **Flour** and **Gluten**.

Hartshorn—See **Ammonium carbonate**.

Hazelnut oil—Pressed from **hazelnuts**, this fragrant oil tastes like the roasted nut. It is commonly used in combination with a lighter oil to balance its full flavor. It is used in dessert sauces, fillings, and syrups, and in the preparation of baked goods. In the hot kitchen, it is most commonly used in salad dressings. Most hazelnut oil is produced in France and imported elsewhere, so it can be very expensive. It must be stored in a cool place.

Hazelnut paste—A paste obtained by pressing **hazelnuts**. It has a nutty brown color, a full, nutty flavor, and is used principally in baked goods. Hazelnut paste is fragrant and has the finished flavor of the roasted nut. It can be purchased from food suppliers commercially, or you can make your own. The purchased paste is more concentrated and a smaller quantity is required.

Hazelnut paste is not the same product as the hazelnut-flavored spreads you find at the supermarket next to peanut butter, intended as a topping for toast. Hazelnut paste contains more essence than these spreads. They should not be used as a substitute.

Hazelnut—Hazelnuts, also known as *filberts* and *cobnuts,* are grown throughout Europe; Turkey and Italy are the largest producers. The distinctive flavor is much improved by toasting, which is also the easiest way to remove most of the nut's skin. Hazelnuts are used in cakes, cookies, candies, and pastries; finely ground hazelnuts are used in linzer dough and in place of flour in some tortes. They are also used to make **hazelnut paste**, an important flavoring agent.

Heavy cream—See **Cream**.

Herb—Any of a large group of annual and perennial plants whose leaves, stems, or flowers are used as a flavoring for cooking. Herbs are used primarily for seasoning but can also be used as a garnish. Among the most common are chervil, thyme, rosemary, dill, tarragon, chives, and parsley. The classification technically includes all edible plants that grow above ground, while those that grow below ground are called *roots*. Herbs differ from **spices** in that herbs are the edible foliage (leaves) of plants, while spices are substances derived from other parts of the plant, such as the roots, seeds, berries, buds, and bark. See entries for specific herbs and spices.

Herbsaint—A liqueur with anise flavoring that is made primarily in New Orleans. It is considered an **absinthe** substitute and is similar to **Pernod**.

Hickory nut—Highly favored in baking, the **pecan** is the most popular variety of hickory nut, mainly because of its thin shell, which allows easy access to the nut meat. The common hickory nut has an especially hard, thick shell that is traditionally removed using a hammer swung with great force. It has a rich, buttery flavor due to its high fat content. The word *hickory* is derived from a Virginia Indian name for a food item, made from crushed hickory nuts, called *pawcohiccora.*

Hiki-cha—Japanese powdered green tea concentrate. Also known as *maccha* or *matcha*. See **Maccha**.

Honey—Honey comes from a natural source: It is the nectar collected by bees and deposited in their honeycomb. In addition to its sweetening power, honey also imparts the flavor of the flowers from which it was gathered. Honey is produced in just about every country in the world, and there are hundreds of varieties; most are named for the flower from which the honey derives its fragrance. Popular varieties include orange blossom honey, from Spain, California, and Mexico; sunflower honey, from Greece, Turkey, and Russia; rosemary honey, produced in the Mediterranean countries; and clover honey, which is the type most commonly used in the United States. Honey has been used as a sweetener in cooking far, far longer than sugar. Previous to the nineteenth century, sugar was still considered a luxury for the masses, and honey was one of the most commonly used substitutes.

The color of the honey varies widely, depending on the source. As is true of **molasses** and other sweetening agents, the darker the color of the honey, the stronger its flavor. Two of the most common varieties in this country are clover and orange blossom. Most types of honey are interchangeable, with the exception of some that are very strongly scented. Honey is available in four forms: comb honey, still in its waxy capsules; chunk honey, which contains both the filtered extracted honey and a piece of the honeycomb; extracted honey, the type most familiar for cooking and table use; and whipped or spun honey, which is extracted honey that is processed using controlled crystallization and which has fine, easily spreadable crystals. Honey adds moisture to baked goods and gives a soft, chewy texture to cakes and cookies. All honey will crystallize over time but is easy to liquefy by heating.

Honeydew melon—Honeydews are large, pale green melons with sweet, very juicy, light green flesh. They are used in the pastry kitchen in fruit salads and to make sorbet. Honeydews are shipped when they are hard (unripe), then usually preripened before being sold. If the melon is very hard, leave it at room temperature for up to four days, until it starts to soften slightly at the stem and bottom ends. While the flesh will become softer and juicier, it will not become any sweeter. Avoid honeydews that have a whitish tinge to the skin; they usually never ripen fully. Honeydews are available throughout the year. Ripe and/or cut melons should be refrigerated and used within two days.

Horehound—The juice of this leafy, aromatic plant, *Marrubium vulgare* (a member of the **mint** family), is used in cooking to produce horehound candy, a brittle confection that is shaped into balls, drops, or squares; it has a mildly bitter aftertaste. Horehound extract is also used to make lozenges, cough syrups, and cordials, and has been used to make a country wine. Also spelled *hoarhound*.

Horned melon—See **Kiwano.**

Huile—French for "oil."

Hydrogenated oil—An oil chemically transformed from its normal liquid state at room temperature into a solid, such as in margarine. During the hydrogenation procedure, pressurized hydrogen gas (additional hydrogen atoms) is forced through liquid vegetable oil (unsaturated fat). This process creates trans fatty acids, converting the mixture into a solid or semisolid form with saturated fat and obliterating any benefits it had as a polyunsaturate. This results in a more spreadable product with better keeping qualities.

Hydromel—An ancient beverage made from honey and water. It was held in high esteem by the Greeks and Romans and was also enjoyed by the Saxons, Celts, Gauls, and Scandinavians throughout the Middle Ages and up to the1700s. *Mel* is Latin for "honey," and *hydro* comes from the Greek word *hudōr*, meaning "water."

Hyssop—Any of several herbs (*Hyssopus officinalis*) belonging to the **mint** family. These herbs, with their pungent, dark green leaves, have a slightly bitter minty flavor. Hyssop is used to add flavor to salads, fruit dishes, soups, and stews. It is most commonly grown, however, as an ornamental, and for its oil, which is extracted and used to make liqueurs such as Chartreuse. Additionally, it is also the source of a premier honey. See **Mint.**

I

Icing sugar—See **Sugar.**

Indian date—See **Tamarind.**

Indian nut—Another name for **pine nut.**

Invert sugar—See **Sugar.**

Irish Mist—A liqueur made from a blend of Irish whiskey and heather honey. The Irish version of **Drambuie.**

Isinglass—A transparent and pure gelatin derived from the air bladders of certain fish, such as the sturgeon. It is made into sheets and was used throughout Europe to make jellies, to clarify wine and liquors, and in the preparation of desserts such as blancmange. However, in recent years, its use has been replaced by refined, more modern forms of gelatin.

Izarra—Based on **Armagnac,** this herb-flavored liqueur is available in yellow and green varieties, the green being the stronger and more full-flavored.

J

Jackfruit—Also known as *jac, fenesi,* and *nangka,* this giant tropical fruit grows on a tree native to India. The fruit can be round to oval, and each measures between 1 and 3 feet (30 and 90 cm) in length and 10 and 20 inches (25 to 50 cm) in diameter. Jackfruit generally weigh 15 to 30 pounds (6 kg 825 g to 13 kg 650 g) but some have reportedly grown as heavy as 65 pounds (29 kg 575 g). The skin is pale green to yellowish-brown and completely covered with short, sharp spikes. There are two main varieties: one with soft, sweet flesh, and the other with a crisper texture that is less sweet. In both, the pulp is white to yellow and full of large seeds. The roasted seeds are considered a delicacy all over the tropics.

Jägermeister—A German liqueur; its name translates to "hunt master." It is flavored with 56 herbs, fruits, and spices. The intense flavors of this 70-proof liqueur becomes slightly more mild if it is served ice cold.

Jaggery—See **Palm sugar.**

Jam—See **Preserve.**

Jamberry—Another name for tomatillo.

Japanese gelatin—Another name for **agar-agar.**

Japanese pear—Another name for **Asian pear.**

Japanese plum—Another name for **loquat.**

Japanese medlar—Another name for **loquat.**

Jasmine rice—A very fragrant long-grain rice from Thailand.

Jelly—(1) An aspic; see **Aspic.** (2) Fruit jelly; see **Preserve.**

Jonathon apple—See **Apple.**

Jordan almond—A large Spanish almond varietal. It is also the name of a candy made by coating these almonds with a hard candy covering that is sometimes flavored with anise. The candies are made in a variety of colors and are often served at weddings.

Jujube—This small green to reddish-brown fruit originated in China, although Syria is also said to have planted the first seed. Growing on very attractive trees, the jujube fruit is either round or pear-shaped. The round variety is known as *Li,* while the pear-shaped variety is known as *Lang.* They are often left to dry on the tree and thus resemble a date—hence the nicknames *Chinese date* and *red date.* Jujube is cultivated in Japan and along the parallel all the way to the Mediterranean island of Majorca. When eaten out of hand, the jujube has a crisp and refreshing apple flavor, although the fruit of some varieties is dry and mealy when eaten fresh. Typically, the fruit of all of the varieties is candied or dried.

K

Kadaif; Kataifi—These are actually two names used for a Middle Eastern dessert that includes long, thin strands of pastry dough. Both terms are also used to describe the dough itself, which is a form of **phyllo dough.** The dough strands are sold in coils that resemble dried pasta. Like other forms of phyllo dough, kadaif is sold frozen and must be protected from drying out.

Kaffir lime—The word *Kaffir* has been used to distinguish varieties of several edible plants, including plums, corn, oranges, and lime. However, the original Arabic word could be translated to "nonbeliever" or "infidel," so the name came to be taken as derogatory. Spelled with one *f*, the term *kafir* was used as a racial or religious slur in certain countries. It has therefore become more politically correct to call these *makrut limes,* as they are known in Thailand. See **Makrut lime.**

Kahlúa—A Mexican coffee-flavored liqueur.

Kalamata olive—A large black olive from Kalamata, Greece. It is dark blackish-purple in color, almond shaped, and about 1 inch (2.5 cm) in length. It has a strong, rich flavor and is sold whole or pitted; however, the olives are commonly pitted before marinating in olive oil and wine vinegar. Kalamata olives are delightful baked into bread. Also spelled *Calamata.*

Kamut—A variety of wheat. The name derives from the ancient Egyptian word for "wheat." Kamut is considered one of the oldest types of grain. Grown commercially only in the state of Montana, this high-protein, nutritious wheat has never been crossbred and remains in its original variety. Kamut has a slightly nutty flavor and is used in the United States in processed foods such as pastas, cereals, and crackers. Due to its limited cultivation, products made with kamut can be difficult to find.

Kanten—Another name for **agar-agar.**

Kasha—The Russian term for both the roasted, dehulled, and crushed **buckwheat groat** and dishes made with it, most commonly a dry porridge or mush. These buckwheat groats have a roasted, nutty flavor.

Kaymak; Kaimaki—A Middle Eastern dairy product made from water buffalo or goat's milk. The milk is heated as for clotted cream so that a thick layer of milkfat forms on the top and can be removed.

Kefir—Originally made from fermented/soured camel's milk in the Caucasus region (between the Caspian and Black seas), kefir is now produced from cow's milk. It is thick and frothy, with a slight aroma, and contains about 2.5 percent alcohol. It is similar to a liquid yogurt. Also known as *kefiri.*

Key lime—The botanical name for the Key lime is *Citrus aurantifolia.* Other names for the fruit are *Mexican lime* and *West Indian lime.* These limes originated in Malaysia and are now grown year round all over the globe in areas with a balmy climate. Key limes are more yellow in color than the common Persian lime (*Citrus latifolia,* the type most readily available commercially) and have a rounded shape.

Henry Perrine, a botanist, planted the first of these trees in the Florida Keys in 1835, and the fruit began to be known as the Key lime in the United States. Hurricanes in 1926 wiped out the commercial Key lime production in Florida, and the groves were replanted with the common Persian lime. Most Key limes now found on the market are imported from Mexico and Central America. The zest of Key limes tends to be bitter and should not be used.

Kinako—Japanese for "soy flour."

Kinome—A Japanese herb with a flavor similar to mint.

Kirsch; Kirschwasser—A colorless **brandy** distilled from the juice of a small black cherry found in the southern part of Germany. *Kirsch* is German for "cherry," and *wasser* is German for "water."

Kiwano—A tropical fruit from New Zealand. It is also known as *horned melon* and as *cucumber horned melon.* Kiwanos are a member of the cucumber family. They are oval in shape, 3 to 5 inches (7.5 to 12.5 cm) long, and have bright orange-yellow skin that is studded with small soft horns, giving the fruit a very interesting and unusual appearance. For the most part, kiwanos are used more for decorative purposes than for their flavor.

Kiwi; Kiwifruit—This barrel-shaped fruit is covered with a thin layer of brown skin and fuzz. Beneath the skin is a soft green interior, with the fruit's small edible black seeds surrounding the pale green center. The taste is said to resemble that of strawberry, pineapple, and melon. Because kiwis are harvested in both California and New Zealand, two locations where the seasons are opposite, one can find this fruit in season almost year round. Kiwis are used in salads, desserts, and as a garnish. Pavlova, the famous meringue creation of Australia and New Zealand, is probably the best-known dessert showcasing the kiwi.

Kiwis are native to China and were originally known as *Chinese gooseberries.* The commercial crop was primarily exported from New Zealand until the fruit was cultivated successfully in California. Firm kiwis can be ripened at room temperature but should be kept out of direct sunlight. Once ripe, they can be stored in the refrigerator for up to two weeks. Kiwis should not be stored next to other fruits because they are very sensitive to the ethylene gas that other fruits may emit.

Kumquat—This small fruit—no bigger than a large olive—looks like a miniature oblong orange. Kumquats originated in China, where the name means "golden orange." The fruit is eaten whole—peel, pits, and all. The unusual twist here, however, is that the peel is sweet and the flesh fairly tart. Kumquats are wonderful to use for decorating, whether fresh, pickled, or candied, and they are also used in salads and made into preserves. Fresh kumquats are readily available from November through March, but the fruit can hang on the tree for many months without negative side effects. Kumquat hybrids can be found in the market starting in September. These are sweeter and slightly larger than the bona fide version. Orangequat and Calamondin are the two most similar to kumquats. These two are also hardy, easy to grow, and the best suited for indoor cultivation of the entire citrus family. Store kumquats at room temperature for one week or so and in the refrigerator for four to six weeks.

L

Lactic acid—The natural acid found in sour milk. The acid forms when particular bacteria come in contact with **lactose** (milk sugar). Lactic acid is used as a preservative, to give a tart flavor to foods or beverages, and in the production of fermented or pickled food products.

Lactose—The natural sugar found in milk.

Lady apple—See Apple.

Lambert cherry—See Cherry.

Lard—Refined pork fat, either natural or hydrogenated. The highest-quality lard is pork leaf fat; lard from other sources must be labeled "rendered pork fat." Lard is excellent for frying and is unbeatable for making flaky pie dough because of its elasticity and shortening power. It can be kept for months if stored, covered, in a cool place; it does not require refrigeration. The word *lard* is also used in the kitchen as a verb meaning to insert strips of fat inside a piece of meat to add flavor and moisture as it cooks.

Lavender—Lavender is an herb with an ancient past. The word itself is derived from the Latin *lavare,* meaning "to wash," due to the fact that the Romans used it in their public baths. The lavender family includes about 30 species and countless varieties. It belongs, in turn, to the *Labiate* family, all of which are aromatics and include **mint, sage,** and **thyme.** Lavender came to England and France from Rome; in both countries, it became a common garden plant during the Middle Ages. At different times throughout history, lavender was used by monks as a medicine, sold in the streets as a plague remedy, used as a charm against evil, and considered both an aphrodisiac and an aid to chastity. Today its antiseptic properties and calming qualities are scientifically accepted. The Provence region of France produces the largest amount of lavender.

Lavender is used in the pastry kitchen fresh and dried as a flavoring and for decorative purposes.

Lavender gem—A hybrid citrus fruit created by crossing a white grapefruit with a tangelo. The result has pale pink skin and flesh.

Leaf gelatin—Another name for sheet gelatin. See **Gelatin.**

Leavener; Leavening agent—Leaveners are used to add volume to baked goods, imparting a lighter texture. The most common examples are **baking soda, baking powder,** and **Yeast;** however, natural elements, such as air and steam, play the same role. Chemical leavening agents work by producing carbon dioxide.

Leche—Spanish for "milk."

Lecithin—A fatty substance that naturally occurs in the membranes of cells and particularly in egg yolks. It is used in baked goods as an **emulsifier** (it keeps water and oil from separating) and antioxidant.

Lemon balm—A member (*Melissa Officinalis*) of the **mint** family. This herb is native to Europe but was introduced to North America, where it has since begun to grow wild. The name *lemon balm* reflects the lemony aroma of its leaves. It can be used fresh in soups; sauces; stuffings for meats, fish, and poultry; fruit salads; jellies; for flavoring both hot and cold drinks; and to make **Chartreuse.** Widely available and used throughout Europe, it is also known simply as *balm* or

as *melissa*—from the Latin word for "honey," because of its attractiveness to bees.

Lemongrass—See Citronella.

Lemon verbena—Lemon verbena, as we usually refer to it in the United States, is also known simply as *verbena.* It is native to Chile and common all through South and Central America, where it can reach heights of 25 feet (7 m 50 cm), though it rarely grows higher than 6 feet (1 m 80 cm) in temperate climates. Like so many herbs and spices, verbena was originally brought to Europe by early explorers returning from sea voyages. This graceful perennial, deciduous shrub has long, pale, pointed leaves with light lilac to purple flowers that grow in clusters. Verbena can be planted as a hedge. The sweet lemon-scented leaves can be used at any time but are most fragrant when the plant is in bloom.

Verbena has many uses in the pastry kitchen, where it gives ices, pound cakes, and creams a special flavor. Tea made from verbena is said to have a soothing, sedative effect and to help bronchial and nasal congestion. Verbena has become increasingly popular in recent years.

Lemon—There are two types of lemons: sweet and acid. The latter are the more popular of commercially grown lemons, the bulk of which are either Eureka (recognizable by a short neck at the stem end) or Lisbon (on which the blossom end appears as a pointed nipple). Lisbons are just about seedless as well, which is also true of the sweet, roundish (no neck or nipple), thin-skinned **Meyer lemon.** Lemons originated in India and are a member of the **citrus** family. Today they are grown in the Mediterranean, the United States, Canada, South America, Asia, Australia, and Africa.

Lemons, lemon juice, and lemon zest are all used frequently in dessert preparations as well as in other types of cooking, as lemon enhances many flavors, both sweet and savory. Lemon juice is used not only as a flavoring agent but also, because of its acidic quality, as an agent that prevents oxidation (it is rubbed onto cut fruit and used to make **acidulated water**). A few drops are used in caramelizing sugar to help prevent both recrystallization and premature darkening. Some lemon juice is added to egg whites when whipping meringue to increase the volume, and, in making puff pastry, lemon juice is worked into both the butter block and the dough to make them more elastic. As a flavoring, lemon juice is almost as widely used as vanilla and chocolate in the pastry kitchen. Lemons are used in lemon curd and other fillings, fruit sauces, doughs, cakes, cookies, mousses, candies, sorbets and ice creams, candied citrus peels, and pies. Soaking lemons in hot water for about an hour before juicing them increases the amount of juice that can be extracted. Rolling the fruit firmly against the table also helps. One medium lemon produces approximately ¼ cup (60 ml) juice and approximately 1 teaspoon (6 g) compacted, grated zest. Lemons keep at room temperature for two weeks and can be stored in the refrigerator for up to six weeks.

Meyer lemon—Biologically not a true lemon, this hybrid

was discovered in the early twentieth century by Frank Meyer, a plant explorer working for the U.S. Department of Agriculture (USDA) in Peking, China (now known as *Beijing*). The Meyer lemon is a cross between an **orange** and a **lemon**. This highly fragrant fruit has a thin, smooth skin and a lower acidity level than the common Eureka and Lisbon varieties. Since its introduction to the United States, the Meyer lemon tree's compact size and shape have made this citrus variety the most popular among home growers and many chefs. In November, when Meyer lemons start to become plentiful in the market, they trigger a rush among the chefs who can not wait to use them for their creations before they become scarce in March.

Levulose—See **Fructose**.

Liaison—An ingredient used as a thickening or binding agent. See **Binding agent** for examples.

Licorice—A flavoring extracted from the feathery plant *Glycyrrhiza glabra,* which grows in the Middle East and throughout southern and parts of central Europe. The bittersweet roots are used to make a distinctive chewy black candy or dried and ground to create a flavor with characteristics similar to but more intense than **anise** and **fennel**. Additionally, juice can be extracted from the root. Licorice is used to flavor liqueurs, medicines, cough lozenges, and in the preparation of tobacco products. It has been utilized for thousands of years both as a sweet flavoring and for medicinal purposes. The term *licorice* can also refer any of several types of candy (usually colored black) flavored with licorice extract.

Lié; Lier—A binding agent, such as egg yolks or cream, used to thicken a sauce. See **Binding agent.**

Light cream—See **Cream.**

Lime—Limes are a member of the citrus family closely related to **lemons**. Limes are not used as extensively but can be substituted for lemons in many cases. They turn from green to yellow when fully ripe; however, immature green limes are the ones that have the desirable tart juice and, because of its bright green color, lime zest is often used as a garnish. Unlike lemons, limes should always be kept refrigerated; they will keep this way for up to six weeks.

Lingonberry—For good reason, lingonberries are known in my native Sweden as "the red gold of the forest." Although they are cultivated to some extent, the majority grow wild all over the country, especially in the north. Lingonberries ripen in September. It is a popular recreational activity for many Swedish families to invade the forest at this time and harvest their plot of berries, the location of which is kept secret throughout the year. Lingonberries thrive in partly sunny openings in the woods and where moss is abundant.

Lingonberries look and taste a bit like small **cranberries**. Lingonberry preserves are a very popular condiment in Scandinavia. Fresh lingonberries are not usually available in the United States, but the preserves are sold in most grocery stores. Lingonberries are used as a topping, in sauces, in parfaits, and in mousses. In Sweden (and in my home in the United States), lingonberry preserves are traditionally served with dinner as an accompaniment to mashed potatoes.

Lingonberries contain a natural preservative, benzoic acid (also found in cranberries, prunes, and cinnamon), which makes it unnecessary to add any other preservative, or even sugar, for storage, nor do they have to be refrigerated. This also makes it possible to market a product called *rårörda,* which is made from raw lingonberries simply crushed and minimally sweetened.

Liqueur—A sweet, usually strong alcoholic spirit flavored by a fruit or herb. See **Alchermes, Amaretto di Saronno, Anisette, Bénédictine, Chambord, Chartreuse, Cointreau, Crème d'abricots, Crème d'amande, Crème d'ananas, Crème de banane, Crème de cacao, Crème de cassis, Crème de cerise, Crème de menthe, Crème de noyaux, Crème de rose, Crème de violette, Frangelico, Goldwasser, Grand Marnier, Kahlúa, Kirschwasser, Mandarine liqueur, Maraschino liqueur, Midori liqueur, Pastis, Pernod, Ratafia, Sabra liqueur,** and **Sambuca.**

Liquor—Any distilled alcoholic beverage.

Litchi—See **Lychee.**

Loaf sugar—See **Sugar.**

Loganberry—See **Blackberry.**

Longan—A small, round fruit cultivated from a southeast Asian tree (*Euphoria longana*). It is somewhat similar to its relative, the **lychee,** but not as sweet. It has a thin, brown shell that must be removed before the fruit is eaten. The crisp, translucent white flesh has a single center seed and a delicate, sweet, and slightly aromatic flavoring. It can be found dried or canned and is eaten either as a snack or used in savory dishes and desserts. Also known as *dragon's eye.*

Loquat—The loquat originated in China. It belongs to the large rose family and looks something like a small oval apple, 2 to 3 inches (5 to 7.5 cm) in diameter. The flesh is sweet, with a hint of acidity, and ivory to orange in color. In addition to being cultivated for its fruit on a small level all around the Mediterranean, Australia, and parts of South America, the loquat tree is popular as an ornamental or shade tree; its long leaves are shiny on top and light green on the underside, which is also covered with a soft down. The fruits grow in clusters of three to five. Unfortunately, loquats are not common in the market, as they spoil quickly after being picked. If you can find them (or grow them, which is easy), they make unusually flavored creams and tarts and can be preserved as jams and jellies (include the few seeds they contain; they have a nice almond flavor).

Lovage—A tall herb (*Levisticum officinale*) of the Old World whose leaves, stems roots, and seeds are all edible and have been used for every purpose, from a seasoning to a medicinal cure for a variety of ailments to an aphrodisiac. This plant grows up to 7 feet (2 m 10 cm) high. The roots can be candied and used in the same fashion as **Angelica.** The dark green leaves, which appear similar to celery leaves, can also be used in savory items to flavor soups, stuffings, and salads; the flavor is especially nice with poultry. The seeds (also known as *celery seed*) can be used in pickling brines and in baked goods. The taste is similar to a concentrated version of celery, with a hint of lemon. The stalks may be prepared as a vegetable. The French refer to lovage as *celeri batard,* meaning "false celery."

Lychee—The lychee (also spelled *litchi* and *lichee*) is most popular in China, where it is eaten as a fruit, often chilled in syrup, dried and sold as *lychee nuts,* and cooked in meat dishes. Fresh lychees can be difficult to find, but the fruit is commonly available canned in syrup. The wide-spreading lychee tree has dense green foliage and loose clusters of fruit growing on long stems. The fruit grows in bunches; each lychee is about the size of an unshelled walnut and is enclosed in a scarlet-colored knobby shell enclosing a firm, translucent, white or pinkish juicy pulp, which in turn surrounds a large, brown inedible seed. To enjoy a lychee fresh, peel from the stem down to keep the fruit in one piece. If the lychee is not freshly picked, the knobby shell will be brittle and brown, but this does not mean the quality has deteriorated. The flesh is juicy and has a sweet, almost perfumed flavor and aroma. Fresh lychees are at their peak in June and July, and can be stored in the refrigerator for several weeks or frozen. Lychees can be used in mousses, charlottes, ice creams, and sauces.

M

Macadamia nut—Macadamias, the king of all nuts, are indigenous to Australia and were named for a chemist from that country, Dr. John Macadam. In the late 1800s, the nuts were brought to Hawaii and planted at Kukuihaele on the big island. It was not long before the macadamia industry was in full bloom. Today macadamias comprise the island's third most important agricultural commodity, exceeded only by sugar and pineapple, and Hawaii accounts for approximately 90 percent of the world's macadamia nut production.

Macadamia nuts have a delicious buttery flavor that is good in cookies and ice cream, where their taste is not overshadowed by other ingredients. Because the shells are very difficult to crack, the nuts are almost always sold shelled, and usually roasted as well. If you are able to find only roasted and salted nuts, thoroughly blanch and dry them before using them in dessert recipes. Macadamia nuts can be substituted for other nuts in some recipes to give a dessert a tropical feeling.

Macaroon coconut—See Coconut.

Maccha—Powdered green tea from Japan. Because it is very concentrated, maccha can be used to impart a strong green tea flavor and celadon green color in syrups, mousses, meringues, and so on without adding additional liquid.

Mace—Mace is the fibrous, bright red covering that enshrouds the **nutmeg** seed. The name is borrowed from the Greek word *markir,* indicating an East Indian tree bark that is used as a spice. Mace is prepared for sale by being flattened and dried in the hot sun, during which time it takes on a yellowish tint. Mace is usually sold and used in a dried ground form, but it can also be obtained whole, in which case it is known as *blade mace.* Not surprisingly, the flavor of mace is similar to that of nutmeg, although not as intense. Mace is not used as much for flavoring sweets as it is in savory dishes, where it is commonly found in pâtés and terrines. Mace should be stored in an airtight container in a dark, cool, dry place.

Madeira—A fortified sweet wine from the island of Madeira.

Makrut lime—A somewhat bitter member of the **citrus** family, these limes are pear-shaped, with bumpy-textured, bright yellow to green skin. The acidic juice is used in Asian cuisine, but the leaves, fresh or dried, are considered even more important, especially in Thai cooking. The leaves have a distinctive shape—something like two leaves joined at their broad ends or a figure eight. Makrut limes are cultivated in Hawaii and all over Southeast Asia. At one time known as Kaffir limes, Makrut limes are still sold under this name (both the limes and the leaves) in many Asian markets in the United States.

Malic acid—An acid that occurs naturally in some fermented fruit. Malic acid is used as an **acidulant** and as a flavoring agent in some prepared food items. When malic acid (present in grapes) becomes **lactic acid** during wine making, the process is called *malolactic fermentation.*

Malt—A germinated (sprouted) grain that is kiln-dried and ground into a fine powder. In the West, malt it is most commonly derived from **barley**. It is used to prepare malt vinegar, in brewing beer and distilling liquors (chiefly **whiskey**), and to add nutrients to many foods. The malting process is carried out to bring about chemical changes, the most important of which is the secretion of amylase, which converts the starch in the grain to maltose, a sugar. The resulting malt (also referred to as *malted grain*) can then be used for fermentation. Malt is important in bread baking, where it converts the starch in the flour to sugar. This sugar provides food for the yeast, helping the bread rise; it also adds to the flavor of the finished product.

Malt extract—A highly nourishing extract derived from sprouted barley that has been dried and ground. It is added to yeast breads to aid in fermentation by converting starch to sugar, which provides food for the yeast. Malt also helps to retain moisture in baked goods, and it adds color to the crust, as it caramelizes at a very low temperature. Diastatic malt contains the enzyme diastase, which, like amylase, converts starch into sugar. Diastatic malt should not be used in products with a long fermentation period, however, as too much of the starch will be broken down. Nondiastatic malt is processed at a higher temperature, which kills the diastase. Malt extract is sold in both a dried, powdered form (sometimes labeled *malt sugar*) and as a syrup. When granulated malt extract or malt sugar is called for in recipes in this book, you should use the nondiastatic formula. If malt sugar or malt extract is not available, in most cases, you may substitute honey at a 2:1 ratio.

Malt sugar—A disaccharide (double sugar) that is formed when starch is broken down by enzyme action and during the barley malting process. It is only one-third as sweet as sucrose (ordinary sugar), but it does have the same energy values. Also commonly referred to as *maltose*. When enzymes react with starches, carbon dioxide gas is produced (this is what makes most bread doughs rise). Starch is converted into sugar during alcohol fermentation. The name *malt sugar* is also used to label granulated malt extract used in baking

Maltose—Another name for **malt sugar.**

Mandarin orange—This small, somewhat flattened variety of orange is distinguished by its loose, easily peeled, "kid glove" skin (although, if the skin is too loose and puffy, the fruit should be avoided, because this is a sign it is overripe and dry). Mandarins originated in China dating back as far as 2000 B.C. The tangerine member of the mandarin family was introduced to Europe early in the nineteenth century and reached the United States a few decades later. Mandarins and their hybrids are among the most versatile fruits around, low in calories and high in both vitamins and minerals, and easy to section with your hands. Mandarins are divided into three classifications: the strictly Japanese *satsumas; tangerines;* and a range of hybrids. Retailers (and wholesalers) tend to generalize and market all of the smaller, deep orange fruits that have a short neck and puffy skin as tangerines, including the satsumas (however, the larger tangelos, a hybrid discussed below, are usually identified correctly).

The most popular mandarins for culinary use are the satsumas—and for good reason, as they are virtually seedless; these are the mandarins most frequently used for canning. The most common commercial variety in this country, however, is the tangerine, named for the city of Tangier. The hybrids **Tangor** (a cross between a tangerine and an **orange**), Temple, and Murlott (also called *honey tangerine*) are the best-known tangerine varieties. Also found in the complex hybrid category is the **tangelo,** which is a cross between a **pomelo** and a tangerine; these have a distinctive nipple-shaped stem end. Minneola and Orlando are the most common types of these. The majority of the commercial mandarin crop is grown in Florida, with California a distant second. Mandarin oranges are available from November through May. Mandarins and all of their hybrids should be stored in the refrigerator, where they will keep for one or two weeks.

Mandarine liqueur—Made with **Cognac** and mandarin oranges, this liqueur has a distinctive orange flavor.

Mango—Mangoes grow on evergreen trees in tropical climates. They are widely used in India in chutneys and curries and are eaten fresh as well. Varieties of mango vary in color from yellow to green and red. When ripe, mangoes have a very strong and sweet fragrance. They are available fresh from spring to late summer and are also available canned.

Mangoes have a large pit and are one of the most difficult fruits when it comes to removing the peel and stone, if you're hoping to keep the flesh intact for cubing or slicing as opposed to making a puree. The best method is to simply cut the two halves free of the stone lengthwise, as close as possible to the large, flat seed, then scoop out the flesh from these halves and discard the skin. To serve mango with the peel on, follow the same method but instead of scooping out the flesh, use a small, sharp knife to cut through the flesh down to the peel in both directions on each cut half. Then turn the halves inside out to raise the scored flesh in a hedgehog pattern (see Figure 14-2, page 727).

Mangoes are used in fruit salads, as a garnish, in ice cream, and in sauces. Fresh mangoes contain an enzyme that will inhibit gelatin from setting, but bringing the fruit pulp to a quick boil will neutralize it. Unripe mangoes can be softened and will become sweeter left at room temperature, away from direct sunlight, for a few days. To speed up the process, place two or more mangoes in a paper or plastic bag. Store ripe fruit, covered, in the refrigerator for up to one week.

Mangosteen—Native to Malaysia, the mangosteen is cultivated in areas all along what is known as the Asian Monsoon Belt, including Indonesia, Burma, Thailand, Sri Lanka, the Philippines, and Vietnam. The reddish-brown fruit is about the size of a mandarin orange, round and flat on both the top and the bottom. The fruit is unusual-looking, with sepals curving in on top around a thick stem. It is not, however, until the fruit is cut open (the rind is very thick and tough and has to be cut open with a sharp knife from end to end) that the real beauty of this fruit is revealed. Inside, five to seven white segments are positioned not unlike citrus segments. The segments look very similar to the flesh of the **lychee,** while the interior of the rind looks like that of a **passion fruit** (pinkish red studded with yellow). The pulp has a melt-in-your-mouth texture and a flavor that is very hard to describe—perhaps "indescribably good" would do it justice. Mangosteens are eaten out of hand (should you be lucky enough to have this opportunity, be aware that the juice will cause quite ugly stains). In desserts, the fruit produces fabulous-tasting bavarian creams and sorbets.

Manufacturing cream—See **Cream.**

Maple syrup—Maple syrup is derived from the sap of the hardwood sugar maple, the black maple, and their relatives, which are all indigenous to the Americas. The trees were first tapped by Native Americans who settled in the eastern portion of North America. Lacking other sweeteners, they used the sap to sweeten beverages, mix with berries and grain, and make hard cakes. Two methods were used by the Native Americans to concentrate the sap into syrup: freezing and the use of hot stones. They passed on their knowledge of maple syrup extraction to the European settlers and, over time, maple syrup became a standard in most kitchens.

Maple syrup is collected mainly in Vermont and the surrounding states. The season for harvesting the sap that becomes maple syrup and its derivatives lasts from two to six weeks. The start of this season depends entirely on weather. The sugarers wait until the end of winter for the first thaw, when the sap begins to flow through the sugar maple trees. It takes a day that warms to a minimum of 40°F (4°C) after a freezing-cold night to cause the sap to run. Trees should be at least 40 years old and/or 10 inches (25 cm) in diameter to be tapped.

Old-fashioned tapping consisted of boring a small tap hole about 2 inches (5 cm) into the trunk. The spout was driven in and a sap bucket hung under the spout. Slashing the trunk is another method that has been used to collect the syrup. Today, modern machinery and huge hoses have taken the place of the bucket method, but essentially, the idea is the same. Once a tree has been tapped, it can produce several gallons of sap a year and can be tapped up to five times a season without harm.

Approximately 40 gallons (153 L 600 ml) of sap are necessary to make 1 gallon (3 L 840 ml) of maple syrup. While the sap was originally boiled in kettles out in the groves, the process has moved inside to what is known as the *sugar house*. The raw sap is boiled in evaporation pans that serve as a water bath. The pans have several sections into which the sap flows, changing direction every few hours to prevent the buildup of niter (potassium nitrate), a byproduct of the syrup making process. The syrup is then filtered and ready for consumption.

The syrup is graded by color: the darker the syrup, the stronger the flavor. Grade AA maple syrup is light amber in color and mild in flavor. Grade A is medium in color but is still mellow in flavor. Grade B is darker amber in color and stronger in flavor. Grade C is very dark, almost molasseslike in flavor, and primarily used for commercial purposes.

Maple syrup, with its wonderful rich flavor, can be used in the pastry kitchen to make candies, flavor ice cream and dessert sauces, and, of course, it is traditional in the United States to use it to top pancakes. There is no excuse to use anything but the real thing—pure maple syrup. While some blends of maple and corn syrups approach pure maple syrup in quality, artificially flavored pancake syrups and other maple-flavored substitutes are absolutely unacceptable and simply will not produce that distinctive, deep, unmistakable taste. Real maple syrup is actually not all that expensive if you consider that it takes about 3 gallons (11 L 520 ml) of boiled sap to produce the amount of syrup used in most recipes. Maple syrup should be refrigerated after opening.

Maple sugar—Made by boiling maple sap until the liquid evaporates almost entirely. Maple sugar is almost twice as sweet as granulated white sugar. It is not feasible to make a completely dry sugar crystal from maple sap because of its content of both **dextrose** and **sucrose**, which are averse to crystallization. Maple sweeteners, which were already popular due to their inexpensive cost compared to cane sugar, were made even more popular by the 1764 Sugar Act, which imposed a high tax on imported cane sugar. Maple sugar remained the main product of maple sap until the late nineteenth century, when inexpensive cane sugar once again became available. Maple syrup then became the main product of the sap, and it remains that way today.

Maple cream—A sweet, creamy, thick spread with a buttery flavor, made from maple syrup. The basic procedure calls for heating the syrup, cooling it over ice water, then beating it with a wooden spoon until the consistency thickens. The process is similar to making fudge or fondant; the mixture turns opaque and thickens as the sugar crystallizes.

Maraschino cherry—See **Cherry**.

Maraschino liqueur—A liqueur made from the Marasca cherry. It can be used as a substitute for **kirschwasser**.

Margarine—A butterlike spread made up of about 80 percent fat, 18 percent water, and 2 percent salt (unless it is unsalted). There are two types of margarine: oleomargarine, which is made from beef and veal fat with vegetable and/or other oils added, and vegetable margarine, which was created as a substitute for butter and is made from corn or soybean oil. Oleomargarine is made primarily for the baking industry and was developed to meet various demands of baking professionals. Some oleomargarines are purposely made tough and with a high melting point; others cream well and are best in baked goods. If kept for a long time, margarine should be stored in a dark, dry place below 70°F (21°C).

Marigold—See **Flowers, edible**.

Marmalade—See **Preserve**.

Marron glacé—*Marron* is French for chestnut. Marron glacé are whole chestnuts, peeled and steeped in a sweet vanilla-flavored sugar syrup of increasing concentration (the syrup becomes more concentrated the longer it cooks) until the sugar penetrates the entire chestnut. This process can take a week. Once the chestnut is removed, it is glazed with a final coat of sugar syrup to give it a shiny, clear gloss. A choice delicacy, marrons glacés are enjoyed as a confection and are used as a garnish. Candied chestnuts are available in cans or jars in most supermarkets; there is also a recipe on page 8, if you would like to make your own.

Marsala—A fortified Sicilian wine made from local grapes, this wine is essentially the Italian equivalent of **Madeira** in French cooking. It has an alcohol content of 17 to 19 percent. The rich, smoky flavor can range from sweet to dry in this dark amber-colored liqueur. The taste can be loosely compared to **sherry**. Sweet Marsala is used as a dessert wine as well as to add flavor to many desserts, including zabaglione and sabayon. Dry Marsala is commonly enjoyed as an apéritif. Marsala is an ideal cooking wine. One can also find special blends of Marsala wine that have been fortified with cream, eggs, and almonds. Marsala was first made in 1773 in the city of Marsala by an Englishman who wanted to improve the staying power of good Sicilian wine.

Marshmallow—A confection originally made from the root of the marshmallow plant, *Althaea officinalis,* a perennial herb so named because it is related to the common mallow and grows in marshes throughout Europe and Asia. The wild plant can still be found today mainly along the east coast in the United States. The leaves and flowers are used both medicinally and for culinary purposes; the root is cooked as a root vegetable, producing a spongy sweet product that dates back to at least 1880 and was the forerunner of the marshmallow confection we know today.

Modern marshmallows are made with egg white, sugar, water, and gelatin. A similar substance, found in France, is called *pâte de gumimauve* and is flavored with rosewater or vanilla.

Marzipan—Marzipan is used extensively in European pastry shops, particularly in Germany, Austria, Switzerland, and Scandinavia. It is made of **almond paste** and **powdered sugar,** with the addition of a moistening agent such as **glucose** or **corn syrup.** Some recipes substitute egg whites or even **fondant,** but the purpose is the same. Marzipan, plain or tinted, is rolled into thin sheets and used for covering cakes and pastries. It is also sculpted into ornamental figures such as animals and flowers.

Due to its large sugar content (60 to 70 percent), marzipan dries very quickly when exposed to air and should be kept covered at all times. If marzipan becomes dry (but it has not dried all the way through), you can reconstitute it by kneading in a small amount of water, although this will shorten its shelf life considerably. Keep your tools and workplace scrupulously clean, and always wash your hands immediately prior to rolling or molding marzipan. The almond oil, which is brought to the surface as you work the marzipan, will pick up and absorb even a small trace of dirt on your hands, which not only ruins the off-white color of the marzipan but can lead to spoilage. If marzipan becomes oily while you are working with it, it generally means it is too firm, causing you to handle it more forcefully than is desired, which brings the oil to the surface. Gently work in a small amount of water to correct the problem. Then add a small amount of powdered sugar if the dough is too sticky. Adding powdered sugar alone, without the water, will simply make the marzipan firmer and will not solve the oily problem.

Marzipan will keep almost indefinitely if you take proper care in the mixing and handling. It should be placed in airtight containers and stored in a very cool place or the refrigerator. It can also be stored in the freezer, should you need to keep it for a long time. If the oil separates from the marzipan after it has thawed, making it crumbly and hard to work with, add a small amount of water and some powdered sugar as described above. Continue to knead the marzipan until it is smooth and elastic.

Mascarpone cheese—See **Cheese.**

May apple—A member of the **Barberry** family and not a true apple. May apples are oblong in shape and about the size of a large olive; they turn yellow when they are ripe. The flesh is lightly sweet to acidic. If eaten when green (and unripe), May apples can be poisonous. They are most common in the eastern United States, where they are often homegrown, but they are rarely found for sale in the commercial market. May apples are great for preserving.

McIntosh apple—See **Apple.**

Mead—Also known as *honey wine* or *sima,* this drink is made from fermented honey or sugar mixed with water, yeast, raisins, and, sometimes, lemon. It is one of the world's most ancient alcoholic drinks. It was favored in Old England and many Indo-European languages contain a similar word with a meaning comparable to "sweet alcoholic drink."

Meringue powder—A fine white powder made from sugar, gum, and dried egg whites. It is used to replace fresh egg whites when making meringues and icings.

Metaxa—A dark Greek **brandy** with a slightly sweet flavor.

Mexican chocolate—A sweet variety of chocolate that is flavored with cinnamon. It has a much grainier texture than other chocolates with visible sugar crystals. It is used to prepare the Mexican hot chocolate beverage and to create Mexican specialty dishes such as *mole poblano.* As a substitute for 1 ounce (30 g) Mexican chocolate, use 1 ounce (30 g) semisweet chocolate, ½ teaspoon (1 g) ground cinnamon, and 1 drop almond extract. The best-known brand is *Ibarra,* packaged in a familiar hexagonal box.

Meyer lemon—See **Lemon.**

Midori liqueur—A green liqueur from Japan flavored with honeydew melon.

Milk—Milk, in addition to being a nourishing beverage, is one of the most frequently used ingredients in the bakeshop. It contributes to the gluten structure in bread dough and gives baked goods a nice crust, color, and flavor. Whole milk, fresh from the cow, contains almost 4 percent fat (usually referred to as *butterfat*) and 8 percent nonfat milk solids; the remaining 88 percent is water. When freshly drawn milk is left undisturbed for several hours, the fat portion rises to the surface, where it can be skimmed off and used as heavy **cream** or for making **butter.** The remaining milk is very rich and probably tastes closer to what we know as half-and-half than the milk we are used to drinking. This raw milk, even if kept cold, has to be consumed within approximately 48 hours and cannot be sold because it has not been pasteurized. Pasteurization is the process of heating the milk to 160°F (71°C) and holding it at that temperature for 15 seconds, which kills harmful bacteria. This process was invented by and named for Louis Pasteur, a French scientist who, in the mid-1800s, demonstrated that wine and beer could be preserved by heating them above 135°F (57°C). Milk is usually homogenized after being pasteurized to ensure that the milkfat is evenly distributed throughout and will not rise to the surface, as previously described. Homogenization is achieved by forcing the milk through tiny holes, which breaks up the fat globules into small particles that remain dispersed throughout the liquid.

Milk is available for purchase in many varieties, the names of which, like cream, are based on the fat content of the product. Some of the names are confusing, as different manufacturers and states have their own names for certain grades. Examples include extra-rich or premium milk, which has slightly more butterfat than regular whole milk, and low-fat milk, which has a little more fat than skim or nonfat milk. There are also variations in the middle, such as extra light, which falls between low-fat and skim. Low-fat, skim, light, or nonfat milk should not be substituted for whole milk in a pastry recipe in most cases. See **Buttermilk, Dry milk, Cream, Crème fraîche, Evaporated milk, Half-and-half, Heavy cream, Light cream, Manufacturing cream, Sour cream, Sweetened condensed milk, Whipped cream, Whipping cream,** and **Yogurt.**

Milk chocolate—See Chocolate.

Milk sugar—Also known as *lactose,* the sugar naturally occurring in milk. Used in candies, milk sugar is the least sweet of all sugars.

Mint—A large perennial herb family known for aromatic leaves. Many varieties have a fragrance or flavor similar to fruit (e.g., lemon or pineapple) or other flavorings (e.g., chocolate). There are over 30 species of mint and 600 known varieties; the most widely available are **spearmint** and **peppermint**. Mint has a strong aroma, a sweet, slightly hot flavor, and a cool aftertaste. In small quantities, it can promote sleep, but in large quantities, it may cause insomnia. Mint can be found in most supermarkets and is available fresh, dried, or in the form of an extract. See **Hyssop.**

> **Peppermint**—A peppery mint, one of the most pungent, and quite easily identified by its bright green lace-shaped leaves and stems tinged with purple. It is used for flavoring candies and in making **crème de menthe.** Peppermint owes its distinctive flavor to menthol, which leaves a fresh taste in the mouth.

> **Spearmint**—The most widely known and used of the mints, spearmint has closely set green leaves with toothed edges. It is native to southern Europe and known as both *common mint* and *garden mint.* Spearmint does not contain menthol like peppermint. It is most commonly used for making mint sauces and jellies.

Mirabelle—See **Plum.**

Molasses—Molasses is produced in the first stages of refining raw sugar. Used in breads and cakes, it adds a distinctive flavor and improves shelf life. Molasses is available in three grades—light, dark, and blackstrap—which are produced from the first, second, and third sugar boilings respectively. Molasses may be labeled as *sulfured* or *unsulfured,* depending on whether or not sulfur was used in the sugar refining procedure.

Montmorency cherry—See **Cherry.**

Morello cherry—See **Cherry.**

Mountain cranberry—A scrubby, woody plant from the same family, *Vaccinium,* as the common **cranberry.** Mountain cranberries, as their name tells you, grow on mountainsides, unlike the common cranberry, which growns in bogs. See **Cranberry.**

Mulberry—There are three varieties of mulberry. The white and the black types are of Asian origin, while the red hails (mainly) from the eastern United States. Although both black and white mulberry trees are cultivated commercially in China and surrounding countries (primarily for their leaves, which are used a food source for silkworms), they grow wild only in Europe. The trees, of medium size, are bushy and somewhat disheveled-looking, yet attractive in their own way. Mulberries somewhat resemble blackberries in appearance, but they grow differently; mulberries develop in clusters rather than individually. The berries must be left to become fully ripe before they are picked. However, instead of being picked off the tree, they are typically allowed to fall to the ground and are gathered there. For this reason, mulberry trees are typically planted in grassy areas. Fully ripe mulberries are both sweet and sour in taste and, when unripe, are so sour as to be practically inedible. In the United States, the berries are used for jams and mulberry wine, sorbets, and ice creams.

Mulled wine—An aromatic alcoholic drink made with red wine, citrus fruit, sugar, and spices; it is served very hot and usually as a winter refreshment. In some cases mulled wine is fortified with the addition of **brandy** or another spirit. Popular in mountain regions in Germany, mulled wine is prepared traditionally with Bordeaux or Burgundy wine. Mulling is a process whereby wine, ale, or cider is warmed, sweetened, and spiced. A popular mulled wine made at Christmastime in Sweden is called *glögg.* Glögg is fortified with **aquavit** and served with whole almonds and raisins in each glass.

Muscatel wine—A sweet dessert wine made from **Muscat grapes.** Muscat grapes are grown in a few places in the Mediterranean region, California, Australia, and near the village of Beaumers-de-Venise, France. The color of the Muscat grape can range from golden to pale amber-red to black as can the wine depending on the grape it is made from. Muscatel wine has the same musty flavor associated with the muscat grapes.

Muscavado sugar—See **Sugar.**

Muskmelon—One of the two categories between which all melons are divided (**watermelon** is the other), this large classification includes many of the most familiar varietes, including the **cantaloupe, Persian, casaba, Crenshaw,** and **honeydew** melons. Muskmelons may have either netted or smooth skin and always contain seeds in a semihollow, fibrous center.

N

Napoleon cherry—See **Cherry.**

Nasturtium—See **Flowers, edible.**

Navel orange—See **Orange.**

Nectarine—Nectarines are one of the oldest fruits and are said to have grown more than 2000 years ago. Their flavor is so fine that the ancient Greeks called them *necter*, meaning "drink of the gods." They are part of the large **stone fruit** family, which includes **plums, peaches,** and **cherries.** The early commercially grown nectarines were small, softened fast, and did not travel well. Newer varieties contain part "peach blood" from crossbreeding in an attempt to get a larger and firmer fruit. However, a nectarine is not, as many believe, a cross between a **peach** and a **plum,** or simply a fuzzless peach. Nectarines are typically smaller than peaches, with a sweeter and more distinctive flavor. Otherwise, nectarines share many characteristics of peaches and, in most cases, can be substituted for peaches. Follow the instructions given with peaches for ripening and storage. Just as with peaches, there are hundreds of varieties; the following are some of the most common:

> **Fantasia**—Originated in California. This medium to large fruit is slightly oval. Up to two-thirds of its skin is covered with red blush. The yellow flesh is firm and smooth. Freestone. Season: Midseason.

> **Silver Lode**—A white nectarine originating in California. The skin is two-thirds red over creamy yellow, with many red dots. It has fine white juice and fiberless flesh. This nectarine ripens over a long period. Freestone. Season: Early to midseason.

> **Gold Mine**—A white nectarine originating in New Zealand. This is a large white fleshed fruit blushed with red over a white skin. It is juicy, with an excellent taste. Freestone. Season: Late.

Newton Pippin apple—See **Apple.**

Nigella seed—Nigella seeds are tiny and black, with a nutty, spicy, peppery flavor. They are most commonly used in Indian and Middle Eastern cooking to flavor savory dishes and breads. They are sometimes mistakenly referred to as *black cumin.* Also known as *black onion seeds.*

Nijisseiki—See **Asian pear.**

Noisette—French for "hazelnut."

Noix—French for "walnut."

Nonpareil—A small sugar pellet available in a variety of colors, used to decorate cakes, cupcakes, confections, ice creams, and cookies. The term also refers to a small chocolate disk covered with tiny white sugar pellets. See **Pastille.**

Non-temp chocolate—Kitchen slang for **coating chocolate.**

Northern Spy apple—See **Apple.**

Northwest Greening apple—See **Apple.**

Nut—Any of a variety of dry fruits that has an edible kernel and a membranous inner casing surrounded by a shell which can be hard, thin, or brittle. Technically speaking, some foods that are commonly referred to as nuts are actually seeds (**Brazil nut**), tubers (**chufa** nut), or legumes (**peanut**). Most nuts are available both shelled and unshelled. The shelled nuts can be found blanched or not, oil-roasted, dry-roasted, salted, whole, halved, candied, broken, chopped, etc. The flavor of most nuts is accentuated with a light toasting. Due to the high fat content in nuts, they can become rancid. To prevent this, shelled nuts should be stored in an airtight container in a cool place or in the freezer. Popular byproducts of nuts include oils, butters, meal, and flour. Nuts are high in calcium and other minerals, vitamin E, and fiber. They have a high protein content and, while they are high in fat, the fat in nuts is 50 to 80 percent monounsaturated. Nuts have been part of the human diet since the beginning of mankind and are still greatly enjoyed. They can be eaten out of hand and are used to a great extent in baking and pastry. See individual listings for specific varieties.

Nutmeg—Nutmeg is the kernel or pit of the fruit of the tropical evergreen nutmeg tree. The fruit has a red or yellow skin, is about 2 inches (5 cm) long, and resembles a cross between an apple and pear in shape. When mature, the outer flesh splits in two, exposing a red web of fibers that almost completely cover the small, hard pit. (When the red fibers are removed, dried, and ground, they become the spice **mace.**) Nutmeg is native to the Spice Islands (the Moluccas). When the islands were seized by the Dutch in 1621, the conquerors monopolized the sale of nutmeg, like so many other spices, and, for a long time, kept the trees from spreading by simply eradicating the spice from other islands. Eventually, the cultivation of nutmeg was spread by enterprising traders. Today nutmeg can be found on many tropical and subtropical islands, including those in the West Indies.

The nutmeg tree does not yield fruit (or the nuts contained within) until it is eight years old, but will then continue to bear for half a century or so. Although the trees contain ripe fruit throughout the year, the three major harvesting months are July, November, and March, with March being the largest harvest. This is the time that both nutmeg and mace are at their prime, while in the other two months one or the other is superior. After the flesh and mace are removed, the nutmeg pits are slowly dried until the kernel shrinks and rattles free inside the shell. The shells are then cracked and the nuts are removed. The nuts are treated to protect them from insects and to ensure that they will not start to germinate when they are stored. If this is done properly, the nuts will keep indefinitely.

Freshly ground nutmeg is far superior to the commercial preground variety. Its sweet, spicy flavor and aroma has long been popular not just in the bakeshop but also in many savory dishes, where nutmeg is used to flavor vegetables and sauces, and nutmeg is, of course, considered a must in egg nog. A fashionable trend in the seventeenth century was for a gentleman to carry a small silver box containing a nutmeg and a grater, which were used to grate fresh nutmeg on top of hot chocolate. Store purchased ground nutmeg in an airtight container in a cool, dry location. If grinding (or grating) it yourself, do not prepare more than you need at one time.

O

Oat—The edible seed of a cereal grass, *Avena sativa,* native to central Europe. For a long time, oats were used only as animal feed and were considered a weed when they sprouted up in wheat fields. Only relatively recently have oats received due credit for their high content of soluble fiber as well as vitamins B_1, B_2, and E. Whole oats are still commonly used for animal feed, however. Oats can be made into a flour, but they are devoid of **gluten** and thus of little help in bread baking. Oats are available in a variety of produced forms that can be added to cookies, crackers, and breads. The various forms are generally not interchangeable.

Oat groats—Oat kernels that have been cleaned, toasted, hulled, and cleaned a second time. In this form, oats retain most of their nutritional value.

Oat flour—Produced from oat groats, which are further broken down and ground into a powder. Like all oat products, it is lacking in gluten, so it is relatively useless as the sole flour used for baked goods that need to rise.

Oat bran—Oat bran does not contain any gluten, so in baking, oat bran must always be combined with flour that does have gluten. It has always been prized as a prime source of dietary fiber, and has been shown to lower cholesterol levels.

Oatmeal—A thick porridge made from hulled, sliced (steel-cut oats are considered the best), and cooked oats. Instant oatmeal is produced from instant oats (groats that have been precooked and dried before they are rolled), which turn into mush with the addition of a liquid. Instant oatmeal is usually flavored with salt, sugar, and other flavoring agents and is often sold in individual serving packets.

Pinhead oatmeal—Hulled oatmeal that is broken down and given one pass beyond groat level.

Quick oat—An oat groat that is cut, steamed, and rolled to decrease cooking time. While quick oats cook in about five minutes, many critics argue that their taste and texture is not quite the same.

Rolled oat—A large oat flake produced when the cut oat groats are steamed, then flattened with rollers.

Scotch oats—Also known as *Irish oats* and *steel-cut oats,* Scotch oats are made by cutting oat groats into two or three pieces; these are neither rolled nor steamed. This type of oat product takes longest to cook.

Oblaten—A thin wafer most commonly known as that given during Communion in the Catholic Church. The word comes from the Latin *oblate,* meaning "flattened or depressed." Oblaten wafers are used to line pans in making candy such nougat or sweets such as panforte. The thin, paper-like wafer is completely edible. **Rice paper** is often used as a substitute.

Oeuf—French for "egg."

Oil—An unsaturated fat that comes mainly from plants and that remains a liquid at room temperature (the most notable exception to this rule being coconut oil, which remains solid and is a saturated fat). Oils are generally a combination of monounsaturated and polyunsaturated fats. They vary by type in taste and nutritional benefit. Oils can be extracted by one of two methods. With solvent extraction, the ground ingredient is immersed in a chemical solvent compound that is later extracted during boiling. With cold pressing, despite the name, the mixture is heated before the oil is pressed out. Refined oils (most commonly found in markets) are treated to make them lighter in color and increase the smoke point and shelf life. Unrefined oils, because they are not treated, turn rancid quickly and should be kept, covered, in the refrigerator. Common types of oil include almond, canola, coconut, corn, cottonseed, olive, peanut, safflower, sesame, soy, and walnut. Oils are used to add moisture and a desireable texture to baked goods and confections and for frying.

Okashi—Japanese for "sweets," "pastry," and "confections"; sometimes simply *kashi.*

Olallieberry—See **Blackberry.**

Oleomargarine—See **Margarine.**

Olive oil—A popular oil throughout the world, olive oil is obtained by pressing tree-ripened olives. While it is most commonly used in the hot kitchen and to prepare salads, it is often used in baking as well. Grades of olive oil are based on the level of acidity. The acidity level of the first press of the olives ranges between 1 and 4 percent. Cold-pressed extra-virgin olive oil, which is light and ranges from a golden yellowish to a pale green shade, is obtained from the first pressing of the olives. Naturally, it is the lowest in acidity, at 1 percent. It is the most aromatic, fruity, and smooth and therefore the most expensive. In descending order, the other grades of olive oil are superfine, fine, virgin, and pure. These are extracted with the use of solvents and result in a paler, weaker-tasting olive oil. A second or third press is pressed hot and is not as fruity and aromatic as the first press.

Olive oil is cholesterol free and high in monounsaturated fat. It can be substituted for other vegetable oils, including canola, corn, peanut, safflower, and sunflower, although because olive oil does have a distinctive flavor, it might alter the taste of the finished product. Olive oil has a low smoke point that makes it unsuitable for frying. It can be stored, covered, in a dark place, or kept, sealed, in the refrigerator. If kept in the refrigerator, it becomes cloudy and thick, but it clarifies and liquefies once it comes to room temperature.

Olive—Olives are found all over the Mediterranean; over 90 percent of the world's cultivated olives are grown in that region. The ragged-looking trees are among the hardiest species and can live to be hundreds of years old. Their main harvest, of course, is olive oil, but what would we do without the popular small pitted fruit? It is hard to imagine a salade niçoise without the dark olives of Provence, or a martini without a pimiento-stuffed green olive (or my favorite martini olive—stuffed with anchovy). The dozens of varieties, sizes, and colors have one thing in common: They are all green before they are ripe and turn black when left on the tree to ripen. Either way, when first picked, olives are very bitter, and, if they are not pressed for oil, they are always cured in brine or oil before they can be eaten. Olives are used in bread baking.

Onion—An underground bulb (*Allium cepa*) belonging to the lily family. Onions are native to Asia but are now grown throughout the world. They contain vitamin C and traces of other vitamins and minerals. The onion is edible at all stages of its development, from the green root to the mature bulb. Onions have two main classifications: green and dry (mature onions with a thin, papery skin covering). They can range in color from white to yellow to red. The types most often used in United States cuisine are the white and yellow globes and the green onion (scallion). Almost all types carry a strong flavor and aroma, and a crisp texture. Onions are used in the bakery in loaf breads, flatbreads, bagels, and other rolls.

Orange flower water—Also known by the Italian name *fiori di sicilia*, orange flower water is a clear, sweet aromatic liquid that is distilled from the blossoms of bitter oranges. It has been used since the Middle Ages and is most popular in Indian, Greek, and Middle Eastern foods. It is very strong and should be used in moderation. It is used to add flavor and essence to cold drinks and savory items as well as various desserts, pastries, and confections.

Orange—Oranges are probably second only to **apples** in popularity among fruits. They are the most commonly used member of the **citrus** family for eating and cooking, and their sweet juice is a typical breakfast beverage. Oranges are grown commercially in the United States in Florida, California, Texas, and Arizona. Fresh oranges are available year round. The trees are everbearing (as are other types of citrus and also the coconut palm, cocoa tree, and coffee plant), meaning that they produce buds, flowers, immature and ripe fruit at the same time. Oranges are used in many of the same dessert preparations as **lemons,** such as sorbets, sauces, fruit salads, and custards. **Blood oranges** are a variety of orange with red flesh, juice, and rind. Their distinctive color adds a nice touch. Bitter oranges, such as **Seville**, are used in marmalades and to make **Curaçao** and **Grand Marnier**. Commercial oranges (and many other fruits) are almost always dipped in or sprayed with an edible wax to enhance their appearance and preserve freshness; often, an orange-colored vegetable dye is added to the wax. The colored wax is absolutely harmless, and there is no need to wash it off before using the fruit. Oranges will yield more juice if stored at room temperature; they can be kept this way for up to two weeks. They can be stored about twice as long in the refrigerator. It is not necessary to wrap or cover oranges in either case, as their sturdy skin offers enough protection.

There are four distinct groups of oranges: (1) the **navel orange;** (2) the so-called **common orange** (both navel and common are also known as *sweet oranges*); (3) the **sour orange** (also known as *bitter orange*); and (4) the **blood orange.**

Orange Varieties

Navel orange—The folded protrusion, the navel, at the blossom end is the development of a secondary fruit at the end of the main fruit, which is the odd-looking top-shaped portion that is so evident both before and after peeling and separating the navel orange. As a group, these oranges are known for crisp, rich flavor and ease of peeling and separation.

Robertson navel—A bud sport of **Washington navel.** Identical to it except that the fruit is smaller and grows in tight clusters on the outside of the tree. It ripens up to two weeks earlier. Season: Early.

Trovita—This is the exception to the rule—a navel orange without a navel but still thought to have the other advantages of the variety. A **Washington navel** seedling also sold under the name *Arizona Sweet*. Season: Midseason.

Washington navel—This is the standard navel fruit—large and flavorful, with no seeds. It is the orange of choice for eating. Season: Early.

Common orange—Sometimes called *juice oranges,* this variety is divided into two groups: those grown in the Southwest and those adapted to the Southeast, with the exception of **Valencia** (the most widely grown and important sweet orange in the world), which is grown in both regions. As their alternate name suggests, common oranges are typically used to make fresh juice, as they all are very sweet and have an abundance of juice.

Diller—Another orange also known as *Arizona Sweet*. The fruit is juicy, small to medium in size, and may contain from very few to many seeds. Season: Early to midseason.

Hamlin—A fairly small fruit that is practically seedless, with a pretty colored skin. This excellent juice orange is another that is also called *Arizona Sweet*. Very similar to **Diller,** but ripens earlier. Season: Early.

Valencia—The standard juice orange and a very important member of the commercial orange crop. Medium to large in size. The trees are quite adaptable and grow worldwide. Valencias are vigorous bearers. Ripe fruit may be left on the tree for up to 5 months. When this is done the rind may become green again. There are both seedless fruits and those with seeds.

Sour orange—Also known as *bitter oranges*. Although well known throughout the Western world, especially in the Mediterranean region, sour oranges are not usually available in the produce market partly due to their much more pungent flavor compared to the sweet varieties. Although all citrus is rich in pectin (the pith of oranges is a major source for commercially produced pectin), the sour orange stands out here—hence its popularity for use in marmalades, not only for the tangy flavor but also because it is possible to make a fine, firm marmalade without the addition of pectin.

Bergamot—A variety of bitter orange, shaped a bit like a pear, with a peel that produces an oil known as *essence of bergamot*. This essential oil is used as a flavoring in food and as a component of perfume. The best-known use of the flavoring is in Earl Grey tea. Although not as well known, there are two other plants with the name *bergamot*: wild bergamot (*Monarda fistulosa*), which is also known as *horsemint* and is used in tea; and Bergamot mint (*Mentha aquatica*), yet another member of the mint family. Season: Year round.

Bouquet; Bouquet de Fleurs—Prized for ornamental use, with bright colored fruit, thornless branches, and profuse blooms of large, clustered, and very aromatic flowers. Adding to its value, the fruit (if not used for making marmalade) will stay on the tree for up to twelve months. Season: Year round.

Chinotto—Just as useful and handsome an ornamental tree as **Bouquet**. Grows into a round and symmetrical tree with thornless branches, small, bright green, densely foliated leaves, and profuse blossoms. It has small, flattened, deep orange fruit held in clusters that will stay on the tree for up to 12 months. It is also known as the *Myrtle Leaf orange*. Season: Year round.

Seville—The most famous of the unimproved (bitter) oranges, this historic orange of ancient and European courtyards is widely used as a decorative plant in Europe as well as in the United States, especially in the Southwest. It has thorny branches with long, dark green leaves that taper into a point. Besides being used for marmalades and certain liqueurs, including **Curaçao** and **Grand Marnier**, this very sour fruit's peel is popular for making into candied orange peel.

Blood orange—This hybrid fruit first appeared in the Mediterranean region in the mid-1800s. Today, one-third of all oranges consumed in that area of Europe, especially in Spain, Italy, and the North African countries, are blood oranges. The name *blood*, of course, describes one of the fruit's distinctive qualities, its red interior, which can vary from just a hint of color to a deep blood-red. Generally speaking, the color of the flesh is more consistently deep red in the hotter growing regions. Do not judge the color of the flesh by the color of the rind, as the two do not have anything to do with each other. Surprisingly, the rind shows a more dramatic effect on fruits grown on the northern part of the citrus tree, where they are somewhat protected from the southern exposure of the sun.

Blood oranges are known in the culinary world as the connoisseur's citrus due not only to their dramatic color but also their distinctive rich flavor. Despite being hard to peel, and although no seedless variety has yet emerged, blood oranges cut into wedges make a colorful and dramatic garnish not only for sweet dishes but savory dishes as well. The juice, of course, lends itself to great-looking and great-tasting sorbets and sauces. The savory Maltaise sauce, for example, a variation of the classic lemon-flavored hollandaise sauce, is made with the juice and zest of the blood orange.

Orgeat syrup—A syrup made from almonds and sugar and flavored with rosewater or orange flower water. With its distinctive almond taste, it is used to add flavor and aroma to cocktails and pastries. In its original composition, it was made with an almond-barley blend.

Ostia—An Italian wafer produced from wheat starch. It is light and paper-thin and can be replaced with Asian **rice paper** if necessary. It is used to line molds and pans for confectionery items such as panforte and torrone.

Ouzo—A Greek alcoholic beverage with an **anise** flavor and clear color, ouzo turns milky white when it is mixed with water. This sweet apéritif is of the **absinthe** type.

P

Palm oil; Palm kernel oil—Palm oil comes from the fruit of the African palm tree; palm kernel oil is extracted from the nut or kernel of other types of palms. Both oils are vegetable sources of cholesterol-raising saturated fatty acids. Although palm oil is a common ingredient in African and Brazilian cuisine, it is not readily found in supermarkets. Palm kernel oil is pale yellow in color and more mild in flavor than the reddish-brown palm oil. Palm kernel oil is used in cosmetic preparations.

Palm sugar—Also called *jaggery*, palm sugar is made from the sap of the Palmyra palm tree. It is an unrefined brown sugar with a coarse texture that is sold in lumps or cakes. Typically, palm sugar is called for in Indian, southeast Asian, and Indonesian recipes.

Papaw—A fruit-bearing tree found in the United States from Massachusetts to Mississippi. The tree, native to Central America, produces fruit known as *dog apple, custard apple,* and *Michigan banana.* The fruit is edible, large, kidney-shaped, dark-colored, sweet, and highly aromatic. The taste has been described as a cross between **banana** and **pear**, and the name is often confused with **pawpaw**. The term *custard apple* is also used for the **cherimoya**; however, the two are unrelated.

Papaya—Papayas are a delicious tropical fruit, Mexican in origin, now grown in tropical climates all over the world. Their green skin turns yellow or orange when the fruit is ripe; the flesh is a pretty salmon color. Papayas are popular for breakfast and are used in ice cream, fruit salads, fruit tarts, and sauces. Papayas contain the enzyme papain, which aids in digestion (in fact, papayas were called *the tree of health* in the Caribbean because the fruit is so beneficial to people with stomach problems). Because of this enzyme, papayas can be used as a meat tenderizer, and, for the same reason, raw papaya will inhibit **gelatin** from jelling. Bringing the fruit to a quick boil will kill the enzyme. Papayas that are about half yellow will ripen in approximately three days if left at room temperature. The process can be greatly accelerated by placing the fruit in a paper bag with a banana. Ripe papayas should be stored, covered, in the refrigerator. They will keep this way for up to one week, but their delicate flavor will fade after a time.

Paprika—A blend of dried red-skinned chilies; very often the **pimiento pepper** is used to produce paprika. The flavor of paprika ranges from mild and slightly sweet to strong, pungent, and a little spicy. The color also varies from a deep orange to a bright or dark red. It is found mainly in the cuisines of Central Europe and Spain, both as a spice to add flavor and as a garnish. It is sometimes referred to as *Hungarian pepper* and paprika from Hungary is considered by many to be the finest available.

Passion fruit—Although the name makes this fruit sound like an aphrodisiac, passion fruit was named by Spanish missionaries who said the appearance of the flowers had a significance to the Crucifixion. The missionaries used the flowers to illustrate the Crucifixion, explaining that the three styles (a portion of the center of the flower) represented the three nails that were used, and the five flower stamens represented the five wounds. Passion fruits are round, about 2 inches (5 cm) in diameter, and have a hard, wrinkled, dark purple skin when the fruit is ripe. The skin, which is almost like a shell, is not eaten. The flesh consists mostly of seeds, which can be eaten, or the flesh can be forced through a sieve to extract the juice. Passion fruit juice can be used in ice creams (fortunately, neither the scent nor the flavor dissipates through storage or freezing), soufflés, sauces, and beverages. Passion fruits are native to Brazil but are also grown now in California, Hawaii, Florida, Africa, India, and New Zealand. Ripe passion fruits can be stored in the refrigerator for about one week.

Pastille—The name comes from the Latin word *pastillus,* meaning "little loaf roll." A pastille is a small, round confection. Pastilles come in two types. The first is a hard ball made of water, sugar, and various fruit flavorings, often sold in small metal tins; the other is a flat drop, usually chocolate flavored and sprinkled with **Nonpareils.**

Pastis—An anise-flavored liqueur.

Pastry flour—See **Flour.**

Pawpaw—This term is used for a number of different fruits, but most often it is used for the **papaya.** *Pawpaw* is often confused with **papaw.**

Peach—Peaches are a member of the rose family, along with apricots, plums, and nectarines, and, like those, are classified as **drupe fruits,** meaning the fruit contains one hard stone in its center. There are both **clingstone** and **freestone** varieties. Peaches, which are referred to by many as *the queen of the temperate-zone fruits,* are available in the United States from early May through October (and in the remaining months, you can find imports from the Southern Hemisphere). Peaches are a fitting fruit partner to the king of fruits, the apple. They are very sweet and juicy when ripe, and are one of the favorite summer fruits for ice creams and cobblers. Peaches

are also often used to make jam. They need a warm climate with no frost and are grown in both North and South America, Australia, Africa, and many parts of Europe. Early settlers in America planted peach trees all along the eastern seaboard, establishing the fruit so thoroughly that botanists in the mid-eighteenth century assumed peaches to be native to the New World. History tells us that, in actuality, peach trees originated in China and from there were introduced to the Middle East, Europe, and subsequently to the Americas. Because peaches were first imported from Persia (more than two millennia ago), the Romans, knowing only that they received the fruit from Persia, gave them the botanical name *Prunus persica* and thus, for many years, they were known as the *Persian apple.*

Unfortunately, tree-ripened peaches do not travel very well, so the commercial crop is almost always picked and shipped hard and unripe. They will soften if left at room temperature. This can be accelerated by placing the fruit in a paper bag. Make several small holes in the bag and leave the fruit this way at room temperature for a few days. (You can turbocharge this process by including an apple in the bag, because ethylene gas produced by the apple aids the ripening process.) The flavor is never as good as that of the tree-ripened variety, though. Ripe peaches will keep four to five days if refrigerated. (Keep them in a plastic bag, if possible.)

In Europe, peaches are cultivated mainly in the Mediterranean region. Even though commercial cultivation in the United States began in the east, mainly in the so-called Chesapeake Peach Belt, today half of the commercial peach harvest comes from California, although the one-time leading peach-producing states of Virginia and, of course, Georgia (it is not called the Peach State for nothing) still produce their fair share. Some 20 years ago, the **Red Haven** variety was probably the most common peach sold. The life of a peach tree is only 20 years, however, so popularity tends to change with new generations of peach lovers. Here, listed in seasonal order, are the more common varieties of the many hundreds of peaches.

Dixired—Originated in Georgia. This is a medium fruit with bright red skin, yellow flesh, and good flavor. It was developed from Halehaven. Semiclingstone. Season: Early.

Redhaven—Originated in Michigan. This fruit is medium in size, with brilliant red over yellow skin. It has sweet and juicy fine-textured meat and is one of the best early peaches. Freestone. Season: Early. (Early Red Haven is almost identical, but it ripens a few weeks earlier.)

Elberta—Originated in Georgia. This is one of the standard commercial peaches. The fruit is large, slightly oval, with a combination of deep golden and blush-red skin. It has firm, juicy yellow flesh. Freestone. Season: Midseason. (There is also an *Early Elberta* and the old variety, *Fay Elberta,* both with a resemblance to the Elberta.)

J. H. Male—Originated in Connecticut. This is a large fruit with yellow skin, blushed with red, and very little fuzz. Once a top commercial variety, it transports very well and is still the most common variety for distant commercial shipping. It has good flavor and nonstringy, juicy flesh. Freestone. Season: Mid to late.

Rio Oso Gem—Originated in California. This has very red skin (especially the larger fruits) and a fine-textured melt-in-your-mouth yellow flesh. It is very close to **Elberta** in popularity. Freestone. Season: Mid to late.

Nectar—Originated in California. This is a large fruit with blushed pink to red skin and white flesh that is tinged with red. It is juicy and full of aroma and generally too soft for commercial use, but what a treat for the home garden! Freestone. Season: Early to midseason.

Babcock—Originated in California. This is a fairly small fruit with light pink skin blushed with red and very little fuzz. The skin is especially easy to peel when perfectly ripe. It has an almost pure white flesh, with a red area around the stone. Semifreestone. Season: Early to midseason.

Melba—Originated in Texas. This is a large fruit with a pale yellow skin and sweet white flesh with a honey overtone. Freestone. Season: Mid to late.

Peanut—Peanuts are a member of the legume family (as are beans, lentils, peas, and soybeans) and are not actually classified as a nut. They are also called *goobers, goober peas, groundnuts,* and *grass nuts.* The most common varieties are the Virginia and the Spanish peanut. Native to South America, the peanut plant was introduced to Africa by European explorers and reached North America with African slaves. Although peanuts form underground, they are not tubers but seeds that are enclosed in a nutlike shell. Peanut farming in the United States began after the Civil War as a result of Southern farmers looking for a crop that would not be subject to the pests associated with cotton. The most famous researcher into the many uses of peanuts was George Washington Carver, whose discoveries helped establish peanut farming as a major industry. In the United States, **peanut butter** is the most important peanut product, but very little peanut butter is consumed in other countries. About two-thirds of the peanut crop worldwide is used for peanut oil. Peanuts, including peanut butter, are mostly used in cookies in the pastry kitchen; peanuts are also found, of course, in peanut brittle.

Peanut butter—A common sandwich spread, peanut butter is also used as an ingredient in candy. Originally intended as a protein substitute for people with poor teeth, peanut butter was invented in 1890 by a physician. Peanut butter is processed by blending peanuts into a butter and separating the oil from the butter as a byproduct. By law, any product labeled *peanut butter* in the United States must contain at least 90 percent peanuts, with the remaining 10 percent restricted to salt, sweeteners, and stabilizers. If labeled *natural peanut butter* it can not contain any ingredients other than peanuts, oil, and salt.

Peanut oil—An oil made from peanuts that is widely used for cooking and deep-frying. Also known as *groundnut oil.* Peanut oil has a neutral flavor. The same oil can be reused for frying several times because the oil can withstand high temperatures without losing quality. Peanut oil is also used in canning as well as the manufacturing of **margarine.**

Pear—Pears are native to Western Asia. From there, they made their way to Greece, then gradually spread throughout the Old World due, in large part, to the assistance of the Romans. In fact, during the time of the Roman Empire, the number of pear varieties cultivated grew from as few as 6 to nearly 60. Pears not only rival the **apple** in popularity, but the two are actually closely related. Both are members of the rose family and are classified as pome fruits, meaning they have a distinct seeded core. Pears are very low in acid and quite high in minerals; they even outdo the hearty apple in that regard. Pears contain an abundance of calcium, iron, phosphorus, and potassium.

Pears come in many sizes and colors, from pale green to yellow, brown, and red. Some are best for cooking and others for eating raw. One variety or another is available year round. Pears are used in many desserts, such as the well-known Pears Belle Hélène, as well as in tarts, charlottes, and ice creams; they are also poached in wine and served with cheese. Pears can be made into pear brandy and jam. They are harvested and shipped before they are ripe; the fruit actually develops a better flavor and texture if ripened off the tree. Pears served raw should be fully ripe. For baking and cooking, however, it is preferable to have them just a little underripe. Pears can be left at room temperature to ripen, then transferred to the refrigerator for two or three days, or they can be refrigerated from the start, which will cause them to ripen more slowly. In either case, do not store in a sealed plastic bag. Pears yield to light pressure when ripe.

Following are some of the more common varieties, listed alphabetically.

Anjou—Originated in France (also said to have first rooted in Belgium). This is a large fruit with green skin that turns to cream when the fruit ripens. It is distinguished by its stocky neck and mild-flavored, juicy, fine-textured flesh. It is best for eating out of hand and other fresh uses. Season: Midseason.

Bartlett—By large account, the most popular pear in the United States. Known as *Williams* in Europe, it was developed in eighteenth-century England and brought across the Atlantic to the Colonies by the early settlers. Here it was named after Enoch Bartlett, a Massachusetts resident who promoted and popularized the variety. Bartlett pears turn from dark green to light golden yellow when they are perfectly ripe. A pretty red-skinned strain of Bartlett has also been developed. These are great for use in a fruit display or fruit basket, or served fresh with cheeses. Red Bartletts are of no significance for peeling and cooking, as the flavor is no different from the original. Season: Midseason.

Beurre—Also known in the United States as *French Butter* *pear,* its many varieties are especially soft and juicy, having none of the grainy texture that can be experienced with others. The two main varieties are the **Anjou** and the Long-Necked **Bosc.** Season: Midseason.

Bosc—This variety originated in either Belgium or France, depending on who is talking. The fruit is large and narrow, with a distinct long and elegant neck that sets it apart from all other pears. It has a yellow-green, heavily russetted skin and a white, firm, actually crisp aromatic flesh. One of the best all-around pears. It should never be placed in the refrigerator. Season: Late.

Comice—Orinsgated in France. The name is an abridgement of the French *doyenne du comice,* which means "top of the show." The large, roundish fruit has a green-yellow skin that can be rather tough. The flesh is unequalled in aroma and flavor, making it one of the best dessert pears. Season: Late.

Seckel—Originated in New York in the mid-1700s. This is a very small fruit, reddish-brown blushed over yellow. Its best feature is its unusually small size. Though it can be poached, it is great for eating fresh, it looks (and tastes) especially good served with cheese. Seckel pears do not keep well. Season: Midseason.

Winternelis—Originated in Belgium (by Jean-Claud Nelis). The fruit is medium in size, and the skin is green-yellow with russet and rather unattractive and rough. It has a spicy, fine-textured flesh, although it can be gritty toward the center. Its best feature is its long keeping ability. Season: Late.

Pecan—Pecans (as well as **walnuts**) are indigenous to North America, and both are a type of **hickory nut.** Pecans are generally purchased already shelled, in halves or pieces. They are more expensive than most other varieties of nuts and are especially suitable for decorative purposes. Pecans are used in some candies and breakfast pastries and, of course, the American favorite, pecan pie.

Pectin—Pectin is a natural gelling agent that is present in varying amounts in certain types of fruit. **Apples, blueberries, cranberries, lingonberries,** and most **citrus** fruits are particularly high in pectin. Pectin is used to thicken marmalades, jams, and jellies. Commercial pectin can be purchased in either powdered or liquid form.

Pepino—Pepinos originated in the temperate parts of the Andean region of Chile and Peru and are cultivated today in New Zealand, California, and other subtropical regions. *Pepino* is Spanish for "cucumber," and the Rio Baba variety does resemble this vegetable. It is exotic-looking, having smooth golden and glossy skin streaked with violet. The size of the fruit varies from that of an apricot to a large papaya. Because its shape often resembles that of a melon, the pepino is known as *melon pear, melon shrub, pepino melon,* and *tree melon.* Other names include *mellowfruit* and *mellow pear.* Their flavor is rather bland eaten out of hand, so the fruit is mostly used in fruit salads or as a vegetable. In any case, and unfortunately, the pretty skin must be peeled.

Pepita—Spanish for "seed," referring almost exclusively to the pumpkin seed. A favorite Mexican snack food, pepitas can be eaten raw or roasted and salted. Ground to a coarse powder, pepitas are used to add texture and flavor to sauces.

Peppercorn—Pepper is the world's most important spice, and, like **salt,** it was once used as a form of currency. It is native to India's Malabar Coast, where it grows wild. The smooth, woody vines of the pepper plant (*Piper nigrum*) can climb 20 feet (6 m) up tree trunks. Pepper is cultivated in many tropical regions, including Malaysia and parts of South America. One of the first spices to be merchandised, pepper was the most important commercial article traded between East India and Europe for hundreds of years. Pepper most likely changed the course of history, given that the demands for it were so great that they inspired the many efforts by the Portuguese to find a way to reach India by sailing around Africa (they finally succeeded in 1498). The goals was to obtain the spice without having to pay the exorbitant prices for overland transport through the so-called Ottoman Barrier on the way to Europe. Peppercorns are obtained from long grapelike clusters of about two dozen small berries each. These gradually turn from green to pink and, finally, to red as they ripen.

Black peppercorn—Black peppercorns are picked when the berries are almost but not quite ripe. They are then dried until the skin shrivels and turns dark brown to black. Black pepper has the strongest flavor and is usually what is meant when one simply speaks of pepper in the kitchen. Because it loses its flavor rather quickly once it is ground, black pepper should always be freshly ground as needed.

Green peppercorn—Harvested before they are ripe; green peppercorns have a milder and fruitier flavor than black peppercorns, but they are still peppery. Green peppercorns are difficult to obtain fresh and are usually sold packed in brine; freeze-dried are also available.

Pink peppercorn—Pink peppercorns are not actually a form of pepper; they are the dried berries of a type of rose plant (*Baies*). They are grown in Madagascar and imported through France, making them very expensive and something of a gourmet novelty.

Red peppercorn—Red peppercorns are vine-ripened and usually not sold as red peppercorns other than for decorative use. They are generally processed to make white pepper.

White peppercorn—White peppercorns are obtained by allowing the berries to ripen fully and turn red. The red skins are removed before the peppercorns are dried, which produces smooth, slightly smaller off-white peppercorns, with a mild flavor.

Peppermint—See **Mint.**

Peppermint schnapps—A peppermint-flavored liqueur. See **Schnapps.**

Pernod—An anise-flavored liqueur made in France. The name came from the family Pernod, which originally produced **absinthe.** The Pernod factory was used to produce absinthe until it was closed for use as a field hospital during World War I. After the war, absinthe was banned, and the business closed. In 1917, the original factory was sold to Nestlé. The Pernod family then began making the current version of the liqueur under their own name.

Persian melon—A **muskmelon** variety, the Persian melon is similar to the **cantaloupe,** but is larger. It has a finely netted yellowish-green rind and fragrant salmon-colored flesh. Season is mid-July to late October.

Persian apple—The ancient name for "peach." See **Peach.**

Persian walnut—An edible nut from a tree (genus *Juglans*) native to southeastern Europe. More commonly known today as the *English walnut,* these nuts have a sweet flavor that makes them desirable for enjoying alone or for using in candies, ice cream, and baked goods. The name *Persian walnut* stems from the fact that the nuts were originally used for trade in the Persian Empire. Many cultures in ancient times believed that the consumption of these walnuts would help to make couples fertile.

Persimmon—Early settlers in the Midwest and southeastern portions of what was to become the United States found they were in for quite a culinary experience upon encountering native persimmons for the first time. For as delicious, creamy, and sweet as the perfectly ripe fruit can be (they should be so ripe, in fact, that they are just about falling apart), taking a bite of an unripe persimmon will surely make you pucker and reach desperately for a glass of water to wash away the unpleasant sour and bitter taste and the peculiar dry feeling it leaves in your mouth. But through trial and error, and from seeing that the Native Americans used persimmons extensively (to make puddings and breads, among other foods), the settlers were soon supplementing their diet with the bountiful wild persimmon. Wild persimmons have a different flavor and are much smaller than the Asian variety, usually known as *Japanese persimmons,* which are found in the markets in the fall.

Two varieties of persimmon are found in the United States: Hachiya and Fuyu. Both are orange in color and available during the winter months. Persimmons are used in many traditional holiday recipes, the most popular being persimmon pudding. Hachiya, the persimmon most commonly found in stores, has a slightly oblong shape and is pointed at the bottom. The Hachiya persimmon is very high in tannin and can be eaten only when fully ripe (the fruit should be almost jellylike throughout). Instead of trying to peel the skin off the Hachiya, it is easier to cut the fruit in half and use a spoon to scoop out the flesh; discard the stem, seeds, and skin. The smaller Fuyu persimmon is shaped like a small beefsteak tomato. It has very little tannin and can therefore be eaten before it is completely ripe and soft. This persimmon is easy to peel with a vegetable peeler. A too-firm Fuyu persimmon can be ripened at room temperature in a few days. An unripe Hachiya is a different story, however, requiring as long as a few weeks to lose its astringent, mouth-puckering tannin. To speed up the process, the fruit can be placed in a paper bag with an apple; this produces ethylene gas, which makes the fruit ripen. Another alternative is to expose the fruit to a small amount of alcohol (place the persimmons in a plastic container, place a few drops of alcohol on each of the leaflike sepals, and close the container tightly), which also encourages the fruit to produce more ethylene gas.

The unpleasant dry taste associated with an unripe Hachiya will disappear when the fruit is cooked, so it is acceptable to use unripe fruit in a recipe such as persimmon pudding if necessary. Unripe Hachiyas must first be frozen solid, then thawed, to make them soft enough to puree. (After freezing and thawing, the fruit will be as soft as when perfectly ripe, but it will still have the dry astringent taste before cooking.) To make persimmon puree with either variety when it is very ripe and soft to the point of falling apart, just remove the stems, puree with the skin on, then force the puree through a fine strainer to remove the small pieces of skin. Persimmon puree freezes well. Add 1 tablespoon (15 ml) lemon juice for every 2 cups (480 ml) puree. Because persimmons are not available year round, it is a good idea to prepare some persimmon pulp to store in the freezer. Pack in freezer containers, cover, and freeze. (If you are using the puree in a recipe that calls for lemon or lime juice, leave it out, as it is already in the persimmon pulp.)

Phyllo dough—Phyllo dough (also called *filo* or *fillo,* which, appropriately enough, is Greek for "leaf"), has been used in the Mediterranean since ancient times for both savory and sweet recipes. Phyllo dough originated in Greece and is very similar to strudel dough, but it is much thinner and even more delicate. Phyllo dough is not a dough at all, in the traditional sense. It is prepared and purchased as paper-thin, leafy sheets made from flour and water. These sheets dry out very quickly once exposed to air, so it is very important to cover them with a damp cloth to keep them somewhat moist as you are working.

When brushed with melted butter and stacked together, the multiple leaves proved a layer structure very similar to puff pastry, but phyllo sheets are virtually fat-free, making the dough suitable for the preparation of low-fat or low cholesterol desserts. Naturally, you must take into consideration the butter that is brushed onto the leaves of dough, but this can be cut down if desired, and vegetable oil can be used if cholesterol is a concern. One option is to spray the melted butter—clarified butter must be used for this purpose—or oil onto the dough instead of using a brush. Some people spray the sheets with a pan coating instead of butter to reduce the fat.

Phyllo sheets vary in size from 12 x 14 inches (30 x 35 cm) to 16 x 18 inches (40 x 45 cm), depending on the brand. Each 1-pound (455-g) package typically contains about 24 sheets. Frozen phyllo dough must be allowed to defrost slowly in the refrigerator overnight before it is used. If it is thawed too quickly, the thin sheets tend to break. See **Kadaif.**

Physalis—This rather unusual-looking fruit, known also as *cape gooseberry,* is surrounded by a loose, beige, ballooning, parchmentlike husk called a *calyx.* The seedy yellow berry inside is about the size of a cherry and has a sweet orange flavor, but with more acidity. There are two main varieties of physalis: the edible one discussed here (*physalis pruinosa*), also known as *ground cherry* and *strawberry-tomato,* and the ornamental variety (*physalis franchetii*), usually known as *Chinese lanterns* because of the bright orange-red lantern-shaped calyx that forms around the ripened berries. The ornamental physalis are often used in late-fall floral arrangements.

Cape gooseberries are great for pies and preserves (with their papery husk removed), but their price is usually prohibitive for this type of application. A better way to utilize these eye-catching berries is in decorating, with the attractive husk left on. Begin by snipping the husk open from the tip with a small pair of pointed scissors. Loosely spread the petals of the husk open like a flower about to bloom, or spread them all the way back to the stem. Dip the fruit into chocolate or fondant flavored with **Cointreau** or **kirsch** and use as a candy or unusual mignardises (another name for an assortment of petits fours). Cape gooseberries will keep fresh for many weeks, stored in the refrigerator. If stored too long, however, the berry begins to dry up, and eventually just the empty husk is left.

Pignolia—The Italian name for **pine nut.**

Pimento—The tree that **allspice** comes from. This is not the same as **pimiento.**

Pimiento—Any of several large sweet red peppers. Pimientos are often found canned or bottled and are well known as the stuffing in green martini olives. The pimiento pepper is dried to produce **paprika.** *Pimiento* is also Spanish for "pepper."

Pine nut—Known as *pignolia* in Italy and *piñon* in Spanish, pine nuts are the edible seed of the stone pine. Their rich flavor is increased by light toasting. Pine nuts are not used as much in baking as they are in other types of cooking. They are popular in savory dishes from Italy and the Mediterranean and are also used in Chinese preparations. Because pine nuts are quite high in oil and turn rancid very quickly, they should always be stored in the refrigerator or freezer. Pine nuts are good in cookies, and their petite, uniform size makes them attractive as a decoration on cakes as well.

Pineapple guava—Another name for the **feijoa.**

Pineapple—This handsome tropical fruit got its English name from its vague resemblance to a pine cone. In most European countries, pineapples are known as *ananas,* derived from the Paraguayan word *nana,* meaning "excellent fruit." Pineapples are native to Central and South America. They did not reach Hawaii until 1790, when they were brought there by Captain James Cook. Hawaii is now the biggest producer of pineapples in the world.

Pineapple is one of the most widely eaten tropical fruits, probably second only to the **banana,** and, like the banana, it is available all year. Pineapples generally grow one to a plant, growing out of the crown (the leafy part that is attached to the top when the fruits are marketed). The fruit develops from a bunch of small, lavender-colored flowers on a short stalk that grows from the center of the leaves (the stalk becomes the core that runs vertically inside the mature pineapple). When developed, a pineapple is actually composed of many small hexagonal fruits merged together, which can be seen from the pattern on the tough skin. The skin is not edible. Being able to distinguish a sweet, ripe pineapple for harvest can be difficult, as color is not a reliable indicator, but the job is quite important because the starch in the fruit will no longer convert to sugar once it is removed from the plant. Some sources say a good test is to see if one of the smaller leaves will pull easily from the crown, but a sweet fragrance is probably the best indicator, just as it is in choosing a harvested pineapple in the market. Pineapples, like many other tropical fruits, contain an enzyme (bromelain) that is beneficial to digestion but not to protein-based **gelatin,** where it inhibits or prevents coagulation. The way around this is to use **agar-agar** or **cornstarch** for thickening, or simply to bring the fruit to a quick boil (which will destroy the enzyme) before using gelatin.

To remove the rind from a pineapple, begin by rinsing the fruit and twisting off the crown, which may be discarded or used for decorating. Cut off the base of the pineapple to make it level. Stand the fruit on end and remove the rind by cutting from the top to the bottom, following the curve of the fruit. Once all of the peel has been removed, you will see that the eyes follow a spiral pattern. Remove them by cutting spiral grooves that wind around the pineapple from the top to the bottom. This extra effort not only adds to the appearance but it saves a great deal of flesh that would be lost if you cut away enough of the entire surface to remove all of the eyes. Cut the pineapple crosswise into slices of the desired thickness and remove the core from each slice, using a cookie cutter. Alternatively, cut the pineapple lengthwise into quarters after removing the eyes and slice the core off each quarter with a knife. A large part of the core can be eaten and makes a nice chewy treat. Pineapples become softer and juicier (but not sweeter) if left at room temperature for a few days. Ripe pineapples should not be stored in the refrigerator longer than four to five days, as the cold can damage the fruit.

Pink peppercorn—See Peppercorn.

Piping chocolate—Melted chocolate that has been thickened with the addition of a small amount of simple syrup or liqueur. The thicker consistency helps keep the chocolate in precise lines as it is piped out with a piping bag for making figurines, writing a message on a cake, decorating the tops of pastries, or streaking.

Piping gel—Piping gel is purchased ready to use. It is made from sugar, corn syrup solids, and vegetable gum, such as gum arabic. It is very sweet and not very pleasant to eat by itself (as you can probably imagine from the ingredient list), but it is one of the most practical decorating materials in today's pastry shop. Although it looks artificial next to a chocolate decoration (for special petits fours or showpieces, you should use piping chocolate), because piping gel is so inexpensive and easy to work with it makes a useful tool for everyday decorating or to add just a small touch of color. For example, you can use it to fill in some of the small loops in a design piped in chocolate. Piping gel is available in a clear, colorless form as well as in various colors. Because many of the colors are a bit bright, I recommend buying the clear gel and coloring it yourself to pastel shades, or, if you are using quite a bit, add clear gel to the colored product to soften the shade.

Pisco—A grape **brandy** from Peru. The mixture is aged in a wax-lined container so that the beverage does not absorb any color or flavor from the wooden cask.

Pistachio—Pistachios are popular for their distinctive green color and are usually used as a garnish on petits fours or candies—and, of course, to make pistachio ice cream. Pistachios need hot, dry summers and cold winters. The largest share of the nuts are grown in the Middle East, although the United States, which has been producing a commercial crop only since 1976, is now the second-largest producer in the world. The nuts have two shells: a red outer shell, which is removed before packing, and a thin inner shell, beneath which a thin skin surrounds the nut. The practice of dyeing the inner shell red is said to have been started by a New York street vendor, and the red color became so expected and associated with the nuts that at one time most pistachios were sold this way. Dyeing the shells is no longer so popular today. When pistachios are purchased in the shell (the thin inner shell), the shells should be partially opened. If they are completely closed, it means the nuts were harvested before they were fully mature. To show off the green color to its fullest, remove the skins by blanching the nuts in boiling water, then pinching them between your fingers or rubbing them in a towel. Adding a pinch of salt to the water helps heighten the color.

Plantain—See **Banana.**

Plum—Plums are a **drupe** or **stone fruit,** meaning that they contain a pit. They are related to other common stone fruits, including **apricots, peaches, nectarines,** and **cherries.** The relation to cherries is especially close, the primary difference being that plums are larger. Plums, like other drupe fruits, are found in both **clingstone** and **freestone** varieties. Plums are far more varied than some of their relatives, however; in fact, there are so many varieties (possibly up to 2000) that sometimes even experts have trouble distinguishing among them.

There are three main categories of plums: Japanese, European, and American, and there are several cultivars (cultivated varieties) within each group. Developing and cultivating new varieties of plum is done through hybridization (creating a new plant by breeding two different plants) and cross-pollination (transferring pollen from one plant to another).

Japanese plums are actually native to China, but they were first cultivated in Japan. Luther Burbank, an American horticulturist, introduced the Japanese plum to California in 1885 and is the person most responsible for the fruit's tremendous success. In his lifetime, Burbank introduced and developed over 250 varieties of fruit, including 113 kinds of plums. The most famous was the **Santa Rosa** plum, named for the city of Santa Rosa, California, where he lived. (Burbank also developed vegetables, flowers, and grasses, and was the inventor of the Burbank potato—a strain of which, the Russett Burbank, is the most commonly grown variety of potato in the United States—and the Shasta daisy, which he created from crossings involving four species of chrysanthemum.) The Japanese plum varieties are generally medium to large in size and very juicy. They are found in many shades of red, yellow, and purple, but very few have the bluish skin associated with European plums. Japanese plums are usually eaten fresh. Cultivated varieties include Abundance, Burbank, Santa Rosa, and **Shiro.**

European plums originated in southwestern Asia, but they have been grown in Europe for more than 2000 years. European plums were first brought to the eastern part of the United States in the 1600s. In the 1700s, Spanish missionaries brought the fruit to California. Cultivated varieties of European plum include Bradshaw, Grand Duke, Jefferson, Lombard, Reineclaude, and Stanley. Some European plums with a high sugar content are used primarily for drying to make prunes. Most European plums are blue or purple; they are usually smaller in size than Japanese plums, round or oval in shape, and have a firmer texture.

American plums developed from wild plum trees of North America. These plums are nowhere near as widely cultivated as the European and Japanese varieties and play a small role commercially. Cultivars of American plums include Cheney, De Soto, Golden Beauty, and Monitor.

Approximately 6 million metric tons of plums are produced in the world annually. The top plum-producing countries are China, Germany, and the United States. The United States produces approximately 9 million metric tons of plums each year, with California contributing far more than all the other states combined. Plums are available from spring to early fall.

Plums are used in ice cream, cobblers, sauces, tarts, and fruit salads. They are also used to make brandy and jam. As with many other fruits, the ripening process for immature plums can be quickened by placing the fruit in a loosely closed paper bag and leaving it at room temperature for a day or two. Store ripe plums in the refrigerator for up to ten days.

Following is an alphabetical list of the best-known European and Japanese plum varieties.

Beauty—Developed in California. This heart-shaped fruit is one of the first on the market. It has bright red skin with amber flesh and is good for eating out of hand and for cooking. Variety: Japanese; early season.

Casselman—Originated in California. A large cone-shaped fruit with red to bluish skin speckled with yellow. The flesh is firm and yellow. Variety: Japanese; late season.

Damson—Originated in Syria. *Damson* is a shorted version of this plum's original name. When the Crusaders brought it to Europe, they called it *Damascene,* meaning "the plum from Damascus." This small bluish to purple fruit has golden flesh that is juicy, with a slightly acidic flavor. This is a traditional antique plum for jams and preserves. Variety: European; midseason.

Greengage—Originally bred in Italy, this plum came to France in the sixteenth century. Claude, wife of François I, gave her name to the fruit, and it is still known in France as the *reineclaude.* The English name comes from Sir William Gage, who is credited with bringing the plum to England. The fruit is round and medium in size. It has greenish-yellow skin with a touch of red. The flesh is green. This plum is a good choice for eating fresh and for cooking. Variety: European; early season.

Kelsey—One of the few Japanese plum varieties that was actually developed in Japan. The fruit is large and heart-shaped, with green to yellow skin and firm and sweet flesh. Variety: Japanese; midseason.

Laroda—Originated in California. This large cone-shaped to round fruit has a deep reddish-purple skin with light amber, firm, and aromatic flesh. It is best used fresh rather than cooked. Variety: Japanese; midseason.

Mirabelle—Originated in Syria. This very small and round cherry-sized fruit has yellow skin with a red flesh. The flesh is firm, juicy, and sweet and can be seen through the thin, fine skin. It is one of the classic European plums used for cooking and for making the famous German **eau-de-vie** Mirabellan Geist. Variety European: midseason.

Prune—Prune-plums are too sweet to have a real plum taste when baked but are great to eat fresh; they are used for garnish and, of course, they are dried to make prunes. Their flesh has a very attractive slight green tint before being fully ripe (at this point, they are also less sweet, and it is a great time to use them fresh for garnish or salad).

> *French prune*—Originated in France. This small fruit has red to dark purple skin and yellow, very sweet flesh. It is probably the most common of the prune-plum varieties. Variety: European prune; late season.

> *Italian prune*—Originating in Germany (oddly enough), this large, long fruit has a dark blue skin with a very attractive matte finish that is lost once the fruit is handled. Variety: European prune; late season.

Queen Ann—Originated in California. This large, heart shaped fruit with a dark purple skin and amber, sweet flesh is a good choice for using fresh or for cooking. Variety: Japanese; midseason.

Santa Rosa—The most famous of the plums created by Luther Burbank, who lived and worked in Santa Rosa, California. This large fruit has crimson skin and yellow flesh that is purple near the skin. It is firm and has a juicy, slightly tart flavor. Variety: Japanese; early season, although there is also a late Santa Rosa variety.

Shiro—Developed in California. This beautiful, medium-sized fruit has both yellow skin and flesh. It is one of the best yellow plums to use fresh or for cooking. Variety: Japanese; early season.

Wickson—Originated in California. This fruit is large and heart-shaped, with a green to yellow skin. The yellow flesh has a great flavor and is better suited to eating fresh than for cooking. Variety: Japanese; midseason.

Poaching syrup—A sugar syrup used to poach fruit. The basic ratio of water to sugar in a poaching syrup is 2:1 by weight. This can be modified depending on the desired sweetness of the finished product. Flavorings such as vanilla, citrus, saffron, cloves, cinnamon, wine, or liqueur may be added.

Poha—Hawaiian for "cape gooseberry." See **Physalis.**

Poire—French for "pear."

Poire Williams—A pear-flavored **eau-de-vie** from Switzerland. This clear, colorless liqueur is used to add flavor to numerous pastries and confections. Some brands of Poire Williams actually have a whole pear inside the bottle. To achieve this, the bottle must be placed over the budding pear; the pear then grows inside the bottle.

Poivre—French for "pepper." *Poivre blanc* translates to "white pepper" and *poivre noir* means "black pepper."

Pomegranate—Pomegranate trees are often planted for ornamental use, and it is easy to see why. In spring, their small, vibrant red carnationlike flowers bloom for two to three weeks; then, in the early fall, the fruit-bearing varieties produce large, bright red round fruit that are 3 to 5 inches (7.5 to 12.5 cm) in diameter and very showy. Pomegranates are grown widely, both in home gardens and commercially, in subtropical areas throughout Asia, the Mediterranean, and in southern California, where they are in season from September to mid-December. This is much too short a time to be able to take advantage of this decorative, juicy fruit. Luckily, whole pomegranates can be kept in the refrigerator for up to three months, and the seeds can be frozen indefinitely. The most common commercial variety of pomegranate is called *Wonderful.*

The name *pomegranate* comes from the French, *pome grenate,* which is further traced back to the Latin, *pomum granatum,* meaning "apple with many seeds." Each round fruit contains hundreds of small edible seeds about the size and shape of a kernel of corn. These are made up of a smaller seed that is surrounded by translucent reddish pulp. The seeds are enclosed in pockets that are divided by a pale, bitter-tasting membrane. Removing the seeds from these pockets without crushing the pulp is quite labor intensive.

Pomegranate seeds are eaten fresh sprinkled over salads, used as a bright and unusual garnish, and added to many sweet dishes. For a quick, easy, and refreshing juice drink, roll a chilled pomegranate between your palms and the table to rupture the seeds inside, cut a small slit, insert a straw, and suck out the juice. **Grenadine,** a very sweet red syrup used in cocktails, is made from pomegranates; it gets its name from the French word *grenate,* discussed above. Interestingly enough, this is also the origin of the word *grenade.* These small explosives not only have a similar round shape and a protruding fuse on top (which looks something like the stem end of the fruit) but they too are filled with tiny bursting pellets. Whole pomegranates can be refrigerated for two to three months; the seeds and/or juice can be frozen for longer storage. Ten small to medium pomegranates, or 2 pounds 8 ounces (1 kg 135 g) whole pomegranates, will yield approximately 2 quarts (1 L 920 ml) seeds.

Pomelo; Pommelo; Pummelo—This **citrus** fruit, which grows abundantly in Malaysia, is an ancestor of the **grapefruit.** It has a similar soft, thick rind, yellowish to pink in color. The flesh also varies from a light yellow to pink. The size of this largest of the citrus fruits can range from approximately that of a honeydew melon to as heavy as 25 pounds (11 kg 375 g). This fruit is also called *shaddock* in reference to the English sea captain who brought the seed to the West Indies. It is also known as *Chinese grapefruit* and *jeruk bali;* the French name for pomelo is *chadec.* The fruit should be heavy, free of blemishes, and slightly fragrant.

Pomme—French for "apple."

Poppy seed—Poppy seeds are the dried, ripened seeds from the pod of the opium poppy, a tall annual with beautiful lilac or white flowers that is native to the Middle East. From the Middle East, poppies spread to China some ten centuries ago, and from there through the famous spice route to Europe, where today, poppy seeds are immensely popular. This is especially true in Germany and Scandinavia, where they are used to flavor and decorate a multitude of baked goods. The crunchy texture and nutty flavor of the tiny seeds (1 pound/445 g contains almost a million seeds) is also popular in many savory dishes in the Western kitchen, but even more so in Middle Eastern and Indian cuisine.

The opium poppy is grown throughout the temperate regions of the world, illegally in most cases, to obtain the drug opium, which was used medicinally for thousands of years (opium did not become an abused narcotic until the nineteenth century, when opium dens began to appear in China). Opium poppies are also cultivated legally to produce several important drugs, including Demerol, morphine, and codeine. The opiates are obtained from the thick juice that oozes out when an incision is made in the unripe seed capsule. Although poppy seeds come from the same pod, they are not narcotic. The majority of poppy seeds are bluish black, but pale yellow (also called *white*) and brown varieties are also available. Poppy seeds should be stored in a cool, dark place, as they can become rancid.

Port—Originating in northern Portugal, port or Porto, as it is also called, is a sweet **fortified wine.** The name *Porto* is derived from the original shipping area in Portugal, a city called Oporto. The highest quality ports are vintage ports, meaning they are made with grapes from a single vintage, or year. Tawny ports are blended with grapes from different vintages. Vintage and tawny ports may be aged anywhere from 5 to 50 years. Ruby ports are the least expensive; they are produced from different vintages as with the tawny variety, but are aged for only a short time.

Pot cheese—See Cheese.

Potash—Potash is a potassium compound that produces carbon dioxide when it comes in contact with an acid. It is an uncommon leavening agent, used mostly in cookies with spices and honey.

Potato flour; potato starch—Potato flour, also known as *potato starch,* is made from cooked, dried, ground potatoes. It is most frequently used as a thickening agent but can also be used in baking to reduce the **gluten** strength of bread flour, for example (in much the same way as **cornstarch** is), as it does not contain any gluten. Potato flour, or potato starch, can be substituted for cornstarch and actually produces a better result. It gelatinizes at 176°F (81°C), leaves no unpleasant taste, and, when used as a thickener, does not break down, causing the product in which it is used to become watery.

Powdered sugar—See Sugar.

Praline paste—A thick paste made by grinding praline (caramelized nuts). It is used as a flavoring agent.

Preserve—Technically, a preserve can be any food product that has been treated to extend its shelf life—the period during which it is fresh and edible. **Jams, jellies, marmalades,** and **conserves** all fall under this heading if they are canned, which is usually the case, and the term *preserves* is sometimes used generically to refer to any and all of these fruit spreads. While there are many similarities—they are all made from boiled fruit and sugar—and some products or recipes are really hybrids of two or more categories, the basic distinctions are as follows. Definitions for each are listed below to allow for comparison and contrast. Figure A-3 shows the natural pectin content in fruit typically used for preserves.

Conserve—This seems to be the category with the least consensus when it comes to a clear definition. Like *preserve,* the word *conserve* literally means "to protect" or "to maintain" and, like *preserve,* it is also used generically to refer to **jam** or any cooked fruit mixture. Cookbooks and reference books give conflicting definitions, but all seem to agree that when the term *conserve* is used to describe a cooked fruit mixture, the mixture is not as firmly set as jam, and it contains larger pieces of fruit than the average jam, having a lumpy or chunky consistency. Some sources say that a conserve is a jam made with two or more kinds of fruit, and other sources describe it as containing a mixture of fruits and nuts.

Jam—Jam is fruit that is boiled with sugar until it is has reached the jell stage. The fruit may jell on its own from the naturally occurring pectin in combination with the sugar cooked to approximately 220°F (104°C), or addi-

Uses and Pectin Content of Fruit for Conserves, Jams, Jellies, Marmalade, and Preserves

Fruit	Natural Pectin Content	Commonly Used For
Apples, tart	Strong	Jam and jelly
Apples, sweet	Medium	Jam and jelly
Apricots	Medium	Marmalade and preserves
Blackberries	Medium	Jam and jelly
Black Currants	Strong	Jam, jelly, and marmalade
Blueberries	Strong	Jam, jelly, and marmalade
Cherries	Unsubstantial	Jam, jelly, and whole preserves
Elderberries	Strong	Jam and jelly
Figs	Unsubstantial	Conserves and preserves
Gooseberries	Strong	Conserves, jam, and preserves
Grapes	Unsubstantial	Jelly and whole preserves
Lemons	Strong	Jelly and whole preserves
Limes	Strong	Jelly and marmalade
Loganberries	Medium	Jelly and marmalade
Mulberries	Medium	Jelly and preserves
Nectarines	Unsubstantial	Jelly and jam
Peaches	Unsubstantial	Jelly, jam, and whole preserves
Pineapple	Unsubstantial	Jam, marmalade, and whole preserves
Plums	Strong to Medium	Jam, jelly, and marmalade
Quinces	Strong	Jam, jelly, and marmalade
Raspberries	Medium	Jam, jelly, and marmalade
Red Currants	Strong	Jam, jelly, and marmalade
Rhubarb	Unsubstantial	Jam and jelly
Seville Oranges	Strong	Marmalade
Strawberries	Unsubstantial	Jam and marmalade

FIGURE A-3 Uses and pectin content of fruits used for preserves

tional commercial pectin may be added to fruits that are naturally low in pectin; sometimes a low-pectin fruit is combined with one that is higher in natural pectin. The pectin reacts with acid (the natural acid found in the fruit plus additional acid that is added to low-pectin fruits) and the sugar (again, both what is in the fruit naturally and the added sugar) to create the jell or thickening process. The high sugar content (most jams are 50 to 65 percent sugar) also plays a large role in preventing spoilage. Jam is made with whole or chopped fruit and is never strained. Small pieces of fruit should be suspended evenly throughout. Jam is used in the pastry kitchen to fill cakes, cookies, and pastries.

Jelly—Jelly is made the same way as **jam,** by cooking fruit and sugar, sometimes with pectin, the difference being that jellies are made from only the strained fruit juice. They should be completely clear and bright in color, and they never contain chunks or pieces of fruit. **Apples** are often used as the base to create jellies that are flavored

with herbs, such as **mint** or **rosemary.** Some jellies, such as red currant, are used in the pastry kitchen to make sauces and glazes.

Marmalade—Marmalade is made in the same way as **jam,** but it always contains fruit peel. Today, the term almost always refers to a mixture made from one or more **citrus** fruits. Marmalades are clearer than jams and closer in consistency to jellies, but unlike jellies, they always contain pieces of rind or peel. The best-known marmalade is made from **Seville oranges,** but other citrus fruits—**lemon, lime, grapefruit**—are used as well.

Prickly pear—This unusual-looking fruit is oval in shape and has a thick greenish-purple to greenish-yellow skin that is full of thorns. The thorns are always removed, usually by singeing them off, before the fruit is shipped to market. The watermelonlike flesh inside is a vibrant purple-red and has small black seeds throughout, which are not eaten. Prickly pears are very popular in many parts of the world, especially in the Mediterranean region. From Mexico all the way to South America, they are known as *cactus pears,* which makes sense, as they grow on several varieties of cactus. The fruit has become better known and more available commercially in some areas only recently. The low-calorie pulp is eaten raw, made into desserts, and stewed; it makes a beautiful sorbet. Allow prickly pears to ripen at room temperature for a few days; they should be soft but not mushy. Store ripe fruit in the refrigerator.

Prune—See Plum.

Puerto Rican cherry—See Acerola.

Pumpernickel flour—See Rye flour.

Pumpkin—Pumpkins are one of several squashes that were eaten as a staple food by the Native Americans at the time the colonists landed in America. The European settlers quickly learned to appreciate the numerous favorable attributes of this large, round, yellow to orange vegetable. One important consideration was that due to their protective shells, pumpkins kept fresh for several months in the cool climate of the Northeast. The colonists made beer and soup from the pumpkin flesh and toasted the seeds to enjoy as a snack. Even the shell made a convenient bowl—if only temporarily. Pumpkin pies were originally served at the settler's second Thanksgiving feast and continue to be the traditional Thanksgiving dessert hundreds of years later. Pies are by far the most widely known and widely consumed sweet made from pumpkin; however, pumpkins are also used in quick breads and cookies and can be used to flavor ice cream, cheesecake, mousse, and the like for holiday menus.

Pumpkins are a member of the winter squash family, which includes the well-known varieties acorn, butternut, and Hubbard. The hundreds of winter squashes vary in size from the small acorn, weighing about 1 pound (455 g) to the giant pumpkin varieties, which can reach over 200 pounds (910 kg). In contrast to the soft-skinned, young summer squashes, winter squashes are harvested only after they have reached maturity and their shells and seeds have grown hard. It is due to the protective property of their hard shells that winter squashes can be stored for many months after harvest. Unlike the other winter squash varieties, which are almost always prepared for consumption, over 90 percent of the pumpkins grown commercially in the United States are sold as jack-o'-lantern pumpkins for Halloween. Most of these are the Connecticut Field variety, which are quite large and bright orange, making them well suited for carving, but they tend to be too stringy to eat. The much smaller sugar pumpkin is the one used almost exclusively for pies and other types of cooking. There are also miniature pumpkin varieties, about the size of an apple, that can be eaten whole after cooking; the best known of these are Jack Be Little and Munchkin. The flat, green pumpkin seeds are popular toasted as a snack or added to breads or cookies. With the exception of spaghetti squash, most winter squash varieties may be substituted for pumpkin for use in cooking, including the preparation of pumpkin pies. Store pumpkins in a cool, dry place, but do not refrigerate more than one week or they will deteriorate more rapidly.

Q

Quark—See **Cheese.**

Queso—Spanish for "cheese."

Quince—Quinces have been growing in the Mediterranean for more than 4000 years; the trees are said to have originated in Greece. The Romans used the flowers and the "golden apple" itself for many purposes, including scenting honey and perfume and as a symbol of love. The long-lived trees are popular in gardens throughout Europe, both for their fruit and for their decorative quality. Besides the flower show of pink and white in the spring, the leaves have a bright autumn hue when the weather begins to get cold, and the twisted branches provide a spectacular silhouette in winter. Quinces have never gained this kind of recognition in America, possibly because this yellow-skinned fruit, which looks something like a cross between an apple and a pear, has a rather astringent, bitter, acidic flavor and numerous hard seeds throughout. Because quinces are high in pectin, they are prized for making jellies and preserves, but they are also excellent in pies, tarts, and custards. The most popular commercial variety is the pineapple quince, but Champion is also a good choice. In commercial nurseries, quince trees are used as dwarfing stock for grafting pears. The fruit will keep for months, stored in the refrigerator and wrapped in plastic. Quinces have a strong, sweet fragrance and help keep the air fresh when placed, unwrapped, in a closet or cupboard. You can add a few slices of raw quince to a cookie jar as you would apple, to soften hard cookies.

R

Raisin—When raisins are called for in cooking and baking, it is generally the dark variety—a dried seedless grape, for the most part **Thompson Seedless**—that is being referred to. However, golden raisins, also called *sultanas* and **dried cur-** rants, are also used frequently in food preparations. The word *raisin* comes from the Latin word *rasemus,* which refers to "a cluster of berries." Most types of raisins originated in the Middle Eastern region of the Meditteranean. Today, the San Joaquin Valley in California produces nearly 50 percent of the world's raisin crop.

The transformation from fully ripened grape to dried raisin takes place naturally. After harvest, the fresh grape clusters are placed on trays that are then set between rows of grapevines. Here, the sun dries the grapes for approximately 2 weeks, during which time the clusters are turned regularly. Once dried, the raisins are removed from the stems and placed in large wooden bins, also known as *sweat boxes.* The bins are left in the sun to heat the dried fruit, which causes the moisture content of the raisins to equalize within the closed boxes; the drier raisins draw moisture away from the jucier ones. After this process the raisins are ready to be shipped to a packaging facility.

The addition of raisins to any baked good will retard staling because the little fruits, which are high in sugar, retain moisture. For many recipes, raisins should be soaked in water or spirits to plump them prior to use. This not only adds flavor but makes the raisins easier to slice through, enabling you to make a clean cut through a cake or pastry. If the raisins are to be frozen (in an ice cream, for example), soaking them in alcohol will prevent them from freezing rock-hard. Raisins can be stored at room temperature for many months without becoming too dry or having the sugar crystallize on the surface, provided they are placed in an airtight container. If refrigerated, they will keep for over a year.

Rambutan—A fruit related to the **lychee**, originally from Malaysia and prevalent throughout southeast Asia. Quite unusual-looking, rambutans are covered with a thick, leathery red shell that is, in turn, covered by spiked strands that resemble hair. The name *rambutan* comes from the Malaysian word *rambut,* which means "hair." Like the lychee fruit, the edible pulp of the rambutan is a translucent white and surrounds a large stone or pit. The flavor is similar as well, although rambutans are not quite as sweet.

Rapeseed oil—See **Canola oil.**

Raspberry—Raspberries originated in Asia and Europe and grow wild in many parts of the United States. They are very popular for decorating and garnishing cakes, pastries, and tarts because of their uniform petite size and bright red color (although there are also black raspberries, which are not very common, as well as a hybrid golden raspberry). Raspberry sauce is used extensively in the pastry kitchen, and raspberries are also used in fruit salads, ice creams, and sorbets. Fresh raspberries, previously available only during the summer, are now obtainable year round due to imports from New Zealand and Chile. The prices, of course, are higher when the fruit is imported. Frozen raspberries may be used to make sauces and sorbets. Refrigerate raspberries in a single layer to extend their shelf life and prevent them from becoming moldy prematurely.

Ratafia—A type of liqueur made from any one of several **stone fruits**. The name is often used for an Italian cherry liqueur that is made using whole cherries, including the pits, for flavoring. *Ratafia* also refers to a liqueur made with an infusion of bitter almonds and apricot or peach kernels (the seeds inside the fruit pits). The name for the liqueur is said to have derived from the Latin saying *Res rata fiat,* which was used when a treaty or settlement was ratified (formally confirmed and agreed to by both sides). Because these occasions usually called for a liqueur toast, the phrase was shortened and came to refer to the liqueur itself. Another explanation says that the word *ratafia* comes from the French West Indian creole dialect where it was also used in toasting, but with **rum,** the ratification of an agreement, again derived from the Latin phrase *rata fiat,* meaning "let the deal be done."

Ratafia essence made from **bitter almonds;** it is used as a flavoring agent. The term *ratafia* is additionally used as a generic name for any type of liqueur, and, lastly, is also the name of a type of macaroon cookie.

Raw milk—See **Milk.**

Raw sugar—See **Sugar.**

Red banana—See **Banana.**

Red currant—Red currants originated in Europe and are very popular in Scandinavia and Germany. They grow in bunches like grapes on large bushes and are harvested in the early fall. Red currants are not as tart as **black currants** and can therefore be eaten raw. Fresh red currants are very pretty and look great as a garnish and in fruit salads. Unfortunately, they are not widely available fresh in the United States. It is actually illegal to grow red currants in many parts of the country, as the plants can harbor a parasite that kills the white pine tree. Red currants are used to make red currant jelly, which is used in Cumberland sauce, to fill cakes and pastries, and to make a glaze for fruit tarts. Berries are among the most perishable of all fruits, and red currants are no exception. Place them in a single layer on a pan or tray, cover, and store in the refrigerator; they will keep for up to two days.

Red date—See **Jujube.**

Red Delicious apple—See **Apple.**

Rennet; Rennin—Rennet is an extract obtained from the lining of a young (unweaned) animal's stomach, usually that of a calf, which contains the enzyme rennin. This enzyme causes milk to curdle; it is used commercially to make cheese. The most common use for rennet other than in the manufacturing of cheese is in making junket, a type of pudding or eggless custard that was very popular in the United States in the early to mid-1900s. Junket dates back as early as the sixteenth century, when the word was used in a generic way to describe any sweet dish. Rennet is sometimes sold in grocery stores labeled as *junket tablets.* The dessert form of junket is made by combining warm milk with sugar and rennet and letting it stand until the rennet coagulates (thickens) the mixture to a jellied consistency. Early recipes were said to use the warm milk straight from the cow after milking. In several British cookbooks and in *The Joy of Cooking,* the recipe for junket is called *Rennet Pudding.* The word *junket* comes from an old French word, *jonquette,* referring to both a reed basket and a type of cheese that was formed and drained in such a basket. The second meaning led to today's use of the word to describe the coagulated dessert.

Forms of vegetable rennet are used to make kosher and vegetarian cheeses. Vegetable rennet comes from plant enzymes that have a similar coagulating effect on the proteins found in milk; one example is the cardoon, a relative of the artichoke. Other sources include **agar-agar** and some varieties of mushroom.

Rhubarb—In botanical terms, rhubarb is a vegetable, but we tend to use it more as a fruit in cakes, pies, and dessert sauces. It is, in fact, actually referred to as *pie plant.* Rhubarb is great in desserts that are topped with meringue because its tart flavor contrasts beautifully with the sweetness of the meringue. Rhubarb leaves are potentially poisonous (in excessive amounts) because their oxalic acid content is high enough that it can interfere with calcium and iron absorption; only the stalks of the plant are used. Rhubarb stalks look something like overgrown red celery. Rhubarb is very tart and is almost always sweetened. It is quite juicy and will actually dissolve if overcooked. Rhubarb is used mostly in pies (sometimes combined with other fruits; strawberry and rhubarb is a common pair) and in cobblers.

Ribier grape—See **Grape.**

Rice—Rice is the most extensively utilized grain in the world; it serves as the principal food for more than half of the world's population and, since ancient times, has been the most commonly used food grain. Although it is not one of the most nutritious grains, consisting of over 80 percent carbohydrate, it still provides enough vitamins and minerals to mean the difference between survival and starvation in many Third World countries. A member of the grass family, *Gramineae,* rice can be grown successfully under climatic conditions ranging from tropical to temperate. When cultivated properly, rice produces higher yields than any other grain with the exception of corn; although the total area planted in rice is much smaller than that devoted to wheat, the rice crop feeds a far greater proportion of the world's population.

As it grows, the rice strand looks very much like wheat; its seed head, however, is completely different. The most common cultivation method is to flood the fields (rice paddies) that are planted with the appropriately named and high-yielding aquatic rice. Rice plants require a steady supply of water; therefore, in addition to flooding the fields through irrigation, rice is often planted during periods of excessive rainfall. Rice fields are kept flooded until just before harvest. Rice plants start from a single shoot, then develop many tillers and pointed, flat leaves. The plants grow from 2 to 6 feet (60 cm to 1 m 80 cm) tall and are usually self-pollinating. The kernel consists of bran layers, germ, and endosperm. More than 7000 botanically different varieties of rice have been identified.

Rice is known to have been consumed almost 7000 years ago in the Far East. It later spread to the Middle East and southern Europe, where it became a popular food during the Renaissance. Today, the Italian arborio rice (the rice used to make risotto) is cultivated exclusively in the Po and Ticino valleys of northern Italy. The United States is the leading exporter of rice but produces only about 2 percent of the total world crop. Most of this is grown in the southern states and, to a lesser extent, in California. In most of the world, rice is harvested by hand, using knives or sickles. The stalks are cut, tied in bundles, and left in the sun to dry. Various means are used to thresh the grain, ranging from the weight of animals or tractors to threshing machines.

The most popular varieties of rice in the United States are white long-grain and white medium-grain, but all rice is pale brown to begin with. Before it reaches the consumer, it goes through a complex process, the first part being the threshing and milling, which strip the kernel of its husk, bran, and germ. Unfortunately, most of the nutritional fiber is lost as well, but this process does serve to increase the shelf life because (just as in removing the germ from wheat in making flour) it prevents the rice from becoming rancid.

There are three basic types of rice available for the commercial market: long-, medium-, and short-grain. In the long-grain category, regular milled white rice is the most common variety. Its kernel is about 4 times as long as it is wide. When cooked, this rice has a fluffy appearance, and the grains separate easily. It is usually enriched with iron, calcium, and vitamins to make up for the loss incurred in making the rice white; therefore, from a nutritive standpoint, the rice should not be parboiled or washed before it is cooked. Brown long-grain rice is simply the entire unpolished grain with only the outer husk removed. Basmati rice is a highly aromatic long-grain variety imported from the foothills of the Himalayas in India. Jasmine rice, from Thailand, is another fragrant long-grain rice.

Medium-grain rice, besides being shorter and plumper, is also more moist and tender when cooked, although it is not as starchy as short-grain rice. Medium-grain rice has a tendency to become sticky as it cools. Short-grain rice appears almost round and opal white. Although it does not contain gluten, it is known as *glutinous rice* in Japan and China. It is extremely starchy, which makes it easier to handle with chopsticks and, therefore, it is preferred in Asia. Converted or parboiled rice, generally known by the brand name Uncle Ben's, has been treated with pressurized steam to flush the minerals and vitamins out of the bran and concentrate them in the kernel. The rice is then dried before it is milled. This treatment also gelatinizes the starch, yielding a rice that is very fluffy after cooking, with distinctly separate grains, which makes this a popular rice for use by culinary institutions using steam tables.

Minute, instant, or quick rice is rice that has been completely or partially cooked before being dehydrated and packaged for the consumer. So-called wild rice comes from a completely different plant and bears very little relation to regular rice. Raw rice grains should be stored in airtight containers in a cool, dry place. Stored this way, white rice will keep indefinitely.

Rice flour—Rice flour is prepared from broken rice grains and is used as a thickening agent. It does not contain any gluten and is therefore not used for baking bread. Glutinous rice flour, also known as *sweet rice flour,* is made from short-grain rice with a high starch content. It is used in Asian cooking as a thickening agent and to make the dough for some types of dumpling wrapper.

Rice paper—An edible translucent paper made either from a mixture of **rice flour** and water or from the pith of the rice paper plant and water. It is usually flavorless and packaged in rectangular, square, or round sheets. Rice paper should be kept dry or it will dissolve. It has many uses in the kitchen: baking sheet liner, separator for the stacked tiers of wedding cakes, to wrap foods that are to be deep-fried.

Ricotta cheese—See Cheese.

Riesling—A grape used to make white wine. Native to Germany, Riesling wines are delicate but characterized by a fruity, spicy taste and floral bouquet. The style ranges from dry to sweet. Reislings are made in Germany and California.

Rock salt—See Salt.

Rock sugar—See Sugar.

Rolled oat—See Oat.

Rome Beauty apple—See Apple.

Rose hip—The ripe reddish-orange fruit of a rose (most often the dog rose or wild rose). While tart when raw, rose hips are often cooked and used to make syrups, jelly, tea, and wine. Rose hips are high in vitamin C and are sometimes dried and ground into a powder.

Rosewater—An extract distilled from water steeped with rose petals. The petals impart their oil to the water, giving the extract a perfumed flavor and fragrance. Rosewater is often used to scent pastries, desserts, and confections, and is used in Middle Eastern cuisine.

Rosemary—The Latin name for rosemary, *Rosmarinus officinalis,* means "dew of the sea." This versatile aromatic herb is native to the Mediterranean area, where it grows wild, thriving in the calcium-rich soil and dry climate. Its hardiness makes it a frequent addition to many home gardens, where it will grow for many years with little attention. Rosemary is related to **lavender,** but unlike lavender, it is evergreen, producing thin, dark green needlelike leaves all year and pale blue flowers in the summer. Whole sprigs are sometimes used as a garnish, and the highly aromatic rosemary leaves impart a delicious yet very strong flavor when this herb is used in cooking. Rosemary can easily overpower and dominate a dish and is most often used to flavor strong game dishes, poultry, and stews, and it is very often used with lamb. It is quite popular as a flavoring in bread in Italy and in some other countries as well. Rosemary is said to soothe

the nerves, help digestion, and make the heart stronger. Herbal preparations containing rosemary are also made to stimulate hair growth. Keep dried rosemary in an airtight container away from light. Fresh sprigs of rosemary will keep for several days, stored in a plastic bag in the refrigerator.

Royal Ann cherry—See Cherry.

Rum—A spirit distilled from fermented sugarcane juice and/or **molasses**. The islands of the Caribbean Sea produce most of the world's rum supply. The lighter amber or golden-colored rums are produced, for the most part, in Puerto Rico and the Virgin Islands, while the heavier and darker varieties come primarily from Jamaica, Cuba, and Barbados. Sugarcane grown along the banks of the Demerara River in Guyana is used to make the strongest and darkest rum. Rum must be at least 60 proof by law (30 percent alcohol), but most brands are 80 proof, with the extreme being 151-proof rum, which is very convenient for flambé work, as it will ignite without being heated. Rum is used extensively in the pastry shop.

The rum trade played an important role in shaping world events during Colonial times through the 1600s and 1700s as it developed in conjunction with the growth of sugar plantations in the West Indies. Starting in the 1600s, distilleries operating in New York and New England produced rum made from molasses that was imported from the West Indies. Rum became part of a trade cycle in which the profits from American rum were used to buy slaves in Africa, and the slaves were then traded in the West Indies for more molasses, which became New England rum. During this era, rum was the prevailing alcohol of the poor in the Colonies, and it was not uncommon for some to enjoy it with breakfast, lunch, and dinner. By the year 1775, Americans were reportedly consuming an astonishing 4 gallons (15 L 360 ml) per person per year. This exorbitant consumption declined sharply with the decrease in sugar and molasses importation brought about by the passage of the Molasses Act and the Sugar Act, which virtually wiped out rum production in the Colonies. The heavy duties levied on imported molasses were an important factor in creating the unrest that ultimately led to the Revolutionary War.

Rye flour—Rye flour is one of the best-tasting flours for making bread. It is divided into light, medium, and dark categories, as well as pumpernickel flour. As with wheat flour, these grades are determined by the part of the grain that the flour is milled from. The medium grade is the one most commonly used. Pumpernickel flour is made in much the same way as whole wheat flour; it is milled from the entire rye grain, including the bran. Rye flour is almost always mixed with some wheat flour to give it added gluten strength and rising power in a bread recipe because the protein in rye flour forms a very weak gluten structure. Therefore, unless you want a very dense and flat bread, the amount of rye flour in any rye bread dough should not exceed 30 to 35 percent of the total flour weight. This lack of gluten-producing help from the rye flour gives extra responsibility to the wheat flour, so it is even more important to pay close attention to the dough's temperature and consistency. A small amount of vinegar added to rye bread dough helps bring out the rye flavor.

S

Sabra liqueur—A liqueur made in Israel flavored with chocolate and orange.

Safflower oil—Oil pressed from the seeds of a safflower, also called *saffron thistle* and *bastard saffron*. This flavorless, colorless, cholesterol-free oil is good for deep-frying because it has a high smoke point. It is also popular for use in salad dressing because it does not solidify when it is cold. Safflower oil can be used interchangeably with other vegetable oils, including sunflower, soy bean, olive, corn, and canola.

Saffron—Saffron is by far the most expensive of all spices. The saffron threads used for flavoring are the bright orange three-pronged stigmata, as well as a portion of the style that comes with it, of a small variety of purple crocus. The facts that they can only be harvested by hand and that it takes around 75,000 flowers to produce 1 pound (455 g) of saffron, explains the high price. Several varieties of this spice grow wild in the Mediterranean area of Europe; however, true cultivated saffron can best be distinguished by its large, loosely hanging stigmata. Saffron has been used since ancient times; it was introduced to northern Europe by the Romans. Later, in the eighth century, the Muslims brought it west to Spain, which today is the largest producer. Saffron is indispensable for making Spanish paella, French bouillabaisse, and Milanese risotto, and it is used to a great extent in Middle Eastern cuisine as well as in a number of European baked specialties, such as the traditional saffron buns and breads. Saffron should always be purchased as threads, as the ground form can be easily adulterated with other yellow to orange foods, such as safflower and marigold petals or ground turmeric. Ground saffron also loses its aroma more quickly. Containers of saffron sold to the foodservice industry are generally 1 ounce (30 g) and are marked with an expiration date. The saffron is still viable well past that date in most cases, provided it has been stored in an airtight container, protected from light.

Sage—A dull greyish-green perennial herb, commonly used in sauces, it is also used in stuffings and commonly paired with onions. Sage is part of the mint family. The word is derived from the Latin word *salvus,* meaning "safe"; it was once commonly used for medicinal purposes. The French word for sage is *sauge.* Sage is available in fresh leaf form, dried and ground, or crumbled.

Sago—Sago is very similar to **tapioca** and is used in much the same way—as a thickener for puddings and fillings. Sago is obtained from the pith of the sago palm, whereas tapioca is extracted from the root of the tropical cassava plant. Sago is sold as small dried granules of starch.

Salt—The salt measurements given in the recipes in this text are based on common **table salt**. If you are using another type of salt, such as **kosher salt,** you may substitute the same amount by weight without adjustment. For volume measures, however, such as measuring by the teaspoon or tablespoon, the amount must be modified. Kosher salt has larger crystals that do not pack together as tightly, so the same volume of kosher salt weighs less than an equal volume of table salt. Four tablespoons of table salt weighs 60 grams, whereas 4 tablespoons of kosher salt weigh 40 grams, making kosher salt one-third lighter. You therefore need to substitute 1 tablespoon plus 1 teaspoon kosher salt for every 1 tablespoon table salt. Kosher salt is great in bread baking and especially for use in sprinkling over flatbreads, pretzels, and bagels. There is really no sense, however, in using some of the more exotic salt varieties discussed below in baking. It simply does not make sense, from an economic standpoint.

Salt has been valuable for centuries around the world. It is an essential ingredient that gives life and character to the food we consume. At times throughout history, it has even been used as currency (the word *salary* is derived from the Latin word for "salt"). While the food we consume would lack much of its flavor without salt, humans are grateful for the salt additive for another reason: The body requires salt to regulate fluid balance.

Common salt, sodium chloride, occurs naturally in pure, solid form as the mineral halite and in deposits of rock or mineral salts. Almost 80 percent of the total dissolved solids in ocean water are salt, and even greater amounts are found in inland saltwater lakes and seas. Salt remains the most commonly used mineral in the world. When it is mixed with crushed ice, it acts as a cooling agent and, conversely, when it is spread on icy streets, it melts the ice. Today, potassium iodine is often added to table salt (then called *iodized salt*) in order to supplement iodine intake in diets. Although most people are familiar with white table salt, salt in its original form can be white, pink, brown, gray, or orange in color. Depending on the type of salt and its geographical origin, the flavor can vary dramatically.

Salt plays a crucial role in almost all cooking and baking as a flavor enchancer. While we may not always be able to identify its presence easily, we definitely know when it is absent. The abilities of salt to draw out the water and enhance the flavors of food are unparalleled. The benefit of salt in cooking is that it can intensify and set colors, as when cooking green vegetables or blanching shelled pistachio nuts. In the case of bread, it is crucial to retard yeast development, strengthen the gluten structure, aid in browning, and, as always, add flavor. Salt is also used to actually "cook" food, by a means known as *curing*. This method can be traced all the way back to ancient Egypt. Salt is used to draw the moisture out of foods, making them less susceptible to bacterial growth and thereby retarding or preventing spoilage. Before refrigeration, this technique was an essential method of food storage. Today, many cured foods are still popular, such as prosciutto, gravlax, beef jerky, and all types of pickles.

Salt is produced commercially by three methods: rock-salt mining; solar evaporation; and solution mining. Rock-salt mining occurs in salt domes or underground salt strata. After the rock salt is brought to the surface, it is crushed into the desired commercial sizes. Solar salt is made by using the heat of the sun to evaporate water from the ocean or from inland salt lakes; it is coarser than other varieties. In solution mining, water is forced into an underground salt deposit through a pipe. The brine is pumped to the surface through another pipe, purified by the addition of chemicals, and condensed in a series of vacuum evaporators. The world's production of salt averaged 1700 million metric tons annually in the 1980s and early 1990s. The United States is the world's largest salt producer. Countless varieties of salt are available today, with the most common including the following:

Curing salt—Used for numerous charcuterie items, especially those that are cold smoked. It is a blend of 94 percent salt and 6 percent sodium nitrite and commonly colored pink to differentiate it from other salt varieties. An acceptable replacement for curing salt is saltpeter, which is simply sodium nitrite.

Iodized salt—Plain salt with iodine added. Iodine was initially introduced as an additive to salt in the American Midwest to help curb and eliminate goiter, a thyroid affliction caused by iodine deficiency. It was found that iodine easily bonds with sodium molecules and could easily and delicately be administered to the general public in minimal amounts. With this addition, however, the salt clouds clear water. The iodine also leaves a slight aftertaste. The salt taste of iodine salt is detected on the front and the sides of the tongue.

Korean yellow salt—A light gray salt with a medium coarse grain. It remains very moist to the touch—in fact, almost wet. The salty flavor is only medium and leaves a slightly unpleasant aftertaste.

Kosher salt—This pure refined mined rock salt is coarse-grained and without additives. It does not contain magnesium carbonate and thus will not cloud items it is added to. It is excellent for use in cooking and as a table seasoning. It is commonly used in commercial kitchens because of its flaked rather than granulated form, which allows more even distribution over food. Kosher salt has a crisp, clean taste and dissolves readily. It is chemically identical to table salt but it contains no additives. As its name implies, kosher salt is the only allowable salt for people who observe strict Jewish dietary guidelines. It is also known as *coarse salt* and *pickling salt*.

Light salt; Salt replacement—Salt substitutes that are either partially or entirely formed from potassium chloride.

Marsh salt—A medium coarse-grain salt that remains moist to the touch. It has a fresh flavor and lacks a distinctive salty flavor. This is an excellent choice for vegetables and salads because it accentuates the fresh flavors. Because of the natural residue or algae that is left in the salt, marsh salt has a light green, grayish look.

Popcorn salt—A very fine-grain salt meant to cling to the oils or the butter used in making popcorn. Popcorn salt usually contains tricalcium phosphate, an anticaking additive used because of the fine grade of the salt grains. This addition gives the popcorn salt a slightly bitter, off flavor. As a result, popcorn salt is not recommended for cooking, simply for popcorn making. The flavor of popcorn salt is detected on the top center of the tongue and, in comparison to other varieties, has a mild salt flavor.

Rock salt—Unrefined salt that is used in preparations and occasionally, presentation, but not directly added to food. One of the most popular uses of rock salt is in ice cream making, in which it is added to the ice to retain the cold temperature.

Sea salt—Achieved by the time-honored traditional method of gathering the ocean water in small ponds and allowing the water to evaporate, leaving behind the mineral-enriched salt crystals. While the crystals are dried, they are not completely dried. If you wish to achieve a drier salt, spread the sea salt on a sheet pan and allow it to air-dry. Sea salt is available both refined and unrefined, in whole crystals or ground. When unrefined, it is often referred to as *sel gris,* French for "gray salt." Depending on the refinement and the point of origin of the sea salt, the colors range from opaque to gold to brown. An increasingly popular form of salt, sea salt is now harvested from waters all over the world. The most highly prized and esteemed salt is the Fleur de Sel de Camargue, which is hand panned from the surface of the ocean in the Camargue region in the south of France. Another highly regarded sea salt is the Fleur de Sel, which is obtained from the top ocean surface off the Brittany coast of France. Other popular varieties include those from Hawaii (with a pinkish tint), the Mediterranean Sea (in both fine and coarse grades), Utah's Great Salt Lake, Maldon sea salt from Essex, England, and Atlantic (with a green hue).

Table salt—The most common, all-purpose fine-grain salt. It is achieved by grinding refined mined rock salt. Table salt is often fortified with iodine and treated with iodine, magnesium carbonate, or calcium silicate (and even, sometimes, small amounts of sugar) to prevent clumping. When it contains magnesium carbonate, salt will cloud the food item if it is dissolved in water. It is not an ideal choice for pickling or consommés despite dissolving quickly. The salty taste of table salt is detected on the front of the tongue. The recipes in this book call for table salt unless otherwise specified.

Sambuca—A colorless, anise-flavored liqueur from Italy. *Sambucas nigra* is the Italian name for the elder shrub, an attractive bush with honeysuckle-shaped leaves, clusters of tiny scented white flowers, and violet-black berries—elderberries. The name *sambuca* was given to the liqueur because elder was originally used as a flavoring agent. The traditional way of serving sambuca in Rome is flambéed, with one or two dark-roasted coffee beans floating on top (referred to in Italian as *con la mosca,* "with the fly"). This is said to bring good luck. Sambuca has a sweet licorice taste and is very strong for a liqueur, 42 percent alcohol or 84 proof.

Sanding sugar—See **Sugar**.

Sassafras—Usually refers to the leaves of the sassafras tree, native to North America. The leaves are dried and used to make tea and filé powder, while the root bark is used as a flavoring agent for root beer.

Satsuma—See **Mandarin orange**.

Saturated fat—See **Fat**.

Sauternes—A French village south of Bordeaux whose five neighboring towns all produce the white dessert wine of the same name. Sauternes grapes are part of a late harvest that allows them the maximum amount of time to develop a high sugar content. The resulting wine is often characterized as having an intense buttery, fruity, golden taste.

Schnapps—A broad term covering a variety of spirits distilled from grain in northern Europe; they are usually colorless and are made with a range of flavorings; peppermint is probably the best known. *Schnapps* is a derivative of the Dutch verb *snappen,* meaning "to gulp."

Sea salt—See **Salt**.

Seckel pear—See **Pear**.

Seed—(1) The fertilized bud of a plant, and its covering. A seed contains a miniature plant that is capable of independent development into a plant similar to the one that produced it. (2) To seed something is to remove its seeds—to seed a grapefruit, for example. (3) Seeding is a process used to temper chocolate.

Self-rising flour—Flour that is premixed with **salt** and **baking powder**.

Sémillon—A white wine grape grown in Chile, France, Australia, and California; the primary grape used in **Sauternes** wine and a blending grape in wine production. White wines with low acidity are made from this grape.

Semisweet chocolate—See **Chocolate**.

Semolina—In the United States, any product labeled *semolina* must, by law, be made from **durum wheat;** it may also contain a maximum of 3 percent other flour. Durum wheat is a **hard wheat flour;** the wheat grains are quite solid and resistant to breaking, and the flour has a higher protein content than any other wheat variety. To make semolina the wheat is chipped or sliced, it is not ground, making the finished product similar in texture to **cornmeal.** Semolina is available for purchase in different textures from very coarse to almost as fine as regular wheat flour. The finer varieties are not as prevalent and are sometimes labeled *semolina flour.* The word *semolina* is also used to refer to other grains—rice, corn, or buckwheat—that are processed in the same way, however it is illegal in the United Stated to label these as semolina.

Semolina is most often used to make pasta and is sometimes called *pasta flour.* Pasta made from semolina, unlike those made with other types of flour, does not become sticky and starchy during cooking as the starch in durum wheat is contained within a hard protein shell.

Sesame seed—Sesame seeds, also known as *benne seeds,* come from a tall plant that originated in Africa. The plants are still widely grown there and throughout the Far East. The small, flat, oval seeds have a nutty flavor and come in black and brown varieties as well as the more common ivory variation. African slaves brought sesame seeds to the United States, and the seeds became especially popular in the South. Today, sesame seeds and sesame seed oil are used throughout the world and are very much associated with Asian cuisines. In the Middle East, white sesame seeds are made into a paste called *tahini* and a confection called *halvah.* Sesame seeds are mostly used in or on top of cakes, cookies, breads, and rolls in Europe. Sesame seeds contain about 50 percent oil, so they can turn rancid very quickly. They can be kept in an airtight container in a cool, dark place for up to two months but should be refrigerated or frozen for longer storage.

Seville orange—See **Orange.**

Sherry—A **fortified wine** originally produced in the Spanish city of Jerez, for which sherry is named. Sherry is produced using a blend of grapes and is classified in categories including fino (a pale and dry variety that is matured with yeast), amontillado (a medium sherry; darker and older than fino), and oloroso (either dry or sweet; dark in color and aged as with fino, but without yeast; sometimes labeled *cream* or *golden*.)

Shortening—See **Vegetable shortening.**

Sieve—"To sieve" means to sift or to use a sieve to separate a substance into finer and coarser particles. *Sieve* is also the name of a utensil; see Appendix B.

Silver leaf—Very thin edible sheets made from pure silver. Silver leaf comes in packages, with each sheet separated by a sheet of tissue or parchment paper. Silver leaf has no taste. See **Gold leaf** for instructions on applying and using silver leaf. Both must be handled very carefully. Store in a cool, dry location.

Silver powder—Edible silver powder is made from pure silver that is ground into dust. Silver powder has no flavor. It is used to decorate desserts, pastries, and confections. It is very lightweight and, just like **gold powder,** has a tendency to fly with the slightest breeze. Store in an airtight container in a cool, dry place.

Slurry—A mixture of **flour** or **cornstarch** with enough water to make a thin paste. The slurry is added to a liquid and heated to act as a thickener.

Soft flour; Soft wheat—Soft wheat grows in warm climates. Soft wheat flours are ideal for quick breads such as scones, muffins, and soda bread. The terms *hard flour* and *soft flour* refer to the flour's protein content; hard flours have more protein and therefore produce more gluten, soft flours have less protein and produce less gluten. See **Flour** and **Gluten.**

Sorghum—A sweet, rich, tangy syrup produced from the stems of the sorghum (sorgo) plant. Also called *sorghum molasses* and *sorghum syrup.* The juice is boiled down to produce a sweet, strong syrup that has a thinner consistency than **molasses.** Often confused with light molasses and wild honey, sorghum can be used as a substitute for molasses in baked goods and desserts.

Sour cream—See **Cream.**

Soy flour—Soy flour is made from the soybean rather than from a cereal grain. It is not commonly used in the pastry shop, but it is very nutritious and can be mixed with other flours in cakes for consumers with restricted diets.

Soy milk—A popular alternative for people who are allergic to cow's milk or follow a vegan diet. Soy milk is often used in infant formulas. It is made by pressing ground, cooked soybeans. It can be purchased plain or flavored.

Spanish melon—A member of the muskmelon family, this is a large oval or egg-shaped melon with a decoratively ribbed green rind. The flesh is pale green, with a juicy, sweet flavor similar to the **Crenshaw.** Season is July through November.

Spearmint—See **Mint.**

Spice—Any of a large group of aromatic plants whose bark, roots, seeds, buds, or berries are used as a flavoring. Spices are usually available dried, either whole or ground. They are differentiated from **herbs,** which are the edible leaf portion of a plant only. See listings for individual spices and herbs.

Star fruit—See **Carambola.**

Stone fruit—Any fruit with a thin skin, soft flesh, and a hard pit or stone in the center. Examples are peaches, plums, apricots, nectarines, and cherries; these are also classified as **drupe fruit.**

Stone-ground flour—Flour produced by grinding the grain between two slowly moving stones; the grain is crushed without generating excess heat or separating the germ. See **Flour.**

Strawberry—Strawberries are one of the most popular fruits. The vines grow wild in many areas, but the berry grown commercially today is the result of much experimentation and cross-breeding. Strawberries are delicious served plain or with just a simple topping of cream and sugar. They are used in tarts, fruit salads, cakes, mousses, and strawberry shortcake. Fresh strawberries are available all year, although their flavor is at its peak in the summer. Frozen strawberries can be used in sauces and ice creams. Store or freeze strawberries as instructed for **blackberries.**

Sucrose—The most common form of sugar, produced from sugarcane or sugar beets. Sucrose contains both **fructose** and **glucose,** making it a complex or double sugar known as a *disaccharide.* Sucrose is pure carbohydrate. See **Sugar.**

Sugar—Sugar is a truly amazing commodity and is one that is indispensable to the baker. The term *sugar* can be applied to more than 100 naturally occurring organic compounds that, by definition, form white or clear crystals when purified, are sweet in flavor, and are water soluble. All forms of sugar are part of the carbohydrate food group. Sugar, as we know it in the kitchen—**granulated, powdered, confectioners', or brown**—is **sucrose** and is the product of an extensive refining process that begins with sugarcane or sugar beets. Although these two plants are totally different in their botanical composition and are often cultivated on opposite sides of the globe, you cannot identify by taste alone whether the sugar you use to sweeten your coffee came from sugarcane or sugar beets; their chemical composition and their flavor are identical after refining. While sugar in different forms has been commercially important since ancient times—in fact, it affected the world as much as any other single commodity during a period that lasted several hundred years—only in the last 150 years have its chemistry and biochemical distinctions been studied. Nobel prizes for studies in sugar chemistry were awarded in 1902, 1937, and 1970.

Sugar consumption, as it relates to nutrition, has been the topic of much debate, and there are those who feel that eating sugar can produce negative side effects running the gamut from depression to hyperactivity, especially in children. While it is accepted that consuming sugar can lead to dental problems and raised insulin levels, no other physical or emotional detriments have been substantiated by research. The Food and Drug Administration (FDA) has stated that "there is no conclusive evidence on sugars that demonstrates a hazard to the general public when sugars are consumed at the levels that are current and are now practiced." In other words, as with everything else, moderation is the key. Of course, there are individuals with specific health concerns that require them to monitor their intake of sugar or abstain from it altogether.

All sugars are converted to **glucose** in the body in the same way, whether the source is refined sugar or naturally occurring sugar—in fruit, for example. Sugar, like all carbohydrates, provides 4 calories per gram, the same as protein, and is obviously fat-free. With today's focus on reducing fat consumption, sugar can play an important role in providing flavor and appeal without fat. However, while carbohydrates are the body's primary source of energy, sugar calories are basically empty calories, containing only trace amounts of vitamins and minerals.

The word *sugar* is most commonly used to refer to granulated table sugar. However, many other types of sugar, with different chemical structures, are used in the pastry shop. The specifics and distinctions between various sugar products, such as granulated sugar, brown sugar, confectioners' sugar, maple sugar, invert sugar, turbinado sugar, and so on, are discussed below.

Sugars are divided into two basic groups: double sugars, called *disaccharides,* which consist of two simple sugars linked together—these include sucrose (beet and cane sugar), maltose (known as *malt sugar*), and lactose (the sugar found in milk); and single sugars, or simple sugars, which are called *monosaccharides.* Simple sugars include glucose (also called *dextrose*) and fructose (also called *levulose*). In sugarcane and sugar beets, glucose and fructose, both monosaccharides, or simple sugars, combine chemically to form the disaccharide, or double sugar, sucrose. Glucose is used as a sweetener in wine and drug production and is added to boiled sugar for many of the techniques used in decorative sugar work. Glucose is also the form of sugar into which digested carbohydrates are metabolized in the body. Fructose is used as a food preservative as well as a sweetener. These types of sugar vary a great deal in their sweetness. Lactose is less sweet than sucrose, and fructose is sweeter than both lactose and sucrose.

The production of sugar has a long and interesting history and has been responsible for changing the course of many nations, and indeed world history, through sugar's commercial exchange and consumption. Though sugar has brought pleasure and riches to many, thousands of people were sacrificed during the evolution of its production, as nearly all of the early mass sugar trade was supported by slavery.

Europeans first tasted sugar at the time of the Crusades. Until then, **honey** had been the only sweetener known in that part of the world, but sugar (although not in the form we know it) had already existed in the tropical parts of the world for many hundreds of years. Presumably, sugarcane and, therefore, its early refinement originated in New Guinea, then spread through the islands of the South Pacific to southeast Asia and India. From there, it went to China and the ancient Arab world, all long before reaching Europe, and much longer still before it came to the Americas. Over time, the taste of red honey, as sugar was once called, improved with better refining techniques, although the process used all the way from the Middle Ages up to the 1800s (when machinery changed the manufacture) was fundamentally the same—extracting the sugarcane juice, boiling the juice, clarifying (this was done using egg white or animal blood), and crystallizing. The methods used to accomplish these tasks have simply become more modern over time. The partially purified sugar that was originally introduced to Europe from the East had a bitter aftertaste and was very expensive compared with honey, which had a better flavor. Sugar, therefore, was definitely a luxury item at first, more common as a status symbol and as a medicinal agent than as a sweetener. It was some time before the craft of the confectioner, or sugarbaker (as it was appropriately called at one time), came into being.

In the 1400s, European explorers, including Columbus, brought sugarcane cuttings to the Caribbean and South America, and the plants flourished in the moist, warm climate. When the explorers returned with news of these desirable and unprotected lands, perfect for growing sugarcane, the possibilities for production and the end to dependence on Eastern sugar sources were immediately evident. By the middle of the 1500s and early 1600s, sugar had become a major trade commodity and a form of currency. Europe was importing several tons annually, and a person with a large chunk of sugar (a sugarloaf) in his kitchen was considered very well-to-do. Sugar production in South America and the Caribbean islands had become the largest, most lucrative industry in the world at the start of the 1600s, supported, for the most part, by slave trade. Many of the Caribbean islands, as well as the coasts of western Africa, Brazil, and Mexico, had been colonized first by Portugal and Spain, then by the English, Dutch, and French. Hundreds of sugar factories were in production, and native island populations were virtually exterminated through forced labor on the plantations. Soon, Africans were abducted and brought as slaves to the islands, resulting in a trade network between the islands, the North American colonies, and Europe, and paving the way for the future slave era in the southern United States.

Sugar trade continued to affect the world for the next century: Numerous land exchanges and political decisions were based on its production, and the wealth it brought shifted the balance of power. When France lost the Sugar Islands in the West Indies to England in the late 1700s, its economic standing was severely affected. This was one of the reasons France supported the American colonists in the Revolutionary War. The huge fortunes made by English plantation owners contributed, in large part, to the financing of the Industrial Revolution. Abolitionists, meanwhile, especially in Britain, were fighting for a ban on sugar products because of the slave labor used in its production; sugar manufacturers in East India, who made their product without slaves, as well as the retailers offering East Indian sugar, made sure that that point was known. Eventually, as the European countries gradually outlawed slavery in the West Indian colonies, sugarcane production in the areas declined. This era of sugar virtually controlling the world lasted approximately 200 years, during which millions of human beings lost their lives to its cause. In *A History of Food* by Maguelonne Toussaint-Samat (1987), Werner Sombart is quoted on this subject: "We grew rich because whole races died for us. For us, continents were depopulated." The same source quotes Bernardin de Saint-Pierre expressing a similar sentiment: "I do not know whether coffee and sugar are necessary to the happiness of Europe, but I know very well that those two plants have brought misfortune on both parts of the world."

Because the majority of the sugarcane was grown far away, required transportation, and its availability and price in Europe continued to be dependent on world conditions, Europeans attempted to cultivate sugarcane at home, although without success. A breakthrough occurred in the mid-1700s when a German pharmacist, Andreas Marggraf, discovered that the sucrose in beets was identical in chemical composition to the sucrose in sugarcane. In 1787, he perfected a way to boil the sap from a particular variety of beet that rendered a coarse grain with the look and taste of cane sugar. With this, the sugar beet industry was born. The trend then spread to France, Russia, Sweden, and Austria-Hungary. The first sugar beet factory was opened in Germany in 1803. Today, the sugar beet industry is responsible for more than

one-third of the world's sugar production.

Sugarcane production in North America began during the 1600s; the first sugar refinery was built in New York City in 1689. Sugar production did not become a major industry in the United States, however, until the 1830s. In 1868, Claus Spreckels of San Francisco invented a new, faster method for refining sugar and opened a major refinery in California. Finally, by the late 1800s, sugar had become the affordable, much-used product we know today. Since 1979, the world has made more sugar than can be sold. Consumption in the United States now stands at about 9 million pounds (4 million kg) per year.

The ratio of sugar used in the food industry to that used by consumers has changed drastically in the last several decades. In the early to middle part of the twentieth century, when most food was prepared at home, consumer use accounted for about two-thirds of total sugar consumption, and food manufacture was responsible for about one-third. Now, with much less of the food production requiring large amounts of sugar being done at home—baking, canning fruit, curing meat, and preparing jams and preserves—those numbers have almost exactly reversed; the food industry currently uses a bit more than two-thirds of total production in the manufacture of processed products.

Sugarcane and sugar beets are the primary sources for commercial sugar production, which consists of harvesting these sucrose-rich plants and converting the sucrose into crystallized sugar. Other sources that yield sucrose are maple sap, sorghum cane, some date and palm trees, watermelons, and grapes, but their cultivation for the purpose of sugar production is negligible in comparison. The world's largest producers of cane sugar are Brazil, India, Cuba, Mexico, the United States, and Pakistan. Producers of beet sugar include the Ukraine, Russia, Germany, France, and the United States.

All green plants manufacture glucose in their leaves through a process called *photosynthesis,* by which plants transform the sun's energy into food. In the leaves, the glucose is converted to sucrose before being transported to the roots and stems. Most plants convert the sucrose a step further, making it into starch for storage. Sugarcane and sugar beets manufacture sucrose in great quantities but, unlike most other plants, they store it unchanged. Figure A-4 illustrates the process for refining sugarcane and sugar beets.

Refining and processing sugarcane

Sugarcane is a tropical grass that is cultivated in warm, moist climates. The canes grow from a little less than a year to close to three years before harvest, each cane growing to between 10 and 20 feet (3 and 6 m) high. Raw cane sugar contains 12 to 14 percent sucrose. Sugarcane is produced in the United States in Florida, Louisiana, Hawaii, and Texas. The production process occurs in two locations: at sugar mills and sugar refineries. The plants are harvested by cutting the cane off close to the ground with machines or, in

Sugar Production and Refinement

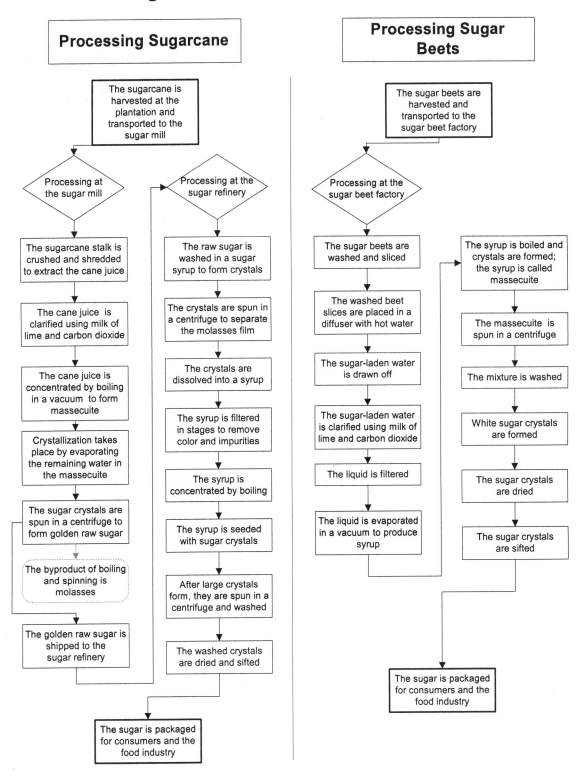

FIGURE A-4 The production and refinement processes for sugarcane and sugar beets

some areas, by hand, using a machete. The leaves are stripped off the stalks, which are transported to a sugar mill. The refining process begins by crushing and shredding the stalks. The resulting material is passed through and pressed under a series of heavy rollers to extract the cane juice. The waste product left from this process is called *bagasse* and is most often used as fuel to run the mills; it is also processed into paper. The cane juice is clarified by adding milk of lime (made from limestone) and carbon dioxide. As the carbon dioxide creates bubbles, the lime forms calcium carbonate. These chalklike crystals bubble through the mixture, attracting the nonsugar matter such as wax, fats, and gums away from the juice. The calcium carbonate and other materials then settle to the bottom, leaving the clarified sugarcane juice. The juice is next concentrated by boiling in several stages under a vacuum, which allows the syrup to boil at a lower temperature to protect it from caramelizing. At this stage, it becomes a thick, brown syrup called *massecuite*. The syrup is crystallized by evaporating the last amount of water and is then passed into a centrifuge with a perforated basket at the center. After spinning and drying, the result is golden raw sugar; this is not the same as the product labeled raw sugar, which is sold commercially.

The raw sugar is approximately 96 to 98 percent sucrose. The crystals are light brown because they are covered by a thin film of molasses. The molasses film contains sugar, water, and impurities such as plant materials. At this stage, the raw sugar is transported from the sugar mill to a sugar refinery, almost always by ship, which is the reason that major refineries are located at seaports.

At the refinery, the raw sugar is transformed into granulated sugar, brown sugar, and other products for both consumers and the food industry. The raw sugar is first mixed with a warm syrup made of water and sugar, which essentially washes the raw sugar to loosen the molasses coating. The mixture is spun in large centrifuges again, separating the molasses film from the crystals. The crystals are washed and dissolved into a syrup that is filtered to remove any remaining molasses and impurities. The sugar is now a clear golden liquid. Further filtering removes the remaining color, leaving a transparent white syrup (whiteners and bleaches are not used to remove color). Some of the water content is removed and the concentrated syrup is conveyed to a vacuum, where fine sugar crystals are added. As evaporation occurs, larger sugar crystals form around the fine crystal seeds, resulting in crystals of the proper size. The sugar goes to a centrifuge again, where any noncrystallized syrup is spun off and the crystals are washed. The damp crystals then go to dryers. After drying, the sugar granules are sifted through screens to separate the crystals by size for packaging.

Refining and processing sugar beets

Sugar beets grow in temperate climates and store sugar in their roots. Sugar beets are raised in many of the United States, including California, Colorado, Idaho, Michigan, Ohio, Oregon, Washington, and many of the Great Plains states. The sugar beet crop contributes slightly less than half of the total U.S. sugar crop. Sugar beets weigh about 2 pounds (910 g) each and contain 16 to 18 percent sucrose in their raw form. Their growing season is about five months long. Unlike sugarcane, the process for refining sugar beets takes place all at one location, generally near the growing area, as the beets do not travel well. Sugar beet factories operate seasonally in response to the harvest; during the time of operation, the facilities may be in production continuously day and night, seven days a week.

The refining process is basically the same as for sugarcane, although not as many steps are involved. The first step at the factory is to wash and slice the beets; which then go into a tank known as a *diffuser,* where they are agitated as hot water washes over them. The sugar-laden water is drawn off, and the remaining beet pulp is processed separately, usually for livestock feed. The watery beet juice is treated with milk of lime and carbon dioxide in carbonation tanks. After the juice is filtered, it is thin and light brown. This is evaporated under vacuum, where it becomes a syrup. The syrup is filtered again, boiled again, and crystals now begin to form. The crystal and syrup combination, as in cane sugar production, is called *massecuite*. The massecuite is sent to a centrifuge and, after spinning, is washed to produce pure white crystals of sugar. These are dried and sifted to separate the crystals by size before they are packaged.

By looking at the ingredients listed in most pastry recipes, you can clearly see that a pastry chef would find it almost impossible to produce the majority of traditional bakery products (keeping the desired flavor and appearance) without using some type of sugar. In addition to providing a sweet flavor that seems to be universally popular, sugar acts as an emulsifying (creaming) agent when mixed with fat by incorporating air; becomes a foaming agent when mixed with eggs; weakens the gluten structure of flour, contributing to a tender and fine-textured product; provides food for developing yeast; enhances the smoothness and mouth feel of frozen ice cream; caramelizes when heated to give an appetizing color and crust to just about all baked items; delays coagulation of egg proteins in custards; helps prevent jams and preserves from spoiling; and, last, by retaining moisture, increases the shelf life of baked goods.

Sugar can be used to make decorations by boiling it into a thick syrup and turning it into a variety of shapes by casting, blowing, or pulling, or it can be spun into delicate threads. With the addition of **gum tragacanth** or **gelatin,** sugar can be made into a paste to be rolled, formed, or molded in almost any way imaginable. Caramelized sugar is used to coat fruit and nuts for dessert garnishes; it can be made into fragile cages to showcase a simple dessert like ice cream and make it special; or it can be piped out into ornaments, figurines, and even flexible spirals. When nuts are added to caramelized sugar, it becomes nougatine, which has many decorative uses. Royal icing is made by mixing powdered sugar and egg whites, and it too can be used to create decorative ornaments to garnish cakes and pastries, or it can be used for showpieces.

Varieties of Sugar

6X sugar—The standard pulverized sugar, commonly known as *powdered sugar.* The particle size found in this type of **powdered sugar** is that typically available to the nonprofessional. This product contains 3 percent cornstarch to prevent clumping.

10X sugar—A finely pulverized **powdered sugar** typically used when it is important that the sugar melt quickly. This product contains 3 percent cornstarch to prevent clumping.

12X sugar—Also known as *fondant sugar,* this sugar offers the finest particle size of the **powdered sugars.** As the alternate name suggests, it is designed for use in fondants and icings. This product contains 3 percent cornstarch to prevent clumping.

Brown or golden sugar—Brown sugar is cane sugar that is not fully refined or beet sugar that has been fully refined with cane molasses added to it. All brown sugar contains molasses and many more impurities than granulated sugar. A mixture of **granulated sugar** and **molasses** can be used as a substitute for brown sugar in most recipes. Brown sugar is available to the professional in a variety of grades from light to dark brown; the darker sugars have more impurities and a more bitter taste. Brown sugar contains a great deal of moisture and must be stored in airtight containers to keep it from drying out and hardening. If the sugar should become hard or lumpy, sprinkle a few drop of water lightly on top and warm it in a low oven, or place a slice of apple or bread in the sugar bin to add moisture.

Castor sugar—Also spelled *caster,* castor sugar is a **granulated sugar** that has been ground more finely than regular table sugar but not as fine as **powdered sugar.** It is actually the British equivalent of American powdered sugar. Castor sugar is used when it is necessary to use a sugar that will dissolve very quickly. The name derives from its association with the tall cylindrical vessel with a perforated lid, known in England as a *castor,* often used to store and dispense it.

Confectioners' sugar—Another name for **powdered sugar.**

Crystal sugar—The coarsest variety of **decorating sugar.** The sugar is formed into pellets that are 4 to 6 times larger than the grains of **granulated sugar.**

Cube sugar—Sugar cubes are made by pressing damp, **granulated sugar** in molds, drying it, then cutting it into the desired shapes.

Decorating sugar—The granules of this sugar are larger than those of standard **granulated sugar** and available in a variety of textures and colors. It is commonly used for decorating cookies, cakes, and confections. **Sanding sugar** and **crystal sugar** are both varieties of decorating sugar that are named for the granule shape and size.

Demerara sugar—A popular raw cane sugar native to the Demerara region of Guyana. The light brown, dry sugar has coarse crystals that dissolve slowly. Because of this, it is a popular additive for sweetening hot cereal and coffee and for sprinkling on top of baked goods to add texture. Commonly used much like **turbinado sugar.**

Fondant sugar—The same as **12X sugar.**

Glazing sugar—A **powdered sugar** with very fine particles, usually **12X.** Depending on the brand, this sugar may have added maltodextrin as a stabilizer to help it absorb and retain moisture so that glazed products will retain their gloss over a longer period.

Granulated sugar—White granulated sugar is the most commonly used sugar variety and is what is meant when a recipe simply calls for sugar. It is produced for both cooking and table use. Granulated sugar is made from either sugar beets or sugarcane; both varieties are slightly more than 99 percent pure sucrose. Granulated sugar is perfect for making cakes because the sugar granules are intentionally made the right size for incorporating the proper amount of air into cake batters and to melt and dissolve at the required speed and temperature during baking. In a professional setting superfine sugar (not always available to the general public) gives an excellent result when used in cakes.

Icing sugar—The same as **12X sugar.**

Invert sugar—A product of sugar refining, invert sugar is a chemically processed heavy syrup that will not crystallize, thereby extending the shelf life of products in which it is used. It is used mostly in icings and flavorings.

Loaf sugar—Used to make sugar sculptures. It is produced in the same way as **cube sugar.**

Malt syrup—See **Malt sugar.**

Muscavado sugar—Minimally refined, with a dark, sticky, and strong bittersweet flavor. Used like **molasses** in goods such as gingerbread and chutney.

Powdered sugar—Also called *confectioners' sugar,* this sugar is produced by grinding **granulated sugar** to a powder. Starch is always added to prevent caking and lumping. Powdered sugar is used mostly for uncooked icings, decorating, and some meringues.

Raw sugar—Actual raw sugar is inedible. In the United States, the product called *Sugar in the Raw* is actually **turbinado sugar.** Many people feel that this form of sugar looks more natural than refined **granulated sugar.**

Rock sugar—Not a sugar used as an ingredient, this is a decorative product named for its porous, rough, rocklike appearance. Rock sugar is made by adding royal icing to a sugar syrup cooked to 285°F (141°C). This causes the syrup to turn opaque and bubble up in the pan. The eruption (swelling) and recrystallization occur as a reaction to quickly beating the egg white and sugar in the icing into the hot syrup. The mixture is then poured into a large bowl, where it continues to foam and expand; eventually, it hardens.

Sanding sugar—The most common coarseness of **decorating sugar**, composed of granules larger than **granulated sugar** but smaller than pellets of **crystal sugar**.

Superfine sugar—Sometimes called *bakers' grade sugar,* this sugar has smaller granules than standard **granulated sugar** and melts and dissolves more quickly. It is used for high-end products where the texture and melting qualities of the sugar are very important. This product is new to the consumer market but is becoming more readily available at many retailers.

Turbinado sugar—A type of **granulated sugar** that is slightly less refined than common granulated white sugar. Although it is also known as *washed sugar,* turbinado sugar actually goes through slightly fewer washing and refining procedures than regular granulated sugar. It retains a small amount of **molasses** both on the surface and in the crystal itself. It is about 3 times coarser than granulated sugar and has a pale brown color and a light molasses flavor.

Sugar apple—See **Cherimoya.**

Sugarplum—A small, sugary candy made with dried fruits and fondant.

Sugar substitute—See **Artificial sweetener.**

Sultana—The Australian name for the Thompson Seedless grape. These grapes are dried to make **raisins**, served as table grapes, and made into a neutral wine used in blending inexpensive white wines.

Sumac—A shrub native to Turkey. Several parts of the plant are used to season food. The petals and berries are dried and ground to produce a purple powder with an acidic flavor. The leaves have a sour, slightly peppery taste and are steeped in water before use. Dried sumac seeds are used as a flavoring ingredient as well as a topping in a way comparable to **poppy seeds.**

Summer coating; Summer icing—Old-fashioned names once used for **coating chocolate. See Chocolate.**

Sunflower seed—Sunflower seeds contain up to 47 percent fat by weight; the plants are cultivated primarily for oil production. Sunflowers (genus *Helianthus*) were grown by the natives of both North and South America before they were exported to Europe and Asia. In the eighteenth century, Peter the Great introduced the sunflower to Russia, where it was embraced because the Church had banned the eating of oily plants on fast days. The sunflower, however, being new to the country, was not listed as a forbidden food, and soon people were enjoying the roasted seeds and, later, extracting the oil from them. Russia continues to be one of the largest producers of the crop to this day. Sunflower seeds, in addition to being a snack food that is particularly well liked by the Russian people, is also used extensively in Russian confectionery.

With bright yellow petals that extend from a dark center tightly packed with seeds, a single sunflower can measure more than 12 inches (30 cm) in diameter and contain as many as 2000 seeds. Most of the cultivation in North America is concentrated in the Great Plains and in California, but the sunflower is the official state flower of Kansas. Jerusalem artichoke is another plant of genus *Helianthus.*

Sunflower oil—Oil pressed from **sunflower seeds.** It is pale yellow in color and very mild in flavor, almost tasteless. Due to its low smoke point, sunflower oil is not a good choice for frying; it is better suited to baking and in making salad dressings. It is low in saturated fat and, like all vegetable oils, does not contain cholesterol.

Superfine sugar—See **Sugar.**

Sweet dark chocolate—**Dark chocolate** is cocoa paste finely ground and conched, with the addition of extra cocoa butter, sugar, and vanilla. Dark chocolate should contain a minimum of 20 percent total cocoa butter and approximately 50 percent sugar. It is used in fillings such as ganache and in a multitude of chocolate desserts. Tempered dark chocolate is used for decorations and coating candies and pastries.

Sweet light chocolate; light chocolate—**Milk chocolate.**

Sweetened condensed milk—A thick, sweet, slightly caramel-flavored milk product made from sweetened whole milk from which 60 percent of the water has been evaporated. Gail Borden invented sweetened condensed milk in 1853. Borden (1801–1874) was an American dairyman, surveyor, and inventor. In 1856, he also patented the process of evaporating milk, and the Borden Milk Company (now the Borden Family of Companies, including Borden Foods Corp. and Borden Chemicals, Inc.) continues to be an economic giant in the business industry. Sweetened condensed milk cannot be used as a substitute for **evaporated milk** because of the added sugar. However, it is also known simply as *condensed milk,* which can lead to confusion.

Sweet potato—Sweet potatoes have deep ties to the American South and southern regional cooking. They are an important agricultural crop in the southern states, though they are grown elsewhere in the country (New Jersey and California being the other top producers) as well. The flesh is naturally sweet due to an enzyme in the potato that converts the majority of its starches to sugar as the potato matures. Still, most traditional American recipes call for generous quantities of additional sweeteners such as maple syrup, brown sugar, molasses, and, of course, marshmallows for the odd, but apparently essential, candied sweet potatoes served for Thanksgiving dinner. This strange combination was popularized in the 1920s, and though it is doubtful that anyone other than young children actually likes it, the dish is so ingrained in the holiday menu we will probably never be rid of it.

The sweet potato is not related to the common white potato but is part of the morning glory family. Native to America, it was brought back to Europe by Columbus in the late 1400s. By the middle of the sixteenth century, the sweet potato was cultivated in Spain and had been introduced to

England, and sweet potato pie had became popular enough in England by the turn of the century to be mentioned by Shakespeare in *The Merry Wives of Windsor.* Sweet potatoes were so widely cultivated by the American colonists that this high-energy tuber was actually the main food source for some of the early settlers and soldiers in the Revolutionary War. Sweet potatoes are, in fact, one of the most nutritious of all vegetables, containing in a single small potato only trace amounts of fat and approximately 5 times the recommended daily allowance (RDA) of vitamin A as well as substantial amounts of vitamins B$_6$ and C. The term *sweet potato* was not used in the United States until the mid-1700s, when a new term was needed to distinguish sweet potatoes from the white potatoes that had come to North America with the Irish immigrants.

There are two different varieties of sweet potato. The moist, orange-fleshed type has a darker skin and is long and narrow in shape. The dry-fleshed variety has a slightly lighter skin, closer to the color of a russet potato, and is rounder, shaped something like a football. Darker moist-fleshed sweet potatoes are often erroneously called *yams.* Genuine yams are from a different botanical family and are much larger—growing up to 7 feet (2 m 10 cm) in length and weighing up to 100 pounds (44.5 kg). Yams are found in Asia and Africa; they are seldom available in the United States. However, because of its widespread usage, this misnomer has become generally accepted.

Sweetsop—Another name for the **cherimoya** or sugar apple.

T

Tahini—A thick, oily paste made from crushed raw sesame seeds. It is used most often in Middle Eastern cuisine as a flavoring agent and in making candy.

Tamarind; Tamarind paste—Tamarinds, originally from the Asian and African rain forests, are cultivated today in the tropics and subtropics all over the world. They are also known as *sour dates* and *Indian dates.* Tamarind pods, which have a reddish-brown hard shell, can grow up to 8 inches (20 cm) long; the pods hang in clusters from the tall evergreen trees. The white flesh surrounding the black seeds turns light brown and dries up when the fruit is ripe. Tamarinds have a distinctive sweet-sour taste. They can be obtained fresh beginning in the late fall and into the winter; they are also available throughout the year, either dried or as a sticky paste, in many grocery stores specializing in Asian foods. In addition to being used in desserts such as parfaits, mousses, and ice cream, tamarinds are most often used in Asian cooking and in the preparation of curries. Store tamarind pods in a plastic bag placed in the refrigerator.

Tangelo—Tangelos are, as the name suggests, a cross between a **tangerine** and a **pomelo.** This loose-skinned hybrid in itself has many varieties. One of the more common ones in the United States is the Minneola, which is distinguished by its large nipple-shaped neck. Colors of the tangelo range from light yellow all the way to deep orange;

size and flavor are also widely variable. Season: Early November through March.

Tangerine—See **Mandarin orange.**

Tangor—Tangors are hybrids of the **tangerine** and the **orange;** the best-known variety is the Temple Orange (others worth mentioning are King and Dweet). The flavor varies in degrees between the two parent fruits; however, they can all be described as oval, loose-skinned oranges with a fair number of seeds, especially the Temple Orange. Season: December to March.

Tannin—A chemical compound, present in the stems and seeds of grapes, that imparts a puckery quality to wines. Tannin is most pronounced in young red wines.

Tapioca—Tapioca is virtually pure starch. Extracted from the root of the tropical **cassava** or manioc plant, an important food source in South America, the word *tapioca* comes from a term used by Brazilian natives that loosely means "to press or squeeze out dregs or residue." This is in reference to the way the starch is extracted: The roots are crushed and steeped in water, and the liquid is then pressed out.

Tapioca is available in several forms, including pure starch or flour, quick-cooking granules, flakes, and pearls (also known as *beads* or *pellets*). When cooked, this last type of tapioca does not dissolve completely; instead, the small particles become translucent and soft. Pearl tapioca is used to make tapioca pudding, a custardlike dessert, and, in some cases, as a thickener for pie fillings. Pearl tapioca must be soaked before cooking. It is best to follow the instructions on the package if you buy them at your local grocer. If you have access to an Asian market, tapioca can usually be obtained in bulk at very low cost. Tapioca flour, also called *tapioca starch,* is used in the same way as **arrowroot, cornstarch,** and **potato starch,** but it is preferable for products that are to be frozen because it will not break down when thawed. Uncooked tapioca can be kept indefinitely if stored in a cool, dry place.

Tartarian cherry—See **Cherry.**

Tartaric acid—Some tartaric acid is a natural constituent in most fruits, but the commercial product is extracted from **grapes.** Despite the somewhat poisonous-sounding name, tartaric acid is used for a number of purposes in cooking. **Cream of tartar** is made from it, and it is used to acidulate **baking powder** and **ammonium carbonate.** When used in sorbets and fruit desserts, it augments the fruit flavor. Tartaric acid can be used whenever **acidulated water** or citric acid is called for (providing, of course, that the citrus flavor is not a necessary addition). Tartaric acid is not usually available in grocery stores but can be purchased or ordered from a drugstore in a granular form; it is quite inexpensive and lasts a very long time. Tartaric acid also acts as the catalyst for pectin glaze.

Tea—Although second to **coffee** in commercial importance, tea ranks first as the most popular beverage in the world. The origin of the tea plant and the infusion of dried tea leaves is a bit uncertain. Experts believe that the plant hails from western China. An ancient legend has it that Shen-nung, a famous scholar and philosopher, in making a fire from the branches of the tea plant, accidentally spilled some leaves into the boiling water he was preparing. The flavor proved to be so exhilarating that, in a short time, the preparation became a common habit of the whole empire. The first European record of tea was made by Marco Polo, who wrote of the stimulating beverage and of the many teahouses in China. Tea was introduced to Europe in the sixteenth century by the Dutch East India Company and subsequently became very popular in England. The English implemented new growing areas in the Darjeeling and Assam valleys of northeastern India, which would later become known as the world's premier tea-growing regions, and on Ceylon (now Sri Lanka), an island that became well known for Lipton Tea, produced by the famous tea baron Sir Thomas Lipton. Another Thomas, with the surname of Twining, also made his fortune in the tea business, having the foresight to realize just how popular the drink was to become. Tea was (and still is) so enjoyed by the English that they developed a meal to go with it. The term *tea* is used by the British to refer to an elaborate meal in which tea is served along with small cakes, pastries, scones, savory tea sandwiches, and the like. However, *high tea* (though the term is often misused) simply refers to the midday meal rather than the ornate repast.

Tea also played a big role in American history. The tax on tea led to the Boston Tea Party on 16 December 1773, when colonists, opposed to the Tea Act of May 1773, dumped into the water of Boston Harbor over 300 chests of British tea, valued at 9000 pounds. The destruction intensified the controversy between Britain and its American colonies and helped to trigger the War of Independence. The United States is credited with the invention of the tea bag and iced tea, both in 1904, the latter at the St. Louis World's Fair.

The tea shrub, of which there are many varieties, is a member of the camellia family. It needs rich, loamy soil, and the best teas are produced at altitudes between 3000 and 6000 feet (900 to 1800 m), as the plant grows slower in the cool air, yielding a better flavor. The cultivated tea plants are kept to about 3 feet (90 cm) in height and are constantly pruned to stimulate the growth of young shoots, or *flushes* as they called, which furnish the tender young leaves that are desired. The plants are pruned and picked regularly for about two years and are then cut down to about 1 foot (30 cm) or less to allow them to rest. Under proper conditions and care, tea plants will bear for as long as half a century.

Tea leaves are handpicked by experienced workers, generally at four significant times per year, starting in April or May. This first picking, or flush, produces the finest and most expensive teas. The quality produced from the subsequent flushes becomes lower as the season progresses. The three major types of tea are black (fermented), oolong (semifermented), and green (unfermented). All three are made from the same plant. The main difference between them is that black teas are oxidized or fermented.

In producing black tea, harvested leaves go through four main processes: withering, rolling, fermentation, and firing. Withering is accomplished by spreading the leaves out on bamboo or wire racks to dry. The purpose is to make the leaves soft and pliable for twisting in the rollers, which is done to break down the cell walls and release the enzyme that gives the tea its flavor. The roll or, more accurately speaking, the mashed lumps, are then passed through a roll-breaker before the young leaves and stems are sifted through a wire mesh. The tea leaves are then spread out in a fermentation room where they oxidize, turning a copper color, and are allowed to ferment. Next comes the firing: The tea is spread out in a thin layer on broad, perforated metal bands, which move slowly while a current of hot air passes through them. This stops the fermentation and turns the leaves black. The dried and brittle tea leaves are then sifted through a series of sieves to determine the various grades. Tea grades reflect the size of the tea leaf. Orange pekoe has a fairly large leaf; if it includes the leaf bud as well, it is called *flowery orange pekoe*. Pekoe leaves are smaller; souchong leaves are round. Broken teas—tea leaves that have broken during processing—are graded as broken orange pekoe, and these make up the largest segment. Broken teas are further graded in descending size as broken pekoe; pekoe fannings; and dust, the last being the smallest leaf particles. Fannings are used to fill tea bags.

Oolong tea begins in the same way as black tea. Its fragrance, however, develops more quickly, and when the leaf is dried, it turns a coppery color around the edges while the center remains green. Oolong teas are fruity and pungent.

Green tea is produced like the others, except that the leaves are heated before rolling and are not fermented or made to oxidize. The tea remains green throughout processing, and the fragrance associated with black tea does not develop. Green teas are graded by age and style.

Although modern methods and equipment have taken over many of the tasks, tea leaves today are picked and, to a great extent, produced in much the same way as they were hundreds of years ago.

Some of the most famous teas are Darjeeling, produced in India; the Ceylon teas, from Sri Lanka, which have a smooth, flowery flavor; and Keemun, a dark China black tea that is also known as *English Breakfast tea*. Various blended teas that have become popular are Irish Breakfast (made from Ceylon and Assam teas); Russian style, a China Congou that can contain other teas or flavorings; and Earl Grey, a black tea scented with **bergamot** or **lavender** oil.

India, China, Sri Lanka, Kenya, Indonesia, Japan, and the republics of Georgia and Azerbaijan are among the top producers of tea. Approximately 2.5 million metric tons of tea were produced annually in the early 1990s; of this amount, India accounted for about one-third.

10X sugar—See Sugar.

Thickening agents—See **Arrowroot**, **Binding agent**, **Cornstarch**, **Potato flour**, **Potato starch**, and **Tapioca starch**.

Thimbleberry—Any of the thimble-shaped raspberries, especially the black variety. See **Raspberry**.

Thompson Seedless grape—See **Grape**.

Thyme—An herb with a pungent mint and lemonlike flavor and aroma (there are also separate lemon thyme and lime thyme varieties). Thyme is native to southern Europe. The ancient Greeks favored thyme blossom honey, and thyme is commonly used in Creole cuisine. It is a low-growing plant with small purple flowers and tiny, round gray-green leaves. It is used both fresh and dried.

Tofu—Japanese for "bean curd." It is known as *dofu* in China, where it said to have been invented due to a culinary mistake around the second century B.C. This incredibly versatile food is a thick, creamy, cheeselike substance obtained from ground, cooked, and strained soybeans (of which there are more than 1000 varieties in a wide range of colors; however, the yellow soybean is the one used to make tofu). The resulting soybean milk is curdled using heat and Epsom salt. (Although **rennet** is commonly used to curdle dairy milk when making cheese, it will not work with soybean milk.) The curds are drained and processed in much the same way as when making **cheese**. Tofu has a bland and neutral flavor and, though it can be eaten on its own, it is generally added to other ingredients because it has a great capacity to absorb the flavor of the food to which it is added. Tofu is used in every meal of the day in some cultures—from breakfast to dessert—fried, grilled, and poached. In the pastry kitchen, it is used to make ice cream and as a substitute for some dairy products. Tofu is a dream come true for those wishing to cut down on fat and cholesterol. It is unique among high-protein foods in being low in calories and saturated fat and entirely free of cholesterol. Tofu is also an excellent source of calcium and other minerals.

Just as meringue can be used as a substitute for a portion of the whipped cream in some recipes, tofu can sometimes be used to replace cream cheese to create a lighter dessert. Using tofu in this manner requires a bit of experimentation. Begin by pureeing soft tofu and forcing the puree through a fine mesh strainer. The mixture may need to be drained in a colander lined with cheesecloth, depending on its intended use. To get an idea of just how significantly the fat and calories in a dish can be lowered, consider that 1 pound (455 g) of tofu has about 350 calories and 23 grams of fat (3.5 grams of saturated fat), whereas the same amount of cream cheese boasts about 1600 calories and 160 grams of fat (100 grams of saturated fat).

Fresh tofu can be purchased in many forms, including soft or firm curds, packaged in water, and vacuum packed. All are highly perishable and should be kept refrigerated in water, and the water should be changed daily. In this way, tofu can be kept for up to one week; it can be frozen for two to three months, but the texture becomes a bit chewy.

Treacle—A very sweet, thick sugar syrup originating in Great Britain. There are two types of treacle: regular treacle, which is also called *dark treacle* or *black treacle,* and light treacle, which is usually known as *golden syrup.* Treacle is similar to **molasses** but it undergoes more refinement. Dark treacle can be substituted for molasses. Treacle is used in making puddings and baked goods, where it adds moisture as well as a distinctive sweet flavor.

Tree melon—See **Pepino**.

Triple-crème—See **Cheese**.

Triple sec—Name used by various French manufacturers for white **curaçao**, an orange liqueur. The literal translation from the French is "thrice dry." Triple sec was originally introduced as the highest grade of liqueur produced by the Cointreau firm in France, but the name is now used generically to refer to any clear orange-flavored liqueur, often the least expensive variety.

Triticale—A hybrid of wheat and rye developed in 1876 by Scottish botanist A. Stephen Wilson. (The commercial crop was not perfected and available in the market, however, until 1970.) Triticale is very nutritious, containing more protein and less gluten than wheat. It has a sweet, nutty flavor. Triticale is sold as whole berries, flakes, and flour, and is often available in health food stores. Because of its low **gluten** content, triticale is combined with wheat flour for use in bread baking.

Turbinado sugar—See **Sugar**.

Turkish coffee—A very strong coffee made by boiling finely ground coffee, sugar, and water three times, cooling the mixture briefly between each boiling. It is served in small cups immediately following the third boil. Also known as *Greek coffee.*

Turmeric—A spice obtained from the dried and ground rhizome of a tropical plant related to **ginger.** Turmeric has a strong, spicy flavor and yellow color and is used in Indian and Middle Eastern cuisines. Turmeric is also an important ingredient in mustard and most blended curry powders. Also known as *Indian saffron* because of its strong color, it is used even today for dyeing cloth and dairy products such as margarine.

12X sugar—See **Sugar**.

U

Ugli fruit—Native to Jamaica and also known simply as *ugly* (quite unfairly), this is a hybrid of the **tangerine** and the **grapefruit**. An ugli fruit can be as big as a **pumelo** (6 inches/15 cm in diameter and 2 pounds/910 g in weight). The "ugly" part has to do with the thick, baggy rind, which has the look of the shar-pei dog, the Chinese wrinkled dog with a pulled-up neck (much like a kitten pulled up by the scruff of its neck). The ugly is easily peeled and its segments are easy to separate. Its unique aroma and flavor hint at both orange and grapefruit. Although in limited supply, the fruit is available in stores from January to spring, usually with the slogan "I am ugly but good."

V

Vanilla; Vanilla bean—Vanilla, sometimes called *the orchid of flavor,* is the most widely used flavoring agent in the pastry kitchen. Its uses are endless because its taste complements just about every other flavor and improves many. Vanilla also has the distinction of being more expensive than any other flavoring or spice, with the exception of **saffron,** due in large part to its long growth and production process; it can take up to one year, from blossom to cured vanilla bean, to produce a product of the highest quality.

Vanilla is the fruit of a tropical vine that is part of the orchid family. It requires a humid tropical climate and thrives around the equator from sea level to approximately 2000 feet (610 m). The vine grows wild, climbing to the top of the tallest trees in the jungle, but as long as the vines can continue to grow upward, they will not flower. For this reason, the vines of *Vanilla planifolia,* the species most widely used for commercial cultivation, are pruned regularly and bent into loops to keep the beans within easy reach of the workers.

Clusters of buds are produced on the vines, taking many weeks to develop into orchids, which then bloom from early morning to late afternoon. If the flowers are not pollinated, they will drop from the plant by the early evening. Although a healthy vine produces up to 1000 flowers, only about 10 percent are pollinated naturally. Therefore, when grown commercially, the flowers are always hand-pollinated and, in the process, thinned to guarantee a good-quality bean. After pollination, the flowers develop into long, thin, cylindrical green beans that can reach a length of 12 inches (30 cm), although the more common size is around 8 inches (20 cm). The beans are ready for harvest after approximately eight months.

There are different ways of curing the bean once it is harvested. The most common and the ideal way is to use the sun to finish the ripening process. After a few days of storage, the beans are spread out on blankets and left in the sun for several hours. The blankets are then folded over to cover the beans for the rest of the day, then wrapped around them and stored in airtight containers, where the beans sweat all night. This procedure is repeated for about two weeks until the beans have turned from green to dark brown. In the final step, the beans are spread out on mats to dry every day for about two months. They are then stored indoors until they are dry enough to be packed and shipped.

According to history, the Spanish stole vanilla cuttings from Mexico and planted them on the island of Madagascar. Madagascar had a monopoly on the crop for hundreds of years and today is still the major producer of vanilla, with Mexico a close second. The same species (sometimes referred to as *Bourbon vanilla,* from the name of one of the Madagascar islands) is grown in both Mexico and Madagascar. Tahiti is also an important growing area, producing a sweeter and more flowery-tasting bean.

Vanilla sugar—**Granulated sugar** infused with the flavor of **vanilla beans.** It is produced commercially or you can make it easily by burying vanilla beans in a container of granulated sugar. The longer the beans are left in the sugar, the stronger the flavor; approximately one week is a minimum.

Vanilla sugar is used in baked goods and pastry fillings and can be served with fruit.

Vanilla extract—A flavoring agent made by aging a mixture of **vanilla beans** and alcohol. If a product is labeled *pure vanilla extract,* it must contain a specified ratio of vanilla beans to alcohol, as regulated by the Food and Drug Administration.

Vanillin—Fragrant, powdery white crystals that form on the outside of **vanilla bean** pods during their curing process. Vanillin is also made synthetically and is produced as a byproduct of the paper industry. Synthetic vanillin is used to flavor artificial **vanilla extract.**

Vark—The name used in India for gold leaf. See **Gold leaf.**

Vegetable oil—Any nonpoisonous oil derived from a plant source, such as nuts, seeds, or vegetables. Examples include almond oil, **canola oil, corn oil, cottonseed oil, grapeseed oil, hazelnut oil, peanut oil,** sesame oil, and walnut oil.

Verbena—See **Lemon verbena.**

Vermouth—A fortified white wine flavored with herbs and spices. The name *vermouth* comes from the German word for wormwood, *wermut.* Several types of this wine are available. The best known is dry white vermouth, used most often in cocktails like the Martini. Sweet vermouth, which gets its reddish brown color from caramel, is used in cocktails such as the Manhattan. In the pastry kitchen, sweet vermouth is used to flavor desserts and sauces.

Violet—See **Flowers, edible.**

V.S.; V.S.O.P.; V.V.S.O.P.—See **Cognac.**

#

Wagashi—Japanese confections, cakes, cookies, and candies. Some of these are actually more of an art form than a food, and design is often more important than flavor.

Walnut—California produces about 90 percent of the world's supply of the most common commercial walnut, the English variety. Walnuts are second only to **almonds** in their numerous uses in baking. They are used in many types of breakfast pastries and muffins, cookies, breads, brownies, ice creams, and tortes. Walnuts are always purchased shelled for use in commercial production; they are available in halves for decorating and in broken pieces at a less expensive price. Because of their high oil content, it is difficult to grind walnuts without them turning into a paste. Grinding them with some of the granulated sugar in a recipe helps alleviate this problem. Also because of the oil, it is preferable not to chop the nuts in a food processor; chop them by hand with a sharp knife instead. Be sure to store shelled walnuts in the refrigerator or freezer.

Watermelon—One of the two categories in which all melons are grouped (**muskmelon** is the other); also the name of a particular fruit. Watermelons differ distinctively from the other sweet melons. They are characterized by their unusually thick and smooth rind and their granular, extremely juicy flesh. Edible, somewhat oily seeds are typically found throughout the flesh, while in the muskmelon category, the seeds are found in the hollow center. There are countless types of watermelons in various sizes, shapes, flavors, and colors. The largest and probably the most widely distributed is the Charlton Gray. It has an elongated shape, a marbled and/or striped skin in pale green to gray green, and a typical weight between 15 and 30 pounds (6 kg 825 g to 13 kg 650 g). The flesh is pink to red and studded with seeds. Some varieties of watermelon have white or yellow flesh. The same goes for the seeds, which are typically black but can be white, brown, red, green, or speckled.

The so-called seedless watermelons are really not completely seed-free; most have a few stowaway seeds scattered throughout. Roasted watermelon seeds taste good and are popular in many countries. The pickled rind of the watermelon is also enjoyed by some. Although watermelons are best in quality from June through August, they can be found in grocery stores almost year round, sold whole and in halves or quarters.

Watermelon flesh tastes best when cold. The watermelon's large size and smooth skin makes it popular as a serving vessel for fruit salads and such in buffet presentations; a decorative design is often carved into the skin. Watermelons are native to Africa and were cultivated by the Egyptians long before 2000 B.C. Perhaps unjustly, they were at one time looked upon as less sophisticated than the sweet muskmelon variety, largely due to their lack of distinct and complex flavor, the watermelon taste being somewhat bland and, as the name implies, watery.

West Indies cherry—See **Acerola.**

Whey—In cheese making, the liquid portion of coagulated milk, as opposed to curds, which are the semisolid portion.

Whipped cream—Heavy cream beaten to incorporate air and change the texture of the cream from liquid to semisolid.

For cream to be whipped successfully, it must contain a minimum of 30 percent fat. This is the reason you can not whip whole milk or half-and-half, for example, as they contain 4 and 18 to 20 percent fat, respectively. As air is beaten into the cream, tiny bubbles of air and fat become encased in a thin film of water. This is an example of an **emulsion.**

As more air is incorporated, the coating of water around each bubble of air and fat becomes progressively thinner. Eventually, the water coating becomes so thin that the fat globules break through and start to stick together. At this point, the cream starts to become thicker and firmer. If this process is taken to the extreme, all of the fat particles become attached to one another to the point where most of the air and water are forced out; the result is a solid mass of fat, also known as *butter.*

Even if the cream is not overwhipped to this extreme, whipping beyond a certain point causes it to break as the water is pushed out. When cream is perfectly whipped, each air bubble is surrounded by fat, and the fat coating sticking together is what holds the bubbles together in a mass.

Cream can become overwhipped when it is combined with other ingredients or simply by the process of forcing it through a pastry bag or spreading it back and forth over a cake. For any of these uses, the cream should initially be whipped only to soft peaks to prevent overmixing as it is manipulated in the final process.

Another cause for whipped cream breaking or separating is heat. For the fat in the cream to form a secure shell around the air bubbles, it must be cold. When fat becomes warm or hot, it melts. When this happens to the fat in whipped cream, the bubbles deflate. For the same reason, temperature is critical as the cream is whipped initially, as warm fat cannot form the coating around the air bubbles that is needed. It is best to use a chilled bowl and a chilled whisk or whip attachment when whipping cream, especially in warm weather or if your kitchen is warm.

Even perfectly whipped cream, kept cold, will eventually break down. A stabilizer is added to whipped cream to give it a longer life and delay this process. Commercial stabilizers are made from modified starch or gum. **Gelatin, pectin,** and pasteurized egg whites are often used in professional kitchens.

Whipping cream—See **Cream.**

Whiskey—An alcoholic beverage made from distilled grain, usually rye, corn, wheat, or barley. Different styles are produced depending on the grain used and where it was grown, how it is processed, and how long the final product is aged. Bourbon, rye, and scotch all fall under the whiskey classification, as do, of course, the popular Canadian and Irish whiskeys.

White chocolate—See **Chocolate.**

White pepper—See **Pepper.**

Whole wheat flour—See **Flour.**

Wild rice—See **Rice.**

Wild strawberry—See **Fraise des bois.**

Wineberry—One of the most decorative and unusual food plants, Japanese wineberries are small and golden in color, ripening to a light red shade. These raspberry lookalikes are juicy and refreshing, with a flavor similar to grapes. If Japanese wineberries are not in season or are unavailable to you, use one of the many similar berries on the market, such as red, black, or yellow **raspberries, blackberries,** and the numerous hybrids that have been developed as a result of crossing various *Rubus* species. **Loganberries, boysenberries,** and dewberries are examples of these.

Wintergreen—An evergreen plant with small red berries and white flowers. The leaves of the plant produce a strong aromatic oil that is used in jellies and to flavor candies and medicines; also known as *checkerberry* and *teaberry.*

Winter melon—A **muskmelon** variety, this large, frosted green melon has the appearance of an overgrown **honeydew.** A fruit by genus, this melon is largely used as a vegetable in Asian cooking. The white flesh tastes somewhat like a zucchini. Winter melons are available year round in Asian and specialty markets. The flesh is usually parboiled before being stir-fried or used in soups.

Winter Nelis pear—See **Pear.**

X

X—Used to label various grades of **powdered sugar** to indicate the degree of coarseness. See **Sugar**.

Xanthan gum—A food additive, produced from **corn syrup**, that is used as a thickener, emulsifier, and stabilizer in commercial food products.

Y

Yam—Often confused with the **sweet potato**, a yam is a vegetable with an off-white to almost dark brown skin and flesh that can range from creamy white to a deep red; it is less sweet than a sweet potato. See **Sweet potato**.

Yeast—Yeast is an essential ingredient for the baker. It is a living microorganism, actually a fungus, that multiplies very quickly in the right temperature range (78° to 82°F/25° to 27°C). In a bread dough, the yeast feeds on the sugars (both the actual sugar added to the dough and the sugar produced from the wheat starch in the flour), fermenting them and converting the sugars to carbon dioxide and alcohol. As the bread bakes, the carbon dioxide is trapped within the dough, causing the bread to rise; the alcohol evaporates during baking. Besides the yeast naturally present in the air, three types are available commercially: fresh (or compressed) yeast, dry yeast, and brewer's yeast. As the name implies, this last product is used mainly in the production of wine and beer; only fresh and dry yeast are used in baking.

All of the recipes in this book use fresh yeast. To substitute dry yeast for fresh, reduce the amount called for in the recipe by half. Dissolve the dry yeast in the warm liquid called for in the recipe, adding a small amount of sugar if the liquid is water rather than milk. If the recipe calls for cold liquid rather than warm, warm a portion of the liquid and use this to dissolve the yeast. Fresh yeast should have a pleasant smell (almost like apple) and a cakey consistency; it should break with a clean edge and crumble easily. Fresh yeast can be kept up to two weeks in the refrigerator before it starts to lose its strength. Fresh yeast that is too old will begin to break down into a sticky, brown, foul-smelling substance and should not be used. To test fresh yeast, dissolve a small amount (1 teaspoon/5 g) in a mixture of ½ cup (120 ml) warm water, 2 teaspoons (10 g) sugar, and 1 ounce (30 g) flour. If the yeast is active, it will expand and foam within 10 minutes. Fresh yeast can be frozen; however, it will lose about 5 percent of its strength. Frozen yeast must be thawed very slowly and used the same day.

In working with yeast, it is important to pay close attention to the temperature of the product. Yeast fermentation is damaged in temperatures above 115°F (46°C), and the yeast is killed at 145°F (63°C). Yeast fermentation is slowed but not damaged at temperatures below 65°F (19°C) and is nonexistent at 40°F (4°C) or lower. Mixing the yeast directly into large amounts of sugar or salt will also damage or actually kill it.

Yogurt—Yogurt is made by adding a special bacteria to milk and holding it at a warm temperature, which causes the milk to ferment, coagulate, and develop a tangy flavor. Yogurt has a thick, custardlike consistency and is eaten plain as well as flavored with berries or other fruits. It is used in the pastry kitchen to prepare churned frozen yogurt and in fillings and sauces, usually in an effort to reduce the fat content of a particular recipe. Fermented milk is known to have been consumed some form as early as 6000 B.C., invented most likely by accident, then used as a convenient way to preserve milk (see **Cheese**).

Yogurt cheese—Another name for drained yogurt. It is made by placing yogurt in a strainer lined with cheesecloth and setting the strainer over a bowl to catch the liquid. The yogurt is left to drain (in the refrigerator) for a minimum of 24 hours. The liquid is discarded. In some recipes, the resulting thickened cheese can be substituted for **sour cream, crème fraîche,** or **cream cheese** to reduce fat and calories. The substitution can be made in an equal quantity in recipes where the ingredient is not cooked—for example, in a mousse or a sauce served to accompany a dessert.

Yuba—Film produced from dehydrogenated soybean milk and used in Asian cuisine; also known as *bean curd sheets*.

Yuca—Also known as **cassava**, the yuca is a root native to South America, although now primarily imported from Africa. The root can range from 6 to 12 inches (15 to 30 cm) in length and 2 to 3 inches (5 to 7.5 cm) in diameter. When its tough, brown skin is peeled, a white, crisp flesh is revealed. The bitter form of this root is poisonous unless cooked, unlike the sweet version, which is used to make tapioca. Yuca should be stored in the refrigerator and for no more than four days.

Z

Zante grape—See **Grape**.

Zest—The skin of the **citrus fruit**. The white part of the peel underneath the zest is called the *pith* and, as this can be bitter, it is usually avoided. For instructions on making zested citrus peel, grated citrus zest, and strips of citrus zest, see pages 40 to 41.

Equipment

A

Aebleskiver pan—A cast-iron pan made for cooking the traditional Danish sweet called *Aebleskiver* or *Danish doughnuts*. The pan has seven deep half-sphere indentations arranged in a circle of six with one in the center; the indentations measure 2 inches (5 cm) in diameter and are 1 inch (2.5 cm) deep. A pancake-style batter is added to the indentations in the hot buttered pan, filling each about two-thirds full. Once the doughnuts have set on the bottom, they are turned over and cooked on the other side, producing a round ball at the end of the cooking process. A slice of apple is usually inserted into the center of the pastry before it is turned; the word *aebleskiver* translates to "apple slice."

Acetate sheet; Acetate strip—Cellulose acetate, which refers scientifically to any of several compounds, insoluble in water, that are formed by the action of acetic acid, anhydride of acetic acid, and sulfuric acid on cellulose, is used for making fabric fibers, packaging sheets, photographic films, and varnishes. In the pastry kitchen, *acetate* refers to a type of transparent, flexible, yet sturdy plastic sheeting used for several applications. Acetate is available in sheets of various sizes and in precut strips or continuous rolls of different lengths and widths, designed for lining the sides of cake pans or molds, but it has many other uses as well. Acetate strips are used to prevent a chilled filling from sticking as it sets up. Acetate is not and cannot be used for baking. Acetate strips are also used to create three-dimensional chocolate decorations and edible chocolate dessert containers. Melted chocolate is spread over an acetate strip in a thin layer. The strip is then formed or bent into a particular shape and secured until the chocolate hardens; the acetate is then peeled away from the chocolate. Precut acetate strips are handy for covering the side of a baked cake, such as a cheesecake, to keep it from drying out, should you need to remove the cake from the springform to reuse the pan, for example.

Adjustable frame—A frame, 2 inches (5 cm) in height, that adjusts to different widths and lengths. The frame is usually placed on a sheet pan, within the perimeter, to contain a fluid filling (for example, one that is thickened with gelatin) until it becomes firm. It is also used in shaping layers of cake and filling in a uniform manner when creating a tall dessert. The frame is also useful for customizing the size of the sheet pan to bake an odd-size cake. The adjustable frame is also known as a **sheet pan extender** and can be used for the same purpose; however, not all sheet pan extenders are adjustable.

Adjustable ring—A metal ring, 2 inches (5 cm) in height, that typically adjusts from 6 to 14 inches (15 to 35 cm) in diameter. It is used to hold a liquid or soft filling while it sets, and it is useful for baking odd-size cakes.

Air pump—A hand tool used in blown sugar work; also called a *bulb pump*. The pump consists of a small rubber hose with a metal or plastic nozzle on one end, which is inserted into a ball of sugar, and a rubber bulb on the opposite end, which is squeezed to force air into the sugar. The higher-end models have a one-way valve to prevent the air from flowing back into the bulb after it has been blown into the sugar. Another version has a foot-operated pump, which leaves both hands free to work on the sugar.

Almond mill—A commercial machine that was once indispensable in the bakeshop and still has many uses. It consists of two marble or granite rollers that turn at a low speed to prevent a buildup of heat from friction. The distance between the rollers can be adjusted as desired. An almond mill can grind almonds as fine as flour, and its main function in the past was making almond paste by grinding almonds and sugar together. It is also useful for softening marzipan or almond paste that has dried or formed a crust, and to produce bread crumbs.

Aluminum—A lightweight, flexible metal used in the kitchen in the form of aluminum foil and disposable aluminum pie tins. Aluminum is the most abundant metal in the earth's crust. It never occurs alone but rather is an important part of many minerals, including clay, bauxite, mica, feldspar, alum, cryolite, and the several forms of aluminum oxide (alumina). Aluminum is prepared for commercial use using a process involving heat and chemicals to separate and purify it. Aluminum is used to make baking pans and other cookware. Aluminum foil is widely used in the pastry kitchen as a wrapping material for the storage of baked goods and, in some cases, as a pan liner. Aluminum pie tins are available in both individual and larger sizes and, in addition to their intended use as disposable containers for desserts, they are used as a decorating tool in creating plate presentations.

Apple corer—A hand tool used to remove the core and seeds from fruits such as apples and pears.

Apple peeler—This tool can peel, core, and slice an apple in

10 to 15 seconds, making it well worth the investment for a bakery that uses a large amount of fresh apples. The device usually attaches to the worktable with a screw clamp, although some models are held in place with suction cups. A rotating horizontal shaft runs the length of the device. A hand crank is attached to one end and three sharp prongs protrude from the other. The apple is pushed onto the prongs. Two cutting blades positioned at the end hold the apple. Turning the crank causes the apple to rotate, pushing it against the blades and moving it forward. Some peelers can be adjusted to peel and core only without slicing. The apple peeler can also be used to peel, core, and slice pears, provided they are fairly round and not too tapered.

Aspic cutter—See **Decorating cutter.**

B

Baba mold—Small, thimble-shaped metal baking forms with rolled edges, used for making rum baba pastries. The forms are made of aluminum or tinned steel. They measure 2¼ to 2¾ inches (5.6 to 7 cm) across the top, 1¾ to 2¼ inches (4.5 to 5.6 cm) across the bottom, and 2¼ to 2¾ inches (5.6 to 7 cm) in height. Their capacity is 5 to 7 fluid ounces (150 to 210 ml).

Baguette form—Baguette forms are baking pans used for baguettes loaves; they are also known as *French bread pans*. The pans are made up of several long half-spheres joined together side by side. The pans are designed to produce round loaves rather than loaves that are flat on one side. They are made from either metal or silicone. Both types are perforated to allow air to circulate around the loaves as they bake and to allow steam to escape. The silicone pans, such as Flexipans, are placed on a perforated sheet pan during use. Metal baguette pans are placed directly on the hearth of the oven or on the oven rack during baking.

Bain-marie—The French name for a water bath—*bain* translates to "bath" and *marie* means "married." Some sources report that the name first came about as *bain de Marie,* meaning "Mary's bath," with Mary being either the sister of Moses or the Virgin Mary.

The purpose of a bain-marie is to protect delicate foods from high heat during cooking or to maintain food at a consistent temperature. A bain-marie can be used in any of three ways:

1. A container may be placed over a pan of hot water on the stove to cook a delicate sauce or to melt chocolate (like a double boiler).

2. A bain-marie may be used to keep cooked foods warm until they are served, as in a steam table.

3. A container—a ramekin filled with custard, for example—can be placed in a pan of water during baking to help ensure that the custard does not get too hot, which can cause it to curdle.

In each case, the water bath provides constant, even heat and protects the food from getting too hot, overcooking, or drying out, as the bath can never get hotter than 212°F (100°C), the boiling point of water.

Baker's blade—A tool used for scoring or cutting slashes on top of bread loaves before baking. The French name for this tool is *lame.* It consists of a small, narrow handle, a removable blade, and a cover that slips over the blade while not in use. The blade slips onto the handle and locks into place so that it is bent at a slight curve. Small metal sticks that are bent at a right angle on one end to form a handle are sold for the same purpose; these are sized to hold standard razor blades. The metal stick is woven in and out through the center of the blade, bending the blade into a curve. A small wooden stick that looks like a miniature wooden popsicle stick (5¾ inches x ¼ inch/14.5 cm by 6 mm) can be used in the same way by trimming the long edges slightly to make the stick a bit narrower. See also **Bread-slashing knife.**

Baker's peel—Also known as *pizza peel, pizza shovel, oven peel,* and *bread peel.* A thin, flat tool that is used like a shovel to transfer loaves of bread or pizzas in and out of the oven when these items are baked directly on the hearth and not on sheet pans. Until recently, peels were always made of wood, but they can now be found in stainless steel and in the combination of a wooden handle attached to a metal blade. The blade of a wooden peel is most often square, with rounded corners on the side nearest the handle, and is tapered to be thinner in front, making it easier to slide under the product. Wooden peels are also made in round shapes for use with pizzas and round bread loaves. Stainless steel peels are made in both round and square shapes and are thin enough that the blade does not need to be tapered. For the most part, peels with round blades are called *pizza peels.* The blades of peels made of either material are made in many sizes and the handles in many lengths. The length of the pole or handle varies in accordance with the depth of the oven and can be up to 16 feet (4.8 meters).

Baker's rack—Baker's racks are also known as *speed racks.* These metal racks are available in several sizes that hold 8 to 24 full-size sheet pans. These racks are indispensable in a professional kitchen: Stationary racks are used for storage and for holding items during preparation to save table space; portable racks are used for unloading deliveries and transporting goods to and from the walk-in, the work area, and the retail area. The rolling racks are available with locking wheels and a bar that runs from top to bottom in the center on the back to keep the sheet pans from sliding out. Plastic covers that fit over the racks are also available. Some speed racks are enclosed on the top, bottom, and sides and have a hinged door in front so that the rack can be used for storage. When the enclosed racks are used to store food products such as cookies or meringues that do not require refrigeration, they are known as *dry boxes.*

Baker's scale—See **Scale.**

Baking bean—See **Pie weight.**

Baking cup—The same as a **muffin cup.** These are fluted paper cups used to line muffin tins when baking muffins and small cakes.

Baking paper—Also called *parchment paper* and *silicone-coated paper,* baking paper is a specially treated nonstick paper. Its primary use is for lining sheet pans to keep baked goods from sticking to the pan, but baking paper has many other uses in the kitchen, including to make piping bags. The sheets of paper measure 16 x 24 inches (40 x 60 cm) to fit a full-size sheet pan and are available in two degrees of thickness; the thicker paper can be used more than once, in some instances. See **Silicone baking mat.**

Baking sheet—See **Sheet pan.**

Baking stone—Baking stones, also called *pizza stones,* are used in a regular rack oven to produce some of the conditions associated with baking in a commercial brick oven or deck oven, in which the bread loaves are baked directly on the hearth. Baking stones are heavy, thick disks or rectangles made from stone or clay. They are placed on the oven rack (a single stone might be used to bake one loaf in a home oven, or the entire rack could be lined with rectangles placed side by side in a commercial setting) and preheated until they are very hot. The bread loaf or pizza is then transferred to the heated stone, using a **peel,** so that it bakes directly on the stone surface instead of a sheet pan. The hot stone produces intense, reflective heat that boosts the oven-spring and promotes a crisp, crusty exterior. In addition, the clay or stone absorbs moisture from the dough, another factor that is beneficial in creating an optimum crust. Unglazed quarry tiles can be used in the same way. In selecting a baking stone, keep in mind that the thicker the tile or stone, the more heat it will retain and the less likely it will be to break.

Balance scale—See **Scale.**

Balloon whisk—See **Whisk.**

Banneton—Bannetons are coiled reed or willow baskets available in round, oval, and rectangular shapes. The baskets are used to imprint a rustic-looking beehive pattern on loaves of bread as they rise. The baskets are floured before the formed bread loaves are left to proof inside. The flour not only keeps the bread from sticking to the basket but also forms a distinct spiral pattern on the dough from where it was pressed into the crevices of the basket. The loaves are then carefully turned out onto a paper-lined sheet pan or a **baker's peel** to be transferred to the oven. As an alternative, you can use any type of woven basket approximately 8 inches (20 cm) in diameter and 3 to 4 inches (7.5 to 10 cm) deep. If you use a basket that is not specifically made for this purpose, be certain that it has not been coated with lacquer or paint, and cover the interior with a piece of cheesecloth before dusting with flour.

Barquette mold—The mold used to form small boat-shaped tartlets called *barquettes.* Barquette molds are elongated ovals with sloping sides and pointed ends that are typically 3 inches (7.5 cm) long by ¾ inch (2 cm) high. The word *barque* means "boat" in French; *barquettes* are "small boats."

Baumé thermometer—See **Thermometer.**

Bear-claw cutter—A round cutter with multiple blades attached to a handle. After a band of bear claw filling is placed along one edge of a sheet of Danish dough and the dough folded over the filling, the bear-claw cutter is rolled along the opposite edge to cut slits in the dough. Also called a *strudel roller.* In making German-style strudel, the tool is rolled down the center of a dough sheet to cut evenly spaced slits in the dough. The sheet is then placed on top of the filling, which stretches the dough slightly and causes the slits to expand.

Bench scraper—See **Scraper.**

Bismarck piping tip—Also known as a *doughnut piping tip* or a *Berliner piping tip.* A Bismarck tip is used in conjunction with a pastry bag to fill pastries such as Berliners, jelly doughnuts, and cream puffs. A thin tube, cut at an angle at the end, extends about 3 inches (7.5 cm) from the end of the pasty tip. The angled end on the tube makes it possible to puncture the pastry without making a large hole in the shell; the tube can then be pushed into the pastry as needed so that the filling can be piped in the center.

Blender—See **Electric blender** and **Immersion blender.**

Bloom gellometer—A tool used to measure the strength or firmness of set gelatin; it was invented by a French scientist named Bloom. It is a calibrated rod with markings from 50 to 300 bloom; 225 to 250 bloom is the average reading for most set gelatin products. The tool is plunged into the set gelatin to obtain a reading. See **Gelatin,** Appendix A.

Blowtorch—A piece of equipment that has become so commonplace in the pastry shop as to be almost indispensable. Two types of torches are used: the propane-powered industrial torch, which is also used for soldering, and a smaller, more manageable torch powered by butane cartridges. In a large production kitchen, the propane version is more practical because the butane torches run out of fuel quickly when used frequently. With either type, the top models do not need to be lit to produce a flame; these are the only types to consider for kitchen use. The lower, squatter style of propane can is safer to use because it is less likely to tip over than the tall, narrow canister type.

Blowtorches are used to caramelize the sugar on top of a crème brûlée, to brown meringue on Baked Alaska and other desserts, to caramelize marzipan placed on a cake or pastry, and to brown and caramelize the edges of a marzipan plaque. A torch can be helpful in loosening molded, chilled desserts that are stuck in their forms by warming the outside of the pans gently. A torch can also be very useful when using the creaming method to make a cake or cookie batter, should the butter you are using be too cold. By using the torch to apply heat to the outside of the mixing bowl while the mixer is running, you can gently and evenly warm the butter to just the right temperature. A broken buttercream can be repaired using the same warming technique. Slices of very ripe fresh fruit to be used in a dessert presentation and fruit that is arranged on top of a tart and brushed with glaze can be caramelized around the edges with a blowtorch, giving it an interesting, elegant look and a nice caramel flavor.

Bombe mold—The mold in which the frozen dessert called a *bombe* is formed. Authorities disagree on the origin of the name; some say it is named because the round shape resembles a cannonball-style bomb, but others say the name refers to the hidden center of the dessert, which is different from its outer shell. The ideal bombe mold is made from lined copper and has a thin screw at the bottom that can be loosened to release the suction holding the ice cream layer in place, allowing the bombe to unmold easily.

Bouchée cutter—See **Vol-au-vent cutter.**

Bowl knife—A flexible metal spatula that can be used to scrape down the contents of a mixing bowl, although a bowl scraper is usually a better choice for this job. See **Scraper.**

Bowl scraper—See **Scraper.**

Bread basket form—A form used as a guide when weaving a basket out of bread dough ropes. These forms are not sold commercially, as are the similar forms used to make sugar baskets, but a large-size sugar basket form can be used for bread as well. See **Sugar basket form.**

Bread pan—See **Loaf pan.**

Bread-slashing knife—A small, thin, sharp knife with a serrated or plain blade that is used to cut slashes on the top of proofed bread loaves before baking. See **Baker's blade.**

Brioche pan—A round, fluted metal baking form with slanted sides. The small individual pans measure 3¼ inches (8.1 cm) across the top, 1½ inches (3.7 cm) wide on the bottom, and 1¼ inches (3.1 cm) high; larger forms are available in several sizes. In addition to being used for baking brioche, the pans can be used to mold charlottes and custards.

Bronze stamps for sugar and chocolate—These are made in France and sold in sets containing different sizes of flower, leaf, and star designs molded in bronze. Each stamp has a short handle used for dipping. The stamps are rather expensive. To produce decorations, the stamps are first chilled, then just the surface of the stamp is quickly dipped into melted chocolate or hot boiled sugar. The liquid hardens immediately because the stamp is cold, creating a very thin shell of chocolate or sugar in the shape of the stamp's design. The stamps need to be kept chilled during use.

Brush—A tool composed of bristles that are tightly gathered and set into a handle. Brushes are used for painting (applying a liquid) and sweeping (removing excess flour from a pastry dough on a work surface). Cleaning brushes are designed for scrubbing.

    Pastry brush—Pastry brushes are available in several sizes and with plastic or wooden handles and natural (boar's-hair) or nylon bristles. A good-size pastry brush for everyday uses, such as applying egg wash, glaze, or melted but-

ter to food products, should have flat bristles and measure ½ to 2 inches (1.2 to 5 cm) wide. For greasing forms, a brush with either flat bristles or a rounded head of bristles can be used (the round brush makes it easier to get into corners and crevices inside a mold), but round brushes should not be used on soft food products (applying egg wash to a proofed croissant, for example) because the rounded brush will damage the dough. Brushes made with natural bristles rather than nylon are preferable overall and are a must when brushing butter or oil on a hot pan. Brushes with plastic handles (regardless of the type of bristle) are considered more sanitary because the bristles are molded directly into the handle, eliminating spaces where bacteria can grow.

    Oven brush—Also known as *hearth brush* and *oven broom.* These brushes are used to sweep out the oven after baking to remove crumbs, seeds, excess flour, and so on. The have detachable handles that fit into the top of brush from the side. The length of the handle required depends on the depth of the oven. The brush itself is about 12 to 14 inches (30 to 35 cm) long and 2 to 3 inches (5 to 7.5 cm) wide.

    Table brush—Also known as a *bench brush.* This brush is used to sweep excess flour or powdered sugar off the surface of a sheet of dough and/or from the table as the dough is rolled out.

Bundt pan—A tube-shaped cake pan with decorative fluted sides and a rounded base. A typical size is approximately 4½ inches (11.2 cm) tall and 9 to 10 inches (22.5 to 25 cm) in diameter, with a capacity of 10 to 12 cups (2 L 400 ml to 2 L 880 ml) of batter. *Bundt* was originally a trademarked name but has now come to refer to any pan of this shape. Bundt pans are very similar to **gugelhupf pans** and are used to bake dense, heavy batters that benefit from the tube shape, which allows the cake to bake from the center and the outside simultaneously. Mini Bundt pans look like muffin pans; each contains 6 or 12 indentations with the same fluted shape and center stem of the original large version.

C

Cake cardboard; Cake circle—See **Cardboard cake round and sheet.**

Cake-decorating comb—A hand-held tool made from plastic or metal, with serrated edges; it is used to make decorative designs and patterns on the tops and sides of frosted cakes, pastries, and chocolates. Cake combs are made in both square and triangular shapes and also in the shape of a long ruler. The most common pattern features sharp, pointed teeth on the edge to make parallel lines, but combs with rounded notches or a combination of patterns are also available. Cake-decorating combs are also called *pastry combs, icing combs,* and *comb scrapers.*

Cake-decorating turntable—A flat, rotating disk, 12 inches (30 cm) in diameter, that fits into a heavy cast-iron base, 4¾ inches (12 cm) high. The disk can be rotated with one hand while applying decorations or buttercream to a cake with the other hand. The turntable can also be used upside down when icing small cakes by placing a cake (on a cake cardboard) on the bottom of the stand instead of on the disk. Turntables made of plastic should be avoided, as they are too lightweight to be stable.

Cake knife—See **Knife.**

Cake marker—A device made from metal or plastic that is shaped like a wheel with spokes. To use a cake marker, place it on top of the cake and press it gently into the surface to mark lines that can be followed to cut equal portions. For professional use, markers are available in configurations to portion 10, 12, 14, 16, or 18 slices. Some markers are double-sided, with a different formation on each side.

Cake pan—Generally speaking, any container used for baking a cake batter. Cake pans are flat containers, 1 to 4 inches (2.5 to 8 cm) deep, available in varying diameters. They are found in a number of shapes and sizes, including round, square, hexagonal, teardrop, and heart-shaped. The size used most often in a professional bakeshop is 2 inches (5 cm) deep and 10 inches (25 cm) in diameter. Cake pans are made out of several types of metal (although the silicone Flexipans are catching up fast), most often aluminum. Traditionally, cake pans were made from tin, hence the name *cake tin*. Most cake batters can be baked in pans that are a different shape than the recipe calls for, as long as the volume of the pans is the same.

Cake rack; Cake cooler—See **Cooling rack.**

Cake ring—A metal or aluminum ring. Cake rings are made in varying sizes ranging from 2 to 3 inches (5 to 7.5 cm) high and from 2¾ to 14 inches (7 to 35 cm) in diameter. Cake rings and **entremet rings** are basically the same thing; however, **entremet rings** are not as tall, typically only 1⅓ inches (3.3 cm) high. A cake ring can be used as a mold when assembling a cake or individual desserts with multiple layers of fillings; it is especially appropriate for use when a filling needs to set before the dessert can stand on its own. Cake rings are also used to bake cake batters. Whatever the use, the cake ring should be placed flat on a lined baking sheet that will serve as the base.

Candy cutter with wire frame—This is a two-piece tool that very quickly cuts sheets of ganache, nougat, caramel, fruit jelly, and other candies and/or candy centers into precise individual pieces. The base consists of a rectangular elevated platform with very narrow, evenly spaced parallel slits running top to bottom across the entire surface. The second piece (the top) is a rectangular metal frame, just slightly larger than the base, which has tightly stretched parallel wires set into it lengthwise. The spacing between the wires determines the size of the candies, and most units come with several frames, each with a different amount of space between the wires. The frame attaches to one short side of the base so it can be raised and lowered on a hinge. The sheet of candy or filling is placed on the platform and the frame is lowered quickly so that the wires slice through the candy and into the slits on the platform. Once the candy sheet has been cut into strips, it can be turned halfway around on the platform and cut again, using the same frame, to make even squares, or it can be sliced with a frame of a different size to make rectangles. By turning the sheet to different angles, the pieces can also be cut into diamonds or triangles. These cutters are also known as *guitar-style candy cutters* because the tightly stretched wires look like guitar strings.

Candy rulers—See **Metal bar.**

Candy thermometer—See **Thermometer.**

Canellé knife—See **Channel knife.**

Cannelé mold—An individual portion-sized heavy copper mold with a rounded fluted top and fluted sides. These molds are made specifically for baking *cannelés* (a type of French pastry), which require the heavy copper molds (the classic technique calls for coating them with beeswax), to achieve the proper crust. The forms can certainly be used for baking individual portions of other cake batters as well. Cannelé forms come in sizes that hold 1 to 3 ounces (30 to 90 ml) of batter. The copper molds must be seasoned before they are used for the first time.

Cannoli form—Tinned steel or aluminum tubes in sizes from about ½ to 1 inch (1.2 to 2.5 cm) in diameter and 4 to 6 inches (8 to 12.5 cm) in length, used to form the shells for filled cannoli pastries. Thin sheets of dough are wrapped around the forms and deep-fried. Once the shells are firm enough to hold the tube shape, the forms are removed. The crisp tube-shaped shells are filled to complete the pastry.

Caramelizer—See **Salamander.**

Cardboard cake round and sheet—These sturdy sheets can be made from regular cardboard or corrugated cardboard. They are available in several round sizes as well as square and rectangular sizes that are designed to hold cakes baked in standard half- or full-size sheet pans. The larger sizes are available in either single or double thickness; the thicker style is preferable because they lie flatter. Finished cakes are placed on doilies on the sheets to transport them from the bakery. The cardboard is also used to support cake layers or short dough cake bottoms, making it much easier to move them during assembly and decorating.

Cassata mold—An elongated mold made of stainless steel or another metal. The forms are rectangular on the open top and have a rounded base, so they produce a long half-sphere dessert after it is unmolded. The molds are usually available with scrapers that have the same rounded shape as the base of the mold. The scrapers are made in graduating sizes, each one about ½ inch (1.2 cm) smaller in diameter. Different flavors of ice cream, sorbet, and/or parfait filling are layered in the mold. The scrapers are used to create an even, smooth layer each time by using the largest scraper after making the first layer, then using a smaller size after making each consecutive layer. Traditionally, three or four layers are made. This style of cassata is known as *Cassata Napoletana*. Among the several other versions of cassata are a round sponge cake layered with a filling made from ricotta, candied fruit, and chunks of chocolate, and a dessert that is made in the mold above using the same ingredients as the cake; this version is chilled but not frozen.

Cat's-tongue mold—A flat, rectangular steel pan with ten shallow indentations, 3 inches (7.5 cm) long, used to form the finger-shaped Cat's Tongue cookies. The pan can also be used to make ladyfingers and éclairs. Also known as a *langues de chat plaque*.

Champignon—French for "mushroom." In the kitchen, a mushroom-shaped wooden pestle. See **Tamis.**

Channel knife—Also known as a *canellé knife, lemon decorator, lemon stripper, mushroom fluter,* and *citrus decorator.* This tool is looks very similar to a **citrus stripper,** and many people use them interchangeably or do not seem to realize there is any difference between the two. However, the channel knife has a *V*-shaped cutting notch positioned at the end of the blade, whereas a citrus stripper has a rounded notch positioned on the side of the blade. A channel knife is designed as a decorating tool. It cuts deep strips of rind, including much more of the white pith than is removed with a citrus stripper. A channel knife is used to carve decorative lines in citrus fruits and cucumbers before they are sliced to give the slices a fluted edge.

Charlotte mold—Metal forms used to make charlottes. The forms vary in size, but the classic style is plain, round, and flat on the bottom, with slightly slanted sides and heart-shaped ears or handles. The molds are made in individual serving sizes and large sizes to serve 10 to 12 guests.

Charlotte comb—See **Ladyfinger comb.**

Cheesecake pan—See **Springform pan.**

Cheesecloth—A light, fine mesh gauze used in the pastry kitchen to strain sauces and to drain off the whey from cheese in making *coeur à la crème,* for example, or in draining yogurt.

Chef's knife—See **Knife.**

Cherry pitter—A utensil used to remove pits from cherries (it can also be used to pit olives, although a separate tool is specifically designed for olives). A cherry pitter looks something like a large pair of tweezers or pliers with a plunger on one end that sits above a small cup on the other end, which holds the cherry. When the handles are squeezed together, the plunger pushes into the cherry and forces the pit out. An automatic version is available wherein the cherries sit in a funnel container above the plunger mechanism. When the plunger is raised, a cherry drops into the proper position. The plunger then pushes the pit out of the cherry into a bottom receptacle and releases the pitted cherry into a separate container.

China cap—See **Conical strainer.**

Chinois—See **Conical strainer.**

Chocolate cutter—A cone-shaped metal tube about 2¾ inches (7 cm) high with a shaped opening (such as round, half-moon, diamond, triangle, or oval) at one end, used to

cut out individual candy centers once the filling has become firm, and a rolled edge at the other end. It looks very much like a pastry tip in that it is tapered, unlike most other cutters which are uniform in shape from top to bottom.

Chocolate funnel—See **Fondant funnel.**

Chocolate mold—Two types of chocolate molds are available. One is a hollow mold used for making standing three-dimensional chocolate figures. These molds are made of two pieces that can be clamped together, leaving a small hole in the bottom through which to add the melted chocolate. The molds can be made of plastic or metal and come in numerous sizes and special shapes such as animals, Santa Claus, and Easter eggs and rabbits. The second type of mold consists of a flat plastic or metal tray with shallow indentations in various designs; this type is used to produce solid chocolate figures that are flat on one side. These molds are also used to make other types of candy, such as hard sugar candies and soft-center filled chocolates.

Chocolate thermometer—See **Thermometer.**

Citrus juicer—This tool comes in several designs; the most basic types are a pointed ridged cone set in the center of a wide shallow base with a pouring lip and a pointed ridged cone attached to a perforated base that locks in place on top of a shallow bowl. The citrus fruit is cut in half and pressed firmly onto the cone with a twisting action to extract the juice. These types of juicers are made of plastic, glass, ceramic, or aluminum and are operated manually.

Electric citrus juicers have the same type of ridged cone described above. Pressing a cut fruit half down on top of the cone activates the motor, which makes the cone spin rapidly to extract the juice. When the juiced fruit half is removed, the motor stops. These machines have a spout to direct the flow of juice into a container placed beneath the spout.

Another type of hand-operated citrus juicer, also known as a *mechanical juicer,* is made of cast aluminum or chromed steel. It has two parts: a rounded top and a bowl-shaped base with a ridged cone in the center and a pour spout on the side. The top is raised and lowered with a rotating lever-style handle. The fruit half is placed on the base on top of the cone and the top piece is brought down with the lever, squeezing the juice from the fruit. The juice runs out through the spout into a container placed underneath. Citrus fruits can also be juiced using a **citrus reamer.** See also **Juice extractor.**

Citrus reamer—A hand-held utensil with a ribbed, ridged cone that is pressed into a cut citrus fruit half and twisted to extract the juice. Reamers are made of wood or plastic.

Citrus stripper—A small hand tool used to cut long, thin strips of citrus zest. The tool has a rounded notch in the blade to remove the zest in uniform strings. See **Channel knife.**

Citrus zester—See **Zester.**

Colander—A bowl-shaped utensil (metal, plastic, or ceramic) perforated on the bottom and the sides. Some colanders sit on an elevated base and others have short legs. Colanders are used to strain quantities of food that are too large to fit in a hand-held **strainer.**

Comb scraper—See **Cake-decorating comb.**

Cone roller—Also known as *pizelle cone roller* and *Krumkake roller.* This is a wooden cone with a short, round handle that is used to form warm pizelle (Italian wafer cookies), Florentina, or tuile paste cookies into cones that look like ice-cream cones. In Scandinavia, cookies made in this shape are called *krumkakes.*

Conical strainer—**Strainers** are also known as sieves. A conical strainer is cone-shaped, with a pointed end. The different types of conical strainers used in the professional kitchen are also known as *chinois, China cap, bouillon strainer,* and *étamé.* The names *chinois* and *China cap* come from the resemblance of the cone shape to that of a Chinese coolie hat.

While the names and terminology can get confusing, there are really just two types of conical strainers: those with a fine flexible mesh and those made from ridged and perforated stainless steel. The flexible mesh strainers are made with superfine, very fine, or fine mesh. Some have reinforcing rods or metal bands welded to the frame to protect the mesh from becoming misshapen or damaged. Very fine mesh strainers are used in the pastry kitchen to strain sauces—raspberry, for example—so they are completely free of tiny seeds. Medium-fine mesh strainers are used for straining custard sauces and for making purees by forcing a soft fruit through the mesh. The other type of strainer, made from perforated stainless steel, is available with fine, medium, and large perforations or holes.

Convection oven—An oven whose built-in fan continually distributes and circulates hot air evenly throughout the interior of the oven during baking. This promotes browning and helps bake food more evenly and quickly than a conventional oven. When using a convection oven, you can generally decrease the recommended baking temperature by about 25°F (14°C).

A convection oven is not the best choice for use in a bakeshop, however, and should not be used, unless you have no alternative, when baking on sheet pans lined with baking paper. The fan causes the edges of the baking paper to lift and fold over, often ruining the product being baked. If you must use a convection oven when baking light products such as pâte à choux and meringue on baking paper, you must weight down the corners securely, a task that takes a ridiculous amount of time in a professional setting. If you are using Silpats to line the sheet pans, the problem is usually avoided, although some convection ovens have fans so strong that I have seen small pâte à choux pastries actually flying around inside the oven once they have dried out!

Cookie cutter—A utensil, made of plastic or metal, used to cut cookies out of rolled cookie dough. One side of the cutter has a thicker, usually rolled edge for handling, and the other side is thinner but not particularly sharp, for cutting.

Dipping the thin edge of the cutter in flour before pressing it through the dough facilitates cutting. Cookie cutters are available in an endless variety of shapes and sizes and are sold separately and in sets. Professional cookie cutter sets are known as **pastry cutters.** See also **Decorating cutter.**

Cookie-cutting sheet—A professional tool that allows the chef to cut out a full baking sheet's worth of cookies at once. The sheets are made of plastic (polystyrene) and measure just slightly smaller than a full-size **sheet pan.** They feature cutouts of various classic designs such as rounds, fluted rounds, stars, crescents, teardrops, and so on. Depending on the size of the cutout, each sheet produces anywhere from 20 to well over 100 cookies. To use, roll out cookie dough to the proper thickness and placed on a lined sheet pan. Place the cutting sheet on top and press it into the dough by rolling a rolling pin over the top. Lift off the cutting sheet and remove the scrap dough; the cookies remain on the pan, perfectly lined up and ready for the oven.

Cookie gun—See **Cookie press.**

Cookie mold—A utensil used to press cookie dough into a desired shape and/or leave a decorative pattern. The dough is pressed into the mold and leveled off with a knife; then the mold is inverted and tapped to release the dough. Cookie molds are made of wood, plastic, metal, or ceramic and are available in various shapes and sizes. Springerle and Scottish shortbread are well-known examples of cookies made using a mold. See **Springerle mold.**

Cookie press—Also known as a *cookie gun.* The device consists of a long, hollow cylinder that is filled with soft butter cookie dough. The back end features either a screw-operated plunger or a trigger and a ratchet-activated plunger that forces the cookie dough out the opposite end, which is first fitted with any one of numerous plates containing holes and patterns to produce various designs. The cookie dough is pressed out directly onto the baking sheet. Some cookie guns can also be fitted with icing nozzles to pipe out buttercream and other frostings. A more professional model features wheels and is operated with a crank. As you roll it along the work surface and turn the crank, the dough is extruded in a rope with the desired pattern. You can then cut the rope of dough into even lengths and form the pieces into rings, for example, or simply place them on the baking pan.

Cookie stamp—Cookie stamps can be made from glass, plastic, wood, or ceramic. A design is carved or imprinted on a flat disk that is attached to a knob-shaped handle. To use, press the stamp firmly on a rolled ball of cookie dough, leaving the dough flattened and marked with the decorative design on top. Stamps can be used successfully only with cookie dough that does not change shape during baking.

Coolant for chocolate and sugar—Food-grade coolant in an aerosol spray made specifically to rapidly cool and set melted chocolate and hot sugar. It is used in creating showpieces when attaching one piece to another and in plating desserts. The advantage of this product is that the chef does not have to wait for the chocolate or sugar that is being used as glue to cool and harden before moving to the next step.

For example, a small amount of melted chocolate may be piped onto a dessert plate for the purpose of attaching a vertical decoration. By quickly spraying the melted chocolate with coolant while holding the decoration upright, the chef secures the decoration immediately and does not have to hold the decoration in position for the time it would take for the piped chocolate to become hard naturally. This can save a great deal of time during service, especially when plating a large banquet. The can sprays very cold air and does not leave any film, taste, or odor on the product. Take care when using the coolant on very fragile (thin) sugar or chocolate pieces; the spray can cool the material to the point where it freezes, causing it to crack or break.

Cooling rack—A metal rack composed of closely spaced parallel or crossed rows of metal that rest on short legs (½ inch/1.2 cm) that allow the rack to sit above the work surface. A cooling rack allows air to circulate completely around warm baked goods after they are removed from the oven, preventing steam buildup and keeping the product from becoming soggy. Cooling racks can be found in circles, squares, and rectangles and in a variety of sizes. They should be sturdy enough to sustain the weight of the baked good they hold. They are also known as *icing racks* and *glazing racks* because they can be used to support cakes being iced; it is a good idea to place a sheet pan under the rack to collect the runoff.

Copper bowl—A popular choice for whipping egg whites by hand with a wire whisk. Some believe a chemical reaction between the copper in the unlined bowl and the protein in the egg whites stabilizes the whites and allows more air to become incorporated; however, current research data are mixed. Copper bowls have a round bottom and sloping sides with a rolled edge. They are available in sizes ranging from 9 to 14 inches (22.5 to 35 cm) in diameter.

Corer—See **Apple corer**.

Cornstick pan—A cast-iron pan used to bake individual portions of cornbread batter. The pans have shallow indentations that are shaped like an ear of corn.

Couche—In French, *couche* means "couch" or "a place to sit or rest." In the bakeshop, the term refers to a piece of cloth—burlap, linen, or canvas—that is used to hold bread loaves, particularly baguettes, as they proof. The well-floured cloth is placed on the work surface and pleated to create a fold of fabric between each loaf. This allows the loaves to be placed close together without touching and keeps the bread in the desired shape as it rises. It is necessary to place a weight against the loaf on each end.

Counterweight—A weight, usually made of cast iron or brass, that is used when operating a balance scale. Counterweights are made in weights of 1, 2, 4, and 8 pounds (455 g, 960 g, 1 kg 820 g, and 3 kg 640 g). See **Scale**.

Coupler—A two-part plastic implement that is used with a pastry bag to attach the pastry tip. The coupler allows the chef to change from one pastry tip to another without emptying the bag. First, a hollow conical nozzle with a band of threading around the outside; is placed in the pastry bag so that it protrudes from the opening (in the same way as a standard tip) before the filling is added. A pastry tip fits over the end of the nozzle, leaving the threading exposed. The second piece of the coupler is a round cap that has threading on the inside and a hole in the center. This piece slips over the pastry tip and screws onto the nozzle inside the bag, holding the tip in place.

Cream horn mold—A tinned-steel cone-shaped baking form. They come in sizes from 4 to 6 inches (10 to 15 cm) in length and with openings from 1 to 2 inches (2.5 to 5 cm) in diameter. Also called *cornet molds* and *ladylock forms*. A strip of puff pastry is wound around the outside of the mold, beginning at the narrow end. The dough-covered molds are placed on their sides on a sheet pan and baked. After the forms are removed and the pastries shells have cooled, the cones are filled with whipped cream.

Crème brûlée mold—Traditional crème brûlée dishes are made of china, have a fluted pattern on the sides, and are 4½ inches (11.2 cm) in diameter and ¾ inch (2 cm) deep. They are made in both oval and round shapes with the oval molds being a bit longer.

Crepe pan—The design of the traditional crepe pan has remained the same for hundreds of years: a round, flat base with shallow, sloping sides. The pan is typically made of carbon steel, with a flat, wide handle that is easy to hold in a firm grip when rotating the batter and flipping the crepes. Sizes range from 5 to 10 inches (12.5 to 25 cm) in diameter, but the standard is about 6 inches (15 cm).

Crimper—A flat metal tool, similar to a pair of tweezers but with much wider sides. A crimper is used to imprint and seal pastry edges. The grooved, ridged ends leave a decorative design when pressed together around the pastry dough. Miniature crimpers are available for extra-fine decorative work on marzipan, gum paste, and rolled fondant. *Crimper* can also refer to a different hand-held utensil, similar to a pastry wheel, with two crimping disks set against one another on either side of a cutting wheel. The tool can be used to seal, crimp, and cut off the remaining scraps of dough simultaneously. It is used to achieve the crimped edge on ravioli, empanadas, and turnovers, and it serves various other pastry applications.

Croissant cutter—A hand-held kitchen utensil, made of steel, with wooden or steel handles. It is a rolling device with four blades, set on a slant, that rotate around the axle. This tool cuts uniform and precise triangles as it is rolled across a sheet of croissant dough. Croissant cutters are made in different sizes to produce smaller and larger triangles. Some cutters even cut a slit in the base of the dough triangle as they cut the dough. A large model cuts three rows of triangles simultaneously. The dough triangles are then rolled up by hand and formed into the traditional croissant shape before baking.

Croquembouche mold—Cone-shaped molds that are flat on the top, used as a guide to form the famous *pièce monté* the name comes from. The molds can be made of tinned or stainless steel. Some have a small lip at the base on which to rest the first row of profiteroles as they are attached to one another around the form. Once the sugar on the caramel-coated cream puffs has hardened, the croquembouche is lifted off the mold and served. Croquembouche molds come in sizes from 7 to 12 inches (17.5 to 30 cm) wide at the base and 10 to 20 inches (25 to 50 cm) in height.

Crumpet ring—Metal rings, approximately 3 inches (7.5 cm) in diameter, with rolled edges. Used to shape crumpet batter as the crumpets bake on a griddle. Once the batter is set and the bottoms have browned, the crumpets are flipped over and the rings are removed.

D

Dariole mold—Thimble-shaped aluminum molds, sized for individual servings, with a rolled edge on top. They are the same size and shape as **Baba molds.** The name comes from an old-fashioned pastry baked in forms of this shape.

Deck oven—A widely used oven in which a sheet pan holding the item to be baked, or the item itself (in the case of some breads, for example), is placed directly on the **hearth** (floor) of the oven. The inside of the oven is about 12 inches (30 cm) high; deck ovens do not have racks inside. Deck ovens are the oldest and most commonly used type of oven in commercial operations. They are made to hold from 2 to over 16 sheet pans side by side (in the larger-size oven, the configuration of the pans is usually 4 across by 4 deep). Because two or more ovens are often placed on top of one another, they are also known as *stack ovens.* Deck ovens can be equipped with **steam injectors.**

Decorating comb with frame—A two-piece tool used in combination with a **silicone baking mat** in the production of decorated sponge sheets. The tool consists of a stainless-steel frame sold in a set with several interchangeable rubber blades called *combs* or *trowels.* The combs have square notches on the edges in assorted designs. The width, depth, and spacing of the notches determine the pattern that they produce. Each comb has two patterns, one of each long edge. To use the comb, it is attached to the frame. Tuile decorating paste is spread over a silicone mat in a very thin, even layer. The comb is pulled across the mat through the paste, and the notches remove rows of decorating paste, leaving a pattern of parallel lines on the mat. The combs are 28 inches (70 cm) long so they can cover a full-size mat in a single pass. Straight lines can be formed lengthwise, crosswise, or at an angle, or the comb can be moved in a wavy motion to produce a pattern of curved lines. After the lines are formed, sponge batter is spread on top and the sheet is baked. When the baked sheet is inverted, the tuile paste pattern appears on the sponge.

> **Plastic decorating comb**—These combs are used in the same way and for the same purpose as the rubber combs described above, but they are made of rigid plastic with rubber notches and do not need to be attached to a separate frame. The plastic combs come in both 14-inch (35-cm) lengths (so you have to make more than one pass over the mat) and 28-inch (70-cm) lengths.

A notched plastic trowel designed for applying glue can be purchased at a hardware store and used as a substitute for the professional square-notched tool, but it is not practical for use in mass production. See **Ladyfinger comb.**

Decorating cutter—These are very small cutters, ¼ inch to 1½ inches (6 mm to 3.7 cm), made in just about every shape you can think of, from geometric shapes to animals, letters of the alphabet, numerals, flowers, holiday designs such as four-leaf clovers and Christmas trees, etc. They are sold in sets and are also called *truffle cutters* and *aspic cutters,* as this is what they are used on in the garde manger kitchen. In the pastry kitchen, they are used to make cutouts on the top of a pie crust for a decorative effect, or to cut out small shapes from marzipan, rolled fondant, or thin sheets of chocolate to use in decorating pastries or petits fours.

Decorating grill—A stencil made of stainless steel or plastic that is used for creating decorative sponge sheets. These thin, flat sheets measure approximately 23 x 15 inches (57.5 x 37.5 cm) and are designed to just cover a full-size Silpat. The grills are available in many patterns. The grill is placed on top of a Silpat, then tuile decorating paste is spread over it in a thin, uniform layer, filling in the pattern. The grill is removed, cake batter is spread over the tuile paste design, and the sheet is baked. The grills should be handled and stored with care to avoid bending them. If they become misshapen and do not lie perfectly flat, it will be difficult to create a pattern with precise edges.

> **Decorating grill strip**—These strips are the same as **Decorating grills** but made in rectangles that measure 22½ inches (56.2 cm) long and are either 1½ or 2⅜ inches (3.7 or 6 cm) wide. They produce individual strips of decorated sponge that are designed to fit around the outside of cakes, 8 inches (20 cm) in diameter and of varying heights.

Decorating nail—See **Rose nail.**

Decorating stencil—A stencil featuring a cutout design, pattern, or shape that can be reproduced precisely by holding the stencil flat against a surface and filling in the cutout with the desired medium. In the pastry kitchen, stencils are used most often to make tuile paste decorations and containers. Throughout this book, many recipes feature actual-size drawings that can be copied or traced and used as a guide to cut out a stencil used for that recipe. Decorating stencils made of plastic or metal can also be purchased. These are typically available in shapes such as fluted circles, stars, and flower designs with pointed or rounded petals. They range in size from approximately 2 to 6 inches (5 to 15 cm) in diameter and are often sold in sets.

Deep-frying thermometer—See **Thermometer.**

Dehumidifying agent—Any of several products that absorb moisture in the air; also known as *desiccants*. They are used to help protect items such as decorative sugar pieces and baked tuile paste decorations from deteriorating as a result of exposure to moist air. The desiccant is placed inside an airtight container together with the item being stored. Silica gel and quicklime are the most common dehumidifying agents used. Both are available under various brand names. Indicator cards that change color based on the relative humidity within a confined space are sold with some dehumidifying agents. These allow you to judge if a desiccant is needed or when it needs to be replaced.

Silica gel—Silica gel is a polymer that changes color depending on its water content. When dry, the crystals are blue; when it has absorbed the maximum amount of moisture possible, the color changes to pink. When this happens, the crystals can be dried out in a 300°F (149°C) oven for a few minutes until they return to the original blue color. Silica gel crystals are reusable indefinitely.

Quicklime—Quicklime is made from a type of sedimentary rock that forms and solidifies over million of years. The rock is quarried, crushed into smaller pieces, then burned for many hours at an extremely high temperature. This process causes a chemical reaction whereby it becomes CaO, calcium oxide. Three areas in Europe where quicklime is found are the White Cliffs of Dover in Great Britain, White Stone of Ulm in Germany, and Champagne in France. Quicklime is also known as *burnt lime* and simply *lime*. Many industrial chemicals require its use, and quicklime is used in the processing of cane and sugar beet juices. When cold water comes in contact with quicklime, it produces an impressive reaction of steam and heat—up to 212°F (100°C). Quicklime is strongly caustic and can severely irritate skin and should therefore never be touched, especially with wet hands. As the quicklime absorbs humidity, it turns to powder and must be replaced. This can take from a few days to one year, depending on the percentage of humidity and the amount of quicklime used. In most cases, only a few small chunks are needed. The quicklime should be kept apart from the item it is protecting (a sugar, tuile paste, or florentina decoration, for example) in a small container with air holes to prevent any mess as it disintegrates.

Desiccant—See **Dehumidifying agent.**

Digital thermometer—See **Thermometer.**

Dipping fork—Dipping forks are small utensils used for dipping candies or petits fours into chocolate or icing. They are usually sold in sets containing several shapes. Each tool is about 8 inches (20 cm) long and has a wooden or plastic handle fitted with a plain or twisted sturdy wire that leads to the end that holds the food item. Chocolate dipping forks are made in fork shapes, as the name suggests, with two, three, or four thin prongs; they are also made with other shapes on the end, such as open rounds or ovals, flat spirals, and tiny square screens. The candy is balanced on the end of the tool and immersed in chocolate, or the candy is immersed in chocolate and removed with the tool; the pronged forks are never inserted into the candy. The various shapes are used to mark different patterns on the top of the chocolate as it sets up. This has to be done at just the right time so that the imprint will stay. The prongs are used to make raised lines, and the screen is used to create the classic ruffled truffle finish by rolling the dipped candy between the screen on the tool and a **truffle screen.** Petit four dipping forks are made in the same pronged styles as well as the style with the small screen. The pronged styles are inserted into the petit four or pastry to dip it into the chocolate or icing, or the pastry can be added to the chocolate by hand and the screen-end fork used to remove it and place it on a rack or paper.

Docker—Dockers, also called *prickers,* are tools used to pierce holes in rolled dough before baking to eliminate air bubbles, to allow steam to escape during baking, and, in some cases, to prevent the dough from rising too much. The last instance is important when baking puff pastry sheets for Napoleon pastries, for example, when you do not want the dough to rise unevenly or get too high, which would make the finished pastry impossible to slice neatly. Rolling dockers have spikes that protrude from a tube-shaped base attached to a handle; they can easily be rolled over a large sheet of dough. Hand-held dockers feature a group of sharp spikes set into a handle and come in various sizes.

Double boiler—A pot made up of two pans, with one fitting securely on top of and just inside the other. The bottom pan is filled with water and the top pan holds the food item. In a professional kitchen, a makeshift version is more common. By placing a bowl over a pan of water or setting a smaller pan inside a larger one, the same effect is created. See **Bain-marie.**

Dough cloth—See **Couche.**

Dough divider—See **Multiple pastry wheel.**

Dough hook attachment—See **Mixer.**

Dough scraper—See **Scraper.**

Dough sheeter—A large machine used in professional kitchens that quickly produces evenly rolled dough sheets. It operates on the same principle as a hand-cranked pasta machine—that is, the dough is passed repeatedly between two rollers that are set closer and closer together as the dough becomes thinner. The rollers on the dough sheeter are in the center of the machine, and wide loops of canvas (like two conveyer belts) extend out on both the left and the right sides on top of flat surfaces. The canvas on the left side moves clockwise and the canvas on the right side moves counter-clockwise, so that each side moves toward the rollers. The dough is placed on the canvas on one side of the rollers. When the machine is turned on, the canvas moves the dough up to the rollers, where it passes through and is deposited on the sheet of canvas on the opposite side. This operation is repeated until the dough reaches the desired thickness. In addition to being much faster than rolling dough by hand, the machine can produce extremely thin sheets of dough that are completely uniform in thickness, which cannot be done by hand. Some dough sheeters require the user to stop and start the machine with each pass of the dough and to adjust the distance between the rollers as needed. More elaborate and expensive machines are fully automatic; the dough passes through the rollers, which move back and forth from one side to the other automatically until a preset thickness is reached.

Doughnut cutter—A utensil made from aluminum or stainless steel consisting of two rings—one smaller and one larger—held together with a *U*-shaped handle or molded from a single piece of metal with a rounded top. The latter is more common in a professional kitchen. The tool is used to cut out doughnut rings. To prevent sticking, dip the doughnut cutter in flour periodically as you cut the dough. Alternatively, cut the doughnut rings with plain round pastry cutters of the appropriate size, first cutting the rounds, then going back and cutting out the centers.

Dowel—Also known as a *straight rolling pin*. Dowels are cylindrical in shape, from 16 to 20 inches (40 to 50 cm) long and ¾ to 2 inches (2 to 5 cm) in diameter; they do not have handles. Dowels can be made of hardwood or treated aluminum; wooden dowels are sometimes tapered at the ends. Narrow dowels are not intended for use in rolling out dough like a rolling pin. You use them to pick up and move a thin sheet of dough or marzipan without tearing it by rolling the sheet around the dowel, then unrolling it off the dowel in the new location—on top of a cake or inside a tart pan, for example. A dowel is also handy to use as straight-edge when cutting dough, as you would use a ruler.

Dredger—A container with a perforated or screened lid. It is used to apply a light coating or a sprinkling of flour or sugar.

Drum sieve—See **Sieve**.

Dutch oven—A large, heavy cast-iron pot used for slow, moist cooking of items such as stews. It is not used by bakers or pastry chefs but is mentioned here to clear up any confusion about the word *oven* in the title.

E

Eggs-in-aspic form—An oval metal form, 3¼ inches (8.1 cm) long and 2½ inches (6.2 cm) wide at the top, with sloping sides that make it slightly narrower at the bottom. The form is named for the classic cold egg dish made in the garde manger kitchen, but it is a nice size for molding custards and charlottes as well.

Electric blender—Commercial blenders are made in the same design as the household type that most people are familiar with using to make frozen drinks and such. Both blenders consist of a base unit that contains the motor and a food canister with propeller-style blades that locks in place on top of the base.

Compared to the household units, commercial blenders approved for foodservice use have much more powerful motors and larger canisters (up to ½ gallon/1 L 920 ml). The canisters are usually made of stainless steel rather than glass or plastic, and they operate at only two speeds, low and high, whereas home blenders often have as many as a dozen speed settings.

In most cases, a high-speed electric blender produces a finer puree than a food processor, and many chefs prefer to use a blender for that reason. In the pastry kitchen, blenders are used to puree fruits and berries for sauces and sorbets, and can be helpful for reemulsifying a sauce such as crème anglaise if it breaks. See also **Immersion blender**.

Electronic scale—See **Scale**.

Entremet ring—Entremet rings are very similar to **cake rings**, just not as tall. The rings have straight sides and are set on a pan lined with baking paper to serve as the bottom. They are used to hold and shape cake layers and fillings as they are being created and as the filling sets up, and the rings are also used to bake cake batters. Entremet rings are typically 1⅓ inches (3.3 cm) tall and range from 2¾ to 12 inches (7 to 30 cm) in diameter.

Étamé—See **Conical strainer**.

F

False-bottomed tart pan—See **Tart pan**.

Fixative syringe—A hand tool used to apply color to finished pieces in sugar work; also known as a *hand sprayer*. The syringe consists of two tubes connected by a hinge; one is slightly longer and thinner than the other and is cut on an angle at the bottom so that it can be placed in the liquid without blocking the flow. The tubes are bent at a 90-degree angle when the tool is in use, and they fold flat for storage. The liquid coloring is sprayed (blown) on the sugar by submerging the end of the thin tube in the color and placing the end of the other tube in your mouth. By blowing air into the syringe, the color is sprayed in a very fine mist. Although designed for the application of coloring, the tool can be used for spraying a fine mist of other liquids as well.

Flan ring—A thin metal ring, usually made of tinned steel with rolled edges, that is 1 to 1½ inches (2.5 to 3.7 cm) high and comes in various diameters. The ring is placed on a sheet pan, which serves as the bottom, and is used for baking tart shells.

Flexipan—The brand name of nonstick flexible pans and molds made of glass fabric impregnated and covered with food-grade silicone. Flexipans are used both for baking and for molding cold or frozen desserts (they can withstand a temperature range of (-40° to 500°F/-40° to 260°C). Each pan is made from a single sheet of material with multiple indentations (like a muffin tin). The pans fit on top of standard-size half and full sheet pans. The shapes and sizes of the molds are extremely varied, from tiny molds to bake cakes for petits fours up to large sizes for individual dessert servings. Shapes include half-spheres, squares, rectangles, pyramids, ovals, and many others. Flexipans are also made in shapes for baking traditional madeleines, ladyfingers, individual brioche, individual savarins, and muffins. Flexipan molds for baking standard sizes of sponge layers, tarts and tart shells, gugelhupf, tube cakes, loaf cakes, and bundt cakes are also available. Like **silicone baking mats** (Silpats), Flexipans have a permanent nonstick surface, so they never require coating with butter and flour or lining with baking paper. They also have the advantage of producing baked goods with a completely uniform appearance. Flexipans are manufactured in France by the Demarle Company, which was founded in the 1960s by Dr. Guy Demarle. The Silpat baking sheet was introduced in 1982 and Flexipans were first produced in the 1990s. Both Silpats and Flexipans conform to Food and Drug Administration (FDA) regulations, are NSF certified, and kosher certified.

Flower nail—See **Rose nail.**

Foil candy cup—A small foil cup with tightly fluted sides that is approximately 1 inch (2.5 cm) in diameter and ⅝ inch (1.5 cm) tall. These cups are used as decorative holders for truffles and other candies and confections. They are sturdy enough that they can also be used to mold a liquid candy filling as it sets up. Foil candy cups are available in gold, silver, and assorted colors.

Fondant funnel—Also known as *chocolate funnel, portion funnel,* and *sauce gun.* This is a conical-shaped tool with a hinged, spring-loaded attachment on the handle that controls a cover that slides open and closed at the bottom. The tool allows you to stop and start the flow of liquid from the funnel using only one hand. Different sizes of tip can be attached to the opening to produce a thin or more ample flow of liquid. Fondant funnels are used to dispense fondant or other icings or glazes onto petits fours and pastries and to fill chocolate truffle shells. They can also be used to portion sauce onto a serving plate. Stands that hold a filled funnel in an upright position between uses are available. A less expensive and less sophisticated model is also available that does not have the spring trigger mechanism to open and close the aperture. Instead, a long, cone-shaped wooden stick is moved up and down by hand to open and close the hole at the bottom.

Food lacquer—Food-grade lacquer in an aerosol spray that is used to protect and add shine to showpieces made from chocolate, pulled and blown sugar, nougat, and marzipan. Depending on the product it is used on, food lacquer is used either to seal the product and prevent it from absorbing moisture from the air or to keep the product from drying out. Food lacquer is available in both glossy and matte finish.

Food mill—A hand-operated kitchen utensil that acts as a mechanical sieve and is used for mashing, pureeing, and ricing food. A food mill has sloped sides like a bowl and a flat sieve on the bottom. Some models feature interchangeable disks with varying sizes and styles of perforation (some are simply smaller or larger holes; others are shaped more like a grating blade) that can be fitted over the base. Other food mills have just one built-in sieve on the base, these are sold with perforations from 1/32 to 1/8 inch (1 to 3 mm). The food mill is set over a receptacle to collect the extruded product. The food item is placed inside. The utensil has a hand crank mounted across the top that turns a curved metal blade or paddle at the base, forcing the food through the sieve. In the process, skin, seeds, and fiber remain in the food mill, and a smooth puree is created.

Food processor—First introduced to the United States by a French company in the 1970s, this heavy-duty kitchen appliance is now a staple item in most household and commercial kitchens. A sturdy plastic bowl with a handle on its side fits on top of the motor unit, and the S-shaped chopping blade (or any of several other disk-shaped attachments for grating, slicing, or shredding) is placed in the bowl on top of the drive shaft. The lid that fastens to the top of the work bowl has a feed tube that allows food to be added while the machine is running; the user can also force the food against any of the disk attachments with the use of a plunger. The motor operates with an on/off switch or a pulse switch; the pulse switch lets the user stop and start the machine quickly, which gives more control. When the motor is turned on, the blade or attachment disk spins very rapidly, so food is chopped, sliced, shredded, or pureed quite quickly. Larger machines can be used to knead bread or pasta dough. Food processors vary in bowl capacity and motor size.

Four-hundred pan—See **Hotel pan.**

Freezer—The type of freezer used in a commercial kitchen depends on the size of the operation, available space, and budget. The three basic styles used in a pastry shop, bakery, or restaurant kitchen are walk-in freezers, reach-in upright models with one to four doors and adjustable racks that accommodate full-size sheet pans, and the built-ins that fit under the worktable. Upright reach-in freezers are the most common, but the drawback can be the floor space they take up. The under-the-table type saves space, but they can be very impractical and downright annoying in a busy kitchen, where it becomes necessary to ask the person working at the table in front of the freezer door to stop and move aside each time someone needs access. This style makes sense only for a small operation with few employees, or for use in combination with one of the other freezer styles.

Whichever style of freezer you use, it is pretty much impossible to operate a pastry shop without one, but it is equally important that you know how to use the freezer efficiently. Many food products, both raw ingredients and partially or fully prepared items, can be frozen with no loss in quality, while others should never be placed in the freezer or can be frozen only under specific circumstances. A good example is the difference between freezing puff pastry and pâte à choux. Puff pastry can be frozen as a block of dough, in unbaked prerolled sheets, or still unbaked but made up into products—turnovers, for example. Pâte à choux, on the other hand, should never be frozen as a raw paste, but if piped out into shapes as soon as it is made, frozen quickly, and placed in the oven without thawing, the freezing process actually seems to accelerate expansion in the oven. If, however, you were to freeze a bowl of raw pâte à choux, thaw it, then pipe it out and bake the pieces, they would not expand satisfactorily.

It is critical that you check to be certain that the freezer maintains a consistent temperature (see **Thermometer**), and that food stored in the freezer is always well wrapped and labeled. Because the temperature in the freezer fluctuates every time the door is opened, ideally, a kitchen should have two freezers: a storage freezer, to be opened only once or twice a day to remove what is necessary for use that day, and a production freezer, where the ingredients being used throughout the day are stored. In this scenario, the storage freezer maintains a colder and more consistent temperature, making it less likely that the items stored in it for long periods will deteriorate. The production freezer will be opened and closed dozens of times over the course of a day, but because the items inside will not be kept there for more than a day or two, there is less chance of the food becoming damaged or spoiled.

Using a freezer correctly can greatly improve productivity. Items can be prepped during a slow time and frozen for future use. When making many types of dough—cookie dough, for example—it does not take any more time to make a double or triple batch than it does to produce a single recipe. By rolling the extra cookie dough into logs and storing them, well wrapped, in the freezer, you will be ready to slice and bake fresh cookies as needed. Fresh berries can be frozen whole or as a puree when they are at the peak of their season. I could offer hundreds of other examples. I sometimes say that having a properly used freezer is like having an extra employee who shows up every day of the year, works quietly and efficiently, and never complains!

G

Gooseneck spatula—See **Spatula**

Grapefruit knife—A slightly curved, flexible, thin knife with a serrated edge on both sides of the blade. It is used to detach individual segments of fruit from the membrane in a halved grapefruit.

Grater—A utensil used to transform a hard food product into small pieces or shreds by moving the food over holes or slots with a sharp cutting edge.

> **Box grater**—The type most often found in home kitchens. The grater has four perforated sides, is open on top and bottom, and has a handle attached to the top. The small, sharp holes on each of the sides is a different size.

> **Folding or slide grater**—A professional-quality grater consisting of a large rectangle attached to folding legs, allowing it to be set up at angle (like a **Mandoline**). It has two grating surfaces with small and large openings. Some grate the food as it moves in both directions.

> **Grater and zester combination**—A fairly new hand-held tool with small, extremely sharp perforations for grating hard cheeses or vegetables as well as citrus zest. This tool is made with a stainless-steel blade about 12 inches (30 cm) long and 1½ inches (3.7 cm) wide, or with a slightly smaller blade that is attached to a handle.

> **Ginger grater**—A small ceramic plate with very small raised spikes. It is used to grate fresh ginger.

> **Nutmeg grater**—A hand-held utensil with a curved surface with sharply grooved ridges. A whole nutmeg is pressed against the steel surface, grating the nutmeg. There is usually a hole in the back or a small casing in which to hold the nutmeg.

> **Rotary grater (hand-held)**—Commonly known as a *Mouli grater,* this grater is used for small quantities of hard food such as chocolate, nuts, and hard cheeses. It comprises two metal sections that are hinged together at the handles. One section is made up of a food hopper, a grating cylinder, and a crank to make the cylinder spin. The other section is a flat or curved piece of metal that holds the food in place and presses it against the grating cylinder. The device is hand-held. The crank can sometimes be switched around so that it is easy to use by both left- and right-handed people.

> **Rotary grater (with table clamp)**—This grater works like the hand-held rotary version, but it clamps to the table and features a feeding tube for adding the food item. This version is better suited to a professional kitchen, as it can grate a larger quantity of food.

Griddle—A flat pan without sides that is used to cook food with little or no fat or oil. Griddles are usually made of iron or some other thick, heavy metal that is a good heat conductor. Some griddles have a nonstick coating. They are placed over direct heat and commonly used to cook pancakes and griddle cakes. A variation of the griddle has three legs to place over a campfire and is known as a *spitfire.*

Grill—A metal grate set over flames, embers (especially charcoal), or another heat source, to cook food upon. Also commonly referred to as a *barbecue.*

Guéridon—A small serving cart on casters that is used in restaurants to cook food at the table. The carts have two or more burners and are most often used for flambé work.

Gugelhupf pan—A tube pan with a rounded bottom and a decorative pattern on the sides. The typical size has a capacity of just over 1 quart (960 ml). The gugelhupf pan is designed not only to produce an attractive presentation but also, like any tube pan, the hole in the center allows the heat to penetrate and bake the cake from all sides. Gugelhupf is a type of coffee cake.

H

Hearth—The the floor of a deck oven. When instructions specify placing a loaf of bread directly on the hearth, it means the bread is to be set directly on the bottom of the oven without using a sheet pan. The bread is positioned in the desired area of the hearth by sliding it from a **Baker's peel** (the placement is critical because once the bread is placed on the hearth, it cannot be moved until a crust has formed). Baking directly on the hearth makes a big difference in the taste and appearance of the bread. Because there isn't any pan, the bread dough is immediately hit with intense heat that creates a much more pronounced oven-spring and, in turn, a higher loaf with a better crust. If your oven does not have a hearth or ceramic bottom, **Baking stones** or pizza stones can be purchased and used in the same way, but these are more suitable for home use, as they usually accommodate only a few loaves of bread. A second alternative is to cover an oven rack with terra-cotta tiles, 6 inches (15 cm) square, then position the rack in the center of the oven. Just as with a baking stone or pizza stone, the tiles must be seasoned the first time they are used by heating and cooling them so they will not crack. Refractory bricks (1½ inch/3.7-cm bricks used to build furnaces) can be used in the same way. Once any of these homemade hearths is in place in your oven, you need not remove it when the oven is used for other baking or roasting; the stones will actually improve the oven's performance and contribute to more even heating. To clean any hearth surface, let it cool completely, then scrub with plain water. Do not use soap.

Heat lamp—See **Sugar lamp.**

Hotel pan—A stainless-steel pan that is available in numerous standard sizes and depths. The pan has a lip all around so that it can be placed on top of a basin of hot water (**Bain-marie** or steam table) to keep food warm. Hotel pans are also useful for marinating and storing food and for baking custards and soufflés in a water bath. The standard-size pan is approximately 10 inches (25 cm) wide by 20 inches (50 cm) long and 2 inches (5 cm) high. These are referred to as *two-hundred pans* in the food industry. When the pans are 4 inches (10 cm) deep, they are known as *four-hundred pans*, 6-inch- (15-cm-) deep pans are known as *six-hundred pans*, and 8-inch- (20-cm-) deep pans are called *eight-hundred pans*.

Hydrometer—See **Thermometer.**

Ice cream machine—Also known as *ice cream freezer.* These machines really run the gamut in terms of size (capacity), price, and ease of use. Generally speaking, ice cream machines can be divided into two broad categories: manual and electric, each of which includes numerous variations. Both manual and electric ice cream makers operate on the same basic principle. A canister with a paddle (known as the *dasher*) holds the ice cream base. This canister is placed inside a container that holds the freezing agent (be it ice and rock salt, a chemical coolant, or a self-contained electric refrigeration unit). The paddle stirs the ice cream mixture as it freezes, incorporating air and preventing the formation of ice crystals to produce a smooth product.

The most basic manual ice cream maker is the old-fashioned type, consisting of a wooden bucket filled with ice and rock salt and a canister that fits inside. The dasher inside the canister is rotated using a hand crank. These machines produce about 1 gallon (3 L 840 ml) of ice cream in 15 to 20 minutes. They are relatively inexpensive and fun for outdoor parties and picnics where there are plenty of helpers to take turns with the crank, but they are not appropriate in a professional kitchen. A newer variation of the manual machine uses a prefrozen outer chamber that is filled with coolant. This chamber is chilled in your freezer for 12 hours before use. The ice cream base is poured into the center canister, which is fitted with a paddle. The crank is turned every 2 to 3 minutes over a period of 20 minutes, so it is nowhere near as strenuous as the larger ice and rock salt version. This model produces just 1 quart (960 ml) of ice cream, and the freezing chamber must be frozen for 12 hours again before a second batch can be produced. Again, this is not appropriate for a restaurant, but very inexpensive, easy to use, and an excellent choice for kids.

Electric ice cream machines start with variations of the two manual models described above—the ice and salt version and the prefrozen outer chamber version. The electric machines operate the same way, but they contain a motor that turns the crank. Of course, the price is higher.

The next level of electric machine is one you will find in many small restaurant kitchens. These are self-contained countertop machines with built-in freezing units. A bowl or chamber with a dasher fits into the top of the machine. All that is required is to pour the ice cream base into the container and turn the machine on. These models come in two sizes. The smaller produces 1 to 1½ quarts (960 ml to 1 L 440 ml) of ice cream per batch in 30 minutes. It has a plastic dasher and a removable bowl, which makes it easy to scrape out the finished ice cream. These machines are designed for household use. (This does not mean it is illegal to use them in a commercial setting; it simply means the manufacturer does not offer a warranty for use there.) The larger size has a more powerful motor and a larger capacity. It produces 2 quarts (1 L 920 ml) in about 15 minutes and is approved for commercial use. Some of these machines do not have a removable canister, making them inconvenient when it comes to removing the finished ice cream and cleaning the machine.

The ice cream freezer used in most larger restaurants is an upright version of the countertop machine discussed above, with a stronger motor and compressor, a larger capacity, and a canister that fits into the machine horizontally instead of vertically. The churning blade is placed in the canister and a hinged cover is closed tightly. The ice cream based is added through a small spout, usually with the help of a funnel. A typical machine produces 3 to 4 quarts (2 L 880 ml to 3 L 840 ml) of ice cream in 5 to 10 minutes. These machines have three settings: off, production, and extraction. When the production setting is turned on, the paddle inside the canister rotates to incorporate air and the unit around the canister freezes. When the ice cream is ready, the extraction setting is selected. This causes the unit to stop freezing, but the churning blade continues to rotate. The cover to the canister is opened and the ice cream is extruded into a storage container. This is helped along by the rotating blade and the fact that the sides of the canister warm slightly once the freezing mechanism is turned off, which keeps the ice cream from sticking to the canister. This type of machine comes in various sizes. The one described above sits on a table and, although not really designed to be portable, can be moved a short distance by two strong people. Larger floor machines are either fixed in place or sit on a wheeled platform. Some of the larger machines have two or more chambers and can produce more than one flavor at a time.

With all of the electric machines, the first batch of ice cream always takes extra time to complete because the machines are not prechilled. Once the machine is cold inside, successive batches are produced more rapidly.

The Rolls Royce of ice cream machines (or perhaps Ferrari is a more appropriate analogy, as it is made in Italy) is actually a food processor that purees frozen food under pressure. These machines are very expensive and have only been available in the United States since 1998. They are small, taking up no more space than a home-style drip coffee machine, but extremely powerful, with a processing blade that runs at 2000 revolutions per minute (rpm) and can produce four made-to-order servings of wonderful ice cream in one minute using a block of prefrozen base. To make a typical custard ice cream, for example, the cooked custard base is poured into one or more of the beakers that come with the machine; each holds about 1 quart (960 ml) of base. When you are ready to produce a serving or servings of ice cream, you simply snap the filled frozen beaker in place, push the appropriate buttons indicating the desired quantity, consistency, and type of product, and the high-speed blade shaves off the top of the frozen custard block, incorporating air and producing silky, soft fresh ice cream servings just as fast as you could scoop them from the container the old fashioned way. Once the desired number of servings have been produced, the beaker is returned to the freezer. Several beakers come with the machine, but you will most likely want to buy extras so that you can stockpile several flavors of base in the freezer. The ice cream base can be stored frozen in the beakers without deteriorating in quality for a much longer time than churned ice cream can be stored. On top of all this, these machines are easy to clean. So, if you are selling enough ice cream to recoup the large investment, this is a great way to go.

Ice cream mold—Used to mold ice cream into a specific shape, design, or size, ice cream molds are found in a wide assortment—square, rectangular, loaf, log, dome, and seasonal shapes such as Santa Claus and other characters. Some have a three-dimensional design on the bottom that

leaves an impression on the surface of the ice cream once it is released from the mold. They range in size from a single serving to those accommodating up to 3 quarts (2 L 880 ml) of ice cream. Ice cream molds are made from stainless steel, other metals, or plastic. Some come with covers.

Long rectangular molds are among the most commonly used. These are 14 to 20 inches (35 to 50 cm) long, 3 to 4 inches (7.5 to 10 cm) wide, and 2 to 3 inches (5 to 7.5 cm) high. The top of the mold is rectangular, and the sides and/or base are made in a half-sphere, triangular, square, or tapered rectangle shape. With this type of mold, the finished product is sliced into portions after it is unmolded.

Ice-cream molds are made for specific desserts. See **Bombe mold, Cassata mold,** and **Parfait mold.**

Ice cream scoop—A hand tool used to form ice cream into a ball as it is removed from its storage container. Ice cream scoops are available in a wide variety of shapes and styles.

Commercial disher—Probably the most familiar model. These tools have been made by the same company for almost a century and are also known as *trigger scoops* and *half-sphere scoops*. They consist of a stainless steel half-sphere scoop attached to a plastic handle with a thumb-operated trigger. The trigger moves a thin, curved band of metal from side to side along the inside perimeter of the scoop to release the ball of ice cream. The only drawback to this model is that it is not available in a left-handed version. Commercial dishers are made with color-coded plastic handles (usually the entire handle is a solid color, but some have only a color-coded cap on the bottom of the handle) that correspond to a standardized portion size. The portion size for each scoop is also classified by a number that is based on (but not the same as), the number of ice cream scoops produced per gallon of ice cream. The precise number of scoops will vary, of course, depending on how firmly the scoop is packed. Standardized sizes and color codes, from largest to smallest, are as follows:

Number	Color	Diameter (across top)	Scoops per Gallon
6	White	3 inches (7.5 cm)	16
8	Gray	2¾ inches (7 cm)	22
10	Ivory	2⅝ inches (6.5 cm)	24
12	Green	2½ inches (6.2 cm)	26
16	Blue	2¼ inches (5.6 cm)	35
20	Yellow	2⅛ inches (5.3 cm)	42
24	Red	2 inches (5 cm)	51
30	Black	1¾ inches (4.5 cm)	62
40	Purple	1½ inches (3.7 cm)	70

Stainless steel scoop—A more modern version of the disher, this scoop features the same type of stainless steel half-sphere bowl, but the handle is stainless steel as well, instead of plastic. This type uses a spring and ratchet mounted in the center of the handle rather than a trigger on the side. The handle itself is made up of two narrow vertical pieces that meet at the top and are connected at right angles at the bottom. To use, the two sides of the handle are squeezed together, and the spring action sweeps a metal band from side to side within the scoop to release the ice cream. Because the spring is positioned inside the handle, this type of scoop can be used with either the left or the right hand. These scoops are sold in varying sizes with numbers that are most often based on the number of scoops they will portion per quart (960 ml) of ice cream, but these are not standardized in the same way as the numbers for the **commercial dishers** above.

Professional stainless steel scoops are also available that produce ice cream portions in shapes other than rounds. These include ovals (sometimes called *quenelle-shaped scoops*), squares, and hearts.

Dipper—Also called *roll dipper*. This is a one-piece tool that does not have any moving parts. It has a thick, round slightly tapered handle with a crescent-shaped bowl at the top that is used for scooping. Dippers are made from cast aluminum, and some models feature a nonstick coating. The handles are hollow and filled with a safe defrosting fluid (similar to antifreeze) that transmits the heat of your hand to make it easier to push the scoop into very hard ice cream.

Spade—As the name suggests, this type of scoop looks a bit like a small shovel. It is constructed in one piece, without any moving parts. Like the **dipper**, spades are made from cast aluminum, with or without a nonstick coating. They also feature the same hollow handles filled with defrosting fluid to transfer the heat from your hand to the blade. The blade is shaped like a very flat, shallow spoon, with a straight edge across the front like a shovel. Spades do not produce the classic ball-shaped scoop, but some people find them very easy to use and prefer the less defined shape of the portion.

Icing comb—See **Cake-decorating comb.**

Icing spatula—See **Spatula.**

Immersion blender—Immersion blenders perform the same functions as standard **electric blenders** that have a food canister—blending, pureeing, and emulsifying sauces, soups, and dressings. With this tool, however, as its name implies, the blender itself can be immersed directly into the mixture—for example, a container of fruit sauce—instead of adding the mixture to the blender jar in batches and then pouring each batch back into a container for storage or service. You can imagine the time saved when dealing with several gallons of product.

Immersion blenders have a handle on the top end that contains the motor and the control switch; at the opposite end is a rotating propeller-shaped blade, and an immersible shaft connects the two. Immersion blenders come in sizes and models for either household or commercial use. The smallest of these tools is 12 to 14 inches (30 to 35 cm) long. It is known as a *hand blender* and is designed for household use. This type is, however, used in many restaurant kitchens for small jobs and is great for quickly reemulsifying a previously prepared sauce during service, for example.

Commercial immersion blenders start at a size just slightly larger than the household models—18 inches (45 cm) long, 200 watts, with a blade that turns at 6000 revolutions per minute (rpm). This size is also made in a cordless version with a rechargeable battery. Immersion blenders increase in size to 22½ inches (56.2 cm) long, 200 watts, with a blade that turns at 8000 rpm, for use with quantities up to 50 quarts (48 L); to 28 inches (70 cm) long, 280 watts, with a blade that turns at 8300 rpm and can process up to 100 quarts (96 L); all the way to a 30-inch (75-cm) model, 500 watts, and a blade that turns at 10,000 rpm, which can be used to blend or puree 100 to 200 quarts (96 to 192 L) of product at one time. These larger units are used more often in the hot kitchen than in the pastry shop of an average restaurant, but may be used for pastry applications in a large hotel or in an industrial foodservice operation.

Induction burner—A cooking instrument that heats cookware using magnetic energy. It features a special smooth ceramic cooktop with induction energy coils directly beneath the surface. These coils produce high-frequency alternating current from regular low-voltage direct current. When cookware made of a magnetic-based material is placed on this special stovetop, the molecules in the vessel begin to move so rapidly that the pan (not the cooktop induction burner) becomes hot.

Infuser—A perforated container used to contain tea leaves, spices, herbs, or other flavoring agents when they are placed into a hot liquid to impart flavor. This is called *infusing the liquid with flavoring* or *creating an infusion*. Placing a flavoring agent, such as herbs, in the infuser makes it easy to remove them instead of having to skim or strain the liquid.

Instant-read thermometer—See **Thermometer.**

J

Jagging wheel—See **Pastry jagger.**

Jelly bag—A bag made from flannel or felt that is used in making jelly. Fruit pulp is placed in the bag, which is then suspended (using attached loops) over a bowl to allow the juice to drip out. Because the juice is extracted slowly and without agitation, and because it filters through the bag, it does not become cloudy. The fibers of the flannel or felt help trap the smaller particles of fruit that would otherwise taint the fruit juice and, basically, the finer the mesh of the fabric, the clearer the juice will be. A properly prepared jelly is completely clear. You should never squeeze the jelly bag in an attempt to speed up the process or to get every bit of juice out, as this will make the juice cloudy and defeat the purpose. Jelly bags are capable of holding several pounds of fruit pulp.

Jelly roll pan—A sheet pan used to make jelly roll sponge cakes and sheet cakes. These are no different than professional **sheet pans.** Jelly roll pans are given a separate designation for the home baker to differentiate this pan from a flat cookie sheet with no sides. Jelly roll pans have sides 1 inch (2.5 cm) high to contain cake batter when baking a sponge cake, the same as professional sheet pans.

Juice extractor—An electrical appliance with a strong motor, used for high-speed extraction of juice from whole fruits and vegetables via centrifugal force. The machine has a feed tube on top for adding the product, a spout where the juice runs out, and a waste container that holds the remnants after the juice is extracted. Most fruits and vegetables can be added without peeling. The skin, seeds, and pulp go into the waste container and the juice runs out the spout. Because the whole food is used, juices produced in this manner are very nutritious.

Juicer—See **Citrus juicer** and **Juice extractor.**

Knife

Bread knife—A knife used to slice baked bread. It has a serrated blade, generally 8 to 10 inches (20 to 25 cm) in length.

Cake knife—A tool that is a combination of a **flexible spatula** and a serrated knife. The blade is 12 inches (30 cm) long, 1⅜ inches (3.4 cm) wide, and has a rounded tip. The serrated edge of the blade is used for cutting sponge layers and other pastry products, and the smooth edge is used like a flexible spatula to apply buttercream, glazes, and so on. The width of the blade facilitates cutting and transferring horizontal sponge layers.

The term **cake knife** can also refer to a standard serrated knife used for cutting sponge layers; however, cake knives always have rounded blade tips, whereas serrated knives for general purpose or bread slicing can have either an angled or a rounded blade tip.

Chef's knife—An all-purpose knife with a tapered blade, 8 to 12 inches (20 to 30 cm) long. It is used for chopping, mincing, and slicing. Also called a *French knife.*

Paring knife—A small knife with a tapered blade, 3 to 5 inches (7.5 to 12.5 cm) long.

Pastry chef's knife—A very practical tool for the pastry kitchen, a pastry chef's knife is something of a cross between a knife and a metal serving spatula. The blade is 6½ inches (16.2 cm) long, wide near the handle, and tapered to a point at the end. One side of the blade has a sharp edge and the other a serrated edge. It is designed to make it easy to cut and transfer cake slices without switching tools, but its size and shape lends it to many other applications as well.

Krumkake iron—The cooking utensil used to create krumkakes, which are thin Danish wafer cookies. This hand-held iron consists of two flat, round, engraved plates, 5 inches (12.5 cm) in diameter, attached with a hinge. It is used in the same way as a waffle iron. The krumkake iron

is heated, the batter is placed in the center of the bottom plate, and the two plates are joined. Then the iron is placed on a ring that rests on a stovetop burner. Once the krumkake is completely cooked through, it is removed from the iron; the engraved pattern from the plates is imprinted on both sides of the cookie. The cookies may be left flat or rolled into a cone shape while still warm (see **Cone roller**) and filled with cream.

L

Ladyfinger comb—Also known as *charlotte comb.* A ladyfinger comb is a thin tool like a ruler, 22 inches (55 cm) long and 4 inches (10 cm) tall, with half-sphere notches cut out of one of the long sides and pointed notches cut out of the other. Ladyfinger batter is spread ½ inch (1.2 cm) thick on a paper-lined sheet pan or over a Silpat. The comb is then pushed through the batter across the width of the sheet, creating a pattern that looks like the batter was piped out of a pastry bag in straight lines, one next to the other. The reference to charlotte in the other name for this tool comes from the tradition of lining charlotte molds with ladyfingers, as in Charlotte Russe, for example.

Ladyfinger mold—Used for baking ladyfinger batter, this thick pan has shallow indentations that, when filled, form ladyfingers, 3½ inches (8.7 cm) long and 1 inch (2.5 cm) wide. The pan can also be used to make langues de chat cookies and small éclairs.

Ladylocks mold—See **Cream horn mold.**

Latex glove—Disposable gloves should be worn whenever it is necessary to pick up chocolate candies or chocolate decorations to prevent leaving fingerprints on the chocolate. Latex gloves are also used for pulled sugar work, both to protect the user's hands from the hot sugar and to protect the sugar from perspiration, which often occurs as a result of touching the hot sugar. Gloves are also useful when it is necessary to pick up pastries, cookies, or candies with your hands instead of tongs or a spatula—when making up a buffet platter, for example. Restaurant suppliers sell disposable latex gloves especially designed and approved for food-service use.

Lattice dough cutter—A flat, round two-piece tool that is 12 inches (30 cm) in diameter, used to cut a lattice pattern into pie dough. Both pieces have diamond-shaped cutouts. A rolled sheet of dough is placed over the bottom cutter and the top round is pushed down on top, cutting through and removing the diamond-shaped holes.

A one-piece version of the lattice cutter is also available. This is a raised circular metal grill imprinted with the lattice design. A sheet of dough is placed on top and a rolling pin is rolled over the dough to cut out the diamond shapes.

Lattice dough roller—This tool can be made from plastic or stainless steel, with a wooden handle. It is a rolling cutter, 5 inches (12.5 cm) wide, with 17 blades. As the tool is rolled over a sheet of pie dough or puff pastry, it cuts a precise pattern of slits in the dough. When the dough is lifted and stretched, the slits open up into diamond-shaped openings, creating the lattice pattern. Figure 7-4 (page 340) illustrates the use of a lattice dough roller.

Loaf pan—A rectangular metal baking form, also known as a *bread pan*. In the pastry kitchen, loaf pans are used for baking breads, pound cakes, and fruitcakes, and for molding frozen desserts. They come in many sizes; a standard pan measures approximately 5 inches (12.5 cm) wide across the top, 9 inches (22.5 cm) long, and 3 inches (7.5 cm) high.

M

Madeleine pan—A special pan with small, shallow, scalloped indentations, used to bake madeleines, which are small, light sponge tea cakes eaten like cookies. The finished cakes are shaped like scallop shells. Madeleine pans are made from metal or silicone (Flexipans).

Mandoline—A hand-operated kitchen utensil used to slice and julienne firm fruits and vegetables. It has adjusting blades to cut slices of varying thickness and allows the user to cut paper-thin uniform slices that would be impossible to produce with a knife. Different blades and combinations of blades can also produce ridged slices and waffle-cut slices. Julienne blades cut matchstick strips in different widths. The mandoline is about 16 inches (40 cm) long and 5 inches (15 cm) wide. It has folding legs, sits at a 45-degree angle during use, and folds flat for storage. A separate piece acts simultaneously to guard the fingers, hold the product, and push the product over the sharp blades. The original models were made from stainless steel. A newer version has carbon stainless-steel blades that can be removed and sharpened and features a fiberglass frame and finger guard.

Marble—A stone used for countertops and other work surfaces in the pastry kitchen; a sheet of marble is called a *marble slab*. Because the stone stays cooler than other materials, it is useful for working with chocolate and sugar in certain applications and for rolling out dough.

Marzipan modeling tool—One of a set of hand tools about 5 inches (12.5 cm) long, used to mark and form marzipan figures. The ends of the tools have surfaces that are blunt, round, pointed, flat, ball-shaped, or engraved to make the various imprints; each tool has a different shape on both ends. A professional set usually includes 12 tools. The set is fairly expensive but a necessary investment if you make marzipan figures frequently. For occasional marzipan work, a set of small tools intended for use with modeling clay can be purchased at an art supply store at a considerably lower price.

Mazarin form—Small, round tartlet form, used for making mazarin pastries. It looks like a miniature pie tin and has smooth, slanted sides (not fluted), and is typically 2½ inches (6.2 cm) in diameter on top, 1½ inches (3.7 cm) across the bottom, and 1¼ inches (3.1 cm) high.

Melon ball cutter; Melon ball tool—A hand tool used to scoop fruit into uniform balls. The tool has a half-sphere scoop on the end of a handle; some models have a scoop on both ends of the handle, each a different size. The scoops range from ⅜ to 1 inch (9 mm to 2.5 cm) in diameter. This tool is also referred to as a *vegetable scoop*, a *ball cutter*, and a *Parisienne cutter* in kitchen jargon (the last stemming from the tool's usefulness in shaping potato spheres for *pommes Parisienne*, a classic dish of roasted balls of potato). A melon ball cutter is also used to make small, curled chocolate shavings and is very handy for removing strawberry hulls and the core from pear halves. The cutters are now being manufactured to produce ovals as well as rounds.

Metal bar—Also called *candy ruler* or *candy bar*. These bars, made of aluminum or steel, are available in varying thicknesses and lengths. Two bars are used as a guide to roll out firm candy fillings or dough to a precise thickness. Four bars can be placed together to create a square or rectangle of the desired size and used to hold a liquid such as boiled sugar, fondant, or a candy filling while the mixture sets up. In this case, a weight is often placed against the outside, or on top of, each bar to hold it in position. A metal bar can also be useful as a guide (like a straightedge) when using a trowel or comb to create straight lines of chocolate or batter. A typical bar is 18 to 32 inches (45 to 80 cm) long and ½ to ¾ inch (1.2 to 2 cm) wide on all sides.

Mixer—Electric mixers are essential to the baking and pastry department. As a fundamental piece of equipment, the mixer ranks next in line after the oven and refrigeration. Mixers are used to knead bread dough and in making the base for laminated doughs such as croissant, Danish, and puff pastry. They are used for mixing cookie dough, cake batters, and muffins; for whipping meringue, heavy cream, and buttercream; and for hundreds of other tasks throughout the day. Commercial mixers come in a range of sizes that vary according to mixer bowl capacity and size of motor. The descriptions and information in Figure B-1 are based on the mixers produced by the leading commercial U.S. manufacturer. Specifications for mixers made by other companies are the same, in many cases, but may vary with respect to material used, interchangeability of bowl sizes, exact names used for various attachments, and so on.

Electric Mixer Terminology

Tabletop mixer—Mixers that are placed on a worktable as opposed to those that sit on the floor. They are portable, but the larger sizes require two people to move.

Floor mixer—Mixers that are large (tall) enough to be placed on the floor. These are not portable and are often bolted to the floor or the wall.

Planetary mixer—Mixers in which the mixing bowl remains fixed in place while the mixer is in operation. This category includes all mixers, tabletop and floor models, other than spiral mixers. Planetary mixers always have removable mixing bowls.

Spiral mixer—Mixers in which the mixing bowl rotates (in addition to the rotation of the attachment arm) during operation. Two separate motors power the mixer

Standard Mixer Specifications

Bowl Capacity	Motor Size (motor size on all planetary mixers refers to the arm motor)	Tabletop or Floor Model	Planetary or Spiral (all planetary mixers have removable bowls)	Other Bowls Usable with an Adapter
5 quarts (4 L 800 ml)	⅙ horsepower	Tabletop	Planetary	None
12 quarts (11 L 520 ml)	⅓ horsepower	Tabletop	Planetary	None
20 quarts (19 L 200 ml)	½ horsepower	Tabletop	Planetary	12 quart (11 L 520 ml)
30 quarts (28 L 800 ml)	¾ horsepower	Floor	Planetary	20 quart (19 L 200 ml)
30 quarts (28 L 800 ml)	1.25 horsepower	Floor	Planetary	20 quart (19 L 200 ml)
40 quarts (38 L 400 ml)	1.5 horsepower	Floor	Planetary	20 and 30 quart (19 L 200 ml and 28 L 800 ml)
60 quarts (57 L 600 ml)	2 horsepower	Floor	Planetary	30 and 40 quart (28 L 800 ml and 38 L 400 ml)
60 quarts (57 L 600 ml)	2.5 horsepower	Floor	Planetary	30 and 40 quart (28 L 800 ml and 38 L 400 ml)
80 quarts (76 L 800 ml)	2 horsepower	Floor	Planetary	30, 40, and 60 quart (28 L 800 ml, 38 L 400 ml, and 57 L 600 ml)
80 quarts (76 L 800 ml)	3 horsepower	Floor	Planetary	30, 40, and 60 quart (28 L 800 ml, 38 L 400 ml, and 57 L 600 ml)
120 quarts (115 L 200 ml)	Arm - 6.5 horsepower Bowl - 1 horsepower	Floor	Spiral with Fixed Bowl	N/A
140 quarts (134 L 400 ml)	5 horsepower	Floor	Planetary	30, 40, 60, and 80 quart (28 L 800 ml, 38 L 400 ml, 57 L 600 ml, and 76 L 800 ml)
190 quarts (182 L 400 ml)	Arm - 5 horsepower Bowl - 1.5 horsepower	Floor	Spiral with Fixed Bowl	N/A
190 quarts (182 L 400 ml)	Arm - 7.5 horsepower Bowl - 1.5 horsepower	Floor	Spiral with Removable Bowl	N/A
250 quarts (240 L)	Arm - 8.5 horsepower Bowl - 1.5 horsepower	Floor	Spiral with Fixed Bowl	N/A
250 quarts (240 L)	Arm - 8.5 horsepower Bowl - 1.5 horsepower	Floor	Spiral with Removable Bowl	N/A

FIGURE B-1 Standard mixer specifications

bowl and the attachment arm. These mixers are used exclusively for kneading bread and bagel dough and are also known as *bagel mixers*. Spiral mixers do not have interchangeable bowls or attachments. Models may feature either attached or removable mixing bowls. These mixers are very heavy (1000 to 2000 pounds/455 to 910 kg) but come equipped with front casters and rear wheels so that they can be moved for cleaning.

Mixer Accessories

Bowl—Mixer bowls are classified by volume capacity and, as shown in Figure B-1, range in size from 5 to 250 quarts (4 L 800 ml to 240 L). The bowls that come as standard equipment with planetary mixers are made of heavy-gauge metal. Tinned-finish or stainless-steel bowls can be special-ordered in many sizes. Spiral mixers always come with stainless-steel bowls.

Bowl truck—A heavy metal ring on wheels that is used to transport the mixing bowl from one location to another by rolling it instead of lifting it. These trucks are made in sizes to fit all planetary floor model mixers. The ring fits both the base of the bowl and between the front legs of the mixer, where it can easily be stored out of the way. When using one of the larger floor mixers, it is not uncommon to be working with as much as 100 pounds (45.5 kg) of bread dough in the bowl. A manual or electric lever is used to lower the filled bowl directly onto the ring so the bowl of dough can be rolled over to the work-table where the bread is to be formed. The empty bowl can later be wheeled to the dishwashing station, and the clean bowl can be wheeled back to the mixer.

Mounted bowl scraper—This accessory can be mounted to the drive shaft that rotates the mixer attachments. It is a wide, heavy plastic scraper that fits tightly against the curve of the mixer bowl from top to bottom. It rotates simultaneously with whatever attachment is being used, automatically scraping down the sides of the mixer bowl. In a busy kitchen where the mixer is used continuously throughout the day, the time saved by not having to stop the machine, manually scrape down the sides of the bowl, and restart the machine over and over can be significant.

Mixer attachments

Following are descriptions of the various attachments available for electric mixers and what each is used for. The average restaurant baking and pastry department will most likely not have all of these variations. The three essentials are a dough arm (dough hook), a beater (paddle), and a wire whip.

Arm—This is more commonly known as a *dough hook* or *dough arm*. Arms come in three styles, the most familiar of which is shaped like the letter J. This arm, or dough hook, is used in 5- to 40-quart (4 L 800 ml- to 38 L 400 ml-) mixers. The other style of dough arm looks very similar but has a more pronounced curl; rather than just curving up at the end, this arm is slightly twisted all along its length before turning up at the tip like the other. These arms are used in 20- to 140-quart (19 L 200 ml- to 134 L 400 ml-) mixers. The third style of arm is called a *sweet dough arm*. It is shaped as an open loop made in an irregular winding shape.

The first two styles of dough arms are used for mixing and kneading bread dough and mixing other types of dough in which the ingredients should be combined without incorporating air. The sweet dough arm is designed for mixing cookie dough, short dough, Danish pastry dough, and other products that, like the mixtures that the hook is used for, should be blended without incorporating air. The sweet dough arm, however, provides more of a creaming action, whereas the two types of dough arms create a kneading action.

Pastry knife—This attachment is similar to the sweet dough arm; it is also shaped as an open frame but, rather than the irregular, wavy edge of the sweet dough arm, the pastry knife has a smooth edge, and the bottom of the loop ends in a slightly curved point. The pastry knife is designed for making pie dough and other doughs where the fat should be cut into the flour and/or sugar and remain in small, separate pieces, as opposed to the fat and flour or sugar being creamed together. The pastry knife creates less agitation than the sweet dough arm.

Beater—This attachment is commonly known as a *paddle*. It is used to mix heavier batters, such as those for tea cakes, pound cakes, and muffins. Paddles consist of a flat, rounded frame with six evenly spaced parallel bars attached vertically inside.

Whip—As the name suggests, whip attachments are used when it is desirable to incorporate a maximum amount of air into a mixture, such as when making a sponge cake or whipping cream. Whips come in three styles. The basic wire whip, which is the one most chefs use, is made of multiple loops of thin wire that are bent into a round shape. The center of each wire overlaps the others at the base of the whip, and the ends of the wire are attached, evenly spaced, all around the top of the tool in a ring. This whip is designed for whipping cream and whipping egg whites. Another style of whip is the heavy wire whip. It is made in the same design as the basic wire whip, but it uses thicker wires and is reinforced with three thin bands of metal—one that wraps around the center of the whip horizontally and two others that wrap around vertically, evenly spaced, on four sides. This whip is for use with slightly heavier mixtures such as cake batters, buttercream, and Italian meringue. The third whip is called a *wing whip*. This shape of this whip is more triangular than the others, which are rounded. It is made from both thin curved wires and thin flat metal bands. The wing whip is for whipping the heaviest mixtures, such as thick icings, mayonnaise, and butter.

Mixer bowl—An essential piece of kitchen equipment. Mixing bowls are used throughout the day in the pastry kitchen for jobs such as mixing doughs and batters that are not made with an electric mixer, melting chocolate over hot water, storing finished creams or fillings in the refrigerator, holding ingredients after they have been weighed out, portioning mise en place items for a recipe, separating eggs, holding dough while it is proofing—the list is endless. Mixing bowls come in a vast array of sizes and materials. A heavyweight stainless steel bowl with a rolled edge and a flat base is best. Bowls for professional use range in size from approximately 6 to 16 inches (15 to 40 cm) in diameter and have a capacity of 1 quart (960 ml) to 4½ gallons (5 L 760 ml).

Mold—A container used to form or shape a particular item. The term *mold* is also used as a noun both to describe a molded food product and also to refer to a fungus. Mold can also be used as a verb meaning "to shape."

Mouli grater—See Grater.

Muffin cup—A fluted paper cup that is placed inside the indentations of a **muffin pan**, filled with batter, and baked. Muffin cups facilitate removing the muffins from the pan and eliminate the need for greasing the pans or using pan spray to ensure that the muffins (or whatever baked good the muffin pan is being used for) can be unmolded easily.

Muffin pan; Muffin tin—A metal baking pan with deep indentations or cups to hold and shape muffins as they bake. Pans for professional use come in standard full- and half-sheet pan sizes usually holding two to four dozen muffins, depending on size. Flexipan also makes muffin forms in several sizes.

Multiple pastry wheel—Also called *dough divider*. This tool consists of four or five pastry wheels, fluted or plain, connected to an expandable frame so that multiple strips of dough can be cut simultaneously. The distance between the wheels is adjusted by expanding or collapsing the frame, then turning a screw to lock the wheels in place. This allows you to cut strips from ½ inch to 5 inches wide (1.2 to 12.5 cm). Some models feature two sets of cutters, both plain and fluted, one on either side of the frame.

This tool can also be used to mark a sheet of pastry, such as brownies or an assembled petits fours sheet, to help you cut straight, uniform portions with a knife. Mark each end of the pastry sheet with the wheels, keeping the wheels set in the same position (and be sure you start with the first wheel lined up exactly at the trimmed edge for both the top and the bottom). You can line up a ruler from the top mark to the corresponding mark at the bottom and cut along the ruler to create straight, evenly spaced strips.

Muslin—See **Cheesecloth**.

N

NSF—NSF International, formerly known as the National Sanitation Foundation, is an organization that develops and publishes standards regarding safety and sanitation for design, construction, and installation of foodservice equipment. These guidelines are updated every five years and, although NSF International is not a government agency like the FDA or the USDA, its standards are widely accepted in the industry. NSF International also evaluates all types of foodservice equipment, from small hand tools to large machines, and publishes a list of the equipment that meets their standards; this list is updated every six months. Equipment that is listed can be labeled with the NSF mark and can be categorized as "NSF listed" or "NSF approved."

Underwriters Laboratories, Inc. (UL) also provides listings of foodservice equipment that meets NSF International sanitation standards, and labels such equipment with a UL Sanitation Classification mark. Further, Underwriters Laboratories evaluates electrical equipment (for either household or commercial use) and lists that which is in compliance with its own safety requirements. If the equipment is listed, it is given the UL mark. Just as with NSF International, equipment that meets Underwriters Laboratories standards is categorized as "UL listed" or "UL approved."

Noncorrosive cookware—Cookware that is made from or lined with a noncorrosive material such as stainless steel, glass, or ceramic, as opposed to a corrosive material such as aluminum or iron. To cause corrosion means to cause something to wear away or to break down. When reactive ingredients such as acids, alkalis, or hydrogen sulfide (which is produced by cooking eggs) come in contact with

aluminum, they penetrate the surface of the metal and form oxide and hydroxide complexes, some of which are gray or black. What this means is that both the food and the pan become discolored, and the food can acquire a metallic taste.

Nonreactive cookware—Cookware made from or lined with a nonreactive material such as stainless steel, glass, or ceramic rather than a reactive material such as copper. Nonreactive cookware is used for the same reason as **noncorrosive cookware** is: to prevent the cookware from having a negative effect on the flavor or color of the food. *Nonreactive* is broader term, however, meaning cookware that will not react in any way when it comes into contact with the food, as opposed to cookware that simply will not corrode. In other words, all noncorrosive cookware is nonreactive, but the possible reactions cookware can have are not limited to corrosion.

Copper, for example, is a reactive metal. When it comes into contact with food, copper ions can easily leach into it. This is not necessarily a bad thing—copper can intensify the green color of cooked vegetables, for example, and copper is excellent for cooking sugar (see **Sugar pan**) and whipping eggs and egg whites. However, it can also react in a negative way by changing the color of a food or changing its flavor when it is used with acid ingredients. Further, ingesting copper can cause medical problems if too much is consumed, because the body is able to excrete copper in very small amounts only.

Nutmeg grater—See **Grater**.

Nutmeg grinder—A hand-held kitchen tool used to grind whole nutmeg into a powder. These grinders come in a variety of shapes and sizes and are made in materials ranging from sterling silver to stainless steel. The grinder is similar in appearance to a pepper mill, except the interior canister is designed to accommodate a whole nutmeg. When the top crank is turned, the nutmeg is grated. A spring inside the center canister presses the nutmeg toward the bottom where it comes in contact with the sharp blade.

Nut mill—A piece of kitchen equipment that pulverizes shelled nuts without releasing their natural oil. Nut mills are usually made of enameled cast iron and attach to the work surface with a clamp and screw mechanism.

O

Oven—The most common and frequently used appliance in any kitchen. It is used to bake, roast, and heat at a particular steady temperature that can be adjusted by using buttons (as in some modern ovens) or a dial with temperature markings on it. The temperature is listed in Fahrenheit or centigrade, depending on the manufacturer, and can be powered by gas, electricity, or fire. See **Convection oven, Deck oven, Hearth, Rack oven, Rotating oven,** and **Tandoor oven.**

P

Paddle attachment—See **Mixer**.
Palette knife—See **Spatula**.

Parchment paper—See **Baking paper**.

Parfait mold—Tall, tapered, cylindrical molds used to freeze individual servings of parfaits, a type of still frozen dessert. Some parfait molds have a rounded dome shape on top, in which case they have tightly fitting lids so that they can be frozen, right-side up, on their flat base. Others are thimble-shaped—flat on both the top and bottom, so they can be filled and frozen upside down without the need for a lid. Parfaits are unmolded and decorated before serving. The word *parfait* is French for "perfect." Parfaits are made from a mixture of egg yolks and sugar syrup whipped to the ribbon stage, with the addition of whipped cream and flavoring.

Pastry bag—A cone-shaped plastic, nylon, or cloth bag that comes in lengths from 7 inches (17.5 cm) to over 20 inches (50 cm). When fitted with a **piping tip**, or pastry tip, it is used to pipe out batter, dough, whipped cream, soft fillings such as lemon curd or ganache, and for portioning mixtures into molds or forms. For information on filling, working with, and caring for pastry bags, see pages 52 and 53.

Pastry bag rack—A rack for drying pastry bags after washing. Pastry bags should never be left flat to dry. After washing, they need dry on the inside as well as the outside as quickly as possible to prevent bacteria from growing; therefore, they need air circulation around both sides. A drying rack usually comprises between four and eight *V*-shaped arms that the bags can be hung on by sliding them on top. Most racks also have holders for piping tips and sometimes pastry brushes as well.

Pastry blender—A hand-held kitchen utensil used to blend cold fat into flour while preparing pastry dough. It is *U*-shaped, with the handle connecting the ends. The round bottom has several parallel wires. This tool facilitates working the fat into the flour until it is in small pieces and not completely blended.

Pastry brush—See **Brush**.

Pastry chef's knife—See **Knife**.

Pastry cloth—A large piece of lightweight material (usually canvas or plastic-coated cotton) that is used as a nonstick surface when rolling out pastry dough. The cloth needs to be brushed with flour before the dough is rolled out to prevent sticking. These cloths are rarely used in a professional kitchen.

Pastry comb—See **Cake-decorating comb**.

Pastry cutter—Professional pastry cutters or cookie cutters come in round, oval, square, triangular, rectangular, star, and heart shapes in sets of graduating sizes, in both plain and fluted styles. They are typically made of stainless steel or coated sheet metal.

A newer version is now being made from a composite plastic and fiberglass material; Exoglass is one trademarked name of this substance. These cutters have multiple advantages: They are nonstick and do not need to be dipped into flour between cuts; they are seamless, so there are no crevices in which bacteria can grow; they can withstand temperatures over 400°F (205°C), so they can be cleaned in a commercial dishwasher; and, because they are not made out of metal, they are rust-proof. Other cutters, for both professional and home use, are available in a multitude of shapes and sizes for special occasions and specific recipes. See **Cookie cutter**.

Pastry jagger—A **pastry wheel** with a fluted edge that creates a decorative design in pastry dough.

Pastry ribbon—PVC or acetate sold on a roll in a continuous strip. The ribbon is typically available in widths between 1½ and 2¾ inches (3.7 and 7 cm). It is used line pastry forms. See **Acetate strip**.

Pastry scraper—See **Scraper**.

Pastry tip—See **Piping tip**.

Pastry wheel—A sharp, round disk, fluted or straight, attached to a handle. It is rolled over a sheet of dough to cut straight lines. The best and most expensive models have a small attached wheel that follows the cutting blade to keep the dough flat and prevent it from curling up as a result of the cutting motion. Pastry wheels with plain blades are also known as *pizza wheels* and *pizza cutters*.

Peel—See **Baker's peel**. The word *peel* also means the outer skin of fruits and vegetables.

Perforated sheet pan—A metal baking sheet with tiny holes, used to promote a crisp crust and ensure proper baking on the bottom of breads and rolls baked in a **rack oven**. In a steam oven, perforated pans also help distribute the steam. The pans are used without **baking paper** and must be completely dry when the product is placed on top or it will stick. The pans are not used in regular shelf-type ovens because the product could become too dark on the bottom.

Petits fours cup—A small paper cup with fluted edges, made to hold individual pastries for display on a buffet or in a showcase.

Petits fours cutter—Any of the small metal cutters made in many classic shapes such as hearts, fluted circles, teardrops, diamonds, and hexagons. They are usually sold in sets. Petits fours cutters measure 1 to 2 inches (2.5 to 5 cm) high and 1 to 1½ inches (2.5 to 3.7 cm) in diameter. They are used to cut out individual petits fours from assembled petits fours sheets (alternating layers of thin sponge and filling).

Petits fours mold—A kind of miniature shallow metal form, available in numerous shapes such as oval, round, triangular, diamond, and boat, used to form a style of petit four that is like a tiny tartlet; these are known as *Viennese petits fours*. The molds have either smooth or fluted edges, range in size from 1¼ to 1½ inches (3.1 to 3.7 cm) in diameter, and are typically ½ inch (1.2 cm) deep. They are often sold in sets of assorted shapes. The molds are also made in configurations in which several forms are soldered to a metal bar. This makes it possible to move the molds from the table to the oven more efficiently. The forms can also be used for molding chocolates.

Pie weight—Pie weights are small aluminum or ceramic pellets used to weigh down a dough or crust to prevent it from expanding too much during baking. Dried beans are a common substitution.

Pincer—A hand tool with two flat, springy arms that have a fluted pattern on the edges. Pincers are available in several widths and shapes and are used for decorating the edges of pie crusts and to pinch designs on marzipan.

Piping bag—A small paper cone, approximately 5 inches (12.5 cm) long, used to pipe out precise and delicate decorations. Piping bags are held using the fingers only; they also called *cornets*. See page 56.

Piping bottle—A small plastic squeeze bottle with a capacity of 1 to 2 cups (240 to 480 ml) and a narrow opening, used mostly to portion sauce onto dessert plates.

Piping tip—Also known as a *pastry tip, pastry tube, icing tube,* and *decorating tube*. A piping tip is a small, hollow cone made of metal, plastic, or a plastic composite; it is used in conjunction with a pastry bag to shape the mixture as it is piped out of the bag. The tips come in various designs and sizes for specific uses, but the basic styles are plain, which produces a smooth edge, and star, which makes a fluted pattern. Star tip variations include open star tips, closed star tips, and French star tips. On an open star tip, the teeth or points at the end of the tip are straight; a closed star tip is not actually closed, but the teeth are bent in toward the center. A French star tip has a greater number of smaller teeth, so it produces a more finely fluted pattern.

There is no standardized sizing when it comes to pastry tips, which can be very confusing. They are made by a multitude of companies all over the world, and each one seems to have its own numbering system. Many of the European-made tips have the size of the opening stamped on the side of the tip—for example, the numeral 6 may indicate that the tip opening is 6 mm; in some cases, the number might be printed as *6 mm,* which makes it easy. However, another company might make a set of tips in which the number 6 happens to measure 4 mm or 10 mm; in other words, the number printed on the tip (if there is one) may or may not have to do with the actual size. In many cases, it is simply a catalog number.

What I consider basic production tips, and the tips that are specified in the recipes throughout this text, are plain and open star tips with openings that range in size from 2 mm to 18 mm. Star tips are measured across the diameter of the opening with the points straight, not bent. I refer them by number as follows:

No. 1	2 mm	No. 4	8 mm	No. 7	14 mm
No. 2	4 mm	No. 5	10 mm	No. 8	16 mm
No. 3	6 mm	No. 6	12 mm	No. 9	18 mm

Figure B-2 shows the actual size of the tip openings. If you are uncertain of the size of a particular tip, you can hold the opening of the tip against the chart for comparison. If you not have the precise number or size specified in a recipe, in most cases, as long as the size is close, it will do.

Other useful tips are:
- Flat tips in both plain and star styles; these resemble regular tips that have been smashed or flattened and, as a matter of fact, instead of buying them, you can make them yourself by doing just that using a heavy object.
- A flat tip that has one plain and one fluted side; these are used to make basketweave patterns.
- Different sizes of square tip, which you can also make yourself from a plain tip.
- **Saint-Honoré tips**, which come in two or three sizes—and yes, you can even make this tip yourself by taking a No. 6 to No. 8 (12 to 16 mm) plain tip and, using a metal cutter, cutting a narrow wedge, approximately ¾ inch (2 cm) long, starting from the opening.
- Curved and straight rose petal tips.
- Leaf tips.

For the most part, a pastry tip goes inside the pastry bag before the filling is added. There are occasions where a tip might be placed on the outside of the bag and held in place using the fingers of one hand while applying pressure to the bag with the other hand, but that is a special circumstance. There are also very small, specialized tips used for making flowers, leaves, and precise decorations. These are used by attaching them to the outside of a bag using a **coupler**. They are almost always sold in sets.

Pitter—See **Cherry pitter**.

Pizza pan—A round metal sheet pan used to bake a circular pizza. It is shallow, with a slightly raised, ringed rim. Some varieties of pizza pan have perforated bottoms that allow moisture to escape during baking.

Pizza peel—See **Baker's peel**.

Pizza stone—See **Baking stone**.

Pizza wheel—See **Pastry wheel**.

Pizelle iron—The kitchen utensil used to create pizelles. This hand-held iron consists of two flat, round engraved plates, 5 inches (12.5 cm) in diameter, attached with a hinge. The batter is placed on the center of one plate and the two plates are joined. Then the iron is placed on a ring that rests on a stovetop burner. Pizelle irons are available with various etchings to imprint the cookies (stars, flowers, ribbons, etc.). One type of pizelle iron is capable of making four small pizelles at once. In addition to the traditional iron that is placed on top of the stovetop burner, an electric iron is available.

Plastic squeeze bottle—See **Piping bottle**.

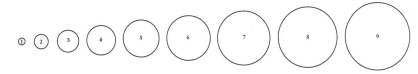

FIGURE B-2 Actual size of tip openings

Plastic strip—See **Acetate strip** and **Pastry ribbon.**

Plastic wrap—An extremely thin, transparent film of plastic sold on a continuous roll. The film clings to both food and containers, creating an airtight seal that protects food from drying out and from spoilage. The majority of plastic wraps are made from polyethylene, which is not absorbed by food to any degree. Plastic wrap is sold in different widths and thickness.

Plate holding rack—These are fairly new to the industry and rather expensive, but they save a great deal of time and space when plating cold or room-temperature food for large banquets. The racks have a central pole attached to a metal frame base, which has locking wheels. The pole has horizontal support posts that extend from all sides and go from top to bottom. These can be adjusted and locked into place to accommodate the diameter of plate and the height of the contents. As the plates of food are made up, they are placed on the rack, where they are suspended in a flat position. Depending on the size of the plates and how close you can place them (if the presentation is flat, you can place them very close together without damage), one rack can hold close to 100 plates in only about 2 square feet (60 square cm) of floor space. The rack can be rolled into the walk-in to keep the plates and their contents cold until needed. In some operations, it is helpful to be able to move the rack closer to the dining room so the servers can make shorter trips back and forth.

It is important to consider the quality of the final product before plating too far in advance. Obviously, some items must be finished at the last moment or they will dry out, become soggy, or sauces will run together, etc. However, many desserts can hold up just fine for 30 minutes to an hour, and often, when there is a large banquet, all the table space is in use until it is time to plate the dessert course because the other courses are being plated and served first (it is our fate to always be the last ones out of the kitchen). Another use for the plate rack is to be able to make up all of the plates partway, then finish each one to order. For instance, the main components can be arranged on the plates and placed on the rack; a sauce and garnish can be quickly added to each as the servers pick up.

Plättiron—See **Small Swedish pancakes pan.**

Pots-de-crème form—Small ceramic forms with tight-fitting lids, used to bake and serve individual portions of custard. Each lid has a small hole to allow steam to escape.

Pricker—See **Docker.**

Proof box—A cabinet or room in which heat and humidity are controlled to create the correct environment for a yeast dough to proof (rise). Ideally, the temperature is about 80°F (26°C), with 85 percent humidity.

Prover—Another name for a **proof box.**

Pullman pan—A baking pan used to make pullman bread loaves. The pan has a sliding top so the loaf is enclosed on all four sides during baking. Pullman pans have a larger capacity than the average bread pan. The typical size measures 16 inches (40 cm) long, 4 inches (10 cm) high and across the base, and just slightly wider across the top.

R

Rack oven—A large convection oven holding one to four **baker's racks** at a time. The ovens are very expensive but save time by producing a large quantity of evenly browned breads, rolls, or other baked goods at once. The ovens come with racks specifically designed to fit each oven. The rack is rolled into the oven and locked onto an arm that rotates the rack during baking. Each rack holds about 15 full-size **sheet pans.** Rack ovens are usually equipped with **steam injectors.** Because the sheet pans do not come in contact with the bottom of the oven, as they do in **deck** and **rotating ovens,** it is necessary, with some recipes, to use **perforated sheet** pans so the product will brown on the bottom; this is especially true of bread products.

Ramekin—A shallow earthenware dish in which a single portion (e.g., an individual soufflé) is baked and served. Ramekins are also used to mold chilled custard desserts. The most common size measures about 3¼ inches (8.1 cm) across and 1½ inches (3.7 cm) high and holds 5 ounces (150 ml).

Reamer—See **Citrus reamer.**

Rectangular fluted pan—A metal baking pan, generally used for tea cakes. The pans are rectangular on the top but they slope down to a rounded, deeply fluted design on the bottom. The pans measure 10 to 14 inches (25 to 35 cm) long, 4½ inches (11.2 cm) wide, and 2½ inches (6.2 cm) deep, and are usually made of tinned steel or aluminum. They are also known by the German name of *Rehrücken,* or "saddle-of-venison" pans, because these molds are used to bake the classic Austrian cake by that name that is designed to look like a saddle of venison. Some pans not only have fluted sides but also a deep groove down the center to represent the center bone of the saddle of the venison.

Rehrücken pan—See **Rectangular fluted pan.**

Rolling pin—Rolling pins are available in a wide array of sizes and are made from materials such as brass, plastic, marble, and porcelain in addition to wood. There are even hollow rolling pins made of glass that are designed to be filled with ice to keep dough cold as it is rolled out. Some rolling pins are more suited for decorative use than actual production, especially in a professional kitchen. A solid cylinder made of hardwood, 12 to 16 inches (30 to 40 cm) long and 3 to 4 inches (7.5 to 10 cm) in diameter, is preferable. Such cylinders are made in two styles; the more common has a steel rod and ball bearings inside with handles on both ends. The other very practical version has a removable wooden or treated aluminum **dowel** inserted through the center of the rolling pin that extends about 4 inches (10 cm) on either side to act as a handle. The dowel can also be used separately to assist in transferring dough sheets and as a guide when cutting dough sheets. The latter is unbreakable, whereas the former can be bent if dropped accidentally, for example, making the pin unusable.

Adjustable rolling pin—This type of rolling pin is used for rolling out fillings for chocolates and candies to a precisely even thickness. The pin comes with several sets of detachable round caps in varying diameters that can be snapped onto the ends of the pin so that it sits closer to or farther from from the work surface. The thickness can be adjusted from $1/16$ inch to 4 inches (2 mm to 10 cm).

Basketweave rolling pin—A decorating tool made of a textured plastic cylinder with attached handles. When rolled over a sheet of marzipan or rolled fondant, it imprints a basketweave pattern. Different pins produce deeper and more defined patterns than others.

French rolling pin—A thin wooden cylinder, about 18 inches (45 cm) long without handles. It is 2 inches (5 cm) in diameter at the center and tapers from there toward each end; it is used for rolling out circular shapes.

Marzipan rolling pin—A decorating tool in the shape of a hollow plastic tube that creates a pattern when it is rolled over a sheet of marzipan. Of the two most common pins, one marks a pattern of fine parallel lines (this is sometimes called a *tread rolling pin*) and the other produces a checkered (waffle) design. Marzipan rolling pins are also used to decorate sheets of rolled fondant.

Pastry or pizza rolling pin—Also called a *broom-handle* or *speed rolling pin*. It is intended for small pieces of dough. These rolling pins have only one handle, which is either attached at a 90-degree angle to a frame suspended over and parallel to the pin and attached at each end or is itself suspended over and parallel to the pin and attached to each end of the pin at a right angle. Because only one hand is required when working with this type of pin, the other hand is free to turn the dough. These rolling pins are made of wood and are 4 to 10 inches (10 to 25 cm) long and 2 inches (5 cm) in diameter.

Springerle rolling pins—See **Springerle mold**.

Rose nail—A flat disk, about 1 inch (2.5 cm) in diameter, attached to a thin pinlike handle. The pastry chef pipes icing roses onto this tool, then removes them with a small spatula or scissors.

Rosette iron—A tool used to prepare a type of deep-fried cookie from Sweden. Rosettes are called *Sockerstruvor* in Swedish. They are fragile, crisp fried shells made in several shapes.

The rosette iron consists of an *L*-shaped metal rod with a handle and several interchangeable metal forms that fasten to the end of the rod. The forms are made in a variety of cutout designs such as snowflakes, butterflies, hearts, trees, wheels, and stars. To make the cookies, attach the chosen design to the shorter end of the *L*-shaped rod and heat the form in oil for deep-frying. Dip the bottom and sides of the form into the cookie batter (made of eggs, cream, sugar, and flour) and return the iron to the oil until the cookie is cooked through and golden brown. It is important to not let the batter go over the top of the form as you dip it in the batter. If it does, you will not be able to remove the cookie from the iron once it is cooked. The fried cookies are drained on paper toweling, then coated with sugar.

Rotary beater—Used in the same fashion as an electric beater, except a rotary beater is operated by hand. Two long metal beaters are connected to a center shaft and operated by a hand crank on the side of the shaft. The chef steadies the device by holding the handle on the top with one hand while operating the crank with the other. The speed of the beaters is determined by how fast one rotates the crank.

Rotary slicer—Also called a *spin scraper*. This slicer was originally made for shaving off thin slices of cheese; the best-known brand name is Girolle. The machine consists of a heavy round base with a vertical spike in the center, a sharp horizontal blade with a loop to fit over the spike on one end, and a handle with a knob used to turn it on the other end. A wheel of cheese is placed on the spike, the blade is placed on top, and the blade is rotated with light downward pressure to scrape off thin slices.

Chocolate manufacturers are now selling disks of chocolate that are made to fit this tool so that it can be used to create chocolate ruffles and fans. By rotating the crank and scraping the blade over the surface of the chocolate, you can produce a ruffled chocolate fan very quickly and easily. The chocolate disks have a hole in the center to fit over the spike on the machine. They are available in solid-colored wheels of dark, milk, or white chocolate, and wheels made from dark, milk, and/or white chocolate in various combinations to produce striped and marbled fans.

Rotary grater—See **Grater**.

Rotating oven—Also known as a *revolving oven*. Rotating ovens are large and bulky. The shelves that hold the sheet pans move around inside the oven like a Ferris wheel. The amount of space required makes them impractical, but, on the positive side, they eliminate the potential for hot spots because the products are in constant rotation. The modern version of the rotating oven is the smaller, more efficient **rack oven**.

Rubber spatula—See **Spatula**.

S

Saccharimeter—The instrument used to measure the sugar concentration in a liquid. See **Thermometer**.

Saccharometer—See **Thermometer**.

Saddle-of-venison cake pan—See **Rectangular fluted pan**.

Saint-Honoré pastry tip—A special **piping tip** used to make the classic decoration on the top of the gâteau Saint-Honoré. The item piped through the tip (a custard, buttercream, mousse, etc.) in formed into an interesting wedge shape. In the case of the gâteau Saint-Honoré, the tip is used to pipe cream chiboust over the top of the cake in a pattern that looks a bit as if two spoons were used to distribute quenelle-shaped dollops of the mixture. The Saint-Honoré tip is currently enjoying something of a rebirth, as chefs have discovered it is an easy way to make an unusual design on the top of other cakes and pastries as well. It can be used to pipe whipped cream, for example, in a single interesting curved wedge for a more modern look than the classic rosette; it can be used to pipe buttercream in interlocking curved lines across or around a cake; and it gives a very good result when used to pipe curved lines radiating from a central point. A Saint-Honoré tip looks like a regular plain (not fluted) tip with a wedge cut out of one side extending from the opening to about halfway down the length of the tip. The traditional size has a ³/₄-inch (2-cm) opening, but today the tips are made in a variety of smaller sizes and, like other piping tips, in both stainless steel and plastic.

Sajj—A convex, dome-shaped pan or griddle that is placed over a fire or burner on a stovetop. It is traditionally used for cooking several types of flatbread. An inverted heavy-duty wok, used in the same fashion, makes a fine substitute.

Salamander—A gas-fired broiler with the heat source at the top. It is used to brown or caramelize food, such as the sugar on top of a crème brûlée or the Italian meringue on top of a tart. The name is also used for a hand tool made of a thick iron disk suspended from a long metal shaft with a metal or wooden handle. This type of salamander is also called a *caramelizer*. To use it, heat the disk in a gas flame until is extremely hot, then hold it just above the food item to brown it. While the original caramelizer is a very old-fashioned tool, both an electric version and one that can be attached to and heated by a portable propane tank are also available.

Sauce gun—See **Fondant funnel.**

Savarin mold—Made in individual-serving sizes, about 2³/₄ to 3¹/₂ inches (7 to 8.7 cm) in diameter, and in larger sizes of up to 10 or 12 inches (25 to 30 cm) in diameter. Savarin forms are shallow rings used for baking savarins, as the name suggests, but they can also be used for baking or molding many other pastries and desserts. The molds are not too tall (³/₄ inch/2 cm for the individual size to 1¹/₂ to 2 inches/3.7 to 5 cm for the larger sizes), and they have a relatively large open hole in the center when compared to a tube pan, for example.

Scales

Balance scale—Also known as *baker's scale* and *balance-beam scale*. The balance scale uses an added weight counterbalancing system with two platforms, one on the left and one on the right, attached to a horizontal balance beam. Counterweights, sized at 1, 2, 4, and 8 pounds, are used to set the scale to the amount of weight you want to measure. An ounce bar on the front of the balance beam has a sliding weight that can be set between 1 and 16 ounces to add ounce increments. Balance scales are designed for use with a specific container (the scale bowl) to hold the ingredient to be weighed and a scale-bowl counterweight (a special weight that is the same weight as the bowl) to compensate for the weight of the bowl. If you use the scale bowl without the scale-bowl counterweight in addition to the counterweights that add up to your desired measurement, you will not get an accurate reading.

The advantage to the balance scale is that it can accommodate a large amount of product to be weighed because it is not limited to the capacity of a spring. This type of scale is not very accurate for measuring quantities less than 1 ounce (30 g), however.

How to Use a Balance Scale

1. Be certain that the scale is resting on a level surface.
2. Place the scale bowl on the left platform and the scale-bowl counterweight on the right platform. Set the weight on the ounce bar to zero; the scale should be balanced.
3. Set the scale for the amount of product you want to measure. For example, to weigh out 6 pounds 10 ounces of flour, place the 4-pound and the 2-pound counterweights on the right platform (along with the scale-bowl counterweight) and move the sliding weight on the ounce bar in front to 10 ounces. The balance beam will tilt down to the right.
4. Begin adding flour to the scale bowl and stop when the balance beam is level.
5. If you do not use the scale bowl or another container and instead place the ingredient directly on the platform, the product to be weighed must still be placed on the left platform and the counterweights on the right or you will not be able to use the ounce bar.

If you use a container other than the scale bowl to hold the ingredient to be measured, you must compensate for the weight of the container, just as with the scale bowl, in order to obtain an accurate reading. If you know the weight of your container, set the ounce bar and/or add counterweights in that amount before adding the amount of counterweights and/or moving the ounce bar in Step 3. Example: You are using a container that weighs 1 pound 4 ounces. You want to weigh out 4 pounds 6 ounces of flour. Place your container on the left platform. Add the 1-pound counterweight to the right platform and move the sliding weight on the ounce bar to 4 ounces. The scale is now balanced. Next, add the 4-pound counterweight to the right platform and move the ounce control to 10 (because it was already at 4 to balance the scale and you want to add 6 ounces for your measurement, which equals 10). Add flour to the container until the scale is balanced.

If you do not know the weight of your container, place it on the left platform and set the ounce bar and/or add counterweights until the scale balances. If the ounce bar is set all the way to 16, place a 1-pound counterweight on the right platform instead and set the ounce bar back to zero so you will be able to use it in setting the desired measurement.

The same principle applies anytime you can not set the ounce bar to the desired number because it has been set too high for the initial balance. Example: You have used a 1-pound counterweight and set the ounce bar to 10 to compensate for your container. You need to weigh out 1 pound 12 ounces of flour. You add a 1-pound counterweight to the right platform, but you cannot move the ounce device another 12 places because it is already at 10. Instead, you would add a second 1-pound counterweight to the right platform (placing you 4 ounces over your desired target) and subtract 4 ounces on the ounce bar by setting it down from 10 to 6.

Electronic scale—This is the most convenient and efficient type of scale to use. It uses a spring mechanism like the spring scale but has a digital readout that can be zeroed. This allows you to weigh one ingredient on top of another without adding the measurements together, or to compensate for the weight of a container by placing the empty container on the scale, setting the readout back to zero, then adding the product to be weighed. Electronic scales are by far the most expensive of the three types discussed here, but they pay off in the long run by contributing to efficiency and reducing human error.

Spring scale—Also known as *portion scale.* This is, indeed, best suited for portion control in a professional kitchen rather than for use in weighing ingredients. It uses a spring mechanism with a round dial and has one small, flat tray. Spring scales are available calibrated in ounces, pounds, or grams.

Scraper—See also **Spatula.**

Bench scraper—Also called *baker's helper* and *dough scraper.* A hand tool designed for cleaning and scraping the surface of a wooden workbench in the kitchen where doughs are rolled out and formed. Bench scrapers consist of a thin, rectangular stainless-steel blade, approximately 6 inches (15 cm) wide by 4 inches (10 cm) tall, with a wooden or plastic handle; they can also be made from a solid piece of stainless steel, with one long edge rolled to form the handle. In addition to being used to clean the top of a worktable, they are used for cutting and portioning dough, cutting baked goods, such as cookies, into pieces, and can be used like a spatula to transfer items.

Bowl scraper—Also known as a *pastry scraper,* this hand tool is made from a thin and flexible yet sturdy piece of plastic that measures approximately 5½ inches (13.7 cm) long by 3½ inches (8.7 cm) tall and has a curved edge on one long side. The tool is flexible enough to bend so that it can be pressed tightly against interior of a mixing bowl to scrape down the contents. Bowl scrapers are also handy for removing dough from a rolling pin because they can be bent to fit the curve of the pin, and they are used for some of the same purposes as bench scrapers.

Dough scraper—See **Bench scraper.**

Pastry scraper—See **Bowl scraper.**

Sheet pan—A metal baking sheet used in professional kitchens. The full-size pan measures 24 x 16 inches (60 x 40 cm) and has 1-inch (2.5-cm) sides. Half-sheet pans are 16 x 12 inches (40 x 30 cm); quarter-sized sheet pans measure 12 x 8 inches (30 x 20 cm). Half- and quarter-sized pans will fit the home oven.

Sheet pan extender—A stainless steel frame made to fit within standard-size full- or half-sheet pans. The frames are 2 inches (5 cm) tall, whereas sheet pans have sides 1 inch (2.5 cm) high. Placing the frame on top of the sheet pan allows the pan to be used to bake taller cakes or mold taller products than would be possible without it.

Sheeter—See **Dough sheeter.**

Shortbread mold—A wooden mold, about 7 inches (17.5 cm) in diameter and with a distinctive thistle imprint, in which shortbread is baked. When the cookie disk is unmolded, the pattern is revealed.

Sieve—Any type of **strainer** is technically a sieve, but, for the most part, the term *sieve* is used for a circular freestanding wooden, metal, or plastic frame about 4 inches (10 cm) high, with a mesh screen stretched across the interior. This is also called a *drum sieve* and by the French term **Tamis.** The mesh is usually metal, but some very fine mesh sieves use a nylon mesh. Metal or wire mesh chosen for use can be very fine to very coarse, depending on the application. Sieves are used for sifting dry ingredients, such as flour or powdered sugar, for removing small pieces of skin from chopped nuts, and for removing lumps from soft food products, which can be forced through the mesh to make the product smooth. Sieves for the professional kitchen are generally 12 to 14 inches (30 to 35 cm) in diameter and can be purchased with fine, medium, or coarse mesh. The word sieve is also used as a verb meaning "to use a sieve" or "to strain."

Sifter—A tool used to aerate (add air to) flour and/or other dry ingredients such as cornstarch, powdered sugar, and cocoa powder. Sifting is also done to remove or break up lumps in the dry ingredient, and may also be done to combine two or more dry ingredients evenly. Sifters come in many sizes. Often, a **strainer** is used for the same purpose.

Silicone baking mat—Referred to in this text by the brand name *Silpat.* This is a nonstick pan liner made from glass fabric covered with food-grade silicone. Silpats are made in sizes that fit full- or half-sheet pans and are used instead of **baking paper** or greasing and flouring the pan. These thin (approximately ⅛ inch/3 mm) soft, flexible sheets are able to withstand temperatures from –40° to 480°F (–40° to 250°C) and can be reused thousands of times. Silicone mats are also used for sugar work because they can tolerate high temperatures and do not need to be greased or oiled. Silicone mats should be washed using a soft, nonabrasive sponge or cloth and hot water or just wiped clean. See **Flexipan.**

Silicone baking mold—See **Flexipan.**

Silicone decorating stamp—These stamps are also called *silicone presses.* They are two-piece rubber molds with a concave pattern on one piece and convex pattern on the other. The molds are most often made with a leaf or flower design. A small portion of marzipan, modeling chocolate, pulled sugar, or rolled fondant is firmly pressed between the two pieces to produce a three-dimensional decoration.

Silk screen—Silk screens are used to create incredibly

detailed images on thin sheets of sponge cake. These are most often cut into strips and used to decorate the sides of cakes or pastries. Alternatively, silk screens can be used to print a design on thin sheets of rolled marzipan, in which case the decorated marzipan is usually placed on the top of a cake. Silk screens come in many patterns; some are abstract, such as marbled or swirled designs, while others depict musical notes, fruits, or flowers, and there are even some that portray hobbies such as boating, golfing, and fishing. Custom-made patterns with a business name or logo may also be specially ordered.

Each screen is made up of material that is tightly stretched within a permanent frame. The pattern that you will see on your finished product is imprinted on the material as a negative image, just as with other printing processes. In addition to the screen, you need a special long rubber scraper that is used to push the decorating paste through the fabric evenly without damaging the thin material. The screens come in sizes to fit standard full- and half- sheet Silpats and sheet pans.

To use the screen to create a decorated sponge sheet, place it on top of a Silpat. Pour a ribbon of cocoa-paste along the top short edge. Pull the rubber scraper evenly along the length of the screen, pushing the cocoa paste through the silk and transferring the pattern onto the Silpat (baking paper can be used too, but it tends to wrinkle when the sponge batter is added). Allow the design dry , then spread a sponge cake batter (specially formulated for this use) on top of the cocoa pattern and bake the sheet. When you unmold the sponge sheet, the pattern appears on the surface. Cut the thin sponge into strips of the desired width to line a dessert mold or to wrap around the side of a finished cake.

To use the screen to decorate marzipan, follow the same procedure, but place the screen directly on a sheet of thinly rolled marzipan. After printing, allow the sheet to dry (do not bake the marzipan as is done with the sponge cake). Cut the marzipan into a round to fit the top of a cake or into strips, as described above. Silk screens must be handled and cleaned very carefully, as even the smallest tear in the fabric will make the screen unusable.

Silpat—The brand name of a type of **Silicone baking mat.**

Silpain—The brand name of a baking mat made especially for baking bread. It has the same nonstick properties discussed under **Silicone baking mat** but is made with an open mesh for better air circulation and with a dark-colored surface to enhance browning. Silpain mats are made by the Demarle Company, which also makes **Silpat** and **Flexipans.**

Skimmer—A flat, finely meshed strainer (or one with small holes) attached to a handle, used to remove particles or scum from a boiling liquid, to poach, and to deep fry.

Small Swedish pancakes pan—A round cast-iron skillet measuring 9 to 10 inches (22.5 to 25 cm) in diameter. The skillet has five to seven round depressions, 2½ to 3 inches (6.2 to 7.5 cm) in diameter, to form pancakes as they are cooking. In addition, the pans are great for making blini. Called *Plättiron* in Swedish.

Soufflé dish; Soufflé ramekin—A round ceramic form with straight sides. Soufflé dishes generally have a fluted pattern on the outside. Soufflés are baked and served in the same form. The two most common sizes for individual servings are 3¼ inches (8.1 cm) in diameter, with a capacity of approximately 5 ounces (150 ml), and 4¼ inches (11.2 cm) in diameter, which holds about 1 cup (240 ml). The largest size has a capacity of 2 quarts (1 L 920 ml) and serves eight to ten.

Spatula—Spatulas are made from any of a variety of materials, including rubber, stainless steel, plastic and plastic composites, silicone, and wood. They vary widely in shape and size, depending on their purpose, which is generally transferring, smoothing, or scraping. In the pastry kitchen, several types of spatulas are used. See also **Scraper.**

Flexible spatula—Elongated spatula also known as *icing spatula* and *palette knife*. These spatulas have stainless-steel, wood, or plastic handles and stainless-steel blades in lengths from 4 to 14 inches (10 to 35 cm); the width of the blade generally increases in proportion to the length. The blade is always a long rectangular shape with a rounded tip. The most practical size for everyday use has a 10-inch (25-cm) blade that is 1½ inches (3.7 cm) wide. Flexible spatulas have a multitude of uses in the pastry kitchen, including applying icings, glazes, and buttercream; spreading batters or melted chocolate into sheets and/or within templates; and moving cake layers.

Offset flexible spatula—Offset spatulas are like plain flexible spatulas except that the blade is bent at almost a 90-degree angle about 2 inches (5 cm) from the handle, then bent again to become parallel to the handle. The advantage to this shape is that it allows you to spread a product very thin without the edge of the baking pan, the handle of the spatula, or your hand getting in the way. Offset flexible spatulas are also known as *gooseneck spatulas, offset icing spatulas,* and *offset palette knives*. Offset flexible spatulas are made with blades that range in size from 3½-inch (8.7-cm) blades to 10-inch (25-cm) blades.

Rubber spatula—Also called a *bowl scraper*. Rubber spatulas have a flat or slightly cupped blade that is straight across the bottom next to the handle and rounded at the top; in some styles, one top corner is round and the other is square to make it easier to get into corners. The blades are made of rubber or one of the new heat-resistant and nonstick composite materials that contain food-grade silicone, fiberglass, polyamide, or polytetrafluorethylene; these can withstand temperatures up to 500°F (260°C). Attached handles can be from plastic or wood. Some of the heat-resistant spatulas are made from one solid piece of material, which is beneficial, from a hygiene standpoint. Rubber spatulas typically have a 12-inch (30-cm) handle and a blade that measures 2 x 3 inches (5 x 7.5 cm). The heat-resistant spatulas, commonly referred to as *silicone rubber spatulas,* are excellent for use in the pastry kitchen. They not only can be used with very hot sugar or used to scrape the bottom of a hot pot with no danger of melting but they also do not absorb flavorings and odors they way conventional rubber spatulas do.

Triangular spatula—Triangular spatulas look like putty knives. They have rigid triangular blades with the wide edge in front and the tapered end attached to the handle. The blades are stainless or forged steel, and the handles are usually made of a rubber or plastic composite for a nonslip grip. The width of the blade is between 1 and 4 inches (2.5 to 10 cm). Triangular spatulas are used for scraping a pool of chocolate together in one form of chocolate tempering, for lifting and scraping boiled sugar or fondant as it cools, and for making chocolate ruffles and chocolate cigarettes.

Turning spatula—Turning spatulas have offset blades that are much shorter and wider than those of flexible spatulas. The blades are made from stainless steel or steel coated with a nonstick material, and they may be slotted. This type of spatula is used for transferring baked cookies from a sheet pan, for example.

Spring scale—See Scale.

Springerle mold—A very intricate cookie mold, originally carved from wood and now also made by casting a resin and wood composite. These molds are used to make the Swiss and German Christmas cookies called **springerle**, which are beautifully molded, anise-flavored cookies that have been closely associated with Christmas festivities in Europe for centuries. The molds are firmly pressed into the rolled dough, then lifted off to reveal the pattern. Springerle dough is formulated so that it does not change shape during baking (it is also baked at a very low temperature for the same reason), so even the tiniest details of the impression remain visible. Some of the very old and elaborately carved springerle molds are now on display in museums. Horses and other animals were popular ancient design themes, and other classic motifs include hunting scenes, baskets of fruit or flowers, which were symbols of prosperity, and biblical images. Many of these original molds are still passed down from generation to generation in Swiss and German families.

Springerle molds can also be used to press designs into rolled marzipan in much the same way as they are used to shape the cookies (of course, the marzipan is not baked as the cookies are). The marzipan pieces may be used as ornaments or placed on top of a cake or pastry. They can be left plain, lightly caramelized around the edges by using a blow torch, painted, or coated with a thin film of melted cocoa butter. Use marzipan that is quite firm so that it will hold the image from the mold.

Springerle rolling pin—Carved rolling pin used for making springerle cookies or decorative marzipan pieces. The same types of designs that appear on individual **springerle molds** are carved into a rolling pin instead. When the pin is rolled firmly over the dough, the designs are imprinted. The cookies are cut apart before baking.

Springform pan—A baking pan with removable sides, also called a *chesecake pan* as it is used mostly for baking cheesecakes. A clamp tightens the sides against the bottom.

Stencil grill—See Decorating grill.

Steam injector—A device on some commercial ovens that transmits steam into the oven during part of the baking time. The steam is used to create a crisp crust on bread and rolls. See pages 97 and 98.

Steamed pudding mold—A deep container, made of tinned steel or earthenware, used as a mold for making Christmas plum pudding or other traditional steamed puddings. The tinned-steel molds are commonly formed with fluted and sculpted sides, or with plain sides and a scalloped top. The earthenware molds are deep, glazed bowls with a pronounced rim. Some molds have a tube in the middle and a lid or cover that may be clamped onto the base.

Strainer—A mesh basket with a handle attached to the rim; available in a variety of designs for a variety of uses. Strainers are used to separate the solids from a liquid or the liquid from solids, and for sifting dry ingredients.

Strawberry huller—A small, wide piece of metal or plastic bent into a V-shape, with a textured gripping area on the tip. It is similar to a large pair of tweezers and is held in an open position by a spring or simply the tension of the bent material. It is used to remove the green stem and core (hull) from strawberries. A **melon ball tool** works just as well for this purpose.

Stripper—See Citrus stripper.

Sugar basket form—A form used as a guide when weaving ropes of pulled sugar into a basket. The form consists of a thick base made of wood or food-grade plastic, with a pattern of drilled holes and removable brass or steel dowels. Some models have several patterns of holes on the same base, allowing the user to form round, oval, diamond, or square baskets. Less expensive models produce a single size in either a round or oval shape, and other forms can be used to produce multiple sizes of either rounds or ovals; in these, the patterns of holes are arranged concentrically. The holes are drilled at a specific angle and spaced accurately to produce a particular shape. After the dowels are inserted into the holes, the sugar ropes are woven in and out around them. Once the sugar hardens, the dowels are pulled out and replaced with dowels made of sugar.

Sugar lamp—Also commonly referred to as a *warming lamp,* a sugar lamp is an essential component in sugar pulling and sugar blowing. The lamp is used to warm and soften hard portions of precooked and stored sugar and to keep the sugar mass malleable while the chef is forming it. A sugar lamp is generally composed of a large infrared bulb of 250 watts and 125 volts, attached either to the top of the **sugar warming case** or a flexible gooseneck stem. The opaque top of the bulb drives the light and its corresponding heat down to the round bottom surface of the bulb and onto the work surface below. The position of the bulb can be moved up and down to adjust the intensity of the heat, still leaving room between the work surface and the lamp where the sugar can be worked on by the chef.

Sugar pan—A heavy, unlined copper pan made especially for cooking sugar. The thickness of the pan helps the sugar to cook evenly without hot spots, and the acidity of the copper produces a chemical reaction that causes some of the sugar to break down into invert sugar (which is more resistant to recrystallization) during cooking. The sugar also cooks faster in this type of pan. A sugar pan has a small spout on the rim, which makes it easy to pour out the boiled sugar. The pans are available in sizes ranging from 2 cups to 5 quarts (480 ml to 4 L 800 ml). Most have hollow handles, sometimes made of a different material, such as stainless steel, to make the handle resistant to heat, and some are made with a metal ring attached about halfway up the side of the pan that sticks out to catch drips. Another helpful accessory sold with some pans is a lid with a hole designed to accommodate a sugar thermometer, allowing the chef to monitor the temperature of the sugar even when the pan is covered.

Sugar thermometer—See **Thermometer.**

Sugar warming case—A large box with solid top and bottom and transparent panels on the back, left, and right sides, leaving the front open. The top of the box accommodates a **sugar lamp;** a removable elevated work surface fits inside the base. The box is used for the procedures described under sugar lamp. The case is large enough that the chef can work on the sugar with his or her hands inside the box, protecting the sugar from air drafts and foreign particles.

Syrup density meter—See **Thermometer.**

T

Table brush—See **Brush.**

Tamis—The French name for a wooden or metal drum-shaped **sieve**, with metal or nylon mesh stretched tightly across the interior (*tamis* is French for "drum"). The fineness of the mesh varies. A tamis is typically used for removing seeds or fibrous material from food and for sifting larger quantities of ingredients. It is sometimes used in conjunction with a **champignon,** which is a mushroom-shaped wooden pestle that is used to push or mash the food through the mesh. Tamis can range from 6 to 16 inches (15 to 40 cm) in diameter. Those made with nylon mesh are more durable than those with metal mesh, and the nylon retains its shape better. A metal mesh is sharper and stronger but can rust if it is not dried and stored properly. The metal may also react with and discolor fruit purees.

Tandoor oven—The word *tandoor* and its many variations, including *tannur, tennur, tandir, tandore, tamdir, tandur, tanir,* and *tanoor,* all translate to "oven" in various languages of the Middle East and Central Asia. The basic tandoor design seems to have first been used in Iran. From there, it spread east to China and India, west to Tunisia and Morocco, and north to Turkey and Georgia. Every tandoor, regardless of size or the country it is used in, works on the same basic principle. Tandoors are round and stand vertically. They are encased in mud, concrete, or another insulating material and lined with clay. They are heated by fire, which is produced by burning wood, dung, coal, or gas at the base of the oven. Before the oven is used for cooking, it is preheated until the oven walls are extremely hot (approximately 500°F/260°C). Once the oven is hot, a damper is opened or the gas is lowered to create a steady heat that won't burn the outside of bread. Thin flatbread dough is placed on a baker's pillow, similar to an oven mitt with a handle on the back, and quickly slapped against the inside wall of the hot oven. The bread cooks very quickly. Breads cooked in a tandoor have a brown bottom with a lighter-colored top due to the one-sided baking technique. Other foods cooked in the tandoor include tandoori-style meat and poultry dishes, in which the meat or poultry is speared on long metal skewers and placed into the tandoor to cook.

Tart pan—A metal baking pan used for baking a tart for multiple servings. The tart pan most often used professionally is an 11-inch (27.5-cm) round that is 1 inch (2.5 cm) deep, but tarts are also made in square and rectangular shapes. Tart pans can be one solid piece or made in two pieces; these are called *false-bottomed pans.* The pans have straight, usually fluted sides.

False-bottomed tart pan—A tart pan with a removable bottom to simplify the removal of the baked tart. These pans are especially advantageous for custard-based tarts and quiches, which cannot be inverted for removal. However, any tart is less likely to be damaged if you can avoid inverting it, so false-bottomed tart pans are used for tarts with firm fillings as well.

Tartlet pan—Pans used for making small, individual tarts that are usually filled with fruit or custard. Tartlet pans can be plain or fluted. The fluted pans have straight sides, and the larger sizes are sometimes made in the false-bottomed style. The plain pans have sloping sides. Both styles are made in sizes from 2 to 4 inches (5 to 10 cm) in diameter and $^3/_8$ to 1¼ inches (9 mm to 3.1 cm) high. The deeper plain tartlet pans are also called *mazarin pans* in this text.

Thermometer—An accurate thermometer is an invaluable tool in the professional kitchen. Thermometers are essential for certain types of food preparation—checking the temperature of bread dough, tempering chocolate, and cooking sugar are examples in the pastry kitchen. They are equally important when it comes to food safety and sanitation. To this end, they are used to test the temperature of raw and cooked food products in storage units and the temperature of food that has been removed from storage to be served from the kitchen or on a buffet table.

Thermometers are also necessary to check that equipment such refrigerators, freezers, and dishwashers are operating at the proper temperature.

Thermometers are made of many materials in different shapes and sizes for specific uses. One of the most common types of thermometer used for cooking consists of a mercury-filled glass tube, with or without a stainless-steel casing. Although these are frequently used in residential kitchens and are found in most retail kitchen equipment stores, it is important to note they are, in fact, illegal for use in professional kitchens in some states.

Thermometers should always be handled carefully; glass thermometers are very fragile and can break easily, and almost all types of thermometers can give inaccurate readings if they have been dropped, handled roughly, or jostled in a drawer full of other tools. Mishandling can also cause the mercury to separate in a mercury thermometer and can cause air bubbles to form in the liquid in the case of a thermometer that uses an alcohol solution to register temperature.

Thermometers used for measuring the temperature of food products must be kept impeccably clean, and you should follow the manufacturer's instructions for doing so. Food residue left on a thermometer not only poses the risk of bacterial contamination but also, in working with boiled sugar, any foreign particle can cause the sugar to recrystallize.

Testing and Calibrating Thermometers

One-piece probe-type thermometers (both digital and manual), as well as glass thermometers, can be tested using the ice-point method or the boil-point method. The probe types can be calibrated, should they give an inaccurate reading. When a glass thermometer fails the test, your only choice is to compensate for the discrepancy when you use it by adding or subtracting the difference in degrees. This assumes it is off by a few degrees only; if the reading is way off, the thermometer should not be used.

To test using the ice-point method, fill a clean container with ice and water and place the thermometer in the liquid without allowing it to touch the container. It should register 32°F (0°C). If the reading is incorrect, you can calibrate a bimetallic stemmed probe thermometer in the following way. Keep the stem in the ice water and use a pair of pliers to firmly hold the adjusting nut located under the head. Turn the thermometer head until the pointer reads 32°F (0°C). Some one-piece digital thermometers have a reset button. These can be calibrated by pushing the reset button while the thermometer tip is still submerged in the ice water.

To test using the boil-point method, bring water to a boil in a clean pan and keep it boiling. Place the thermometer in the water without letting it touch the pan. It should read 212°F (100°C). If needed, you can calibrate following the same instructions given for the ice-point method, in this case making the adjustment or using the reset button while the stem is submerged in the boiling water.

Regulations Regarding the Use of Mercury-Filled Glass Thermometers in Professional Kitchens

In California, it is illegal to use mercury-filled glass thermometers in a professional kitchen. The California Uniform Retail Food Facility Law governs such practices, and the law is clear that mercury thermometers are not approved for use in commercial or public food preparation facilities. The reasoning behind this is the risk of contaminating food with mercury, which is poisonous, should the glass break. Glass thermometers that use alcohol to indicate the temperature may be used; however, the state recommends that restaurant and commercial kitchens use bimetallic stem probe thermometers (commonly called *instant-read thermometers*) or digital probe thermometers instead. With these, not only is the risk of mercury poisoning eliminated, there is no potential for broken glass and, in the case of thermocouple digital probe thermometers, because different probes are used for different types of food products, there is less risk of cross-contamination. If you are unsure as to whether a thermometer contains mercury or alcohol, note that the alcohol solution is generally tinted red or blue, whereas mercury is a dull silver-gray color. For the record, California state law does not prohibit the use of glass mixing bowls, measuring cups, or other glass tools or utensils in commercial kitchens, but these items are impractical and really have no place in a professional setting. Because state law, not federal, governs these practices, you should contact the proper authority to determine the regulations for the state you work in.

Baumé thermometer—This tool is also known as a *saccharometer, syrup-density meter, sugar densimeter, hydrometer,* and *Baumé hydrometer.* It is used to determine the concentration of sugar in a liquid, which affects the density of the solution. By technical definition, it is not actually a thermometer because it does not measure heat. However, *Baumé thermometer* is the term typically used in the industry. A saccharometer is a thin glass tube with a graduated scale that ranges from 0° to 50° BE. The weights at the bottom of the saccharometer are precisely adjusted by the manufacturer so that it will read 0° BE when placed in water that is 58°F (15°C). The mixture being measured must therefore be at or close to this temperature (tepid room temperature) for the reading to be accurate. Before using the instrument for the first time, it is a good idea to test it and, if necessary, compensate for any discrepancy, plus or minus, when using it. The weights at the bottom also allow the instrument to remain in a vertical position in the liquid. To use the saccharometer, a high narrow container, preferably a laboratory glass, must be filled with enough of the liquid that is to be measured so the saccharometer will float. The scale is read at the point where the instrument meets the surface of the liquid. For example, if the saccharometer settles at 28°BE, the density of the solution is 1.28, which means that 1 liter (33.8

ounces) of the solution will weigh 1 kg 280 g (2 pounds 13 ounces). The calibration on the scale refers to degrees of Baumé, named for the Frenchman Antoine Baumé. For a list of Baumé readings relative to various levels of sugar concentration, see Appendix C.

Another instrument with a very similar name—*saccharimeter*—also measures sugar concentration in a liquid but does so by measuring the angle through which the plane of vibration of polarized light is turned by the solution. The names of both instruments come from the Greek words *sakcharon* ("sugar") and *metron* ("measure").

Brix hydrometer—This is the same instrument as the **Baumé thermometer** (again, this is not technically a thermometer); Brix is simply the name of a different scale of measurement. Both the Brix and Baumé scales use a hydrometer although, when using the Baumé scale, the tool is more commonly known by the name of saccharometer. The only difference is that the Baumé scale is expressed in degrees and the Brix scale is based on the decimal system. A different tool that uses the Brix scale to measure sugar concentration is called a *sugar density refractometer*. This instrument works on the same principle as the saccharimeter.

Candy thermometer—Also known as a *sugar thermometer* or a *confection thermometer,* this is a glass thermometer used to determine the temperature during the cooking process of boiled sugar, fondant, candies, jams, and jellies. A thermometer is essential during the preparation of these items, where miscalculating by a few degrees in either direction can significantly alter the outcome. Candy thermometers register from 100° to 400°F (38° to 205°C) and are marked to indicate the various standard cooked sugar stages—soft ball, hard ball, soft crack, and so on. It is especially important for a candy thermometer to be marked in at least 2-degree increments (either Fahrenheit or centigrade) so that any slight change in the temperature of the sugar can be detected. Candy thermometers made for professional use are suspended inside a metal cage to protect against breakage and to elevate the glass so it does not rest on the bottom of the pan.

Chocolate thermometer—This thermometer is specially designed for use with chocolate, primarily while tempering it. The thermometer reads in 1-degree gradations (in both Fahrenheit and centigrade) for precise measurement and has a range of 40 to 130°F (4 to 54°C). One chocolate thermometer is designed with a temperature dial on top that is attached to a silicone spoon. The sensor is located inside a round cutout in the bowl of the spoon. With this tool, you can measure the temperature of the chocolate while continuing to stir constantly. This is also a good thermometer to use for warming fondant.

Deep-frying thermometer—A glass thermometer very similar to the **candy thermometer** but specifically designed to read the temperature of hot fat for deep-fat frying. Dual-purpose thermometers that are marked with readings for both candy and deep fat frying are available.

Digital thermometer—Digital thermometers measure temperature through a metal probe or a sensing area and display the temperature on a digital readout. They may use either a thermocouple sensor or a thermistor sensor to detect temperature. Most allow you to switch between centigrade and Fahrenheit. They are made in a variety of models, from small one-piece pocket styles to those in which a probe attached to a flexible wire leads to a separate base unit placed on the work surface. The most sophisticated of these are computerized and capable of storing data. The base contains the on/off switch and the digital display as well as, on the higher-end models, other switches and display panels that give further information. These two-piece digital thermometers are available with a single probe attached to the base by the wire or with a connector on the base that allows the user to plug in different kinds of probes.

Detachable probe—Basic types of probes include surface (used to measure the temperature of flat cooking equipment), immersion (used to measure the temperature of liquids), penetration (used to measure the internal temperature of food products), and air (used to measure the temperature inside an oven or a refrigerator). Almost all digital thermometers that can be used with multiple types of detachable probes use the thermocouple sensor system. However, the term *thermocouple* itself does not refer to the ability to plug in different probes. Digital thermocouple thermometers with detachable probes, although relatively expensive, are extremely fast and accurate and are the type of thermometer recommended for use in commercial kitchens by the Food and Drug Administration and the U.S. Department of Agriculture. The temperature range varies with the model; some thermocouple thermometers can measure as wide a range as –112° to 1999°F (–80° to 1100°C).

Digital recording thermometer—Thermometers that can produce digital recordings are made for commercial foodservice establishments. Like other digital thermometers, they are made with a single attached probe or with a connector to allow the user to attach different probes. The base of the tool stores temperature readings that can be read and reviewed on the digital display or downloaded to a computer to be printed. Some instruments can be programmed to take and record temperature readings at time intervals from 1 second to every 12 hours and to store several thousands readings in memory. Others can record not only temperature readings but also the date, time, and location of each reading. Some of these can store over 500 hundred readings at more then 100 locations.

Digital waterproof thermometer with minimum-maximum temperature recording—Made for the food industry, this is a great tool for checking the temperature in dishwashers, refrigerators, and freezers. It is a probe-style thermometer that records both the highest and lowest temperature reached over a specified period. Although commercial dishwashers are required to contain built-in thermometers, one would have to stay and read the thermometer throughout the entire cycle to be certain that the water reached the minimum sanitation temperature required by NSF standards. Because this thermometer is waterproof, it can be placed in an automatic dishwasher along with the dishes; when the cycle is finished, the device will show the highest and lowest temperatures reached throughout. Along the same lines, this thermometer can be placed in the walk-in or freezer to check temperature fluctuation over a specified period.

Instant-read thermometer—Also called a *probe thermometer,* this is technically classified as a *bimetallic stemmed thermometer.* It measures temperature through a metal probe that has a sensor in the end and typically is scaled from 0° to 220°F (–18°C to 104°C). The indicator head has a round face with a needle that registers at the numbered temperature markings. Most models have an adjustable calibration nut and slip into a thin tube with a holding clip, which allows you to attach the thermometer to your chef's jacket.

Oven thermometer—This thermometer is used for checking the accuracy of the oven thermostat and for locating temperature fluctuations within an oven. It is configured with a pointer and dial set in a metal frame or as a mercury- or alcohol-filled glass tube attached to a metal backing. Both styles generally have a lip or hook to easily hang from the oven rack and are available with both Fahrenheit and centigrade readings ranging from about 100°F to 650°F (38° to 324°C).

Refrigerator or freezer thermometer—These thermometers are made for measuring the temperature inside a refrigerator or freezer and are available in the same two styles as the **Oven thermometer.** These register a temperature range from (–20° to 80°F (–29° to 26°C). Refrigerated foods should be maintained at 41°F (5°C) or below. Frozen foods should be kept at 0°F (–18°C) or below.

Sugar thermometer—See **Candy thermometer.**

Torch—See **Blowtorch.**

Transfer sheet—Transfer sheets are available for purchase from bakery supply and chocolate companies and are used to transfer designs onto chocolate. The sheets are made from clear acetate that has been imprinted with a design or pattern made from cocoa butter or vegetable fat colored with food dye. The patterns typically include symbols such as musical notes, dots, stars, or coffee beans; others have intricate swirls, stripes, or a marbleized pattern or crosshatch lines. Special-order monograms or logos can be ordered with the name of the restaurant or the name of dessert or type of candy. The designs are rarely printed in the typical brown chocolate color. Instead, they are generally gold, silver, white, or red so that the pattern will contrast and be visible on dark chocolate, although some patterns are made in dark or milk chocolate for use on white chocolate.

Transfer sheets can be used in several ways. To make flat decorations, place the transfer sheet on a work surface with the design facing up. Spread melted chocolate or coating chocolate over the sheet in a thin, even layer. When the chocolate has set for a few seconds and is no loger sticky, place a piece of baking paper or plastic on the chocolate and top with a weight. Chill for a few minutes, remove the weight and invert. Carefully peel the acetate transfer sheet away from the chocolate. The pattern will appear on the surface of the chocolate. The decorated chocolate sheet can be cut into a particular shape, or randomly broken pieces or shards can be used as a garnish. Using the same technique, transfer sheets can also be used to decorate a chocolate strip to wrap around the side of a cake. Simply cut the transfer sheet to the desired length and width before spreading the chocolate on top. Another option is to place a rubber stencil sheet on the transfer sheet, then spread chocolate over the stencil sheet and into the indentations. When the chocolate has set, remove the template and lift the decorated chocolate shapes off the transfer sheet.

Tread rolling pin—See **Rolling pin.**

Trois Frères cake pan—A shallow tube pan that has a decorative fluted pattern on the bottom and lower portion of the side and a plain band around the top, which is just slightly larger in diameter than the patterned portion. Trois Frères pans look very much like **gugelhupf pans,** but they are only about half as tall. The pans are approximately 8 inches (20 cm) in diameter and 2 inches (5 cm) high. The pan is named for a cake created in the 1800s by the three Juliene brothers, who were highly regarded Parisian pastry chefs. *Trois frères* is French for "three brothers."

Trowel—See **Decorating comb with frame.**

Truffle screen—This screen looks something like a **cooling rack,** but the screen does not have feet so it must be suspended for use. It is made of heavy woven wire mesh, which gives it an uneven surface. After truffles are dipped into melted chocolate to coat them, they are transferred to the truffle screen, where they are rolled around with the aid of a truffle **dipping fork,** which is made with the same screen material on the end. Rolling the candies between the two screens produces the classic rough spiked surface.

Truffle shell sealing stencil—A tool available from bakery supply companies and chocolate manufacturers. It is made for use with purchased hollow chocolate truffle shells that are sold in plastic trays, ready to be filled. The stencil is made to fit perfectly over the top of the shells after they are filled. The stencil's round openings expose only the small hole on each truffle where the filling was added. Melted chocolate is spread over the stencil to fill the holes and seal the truffles with no chance of getting melted chocolate on the outside of the shells.

Tube pan—A round cake pan with a hollow tube in the center that produces a ring-shaped cake. Angel food cake pans,

Gugelhupf pans, and **Bundt pans** are all examples of tube pans. Except for angel food cake, tube pans are used to bake heavy cake mixtures, such as a pound cake or fruitcake, that will benefit from receiving heat from both the center and the outside during baking.

Tuile sheet—A steel or tin mold used to form warm tuile cookies into the traditional curved shape as they cool. The sheets usually have six half-sphere channels side by side, each one about 1½ inches (3.7 cm) wide, 1 inch (2.5 cm) deep, and about 14 inches (35 cm) long.

Two-hundred pan—See Hotel pan.

U

Underwriters Laboratories, Inc. (UL)—See NSF.

V

Vegetable peeler—This hand tool, used to remove the skin or peel from fruits and vegetables, is sometimes called a *fruit and vegetable peeler* and also a *potato peeler*. Several designs in different shapes are available. All consist of a blade that is slit in the center, allowing the peelings to pass through. The blade usually swivels within the frame and/or handle to follow the shape of the item being peeled.

Viennese roll marker—This tool is used to mark the traditional imprint found on top of Viennese rolls and kaiser rolls. The portion that creates the pattern is a half-sphere of plastic with rounded fan-shaped blades. This piece is attached to the handle by a spring-loaded axle made in a precise length so that when you press the marker into the roll, the top of the tool twists approximately 45 degrees as it creates the design. Also sold under the name *Twirling Stick*.

Vol-au-vent cutter—A special cutter used to cut out puff pastry circles for vol-au-vents (puff pastry shells). This cutter allows you to score a ring just inside the perimeter of the dough at the same time that you cut out the dough circle. The tool consists of a small round cutter that is attached inside a larger cutter, with the smaller ring positioned slightly higher. As you press down on the dough, the larger ring cuts out the round base and the smaller ring presses halfway into the dough to score the ring that will define the sides of the vol-au-vent. The cutters come in sizes of approximately 1½ to 4 inches (3.7 to 10 cm) in diameter (measuring the ring that does the cutting); the smaller sizes are suitable for making bouchées as well. One style of cutter is made from two of these cutters soldered side by side

so you can cut out two circles and mark two rings in one quick movement.

A different tool sold under the same name consists of a set of 12 tinned-steel rounds in graduating sizes that are used as a guide when you cut puff pastry with a knife; they do not have a cutting edge. The metal rounds are slightly domed (like a pan lid), and each has a hole in the top where you can insert your finger to hold onto the guide as you cut with your other hand.

W

Waffle rolling pin—See Rolling pin.

Water bath—See Bain-marie.

Whip—Another name for *whisk*. Also used a verb meaning "to whip."

Whip attachment—See Mixer.

Whisk—A hand tool used for mixing and incorporating. Whisks are made of metal wires bent into a rounded hollow and attached to a handle. Different whisks are made for different jobs, but their most common uses in the pastry kitchen are for whipping egg whites and creating whipped cream. For both of these, a **balloon whisk** is preferable. To mix a heavy batter, a whisk with stiff, heavy wires is used. Like balloon whisks, these come in a variety of sizes. These heavier whisks are known as *sauce whisks*. A third type of whisk is a flat whisk known as a *batter whisk*. It has a rounded end, like the others, but is flat and two-dimensional. Flat whisks are useful for mixing or beating batters to make them smooth, but they do not incorporate air like the others. The term *whisk* is also used as a verb meaning "to whisk."

Balloon whisk—The most commonly used whisk in the pasty kitchen. Balloon whisks are also known as *egg whisks*. They have a very round (balloon) shape at the end, and the wires are light and flexible. They are especially useful for incorporating the maximum amount of air into batters and egg whites. Balloon whisks come in various sizes.

Z

Zester—A hand tool used to cut the zest (the colored part of the rind without the white pith) from citrus fruits. About the size of a paring knife, a zester has five small holes at the end to remove the skin in small threads. See also **Citrus Stripper** and **Grater**.

APPENDIX C

Weights, Measures, and Yields

The Metric System

Accuracy of measurement is essential in achieving a good result in the pastry shop. Ingredients are therefore almost always weighed or *scaled,* to use the professional term. The few exceptions are eggs, milk, and water; for convenience, these are measured by volume at the rate of 1 pint to 1 pound, 1 liter to 1 kilogram, or, for a small quantity of eggs, by number. The system of measurement used in the United States is highly complicated and confusing compared to the simple metric system used just about everywhere else in the world. Under the U.S. system, the number of increments in any given unit of measure is arbitrarily broken down into numbers that have no correlation with each other. For example, there are 12 inches in 1 foot, 32 ounces in 1 quart, 4 quarts in 1 gallon, 3 teaspoons in 1 tablespoon, and so on. Adding to the confusion is the fact that ounces are used to measure both liquids by volume and solids by weight; so if you see the measurement "8 ounces melted chocolate," you do not really know if this means to weigh the ingredient or measure it in a cup. This can make a big difference in a particular recipe, as 1 cup (8 liquid ounces) melted chocolate weighs almost 10 ounces. The metric system, on the other hand, is divided into three basic units, one each for length, volume, and weight. (Centigrade and Fahrenheit, the temperature scales, are not part of the metric system.)

Meter is the unit used to measure length. It is divided into increments of millimeters, centimeters, and decimeters.

- 10 millimeters = 1 centimeter
- 10 centimeters = 1 decimeter
- 10 decimeters or 100 centimeters = 1 meter

Meters, centimeters, and millimeters are abbreviated as m, cm, and mm, respectively, throughout *The Professional Pastry Chef.* The decimeter measure is rarely used in the United States and is not used in this text.

Liter is the unit used to measure volume. A liter is divided into milliliters, centiliters, and deciliters.

- 10 milliliters = 1 centiliter
- 10 centiliters = 1 deciliter
- 10 deciliters or 100 centiliters = 1 liter

Liters, deciliters, centiliters, and milliliters are abbreviated as L, dl, cl, and ml, respectively, throughout the text.

Kilogram is the unit used to measure weight.

- 100 grams = 1 hectogram
- 10 hectograms = 1 kilo

The hectogram is rarely used in the United States. Instead, the kilo is divided into 1000 grams. Kilograms and grams are abbreviated as kg and g, respectively, throughout the text.

The following approximate equivalents will give you a feeling for the size of various metric units:

- 1 kilo is slightly over 2 pounds
- 1 liter is just over 1 quart
- 1 deciliter is a little bit less than ½ cup
- 1 centiliter is about 2½ teaspoons
- 1 meter is just over 3 feet

Units of measure in the metric system are always in increments of ten, making it a precise system and easy to follow once you understand the principles. Nevertheless, many people who did not grow up using this method are reluctant to learn it and think it will be difficult to understand. Reading that there are 28.35 grams to 1 ounce looks intimidating, but this actually shows how the metric system can give you a much more accurate measurement. When measuring by weight any ingredient that is less than 1 ounce, use the gram weight for a precise measurement, or convert to teaspoons and/or tablespoons if necessary.

The equivalency tables that follow have been used to convert the measurements in *The Professional Pastry Chef* and provide both U.S. and metric measurements for all ingredients in the recipes. However, they do not precisely follow the conversion ratio; instead the tables have been rounded to the nearest tenth. For example, 1 ounce has been rounded up to 30 grams rather than using 28.35, grams which is the actual equivalent; 2 ounces has been rounded down to 55 grams instead of 56.7 grams, and so on. As the weight increases, every third ounce is calculated at 25 g rather than 30 to keep the table from getting too far away from the exact metric equivalent. Preceding these tables are the precise conversion measures, should you require them.

Precise Metric Equivalents

Length

1 inch	25.4 mm
1 centimeter	0.39 inches
1 meter	39.4 inches

Volume

1 ounce	(2 tablespoons) 29.57 milliliters
1 cup	2 dl, 3 cl, 7 ml (237 ml)
1 quart	9 dl, 4 cl, 6 ml (946 ml)
1 milliliter	0.034 fluid ounce
1 liter	33.8 fluid ounces

Weight

1 ounce	28.35 grams
1 pound	454 grams
1 gram	0.035 ounce
1 kilogram	2.2 pounds

Precise Metric Conversions

Length

To convert:	Multiply by:
inches into millimeters	25.4
inches into centimeters	2.54
millimeters into inches	0.03937
centimeters into inches	0.3937
meters into inches	39.3701

Volume

To convert:	Multiply by:
quarts into liters	0.946
pints into liters	0.473
quarts into milliliters	946
milliliters into ounces	0.0338
liters into quarts	1.05625
milliliters into pints	0.0021125
liters into pints	2.1125
liters into ounces	33.8

Weight

To convert:	Multiply by:
ounces into grams	28.35
grams into ounces	0.03527
kilograms into pounds	2.2046
pounds into kilograms	0.4535924

Metric and U.S. Equivalents: Length

In the tables that follow, metric amounts have been rounded to the nearest tenth. These conversions should be close enough for most purposes.

U.S.	Metric	U.S.	Metric
$\frac{1}{16}$ inch	2 mm	7$\frac{1}{2}$ inches	18.7 cm
$\frac{1}{8}$ inch	3 mm	7$\frac{3}{4}$ inches	19.5 cm
$\frac{3}{16}$ inch	5 mm	8 inches	20 cm
$\frac{1}{4}$ inch	6 mm	8$\frac{1}{4}$ inches	20.6 cm
$\frac{1}{3}$ inch	8 mm	8$\frac{1}{2}$ inches	21.2 cm
$\frac{3}{8}$ inch	9 mm	8$\frac{3}{4}$ inches	22 cm
$\frac{1}{2}$ inch	1.2 cm	9 inches	22.5 cm
$\frac{5}{8}$ inch	1.5 cm	9$\frac{1}{4}$ inches	23.1 cm
$\frac{2}{3}$ inch	1.6 cm	9$\frac{1}{2}$ inches	23.7 cm
$\frac{3}{4}$ inch	2 cm	9$\frac{3}{4}$ inches	24.5 cm
$\frac{7}{8}$ inch	2.1 cm	10 inches	25 cm
1 inch	2.5 cm	10$\frac{1}{4}$ inches	25.6 cm
1$\frac{1}{4}$ inches	3.1 cm	10$\frac{1}{2}$ inches	26.2 cm
1$\frac{1}{2}$ inches	3.7 cm	10$\frac{3}{4}$ inches	27 cm
1$\frac{3}{4}$ inches	4.5 cm	11 inches	27.5 cm
2 inches	5 cm	11$\frac{1}{4}$ inches	28.1 cm
2$\frac{1}{4}$ inches	5.6 cm	11$\frac{1}{2}$ inches	28.7 cm
2$\frac{1}{2}$ inches	6.2 cm	11$\frac{3}{4}$ inches	29.5 cm
2$\frac{3}{4}$ inches	7 cm	12 inches (1 foot)	30 cm
3 inches	7.5 cm	12$\frac{1}{2}$ inches	31.2 cm
3$\frac{1}{4}$ inches	8.1 cm	12$\frac{3}{4}$ inches	32 cm
3$\frac{1}{2}$ inches	8.7 cm	13 inches	32.5 cm
3$\frac{3}{4}$ inches	9.5 cm	13$\frac{1}{2}$ inches	33.7 cm
4 inches	10 cm	13$\frac{3}{4}$ inches	34.5 cm
4$\frac{1}{4}$ inches	10.6 cm	14 inches	35 cm
4$\frac{1}{2}$ inches	11.2 cm	14$\frac{1}{2}$ inches	36.2 cm
4$\frac{3}{4}$ inches	12 cm	14$\frac{3}{4}$ inches	37 cm
5 inches	12.5 cm	15 inches	37.5 cm
5$\frac{1}{4}$ inches	13.1 cm	15$\frac{1}{2}$ inches	38.7 cm
5$\frac{1}{2}$ inches	13.7 cm	15$\frac{3}{4}$ inches	39.5 cm
5$\frac{3}{4}$ inches	14.5 cm	16 inches	40 cm
6 inches	15 cm	16$\frac{1}{2}$ inches	41.2 cm
6$\frac{1}{4}$ inches	15.6 cm	16$\frac{3}{4}$ inches	42 cm
6$\frac{1}{2}$ inches	16.2 cm	17 inches	42.5 cm
6$\frac{3}{4}$ inches	17 cm	17$\frac{1}{2}$ inches	43.7 cm
7 inches	17.5 cm	17$\frac{3}{4}$ inches	44.5 cm
7$\frac{1}{4}$ inches	18.1 cm	18 inches (1$\frac{1}{2}$ feet)	45 cm

U.S.	Metric
18½ inches	46.2 cm
18¾ inches	47 cm
19 inches	47.5 cm
19½ inches	48.7 cm
19¾ inches	49.5 cm
20 inches	50 cm
20½ inches	51.2 cm
20¾ inches	52 cm
21 inches	52.5 cm
21½ inches	53.7 cm
21¾ inches	54.5 cm
22 inches	55 cm
22½ inches	56.2 cm
22¾ inches	57 cm
23 inches	57.5 cm
23½ inches	58.7 cm
23¾ inches	59.5 cm
24 inches (2 feet)	60 cm
24½ inches	61.2 cm
25 inches	62.5 cm
25½ inches	63.7 cm
26 inches	65 cm
26½ inches	66.2 cm
27 inches	67.5 cm
27½ inches	68.7 cm
28 inches	70 cm
28½ inches	71.2 cm
29 inches	72.5 cm
29½ inches	73.7 cm
30 inches (2½ feet)	75 cm
30½ inches	76.2 cm
31 inches	77.5 cm
31½ inches	78.7 cm

U.S.	Metric
32 inches	80 cm
32½ inches	81.2 cm
33 inches	82.5 cm
33½ inches	83.7 cm
34 inches	85 cm
34½ inches	86.2 cm
35 inches	87.5 cm
35½ inches	88.7 cm
36 inches (3 feet/1 yard)	90 cm
36½ inches	91.2 cm
37 inches	92.5 cm
37½ inches	93.7 cm
38 inches	95 cm
38½ inches	96.2 cm
39 inches	97.5 cm
39½ inches	98.7 cm
40 inches	100 cm (1 meter)
40½ inches	1 m 1.2 cm
41 inches	1 m 2.5 cm
41½ inches	1 m 3.7 cm
42 inches	1 m 5 cm
42½ inches	1 m 6.2 cm
43 inches	1 m 7.5 cm
43½ inches	1 m 8.7 cm
44 inches	1 m 10 cm
44½ inches	1 m 11.2 cm
45 inches	1 m 12.5 cm
45½ inches	1 m 13.7 cm
46 inches	1 m 15 cm
46½ inches	1 m 16.2 cm
47 inches	1 m 17.5 cm
47½ inches	1 m 18.7 cm
48 inches (4 feet)	1 m 20 cm

Metric and U.S. Equivalents: Volume

U.S.	Metric	U.S.	Metric
¼ teaspoon	1.25 ml	33 ounces (4⅛ cups)	990 ml (9 dl 9 cl)
½ teaspoon	2.5 ml	34 ounces (4¼ cups)	1 L 20 ml
1 teaspoon	5 ml	35 ounces (4⅜ cups)	1 L 50 ml
1 tablespoon (3 teaspoons)	15 ml (1 cl 5 ml)	36 ounces (4½ cups)	1 L 80 ml
1 ounce (2 tablespoons/⅛ cup)	30 ml (3 cl)	37 ounces (4⅝ cups)	1 L 110 ml
1¼ ounces	37.5 ml	38 ounces (4¾ cups)	1 L 140 ml
1½ ounces (3 tablespoons)	45 ml	39 ounces (4⅞ cups)	1 L 170 ml
1¾ ounces	52.5 ml	40 ounces (1 quart 1 cup)	1 L 200 ml
2 ounces (4 tablespoons/¼ cup)	60 ml (6 cl)	41 ounces (5⅛ cups)	1 L 230 ml
3 ounces (6 tablespoons/⅜ cup)	90 ml (9 cl)	42 ounces (5¼ cups)	1 L 260 ml
4 ounces (8 tablespoons/½ cup)	120 ml (1 dl, 2 cl)	43 ounces (5⅜ cups)	1 L 290 ml
5 ounces (10 tablespoons/⅝ cup)	150 ml (1 dl 5 cl)	44 ounces (5½ cups)	1 L 320 ml
6 ounces (12 tablespoons/¾ cup)	180 ml (1 dl 8 cl)	45 ounces (5⅝ cups)	1 L 350 ml
7 ounces (14 tablespoons/⅞ cup)	210 ml (2 dl 1 cl)	46 ounces (5¾ cups)	1 L 380 ml
8 ounces (16 tablespoons/1 cup)	240 ml (2 dl 4 cl)	47 ounces (5⅞ cups)	1 L 410 ml
9 ounces (1⅛ cups)	270 ml (2 dl 7 cl)	48 ounces (1 quart 2 cups)	1 L 440 ml
10 ounces (1¼ cups)	300 ml (3 dl)	49 ounces (6⅛ cups)	1 L 470 ml
11 ounces (1⅜ cups)	330 ml (3 dl 3 cl)	50 ounces (6¼ cups)	1 L 500 ml
12 ounces (1½ cups)	360 ml (3 dl 6 cl)	51 ounces (6⅜ cups)	1 L 530 ml
13 ounces (1⅝ cup)	390 ml (3 dl 9 cl)	52 ounces (6½ cups)	1 L 560 ml
14 ounces (1¾ cups)	420 ml (4 dl 2 cl)	53 ounces (6⅝ cups)	1 L 590 ml
15 ounces (1⅞ cups)	450 ml (4 dl 5 cl)	54 ounces (6¾ cups)	1 L 620 ml
16 ounces (2 cups/1 pint)	480 ml (4 dl 8 cl)	55 ounces (6⅞ cups)	1 L 650 ml
17 ounces (2⅛ cups)	510 ml (5 dl 1 cl)	56 ounces (1 quart 3 cups)	1 L 680 ml
18 ounces (2¼ cups)	540 ml (5 dl 4 cl)	57 ounces (7⅛ cups)	1 L 710 ml
19 ounces (2⅜ cups)	570 ml (5 dl 7 cl)	58 ounces (7¼ cups)	1 L 740 ml
20 ounces (2½ cups)	600 ml (6 dl)	59 ounces (7⅜ cups)	1 L 770 ml
21 ounces (2⅝ cups)	630 ml (6 dl 3 cl)	60 ounces (7½ cups)	1 L 800 ml
22 ounces (2¾ cups)	660 ml (6 dl 6 cl)	61 ounces (7⅝ cups)	1 L 830 ml
23 ounces (2⅞ cups)	690 ml (6 dl 9 cl)	62 ounces (7¾ cups)	1 L 860 ml
24 ounces (3 cups)	720 ml (7 dl 2 cl)	63 ounces (7⅞ cups)	1 L 890 ml
25 ounces (3⅛ cups)	750 ml (7 dl 5 cl)	64 ounces (2 quarts)	1 L 920 ml
26 ounces (3¼ cups)	780 ml (7 dl 8 cl)	65 ounces (8⅛ cups)	1 L 950 ml
27 ounces (3⅜ cups)	810 ml (8 dl 1 cl)	66 ounces (8¼ cups)	1 L 980 ml
28 ounces (3½ cups)	840 ml (8 dl 4 cl)	67 ounces (8⅜ cups)	2 L 10 ml
29 ounces (3⅝ cups)	870 ml (8 dl 7 cl)	68 ounces (8½ cups)	2 L 40 ml
30 ounces (3¾ cups)	900 ml (9 dl)	69 ounces (8⅝ cups)	2 L 70 ml
31 ounces (3⅞ cups)	930 ml (9 dl 3 cl)	70 ounces (8¾ cups)	2 L 100 ml
32 ounces (1 quart)	960 ml (9 dl 6 cl)	71 ounces (8⅞ cups)	2 L 130 ml

U.S.	Metric	U.S.	Metric
72 ounces (2 quarts 1 cup)	2 L 160 ml	101 ounces (12⅝ cups)	3 L 30 ml
73 ounces (9⅛ cups)	2 L 190 ml	102 ounces (12¾ cups)	3 L 60 ml
74 ounces (9¼ cups)	2 L 220 ml	103 ounces (12⅞ cups)	3 L 90 ml
75 ounces (9⅜ cups)	2 L 250 ml	104 ounces (3 quarts 1 cup)	3 L 120 ml
76 ounces (9½ cups)	2 L 280 ml	105 ounces (13⅛ cups)	3 L 150 ml
77 ounces (9⅝ cups)	2 L 310 ml	106 ounces (13¼ cups)	3 L 180 ml
78 ounces (9¾ cups)	2 L 340 ml	107 ounces (13⅜ cups)	3 L 210 ml
79 ounces (9⅞ cups)	2 L 370 ml	108 ounces (13½ cups)	3 L 240 ml
80 ounces (2 quarts 2 cups)	2 L 400 ml	109 ounces (13⅝ cups)	3 L 270 ml
81 ounces (10⅛ cups)	2 L 430 ml	110 ounces (13¾ cups)	3 L 300 ml
82 ounces (10¼ cups)	2 L 460 ml	111 ounces (13⅞ cups)	3 L 330 ml
83 ounces (10⅜ cups)	2 L 490 ml	112 ounces (3 quarts 2 cups)	3 L 360 ml
84 ounces (10½ cups)	2 L 520 ml	113 ounces (14⅛ cups)	3 L 390 ml
85 ounces (10⅝ cups)	2 L 550 ml	114 ounces (14¼ cups)	3 L 420 ml
86 ounces (10¾ cups)	2 L 580 ml	115 ounces (14⅜ cups)	3 L 450 ml
87 ounces (10⅞ cups)	2 L 610 ml	116 ounces (14½ cups)	3 L 480 ml
88 ounces (2 quarts 3 cups)	2 L 640 ml	117 ounces (14⅝ cups)	3 L 510 ml
89 ounces (11⅛ cups)	2 L 670 ml	118 ounces (14¾ cups)	3 L 540 ml
90 ounces (11¼ cups)	2 L 700 ml	119 ounces (14⅞ cups)	3 L 570 ml
91 ounces (11⅜ cups)	2 L 730 ml	120 ounces (3 quarts 3 cups)	3 L 600 ml
92 ounces (11½ cups)	2 L 760 ml	121 ounces (15⅛ cups)	3 L 630 ml
93 ounces (11⅝ cups)	2 L 790 ml	122 ounces (15¼ cups)	3 L 660 ml
94 ounces (11¾ cups)	2 L 820 ml	123 ounces (15⅜ cups)	3 L 690 ml
95 ounces (11⅞ cups)	2 L 850 ml	124 ounces (15½ cups)	3 L 720 ml
96 ounces (3 quarts)	2 L 880 ml	125 ounces (15⅝ cups)	3 L 750 ml
97 ounces (12⅛ cups)	2 L 910 ml	126 ounces (15¾ cups)	3 L 780 ml
98 ounces (12¼ cups)	2 L 940 ml	127 ounces (15⅞ cups)	3 L 810 ml
99 ounces (12⅜ cups)	2 L 970 ml	128 ounces (16 cups/4 quarts/1 gallon)	3 L 840 ml
100 ounces (12½ cups)	3 L		

U.S. Volume Equivalents

3 teaspoons	=1 tablespoon
2 tablespoons	=1 ounce
8 ounces (16 tablespoons)	=1 cup
2 cups	=1 pint
2 pints	=1 quart
4 quarts	=1 gallon

Note: 1 pint (2 cups) of water, or any liquid of similar viscosity, will weigh 1 pound.

Metric and U.S. Equivalents: Weight

U.S.	Metric	U.S.	Metric
½ ounce	15 g	22 ounces (1 pound 6 ounces)	625 g
⅔ ounce	20 g	23 ounces (1 pound 7 ounces)	655 g
¾ ounce	22 g	24 ounces (1 pound 8 ounces)	680 g
1 ounce	30 g	25 ounces (1 pound 9 ounces)	710 g
1½ ounces	40 g	26 ounces (1 pound 10 ounces)	740 g
2 ounces	55 g	27 ounces (1 pound 11 ounces)	765 g
2½ ounces	70 g	28 ounces (1 pound 12 ounces)	795 g
3 ounces	85 g	29 ounces (1 pound 13 ounces)	825 g
3½ ounces	100 g	30 ounces (1 pound 14 ounces)	855 g
4 ounces	115 g	31 ounces (1 pound 15 ounces)	885 g
4½ ounces	130 g	32 ounces (2 pounds)	910 g
5 ounces	140 g	33 ounces (2 pounds 1 ounce)	940 g
5½ ounces	155 g	34 ounces (2 pounds 2 ounces)	970 g
6 ounces	170 g	35 ounces (2 pounds 3 ounces)	1 kg (1000 g)
6½ ounces	185 g	36 ounces (2 pounds 4 ounces)	1 kg, 25 g
7 ounces	200 g	37 ounces (2 pounds 5 ounces)	1 kg 50 g
7½ ounces	215 g	38 ounces (2 pounds 6 ounces)	1 kg 80 g
8 ounces	225 g	39 ounces (2 pounds 7 ounces)	1 kg 110 g
8½ ounces	240 g	40 ounces (2 pounds 8 ounces)	1 kg 135 g
9 ounces	255 g	41 ounces (2 pounds 9 ounces)	1 kg 165 g
9½ ounces	270 g	42 ounces (2 pounds 10 ounces)	1 kg 195 g
10 ounces	285 g	43 ounces (2 pounds 11 ounces)	1 kg 220 g
10½ ounces	300 g	44 ounces (2 pounds 12 ounces)	1 kg 250 g
11 ounces	310 g	45 ounces (2 pounds 13 ounces)	1 kg 280 g
11½ ounces	325 g	46 ounces (2 pounds 14 ounces)	1 kg 310 g
12 ounces	340 g	47 ounces (2 pounds 15 ounces)	1 kg 340 g
12½ ounces	355 g	48 ounces (3 pounds)	1 kg 365 g
13 ounces	370 g	49 ounces (3 pounds 1 ounce)	1 kg 395 g
13½ ounces	385 g	50 ounces (3 pounds 2 ounces)	1 kg 420 g
14 ounces	400 g	51 ounces (3 pounds 3 ounces)	1 kg 450 g
14½ ounces	415 g	52 ounces (3 pounds 4 ounces)	1 kg 480 g
15 ounces	430 g	53 ounces (3 pounds 5 ounces)	1 kg 505 g
15½ ounces	445 g	54 ounces (3 pounds 6 ounces)	1 kg 535 g
16 ounces (1 pound)	455 g	55 ounces (3 pounds 7 ounces)	1 kg 565 g
17 ounces (1 pound 1 ounce)	485 g	56 ounces (3 pounds 8 ounces)	1 kg 590 g
18 ounces (1 pound 2 ounces)	510 g	57 ounces (3 pounds 9 ounces)	1 kg 620 g
19 ounces (1 pound 3 ounces)	540 g	58 ounces (3 pounds 10 ounces)	1 kg 650 g
20 ounces (1 pound 4 ounces)	570 g	59 ounces (3 pounds 11 ounces)	1 kg 675 g
21 ounces (1 pound 5 ounces)	595 g	60 ounces (3 pounds 12 ounces)	1 kg 705 g

U.S.	Metric	U.S.	Metric
61 ounces (3 pounds 13 ounces)	1 kg 735 g	71 ounces (4 pounds 7 ounces)	2 kg 20 g
62 ounces (3 pounds 14 ounces)	1 kg 765 g	72 ounces (4 pounds 8 ounces)	2 kg 45 g
63 ounces (3 pounds 15 ounces)	1 kg 795 g	73 ounces (4 pounds 9 ounces)	2 kg 75 g
64 ounces (4 pounds)	1 kg 820 g	74 ounces (4 pounds 10 ounces)	2 kg 105 g
65 ounces (4 pounds 1 ounce)	1 kg 850 g	75 ounces (4 pounds 11 ounces)	2 kg 130 g
66 ounces (4 pounds 2 ounces)	1 kg 875 g	76 ounces (4 pounds 12 ounces)	2 kg 160 g
67 ounces (4 pounds 3 ounces)	1 kg 905 g	77 ounces (4 pounds 13 ounces)	2 kg 190 g
68 ounces (4 pounds 4 ounces)	1 kg 935 g	78 ounces (4 pounds 14 ounces)	2 kg 220 g
69 ounces (4 pounds 5 ounces)	1 kg 960 g	79 ounces (4 pounds 15 ounces)	2 kg 250 g
70 ounces (4 pounds 6 ounces)	1 kg 990 g	80 ounces (5 pounds)	2 kg 275 g

Temperature Scales

Centigrade Scale

The centigrade scale is the temperature scale used throughout most of the world outside the United States. Temperatures are expressed in degrees Celsius, with 0° as the freezing point of water and 100° as its boiling point. The name *Celsius* comes from the inventor of the scale, Anders Celsius, a Swedish astronomer who developed the system of measurement in 1742. Degrees Celsius are abbreviated as ˚C throughout this text.

Fahrenheit Scale

The Fahrenheit temperature scale is used almost exclusively in the United States. It was developed in 1714 by German physicist Gabriel David Fahrenheit. The Fahrenheit scale uses 32˚ as the freezing point of water and 212˚ as its boiling point. Degrees Fahrenheit are abbreviated as ˚F throughout this text.

Temperature Equivalents

Fahrenheit	Celsius	Fahrenheit	Celsius
-50°F	-45°C	2°F	-17°C
-45°F	-43°C	5°F	-15°C
-40°F	-40°C	7°F	-14°C
-35°F	-37°C	10°F	-12°C
-30°F	-35°C	12°F	-11°C
-25°F	-32°C	15°F	-10°C
-20°F	-29°C	17°F	-9°C
-17°F	-27°C	20°F	-7°C
-15°F	-26°C	22°F	-6°C
-12°F	-25°C	25°F	-4°C
-10°F	-24°C	27°F	-3°C
-7°F	-22°C	30°F	-1°C
-5°F	-21°C	32°F	0°C (freezing point of water)
-3°F	-20°C	35°F	2°C
0°F	-18°C	38°F	3°C

Fahrenheit	Celsius	Fahrenheit	Celsius
40°F	4°C (yeast is dormant)	128°F	53°C
43°F	6°C	130°F	54°C
45°F	7°C	133°F	56°C
48°F	9°C	135°F	57°C
50°F	10°C	138°F	59°C
53°F	12°C	140°F	60°C
55°F	13°C	143°F	62°C
58°F	14°C	145°F	63°C (yeast is killed)
60°F	16°C	148°F	64°C
63°F	17°C	150°F	65°C
65°F	19°C	153°F	67°C
68°F	20°C (gelatin begins to set)	155°F	68°C
70°F	21°C	158°F	70°C
73°F	23°C	160°F	71°C
75°F	24°C	163°F	73°C
78°F	25°C	165°F	74°C
80°F	26°C (ideal temperature for yeast to multiply)	168°F	76°C
83°F	28°C	170°F	77°C
85°F	29°C (lowest working temperature for tempered chocolate)	173°F	78°C
		175°F	80°C
86°F	30°C (gelatin dissolves)	178°F	81°C
88°F	31°C	180°F	82°C
90°F	32°C (highest working temperature for tempered chocolate)	183°F	84°C
		185°F	85°C
93°F	34°C	188°F	87°C
95°F	35°C	190°F	88°C
98°F	37°C	193°F	89°C
100°F	38°C (lowest working temperature for coating chocolate)	195°F	91°C
		198°F	92°C
103°F	39°C	200°F	94°C
105°F	40°C (working temperature for coating chocolate)	203°F	95°C
		205°F	96°C
108°F	42°C	208°F	98°C
110°F	43°C (highest working temperature for coating chocolate)	210°F	99°C
		212°F	100°C (water boils at sea level)
113°F	45°C	215°F	102°C
115°F	46°C	218°F	103°C
118°F	48°C	220°F	104°C
120°F	49°C	223°F	106°C
123°F	51°C	225°F	108°C
125°F	52°C		

Fahrenheit	Celsius		Fahrenheit	Celsius
228°F	109°C		328°F	164°C
230°F	110°C		330°F	166°C
233°F	112°C		333°F	167°C
235°F	113°C		335°F	168°C
238°F	114°C		338°F	170°C
240°F	115°C (sugar syrup for Italian meringue/soft ball stage)		340°F	171°C
			343°F	172°C
243°F	117°C		345°F	173°C
245°F	118°C		348°F	174°C
248°F	120°C		350°F	175°C
250°F	122°C		355°F	180°C
253°F	123°C		360°F	183°C
255°F	124°C		365°F	185°C
258°F	126°C		370°F	188°C
260°F	127°C		375°F	190°C
263°F	128°C		380°F	193°C
265°F	130°C		385°F	196°C
268°F	131°C		390°F	199°C
270°F	132°C		395°F	202°C
273°F	134°C		400°F	205°C
275°F	135°C		405°F	208°C
278°F	137°C		410°F	210°C
280°F	138°C		415°F	212°C
283°F	139°C		420°F	216°C
285°F	141°C°		425°F	219°C
288°F	142°C		430°F	222°C
290°F	143°C		435°F	224°C
293°F	145°C		440°F	226°C
295°F	146°C		445°F	228°C
298°F	148°C		450°F	230°C
300°F	149°C		455°F	235°C
303°F	151°C		460°F	237°C
305°F	152°C		465°F	240°C
308°F	153°C		470°F	243°C
310°F	155°C		475°F	246°C
313°F	156°C		480°F	248°C
315°F	157°C		485°F	251°C
318°F	159°C		490°F	254°C
320°F	160°C (sugar begins to caramelize)		495°F	257°C
323°F	162°C		500°F	260°C
325°F	163°C		550°F	288°C

Fahrenheit	Celsius		Fahrenheit	Celsius
600°F	315°C		850°F	454°C
650°F	343°C		900°F	482°C
700°F	371°C		950°F	510°C
750°F	398°C		1000°F	537°C
800°F	426°C			

Temperature Conversions

To convert centigrade to Fahrenheit, multiply by 9, divide by 5 (centigrade x 9 ÷ 5), then add 32.

Example: 190°C x 9 ÷ 5 = 342 + 32 = 374°F

To convert Fahrenheit to centigrade, subtract 32, multiply by 5, then divide by 9 (Fahrenheit –32 x 5 ÷ 9).

Example: 400°F – 32 = 368 x 5 ÷ 9 = 204.4°C

Volume Equivalents of Commonly Used Products

Product	U.S.	Metric
1 pound bread flour (unsifted)	4 cups	960 ml
1 pound cake flour (unsifted)	4⅓ cups	1 L 40 ml
1 pound cornstarch	3¼ cups	780 ml
1 pound semolina flour	2½ cups	600 ml
1 pound cornmeal	3 cups	720 ml
1 pound butter	2 cups	480 ml
1 ounce butter	2 tablespoons	30 ml
1 pound granulated sugar	2¼ cups	540 ml
1 pound powdered sugar	4 cups	960 ml
1 pound brown sugar	2⅔ cups	640 ml
4 tablespoons table salt	1¾ ounces	52 g
4 tablespoons kosher salt	1½ ounces	40 g
1 pound unsweetened cocoa powder	4¾ cups	1 L 140 ml
1 pound honey	1⅓ cups	320 ml
1 pound rolled oats	5⅓ cups	1 L 280 ml
1 pound macaroon coconut	5 cups	1 L 200 ml
1 pound rice (jasmine)	2 cups	480 ml
1 pound peanuts (shelled)	3 cups	720 ml
1 pound pistachios (shelled)	3⅓ cups	800 ml
1 pound hazelnuts (shelled)	3½ cups	840 ml
1 pound almonds (whole)	3 cups	720 ml
1 pound sliced almonds	6 cups	1 L 440 ml
1 pound almonds (slivered)	4 cups	960 ml
1 pound almonds (finely ground)	4 cups	960 ml
1 pound walnuts (shelled, halves)	4½ cups	1 L 80 ml
1 pound pecans (shelled, halves)	4⅓ cups	1 L 40 ml
1 pound pine nuts	3¼ cups	780 ml
1 pound black or golden raisins	2¾ cups	660 ml
1 pound dried currants	2⅔ cups	640 ml

Approximate Prepared Yields of Commonly Used Products

Item	Prepared Yield
1 cup (240 ml) heavy cream whipped to stiff peaks	2 cups (480 ml)
5 pounds (2 kg 275 g/15 medium) whole apples	13¾ cups (3 L 300 ml), chopped or sliced
5 pounds (2 kg 275 g/40 to 60) fresh apricots	12½ cups (3 L), sliced or halved
5 pounds (2 kg 275 g) dried apricots	13¾ cups (3 L 300 ml)
5 pounds (2 kg 275 g) dried apricots, reconstituted	27½ cups (6 L 600 ml)
5 pounds (2 kg 275 g/15 medium) whole oranges	4 cups (960 ml) strained juice
5 pounds (2 kg 275 g/20 to 25 medium) whole lemons	3 cups (720 ml) strained juice
5 pounds (2 kg 275 g/30 to 40 medium) whole limes	2½ cups (600 ml) strained juice
5 pounds (2 kg 275 g) unhulled strawberries	5 cups (1 L 200 ml) strained juice
2 pounds (910 g) raspberries	3 cups (720 ml) strained juice
5 pounds (2 kg 275 g/15 to 20) fresh bananas	10 cups (2 L 400 ml), sliced
1 pound (455 g) frozen blueberries	2½ cups (600 ml)
5 pounds (2 kg 275 g) fresh carrots (without tops)	5 cups (1 L 200 ml), chopped or sliced; 12½ cups (3 L), shredded
5 pounds (2 kg 275 g) fresh cherries	12 to 15 cups (2 L 880 ml to 3 L 600 ml), pitted
5 pounds (2 kg 275 g) whole dates	10 cups (2 L 400 ml), unpitted; 13¾ cups (3 L 300 ml), pitted and chopped
5 pounds (2 kg 275 g) seeded grapes	12 to 15 cups (2 L 880 ml to 3 L 600 ml)
5 pounds (2 kg 275 g/20 medium) fresh peaches	14 cups (3 L 360 ml), sliced; 12½ cups (3 L), chopped
5 pounds (2 kg 275 g/15 medium) fresh pears	10 cups (2 L 400 ml), sliced
5 pounds (2 kg 275 g) fresh plums	10 cups (2 L 400 ml), pitted and quartered
5 pounds (2 kg 275 g) fresh whole pumpkin	5 cups (1 L 200 ml), cooked and mashed
5 pounds (2 kg 275 g) fresh rhubarb	10 cups (2 L 400 ml), chopped and cooked

Volume Equivalents for Shelled Eggs, Average Size

These numbers have been rounded for convenience and ease of multiplication.

Egg Whites

2	¼ cup/60 ml
4	½ cup/120 ml
5	⅝ cup/150 ml
6	¾ cup/180 ml
8	1 cup/240 ml
10	1¼ cups/300 ml
12	1½ cups/360 ml
14	1¾ cups/420 ml
16	2 cups/480 ml

Egg Yolks

3	¼ cup/60 ml
4	⅓ cup/80 ml
6	½ cup/120 ml
8	⅔ cup/160 ml
9	¾ cup/180 ml
10	⅞ cup/210 ml
12	1 cup/240 ml
16	1⅓ cups/320 ml

Whole Eggs

1	¼ cup/60 ml
2	½ cup/120 ml
3	¾ cup/180 ml
4	1 cup/ 240 ml
5	1¼ cups/300 ml
6	1½ cups/360 ml
7	1¾ cups/420 ml
8	2 cups/480 ml
9	2¼ cups/540 ml
10	2½ cups/600 ml
11	2¾ cups/660 ml
12	3 cups/720 ml
13	3¼ cups/780 ml
14	3½ cups/840 ml
15	3¾ cups/900 ml
16	1 quart/ 960 ml

Gelatin Equivalents and Substitutions

- Unflavored gelatin powder and gelatin sheets can be substituted one for the other in equal weights.
- 1 sheet of gelatin (most brands) weighs ¹⁄₁₀ ounce (3 g).
- 1 tablespoon (15 ml) unflavored gelatin powder weighs just under ⅓ ounce (9 g).
- 1 ounce (30 g) unflavored gelatin powder measures 3 tablespoons plus 1 teaspoon (50 ml) by volume.
- A consumer packet or envelope of unflavored gelatin powder weighs ¼ ounce (just over 7 g) and is equivalent to 2½ teaspoons (12.5 ml) when measuring by volume.

Examples of Substituting Unflavored Gelatin Powder in a Recipe That Calls for Sheet Gelatin

Recipe calls for	Use
5 sheets of gelatin	½ ounce (15 g) gelatin powder
5 sheets of gelatin	5 teaspoons (25 ml) unflavored gelatin powder
1 sheet of gelatin	¹⁄₁₀ ounce (3 g) gelatin powder
1 sheet of gelatin	1 teaspoon (5 ml) unflavored gelatin powder

Examples of Substituting Sheet Gelatin in a Recipe That Calls for Unflavored Gelatin Powder

Recipe calls for	Use
1 ounce (30 g) unflavored gelatin powder	10 sheets of gelatin
3 tablespoons (45 ml) unflavored gelatin powder	9 sheets of gelatin
1 packet or envelope of unflavored gelatin powder	2½ sheets of gelatin

Note: When substituting sheet gelatin for powdered, soak the sheets in water as directed on page 889, remove the sheets from the water without squeezing, and melt the sheets in a bain-marie or in a saucepan over low heat. Add to the recipe as directed including whatever liquid was called for to soften and dissolve the gelatin powder.

Yeast Equivalents and Substitutions

- Some nonprofessional recipes specify the amount of yeast in a recipe by the envelope or packet. A consumer packet of active dry yeast weighs ¼ ounce (just over 7 g) and measures 2¼ teaspoons (11 ml) by volume.
- To substitute active dry yeast for fresh compressed yeast, use half the amount of dry yeast by either weight or volume.
- To substitute fresh compressed yeast for active dry yeast, use twice the amount by either weight or volume

Examples

Recipe calls for	Use
1 tablespoon (45 ml) fresh compressed yeast	1½ teaspoons (7.5 ml) active dry yeast
1 ounce (30 g) active dry yeast	2 ounces (55 g) fresh compressed yeast
2 tablespoons (30 ml) active dry yeast	4 tablespoons (60 ml) fresh compressed yeast
1 package active dry yeast	½ ounce (15 g) fresh compressed yeast

Gram Weight of Commonly Used Products

Item	Grams per Teaspoon	Grams per Tablespoon
Ammonium carbonate	3.5	10
Baking powder	4	12
Baking soda	4	12
Bread flour	2.5	8
Butter	5	15
Ground cinnamon	1.5	5
Unsweetened cocoa powder	2.5	8
Cornstarch	2.5	8
Cream of tartar	2	6
Granulated sugar	5	15
Grated citrus zest	6	18
Ground spices (except cinnamon)	2	6
Kosher salt	3.5	10
Malt sugar	3	9
Mocha paste	4	12
Powdered gelatin	3	9
Powdered pectin	3	9
Powdered sugar	3	9
Table salt	5	15

Volume and Weight Equivalents for Honey, Corn Syrup, and Molasses

Volume	Weight
¼ cup/60 ml	3 ounces/85 g
⅓ cup/80 ml	4 ounces/115 g
½ cup/120 ml	6 ounces/170 g
⅔ cup/160 ml	8 ounces/225 g
¾ cup/180 ml	9 ounces/255 g
1 cup/240 ml	12 ounces/340 g
1¼ cups/300 ml	15 ounces/430 g
1⅓ cups/320 ml	1 pound/455 g
1½ cups/360 ml	1 pound 2 ounces/510 g
1¾ cups/420 ml	1 pound 5 ounces/595 g
2 cups/480 ml	1 pound 8 ounces/680 g
3 cups/720 ml	2 pounds 4 ounces/1 kg 25 g

Calculating a Cake Circumference

To calculate the circumference (the perimeter) of a cake using *pi* (3.14), multiply the diameter of the cake times *pi* (or simply multiply by 3 and add a little). You may need to calculate the circumference to cut out strips of paper to line the inside of a cake pan, for example, or if you are making a chocolate band to wrap around a finished cake. The chart below shows the basic math using *pi*.

Diameter	Calculation	Circumference
8-inch (20-cm) cake	8 × 3.14 *or* 20 × 3.14	25.02 inches (62.6 cm)
10-inch (25-cm) cake	10 × 3.14 *or* 25 × 3.14	31.4 inches (78.7 cm)
12-inch (30-cm) cake	12 × 3.14 *or* 30 × 3.14	37.68 inches (93.8 cm)

Cake Pan Capacities by Volume

The volume listed for pan sizes below takes into consideration that you would not want to fill the pan to the top with batter. So, more accurately speaking, these numbers are not the precise volume of the pan; they are the amount of batter that would be baked in that size pan.

Pan (all pans are 2 inches/5 cm high)	Volume Size (allowing for expansion in oven)
5 inches (12.5 cm) round	2½ cups (600 ml)
6 inches (15 cm) round	3½ cups (840 ml)
7 inches (17.5 cm) round	5 cups (1 L 200 ml)
8 inches (20 cm) round	6¾ cups (1 L 620 ml)
9 inches (22.5 cm) round	8½ cups (2 L 40 ml)
10 inches (25 cm) round	9 cups (2 L 160 ml)
12 inches (30 cm) round	13 cups (3 L 120 ml)
14 inches (35 cm) round	20 cups (4 L 800 ml)
16 inches (40 cm) round	28 cups (6 L 720 ml)
8 inches (20 cm) square	7 cups (1 L 680 ml)
10 inches (25 cm) square	11 cups (2 L 640 ml)
12 inches (30 cm) square	14½ cups (3 L 480 ml)
14 inches (35 cm) square	22½ cups (5 L 400 ml)

Wedding Cake Yields

Calculating the Number of Servings per Tier

The chart below explains the number of servings you can plan on per tier from the average wedding cake. Very rich cakes, such as cheesecakes and cakes like chocolate decadence, yield more servings than a lighter cake, as the pieces can be cut smaller. These figures are based on round tiers that are 3 to 4 inches (7.5 to 10 cm) high after being filled and iced.

Round Cake Size	Number of Servings
5-inch (12.5-cm)	6
6-inch (15-cm)	8
7-inch (17.5-cm)	10 to 12
8-inch (20-cm)	12 to 14
9-inch (22.5-cm)	16 to 20
10-inch (25-cm)	24 to 28
12-inch (30-cm)	36 to 42
14-inch (35-cm)	48 to 64
16-inch (40-cm)	72 to 84
18-inch (45-cm)	92 to 108

Calculating the Number of Servings per Tier Combination

Putting together the best combination of tier sizes to produce both the correct amount of cake and a balanced presentation requires some calculation. Following are some successful combinations. These totals assume that the top tier is not going to be served (if it is, increase the total accordingly).

Tier Combination	Number of Servings
6, 9, and 12 inches (15, 22.5, and 30 cm)	52 to 62 (6-inch/15-cm saved)
6, 10, and 14 inches (15, 25, and 35 cm)	72 to 92 (6-inch/15-cm saved)
6, 8, 12, and 14 inches (15, 20, 30, and 35 cm)	96 to 120 (6-inch/15-cm saved)
6, 10, 14, and 16 inches (15, 25, 35, and 40 cm)	144 to 176 (6-inch/15-cm saved)
6, 10, 14, and 18 inches (15, 25, 35, and 45 cm)	164 to 200 (6-inch/15-cm saved)

Baker's Percentage

The term *baker's percentage* refers to a mathematical system or formula that is used to compare the proportion of each ingredient to the others in a baking recipe. However, this formula does not take the total of all of the ingredients in a given recipe and express this amount as a 100 percent yield. Instead, flour is always "100 percent" and the other ingredients are calculated in relationship. When using this method, all of the ingredients must be expressed in the same unit (ounces, pounds, etc). To find the percentage of an ingredient, divide its weight by the weight of the flour, then multiply by 100.

Example:

4 pounds (1 kg 820 g) flour	100 percent
1 pound (455 g) sugar	25 percent
2 pounds (910 g) butter	50 percent
8 ounces (½ pound/225 g) yeast	12.5 percent
1 quart (960 ml/2 pounds/910 g) water	50 percent

The intention of the baker's percentage formula is to provide a tool for comparing the amount of one ingredient to another in a recipe to achieve a better understanding of the particular formula balance. It can also be used to scale a recipe up or down. For a small recipe that you simply want to halve or double, there would be no real advantage to converting all of the ingredients from weight to percentage, multiplying or dividing the percentages, then converting these figures back to pounds and ounces. In a large commercial operation where you are making hundreds of pounds of bread dough, for example, using the percentage method rather than simply multiplying assures that the ingredients will remain in balance. Also, if substitutions are to be made, they can be made based on an equal percentage. A word of caution, however: This is not to say that any recipe can be scaled up or down successfully just by using the correct math!

Gram Measurements in Rounded Percentages as They Relate to 16 ounces (1 pound) as 100 Percent

Weight (in grams)	Rounded Percentage	Weight (in grams)	Rounded Percentage	Weight (in grams)	Rounded Percentage	Weight (in grams)	Rounded Percentage
1 g	0%	23 g	5%	45 g	10%	67 g	15%
2 g	0%	24 g	5%	46 g	10%	68 g	15%
3 g	1%	25 g	5%	47 g	10%	69 g	15%
4 g	1%	26 g	6%	48 g	11%	70 g	15%
5 g	1%	27 g	6%	49 g	11%	71 g	16%
6 g	1%	28 g	6%	50 g	11%	72 g	16%
7 g	2%	29 g	6%	51 g	11%	73 g	16%
8 g	2%	30 g	7%	52 g	11%	74 g	16%
9 g	2%	31 g	7%	53 g	12%	75 g	16%
10 g	2%	32 g	7%	54 g	12%	76 g	17%
11 g	2%	33 g	7%	55 g	12%	77 g	17%
12 g	3%	34 g	7%	56 g	12%	78 g	17%
13 g	3%	35 g	8%	57 g	13%	79 g	17%
14 g	3%	36 g	8%	58 g	13%	80 g	18%
15 g	3%	37 g	8%	59 g	13%	81 g	18%
16 g	4%	38 g	8%	60 g	13%	82 g	18%
17 g	4%	39 g	9%	61 g	13%	83 g	18%
18 g	4%	40 g	9%	62 g	14%	84 g	18%
19 g	4%	41 g	9%	63 g	14%	85 g	19%
20 g	4%	42 g	9%	64 g	14%	86 g	19%
21 g	5%	43 g	9%	65 g	14%	87 g	19%
22 g	5%	44 g	10%	66 g	15%	88 g	19%

Weight (in grams)	Rounded Percentage	Weight (in grams)	Rounded Percentage	Weight (in grams)	Rounded Percentage	Weight (in grams)	Rounded Percentage
89 g	20%	129 g	28%	169 g	37%	209 g	46%
90 g	20%	130 g	29%	170 g	37%	210 g	46%
91 g	20%	131 g	29%	171 g	38%	211 g	46%
92 g	20%	132 g	29%	172 g	38%	212 g	47%
93 g	20%	133 g	29%	173 g	38%	213 g	47%
94 g	21%	134 g	29%	174 g	38%	214 g	47%
95 g	21%	135 g	30%	175 g	38%	215 g	47%
96 g	21%	136 g	30%	176 g	39%	216 g	47%
97 g	21%	137 g	30%	177 g	39%	217 g	48%
98 g	22%	138 g	30%	178 g	39%	218 g	48%
99 g	22%	139 g	31%	179 g	39%	219 g	48%
100 g	22%	140 g	31%	180 g	40%	220 g	48%
101 g	22%	141 g	31%	181 g	40%	221 g	49%
102 g	22%	142 g	31%	182 g	40%	222 g	49%
103 g	23%	143 g	31%	183 g	40%	223 g	49%
104 g	23%	144 g	32%	184 g	40%	224 g	49%
105 g	23%	145 g	32%	185 g	41%	225 g	49%
106 g	23%	146 g	32%	186 g	41%	226 g	50%
107 g	24%	147 g	32%	187 g	41%	227 g	50%
108 g	24%	148 g	33%	188 g	41%	228 g	50%
109 g	24%	149 g	33%	189 g	42%	229 g	50%
110 g	24%	150 g	33%	190 g	42%	230 g	51%
111 g	24%	151 g	33%	191 g	42%	231 g	51%
112 g	25%	152 g	33%	192 g	42%	232 g	51%
113 g	25%	153 g	34%	193 g	42%	233 g	51%
114 g	25%	154 g	34%	194 g	43%	234 g	51%
115 g	25%	155 g	34%	195 g	43%	235 g	52%
116 g	25%	156 g	34%	196 g	43%	236 g	52%
117 g	26%	157 g	35%	197 g	43%	237 g	52%
118 g	26%	158 g	35%	198 g	44%	238 g	52%
119 g	26%	159 g	35%	199 g	44%	239 g	53%
120 g	26%	160 g	35%	200 g	44%	240 g	53%
121 g	27%	161 g	35%	201 g	44%	241 g	53%
122 g	27%	162 g	36%	202 g	44%	242 g	53%
123 g	27%	163 g	36%	203 g	45%	243 g	53%
124 g	27%	164 g	36%	204 g	45%	244 g	54%
125 g	27%	165 g	36%	205 g	45%	245 g	54%
126 g	28%	166 g	36%	206 g	45%	246 g	54%
127 g	28%	167 g	37%	207 g	45%	247 g	54%
128 g	28%	168 g	37%	208 g	46%	248 g	55%

Weight (in grams)	Rounded Percentage	Weight (in grams)	Rounded Percentage	Weight (in grams)	Rounded Percentage	Weight (in grams)	Rounded Percentage
249 g	55%	289 g	64%	329 g	72%	369 g	81%
250 g	55%	290 g	64%	330 g	73%	370 g	81%
251 g	55%	291 g	64%	331 g	73%	371 g	82%
252 g	55%	292 g	64%	332 g	73%	372 g	82%
253 g	56%	293 g	64%	333 g	73%	373 g	82%
254 g	56%	294 g	65%	334 g	73%	374 g	82%
255 g	56%	295 g	65%	335 g	74%	375 g	82%
256 g	56%	296 g	65%	336 g	74%	376 g	83%
257 g	56%	297 g	65%	337 g	74%	377 g	83%
258 g	57%	298 g	65%	338 g	74%	378 g	83%
259 g	57%	299 g	66%	339 g	75%	379 g	83%
260 g	57%	300 g	66%	340 g	75%	380 g	84%
261 g	57%	301 g	66%	341 g	75%	381 g	84%
262 g	58%	302 g	66%	342 g	75%	382 g	84%
263 g	58%	303 g	67%	343 g	75%	383 g	84%
264 g	58%	304 g	67%	344 g	76%	384 g	84%
265 g	58%	305 g	67%	345 g	76%	385 g	85%
266 g	58%	306 g	67%	346 g	76%	386 g	85%
267 g	59%	307 g	67%	347 g	76%	387 g	85%
268 g	59%	308 g	68%	348 g	76%	388 g	85%
269 g	59%	309 g	68%	349 g	77%	389 g	85%
270 g	59%	310 g	68%	350 g	77%	390 g	86%
271 g	60%	311 g	68%	351 g	77%	391 g	86%
272 g	60%	312 g	69%	352 g	77%	392 g	86%
273 g	60%	313 g	69%	353 g	78%	393 g	86%
274 g	60%	314 g	69%	354 g	78%	394 g	87%
275 g	60%	315 g	69%	355 g	78%	395 g	87%
276 g	61%	316 g	69%	356 g	78%	396 g	87%
277 g	61%	317 g	70%	357 g	78%	397 g	87%
278 g	61%	318 g	70%	358 g	79%	398 g	87%
279 g	61%	319 g	70%	359 g	79%	399 g	88%
280 g	62%	320 g	70%	360 g	79%	400 g	88%
281 g	62%	321 g	71%	361 g	79%	401 g	88%
282 g	62%	322 g	71%	362 g	80%	402 g	88%
283 g	62%	323 g	71%	363 g	80%	403 g	89%
284 g	62%	324 g	71%	364 g	80%	404 g	89%
285 g	63%	325 g	71%	365 g	80%	405 g	89%
286 g	63%	326 g	72%	366 g	80%	406 g	89%
287 g	63%	327 g	72%	367 g	81%	407 g	89%
288 g	63%	328 g	72%	368 g	81%	408 g	90%

Weight (in grams)	Rounded Percentage	Weight (in grams)	Rounded Percentage	Weight (in grams)	Rounded Percentage	Weight (in grams)	Rounded Percentage
409 g	90%	421 g	93%	433 g	95%	445 g	98%
410 g	90%	422 g	93%	434 g	95%	446 g	98%
411 g	90%	423 g	93%	435 g	96%	447 g	98%
412 g	91%	424 g	93%	436 g	96%	448 g	98%
413 g	91%	425 g	93%	437 g	96%	449 g	99%
414 g	91%	426 g	94%	438 g	96%	450 g	99%
415 g	91%	427 g	94%	439 g	96%	451 g	99%
416 g	91%	428 g	94%	440 g	97%	452 g	99%
417 g	92%	429 g	94%	441 g	97%	453 g	100%
418 g	92%	430 g	95%	442 g	97%	454 g	100%
419 g	92%	431 g	95%	443 g	97%	455 g	100%
420 g	92%	432 g	95%	444 g	98%		

Ounce Measurements in Rounded Percentages as They Relate to 16 ounces (1 pound) as 100 Percent

Weight (in ounces)	Rounded Percentage	Weight (in ounces)	Rounded Percentage	Weight (in ounces)	Rounded Percentage	Weight (in ounces)	Rounded Percentage
¼ ounce	2%	4¼ ounces	27%	8¼ ounces	52%	12¼ ounces	77%
½ ounce	3%	4½ ounces	28%	8½ ounces	53%	12½ ounces	78%
¾ ounce	5%	4¾ ounces	30%	8¾ ounces	55%	12¾ ounces	80%
1 ounce	6%	5 ounces	31%	9 ounces	56%	13 ounces	81%
1¼ ounces	8%	5¼ ounces	33%	9¼ ounces	58%	13¼ ounces	83%
1½ ounces	9%	5½ ounces	34%	9½ ounces	59%	13½ ounces	84%
1¾ ounces	11%	5¾ ounces	36%	9¾ ounces	61%	13¾ ounces	86%
2 ounces	13%	6 ounces	38%	10 ounces	63%	14 ounces	88%
2¼ ounces	14%	6¼ ounces	39%	10¼ ounces	64%	14¼ ounces	89%
2½ ounces	16%	6½ ounces	41%	10½ ounces	66%	14½ ounces	91%
2¾ ounces	17%	6¾ ounces	42%	10¾ ounces	67%	14¾ ounces	92%
3 ounces	19%	7 ounces	44%	11 ounces	69%	15 ounces	94%
3¼ ounces	20%	7¼ ounces	45%	11¼ ounces	70%	15¼ ounces	95%
3½ ounces	22%	7½ ounces	47%	11½ ounces	72%	15½ ounces	97%
3¾ ounces	23%	7¾ ounces	48%	11¾ ounces	73%	15¾ ounces	98%
4 ounces	25%	8 ounces	50%	12 ounces	75%	16 ounces	100%

High-Altitude Cake Baking

Because most recipes are developed for use at sea level (including those in *The Professional Pastry Chef*), when baking cakes—sponge cakes, pan cakes, tea cakes, muffins, and the like—at higher altitudes, where the atmospheric pressure is much lower, you must make some adjustments to produce a satisfactory result (these changes do not apply to baking bread or other yeast items; only those formulas that use a chemical leavening agent). Although some experimental baking has to be done to convert a sea-level recipe to a particular local condition and altitude, certain manufacturers supply the rate of adjustment for some of their products.

At high altitudes, the lower air pressure causes water to boil at a lower temperature. Thus, more evaporation takes place while a cake is baking, because the liquid begins to boil sooner. This results in insufficient moisture to fully gelatinize the starch, which weakens the structure. The lower air pressure also causes the batter to rise higher; however, it later collapses due to the lack of stabilizing starches.

It is necessary to make adjustments with cake baking starting at altitudes from 2500 feet (760 m). In general, the changes consist of:

- reducing the amount of baking powder or baking soda
- increasing the amount of liquid, sometimes with additional eggs, egg whites, or yolks
- increasing the flour
- using a higher baking temperature

These changes are applied to a greater degree as the altitude gets higher. Although the changes help protect the shape and consistency of the cake, they reduce its quality and flavor.

Adjustments for specific ingredients are as follows:

Leavening agents—Baking powder or soda, and any other substitute that reacts with heat, must be reduced by 20 percent starting at 2500 feet (760 m) and gradually be reduced up to 60 percent at 7500 feet (2280 m). For example, if a recipe calls for 10 ounces (285 g) baking powder, only 4 ounces (115 g) should be used at 7500 feet (2280 meters). In a dark cake or muffin recipe that calls for both baking powder and baking soda together with buttermilk, it is best to change to sweet milk and use baking powder only (add the two amounts together) to save having to convert both leavening agents.

Eggs—At 2500 feet (760 m), add 3 percent more whole eggs, egg whites, or egg yolks. Progressively increase the amount of eggs until, at 7500 feet (2280 m), you are adding 15 percent more eggs. For example, if your recipe calls for 36 ounces (1 kg 25 g) eggs (which is 1 quart/960 ml), you must use an additional 5.4 ounces (150 g) or ¾ cup (180 ml) at 7500 feet (2280 m).

Flour—Beginning at 3000 feet (915 m), add 3 percent more flour, gradually increasing the amount up to 10 percent more at 8000 feet (2440 m). For example, if your recipe calls for 40 ounces (1 kg 135 g) flour, you should use 1¼ ounces (35 g) more at 3000 feet (915 m).

Oven—Starting at 3500 feet (1065 meters), increase the baking temperature by 5 percent. For example, if your recipe calls for baking at 400°F (205°C), you should increase the temperature to 420°F (216°C) at 3500 feet (1065 m). The baking time should remain the same as at sea level, but you need to take care not to bake any longer than necessary to prevent the rapid evaporation that takes place at high altitudes.

Storage—Everything dries more quickly in thin air, so to ensure maximum moisture and freshness, cakes should be removed from the pans, wrapped in plastic, and stored in the refrigerator as soon as they have cooled. It is actually preferable not to keep any sponges in stock at high altitudes; instead, make them up as you need them.

Baumé Scale Readings

The Baumé scale of measurement is used to describe the concentration of sugar in a liquid by measuring the density. It is named for a French chemist, Antoine Baumé. Following are the Baumé readings for certain percentages of sugar solutions based on 2 cups (480 ml) water and varying amounts of sugar when the mixture is brought to a boil to dissolve the sugar and the solution is then measured at room temperature (65°F/19°C). When measured hot, the BE° will read 3° lower. If the syrup is boiled for any length of time, these readings will no longer apply because the evaporation that will take place will increase the ratio of sugar to water.

Baumé Readings at Room Temperature for Sugar Solutions Relative to 2 cups (480 ml) Water

Water	Granulated Sugar	Baumé Reading
2 cups (480 ml)	5 ounces (150 g)	14° (sorbet syrup)
2 cups (480 ml)	6 ounces (170 g)	15°
2 cups (480 ml)	7 ounces (200 g)	17°
2 cups (480 ml)	8 ounces (225 g)	18° (baba syrup)
2 cups (480 ml)	9 ounces (255 g)	20° (candied citrus peel)
2 cups (480 ml)	10 ounces (285 g)	21°
2 cups (480 ml)	12 ounces (340 g)	25°
2 cups (480 ml)	14 ounces (400 g)	27°
2 cups (480 ml)	1 pound (455 g)	28° (simple syrup)
2 cups (480 ml)	1 pound 2 ounces (510 g)	29°
2 cups (480 ml)	1 pound 4 ounces (570 g)	31°
2 cups (480 ml)	1 pound 6 ounces (635 g)	32°
2 cups (480 ml)	1 pound 8 ounces (680 g)	33°
2 cups (480 ml)	1 pound 10 ounces (740 g)	34°
2 cups (480 ml)	1 pound 12 ounces (795 g)	35° (liqueur candies)

Saccharometers that are calibrated to measure density using a decimal scale are becoming more popular. The range of measurement varies with brand and price. A typical range is from 1.1 to 1.4, equivalent to 13° to 37°BE. Following are conversions from Baumé to the decimal system, rounded to the closest even number.

Degrees Baumé	Decimal Reading	Degrees Baumé	Decimal Reading
5°BE	1.03	19°BE	1.15
6°BE	1.04	20°BE	1.16
7°BE	1.05	21°BE	1.17
8°BE	1.05	22°BE	1.18
9°BE	1.06	23°BE	1.19
10°BE	1.07	24°BE	1.20
11°BE	1.08	25°BE	1.21
12°BE	1.09	26°BE	1.22
13°BE	1.10	27°BE	1.23
14°BE	1.11	28°BE	1.24
15°BE	1.12	29°BE	1.25
16°BE	1.12	30°BE	1.26
17°BE	1.13	31°BE	1.27
18°BE	1.14	32°BE	1.28

Brix Scale

The Brix scale was invented by a German scientist named Adolph Brix. It is used for the same purpose as the Baumé scale: to measure the sugar content in a liquid. The Brix scale is used only with pure sucrose solutions; it cannot be used with other solutions. Both the Brix and Baumé methods use a hydrometer (see Appendix B), although, when using the Baumé scale, it is more commonly known as a *saccharometer*. The Baumé scale is expressed in degrees and the Brix scale is based on the decimal system. The Brix scale is calibrated to read 0.1° Brix at 68°F (20°C). A solution containing 20 grams sucrose per 100 grams liquid will read 20° Brix.

The Brix scale is used in the wine-making industry to measure the sugar content in fresh or fermenting grape juice; by farmers, in conjunction with other tools, to measure the sugar-to-acid ratio in determining when to harvest fruits; and in the commercial fruit canning industry in the preparation of sugar syrups.

Following are equivalent measures for degrees Baumé and degrees Brix, with the solution measured at 68°F (20°C).

Degrees Baumé	Degrees Brix	Degrees Baumé	Degrees Brix
5°BE	3.5°Brix	21°BE	37.9°Brix
6°BE	5.4°Brix	22°BE	39.6°Brix
7°BE	7.4°Brix	23°BE	41.5°Brix
8°BE	9.3°Brix	24°BE	43.5°Brix
9°BE	11.3°Brix	25°BE	45.4°Brix
10°BE	14.2°Brix	26°BE	47.4°Brix
11°BE	16.2°Brix	27°BE	49.4°Brix
12°BE	18.1°Brix	28°BE	51.3°Brix
13°BE	20.1°Brix	29°BE	53.3°Brix
14°BE	23.1°Brix	30°BE	55.2°Brix
15°BE	25.0°Brix	31°BE	57.1°Brix
16°BE	27.0°Brix	32°BE	59.1°Brix
17°BE	29.1°Brix	33°BE	61.0°Brix
18°BE	31.1°Brix	34°BE	63.0°Brix
19°BE	33.0°Brix	35°BE	64.9°Brix
20°BE	35.9°Brix	36°BE	66.9°Brix

Sugar Boiling Conversions

If you were to compare the sugar conversion tables in ten cookbooks, you would probably find ten different temperatures and almost as many names used to describe the same stage. Some charts have 14 separate stages, which can really make your head spin! All of these names and stages are, in a way, misleading and unrealistic for use by anyone who does not have years of experience. For example, by the time you have tested and determined that the boiling sugar is at the crack stage, it has probably already reached hard crack. What is important is not what a particular stage is called and how to test for it, but what temperature is required for the sugar syrup based on what it is to be used for. I suggest you rely on an accurate sugar thermometer rather than your poor index finger and ignore all the different names; however, the testing procedures are listed below should you want to use them.

Special thermometers for boiling sugar are calibrated according to the temperature range needed. Professional thermometers have a wire screen that protects the glass and should be stored hanging up, using the handle that is part of this screen (see page 968 for more information). Although centigrade is used more and more for measuring sugar in European countries, I have included the old Réaumur system here because it is still part of the scale on professional European thermometers.

Required Temperature and Testing Procedures for Sugar Stages

Sugar Stage	Fahrenheit Reading	Celsius Reading	Réaumur Reading	Manual Testing Procedure
Thread	215 to 230°	102 to 110°	82 to 88°	Pull a small amount of sugar between your thumb and index finger; shorter or longer threads will form depending on the temperature.
Soft Ball	240°	115°	92°	Place your index finger in ice-cold water, dip it very quickly into the hot syrup and immediately plunge it back into the ice water. The sugar will fall off your finger and you will be able to roll it into a ball.
Firm Ball	245°	118°	94°	The test is the same as for the soft ball stage, but here the ball will be firmer.
Hard Ball	250 to 260°	122 to 127°	97 to 101°	The test is the same as for the soft ball stage, however here the sugar will be more resistant to forming a ball and the ball will not be malleable.
Small Crack	265 to 270°	130 to 132°	104 to 105°	Dip your finger into ice water and then into the sugar syrup as for the soft ball test; at this stage you will be unable to form the sugar into a ball. The sugar will also show small cracks.
Crack	275 to 280°	135 to 138°	108 to 110°	The test is the same as for the small crack stage, however, at this stage, the sugar will break apart.
Hard Crack	295 to 310°	146 to 155°	116 to 123°	The test is the same as for the small crack stage, however, at this stage, the sugar will shatter when placed in the ice water.
Caramel	320°	160°	128°	Test by observing the color of the sugar: The syrup will change from amber to golden, and then become light brown.